THE HIDDEN TRUTH OF YOUR NAME

THE HIDDEN TRUTH OF YOUR NAME

A Complete Guide to First
Names and What They Say
About the Real You

❦

THE NOMENOLOGY PROJECT

Ballantine Books • New York

A Ballantine Book
Published by The Ballantine Publishing Group

http://www.randomhouse.com

LIBRARY OF CONGRESS CATALOGING-IN-PUBLICATION DATA
The hidden truth of your name : a complete guide to first names and
what they say about the real you / The Nomenology Project. — 1st ed.
    p.   cm.
    ISBN 0-345-42266-X (alk. paper)
    1. Names, Personal—Psychological aspects.   2. Cabala—Miscellanea.
3. Runes—Miscellanea.   4.Numerology.   I. Nomenology Project.
CS2377.H53   1999
929.4′01′9—dc21   98-29795
                                                                CIP

Text design by Holly Johnson

Cover design by Dreu Pennington-McNeil

Cover illustration by Christina Balit

Manufactured in the United States of America

First Edition: March 1999

10 9 8 7 6 5

Contents

Part I

The Mystery and Science of Names

The Forgotten Power of Names

This is the million-dollar question: Did Hercules start out with a great name, or did he make his name great by making the most of it? Your name is a suit of clothes you are given at birth, a suit you grow into or out of, strain at the seams, or wear elegantly and effortlessly like a custom-made affair. Our parents give us our names, and we do our best or our worst with them without ever really understanding how our names influence our lives. But what if you could actually know what powers and personality traits a name possessed?

For example, think of a little girl named Brittany. The influence of the name Brittany is monumental: In a nutshell, Brittany is tenacious, independent, single-minded, and very, very direct. That's all well and good for Brittany herself, but what about her parents? There may be little harmony in that house until Brittany packs up and goes off to college. That's a long time for everyone in Brittany's family to wait for a little peace and quiet. But if her parents understood the effect Brittany's name has on their daughter, her parents could be empowered with knowledge that would allow them to see their daughter in a new light. Instead of engaging in a continual battle of wills with Brittany, her parents could work with her to enhance her strengths and mitigate her weaknesses as she matures.

This book is the key that unlocks the mystery of names so you can deal with the Brittanys in *your* life and improve your understanding of yourself and others by arming yourself with the knowledge that comes from truly understanding the personality traits inherent in a name—what a name gives you, what it takes away from you, and what it can really do for you if you give it a chance. Once you have brushed up on your own name's strengths and weaknesses, there are 717 other name interpretations in this book to check out. Reading a name's entry will tell you whether or not a new boss named George could be supportive, or a new lover named Kathy might be inclined to want children.

What's to know about a name, besides the origin or derivation of the thing? Plenty. There are powers that are inherent in a name, and there are very distinct ways in which a name can control one's destiny, for good and bad. The powers associated with names have been studied by mystics for centuries, but this is the first book to digest their findings for the layperson. By reading the expert interpretations in this book, anyone can understand the influences of their name as well as the influences of the names of people in their life, whether they are already familiar with the work of numerologists, rune masters, and kabbalists or are reading about these arts for the first time right now.

Your name is not only your calling card, it is also something that uniquely distinguishes you from everyone else and may even determine, to a large extent, who you turn out to be in your lifetime. The name you "wear" affects not only how others perceive you but also how you perceive yourself. If you truly understood the meaning of your name in all its mysterious and hidden aspects, could you use that knowledge to affect your own destiny? Would it be possible to take advantage of the inherent power of your name to alter the direction of your life for the better?

With a bit of effort and the information available in this book, you'll be able to learn enough about the meaning of your name to be able to truly embrace its secret powers. By knowing and comprehending the meaning and significance of your name, you will come to understand yourself more clearly and more fully. Armed with this understanding, you will be able to develop a deeper self-knowledge that will help you make the most of your life by utilizing the strengths and influences of your name to your benefit.

After you've learned how to analyze and understand the significance of your name and how it shapes your personality, you'll be able to work out the meanings of the names of your coworkers, friends, family, or anyone else you want to understand better. As you learn the deeper meanings of their names, you'll be more in tune with the temperaments and tendencies of the people in your life. And by considering how the personality characteristics of others correlate with your own traits, you will be able to deepen your relationships by building upon things you have in common with others and by avoiding areas of potential discord. If, for example, you discover that someone you will soon be working with has a name that indicates a feisty, argumentative temperament, you will know what to expect when dealing with them. By deepening your understanding of others, you will be able to create stronger and more lasting relationships in all areas of your life, from your work and social relationships to your intimate relationships with family, friends, and lovers.

In addition, by understanding the power and deep significance of names, you will be better equipped to choose names for your children when the time comes for you to do so. Choosing a name for your child can often be a daunting task with few guidelines for the decision other than your own preference or sensibility. How do you know if a girl named Grace really will be poised or if a boy named Clint will be adventurous? By understanding the meanings and energies that a particular name bears, you will be able to choose a name for your child that will equip her to embrace the challenges of life with strength and certainty. By giving your child a powerful and meaningful name, you will help her begin life with one of the greatest gifts you can give, a good name.

Finally, this book will teach you how to create name interpretations of your own based on the ancient arts of the Kabbalah, numerology, and runes. These mystical forms of divination have been used for centuries to glean insights into a person's destiny. In the pages that follow, you will learn from experts how to begin to use these techniques yourself to create original interpretations of not only first names but *any* name. Your first name plays the most powerful role in determining your destiny because this is the name most associated with you. However, middle names and last names also have an impact on your life, and by interpreting these, too, you can gain a fuller understanding of your personality and the personalities of others. If you have a friend with a very unusual name not interpreted by the experts in part II of this book, you will still be able to determine the key characteristics of his name by doing your own analysis. As you become more adept at creating your own interpretations, you will also gain additional insights into almost any name you choose to study, whether it is already listed here or not, for as you will see, name interpretation is a science based on instinct. Like reading tarot cards or astrology charts, there is no one right or wrong way to define a name's characteristics, and everyone's analysis of a name will vary a little bit according to the methods of interpretation they use. These methods are thousands of years old, and the mysteries they reveal are constantly changing as new practitioners learn to unlock their magic.

THE EVOLUTION OF NAME ANALYSIS

In ancient times the symbolic meaning of names was an assumed part of their overall significance. For people in most ancient cultures, a name was far more than simply an identifier; it was a way of truly and essentially knowing the person or thing named. Choosing a name for a child was not taken lightly, as that name would necessarily prove to be a source of strength or weakness for that individual throughout his or her life. As an example of the powerful influence of names in ancient cultures, consider that in ancient Egyptian society, one's name was thought to be integral to the very essence of a person's existence. In fact, according to Egyptian beliefs, the name was a living part of the person as much as the body, soul, or personality of that individual. It was therefore critical in ancient Egypt that a child be named immediately at birth so the "coming into existence" of the infant would be properly accomplished; a child without a name was almost as terrible to imagine as a child without a soul!

In part, the importance of names was based on the theology of the Egyptians. According to one of the Egyptian creation myths, the god Ptah created the universe by pronouncing the names of all things; the very act of speaking the names of things brought them into existence. Since the name of someone or something was so intimately tied to its very being, the preservation of an individual's name was an important part of his or her ability to survive both in this life and in the next. For example, an important aspect of Egyptian funerary theology involved the nightly reunion of the *ba*, which is loosely translated to mean "personality" or "spirit," with the physical body of the deceased. One question the Egyptians faced was where the ba would go if the body were destroyed. The solution was to provide a statue or likeness of the person to which the ba could return. But as anyone who has seen Egyptian statuary might wonder, how would the ba know which statue to return to? The answer was simple: A statue would have the *name* of the individual carved into it. The name would effectively transform the lifeless image into an appropriate nightly resting place for the ba by imbuing it with the very essence of the person whose name was carved into it. A nasty consequence of using a name to "claim" a statue, however, was that once you were gone, someone else might come along and usurp that statue for himself by cutting out and replacing your name with his own! And it was critical for a person to ensure the continuation of his or her name because if that name were wiped out or entirely forgotten, there was a distinct and terrifying possibility that he or she would simply cease to exist.

Although other ancient cultures differed in their specific views of the significance of names, most of them shared a common perspective that the name was a crucially important part of who a person was. The choice of an appropriate name was so vitally significant in ancient societies that parents would often consult oracles or religious authorities for assistance in assigning a name befitting their child. If an oracle was not consulted, parents might name their children on the basis of their physical characteristics, their place of birth, their relationships, or even the expectations parents had for their future achievements. Illustrious parents would pass down the power and significance of their names by using prefixes such as "son of" or "daughter of" to indicate that the child was expected to continue, and even reinforce, the glory of the parents' name. Religious customs also played an important part in the naming conventions of many cultures; children in pagan societies were often named after the favorite family gods just as children in monotheistic societies were given names to inspire religious sensibilities and an awareness of the fact that there was only one God (for example, Elihu, which means "my God is He," or Elijah, meaning "my God is Jehovah").

The name was not only essential to truly understanding a person but could also provide tremendous power over that person. In many ancient religions, including the Israelite and Egyptian religions, God or the gods had many different names, some of which were more powerful than others. Many of these names were hidden or secret names that were rarely, if ever, pronounced. Speaking a name with the appropriate accents and sound quality would literally provide power to move the gods to do one's bidding, and the secret names of the divine being or beings were known only by a select few among royalty or the priesthood. Because of the power inherent in divine names, knowledge of the secret names of gods was also a key element in magical and religious rites. By knowing the various names of gods, one could literally manipulate them to obtain favors or gifts, or to guarantee an appropriate harvest or a victory in battle. But the inappropriate use of a name could bring down divine wrath to such an extent that the universe itself could be devastated, and it was considered blasphemous to inappropriately utter the name or names of divinities.

The symbolism of names did not involve only the use of whole words. The ancients also believed that individual letters contained intrinsic meaning that, when combined to form words, produced varied textures and layers of significance that would provide clues to the mystical or hidden meanings of those words. When the words were names of people, the meanings would reflect not only the physical aspects of a person's life but also the complexities of an individual's personality and spirituality. The philosophy of the critical importance of letters as mystical manifestations of the thoughts or intentions of the divine was expressed powerfully in the arcane tradition of the Kabbalah, which was the name given in the twelfth century to the ancient mystical traditions of the Jewish people. According to kabbalistic teachings, God created the universe from the letters of the Hebrew alphabet, in much the same way as the Egyptian god Ptah created the universe by his spoken word: "Twenty-two elemental letters. God engraved them, carved them, weighed them, permuted them, and transposed them, forming with them everything formed and everything destined to be formed."[1]

Each of the letters of the Hebrew alphabet was thought to contain a kernel of mystical truth that, when meditated upon individually and in combinations, could bring the spiritual seeker to union with God, the source of all things. By deeply understanding the meanings of letters and words, the student of Kabbalah was able to penetrate into the mysteries of the universe by entering into communion with the mind of the divine. And by uttering or writing words and letters, the mystic could literally attune his vibrations with the higher vibrations of the energy that sustained the entire universe. In Kabbalah, each letter contains within itself the potential to be a path of ascent from the microcosm of the individual human life to the macrocosm of all existence and ultimately to the divine spirit. Since each letter of an individual's name was so pregnant with meaning and significance, analyzing a name using kabbalistic methods could yield a tremendous amount of insight into a person's character and personality. Today this ancient form of name analysis is gaining in popularity once again, and using the techniques described in this book, one can gain valuable insight into the hidden meanings of hundreds of names.

The letters of other ancient languages such as Egyptian and Chinese were also considered to have intrinsic meaning that extended far beyond their mere use as the building blocks of words. [One such collection of symbols that has enjoyed a modern renaissance is the Futhark, the letters of which are known as runes. The Futhark is a northern European alphabet whose origins are uncertain but which was known to have been used throughout Europe since at least 200 B.C.E.] The runes are widely used today as an oracle, and "casting runes" has become a popular method of divination as well as a means of gaining deeper self-knowledge. By analyzing the ancient symbolic characters of one's name in the Futhark, an individual might be able to obtain a greater understanding of his or her own personality. By looking at *both* the runic and kabbalistic interpretations of a name, an even more detailed picture of a particular name will be revealed.

Ancient peoples not only saw meaning in letters and words but also considered numbers to be extremely significant as aspects of the universal order. Each number represented a concept that reflected the essential nature of a particular attribute of the universe. According to some ancient philosophical systems, the analysis of numbers was the key to a complete knowledge of the mysteries of existence. The most famous ancient philosopher of numbers, Pythagoras, lived in Greece circa 550 B.C.E. and taught that all things could be reduced to a numerical value that would provide the means to understanding their nature. Because numbers were a fundamental building block of the universe, they were obviously associated with all things that existed, including, of course, words and letters. In the kabbalistic tradition, the study of the correspondences between letters and numbers was known as *gematria*. According to the science of gematria, each letter in the Hebrew alphabet corresponded to a specific number. When words were analyzed for their numeric values, hidden meanings could be unearthed that would shed light on mysteries that were normally beyond the grasp of ordinary intellectual comprehension. Of course, the letters of other alphabetic systems, such as Greek, Egyptian, and the Futhark, also contained numerical correspondences that could be used to analyze the hidden meanings of words and names, and the people who used these languages were well aware of the depths of their significance.

By combining divination and the consultation of oracles with the analysis of words, letters, and numbers, ancient peoples were able to create names for themselves and their children that were extraordinarily rich in symbolic value. A person in ancient society would have little doubt about the meaning of his or her name, as this knowledge would be deeply ingrained from an early age. And by deeply understanding how their names affected their lives and destinies, the ancients were able to possess the great depth of self-knowledge and per-

1. Daniel C. Matt, *The Essential Kabbalah* (San Francisco: HarperSanFrancisco, 1995).

sonal strength that was the natural result of being in tune with the energy of their names. By taking advantage of the power of one's name and avoiding the pitfalls associated with any weakness of that name, a person could literally shape his or her life into a true reflection of the destiny implied by that name, and thus live in greater harmony with the natural order of the universe.

THE CONTEMPORARY SIGNIFICANCE

Although the significance of words and names has largely been obscured in the modern age, which tends to discount mystical and spiritual phenomena, the fact remains that our names continue to have significant power to influence us. One's name evokes a reaction from his or her companions and can powerfully affect a person's self-esteem. For example, in every society throughout the world, children with unusual names are often ridiculed by their peers. The contemporary significance of a name, however, is much more than simply whether or not it leaves us open to embarrassment. Over the past few years there has been a tremendous resurgence of interest in traditional spirituality and religion. For example, people of Western religious traditions such as Christianity, Judaism, and Islam now choose names for their children based on favorite saints, biblical personages, or sages from their respective traditions. People from many other cultural backgrounds have rediscovered the power and meaning of using names that reflect their pride in their roots, their families, and their national or cultural origins. By using and understanding the meaning of these names, they've found a way to maintain a living link with their own histories that adds richness and depth to their contemporary lives.

In addition to a reawakening of traditional forms of religion and spirituality, there has also been a tremendous growth of interest in mysticism, divination, and other methods of gaining deeper self-awareness such as numerology, runes, tarot, and the Kabbalah. Because of the revival of interest in these metaphysical disciplines and philosophies, the ancient ideas about the meaning and significance of names have become popular again. An increasing number of people are making efforts to consider a wider variety of options for their children's names based on the metaphysical and spiritual consequences of those names. More and more, people are beginning to realize that their own names possess power that they can tap into for personal strength and growth, and that the names of others can be used as tools for improving their relationships. There is a growing suspicion that perhaps the ancients weren't as far "off the wall" as the modern scientific mind-set has always assumed. The renewed interest in matters long ago written off by science as irrelevant superstition has led to a newfound respect for the wisdom and knowledge of ancient cultures and a rediscovery of many of their forgotten secrets.

And as science itself continues to discover that things in the world are more intimately connected than ever before thought possible, the idea that a name, a birth date, or a place of birth can have a significant influence upon a person's life and destiny becomes more and more feasible. The belief in a deep existential connection among all things allows for the possibility that our name is fundamentally correct for us. If all things intimately affect and are intimately related to all other things, and if there is a deep well of spiritual life from which we all draw our existence, then the idea that the name we ended up with is the *right* name for us becomes a plausible concept indeed. Because of the amazing and paradoxical discoveries in fields such as quantum physics, many rational and intelligent people are replacing an overt skepticism with a willingness to accept that there are things we simply may never understand but that are nonetheless quite real and affect our lives in ways we have yet to imagine. To conceive that the name we are assigned to "wear" throughout our lifetime has meaning for us should seem a small leap of the imagination when compared to some of the incredible truths science has discovered in this century about the workings of the universe on both the micro and the macro levels. And to imagine that a name contains power in its own right as a bundle of energy or a set of vibrations should not be any more of a challenge to an open mind.

To get a sense of how a name possesses a certain "feel" or energy, consider the fact that everyone has at one time or another heard phrases such as "you don't look like a Tom" or "I think you're more of an Ellen than a Mary." We tend to associate stereotypes with certain names based on our experiences of people bearing those names. However, despite our tendency to stereotype, there are certain energies associated with names and words, just as the ancients taught for thousands of years. Although the way people respond to your name is typically caused by personal impressions and experiences, there is a certain "truth" to your name, and you probably identify very strongly with it because you have a sense that it is "right" for you. As you use this book to become more conscious of the symbolism and meaning of names, you will be able to utilize their power to influence your destiny more directly as well as gain valuable insight into the character and personality of others whose names you analyze. If you find that your name doesn't quite "fit" you in some way, you may need to analyze it in light of your personality to see just where discrepancies can be uncovered and dealt with. The problem may simply lie in the fact that you haven't taken full advantage of the power of your name and therefore you aren't drawing strength and energy from it as you should. On the other hand, you may find after careful analysis of the meaning of your name that it simply doesn't feel right to you, in which case you may need to consider the possibility of either changing your name outright or changing the name you allow people to use when addressing you. For example, a good nickname or a variant on your given name might fit your personality more closely, and using this means of referring to yourself will give you the opportunity to take advantage of the power of your name in a way that suits you.

While many people are discovering that names have a tremendous significance on a mystical or spiritual level and are therefore drawn toward a more in-depth study of their many meanings, others simply find that they identify closely enough with their name on an intuitive or feeling level to make the most of that name in their lives. For example, you may know that your parents named you after a great king, a saint, a sage, a famous actor or sports hero, or even a beloved relative or relatives. You don't have to walk in that person's footsteps to draw inspiration and power from his or her name because you can consciously adopt a certain grace or finesse for yourself based on the power of that name. Someone named Alexander (or Alexandra) doesn't necessarily have to be a world conqueror to take advantage of the power of that illustrious name! However, an Alexander may find that he is comfortable with a leadership role in his work or daily activities, and he should easily be able to draw strength from his name in his leadership position.

To say that a name has a certain specific influence or effect on one's life isn't to say, of course, that because someone is named Alexander at birth he will become a powerful leader simply by virtue of that name. A good name is analogous to a talent that someone is born with: An individual may have a particular gift for music, for example, but if that innate ability is not developed and exercised, it will simply go to waste. To truly take advantage of a congenital musical talent, an individual must spend many painstaking hours learning the techniques required to play a musical instrument or working out a range of vocal skills that will transform a naturally beautiful voice into a magnificent instrument. In much the same way, a name gives a person certain potentials and characteristics that must be understood, embraced, and developed by that person if the power of the name is to be fully utilized. So while an Alexander may have a gift for intelligence and leadership, if he squanders his talents by not pursuing a path that enables him to take advantage of these strengths, the power of his name will never be completely expressed in his lifetime.

Another issue to consider in regard to the inherent qualities of a name is that even a good name can have both positive and negative influences on a person's life. While the natural leadership strengths of an Alexander may be a positive characteristic in many respects, there is always potential for the abuse of that power. There is a danger that Alexander's great pride and tremendous ego may become overbearing to others or that his ambition will lead him to harm others as he continues his pursuit of self-aggrandizement. By learning both the strengths and weaknesses of your name, you will be able to improve your areas of weakness and exploit your areas of strength by intentionally choosing to build skills that match the influences of your name. And by learning the strengths and weaknesses of other people's names, you will be able to work off *their* names' powers to improve your relationships with them. As with any tool that can help you improve yourself and your future prospects, the benefits you receive from an in-depth knowledge of a name depend upon your own level of awareness and your willingness to make positive changes in your life to achieve your goals when necessary. You must be willing to find ways to use the power of names creatively and constructively before those names will be able to impart their power to you.

If you acknowledge the tremendous power inherent in names and are inclined to learn more, keep reading. In this book you will learn how to discern and understand the many meanings of your name so you can use that knowledge to increase your personal power. You'll also be able to use the information in this book to help you name a child appropriately and in such a way that he or she will be able to draw strength from that name throughout his or her lifetime. Equally important, you will learn to analyze the names of your friends, lovers, and coworkers to gain a better understanding of what makes them tick. For example, you may feel uncomfortable asking for a new boss's astrological sign, but once you know her name, you'll be able to use this book to get immediate access to the information you need best to interact with her.

Regardless of whether you accept the ancient teachings about the meanings of letters, words, numbers, and sounds, the fact remains that our names are a fundamentally important part of who we are. By learning as much as possible about your name and the names of those you know, not only will you have a better understanding of the influences and energies that affect you and others, but you'll also know more about how other people see you and react to you because of the name you bear. Armed with this knowledge, you'll have the opportunity to take steps to improve the quality of your life by developing skills that allow you to fully embrace the power and energy of your name.

DIVINING WITH NAMES:
THE ANCIENT ART OF ONOMANCY

Because ancient cultures believed that words could manifest power in the world, the counsel of the wise often recommended that people keep silent as much as possible and speak only when necessary: "Even a fool, when he holdeth his peace, is counted wise: and he that shutteth his lips is esteemed a man of understanding."[2] With words, a person could literally create effects in the world that might have disastrous consequences not only for that individual but also for the society as a whole. Not all words were considered equally powerful, however, and there were certain magical words that could have greater effect. The secret names of gods or other spiritual beings such as angels were not only used in magical rites to obtain favors but were also key to understanding future events through the process of name divination, which is also called onomancy. By analyzing the names of gods or spiritual beings associated with places, people could determine whether it would be beneficial to the society at large to construct a temple or other building on that site. For instance, if a particular place was associated with a god or an angel whose name meant "gracious provider," a diviner or priest might determine that the land would benefit from that god's favor if a temple dedicated to that god were built on the site. Similarly, divination using a person's name was believed to be able to reveal a great deal about that person's overall life path. Knowing one's potential and the influences expected to affect one's life as implied by his or her name gave someone a distinct advantage because he or she could consciously make use of the power of that name to avoid its pitfalls and embrace its strengths. By working with a name's strengths and attempting to lessen the impact of any negative characteristics of the name, a person could positively affect his or her life's course for the better.

These days, the same techniques of name analysis and name divination can be used to determine the general path of someone's life just as astrology is frequently consulted for

2. Prov. 17:28.

guidance. If you understand the subtle nuances of meaning in your name, you will be better able to determine your life's purpose. Consider again, for example, the name Alexander. If you think of some of the qualities of Alexander the Great (perhaps the most famous person bearing this name), you should get an immediate sense of the energies behind it. Someone given Alexander as a birth name is likely to have a natural propensity for leadership roles in his life, whether that means an executive or managerial position in a company or a preeminent position in some other career or activity. Alexanders are very adept at mental activity and deep thought, and they are quite willing and able to act on their ideas. This name bears a tremendous amount of creative energy and potential that, if tapped into with wisdom and self-awareness, can result in success in any chosen field. A simple divination based on this name indicates that an Alexander should consider putting his energy into developing his leadership and interpersonal skills so that he can better fulfill his destiny as a thinker, creator, and person of action.

Understanding Your First Name

Your first name is the name you use as your primary identifier on a day-to-day basis, and therefore it expresses your personality traits and destiny most powerfully. The sound of your name carries certain vibrations that, when spoken, release your energy into the presence and awareness of whoever has spoken it. However, the very sound of your name has power associated with it because it is composed of different letters that not only have meaning individually but also have meaning when combined to form your specific name. To understand your first name enables you to take advantage of its energy so you can assimilate it into your personality and your life and thereby positively affect your destiny. Again, by consciously trying to improve yourself through the process of integrating the strong points of your name with your personality and shunning its weaker points, you'll be able to utilize its power to your long-term benefit.

Your middle name complements and adds energy to your first name and is therefore also very important to understand in terms of its influence upon the energies of your first name. However, if you tend to "go by" your middle name, that name will be the "sound" or energy associated with you, and will therefore have a stronger influence on your personality than your first name.

Also, you need to consider how you use your name to get a better sense of how the energy associated with it plays upon your life. For example, if your name is Thomas and the most common way people address you is to call you Tom or Tommy, then the influence of the name Thomas is altered because you are shortening or modifying its spelling and its sound, and therefore its energy. You also may use different forms of your name at different times and in different circumstances, depending on who is addressing you and your relationship to that person. Using different forms does not necessarily lessen the influence of the "primary" form of the name in your life (Thomas, in this example) but rather allows you to express the diverse aspects of your personality, depending on the contexts in which the name is used to address you. For example, Thomas may be an appropriate form of address in your professional life or career, whereas Tom might be the form your friends use, and Tommy the form used by intimates such as your wife or family members. The variant you use most of the time will have the strongest influence on your life and personality, and if you choose to change the forms of address people use with you, you'll be able to modify the energies and vibrations they receive from their interactions with you.

Your last name, of course, carries the energies of your family and your national and cultural heritage. While the influence of your last name is typically less powerful on you than the influence of your first name because you are primarily associated with your first name in your day-to-day life, your last name nevertheless affects the energies available to you in your first and middle names by bringing its power to bear on those names.

HOW TO USE THIS BOOK
TO ANALYZE NAMES

The information in this book is designed to teach you how to interpret and analyze names from the perspective of three of the most popular metaphysical systems used today: the

Kabbalah, the runes, and numerology. In the following sections you'll be given an overview of the process of working out an analysis of any name using methods from each of these systems so you can begin to work with the various meanings of your name and the names of other people in your life to learn more about how these names affect your life. With this basic information, you should also be able to begin a preliminary analysis of the meaning of your last name on the basis of the inherent meanings and numerical correspondences of its letters.

In part II you will find a comprehensive listing of interpretations for 718 of the most popular names in use today. One of the most fascinating aspects of name interpretation is the variety of results each system offers. While the three systems you read about in this book often complement one another, it is not uncommon for there to be significant differences in the interpretation of a name. You may want to weight more heavily the system of thought that seems most reflective of you and your personality. If you're doing your own basic name analysis with the information provided in this section, you'll be able to use these analyses to check your work. Keep in mind that much of the information you'll discover on your own about a name will be very personal, and your interpretation may include different nuances and meanings from the analyses in part II. That's not necessarily an indication that your work is incorrect as much as it may simply show that you've considered your current situation and personality traits when working on your own analysis. Each of us is subject to many influences that affect our personality and the way we express the energies of our name, so if you find that your name analysis in part II isn't a precise reflection of who you know yourself to be at this stage in your life, there's no reason to think that it is entirely inaccurate. If you carefully consider the details of the analysis, you should find that the general sense of the interpretation is an accurate picture of traits and characteristics that define your personality and behavior tendencies.

Consider again the name Alexander. A person named Alexander will tend to have strong leadership qualities as a primary personality trait, but if your name is Alexander and you don't happen to be an all-powerful military leader, it doesn't mean you've disgraced the power of that illustrious name! To find how your name's influence acts upon and shapes your character, you need to consider other areas in your life where you naturally bring leadership skills to bear. If you're a father, for example, are you doing your best to foster your child's character and good behavior? Are you leading by example or just by words and rules? Are you, in a positive and nurturing sense, the true head of your household? In your career, even if you aren't a manager or executive by title, do you often find yourself in situations where you're called upon to provide help or guidance to other people because of your skills and ability to lead others toward their own success? Remember that leadership is more than simply the act of taking charge and manipulating things to your own benefit. Leadership also involves helping others achieve their goals and facilitating success for the entire group; Alexander the Great may have been a pretty amazing fellow, but without a cadre of talented generals, he probably wouldn't have gone nearly as far.

With the extensive information available in part II, you'll have information at your disposal that will give you important insights into the character and personality of other people in your life. You will also have a tremendous selection to choose from when you need to find an appropriate name for a child or for yourself if you should decide to change your birth name. Remember that selecting a name is much more than simply picking a label with which to identify someone. A name carries great power in a person's life, influences his or her personality and development, and becomes part and parcel of a person's overall identity, for better or worse. The energies associated with a particular name can provide strength to bolster the confidence of someone who may naturally lack it, or further weaken someone who may be in need of additional strength. With a good name and an understanding of the meanings and energies behind that name, a person can make great strides toward improving his or her situation in life.

A KABBALISTIC SYNOPSIS
The Philosophy of Kabbalah

Kabbalah is the mystical philosophy of the Jewish religion that, according to tradition, traces its origins to biblical times. Historically, the movement known as Kabbalah can be traced to twelfth-century Europe, where great teachers such as Moses de Leon, Abraham Abulafia, and their followers spread the mystical teachings throughout Europe and the Middle East. These teachings were based primarily on the collection of writings known as the Zohar, but they were also influenced by a much earlier work called the Sefer Yetsirah, which is thought to have been written in Palestine between the third and sixth centuries. The Hebrew word *kabbalah* can be translated as "to receive" or "what has been received" and refers to both the spiritual knowledge revealed directly to the mystics by the divine spirit, and the secret traditions passed down through generations of mystics and teachers over the centuries. Kabbalah is a mystical system that allows adepts to receive the light of truth and inspiration directly from the mind of God if they follow a specific path of knowledge that leads to the clear apprehension of the divine.

According to kabbalistic tradition, the prophets of old were the first kabbalists because they received their knowledge and teachings via direct inspiration and communication with the divine spirit. For example, Moses was said to have met God "face-to-face" (Exod. 33:20; Deut. 34:10). He received great knowledge and wisdom directly from the divine spirit that was able to guide his people toward truth, righteousness, and ultimately, the Promised Land.

As the mystical traditions deepened and developed over the centuries, the ascent to the throne of God became so clearly defined that a follower of Kabbalah could be assured that the path was well marked. The Kabbalah ultimately systematized the mystical journey by combining elements of many different schools of thought and mysticism into a coherent, though complex, methodology. By expanding upon elements of the Sefer Yetsirah, the Zohar, which is considered the principal text of Kabbalah, presented a road map for the spiritual odyssey of an individual soul seeking to attain union with the divine. According to the Sefer Yetsirah, God created the universe by his manipulation of the twenty-two letters of the Hebrew alphabet and the ten *sephirot*, which are nodes on the mystical Tree of Life. The sephirot are treated in the text as living entities, elements of the divine personality of God that embody

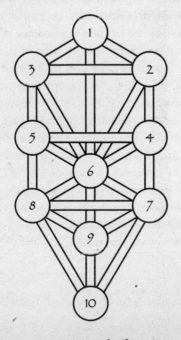

The Tree of Life

NAMES OF THE SEPHIROT

Sephirah	Hebrew Name	English Name	Personality and Psychological Traits
1	Kether	Crown	Highest self, transpersonal consciousness, union with the Supreme Being
2	Chockmah	Wisdom	Spiritual purpose, will, devotion
3	Binah	Understanding	Spiritual awareness, deeper knowledge
4	Chesed	Mercy	Love, kindness, mercy
5	Geburah	Judgment	Personal power, will
6	Tiphareth	Beauty	Self-identity, ego, personality, self-awareness
7	Netzach	Victory	Emotions, feelings
8	Hod	Splendor	Mind, intellect, thoughts
9	Yesod	Foundation	Sexuality, sexual energy, subconscious mind
10	Malkuth	World	Physical body, material aspect, the senses, external world

the metaphysical values of the numbers one through ten, and through which God emanates his presence down from the spiritual world of heaven into the physical world of matter. The letters of the Hebrew alphabet correspond to twenty-two "paths" that connect the various sephirot on the Tree of Life. The Zohar expands upon the idea of the sephirot and sees the Tree of Life not only as the means for the divinity to extend itself into the material world through the process of creation but also as a ladder for the mystic to climb back to the realm of God. Thus the Kabbalah, as expressed through its fundamental text, the Zohar, not only explains the creation of the universe but also offers the spiritual seeker a path to return to the source from which his or her life originated.

Because the divine being is seen as the fountainhead of all existence, the Kabbalah reveals the notion of the "oneness" of God in such a way as to assert that nothing in the universe exists except for the Godhead. Considered this way, all things in the universe are but aspects of the one God and exhibit the richness and potency of the creative nature of the divine spirit. And if all things are but aspects or expressions of the divine energy, then all things are intimately related to one another because they all share a common energy, which is the energy of God. In Kabbalah, these interrelations of things are known as correspondences. The correspondences include the numerical values and meanings of each sephirah as well as the mystical meanings of the twenty-two letters of the Hebrew alphabet. The letters, in turn, correspond to the twenty-two paths or connections between the ten sephirot on the Tree of Life. Thus, by understanding the meanings of the letters and numbers in the Tree of Life, one might be able to climb the Tree back to the source of all things. The table above shows the names of the sephirot by their number as displayed on the image of the Tree above. By using the techniques that follow, you'll learn to calculate the numerical value of your whole name as well as the individual letters in your name, and you'll be able to make associations between the energies of the sephirot and the numerical values of your name.

A Brief Introduction to the Mathematics of Your Name

According to kabbalists, because of the associations between the elements of the Tree of Life, the letters of the alphabet, and the corresponding numbers, an analysis of your name based on the numerical values of the letters composing that name will yield significant insight into your personality and deeper spiritual traits. With the ancient Hebrew system of letter and number analysis known as gematria you can not only discover the numerical value of your whole name but you can also associate your name to the paths between the sephirot on the Tree of Life by using the values of its individual letters as well as the reduced value of your whole name number. Gematria, in a nutshell, is the process of adding the numerical values of the letters in a word, name, or sentence to obtain the complete value of that word or collection of words. Once the number is known, correspondences can be drawn between that word's numeric value and other words with an equivalent numeric value to gain deeper insight into both words. For example, many Christian mystics use gematria to correspond the name Jesus to the name Adam. Checking the Hebrew letter table that follows (page 16), you can see that the name Jesus adds up to a total of 621 (Yod = 10 + He = 5 + Shin = 300 + Vau = 6 + Shin = 300), and the reduced value of 621 is 9 (6 + 2 + 1 = 9). The name Adam totals 45 (Aleph = 1 + Daleth = 4 + Mem = 40), and the reduced value of this is also 9 (4 + 5 = 9). Significantly, Jesus frequently referred to himself as the "Son of Man" in the texts of the New Testament, and Adam was, of course, the first man. Later in the book as you begin to study techniques of numerology, you'll be able discover some of the meanings of the number nine that will give you further insight into the meanings of this example.

Working with individual letters is also part of the science of gematria, and by corresponding the individual letters of your name to the various paths connecting the sephirot and the various meanings of individual Hebrew letters, you can deepen your understanding of the different cosmic and universal energies that bear an influence upon your life and personality. Keep in mind that the primary practice of gematria revolves around the process of making connections between your whole name, the letters of your name, and other words and symbols. The more connections you can find, the more insight and depth you can glean from your efforts to analyze your name. As you work through these sections, don't worry about which technique or method might be more valuable than another; simply remember that the process of making connections is the important part.

To find the numerical value of your name using gematria (as you saw in the example above), you'll first need to transliterate your name's letters into the equivalent letters in Hebrew. Using the following table that associates the Hebrew alphabet with the English, you can come up with your name's numeric value. Keep in mind that not every letter in English has a directly corresponding value in Hebrew, so you'll have to make adjustments. For example, some letters appear twice, such as the letter *j*. This can be resolved by finding the pronunciation of that letter that most clearly matches your name. For example, the name Johann is pronounced like "Yohan," so the *j* in this name would correspond to the letter Yod rather than Gimel. You'll also notice that some of the Hebrew letters correspond to sounds in English that are created by combining letters, as in *ch* or *sh*. In these cases use the appropriate sound for your name if it exists rather than combining letters as in English.

There is no straightforward route to transliteration for every name, for one of gematria's complexities lies in the absence of vowels from the Hebrew alphabet. In addition, certain letters share sounds. However, as a general rule one should rewrite the name in English in as simple and phonetic a manner as possible—so Christopher becomes Kristufa, for instance. We then look to see if we have superfluous vowel sounds. We can remove the second *a* in Adam, for instance. Finally, we replace the remaining letters with Hebrew. Where we have a choice of letters, we can either look at other words with similar phonetic structures for advice or, since this is an esoteric approach, we look at the effect on meaning of the alternatives. A combination of these approaches is often the best way to approach the situation.

The table that follows not only associates the Hebrew letters with the English but also indicates the corresponding paths on the Tree of Life so you can associate the letters of your name to the paths between the sephirot. It also provides a basic one- or two-word meaning as well as correspondences to the tarot cards if you wish to dig deeper into the possible meanings of the letters. You can check your transliteration by using the name references in part II of this book.

THE HEBREW LETTER TABLE AND THE
ENGLISH LETTER EQUIVALENTS

Hebrew Letter	Hebrew Name	Path	Number	English	Significance	Tarot Card
א	Aleph	1–2	1	A	thinker	Fool
ב	Beth	1–3	2	B, V	domestic	Magus
ג	Gimel	1–6	3	C, G, J	travel	High Priestess
ד	Daleth	2–3	4	D	opportunity	Empress
ה	Heh	2–6	5	E, H	observer/control	Emperor
ו	Vau	2–4	6	U, V, W	choice	Hierophant
ז	Zayin	3–6	7	Z	aggression/conflict	Lovers
ח	Cheth	3–5	8	Ch	defensive	Chariot
ט	Teth	4–5	9	T	revenge	Strength
י	Yod	4–6	10	I, J, Y	energy	Hermit
כ	Kaph	4–7	20	K	wise	Wheel of Fortune
ל	Lamed	5–6	30	L	driven/just	Justice
מ	Mem	5–8	40	M	caring	Hanged Man
נ	Nun	6–7	50	N	introspective	Death
ס	Samech	6–9	60	S	supportive	Temperance
ע	Ayin	6–8	70	O, Oo, Ou	business mind/athletic	Devil
פ	Peh	7–8	80	P, F	talkative/social	Tower
צ	Tzaddi	7–9	90	X, Tz	crafty/dogged	Star
ק	Qoph	7–10	100	Q	thinker (emotional)	Moon
ר	Resh	8–9	200	R	thinker (rational)	Sun
ש	Shin	8–10	300	Sh	judgmental/drive	Judgment
ת	Tau	9–10	400	T, Th	honest/altruistic	Universe

Many kabbalists attribute different number values to the "final forms" of certain letters. In Hebrew, some letters have a slightly different spelling or emphasis if they appear at the *end* of a word than if they appear at the beginning or middle of a word. The following table displays the values used for the letters listed when they appear at the end of a word or name.

VALUES FOR "FINAL FORM" LETTERS

Hebrew	Hebrew Name	Path	Number	English
ך	Kaph	4–7	500	K
ם	Mem	5–8	600	M
ן	Nun	6–7	700	N
ף	Peh	7–8	800	P
ץ	Tzaddi	7–9	900	X, Tz

Other correspondences you can work with involve the four primary elements, the planets, and the signs of the zodiac. You can learn much about the significance of a name by learning about the meanings of these different items as they appear in the individual letters of that name. The following tables list these correspondences:

THE ELEMENTS

Element	Hebrew	Name of Hebrew Letter	Personality Trait
Fire	ש	Shin	energetic, inventive, rash
Water	מ	Mem	emotional, caring, creative
Air	א	Aleph	intellectual, logical, organized
Earth	ת	Tau	physical, practical, homely

THE PLANETS

Planet	Hebrew	Name of Hebrew Letter	Personality Trait
Mercury	ב	Beth	quick-witted, communication
Moon	ג	Gimel	creativity, the supernatural
Venus	ד	Daleth	love, health issues
Jupiter	כ	Kaph	jovial, good fortune
Mars	פ	Peh	warlike, physically active
Sun	ר	Resh	paternal, generous
Saturn	ת	Tau	melancholy, family-centered

THE ZODIAC

Zodiac	Hebrew	Zodiac Sign
Heh	ה	Aries
Vau	ו	Taurus
Zayin	ז	Gemini
Cheth	ח	Cancer
Teth	ט	Leo
Yod	י	Virgo
Lamed	ל	Libra
Nun	נ	Scorpio
Samech	ס	Sagittarius
Ayin	ע	Capricorn
Tzaddi	צ	Aquarius
Qoph	ק	Pisces

By using these correspondences, you'll be able to explore ways in which your name relates to other words, and with this information you can draw parallels to your own life and personality. For example, consider the name Irv. The numerical value of this name when transliterated to Hebrew is 216 (Yod = 10 + Resh = 200 + Vau = 6). Other words that add up to 216 include the Hebrew word GBVRH, which means "strength," and the word ARIH, which means "lion." When you consider the connections between these different words, you can see that the traits of Irv include personal strength and tenaciousness. By finding associations like these among different words, you should be able to make connections between your name and other words that have the same numeric value. Of course, most people won't know the Hebrew words as used in this example, but if you use English words and transliterate them to Hebrew (as we've done earlier through the table on page 16), you should be able to find your own correspondences by using the techniques in the same manner. As you apply the same techniques of gematria to determine the numeric value of other words that are similar to the numeric value of your name, you'll learn more and more about the meanings of your name based on the meanings of words that have the same numeric value. The process of discovering these connections is perhaps the most exciting and interesting part of working with gematria, but the work requires effort and concentration. As you continue your practice of these techniques, however, you'll learn more about yourself each time you find a connection.

There are many ways to manipulate the numeric values of names in gematria, and each one brings added nuances of meaning to your name's significance. For instance, another way of interpreting the numeric value of a name consists of taking the total you've calculated for that name and then figuring out which other letters add up to that number. These other letters will also have an influence on you, and you'll need to study them to find just how they fit in with your personality. For example, consider the numeric value of the name Adrienne. To obtain its total value, first transliterate the name into Hebrew, then add the values of those letters as follows: Aleph + Daleth + Resh + Yod + Aleph + Nun (ADRYAN = 916, using the value of 700 for the letter Nun because it appears at the end of the name). The other letters in the alphabet that add up to 916 are Tzaddi (final form) + Yod + Vau. By understanding this equivalence, you can associate the letters Tzaddi, Yod, and Vau with the paths on the Tree of Life to discover even more influences on the life and personality of Adrienne. You could also work with the individual single digits that comprise the total value of your name. For Adrienne, these numbers are nine, one, and six, which are represented by the letters Teth, Aleph, and Vau, respectively. Each time you discover another letter, word, or combination of letters that adds up to the same numeric value as your name, you've in effect discovered another correspondence that may have influence on your personality. Your job as you find these many connections is to use your insight and intuition to see how the corresponding letters fit within the overall context of your personality and the other correspondences you've discovered for your name.

Yet another method of working with your name's numeric value is to reduce the total calculated value for your name into another number by adding the individual numbers together. This method was used in the example connecting the names Adam and Jesus earlier in this section. You can continue to reduce until you arrive at a single number in the range of one to ten (although ten can be further reduced to one) to find which sephirah corresponds to your name. Each value arrived at along the way as you reduce the number bears significance for your name's analysis. This method of reducing numeric values is also used in numerology, and you'll learn more about how that works later. To reduce the value for Adrienne, for example, you can add up the numbers that make up 916 as follows: $9 + 1 + 6 = 16$ and $1 + 6 = 7$. Once you've reduced your name's value to a single digit, you can associate that digit with a particular sephirah on the Tree of Life to see which of the nodes bears the most influence upon you by virtue of the reduced numeric value of your name. By using these methods as well as the other methods of analysis you learned earlier, you should be able to find additional equivalences for Adrienne by finding other words that reduce to these values.

The process of using gematria to determine the significance of your name can be quite complex, and there are many more ways to calculate the number value of your name in the kabbalistic system. This overview gives you a brief look at how to calculate these values using two or three commonly used approaches, but there are other ways to work with your name with gematria that you can learn more about by consulting some of the books that describe these techniques and many of the correspondences in greater detail. By "playing" with different methods of calculation and discovering connections between your name and other words, you'll have a means of gaining knowledge of the deeper workings of your spirit and psyche. Because one of the primary aspects of using gematria is doing as many permutations as possible to find all manner of correspondences, you should experiment with as many methods as you like to find different nuances of meaning that might have an influence in your life. While it may initially seem confusing to work with so many different techniques, you'll probably be surprised at all the things you can learn by trying some of them. If you find that you enjoy working with these techniques and want to learn more about Kabbalah, there are a number of books that provide much more detail about different analytical methods and correspondences. The primary techniques used to analyze names in this book involve transliterating a name into Hebrew, then analyzing the value of the number of the whole name as well as the numbers of each individual letter for their meanings. By considering the meaning of all these elements, you should be able to create your own basic name analyses using gematria. But remember that in many ways these techniques are quite open-ended. As you delve further into the use of Kabbalah for name analysis, you will probably want to consult other books for more information on additional correspondences and meanings to add more richness and depth to your interpretations.

Your Name and Your Health

The thirty-two elements in the Tree of Life (ten sephirot and twenty-two paths) can be corresponded to all manner of different things in the universe. For example, they can be associated with the signs of the zodiac, plants and herbs, the tarot cards, and even parts of the body.

Finding these correspondences and studying how they associate with the numeric values you've determined for your name will provide you with a wealth of information about the influences that affect you.

To find how the numeric values of your name correspond to these elements in the Tree of Life, you first need to work out the numbers for both the individual letters in your name and your whole name, as you learned above. If you come up with a number that is greater than 32, you can reduce that number by adding each single digit of that number together (as described earlier) until you arrive at a number that can be associated with an element on the Tree. Of course, you can further reduce double-digit numbers to make even more connections so that, for example, the number 25 can be further reduced to the number 7 (2 + 5 = 7). If your name reduces in this way to 25 and 7 respectively, you can see from the following chart (page 22) that you are influenced by both the path between sephirot 6 and 9 and also by the seventh sephirah itself. You should also examine the numbers of individual letters in your name to find their connections to the elements on the Tree as discussed in the previous sections. Of course, only you can determine, as you find more and more connections in this way, which influences are the strongest in your life. By working with different numbers and combinations of numbers, you'll find correspondences that you never may have considered, and the experience of discovering these connections can be a source of great fun as well as insight. Remember, an important aspect of using these techniques of name and word analysis is simply being able to find as many varied correspondences as possible by using different permutations of the names and letters. Each time you make a new connection, you'll find that your analysis takes on greater depth.

As an example of making a connection between the Tree and your name, consider again the name Alexander. Because you know from looking at the Hebrew alphabet table on page 16 that the value of the first letter is the number one, you know it corresponds to the sephirah known as Kether. Kether corresponds to your higher spirituality, intellect, and consciousness. With this knowledge, you should realize that one of the greatest influences on your life is your higher self, and you should work to improve your understanding of that aspect of your life and spirituality. By doing additional work with the name, you'll find that the numeric value for the full name Alexander is 300, based on the following transliteration:

Aleph = 1
Lamed = 30
Cheth = 8
Zayin = 7
Nun = 50
Daleth = 4
Resh = 200
(1 + 30 + 8 + 7 + 50 + 4 + 200 = 300)

The number 300 can be further reduced to 3 (3 + 0 + 0 = 3), which corresponds to the sephirah called Binah, whose influence is the right side of the head and the right brain, the area of the brain known to be the source of creativity and intuitive energy. For a person named Alexander, these two correspondences may indicate that more effort should be put toward developing spiritual, intuitive, and creative skills for which he already has a natural propensity.

Knowing the correspondences between the number values of your name, the Tree of Life and its energies, and your body's physical systems can help you keep your physical self in better condition. Although ignoring the energies that affect you because of your name won't necessarily cause you harm, you may leave yourself open to potential dangers or problems in the areas in which you are the most heavily influenced if you aren't aware of the fact that those energies play a powerful role in your destiny. For example, if your name reduces to one, you very likely have a powerful intellect and spirituality but may find that you often suffer from headaches. If your name reduces to six, you'll have more energies around the chest and heart areas. Depending on your personal circumstances, this may indicate either that you have a strong heart that needs very little extra effort to keep in shape, or that you have a vulnerability in your circulatory system that needs to be strengthened either by exercise or better dietary habits. Because each individual is entirely different, the energies that influence you in one way may influence someone else in an entirely different way, and only you can know if you have a strength or a weakness in a particular area. But by using these techniques, you can discover what physical aspects of your life need greater attention in one way or another, and you should be willing to do a bit of self-exploration as you discover them. Knowing what your strengths are or where potential weaknesses may appear gives you the ability to work out a health regimen that is built around this knowledge. By not working with the influences of the sephirot and paths that your name corresponds to, you may not be able to affect those areas of your life as directly or powerfully as you could if you knew about these connections and seriously considered the influences they bring to bear on you. However, if you choose to work with the strengths of the sephirot and the paths that your name is associated with, you can improve the energies in those areas and perhaps even avoid problems or heal them if they have already begun to appear.

The following table shows the correspondences between the sephirot, the paths between them, and the physical areas of the body with which they correspond. For more in-depth information about the connections between the elements of the Tree of Life and your physical systems, the book *The New Living Qabalah: A Practical Guide to Understanding the Tree of Life* (Rockport, MA: Element Books, 1995) by Will Parfitt will prove to be an excellent reference. Keep in mind that if the various numbers of your name (whole name as well as individual letters) correspond to paths between two sephirot, you are probably also affected to some degree by the energies of those two sephirot as well as the energies of the specific path that connects them. The more you work with gematria and the correspondences, the more you will find connections and associations that you should consider influential in your life and health. And as you work with the specific energies and the areas of your body that correspond to the various numeric values of your name, you will be able to improve the quality of your physical health by strengthening weak areas and taking advantage of your inherent strengths.

THE CONNECTIONS BETWEEN THE TREE OF LIFE
AND YOUR BODY

English Letter	Hebrew Letter	Number	Sephirah, Path	Physical Influence
		1	Kether	Top of the head, consciousness
		2	Chockmah	Left brain, left side of head
		3	Binah	Right brain, right side of head
		4	Chesed	Left shoulder, left adrenal gland
		5	Geburah	Right shoulder, right adrenal gland
		6	Tiphareth	Sternum, heart
		7	Netzach	Left hand, arm, and kidney
		8	Hod	Right hand, arm, and kidney
		9	Yesod	Sexual organs
		10	Malkuth	Base of spine, feet, lower body
A	Aleph	11	1–2	Left eye and ear, pituitary gland
B, V	Beth	12	1–3	Right eye and ear, pineal gland
C, G, J	Gimel	13	1–6	Backbone, spinal cord
D	Daleth	14	2–3	Nose, mouth
E, H	Heh	15	2–6	Left front of neck, arteries
U, V, W	Vau	16	2–4	Back of neck on left side
Z	Zayin	17	3–6	Right front of neck, veins
Ch	Cheth	18	3–5	Back of neck on right side
T	Teth	19	4–5	Breasts, chest, lymph, spleen
I, J, Y	Yod	20	4–6	Left upper back and sides, lung
K	Kaph	21	4–7	Left middle back and sides, rectum
L	Lamed	22	5–6	Right upper back and sides, lung
M	Mem	23	5–8	Right middle back and sides, large intestine
N	Nun	24	6–7	Left lower back, stomach
S	Samech	25	6–9	Solar plexus
O, Oo, Ou	Ayin	26	6–8	Right lower back, liver, gall bladder, pancreas
P, F	Peh	27	7–8	Middle abdomen, small intestine
X, Tz	Tzaddi	28	7–9	Lower abdomen, left side
Q	Qoph	29	7–10	Left leg, skeletal and muscular systems
R	Resh	30	8–9	Lower abdomen, right side
Sh	Shin	31	8–10	Right leg, skeletal and muscular systems
T, Th	Tau	32	9–10	Buttocks, perineum, bladder, skin

By using the tools of Kabbalah and gematria, you should be able to discover hundreds of associations between the different alphabetic and numeric values in your name and other words, phrases, and names. For practice, try working with names other than your own, and check your discoveries against the interpretations provided in part II. If you continue to develop your skills, you will find that you'll be able to work out numeric values for words almost by intuition, and that connections will appear more quickly and easily. As you improve your ability to find numeric correspondences among different things, you'll be amazed at the different ways you can apply the basic techniques you've learned so far. The more you practice these techniques, the more your insight into the web of interrelations among all things will grow, and you'll soon start finding connections you would never even have thought to consider before. The following is a worksheet you can fill out with the connections you start uncovering.

KABBALISTIC NAME WORKSHEET

Name	Hebrew Letters	Number Value	Reduced Numbers	Sephirot/Path	Personality Correspondences for Letters	Physical Body Correspondences
Andy	Aleph (1), Nun (50), Daleth (4), Yod (10)	1 + 50 + 4 + 10 = 65	6 + 5 = 11, 1 + 1 = 2	Path between first and second sephirot, Chockmah (second sephirah)	Thinker, logical, intellectual, organized, introspective, Scorpio, opportunity, love, health issues, energy, Virgo	Top of head, left side of head, and left brain

THE RUNIC INTERPRETATION

The Hebrew language is by no means the only one whose letters are considered symbolic and meaningful. However, certain languages and alphabets, such as ancient Egyptian, Hebrew, Sanskrit, and the Futhark, have long been considered exceptional because of their inherent symbolic value and historical use in religious and magical rites and rituals. By translating English-language words into the characters and words of these special languages, you can analyze the meaning of the words more readily because of the inherent symbolism of the letters of these alphabets. Thus, with a method such as gematria that requires you to transliterate your name into Hebrew, you can find correspondences that you would never discover using the English letters. Similarly, you can transliterate your name into any of these other symbolic languages to gain additional insight into the hidden meanings that may be contained within that name.

One alphabet that is now widely used for the purposes of divination, name analysis, and self-discovery is the Futhark, which is the name commonly used to refer to the letters or symbols known as the runes. Although there are different runic alphabets in existence, the most popular alphabet is known as the Germanic Futhark or the Elder Futhark. The Elder Futhark is a collection of twenty-four very simple symbols or letters that are made up of adjoining straight lines, as well as a twenty-fifth "blank" rune that represents that which is unknowable and inexpressible. Historically runes were most often carved into wood or stone or etched into metal pieces, and only rarely, if ever, written on paper or parchment. Individual runes were carved onto flat stones or pieces of wood that could then be "cast" for purposes of divination. Different materials such as birch, ash, and oak empowered the runes with different strengths. When used as an oracle, rune stones or sticks were thrown to the ground or onto special pieces of cloth and then interpreted by shamans or runemasters who intuitively grasped the significance and meaning of the symbols because of their long practice with them.

A History of Runes

The origins of the runes are lost in an obscure history that, nonetheless, can be traced back at least as far as 200 B.C.E., and possibly much further. The Celtic runes, for example, are believed to date back to the Bronze Age. Evidence of the use of runes extends throughout Europe, from as far north as Iceland to as far south as the Mediterranean Sea. Scholars have proposed many theories about their origins, though no certainty as yet exists as to how or by whom they were first developed. Some suggest that the language is based on Greek, Latin, or some other early Italic script that moved north with groups of wanderers as they traveled throughout the European continent. However, although evidence of rune carvings has been found as far south as Romania and southern Austria, most runic evidence that has been discovered exists in the northern parts of Europe in countries such as England and Germany, and throughout Scandinavia. This geographical evidence has led to other theories that connect the runes with a much earlier form of inscribed communication known as the *hällristningar*. This "script" is actually a collection of pictorial symbols that were carved into rocks as early as 1300 B.C.E. and were probably used for ritual purposes.

Though the precise origins of the runes may never be known, the most plausible scenario is that the runes developed and changed over time as cultures that used certain alphabetic systems came into contact with other societies with different forms of written communication. This idea is supported by the fact that different sets of runes developed in different countries over the centuries. By the Middle Ages, there were English, Celtic, German, and Viking rune alphabets. Each contained different combinations of letters, with some alphabets containing as many as fifty-four letters and others containing as few as sixteen. In addition, various uses of the symbols probably developed over time as they evolved from strictly practical tokens used for commerce and communication to quasi-religious symbols that were used for divination and ritual purposes. In contrast, the collection of symbols known as the hällristningar is generally believed to have always been used for ritual purposes.

Despite their ambiguous history, the fact remains that the runes, in the forms known to us today, served the dual purpose of being both a practical and a spiritual language. Inscriptions found on stone monuments and excavated wooden tablets throughout Europe indicate that runes were a widely used means of communication for such mundane purposes as merchants' inventories, letters, and almanacs. Of course, magical uses were quite common as well, and many rune stones are inscribed with magical spells and religious or cultic stories and poetry. Each rune is not only a single letter that can be used in combination with other letters to form words, but is also a complete word in itself, as you'll see from the following table (page 26). Because each letter had a complete meaning and literally contained and manifested the power of that meaning, it could be inscribed onto a talisman or an amulet that would impart its power to the bearer of that charm. Magical spells composed of combinations of letters were used in rituals to invoke the assistance of the gods, inscribed on weapons of war to bring victory to the warrior, and carved into gravestones to assure the peaceful journey of souls in the afterlife.

Runes became such an important part of the life of northern European societies because of their use as a practical means of communication as well as their magical and religious value that those who knew the runic languages were in tremendous demand. Two primary classes of skilled workers who were proficient with the runes arose to fill that need. The first class was the runemaster class, and it was this group of people that possessed the most in-depth knowledge of the runes and their meanings. Runemasters not only knew how to carve their own runes, but they also understood how to use runic grammar for various types of contracts and documents. The runemasters also knew the hidden, magical meanings of the runes, and for this reason they were both respected and feared as shamanlike figures who could manipulate the powers of the natural world and bring either blessings or curses down upon their people. The second class of rune experts were known as runecutters. This group could read runic inscriptions and were skilled in the physical techniques of actually carving rune symbols into wood, stone, or metal. They were frequently called upon to engrave messages for people who were not able to read or write but who did not need the specialized skills of the runemaster. Of course, the wealthy and well-educated people might also have possessed reading and carving skills appropriate to his or her station in life, but the specialist classes were very much a part of the ancient northern European cultural elite.

Mythical Origins

Of course, if you had the opportunity to ask a Viking from the third century whence the runes originated, you'd get an entirely different story from the rough historical outline given here. The legend of the discovery of the runes is associated with the god Odin, who was one of the primary gods in Norse mythology, the "father god" who dwelled in the heavenly mansion known as Valhalla. Depicted as tall and thin with a patch over one eye, Odin is a healer and a trickster who can fly. He corresponds to the Hanged Man in the tarot deck. Odin was also the father of the great Thor, god of thunder and protector of the universe. The story of the runes' origin comes to us through the collection of poems known as the Poetic Edda that dates from about 1000–1200 C.E. According to one of the stories in the Poetic Edda, Odin sought to find wisdom and the knowledge of life and death by offering himself as a sacrifice to himself. He wounded himself with his own sword, then hung upside down from the cosmic world-tree known as Yggdrasil as an act of initiation and self-sacrifice. Odin remained suspended from the tree for nine nights without food or drink until, at the culmination of his lengthy torment, he had a vision of the runes, which he was able to seize just before falling from the tree to his freedom. His sacrifice earned him not only wisdom and knowledge of the runes but also strength, well-being, and great power. Because the word *rune* means "whisper" or "secret," it was clear to the ancient northern consciousness that Odin was the possessor and master of the great mysteries contained within the runes. For this reason he was the patron of all runemasters and runecutters, and hardly a rune would be cut without a prayer or gift being offered to Odin.

A Guide to the Futhark

The word *futhark* is derived from the first few letters of the runic alphabet just as our word *alphabet* is derived from the first two letters of the Greek alphabet (alpha + beta). The Elder Futhark or Germanic Futhark is the most popular of the runic alphabets used today, and will therefore be the alphabet you'll work with the most in this book, as well as if you choose to pursue additional study of the runes. If you look at the runic alphabet in the following figure, you'll see how the word *futhark* was derived from the letters themselves:

THE RUNIC ALPHABET

Runic Group	Specific Runes							
FREYR'S AETT								
Name	Fehu	Uruz	Thurisaz	Ansuz	Raido	Kano	Gebo	Wunjo
English Letter	(F or V)	(U or W)	(Th)	(A)	(R)	(C, K, or Q)	(G)	(W)
HAGAL'S AETT								
Name	Hagalaz	Nauthiz	Isa	Jera	Eihwaz	Perth	Algiz	Sowelu
English Letter	(H)	(N)	(I)	(J)	(Y)	(P)	(X or Z)	(S)
TYR'S AETT								
Name	Teiwaz	Berkana	Ehwaz	Mannaz	Laguz	Inguz	Othila	Dagaz
English Letter	(T)	(B)	(E)	(M)	(L)	(Ng)	(O)	(D)

Runes could be read from left to right, right to left, vertically, or even back and forth from one row to the next in the manner of an animal plowing a field. For magical purposes, the Futhark was divided into three groups of eight runes each, with each group being dedicated to a particular deity, and the twenty-fifth or blank rune standing apart on its own. This division is important primarily because of the sacred and magical significance of the numbers three and eight in early northern cultures. The groups are called *aettir*, which means a number of things, including family, gender, lineage, and, quite simply, the number eight. Though each aett was protected or influenced by a specific god, the overall collection of runes was nevertheless always under the control of the chief god, Odin.

The aettir possessed powerful qualities derived from the attributes of the gods from which they were named, in addition, of course, to the meanings of the individual letters themselves. Freyr, the god of the first aett, was the potent god of fertility and the summer sunshine. The runes in Freyr's aett therefore represent qualities of growth, fertility, increase, and the emergence of new life. Hagal (or Heimdal), the god of the second aett, was the guardian of the rainbow-bridge that led from the earth to Asgard, the realm of the gods where the great palace of Valhalla was located. Because of Hagal's rulership of the expanse between heaven and earth, his aett is associated with the four elements from which everything in the world was created. The third aett is named for Tyr, who was the great god of war and battle. Tyr was the "general of the gods" who was responsible for courageously leading them in their battles. For this reason, the third aett represents courage and strength in the face of adversity. As you work through this section and begin to analyze your name by transliterating it into the runes and working with the meanings of the individual letters, don't forget that you'll need to be aware of the meanings of the aettir and how they influence the meanings of the letters in your name. Consider that if you have multiple occurrences of the same letters in your name, for example, you will need to work with the influence of the aett from which those letters are derived, as well as the influence of the individual letters making up your name.

To analyze your name using the runes, then, first work out a translation using the rune chart above. You may want to analyze the letters in your name from right to left (as we do throughout this book), which was the most common usage. Once you've got the transliteration down, you can look over the general pattern of runes that make up your name to see, first of all, whether you have a strong influence from one or more of the aettir due to multiple occurrences of particular letters. Then use the meanings and interpretations below to work through each letter to get a broad sense of all the different influences that play upon your life. As you analyze the letters that make up your name, you will notice patterns among the different meanings and interpretations that will paint an overall "picture" of your name's influence on your life and personality. By working with these interpretations and by striving to understand how they complement or contradict one another, you'll find relationships between the letters that will provide you with insight into the power of your name.

Runic Meanings and Interpretations

Rune	Literal Meaning	Divinatory Interpretation
Fehu	Cattle, possessions, material gain	Prosperity, financial success, increase in possessions or resources, fulfillment of a dream, nourishment
Uruz	Aurochs (oxlike animal, now extinct)	Physical strength and speed, power in both the physical sense and the spiritual sense, new opportunities
Thurisaz	Giant, troll, thorn	Challenge or conflict that leads to change; aggression, difficulties, unreliability
Ansuz	God or deity (usually Odin)	Spiritual strength; religious sensibilities, blessings, and inspiration
Raido	Cart, chariot, wheel	Journeys or travel both in the literal sense and in the inner, spiritual sense. Movement, changes in location or attitudes
Kano	Torch, light, bonfire	Opening, enlightenment, breakthrough, or success; a new understanding or positive energy, the "light at the end of the tunnel"
Gebo	Gift	Gifts, generosity, abundance, new relationships or partnerships
Wunjo	Joy, happiness, bliss, glory	Pleasure, enjoyment, or joy with the potential of excess; success, happiness, domestic and marital bliss
Hagalaz	Hail (noun form)	Difficult or unexpected circumstances, possibly related to the weather; also concerns disruptive influences or delays both internal and external
Nauthiz	Need, constraint, necessity	Financial or emotional strain, insufficient resources, work issues
Isa	Ice	Psychological, emotional, or financial blockage, stress in relationships or separation; Isa also reinforces the meaning of runes adjacent to it
Jera	Harvest	Fulfillment of previous efforts, success, culmination of a vision, good fortune and reward for hard work, completion
Eihwaz	Yew tree	Motivation, ambition, progress in carrying out plans; power to avoid troubles and overcome obstacles, forward movement
Perth	Initiation, womb, female fertility	Warmth and comfort, creativity and generative energy, inner transformation or secret wisdom
Algiz	Defense, protection	Shelter, protection, and healing; the ability to keep what one has gained
Sowelu	Sun, wholeness, life force	Good health, positive energy and circumstances, harmony; spiritual strength, clarity and understanding, love
Teiwaz	The god Tyr, war, victory at war	Leadership, power and authority, success in overcoming conflicts or adversaries, clarity of purpose

Rune	Literal Meaning	Divinatory Interpretation
Berkana	Birch tree, fertility, vigor, growth	Prosperity, fertility, personal growth and spiritual consciousness; also newness, change, or regeneration
Ehwaz	Horse	Social status, improvements in one's personal situation, transitions, steady progress; strongly influences meanings of adjacent runes
Mannaz	Mankind, human being	Personal relationships, interactions; one's self-image as well as the opinions of others about oneself
Laguz	Water, lake, ocean	Material or financial issues, whether success or failure. Overseas travel or journeys by boat. Also relates to psychic abilities or spiritual matters
Inguz	Male fertility	Family, procreation, creative energy, positive change and growth, new beginnings
Othila	Inheritance	Inheritance or financial well-being, property, family heritage, traditional values; also concerns marriage and children as well as spirituality or your "inner home"
Dagaz	Day, daylight, breakthrough	Clarity, certainty, security, enlightenment; enthusiasm for new projects or adventures, planning

Keep in mind that the meanings for the letters and the divinatory interpretations given above are frameworks for you to use as you analyze the letters of your name. Also remember that adjacent runes tend to influence each others' meaning so that if you have a rune meaning "strength" next to one meaning "prosperity," you can assume that you will have powerful financial influences in your life that may ultimately guide you to an experience of prosperity if you can harness those energies and pursue an appropriate life path.

As an example of using the runes to analyze a name, consider the name Adam. This is a simple, four-letter name that should be easy enough to work with as a starting point. First of all, from the chart above you can easily determine that the transliteration of the name appears thus: Mannaz, Ansuz, Dagaz, Ansuz. First off, you'll notice that the letter Ansuz appears twice in the name and that it is also the first letter of the name, thus giving it greater overall influence on the name than the other letters. Ansuz is a member of Freyr's aett and, as you'll recall, this family of eight runes relates particularly to qualities of growth, fertility, increase, and the emergence of new life. Interestingly, Adam is the name given in the biblical creation story to the first man created by God, and so the dual appearance of Ansuz along with this biblical correspondence indicates very powerfully that Adam represents newness, fertility, and growth, and is heavily influenced by these energies. Ansuz by itself relates to spirituality and inspiration, so with this letter appearing twice, it should be clear that Adam will be a very creative person with lofty goals both in terms of spiritual attainment and material accomplishments. Dagaz, which is surrounded by the powerful creative and spiritual energy of Ansuz, indicates clarity and certainty, as well as enthusiasm for plans and projects. Of course, with this energy being surrounded by Ansuz, we can see that Adam is likely to be somewhat ambitious and will aspire to great achievements both on the spiritual and the material levels. With the final letter of Mannaz, we again encounter a correspondence linking Adam to the biblical story of creation. In its broadest sense, Mannaz means "mankind" or "humanity" and thus is entirely appropriate as a letter in the name of the first man. Mannaz also relates to interpersonal relationships as well as one's relationship to oneself. By combining the creative and spiritual strength in the energies of the first three letters of the name Adam with the social aspects of Mannaz, we find that Adam will very likely be a good, strong leader who can bring balance to his authority and guide others toward fulfilling the plans and goals he has designed. Overall, Adam will be a person of lofty objectives and principles, and these strengths will guide him throughout his lifetime.

Relation to the Elements

If you're even the slightest bit familiar with ancient history, you're well aware that most ancient societies believed there were four primary elements—earth, air, fire, and water—from which all material things were created. Each element had specific properties and characteristics that determined its behavior and influence upon other things. Although every object was composed of a blend of the four elements, it also had a primary element whose energies dominated the qualities of that thing. People were associated with the elements by virtue of their behavior or personality, and each astrological sign corresponded to one of the elements as well. Because the elements were such an important part of the nature of the universe, nearly everything could, in some way, be corresponded to them. By discovering the primary elements from which something was created, one could gain tremendous insight into its fundamental nature.

In addition to the fact that Hagal's aett was broadly associated with all the elements, each individual rune in the whole Futhark corresponded to one or more of the elements as well. Because most of the runes have a number of possible interpretations and corresponding energies, some of them can correspond to more than one element simply because they bear the energies of both. In the context of a name reading, you should be able to tell which element is the most influential because of the effect of the surrounding runes and the general interpretation of the runic meaning of the name. But if a rune has two elemental connections, you should still take both of them into account when analyzing a name containing such a rune. For example, if a rune corresponds to both fire and water, the power of the fire element might be somewhat subdued or (literally) dampened by the power of the water. However, if a rune has both air and fire connections, then the power of both will be increased because fire is strengthened and increased by air. The table below indicates the general influences and meanings of the elements and corresponds the appropriate runes to each element.

CONNECTIONS OF THE ELEMENTS TO THE RUNES

Element	Meaning or Energy	Associated Runes
Earth	Groundedness, stability, material possessions or money, strong foundations	Eihwaz, Uruz, Wunjo, Berkana, Othila, Isa, Jera
Air	Intellect, judgment, rationality, activity, action and energy, dispassion	Ansuz, Teiwaz, Berkana, Ehwaz, Algiz, Sowelu, Mannaz
Fire	Creative energy, life force, momentum, potentiality	Dagaz, Othila, Fehu, Thurisaz, Nauthiz, Eihwaz
Water	Intuition, emotion, matters of the heart, secret wisdom, passive energy	Kano, Perth, Laguz, Inguz, Raido, Gebo, Hagalaz

In part II of this book, you will see that both elements are listed for those runes that have two elemental connections.

In using the runes to analyze and interpret your name, you will discover a great deal about yourself by simply working with the combinations of letters from which your name is assembled. By combining the meanings of the aettir with those of the individual runes and their elements, you will be able to create a complete interpretation of a person's general character on the basis of his or her name. As you become more fluent in the use of the runes for name analysis, the patterns and interactions among the different meanings will become much easier to find and understand, and soon you'll have no trouble using the runes to create complex personality profiles from the simple knowledge of someone's name. As you continue this process of discovery, don't forget to take advantage of the techniques of kabbalistic name analysis you've already learned. With these two methods, in addition to the numerological method about which you'll learn momentarily, you'll have a complete set of tools for creating detailed interpretations of the hidden meanings and nuances of any name.

The more you work with the runes, the more you will discover their power and their ability to reveal hidden truths to you. Because of the traditional uses of the runes for magic using casting cloths, however, a word of caution is in order. Although many runemasters use the runes for ritual or magical purposes such as amulets or talismans, you must respect the fact that if you aren't well versed in all the details and implications of using the runes for such purposes, you should not engage in these kinds of activities. Many people ascribe tremendous power to the runes, and if you attempt to cast spells, do healings, or work other feats of power, you should know you may be playing with fire. As an example, imagine that you know someone who is sick, so you decide you want to create a rune amulet to bring healing and strength back to that person. You might choose Sowelu and Perth for your charm because of their associations with health, vitality, growth, and the like. However, because there are very specific ways to use the runes for healing, you may end up making the sick person worse and strengthening or adding additional vitality to the disease by using these runes! In short, if you are interested in working with rune spells and ritual applications of the runes, you should proceed with extreme caution and make sure to study the details of these uses in depth. If possible, consult with someone who is already adept at using the runes before you venture out into the unknown. The runes are not only excellent tools for gaining wisdom and insight, but they are considered by many to be instruments of tremendous power. It is in your best interest to respect that power and steer clear of uses that might make you vulnerable to forces beyond your control.

The following is a worksheet for you to use as you come to understand the connections of the runes with your name or that of others.

RUNIC NAME WORKSHEET

Name	Runic Letters	Influential Aettir	Elements	Primary Meanings
Bill	Berkana, Isa, Laguz, Laguz	Tyr's aett (three letters), Hagal's aett (one letter)	Air/earth, earth, water, water	Leadership, intuition, prosperity, emotion, intellect, action .

THE NUMEROLOGICAL INTERPRETATION

Another popular and powerful method of gaining insight into your name and personality is numerology, the systematic study of numbers and their meanings and interrelationships. Similar in many ways to gematria, numerology assigns a unique numeric value to each letter of the alphabet (whether that alphabet is the English, Greek, Hebrew, or any other doesn't matter because each one will have its own numeric correspondences) and then analyzes the numeric values of the individual letters and the combined letters in a word or name, based on the different meanings of each number. The philosophy of numerology, just as with Kabbalah and the runes, is that all things in the world are interrelated and nothing occurs simply by chance. That you were born at a particular time, in a particular place, and were given a certain name when you came into the world is seen in this philosophy as much more than a series of interesting coincidences. The particulars of your birth and your name are unique aspects of your existence that stamp an indelible mark upon your life and that create the initial influences under which you grow and develop. Thus, if you understand the hidden meanings of your name and your time of birth, you can gain significant insight into your character and personality. To find these hidden meanings, of course, you need to take advantage of the techniques designed to provide access to these truths, and numerology is one of these techniques.

A History of Numerology

The science of numerology is extremely ancient, and different numerological systems can be traced to the beginnings of nearly every culture in the world. The Egyptians, Babylonians, Assyrians, Greeks, Hindus, and, of course, the Hebrews, all developed complex numerological systems based on the belief that wisdom and knowledge of the nature of the universe could be derived from studying the numeric values and correspondences of all existing things. Modern numerology takes bits and pieces of many of these systems and combines them into a comprehensive structure that corresponds numbers to specific meanings. Western numerology developed primarily from the Hebrew methods of gematria and the Pythagorean techniques of analyzing the meanings of individual numbers. From gematria came the idea and methodology of corresponding letters to specific numbers. Just as each letter in the Hebrew alphabet was associated with a particular number, so could the letters of other alphabets be associated with numbers and then analyzed. By finding the numbers of things through the application of gematria or similar number-letter correspondences, the nature of things could be understood more clearly and hidden wisdom brought to light.

From Pythagoras came the notion that each number not only possessed meaning as a measurement of quantity, but also had intrinsic meaning that represented a broad range of philosophical, psychological, and cosmological concepts that could be applied to things on the basis of their numeric values. Pythagoras is considered by many to be the greatest philosopher of numbers in history. He is known as the father of geometry, and is in many ways the father of numerology. Even during his lifetime Pythagoras was revered and honored as a sage, and his philosophical ideas had tremendous influence on science, mathematics, and philosophy for centuries after his death. Plato, one of the greatest Greek philosophers, was so greatly influenced by the ideas of Pythagoras that many elements of Pythagorean thought that have survived the ages have come down to us through the works of Plato.

According to Pythagoras, everything in the universe could be reduced to numbers, and the fundamental nature of all things could then be explained by understanding these numbers. For example, Pythagoras was the first to discover the relationship between numbers and sound. In his experiments he found that the octaves were related to each other in the ratio of 2 to 1. He further postulated that everything in the universe emitted a certain vibration or sound and that each planet and each star produced a different sound depending on its distance from the center of the universe, around which all things revolved. These sounds were referred to as "the music of the spheres," and the combined sounds of all the objects in the universe were thought to produce a musical harmony that was a reflection of the perfection and order of the universe. The music of the spheres was also believed to affect the lives of individuals on earth, and the particular tone or vibration of the universe at the moment of a person's birth was said to influence that person's destiny and character for the rest of his or her life. By knowing the numbers of a person's birth, that destiny could be discovered and embraced because each number contained within itself a deep significance that would open the secrets of the universe to anyone who could learn and understand that meaning.

Most of the additional developments in numerology that took place over the centuries following the discoveries of Pythagoras were enhancements of his original findings. For example, occultists and philosophers over the centuries worked out additional correspondences and details of the connections between numbers and philosophical or magical concepts. In addition, different systems that relied on the meanings of numbers, such as the Pythagorean system and the Hebrew system of gematria, were combined through the efforts of philosophers, alchemists, scientists, and occultists throughout Europe. Renaissance magicians such as Henry Cornelius Agrippa (ca. 1486–1555) worked out complex theories of the correspondences between numbers and the physical body, many of which were enhancements of and additions to the much earlier theories of Pythagoras himself. And in the late nineteenth century and the early part of the twentieth century, a resurgence of interest in magic and occultism led to the formation of secret societies that did much to further the use of numbers and numerology as tools of divination and magic. One of the most influential of these societies was the Order of the Golden Dawn, whose members explored such systems as Kabbalah, the tarot, and numerology in a further attempt to uncover the mysteries of the universe. Ultimately, however, the greatest contribution to the philosophy of numerology must be credited to the ancient master, Pythagoras himself.

A Guide to the Key Numbers

Numerologists typically work with only the single-digit numbers from one to nine and the so-called "master numbers," eleven and twenty-two. To arrive at a single-digit number on the basis of a word or name, a technique is used in which numbers are reduced to single digits or one of the master numbers. To reduce the numeric value of a name to a single digit, you simply add the numbers of the letters of a name repeatedly until you end up with a single digit, as you learned in the discussion of gematria. The first step, of course, is to associate the letters of the alphabet with numbers. Though there are different methods for doing this, the most commonly used simply associates the letters of the alphabet in their normal order with the numbers one through nine, as shown in the following table.

INDIVIDUAL LETTERS AND THEIR NUMERIC EQUIVALENTS

1	2	3	4	5	6	7	8	9
A	B	C	D	E	F	G	H	I
J	K	L	M	N	O	P	Q	R
S	T	U	V	W	X	Y	Z	

To reduce a name value to a single digit, you first correspond the letters of that name to their appropriate numbers. So, for example, if the name you're working with is Mary, you find the numeric values in the table to be the following: M = 4, A = 1, R = 9, Y = 7. Then you add these values to come up with a total value: 4 + 1 + 9 + 7 = 21. Because the number twenty-one is neither a single digit nor a master number (eleven or twenty-two, which are usually not reduced further for reasons you'll learn about momentarily), you can further reduce the number by adding the two and the one to arrive at a value of three. Thus, for the first name Mary, the whole-name numeric value is three. As you'll see later, you can work with not only the whole-name value but also the reduced value of the vowels in the name as well as the reduced value of the consonants in the name. Each of these methods will give you a different level of insight into the meaning of the name you are working with.

Once you've reduced the name value to a single digit, you can begin working with the meanings of the numbers to arrive at a character analysis of the name you are examining. Use the interpretations given in the section below to begin working with numerical values. As you work more with numerology, you may want to consult additional references to find more in-depth discussions of the meanings of each number. When you've gotten the sense of a name from a number arrived at by reducing the whole-name value, you can start working with variant methods of analysis such as the vowel value, the consonant value, and the first-letter value.

Number One

The number one represents the beginning or the origin of all things. As such, it is associated with God or the First Principle of the universe that sets all things in motion. One is the creative principle of the divine spirit, a number that represents unity, wholeness, and self-sufficiency. One is also the representation of masculine energy because according to Pythagoras, all odd numbers reflect masculine, active, creative qualities. One can also indicate aggression, which can be either positive or negative, depending on the circumstances and the way it is expressed. Individuals influenced by the number one as their primary or whole-name number are often outgoing, aggressive, and achievement oriented. Ones are leaders and typically have very dynamic and expressive personalities that enable them to accomplish much. On the negative side, ones can occasionally be obstinate and overbearing, so care must be taken to balance the aggression with thoughtfulness.

Number Two

Two represents duality, polarity, and the interaction of opposites. Two is also an expression of feminine energy, as the even numbers were considered by Pythagoras to reflect feminine, receptive qualities. Because of the influence of opposing forces in the number two, people whose names resonate to the number two are good at reconciling and negotiating between conflicting interests. Unlike ones, who are outgoing and aggressive, twos are compromising, passive, and more likely to follow than to lead. This can have both positive and negative consequences, of course; being too passive can not only leave one vulnerable to abuse, but it can also make for a passive-aggressive personality. The number two also represents creativity, because the joining of the opposites (as in male and female, for example) creates a third element as the result of the union.

Number Three

The number three represents the completion or fulfillment of the union of opposites expressed in the two. Thus, threes represent family and family values. Three also symbolizes time because of the threefold nature of time as we understand it, which includes the past, the present, and the future. Three is a sacred mystical number in nearly all cultures, and Pythagoras himself considered three to be a number of perfection. In Christianity, three represents the Trinity or the threefold nature of God and therefore also represents heaven and the ethereal realms. Those under the primary influence of the number three tend to be assertive and generally positive people with a good deal of luck on their side. On the negative side, the assertiveness of the three can become brusque, and this bluntness can lead to trouble if not controlled.

Number Four

The number four is also a sacred number. Four represents stability, foundations, solidity, the earth, and the four elements. According to Pythagoras, four is the number of equilibrium and balance. People who resonate to the energy of four are therefore very reliable, stable individuals who can be counted on to be efficient, well organized, calm, and respectable. Fours are certainly not impulsive, and they usually think things through carefully before embarking on a course of action. On the negative side, the four can be dull or slow, and even boring if the energies of stability and solidity are not balanced with the more creative fire.

Number Five

Five represents the material world, humanity, the five senses, instability, or distraction. Unlike four, which has stability and foundation as its primary characteristics, the five includes an additional destabilizing element that makes it representative of uncertainty and chance rather than the certainty of the four. However, as a masculine number, five represents activity and energy. People under the primary influence of the five tend to be adventurous and willing to try new things. Because of the apparent unstable nature of this number, people who resonate to five are also risk takers who are willing to take chances that others might consider unwise. But fives are resilient and can bounce back from any failure their impulsive nature might cause them.

Number Six

Six represents health, the restoration of the balance lost by the five, equilibrium, and harmony. Although six is a feminine number because it is even, there is an androgynous quality about this number because it is divisible by both an even number (two) and an odd number (three). Six combines aspects of feminine and masculine energies and is thus considered a perfect number and a number of harmony. Because of the combination of the energies of both odd and even numbers, sixes tend to be very creative and artistically oriented but also willing to take action to accomplish goals. Balance and harmony surround the six in much the same way as the four but without the negative tendency toward inertia or dullness that can sometimes afflict the four. However, on the negative side, if the desire for harmony in all things becomes excessive, sixes may become nitpicky or fastidious, and this may strain their relationships.

Number Seven

The number seven is one of the most significant numbers in nearly every religion and spiritual system, and can be found in sacred writings and teachings throughout the world. Seven represents spirituality, mysticism, perfection, order, and good fortune. There is also an element of the union of opposites in seven because it is the result of adding three, the number of the heavens, with four, the number of the earth. People under the primary influence of seven are often endowed with psychic abilities and tend to be very interested in spirituality and mysticism. They are also inclined toward artistic pursuits, and they are usually very intuitive and prone to thinking and meditation. Although sevens are usually empathetic because of their sensitivity and depth of feeling, the negative side of their nature can lead to aloofness, moodiness, or depression because of their potential to become entirely too wrapped up in their own thoughts and feelings.

Number Eight

The qualities of the number eight include regeneration, stability, new life, eternity, and the cycle of time. According to the ancient Greeks, eight represented justice because each time it was halved, it would continually result in two equal parts: the eight halves to four, the four to two, and the two to one. Eight also signifies equilibrium and balance not only because of its behavior when halved but also because its very appearance consists of two equal circles adjoining along a vertical axis. Eight is a number that indicates materialism and worldly interests for those who are influenced by it. People under the influence of the number eight tend to exhibit extremes in terms of their material success, either possessing a great deal of good fortune or none at all. However, another of the characteristics of eights is tenacity and the willingness to keep trying, which, in the positive sense, can lead to success for those whose luck isn't the best, but in the negative sense can lead to hardheadedness and the continuance of difficulties because of an unwillingness to move on to better things.

Number Nine

Nine is the final number of the single digits and therefore represents completion and fulfillment. As the embodiment of three sets of three, nine is also a very mystical number that is associated with the heavens and with spirituality. Another interesting property of the number nine is that when it is multiplied by any other number, it can always be reduced back to nine (e.g., $3 \times 9 = 27, 2 + 7 = 9; 37 \times 9 = 333, 3 + 3 + 3 = 9; 9 \times 6 = 54, 5 + 4 = 9$). Because of this property, people whose primary number is nine may have a tendency to be rather self-centered and egotistical. On the positive side, nines can have lofty goals and high ambition that leads them to great temporal accomplishments as well as spiritual attainments.

Number Eleven

The numbers eleven and twenty-two are, as mentioned previously, considered "master numbers" by numerologists and are therefore not usually reduced further when encountered in an analysis. People who have one of these as their primary number tend to be extraordinary individuals to whom the numbers two and four (the reduced values of eleven and twenty-two, respectively) would not normally apply. The master number eleven indicates a need, for those who fall under its influence, to balance temporal interests with a strong natural attraction toward self-sacrifice and a giving of themselves for the benefit of others. Eleven is a transcendental number that relates to enlightenment and spirituality as well as martyrdom. The eleven tends to be someone who naturally uses his or her innate abilities to help others, whether that be through a life of sacrifice and giving, through the arts, or through a leadership role of some sort. The negative aspect of eleven indicates that a person who is an eleven may be so wrapped up in trying to "save the world" that their immediate relationships suffer from coldness or neglect. Another negative is that if the individual chooses to ignore his or her mission of seeking and sharing enlightenment, he or she may simply become entirely materialistic or uncaring in an extreme way. This number requires that powerful forces be balanced, so as to avoid the extremes of martyrdom on the one hand and complete lack of care for others on the other.

Number Twenty-Two

The number twenty-two is a powerful sacred number for a number of reasons. First of all, there is a kabbalistic correspondence here; the Hebrew alphabet, which is what God used to create the world, consists of twenty-two letters. Another reason twenty-two is considered sacred and powerful is because when you divide it by the mystical number seven, you arrive at the value of pi, the mathematical value that represents the relationship of the circumference of a circle to its diameter. People who are influenced by the number twenty-two are often considered to be ahead of their time, and their intelligence and brightness will enable them to achieve great things in their lifetime if they can harness the energy of this number. However, living up to the power of the number twenty-two may be the most difficult task of a person under this numeric influence, and the negative aspect of this challenge is that they may give up the struggle or even turn their intelligence and creativity toward evil ends. Anyone with this number as a primary influence is very likely to be tremendously successful in any venture or vocation she chooses to pursue, if she can find ways to harness and express the energy the number implies.

What You Can Learn

Using numerology to analyze your name can become rather complex because of the many different correspondences that can be drawn between numerology and other methods of divination and analysis such as astrology. As you delve deeper into the study of numerology, you'll undoubtedly want to consult additional books and resources to explore these connections in greater depth. However, to give you an introduction to the different possibilities, the next few sections will briefly discuss some of the basics of these different methods of analysis. Keep in mind that this is by no means a complete or comprehensive reference to the various disciplines involved but rather a "primer" to whet your appetite for learning more. For example, while you'll read an overview of how color, number, and name relate to one another and affect your life in general terms, you should consult other references on color and the effects of the vibrations of color if you want to learn more details about the psychological and metaphysical implications of color. In addition, you'll see in the charts below that the master numbers (eleven and twenty-two) don't have specific color, stone, or herb correspondences as do the single-digit numbers, so if one of your numbers is a master number, simply reduce the number to a single digit ($11 - 1 + 1 = 2$ or $22 = 2 + 2 = 4$) to find the corresponding element in the appropriate chart.

The name analyses you'll read in part II of this book include the numbers arrived at by reducing the vowel values (referred to as VV in part II) in your name, the consonant values (CV), the whole-name value (NV), and the first-letter value (FL). If you turn to some of the names in part II, you'll see the reduced totals for each of these values for the names listed so that, for example, under the numerological interpretation for the name Austin you'll see the following values displayed: (NV = 3, CV = 8, VV = 4, FL = 1). By using the letter-to-number correspondence table on page 34, you'll see how these values were arrived at for the analysis of the name Austin. As you read through the next few sections, you'll learn more about how these different values affect you and what significance they bear upon the numerological interpretation of your name.

The Vowels

The vowel value (VV) of your name is arrived at by simply adding together the numbers corresponding to the vowels in your name and then reducing them to either their single-digit or master number value. So for Austin you can determine the vowel value like this: $(A = 1) + (U = 3) + (I = 9) = 13$ and $1 + 3 = 4$. According to numerologists, the vowel value relates primarily to inner life and spirituality. This value also relates to one's soul purpose or life path in the spiritual or inner sense as well as a person's higher self. For those numerologists who believe in reincarnation, the vowel value also reflects the character and personality that was developed over previous lifetimes as well as the level of wisdom attained during those lifetimes. By analyzing the vowel value of your name, you will be able to gain deeper insight into your inner nature and your spiritual purpose in life, as well as your hidden motivations and deeper desires (as opposed to your more mundane or worldly interests).

The Consonants

The consonant value (CV) is arrived at by adding together the numeric values of the consonants in a name. For the name Austin, the CV is calculated as follows: $(S = 1) + (T = 2) + (N = 5) = 8$. The consonant value, according to numerologists, represents your external image or the "mask" you wear as your outward persona. The consonant value, then, relates to how you project your personality into the world, including all aspects of your social life. When attempting to understand the influence of the consonant value in your life, you need to consider how the number you arrive at coincides with the image of yourself that you project into the world and make public.

The Whole Name

The whole-name value (NV) is, as you might expect, derived by adding the numeric values of all the letters in your name and then reducing them to either a single digit or a master number. For our example name, Austin, the whole-name value comes to 3. The name value is also referred to as the "life path" or "path of destiny." This number is probably the most important value for the numerological analysis of your name because it represents you as a complete person. The name value integrates your inner life (as signified by the vowels in your name) with your outer life or personality (as signified by the consonants). Because of the integration of your inner and outer life in the name value, it is considered by numerologists to be the best indicator of your overall destiny or direction in life and therefore is most often used in working with name analysis. With an understanding of the name value, you will be able to get a clear picture of your purpose in life and your strengths and weaknesses as a complete individual.

The First Letter

The first-letter value (FL) is simply the numeric value of the first letter of your name. For Austin, the FL value is 1. The FL acts as an emphasis to the other numeric values in the name. So if the value of the first letter seems to contradict or be the opposite of the other values in the name in terms of its meaning, it might simply indicate that the other meanings are tempered or balanced by the first-letter value and therefore not quite as intense or powerful as they otherwise might have been. However, if the first-letter value is the same as or has the same general meaning as the other values, it will serve to strengthen the influence of those values in your life.

An Example

Using the example of Austin, then, we find that the numeric values pertaining to this name are (NV = 3, CV = 8, VV = 4, FL = 1). To do an elementary analysis of this name, first start with the whole-name value of three, which is the most powerful number influencing a person. The number three, as you'll recall, relates to family issues and the triune nature of time. Three is also an important mystical number. More practically, people whose NV is three tend to be assertive, positive people with a great deal of good luck on their side. A three individual is quite likely to be successful in life in whatever endeavor he or she chooses to pursue.

After getting a basic outline from the whole-name value, you'll want to consider the other numeric values of the name. For Austin, the CV was eight. The consonant value relates to one's external persona or image. The number eight relates to stability and equilibrium but also indicates an attraction to material things and outward signs of success. Combining this with the good luck and assertiveness implied in the NV of three, one can begin to see that Austin will be a rather practical person who is driven to succeed and create a sense of worldly stability and prosperity for himself.

The vowel value relates to the inner life or spirituality of an individual, and for Austin this number was four. Four relates to solidity, foundations, and, like eight, stability. Because of the influence of four, combined with the influence of eight, you can see that Austin will very likely be a stable, efficient, and reliable person in both his external and his internal pursuits. The four also indicates that Austin is the type to think things through and not act impulsively, so you can see that whatever good fortune comes his way will be due to his own clarity of thought, combined with the good luck that overshadows him because of the number three as his whole-name value.

Finally, the first-letter value, which serves to add emphasis to the other values, is the number one for Austin. The number one indicates creativity, energy, expressiveness, and achievement. When added as an emphasis to the other numbers, the one simply serves to confirm what we've already learned about Austin: He will tend to be a thoughtful and meticulous person who strives to accomplish his goals, both inner and outer, with clarity and purpose, and he will have a good deal of luck to help him along the way.

Principal Colors

Although the study of numerology is primarily concerned with numbers, there are correspondences between the numbers and other things that you should be aware of as you work on a name analysis. One of the things very closely associated with numbers is color. Have you ever noticed how some colors just feel "right" to you? Most everyone has a favorite color or colors that they look best in. Color, like number, has certain vibrations that we either resonate with or conflict with. Because color and number both have strong vibrations that affect our personalities, numerologists believe we can make associations between the numbers that we resonate with and color.

According to the late-nineteenth-century numerologist Count Louis Hamon (1866–1936, also known as Cheiro), each number corresponds to a specific color frequency that properly harmonizes with that number's vibrations. If you learn these correspondences, you can surround yourself with the colors that correctly resonate with the numbers that you are most closely associated with. By doing this, you will be able to create a more peaceful existence surrounded by the vibrations that most closely match your personal energies. To find the colors that vibrate in tune with your name, first calculate the various name values for your name as you learned above, then refer to the correspondences provided in the chart that follows. Consider the whole-name value to be the most influential in terms of choosing colors unless you feel more strongly attracted to colors that vibrate to one or the other of your name values. Remember that each individual is different and that some people are more strongly influenced by their vowel or consonant values than their whole-name value. Also keep in mind that the principal colors listed here are really ranges of color and that you can use any color that is in the same color "family." So, for example, if your number is one, your principal colors are the yellows, but that also includes orange, gold, and golden brown shades. By applying your knowledge of yourself and your tendencies to this analysis, you'll be able to find the correct colors to match and enhance your energies.

COLOR CORRESPONDENCE

Number	Principal Color or Colors
1	All yellows, ocher, bronze, gold, orange
2	All greens, white and shades of white such as cream
3	All shades of purple, violet, mauve, and lilac
4	All shades of gray, also bright blues
5	Light gray, also light shades of nearly any other color
6	All varieties of blue except the very bright blues
7	All shades of yellow, gold, and green
8	Dark colors such as dark blue, gray, purple, or black
9	Red and pink, also crimson and other deep shades of red

Gemstones and Precious Metals

We usually surround ourselves with color by changing the clothing we wear, by painting or decorating our houses in certain ways, or by hanging artwork on our walls. Another way to take advantage of the vibration of color is to use gems or stones that reflect the colors whose vibrations we want to be in tune with. In addition to reflecting colors, gems are also considered by many to vibrate to other energies in the universe, so that if we place the stones on our skin, we'll be able to harness those energies and take advantage of their benefits. Each of the single-digit numbers corresponds to a particular stone or stones. By using the numbers of your name, you'll be able to find the appropriate stones for yourself on the basis of the table below.

GEMSTONE AND PRECIOUS METAL CORRESPONDENCES

1	Yellow diamond, citrine, amber, and topaz
2	Pearl, jade, cat's-eye, moonstone
3	Garnet, amethyst
4	Sapphire
5	Light-colored stones, also "grayish" metals such as platinum or silver
6	Emerald, turquoise
7	Moonstone, cat's-eye, pearl, any white stone
8	Black diamond or pearl, any dark-colored stone
9	Bloodstone, garnet, ruby

Botanicals

Numerologists and astrologers have long believed that plants and herbs also correspond to particular numbers. Of course, plants have medicinal and healing value even apart from their numerological or astrological correspondences. But if you can combine the power and influence of your numbers with gemstones and beneficial herbs, you can create a more harmonious and well-balanced lifestyle for yourself that takes advantage of many different sources of energy. To best harness the power of the herbs that correspond to your numbers, you'll need to learn as much about their uses as you can by consulting other books or references on the appropriate uses for plants and herbs in a holistic lifestyle. Some plants are suitable only for external use, such as application to the skin or hair, or as an oil or essence for fragrance or incense. Others are wonderful spices that you can ingest as complementary flavors to your favorite foods, while still others are best in teas or other drinks. The table below gives a few of the herbal correspondences that will get you started exploring the uses of plants for health and spiritual energy. Keep in mind that this is only a starting point; once you have the correspondences you need, you should pursue further study on the appropriate uses of these herbs for different purposes. Again, you should focus on your whole-name value because that provides the key to your overall personality, health, and well-being.

HERBAL CORRESPONDENCES

Number	Primary Herbs or Plants
1	Borage, chamomile, eyebright, lavender, Saint-John's-wort, sorrel, thyme
2	Cabbage, chicory, lettuce, plantain, melon, turnips, cucumber
3	Apple, barberry, bilberry, cherry, dandelion, lungwort, mint, strawberry, pomegranate
4	Lesser celandine, sage, spinach, wintergreen, medlar
5	Hazel, marjoram, oats, parsley, mushrooms, parsnips, all types of nuts
6	Verbena, dog rose, violets, walnuts, all types of beans, apricots, almonds
7	Elder, blackberry, hops, juniper, linseed, grapes, all types of fruit juices
8	Marsh mallow, angelica, shepherd's purse, ragwort, celery, gravel root
9	Garlic, broom, nettle, onion, wormwood, leeks, mustard seed, pepper

Pulling It All Together

As you can see, analyzing your name by using the techniques, tools, and correspondences of numerology can become rather involved and complex. However, using all the tools available to you doesn't necessarily have to be difficult or overwhelming. Although you can certainly spend years studying and mastering all the correspondences and their effects, it isn't necessary to dive that deep into these matters to take advantage of their strengths. There are some simple ways to take advantage of the energies and vibrations inherent in your name's numbers, and you don't have to become an expert in all the arcane details of every field of study associated with numerology. As an example, suppose your whole-name value is one. First make an inventory of the various influences and correspondences that relate to that number. One, as you'll recall, is a number of great power, vitality, energy, and creativity, but it may be overbearing if its negative aspects become too strong. The colors of the one are the entire family of yellows and variants of yellow. The stones of the one are yellowish stones such as amber and topaz. The herbs that can be helpful to a one include chamomile, among others.

To enhance the influence of the vibrations of the number one in your life, you can take advantage of your color by painting one or more rooms in your home with an attractive shade of yellow or applying a wallpaper with golden highlights. If you're not interested in making yellow a primary color in your home-decoration scheme, you may consider artwork or prints that contain yellows and are attractive enough to draw your attention to them. A piece such as one of Van Gogh's sunflower series might be a tasteful way to add yellow to your home environment. Of course, you must decide for yourself how to apply the colors in an interesting and attractive way. The point is simply to place well-chosen shades of this color throughout your home to enhance the energy of the color because it resonates so well with your number. You might also consider getting a yellow car; something like a bright yellow Ford Mustang would be a powerful expression of the energies of the number one!

In addition to using yellow in your home or for your car, you should consider wearing the gems that resonate to the appropriate vibrations for you, or simply putting them in places in your home such as on a mantel or shelf. If you enjoy wearing jewelry, you could wear amber or topaz that is set in gold or another metal as a ring, necklace, or pin. If you're not particularly fond of wearing jewelry, a gold watch would work well to bring the influence of the color into your daily activities. Finally, a one might enjoy a cup of chamomile tea on occasion to bring the strength of that herb to bear on his or her life. Chamomile is considered useful for healing and soothing, so it might be a good way to calm the energies of the number one so as to avoid falling into the potentially negative aspects of excessive aggressiveness that ones may be subject to.

Of course, because colors, stones, and herbs influence other people as much as they affect you, you may want to consider how you can use these elements to improve your relationships with people such as your mate, your boss, or your coworkers. For example, you can calculate the numeric values of your boss to find which colors he or she will resonate with most strongly. If you want to take advantage of this information, you might consider wearing clothing that matches his primary color so you can positively influence your interactions with him. Because a person feels more in harmony when surrounded by his or her numerologically correct color, you might be able to affect the mood of a meeting, for example, by wearing a color or a stone that resonates well with your boss. However, be careful not to overdo it! By wearing a color or stone that clashes with your own color, you may be setting yourself up for disappointment because the positive effect on other people might be outweighed by the negative effect on *you*. Generally speaking, you are better off by concentrating on the colors, stones, and herbs that affect you personally, but you can certainly share your insights with others to help them find items that work well with their energies and vibrations.

By doing small things as suggested here, you will be able to organize your day-to-day life to take full advantage of the meaning and power of your name and the many things that bear a numerological correspondence to your name. When you begin working on the analysis of the numeric values of the letters of your name, remember that there are a number of different values you should consider, such as the whole-name and first-letter values, and the vowel and consonant values. Also, though you can learn a great deal about your name's influence on your personality by simply studying the numbers of your name and the way they relate to one another, using the correspondences of colors, stones, and herbs provides you with practical ways to utilize your knowledge of the numeric influences in your life and in your relationships with others. There are a number of excellent books available on the subject of numerology and its different techniques and correspondences that you might want to read for more in-depth information. One good example is *The Numerology Workbook: Understanding and Using the Power of Numbers* (New York: Sterling, 1985) by Julia Line. This book provides a good overview of numerology and many of the correspondences. When you combine these techniques with the analysis of your name using the Kabbalah and the runes, you'll have at your disposal a powerful collection of tools to gain insight and deeper knowledge of yourself and the energies that affect you.

The following is a numerological name worksheet for you to fill out for the whole-name, first-letter, vowel, and consonant values of your name.

NUMEROLOGICAL NAME WORKSHEET

Name: _Carol_

Four Primary Numeric Values	Primary Meanings	Colors	Stones	Herbs
NV = (C = 3) + (A = 1) + (R = 9) + (O = 6) + (L = 3) = 22. 2 + 2 = 4	Stability, foundations, solidity, the earth, the four elements, equilibrium and balance	Grays, bright blues	Sapphire	Lesser celandine, sage, spinach, wintergreen, medlar
FL = C = 3	Family, time, mysticism, spirituality	Purple, violet, mauve, and lilac	Garnet, amethyst	Apple, barberry, bilberry, cherry, dandelion, lungwort, mint, strawberry, pomegranate
VV = (A = 1) + (O = 6) = 7	Perfection, order, good fortune	Yellow, gold, and green	Moonstone, cat's-eye, pearl, any white stone	Elder, blackberry, hops, juniper, linseed, grapes, all types of fruit juices
CV = (C = 3) + (R = 9) + (L = 3) = 15. 1 + 5 = 6	Health, balance, equilibrium, harmony	Blue	Emerald, turquoise	Verbena, dog rose, violets, walnuts, all types of beans, apricots, almonds

NUMEROLOGICAL NAME WORKSHEET

Name: _____

Four Primary Numeric Values	Primary Meanings	Colors	Stones	Herbs
NV =				
FL =				
VV =				
CV =				

Getting the Whole Picture: Other Factors That Influence Your Personality

ALL OF YOU: SURNAME, MIDDLE NAME, BIRTH DATE

Though your first name is the most influential part of your whole name because of its constant and abiding effect on your daily life, there are a number of other factors to consider when trying to understand the things that affect your overall personality. For example, you've already seen that your middle name and last name (or surname) have the effect of acting as enhancing factors on the energy of your first name. You can use the techniques of Kabbalah, the runes, and numerology as described in this book to analyze those parts of your name to see how they interact with the energies of your first name. For some people, the three parts of their name will all have similar qualities or similar vibrations in terms of their inherent meanings and correspondences. In these cases, the individual's personality should rather clearly express the energies implied by those names because of the increase in their influence on that person. If the middle and last names have somewhat different meanings, they may have the opposite effect: These names may lessen the influence of the first name or add a different twist to its overall significance in a person's life.

In ancient Roman times, the middle name was used as a means of identifying one's *gens*, which referred to the clan or family "subgroup" as opposed to the last name, or *cognomen*, which identified one's broader ancestry or overall family membership. In modern times, however, this custom is no longer popular, and the middle name is used simply as an extension of the first name or as a way to further distinguish one person from another. Because of this relationship between the first and middle name, you should consider the two as a "team" if you decide to go beyond the simple analysis of your first name. The first and middle names are, in today's society, given to us by our parents primarily to distinguish us from other members of our family. Metaphysically speaking, however, there are no accidents, so the names you've been given in your life have an influence on your personality whether you like it or not! You can make the most of the middle name you've been given by learning its meaning and trying to work with its influence in your life rather than struggling against it or simply ignoring it altogether.

Your last name brings the energies of your family and ancestry to bear on your life. In the same way as your first and last names influence your personality, your last name also has an effect on you, though perhaps not as powerful because it does not so clearly signify *you* as a unique individual as much as it associates you with the vibrations of a certain family. By using the analysis techniques you've learned in this book to determine the significance of your last name, you'll be able to see more clearly how the energies of your family (or your spouse's family, if you've changed your name) have come down to you through the generations. You'll also be empowered to find ways to work with those energies just as you've worked with the energies of your first name to create a more holistic lifestyle that is "tuned-in" with the vibrations of your whole name.

Your name isn't the only factor that influences your personality, of course, as anyone who has even a cursory knowledge of astrology will tell you. Your birth date also plays a significant role in determining your destiny and your personality. In fact, many numerologists and astrologers might argue that a birth date is an even more potent factor in the analysis of personality primarily because it is something we can neither choose nor change. Analyzing your birth date can become quite complex because of the fact that you use not only numerology to determine its meaning, but also astrology. To dive deep into the astrological interpretations of a birth date can become quite a daunting task because of all the nuances and details of the planets, stars, and other heavenly bodies, and their precise positions at the very moment of your birth. However, you can always consult one of the many good books on astrology or even spend an hour or so with a professional astrologer who can analyze and interpret all the complexities for you. To use numerology in order to better understand the influence of your birth date, simply reduce the full date to a single number or master number, then consult the brief meanings given in this book. As with the analysis of names, you can also analyze the birth dates of important people in your life to learn more about their personalities and how they interact with you by using these techniques as well.

As an example of how to reduce the birth date, consider someone whose birth date is July 23, 1963. The numeric values of this date are (7) + (2) + (3) + (1) + (9) + (6) + (3) = 31, which can be further reduced to (3) + (1) = 4. The person with this birth date, then, should look up the meanings given for the number four and compare it with the numeric values of his or her name to see how the influences interact and either complement or contradict one another. If the numeric value of the first name reduces to four or a complementary number (for example, eight, because it is a multiple of four), then the influences of both of these factors should be somewhat consistent in that person's life because of the strength of that number's influence on that person. However, if the name and the birth date seem to conflict, you may want to examine the individual's personality to determine which value seems to have the strongest potency in his or her life. Some names and numbers simply have a stronger energy than others. When you consider the various numeric values that affect you in light of what you already know about yourself, you should be able to determine readily which factor has the greatest "pull" in your life. Again, just as with the interaction between your first, middle, and last names, there is a give-and-take of complementary and contradictory energies that play upon your personality. Working through the different influences to create a comprehensive profile of yourself will take a little effort on your part.

WHAT YOUR PARENTS INTENDED

If your name has an effect and influence on your destiny because of the metaphysical connection that exists among all things, it would seem irrelevant to consider your parents' intentions when they selected your name for you at your birth. However, there's no doubt that one's parents are very intimately a part of his or her destiny, and their influence can play a powerful role in the development or failure to develop that destiny to its fullest extent. When your parents choose the name *you* will bear, they are in essence making a choice that will affect you intimately and powerfully for your entire life, for better or worse. If your parents' intent was to give you a name that would help you achieve a position of status and authority (the example used earlier, Alexander, comes to mind), and if that goal is something you decide you want to pursue, you'll have a head start and the power of a good, strong name behind you. However, if you should choose to follow the path of an artist to the possible dismay of your parents, you can still utilize the energies of your name to your benefit.

As you have seen, Alexander is a name of leadership and power. Just because an Alexander chooses a career or life path that seems (by ordinary conventions, at any rate) to have little to do with power and authority doesn't mean that the power of that name will be to no avail in that person's life. Consider Alexander Calder, for example. Here was an artist whose works were considered by many to be powerful expressions of artistic energy and creativity. His sculptures conveyed a sense of power and authority, and many were very large pieces that were placed in conspicuous public places—certainly an assertive and powerful way to express one's talent and energy, and an absolutely appropriate form of expression for the authoritative name of Alexander.

The reasons people give for choosing a name for a child can range from the sublime to the ridiculous, but there is usually an attempt on the part of conscientious parents to select a name that is attractive, at the very least. Many people choose names on the basis of famous or not-so-famous people they know and honor or respect, while others choose names in hopes that their children will adopt the qualities of people they know who bear those names. Still others choose names for spiritual reasons, such as honoring a saint or sage, while others choose the name of an ancestor as a way to remember that individual. Regardless of the reasons your parents chose your name and their conscious intentions, the energies of that name are yours unless you choose to alter it. If you find that the names you have been given simply do not "work" for you or resonate with your personality, you can choose to make a change, and you'll read more about this process later. But a change like this is something you should think about carefully; this isn't something to jump into without clear knowledge of your intentions. Perhaps instead of changing your name, you should first see if you can find ways to work with rather than against its energies. If there is in fact a cosmic or "higher" reason for the names we bear, as the ancients and many contemporary people strongly believe, then changing a name without a very powerful desire or genuine need can be potentially harmful in the long run.

MARRIAGE, ADOPTION, AND OTHER NAME/LIFE-ALTERING EVENTS

If the energies of our names have such a clear and abiding effect on our lives, what happens to people whose names are changed by events or circumstances that are, at least to a certain extent, beyond their control? For example, many women who get married still follow the custom of adopting the family name of their husband. Certainly women who change their names after marriage experience a much more difficult adjustment than their husbands, whose names haven't been altered. Even if the spiritual and energetic effects of the name change are discounted, the process of making the change legal, and the efforts required to change bank accounts, Social Security information, medical records, and employment information, not to mention the challenge of changing the way people address you, all add up to many months of difficulties that can be mildly traumatic. And if you do consider the energetic and vibrational aspects of the new name, it becomes clear that the person with the new name will have to undergo a period of psychological readjustment while she tries to absorb and "tune into" the energies of the new name. By taking on a new last name, in fact, a person literally merges her ancestral heritage with the influences of her husband's family energies, thereby truly "entering into" the new family in a very literal and powerful way. If you're a woman who's about to be married, you may need to consider very carefully the influences and effects of adopting a new family name before changing your last name. Many women these days opt to keep their own names simply because of the inevitable difficulties that result from changing their names and because they wish to maintain their spiritual and energetic connection to their own family's heritage. Other couples are choosing to hyphenate both last names to symbolize the joining of two families, but this raises the question of what name to pass on to their children. Occasionally, husbands opt to take the wife's name. This book can help you decide what will be the best course of action for you.

What of divorce, then? Should a woman who becomes separated from her husband change her name back to her premarriage last name? Again, careful consideration must be given to this decision because of the efforts required to make another change. If you have taken on your husband's name and have completely and fully adopted its energies as your own, there may be no reason to change back to your prior name. However, if there is a certain amount of tension surrounding the name or the memories associated with the name, or if the name never quite seemed to fit, there is probably good cause to change back. The inevitable challenges will, of course, be the same as when you changed your name in the first place, but the psychological "letting go" of the energies of the married name to reembrace your own family's name might be worth the effort required. Again, you need to make a determination on the basis of your own situation and your own sense of what is the right course of action for you.

In cases of adoption, the child typically has no choice in the matter, so it is up to the new parents to ensure that if the first name is changed, it carries a positive energy that will help the child grow. Especially if the child is older, the first name should not be changed without the clear and intentional consent of the child because of the challenges involved with a name change that is beyond one's control. The inevitable change in the last name that results from adoption very clearly has the effect of altering the child's ancestral bonds and associating him or her with the familial energies of the new family. Although you might consider *not* changing the child's last name, this can have a negative impact as well. The child may never feel entirely assimilated into his or her new family. When you adopt a child, you are literally bringing that child into your "fold," and changing his or her last name to match yours ensures that he or she will adopt the energies and strengths of your family.

Changing Your Name

CAN YOU REALLY CHANGE YOUR DESTINY?

While some people experience a name change because of changes in their circumstances, others consciously choose to alter their name for one reason or another. Does changing your name truly allow you to change your destiny? If, for example, you strongly desire a position of leadership but are not currently in such a situation, can you give your career a boost by changing your name to Alexander? Certainly the change in your name will create an entirely different set of energies and influences in your life, and others will very likely respond to you differently if you have a different name. But there is something of a chicken-and-egg dilemma involved in making a choice to alter your given name or names. Those who believe in a strong metaphysical or even karmic reason for the names we bear will likely argue that your name is truly *your* name and that you were destined to have this particular name, whether you necessarily like it on a conscious level or not. This perspective might point to the idea that your name actually *reflects* something of your inherent nature, rather than creates or modifies that nature; you were born into the world with a very specific purpose, and your name is an expression of that purpose, not the creator of that purpose.

However, you've already seen that your name does have an effect on your life and personality. If you change your name to match characteristics that you want to enhance in yourself, you may very well be able to add strength to those personality traits you wish to develop. That is not to say, of course, that if you name yourself Alexander you will become a great world leader; that kind of thinking is far too literal and simplistic, and changing your name in hopes of such a miracle would be ludicrous. But if you feel that perhaps you truly resonate more strongly with a different name or that your given name somehow does not quite *feel* right, you may want to examine some of the techniques given here for finding a more appropriate name.

WHY DO YOU WANT TO CHANGE YOUR NAME?

The first question to ask yourself, then, is why do you feel the desire to change your name? Your name is a reflection of your mission and purpose in this lifetime. To change it, you must have a strong belief that your name is inappropriate for that mission or that another name might be better suited to you in the long run. Changing a name is a rather serious decision, so you need to be very clear and honest with yourself about your reasons. You may want to perform a personal inventory of the reasons you've been mulling over when you think about selecting a new name. Are you ashamed of your name or proud of it? If you lack pride in your name, it may be due to low self-esteem rather than the fact that your name is inappropriate for you. Perhaps the first thing to do is to work on improving your self-image, then reassess your name in light of your stronger, more confident self. Do you tend to go by a nickname or shortened form of your name? If so, that doesn't necessarily require a wholesale change of the name you've been given. Some people simply feel more comfortable with different versions of their name, so that a Timothy feels better "wearing" the name Tim instead. You might also choose to go by your initials or your middle name if that feels more appropriate to you. If you do this, you are intentionally choosing to be more strongly influenced by your middle name or initials rather than your first name.

Is there something about your name that you simply don't like? Or is there some connection to your past that is providing the impulse to change your name? When you are considering a dramatic move like changing your name, try to focus on the positive reasons for your choice and not on negative factors that may be an influence. If you are changing your name because you are, in some sense, running away from a part of yourself or your past, you may be intentionally discounting a very important part of your own spiritual and psychological development. If your name is a reflection of your purpose in this life, it may be to your benefit to do an in-depth study of its meanings so you can understand it more fully before you decide to change it. If you discover that your middle name connects you deeply to a significant group of people in your family's history, you may ultimately decide to keep that name both out of respect and because it provides fertile ground for further analysis of the names from which it was created. By finding out as much as possible about the meanings and influences of your name, you will be able to take a more active role in adopting that name as truly your own because you will understand its significance and be able to apply that significance to your own life.

MAKING A STRATEGIC CHOICE

When deciding to take on a new name, you must make a strategic choice that is carefully thought out and well analyzed. Choosing a name for yourself should certainly be at least as serious a choice as choosing a name for your child, and you'll want to make sure that the name you select really works for you. There are many ways to select a new name for yourself, not the least of which is simply finding a name that feels or sounds right or is attractive and interesting to you. If you're choosing a name for religious or spiritual reasons, you should have no problem finding the names of the saints and sages of your faith that can help guide you toward your goal of a deeper and more authentic spirituality. Other strategic methods of choosing a name involve creating a list of names that you like for whatever reason, then performing a complete kabbalistic, runic, and numerological analysis of each of them to determine which one most closely resonates with the energies that you know are most important or powerful in your life. When you make the decision to change your name, you will want to find a name that has qualities and characteristics that will not only complement your personality but that will also serve to inspire you as you strive to improve areas of weakness. By choosing a name that exudes confidence and strength, for example, a generally shy person might be able to increase his or her capacity for outward expression, just as a very aggressive person might be able to find a name that will help tone down the negative aspects of that aggression with a more peaceful or balanced energy.

TECHNIQUES FOR CHANGING
OR CREATING A NAME

If, after careful consideration, you've decided you definitely want to change your name, where do you begin? One good place to start looking for a new name is in the listing of names in part II of this book. There you will find an excellent collection of hundreds of interesting names that you can browse through for initial impressions and ideas. And if you find one that "clicks" or seems attractive to you, you can read the interpretation provided to find out whether your initial impression was correct on the basis of the analysis provided. You may very well discover a name that you hadn't considered before but that suddenly seems just right. If you don't happen to find a name that seems quite right to you, you can try some of the techniques described below to find or create a name for yourself based on interpretations of variations of common names. You may also want to consider doing some research into names that were used in your family by long-gone relatives, or you may want to find names that were used in the country of your parents' or grandparents' origin to see if something from that culture works for you. There are plenty of names out there and plenty of ways to analyze the meanings of those names, so you shouldn't have too much trouble coming up with something that is appropriate for you.

Interpret Unique Spellings

One method of coming up with a new name for yourself is simply to spell your current name differently and then analyze the meanings of the new name. As a simple example, if your name is Thomas and you've always been addressed as Thomas throughout your life, you might consider using a variant like Tom or Thom. You might also consider using a spelling of your name that is common in another culture; in this case, something like Tomas. By adding or dropping a letter here or there, you will be able to create an entirely different energy for yourself, especially if you embrace that new version of your name. Consider the differences from a numerological standpoint if you change your name from Thomas to Tomas. Thomas reduces to four whereas Tomas reduces to five. If you consider the respective meanings of each of those numbers, you'll find that four represents stability, firmness, and solidity and can potentially become stodgy or boring. Five, on the other hand, tends to be less stable, perhaps somewhat impulsive, careless, or even unstable. By altering the name in this way, you can create an entirely different perception of yourself among other people, and you can bring a complete new set of energies and vibrations into your life.

Interpret "Related to" Names and Nicknames

In the same way, you can analyze variants of names and even nicknames to find out whether one of these alterations would suit you better. If you don't want to change to an entirely different name, you might want to consider this option. For example, if your name is Edwin, you may want to examine the interpretations and meanings of the names Edward, Edgar, Edmund, Ed, or even Eddie. (Daggers following names in the "Related to" section of a profile indicate names that are profiled elsewhere in the book.) You could also try a spelling variant such as Edouin or Eduard to see if the alteration brings about a positive change in the energies of the name that you might feel more comfortable with. Remember that changing the spelling of a name brings a whole new vibration to that name. If you aren't entirely comfortable with your current name but don't necessarily feel an aversion to it, all you may need to do is modify the spelling somewhat or use a common variant of the name to bring the proper energies to bear on your personality. Also, because different name variants affect the energies implied by those names, you can interact how others interact with you by changing how you address them. Clearly, if you address your friend Tom as Tommy, you're going to draw a different response from what you are accustomed to, but it might not necessarily be pleasant! When addressing other people by name, be sure to respect their desires and their energy by using a form of address that is both appropriate for the circumstance and acceptable to the individual you are addressing.

Study the Etymology of Names

Learning about the history and origin of names is an excellent way to find a name that has appropriate energies and influences for you. Understanding the etymology of a name enables you to embrace the historical significance of the name and establish a connection with the past that may provide a deeper sense of satisfaction and fulfillment. Knowing a name's etymology also gives you another tool that you can use when analyzing names you may be considering. If the kabbalistic correspondences, runic interpretations, and numerological meanings all seem right to you for a particular name, and the etymology strikes you as interesting, romantic, or in some other way attractive, you've probably found a name that will be a strong positive influence in your life should you choose to adopt it. For example, if you're considering the name Claire and have found the meanings and interpretations to be suitable for yourself, also knowing that the name is of French origin and that it means "shining and bright, gentle and famous" may be significant enough to help you make your final decision. Knowing the etymology of a name will also help you feel more in tune with that name because you will have a clearer sense of the origins of the name and the meanings that were associated with it by the people who first used it.

MAKING IT LEGAL

Once you've carefully selected an appropriate name that will carry you through your life with the proper energies you want to embrace and project into the world, the last step is to make it legal. To change your name legally does not, according to current law in most states, require that you file forms in court, but having a court-ordered or -approved name change will very likely make changing other documents easier. In most states, you can change your name by simply adopting and using that name in all aspects of your professional, personal, and social life. However, it may be difficult for you to have legal documents such as passports and your birth certificate changed without a court order. To find out if your state's laws require a court order, you should contact your local clerk of court or consult your state's statutes at a local law library. Each state has its own laws on the books, and you'll need to do some digging to find out exactly what the requirements are in the state in which you reside.

In addition to the potential requirement of getting a court order to legally change your name, you must consider that you will also have to change things like your employment records, credit cards, bank accounts, mortgage information, and other registrations and/or legal commitments that keep your name on record. And even if your state does not legally require you to obtain a court order, you will certainly have to contact the state government to change your driver's license or state identification card information. Of course, you'll also need to file changes with federal government agencies such as the Social Security Administration and the IRS. If you intend to alter your birth certificate to reflect your new name, you should again contact your city or local government for more information about the specific requirements and forms you'll need to fill out. In many cases, in order to change your birth certificate you will need a court document that you've properly filed and had signed by a judge. Remember that each state has its own unique set of requirements and that it is imperative for you to get everything done correctly if you truly wish to embrace your new name as the standard-bearer of your new life.

Finally, you should be aware of the fact that although it is entirely legal and acceptable to change your name, there are a few restrictions on the names you can use. Most of these restrictions are simply expressions of common sense and good taste, but they are legal restrictions that you should at least know about. One restriction is that you cannot change your name to avoid your obligations or to carry out any other kind of fraudulent activity. In other words, if you owe the government thousands of dollars in back taxes, you can't change your name in order to avoid paying them. You cannot use a name that interferes with someone else's rights. This restriction usually applies to the inappropriate use of the name of a famous person, although other circumstances may apply as well. Other restrictions include not using names that are intentionally confusing (by putting punctuation marks or numbers in your name, for example), not using names that are racially insulting or degrading, and not using names that might be offensive, threatening, or obscene.

Although it may seem like an arduous and time-consuming process, changing your name can be done and is done daily across the country by thousands of people. Your primary consideration, of course, should not be whether the red tape of making it official would be too much of a hassle to bother with, but rather whether the name you will bear for the rest of your life is a good name that is appropriate for you as a unique individual. Your name is much more than simply a label that distinguishes you from others; it is a powerful source of energy that influences nearly every aspect of your life. To ensure that you go through life with the best possible name for you is a task that should not be taken lightly. A properly chosen name can provide a great deal of personal satisfaction and power, so be sure you are clear in your intentions and thorough in your research. And when the time comes to fill out the inevitable paperwork, just try to smile and remember that you are choosing to alter an integral part of yourself for your own long-term benefit, and that you'll probably do it only once in your lifetime anyway!

Part II

~

NAME PROFILES

Aaron

A Kabbalistic Synopsis

עָרוֹן —A'ARVN (Ayin, Resh, Vau, Nun)

Aaron has a strong, self-possessed character. He is seen by many (quite rightly) as a safe pair of hands, in that he can be trusted with pretty much any task or responsibility. An unlikely leader, he is happiest when working on his own terms. Aaron adds up to 976, which can be represented by the letters Tzaddi, Ayin, and Vau, meaning fishhook, eye, and nail, respectively. These letters reveal certain major aspects of Aaron's personality and skills, as shown below. We can see that Aaron would be ideally suited to a role, say, in purchasing or acquisitions, since he has an eye (from Ayin) for the best deal, which allows him to pin down (from Vau) and then reel in (from Tzaddi) whatever he covets at bargain rates through his hardnosed negotiating skills. His head for business is enhanced by the influences of Capricorn, a star sign that relates to an enjoyment of and skill in moneymaking schemes. There is another more personal side to Aaron. His name reduces to twenty-two, the number of the Fool in the tarot. On one level this suggests that Aaron enjoys a good laugh and may even be something of a practical joker. However, the Fool also signifies the "wise fool" of mysticism. The concept of the fool as enlightened can be found in most religions, from the words of Lao-tzu to the New Testament. Aaron is likely to have a clear and optimistic faith in the hereafter, which influences his day-to-day dealings.

The Runic Interpretation

ᚾᛟᚱᚨᚨ (Nauthiz, Othila, Raido, Ansuz, Ansuz)

Aaron can be childlike and amusing, and he is a born performer. This kid can dance, act, and sing. If he chooses to follow the limelight in later years, he certainly will help launch other budding talents because he will remember how he got his own start. Aaron likes to help people, and he likes *you* to hear how he helped people. If he turns his considerable acting talents to other careers, he can enjoy religion, sales, or teaching. He'd be a great speechwriter or could do most anything in politics. Aaron is wonderful to have at parties and will always remember Mother's Day.

Elements: Fire, earth/fire, water, air, air

The Numerological Interpretation

Aaron (NV = 4, CV = 5, VV = 8, FL = 1)

A name that promises success and material comfort through self-initiated plans and projects, Aaron denotes a person who is curious, ambitious, and eager to make every action count for something special. Aaron is hardworking and expansive by nature. This name contains a great deal of potential for positive, practical outcomes. Never one to avoid the many adventures of life, Aaron not only takes what comes his way but initiates many new experiences, thanks to his active mind.

DERIVATION: Egyptian, the name of Moses' brother, who was chosen by God as Moses' spokesman. Aaron subsequently became the first high priest of the Israelites. Especially common in the late twentieth century.

PRINCIPAL COLORS: Electric colors

GEMSTONES AND PRECIOUS METALS: Sapphires

BOTANICALS: Celandine, sage

UNIQUE SPELLINGS: Aaran, Aaren, Aarron, Aeron, Aharon, Ahren, Ahron, Aihron, Airon, Aren, Aron, Arran, Arron

RELATED TO: Arke, Arn, Haroun, Ron, Ronnie, Ronny, Yaron

DERIVATION: Yiddish, from the
word *abba*, meaning "father."
Existed as an independent name
in Talmudic times; now often a
nickname for Abraham.

PRINCIPAL COLORS: Black, the
darker shades of blue and purple

GEMSTONES AND PRECIOUS
METALS: Black pearls and
diamonds, sapphires

BOTANICALS: Angelica, shepherd's
purse

UNIQUE SPELLINGS: Aibe,
Aybe, Eibe

RELATED TO: Abel, Abey, Abiah,
Abner, Abraham†, Abram,
Absalom

Abe

A KABBALISTIC SYNOPSIS
בי —AYB (Aleph, Yod, Beth)

Abe is the kind of guy likely to be found huddling in the corner of the local bar with his few closest friends. He will probably be regaling his company with tales of his latest catch—which is never quite as big as he claims. To Abe, life is all about this sort of social get-together. Sure, he does his day job, and is likely to be quick and efficient at it, too, but that is simply the means to a more enjoyable end. Abe adds up to thirteen, and among other words is equivalent to the Hebrew word AChD, pronounced "Achad," meaning "unity." In personality terms this tells us that Abe likes his life to be controlled and compact; this goes for his job and also his love life. If things ever change, it is at an acceptably slow pace. Abe flourishes in small communities where everyone knows his name. Beware of Abe at parties, though. Another equivalence to his name is "locust," and you can be sure that he will always have more than a healthy appetite! Next to making cash, eating is Abe's favorite pastime.

THE RUNIC INTERPRETATION
MBᚠ (Ehwaz, Berkana, Ansuz)

Abe's life lesson is learning to say no. Relinquishment precedes growth, but letting go is hard for us all. Abe may have old habits to shed, or he may need to consider new avenues for expressing his talents when his work is panned by the critics. Over the course of his life, he may surrender property or birthright. These are hard lessons. During a Saturn transit in astrology or a corporate takeover in business, for example, Abe feels insecure through it all. But after these trials he emerges polished by the fire and pure. He can now function on a higher frequency than the rest of us and is able to live in the moment and to love. When Abe is one with the spirit, he feels he has all he will ever desire.

Elements: Air, air/earth, air

THE NUMEROLOGICAL INTERPRETATION
Abe (NV = 8, CV = 2, VV = 6, FL = 1)

The name Abe implies a practical person who is very cooperative, loving, and caring. Responsibility to family, friends, coworkers, and society in general is a very important characteristic associated with this name. A peacemaker at heart, Abe will always endeavor to promote harmony between himself and others. Calm and usually self-contained, Abe is faithful and loyal, and offers keen insights into other people's true nature.

Abigail

A KABBALISTIC SYNOPSIS

אבגאיל —ABGAYL (Aleph, Beth, Gimel, Aleph, Yod, Lamed)

The value of Abigail is forty-seven, a number that symbolizes the marriage of the material with the mystical. Her name is associated with the tarot card the Fool and suggests an idealistic, almost childlike, view of the world. In short, Abigail is a dreamer, and this is further shown by her name's equivalence to the Hebrew word for "cloud." With her awesome power of imagination, regardless of her job, Abigail always shines in the creative roles. The presence of L, or Lamed, signifies that she has the driving force needed to pursue an ideal in the face of pressure to conform. In relationships, Abigail is often confusing to her partners. She can have unrealistically high expectations of romance, which cause her to experience disappointment, while at the same time her idealistic nature makes her ever ready to believe that the great times are just around the corner.

THE RUNIC INTERPRETATION

ᛚᛁᚨᚷᛁᛒᚨ (Laguz, Isa, Ansuz, Gebo, Isa, Berkana, Ansuz)

Abigail knows that we have many lives within one lifetime, and that our selves change often with every new connection. These connections come to us in our dreams, through our talents, and through opportunities and chance encounters. The name Abigail uses the energy of double Ansuz, meaning "message." Thoughtful Abigail notices people who come her way and ideas that lift her up to new levels of engagement with the world. She has disciplined herself to become receptive to these intuitions; they are divine messages for patient Abigail. She is modest and allows these angel thoughts to direct her. In this simple way, her life unfolds in harmony.

Elements: Water, earth, air, water, earth, air/earth, air

THE NUMEROLOGICAL INTERPRETATION

Abigail (NV = 5, CV = 3, VV = 2, FL = 1)

At her inner core, Abigail is a peaceful person, eager to find harmony and balance in life. Yet on the surface, she is a very active woman, and mentally alert with an eager curiosity to match! Abigail is usually quite at home in an academic or intellectual environment. She is a storehouse of information and has no problem communicating what she knows. Her name implies that she will put this information to good use, not only for her own benefit but as an expression of her urge for cooperation and shared success. She's invariably a star in brainstorming meetings or client presentations; she makes everyone look good. This name indicates one who can achieve a positive rapport with almost anyone and doesn't hesitate to use her sensitivity and natural charm.

DERIVATION: Hebrew, from the word *abigal*, meaning "my father rejoices." In the Old Testament, the wife of King David. Common among the Puritans, it became fairly common in the United States with the rise of such prominent name bearers as Abigail Adams and advice columnist Abigail Van Buren.

PRINCIPAL COLORS: The full spectrum of light hues

GEMSTONES AND PRECIOUS METALS: Silver, platinum, diamonds

BOTANICALS: Oats, sweet marjoram

UNIQUE SPELLINGS: Abagael, Abagail, Abagale, Abagayl, Abbigail, Abbigaile, Abbygail, Abbygaile, Abigael, Abigaele, Abigale, Abigayl, Abigayle

RELATED TO: Abbe, Abbi, Abbie, Abby, Gael, Gail, Gaila, Gayla, Gayle

"I am but God's finger, John."
—ABIGAIL IN *THE CRUCIBLE* BY ARTHUR MILLER

DERIVATION: Hebrew, name of the first Jewish patriarch, who was originally called Abram. His name was lengthened to Abraham after he made a covenant with God, which stated that his descendants would inhabit the land of Canaan. Especially common among seventeenth-century Puritans.

PRINCIPAL COLORS: Darkest shades of purple, blue, and gray

GEMSTONES AND PRECIOUS METALS: Rubies, amethysts, black pearls

BOTANICALS: Marsh mallow, angelica

UNIQUE SPELLINGS: Abrahamm, Abreham, Abriham

RELATED TO: Abet, Abram, Ahe, Avraham, Bram

Abraham

A KABBALISTIC SYNOPSIS
אברהם —ABRHM (Aleph, Beth, Resh, Heh, Mem)

Abraham is a hugely significant name in the Kabbalah, being the name of the founder of Judaism. It is not surprising, then, that the name Abraham can yield a wealth of interpretation, though much of it relates to mysticism rather than personality. Abraham is, as you would expect, a dutiful man. He holds his beliefs strongly and is a man of principle rather than pragmatism. His concern with moral action may lead him to be somewhat distant from his wife and children, but he will be a great protector figure for them. Abraham may well have a job that requires him to travel, possibly over considerable distances. In the Old Testament it is Abraham who first leaves the city of Ur and wanders in search of a new homeland.

THE RUNIC INTERPRETATION
ᛗᚨᚺᚨᚱᛒᚨ (Mannaz, Ansuz, Hagalaz, Ansuz, Raido, Berkana, Ansuz)

An inner knowledge of the extremes of darkness and light follow Abraham throughout his earthly journey. Life's tapestry, for Abraham, is woven from subtle threads of mystery and wonder. Abraham makes a clever detective, researcher, physicist, astronomer, judge, social worker, or spiritual leader. His keen, analytical mind seeks balance with the quiet, poetic side of his nature. Prone to drama and passion, Abraham needs to learn to seek moderation and balance in his affairs. His ideals are so high that he demands much more of himself than anyone else does. Should he find himself compromised in his achievements, he will forgive himself and learn a lesson from the pain. His strong sense of personal power is based on surrender of his will to God.

Elements: Air, air, water, air, water, air/earth, air

THE NUMEROLOGICAL INTERPRETATION
Abraham (NV = 8, CV = 5, VV = 3, FL = 1)

This name carries the energy of a very productive person, a man of vivid mental activity and endless curiosity about life. Abraham implies an intense intelligence and the capacity to use it toward material success. He can be a productive businessman, but he has to be careful not to lose compassion when dealing with others. His personality centers around the many opportunities life brings him as well as those he creates and initiates for himself. Abraham will never be bored.

Adam

A KABBALISTIC SYNOPSIS
אדם —ADM (Aleph, Daleth, Mem)

Adam is a complex individual. He will have many friends who think they know him well, and yet his true nature will be known by only a select few. On the outside Adam is the definitive "everyman." In other words, he is a man completely at home in a world of practical considerations while at the same time having a definite faith in the spiritual side of things; his personality tends to be unusually well balanced. If he is born under an earth sign, this factor will predominate, and we will find Adam in a career that involves a great deal of interpersonal contact and requires strong communication skills. His interest in people may lead him to an interest in history. In direct contrast to his outwardly common appearance, Adam also has a mysterious side. His name adds up to forty-five, which is the secret number of Yesod, the sphere on the Tree of Life that represents, among other things, the astral plane. Adam may have some psychic ability himself, and he will certainly have a natural gift for exploring the unexplained.

THE RUNIC INTERPRETATION
ᛗᚨᛞᚨ (Mannaz, Ansuz, Dagaz, Ansuz)

Adam stands for the human race. His is the profound concept that All Is One. There is no sense of emptiness or void in the energy of this name. Adam knows that he can love others as an art and discipline, for loving is an art in itself. Keeping a journal of what he reads and learns helps him dialogue with his many selves and keep in touch with his lofty spiritual and materialistic goals. He aspires to clarity of thought. He may be particular about his diet and the air he breathes. Adam enjoys the outdoors and prefers things like fishing and hiking to competitive sports. He handles positions of power and authority with grace and is willing to change to bring balance to his life. As a boss, Adam is modest and tends not to criticize anyone unless a high principle is violated. He is unlikely to engage in petty arguments; instead, he answers to the spirit within, and his values are much higher than those of most of us. This sets him apart.

Elements: Air, air, fire, air

THE NUMEROLOGICAL INTERPRETATION
Adam (NV = 1, CV = 8, VV = 2, FL = 1)

Adam is a name that implies a person who is very sure of himself. His sense of individuality is usually quite strong, and Adam is determined to establish his place in the world around him. The energy Adam carries is ambitious; he is determined and eager for material success. He is bold and unafraid to create new adventures and enterprises, lending an original slant to all that he may do. Yet at his core he longs for intimate human relationships. This deep need for harmonious contacts with others can conflict with the other, more egocentric qualities indicated by this name.

DERIVATION: Biblical, probably from the Hebrew word *adama*, meaning "earth." In Genesis, God sculpted the first man, Adam, from clay and then breathed life into him. Very popular in the United States since the 1960s.

PRINCIPAL COLORS: Shades of yellow and brown, gold

GEMSTONES AND PRECIOUS METALS: Topaz, amber, yellow diamonds

BOTANICALS: Borage, lavender, thyme

UNIQUE SPELLINGS: Adem, Adim, Adom, Ahdam, Ahdem

RELATED TO: Adamo, Adan, Adriant, Aidan

Adele

DERIVATION: English, from the French Adèle. Germanic in origin, associated with nobility. The name of a character in Johann Strauss's opera *Die Fledermaus*. Gained further popularity as a character in Dornford Yates's novels of the 1930s.

PRINCIPAL COLORS: The darker shades of pink, red, and reddish-purple

GEMSTONES AND PRECIOUS METALS: Garnets, bloodstones, and rubies

BOTANICALS: Nettle, broom, wormwood, garlic, and onion

UNIQUE SPELLINGS: Adell, Adelle

RELATED TO: Adela, Adelaide, Adelia, Adelinda, Adeline, Adella, Adellah, Adelpha, Delina, Deline, Delly, Edelie

A KABBALISTIC SYNOPSIS
אדאל —ADAL (Aleph, Daleth, Aleph, Lamed)

Adele goes through a number of distinct stages in her life, and she will grow and develop during each one. We all change in the process of a lifetime, but with Adele each change represents an almost total break from her past. The letter Daleth (D) in her name means "door" in Hebrew, and the letter Aleph (A) represents force and direction. In other words, Adele will follow a given direction with considerable energy and then suddenly change to follow a different path with equal commitment. Adele is not flighty, but she ardently believes in the virtues of whichever lifestyle she happens to be following at the time. Adele is very expressive, and whoever she is with will definitely know exactly how she feels about them. The value of her name is thirty-six, which reduces to nine, the number of the letter Teth, meaning "serpent"—so it's not a good idea to let Adele down emotionally, as she knows how to wreak her revenge. The final letter in Adele's name is Lamed, meaning "ox goad." It represents a force driving the individual which may not be of the individual's choosing. It has more to do with feelings of duty and obligation than the energy of Aleph. Its position at the end of her name suggests that ultimately Adele will find a partner and a lifestyle with which she will be permanently happy.

THE RUNIC INTERPRETATION
ᚱᛗᛞᚨ (Laguz, Ehwaz, Dagaz, Ansuz)

Adele can usually be found standing in the sunlight near an open window. She absorbs information from the light. Adele has somehow learned the valuable lesson that as we cultivate our own strengths, all else follows. This lesson applies to relationships and helps Adele focus on goals for her life. The Dagaz rune indicates that Adele will have many opportunities to change the direction of her life. With intuition strongly aspected in her name, Adele is receptive to opportunities as they come her way. Adele is flexible and allows herself to be "reinvented" the more she risks and grows.

Elements: Water, air, fire, air

THE NUMEROLOGICAL INTERPRETATION
Adele (NV = 9, CV = 7, VV = 11, FL = 1)

A very compassionate woman who has wide and inclusive views about life, Adele is someone who truly cares. She is possessed of deep insights into human nature and is willing to do her share to improve the lives of the people around her. However, she has to take care not to expect too much from others too soon. Adele is an idealist whose visionary quest can sometimes get the better of the more practical issues that face her. She will be faced with having to balance her hopes and aspirations for tomorrow with a careful assessment of what is happening in the world around her today. Adele is quietly graceful, a bit introverted, and sometimes reluctant to speak. She enjoys the times when she can be alone to contemplate the things that most interest her.

Adrian

A Kabbalistic Synopsis
אדריון —ADRYVN (Aleph, Daleth, Resh, Yod, Vau, Nun)

Adrian is a very deep and often philosophical individual. Career and money are not driving forces for him. His focus is on the bigger questions in life, and he is looking for some form of spiritual or emotional fulfillment. He begins in the element of air (A) and is completed in the element of water (N). Consequently, he is likely to be a dreamer in early adulthood but will ultimately realize his goals, not the least because of the fire energy in his name. To his friends, Adrian will be a quiet and reliable source of support. The value of his name can be compressed to twelve, which is the number of the Hanged Man in tarot, representing self-sacrifice. If an Adrian is your friend, you are in luck, as this individual always tends to put the needs of others above his own. Adrian will be particularly at home in any of the caring professions.

The Runic Interpretation
ᚾᚨᛁᚱᛞᚨ (Nauthiz, Ansuz, Isa, Raido, Dagaz, Ansuz)

Adrian is the poet and bard who searches the shadow side of himself in order to integrate subconscious thrashings into balance with his practical, conscious self. He will tell you that he feels things with such depth of emotion that he exhausts himself. He cries on dates and he cries at happy movies because it's all so wonderful. Give him reams of paper as a child, and let him draw and write and stay connected to the wisdom buried within. Adrian knows that art gives voice to the powerful mysteries that motivate us all. He would appreciate hearing Bach in the cradle and Beethoven on the swing set. He needs to laugh and run and play and feel the safety of a father's arms.

Elements: Fire, air, earth, water, fire, air

The Numerological Interpretation
Adrian (NV = 2, CV = 9, VV = 11, FL = 1)

A complex individual, Adrian is a man of deep feelings with many facets to his personality. This is a name that can easily belong to a very physically compelling man, one possessing charisma and magnetism. An individual who is both original and full of surprises, Adrian is not content to take the established road in life, but will seek instead to carve out his own direction. Usually philosophical by nature, Adrian is a man who will seek to develop his inner, spiritual nature. Travel will also be a favorite activity, as Adrian's eye is always on the next horizon.

DERIVATION: Latin, referred to someone from the town of Hadria, after which the Adriatic coast was named. This name gained fame after the Roman emperor Publius Hadrianus and several early popes bore the name as well. Popular in the late nineteenth century.

PRINCIPAL COLORS: White, the full spectrum of greens

GEMSTONES AND PRECIOUS METALS: Pearls, jade, moonstones

BOTANICALS: Cabbage, lettuce, plantain

UNIQUE SPELLINGS: Adrien, Adryan, Adryen, Aedrian, Aedryan

RELATED TO: Adamt, Adren, Adriano, Adrio, Hadrian

Adrienne

DERIVATION: French, the feminine form of the Latin name Adrian, which referred to someone from the ancient town of Hadria. Increasingly popular in Britain and the United States since the 1950s.

PRINCIPAL COLORS: All green and yellow hues, gold

GEMSTONES AND PRECIOUS METALS: Pearls, moonstones, all other white stones

BOTANICALS: Blackberry, juniper

UNIQUE SPELLINGS: Adriant, Adriane, Adrianne, Adrien, Adriene

RELATED TO: Ada, Addie, Adra, Adrea, Adria, Adriana, Adrianna, Adriena, Adrienna

❧

"The awakening of consciousness is not unlike the crossing of a frontier—one step and you are in another country."
—ADRIENNE RICH (POET)

A KABBALISTIC SYNOPSIS
אדריאן —ADRYAN (Aleph, Daleth, Resh, Yod, Aleph, Nun)

Adrienne is one of the most adaptable people you could hope to meet; she will learn to deal with enormous change throughout her life. ADRYAN, the Hebrew version of Adrienne's name, can be compressed to the number sixteen, which is the House of God card in the tarot. The House of God, also known as the Crumbling Tower, represents catastrophic or traumatic change. The total value of her name also contains the number sixteen and again refers us to the Crumbling Tower card, suggesting significant traumas in Adrienne's life. It is in the meaning of nine hundred that we find Adrienne's means of dealing with the constant upheaval in her life. Nine is a mystic number of the moon, of intuition and the sixth sense. Adrienne has an unusually developed sense of intuition, which enables her to anticipate changes before they arrive. A further benefit is that the Aquarian influence in her name means that she actually quite enjoys the unpredictability of her lifestyle. The name's generally positive nature ensures that for the most part the events in her life, while they may seem traumatic at the time, have a knack of turning out for the best.

THE RUNIC INTERPRETATION
ᛗᚾᚾᛗᛁᚱᛞᚨ (Ehwaz, Nauthiz, Nauthiz, Ehwaz, Isa, Raido, Dagaz, Ansuz)

The feminine counterpart to the name Adrian contains earthier, less poetic, energy. Adrienne is able to remain focused in the face of fluctuating circumstances, and family, friends, and colleagues are drawn to this quality. She's a natural at on-the-spot troubleshooting; she could produce a movie, run a political campaign, or raise a houseful of children with equal aplomb. And Adrienne isn't shallow. *Mais, non!* Instead she is pragmatic. She realizes that hard knocks come with the territory, and therefore she believes in doing her best and taking comfort in good food, friends, and love.

Elements: Air, fire, fire, air, earth, water, fire, air

THE NUMEROLOGICAL INTERPRETATION
Adrienne (NV = 7, CV = 5, VV = 2, FL = 1)

Adrienne connotes a person who is seeking to find the answers to life. Her tendency is to do this more intellectually than metaphysically. Thus she will find that higher education is a very important goal in her life. This urge "to know" may be so profound that Adrienne may spend hours alone in reclusive contemplation. Yet deep within her is a very profound need for the beauty of intimate human relationships. She is, at her core, a romantic. These two tendencies—the analytical mind of the intellectual and the heart of the lover—can create definite challenges. Her struggle will be to integrate and balance the two tendencies that her name implies.

❧

Agnes

A Kabbalistic Synopsis
אגנס —AGNS (Aleph, Gimel, Nun, Samech)

Agnes is a deeply rational and highly intelligent woman. By kabbalistic analysis her very name means "science" and "brains." From an early age Agnes will be outstripping her classmates, and not just by little steps but in giant leaps and bounds. As an adult Agnes will continue to impress with her intellectual superiority; she is ideally suited to a high-profile academic role. You might also find her hard at work in a large and prestigious research-and-development facility. However, Agnes has a very strong moral conscience, and if she is born under Pisces, it is likely that this moral streak will be very strong indeed. Agnes's sense of responsibility is also shown in her work, as ideally she wants to do something with her life that will benefit the planet and all the people on it. In her personal relationships Agnes is equally generous and caring. It is important, though, that Agnes's friends keep a close eye on her, as she can be emotionally naive and may allow herself to be exploited by more unscrupulous partners.

The Runic Interpretation
ᛋᛖᚾᚷᚨ (Sowelu, Ehwaz, Nauthiz, Gebo, Ansuz)

Agnes loves to be in love. Agnes loses herself in blissful unions, and separations cause her heart to break. She enjoys the company of children and is happiest with one snuggled on her lap. She entertains freely and her friends are always popping in for a cup of coffee. (Of course, true friends know what to expect: Dogs, cats, and wild birds being nursed back to health are all likely to greet them at the door.) Agnes most enjoys the company of bright friends and colleagues who will challenge her intellectually and keep her on course. The many people in her life help her to love herself and to question her life. Agnes needs a partner she can awaken during the night with urgent or profound thoughts, and who will then lull her back to sleep with affirmations and reassurances, for that is really all she asks.

Elements: Air, air, fire, water, air

The Numerological Interpretation
Agnes (NV = 1, CV = 4, VV = 6, FL = 1)

The name Agnes indicates a woman who will work with great determination to secure her place in the world. Practical considerations are usually very important to Agnes, and she has the capacity to ensure that her sense of material security is firmly anchored. Taking risks where money is concerned is not one of her personality characteristics. Yet Agnes is not afraid to express a definite sense of her own individuality. People named Agnes often find that home and family are at the center of their lives. Agnes enjoys the comfort of familiar faces and settings, and will do her best to help those in her immediate surroundings.

DERIVATION: Greek, from the root meaning "pure" or "virginal." Name of a young Roman martyr who was a popular saint during the Middle Ages.

PRINCIPAL COLORS: All shades of yellow and orange, brown and gold

GEMSTONES AND PRECIOUS METALS: Citrine, topaz, amber

BOTANICALS: Chamomile, lavender, sorrel

UNIQUE SPELLINGS: Agnese, Agness, Agnesse, Agnis, Agnys, Agnyse, Agnysse

RELATED TO: Aggi, Aggie, Agna, Agnetta, Aina, Anais, Annis, Inat, Ines, Inezt, Nessa, Una

DERIVATION: English, the short
form of many names beginning
with this syllable, including Alan,
Albert, Alexander, Alfonso,
Alfred, and Alvin.

PRINCIPAL COLORS: Electric
shades of blue, gray

GEMSTONES AND PRECIOUS
METALS: Sapphires

BOTANICALS: Sage, wild spinach

UNIQUE SPELLING: Ael

RELATED TO: Alan†, Alastair,
Albert†, Albie, Alec, Alejandro†,
Alex†, Alexander†, Alfonso†,
Alfred†, Allen†, Alonso, Alphonse

A KABBALISTIC SYNOPSIS
אל —AL (Aleph, Lamed)

Al is a powerful figure who will naturally carry an air of great authority wherever he goes. AL is one of the many Hebrew names for God, and it represents God in terms of the divine power over the material universe. In Al this may manifest itself as impressive organizational and managerial skill; at the same time, this power could relate to a skill such as carpentry or masonry. So whether a mover and shaker in the world of business or a skilled craftsman, Al will always be convinced of his own ability and sound judgment. This characteristic makes him very attractive to people looking for a self-assured and decisive lover. However, if Al is a Scorpio or Leo, this authoritative manner may spill over into a dictatorial attitude toward those around him. But an Al born under the sign of Capricorn will definitely go into business . . . and will most likely make a killing!

THE RUNIC INTERPRETATION
ᛚᚨ (Laguz, Ansuz)

Al isn't here to experience suffering and sorrow. Compared to more burdened souls, one could fairly say that Al is just passing through. He isn't a worrier; yet, he has challenges like the rest of us. His approach is to increase his effort for a while and then, if things are still blocked, take another, more scenic route. Al also knows (without being aware of how he knows) that as we fine-tune our bodies, our thoughts become more disciplined. So Al works out and is able to focus his mind with great precision. He lives life with courage, but if you told him that, he'd just laugh. Al likes to keep things simple.

Elements: Water, air

THE NUMEROLOGICAL INTERPRETATION
Al (NV = 4, CV = 3, VV = 1, FL = 1)

Al brings a direct and forthright energy to life. This is a person who has simple tastes and is usually uncomplicated. A man who does not avoid hard work, Al is a person who goes after what he seeks to achieve with strength and determination. This name indicates practicality, dependability, and careful attention to the material concerns of life. Al connotes a person with much common sense who is more concerned with the values of the world around him than with conjectures about impossible dreams.

Alan

A KABBALISTIC SYNOPSIS
אלן —ALN (Aleph, Lamed, Nun)

Alan is a man looking for peace of mind. He may well feel ill at ease in social settings, as he has never quite fit in with the norm. Alan is not necessarily a nonconformist, but he really does perceive the world in a completely different way from his peers. The number of his name, eighty-one, is one of the mystic numbers of the moon, making Alan prone to idealism and suspicious of pat explanations. Alan has a great love of reading, particularly the more serious literature of the imagination. Indeed, he may even be a poet himself. Alan's quest for inner peace is all-consuming, and in itself this is not a bad thing; a search for some form of higher truth is highly commendable. However, the presence of N, or Nun, in his name may, in Alan's case, lead to a dangerous and potentially self-destructive obsession with death and a fascination with the possibilities of a life beyond.

THE RUNIC INTERPRETATION
ᚾᚨᛚᚨ (Nauthiz, Ansuz, Laguz, Ansuz)

Alan is a Renaissance man comfortable in the world of ideas who quickly moves from one important insight to the next. He is a born teacher, healer, inventor, artist, and statesman, but he subverts these gifts by procrastinating or choosing the wrong partners. Alan must be careful in affairs of the heart because of his open and trusting nature. A large chunk of Alan's life must be spent in solitary pursuits. This is because he is a Way Shower and his guidance comes from within. He is well loved because he laughs easily at himself and helps others see the humor in it all.

Elements: Fire, air, water, air

THE NUMEROLOGICAL INTERPRETATION
Alan (NV = 1, CV = 8, VV = 2, FL = 1)

Bold and direct as well as highly individual, Alan indicates a person who is not afraid to be himself. In fact, he has little choice! Yet as he moves out into life, exploring his creative possibilities, Alan is at his core a person eager for the closeness of human relationships. The name implies a man who, in his own individualistic way, seeks to bring about a sense of unity among people separated by differences in ideology and belief, as well as to provide the possibility for harmonious communication in all social situations so that even more impressive creative goals may be achieved.

DERIVATION: Celtic, possibly derived from words meaning "noble" or "rock." Became common in England after William the Conqueror invaded the nation and declared his follower Alan the Earl of Brittany. Very common in the United States during the 1950s.

PRINCIPAL COLORS: All shades of brown and yellow, gold and orange

GEMSTONES AND PRECIOUS METALS: Topaz, amber, all other yellow stones

BOTANICALS: Lavender, Saint-John's-wort, thyme

UNIQUE SPELLINGS: Alen, Alin, Allan, Allen, Allin, Allon, Allun, Allyn, Alon, Alun, Alyn

RELATED TO: Ailain, Ailean, Alt, Alain, Allent, Lanny

DERIVATION: German, from the words for "noble" and "bright." Popular in Western Europe, especially among noble families. Had a tremendous upsurge in popularity after Queen Victoria married Prince Albert in 1840.

PRINCIPAL COLORS: Lighter shades of blue and gray

GEMSTONES AND PRECIOUS METALS: Sapphires

BOTANICALS: Celandine, sage

UNIQUE SPELLINGS: Aelbert, Ailbert, Alburt

RELATED TO: Alt, Albie, Bert, Bertie, Burt, Burtie

❧

"God does not play at dice with the universe."
—ALBERT EINSTEIN (PHYSICIST)

Albert

A KABBALISTIC SYNOPSIS
אלבת —ALBTh (Aleph, Lamed, Beth, Tau)

Albert will always open a door for a lady and give up his seat on a train or bus. He refuses to believe that the age of chivalry is dead and cannot understand why others don't follow his example. But while Albert may treat women well, he also has a tendency to put them on an unrealistically high pedestal, which may prove difficult for any partner. Not only will Albert's expectations be far in excess of what his partner can realistically accomplish, but she will also have to compete with Albert's mother, with whom no woman can ever hope to compare. His name consists of AL, meaning "God," and BTh (pronounced "Beth"), which represents the feminine aspects of life. In addition his name adds up to 433, showing a concern with women, particularly mother figures, through the predominance of the number three. Three is the number of the Empress in the tarot and relates to the creativity of women. Albert is likely to be the kind of guy who can fall into all kinds of difficulties and yet still come up smelling of roses, since the number three also relates to fortune. At work he will tend to dominate his peers, although this is not perceived as a negative, since this often stems from the fact that he is nearly always first to come up with a creative solution to any given problem in the workplace.

THE RUNIC INTERPRETATION
ᛏᚱᛗᛒᛚᚨ (Teiwaz, Raido, Ehwaz, Berkana, Laguz, Ansuz)

Albert is charming and open-minded, a loyal counselor and friend who facilitates the birth of ideas. He takes a long time to deliberate before he moves, but once he comes on board, he works harder than most. Albert is a born mediator and is patient with people with special needs; he has considerable healing ability and an elegant sense of diplomacy. He will be successful in foreign lands because he steps back to observe the ways of the people and thus is able to blend in graciously. Travel connects him with hitherto untapped aspects of his personality, and Albert always returns from a trip to his day-to-day life refreshed and motivated. Albert reminds many of a teddy bear and so receives plenty of hugs.

Elements: Air, water, air, air/earth, water, air

THE NUMEROLOGICAL INTERPRETATION
Albert (NV = 4, CV = 7, VV = 6, FL = 1)

Albert is a practical name, one that invokes the image of a person of original and significant mental abilities. Home and family are important to him, but he may not be the most openly communicative of people, and he may need many hours to spend alone investigating his special interests. Albert is a name that requires the material comforts and security of life. Material comforts give him the peace of mind that lets him know his loved ones are well taken care of and protected. With this accomplished, he may then peacefully withdraw to his favorite room and pursue his own individual endeavors.

❧

Alejandro

A KABBALISTIC SYNOPSIS
אלינדרע —ALYNDRA'A (Aleph, Lamed, Yod, Nun, Daleth, Resh, Ayin)

Alejandro is enthralled by the past. It may be that he has an enormously and carefully organized photo collection of his childhood, or that he collects some other form of nostalgia. His historical interests can seek a more serious outlet, and he may be employed as an archivist or record keeper of some kind. Alejandro's love of history is primarily sparked by a desire to reveal the hidden and unknown; this may incline him toward a career in prehistory and archaeology. In his personal life, Alejandro wants to love his partner intensely. There is a fiery passion running through Alejandro's soul that any partner should be aware of when trying to comprehend Alejandro's sometimes strange behavior. This is a man who can often come across as quiet on the surface, but he feels with enormous intensity and has the capacity for deep jealousy.

THE RUNIC INTERPRETATION
ᛟᚱᛞᚨᚺᛟᛗᛚᚨ (Othila, Raido, Dagaz, Nauthiz, Ansuz, Jera, Ehwaz, Laguz, Ansuz)

Life presents many challenges for Alejandro, and he has to learn his lessons the hard way until he lets go of the need to push his way through problems. Once he loves himself enough to bring the silver key from his pocket and examine it, his life changes forever. The power of the key is the ability to go anywhere, anytime, thanks to Ehwaz, the rune of movement. Alejandro has a strong laugh and will enjoy the company of many loves. Alejandro's mother, when she first feels him to be a blessing in her arms, utters, "What is yours will come to you."

Elements: Earth/fire, water, fire, fire, air, earth, air, water, air

THE NUMEROLOGICAL INTERPRETATION
Alejandro (NV = 8, CV = 22, VV = 4, FL = 1)

In his own very distinct way, Alejandro may be a bit of an alchemist. This is a name that indicates a person who is very occupied with the material plane and worldly success. Yet behind this ambitious and luxury-loving man is someone who knows how to make things happen, and in ways that are both fascinating and magical! If Alejandro is a more spiritual person, he will use his powers of manifestation, his social position, and his abundant creativity for the well-being of humanity. If, on the other hand, his focus is more egocentric, he may find himself a prisoner of what he has created and limited by the weight of his material concerns.

DERIVATION: Spanish form of Alexander, a Greek name that means "defender of men." Among English-speaking countries, most common in the United States.

PRINCIPAL COLORS: Dark gray and black, dark shades of blue and purple

GEMSTONES AND PRECIOUS METALS: Black pearls and diamonds, deep-toned rubies and sapphires

BOTANICALS: Marsh mallow, shepherd's purse

UNIQUE SPELLINGS: Alahandro, Alajandro, Alehandro, Alijandro

RELATED TO: Alt, Alastair, Alec, Alext, Alexandert, Alistair, Sander, Sandyl

Alex

DERIVATION: Pet form of Alexander, a Greek name that means "defender of men." Alexander has been a long-standing favorite name in all English-speaking countries, and its diminutive forms are frequently used as full names.

PRINCIPAL COLORS: All but the brightest shades of blue

GEMSTONES AND PRECIOUS METALS: Emeralds and turquoise

BOTANICALS: Vervain, violet, and walnut

UNIQUE SPELLINGS: Ahlex, Ailex, Aliks, Alix, Allex, Alyx

RELATED TO: Alt, Alastair, Alec, Aleck, Alexandert, Alick, Alistair; Alexandrat, Alexist

෴

In the absence of any direct equivalent to the letter x in the runic alphabet, the runes Sowelu and Kano are used in conjunction.

A KABBALISTIC SYNOPSIS
אלחס —ALChS (Aleph, Lamed, Cheth, Samech)

Alex is a patient and deeply sensitive person, although he or she tends to put up barriers to all but the closest of friends. Alex adds up to ninety-nine in terms of its Hebrew value, and nine is the number of the moon; it is a symbol of emotions and hidden feelings. In addition, Alex reduces to eighteen, which in the Kabbalah corresponds to the sign Cancer. Alex has a classic Cancerian temperament, ruled by the heart rather than the head; he or she is likely to be more intuitive than most. Be careful what you say to and about Alex, as he or she can be deeply hurt by comments that others would shrug off. Alexes hide this vulnerable side to their natures under a crustacean shell, which in the name is represented by Cheth, meaning "enclosure." If you are lucky enough to get close to an Alex, you will find that it's worth the wait, as the old saying "still waters run deep" could have been written with Alex in mind.

THE RUNIC INTERPRETATION
ᛋᚲᛗᛚᚨ (Sowelu and Kano, Ehwaz, Laguz, Ansuz)

Alex is talkative and imaginative and oh so prone to exaggeration. Because of a love of over-statement, Alex is the brunt of a lot of jokes but only stays mad a week or two. Alex is also prone to extremes. Alex changes gears every few weeks, chasing one windmill after another, and is the type likely to propose on the first date. Alex is a gambler but has a generous heart. If he or she wins the lottery someday, Alex really will share the winnings with lifelong pals. That's because Alex thrives in the spirit of good company. And real friends don't mind the way he or she dresses.

Elements: Air and water, air, water, air

THE NUMEROLOGICAL INTERPRETATION
Alex (NV = 6, CV = 9, VV = 6, FL = 1)

Alex is a highly idealistic name, one that indicates a person who is profoundly concerned with peace, harmony, and proper human relationships. Alex seeks not to harm anyone and can be rather shocked and hurt when people abuse one another. Having the name of a compassionate and artistically talented person, Alex may use his or her talents to evoke beauty and harmony in the immediate environment. This is a name that carries an energy of grace, tolerance, and kindness. It also indicates an interest in using one's talents and skills in helpful and unselfish projects.

෴

Alexander

A Kabbalistic Synopsis

אלחזנדר —ALChZNDR (Aleph, Lamed, Cheth, Zayin, Nun, Daleth, Resh)

Perhaps the greatest leader and empire builder in history was Alexander the Great. His name could not have been more appropriate: Alexander has a value of three hundred, the same as the letter Shin, ש. Shin represents the energies of fire in its purest form and is symbolic of immense creative energy. Even a modern-day Alexander is likely to have a meteoric rise to success in his chosen field. Such an energetic nature has only one danger: that its possessor may literally burn out through too much explosive creativity. Alexander will not only do well but will also be respected. He has very strong principles, which he will not compromise for a speedier advance up the ladder of success. This highly principled nature is emphasized by the name's gematric equivalence to the kabbalistic word for "the spirit of God"; this spirit is called the Ruach Elohim in Hebrew. Alexander is associated with this holy spirit thanks to the value of both words being exactly the same. In Kabbalah, words of the same value have connected meanings.

The Runic Interpretation

ᚱᛖᛞᚨᚺᚾᛋᚲᛗᛚᚨ (Raido, Ehwaz, Dagaz, Nauthiz, Ansuz, Sowelu and Kano, Ehwaz, Laguz, Ansuz)

Alexander shares the gift of expansiveness with the name Alex and adds a tremendous need to travel as well. Alexander loves money, mystery, and intrigue. A romance or two is also valued, as it sometimes can cage the extreme loneliness Alexander can experience. He breaks away from childhood limitations at an early age and often experiences feelings of alienation from family and culture. With energies like Dagaz and Nauthiz in his name, Alexander is born wise. He accomplishes a great deal in this lifetime and sometimes needs to stop striving in order to sit back and enjoy the abundance of life with family and friends. With the energies of this name, Alexander the Great was bound to be a conqueror.

Elements: Water, air, fire, fire, air, air and water, air, water, air

The Numerological Interpretation

Alexander (NV = 3, CV = 9, VV = 3, FL = 1)

A man of great mental activity, Alexander has no problem following through on his ideas, visions, and concepts. He is a thinker, a philosopher, and a man of original act and action. He is propelled through life with a profound desire to learn and to teach others what he has discovered. One caveat, though: This is a name that indicates a person who can be so involved with his own processes and projects that he may engender certain difficulties in his intimate personal relationships.

DERIVATION: From a Greek word meaning "defender of men." Found in the New Testament, the name became famous around the world after the conquests of Alexander the Great around 340 B.C.E. Has been the name of several saints and popes, and is a royal name in Scotland. Very popular in all English-speaking countries.

PRINCIPAL COLORS: All violet and purple hues, including the palest shades of lilac

GEMSTONES AND PRECIOUS METALS: Amethyst, garnets

BOTANICALS: Barberry, dandelion, strawberry

UNIQUE SPELLINGS: Ahlexander, Alecsander, Aleksandr, Alexandder, Alexandr, Alixander

RELATED TO: Alt, Alastair, Alec, Aleck, Alejandro†, Alessandr, Alext, Alexandre, Alic, Alick, Alistair, Sander, Sandy†, Sasha

In the absence of any direct equivalent to the letter x in the runic alphabet, the runes Sowelu and Kano are used in conjunction.

Alexandra

❧

"Should-haves solve nothing. It's the next thing to happen that needs thinking about."
—ALEXANDRA RIPLEY (AUTHOR)

❧

In the absence of any direct equivalent to the letter *x* in the runic alphabet, the runes Sowelu and Kano are used in conjunction.

A KABBALISTIC SYNOPSIS
אלחזנדרא —ALChZNDRA (Aleph, Lamed, Cheth, Zayin, Nun, Daleth, Resh, Aleph)

In kabbalistic interpretation one letter can make a world of difference. Alexandra is a typical example of that aspect of the system. By adding the letter A, or Aleph, to the name Alexander, the character of the name changes completely. Alexandra is a very powerful woman. Her value is 301, which equates to ASh, meaning "fire." However, this is a fire that comes from thoughts, as the name itself is now enclosed by two Alephs, which signify the element of air and the mind. If you are looking for a good strategic planner, Alexandra is your woman. Not only does she have the mental vision needed, but she has the energy to see things through. Ideally suited for senior management roles, Alexandra is able to contain her energy and will always come across as surprisingly calm and at ease, despite dealing with workloads that would have lesser mortals in tears.

THE RUNIC INTERPRETATION
ᚫᚱᛞᚾᚫᛋᚲᛗᛖᚱ (Ansuz, Raido, Dagaz, Nauthiz, Ansuz, Sowelu and Kano, Ehwaz, Laguz, Ansuz)

Alexandra has the curiosity and love of travel that the name Alexander bears. The additional *a* in the name brings the Ansuz energy of signals to heighten her intuition. But while Alexander is guided by his logic, Alexandra makes voyages to her soul. When all is said and done, Alexandra may not have amassed a fortune or conquered civilizations, but she has conquered herself. She has trained her mind to use deep meditative states to gain information and to heal. Through this ability she finds peace and balance, which allows her to enjoy her connections to home and family. The Ansuz energy gives Alexandra the strength to sit in silence, and from this practice she unlocks many mysteries and is protected her whole life.

Elements: Air, water, fire, fire, air, air and water, air, water, air

THE NUMEROLOGICAL INTERPRETATION
Alexandra (NV = 8, CV = 9, VV = 8, FL = 1)

This name endows a person with the motivation to care for the health and beauty of both her physical body and her immediate surroundings. Appearances are very important to Alexandra. Status and social position mean a great deal to her, and she will do her best to maintain them in her life. If she is of a more humanitarian bent, Alexandra will tend to extend this sense of responsibility to her community and even outwardly to the earth. Therefore, she may often be found participating in projects that deal with ecology and energy-resource management.

❧

Alexis

A Kabbalistic Synopsis
אלחסיס —ALChSYS (Aleph, Lamed, Cheth, Samech, Yod, Samech)

Everything about Alexis is larger than life. It may be that the creators of *Dynasty* were secret kabbalists, as the character Alexis Carrington was, in many ways, an archetypal Alexis with all that glamour and passion! Alexis is driven by her emotions and is often guilty of acting before thinking, which accounts for the rapid and unexpected changes in her somewhat hectic life. Her name adds up to 169, which is thirteen multiplied by itself, or the number of change squared. What is more, her number reduces to sixteen, a number signifying major or catastrophic change—so Alexis is quite a tempestuous lady indeed. You won't be bored if you are spending time with Alexis, but watch out; Alexis not only encounters more than her own fair share of change, she is prone to bringing change into other people's lives as well, often with dramatic results. In the rare case of an Alexis with a low sense of self-esteem, she may have a tendency to thrive on the conflicts that she effortlessly causes in other people's relationships, rather than creating explosive passion in her own.

The Runic Interpretation
ᛋᛁᚲᛗᛖᚨ (Sowelu, Isa, Sowelu and Kano, Ehwaz, Laguz, Ansuz)

Alexis takes magic words and weaves them into one entertaining story after another. Her description of a simple ride on the train makes you wish you'd been there, too. Her dreams and her conversation are utterly delightful. Her looks are pleasant enough, but it is her charm that allows her to seduce many suitors with her words. Her voice is well modulated and hypnotic, and she is well read. Alexis has a lot of ambition, so she will achieve her goals and have a good time until midlife. At that point she may become interested in metaphysics, and materialism will no longer be a driving force in her life. Alexis will influence many lives with her prayers because they are well spoken and to the point.

Elements: Air, earth, air and water, air, water, air

The Numerological Interpretation
Alexis (NV = 7, CV = 1, VV = 6, FL = 1)

Alexis is a name indicating a woman who is quite confident. She is unafraid to project her needs and wishes, and then pursue them! A strong person with an analytical mind, Alexis will have an assertive personality with a tendency to prevail over both adversity and adversaries. Yet Alexis is far more complex than she may appear on the surface. This name denotes a person who possesses a very contemplative and philosophical side to her nature, which makes her an astute observer of human character. This can lead to highly developed intuition, a quality that can be used for supporting and encouraging other people with not quite as much confidence and self-assurance as herself.

DERIVATION: English, from the Greek name Alexios, meaning "defender." Originally a male name but now used primarily as a female name.

PRINCIPAL COLORS: Gold, the full range of greens and yellows

GEMSTONES AND PRECIOUS METALS: Pearls, moss agate, any other white stones

BOTANICALS: Blackberry, elder, hops

UNIQUE SPELLINGS: Alexice, Alexiss, Alexys, Alyxice, Alyxis

RELATED TO: Aleka, Alessa, Alessandra, Alessia, Alext, Alexa, Alexandrat, Alexi, Alexia, Alexie, Alexina, Alix, Allexina, Lexi, Lexie, Lexy

∽

In the absence of any direct equivalent to the letter *x* in the runic alphabet, the runes Sowelu and Kano are used in conjunction.

∽

Alfonso

DERIVATION: Spanish, initially from Germanic words meaning "noble" and "ready." Saint Alphonsus was a ninth-century Spanish bishop, and the name became traditional among royal families of the Iberian Peninsula.

PRINCIPAL COLORS: The full spectrum of yellows, including orange and gold

GEMSTONES AND PRECIOUS METALS: Topaz, amber, any other yellowish stone

BOTANICALS: Borage, chamomile, Saint-John's-wort

UNIQUE SPELLINGS: Ahlphanso, Ahlphonso, Alfonzo, Alphonso, Alphonzo

RELATED TO: Alfonxo, Alt, Alanso, Alf, Alfonse, Alfy, Alphie, Alphonse, Alphonsus

❧

"Had I been present at the creation, I would have given some useful hints for the better ordering of the universe."

— ALFONSO X (THE WISE, KING OF CASTILE AND LEÓN)

❧

In the absence of any direct equivalent to the letter *f* in the Hebrew alphabet, the letter Peh is used. Peh can function as either a hard or a soft letter, and as such, is one of the seven "doubles."

A KABBALISTIC SYNOPSIS

אלפנסוה —ALPhNSVH (Aleph, Lamed, Peh, Nun, Samech; Vau, Heh)

Alfonso has trouble keeping his feet on the ground and may fall into the trap of believing his ideas to be greater than they actually are. This is not to say that Alfonso lacks intelligence; in fact, his name suggests great mental activity. Kabbalistically, Alfonso can be placed on the twenty-seventh and twenty-ninth paths of the Tree of Life, which relate to natural and corporeal intelligence, respectively. His problem comes from the fact that his name, under closer analysis, can mean "the limit of God" when centered around the letter N, or Nun, which is concerned with emotions. Alfonso runs the risk of applying his lofty ideas to himself rather than to a greater force outside of himself. If he does decide that he has the next great truth, he will waste no time in telling everyone he can get to listen; the value of Alfonso can also spell QvPh, meaning "mouth." However, if Alfonso can keep his own importance in perspective, he will be a veritable fountain of profound insight and much wisdom.

THE RUNIC INTERPRETATION

ᛟᛋᚾᛟᚠᛚᚨ (Othila, Sowelu, Nauthiz, Othila, Fehu, Laguz, Ansuz)

The Fehu energy in this name is auspicious. Alfonso is a good-luck name. What makes one person win at a game of chance while the rest of us just waste our money? Alfonso knows. He has the ability to create the reality he sees in his mind, and he can envision both opportunities and danger, or health concerns. Chances are excellent that he will better his station in life; money comes to him. He is able to learn to curb reckless tendencies, amass savings, and appreciate what he has. In his golden years he will teach or heal.

Elements: Earth/fire, air, fire, earth/fire, fire, water, air

THE NUMEROLOGICAL INTERPRETATION

Alfonso (NV = 1, CV = 6, VV = 4, FL = 1)

With a name indicating power as well as compassion, Alfonso may use his talents and gifts in the creation of beauty and harmony. A person with a love of the arts, Alfonso is a man who will work diligently to produce the perfection of his visions in the physical world. Original in his thinking, Alfonso is a consummate individualist, a man aware of his needs and eager to go forward and establish himself in the world. Creativity is fundamental to his nature, and perseverance is an integrated aspect of his character.

❧

Alfred

A KABBALISTIC SYNOPSIS
אלפרד —ALPhRD (Aleph, Lamed, Peh, Resh, Daleth)

If you're in a fancy restaurant and there's a bigger-than-life figure with an obvious eye for the best food and wine who's on first-name terms with the maître d'—and possibly even has his own private table—there's a good chance he's an Alfred. Alfred is an unabashed sensualist. He loves the finer things in life, and he wants them by the truckload! Alfred has a definite preference for the exotic, whether it be his clothes or his romances. In extreme cases (particularly with a Scorpio Alfred), his tastes in the art of love may even run to the bizarre. Of course, not every Alfred can afford such a lifestyle, but not to worry. The name Alfred is made up of the full spelling of Aleph, which is the element of mind, and Resh, meaning "head," plus Daleth, for "door." The net result of this is that even without the wallet to suit his tastes, Alfred can still conjure up the most amazing and exotic fantasies to keep himself happy!

THE RUNIC INTERPRETATION
ᛞᛖᚱᚠᛚᚨ (Dagaz, Ehwaz, Raido, Fehu, Laguz, Ansuz)

Alfred reaches out to people all day long, and he feels lost when he is alone for extended periods of time. This is because one of his reasons for living is to interact with people. When he's alone, he's out of a job! Naturally, Alfred is a gracious host. His generosity touches the lives of people, because he helps wherever he can to enhance talents and extend a shoulder of sympathy. He understands that his cup overflows and is eager to share himself with others. But Alfred would do well to step back occasionally, rest, and replenish himself. His physical body is not as strong as his spirit. Offer Alfred appreciation early in life and he will be a loyal friend always.

Elements: Fire, air, water, fire, water, air

THE NUMEROLOGICAL INTERPRETATION
Alfred (NV = 1, CV = 22, VV = 6, FL = 1)

This is a powerful name, as it indicates a person who is very self-assured, with strong motivations and lofty ambitions. Alfred is capable of extraordinary feats of creative self-expression. Here is a man who is undaunted by challenges; in fact, he is encouraged by them. Alfred likes to work on large-scale projects and have an administrative role in directing them. Yet the name Alfred also contains a certain tendency toward harmony and beauty, and a type of sensitivity that allows for peaceful cooperation in everything that he may undertake.

DERIVATION: Old English, from the word *aelfraed*, meaning "elf counsel." Popular during the Middle Ages, its usage subsequently declined, then reemerged in the late eighteenth century.

PRINCIPAL COLORS: All the various shades of yellow and brown, including gold and bronze

GEMSTONES AND PRECIOUS METALS: Citrine, topaz, amber, and any other yellowish stone

BOTANICALS: Saint-John's-wort, sorrel, thyme

UNIQUE SPELLINGS: Aelfred, Aelfrid, Aelfryd, Ailfred, Ailfrid, Ailfryd, Alfrid, Alfryd

RELATED TO: Alt, Alf, Alfie, Alfredo, Alfy, Fredt, Freddie

In the absence of any direct equivalent to the letter *f* in the Hebrew alphabet, the letter Peh is used. Peh can function as either a hard or a soft letter, and as such, is one of the seven "doubles."

DERIVATION: English and French, variant of Adelaide. Gained popularity in the nineteenth century, especially when Lewis Carroll used this name for his child heroine in *Alice's Adventures in Wonderland* and *Through the Looking Glass.*

PRINCIPAL COLORS: The full spectrum of purple and mauve

GEMSTONES AND PRECIOUS METALS: Amethyst, garnets

BOTANICALS: Bilberry, lungwort, mint

UNIQUE SPELLINGS: Ahlice, Ahliss, Ahylice, Alise, Aliss, Alyce, Alys, Alyse, Alyss

RELATED TO: Adelaide, Ali, Aliciat, Alisa, Alison, Alissa, Allie, Allisont, Ally, Allyson, Alycia, Alysa, Alyson, Alyssat, Elise, Elyse, Ilise, Ilyse, Lise, Lissa

A KABBALISTIC SYNOPSIS
אלים —ALYS (Aleph, Lamed, Yod, Samech)

Alice is the epitome of naive modesty; she is the quiet one in the office, always first to blush and last to find a partner. She is likely to be religious in a traditional sense, churchgoing and unassumingly moral. However, she will always be surrounded by friends, as Alice has no desire to preach or convert others to her lifestyle. You won't catch Alice going out on a blind date; she is far more likely to be seen on a charity drive or doing volunteer work. This attitude is shown by gematric analysis, which produces, for example, the Hebrew for "storehouse." This tells us that Alice is storing something for later. Other letters in the name reveal that it is her innocence she is holding on to. While happy with platonic relationships, Alice may have a fear of serious commitment. This is shown by the value of her name, 101; we can see that the possibility of making two is prevented by the zero. The effect of Jupiter, the planet of luck, should reassure Alice that she will ultimately find that for which she has saved herself.

THE RUNIC INTERPRETATION
ᛗᛋᛁᛚᚨ (Ehwaz, Sowelu, Isa, Laguz, Ansuz)

Alice is an iron butterfly. Underneath that beatific smile is one strong woman! Alice prides herself on keeping up with fashion and current events. She's the sort that requires real diamonds, and she will wear them all day long if she gets them. Alice needs her lovers to be smart and fascinating. Marrying is something she acknowledges she'll do someday; however, she does not necessarily relish the thought of limiting her romantic options. She wants to travel but finds it's hard to get away from all she cares for at home. She makes a good critic, and she negotiates with calm authority. Alice will be kind to her aging parents and appreciates being remembered, as well.

Elements: Air, air, earth, water, air

THE NUMEROLOGICAL INTERPRETATION
Alice (NV = 3, CV = 6, VV = 6, FL = 1)

Sweet Alice: The name conjures up flowers and peaceful spring days, and so it should! There is a profound sensitivity contained within the energy of this name, one that extends outward from Alice into the environment. Alice indicates a woman who is constantly seeking to bring comfort and emotional support to those around her. Active and always on the go, Alice is constantly finding ways to communicate her sense of harmony and peace into her surroundings. The home and workplace are especially important to her, and Alice will do what is possible to ensure that these locations are not only aesthetically pleasing but emotionally secure as well.

Alicia

A Kabbalistic Synopsis
אל ישה —ALYShH (Aleph, Lamed, Yod, Shin, Heh)

Alicia knows just what to say to a man and how to say it to make his head turn. Flirting is an exact science for her—a skill developed over the years based not on what she looks like but on the powerful person she knows she is. Alicia is at home in almost any work environment, as she is not only intelligent and capable, but she knows how to apply that little extra touch to get her where she wants to be. Beneath her appealing exterior is a core of steel, and she can cut her way quite happily through the jungle of commerce. Her name refers not only to pleasure but also to willpower. Do not try to outbluff this gal in a poker game; it just can't be done!

The Runic Interpretation
ᚾᛁᛋᛁᛚᚨ (Ansuz, Isa, Sowelu, Isa, Laguz, Ansuz)

Alicia is a born actress. She has the chameleon's ability to blend in and develop an instant rapport with people. Like most actresses, Alicia needs private time to stay in balance. Time spent painting, reading, or praying helps her bounce back to being herself. Friends need to look out for Alicia because although she knows how to attract money, she often doesn't give it much thought. Her life is passionate and she's likely to tell you all the details— that is, if her phone hasn't been turned off this month! Alicia is fortunate to have the Sowelu energy of wholeness to draw on in her name. Sowelu teaches us that what we are striving to become is what we are already. The key is to know ourselves and appreciate the fact that our talents came to us with the implied expectation on the part of the universe that we use these talents for the benefit of all.

Elements: Air, earth, air, earth, water, air

The Numerological Interpretation
Alicia (NV = 8, CV = 6, VV = 2, FL = 1)

A name indicating cooperation and harmony, Alicia evokes a woman for whom balanced and fruitful personal relationships are of the utmost importance. This is a lady who seeks to have a beautiful rapport with everyone and everything. Her artistic sensibility is strong, and she is at her creative best when she knows that her efforts will please others. Alicia also believes in material abundance and worldly success. In this respect, we find that Alicia is a name geared to combining artistic talent with business sense, and the urge for human harmony with a deep sense of practicality.

DERIVATION: Spanish and English, a modern form of Alice.

PRINCIPAL COLORS: Black, as well as the darkest gray, blue, and purple hues

GEMSTONES AND PRECIOUS METALS: Amethyst, black pearls, carbuncles, any other dark stones

BOTANICALS: Angelica, marsh mallow, shepherd's purse

UNIQUE SPELLINGS: Alecia, Aleesha, Alesha, Alisha, Alycia, Eleshia, Elicia, Elisha, Elycia, Ilecia, Ilicia, Ilycia

RELATED TO: Ali, Alice†, Alisa, Alison, Alissa, Allie, Allison†, Allyson, Alyce, Alyse, Alyson, Alyssa†, Elisa, Elise, Elissa, Elyssa, Ilise, Ilyse

~

"To define oneself as authentically as possible from within has become the major female enterprise."
—ALICIA OSTRIKER (POET)

DERIVATION: An alternative spelling of Alan, a name of Gaelic origin. Although this spelling is hardly ever used in Britain and Scotland, it is quite common in the United States.

PRINCIPAL COLORS: Black and gray, darker shakes of blue and violet

GEMSTONES AND PRECIOUS METALS: Dull rubies, black pearls, black diamonds, and all other dark stones

BOTANICALS: Angelica, shepherd's purse, ragwort

UNIQUE SPELLINGS: Alan, Alen, Alin, Allan, Allin, Allon, Allun, Allyn, Alon, Alun, Alyn

RELATED TO: Ailain, Alt, Alain, Alant, Lanny

Allen

A KABBALISTIC SYNOPSIS
אללן —ALLN (Aleph, Lamed, Lamed, Nun)

Allen is reliable. He may not be particularly exciting, but he's always around when you need him. If Allen is born under any of the earth signs—Capricorn, Taurus, or Virgo—he may actually be around even when you don't need him! Still, people really like Allen: He is a reminder of stability in the midst of the ever-changing world we now live in. Most Allens you meet seem middle-aged, even if they are not yet that old. Allen has an aura of having arrived at his proper place in the world, no matter how young he is. The ideal uncle figure, he is one of the few people in life who not only is attracted to a traditional family and lifestyle but genuinely achieves it. However, there is also a hidden side to Allen, a side that no one else ever sees or even guesses at. It will vary from Allen to Allen, but the numerical uniqueness of the name ensures that in some carefully camouflaged way, each Allen is truly individual.

THE RUNIC INTERPRETATION
ᚾᛖᛚᛚᚨ (Nauthiz, Ehwaz, Laguz, Laguz, Ansuz)

Emotional in nature, Allen could pursue a career as a therapist, and he will be a successful healer because he has worked on himself. Allen is also good with children, and may find social work to be another calling. Allen loves to unwind to music and feels restored in the shower. Vacations by the sea are a tonic for him, for he is a kindhearted man with a well-developed affinity for nature. Women respond to this, and Allen never wants for a date. Some of Allen's admirers get more than they'd hoped for when Allen weeps into hundreds of tissues at the movies. But the right woman will appreciate every tear.

Elements: Fire, air, water, water, air

THE NUMEROLOGICAL INTERPRETATION
Allen (NV = 8, CV = 11, VV = 6, FL = 1)

The vibration of this name carries a strong urge for material success as well as a gifted, intuitive nature. Beauty and harmony are also important to Allen, and it is highly likely that he would be involved in some area of communications, the arts, or the media—fields through which he could disseminate his wide and inclusive perspective on life. Allen is in touch with life's physical beauty as well as its spiritual essence, and would be very open to explore the more metaphysical sides to existence. Yet Allen has a very practical side to his nature and would make sure that his creative pursuits include abundant opportunities for social achievement.

Allison

DERIVATION: Scottish and French, originally a diminutive version of Alice. Since the 1930s, it has become increasingly popular.

PRINCIPAL COLORS: All yellows and browns, including gold

GEMSTONES AND PRECIOUS METALS: Topaz, amber, yellow diamonds

BOTANICALS: Borage, eyebright, lavender

UNIQUE SPELLINGS: Alesin, Aleson, Alicin, Alison, Allyson, Alycin, Alysin, Alyson

RELATED TO: Ali, Alicet, Aliciat, Alisa, Alisha, Allie, Alyce, Alyse, Alyssat, Elise, Elyse, Elyssa, Ilyse

A Kabbalistic Synopsis

אלליסון —ALLYSVN (Aleph, Lamed, Lamed, Yod, Samech, Vau, Nun)

Quietly generous, Allison is in many ways similar to her "sister" Alice. Both can be shy, demure, and unassuming. Allison will also devote much of her time to good causes, although in her case they are likely to be friends and relations. However, while Alice keeps all her feelings tightly under lock and key, Allison's emotions sit much closer to the surface. The key to Allison's nature lies in the second half of her name. The two sections are separated by a Y, or Yod, א"ע, the fiery creative energy, which in Kabbalah begins the mystic four-lettered name of God and is the first breath of creation. This Yod energizes the second half of the name, whose letters have strong connections with sensuality based in emotional commitment. Allison, then, is a classic case of still waters running deep. Underneath her modest exterior is a seething core of sensual desires, which the right mate will only be half-surprised to discover, as this current of desire cannot keep itself completely out of sight.

The Runic Interpretation

↑◇ᛋᛁᛚᛚᚨ (Nauthiz, Othila, Sowelu, Isa, Laguz, Laguz, Ansuz)

Allison often feels overwhelmed, as if she must get things done through the proper channels but the people she is dealing with are at odds with her efforts. If she can work through this frustration, her unique administrative skills flourish. What matters is that Allison become her own advocate and get the answers in her own time. Some will value her and some will dismiss her entirely. Regardless, Allison must make her own luck, and her life lesson is to form friendships with positive people. She learns this through the years, and as she mellows, her life becomes as enchanting as summer twilight. Allison uses the Nauthiz energy to reverse feelings of constraint in her life. She can be proud of her many successes because she is truly a self-made woman.

Elements: Fire, earth/fire, air, earth, water, water, air

The Numerological Interpretation

Allison (NV = 1, CV = 3, VV = 7, FL = 1)

Allison is a name that evokes a great deal of mental energy. But Allison is not just a thinker; she is also innovative and original in the application of her thoughts. Some people may think of her as being too abstract and very impractical. She does have a strong philosophical nature as well as a tendency to spend many hours by herself. She needs this time to assure herself about her life direction and to anchor her opinions and concepts deep within herself. When the moment is right, Allison will emerge from her self-imposed exile and begin to communicate her visions and insights to others, inspiring and stimulating them. She is not a born leader but becomes one over time as she grows into her true strengths.

DERIVATION: Spanish diminutive form of Alphonso, which was a common Spanish royal name. This name was somewhat common in Britain during the 1930s.

PRINCIPAL COLORS: All greens, white, cream

GEMSTONES AND PRECIOUS METALS: Jade, pearls, moonstones

BOTANICALS: Chicory, lettuce, plantain

UNIQUE SPELLINGS: Ahlonso, Ahlonsoe, Ahlonzo, Ahlonzoe, Allonso, Allonsoe, Allonzo, Alonso, Alonzoe

RELATED TO: Alfonso†, Alphonse, Alphonso, Alphonsus

A KABBALISTIC SYNOPSIS
אלנזע —ALNZA'A (Aleph, Lamed, Nun, Zayin, Ayin)

Alonzo is a shrewd customer. He is the guy in the bar with plenty of cash in his wallet, and most of the time that is exactly where it stays. It isn't that Alonzo is stingy; he is, in his own words, merely careful and prudent. When considering his career, Alonzo's main concern will always be the paycheck rather than the nature of the work. Alonzos don't tend to be high-fliers but if they are, it is likely to be in the field of accountancy. Alonzo tends toward jobs that are reasonably rewarding, but above all, stable, predictable, and long-term. In Hebrew, the basis for Kabbalah, Al is one of the names of God. Like all whose names begin with "Al," Alonzo has great respect for authority. The remainder of the name determines how this manifests itself, and in Alonzo's case, it guarantees a strong affinity for the work ethic.

THE RUNIC INTERPRETATION
ᛟᛉᚾᛟᛚᚨ (Othila, Algiz, Nauthiz, Othila, Laguz, Ansuz)

Alonzo is quick to absorb the emotions of others. He needs time to let out all the toxic energy he sucks in during the events of the day, but Alonzo is not one to hold grudges or shout and scream. His gigantic reserve of energy is one of his unique characteristics. He has considerable musical ability and is attracted to professions that suit his keen sense of justice. He lives his life with honesty and integrity, and can tell a liar by the sound of his voice. Alonzo is willing to wait some time to marry, as he seeks a woman he can really love. Alonzo's life lessons involve cultivating modesty and feeling gratitude for his many blessings. Although he will admit it only to close friends, Alonzo is very psychic.

Elements: Earth/fire, air, fire, earth/fire, water, air

THE NUMEROLOGICAL INTERPRETATION
Alonzo (NV = 11, CV = 7, VV = 4, FL = 1)

The name Alonzo indicates a highly gifted and intuitive individual, one for whom hard work, determination, and service to others form the core of his being. This is a man who may spend a great deal of time on personal research projects. His efforts are often geared to developing new theories and initiating new concepts, which he may then communicate to the world around him. His orientation is decidedly social, and his aims are fundamentally involved with helping others achieve by expanding their horizons. However, he has to remember that life is not totally centered in the mind, and he may find that his intimate personal relationships require some attention as well.

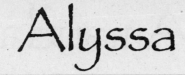

Alyssa

A KABBALISTIC SYNOPSIS
אל יסא —ALYSA (Aleph, Lamed, Yod, Samech, Aleph)

Alyssa has a regal way, carrying herself with a graceful, swanlike air. While she may appear fragile, Alyssa has a resilience few would suspect. This resilient streak is revealed by the central Y, or Yod. Not only tough but canny as well, Alyssa knows what's what and will fiercely defend any incursion into what she regards as her emotional or material property. Although Alyssa is rightly proud of all she owns, which is usually considerable, the dual presence of the A, or Aleph, prevents her from becoming obsessive about material possessions. Motherhood is supremely important to Alyssa; her name adds up to three, which is both the number of the Empress card in tarot and the sephirah (sphere) known as Binah on the Tree of Life. The Empress represents the material instinct, while Binah is the sephirah associated with motherhood and the female creative principle. Despite her generally pleasant nature, Alyssa can at times have a somewhat morbid outlook on life, which is caused by the associations with Saturn in her name. However, these moments of dark doubt and fatalism are minor considerations against the otherwise positive nature of the name.

THE RUNIC INTERPRETATION
ᚨᛋᛋᛇᛚᚨ (Ansuz, Sowelu, Sowelu, Eihwaz, Laguz, Ansuz)

Alyssa loves the heavens. Drawn to psychic realms, she may frequently consult astrologers. Her first question as she looks at her chart will be a disarming one: "Tell me, where do you see the trust fund?" Let's hope it's there! We can attribute Alyssa's artistic nature to the Ansuz energy in her name. Ansuz means "signals" and Alyssa listens to her inner signals. She knows she needs to create and play. Let Alyssa tango under the stars and advise you on a color scheme for your next house. She'll charm you and make you giggle for days with a simple summation of a complicated problem. She's terrible at foreign languages, and that's just another thing that gets you laughing. Whatever you do, treasure her and keep her safe. She is from another time.

Elements: Air, air, air, earth/fire, water, air

THE NUMEROLOGICAL INTERPRETATION
Alyssa (NV = 5, CV = 4, VV = 3, FL = 1)

Alyssa is a name that gives the impression of a person with a very expansive nature. She is a woman who communicates freely with others and enjoys exchanging her views and opinions. You want to work alongside Alyssa, for she's a catalyst for constructive dialogue and has been known to get negotiations moving again after they've sat for a spell at an impasse. Alyssa takes great pleasure in the pursuit of knowledge, which she not only absorbs from books but also cultivates firsthand. Yet, this is a name that is not overly mental and intellectual. Alyssa is hardworking, dedicated, and practical. She pays careful attention to her responsibilities and to the fulfillment of her daily needs. And she is able to accomplish all this with a lighthearted attitude and a sincere appreciation and respect for others.

DERIVATION: English, a popular variant of Alice and Alicia. Has become increasingly common in recent years.

PRINCIPAL COLORS: The full spectrum of light hues

GEMSTONES AND PRECIOUS METALS: Diamonds, silver, platinum

BOTANICALS: Hazel, oats, parsley

UNIQUE SPELLINGS: Alisa, Alissa, Alysa, Elisa, Elissa, Elysa, Ilisa, Ilissa

RELATED TO: Ali, Alicet, Aliciat, Alise, Alisha, Alison, Aliza, Allie, Allison†, Allyson, Alyce, Alyse, Alyson, Elise, Elyse, Ilise, Ilyse

PRINCIPAL COLORS: All green and yellow hues

GEMSTONES AND PRECIOUS METALS: Pearls, moss agate, all other white stones

BOTANICALS: Elder, hops, juniper

UNIQUE SPELLINGS: Amandah, Amenda, Ammanda, Ammenda

RELATED TO: Aimee, Amata, Amey, Amyt, Manda, Mandee, Mandi, Mandie, Mandy

Amanda

A KABBALISTIC SYNOPSIS
אמנדא —AMNDA (Aleph, Mem, Nun, Daleth, Aleph)

The word *mother* can be represented in Hebrew (the language of the kabbalists) by a number of spellings, including "AM." Consequently, any name beginning with "AM" will have strong connections to the theme of motherhood. In Amanda's case this central feature denotes one of inner conflict with the mother figure. It is possible that Amanda's mother found it difficult when Amanda began to blossom into womanhood (perhaps due to feelings of jealousy or resentment). Amanda, as a result, has a deep-seated fear of re-creating this situation with her own female offspring. Amanda has a reflective temperament, but she does not let it interfere with her generally active life. She has a great love of the outdoors and will try any number of activities, from climbing to cycling. Ideally she will work by the sea or, at least, in some water-based endeavor.

THE RUNIC INTERPRETATION
ᚨᛞᚾᚨᛗᚨ (Ansuz, Dagaz, Nauthiz, Ansuz, Mannaz, Ansuz)

Amanda is a woman of keen intelligence who will find a way to pursue higher learning because she is very motivated and her mind is quick and sure. She enjoys being active and is at her best when she engages in such leisure pursuits as skiing or hang gliding with friends. She enjoys the company of witty people, laughing for days over a good joke. Her challenge will be to provide structure for herself and learn to control some compulsive tendencies, which could be about food or men or money. Prayer helps her when she feels out of control. Singing is good for her, as well as public speaking. As she grows older, Amanda will become more comfortable with silence, and this shift is indicative of balance returning to her life.

Elements: Air, fire, fire, air, air, air

THE NUMEROLOGICAL INTERPRETATION
Amanda (NV = 7, CV = 4, VV = 3, FL = 1)

Amanda denotes a person who has a careful sense of order and structure, and an understanding that rewards come only from hard work and personal effort. Although she is very open to communicating with others, Amanda has the tendency to retreat into herself in order to regenerate her energy. A deep thinker, Amanda may not appear to be paying attention to the world outside of herself. This is because her own internal world occupies a great deal of her attention. Yet, it is from this contact with her own internal processes that Amanda derives a great deal of her strength.

Amber

A KABBALISTIC SYNOPSIS
אמבה —AMBH (Aleph, Mem, Beth, Heh)

Amber is as sensual as her name suggests; in fact, she oozes an almost tangible sexuality. Her name has a variety of meanings when explored with kabbalistic methods of analysis, yet almost all point to an awesome level of sexual magnetism. Amber is as fickle as they come, having a strong mercurial influence in her name's construction. In spite of her tendency to flit from one romantic encounter to another, Amber sincerely believes herself to be fully committed for the short time each relationship lasts. What's more, Amber is a delight to be with; the long line of also-rans will not have a bad word to say about her. Her generosity of spirit means she will always have friends and is great fun to be with; one meaning of her name is "warmth." This emotional warmth means that ultimately she will settle down. Her family adores her, as her Mercury influence makes her a great communicator, and even when she has responsibilities, she never loses her immense sense of joy.

THE RUNIC INTERPRETATION
ᚱᛖᛒᛗᚨ (Raido, Ehwaz, Berkana, Mannaz, Ansuz)

Amber is confident and well loved. She dresses with care and enjoys physical comforts and attention. She is very neat and orderly. While Amber has a temper, she's not a screamer; she likes to talk things out and tries hard to be fair. Order helps her relax, and rest is important for Amber, who has a passionate and intense nature. In Amber there is a good writer and student of human nature. She believes that nature is filled with signs to help us guide our lives, and she is one of those individuals who can remember her dreams. Amber is playful and intuitive. The Berkana rune signals that she is nurturing, and Mannaz tells us that she relates well to people.

Elements: Water, air, air/earth, air, air

THE NUMEROLOGICAL INTERPRETATION
Amber (NV = 3, CV = 6, VV = 6, FL = 1)

With a name that comes with a ready and open smile, Amber is a person who exudes joy, peace, and laughter. Art, music, and theater may hold a very special interest for her, and she will be eager to participate in all creative projects that bring beauty into other people's lives. She is especially fond of her home and family, and becomes very distressed when discordant elements enter her door. Amber has a difficult time when communication breaks down between herself and the people she loves. This is a name that encourages dialogue and open contacts between people; Amber may not easily accept that difficult cycles and moods are also part of life.

DERIVATION: English, named after the gemstone amber, which is derived from the French word *ambre*. First became fashionable in the late nineteenth century. Its popularity increased after the 1944 publication of Kathleen Winsor's romance novel *Forever Amber*.

PRINCIPAL COLORS: The full range of purples and violets, including the palest shades

GEMSTONES AND PRECIOUS METALS: Amethyst, garnets

BOTANICALS: Cherry, dandelion, strawberry

UNIQUE SPELLINGS: Ambir, Ambre, Ambur, Ammber, Ammbre, Ammbur

RELATED TO: Amberetta, Ambretta, Ambrosina, Ambrosine

Amelia

DERIVATION: English, originally from the Latin word meaning "industrious." Became popular in Britain with the rise of Princess Amelia in the eighteenth century. Common throughout English-speaking countries during the eighteenth century. Its first use can be traced to the heroine of Henry Fielding's 1751 novel, *Amelia*.

PRINCIPAL COLORS: The full spectrum of very light hues, especially light gray

GEMSTONES AND PRECIOUS METALS: Silver, diamonds

BOTANICALS: Sweet marjoram, oats, parsley

UNIQUE SPELLINGS: Amilia, Ammelia, Ammilia, Amylia, Emelia, Emilia, Emmelia, Emmilia, Emylia

RELATED TO: Amala, Amela, Amelie, Amie, Ammela, Amy†, Emilie, Emily, Milia, Milica, Milla

A Kabbalistic Synopsis
אמליה —AMLYH (Aleph, Mem, Lamed, Yod, Heh)

Amelia is an ideal name for the archetypal mother. It is by no means her only job, but to Amelia the role of mother is completely fulfilling. And that is because to Amelia, the tending to family is in some ways an expression of spirituality. Amelia has a strong faith, and she is eternally optimistic (which must be a source of great comfort when surrounded by hungry kids and dirty laundry!) If Amelia has any faults at all, it is that she can be overindulgent. Under a kabbalistic analysis one derives the phrase "she who ruins." In Amelia's case this is a warning against spoiling the children with too much attention, toys, and candy. Amelia needs a strong and supportive partner in order to really fulfill her potential; she needs a friend who will ensure that, in spite of her giving nature, Amelia remembers to take some time for herself.

The Runic Interpretation
ᚨᛁᛚᛖᛗᚨ (Ansuz, Isa, Laguz, Ehwaz, Mannaz, Ansuz)

Amelia has an analytical and critical mind that can become impatient when operations are slow. She is a born organizer and may choose a career in management, sales, fund-raising, counseling, teaching, or politics. Amelia has a gift for persuasion, and she can charm her way into or out of just about anything. Drawn to the performing arts, she needs plenty of praise and admiration. Amelia is keenly aware of the impression she creates, and dressing well is important to her from an early age. Her temper is a tool she wields skillfully but only as a last resort; she will prosper by her own wits. Mannaz tells us that Amelia can count on others for help.

Elements: Air, earth, water, air, air, air

The Numerological Interpretation
Amelia (NV = 5, CV = 7, VV = 7, FL = 1)

Independence and personal freedom are very important to the name Amelia. Yet for some Amelias this can be exaggerated to the point of social alienation. Amelia can be very withdrawn and may find that her inner world is often a lot more interesting than the outer circumstances that surround her. Although usually more introverted than expressive, Amelia holds strong opinions about life and one's conduct, and is not one to mince words. In fact, her opinions may go right to the heart of any matter, and the strength of her personal expression may be surprising. People should take the time to get to know Amelia; she is a treasure house of deep perceptions and subtle meanings.

Amy

A KABBALISTIC SYNOPSIS
אמי —AMY (Aleph, Mem, Yod)

One kabbalistic equivalent of Amy is HVM, meaning "tumultuously." This word just about sums up Amy's scattered approach to life: Amy is the woman you see with her collar half up and half down, charging around the office like a tornado, throwing down coffee as she flies past her desk. What will immediately strike you about Amy as you watch this human whirlwind in action is that far from looking stressed, she appears to be quite happy—even smiling. Amy is in her element when in a rush; she has literally no time for relaxing or planning. Amy contains two of the three so-called mother letters of the Hebrew alphabet: Aleph and Mem, representing air and water, respectively; and Yod, which signifies an intense fire all its own. What is missing is the element of earth, which is a grounding, consolidating force—hence Amy's behavior. She is a whirling ball of elemental energy rather like a powerful stroke of lightning. However, her frenetic activity will usually yield surprisingly good results, although no one else will have a clue as to the end product until it is finished. For this reason Amy thrives in an environment full of quick decisions and tight deadlines. As for the mother influence? When Amy has had a particularly energetic day, she might phone her mother, who is just about the only one who can slow her down!

THE RUNIC INTERPRETATION
ᛇᛗᚨ (Eihwaz, Mannaz, Ansuz)

Amys are sensitive and trusting souls. In spite of some challenges and responsibilities within the family unit, Amy manages to carve out a sound identity for herself. Amy is attached to one or both of her parents throughout life. She is quick-minded and appeals to the opposite sex because she is emotionally flexible, preferring to play the field as long as possible. Yet she is discriminating in her choice of partners. Amy's spirituality emerges at its own rate like an unfolding blossom. With this growth comes an ability to look into the future and to heal. If Amy works as a healer with the public, she will make quite a name for herself and help many.

Elements: Earth/fire, air, air

THE NUMEROLOGICAL INTERPRETATION
Amy (NV = 3, CV = 4, VV = 8, FL = 1)

People may easily find women with the name Amy to be very mentally stimulating. There is no doubt about it: Amy likes to communicate and share expansive ideas and opinions. Her interests are very varied, and Amy may especially enjoy music and the arts. When Amy is not visiting museums or libraries, you will find her hard at work furthering her career; she's at home practicing public relations, coordinating events, or bringing different sorts of people together to accomplish an ambitious goal. She is very materially oriented and is interested in assuring her place in her chosen profession.

DERIVATION: English, anglicized version of the French word aimé, meaning "beloved." Used in English-speaking countries since the eighteenth century. Its popularity in the United States started to increase in the 1950s, and by the 1970s, it had become one of the most common names.

PRINCIPAL COLORS: All the various shades of violet and mauve

GEMSTONES AND PRECIOUS METALS: Amethyst, garnets

BOTANICALS: Apple, bilberry, mint

UNIQUE SPELLINGS: Aimee, Aimey, Aimie, Amey, Ami, Amie

RELATED TO: Ama, Amanda†, Amata, Amelia†, Amia

DERIVATION: French form of
Andrew, which derives from the
Greek word *andreas*, meaning
"manly."

PRINCIPAL COLORS: All the
various shades of blue, except for
the brightest ones

GEMSTONES AND PRECIOUS
METALS: Emeralds, turquoise

BOTANICALS: Dog rose, violet,
walnut

UNIQUE SPELLINGS: Ahndray,
Ahndre, Ahndrey, Andray,
Andrey

RELATED TO: Anders, Andreas,
Andrew†, Andris, Andy†

Andre

A KABBALISTIC SYNOPSIS
אנדרה —ANDRH (Aleph, Nun, Daleth, Resh, Heh)

Andre has loads of potential, but his main quality is intelligence. He has the sort of mind capable of pulling together diverse elements into a coherent whole. Computer programming would suit Andre as a career, since he can see through complicated requirements and find a way of making things work. While the two in Andre's name stands for wisdom and the six stands for choice-making, these generally useful traits can lead to problems. The desire for truth can lead Andre on idealistic wild-goose chases, and the emphasis in his name on making choices may in fact produce an inability to come down on one side or the other. In such a case, Andre will benefit from relationships with coworkers and friends who demand decisions. In rare cases the potential for indecision may affect his entire life and cause him to become a drifter, unable to stick to anything or with anyone.

THE RUNIC INTERPRETATION
ᛖᚱᛞᚾᛅ (Ehwaz, Raido, Dagaz, Nauthiz, Ansuz)

Andre is a successful businessman with the aesthetic of a poet. It is his fondest dream to make enough money to leave the corporate rat race and reduce the amount of stress in his life. He may achieve that goal through an unexpected gift from someone who has watched him grow and develop, and has spotted his unique talents early on. The money will be used wisely by Andre; he is a careful sort of man. His words and actions come from the heart, but you would hardly guess that at first because he is a reticent and guarded speaker. This nonverbal side of him is just a defense he uses to shield himself from the slings and arrows of criticism. Andre uses the Ansuz energy of his name to hear messages of profound beauty and practicality.

Elements: Air, water, fire, fire, air

THE NUMEROLOGICAL INTERPRETATION
Andre (NV = 6, CV = 4, VV = 8, FL = 1)

This name denotes a person who is very much attracted to the finer things in life. Strongly emotional and sensual, Andre likes to dress well, eat well, and enjoy the material and romantic sides of life. He can be very driven by success and must take care that the intensity of this drive does not endanger his personal and professional relationships. The numbers in his name indicate the need for harmonious social interchange in order to achieve success. Andre is a name that speaks of a man who has a very strong awareness of the steps that it will take to satisfy his aims in life and has the clear determination to get ahead.

Andrea

DERIVATION: English and Italian, feminine form of the name Andrew, which derives from the Greek word *andreas*, meaning "manly." Commonly used since the seventeenth century.

PRINCIPAL COLORS: The full range of greens and yellows

GEMSTONES AND PRECIOUS METALS: Moonstones, pearls, moss agate

BOTANICALS: Blackberry, hops, juniper

UNIQUE SPELLINGS: Andreea, Andreia, Andreya, Andria, Andrya, Anndrea, Anndria

RELATED TO: Andera, Andra, Andreana, Andree, Andrene, Andretta, Andrette, Andrewina, Andrianna, Drena, Reena, Rena

"The creative mind is intelligence in action in the world."
—ANDREA DWORKIN (AUTHOR)

A KABBALISTIC SYNOPSIS
אנדריה —ANDRYH (Aleph, Nun, Daleth, Resh, Yod, Heh)

One might expect some similarity between Andre and his female counterpart, Andrea, but this is not the case at all. In Hebrew, the addition of one letter makes all the difference. Andrea, spelled ANDRYH in Hebrew, adds up to 270, which has special significance in kabbalistic terms, being the equivalent of the inscription above Jesus at the crucifixion—INRI—which also adds up to 270. We can rightly expect Andrea to be more spiritual than most, and this usually is the case. However, her spirituality is likely to change dramatically in her adult life. The particular association of INRI in Kabbalah is of fire followed by water, followed by fire from the sun, and completed by the fire of the spirit. Where Andrea is concerned, this can point to a strong attachment to her family's beliefs, followed by some traumatic event that causes the death of these beliefs; the N, or Nun, in Andrea is itself suggestive of such an event. The R, or Resh, of both INRI and Andrea represents the discovery of a new belief and faith in the world, which brings a reaffirmation of Andrea's generally optimistic outlook. And once she goes through this unsettling experience, Andrea's newfound faith is unshakable.

THE RUNIC INTERPRETATION
ᚨᛖᚱᛞᚾᚨ (Ansuz, Ehwaz, Raido, Dagaz, Nauthiz, Ansuz)

Andrea is very tidy and likes to feel safe and cozy. As a result, she can be a little compulsive about her friends and her possessions. She's drawn to the blue in everything, such as shrubs that take on a bluish cast at twilight. Activities related to horticulture are sure to be successful ventures for Andrea; Andrea would flourish as a landscape architect or gardener. Andrea is a tender romantic and needs good earth-sign friends to help her with the administration of her life. With Raido for journey, Andrea welcomes travel opportunities. The double Ansuz rune encourages communication, and jobs related to this suit Andrea.

Elements: Air, air, water, fire, fire, air

THE NUMEROLOGICAL INTERPRETATION
Andrea (NV = 7, CV = 9, VV = 7, FL = 1)

The essential strength in this name rests in Andrea's ability to focus on her inner thoughts. Introspective and philosophical by nature, this woman seeks to develop a deeper understanding of herself. As a result of these efforts, Andrea will come to know more about people in general, and she will become a person of profound human understanding and insight—insight that she will tend to offer freely to those who come to her for help and advice. In romantic relationships, Andrea must not end up with her opposite; she needs a partner who can match her degree of sensitivity and intuitive perception.

DERIVATION: Greek, from the word *andreas*, meaning "manly." Andrew was the first Apostle in the New Testament, and Saint Andrew is the patron saint of Scotland and Russia. Common name from the seventeenth century on; in fact, since the 1970s, it has been one of the most popular male names.

PRINCIPAL COLORS: The full range of green hues from darkest to lightest, white

GEMSTONES AND PRECIOUS METALS: Jade, pearls, cat's-eyes, moonstones

BOTANICALS: Cabbage, chicory, lettuce

UNIQUE SPELLINGS: Andrewe, Andrue, Anndrew, Anndrue

RELATED TO: Anders, Andret, Andreas, Andy†, Drew†

Andrew

A KABBALISTIC SYNOPSIS
אנדרו —ANDRV (Aleph, Nun, Daleth, Resh, Vau)

Andrew is fiercely loyal to his family, his friends, his employer, and his country. This loyalty is an Arian trait and, consequently, if Andrew is also an Aries or, in Chinese astrology, a Dog, you will find his sense of duty all-consuming, and a career in the military or public service becomes a very strong possibility. In all names, as in all personalities, there is an element of conflict or tension—however small it may be—and Andrew is no exception. When we look at the value of the name, 261, it's clear that the representative of choice acts as a balance between the principle of individuality and that of union. Andrew has many doors open to him in life, and this is the source of tension; he struggles with the option that most favors his own interest and that he sees as best for those to whom he owes his loyalty.

THE RUNIC INTERPRETATION
ᛈᛗᚱᛞᚾᛏ (Wunjo, Ehwaz, Raido, Dagaz, Nauthiz, Ansuz)

When challenged, Andrew displays discipline and fortitude. The trouble is, these qualities only emerge under pressure. In times of peace Andrew's priorities are nonexistent, and excesses flow freely. As a child, Andrew needs a nanny, parents, grandparents, and plenty of siblings to provide loving care. But Andrew doesn't mean to exhaust everyone; it's just that he's physically stronger than most people. His outstanding attribute is physical stamina, and as a child he needs to participate in sports and have tumbling mats and playground equipment nearby for rainy days. As an adult he's drawn to a career with freedom of movement, whether a corporate life that allows for travel or an outdoor vocation such as athletics, ranching, or construction.

Elements: Earth, air, water, fire, fire, air

THE NUMEROLOGICAL INTERPRETATION
Andrew (NV = 2, CV = 9, VV = 11, FL = 1)

There is great potential in this name for the development of intuition. A philosophical tendency is inherent in Andrew, one that may easily lead him to fields of interest that bestow wisdom as well as knowledge. Andrew is capable of working or volunteering in his community, using his special sensitivity for the betterment of others. Andrew has a caring disposition as well as a highly developed sense of feeling for people. A natural-born consultant, Andrew is the man friends and family will often come to for advice and comfort.

Andy

A Kabbalistic Synopsis
אנדי —ANDY (Aleph, Nun, Daleth, Yod)

Andy is a man at one with the world; he has a feel for the natural harmony between the individual and his environment. Andy's sensitivity makes him an excellent practitioner in the areas of alternative health and other forms of therapy. His sympathy for the underlying rhythms of life also may lead him into musical expression. The great sense of balance implicit in the name Andy may also suggest a talent for dance or choreography. Andy is a great teacher, and he has a strong desire to share his perspective on life in order to demonstrate that one *can* find a balance! Most Andys that you come across will have a means by which they maintain their sense of inner harmony, often through meditation or self-hypnosis, or through more unusual means. Andy reduces to eleven, which is the prime number of magic—so don't be surprised to find Andy dabbling in some form of the occult.

The Runic Interpretation
ᛇᛞᚾᚨ (Eihwaz, Dagaz, Nauthiz, Ansuz)

It's difficult for Andy to make decisions that stick because he's so changeable. One day he's certain he's going off in one direction, and the next day he cancels the appointments he just made. He can be a jack-of-all-trades, but he won't find success until he finds one thing to do very well. Andy uses his Isa energy to come to terms with his relationship with money—and over time, he even manages to sew up that hole in his pocket! The Nauthiz represents constraint (or hardship), and many of Andy's hard-won lessons do cause him to have enormous insights. People who know him remark that he seems directed and motivated, and seems to be following a good course in his life. They are right to compliment him; he is spiritual, and his faith shines light on his path. Andy knows that we are keenly observed from the other side, and this faith helps him find satisfaction in today. He doesn't feel he needs to impress anyone. He's good to his family, and in his old age they pamper and spoil him.

Elements: Earth/fire, fire, fire, air

The Numerological Interpretation
Andy (NV = 8, CV = 9, VV = 8, FL = 1)

People who know Andy will probably find him to be a very productive person. Men named Andy are capable of creating material comfort for themselves. They have far-reaching visions and an active creative imagination. These characteristics give them the ability to make the most out of their own resources and reap the rewards that their efforts produce. Andy is eager for social approval and status. His is a name that bestows the ability to manifest whatever life may require of him. Andys walk with pride and self-assurance, and use their strength for success and personal achievement.

DERIVATION: English, short form of Andrew, which derives from the Greek root *andreas*, meaning "manly." Sometimes used as an independent given name. Can also be a female nickname for names such as Andrea or Andrine.

PRINCIPAL COLORS: The darker shades of blue and gray, black

GEMSTONES AND PRECIOUS METALS: Amethyst, black pearls, black diamonds, sapphires

BOTANICALS: Angelica, shepherd's purse, mandrake root

UNIQUE SPELLINGS: Andee, Andey, Andi, Andie

RELATED TO: Anders, Andret, Andreas, Andree, Andrei, Andres, Andrewt, Andreat, Andriana, Andrina, Andrine

"In the future, everyone will be world-famous for fifteen minutes."
—ANDY WARHOL (ARTIST)

DERIVATION: English, from the
Greek *angelos*, meaning "angel" or
"messenger." Used for both males
and females.

PRINCIPAL COLORS: The full
range of violet and purple hues

GEMSTONES AND PRECIOUS
METALS: Garnets, amethyst

BOTANICALS: Lungwort, mint,
strawberry

UNIQUE SPELLINGS: Angil, Angyl,
Anjel, Anjil, Anjyl

RELATED TO: Angelot, Angelat,
Angelicat, Angelina, Angelique,
Angelita, Angie, Archangela

Angel

A KABBALISTIC SYNOPSIS
אנגל —ANGL (Aleph, Nun, Gimel, Lamed)

This name has prominent connections to the world of the mystic and therefore the world of the Kabbalah. Angel adds up to eighty-four and is equivalent to ChLVM, meaning "dream." Our "earth angel" is likely to be quite a dreamer, someone who at times seems out of place in a world of computers, high-rises, and consumerism. Angel is able to retain the innocent wisdom one finds in children and allow this to grow and develop as he or she becomes an adult. If we reduce eighty-four we get twelve, which is the tarot card of the Hanged Man—again appropriate for Angels, since they are forever putting others first. An Angel's self-sacrifice may well be more significant than mere generosity; she may enter a convent, while he may become a monk or priest. Either may become a volunteer worker overseas, or even open a refuge center for the homeless. A male Angel tends to feel strong protective feelings toward parents and siblings. In any event, Angel's life is likely to be ruled by the nature of some chosen sacrifice. The final association is with AGPh, meaning "squadron" or "troop." Angel can lead and inspire a group to work toward a common goal.

THE RUNIC INTERPRETATION
ᛚᛖᚷᚾᚨ (Laguz, Ehwaz, Gebo, Nauthiz, Ansuz)

Angel the woman is hip. She's got *moves*. And with all that Gebo energy in her name, she's more than likely got the voice of an angel. She'll wring every ounce of pleasure from her varied romantic endeavors, but when she's ready to settle down, she'll be happy with a man who wants a simple home and an affectionate family. She's a warm and affectionate woman comfortable in a somewhat chaotic environment, say one peppered with birds and snakes, dogs and cats, and ferrets and butterflies. People drop in and forget to leave. Coffee is always on, and Angel, who has been known to cry along with a friend who's hurting, is always ready to listen. The male Angel is energetic and a good family man. He will excel in careers involving animals or sports. Whether male or female, Angel is a leader and is an asset to any organization or charity foundation.

Elements: Water, air, water, fire, air

THE NUMEROLOGICAL INTERPRETATION
Angel (NV = 3, CV = 6, VV = 6, FL = 1)

Angel is a name indicating a person with a wide variety of interests. An active communicator, Angel exhibits a bright intelligence and a love of others. This name also endows a person with wit, charm, and a desire to make other people happy. Angel can move about freely in social settings, and no one is a stranger to him or her. Angel enjoys making others feel at ease and likes to bring harmony into group situations. Angel can also be the name of a person who is attracted to art and music. He or she has a refined sense of aesthetics and is attracted to beauty in all its forms.

Angela

A Kabbalistic Synopsis
אנגלא —ANGLA (Aleph, Nun, Gimel, Lamed, Aleph)

The fabled Arabian princess with a thousand tales might easily have been an Angela. Her name has the same value as the full spelling of the letter Peh, meaning "mouth," while the double Aleph at the beginning and end ensure that Angela's mouth is often open. Angela may well make it in the field of journalism, or even sales, as her sunny outlook combined with her natural gift for gab ensure her plenty of success in these fields. While she loves to talk, you are unlikely to hear Angela gossiping unkindly. Her connection to Angel ensures that her interest is in good conversation and not malicious rumor. As her name reduces to thirteen, signifying the forces of change, she is likely to enjoy variety. Other aspects of the name suggest movement and travel. So if you have a day to spend with Angela, you can be sure that while you will hardly get a word in, you most certainly will not be bored.

The Runic Interpretation
ᚨᛚᛖᚷᚾᚨ (Ansuz, Laguz, Ehwaz, Gebo, Nauthiz, Ansuz)

Angela's name carries with it the energy of Angel with the addition of double Ansuz, or gifts. She is very connected with sacred knowledge and lets God direct her path. She is also very focused on career goals and developing her talents and abilities. Angela makes an effort to circulate among her colleagues and is appreciative of her good friends. She is willing to change, is receptive to new ideas, and will receive answers to her prayers. One reason for this is because she pays attention to chance encounters, overheard conversations, and people coming her way who support her beliefs.

Elements: Air, water, air, water, fire, air

The Numerological Interpretation
Angela (NV = 4, CV = 6, VV = 7, FL = 1)

This name indicates a person with a great variety of attributes. First and most important, Angela is very responsible and diligent in terms of her chosen field of work. She is fond of the material things in life and is very willing to spend long hours in pursuit of all her goals. Yet this is not a person who takes pleasure only in her career. Art, music, poetry, and theater are all areas of life Angela will find of significant interest. Angela also possesses a more circumspect and introverted side, and she will enjoy spending time alone—especially in natural surroundings.

DERIVATION: English and Italian, feminine form of the Latin word *angelus*, meaning "angel" or "messenger." It has been used widely since the eighteenth century and has steadily grown in popularity.

PRINCIPAL COLORS: Any of the bright, electric hues

GEMSTONES AND PRECIOUS METALS: Sapphires

BOTANICALS: Sage, wild spinach, wintergreen

UNIQUE SPELLINGS: Angella, Angila, Angyla, Anngela, Anngila, Anngyla

RELATED TO: Angeles, Angelicat, Angelika, Angelike, Angelina, Angelique, Angelita, Angie, Archangelica

Angelica

A KABBALISTIC SYNOPSIS

אנגליכא —ANGLYKA (Aleph, Nun, Gimel, Lamed, Yod, Kaph, Aleph)

Cyndi Lauper may well have dedicated her hit "Girls Just Wanna Have Fun" to all the Angelicas of the world. Angelica means "pleasure" in Hebrew in two different spellings, both of which add up to the same value. Angelica does not want to be tied down by anything or anyone, and she is not overly worried about having a successful career. Angelica's life is ruled by the need for *enjoyment*. If you are planning to settle down with Angelica, you'd better have a sense of humor and plenty of energy. Angelica has aspects of both Leo and Jupiter in her name. The influence of Jupiter emphasizes the jolly aspect of this planet and gives her the admirable ability to find the amusing in the most dire circumstances. The influence of Leo gives her a headstrong character, which goes some way toward explaining her unwillingness to slow down.

THE RUNIC INTERPRETATION

ᚨᚲᛁᛚᛖᚷᚾᚨ (Ansuz, Kano, Isa, Laguz, Ehwaz, Gebo, Nauthiz, Ansuz)

Angelica absorbs the energy of Angel and adds the runes of Isa and Kano for standstill and opening. Angelica will not find happiness easily with most of what comes her way because she is very discriminating and may have disappointments in love or career. She often feels that her love for her mate can never be as good as it once was; trying to hold on to worn-out relationships makes her feel shallow or passionless. Hers is a lonely path at times, and the only way out is to accept what is. In order for this to occur, Angelica should be alone for a time and use the Isa rune to seek understanding of what it is that has her blocked. With each ending comes the new love of springtime. The Kano rune supports her new beginning, and she will find happiness, affection, and wholeness in her new cycle.

Elements: Air, water, earth, water, air, water, fire, air

THE NUMEROLOGICAL INTERPRETATION

Angelica (NV = 7, CV = 9, VV = 7, FL = 1)

Angelica is a contemplative person with a deep sense of the inner meanings of life and an urge to deepen this understanding through study and a spiritual orientation. A student of life on both physical and metaphysical levels, Angelica may turn to either religion or science (or both!) to give herself the answers for her many quests. She is very sensitive to other people's living conditions and is oriented to the betterment of humanity.

❧

Angelo

A Kabbalistic Synopsis
אנגלע —ANGLA'A (Aleph, Nun, Gimel, Lamed, Ayin)

Angelo comes close to emulating Angel's considerate nature. We can break down the value of his name to three letters—Qoph, Nun, and Daleth, which mean "head," "water," and "door." Through the process of interpretation this name tells us that Angelo is a man whose thoughts are primarily occupied with emotional matters and that through this sensitivity he is able to open doors for other people. Without doubt Angelo makes an excellent counselor, adviser, or possibly a psychiatrist. Fortunately for Angelo, he can afford to spend his time resolving other people's emotional problems, since he will have few of his own. In fact, Angelo is by nature a lucky individual. While he will not win the lottery or make a million through his career, he will be in the enviable position of being satisfied with his life, and is unlikely to be troubled as much as the average Joe by the usual irritations such as car breakdowns, leaking gutters, and the like.

The Runic Interpretation
ᛟᛚᛖᚷᚾᚨ (Othila, Laguz, Ehwaz, Gebo, Nauthiz, Ansuz)

Angelo makes a good minister, counselor, or children's advocate. The Gebo rune for partnership gives Angelo many loving qualities. His is an idealistic path, and along the way he accumulates inheritances and gifts, blessings and benefits. Angelo is bound to go through times of relinquishment, as indicated by the Nauthiz rune of constraint. In the process of releasing old beliefs that once served him well, Angelo learns to turn inward. This cycle is hinted at by the Othila rune of separation. He evaluates his strengths and his need to be admired. He surrenders his will to the will of the Divine, and great harmony begins to balance his life. Angelo can look forward to beneficial outcomes.

Elements: Earth/fire, water, air, water, fire, air

The Numerological Interpretation
Angelo (NV = 9, CV = 6, VV = 3, FL = 1)

Angelo is a name that reveals a multifaceted and sometimes mysterious person. A very loving and caring individual, Angelo is always surprising people with his large repertoire of unusual stories and interesting bits of information. In this respect, he is an amusing and entertaining person. He is also a born romantic and is quite charming. Yet underneath this very sociable exterior lies the heart of a philosopher. Make no mistake about it: Angelo is more profound than he lets on.

❧

"There is no scientific answer for success. You can't define it. You've simply got to live it and do it."
—ANITA RODDICK (FOUNDER OF THE BODY SHOP)

Anita

A KABBALISTIC SYNOPSIS
אניטא —ANYTA (Aleph, Nun, Yod, Teth, Aleph)

For Anita life seems to be a glass that is always half empty, and we can see this in the gematria of her name. Equivalences to her name include "thy terror" and "lead," which is the metal of Saturn, a planet that has associations with depressive emotions. She suspects the worst in people and often will not give them the chance to disprove her suspicions. Anita spends her days in a state of almost constant apprehension, waiting with a sense of leaden certainty for somebody to slight her or for some event to throw a bucket of cold water over any plans she may have made. On the whole, her conviction that the worst is bound to happen means she doesn't make any plans at all. However, her name also holds the key to her problem: All her fears are self-created by her terror of real communication. If Anita can overcome this, she can live out the meaning of another gematric equivalent of her name, meaning "fullness" and "plenitude." In fact, Anita can have a great time once she shrugs off her paranoia. And in fact, it is probable that Anita will attract genuine friends who will try and bring her out of herself. Once she lets go, Anita can turn all that nervous energy into positive energy and surprise friends and colleagues with her charming manner. Anita's best key to enjoyment is her voice, which is naturally melodic. She is a wonderful singer and is very witty, although she usually keeps her witticisms to herself. When she shares them with others, she keeps them in stitches.

THE RUNIC INTERPRETATION
ᚨᛏᛁᚾᚨ (Ansuz, Teiwaz, Isa, Nauthiz, Ansuz)

Anita is a woman of strength. She works well in organizations because she likes structure and has natural leadership ability. A career in business or the military would suit her, since Anita is a great team player. She loves to laugh at herself, and her quick wit gives her an easy manner that helps her blend easily with diverse groups of people. Anita may have left home at an early age or raised herself for the most part; in either case, she's had more than her share of challenges and has learned patience through it all. A necessary component of her makeup is that she has learned to conquer herself.

Elements: Air, air, earth, fire, air

THE NUMEROLOGICAL INTERPRETATION
Anita (NV = 9, CV = 7, VV = 11, FL = 1)

With a name whose numbers indicate an urge to enlarge the scope of communication, Anita will strive to develop new theories, original ideas, and interesting projects. This is a woman of insight, vision, and wide perspective. She is never satisfied with her achievements and often gets more than one advanced degree in her continual effort to augment her intellectual tools and gifts. Anita is always in search of personal growth and self-improvement, and brings her personal successes to the world around her.

❧

Ann

A KABBALISTIC SYNOPSIS
אן —AN (Aleph, Nun)

One meaning of Ann is "grace," and as such we can expect Ann to have a strongly moral character. This expectation is backed up by the Kabbalah, where the name equates to AShTh. In these Hebrew letters we can see the progress of matter (A) being enflamed with spirit (Sh) and ending on the Cross (Th). This arrangement mirrors the progress of Jesus from incarnation to ascension, and Ann attempts to mirror the example he set as she goes about her business. You will never catch Ann crossing the street to avoid a charity box; she will do whatever she can to help others and rarely allows her personal feelings to get in the way of doing what is right. Ann adds up to 701, which by virtue of being a prime number suggests a unique personality. There is a danger here for Ann in that the strong presence of traditionally holy associations may create a character with delusions of grandeur or possibly an excessively pious attitude to others. At work, Ann is not someone you would want for a boss; she may be more suited to the role of supporter. The negative aspect of this name is effectively counteracted by the value of seven hundred contained within it. Seven hundred is the mystic protective number seven multiplied by a power of a hundred, suggesting that Ann is protected by a greater power.

THE RUNIC INTERPRETATION
ᚾᚾᚨ (Nauthiz, Nauthiz, Ansuz)

Ann finds herself attracting friends with low morals and lack of ambition, people whose limiting beliefs go unchallenged and whose lives are compromised as a result. Ann is able to discover her integrity by challenging these beliefs. If she examines her actions, she will learn how so much negativity has seeped into her life. For a time Ann may feel as if she is discarding one longtime friend after another, but she is making room in her life for fresh, positive friends. Separation from family for a time also brings healing benefits. At last, when she is able to find work she is suited for, friends who can nourish her, and the right distance from her family, Ann reaches optimism.

Elements: Fire, fire, air

THE NUMEROLOGICAL INTERPRETATION
Ann (NV = 11, CV = 1, VV = 1, FL = 1)

Ann is a name that carries a definite sense of assertiveness and independence. Self-assured and striving, Ann also has the talent and ability to inspire others to achieve their goals. The name Ann carries with it the energy of the pioneer; she is not afraid to go it alone in life if she has to. This is a very intuitive and highly original woman with ideas of her own—ideas that she will promote for the benefit of society through meaningful work.

DERIVATION: English, from the Hebrew name Hannah, meaning "grace." Associated with the mother of the Virgin Mary in early Christian tradition and with the mother of Samuel in the Bible. Very common in the nineteenth century.

PRINCIPAL COLORS: White, the full range of green hues

GEMSTONES AND PRECIOUS METALS: Jade, pearls, moonstones

BOTANICALS: Cabbage, chicory, lettuce

UNIQUE SPELLINGS: Ane, Anne, Ayn

RELATED TO: Ana, Anita†, Anna†, Annabel, Annabella, Annabelle, Annet, Annelise, Annetta, Annette†, Annie, Annika, Anya, Bethany†, Nan, Nana, Nancy, Nani

Anna

DERIVATION: Latin variant of Ann, it is in common use around the world. Found in Virgil's *Aeneid* as the sister of Dido, queen of Carthage. Other famous literary examples of the name include Leo Tolstoy's *Anna Karenina*.

PRINCIPAL COLORS: All the various purple and violet hues

GEMSTONES AND PRECIOUS METALS: Amethyst, garnets

BOTANICALS: Apple, bilberry, lungwort, mint

UNIQUE SPELLINGS: Ahna, Ahnna, Ana, Annah, Anneh

RELATED TO: Anita†, Ann†, Annabel, Annabella, Annabelle, Annalisa, Anne†, Annelise, Annette†, Annie, Annika, Anya

❧

"As Anna says about making a quilt, you have to choose your combination carefully. The right choices will enhance your quilt. The wrong choices will dull the colors, hide their original beauty. There are no rules you can follow. You have to go by instinct and you have to be brave."
—FINN IN *HOW TO MAKE AN AMERICAN QUILT* (1995)

A KABBALISTIC SYNOPSIS
אננא —ANNA (Aleph, Nun, Nun, Aleph)

Anna adds up to 102, which is the same value one finds for Alyssa. Like Alyssa, Anna boasts an impressive appearance, a fierce pride, and a good chance of earning a higher-than-average income. However, when analyzing a name, we need to consider not just the final value but the significance of the individual letters that make up the total. The key factor in Anna is the lack of variety of letters in the name—we have only A and N. We can deduce from this that Anna is an intense person with a very definite focus in life. She knows what she wants and she goes after it, in both her professional and her personal life. The letters themselves represent the elements of air and water, the forces of mind and emotion, respectively. By their arrangement—the two N's forming the core of the name—it becomes clear that Anna is profoundly affected by her emotions. The terminal A's tell us that she doesn't allow her emotions free expression; this is not because of repression but because she applies her considerable analytical skills to any emotional problem or situation. Anna, then, is an unusually balanced individual. It is interesting that 102 can be reduced to 3, which is the number of the trinity and a symbol of perfect balance. Even in this name of two letters there is much that can be found.

THE RUNIC INTERPRETATION
ᚨᚾᚾᚨ (Ansuz, Nauthiz, Nauthiz, Ansuz)

Anna's name contains the energies of Ann and adds the additional Ansuz rune of signals. Unlike Ann, who spends a lifetime deciphering her psychological makeup, Anna is keenly aware of her limitations and her family's impact on her. As she goes out into the world, she finds she understands people better than they understand themselves. Once she gains confidence, she will probably go on for higher academic degrees or rise to the top of her profession. However, this high level of success can turn her head for a while, since Anna needs to learn to handle her success with humility and gratitude.

Elements: Air, fire, fire, air

THE NUMEROLOGICAL INTERPRETATION
Anna (NV = 3, CV = 1, VV = 2, FL = 3)

A woman at ease with herself in society, Anna can be a very influential person. This is due largely to two factors. First, she is endowed with a good amount of self-confidence. Second, she really cares about other people and lets them know it. Anna is an easy conversationalist, witty, and actively intelligent. She often surprises and delights people with her vast knowledge, but is not full of intellectual pride. Anna's charm and personal appeal should take her far.

❧

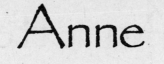

Anne

A Kabbalistic Synopsis
אנן —ANN (Aleph, Nun, Nun)

Given the phonetic nature of Hebrew, it would seem that Anne should produce the same kabbalistic analysis as Ann. However, the addition of the English *e* has the effect of multiplying the emotional focus of Anne, who is far more concerned with affairs of the heart than of the soul. In addition, the resulting value lacks the biblical connections found in Ann. If we consider the earth aspect of A, or Aleph, which means "ox," and the connection of N, or Nun, to Scorpio, we find in Anne a strong interest in the hidden aspects of relationships and a love of secrecy. Thus Anne would be an asset in any job requiring confidentiality. You can tell your burning secret to Anne in the knowledge that it will go no further. If Anne is born under Scorpio, this interest in secrets may take on a supernatural twist, while under Taurus it may well become a fascination with the intimacies of relationships. Whatever her star sign, Anne will always be a listener rather than a talker, which gives her sufficient insight to be a good novelist.

The Runic Interpretation
ᛗᚾᚾᚨ (Ehwaz, Nauthiz, Nauthiz, Ansuz)

Anne is a name bringing the challenges of Ann and the additional lesson of the Ehwaz energy. Anne learns early on that she must work hard to remake herself while kindly but firmly disagreeing with most of the opinions her family holds of her—a process she negotiates with great energy and fortitude. Ehwaz added to the name helps Anne enjoy the fruits of her labors. She takes all this in as a sign of the goodness of God. She has learned to accept herself, and her firm boundaries minimize the impact of negative people in her life.

Elements: Air, fire, fire, air

The Numerological Interpretation
Anne (NV = 7, CV = 1, VV = 6, FL = 1)

Anne is a name that shows a woman who is sure of herself and her way in life and yet, at the same time, is open to the opinions and feelings of others. This should make her well liked and appreciated. She wants to be an expert in her chosen field, and has all the numbers in her name to indicate that success will come with perseverance.

DERIVATION: English, from the Hebrew name Hannah, meaning "grace." Associated with the mother of the Virgin Mary in early Christian tradition and the mother of Samuel in the Bible. Since the 1950s, the Anne spelling has become very popular.

PRINCIPAL COLORS: Greens, yellows

GEMSTONES AND PRECIOUS METALS: Pearls, moonstones, cat's-eyes, any other white stones

BOTANICALS: Elder, hops, juniper, mushrooms

UNIQUE SPELLINGS: Ane, Ann, Ayn

RELATED TO: Ana, Ann†, Anna†, Annabel, Annabella, Annabelle, Annelise, Annetta, Annette†, Annie, Annika, Anya, Bethany†, Nan, Nana, Nancy, Nani

"Where there is hope, there is life."
—ANNE FRANK IN *ANNE FRANK: THE DIARY OF A YOUNG GIRL*

"Power can be seen as power with rather than power over, and it can be used for competence and cooperation, rather than dominance and control."
—ANNE BARSTOW (AUTHOR)

Annette

DERIVATION: French diminutive form of Ann, which derives from the Hebrew name Hannah, meaning "grace." Common in English-speaking countries as well, particularly in the mid-twentieth century.

PRINCIPAL COLORS: The full range of yellows and greens, gold

GEMSTONES AND PRECIOUS METALS: Moonstones, cat's-eyes, moss agate

BOTANICALS: Hops, juniper, linseed, blackberry

UNIQUE SPELLINGS: Anet, Anete, Anett, Anette, Annete

RELATED TO: Anetta, Annt, Annat, Annet, Annice, Annie, Anya, Hana, Hanna, Nan, Nana, Nancy, Nanette, Ninette

A KABBALISTIC SYNOPSIS
אניּת —ANYTh (Aleph, Nun, Yod, Tau)

Annette has a very clear sense of the value of things. Her name is equivalent to all things material, and it is by possessions that she judges herself and others. She'd make a good buyer for a department store. Annette sees the world in terms of "them" and "us." She is not a fan of foreign cuisine or the supernatural; her world is one of solid practicality, full of the familiar. She can be generous to those she sees as "like her," but her name is an equivalent to AThNYM—meaning "strong"—and Annette will get what she wants, no matter who may be harmed along the way.

THE RUNIC INTERPRETATION
ᛗᛏᛏᛗᚾᚾᚨ (Ehwaz, Teiwaz, Teiwaz, Ehwaz, Nauthiz, Nauthiz, Ansuz)

Annette's name has the energy of Anne's with the addition of Teiwaz and Mannaz. Annette may have been an orphan or had to learn the love of family later in life. Her challenges hit her hard and at a tender age. But with time and perhaps the love of a good mate or a rewarding career, Annette comes to realize that she's a capable and responsible adult. No one is causing her life to be disorganized and scattered but herself. Letting go of old memories helps Annette realize that the future is up to her. Once she acknowledges this, Annette can begin to hold her head up and speak more positively.

Elements: Air, air, air, air, fire, fire, air

THE NUMEROLOGICAL INTERPRETATION
Annette (NV = 7, CV = 5, VV = 11, FL = 1)

An independent nature and an urge to explore new experiences in life are two of the characteristics inherent in this name. Annette indicates a woman who is driven by an inner need for change and growth, who definitely does not like to be tied down by established codes of behavior. She is freedom-loving and seeks out those adventures that expand her way of thinking and being. Although she is eager for social contacts, Annette has a contemplative and analytical side to her as well and may spend many hours alone reading and studying. She's an ideal student or researcher.

Anthony

A Kabbalistic Synopsis
אנטוני —ANTVNY (Aleph, Nun, Teth, Vau, Nun, Yod)

Anthony is the name of a craftsman. He is at his most comfortable in his garage or workshop making and fixing—anyplace where he gets to use his hands is preferable. By reduction his name becomes a three-letter word in which there are two letters representing the hand and there is V, or Vau, meaning "nail," "pin," or "hook." This connection of the hand with some well-known tools of trade, such as nails, suggests that the ideal role for Anthony would be carpentry or something in the construction industry. In his personal life, Anthony is cautious and may even feel the need to adopt a mask or alternative persona when getting to know new people, particularly potential lovers. This stems in part from a feeling that his true self, with his love of manual work and methodical approach to life, will appear boring and uninspiring to the outside world. However, if Anthony can maintain his confidence, he has no need to fear, since those practical talents of his have deeper attributes as well. In his relationships Anthony is fair and always prepared to work on weak areas. His approach may lack spontaneity but it is effective.

The Runic Interpretation
ᛇᚾᛟᚦᚾᚨ (Eihwaz, Nauthiz, Othila, Thurisaz, Nauthiz, Ansuz)

Anthony loves to sing and prides himself on his ability to charm people with his music. He likes fast cars and keeps his home in immaculate condition. Anthony is willing to work diligently to get ahead and is able to ride the waves of life this way until his decisions begin to be affected by his reluctance to look within. When he can no longer carry on, he finds himself in chaos, and this is the turning point of Anthony's life. An evolved Anthony thanks the universe for sending him this wake-up call; a less-developed Anthony turns to greater and more dangerous escape routes from himself.

Elements: Earth/fire, fire, earth/fire, fire, fire, air

The Numerological Interpretation
Anthony (NV = 7, CV = 2, VV = 5, FL = 1)

Personal relationships are very important to Anthony. Intimate, emotional contacts with a lover or spouse provide Anthony with the opportunity to utilize his caring nature. In this respect, Anthony can be very creative in partnership arrangements, whether romantic or professional. The number values in this name also suggest a person who has a great zest for life and a strong urge to expand and explore. He can thus be a very stimulating partner, one who will be at his best (and who will also achieve the most freedom within the context of relationships) when supporting the growth of the people closest to him.

DERIVATION: Latin, from the Roman family name Antonius. Was common in the early Middle Ages, declined until the early twentieth century, and has become quite popular once again. It is now popular in all English-speaking countries.

PRINCIPAL COLORS: Greens, yellows

GEMSTONES AND PRECIOUS METALS: Cat's-eyes, pearls, moss agate

BOTANICALS: Blackberry, elder, hops, juniper

UNIQUE SPELLINGS: Annthony, Anthonee, Anthoney

RELATED TO: Anntoney, Antain, Antoine, Anton, Antoni, Antonin, Antoniot, Antony, Tonio, Tonyt

Antoinette

DERIVATION: French, feminine form of Antoine, the French version of Anthony. Made famous by the late-eighteenth-century queen of France, Marie Antoinette. Quite common in the United States during the mid–twentieth century.

PRINCIPAL COLORS: All but the brightest shades of blue

GEMSTONES AND PRECIOUS METALS: Emeralds, turquoise

BOTANICALS: Vervain, violet, walnut

UNIQUE SPELLINGS: Anntoinette, Anntoinnette, Antoinete, Antoinett

RELATED TO: Antionette, Antonette, Antonia†, Antonina, Antwaine, Toni†, Tonia, Tonya†

A KABBALISTIC ANALYSIS
אנטנט —ANTNT (Aleph, Nun, Teth, Nun, Teth)

Antoinette was born to be a star! One particularly appropriate rendering of her name is HNNY, which adds up to 115 and means "Here am I." Perhaps the most famous Antoinette was Marie, and while Antoinette was a surname for her, she typifies the excess of vanity that must constantly be avoided by Antoinette. Antoinette has strong Leo influences, and her name reduces to the number of the Chariot card in tarot. This card means triumph or success but also represents the tendency to ride roughshod over others. Antoinette can be a terror at the office, but if she can keep herself in check, then her style, charisma, and self-confidence will assure success in all her ventures. However, the further she climbs, the harder it will be to keep a sense of perspective and avoid the pitfalls of vanity. If she does fall because of this shortcoming, she is guaranteed an undignified slide back to reality.

THE RUNIC INTERPRETATION
ᛖᛏᛏᛗᚺᛁᛟᛏᛏᚨ (Ehwaz, Teiwaz, Teiwaz, Ehwaz, Nauthiz, Isa, Othila, Teiwaz, Nauthiz, Ansuz)

Antoinette needs stimulation and innovation. She probably does very well with computers and novelties of any sort. Antoinette's lesson involves a period of crisis when she is confused and loses her way for a bit. However, she is protected through this time, which turns out to be life-changing for her. Whereas before she was selfish, now she has compassion. Whereas before she pushed and manipulated people and circumstances, she now judges life from a sense of wonder and acceptance. Antoinette walks the planet to show us that endurance brings us through challenges and purifies the soul. Antoinette lives simply now and is generous and laughs easily. Antoinette is very strong due to her triple Teiwaz energy.

Elements: Air, air, air, air, fire, earth, earth/fire, air, fire, air

THE NUMEROLOGICAL INTERPRETATION
Antoinette (NV = 6, CV = 7, VV = 8, FL = 1)

This name reveals a person of great complexity. Antoinette is very analytical and is keen to use the logical faculties of the mind to resolve life's challenges. At the same time, there is a strong artistic side to her nature, one that is quite idealistic and attracted to music, poetry, and painting. Underneath it all is the heart of a person eager to succeed in the material world: Antoinette wants it all! She is also a woman who cares a lot about her appearance and is usually attractive and quite charming.

Antonia

DERIVATION: Feminine form of Anthony, has been in existence since classical times. Most famous literary use found in Willa Cather's novel *My Antonia*.

PRINCIPAL COLORS: White, all the various shades of green

GEMSTONES AND PRECIOUS METALS: Jade, pearls, moonstones, cat's-eyes

BOTANICALS: Lettuce, plantain, willow ash

UNIQUE SPELLINGS: Anntonia, Anntonya, Antonea, Antonya

RELATED TO: Antoinette†, Antonette, Antonie, Antonina, Toni†, Tonia, Tonya†

A Kabbalistic Synopsis

אנטעניא —ANTA'ANYA (Aleph, Nun, Teth, Ayin, Nun, Yod, Aleph)

Even without any form of kabbalistic analysis, it is clear from this name alone that we are dealing with *class*. For Antonia, work is likely to be something that other people do. If Antonia isn't born into wealth, she will find her way to it; for her it is as natural as a river flowing to the sea. Kabbalistically her name equates to QVPH, meaning "chest" or "repository," which could refer to either the many safety-deposit boxes she is likely to need or possibly to the inherited wealth that she may well acquire by succession. However, Antonia is not particularly concerned with possessions; she is used to them, and their attraction for her has waned. Her name adds up to 191, which reduces to 11. Eleven is the number of magic, and one can then associate QVPH with a hidden treasure chest not of material wealth but of secrets. Antonia will be attracted to matters of an occult or esoteric nature. If she is born under Capricorn, it is possible that this interest may be of a dark nature, as it will combine with her associations with money and could involve a search for secrets that will lead her to greater wealth. Depending on her personality, this search may be for ways to conceal such things as underhanded business methods or shortcuts in production processes. But it may also relate to dabbling in the dark side of the occult and could produce wealth in terms of greater knowledge or understanding of the ways in which people can be manipulated.

The Runic Interpretation

ᚨᛁᚾᛟᛏᚾᚨ (Ansuz, Isa, Nauthiz, Othila, Teiwaz, Nauthiz, Ansuz)

Antonia is filled with contradictions. One day Antonia is in the lotus position, and the next day she's arguing over a dollar. One foot, with polished toenails, is in heaven, and the other is doing a tango step here on earth. She is so persuasive, you're convinced she really means what she's telling you. She does—until the next notion turns her head. She wields a kind of magic and knows how to enchant a suitor into thinking she is the most deserving creature in the galaxy. Antonia isn't here for big life lessons. And with double Nauthiz runes, she'll have some obstacles to overcome, too.

Elements: Air, earth, fire, earth/fire, air, fire, air

The Numerological Interpretation

Antonia (NV = 11, CV = 3, VV = 8, FL = 1)

Antonia is a very powerful name, containing many highly creative elements. The total name value shows a person who can be very spiritually oriented with a profound gift for understanding others (although perhaps misunderstood herself). Antonia can be an inspiration to those around her, for she communicates easily with others and enjoys sharing her insights and thoughts. She likes the challenges of the material world and is eager to prove herself through her chosen career. Antonia also indicates a woman who likes to take care of her physical appearance and enjoys clothing, jewelry, and other finery.

"The true exercise of freedom is—cannily and wisely and with grace—to move inside what space confines—and not seek to know what lies beyond and cannot be touched or tasted."

—ANTONIA SUSAN BYATT (AUTHOR)

PRINCIPAL COLORS: Gold, the full range of green and yellow hues

GEMSTONES AND PRECIOUS METALS: Pearls, moss agate, any other white stones

BOTANICALS: Elder, juniper, grapes

UNIQUE SPELLINGS: Anntonio, Anntonyo, Antonyo

RELATED TO: Anthony†, Antoine, Anton, Antony, Tonio, Tony†

Antonio

A KABBALISTIC SYNOPSIS
אנטעניע —ANTA'ANYA'A (Aleph, Nun, Teth, Ayin, Nun, Yod, Ayin)

Antonio just loves mirrors—his house may well be full of them—although any reflective surface will do just as well. In the eighteenth century Antonio would have been a dandy, draped in the finest brocade, bewigged, and powdered. In our modern times he is an avid label hunter. We have evidence of the importance of power in his name, and in Antonio's case the authority he follows may be the words and images of the fashion world. With Leo prominent in the name's balance, Antonio has the confidence to carry off the most outrageous lifestyle; it is also probable that he will have the looks to match. It comes as no surprise, then, to discover that his name reduces to seven, a sign of great success and triumph. In Antonio's case this transpires as a highly optimistic outlook emphasized by his Leonine confidence. Given these personal qualities, Antonio is found working in any field associated with glamour. Advertising would be an ideal career for him, particularly if he's surrounded by hordes of beautiful extras for those tropical shoots!

THE RUNIC INTERPRETATION
ᛟᛁᚾᛟᛏᚾᚨ (Othila, Isa, Nauthiz, Othila, Teiwaz, Nauthiz, Ansuz)

Antonio's energy is similar to Antonia's, who changes her reality with her thoughts. Antonio's change comes about because fate wills it for him. When Antonio is presented with an opportunity, it is his receptive nature that seizes this gift from the gods. It is his very courage and willingness to step out on air that helps him arrive at a new life—one so unlike the old one that he must use his Dagaz energy to adjust to the change. Once he risks everything, his trust is rewarded and he enters a major period of achievement and prosperity. A great deal of labor is involved during this time of transformation, and Antonio works with discipline and a nonconfrontational attitude to make his heavenly opportunity succeed.

Elements: Earth/fire, earth, fire, earth/fire, air, fire, air

THE NUMEROLOGICAL INTERPRETATION
Antonio (NV = 7, CV = 3, VV = 22, FL = 1)

This is a name that is worth living up to! At its most evolved level, Antonio indicates a man with profound spiritual gifts and a deep philosophical nature. The indications are that this name instills a strong sense of social responsibility and the urge to participate in humanitarian projects. The name Antonio can bestow organizational skills that are at their best when applied to social welfare projects. On a more personal and down-to-earth level, this name indicates a desire to learn and communicate what is learned. No matter on which level he may find himself, Antonio can be an incredible helper and sensitive partner.

April

A Kabbalistic Synopsis
אפריל —APRYL (Aleph, Peh, Resh, Yod, Lamed)

April as a person is ideally suited to her name, which has a variety of meanings all associated with the energies of spring. One can spell April as APRL or APRYL. Taking the former spelling, we find the equivalent of the Hebrew "to make new," along with other phrases emblematic of the creative power of the new year. In adding a Y, or Yod, to the name, we are further emphasizing the creative fire power within this name. April is a joy to have as a friend or colleague, as she is always bursting with energy and new ideas. She makes friends easily, and with her predominant sense of optimism and bright outlook she will never be down for long.

The Runic Interpretation
ᚾᛁᚱᛈᚨ (Laguz, Isa, Raido, Perth, Ansuz)

April is so intuitive that she may have a cottage industry going as a kitchen table psychic. Her kids can't stand this; she always walks in when they're lighting up their first cigarette or trying to rebel in countless other ways. April can't help it. She can smell trouble. She can smell death. She can smell money. April's life lesson is to disentangle herself from all the people who attach to her to use her for her psychic awareness.

Elements: Water, earth, water, water, air

The Numerological Interpretation
April (NV = 2, CV = 1, VV = 1, FL = 1)

April indicates a person who is very much on her own path. It is a name that reveals individuality, confidence, and the urge to meet all of life's challenges with courage. April is very aware of herself. She knows who she is and what she wants to do. She is never down for too long without coming back up with a bang! Partnership and harmonious cooperation with others are also very important to April. Her life lesson involves the integration of her very distinct sense of her own needs and objectives with those of her partners and friends.

DERIVATION: English, from the month April. First appeared during the early twentieth century and became quite common during the 1940s. Other common month names include June and May.

PRINCIPAL COLORS: Greens, white

GEMSTONES AND PRECIOUS METALS: Green and white stones, such as jade and pearls

BOTANICALS: Lettuce, plantain, melon, rapeseed

UNIQUE SPELLINGS: Aprel, Aprill, Aprille, Apryl, Apryll, Aypril

RELATED TO: Aprilla, Avril

DERIVATION: English, short form of Archibald, which derives from the Old German roots *ercan*, meaning "genuine," and *bald*, meaning "brave." Especially common in Scotland.

PRINCIPAL COLORS: The darkest hues, especially deep blue and purple, black

GEMSTONES AND PRECIOUS METALS: Black pearls, black diamonds, richly shaded rubies and sapphires

BOTANICALS: Angelica, pilewort, gravel root, shepherd's purse

UNIQUE SPELLINGS: Archee, Archey, Archi, Archy

RELATED TO: Arch, Archer, Archibald, Archibold, Archimbald

A KABBALISTIC SYNOPSIS
ארחי —ARChY (Aleph, Resh, Cheth, Yod)

Archie is a simple man and a great guy to have around. His relaxed manner is a breath of fresh air to the busy career types who will see him as something of an oasis in a stressful competitive desert. Archie has an abiding interest in the mundane; he may have a vast collection of old cereal boxes or discontinued coinage, for example. Whatever his interest, it will be ordinary, everyday things that really fire his enthusiasm. These hobbies may seem dull to the outsider, but Archie is no slouch. He does have the capacity for intensity. The compression of his name produces both R (Resh) and Y (Yod), which are connected with fire, while the presence of T (Teth) in the name's compression reminds us that Archie can actually have quite a vicious tongue if he is pushed too far.

THE RUNIC INTERPRETATION
ᛖᛁᚺᛋᚱᚨ (Ehwaz, Isa, Hagalaz, Sowelu, Raido, Ansuz)

Archie moves frequently in this lifetime. He'd make a good airline pilot, athlete, explorer, or part of a group that goes from town to town. Archie is a wanderer and his photographs are spectacular. He has a good artistic nature and likes to follow his dream. He has hunches about where the luck is—and he's usually right. Archie makes friends easily but is most comfortable keeping his relationships fairly superficial. He has a perfect smile and a laid-back humor that lovers find satisfying. Don't try to get Archie to the altar, though. He'll only go when he's ready—and that seems to be his motto. All that gets Archie down, really, is exhaustion and the occasional feeling of being overwhelmed. As long as Archie is leading an unconventional lifestyle, he is safe. Archie is just asking for the freedom to be himself. He has sacrificed a lot in life for this simple request.

Elements: Air, earth, water, air, water, air

THE NUMEROLOGICAL INTERPRETATION
Archie (NV = 8, CV = 2, VV = 6, FL = 1)

Archie is someone who is very aware of the need for cooperative living and right social attitudes. These are all very necessary for his success in life—and success is definitely what he is seeking. Archie's name value is associated with the urge for material comforts and increased social status. Yet, Archie would not achieve these objectives ruthlessly. This name also carries the vibrations of cooperation, harmony, and kindness. Home and family are very important to Archie, and the need to bring the comforts of life to those he cares about is a very important underlying factor associated with this name.

Arlene

A Kabbalistic Synopsis
ארלין —ARLYN (Aleph, Resh, Lamed, Yod, Nun)

Arlene loves the sun. She dreams of spending her days on a beach in a designer swimsuit draped in rich jewelry. Associated with gold in all its forms, Arlene craves material possessions; more precisely, she desires expensive decorations and luxurious accessories. And there is a reasonable chance that Arlene will indeed achieve her aims—whether she does so through her own successful career or by finding a partner who is only too willing to adorn her with expensive gifts and affection. This stunning success with romantic relationships is clearly shown when we analyze the kabbalistic reduction of her name to its fewest possible letters.

The Runic Interpretation
ᛖᚺᛖᛚᚱᚨ (Ehwaz, Nauthiz, Ehwaz, Laguz, Raido, Ansuz)

Arlene is a wonderful gardener and a gracious hostess. She loves flowers and likes to have fresh flowers in her home year round. She takes delight in beautiful candles and tasteful china and knows how to create a feeling of glamour and luxury in her home. Arlene is very feminine and tends to be a perfectionist. At work and at home she is extremely well organized. Unfortunately, she is likely to suffer from dental problems.

Elements: Air, fire, air, water, water, air

The Numerological Interpretation
Arlene (NV = 1, CV = 8, VV = 11, FL = 1)

Arlene is a very potent name. The numbers indicate a woman who is very much her own person, one who is clear about her goals and ambitions. She has a sense of authority and enjoys looking healthy and beautiful. Arlene also enjoys the material rewards of life and the challenge of achieving them. She prefers to enlarge upon her list of accomplishments—and this list can be quite extensive. Compassion and understanding of other people's feelings may be important traits for her to cultivate, but if these qualities have already been incorporated into her nature, Arlene makes a wonderful and loyal friend.

DERIVATION: English, of uncertain derivation. Possibly a shorter version of Charlene or Marlene. First seen during the nineteenth century; became popular in the early twentieth century, especially in the United States.

PRINCIPAL COLORS: The full spectrum of yellow, gold, and brown hues

GEMSTONES AND PRECIOUS METALS: Topaz, amber, yellow diamonds, other stones of golden hue

BOTANICALS: Eyebright, lavender, Saint-John's-wort

UNIQUE SPELLINGS: Arlean, Arleane, Arleen, Arleene, Arleine, Arline, Arlyne

RELATED TO: Arla, Arlen, Arlena, Arletta, Arlette, Arlinda, Arlyn, Arlynn, Lenat, Lene

Armando

DERIVATION: Spanish version of the German name Herman, which comes from Old German words meaning "army" and "man." Connected to Armand, the French version of Herman.

PRINCIPAL COLORS: The full range of violet hues, from palest to deepest purple

GEMSTONES AND PRECIOUS METALS: Garnets, amethyst

BOTANICALS: Dandelion, mint, endive, beetroot

UNIQUE SPELLINGS: Armandoe, Armanndo, Armendo, Ermando

RELATED TO: Armand, Harman, Hermant, Hermon

A KABBALISTIC SYNOPSIS
ארמאנדע —ARMANDA'A (Aleph, Resh, Mem, Aleph, Nun, Daleth, Ayin)

Armando is a deeply inquisitive individual; he finds it hard to pass a house without looking through the window. His is not an interfering nosiness, but a genuine curiosity about the lives other people lead. His name has a total value of 365, which is equivalent to PhRYa'aH, meaning "an uncovering" or "exposing." This, combined with his inquiring temperament, strongly suggests that serious journalism would ideally suit Armando. He is a very balanced individual who is more than capable of seeing both sides of every story. This quality is of great use to him in his relationships, since it enables him to avoid the petty squabbles that interfere in the lives of many couples.

THE RUNIC INTERPRETATION
ᛟᛞᚾᛏᛗᚱᚨ (Othila, Dagaz, Nauthiz, Ansuz, Mannaz, Raido, Ansuz)

Armando speaks with a soothing tongue and words of affection, but underneath all this wooing magic is a stalking tiger. Armando likes to travel and take chances. He's a good race-car driver, professional athlete, or high-risk Wall Street trader. Risk is Armando's passion. Passion is Armando's passion as well; he has lovers on a global scale. But he feels as if no one can ever really love him as deeply as Mom, and he needs a mate who understands this.

Elements: Earth/fire, fire, fire, air, air, water, air

THE NUMEROLOGICAL INTERPRETATION
Armando (NV = 3, CV = 22, VV = 8, FL = 1)

Men who carry the name Armando through life possess the urge to accomplish things in a very big way. They are capable of an incredible amount of creative output—output that is very geared to material and social success. Armando is not afraid of money! When more spiritually polarized, men with this name are often very generous. In addition, Armando has an active mind and is eager to share information with others. Numbers indicating a quick wit and an eager intelligence add even more dynamism to this name.

Arnold

DERIVATION: English and German, derived from words meaning "eagle" and "ruler." Popular during the Middle Ages, but virtually died out afterward. Revived in the nineteenth century.

PRINCIPAL COLORS: From golden yellow to deep brown, orange

GEMSTONES AND PRECIOUS METALS: Golden, sunshine-yellow stones, including citrine, topaz, and yellow diamonds

BOTANICALS: Chamomile, ginger, sorrel, thyme

UNIQUE SPELLINGS: Arnald, Arnauld, Arnnold, Arrnold

RELATED TO: Arn, Arnaldo, Arnaud, Arndt, Arne, Arno

A KABBALISTIC SYNOPSIS
ארנעלד —ARNA'ALD (Aleph, Resh, Nun, Ayin, Lamed, Daleth)

If one were looking for a single word to sum up Arnold it would be "conscientious." Arnold has a firm belief that hard work will gradually bring him success. He is also in agreement with the old adage "Virtue is its own reward." Earth-sign Arnolds, particularly Capricorns, may have a strong sense of duty that relates to their immediate work environment. Most Arnolds, in addition, have a very religious side. Arnold adds up to 355, which can be represented as ShHN in Hebrew. Not only does this show Arnold as being driven by Shin, symbol of spirit, but it is a means of spelling Shin in full. This means that Arnold's beliefs and deeply ingrained moral conscience are not rigid or dogmatic. In fact, Arnold is a very adaptable guy who is always open to new ideas. Novel views may well change his perception of the world in which we live, but his core values will remain unshakable.

THE RUNIC INTERPRETATION
ᛞᛚᛟᛏᚱᚨ (Dagaz, Laguz, Othila, Nauthiz, Raido, Ansuz)

Arnold is perceptive and intuitive. He is very mechanical and could do well in engineering or technology. Although he'd never admit this to anyone, he has a superstition that exists in the deep recesses of his mind that machinery can communicate with him. Arnold has a rich imagination and very light sense of humor. He likes himself, and people like this about Arnold. Arnold recognizes the value of love and cooperation. He isn't a serial dater; he marries young and keeps his mate on a pedestal. He is faithful, although he likes to look.

Elements: Fire, water, earth/fire, fire, water, air

THE NUMEROLOGICAL INTERPRETATION
Arnold (NV = 1, CV = 3, VV = 7, FL = 1)

Self-assurance and a strong sense of personal identity characterize the name Arnold. Inherent in this name is a distinct mental curiosity, which may lead Arnold to intense periods of education and study. Arnold is more geared for the sciences than the humanities and is very at home with a logical approach to life. This can make for a highly introspective and contemplative person. Yet Arnold likes to share what he knows and is admired by others for the depth and breadth of his accumulated knowledge.

Arthur

DERIVATION: Celtic, from the root meaning "bear" or "rock." Made famous by King Arthur of Britain during the fifth or sixth century. Became popular during the Victorian era in Britain, and subsequently spread throughout Western Europe.

PRINCIPAL COLORS: The full spectrum of lightly shaded hues

GEMSTONES AND PRECIOUS METALS: Diamonds, any other lightly shaded stone of pale color, silver, platinum

BOTANICALS: Hazel, oats, parsley, sea kale

UNIQUE SPELLINGS: Arther, Arthure

RELATED TO: Art, Artair, Artiet, Artur, Arturot

A KABBALISTIC SYNOPSIS
ארתור —ARThVR (Aleph, Resh, Tau, Vau, Resh)

Anyone with even a passing interest in myths and legends will be aware of King Arthur and the Knights of the Round Table. The kabbalistic meaning of the name Arthur is in full accord with this legendary king. Arthur is a brave and honorable man. His name can be represented by the letters Z (Zayin) and P (Peh), meaning "sword" and "mouth." These letters show his preparedness to voice and defend his beliefs to the utmost. In the modern world we may find Arthur in law enforcement or the military—there not being much call for warrior knights in these days. But wherever one encounters Arthur, one can be sure that he will be standing up faithfully for all that is right and honorable.

THE RUNIC INTERPRETATION
ᚱᚢᚦᚱᚨ (Raido, Uruz, Thurisaz, Raido, Ansuz)

Arthur is a brave warrior and often finds conflict during his lifetime. He is willing to travel, endure hardships, and risk his life for principles he upholds. For Arthur life is made up of the little moments, and he tries to enjoy each day. He loves good food, art, and literature, and is a good storyteller. He also admires an opinionated and original thinker. For Arthur, the mind of a woman is her most seductive attribute. And if she can frolic and make him laugh at life's searing pain, he is willing to be wooed. Arthurs often have large families late in life.

Elements: Water, earth, fire, water, air

THE NUMEROLOGICAL INTERPRETATION
Arthur (NV = 5, CV = 1, VV = 4, FL = 1)

This name contains numbers that indicate its bearer will work hard and persevere in order to succeed. Arthur follows his own track in life and determines his own way. His interests may be wide and varied, but these interests are definitely his own. Arthur enjoys sharing his discoveries and is very pleased when other people wish to participate in his activities, for it is easier for him to integrate others into his realm than vice versa.

Artie

DERIVATION: Pet form of Arthur, which comes from the Celtic root meaning "bear" or "rock." Occasionally used as an independent name.

PRINCIPAL COLORS: Darkly shaded hues, especially gray, purple, blue, black

GEMSTONES AND PRECIOUS METALS: Richly colored rubies, sapphires, and amethysts, black diamonds

BOTANICALS: Mandrake root, marsh mallow, angelica

UNIQUE SPELLINGS: Artey, Arty

RELATED TO: Artair, Arther, Arthurt, Artor, Arturot, Artus

A KABBALISTIC SYNOPSIS
ארטי —ARTY (Aleph, Resh, Teth, Yod)

Artie is something of a firecracker, full of a seemingly boundless life force; he even has an appearance that suggests great activity. One can almost feel the current of powerful nervous energy coursing through his body. In Hebrew the word RVCh stands for the divine life force that rushes through the cosmos. Artie is equivalent to RYCh. This new word is the same as RVCh; it's pronounced "Ruach" and means the life energy that flows through each one of us. The name Artie suggests the sort of person who is on the go almost before he gets out of bed in the morning, and when he is in bed, it is rarely just for sleeping purposes! In career terms Artie needs to be calling the shots—but all that energy can become extremely negative if he feels that he is being constrained in his activities by a boss. However, if Artie is given the right amount of freedom, he will produce any number of immensely creative ideas.

THE RUNIC INTERPRETATION
ᛗᛁᛏᚱᚨ (Ehwaz, Isa, Teiwaz, Raido, Ansuz)

Artie discovers that money comes to him. He finds pennies on the street and dollars on the lawn. His life lesson is to learn to manifest joy. As he grows in his sense of self-love and entitlement, Artie comes to appreciate that unity is the real goal, not just prosperity. When he seeks unity, an urgency overtakes him to make connections with his fellow man by adopting a life of involvement in his family, his community, and spiritual causes. Artie eventually will thank the universe for sending him this wake-up call. As he rebuilds his life, it is on a firm foundation of faith.

Elements: Air, earth, air, water, air

THE NUMEROLOGICAL INTERPRETATION
Artie (NV = 8, CV = 11, VV = 6, FL = 1)

Artie possesses a very perceptive and penetrating understanding of life, one that is free of prejudice and obstinate opinions. At his core, Artie tends to be a bringer of harmony and a lover of beauty. He may easily find himself attracted to the arts, and would also take great pleasure in music. In this respect, he may find himself in a career or business that is associated with beautiful objects or artistic people. Artie enjoys life's sensual pleasures and will gear much of his creative efforts toward obtaining them.

Arturo

A KABBALISTIC SYNOPSIS
ארטורע —ARTVRA'A (Aleph, Resh, Tau, Vau, Resh, Ayin)

If there's an easy way to get something done, you can be sure that Arturo will go by a different route. It isn't that he is pedantic by nature, or that he likes to draw attention to the amount of work he is doing. It is simply that he is incapable of cutting any corners whatsoever—even if there is no impact on the final outcome of the task at hand. Apart from this particular quirk, Arturo is generally a "together" person, who tends to live by the sensible motto that all things should be enjoyed in moderation. It may be due to his perfectionism in the workplace that he has a sensitivity to other people's suffering. He not only has a knack for understanding but is always happy to offer advice to friends going through a difficult time. Most of the time his advice proves useful, as he is an observant individual and a dedicated people watcher. Indeed, it may be his observant nature, signaled by A'A, or Ayin, meaning "eye," that provides him with such a store of valuable insight.

THE RUNIC INTERPRETATION
ᛟᚱᚢᛏᚱᚨ (Othila, Raido, Uruz, Teiwaz, Raido, Ansuz)

Arturo is more aggressive than Arthur, though they share many qualities in common. Arturo has the Teiwaz warrior energy to seize opportunities and wage warlike campaigns. He could be a composer, an inventor, or a research physicist. His mind is like a Swiss watch; his memory is impressive, and his mind is so active that he often runs for weeks on two or three hours of sleep and it doesn't slow him down. Arturo has no time for petty gossip or limiting belief systems. He is fascinating and he has a sixth sense about going where the luck is. And when luck comes his way, he runs with it.

Elements: Earth/fire, water, earth, air, water, air

THE NUMEROLOGICAL INTERPRETATION
Arturo (NV = 8, CV = 2, VV = 6, FL = 1)

Arturo is a name that evokes a close friend, a loyal companion, and a romantic lover. The numbers in Arturo indicate a charming and cooperative person who likes to be appreciated by others, and in this respect, he does all that he can to bring harmony to his social circle. This is a person who loves his home and adores his children. Arturo is also a name that carries a certain amount of ambition, as he has a need for social achievement and a love of beautiful objects. This is a man who can use his charming nature and attractive appearance to achieve his powerful career objectives.

Ashley

DERIVATION: English, from the Old English words for "ash" and "wood." Originally a surname, it has become an increasingly popular name for girls in Britain and the United States.

PRINCIPAL COLORS: Yellow, gold, very pale to deepest green

GEMSTONES AND PRECIOUS METALS: Moonstones, pearls, moss agate, any other white stones

BOTANICALS: Blackberry, hops, linseed, juniper

UNIQUE SPELLINGS: Ashlee, Ashleigh, Ashlie

RELATED TO: Ash, Ashe, Leet, Leight

A KABBALISTIC SYNOPSIS
אשלי —AShLY (Aleph, Shin, Lamed, Yod)

Got a wacky or unusual idea? Then why not find an Ashley and watch him or her turn your brainchild into a great business opportunity. Ashley is the sort of person who can find a market for almost anything, however weird and wonderful—tennis rackets with no strings, glow-in-the-dark furniture, these are the sorts of things that Ashley can turn into winners! This name is dominated by threes and ones, indicating a combination of uniqueness tending toward eccentricity, along with great fortune and creativity. Ashley is a good person and is not one to get an oversized head as a result of success. Ashleys have a strong sense of the things that really matter in life, and friendship is much higher on their agenda than making money. A cautionary note, though, for any Aquarian Ashleys—some ideas are just *too* crazy! If Ashley is a guy, he will probably be more focused than his female equivalent on business schemes. Three is important in this name, and for women this often has associations with motherhood. So a female Ashley may well find that much of her creative energy goes into finding new and outlandish ways to amuse the kids.

THE RUNIC INTERPRETATION
ᛇᛖᛚᚺᛋᚨ (Eihwaz, Ehwaz, Laguz, Hagalaz, Sowelu, Ansuz)

Ashley is a name with feminine or masculine energy. Ashley is high-minded, and beauty, culture, manners, and traditions are important to Ashley. Whatever Ashley's sex, his or her soul is interested in pursuits such as anthropology, poetry, and history. These interests stem from Ashley's longing for more gracious times. It's as if the present were hopelessly flat when compared to the past on some level. Ashley's lesson is to see hope in the present. The present becomes more promising if Ashley considers a new place to live. The energy of a place affects the soul on many levels.

Elements: Earth/fire, air, water, water, air, air

THE NUMEROLOGICAL INTERPRETATION
Ashley (NV = 7, CV = 3, VV = 4, FL = 1)

Ashley is a name that points to an introspective person, one given to inner contemplation and reflection. Ashley can gain a great deal from her areas of expertise, and she will tend to use such knowledge toward her particular career objectives. This is a woman who will work hard and long in order to achieve her ends in life. She has a strong mind and a wide range of intellectual interests. People often hold deep respect for Ashley, as she is ready to offer wise counsel when called upon for advice. A male Ashley will share all these fine traits.

Audrey

DERIVATION: English, derived from the name of a sixth-century saint, Etheldreda. The name declined after the Middle Ages, but in the last century it has become more common.

PRINCIPAL COLORS: Pale grassy to deep forest green, white, off-white

GEMSTONES AND PRECIOUS METALS: Jade, moonstones, pearls

BOTANICALS: Borage, eyebright, chamomile, nutmeg

UNIQUE SPELLINGS: Audree, Audri, Audrie, Audry

RELATED TO: Audie, Audra, Audreen, Audria, Audrina

❧

"I tried always to do better: saw always a little further. I tried to stretch myself."
—AUDREY HEPBURN (ACTRESS)

A KABBALISTIC SYNOPSIS
אודרי —AVDRY (Aleph, Vau, Daleth, Resh, Yod)

Audrey is a firm believer in the Boy Scout motto "Be prepared," and because of this she makes the rest of the office feel woefully inefficient. She has her reports ready early, makes stellar presentations, and never seems to lose her cool. More than merely efficient, Audrey has very clear ideas of what she wants to achieve, and will then methodically set about accomplishing her goal. Anyone who has ever clashed with an Audrey will testify to the feeling of inevitability she carries with her. While her planning expertise makes her a fearsome boardroom opponent, it also serves to make her a wonderful friend. Moreover, Audrey is not at all insensitive in her determination to succeed; the card of the High Priestess is represented in her name in a number of ways, which indicates her good understanding of the needs of those around her.

THE RUNIC INTERPRETATION
ᛇᛖᚱᛞᚢᚨ (Eihwaz, Ehwaz, Raido, Dagaz, Uruz, Ansuz)

Audrey is happiest with a partner to share life's challenges. Should she be widowed, divorce, or remain single, it is helpful for Audrey to abandon herself to her faith and her work. In the best of circumstances, Audrey plays the role of partner and mother. Audrey comes from the heart, which is a very rare quality indeed. She makes a good ally and a fierce opponent. What's impressive is that those she defeats often tell her it was a fair fight, and are proud to bow out graciously. Audrey is special, and her high standards bring her great satisfaction in life.

Elements: Earth/fire, air, water, fire, earth, air

THE NUMEROLOGICAL INTERPRETATION
Audrey (NV = 1, CV = 3, VV = 7, FL = 1)

A highly individual person with a strong sense of her own identity, Audrey takes great pride in what she knows. Very intellectual with a great love of knowledge, Audrey will always have a good book near at hand or be enrolled in some course of higher education. She is not shy with her information and enjoys discussion and a good debate. Audrey is a lively partner and fascinating friend; her vitality comes through her endless need to discover and know.

❧

Austin

A Kabbalistic Synopsis

אוסטין —AVSTYN (Aleph, Vau, Samech, Teth, Yod, Nun)

Austin is a smooth character, to say the least. He is found in the classy wine bars and eateries of the financial district, probably charming his way into yet another deal or yet another bed! Clearly not everyone born to the name Austin will be able to buy his suits from Savile Row, but the general process will be the same. Austin begins with a powerful mind, which he uses to get into his chosen career. Once there he will convincingly play the role of supportive employee or colleague, as shown by S, or Samech, meaning "prop." However, as soon as the opportunity presents itself, he will strike like the serpent represented by T, or Teth. The next letter connects with the Wheel of Fortune and ensures that Austin is able to maintain his position once he achieves it. Finally, after a long career at the top of his chosen field, Austin discovers his deeper emotional self with a vengeance, as shown by the final N, or Nun.

The Runic Interpretation

ᚾᛁᛏᛋᚢᚨ (Nauthiz, Isa, Teiwaz, Sowelu, Uruz, Ansuz)

Austin takes some time to find his way in life and is given to extremes. Many Austins have turbulent teen years, and some even come to have police records that later haunt them. Austins need to take risks, and some of them become gamblers or stunt men. Many others find themselves in the romantic field of acting. Austin is a good speaker and, typical of most actors, is shy in person. Austin can do wonderfully in the martial arts and dance, and he probably had a black belt as a boy. Austin is a late bloomer, but it's worth the wait. Once Austin hits his stride, he is wonderful to his family and becomes a son to be especially proud of. Austin prospers and gives away a lot of money in useful ways.

Elements: Fire, earth, air, air, earth, air

The Numerological Interpretation

Austin (NV = 3, CV = 8, VV = 4, FL = 1)

Life's material rewards are very important to someone with the name Austin. Ambitious by nature, this is a person who will work very diligently in order to achieve his goals in life. His aims are usually very practical, and he pursues his visions with logical precision. He enjoys a career that opens him up to a wide variety of experiences that appeal to his profound interest in learning. Austin takes great pleasure in adding to his rich storehouse of information.

DERIVATION: English, a contracted form of the Latin name Augustinus. Originally used as a surname, it has become increasingly common as a first name in recent years.

PRINCIPAL COLORS: Light to deep purple, mauve

GEMSTONES AND PRECIOUS METALS: Amethyst, garnets

BOTANICALS: Apple, lungwort, mint, strawberry

UNIQUE SPELLINGS: Austen, Austyn, Awsten, Awstin

RELATED TO: Aston, August, Augustus

❧

"Actually, my name is Austin Powers. Danger is my middle name."
—AUSTIN IN *AUSTIN POWERS: INTERNATIONAL MAN OF MYSTERY* (1997)

DERIVATION: English, German, and
Polish, from the feminine form of
the Greek *barbaros*, meaning
"foreign, strange." Not common in
England in the eighteenth and
nineteenth centuries, but very
popular from 1950 on.

PRINCIPAL COLORS: Pale to deep
golden yellow, green, gold

GEMSTONES AND PRECIOUS
METALS: Cat's-eyes, moss agate,
pearls

BOTANICALS: Blackberry, hops,
juniper, linseed

UNIQUE SPELLINGS: Bahrbrah,
Barbarah, Barbra, Barbrah,
Barbreh, Barbyra, Barbyrah

RELATED TO: Bab, Babette, Babs,
Bar, Bara, Barb, Barbie, Barby,
Baubie, Bobbie, Bora

Barbara

A KABBALISTIC SYNOPSIS
ברברא —BRBRA (Beth, Resh, Beth, Resh, Aleph)

Barbara is complex. Effectively, Barbara fluctuates between a solar and a mercurial temperament, or from a proud and dominant presence to that of a loquacious wit. When we look at the value of Barbara's name, we see that the letters B, or Beth, and R, or Resh, mirror each other, one having a value of two, the other of two hundred. Thus the two sides of Barbara's nature are not in conflict with each other but are complementary. The solar, energizing side gives Barbara an enthusiastic and confident air, while the Mercury influence makes her an excellent communicator. Barbara would be good in sales. The Mercury aspect of her name acts as a channel through which she can present the energy and qualities of the sun. The mixture of immense energy with the talkative and sometimes noncommittal nature of Mercury will often produce a person without any sense of direction. However, in Barbara's case, the final A, or Aleph, acts as a controlling force, ensuring that she maintains a constant and definite focus in life.

THE RUNIC INTERPRETATION
ᚨᚱᚨᛒᚱᚨᛒ (Ansuz, Raido, Ansuz, Berkana, Raido, Ansuz, Berkana)

Barbara comes into this life with a pressing need to develop the soul. Men like Barbara because she can take them *and* leave them. She appreciates her independence and is very good at loving as an art form. Barbara is disciplined and needs freedom within the family to study and to seek out spiritual teachers to groom her. She excels in the arts and can make a mark in the world—but doesn't call attention to herself. Barbara loves to meditate and stretch her imagination. Eventually someone kind will come into her life to swing wide the door opportunity has positioned directly in her path. Barbara is very nurturing due to the two Berkanas in her name.

Elements: Air, water, air, air/earth, air, air, air/earth

THE NUMEROLOGICAL INTERPRETATION
Barbara (NV = 7, CV = 22, VV = 3, FL = 2)

Barbara has the ability to communicate directly with people as well as having an acutely analytical mind. A very potent name, Barbara endows a person with a keen judgment of character and also gifts Barbara with a witty and intelligent personality that is highly intuitive. Barbara seeks to achieve lofty ambitions and far-reaching goals. The numbers in this name certainly indicate that she has the possibility for great success in her chosen career.

Barry

A KABBALISTIC SYNOPSIS
בארי —BARY (Beth, Aleph, Resh, Yod)

Barry is a big man, his name in Hebrew is equivalent to "strong" or "powerful," and he is very definitely a man who will make money through his body rather than through his brain. Barry reduces to six, which tells us that he works at keeping himself in peak physical condition. He is concerned with the balance of his body and is more suited to Eastern whole-body approaches than to any Western sport or fitness routine. Barry has an ambition to go places; he sees the world as a treasure trove full of experiences just waiting for him to try them out. However, if Barry has been raised by particularly cold parents, there is a possibility that he will turn his physical prowess to more dubious ventures, although this may still involve considerable travel. The presence of both two and three in his name indicates that despite his life in a world of muscle and power, he still has a great love of the more delicate things in life.

THE RUNIC INTERPRETATION
ᛇᚱᚱᚨᛒ (Eihwaz, Raido, Raido, Ansuz, Berkana)

Barry's life lesson is honesty because Barrys like to bend the law. He likes the good life—and if he can get it for free, it's all the same to him. That being the case, he'd make a rotten bank teller. And when you're out with Barry, you'd best watch your wallet; you can be sure Barry does! Once Barry determines to be a good solid citizen, he can use his talents in music and art to great advantage. The trouble is Barry doesn't edit his schemes according to a yardstick of integrity. He likes the easy way out. Barry thinks it's a dumb idea to go through life wanting for money. So he makes sure he has a comfortable, if not always luxurious, lifestyle. Barry is good in sales and is a very good provider. He's also protective of his family and friends.

Elements: Earth/fire, water, water, air, air/earth

THE NUMEROLOGICAL INTERPRETATION
Barry (NV = 1, CV = 2, VV = 8, FL = 2)

Barry has a very strong sense of himself. Social by nature, he has charm and a great deal of personal magnetism. Relationships are very important to Barry, since he has a strong need to be accepted by others and a fundamental desire to live in harmony with those close to him. Barry also indicates a man who is ambitious for material success and social status. One of the major life lessons for this name is the development of the ability to integrate the strong need for personal attainment with the emotional need for intimate relationships.

DERIVATION: Irish, from the Gaelic *barra*, a shortened form of Fionnbarr. Gained some popularity in the nineteenth century, particularly in Australia.

PRINCIPAL COLORS: Very pale to deep golden shades of yellow and brown, including reddish yellow

GEMSTONES AND PRECIOUS METALS: Any yellow stone, including amber, topaz, citrine

BOTANICALS: Lavender, Saint-John's-wort, sorrel, thyme

UNIQUE SPELLINGS: Bari, Barie, Barrie, Bary, Bayrie, Bayry

RELATED TO: Bairre, Barra, Baz, Bazza, Finbar

DERIVATION: French and Italian form of the Latin *beatrix*, meaning "one who makes happy" or "one who blesses." Especially popular in England during the Middle Ages. The name of Dante's beloved, it is often associated with her.

PRINCIPAL COLORS: The full range of reds, from pink to dark crimson, especially the deepest shades

GEMSTONES AND PRECIOUS METALS: Deep red stones, including rubies, garnets, bloodstones

BOTANICALS: Broom, garlic, nettle, wormwood

UNIQUE SPELLINGS: Beatriss, Beatryce, Beatryse, Beatryss, Beeatrice, Beeatriss, Beetrice, Beetryss

RELATED TO: Bea, Beatrix, Beattie, Beatty, Trissie, Trixie

Beatrice

A Kabbalistic Synopsis

ביאטריס —BYATRYS (Beth, Yod, Aleph, Teth, Resh, Yod, Samech)

Beatrice is looking to settle down. She has a strong urge from young adulthood to nest—not necessarily to start a family or to marry, but to establish herself in the world. Once she has found her home, it will always be a home—never just a house. Beatrice will spend every spare moment working on it until it is exactly to her taste. Beatrice is associated with the field of medicine and may well practice as a doctor. Her name is suggestive of material comfort, so it is likely that she will be operating at the level of a well-paid professional. Given her likely career with its associated stress levels, it is not surprising that Beatrice longs for her own perfect space, where she can properly relax. Beatrice is a very understanding woman by nature, and the dual presence of the number two in her name ensures that she has a great sensitivity to the needs of others. This is a help in both her personal life and, of course, in her career.

The Runic Interpretation

MSIR↑AM↑ (Ehwaz, Sowelu, Isa, Raido, Teiwaz, Ansuz, Ehwaz, Berkana)

Beatrice loves *anything* to do with heaven or the sky. She loves astrology and the TV weather station. She has a lot of hot-air-balloon stories and photographs she carries in her wallet. Beatrice would make a good sky diver. She's out of her body so much, you can't talk to her on the phone without being put on hold. Her family is embarrassed by her escapist tendencies—and the smart ones know they *should* take it personally! Her favorite color is sky blue. She thinks it's a neat idea to fly like an angel, really low, over the Los Angeles freeway at rush hour. On the earth plane Beatrice can make a handsome living in the performing arts, where whimsy and romance are appreciated.

Elements: Air, air, earth, water, air, air, air, air/earth

The Numerological Interpretation

Beatrice (NV = 1, CV = 7, VV = 3, FL = 2)

A strong intellect, a philosophical orientation, and a love of communicating with others characterize Beatrice. The numbers in this name indicate a woman who is very energetic and enthusiastic about her plans and projects. Beatrice tends to be very supportive of others, adding her insights and vital life energy to those who need that special push to get ahead. She's a great friend and a great boss. This is a friendly name, and it denotes a woman who likes to share what she knows and what she has with those close to her.

Becky

A Kabbalistic Synopsis
בכי —BKY (Beth, Kaph, Yod)

It's very difficult, if not impossible, to get bored with Becky. Her name has a value of thirty-two, which can be reduced to five—the number of the Hierophant in the tarot. This indicates a capacity for knowledge as well as a strong, charismatic personality. You may well find Becky succeeding in those careers which require a high degree of intelligence. In her name the letter Beth has a value of two and is ruled by the planet Mercury, which is associated with nimbleness of both mind and body. Thus Becky is especially suited to any line of work which depends not just on brains but on a certain amount of quick-wittedness and the ability to grab opportunities when they arise. Becky would make a great gambling partner, and if you know of one, it might be worth taking her out to a casino; not only is she lucky by nature—thanks to the influence of Jupiter in her name—but she is also extremely good at bluffing. Emotionally Becky has a very fixed idea of the sort of partner she is looking for in a long-term relationship. Fun is high on her agenda, and she will expect any partner to share this attitude to life. The Mercurial influence in her name may make her wonder about other possible liaisons from time to time, but it is unlikely that she would ever be unfaithful.

The Runic Interpretation
ᛇᚲᛖᛒ (Eihwaz, Kano, Ehwaz, Berkana)

Born caretakers like Becky are blissfully codependent. Subjugating her needs comes naturally to Becky, who gladly gives up the most comfortable part of the mattress to her golden retriever. A house filled with plants and a bird with a broken wing is a bit of heaven to this caring soul. Feel free to drop in at Becky's home anytime; there's always a willing ear and coffee on the table. Just don't expect to put up with mess and clutter, because Becky runs a tight ship. Becky can be a bit controlling, but the animals enjoy the strict regimen, and everyone feels safe in her care.

Elements: Earth, water, air, air

The Numerological Interpretation
Becky (NV = 1, CV = 7, VV = 3, FL = 2)

Becky is eager to explore life and quick to act on her decisions. She wants to have many experiences and enjoy all the people she meets and the places she visits. Yet her interests are not purely sensual, and her objectives are not merely to fulfill emotional desires; Becky has a vivid curiosity about life and wants to know the real reasons people act the way they do. Although relationships mean a great deal to her, Becky is in independent person, a woman who has to be in control of her own destiny and direction. She is an engaging conversationalist and will have many friends from all different walks of life. She has to be careful not to be too brusque when dealing with others, as patience is not her most developed quality.

DERIVATION: English, from the Hebrew Rebecca. Commonly used as independent first name. Quite popular in the eighteenth and nineteenth centuries.

PRINCIPAL COLORS: The full spectrum of yellows and bronzes, orange, gold

GEMSTONES AND PRECIOUS METALS: Amber, topaz, citrine, any other yellow stones

BOTANICALS: Lavender, chamomile, sorrel, borage, Saint-John's-wort, eyebright

UNIQUE SPELLING: Beckie

RELATED TO: Beca, Becca, Becka, Bekka, Reba, Rebecca†, Rebecka, Rebeka

DERIVATION: English, of uncertain origin. Possibly from the Germanic *lind*, meaning "snake" or "dragon." Commonly used in literature.

PRINCIPAL COLORS: White, the full range of green hues

GEMSTONES AND PRECIOUS METALS: Cat's-eyes, jade, moonstones, pearls

BOTANICALS: Cabbage, chicory, plantain

UNIQUE SPELLINGS: Balinda, Balindah, Balynda, Belindah, Belynda, Belyndah, Bilinda, Bilynda, Bullinda, Bullynda

RELATED TO: Bella, Belli, Linda†, Lindie, Lindy, Lyn, Lynda, Lyndie, Lynette†, Lynn†, Lynne

"Belinda smil'd, and all the World was gay."
—FROM "THE RAPE OF THE LOCK" BY ALEXANDER POPE

A KABBALISTIC SYNOPSIS

בלינדה —BLYNDH (Beth, Lamed, Yod, Nun, Daleth, Heh)

Belinda is an accomplished watcher of the world and likes nothing better on a sunny afternoon than to sit on a bench in a crowded park and watch the people walk by. However, Belinda could never be accused of having her head in the clouds. Her name totals to one hundred, which is strongly symbolic of an overt concern with the material world. In Belinda's case this does not manifest itself as a desire for financial gain but as an abiding interest in the details of the society in which she lives. Belinda makes a perfect sociologist. She has a very easy way and is happy to talk to almost anyone—although she may not have always been so open. Her contented state is the result of a profound emotional experience that will have significantly altered her view of life. The presence in her name of L, or Lamed, meaning "ox goad," is evidence of her driven character, yet by her early thirties Belinda is happy to kick back and watch other people do the rushing about.

THE RUNIC INTERPRETATION

ᚨᛞᚾᛁᛚᛖᛒ (Ansuz, Dagaz, Nauthiz, Isa, Laguz, Ehwaz, Berkana)

Belinda's name boosts all four of the elements, which give it great power and balance; few names have this attribute. Once Belinda learns her life lesson of diligence, which should happen early in life, she's on her way . . . but she will need good advisers and a strong business plan before leaping into action. She is committed to the long term in her journey to success. In business, Belinda would enjoy being a troubleshooter or a systems engineer, and she will be happiest with a mate who will comfort her when she returns home from battle disheveled. His job is to remind her of how capable she is so she can persevere, and for this she thanks him from the bottom of her heart.

Elements: Air, fire, fire, earth, water, air, air/earth

THE NUMEROLOGICAL INTERPRETATION

Belinda (NV = 11, CV = 5, VV = 6, FL = 2)

This name describes a natural-born communicator, a woman who will reach out to others and enjoy her experiences with great gusto. Belinda is fun-loving, adventurous, and open to all the excitement that life may bring. She has a great affinity for the arts and all forms of beauty. Intimate relationships are very important to Belinda, as she is not a loner. She much prefers to share her enthusiasm and zest with that special someone. Belinda can be a very restless person, as she is not easily satisfied by the status quo and is ever eager to travel and explore.

Ben

A KABBALISTIC SYNOPSIS
בן —BN (Beth, Nun)

Ben is a very important name in the Kabbalah; it means "son" and has connections to the third letter in the mystical four-lettered name of God. This connection associates Ben with V, or Vau, representing the element of air. It is usual for Ben to be a deeply thoughtful, even philosophical, man who can sometimes come across as too serious for his own good. Virgoan and Piscean Bens are the ones most likely to indulge in excessive brow-furrowing. For most Bens, thankfully, the dual nature of "son" as "sun" brings an optimistic and lighter side to their personality. As well as being thoughtful, Ben is a deeply emotional man. On the whole this is a positive factor, as Ben tends to be far more understanding than the average man in both romance and friendship. Occasionally, though, Ben may be somewhat withdrawn. This may stem from his relationship to his mother, with whom he is probably very close. In certain cases the ties may be so strong that to embark on a relationship may seem to him to be a rejection of his mother. Such a Ben feels very intensely; he simply refuses to let it show.

THE RUNIC INTERPRETATION
ᚾᛖᛒ (Nauthiz, Ehwaz, Berkana)

Ben has a lot of energy and ambition. He is multitalented, and unlike lesser souls who are hard put to discover even one talent, Ben excels at whatever he concentrates on. His challenge is knowing what to choose as a career, and he will probably have half a dozen in one lifetime! It is a hard way to live because before he can get deeply involved in any one thing, he is fascinated by the next endeavor. In Ben's case it is important to pray for perseverance and the ability to succeed one step at a time. Eventually Ben learns to stay with one job by developing the playful side of his life.

Elements: Fire, air, air/earth

THE NUMEROLOGICAL INTERPRETATION
Ben (NV = 3, CV = 7, VV = 5, FL = 2)

There are two distinct sides to Ben's nature. The first, and perhaps the more dominant, is the social side. Ben is a man who loves to have a good time with close friends. He is ever ready for the new possibilities that life has to offer him, and he takes great pleasure in being active. The other side to Ben's nature is far more intellectual and reserved. There are times when Ben will much prefer to be by himself, quietly exploring his inner nature, rather than traveling in the fast lane in search of new adventures.

DERIVATION: English, pet form of Benjamin, Bennett, Benson, and related names. Also used independently.

PRINCIPAL COLORS: The full range of purple hues, from lightest to darkest

GEMSTONES AND PRECIOUS METALS: Amethyst, garnets

BOTANICALS: Apple, barberry, dandelion, strawberry

UNIQUE SPELLINGS: Behn, Behnn, Benn

RELATED TO: Benedict, Benjamin†, Benjie, Bennett, Bennie, Benny, Benson, Bentley, Benyamin

Benjamin

DERIVATION: English, French, and German, from the Hebrew *benyamin*, meaning "son of the right hand." Gained usage among English Puritans and was brought to America in the seventeenth century.

PRINCIPAL COLORS: Any hue characterized by a very pale shade, light gray, pastels

GEMSTONES AND PRECIOUS METALS: Any shiny, pale stone, including diamonds, as well as platinum and silver

BOTANICALS: Caraway, marjoram, oats, parsley

UNIQUE SPELLINGS: Behnjamin, Behnjamyn, Bengemin, Benjamen, Benjaminn, Benjamon, Benjamyn, Benjiman, Benjimon

RELATED TO: Ben†, Benjie, Bennie, Benny, Binyamin, Jami, Venyamin

A KABBALISTIC SYNOPSIS
בנימין —BNYMYN (Beth, Nun, Yod, Mem, Yod, Nun)

Understandably Benjamin has many ties to Ben, his name being an extended version of the latter. One could literally translate the name as "son of YMYN." In doing so, we instantly see the effect of this name lengthening, which is to produce a creative conflict of the elements fire and water. Both M (Mem) and N (Nun) are connected with the emotions, while the double Y (Yod) symbolizes raw energy. Benjamin is the product of this opposition, and the traits found in Ben will be colored by its effect. Benjamin is an extremely passionate man in his taste and in his relationships. From time to time this can lead him to make rash decisions without thinking them through in the way that Ben would. He is certainly an exciting guy to be around, as you can never tell which element of his personality is going to dominate; sometimes he is thoughtful, and at other times he is full of a desire to go off and do things. Yet the existence of this friction is in no way negative. In Benjamin we find a man who can translate his musings into direct and creative action. At the same time he retains the emotional receptivity of Ben, and in fact may be more influenced by his heart than by his head.

THE RUNIC INTERPRETATION
ᚺᛁᛗᚨᛜᛏᛗᛒ (Nauthiz, Isa, Mannaz, Ansuz, Jera, Nauthiz, Ehwaz, Berkana)

Poetic Benjamin is optimistic and multitalented, but he must learn to guard his heart. He can be deeply hurt by people, and this can lead to high blood pressure and all sorts of physical ailments. Benjamin is destined for success when he has the love of a good family. Discipline and self-reliance are his life lessons, and a time spent away from home will help Benjamin to realize who he really is. Benjamin is articulate, and his analytical powers are awesome. Once he has made his mark in the world and he returns to his family, he will be much wiser as well. He retains his independence of thought but gains a sense of modesty from facing his dark night of the soul.

Elements: Fire, earth, air, air, earth, fire, air, air/earth

THE NUMEROLOGICAL INTERPRETATION
Benjamin (NV = 5, CV = 8, VV = 6, FL = 2)

Benjamin has an innate sense of beauty and harmony. This is a man who can empathize deeply with other people's feelings. The numbers in this name reveal an individual who can be very caring and supportive, comforting and sensitive. Benjamin brings a certain sense of joy to all that he does—and he does a great deal! An active person with a very curious nature, Benjamin is also busily at work becoming a success in life. His tendency, however, is to share the rewards of his achievements with those he loves.

Bernadette

A Kabbalistic Synopsis
ברנדאט —BRNDAT (Beth, Resh, Nun, Daleth, Aleph, Teth)

Bernadette is a name that seems almost made with the modern woman in mind. The name can be split into two self-contained units. The first half of her name begins with B, or Beth, meaning "house," and Bernadette's thoughts and feelings are likely to be concerned with her home. Her family life is of great importance to her. The introduction to her name ends with the emotional Nun, clearly showing her deep attachment to the domestic world. By contrast, her name is completed by three very active "go-getting" letters. Appropriately enough, the first of these is D, or Daleth, meaning "door." It is once she opens the door and leaves the home that Bernadette reveals her other side. Bernadette has a real sense of focus regarding her career aims and has a solid, supportive home base from which to reach for them. Bernadette is even capable of aggressive tactics when necessary to advance her career, as indicated by T, or Teth, meaning "serpent," which completes her name.

The Runic Interpretation
ᛗᛏᛏᛗᛞᚨᚾᚱᛖᛗᛒ (Ehwaz, Teiwaz, Teiwaz, Ehwaz, Dagaz, Ansuz, Nauthiz, Raido, Ehwaz, Berkana)

Bernadette enters life with a plateful of issues to resolve. Her family doesn't quite understand her, and she needs a good support system of friends to bolster her confidence. Bernadette has a passionate nature and a stubborn streak that helps her hang on to her dreams when all else fails. The life lesson for Bernadette is that she need not stay stuck in the past; we all can create our own reality. For Bernadette this may mean travel or a move, and she will enjoy the adventure of it all. It also may mean finding a job in a large organization that provides her with a sense of belonging and of family. Should she marry, it is of utmost importance for Bernadette to keep a little distance between herself and her mate; Bernadette needs space to stay even-tempered. She also may drive her partner crazy with incessant chatter, but Bernadette talks less when she feels safe. Bernadette needs to love herself, and she learns this lesson well.

Elements: Air, air, air, air, fire, air, fire, water, air, air/earth

The Numerological Interpretation
Bernadette (NV = 4, CV = 6, VV = 7, FL = 2)

A strong and hardworking woman, Bernadette is filled with compassion and understanding for others. This name indicates a person who can be equally content being with others as well as spending hours alone. When she is by herself, she is often very meditative and contemplative. A lover of philosophy as well as science, Bernadette is a woman who is very open to helping others by sharing the knowledge she acquires in life. People find Bernadette a great comfort and look forward to being in her caring presence.

DERIVATION: French, the feminine form of the Germanic name Bernard, meaning "strong bear." Often used by Roman Catholics to honor Saint Bernadette Soubirous, who had visions of the Virgin Mary at Lourdes.

PRINCIPAL COLORS: Bright, vivid colors, and medium tones such as gray

GEMSTONES AND PRECIOUS METALS: Sapphires

BOTANICALS: Celandine, sage, Solomon's seal

UNIQUE SPELLINGS: Birnadet, Birnadett, Byrnadet, Byrnadette

RELATED TO: Bernadetta, Bernardetta, Bernardette, Bernette, Berni, Berniet

DERIVATION: English and French, from the Germanic for "strong bear." Brought to Britain by the Normans in the eleventh century and very popular in England until the eighteenth century.

PRINCIPAL COLORS: Black and dark gray, very deep shades of blue and purple

GEMSTONES AND PRECIOUS METALS: Carbuncles, amethyst, black pearls, black diamonds

BOTANICALS: Angelica, marsh mallow, pilewort

UNIQUE SPELLINGS: Bearnard, Bearnhard, Bernhard, Byrnard, Byrnhard

RELATED TO: Bernadino, Bernardo, Bernat, Bernhardt, Berniet, Bernt

Bernard

A KABBALISTIC SYNOPSIS
ברנעד —BRNA'AD (Beth, Resh, Nun, Ayin, Daleth)

Bernard is a tough cookie indeed. He may lack the chiseled jaw or the John Wayne drawl, and he may even have a deeply "nonmacho" job—Bernard is very suited to interior design, for instance—but this is a man with true *grit*. By kabbalistic analysis of the total value of Bernard, we arrive at three letters meaning "tooth, hand, nail." This could not be more appropriate to the name Bernard, as Bernard will indeed fight tooth and nail in order to get his way. This is not to say that Bernard is aggressive—far from it. It simply means that he has goals and is absolutely determined to achieve them by any means at his disposal. Like Bernadette, Bernard is centered in the home, although in his case it is likely that his career will relate to the home in some way. The presence of Ayin, meaning "eye," suggests that this job is not connected to the building of homes but to what they actually look like, hence the suitability for interior design.

THE RUNIC INTERPRETATION
ᛗᛖᚨᚾᛋᚱᛞ (Dagaz, Raido, Ansuz, Nauthiz, Raido, Ehwaz, Berkana)

Bernard has much of the appeal of Bernadette without her bad temper. Bernard is a way shower who is not coercive or confrontational. Like the best leaders, he inspires the trust of those he would influence, and they willingly follow. Even more important, Bernard has deep trust in the process of creation. He looks at every detour as a way of reshaping his outcome. Bernard has good social skills and can go just about anywhere that a fair and principled leader is appreciated. He is always willing to help, as is indicated by the Raido energy in the name, which implies cooperation and a merging.

Elements: Fire, water, air, fire, water, air, air/earth

THE NUMEROLOGICAL INTERPRETATION
Bernard (NV = 8, CV = 11, VV = 6, FL = 2)

This name points to a man of special gifts. There is a sense of self-confidence that radiates from Bernard's gentle and openly friendly demeanor. Bernard doesn't have to prove himself to anyone, and yet he takes a natural sense of pride in his achievements in life. He likes to take charge but not dominate situations. He likes to get things done without having to manipulate or dominate others. People find Bernard an asset to any mutual plans or projects. He tends to be a loyal friend and a faithful lover.

Bernie

A KABBALISTIC SYNOPSIS
ברני —BRNY (Beth, Resh, Nun, Yod)

If Bernard and Bernie were to team as a company, not only would they have a catchy name, but they would also have a very attractive and unique service to offer to customers. Whereas Bernard is something of an aesthete, Bernie is a definite nuts-and-bolts man. Again we have here strong emotional and mental connections to the home, but thanks to the complexity of Kabbalah and gematric analysis, a single letter makes all the difference! Bernie's name is finalized by the creative energy of Yod, so he is an achiever. In addition the value of the name reduces to ten, suggesting a concern with the material rather than the emotional, and Bernie believes in calling a spade a spade. An analysis of the total value of his name produces the symbol for house. In Bernard's case this refers to structural repair of houses—hence the idea of a partnership with Bernard!

THE RUNIC INTERPRETATION
ᛗᚾᚱᛗᛒ (Ehwaz, Nauthiz, Raido, Ehwaz, Berkana)

The Raido energy in Bernie's name makes him solid as a rock and a welcome addition to any group. Bernie is a born communicator, jovial and optimistic with incredible writing ability. He enjoys puns and he loves crossword puzzles. Because he is fascinated by words, philology is a good field for Bernie, as is linguistics. With the Berkana rune of growth prominently positioned, Bernie is sure to expand his many talents. He courts generous thoughts and high ideals whenever they come to mind. His writing is charming, and it carries a deep message.

Elements: Air, fire, water, air, air/earth

THE NUMEROLOGICAL INTERPRETATION
Bernie (NV = 8, CV = 7, VV = 1, FL = 2)

Bernie has great drive and a strong need to achieve a certain stature in life. With a name that bestows practical insight and a highly astute mind, Bernie has far-reaching plans and good organizational abilities to match. He will need other people to reach his goals, and has to learn to express compassion for coworkers along with his abundant intelligence and strong will. This is a man who has a clear sense of his own individuality and a tremendous urge to make the most out of his many talents and abilities.

∽

"There are many Beths in the world,
shy and quiet, sitting in corners till
needed, and living for others so
cheerfully that no one sees the sacrifices till the little cricket on the
hearth stops chirping, and the
sweet, sunshiny presence vanishes,
leaving silence and shadow behind."
—FROM *LITTLE WOMEN*
BY LOUISA MAY ALCOTT

Beth

A KABBALISTIC SYNOPSIS
בת --BTh (Beth, Tau)

Beth is the full Hebrew spelling of the letter B, which means "house." However, in Beth's case, the home has a more symbolic value, rather than a literal meaning. Beth's name adds up to 402. In this number we can see that the zero, which represents the infinite circle of existence *(orouboros)*, is flanked on one side by four, representing concerns with day-to-day life, and on the other by two, the symbol of higher emotional or spiritual matters. In this number Beth is revealed as the archetypal mother figure. She has to juggle the role of domestic manager, chef, and painter-decorator (the number four) with that of therapist, aunt, and marriage counselor (the number two). This complex role is suited to Beth's altruistic personality. The house reference is, of course, a symbol of where these skills and activities are most commonly located.

THE RUNIC INTERPRETATION
ᚦᛖᛒ (Thurisaz, Ehwaz, Berkana)

Beth is a loner and her thoughts run along the lines of a mystic's. Beth is unusual because she values the care of the soul. She's born understanding that the soul is energy with many frequencies, and that we can advance in our exploration of the soul. Beth may not be physically strong, but she propels the body with her mighty spirit. The Berkana rune makes Beth nurturing and kind. Thurisaz in her name symbolizes the gateway between the human and the divine. Beth learns that she saves time in the long run by listening to her heart before she acts. Ehwaz signifies travel and relocation, and Beth accepts these changes with strength of character and courage. She has the temperament of an artist and a visionary.

Elements: Earth, air, air/earth

THE NUMEROLOGICAL INTERPRETATION
Beth (NV = 8, CV = 3, VV = 5, FL = 2)

A wide variety of talents and a tendency to be open to an ever-widening scope of life experiences are associated with the name Beth. Usually of a cheerful and gregarious disposition, Beth enjoys sharing her many adventures with others. The numbers in Beth show a woman who is very creatively productive. She knows how to establish herself materially and enjoys sharing her comforts and abundance with others. Because social opinion is important to her, Beth likes to look good and cares for her clothing and physical appearance.

∽

Bethany

A Kabbalistic Synopsis
בתני —BThNY (Beth, Tau, Nun, Yod)

In Bethany we find a particularly joyous woman. She is so at ease with herself that all around her feel immediately at home. She will invite a whole host of people over for a fabulous dinner party—and still have the energy to have a good time herself. Every guest will be made to feel special, as Bethany seems to find time to pay some attention to each and every one. She is adored by friends, family, and coworkers. Cynics might regard Bethany as naive or even consciously blotting out the harsher realities of life, but Bethany works hard for her chosen lifestyle. Essentially, Bethany is Beth with the influence of Scorpio and Virgo added. Virgo is the astrological aspect of Y, or Yod. The effect of these additional influences on Bethany is to make her more aware of her own desires and feelings.

The Runic Interpretation
ᛟᚺᚾᛞᛗᛉ (Eihwaz, Nauthiz, Ansuz, Thurisaz, Ehwaz, Berkana)

Bethany is a balanced woman whose path is a healing one; she is intuitive and strong. The name Bethany has a lot of air energy, which is represented by the crash of thunder. While "airy" people can charm you with their whimsy and infectious patter, they can also move mountains when fighting for a cause. So Bethany makes a good reformer. She makes a fine living challenging the system or working in government, medicine, or education. Art therapy is also a good career choice. Bethany has strong family ties and needs to step back from the rescuer role now and then and re-create herself. Bethany's early life's challenges changed her forever; she misses some of the fun in life, and that's just the way it is.

Elements: Earth/fire, fire, air, fire, air, air/earth

The Numerological Interpretation
Bethany (NV = 3, CV = 8, VV = 4, FL = 2)

Witty and intelligent, Bethany always has a ready opinion about any situation she may encounter. This name denotes a woman with a keen intellect and precise points of view. She uses her perceptive gifts for the achievement of her many goals. Bethany is a name that connotes an ambitious person who will work long and hard for what she is seeking to achieve. Careful and responsible, Bethany is known for her loyalty and stability. She realizes that it will take a while to reach her pinnacle, and she is willing to take the time to slowly work her way there.

DERIVATION: English, from the New Testament name for the home of Lazarus. From the Hebrew, possibly meaning "house of figs." Sometimes used to honor Mary of Bethany, sister of Lazarus and Martha.

PRINCIPAL COLORS: The full range of purple hues, including pale bluish violet and lilac

GEMSTONES AND PRECIOUS METALS: Amethyst, garnets

BOTANICALS: Apple, cherry, lungwort, mint

UNIQUE SPELLINGS: Bethani, Bethanie, Bethanni, Bethannie, Bethanny

RELATED TO: Ann†, Annet, Anni, Annie, Anny, Ayn, Beth†, Bethan, Bethann, Bethanna, Bethanne, Betsy†, Betty, Elizabeth†, Hannah†

Betsy

A KABBALISTIC SYNOPSIS
בטסי —BTSY (Beth, Teth, Samech, Yod)

The value of Betsy is eighty-one, which, since it is nine squared, is a highly significant number, nine being the number of intuition and mystery. Betsy can be represented by Peh, meaning "mouth," and Aleph, signifying air. This indicates that Betsy likes to talk and, in particular, loves to talk about her ideas and beliefs. Betsy's personality is enlivened by the energy of Yod, and of all the esoteric arts to which she may be drawn, her name points to Tantric practices as being most appropriate for her nature. There is a slight problem in Betsy's makeup in that S, or Samech, meaning "prop," may suggest a tendency to look for some kind of emotional or mental crutch in life. If this need is not properly kept in check, Betsy's interest in the occult might become a dependence.

THE RUNIC INTERPRETATION
ᛇᛋᛏᛗᛒ (Eihwaz, Sowelu, Teiwaz, Ehwaz, Berkana)

The name Betsy has a lot of air energy. Air equals eloquence, romance, metaphysical inclinations, and noteworthy artistic ability. Making things beautiful is all Betsy wants in life, and she is sometimes overly sensitive to criticism. Betsy can get very angry when faced with jealousy and coldness, and she doesn't know how to handle these situations. Either she loses control like a popping balloon or she gets depressed. Depression is one reason Betsy loses herself in her artwork. It's not only therapeutic for her, but her talents soar while she is creating her quality expressions to share with the world. A partner in life will help Betsy to feel more fulfilled.

Elements: Earth/fire, air, air, air, air/earth

THE NUMEROLOGICAL INTERPRETATION
Betsy (NV = 8, CV = 5, VV = 3, FL = 2)

Betsy knows how to make the most out of the tools and talents with which she was born. In addition to relying on these fundamental aspects of her nature, she is open and ready to acquire even more skills that can help her achieve her many goals. She depends a great deal on her mind and uses it to her advantage—without having to take advantage of others in the process. Education is important to a woman with this name, and Betsy will take her knowledge both from books and from her own varied life experiences.

Betty

A KABBALISTIC SYNOPSIS
בטטי —BTTY (Beth, Teth, Teth, Yod)

Betty has a predominance of nines in her name; in fact, the influence of the unknown could be said to constitute the core of her being. Intuition is Betty's psychic connection, as is suggested by B, or Beth, which, in this sense, is mother to the two Teths in her name. Betty's name adds up to thirty, which is the value of L, or Lamed in Hebrew, and the meaning of this letter is a key to her personality. Lamed represents a powerful driving force, and Betty is likely to come across as someone in a great hurry—possibly even as a woman on a mission. In the case of Aries or Leo Bettys, we have absolutely driven individuals who expend so much energy that they sometimes teeter on the edge of complete burnout. There is no sign in Betty's name of any particular direction for all this fire, but that is where the central letters come into play: Betty can always rely on her intuition to choose the right path, so, paradoxically, it is her "mysterious" nature that keeps her grounded.

THE RUNIC INTERPRETATION
ᛇᛏᛏᛗᛒ (Eihwaz, Teiwaz, Teiwaz, Ehwaz, Berkana)

Betty's early years may be challenging because her approach to strife and humiliation is to face them headlong and alienate lots of people in the process. Once Betty becomes patient and modest, she finds troubles fall by the wayside. Older Bettys are conciliatory and tactful; they have mellowed like fine wine. These Bettys have learned that patience is needed more than words in times of chaos, and that these are times in which to gather more information and speak with good judgment. For Betty, her struggles were worthwhile; now she values order and peace. She's determined that the second half of her life will be more comfortable than the first, and Betty's wish comes true.

Elements: Earth/fire, air, air, air, air/earth

THE NUMEROLOGICAL INTERPRETATION
Betty (NV = 9, CV = 6, VV = 3, FL = 2)

A compassionate person who tends to be broad-minded about life, Betty cares about others in a most sincere way. This is the name of an idealist, a woman who has an inner sense that the world can be a more harmonious and beautiful place in which to live, and is willing to do something to bring her visions into fruition. Human relationships are very important to Betty, both on personal and impersonal levels. She will always do what she can to improve the living conditions around her, and others often admire her for this.

DERIVATION: English, pet form of Elizabeth, which is originally from the Hebrew name *elísheba*, meaning "oath of God." Commonly used as a given name since the eighteenth century. One of the most popular names in the English-speaking world in the 1920s.

PRINCIPAL COLORS: Deep, rich reds; pink

GEMSTONES AND PRECIOUS METALS: Deep red stones, such as rubies and bloodstones

BOTANICALS: Garlic, wormwood, pepper

UNIQUE SPELLINGS: Beht, Behtey, Behtie, Behttey, Behtti, Behttie, Behty, Betey, Beti, Betie, Bettey, Betti, Bettie, Bety

RELATED TO: Bess, Bessie, Beth†, Bethany†, Betsy†, Betty Ann, Betty Jo, Betty Lou, Betty Mae, Betty Sue, Elisabet, Elisabetta, Elizabeth†, Elizabetta, Elsbeth, Elspeth, Lisbet

❧

"Don't compromise yourself. You are all you've got."
—BETTY FORD (FORMER FIRST LADY OF THE UNITED STATES)

DERIVATION: English, originally a
surname and a place-name, with
the Old English roots *beofor*,
meaning "beaver," and *leac*,
meaning "stream." Very common
in the United States from 1920
to 1950.

PRINCIPAL COLORS: Dark blue
hues, purple, gray, black

GEMSTONES AND PRECIOUS
METALS: Black diamonds, black
pearls, amethyst, any dark stones

BOTANICALS: Angelica, shepherd's
purse, ragwort

UNIQUE SPELLINGS: Beverlea,
Beverleigh, Beverley, Beverli,
Beverlie

RELATED TO: Bev, Bevah, Bevi

Beverly

A KABBALISTIC SYNOPSIS
בורלי —BVRLY (Beth, Vau, Resh, Lamed, Yod)

A haven of calm in a mad world—*that* is Beverly. She is the only one who, when stuck in gridlock during rush hour, is sitting happily, humming to herself. Due to her ability to cope well under enormous pressure, Beverly may well find herself rising to managerial positions in her career. However, Beverly is not particularly ambitious, so this may take a few years to happen, and when the promotion does come, Beverly will view it with the same quietly amused eye that she turns on the rest of the rushing, panicking world. The secret to Beverly's temperament is acceptance; she has realized that in life there is very little she can change and that in the long run, true contentment comes from inside. It is in this undemanding and stoic attitude that she mirrors the biblical character Abraham, the value of whose name her own name shares.

THE RUNIC INTERPRETATION
ᛇᛚᚱᛗᚠᛗᛒ (Eihwaz, Laguz, Raido, Ehwaz, Fehu, Ehwaz, Berkana)

Beverly is a romantic who has the courage to change her destiny. This name carries the energy of a deeply spiritual and private woman; Beverly needs to take her coffee out on the deck in the morning and talk to God. She will live modestly, in a peaceful and safe home. Beverly is able to handle difficult and abrasive personalities because she thanks the person inwardly for the opportunity given to her to express tolerance and peace. Her tolerance makes Beverly special.

Elements: Earth/fire, water, water, air, fire, air, air/earth

THE NUMEROLOGICAL INTERPRETATION
Beverly (NV = 8, CV = 9, VV = 8, FL = 2)

Care and respect for the physical body and the material conditions of the world are very important to Beverly, who may use this concern to engage in ecological or conservation work. Whatever career she chooses, it may take her to a prominent position in life, as she strives to ensure that she is successful in her chosen field. Beverly is motivated to express herself creatively in her urge for prosperity, and therefore her work will probably be creative as well.

Bill

DERIVATION: English, pet form of William, which is from the Old German roots *wil*, meaning "desire," and *helm*, meaning "helmet." Used independently since the 1840s.

PRINCIPAL COLORS: Dark gray and blue hues, black

GEMSTONES AND PRECIOUS METALS: Richly shaded sapphires, rubies, amethyst, any black stones

BOTANICALS: Angelica, marsh mallow, pilewort

UNIQUE SPELLINGS: Bhil, Bhill, Bhyl, Bhyll, Bil, Byl

RELATED TO: Billiet, Billy, Guillaume, Guillermot, Wilhelm, Wilkinson, Will, William†, Williet, Willis, Willy, Wilmott, Wilson†

A KABBALISTIC SYNOPSIS
ביל —BYL (Beth, Yod, Lamed)

Bill is a solitary figure who eschews company of any kind. While for Scorpio Bills it may be the case that their isolation stems from misanthropy, it's not usually a dislike of other people that generally prompts this solitude. For the average Bill, it is the result of a desire for complete self-sufficiency. Also, there is a tendency toward agoraphobia suggested by Bill's name. The relationship of the B (Beth) to the L (Lamed) may point to a personality who feels driven back into the home by the outside world. Bill adds up to forty-two, which indicates a love of the sea, and it may well be that Bill makes his home there, possibly by joining the navy or even living on a barge or houseboat. On the whole Bill is happy with his unusual lifestyle, but every now and then he has a crisis of confidence. It is not that Bill ever doubts the suitability of his chosen lifestyle for him as an individual; rather, it is that he wonders about the other possibilities he has not tried.

THE RUNIC INTERPRETATION
ᛚᛚᛁᛒ (Laguz, Laguz, Isa, Berkana)

Bill puts on his earphones and he's in his own world. Bill is a live-and-let-live kind of fellow. Bill's love of music comes from the double Laguz energy of flow. As a child he exhibits a keen intelligence that is somewhat stifled by intense shyness, which is the legacy of the Isa energy of standstill. The arts are an appropriate vehicle to foster Bill's musical ability and encourage his self-confidence. The benefits inherent in the Berkana rune ensure growth and maturation on deep levels for Bill. He can look forward to recognition and accolades in his adult life.

Elements: Water, water, earth, air/earth

THE NUMEROLOGICAL INTERPRETATION
Bill (NV = 8, CV = 8, VV = 9, FL = 2)

Helpful and caring, Bill is a man who is always present when others need him. He can be a very generous person who gives freely of himself and his resources. But do not think that he is free from material preoccupations—not at all! The numbers in Bill's name indicate a person who is very much involved with the acquisition of money and the social rewards that come with financial security. Yet this is not a selfish man. The name Bill denotes an open hand and an open heart.

Billie

DERIVATION: English, pet form of William, which is from the Old German roots *wil*, meaning "desire," and *helm*, meaning "helmet." Occasionally used as an independent name.

PRINCIPAL COLORS: Brilliant azure, gray

GEMSTONES AND PRECIOUS METALS: Lightly to very richly toned sapphires

BOTANICALS: Sage, medlar, wild spinach

UNIQUE SPELLINGS: Bhilley, Bhilli, Bhilly, Bhylley, Bhylli, Bhyllie, Bhylly, Billey, Billi, Billy, Bylley, Bylli, Byllie, Bylly

RELATED TO: Bill†, Guillaume, Guillermot, Wilhelm, Wilkinson, Will, William†, Willie†, Willis, Willy, Wilmott, Wilson†

❧

"If I don't have friends, then I ain't nothing." —BILLIE HOLLIDAY (JAZZ SINGER)

A KABBALISTIC SYNOPSIS
בילי —BYLY (Beth, Yod, Lamed, Yod)

Billie is a people person and, in contrast to Bill, he or she likes nothing more than to be among people talking and laughing together. Very definitely a city person, Billie is drawn to working in large offices—not because of the nature of the work, but due to the vast array of personality types to be found in such an environment. Thanks to their sociable nature, Billies have no trouble finding a date—but will have substantially more difficulty in trying to settle on one in particular! Billie's name reduces to seven, a powerful number indicating great success. The positive effect of this number is usually tempered by a tendency, if unchecked, to ride roughshod over other people's feelings. However, in Billie's case we arrive at the number by a combination of five and two. In kabbalistic terms this tells us that Billie's success is directly related to an understanding of the interactions between people in a social environment.

THE RUNIC INTERPRETATION
ᛖᛁᛚᛚᛁᛒ (Ehwaz, Isa, Laguz, Laguz, Isa, Berkana)

Billies are young at heart, and children love them. Billies are good storytellers; the Ehwaz and Berkana air energies place words at their fingertips. He or she may be a writer or children's book illustrator. Because Billie relishes fast cars, boats, and grown-up toys, Billie could rack up large credit card bills. Billie needs to work at managing money but is fully capable of doing so. Billie's capacity for wonder and joy make us all wish he or she could grow up *just* enough to make his or her dreams come true.

Elements: Air, earth, water, water, earth, air/earth

THE NUMEROLOGICAL INTERPRETATION
Billie (NV = 4, CV = 8, VV = 5, FL = 2)

Billie is the name of a very practical person, the type of individual who goes to work every day, pays bills on time, and plans for the future. Billie gives the appearance of being a responsible person, well organized and under control—and while this may be very true, there is another facet to Billie's life: Deep within Billie is the urge to develop and evolve his or her natural talents into something very special. Billie wants to have freedom from routine but not lose the security he or she has worked so hard to establish. Billies tend, therefore, to have a number of side interests that keep their active minds entertained, and are always open to new opportunities that may come their way.

❧

Blake

DERIVATION: English, from the Old English *blac*, meaning "pale," or *blaec*, meaning "black." Originally a surname, now commonly used in the United States as a given name.

PRINCIPAL COLORS: Bright blue, medium gray

GEMSTONES AND PRECIOUS METALS: Sapphires

BOTANICALS: Lesser celandine, sage, spinach

UNIQUE SPELLINGS: Blaike, Blayke

RELATED TO: Blaine, Blair, Blaise

A Kabbalistic Synopsis
בלאיכ —BLAYK (Beth, Lamed, Aleph, Yod, Kaph)

James Dean, watch out! Blake is a rebel par excellence, and he doesn't grow out of it either. Blake is the guy we all feel sorry for when he's thirty: He still hasn't got a proper job, or a house or a wife and kids. But by the time we are forty, he is the cause of some major envy! While we are worrying about the firm, the mortgage payments, and the kids' school, Blake is still living it up—and looking good, too. There is a strong suggestion in the name that Blake's nonconformist ways stem from conflict in the family home. The central A, or Aleph, lets us know that Blake is an individual and proud of it. It is Blake's confidence in himself that keeps him from settling down. However, Blake is not just some idle bum; he expects to work to maintain his lifestyle. His jobs may not last long, but he is more than willing to try his hand at anything.

The Runic Interpretation
ᛗᚲᚨᛚᛒ (Ehwaz, Kano, Ansuz, Laguz, Berkana)

Blake is a good solid citizen. His health and the health of his family members are of utmost importance to Blake. Mentally and emotionally, Blake is strong and true; you'd trust him with your money, and many do. He likes to dress like a rich man, with silk smoking jackets and expensive cuff links. Blake likes jewelry and cashmere scarves. Yet he is so unassuming that one wonders from where the dapper side of Blake originated. It's in his name, of course: Blake carries the Kano energy of expansiveness. This energy includes expensive taste in clothes and a desire to be noticed. Blake is a teddy bear, and everyone who knows him well gives him a good-natured squeeze now and then.

Elements: Air, water, air, water, air/earth

The Numerological Interpretation
Blake (NV = 4, CV = 7, VV = 6, FL = 2)

Personal relationships, home, and family are very important to Blake. This is a man who takes his responsibilities to others seriously. However, he is also diligent when it comes to fulfilling the demands of his career. He has an artistic side to his nature as well and may have a special love of painting and music. He enjoys and needs the harmony that such interests awaken within him. Blake can be a very introspective person, with a penchant for spending long hours by himself in pursuit of his special interests.

DERIVATION: English, short form
of Robert, which is from the
Germanic roots *hrod*, meaning
"fame," and *berht*, meaning
"bright." Used independently
since the middle of the nineteenth
century.

PRINCIPAL COLORS: Pale yellow to
deep gold, browns, orange

GEMSTONES AND PRECIOUS
METALS: Citrine, topaz, yellow
diamonds

BOTANICALS: Borage, chamomile,
saffron, gentian root

UNIQUE SPELLINGS: Bahb,
Bahbb, Bobb

RELATED TO: Bertie, Bobbie,
Bobby, Riobard, Robt, Robbie,
Robby, Robert, Roberto,
Robin, Robinson, Rupert,
Ruperto

Bob

A KABBALISTIC SYNOPSIS
בעב —BA'AB (Beth, Ayin, Beth)

If you know a Bob, you might consider taking him out for a drink—preferably somewhere a good few miles from home—and leaving him there! Now, this is not because Bob is a bad person, but because he is far too attached to his home for his own good. Most Bobs have a very close relationship with their parents, and would not consider putting Mom and Dad in a nursing home. In spite of this powerful pull toward home life, Bob has an equally powerful desire to escape. In the spelling of his name we see that B, or Beth, meaning "house," surrounds A'A, or Ayin, meaning "eye." This creates the impression of an individual who looks out at the world, wanting to become a part of all that it has to offer, and then is pulled back in by the security of the home.

THE RUNIC INTERPRETATION
ᛒᛟᛒ (Berkana, Othila, Berkana)

Bob has a sense of style and finesse that is inborn. He keeps company with well-mannered people. Coarse speech is deeply offensive to Bob, who never swears. Period. Bob is sentimental about his mother and just doesn't understand how people can be so thoughtless toward their parents. The double Berkana energy affords Bob a healthy, nurturing quality with people. Bob enjoys helping his friends reach their full potential, and personal growth is important to him. He is generous with his time and money. Bob makes a good stylist, and his talents afford him a good standard of living. The four elements present in the name ensure success.

Elements: Air/earth, earth/fire, air/earth

THE NUMEROLOGICAL INTERPRETATION
Bob (NV = 1, CV = 4, VV = 6, FL = 2)

On the surface it might appear that Bob is very concerned—perhaps too concerned—with his own plans and projects. He is an individual by nature and is usually quite enthusiastic about his special interests. Bob is a man who will work hard to achieve his aims in life, and can be quite preoccupied with his material security. But this is not a selfish man. His home and his loved ones mean a great deal to him, and he is always ready to share the financial rewards of his efforts with those around him. Bob may enjoy music as a favorite pastime.

Bonnie

A Kabbalistic Synopsis
בעני —BA'ANY (Beth, Ayin, Nun, Yod)

Bonnie is very smart, although her learning is as likely to come from observing people and her environment as it is from books and formal education. She has an intelligence that is particularly useful when making one's way in the world. Bonnie is extremely pragmatic and will thrive in any work environment where practical application of good business ideas is required. She's a good manager but may prefer the life of a small business owner or entrepreneur. The hobbies that Bonnie selects will also have this practical element to them, whether she chooses gardening or computing. Unfortunately for Bonnie—and to the confusion of all her friends—this approach goes totally out the window when it comes to relationships. We can tell from the presence of N, or Nun, that Bonnie's emotional life is a key factor in her personality. A closer analysis reveals that if Bonnie is searching for anything in life it is true love. The value of Bonnie's name can be reduced to six, the number of the Lovers in the tarot and a card emblematic of choice-making. Bonnie is often unable to choose between romantic alternatives. She may have any number of chances to make a serious commitment, but each time the fear that it may involve sacrificing her own personality causes her to withdraw. Bonnie's best hope of finding the ideal partner is to find someone with almost exactly the same personality.

The Runic Interpretation
ᛖᛁᚾᚾᛟᛒ (Ehwaz, Isa, Nauthiz, Nauthiz, Othila, Berkana)

Bonnie has an earthy and fiery nature. She is organized and responsible, and impatient in groups where people waste time. She prefers to work alone in the middle of the night when the world is quiet and she feels omnipotent. The double Nauthiz energy in her name belies the need for partnership. Bonnie will function best with a tactful and gracious mate who tolerates her blunt and controlling nature. In turn, she will use humor with her partner and know how to insert just enough compliments into their conversations to keep him from balking. She may not be the most glamorous of women, but her energy is passionate and romance is important to her. A good mate teaches Bonnie to use her eyes rather than her mouth. Eyes speak the universal language of love.

Elements: Air, earth, fire, fire, earth/fire, air/earth

The Numerological Interpretation
Bonnie (NV = 5, CV = 3, VV = 2, FL = 2)

An active and vivacious woman, Bonnie has a wide range of interests and a large circle of friends. People enjoy Bonnie. She always has something stimulating to say and is ever willing to bestow a warm smile on others. A generous and supportive person by nature, Bonnie knows how to be a friend. Personal relationships mean a great deal to her. She will devote much of her time to her marriage or partnership.

DERIVATION: English, from the common Scottish word meaning "pretty." Quite popular since the mid-twentieth century.

PRINCIPAL COLORS: Any very pale hues

GEMSTONES AND PRECIOUS METALS: Silver, diamonds

BOTANICALS: Hazel, oats, parsley

UNIQUE SPELLINGS: Bahni, Bahnie, Bahny, Bonnee, Bonni, Bonny

RELATED TO: Bonita, Bunnie, Bunny

"No matter what the competition is, I try to find a goal that day and better that goal."
—BONNIE BLAIR (ATHLETE)

DERIVATION: English, from the
Old English for "broad wood"
or "broad clearing." Originally a
surname, it is mainly used now in
the United States as a given name.

PRINCIPAL COLORS: Brilliant
azure, shades of gray

GEMSTONES AND PRECIOUS
METALS: Sapphires

BOTANICALS: Celandine, sage,
wintergreen

UNIQUE SPELLINGS: Braddley,
Bradlee, Bradli, Bradlie, Bradly

RELATED TO: Brad, Braddick,
Braddock, Bradford, Leet

Bradley

A KABBALISTIC SYNOPSIS
בראדלי —BRADLY (Beth, Resh, Aleph, Daleth, Lamed, Yod)

Bradley will do very well for himself. He has an impressive personality and usually a personable manner, so any career where client service is important will suit Bradley very well. Bradley's name reduces to thirteen, which is associated with change. Bradley is very well suited to fast-moving, high-pressure work environments. Under kabbalistic analysis there are strong indications of a suitability for training others. Bradley has a good brain for moneymaking schemes, and his inventive personality ensures that he can always come up with something new and exciting. One meaning of Bradley is "to overwhelm," and it would be no surprise if Bradley did indeed become a roaring success. Emotionally, Bradley is capable of making a firm commitment to a single person, but his love of change means that his partner will have to be as lively as Bradley to maintain his interest.

THE RUNIC INTERPRETATION
ᛇᛚᛞᛉᚱᛒ (Eihwaz, Laguz, Dagaz, Ansuz, Raido, Berkana)

This name carries the energy of Eihwaz, which is that of defense and the ability to turn events around to one's benefit. Bradley has a mind like a radar screen; he is a brilliant strategist. He seems to know what to say, and his sense of timing is based on a rich inner knowing. Bradley works so well in the outer world because he was born understanding the value of meditation. When he meditates, Bradley gains patience and perspective on his life. Bradley notices coincidences; overheard conversations, numbers that repeat during the day, and all the trivia of life are signals from the universe. He looks for links and patterns and clues to information the universe freely provides to those who see. People ask Bradley the secret of his success, and he says the universe points the way. How honest. But most people miss the point.

Elements: Earth/fire, water, fire, air, water, air/earth

THE NUMEROLOGICAL INTERPRETATION
Bradley (NV = 4, CV = 9, VV = 4, FL = 2)

Bradley is a name that expresses a very practical and down-to-earth man. People see Bradley as very well organized and he is. This is a man who doesn't go off into dreamland to fantasize about things that do not matter to his daily life. He will work to achieve his envisioned goals, and he will accomplish his aims with persistence and diligent activity. Bradley is also very open to helping others in a material sense, and he may be counted on to contribute to and support those charitable endeavors that appeal to the more humanitarian side of his nature.

Brandon

DERIVATION: English, from the Old English *brom*, meaning "broom," and *dun*, meaning "hill." Also a variant form of the Irish Brendan. Commonly used in the United States since the 1930s.

PRINCIPAL COLORS: Gray, very lightly toned hues

GEMSTONES AND PRECIOUS METALS: Shiny, pale stones, including diamonds; platinum

BOTANICALS: Sweet marjoram, parsley, caraway

UNIQUE SPELLINGS: Brandan, Branden, Brandin, Brandyn, Brannden, Branndin, Branndon, Branndyn

RELATED TO: Brando, Brant, Branton, Breandán, Brendan, Brenden, Brentt, Briant

A KABBALISTIC SYNOPSIS

בראנדון —BRANDVN (Beth, Resh, Aleph, Nun, Daleth, Vau, Nun)

Brandon feels rather than thinks, his personality dominated completely by his emotional state. While his emotionally open nature may make him attractive to potential mates, he has a tendency to become far too possessive. Brandon adds up to eighteen, which is the number of the Moon in the tarot. The Moon represents emotional uncertainties and anxieties, and in extreme cases it may even point to neuroses. Brandon is a very insecure individual who needs constant reassurance and approval from his partner, or he will become withdrawn and cold. His name can be represented by the letters Tzaddi, Samech, and Gimel, which between them tell an interesting tale. Tzaddi shows Brandon's need to possess the things that he cares about, including people; Samech tells us that these possessions act as a form of support, enabling Brandon to function happily in the world; and, Gimel reveals that with the right sympathetic and supportive partner, Brandon will be able to move on with confidence.

THE RUNIC INTERPRETATION

ᚾᛟᛞᚾᚨᚱᛒ (Nauthiz, Othila, Dagaz, Nauthiz, Ansuz, Raido, Berkana)

Brandon's name contains the energy of the waning moon, which is a time of black magic. Brandon can protect himself from negativity with honesty, positive friends, and laughter. Light is the vehicle to combat negativity—and laughter surely draws in the light. Women have been known to tease Brandon about his sexual prowess, but Brandon just can't help it: He has fire, earth, air, and water in his name. He creates a rapport with people instantly and has his little black book on computer now. And you can be sure Brandon bought a computer with a lot of memory—memory is another of Brandon's many attributes.

Elements: Fire, earth/fire, fire, fire, air, water, air/earth

THE NUMEROLOGICAL INTERPRETATION

Brandon (NV = 5, CV = 7, VV = 7, FL = 2)

Brandon loves to explore life and is open to what is new and different. His purpose in life is to develop his mind and then increase his worldly experience. Through his travels, he is able to distill the important essence of his encounters and extract the hidden meaning in each of life's many lessons. The numbers in this name give a distinct analytical orientation to Brandon's mind, allowing Brandon to think through every situation and come up with an interesting conclusion or solution.

Brandy

DERIVATION: English, probably from the common English word, but also a possible form of Brandon. Fairly popular in the United States.

PRINCIPAL COLORS: Bronze and russet, the full range of yellow hues

GEMSTONES AND PRECIOUS METALS: Amber, citrine, any pale or brilliant yellow stones

BOTANICALS: Chamomile, lavender, eyebright

UNIQUE SPELLINGS: Brandee, Brandey, Brandi, Brandie

RELATED TO: Brendat, Brenna, Brenne, Brenni

❧

"I keep reminding myself of what I can achieve if I believe and try hard enough. It motivates me to keep going further . . . because I know I can."
—BRANDY NORWOOD
(ACTRESS, SINGER)

A KABBALISTIC SYNOPSIS
בראנדי —BRANDY (Beth, Resh, Aleph, Nun, Daleth, Yod)

Brandy is appropriately named, as she exercises an intoxicating influence on all those who know her. She is a very charismatic woman with a real sense of individuality, and while Brandy has looks that can kill, she also has her own unique style. Brandy is a complex mixture of feminine intuition and good old-fashioned common sense. The presence of the solar R, or Resh, along with Scorpio's influence, means that Brandy is very attracted by power both in herself and in her partners. If she has been born under Scorpio, it may be that this interest in power games and domination extends to the bedroom. Brandy's charisma is such that on a good day she can have an almost hypnotic effect on any number of people. Needless to say, Brandy has her pick of careers, but her magnetism and powers of persuasion are ideally suited to fields such as sales and marketing.

THE RUNIC INTERPRETATION
ᛇᛃᚾᚨᚱᛒ (Eihwaz, Dagaz, Nauthiz, Ansuz, Raido, Berkana)

Completion and accomplishments are important to Brandy. She knows how to put herself together to create a good impression but is far from vain. Rather, Brandy is practical and knows, from the time she is a little girl, that the way we package ourselves affects how people respond to us. Brandy is comfortable singing or speaking before a large audience. Opportunities to be in the public eye abound. If her life involves selling, she will set all kinds of records and then use the money for cruises and luxurious adventures. Brandy is fortunate to have the four elements represented in her name, because this configuration represents wholeness and a balance of power, talents, and abilities.

Elements: Earth/fire, fire, fire, air, water, air/earth

THE NUMEROLOGICAL INTERPRETATION
Brandy (NV = 1, CV = 2, VV = 8, FL = 2)

This name denotes a woman who is very much an individual. Brandy connotes high ideals and long-range goals. Her success in her chosen field of endeavor is very important to her, and she is willing to make every effort to reach the top. Personal relationships are also very important—she does not want to reach the pinnacle alone! Because Brandy is a person who understands the subtleties involved in personal relationships, she is a good friend as well as a caring partner or spouse and, therefore, needn't worry about being lonely at the top.

❧

Brenda

A KABBALISTIC SYNOPSIS
ברנדא —BRNDA (Beth, Resh, Nun, Daleth, Aleph)

You know exactly where you are with Brenda, who prides herself on her absolute honesty. Brenda is frank, sometimes to the point of bluntness, and especially so if she has been born under the signs of Taurus or Sagittarius. Because of her reliability, Brenda makes a good employee. She is a solid investment for any firm, though she lacks any real ambition for advancement. Banking, accounting, and real estate all appeal to her no-nonsense style, and working in the manufacturing industry also suits Brenda's down-to-earth outlook. Brenda likes measurable, attainable goals. She has little time for office intrigue, or the subtlety and pretension of the worlds of media and marketing. Relationships are very straightforward affairs for Brenda, too. She is not one to agonize over her choices, but will simply know if any particular man is right for her or not. If she decides that you are the one, then there is a near certainty that you will end up hers, as Brenda's other primary quality is dogged persistence!

THE RUNIC INTERPRETATION
ᚨᛞᚾᛖᚱᛒ (Ansuz, Dagaz, Nauthiz, Ehwaz, Raido, Berkana)

Brenda is charismatic and sensual. She enjoys expensive fashions and seductive fragrances. She keeps her body well groomed, and her home is clean and sweet smelling. Aromas and fragrances affect Brenda deeply. Brenda has high standards, and only the best wines and food will do for her. She follows a sparse diet, and this way she can indulge when the occasion warrants a splurge. Brenda appreciates the link between smell and memory, and this interest will serve her well in the twenty-first century; aromatherapy and healing with essential oils are being studied with great respect by noted therapists today. Brenda is humble and modest, and highly discriminating.

Elements: Air, fire, fire, air, water, air/earth

THE NUMEROLOGICAL INTERPRETATION
Brenda (NV = 8, CV = 2, VV = 6, FL = 2)

Brenda is a name that indicates a woman who is very social. She enjoys the company of others and will spend a good deal of her time and energy on her relationships. A warm companion and a supportive partner, Brenda considers home and family very important. She has an instinct for what makes others happy but has to realize that she is not responsible for their happiness. Brenda's personal goals in life are sometimes too intimately connected with those around her.

DERIVATION: Scottish, Irish, and English, of unknown origin. Possibly from the Old Norse *brand*, meaning "sword." Always common in Scotland and Ireland, and popular in the United States since the 1940s.

PRINCIPAL COLORS: From gray to black, deep azure, purple

GEMSTONES AND PRECIOUS METALS: Black pearls, black diamonds, carbuncles

BOTANICALS: Marsh mallow, pilewort, shepherd's purse

UNIQUE SPELLINGS: Brehnda, Brehndah, Brehnnda, Brendah, Brennda

RELATED TO: Branda, Brandee, Brandi, Brandy†, Brendanna, Brendanne

DERIVATION: English, originally a surname derived from an English place-name, probably from a Celtic or Old English root meaning "high place" or "hill." Especially popular in Britain in the 1970s and '80s.

PRINCIPAL COLORS: The full spectrum of all the palest shades

GEMSTONES AND PRECIOUS METALS: Silver, platinum, any very lightly shaded stone

BOTANICALS: Hazel, parsnips, mushrooms

UNIQUE SPELLINGS: Brehnt, Brehntt, Brentt

RELATED TO: Brentan, Brenten, Brenton, Brett†, Bryant†

Brent

A KABBALISTIC SYNOPSIS
ברנט —BRNT (Beth, Resh, Nun, Teth)

Brent has an unnerving capacity to make people feel woefully inadequate; he doesn't mean to do this, but people find it difficult to feel that they are quite up to standard after an hour or so in Brent's company. In his appearance Brent is deceptive; the influence of R, or Resh, is likely to give him a cheerful look, which belies the awesome seriousness of his personality. Brent has an enormous sense of moral duty and responsibility. Indeed, many of his life choices are determined by the moral quality of the available options. On the whole you will find Brent working in charitable organizations or the caring professions, as he is unlikely to be comfortable working in business. Brent's morality doesn't give him a judgmental hellfire-and-damnation approach to other people; rather, he is very sympathetic and understanding. Brent's moral sense comes from within.

THE RUNIC INTERPRETATION
↑ᚺᛗᚱᛒ (Teiwaz, Nauthiz, Ehwaz, Raido, Berkana)

Brent calls to mind the tall oak tree with its power and intelligence. This is a name with the water Raido energy prominently positioned. He requires change and movement. Philosophy, anthropology, and history interest him. Brent loves travel and loves to see how people's attitudes are duplicated in the environments they create. Brent is broad-minded and creative in his thinking. He enjoys the company of gifted and original minds. He keeps challenging books on the night table and is able to make himself understood in an elementary fashion in dozens of languages. He would work well in a think tank or as a teacher or writer. Brent understands that we can make our mind into an exquisite garden.

Elements: Air, fire, air, water, air/earth

THE NUMEROLOGICAL INTERPRETATION
Brent (NV = 4, CV = 9, VV = 5, FL = 2)

Brent is a man with his feet on the ground, and he enjoys having them there! Although he loves to explore life and engage in new and different experiences, Brent nonetheless is primarily a practical person. In order to give himself the freedom to break with his usual routine, he first has to assure himself that his routine is secure. Honest and sincere, Brent is endowed with a sense of compassion for others and is a helpful individual by nature.

Brett

DERIVATION: English, from the Latin name Britto, meaning "Breton." A surname in the Middle Ages, it is now used as a given name in the United States and England with some popularity.

PRINCIPAL COLORS: From lightest to deepest green, creamy white

GEMSTONES AND PRECIOUS METALS: Jade, moonstones, white pearls

BOTANICALS: Cabbage, chicory, colewort, moonwort

UNIQUE SPELLINGS: Breht, Brehtt, Bret, Brette

RELATED TO: Bernt, Brentt, Breton, Bretton

A KABBALISTIC SYNOPSIS
ברט —BRTh (Beth, Resh, Teth)

Brett is another man with very firm beliefs, although the absence of the emotional and spiritual N, or Nun, indicates that his main concern is political or philosophical values rather than religious ones. It is highly likely that Brett will go into politics even if it is at a low level. His connection to his home or community is shown by B, or Beth, which suggests that Brett gets excited by local issues rather than more global concerns. If Brett has passionate views, they will be about the new road being planned in a local area rather than the federal deficit. Although he may not be an innately spiritual person, Brett is very altruistic. He genuinely believes in putting his fellow citizens first and is drawn to activities that enable him to put something back into the community. A happily married man, Brett is a very contented husband who thrives in a long-term committed relationship. Unlike some less scrupulous politicians, he is not one to play around.

THE RUNIC INTERPRETATION
↑↑MR8 (Teiwaz, Teiwaz, Ehwaz, Raido, Berkana)

Brett is very social, and if he succumbs to marriage, it will be later in life. He has a double Teiwaz energy in his name that makes him psychically strong and very sexy. His direct manner and command of words, combined with his dignified bearing, let people know that this man likes himself and that he will treat others with sensitivity and good humor. Brett values his freedom, and in his youth likes to keep unattached because he knows he has a lot of living to do.

Elements: Air, air, air, water, air/earth

THE NUMEROLOGICAL INTERPRETATION
Brett (NV = 11, CV = 6, VV = 5, FL = 2)

Brett is a complex man with many levels to his nature. This is a person who possesses a wide scope of vision and a multitude of interests. He is easily bored with the commonplace and avoids routine. He is able to adapt to the changes life brings and looks forward to them. Kind, harmonious, and peace loving, Brett has a very inclusive philosophy, one that is less preoccupied with separatist doctrines and more concerned with humanitarianism.

Brian

DERIVATION: Irish and English, of unknown origin. Possibly from an Old Celtic word meaning "high" or "hill." Very popular in all English-speaking countries in the mid-1900s.

PRINCIPAL COLORS: Dark shades of azure; purple, gray, black

GEMSTONES AND PRECIOUS METALS: Lackluster rubies, amethyst, black diamonds

BOTANICALS: Mandrake, gravel root, shepherd's purse, angelica

UNIQUE SPELLINGS: Brion, Bryan, Bryen, Bryin, Bryon

RELATED TO: Branden, Brandon†, Brenden, Bryant†, Byron†

A KABBALISTIC SYNOPSIS
בריון —BRYVN (Beth, Resh, Yod, Vau, Nun)

Unless you like a really good row, it's not a good idea to get into a fight with Brian, who could win prizes for his ability to verbally crush his opponents! Often small in stature, Brian sees himself as something of a David figure, and all those who disagree with him as the Goliaths. He is never happier than when he is opposing the general view, and this can lead to his taking a somewhat perverse approach to his own beliefs. Brian loves playing devil's advocate—and he usually wins the argument. It should be added that there is no malice in Brian, who is on the whole a friendly chap. The framing of his name with B (Beth) and N (Nun) means that he enjoys a calm and emotionally supportive home life. In fact, Brian hates real arguments, and when it comes to serious personal matters with his family, he is always willing to compromise and be reasonable. However, if you are with a Brian, you will have to accept his love of verbal swordplay.

THE RUNIC INTERPRETATION
ᚾᚨᛁᚱᛒ (Nauthiz, Ansuz, Isa, Raido, Berkana)

Brian is practical and emotionally strong. He is a born negotiator and understands people very well. His peculiar trait is that he loves practical jokes, but Brian's tricks are often misconstrued. Still, Brian needs to play and he loves to see the dumbfounded look on people's faces when he's got them in the palm of his hand. (Be careful of the palm of his hand—he probably has a buzzer there for when you shake!) Brian loves whoopee cushions and flies-in-the-ice-cube tricks. It's all harmless enough, and people could use more fun in their lives.

Elements: Fire, air, earth, water, air/earth

THE NUMEROLOGICAL INTERPRETATION
Brian (NV = 8, CV = 7, VV = 1, FL = 2)

It is important for Brian to individualize his creativity as well as his need for social and material success. This means that he tends to be a man more comfortable being self-employed in a career of his own choosing than being employed by another. This is a name that indicates a strong mind, one that Brian can use to support his vital, creative impulses. Brian will work to distinguish himself from others in order to make a clear and distinctive mark on his environment.

Brittany

DERIVATION: Latin, meaning "from Britain." Very popular in the early 1990s.

PRINCIPAL COLORS: The full set of yellow, brown, and orange hues

GEMSTONES AND PRECIOUS METALS: Pale to brilliant yellow stones, including topaz and yellow diamonds

BOTANICALS: Lavender, Saint-John's-wort, barley, cloves

UNIQUE SPELLINGS: Britaney, Britani, Britany, Briteny, Brittaney, Brittani, Britteny

RELATED TO: Brett†, Brit, Britney, Britni, Britny, Britt, Britta, Brittan, Brittnee, Brittney, Brittni, Brittny

A KABBALISTIC SYNOPSIS
ברימני —BRYTNY (Beth, Resh, Yod, Teth, Nun, Yod)

Teaching is the ideal vocation for Brittany, although there is a side of her that dreams of a more glamorous life—preferably somewhere hot, with a deserted beach! Brittany has a social conscience and wants to help out those less fortunate than she, although not to the extent of making herself a martyr to any particular cause. Her attitude runs more along the lines of choosing to work in the public rather than the commercial sector—in the local government, perhaps, or social services. Intelligent and witty, Brittany has the mental resources to cope with the stress of a job like teaching and to maintain a sunny, patient temperament in the face of thirty or so bored twelve-year-olds. Brittany is a lively conversationalist and will always be happy to chat both in and out of the workplace; she likes working in a city where she can have a large circle of friends and plenty of places to socialize.

THE RUNIC INTERPRETATION
ᛃᚺᚨᛏᛏᛁᚱᛒ (Eihwaz, Nauthiz, Ansuz, Teiwaz, Teiwaz, Isa, Raido, Berkana)

Brittany is bound for recognition and success on many levels. She has the amazing gift of being able to talk to all kinds of people, and if they want to do a favor for her, all the better! Brittany knows which side her bread is buttered on. She epitomizes charm and has considerable acting ability. She is also flexible and resilient. She manages her emotions well and can accomplish a great deal in this lifetime. She has a good sense of self-protection and is not easily fooled. She may not have had all the advantages money can buy, but you'd never guess it to look at her. Brittany is a colorful friend who can make you laugh like no one else. But beware of Brittany as a counselor, because once crossed she can be cold as ice.

Elements: Earth/fire, fire, air, air, air, earth, water, air/earth

THE NUMEROLOGICAL INTERPRETATION
Brittany (NV = 1, CV = 2, VV = 8, FL = 2)

Brittany is a name that connotes a woman with a highly energetic disposition. She is usually very enthusiastic about her involvements and encourages other people in their own pursuits and interests as well. Although very self-motivated, Brittany tends to be supportive rather than competitive. Achieving harmony in her relationships is important to her, and she would much rather have partners with whom she may achieve mutual goals than work against potential adversaries. People admire Brittany for her enterprising spirit and passion for life.

Brooke

DERIVATION: English, once a surname used to indicate living near a brook. Now regularly appears as a given name.

PRINCIPAL COLORS: The full set of purple hues, including maroon

GEMSTONES AND PRECIOUS METALS: Garnets

BOTANICALS: Apples, cherries, strawberries, mint

UNIQUE SPELLING: Brook

RELATED TO: Brookes, Brookie, Brooks

❧

"There is hope if people will begin to awaken that spiritual part of themselves—that heartfelt acknowledgment that we are the caretakers of life on this planet."

—BROOKE MEDICINE EAGLE (NATIVE AMERICAN AUTHOR)

A KABBALISTIC SYNOPSIS
ברוכ —BRVK (Beth, Resh, Vau, Kaph)

Brooke is a relatively modern name, but due to the methods of the Kabbalah, which analyze largely through the value of individual letters, her name can be related to the basis of the Kabbalah itself. The value of Brooke's name is equivalent to עץהיים (or A'ATZ ChYYM, which is Hebrew for the Tree of Life. According to the Kabbalah, all mysteries of the universe and spiritual development are contained within the Tree of Life. It is no surprise, then, that Brooke is a deeply spiritual woman—not in the churchgoing sense, but at a mystical level. Brooke will not be satisfied by material success, and despite her intelligence and capacity to hold down a professional career in law, journalism, or letters, she may well seek out unskilled manual work in order to free up her mind for consideration of higher things. Brooke is a seeker whose main goal in life is to achieve some kind of enlightenment or to locate some kernel of absolute truth. The fact that her name can be reduced to the value of the Hanged Man in tarot indicates that she will go to any lengths to achieve this goal.

THE RUNIC INTERPRETATION
ᛗᚲᛟᛟᚱᛒ (Ehwaz, Kano, Othila, Othila, Raido, Berkana)

Brooke's name contains the Othila energy of separation. She may have been compromised by circumstances growing up, and she gave up a lot of fun and silliness as a young woman to better her life. She may also have overcome a physical disability. But none of this stops Brooke: She has learned to love the ignorant and insulting people she is forced to interact with, and this sense of newfound peace is the one thing in life she appreciates above all else. Brooke has mastered the spiritual lesson of being her highest self in times of stress and alienation. This personal power takes her to new heights and accomplishments both on earth and in other realms. Brooke has learned her lesson well.

Elements: Air, water, earth/fire, earth/fire, water, air/earth

THE NUMEROLOGICAL INTERPRETATION
Brooke (NV = 3, CV = 4, VV = 8, FL = 2)

The name Brooke carries with it a certain amount of ambition for success. Social position and career achievements are indicated through the numbers of this name. Brooke is very communicative and always has something interesting to contribute to any gathering of friends and associates. She is curious and inquisitive in nature and eager to pursue any form of education that will carry her toward the accomplishment of her many plans and projects. People find Brooke mentally stimulating and a storehouse of facts and figures.

❧

Bruce

DERIVATION: Scottish and English, from a Norman place-name. Once exclusively a surname, it was first used as a given name in Scotland. Popular in many English-speaking countries since the 1930s.

PRINCIPAL COLORS: Grays, bright blue

GEMSTONES AND PRECIOUS METALS: Sapphires

BOTANICALS: Medlar, lesser celandine, Iceland moss

UNIQUE SPELLINGS: Brooce, Broose, Brus

RELATED TO: Brice, Brizio, Broz, Bryce

A KABBALISTIC SYNOPSIS
ברעס —BRA'AS (Beth, Resh, Ayin, Samech)

Is it a bird, is it a plane, or is it a speeding bullet? This guy is so energetic, it's downright scary! Bruce is extremely athletic; his name has associations with the tarot trump card, representing strength and force, while the Ayin that occupies center stage in his name signifies the nimble agility and hardiness of the mountain goat. Like all names beginning with BR, Bruce is a man of firm beliefs and definite goals. For him the desire to compete is overwhelming. It is probable that this will be sporting competition, since Bruce has incredible speed. The chances of outstanding sporting success are increased if Bruce is an Aries or a Gemini. If Bruce is not a sporty type, then the corporate world had better look out! The competitive urge in Bruce will still find some form of expression, and it is likely that Bruce will rocket his way to the top. What he lacks in subtlety and understanding, he more than makes up for by his sheer force of will.

THE RUNIC INTERPRETATION
ᛗᚲᚢᚱᛒ (Ehwaz, Kano, Uruz, Raido, Berkana)

Bruce likes to work with his hands, and he is very strong and powerful. The Uruz energy at the center of the name symbolizes the wild ox. Bruce's life lesson is to learn humility and service. His physical prowess affords him vast reserves of energy best channeled into patience, tolerance, and a willingness to change. Yet it is the very nature of personal development that we are always free to resist our own growth. Personal power is the willingness to discipline the self to create goals and to have the discipline to carry out our dreams. Bruce could be a star in sports or a leader in many fields. He is blessed with the prize of physical health and stamina.

Elements: Air, water, earth, water, air/earth

THE NUMEROLOGICAL INTERPRETATION
Bruce (NV = 4, CV = 5, VV = 8, FL = 2)

Bruce works to make sure that his own practical needs and those of his friends and family are securely anchored. He is not one to take unnecessary risks or undertake projects that are beyond his capabilities. The material considerations of life are uppermost in his mind, and he is not averse to spending as much time and effort as possible to achieve his goals and career ambitions. Although he may experiment with different hobbies and pastimes, his priorities are usually quite set.

DERIVATION: English, originally a
surname related to Brian. Popular
in the United States in recent
years.

PRINCIPAL COLORS: Deep azure,
gray, black

GEMSTONES AND PRECIOUS
METALS: Dark sapphires and
amethyst, pearls, black diamonds

BOTANICALS: Marsh mallow,
angelica, ragwort

UNIQUE SPELLINGS: Briant,
Briantt, Bryehnt, Bryont, Bryontt

RELATED TO: Brentt, Briant,
Bryan, Bryon, Byront

Bryant

A KABBALISTIC SYNOPSIS
ברײונט —BRYVNT (Beth, Resh, Yod, Vau, Nun, Teth)

Bryant had better be a good earner because this chap is destined to have a whole houseful of kids! His name adds to 277, which is a direct numeration of the Hebrew for "propagation." In some cases this could be interpreted as referring to general creativity and the ability to come up with an array of new ideas. However, there are a number of aspects to Bryant's name that signify the production of a large family—and not least of these is the presence of T, or Teth, in his name. Teth means "serpent," and from the earliest times the serpent has been a potent totemic sign of fertility. Before Bryant starts to panic, we should add that there is strong evidence of Bryant doing very well for himself financially. There is, for instance, the double presence of the number seven in his name, which is a good indicator of general success. In addition, Bryant begins with B, or Beth, suggesting that Bryant will be more than happy with such a full home life.

THE RUNIC INTERPRETATION
↑ᚺᛀᛇᚱᛒ (Teiwaz, Nauthiz, Ansuz, Eihwaz, Raido, Berkana)

Bryant is blessed with the warrior Teiwaz energy. Bryant's battle, like that of all spiritual warriors, is with the shadow side of the self. He needs to see how he sabotages his success in business and to use his Berkana energy of growth to remain enthusiastic and aware. Bryant is cooperative and a clear communicator, having Ansuz for signals in his name. He is able to stop and evaluate the needs of himself and those around him. The Raido energy of journey ensures prosperity and adventures ahead for lucky Bryant. He is brave, and he is excited to know more about the world and to become involved in making the earth a safe place to be.

Elements: Air, fire, air, earth/fire, water, air/earth

THE NUMEROLOGICAL INTERPRETATION
Bryant (NV = 8, CV = 9, VV = 8, FL = 2)

Bryant is a name that evokes material success and achievement. People working with Bryant in his business ventures find him a definite asset. A definite career man, Bryant has a great deal of practical insight and enough personal magnetism to reach his goals. Self-confidence is another one of the more positive characteristics inherent in this name. Yet Bryant has to take care not to try to overly control and dominate others. People will naturally respond to him when he uses his strength as a source of genuine support and friendship.

Byron

A Kabbalistic Synopsis
בירון —BYRVN (Beth, Yod, Resh, Vau, Nun)

The name Byron has obvious romantic associations, thanks to the eighteenth-century poet Lord Byron. Byron reduces to eighteen, which along with the terminal N, or Nun, emphasizes the importance of creativity and the emotions. However, there are also signs here of anxiety and self-doubt, so we should not expect Byron to have a dashing, devil-may-care approach to life. In fact, Byron has quite a somber outlook, and can often see the world as alien to him, or as a thing that he must contain. Under kabbalistic analysis the symbols of a fishhook and an enclosure are revealed, suggesting Byron has a desire to carefully select and control his experience. On a literary note, these symbols could also refer to the capturing of experience for later recollection or expression.

The Runic Interpretation
ᛏᛟᚱᛇᛒ (Nauthiz, Othila, Raido, Eihwaz, Berkana)

Byron needs to express himself in the arts. His feet are always tapping, and he lives for the clubs. He dances till dawn, and people form a circle around him, clapping, and he loves it. Byron's life lesson is the Eihwaz energy for patience and perseverance, Nauthiz for constraint, and Othila for separation. These rune lessons demand isolation and introspection, which are implied by their meanings. Byron would do well as a choreographer, dancer, or designer in nearly any artistic endeavor. He's a delight to know because he's happy inside and it shows.

Elements: Fire, earth/fire, water, earth/fire, air/earth

The Numerological Interpretation
Byron (NV = 11, CV = 7, VV = 4, FL = 2)

Byron can offer a great deal of aid and comfort to his friends and family. People are attracted to Byron because of his ability to peer beneath the surface of ordinary activity. He has profound insights concerning daily life, yet his advice is very down-to-earth and has a definite practical application. Byron is usually dedicated to an ideal, one that is often connected to helping others find their way. The numbers in this name also bestow a strong willpower and a clarity of intent.

DERIVATION: English, originally a surname derived from the Old English *hyre*, meaning "barn" or "cow shed." Used to honor the Romantic poet Lord Byron (1788–1824). Common since the 1850s.

PRINCIPAL COLORS: Pale grassy to deep forest green, white

GEMSTONES AND PRECIOUS METALS: Creamy-colored pearls, jade, moonstones

BOTANICALS: Plantain, colewort, lettuce

UNIQUE SPELLINGS: Biran, Biron, Byran, Byren, Byrin, Byryn

RELATED TO: Briant†, Bryant†, Bryon, Byford, Byram, Byrom

"All who would win joy, must share it; happiness was born a twin."
—LORD BYRON (POET)

DERIVATION: Biblical, the name of Moses' follower who managed to survive long enough to enter the Promised Land. Related to the Hebrew word for "dog." Especially popular among the Puritans.

PRINCIPAL COLORS: The full spectrum of pale shades, especially light gray

GEMSTONES AND PRECIOUS METALS: All pale, glittering stones, such as diamonds, and platinum

BOTANICALS: Sweet marjoram, oats, parsley

UNIQUE SPELLINGS: Callib, Callyb, Calyb, Kaleb, Kalebh, Kalleb, Kallib

RELATED TO: Cale, Caley, Callum, Calumba

❧

"When you have nothing to say, say nothing."
—CHARLES CALEB COLTON
(AUTHOR)

A KABBALISTIC SYNOPSIS
כאלאב —KALAB (Kaph, Aleph, Lamed, Aleph, Beth)

Whatever Caleb does, he throws himself into it wholeheartedly and with passion. His name begins with K, or Kaph, meaning "hand," which shows that he is a doer rather than a talker. The final B, or Beth, suggests that, despite his capacity for getting things done, he is not hugely ambitious. His main aim is to create a happy domestic situation for himself and his family. The central feature of Caleb is the two Alephs balanced by the L, or Lamed. This arrangement points to the source of his drive and immense energy, as well as the way that he channels that energy. The Lamed is the sheer force of energy, while the two Alephs are connected to practical activities, so we can tell that Caleb is driven to work in areas such as building, machining, or carpentry. The name Caleb may sound somewhat backwoodsy, and it has to be said that there is some justification in this association: Caleb has a great respect for nature and is likely to spend his weekends and holidays out in the country hunting, fishing, or just enjoying the natural environment. Caleb's love of the rugged great outdoors may lead him to live in a remote area of the country.

THE RUNIC INTERPRETATION
ᛒᛖᛚᚨᚲ (Berkana, Ehwaz, Laguz, Ansuz, Kano)

Caleb's name contains the optimistic, invigorated energy of the waxing moon. Laguz figures prominently in the name, bringing a flow of people and ideas to Caleb in effortless fashion. Opportunities often come his way, and people mutter that Caleb has all the luck. Caleb is also excellent at eliminating limiting beliefs from his worldview. He empowers himself by diligently cultivating the art of awareness or the discipline of focused concentration. Caleb fails more than he succeeds, and that is okay because it's important that he tries and takes risks. His friends see only his successes, and they are wrong to assume that they came easily to Caleb. But Caleb enjoys his reputation—and why not?

Elements: Air/earth, air, water, air, water

THE NUMEROLOGICAL INTERPRETATION
Caleb (NV = 5, CV = 8, VV = 6, FL = 3)

The name Caleb is characterized by a very expansive and communicative nature. This is a man who seeks to free himself of those mental limitations that inhibit success in the world. In this respect, Caleb is an adventurer, ever seeking those experiences that will widen his scope of vision and increase his understanding of the world. A lover of the arts, Caleb seeks to bring harmony and beauty into his environment. He is also a man who likes to look good and takes pride in his personal appearance.

❧

Calvin

DERIVATION: English, from the French surname meaning "bald one." Also used as a given name to honor the Protestant religious reformer John Calvin.

PRINCIPAL COLORS: Pale to deep green, yellow, gold

GEMSTONES AND PRECIOUS METALS: Cat's-eyes, moss agate, all cream-colored stones, such as pearls

BOTANICALS: Elder, blackberry, linseed

UNIQUE SPELLINGS: Calven, Calvyn, Kalven, Kalvin, Kalvyn

RELATED TO: Cal, Cale, Caley, Cally, Calum, Calvert, Vin, Vinnie

"The business of America is business."
—CALVIN COOLIDGE (PRESIDENT OF THE UNITED STATES)

"That's the difference between me and the rest of the world! Happiness isn't good enough for me! I demand euphoria!"
—CALVIN, IN *CALVIN & HOBBES* (COMIC-STRIP CHARACTER)

A Kabbalistic Synopsis

כאלוין —KALVYN (Kaph, Aleph, Lamed, Vau, Yod, Nun)

Calvin is a success with a capital *S*. If anybody can make it in business, Calvin can. As well as gematric equivalences, Kabbalah uses "compression," whereby one finds the fewest number of letters that will give the same value as the name being looked at. Calvin's name adds up to 767, which is associated by this process of compression with the World card in tarot. This decidedly positive card represents the successful completion of a major cycle in one's life. Its dominant influence over Calvin indicates that he will experience a whole series of major successes in life. In addition, we have the value of his name both beginning and ending with seven, showing that he begins and ends with good fortune as his companion. Calvin is a hard worker who feels driven to constantly better himself. His ambition is not related purely to a desire for a higher standard of living but to an emotional need to outstrip his colleagues. While he certainly knows how to enjoy himself, Calvin is, in general, quite a serious individual who thinks very carefully about his career choices—hence his repeated successes.

The Runic Interpretation

ᚾᛁᚠᛚᚨᚲ (Nauthiz, Isa, Fehu, Laguz, Ansuz, Kano)

Calvin cannot live in a traditional way because he feels life is mysterious and forceful, and he seeks sights and sounds and personalities that support this belief system. Whatever is unique and well constructed appeals to Calvin; he's distracted by petty details and monotonous people. Calvin needs excitement and a pinch of danger to be happy. Detective work or design work are good fields for Calvin. He needs to travel and search for elusive life mysteries.

Elements: Fire, earth, fire, water, air, water

The Numerological Interpretation

Calvin (NV = 7, CV = 6, VV = 1, FL = 3)

A strong personality with a tremendous urge to be unique, Calvin uses his highly developed mind to focus and promote his talents and abilities. The numbers in this name are indicative of a man in whom creativity is fundamental. He is a person who appreciates beauty in all of its forms and works ceaselessly to bring that sense of aesthetics out into the world around him. Disappointment comes into his life when he feels he is not living up to his own ideas of perfection.

DERIVATION: Scottish, from the Gaelic for "crooked nose." Originally a surname, it became popular as a given name during the Romantic movement. Especially common in Australia and Canada during the 1970s.

PRINCIPAL COLORS: Light to medium blue

GEMSTONES AND PRECIOUS METALS: Emeralds, turquoise

BOTANICALS: Dog rose, violet, walnut

UNIQUE SPELLINGS: Camerin, Cameryn, Cammeron, Kamerin, Kameron, Kameryn, Kammeron

RELATED TO: Cam, Camillus

A KABBALISTIC SYNOPSIS

כמרון —KMRVN (Kaph, Mem, Resh, Vau, Nun)

Cameron is an outgoing guy, and the ideal person in the office to introduce to any new employees. He will welcome them warmly, befriend them, and put them at ease in their new surroundings. There is a strong influence from the sun in his name, which gives him both vigor and a sense of authority—although he expresses this authority in a very low-key way. Cameron knows how to control his natural enthusiasm and has the capacity to take life as a series of separate stages of development. This skill enables him to plan his life carefully, and as he carries this tendency into the office, he is an extremely reliable worker. Cameron's optimistic outlook is particularly appealing to the opposite sex, and he is generally lucky in love. His only problem is that he can sometimes take the same methodical approach to his love life that he applies to other areas. In the case of Virgo and Capricorn Camerons, this lack of spontaneity can become quite trying for his partner. However, Cameron is emotionally very giving and is likely to more than compensate for any failings with his affectionate nature.

THE RUNIC INTERPRETATION

ᚾᛟᚱᛗᛗᚨᚲ (Nauthiz, Othila, Raido, Ehwaz, Mannaz, Ansuz, Kano)

Cameron uses the runes to enrich his experience. He has Nauthiz for constraint, Othila for separation, Raido for journey, Ehwaz for movement, Mannaz for self, Ansuz for signals, and Kano for opening. The Kano and Mannaz runes can make Cameron a bit of a show-off; he likes praise and attention for his accomplishments. Raido and Ehwaz assure Cameron of sales ability, travel opportunities, and the chance to relocate many times. Thus Cameron is a good businessman and is also a wonderful lawyer or mediator. The Othila rune of separation allows him to remain cool and objective during negotiations. Cameron will accumulate material rewards during his career.

Elements: Fire, earth/fire, water, air, air, air, water

THE NUMEROLOGICAL INTERPRETATION

Cameron (NV = 6, CV = 3, VV = 3, FL = 3)

Harmony, balance, music, beauty—all of these are powerfully invoked with the name Cameron. This is a man who is very much involved with the development of his communication skills, and has a profound need to be useful to the world around him. Cameron will tend to be very verbal, using his speaking voice as if it were a musical instrument to convey the many subtleties of meaning he conceives in his very active mind. The name Cameron indicates a very gregarious individual with a wide set of friends and associates.

Candace

A KABBALISTIC SYNOPSIS
כנדאיס —KNDAYS (Kaph, Nun, Daleth, Aleph, Yod, Samech)

Candace is a woman completely at ease with the world. She understands that in order for others to like her, she must first learn to like herself. However, she will not be vain even if she is devastatingly attractive; Candace is in fact comfortable enough with herself not to be overly concerned with her appearance and is as happy with her sexuality as she is with other aspects of her personality. There is strong evidence that she is a highly sexed woman, although she is not remotely interested in short-term, casual relationships. Her name also indicates career success. It is likely that she will run her own business rather than work for someone else, since her ideal career is closely connected to a need to maintain her individuality. As the value of Candace reduces to ten, she generally has good fortune in all areas of her life. Any friends she is especially close to are exceptionally lucky, since Candace has a very generous nature. Within her social circle Candace will always be the one friends visit if they are having a hard time. Her name is completed with S, or Samech, which shows her capacity to provide excellent moral support or a shoulder to cry on.

THE RUNIC INTERPRETATION
ᛖᚲᚨᛞᚾᚨᚲ (Ehwaz, Kano, Ansuz, Dagaz, Nauthiz, Ansuz, Kano)

Candace thinks of life as a superhighway when she's young. But as she matures, she knows it's a winding road. Candace will set out at an early age to improve her station in life; as a young woman she may entertain delusions of grandeur. But when life compromises her dreams, Candace will learn from her mistakes. A few setbacks down the road later, Candace learns to improve her sense of timing. Once she finds her center, Candace begins to enjoy navigating the twists and turns that life has in store for her. Candace ultimately succeeds because she makes every challenge into an opportunity. She has changed the meaning of failure for herself, realizing that missing her goal is not a failure. Candace makes progress in this life both materially, with her artistic talents, and spiritually, as a woman who bears and endures all things.

Elements: Air, water, air, fire, fire, air, water

THE NUMEROLOGICAL INTERPRETATION
Candace (NV = 4, CV = 6, VV = 7, FL = 3)

Candace is a most complex and interesting personality. There are two very distinct sides to her nature: emotional and mental. Her emotional side seeks a peaceful harmony in all of her relationships. She much prefers a long-lasting, monogamous union to a series of passionate and pointless encounters. Mentally, she tends toward introspection and a philosophical approach to life. Candace is prepared to work very consistently toward the achievement of her goals and makes for a very loyal friend and companion.

DERIVATION: English, from the name of a long line of Ethiopian queens. It is found most often in the United States and Canada, among the English-speaking countries. Has become increasingly popular since the 1950s.

PRINCIPAL COLORS: The full spectrum of colors with a medium shade; also, bright azure

GEMSTONES AND PRECIOUS METALS: Dull to brilliant sapphires

BOTANICALS: Lesser celandine, spinach, Solomon's seal

UNIQUE SPELLINGS: Candice, Candis, Candiss, Candys, Candyss, Ka, Kandace, Kandice

RELATED TO: Candy

Carl

DERIVATION: German and English. Variation of Karl, the German version of Charles. From the Old English *ceorl*, meaning "man, husbandman." Very popular in the second half of the nineteenth century.

PRINCIPAL COLORS: The full range of yellow and green tones

GEMSTONES AND PRECIOUS METALS: Cat's-eyes, moonstones, pearls

BOTANICALS: Blackberry, elder, hops

UNIQUE SPELLINGS: Caarle, Carle, Kaarle, Karl, Karle

RELATED TO: Carlo, Carlos†, Carlton, Charles†, Charley, Charlie†, Charlton, Chaz, Chuck†, Kaarle, Karel, Karol, Károly, Séarlas, Siarl

❧

"Show me a sane man and I will cure him for you."
—CARL GUSTAV JUNG (PSYCHOLOGIST)

A KABBALISTIC SYNOPSIS
כעל —KA'AL (Kaph, Ayin, Lamed)

Carl's name has deeply mystical overtones that reach right back to the time of Osiris and Isis, and Carl will have a natural understanding of the nature of these mysteries. He is likely to come across as somewhat withdrawn to his friends and associates, as his concerns are fairly divorced from the day-to-day world of work and family life. In spite of his interest in and feel for more esoteric matters, Carl can be very practical when it is called for. By compression we produce the letters Qoph and Kaph, meaning "head" and "hand," respectively, which indicate a valuable capacity for translating thoughts into actions. Carl is ideally employed in a problem-solving capacity, possibly in the development of prototype products or concepts. Additionally the Qoph and Kaph association of this name has its own significance in that it is suggestive of the process by which one brings the imagined into existence.

THE RUNIC INTERPRETATION
ᛚᚱᚨᚲ (Laguz, Raido, Ansuz, Kano)

Carl is protective and generous. He is also a meat-and-potatoes kind of man. He needs to feel he is at the helm in relationships, and for this very reason he is difficult to love. Carl doesn't like to let his guard down with anyone. Computer science, engineering, and technologies that don't require many social skills are appropriate for Carl, who is most comfortable in the world of logic and numbers. The wise woman will get him out on the dance floor and show him that the beat of the music has a power that defies logic on a moonlit night. Place a kaleidoscope in his hands and show him that color and pattern have much to teach him on an intuitive level. Be gentle with Carl, and his sincerity will lead you to enjoy his company.

Elements: Water, water, air, water

THE NUMEROLOGICAL INTERPRETATION
Carl (NV = 7, CV = 6, VV = 1, FL = 3)

Carl is a man who may spend a great deal of time on his own in order to perfect his vision. Introspective and peace-loving by nature, Carl is focused on his need to develop whatever gifts, talents, and abilities he may possess. Contemplative and reserved, Carl may not be the most communicative of men. He requires relationships that appreciate and support his urge for study and intellectual investigation. He should also be patient with the development of his own creative impulses.

❧

Carla

DERIVATION: Italian, English, and German. Feminine form of Carl. From the Old English *ceorl*, meaning "man, husbandman."

PRINCIPAL COLORS: Dark blue and purple tones, black, gray

GEMSTONES AND PRECIOUS METALS: All deeply hued stones, including amethyst, sapphires, and black pearls

BOTANICALS: Angelica, shepherd's purse

UNIQUE SPELLINGS: Carlah, Carrla, Karla, Karlah, Karrla

RELATED TO: Carlene, Carletta, Carlie, Carlin, Carline, Carlotta, Carly, Carolt, Carole, Caroletta, Carolynt, Karleen, Karlene, Karli, Karlie

A KABBALISTIC SYNOPSIS

כעלא —KA'ALA (Kaph, Ayin, Lamed, Aleph)

If you're working on a business idea and have come to a deadlock, you need the input of a Carla. Whereas Carl is an excellent problem solver, Carla's skill lies in taking that solution and the new problems it inevitably produces and finding the best way to make it all fit together and work. In a sense she provides the next level of ideas and associated application. In terms of romantic relationships, Carla can be a frustrating lover, as she tends not to express her feelings. This is not due to repression of any kind, but rather to her belief that she knows how she feels and assumes that therefore so must her partner. However, it is rare to see a dissatisfied partner to Carla, as she amply compensates for any lack of verbal expression with her actions. Whatever her interest in her work, her partner will always come first.

THE RUNIC INTERPRETATION

ᚨᛚᚱᚨᚲ (Ansuz, Laguz, Raido, Ansuz, Kano)

Carla has much of the logic of the name Carl with the addition of the double Ansuz energy that makes her willing to make leaps of faith beyond what logic would dictate. It is in these artistic jumps that Carla makes new associations and highly creative discoveries. The "Aha!" experience of the artist, inventor, and math whiz is a peak experience for Carla. Carla is a good sport and a good listener. She is modest and kind and ahead of her time. Carla may need some advice on personal grooming because she really is quite beautiful. She must not be allowed to hide from the world.

Elements: Air, water, water, air, water

THE NUMEROLOGICAL INTERPRETATION

Carla (NV = 8, CV = 6, VV = 2, FL = 3)

This is a most romantic name. Carla works to create an environment that is conducive to intimate relationships. Her sense of beauty and aesthetics is very well developed. This is a woman who is very fond of the arts and is a natural-born decorator. She is also very inclusive in her friendships and is much appreciated for her kindness and generosity. Carla's goal is to bring about a greater sense of cooperation between people, and she tries to set a positive example through her own personal conduct.

Carlos

෴

"Brotherhood is the very price and condition of man's survival."
—CARLOS P. ROMULO (PHILIPPINE GENERAL, DIPLOMAT, AND JOURNALIST)

A KABBALISTIC SYNOPSIS
כעלעס —KA'ALA'AS (Kaph, Ayin, Lamed, Ayin, Samech)

The value of Carlos's name points to definite inclinations toward psychotherapy. Carlos adds to 250, which has associations to the letter Samech. Samech indicates the ability to bear the emotional problems of others and is emphasized by the appearance of the letter itself at the end of his name. Compression of the name gives us words meaning "head" and "water"; Carlos's head is bursting with connections of the rational mind acting on his emotional mind in a supportive manner. There are also indications of financial success, due to the influence of Capricorn in the name. Even if Carlos does not practice psychoanalysis in a professional capacity, he will certainly take advantage of his ability to read the behavior of others in order to succeed in his chosen field.

THE RUNIC INTERPRETATION
ᛋᛟᛚᚱᚨᚲ (Sowelu, Othila, Laguz, Raido, Ansuz, Kano)

Carlos may need to learn to let things slide. When he isn't unnerving people with displays of temper, he is singing and joking around. The extremes of his nature put people on alert, and they avoid Carlos for fear of igniting his oh-so-short fuse! Fortunately, Carlos can call on the strength of Ansuz to get him through hard times. Ansuz is the rune of intuition. Carlos would like to have more self-control, and he'll try anything to obtain it. He only wants to be loved, underneath it all. He needs to learn to leave the room and counsel himself before criticizing those around him. Once he finds inner peace, Carlos is an asset in any situation.

Elements: Air, earth/fire, water, water, air, water

THE NUMEROLOGICAL INTERPRETATION
Carlos (NV = 5, CV = 7, VV = 7, FL = 3)

A man with a number of intellectual gifts, Carlos is eager for mental stimulation. His powerful mind allows a clear vision of what he is seeking, and his endeavors center on his urge to improve and transform himself at the deepest level. Carlos sees the possibilities that exist in life and, when called upon, can be a very supportive friend, helping and advising others to make the best out of their lives.

෴

Carmen

DERIVATION: Spanish form of Carmel, derived from a Hebrew word for "garden." Related to the Latin *carmen*, meaning "song." Often associated with the heroine of Bizet's opera *Carmen*.

PRINCIPAL COLORS: Deep reds, crimson, rose, maroon

GEMSTONES AND PRECIOUS METALS: Garnets, rubies, deep-red bloodstones

BOTANICALS: Broom, onions, wormwood

UNIQUE SPELLINGS: Carmin, Carmyn, Karmen, Karmin, Karmyn

RELATED TO: Carmel, Carmela, Carmelita, Carmena, Carmencita, Carmine

"All the great decisions in my life have been made in less than half an hour."
—CARMEN MAURA (ACTRESS)

A KABBALISTIC SYNOPSIS
כעמן —KA'AMN (Kaph, Ayin, Mem, Nun)

Carmen is a classic strong woman, and if you have any pretensions to being her lover or even her friend, you had better be able to justify your claims with some impressive action. In the Hebrew alphabet there are certain letters that have a different form and value when they appear at the end of a word. N, or Nun, falls into this category; normally its value is fifty, but it can also be seven hundred when it appears at the end of a word. Kabbalistic analysis looks at both of these values. If we take Nun to have a value of fifty and then analyze the name by finding the fewest letters that equal the value of the whole name (compression) we reveal Qoph and Peh, meaning "head" and "mouth," demonstrating her readiness to give vent to her thoughts without concern for the effect those words might have. In using the higher value of seven hundred for Nun, we produce Peh and Lamed. This arrangement shows the force with which Carmen can deliver her views, as Lamed represents driving energy. In simple terms, Carmen's name has two possible values, both of which refer to her strong voice—one to her rashness, and one to the sheer power of her voice. It also suggests that Carmen feels driven to express herself freely in all circumstances. One equivalent of Carmen is "fountain," and emotionally that is exactly how Carmen functions: in huge dramatic bursts. Her name draws her to high-profile careers in the arts, the media, or advertising. She's also a gifted adviser, therapist, or counselor.

THE RUNIC INTERPRETATION
ᚺᛖᛗᚱᚨᚲ (Nauthiz, Ehwaz, Mannaz, Raido, Ansuz, Kano)

One of Carmen's problems is that she has a somewhat compulsive nature. She likes to eat, and this is from the Ansuz energy in her name. When Carmen learns to channel her appetite and, most important, to express her opinion and anger in appropriate ways, she begins to bring her life into balance. When she has learned to discipline herself, she will be ready to minister to others, and they will want to follow her example. Carmen is warm and friendly, and is at her best when dealing with the public. Travel and ever-widening spheres of influence are in the future for Carmen.

Elements: Fire, air, air, water, air, water

THE NUMEROLOGICAL INTERPRETATION
Carmen (NV = 9, CV = 3, VV = 6, FL = 3)

Carmen is a name that reveals a woman of deep passion and strong emotional insights. In this respect, Carmen is very supportive. She is a person who is able to look deeply into the hearts of her friends and loved ones. At home, she seeks harmony and is capable of bringing into her relationships a very profound degree of love and caring. Carmen is dramatic, expressive, and openly communicative. Her face tells you what is in her heart, and it is a heart that is always filled with warmth.

DERIVATION: English, anglicized
form of the Latin *carolus*. Related
to the Old English *ceorl*, meaning
"man, husbandman." Also a pet
form of Caroline. Once a male
name, it became popular for
females at the end of the
nineteenth century.

PRINCIPAL COLORS: Electric
colors, bright azure, grays

GEMSTONES AND PRECIOUS
METALS: Sapphires

BOTANICALS: Lesser celandine,
sage, Iceland moss

UNIQUE SPELLINGS: Carel,
Carole, Caroll, Carrel, Carrol,
Carroll, Carryl, Caryl, Karel,
Karol, Karyl

RELATED TO: Cara, Carola,
Carol-Ann, Carolee, Caroleen,
Carolenia, Carolin, Carolina,
Carolinda, Caroline†, Carolyn†,
Carolyne, Carolynne, Carrie†

"Experience is not what happens
to you, but how you manage what
happens."

—CAROL BARTZ
(BUSINESSPERSON)

Carol

A KABBALISTIC SYNOPSIS
כארול —KARVL (Kaph, Aleph, Resh, Vau, Lamed)

Like all those blessed with a name beginning with Kaph, Carol is a woman of action, but this action is undertaken only after considerable deliberation. Carol could never be accused of being rash. At times, this can make her seem overly cautious and frustrate colleagues who simply want to "go for it." However, there is a lot to be said for Carol's approach; the presence of R, or Resh, indicates that her mind is a good one, and that her tendency to delay firm decisions stems from good sense and not lack of will. Carol adds up to fourteen, which further emphasizes her concern with considering all the options, as it is connected to the tarot trump Temperance. There are strong indications of an active interest in justice in Carol's name, so she may pursue a career in law or politics. One equivalent of her name is "ark," and other connections to animals can be found. So we also can expect to see Carol at animal rights protests and in vegetarian food stores. However, due to her balanced nature, she will not be out trying to "liberate" farm animals or engaging in similar, more extreme activities. Carol is far more the letter-writing and petition-signing type.

THE RUNIC INTERPRETATION
ᛚᛟᚱᚨᚲ (Laguz, Othila, Raido, Ansuz, Kano)

Carol has studied philosophy, religion, metaphysics, and psychology. The mysteries of life intrigue Carol, and she is quick to grasp abstract concepts. On a personal level, she is an inspiration to her many friends. Her one problem is her inability to manage money. What Carol needs most is the strength to curb her Kano energy, which is impulsive and expansive as well as expensive. Once Carol establishes boundaries to her spending, she develops trust that her needs will be met. Once her money starts growing, Carol has conquered her shadow side. Then she is free to teach and do research. Her talents abound and her contributions are significant.

Elements: Water, earth/fire, water, air, water

THE NUMEROLOGICAL INTERPRETATION
Carol (NV = 4, CV = 6, VV = 7, FL = 3)

The numbers in Carol indicate a woman who is very strong-minded. Carol takes her time cultivating her values and opinions, and then she sticks to them. A hardworking woman, Carol is very persistent and faithful. She uses her vast storehouse of knowledge to build a solid foundation under her feet. Aware of her own resources and their possibilities, she seeks relationships that are supportive of her practical aims and goals. Her needs are simple but they are well defined, and she is a willing partner to those people who are serious about their life interests. Balance in life and in love underlies her actions.

Caroline

A Kabbalistic Synopsis
כארולין —KARVLYN (Kaph, Aleph, Resh, Vau, Lamed, Yod, Nun)

Do not attempt to fool Caroline by lying to her, as she will find you out every single time! Her name has a value of 317, which can be further reduced to eleven. Eleven is the number of the tarot card Justice and indicates Caroline's overriding concern with truth and honesty. Interestingly, her name is equivalent to the Hebrew word for "iron," which may hint at a somewhat stern approach to those found wanting in the honesty stakes! If we compress her name into the fewest possible Hebrew letters providing the same value, we produce the letters Shin, Yod, and Zayin, which could be taken as pointing to a vocation as a legal prosecutor. While Shin and Yod relate to driving energies in life, Zayin represents a sword—in Caroline's case, a sword of justice. In her relationships Caroline is intensely loyal and expects the same level of loyalty in return. She can be inclined to depressive thoughts and excessive worries about the direction of her relationships, yet on the whole Caroline is a very balanced individual. This is probably due to the central letter of her name, Vau, which represents the element of Air and the central nature of Caroline's life: she is not one to act rashly or in anger.

The Runic Interpretation
ᚺᛁᛚᛟᚱᚨᚲ (Nauthiz, Isa, Laguz, Othila, Raido, Ansuz, Kano)

As a child Caroline had a temper tantrum over the tired-looking clothes she was forced to wear, as even then, she seemed to know that first impressions are lasting ones. Today, Caroline is good at sales and packaging and marketing products, including herself. She is achievement-oriented and hasn't yet learned that who she is intrinsically is enough. Caroline is still trying to justify her existence or self-worth by what she accomplishes. Being held in high regard is important to Caroline. Hopefully somewhere along the way someone will teach her this priceless insight by loving her, really loving her essence.

Elements: Fire, earth, water, earth, water, air, water

The Numerological Interpretation
Caroline (NV = 5, CV = 2, VV = 3, FL = 3)

All the number values in Caroline describe a woman who is usually upbeat and quite focused on the expansion of her personal life experiences. She is driven by an inner need for change and character development. She definitely does not want to be tied down to conventional codes of behavior that restrict her actions and activities. Caroline easily recognizes the "closed boxes" that many people live in, and she does not want that in her life. Her relationships with lovers are at the center of her life, as she finds it very important to have a partner with whom she can share her many adventures. Caroline requires more than just physical attraction in her intimate contacts. This is an intelligent woman who must have a companion who is mentally stimulating as well as emotionally courageous.

DERIVATION: English and French, possibly from the Latin or Italian Carolina, but ultimately descends from the Old Germanic Charles. Suggests royalty. Widely used through the end of the nineteenth century until recent renewal of popularity. Current person of royalty with the name is Princess Caroline of Monaco.

PRINCIPAL COLORS: Light gray, as well as the lightest shades of any other color

GEMSTONES AND PRECIOUS METALS: Silver, diamonds, platinum

BOTANICALS: Marjoram, parsley, oats, hazel

UNIQUE SPELLINGS: Carolyne, Karoline, Karolyne

RELATED TO: Carleen, Carlin, Carly, Carol, Carolina, Carollyn, Carolynt, Carolynne, Cary, Charleen, Lina, Sharleen

DERIVATION: Modern form of Caroline, from the Latin *carolus*. Related to the Old English *ceorl*, meaning "man, husbandman." Very popular in the eighteenth century, disappeared by the end of the nineteenth century, and became common again in the 1950s.

PRINCIPAL COLORS: Gold, all green and yellow hues

GEMSTONES AND PRECIOUS METALS: Moonstones, white pearls, cat's-eyes

BOTANICALS: Juniper, elder, blackberries

UNIQUE SPELLINGS: Caralin, Caralyn, Caralynne, Caroline†, Carolynne, Karolin, Karolyn

RELATED TO: Cara, Carla†, Carol†, Carola, Carol-Ann, Carole, Carolee, Caroleen, Carolenia, Carolina, Carolinda, Caroline†, Carrie†

"Today's shocks are tomorrow's conventions."
—CAROLYN HEILBRUN (AUTHOR)

A KABBALISTIC SYNOPSIS

כארולין —KARVLYN (Kaph, Aleph, Resh, Vau, Lamed, Yod, Nun)

Carolyn has something of a split personality. On the one hand, she is idealistic; she believes firmly that a perfect society can be created if people would only get together and be kind. This idealism is shown by the compression of her name to twenty-two, the Fool in the tarot. In addition to pointing to innocence and naïveté, this symbol connects to the idea of the "wise fool" found in many religions and cultures. The other side of Carolyn is much more pragmatic and is signified by the latter half of her name, where we find both the fiery force of Yod and the driving force of Lamed, meaning "ox goad." Her powerhouse personality is linked strongly to her emotions and to her lofty ideals. As a result Carolyn will fiercely defend her viewpoint against any opposition and may well develop into a committed activist. From a relationship point of view, Carolyn is a very exciting partner, while the influence of the Fool makes her affectionate and deeply trusting of her loved one.

THE RUNIC INTERPRETATION

ᚾᛁᛚᛟᚱᚨᚲ (Nauthiz, Eihwaz, Laguz, Othila, Raido, Ansuz, Kano)

Carolyn has the Sowelu energy of wholeness in her name. Carolyn understands the power of thought, and she is comfortable manifesting her future. Focused thought is *powerful*. Carolyn suggests to her subconscious that her desired goal is already accomplished—and stating her desire in the present causes her subconscious to scramble around and arrange circumstances to bring about the desired outcome. This technique is useful for Carolyn as she pursues a career in sales. Carolyn's spiritual life has richness and depth. Once Carolyn is able to become more relaxed and understand that tomorrow will be good—really good—she lightens up and lives in the present.

Elements: Fire, earth/fire, water, earth/fire, water, air, water

THE NUMEROLOGICAL INTERPRETATION

Carolyn (NV = 7, CV = 2, VV = 5, FL = 3)

The name Carolyn indicates an active and intellectually curious mind. It is not just logic that Carolyn possesses, it is definitely something more: an intuitive ability to see into people's hearts and discover the real issues that are important to them. Carolyn has had to work for this gift, developing her sensitivity through long hours of introspection. Her ideal relationship is with a partner who shares her depth and is eager to discuss life's more profound realities. Carolyn is less involved with style and more concerned with substance, less attracted by glamour and more inspired by truth.

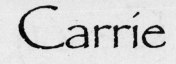

Carrie

A KABBALISTIC SYNOPSIS
כארי —KARY (Kaph, Aleph, Resh, Yod)

It takes an enormous amount of bad luck to get Carrie down. Her whole personality is affected by the strong solar influence in this name, which comes both from the R, or Resh, and the total of her name. By reduction Carrie has connections to the sephirah on the Tree of Life known as Tiphareth. This is often said to be the highest point that a person can achieve in their spiritual and personal development. This ultimate state represents a point where one has overcome all the conflicting desires of the conscious self and is operating solely with regard to one's higher self or "true will." Carrie is never short of friends for exactly this reason. She is sufficiently untroubled by the envy, jealousy, and insecurity that bother most of us in relation to our acquaintances, and she is able to be an understanding and unconditional friend. Carrie is intelligent and emotionally mature, and usually has her pick of careers. Whatever she ultimately chooses, she will be happy—as this is her nature.

THE RUNIC INTERPRETATION
MIRRAK (Ehwaz, Isa, Raido, Raido, Ansuz, Kano)

Travel opportunities begin at an early age for Carrie, who has the Raido energy of movement in her name. It's not long before Carrie has friends around the world. Warm and entertaining, Carrie is eager to learn the ways of a new culture. She is flexible and broad-minded, and keeps voluminous journals of her experiences. The Ansuz energy of communication in her name gives Carrie writing talent. Carrie is also interested in advocacy for children. She may get a Ph.D. or return to a nation that has won her heart and fight for the poor children there. Carrie is spiritually advanced and generous with her time and energy. Carrie has a mission!

Elements: Air, earth, water, water, air, water

THE NUMEROLOGICAL INTERPRETATION
Carrie (NV = 9, CV = 3, VV = 6, FL = 3)

A very open and giving person, Carrie loves to communicate her excitement for life. This is a name that belongs to an idealist, a romantic, and a poet. A sociable woman of high energy and verve, Carrie is happiest when she can share her special interests with those she loves. When people are in partnership with Carrie, they experience the caring she shares with them as something authentic, deep, and beautiful. Her success in life comes from her fine humane qualities.

DERIVATION: English, pet form of Caroline. Commonly used as an independent given name since the end of the nineteenth century. Very popular in the 1970s.

PRINCIPAL COLORS: All shades of red, from pink to the richest crimson

GEMSTONES AND PRECIOUS METALS: Rubies, bloodstones

BOTANICALS: Garlic, nettle, white hellebore

UNIQUE SPELLINGS: Cari, Carie, Carri, Carry, Cary, Kari, Karri, Karrie, Karry, Kary

RELATED TO: Cara, Carolt, Carola, Carol-Ann, Carole, Carolee, Caroleen, Carolenia, Carolina, Carolinda, Carolinet, Carolynt, Carrie-Anne, Kerri

DERIVATION: English, both
masculine and feminine. Used to
honor the train engineer Casey
Jones (1864–1900), who gave up
his life to save passengers on the
Cannonball Express. Also an Irish
surname from a Gaelic word
meaning "vigilant."

PRINCIPAL COLORS: The darkest
gray, purple, and blue hues; black

GEMSTONES AND PRECIOUS
METALS: Carbuncles, black
pearls, black diamonds, any other
very dark stones

BOTANICALS: Angelica, marsh
mallow

UNIQUE SPELLINGS: Cassey,
Kacey, Kacy, Kasey

RELATED TO: Case; Cass,
Cassandrat, Cassie, Kay

Casey

A KABBALISTIC SYNOPSIS
כאסי —KASY (Kaph, Aleph, Samech, Yod)

If you have ever seen a terrier hold tight to a ball or stick and not let go until it decides it has had enough, then you have an idea of Casey's approach to life. Casey is incredibly tenacious and has a habit of making his or her ideas happen. This quality is shown by compression of the name to Tzaddi, meaning "fish hook," and Aleph, which, among other things, can represent the material solidity and inertia of the ox. One equivalence of Casey in Hebrew is "food," and it may well be that Casey's interest in food extends beyond the eating of it although from this name we can discern a good appetite is likely. If Casey goes into cooking in a professional capacity, it is worth noting that this name is also equivalent to "manna," which is of course food from above—so we can reasonably expect Casey to produce more than standard fare.

THE RUNIC INTERPRETATION
ᛇᛗᛋᚨᚲ (Eihwaz, Ehwaz, Sowelu, Ansuz, Kano)

Casey uses the runic energy of Eihwaz (defense), Sowelu (wholeness), Ansuz (signals), and Kano (opening) to pursue lifelong dreams. Casey is a male or female name, and the runic interpretation applies to either sex. As Casey unfolds, using the Kano energy of opening to become a capable and responsible person, many opportunities arise. A career in the performing arts or healing would use the intuitive Ansuz gift of signals. The Sowelu energy of wholeness would also support this career direction for Casey, who is a generous, independent, and productive person. Casey needs to be careful of passion, though, because it's easy to go overboard, and Casey has too much to accomplish to waste time with bedroom dramas.

Elements: Earth/fire, air, air, air, water

THE NUMEROLOGICAL INTERPRETATION
Casey (NV = 8, CV = 4, VV = 4, FL = 3)

Casey is a practical name. It contains numbers that indicate hard workers who will never rest until they have achieved their material goals and ambitions. Casey is responsible and dependable, honest and sincere. Physical health and well-being are uppermost in his mind, and Casey aims to earn enough money to be able to buy the best possible goods, objects, and services. Cautious by nature, Casey tends to think things through thoroughly before acting upon them.

Cassandra

A Kabbalistic Synopsis

כאסאנדרא —KASANDRA (Kaph, Aleph, Samech, Aleph, Nun, Daleth, Resh, Aleph)

Cassandra certainly knows who is boss—she is! There is little evidence in her name of career or business achievement, so it may well be that her authority lies in the realm of politics—her ideal and natural home. If she does not find herself in the most suitable career, she will still rise to the top. Her name can be translated as "ruler of earth" and this is exactly the sort of challenge that Cassandra is looking for. If she is an Aries, this natural power and authority may descend into megalomania and delusions of even far greater importance than the considerable position she will already hold. Not for Cassandra the new management ideals of worker involvement and cooperation; she believes in firm and sometimes harsh rule. Her name can be numerically represented by the letters Shin, Lamed, and Zayin, meaning "tooth," "ox goad," and "sword," respectively. If you intend to tangle with Cassandra in the home or in the boardroom, you had better be prepared for a bloody conflict—and be ready to lose gracefully!

The Runic Interpretation

ᚨᚱᛞᚨᛉ:ᛞᚺ:ᛞᚺᚨᚲ (Ansuz, Raido, Dagaz, Nauthiz, Ansuz, Sowelu, Sowelu, Ansuz, Kano)

Cassandra is influenced by the double Sowelu energy in her name. When we choose a career path or a mate, we can call upon Sowelu energy to indicate the path we must follow. Sowelu helps Cassandra take aim for her target and maintain that aim without swerving. Cassandra goes from job to job for a while because none is a good fit. Finally she stops trying to fit into jobs for which she is poorly suited and begins doing what she loves. The attainment of wholeness comes to Cassandra as she becomes conscious of her essence and brings it into form. Cassandra discovers that what she is striving to become is what she already is.

Elements: Air, water, fire, fire, air, air, air, air, water

The Numerological Interpretation

Cassandra (NV = 8, CV = 5, VV = 3, FL = 3)

This is a highly individualistic person, a woman who means to leave her mark on people and society. Quick-witted and charming, Cassandra has an easy time communicating her wide array of interests and opinions. Cassandra is a very adventurous and curious woman. This love of adventure also extends to her intimate relationships. Cassandra usually prefers to have more than one admirer. There is an unmistakable personal flair in whatever she says or does. A dramatic personality with a wardrobe to match, a woman named Cassandra is very difficult to forget!

Catherine

DERIVATION: English, spelling variation of Katherine. Originally from the Greek *aikaterina*, of unknown meaning. Spelled Katerina by the Romans, who associated it with the Greek *katharos*, meaning "pure." The name of several saints, one of whom was martyred at Alexandria in 307.

PRINCIPAL COLORS: The full range of greens, pale white tones

GEMSTONES AND PRECIOUS METALS: Green jade, white pearls, moonstones

BOTANICALS: Lettuce, plantain, moonwort

UNIQUE SPELLINGS: Catharin, Catheryn, Cathrine, Cathryn, Katherine, Katheryn, Katheryne, Kathrine, Kathryn, Kathryne, Kathyrine

RELATED TO: Caitlin, Caitriona, Catarine, Cateline, Cathaleen, Catharina, Caterina, Catherleen, Cathie, Cathleen, Cathrene, Cathy†, Catrin, Catrina, Catrine, Catriona, Karen, Karin, Katarina, Kate†, Katerina, Katey, Katheleen, Katheline, Kathereen, Katherina, Katherine†, Kathie, Kathileen, Kathleen†, Kathlyn, Kathlynn, Kathrene, Kathryn†, Kathy†, Katie†, Katina, Katleen, Katrena, Katrina†, Katriona, Katryna, Kattrina, Katy, Kay†, Kitty†, Treena, Trina

"For your born writer, nothing is so healing as the realization that he has come upon the right word."
—CATHERINE DRINKER BOWEN (AUTHOR)

A KABBALISTIC SYNOPSIS
כאתאריןKATHARYN (Kaph, Aleph, Tau, Aleph, Resh, Yod, Nun)

In Hebrew there is no difference between C and K; consequently, individuals with the name Catherine and Katherine are of the same basic personality type as far as kabbalistic analysis is concerned. Catherine is an artist by nature even if not by deed; she has a natural instinct for creative expression, which may well be recognized from an early age. The dominance of the letter Shin in the numeration of her name suggests a fiery, go-getting approach to life; she likes to live in a fast-moving environment, one full of people with new and exciting ideas. Catherine wants to be on the cutting edge and is likely to have a taste for the avant-garde. Her ideal community would be Greenwich Village in New York or the Left Bank in Paris. However, she can make a stir wherever she is! One meaning of her name is "joyful noise," so her artistic expression may manifest itself in contemporary music. The central balance of her name, Th (Tau) and R (Resh), suggests an attachment to mythology and religion. This interest relates to both her creativity and her strong, and sometimes dramatic, emotions. Her artistic expression may well be considerable and have heavy spiritual overtones or symbolism. Her grand passions are legendary: photography, music, fine art, design. And her whole emotive response to life's events is likely to be governed by her religious convictions.

THE RUNIC INTERPRETATION
ᛖᚾᛁᚱᛖᚦᛅᚲ (Ehwaz, Nauthiz, Isa, Raido, Ehwaz, Thurisaz, Ansuz, Kano)

Catherine's name implies hard lessons of separation and wholeness that come from standing apart for a time. Catherine is best able to face challenges when she seeks her own counsel. Her life lesson is not to be swayed by the criticism and the opinions of others. She must also learn waiting and patience. When she can maintain a nonreactive stance, Catherine demonstrates great wisdom. She is able to attract teachers and supportive friends that help her along the way. These attributes are greater than any accomplishment in the outer world. On some level, Catherine knows this, but she could still use a gentle reminder now and then. . . .

Elements: Air, fire, earth, water, air, fire, air, water

THE NUMEROLOGICAL INTERPRETATION
Catherine (NV = 11, CV = 9, VV = 2, FL = 3)

Catherine is a name that indicates a woman who can be quite an inspiration to the people around her. People seem to gravitate to Catherine because she demonstrates compassion. The number values in this name open a person to larger, philosophical issues that go beyond the confines of purely personal concerns. In this respect, Catherine reveals an extremely sensitive nature, one that is eager to communicate the hidden meanings beyond life's apparent superficialities.

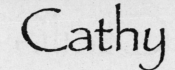

Cathy

A KABBALISTIC SYNOPSIS
כאתי —KAThY (Kaph, Aleph, Tau, Yod)

Like Katherine, Kathy shares her meaning with Cathy since, in the language of the Kabbalah, they are essentially the same name. If you are friends with a Cathy, never invite her to see a show at The Comedy Store. No matter who is onstage, she will not even raise a chuckle. Cathy is a deeply serious individual with a strong, practical intellect. She is very happy with herself and is likely to be surprised that anybody could wish to have a lifestyle different from hers. She finds her own life immensely rewarding. She is a materialist, both philosophically and in terms of her long-term goals, which revolve around work and the gradual amassing of property. Hard work is no stranger to Cathy; her name forms around the central Th, or Tau, meaning "cross," indicating that she will experience some suffering and trials on the road to material comfort. Once she has achieved her required level of success, probably in accounting or some related field, she will enjoy having free time for greater contemplation—but even then it is unlikely that her reflections will be aimed at any spiritual considerations.

THE RUNIC INTERPRETATION
ᛇᚦᚨᚲ (Eihwaz, Thurisaz, Ansuz, Kano)

Cathy is a doer. She wants a successful career and a successful husband. She enjoys all the labor entailed in owning her huge house, and she's polished every brass doorknob by hand. Large projects are grist for Cathy's nervous energy. She's up till the middle of the night organizing a meeting and arrives perfectly coiffed with a larger-than-life grin on her face at 9 A.M. She can go directly to the top of any organization. Her husband and kids think she hung the moon; rumor has it, she did. Cathy accomplishes a lot in the material realm.

Elements: Earth/fire, fire, air, water

THE NUMEROLOGICAL INTERPRETATION
Cathy (NV = 3, CV = 4, VV = 8, FL = 3)

Cathy always has something to say about any life situation that she may encounter. She is generally curious by nature and is open to the exploration of all the many things that interest her. There is also a very strong practical side to Cathy's nature. She is aware of the material considerations of life and will work very steadily at achieving her life's goals and ambitions. She does have to be careful to conserve her energy, as she is prone to doing too many things at the same time. Her real talents emerge as she integrates all her many facets into a structure that allows her both variety and security.

DERIVATION: English, pet form of Catherine. Originally from the Greek *aikaterina*, of uncertain meaning. Related to the Greek *katharos*, meaning "pure." Used independently since the 1950s.

PRINCIPAL COLORS: Pale bluish violet to the deepest of purples

GEMSTONES AND PRECIOUS METALS: Amethyst, garnets

BOTANICALS: Barberry, dandelion, lungwort, mint

UNIQUE SPELLINGS: Cathi, Cathie, Kathi, Kathie, Kathy

RELATED TO: Caitlin, Caitriona, Catarine, Cateline, Cathaleen, Catharin, Catharina, Catherina, Catherine, Catherleen, Catheryn, Cathleen, Cathrene, Cathryn, Catrin, Catrina, Catrine, Catriona, Karen, Karin, Katarina, Kate†, Katerina, Katey, Katheleen, Katheline, Kathereen, Katherina, Katherinet, Katheryn, Katheryne, Kathileen, Kathleen†, Kathlyn, Kathlynn, Kathrene, Kathrine, Kathryn†, Kathryne, Kathy†, Kathyrine, Katie†, Katina, Katleen, Katrena, Katrina†, Katriona, Katryna, Kattrina, Katy, Kay†, Kitty†

⤶

"It seems that we learn lessons when we least expect them but always when we need them the most, and, the true 'gift' in these lessons always lies in the learning process itself."
—CATHY LEE CROSBY (ACTRESS)

⤶

DERIVATION: Latin feminine form of Cecil. Related to the Latin *caecus*, meaning "blind." Especially popular at the end of the eighteenth and beginning of the nineteenth centuries.

PRINCIPAL COLORS: All but the brightest shades of blue

GEMSTONES AND PRECIOUS METALS: Emeralds, sky-blue or greenish blue turquoise

BOTANICALS: Violet, walnut, dog rose

UNIQUE SPELLINGS: Cecelia, Cicelia, Cicilya, Sicilia

RELATED TO: Cecily, Celia†, Céline, Cicely, Sissy

Cecilia

A KABBALISTIC SYNOPSIS

סוסיליה —SVSYLYH (Samech, Vau, Samech, Yod, Lamed, Yod, Heh)

Cecilia is a difficult character to pin down, as she is something of a chameleon. No two people are likely to agree on who Cecilia really is. All things to all men and all women, Cecilia will adjust her behavior to blend into almost any surrounding. This is quite a talent and makes her ideally suited to careers in corporate entertaining, promotional work, and even—in rare cases—covert operations! In the case of Gemini Cecilias, there may be a tendency for this blurring of personality to slip into Cecilia's own sense of identity, and if this happens, it can be quite disturbing for her and those around her. This characteristic is partially suggested by the total value of Cecilia's name, 181, where we can see the symbol of individual identity framing the symbol of eternal change. Within the sum of her name we can also identify a temperament that is balanced and accepting of the trials and tribulations in daily life. As her name reduces to ten, she will on the whole avoid any major upsets in life.

THE RUNIC INTERPRETATION

ᚨᛁᛚᛁᚲᛖᚲ (Ansuz, Isa, Laguz, Isa, Kano, Ehwaz, Kano)

Cecilia loves the celestial and the arts, and she may be psychic with animals. Her name contains a preponderance of water energy. Music speaks to her on a cellular level, and she is attuned to the sacred geometry of nature. Cecilia sees life as a kaleidoscope of energy, and she is able to read currents on water and in the air. Even rock vibrations resonate with her. Cecilia needs time alone to decipher the information coming her way. She is sensitive and can do a lot of good work as a healer, even from a distance.

Elements: Air, earth, water, earth, water, air, water

THE NUMEROLOGICAL INTERPRETATION

Cecilia (NV = 6, CV = 9, VV = 6, FL = 3)

Soft and gentle, sincere and wise, Cecilia is a person who attempts to bring harmony into all her life circumstances. Cecilia tends to be devoted to her home and family. She needs to be in emotionally secure surroundings. When she feels loved, she adds warmth and caring wherever she goes. Art, theater, music, and poetry interest her, and she may express certain talents in one or more of these creative areas. She has to take care not to let her empathy and compassion sway her better judgment, however, as she may be too idealistic in her relationships with others.

Celia

A Kabbalistic Synopsis
סיליה —SYLYH (Samech, Yod, Lamed, Yod, Heh)

Like most people with names that end with an H, or Heh, meaning "window," Celia has a strong interest in the lives of others. The terminal Heh usually indicates a desire to observe the world—not in a prurient, nosy way, but out of eager curiosity. In Celia's case this interest is likely to lead her into working in an environment with the general public. Celia is ruled by Virgo. In the compression of her name, we reveal Qoph, Yod, and Heh; astrologically, this equates to Pisces, Virgo, and Aries. Thus we have the oldest and the youngest separated by the Great Mother, Virgo. Aries is the first sign of the zodiac and represents the young, while Pisces is the old and wise character of the astrological cycle, being the last of the signs. The connection to youth and age is suggested by many of the typical characteristics of people born under these signs. Virgo represents the mother figure in astrological terms. These factors suggest that Celia may be ideally suited to nursing, teaching, or some other caring profession.

The Runic Interpretation
ᚨᛁᛚᛖᚲ (Ansuz, Isa, Laguz, Ehwaz, Kano)

Celia is strongly affected by the phases of the moon and is not herself during a full moon. Her life lesson is to find the Kano energy that will open up her life and lift the darkness and suspicion lurking just below the surface. A large part of Celia runs away from problem solving and harmony. At her center is sunlight and calm air, and it's Celia's task to speak from this center. No matter how rude and cruel people may be, Celia must learn to treat them courteously. It's not easy, but the alternative is worse.

Elements: Air, earth, water, air, water

The Numerological Interpretation
Celia (NV = 3, CV = 6, VV = 6, FL = 3)

As her name is associated with strong creative urges, Celia quickens to all artistic possibilities. Her mind is impressed with an innate sense of beauty, and she is able to perceive the feelings of others. She may express these sensitive insights through her artistic use of color, form, and words. Celia's innermost desire is to be a vehicle that brings joy and beauty into her environment. A very communicative person, Celia finds many ways to express this quality of joy to others. She may also convey joy by the manner in which she decorates a room, serves a meal, or smiles.

DERIVATION: English and Italian, from the Latin root *caelia*, the name of a Roman clan. Possibly related to *caelum*, meaning "sky" or "heaven." First appeared in the English-speaking world in Shakespeare's *As You Like It*. Quite popular in the 1950s, and still used regularly.

PRINCIPAL COLORS: Brilliant blue; medium tones, such as gray

GEMSTONES AND PRECIOUS METALS: The palest to the richest of sapphires

BOTANICALS: Sage, wild spinach

UNIQUE SPELLINGS: Ceelia, Ceelya, Celya, Seelia, Seelya

RELATED TO: Cecelia, Cécile, Ceciliat, Cecily, Céline, Sissy, Sessy, S'le

"No longer will women agree to protect the hearth at the price of extinguishing the fire within ourselves."
—CELIA GILBERT (POET)

"The way to do research is to attack the facts at the point of greatest astonishment."
—CELIA GREEN (AUTHOR)

Cesar

A KABBALISTIC SYNOPSIS
סיסער —SYSA'AR (Samech, Yod, Samech, Ayin, Resh)

Looking for a loan? You could do a lot worse than to ask Cesar. Totaling to four hundred, the name Cesar indicates an uncanny understanding of the world of commerce. While those all around him are experiencing losses, Cesar will have found yet another way to turn a profit. However, Cesar is not some greedy Scrooge figure. His own standing in the world stems from the assistance he received early on, and he is now more than happy to offer that same assistance to anyone who genuinely asks for his help. There is a hidden side to Cesar, too; four hundred is the value of Th, or Tau, meaning "cross." Despite his obvious success, Cesar still suffers from concerns about the ultimate purpose of possessing all this property. In later life he may well become more religious in an attempt to attach some deeper meaning to his life.

THE RUNIC INTERPRETATION
ᚱᚨᛋᛖᚲ (Raido, Ansuz, Sowelu, Ehwaz, Kano)

Cesar's girlfriends think he's a good candidate for the "Am I Thoughtless?" quiz. Sample questions include: (1) Did you say you'll call and forget to do so all week? and (2) Did you say you're just fine, even though no one else agrees? Cesar will either grow old alone, or the Sowelu energy of wholeness in his name will help him unify his words and right his actions. Sowelu energy helps us look within and see that problems in the outer world are magnifications of problems within. Hopefully Cesar will attract a friend who encourages him to aim for loving himself and those around him by copying the example of someone who does it well.

Elements: Water, air, air, air, water

THE NUMEROLOGICAL INTERPRETATION
Cesar (NV = 1, CV = 4, VV = 6, FL = 3)

As this name so clearly indicates, Cesar is a born leader, a man who has a firm sense of himself and seeks to communicate his individuality to others. Cesar has the tendency to assert his thoughts, opinions, and viewpoints very dynamically. He has a firm conviction about his beliefs and lets others know where he stands on all issues. Cesar is also surprising in that he has a gentle and artistic side to his nature as well. Harmony and beauty are important to him, and although he may not be an artist himself, he may easily express a flair in the way he dresses and decorates his surroundings.

Chad

A Kabbalistic Synopsis
חד —ChD (Cheth, Daleth)

Chad cuts a very impressive figure, particularly as he grows older, as he increasingly has the appearance of a traditional patriarch. Solid and reliable, Chad is likely to be deeply loyal to his employer and will be the best bet to receive a gold watch at the end of his twenty-five years with the firm. In spite of his loyalty, Chad is unlikely to receive many promotions, and in reality, he has no desire for a high-profile career. Chad's primary focus is the home, where he sees himself as a protector figure. The letters of his name mean "enclosure" and "door," respectively, so we can see Chad as feeling responsible for everything that comes into or leaves his family home. On the surface this suggests a restrictive, overbearing character, but the compression of his name reveals associations with maternal instincts. It is likely that Chad can be fierce when needed, but on the whole he dotes indulgently on his children and partner.

The Runic Interpretation
ᛞᚨᚺᛋ (Dagaz, Ansuz, Hagalaz, Sowelu)

Chad is well equipped on a spiritual level to face up to difficult challenges. At the same time he is too good and sweet for this problematic realm. The Hagalaz in Chad's name is the rune of elemental disruption. Unfortunately, most of the challenges in Chad's life are beyond his control. Being evolved, as Chad most certainly is, doesn't mean an easy life; quite the contrary. Chad's lessons are brutal ones that would destroy a weaker soul, but he learns from each adversity, and his strength comes from the knowledge he gains.

Elements: Fire, air, water, air

The Numerological Interpretation
Chad (NV = 7, CV = 6, VV = 1, FL = 3)

Chad points to a man who is very complex by nature. A highly analytical person, Chad may sometimes be quite critical of the people and circumstances surrounding him. He sees into life with a penetrating eye and is not satisfied by the status quo. It is not only knowledge that Chad possesses; he is also very intuitive. A curious and versatile person, Chad loves to accumulate knowledge and experience firsthand, and he is not afraid to change his life's direction when required.

DERIVATION: English, from the Old English *ceadda*, the name of a seventh-century saint. Of uncertain meaning. Quite rare until the 1960's, when it became fairly common. Its increased popularity was probably related to the Reverend Chad Varah (b. 1911), who founded the Samaritans.

PRINCIPAL COLORS: Any yellow or green hue

GEMSTONES AND PRECIOUS METALS: Cat's-eye, moss agate, white pearls, any other white stone

BOTANICALS: Blackberry, elder, mushrooms, grapes

UNIQUE SPELLINGS: Chaad, Chadd

RELATED TO: Chadwick, Chuck

DERIVATION: English and French, from the Old English root *ceorl,* meaning "man, husbandman." Made popular by the Frankish leader Charlemagne, who became the Holy Roman Emperor in 800. Also the name of several Holy Roman Emperors and ten kings of France. Generally very popular from the seventeenth century to the present.

PRINCIPAL COLORS: The full range of purples and violets, from pale lilac to deep maroon

GEMSTONES AND PRECIOUS METALS: Garnets, amethyst

BOTANICALS: Apple, lungwort, mint, cherry

UNIQUE SPELLINGS: Chaarles, Chaarlz, Charlz

RELATED TO: Carlt, Carlo, Carlost, Carlton, Charley, Charliet, Charlton, Chaz, Kaarle, Karel, Karl, Karol, Károly, Séarlas, Siarl

Charles

A KABBALISTIC SYNOPSIS
חעלם —ChA'ALS (Cheth, Ayin, Lamed, Samech)

There are very few people who can genuinely say that they really know Charles. A very thoughtful man, he tends to spend his free time alone pondering all manner of things, from the mundane to the great questions of life. It is likely that he will be equally quiet at work, never one to attend the office party or join in the water cooler gossip. Understandably this makes him an object of much speculation and interest, but he will be largely oblivious of this—unless, of course, the select individuals he is close to let him know. The amount of time Charles spends contemplating the world can lead him into depression. A common response for him is to shut out the real world and become increasingly self-involved in order to avoid facing the world's social ills. This reaction may be useful but dangerous for Charles, who may become self-indulgent. Relationships with him may be difficult.

THE RUNIC INTERPRETATION
ᛋᛖᛚᚱᚨᚺᛋ (Sowelu, Ehwaz, Laguz, Raido, Ansuz, Hagalaz, Sowelu)

When Charles takes a wife, she will most likely be respectful of tradition and provide a well-appointed study in the home for her husband. Although he's gracious and charming, Charles needs time at his desk to reflect. A historian by nature, Charles quotes mythology while he's bathing the kids, and sends them off to bed believing they have the greatest father in the world. Charles also has a strong artistic side. He needs textures like nubby wools and raw silk around him, and likes brandy snifters and pipe racks. Charles enjoys anyone who will share his flights of fancy. Imagination is oxygen for Charles.

Elements: Air, air, water, water, air, water, air

THE NUMEROLOGICAL INTERPRETATION
Charles (NV = 3, CV = 6, VV = 6, FL = 3)

Charles will have a very strong artistic sensibility. This may easily and naturally be expressed through involvement in one or more of the arts. This is a man who is very happy at home surrounded by his loved ones. Harmony in partnership is important to him, and he tends to be very idealistic and romantic by nature. Never one to be too staid, Charles is eager to give expression to his many ideas and interests. An avid reader, Charles loves to collect knowledge and takes great pleasure in sharing what he knows with his friends and family.

Charlie

A KABBALISTIC SYNOPSIS
חעלי — ChA'ALY (Cheth, Ayin, Lamed, Yod)

The worlds of high technology, virtual reality, and the Internet are ideal environments for Charlie, who has a passion for invention. Charlie is an idea man par excellence and has the commercially viable ability to see what it is that people want next—quite often before they realize that they want it! The second half of his name indicates both the energy and the driving force that enables Charlie to work long hours playing with various ideas until he hits upon the one that will sell. If Charlie has missed his chance at employment in an area that suits him, he will probably spend his free time in his den scribbling down ideas and plans. Unfortunately, Charlie lacks the staying power to bring any of his ideas to fruition without the right support network. He is very aware of the worth of his inventive mind and, as a result, tends to be very secretive; this is indicated by the presence of Ch, or Chet, meaning "enclosure." Emotionally, he is likely to be just as defensive and somewhat aloof. However, he is likely to have a happy love relationship, as his enthusiasm for life is so infectious that any drawbacks can be forgiven.

THE RUNIC INTERPRETATION
ᛖᛚᚱᚨᚺᛋ (Ehwaz, Laguz, Raido, Ansuz, Hagalaz, Sowelu)

Charlie has the soul of an artist. He is creative, which will help him when he encounters roadblocks that are paralyzing to his career. His talent is considerable, with Laguz, the rune of flow, in his name. The Hagalaz energy of disruption in Charlie's name brings chaos in its wake. The Raido energy of journey and Ehwaz energy of movement hint that Charlie could travel and even live abroad for extended periods of time. The Ansuz energy of intuition predicts that eventually Charlie will overcome any roadblocks and launch a fabulous career.

Elements: Air, water, water, air, water, air

THE NUMEROLOGICAL INTERPRETATION
Charlie (NV = 11, CV = 5, VV = 6, FL = 3)

Charlie denotes a person who is driven by an inner need for change and growth. This is someone who definitely does not want to be tied down by established codes of behavior or confined living conditions. Charlie likes to move through life, experimenting with the possibilities that come his way, and one of his favorite places is the travel agency. Charlie is freedom-loving and very aware that he is at his most creative when he can assert his independence openly and clearly. A lover of education, Charlie respects erudition in others and requires a great deal of mental stimulation in all of his relationships.

DERIVATION: English, pet form of Charles, which is from the Old English root *ceorl*, meaning "man, husbandman." Regularly used as an independent name.

PRINCIPAL COLORS: The full range of green hues, also white

GEMSTONES AND PRECIOUS METALS: Moonstones, cat's-eye, cream-colored pearls

BOTANICALS: Cabbage, chicory, lettuce

UNIQUE SPELLINGS: Charley, Charli, Charly, Charrley, Charrli, Charrlie, Charrly

RELATED TO: Carel, Carlt, Carlo, Carlost, Carroll, Chadt, Charlest, Charlton, Chas, Chaz, Chuck

"They teach you there's a boundary line to music. But, man, there's no boundary line to art."
—CHARLIE PARKER (MUSICIAN)

"All I need to make a comedy is a park, a policeman, and a pretty girl."
—CHARLIE CHAPLIN (ENTERTAINER)

Charlotte

A KABBALISTIC SYNOPSIS
חעלעת —ChA'ALA'ATh (Cheth, Ayin, Lamed, Ayin, Tau)

Mobile phone in one hand, calculator in the other—Charlotte is a sharp-minded business-woman with a love of last-minute deals and fast money. There is a heavy Capricorn influence in her name from the double Ayin, a clear indication of a concern for moneymaking and a love of material accumulation. The central source of her power is the Lamed, which separates the two Ayins and represents a strong, driving force in her life. The initial Ch, or Cheth, suggests that her love of life in the ultrafast lane stems from feeling hemmed in by the normal routine of the nine-to-five job. For an Aries Charlotte there is the potential for a love of risk to be too heavily featured, resulting in a tendency to stay far too long at the gambling tables than is wise. However, the power of judgment is still overriding; a Charlotte is very rarely wrong in her predictions, and applies her cool, calculating analysis to her love life with the same precision that she applies it on the trading room floor.

THE RUNIC INTERPRETATION
ᛖᛏᛏᛟᚱᚱᚨᚺᛊ (Ehwaz, Teiwaz, Teiwaz, Othila, Laguz, Raido, Ansuz, Hagalaz, Sowelu)

Charlotte is optimistic, and people are drawn to her warm personality. However, Charlotte may encounter sadness in life because she is overly empathic and takes on the sorrows of her friends. Charlotte needs to keep a journal and have some good pals in whom she can confide. She is a born negotiator who gets further with difficult people than most of us by keeping conversations pleasant and trying to listen. She isn't good at being hostile, although it's tempting; it just doesn't get her anywhere.

Elements: Air, air, air, earth/fire, water, water, air, water, air

THE NUMEROLOGICAL INTERPRETATION
Charlotte (NV = 3, CV = 9, VV = 3, FL = 3)

A definite communicator by nature, Charlotte has a sincere and innate interest in the world around her, along with a friendly disposition. She is an uplifting companion and friend. People find Charlotte very mentally stimulating. She tends to be very informed on a number of issues, and her bright intelligence allows her to share her knowledge with others in ways that are both original and entertaining. Charlotte is never lacking for a witty remark, and she can be counted on to bring positive energy into any social situation.

Chelsea

A Kabbalistic Synopsis
חאלסי —ChALSY (Cheth, Aleph, Lamed, Samech, Yod)

If you offend Chelsea, you will certainly know about it! Few people are foolish enough to be snide to her more than once, however, as she has a line of verbal assaults that can sting her victim and leave him or her sore for days. Chelsea's name can be compressed into two letters: Qoph and Teth, meaning "head" and "serpent." From this we can see that Chelsea's capacity for verbal spite is backed up by an active brain. It may well be that Chelsea makes money from this ability as a satirist or comic writer. While her words can sting, Chelsea is a brilliantly supportive friend always ready to leap to someone's defense. There are strong suggestions in Chelsea of deep religious or moral convictions, and she applies these values to her friendships. Her pals know that they always have a place to stay and an ear to bend as long as they have Chelsea in their circle.

The Runic Interpretation
ᚨᛗᛋᛚᛗᚺᛋ (Ansuz, Ehwaz, Sowelu, Laguz, Ehwaz, Hagalaz, Sowelu)

Chelsea's life seems to improve with age, and some would say she arrives in her golden years. She accumulates a great deal of money in her lifetime, and yet she is not materialistic; instead, she is saving it for her family. Chelsea surrounds herself with people involved with philanthropy and is a member of various charities in which she voices her wise counsel. Friends admire her judicial mind, for Chelsea appreciates far-reaching consequences. She's serious, but she can also laugh at herself. She's a cultivated and gracious woman, with high principles. Her only regret is that she might have had a bit more fun in life.

Elements: Air, air, air, water, air, water, air

The Numerological Interpretation
Chelsea (NV = 8, CV = 6, VV = 11, FL = 3)

This name can indicate a highly developed spiritual nature. Both sensitive and intuitive, Chelsea seems to be able to experience life's realities with a penetrating depth and clarity that intrigues others. Chelsea might often find that although she understands others, she may not be equally understood in return. She frequently acts as an inspiration, a helper, and a guide. She will feel the need to establish herself in society through her chosen career, a profession that will allow her to combine her interest in people and her urge to bring harmony into her environment.

DERIVATION: English, from the London place-name, meaning "landing place for limestone or chalk." First used as a given name in Australia, but now used in other English-speaking countries.

PRINCIPAL COLORS: Black, dark tones, especially blue, gray, purple

GEMSTONES AND PRECIOUS METALS: Carbuncles, amethyst, black diamonds, sapphires

BOTANICALS: Marsh mallow, ragwort, celery

UNIQUE SPELLINGS: Chellsea, Chellsee, Chellsey, Chelsee, Chelsey, Chelsie, Chelsy

RELATED TO: Elsie, Kelsa, Kelsie

DERIVATION: English, of unknown origin. Possibly a cross between Cherry and Beryl. Not seen until the 1920s, and not popular until the 1940s.

PRINCIPAL COLORS: Deep azure, black, dark shades of gray

GEMSTONES AND PRECIOUS METALS: Black pearls, black diamonds, lackluster rubies, any other stone with a very dark hue

BOTANICALS: Angelica, gravel root, shepherd's purse

UNIQUE SPELLINGS: Cherill, Cherril, Cherrill, Cherryl, Cherryle, Cherryll, Cheryle, Cheryll, Sherell, Sheril, Sherill, Sherrell, Sherryll, Sheryl

RELATED TO: Cheralyn, Cheri, Cherie, Cherilyn, Cherilynn, Cherralyn, Cherrlene, Cherry, Cherrylin, Cherryline, Cherylyn, Sheralyn, Sheree, Sheri, Sherie, Sherilyn, Sherralyn, Sherree, Sherryt, Sherryllyn, Sherrylyn

A KABBALISTIC SYNOPSIS
חאריל —ChARYL (Cheth, Aleph, Resh, Yod, Lamed)

"Graveyards and werewolves and scorpion stings—these are a few of my favorite things." Cheryl would probably appreciate this distortion of the Julie Andrews classic, yet she is not a morbid person. In fact, Cheryl loves to laugh and joke about, and she is always in the thick of it at parties, dancing away with the best of them. In short, her outward behavior gives no indication of her capacity for the most terrible imaginings. But Cheryl also has a very full fantasy life; if she put her daydreams down on paper, she would give Stephen King and Clive Barker a good run for their money. The total value of her name is 249, which is equivalent to the Hebrew for "terror," while the strong influence of M, or Mem, in her name suggests that if she does turn her dark thoughts into fiction, they will contain a depth of emotion unusual in such novels. Potential partners should be aware that her sexuality is equally dark and mysterious; in addition, the associations with the number fifteen in her name indicate that she has an abiding interest in sexuality in all its forms.

THE RUNIC INTERPRETATION
ᛗᛚᚱᛗᚺᛋ (Ehwaz, Laguz, Raido, Ehwaz, Hagalaz, Sowelu)

Cheryl loves minutiae. As a child she believed in gnomes and fairies. As an adult she might like marine biology, genetics, or fastidious research work, all of which appeal to her fascination with the microcosm. She collects miniature villages, has a miniature dog of some kind, and lives in a small house or apartment. She is sentimental to a fault and enjoys collecting Victorian valentines and stories about miracles and angels. Cheryl is highly intelligent and possibly a bit lonely. She would enjoy living in Nova Scotia or places where there is a great deal of peace. Cheryl makes a loyal, responsible, and caring friend. Cheryl will move around a lot during her lifetime.

Elements: Air, water, water, air, water, air

THE NUMEROLOGICAL INTERPRETATION
Cheryl (NV = 8, CV = 5, VV = 3, FL = 3)

Cheryl is highly motivated and has a wide range of interests. She enjoys personal freedom and tends to create a lifestyle that allows her to pursue her own interests while still living up to the responsibilities she has to other relationships. Direct and forceful when it comes to expressing her opinions, Cheryl looks forward to intense discussion with others on any number of topics. Variety is very natural to her, and she rebels against confinement, intellectual and otherwise.

Chester

A Kabbalistic Synopsis
חאסטר —ChASTR (Cheth, Aleph, Samech, Teth, Resh)

If you're feeling low, Chester is definitely someone you should seek out. He has a refreshingly optimistic outlook on life and is the guy who will always find the cloud's silver lining however black the skies may at first appear. Chester's name reduces to seventeen, which is the number of the tarot trump, the Star. The Star represents the guiding light of destiny and the waters of life; it is a protective and hopeful symbol, suiting Chester's personality perfectly. Chester is likely to make a commitment to one partner early on in adulthood and will carry a torch for his chosen loved one faithfully for the rest of his life. Thanks to his take on life, his marriage will be able to weather any storm, and in the inevitable times of trouble he will always be there to comfort his partner, reassuring her that the good times are just around the corner. Chester is an all-around good guy, and anyone who has a Chester in their life will be much better for his presence.

The Runic Interpretation
ᚱᛖᛏᛋᛗᚺᛋ (Raido, Ehwaz, Teiwaz, Sowelu, Ehwaz, Hagalaz, Sowelu)

Chester is generous to a fault. He keeps his checkbook by the phone and likes to donate to whatever cause has his number. Chester collects food for the needy and is determined that his life make a difference. In keeping with this, Chester enjoys social work, the ministry, paramedic work, and mentoring organizations. He may even adopt a child or participate in foster care. Chester has a heart for the children of poverty and answers the call of human suffering, but none of this is done for the accolades. He eschews publicity and recognition, preferring to work long and hard behind the scenes. His needs are modest, and he is very tolerant of people. Divine protection is operating on all levels of Chester's life.

Elements: Water, air, air, air, air, water, air

The Numerological Interpretation
Chester (NV = 6, CV = 5, VV = 1, FL = 3)

The numerological significance of Chester points to a man who may find himself divided between his love of home and family and his need to be independent and consistently self-assertive. A lover of beauty, with a distinct need for peace and harmony, Chester is nonetheless a rugged individualist who enjoys nothing better than to pursue his sense of adventure to the maximum extent possible. In his relationships he will require people who appreciate spending time alone as well as sharing intimate moments together.

DERIVATION: English, originally used as a surname, indicating that one lived in the town of Chester. From the Latin *castra*, meaning "camp, site." Used regularly as a given name in the twentieth century in all English-speaking countries, but most popular in the United States.

PRINCIPAL COLORS: From pale to medium azure hues

GEMSTONES AND PRECIOUS METALS: Emeralds, blue or blue-green turquoise

BOTANICALS: Vervain, violets, walnuts, almonds

UNIQUE SPELLINGS: Chestir, Chestyr

RELATED TO: Chett

"They say married men live much longer than bachelors."
—CHESTER IN *ROYAL WEDDING* (1951)

DERIVATION: English, pet form of
Chester, which is from the Latin
castra, meaning "camp, site."
Occasionally used as an
independent name.

PRINCIPAL COLORS: The full
range of red hues, particularly the
deep, richer tones

GEMSTONES AND PRECIOUS
METALS: Deep red rubies,
garnets, and bloodstones

BOTANICALS: Nettle, onion,
wormwood

UNIQUE SPELLINGS: Cheht,
Chehtt, Chett

RELATED TO: Chestert, Chetwin

"Once you become predictable, no
one's interested anymore."
—CHET ATKINS (MUSICIAN)

Chet

A KABBALISTIC SYNOPSIS
חאת —ChET (Cheth, Aleph, Tau)

Chet is a drifter by nature. He dreams of packing up all his belongings and just heading off into the great blue yonder. For many Chets this desire will remain no more than a dream, as there are strong influences in the name that tie them to their hometowns. Still, you will often see Chet in the local coffee shop with his friends describing his planned route for the day when he finally gets around to setting off on his travels. Chet is not a depressed man; he derives much pleasure from his mental drifting and is likely to be an avid fan of science fiction author J. R. R. Tolkien. In his relationships, Chet is an exciting prospect, as he can bring his roving imagination into play whenever the partnership begins to stagnate. Despite his desire to roam, Chet will take his loved one with him if he ever does set off, and his key priority will be her protection.

THE RUNIC INTERPRETATION
↑ᛗᚺᛋ (Teiwaz, Ehwaz, Hagalaz, Sowelu)

Chet is being groomed for leadership in a world where honesty and integrity are valued. Chet upholds responsibilities with simplicity and strength. He carves out a new destiny for himself with discipline and plenty of introspection. Chet is blessed and could inherit money in his lifetime. He has the Sowelu energy of wholeness in his name, which will help him to surrender limiting beliefs, habits, or cultural biases. He has a willingness and ability to relinquish old patterns, and keeps the peace in troublesome situations.

Elements: Air, air, water, air

THE NUMEROLOGICAL INTERPRETATION
Chet (NV = 9, CV = 4, VV = 5, FL = 3)

Chet has no problem spending time alone. It is not that Chet is antisocial—not at all. He just finds that solitude provides him with great opportunities to explore life philosophically. This introspective side gives rise to a compassionate nature and a life perspective that is broad and inclusive. Chet is a name that gives a person the power of strong convictions and a firm sense of self-confidence.

Chris

A KABBALISTIC SYNOPSIS
כרים —KRYS (Kaph, Resh, Yod, Samech)

Chris can be used for both men and women. Chris has a deeply suspicious nature; "trust no one" could well be his or her personal motto. Of course, most Chrises will not hit extremes of paranoia—although you may find a Scorpio Chris who sees conspiracies and New World Order movements behind the most innocuous incidents. Chris is certainly no dope, though, and tends to be highly intelligent. This name can be compressed to the letters R (Resh) and Tz (Tzaddi), which indicates an active mind with the ability to latch on to a concept and doggedly follow it to its conclusion. This trait accounts in part for the suspicious element in his or her character, but it also makes Chris ideal for academic work in which mental persistence is essential.

THE RUNIC INTERPRETATION
ᛋᛁᚱᚺᚲ (Sowelu, Isa, Raido, Hagalaz, Kano)

Once Chris finds his or her voice, Chris begins to participate in the world, and life takes on a new joy. The Raido rune of good communication combines with the Isa, the rune of standstill, to explain that for a time Chris is more comfortable expressing emotions with written words than with speech. Chris's shyness and hesitation cause discomfort and indicate the effects of Hagalaz, the rune of disruption, in his or her life. Sowelu, the rune of wholeness, helps Chris follow his or her dreams. Whether actively involved in sports or the school drama club, Chris is able to speak up for a cause he or she holds dear. Kano, the rune of openings, ensures that Chris emerges as an expressive and confident individual.

Elements: Air, earth, water, water, water

THE NUMEROLOGICAL INTERPRETATION
Chris (NV = 3, CV = 3, VV = 9, FL = 3)

Chris is a fountain of information, and a reference source on a wide variety of topics of interest. People with this name make very sociable and communicative friends and companions. Chrises are men or women who have to take care that their intense intellect does not overly stimulate the nervous system. People named Chris have so many interests in so many places that they may easily find that their attention drifts and wanders. Chris requires a career and a relationship that give both stability and integration as well as freedom and variety of expression. Male or female, Chris is definitely a likable person with a warm and flexible personality.

DERIVATION: English, a nickname for both males and females. Can be short for Christopher, Christine, and many other names starting with "Christ." Sometimes used as an independent given name as well.

PRINCIPAL COLORS: The complete gamut of purple and violet hues, from palest to deepest

GEMSTONES AND PRECIOUS METALS: Garnets, amethyst

BOTANICALS: Apple, bilberry, mint, asparagus

UNIQUE SPELLINGS: Chriss, Chrys, Chryss, Cris, Criss, Crys, Cryss, Kris, Kriss, Kryss

RELATED TO: Christiant, Christoff, Christophe, Christophert, Chrisanda, Chrissie, Chrissy, Christa, Christabel, Christal, Christella, Christen, Christie, Christinat, Christine, Christy

"You've got to take the initiative and play your game. In a decisive set, confidence is the difference."
—CHRIS EVERT LLOYD
(ATHLETE)

Christian

DERIVATION: English, ecclesiastical Latin form of *christianus*, meaning "follower of Christ." From the Greek word *christos*, meaning "anointed." Common as a female name in the Middle Ages, and used as a male name since the eighteenth century. Very popular in Britain in the 1970s.

PRINCIPAL COLORS: White and off-white, the full range of green tones

GEMSTONES AND PRECIOUS METALS: Jade, cat's-eye, moonstones

BOTANICALS: Chicory, moonwort, plantain, willow ash

UNIQUE SPELLINGS: Christyan, Chrystian, Chrystyan, Cristian, Cristyan, Crystian, Crystyan, Khristian, Khrystian, Kristian, Kristyan, Krystian, Krystyan

RELATED TO: Christ, Christer, Christhard, Christie, Christof, Christoff, Christoph, Christophe, Christophert, Christy, Kris, Kristofer, Kristopher

A KABBALISTIC SYNOPSIS

כריסטיון —KRYSTYVN (Kaph, Resh, Yod, Samech, Teth, Yod, Vau, Nun)

Christian moves the suspicious nature of Chris (page 173) up a gear, into a realm of action. Christian, as one might suspect of such a name, has a very high sense of moral responsibility. His name in kabbalistic terms can be seen as the sephirah of Tiphareth, the highest point of human development, as it manifests itself in the material world. In other words, Christian applies his spirituality to real-world problems. We may find him working for overseas aid agencies or as a missionary or even just as an enthusiastic volunteer for charitable causes. The central position of Teth, meaning "serpent," in his name suggests a desire to expose and vigorously oppose the sources of immorality and injustice. At a personal level Christian comes across as an intense individual for whom any emotional commitment is difficult but highly rewarding.

THE RUNIC INTERPRETATION

ᚾᚨᛁᛏᛋᛁᚱᚺᚲ (Nauthiz, Ansuz, Isa, Teiwaz, Sowelu, Isa, Raido, Hagalaz, Kano)

A period of confusion and chaos in Christian's early manhood is the key to his spiritual awakening. This early experience was a time of trials and tribulations for Christian. Fortunately he will survive this test. In the process he learns that he alone is responsible for his peace and happiness. He has great strength, which stems from having all four elements—air, fire, water, and earth—in his name. Christian enjoys life and he lives modestly, appreciating his health and peace of mind. He knows these attributes are hard-won for us all, and he emerges from his life lesson victorious and more fully alive.

Elements: Fire, air, earth, air, air, earth, water, water, water

THE NUMEROLOGICAL INTERPRETATION

Christian (NV = 2, CV = 1, VV = 1, FL = 3)

Christian is the name of a man who, given the right opportunities, can rise to the top of his chosen professional field. Forthright and courageous, he finds no oppositional circumstances too great for him to tackle. Christian possesses charm and social grace as well as a clear sense of personal identity. This combination allows him to accept the help and assistance of others and to return these same favors to those who may have need of his abundant life energy. Christian moves forward in life, taking other people with him.

Christina

A Kabbalistic Synopsis

כריסטינא —KRYSTYNA (Kaph, Resh, Yod, Samech, Teth, Yod, Nun, Aleph)

In Kabbalah, as with other hermetic practices, a great significance is attached to numbers that reflect key geometric or arithmetic concepts, as it is from these abstractions that the actual world is created. Christina's name adds up to 360, which has importance because it equals the number of degrees in a circle. From this value we can discern that Christina is likely to be a popular individual, since she will rarely be flustered or agitated. This calm stems from an innate recognition of the cyclical nature of existence and an inner balance or equilibrium of the elements as represented by the circle. It is common knowledge that the circle is a key symbol of protection in most occult rituals, and Christina's name acts as a linguistic version of that protective talisman. We can expect her to go through life with few major disasters to endure. Her only problem will be that the circle is, of course, complete in itself, and she may have a tendency to avoid company.

The Runic Interpretation

ᚨᚾᛁᛏᛋᛁᚱᚺᚲ (Ansuz, Nauthiz, Isa, Teiwaz, Sowelu, Isa, Raido, Hagalaz, Kano)

Christina is a sweet soul who loves animals and gardening. She has a passion for growing things and is an accomplished gourmet cook. In fact, she likely owns a trendy restaurant where she loves to spend time singing as she creates her complicated sauces. Christina has all four burners going at once, and this metaphor applies to every area of Christina's life. The Nauthiz rune of constraint indicates that Christina had financial worries early in life. Now money and love grow at an amazing rate for Christina, and she checks the market as often as she waters her plants. She has the power of all four elements in her name and may have some psychic ability.

Elements: Air, fire, earth, air, air, earth, water, water, water

The Numerological Interpretation

Christina (NV = 2, CV = 1, VV = 1, FL = 3)

This name endows a woman with a strong sense of her own destiny. She is very relationship oriented but will make sure that her companions complement her goals. Supportive but frank, intimate but independent, Christina is loyal both to herself and to her loved ones. This is a woman who has clear aspirations and a firm sense of herself. People admire Christina as much for her sense of personal integrity as for her steadfast friendship. This is a woman people can depend on because Christina can depend on herself.

DERIVATION: English, an abbreviated form of the Latin *christiana*. Ultimately from the Greek *christos*, meaning "annointed." Common in English-speaking countries since the early 1950s.

PRINCIPAL COLORS: White, any shade of green

GEMSTONES AND PRECIOUS METALS: Jade, cream-colored pearls, cat's-eye

BOTANICALS: Lettuce, cucumber, plantain

UNIQUE SPELLINGS: Chrystina, Chrystyna, Cristina, Crystina, Crystyna, Khristina, Khrystina, Khrystyna, Krystina, Krystyna

RELATED TO: Christ, Christinet, Khristine, Kirsten, Kirstie, Kirsty, Kirstyn, Kris, Kristie, Kristine, Kristy, Kyrsty

"Better by far that you should forget and smile than that you should remember and be sad."
—CHRISTINA ROSSETTI (POET)

DERIVATION: English and French, variant form of Christina. Ultimately derived from the name Christian, meaning "follower of Christ." First used in English-speaking countries in the nineteenth century. Very popular in the 1950s and 1960s, and remains quite common today.

PRINCIPAL COLORS: All but the brightest shades of blue

GEMSTONES AND PRECIOUS METALS: Turquoise, emeralds

BOTANICALS: Dog rose, daffodils, walnuts

UNIQUE SPELLINGS: Christeen, Christene, Christyne, Chrysteen, Chrystene, Chrystyne, Cristeen, Cristene, Cristyne, Khristeen, Khristene, Khristyne, Kristeen, Kristene, Kristyne

RELATED TO: Christ†, Chrisanda, Chrissie, Christiana, Christianna, Christie, Christina†, Christy, Chrystal, Crista, Crystal†, Kerstin, Kirstie, Kris, Krista†, Kristeen, Kristen†, Kristina, Krystle, Krystyna

A KABBALISTIC SYNOPSIS

כריסטין —KRYSTYN (Kaph, Resh, Yod, Samech, Teth, Yod, Nun)

The name Christine has the root "KRYS," which points to a strong religious influence in her life. Christine is no zealous evangelist, however; the total value of her name is 359, which by virtue of being a prime number (divisible only by itself and one) lets us know that she has a very individual, if not unique, slant on life. Christine's approach to the world does indeed stem largely from her religious background, but hers is a very earthy, human perspective. Within her name we have symbols of both the Empress and the wise old Hermit. All of this indicates a woman whose focus is on the natural riches and joys of the world and the importance of the cycles of birth and death. To most people she comes across as a warm earth mother. She brings a happy atmosphere to any workplace while managing to get her job done effectively and quickly.

THE RUNIC INTERPRETATION

ᛗᚾᛁᛏᛋᛁᚱᚲ (Ehwaz, Nauthiz, Isa, Teiwaz, Sowelu, Isa, Raido, Kano)

Christine's name has much of the energy of Christian's, with the addition of the Ehwaz energy, which represents the waxing moon. Christine has a heartier constitution than Christian. Christine can take on enormous physical challenges and has what it takes to participate in the Olympics and win. She has discipline, vision, and persistence. She is a powerhouse physically and has a driving will that takes her far in life. She is an overachiever and expects more of herself than anyone expects of her. Christine could finish medical school early by taking lots of courses in the summer. Her prescription: One belly laugh a day. Funny videos and the company of amusing friends are a delight for Christine.

Elements: Air, fire, earth, air, air, earth, water, water

THE NUMEROLOGICAL INTERPRETATION

Christine (NV = 6, CV = 1, VV = 5, FL = 3)

Christine will have to work at combining her sense of compassion and understanding for others and their positions in life with her own tremendous need to act independently. She loves to explore life and all of its adventures and possibilities while at the same time avoiding clashes and personality conflicts with others. This balance is not easy to achieve. Christine must cultivate a sense of personal boundaries that permit her the artistic and personal freedom that her mind requires while still allowing her to cultivate the intimate relationships that are so important to her heart.

Christopher

A KABBALISTIC SYNOPSIS
כריסטעף —KRYSTA'APh (Kaph, Resh, Yod, Samech, Teth, Ayin, Peh)

Many people will assume that they know the meaning of this name—that it refers to the saint who carried Christ across the river and means "bearer of Christ." Yet there is an even greater mystical symbolism to be found in this name, which has strong religious overtones due to the "KRYS" root. The total value of the name is 449, which is represented by the letters Tau, Daleth, and Teth. These letters give us "cross," "door," and "serpent," and together they represent an ideal of eternal balance. On the one hand, we have the cross of Christ, Osiris, or any other resurrected god figure; on the other, we have the serpent, an evil figure such as Satan, Apophis, or any similar deity. Between the two we have the door of Daleth. For Christopher, then, truth is found in the balance or space between the forces of order and chaos, or light and dark, rather than by adhering to the values of either extreme. This view is the basis of many deep occult secrets. In practical terms, it means that Christopher is a tolerant and understanding guy, able to see both sides of any argument. He makes an excellent arbitrator or regulator due to his impartial nature. The final Peh in his name indicates an enjoyment of lively conversation and discussion.

THE RUNIC INTERPRETATION
ᚱᛖᚺᚹᛟᛏᛊᛁᚱᚲ (Raido, Ehwaz, Hagalaz, Wunjo, Othila, Teiwaz, Sowelu, Isa, Raido, Kano)

Christopher is visual, and careers such as picture framing, upholstery work, and art could be his specialty. He is also a loner who may spend some of his social time helping people in adversity. He knows pain and suffering and may well have deep regrets that stem from his childhood, which left some scars. But he will in time learn to trust and to laugh at himself. Christopher is interested in the truth, and where truth is present, healing occurs on many levels. He is also a perfectionist who is smart enough to modulate his intense nature when working with other people; for example, he adopts casual dress and the pace of his speech is slow. He works at appearing to be more relaxed than he is on the inside, and people respond well to him.

Elements: Water, air, water, earth, earth/fire, air, air, earth, water, water

THE NUMEROLOGICAL INTERPRETATION
Christopher (NV = 4, CV = 11, VV = 2, FL = 3)

A man of far-reaching vision, Christopher will use his insight and intuition about life in pursuit of his practical aims and ambitions. He usually has his life well organized and under control. Others view him as a man with a strong pragmatic drive but one who also has time to give, especially if it is to people who share his urge for achievement. Christopher can be a very generous person, one who is happy to encourage the possibilities for material prosperity with those supportive of his efforts. He is also a romantic who enjoys partaking in life's more sensual pleasures with his partner.

DERIVATION: English, from the Greek *kristophoros*, meaning "one who carries Christ." The name was given to a saint who carried the Christ child across a river. Quite popular in the seventeenth century, but less common in the nineteenth. Extremely popular from the 1970s on.

PRINCIPAL COLORS: Any moderately shaded tone, bright blue

GEMSTONES AND PRECIOUS METALS: From the palest to the richest sapphire

BOTANICALS: Lesser celandine, wintergreen, medlar

UNIQUE SPELLINGS: Chrystofer, Chrystopher, Cristofer, Cristopher, Crystofer, Crystopher, Khristofer, Khristopher, Khrystofer, Khrystopher, Kristofer, Kristopher, Krystofer, Krystopher

RELATED TO: Christ, Christer, Christhard, Christiant, Christie, Christmas, Christof, Christoff, Christoph, Christophe, Christy, Cristobal, Kit, Kris

Chuck

A KABBALISTIC SYNOPSIS
כוח —ChVK (Cheth, Vau, Kaph)

Chuck is everybody's pal, the first to buy a round or to invite people over to dinner. It is rare for people to refuse an invitation from Chuck, as he knows how to have a good time—with a vengeance! His name adds up to thirty-four, which can be viewed as an indication of the high priority of fun and plenty in his life. From time to time his partner will find his happy-go-lucky attitude frustrating, and demand that he take a more serious approach to life—but it won't be long before he has her in stitches again. Chuck's only real concern is managing the split between work and home. In order to maintain the abundant lifestyle he prefers, Chuck has to work hard. Provided he has some element of responsibility, Chuck is happy in the workplace. But he is usually head over heels in love with his partner, and hates to be away from home any longer than absolutely necessary. There is a strong suggestion that this desire to be at home stems from a need to protect his family, evidenced by the Ch, or Cheth, in his name.

THE RUNIC INTERPRETATION
ᚲᚲᚢᚺᛋ (Kano, Kano, Uruz, Hagalaz, Sowelu)

Chuck has an expansive nature and likes to live for the moment. He likes credit cards and carries a heavy debt load. But Chuck also has the Uruz energy on hand to give him the determination to look within and trust the universe to help him correct his spending habits. Uruz is the energy of strength, and it helps Chuck to create spending boundaries. Chucks needs to feel he has an organized life. This sense of neatness and structure will empower him to inspire the confidence and trust of his friends and business associates. The double Kano suggests that Chuck is open and creative.

Elements: Water, water, earth, water, air

THE NUMEROLOGICAL INTERPRETATION
Chuck (NV = 1, CV = 7, VV = 3, FL = 3)

Chuck is the name of a person who is very energetic and quite enthusiastic about his plans and projects. He has an active mind and often a highly developed intellect. Chuck is happy to help others find direction, but sometimes he can be overly self-involved. This is a man who has a very analytical nature that permits him to go to the core of any issue with speed and precision. Chuck can achieve a great deal with his many talents and abilities but may need to cultivate a bit more compassion in dealing with people.

Cindy

DERIVATION: English, pet form of Cynthia and Lucinda. From the Greek *kynthía*, a name of the moon goddess Artemis, who was supposedly born on Mount Kynthos on the island of Delos.

PRINCIPAL COLORS: The full range of yellows, including gold and bronze

GEMSTONES AND PRECIOUS METALS: Amber, topaz, yellow diamonds, any other yellow stone

BOTANICALS: Chamomile, lavender, cloves, sorrel

UNIQUE SPELLINGS: Cindi, Cindie, Cyndi, Cyndie, Cyndy, Sindi, Sindie, Sindy, Syndi, Syndie, Syndy

RELATED TO: Cinderella, Cinthia, Cinzia, Cynthia†, Lucinda

A KABBALISTIC SYNOPSIS
סינדי —SYNDY (Samech, Yod, Nun, Daleth, Yod)

If Cindy tells you she's engaged to be married, don't rush right out to buy the wedding present. Of course, if you know a Cindy well, you won't need this advice. Cindy has great difficulty committing emotionally but finds it very easy to take the first steps toward such a commitment. A Cindy born under Cancer may get engaged on a frighteningly regular basis! The letter Yod always stands for energy moving a person in a particular direction, and at the end of a name it suggests a pulling away from whatever is suggested in the main body of the name. In this case, it is a movement away from emotional ties. In Cindy's name we see the energies of Yod pushing her toward the emotional bond with another, until the final Yod pulls her away with the same amount of force. In addition her name reduces to thirteen, indicative of change. Luckily Cindy has strength of character and resilience, and will not be permanently damaged by the emotional roller coaster she experiences before finally committing to a partner for good. In work terms Cindy does not have a commitment problem, and will be a useful and reliable employee. As her name has the same value as Ayin, meaning "eye," she will do well in any career requiring good powers of observation, which could range from photography to law enforcement.

THE RUNIC INTERPRETATION
ᛇᛞᚾᛁᛊ (Eihwaz, Dagaz, Nauthiz, Isa, Sowelu)

Cindy is a social climber and likes intrigue. A life of gossip and politics in Washington, D.C., would keep Cindy feeling like she is where events are happening. Cindy makes a good journalist or photojournalist. She has the Dagaz energy of breakthroughs in her name. She engages in little self-pity, so assignments in third world countries with all the hardships entailed would suit her just fine. Cindy is honest and can smell duplicity, and isn't afraid to go for the jugular with a winning smile on her face! She loathes hypocrisy and yet she's cynical. She says it isn't love that makes the world go round; it's power, greed, and injustice. Cindy is out to blow the whistle on the whole world, and she has a lot of fans cheering her on to do just that. She is somewhat introverted and cautious, but Dagaz and Sowelu in her name soften these qualities. She will have obstacles to face, but she will be able to overcome them.

Elements: Earth/fire, fire, fire, earth, air

THE NUMEROLOGICAL INTERPRETATION
Cindy (NV = 1, CV = 3, VV = 7, FL = 3)

Cindy has self-assurance that strengthens her determination to succeed in life. Other people look to her for a sense of direction, and she is very open to guiding and helping her friends with their objectives. Cindy is a dynamic communicator who feels at home in any number of intellectual areas of interest. Always eager to add knowledge to her repertoire, Cindy is the perpetual student. Lighthearted on the outside but profound and philosophical within, Cindy is a multifaceted woman of varied interests.

Claire

DERIVATION: French form of the name Clara. From the Latin *clarus*, meaning "clear, bright, famous." Brought to Britain by the Normans, but not widely used. Became very popular in Britain and Australia in the 1970s.

PRINCIPAL COLORS: The full range of purple hues

GEMSTONES AND PRECIOUS METALS: Amethyst, garnets

BOTANICALS: Cherry, dandelion, beetroot, mint

UNIQUE SPELLINGS: Clair, Clare, Clayre, Klair, Klaire, Klare

RELATED TO: Clarat, Clarette, Claribel, Clarice, Clarinda, Claris, Clarisa, Clarissa, Clarisse, Clarita, Clarrie, Klara

A KABBALISTIC SYNOPSIS
כלאר —KLAR (Kaph, Lamed, Aleph, Resh)

Claire cannot understand why everyone these days is so obsessed with career and work, success and money. In Claire's world these are very much secondary considerations (although the influence of Jupiter in her name suggests that she is unlikely to ever suffer real hardship or poverty). Her main interests are the practical, down-to-earth issues of everyday living. She does have buckets of energy, shown by the driving L, or Lamed, meaning "ox goad." Claire is the sort of woman who accomplishes things that the rest of us keep meaning to do but never seem to find the time for, like building that conservatory, painting the porch, or landscaping the garden. Claire's name has the same value as Uriel, the archangel of the element of earth, and we can expect her to have an affection for all things with a natural connection. She is not one for using modern synthetic materials in her house, and will surround herself with traditional furnishings. Ideally, Claire would love to have an idyllic wood cottage in the forest far away from contemporary distractions.

THE RUNIC INTERPRETATION
ᛖᚱᛁᚨᛚᚲ (Ehwaz, Raido, Isa, Ansuz, Laguz, Kano)

Claire loves music, and Isa in her name makes her a loner. She is fairly high-strung and requires solitude to keep her emotions in balance. She is nearly always happier reading a book than listening to someone's boring jokes. Claire has a good command of languages and loves to read foreign literature and study ancient cultures. Claire also enjoys libraries and museums. A piece of Egyptian linen from 5,000 B.C.E. stays in her thoughts for days. If she marries at all, it will be late in life for security and companionship. Marriage isn't easy for Claire; she needs a separate wing in the house for her books and, most important, her identity.

Elements: Air, water, earth, air, water, water

THE NUMEROLOGICAL INTERPRETATION
Claire (NV = 3, CV = 6, VV = 6, FL = 3)

Harmony, home, and happiness are very important to a woman named Claire. This is a person who tends to be sympathetic and compassionate to all who know her. She often finds herself involved with causes and activities that aim to help others. Claire most easily accomplishes this through her artistic talents and abilities. She is always seeking to bring beauty and peace into her environment, and may be counted on to add her grace to whatever project she takes on.

Clara

A KABBALISTIC SYNOPSIS
כלערא —KLA'ARA (Kaph, Lamed, Ayin, Resh, Aleph)

Some people seem to have a knack of always coming up smelling like roses, no matter what misfortune befalls them. Clara is one of these lucky people, and she knows it. Her name can be compressed to Shin, Kaph, and Aleph. This creates an interesting trio of influences. Shin equates to the power of judgment, while Aleph is the naive innocence of the Fool. Between these two extremes lies the hand symbol of Kaph, associated with Jupiter and the Wheel of Fortune. It appears from this arrangement that Clara oscillates between a sound, rational approach to decision making and a purely instinctive, possibly naive basis for making choices. There is no fixed pattern as to which method she chooses; it is all in the hand of fate. In many jobs this tendency could cause utter chaos, but Clara would be ideally suited to a creative field, such as design. The central presence of Ayion, meaning "eye," points to some kind of visually based career.

THE RUNIC INTERPRETATION
ᚨᚱᚨᛚᚲ (Ansuz, Raido, Ansuz, Laguz, Kano)

Clara gravitates toward Oriental art and religion. She likes delicate watercolors and Japanese prints. Her home furnishings have simple lines, and she enjoys mellow, rich color as a background. Clara is straightforward and dresses in an understated elegant way. She asserts her independence as a young woman and travels during most of her adult life. She would do well with an import-export business or as a global educational consultant. She may marry a foreigner. Clara enjoys working with gifted children and adults, and makes important contributions in whatever way she can. Clara is simple and true.

Elements: Air, water, air, water, water

THE NUMEROLOGICAL INTERPRETATION
Clara (NV = 8, CV = 6, VV = 2, FL = 3)

Clara brings her need for balance, responsibility, and love into all of her relationships. This is a name that indicates a woman for whom material satisfaction and comfort are very important. But they are not important just for her alone; she is very much other-oriented, and her family and intimate circle of friends and loved ones are important to her. In fact, Clara sees no separation between her own life and the lives of the people with whom she is in closest contact. Although this characterizes Clara's special form of kindness, she has to be careful not to compromise herself, as she is not responsible for everyone's happiness.

DERIVATION: English, Italian, and German, from the Latin *clarus*, meaning "clear, bright, famous." Once written and pronounced as Clare, later relatinized to form Clara. Very popular in all English-speaking countries from 1850 to 1900.

PRINCIPAL COLORS: Purple, gray, black, the darkest shades of azure

GEMSTONES AND PRECIOUS METALS: Carbuncles, black diamonds, black pearls, sapphires

BOTANICALS: Marsh mallow, ragwort, angelica

UNIQUE SPELLINGS: Clarah, Klara, Klarah

RELATED TO: Clairet, Clarette, Claribel, Clarice, Clarinda, Claris, Clarisa, Clarissa, Clarisse, Clarita, Clarrie

"Until I die, I'm going to keep doing. My people need me. They need somebody that's not taking from them and is giving them something."
—CLARA MCBRIDE HALE (FOUNDER OF HALE HOUSE, A HOME FOR INFANTS BORN ADDICTED TO ILLEGAL DRUGS)

Clark

DERIVATION: English, originally a surname. Used in the Middle Ages to indicate the occupation of clerk or scholar. Most commonly used in the United States as a given name, largely after the popularity of the actor Clark Gable (1901–1960).

PRINCIPAL COLORS: The full range of red hues from pink to deep reddish purple

GEMSTONES AND PRECIOUS METALS: Reddish stones, such as bloodstones and rubies

BOTANICALS: Garlic, onion, wormwood

UNIQUE SPELLINGS: Clarke, Klark, Klarke

RELATED TO: Clay, Clayborne, Clayton

A KABBALISTIC SYNOPSIS
כלעכ —KLA'AK (Kaph, Lamed, Ayin, Kaph)

Never happier than when surrounded by tools and with a good, long repair or maintenance job ahead of him, Clark is a man with a totally practical mind-set. Almost any job will suit him as long as it involves using his hands. Although he will never be a businessman, Clark is unlikely to be short of money either, as he knows how to work hard and always likes to work at top speed. The value of his name suggests a calm and reasonable manner. He is not a man to get all hot under the collar if his team loses; instead, he is more likely to shrug it off and take a more philosophical outlook. In many ways Clark can appear faultless; he is down-to-earth and unpretentious, he has no temper to speak of, and he is a good worker. When all these aspects are combined in one person, however, it can sometimes lead to a somewhat boring and even irksome personality. Thankfully, the Ayin in Clark indicates that he does have an interest in the outside world.

THE RUNIC INTERPRETATION
ᚲᚱᚨᛚᚲ (Kano, Raido, Ansuz, Laguz, Kano)

Clark gets very focused and develops specific career goals early in life. His work is high-quality and high-concept; the proof is in the details. Clark makes a good labor leader or lawyer, and is able to handle tough and cruel people with velvet gloves and shrewd strategies. He gravitates toward sports that are noncompetitive, such as surfing and yoga, and he uses his considerable athletic talent as therapy to soothe his mind. Keeping his stress at a tolerable level is a full-time goal for Clark. Clark has a belief system that enables him to speak freely with people from all walks of life, and he is not intimidated by powerful people. Instead, he enjoys them because they share the same worldview. Clark is strong and brave, and a man of conviction.

Elements: Water, water, air, water, water

THE NUMEROLOGICAL INTERPRETATION
Clark (NV = 9, CV = 8, VV = 1, FL = 3)

The vibrations in the name Clark reveal a man who is courageous and bold. Many people may think of him as being overly involved with himself. This is true, but when we examine Clark more closely, we see that he uses his strength for the benefit of others, and his generosity is neither superficial nor confined to material goods and services. Clark is there when he is needed. He is both a supportive friend and a faithful companion. His special talent may lie in his ability to uncover hidden resources both in himself and in others.

Claudia

A Kabbalistic Synopsis

כלאודיא —KLAVDYA (Kaph, Lamed, Aleph, Vau, Daleth, Yod, Aleph)

In spite of a slight tendency to ignore the needs or opinions of others, Claudia is generally a well-liked individual. In addition, her self-confidence and self-promotion are tempered by the influence of wisdom and understanding, as represented by the High Priestess in the tarot. Any lover of Claudia will need to be aware that she is a vulnerable person emotionally, although she keeps this well disguised. A close analysis of her name yields a series of contradictory impulses, which are essentially a conflict between her strong professional ambition and her desire for a warm and cozy home environment. Claudia is usually blessed with good looks and is often quite happy to use them to her advantage . . . whether that be in a specific professional context or simply as an assistance to her pursuit of the ideal career.

The Runic Interpretation

ᚨᛁᛞᚢᚨᛚᚲ (Ansuz, Isa, Dagaz, Uruz, Ansuz, Laguz, Kano)

Claudia's name contains the energy of Uruz, the wild ox. Once tamed, this willful creature can be directed to transport weighty cargo. Claudia's life lesson thus involves a death or loss that forces her to bear the weight of enormous pain. One strategy Claudia employs is to muster her strength and acknowledge all the fine qualities she appreciated in the person whom she must now live without. Her task is to grow these attributes within herself, and once this is accomplished, she is free to look to the future. The burden of this heavy load is considerable, but Claudia is equal to the task and fills the void within herself. The four elements represented in her name assure Claudia of victory.

Elements: Air, earth, fire, earth, air, water, water

The Numerological Interpretation

Claudia (NV = 6, CV = 1, VV = 5, FL = 3)

Claudia gives herself the freedom to just be herself. She is excited by life and all of its many possibilities. Claudia has an artistic nature and enjoys experimenting creatively with words, songs, and dances. She loves to bring beauty and harmony into her environment but rebels against being confined. She adds charm and intelligence to any social gathering but refuses to be exclusive to one circle of friends. You can't capture Claudia; she must give herself to you.

DERIVATION: English and German, feminine form of the old Roman family name Claudius. Derived from the Latin *claudus*, meaning "lame." In the New Testament, mentioned in one of Saint Paul's letters to Timothy. Used in many English-speaking countries.

PRINCIPAL COLORS: Pale to medium blue hues

GEMSTONES AND PRECIOUS METALS: Emeralds, blue or blue-green turquoise

BOTANICALS: Violets, apricots, walnuts

UNIQUE SPELLINGS: Claudya, Clawdia, Klaudia, Klaudya, Klawdia

RELATED TO: Claude, Claudelle, Claudette, Claudine

DERIVATION: English, pet form of the English names Clifford and Clifton, meaning "ford near a cliff" and "settlement near a cliff," respectively. Used as a given name since the middle of the twentieth century, partially due to the influence of singer Cliff Richard (b. 1940).

PRINCIPAL COLORS: All shades of red, including pink, bloodred, and maroon

GEMSTONES AND PRECIOUS METALS: Rubies, bloodstones, garnets

BOTANICALS: Onion, nettle, broom

UNIQUE SPELLINGS: Clif, Cliph, Clyf, Clyff, Clyph, Klif, Kliff, Kliph, Klyf, Klyff, Klyph

RELATED TO: Clifford, Clifton, Heathcliff

In the absence of any direct equivalent to the letter *f* in the Hebrew alphabet, the letter Peh is used. Peh can function as either a hard or a soft letter, and as such, is one of the seven "doubles."

A KABBALISTIC SYNOPSIS
כליף —KLYPh (Kaph, Lamed, Yod, Peh)

Although no one but his closest friends would ever guess it, Cliff is a deeply shy guy. He covers for his nervousness in public by talking; he cannot abide any silences at social gatherings, and will talk about almost anything in order to fill the awkward lulls in conversation. In work as well as socially it is Cliff's voice that acts as his main source of support. He may well have a job where negotiation plays a key part, or it may be that his voice more directly supports him, as a singer or television announcer, for example. Cliff tends to have a healthily balanced outlook on the world, in part due to his dual interest in the intellectual and the practical. The practical element is indicated by the initial Kaph, meaning "hand"; its combination with the final Peh, meaning "mouth," may point to an ideal job as a trainer or instructor in some concrete skill.

THE RUNIC INTERPRETATION
ᚠᚠᛁᛚᚲ (Fehu, Fehu, Isa, Laguz, Kano)

With the double Fehu energy of flow, Cliff likes to dance, and if he dances professionally, he'll have quite a following. Cliff is one of those creative people you like to know. He can cut your hair, sew you a shirt, whip up a gourmet dinner, and then tango till dawn. Who cares if the dishes pile up? He'll get out his potter's wheel and spin you a new set. Cliff is versatile, and that describes his love life as well. He looks deep into the heart of his companions, and he appreciates a good soul from any walk of life. Cliff lives modestly. He learned humility early on, and that is one way someone as talented as Cliff keeps things in perspective.

Elements: Fire, fire, earth, water, water

THE NUMEROLOGICAL INTERPRETATION
Cliff (NV = 9, CV = 9, VV = 9, FL = 3)

This is the name of a man with deep compassion. Cliff is a person who possesses a very wide and inclusive view of life. He cares about others and shows it through his actions. Cliff realizes that it takes a great deal of hard work to make any changes in other people's lives, yet he is willing to do whatever it requires to make a contribution to some humanitarian causes. This makes Cliff quite selfless and giving—at times, to his own detriment. He has to take care that he is not swept away by his own idealism and that the more practical side of life is also included in his actions.

Clint

DERIVATION: English, the shortened form of the English place-name Clinton, meaning "settlement near a hill." Used as a given name, especially after the actor Clint Eastwood (b. 1930).

PRINCIPAL COLORS: Blues, grays

GEMSTONES AND PRECIOUS METALS: Pale to deeply hued sapphires

BOTANICALS: Celandine, sage

UNIQUE SPELLINGS: Clintt, Clynt, Clyntt, Klint, Klintt, Klynt, Klyntt

RELATED TO: Clifford, Clifton, Clinton

A KABBALISTIC SYNOPSIS
כלינט —KLYNT (Kaph, Lamed, Yod, Nun, Teth)

Clint is equivalent to the tarot trump card, Strength. This symbol represents the force of the will rather than purely physical strength. Clint's willpower carries with it a high level of self-confidence, which suggests considerable reserves of inner power. If put to good use, this strength of will can be a benefit, whether to fellow workers in the context of Clint's career or to society in general if Clint decides to take a more public role. It is likely that Clint will be a fairly charismatic character. However, the value of Clint is also equivalent to Beelzebub or the Lord of the Flies, one of the key devil figures of early mythology. The existence of a strong negative character is no guarantee of bad behavior or low morality, though. The compression of the name Clint suggests that this fellow can be either well behaved or something of a terror, as the energy of the central Yod is flanked by the symbol of thought and of vengeance.

THE RUNIC INTERPRETATION
↑ᚺᛁᛚᚲ (Teiwaz, Nauthiz, Isa, Laguz, Kano)

Clint has some selfish energy blocks to overcome. Clint is very cautious about money, and so he keeps excellent records. He takes pride in his significant organizational ability: He takes obvious delight in paper clipping, punching the stapler, and running carefully ruled lines through endless columns of numbers filed in the best folders on the market. Clint also has a watch that tells you what time it is in countries you might never see, and which will run at twenty miles under the sea (not that he swims). Clint's life lesson is surrender: We can plan only so much, and then we need to watch and listen to the still small voice within. It may have a plan better than our own.

Elements: Air, fire, earth, water, water

THE NUMEROLOGICAL INTERPRETATION
Clint (NV = 4, CV = 4, VV = 9, FL = 3)

A most practical man by nature, Clint is the name of a person who is reliable and steadfast in his orientation to life. He wants things to be predictable and orderly. Clint does not like surprises and is very uncomfortable when he is taken off guard. This is a man who has to be in control and, as such, is not given to spontaneous gestures. He tends to be a person with his eyes firmly fixed on his goals, and he will work with all of his strength to achieve these objectives. Clint's sense of personal responsibility extends outward into his relationships, and he may be counted on for loyalty and faithfulness.

DERIVATION: From the Old English, meaning "pillow." Used for both girls and boys.

PRINCIPAL COLORS: White, all green tones

GEMSTONES AND PRECIOUS METALS: Jade, creamy white pearls, moonstones

BOTANICALS: Cabbage, plantain, lettuce

UNIQUE SPELLINGS: Codee, Codey, Codi, Codie, Kodee, Kodey, Kodi, Kodie, Kody

RELATED TO: Cuddy

Cody

A KABBALISTIC SYNOPSIS
כעדי —KA'ADY (Kaph, Ayin, Daleth, Yod)

Cody would make an ideal lawyer. He has a very strong intellect, which he puts to good use finding solutions to a variety of complex problems. The framing of his name by Kaph and Yod, the two letters representing aspects of the hand ("hand" and "palm," respectively) suggest that he has an interest in providing solutions that are practically applicable rather than simply theoretically appropriate. And as hands suggest a practical approach, we can expect Cody to be a practical guy. There is a strong influence of Venus in Cody's name, both from the planet itself and its designated sign of Virgo. We can therefore expect Cody to be quite successful in the romance department, as he knows how to woo his lovers and make them feel incredibly special and unique. Cody's name can be reduced to five, which, among other things, represents a strong, if somewhat conservative, moral conscience. This concern for the right behavior will ensure his honorable conduct in relationships as well as further suiting him for a role in the legal profession, where he can put his sense of justice to good use.

THE RUNIC INTERPRETATION
ᛇᛞᛟᚲ (Eihwaz, Dagaz, Othila, Kano)

Cody is a man's man. He wants meat and potatoes, and when he meets a woman, he tips his hat to her John Wayne style and says, "Howdee, ma'am." He knows how to lift her up off that barstool and dance her around the floor until her shoes lift off the ground. Cody is blessed to have the Dagaz energy of transformation and breakthrough in his name. Once the darkness has passed, Cody appreciates his hard-won victories. Cody is a man of principle, and young people need more role models like Cody. He works hard and he loves hard. And you can trust him with your vulnerabilities because he wants only the best for those he respects.

Elements: Earth/fire, fire, earth/fire, water

THE NUMEROLOGICAL INTERPRETATION
Cody (NV = 11, CV = 7, VV = 4, FL = 3)

Cody is a special combination of the visionary and the practical. This name possesses a combination of influences that tend toward a philosophical and spiritual disposition. Yet Cody is neither a monk nor a lofty, unreachable philosopher. What he knows, what he sees, has a distinct pragmatic aim. Cody seeks to bring his noble sense of values into the world around him, improving life and making the world that much better as a result of his participation. Working with others of like mind will be very important to him, as it is through his collective relationships that his goals will be achieved.

Colin

DERIVATION: English and Scottish, pet form of Nicholas. From the Greek, meaning "victorious among the people." Also an anglicized form of the Gaelic *cailean*, meaning "youth." Very popular in Scotland and Ireland.

PRINCIPAL COLORS: Black, gray, dark blue

GEMSTONES AND PRECIOUS METALS: Lackluster rubies, carbuncles, deeply hued sapphires

BOTANICALS: Angelica, shepherd's purse, pilewort

UNIQUE SPELLINGS: Cahlin, Cahlyn, Colinn, Collin, Collinn, Kahlin, Kahlinn, Kahlyn, Kahlynn, Kolin, Kolinn, Kollin, Kollinn

RELATED TO: Calum, Cole, Coll, Nicholast, Nick, Nicki, Nicky

> "Avoid having your ego so close to your position that, when your position fails, your ego goes with it."
> —COLIN POWELL (FORMER CHAIRMAN OF THE JOINT CHIEFS OF STAFF)

A KABBALISTIC SYNOPSIS
כעלין —KA'ALYN (Kaph, Ayin, Lamed, Yod, Nun)

Colin is a man of passionate beliefs whose concerns are likely to be social or political rather than religious, as the Kaph and Ayin in his name suggest a primary interest in the real world and the way that it is lived by society. His name can add up to either 180 or 830, depending on how one treats the final N, or Nun. In both values the letter Peh, meaning "mouth," is featured; this is a strong indication of Colin's urge to speak out on the issues that concern him. In fact, the other letters, Lamed and Qoph, show us that he is actually driven to give vent to his thoughts. Although his passion is politics and his views are the result of much solitary thinking, the driving force behind Colin is his emotional feelings. It is the dominance of his emotions that makes Colin so passionate about his beliefs. This emphasis also suggests that Colin is likely to have a very intense—if at times stormy—love life.

THE RUNIC INTERPRETATION
ᚺᛁᛚᛟᚲ (Nauthiz, Isa, Laguz, Othila, Kano)

Colin is very musical, and his analytical mind could lead him to compose and perform. Or he could go toward the fields of math or law. He's also got a natural talent for science. Colin is highly intuitive and just a bit suspicious by nature. He holds resentments too long for his own good, and may seek revenge on those who have wronged him. His nature is passionate, and lovemaking is terribly important to him. Acting is a good field for Colin because it will allow him to pretend to be naughty but actually lead a life of right action.

Elements: Fire, earth, water, earth/fire, water

THE NUMEROLOGICAL INTERPRETATION
Colin (NV = 8, CV = 11, VV = 6, FL = 3)

Colin possesses a strong sense of compassion and a deep sympathy for others. He tends to be less involved with established doctrines and theologies and more concerned with the underlying humanitarian spirit at the core of all true belief systems. Colin needs to be able to express his values and life philosophy in useful ways. He has a very strong practical side to his nature, and knows that you have to live in your daily life what you feel in your heart.

DERIVATION: U.S. and Australian English, from the Irish word *cailín*, meaning "girl." Popular in many English-speaking countries since the 1940s, especially in the United States.

PRINCIPAL COLORS: The full range of violet hues

GEMSTONES AND PRECIOUS METALS: Amethyst, garnets

BOTANICALS: Cherry, dandelion, strawberry, figs

UNIQUE SPELLINGS: Cahleen, Cahlene, Collene, Kahleen, Kahlene, Kolleen

RELATED TO: Colette, Collette, Colombe

❧

"I like viable women who are out there doing. I don't mean in terms of the working woman versus the nonworking woman, because we all know that ALL women are working, each in their own way. I like women who are very involved with living and who haven't pulled out from life."

—COLLEEN DEWHURST
(ACTRESS)

A KABBALISTIC SYNOPSIS
כעלײן —KA'ALYYN (Kaph, Ayin, Lamed, Yod, Yod, Nun)

What a difference a letter makes! On the surface, all that has changed in the Hebraic version of Colleen from Colin is the addition of a Y, or Yod. Surely the effect of this is simply to increase to an even higher pitch the fervor felt by Colin? However, the Kabbalah is never that straightforward—which is part of its attraction! In adding the Yod we change the total value of the name, thereby shifting the slant to the purely emotional. Colleen is entirely focused on her family life, particularly the welfare of her children. There is a danger that in placing them at the center of her life, she will be unable to let go fully when they are ready to leave the nest. The possibility of this possessive behavior is indicated by the presence of Tzaddi in the compression of her name. Colleen will be a great mom nevertheless and will spend long hours with her kids just listening to them and telling them wonderfully imaginative tales. She is equally committed to her husband, although he will have to be able to cope with her tendency toward morbidity once the children are all in bed. Of course, Colleen has dreams like everyone else, and if she has the time, she will act on them. If she does, you will find her at art galleries and museums, or even starting to paint or sculpt herself. If Colleen doesn't have children, she may follow this interest full-time and become a professional artist. The connection with children will still be there, though, and most probably will be featured in the subjects of her artwork.

THE RUNIC INTERPRETATION
ᚾᛖᛖᛚᛚᛟᚲ (Nauthiz, Ehwaz, Ehwaz, Laguz, Laguz, Othila, Kano)

Colleen must learn how to anticipate danger and not be so gullible. The double Laguz energy of flow may cause Colleen to swim into troubled waters—but she can use this flexible energy to swim right out again. She needs to surround herself with friends of good character and not waste her energy trying to rescue too many lost souls who will pull her down. Instead, she needs to build a solid foundation based on her own strengths and carve out a good, safe life for herself. With all her talents and energy, this is bound to happen. Colleen needs to understand that not everyone is as kind as she is.

Elements: Fire, air, air, water, water, earth/fire, water

THE NUMEROLOGICAL INTERPRETATION
Colleen (NV = 9, CV = 11, VV = 7, FL = 3)

Colleen is a woman who is very intuitive, compassionate, and kind. Inclusive in her love, she finds that all people are her brothers and sisters. This inner orientation may express itself outwardly in her choice of careers, which will usually involve service of some kind. Colleen is a natural teacher and caregiver, a person sensitive to the needs of others and generous in her ability to provide what is required of her. She is also gifted with a strong mind and the perceptive ability to see behind the masks that people wear and into their inner natures.

❧

Connie

DERIVATION: English, pet form of Constance. From the Latin *constantia*, meaning "constancy." Used as a given name since the 1880s.

PRINCIPAL COLORS: All but the most brilliant shades of azure

GEMSTONES AND PRECIOUS METALS: Turquoise, emeralds

BOTANICALS: Vervain, dog rose, apricots

UNIQUE SPELLINGS: Cahnni, Cahnnie, Cahnny, Conni, Conny, Kahnni, Kahnnie, Kahnny, Konni, Konnie, Konny

RELATED TO: Conseja, Consolata, Constance†, Corinne

A KABBALISTIC SYNOPSIS
כעני —KA'ANY (Kaph, Ayin, Nun, Yod)

Connie has a very simple approach to life: total self-indulgence! Her name adds up to 150, which is the number of the Devil in tarot, a figure tied very strongly to the material world. The Devil card does not translate literally to evil; rather, it relates to the indulgence of our so-called lower appetites. So we can expect to find Connie in the best restaurants and bars, dressed in the most expensive labels she can afford. However, for Connie the key form of self-indulgence is sexual pleasure, and as in everything else, she likes to be very much in control! Connie's hedonistic behavior is not mindless gluttony, though; she is a cultured and often well-read woman who is as concerned with quality as she is with quantity. Emotionally, as one would expect, she dominates utterly but can be very generous, too. She is certainly a passionate woman, and despite her tendency toward flirting, she herself is also exceedingly jealous.

THE RUNIC INTERPRETATION
ᛗᛁᚾᚾᛟᚲ (Ehwaz, Isa, Nauthiz, Nauthiz, Othila, Kano)

Connie is lucky to have the double Nauthiz energy of constraint in her name. While this may sound like a negative, it is really helpful and positive. Connie uses any delays or involuntary spare time in her life to throw in a video and work out. No date Friday night? Connie takes a class instead. Connie has a knack for turning setbacks into challenges, and once she realizes this, she gets a rhythm going. She tries harder, and she starts to notice that negative people waste her energy. Connie has learned through adversity that she doesn't have time to waste being negative. Instead, Connie turns her problems over to a higher power, and she has stories to tell about the miracles in her life.

Elements: Air, earth, fire, fire, earth/fire, water

THE NUMEROLOGICAL INTERPRETATION
Connie (NV = 6, CV = 4, VV = 2, FL = 3)

The name Connie denotes a woman who is other-oriented. Personal relationships are very important to Connie. She has a need for harmony and an urge to create a peaceful and beautiful environment. Connie enjoys beauty in all its forms and may often express herself artistically. She finds it necessary to surround herself and her loved ones with not only emotional security but firm economic security as well. The material side of life is of major interest to her. Connie will work hard to achieve success. Spending long hours at her career does not disturb her when she knows that her efforts will bring greater happiness and well-being into the lives of the people she loves.

DERIVATION: Irish, from the Gaelic
Conchobhar, the name of an Irish
king. Means both "desire" and
"lover of hounds."

PRINCIPAL COLORS: Green,
yellow, gold

GEMSTONES AND PRECIOUS
METALS: Anything white

BOTANICALS: Blackberry, juniper,
elder, hops

UNIQUE SPELLING: Conor

RELATED TO: Conan, Conlan,
Conroy

Connor

A KABBALISTIC SYNOPSIS
כנער —KNA'AR (Kaph, Nun, Ayin, Resh)

Connor likes to win—not just at sports, but in every aspect of his life. Thankfully this does not make him insufferable. In fact, Connor is usually great fun to be with, and this is indicated by the value of his name. Connor adds up to 340, and as such his name can be represented by the letters Shin and Mem, which point to Connor's enormous reserves of energy and his warmhearted nature. The tarot card the Chariot can be associated with Connor, and this card indicates triumph and success—sometimes at the expense of others. Although Connor does ride roughshod over other people's feelings, it is usually done unknowingly. Career-wise, despite his competitive nature, Connor would be very suited to any trade that involves a high degree of manual skill and craftsmanship. He has a certain amount of creative ability, although he is unlikely ever to see himself as an artist rather than an artisan. Emotionally Connor can be unpredictable. On the one hand, there is his nurturing side, but on the other, the connection of the outgoing letter Resh with the passionately sexual letter Ayin may create a danger of infidelity—unless Connor's partner knows how to keep his attention in every sense of the word.

THE RUNIC INTERPRETATION
ᚱᛟᚾᚾᛟᚲ (Raido, Othila, Nauthiz, Nauthiz, Othila, Kano)

The danger signal in this name comes from the double Nauthiz rune of constraint. If Connor encounters cruelty in his life, it might arrive in the form of unrelenting demands from his parents or from feeling unacceptable to himself and others. However, the beneficial Othila rune teaches Connor to grow stronger from the onslaughts of fate and consider the uses of adversity. It's vital for this sensitive soul to place himself in nurturing environments where love and support are freely given. Connor needs to be free to become more of who he truly is.

Elements: Water, earth/fire, fire, fire, earth/fire, water

THE NUMEROLOGICAL INTERPRETATION
Connor (NV = 7, CV = 22, VV = 3, FL = 3)

Connor has one of those rare names that possesses the master number twenty-two. As the consonant value in Connor's name, twenty-two adds ambition and drive to Connor's personality. Connor is capable of a tremendous amount of creative output in life, and will not rest until he has accomplished many of the large plans and projects that his active mind envisions. His other name numbers add an interesting combination of influences. On the one hand, Connor is quite a sociable person, much given over to good companionship, friendships, and parties. On the other, he has a certain introverted orientation that requires time alone to study and contemplate life. Connor is a complex person, one who is not easily understood by his friends and associates. His major lesson in life is learning how to use his willpower correctly.

Conrad

A Kabbalistic Synopsis
כענראד —KA'ANRAD (Kaph, Ayin, Nun, Resh, Aleph, Daleth)

If you're in the middle of a heated debate, you need Conrad, who will resolve the matter quickly and calmly. Conrad is a born arbitrator. He excels at making people realize the excessive way in which they are behaving and convincing them to discuss disagreements in a rational and constructive manner. We have the Ayin, meaning "eye," which is the focus of the first half of Conrad, where we see the practical side of Conrad's personality feeding his observations. The letter Kaph shows us his practical side as well, and suggests that in looking at the world around him he is concerned with practical issues such as housing or the economy. His reaction to such issues, though, is governed by his feelings, as shown by the letter, Nun—so his response to seeing poor housing will be an emotive one of sympathy rather than a practical idea of how it could be improved. The second section of Conrad's name reveals the emotional sensitivity he possesses. He is most sensitive to interpersonal conflicts and can notice problems when the rest of us would not realize that a conflict of emotions was going on. Conrad generates ideas that open the door to reconciliation, allowing the positive energies of the sun, shown by R (Resh), to shine through.

The Runic Interpretation
ᛞᚨᚱᚾᛟᚲ (Dagaz, Ansuz, Raido, Nauthiz, Othila, Kano)

Conrad is strong and healthy and a born optimist. He likes to be productive and usually has various income streams trickling in at various rates. He has a whole repertoire of jokes for nearly any occasion, and it's not even a problem that his jokes aren't funny; people laugh anyway because they like Conrad and they just know he's good-hearted. Although Conrad is powerful, he is gentle. Conrad has a love of nature and the wonder of a child. The Raido rune of journey helps Conrad seek harmony and communion with his higher self. Conrad has learned that we love ourselves as we love others. So he carries his harmless little joke book and spreads joy along the way.

Elements: Fire, air, water, fire, earth/fire, water

The Numerological Interpretation
Conrad (NV = 1, CV = 3, VV = 7, FL = 3)

Conrad prides himself on his academic abilities and intellectual accomplishments. He can be a virtual encyclopedia of information and is not at all reluctant to share what he knows with others. In fact, he takes great pleasure in all forms of intellectual debates and discussions. A very individualistic man with a strong philosophical side to his name, Conrad is firm in his opinions and beliefs. He may have to learn, however, to be more open and flexible to other people's points of view.

DERIVATION: English and German, an alternate spelling of the German name Konrad, meaning "brave counsel." Used in the Middle Ages to honor the tenth-century bishop of Constance in Switzerland. Regularly used in the United States in the 1930s and 1940s.

PRINCIPAL COLORS: The full range of yellow hues, gold, russet shades

GEMSTONES AND PRECIOUS METALS: Citrine, amber, topaz

BOTANICALS: Sorrel, nutmeg, thyme

UNIQUE SPELLINGS: Kahnrad, Konrad

RELATED TO: Connort, Conroy, Curt, Kurt†

Constance

DERIVATION: English and French, from the Latin *constantia*, meaning "constancy." Common in Britain in the Middle Ages, and regularly used by the Puritans in the seventeenth century. Most popular at the beginning of the twentieth century.

PRINCIPAL COLORS: Medium tones, gray, medium blue

GEMSTONES AND PRECIOUS METALS: Sapphire

BOTANICALS: Wild spinach, lesser celandine

UNIQUE SPELLINGS: Cahnstance, Kahnstance, Khanstance, Khonstance, Konstance

RELATED TO: Conniet, Constantia

A KABBALISTIC SYNOPSIS

כענסטונס —KA'ANSTVNS (Kaph, Ayin, Nun, Samech, Teth, Vau, Nun, Samech)

One standard interpretation of Constance is that of a loyal and constant individual, and the kabbalist's interpretation is a development of this theme. There are considerable Martian influences in Constance's name. By Martian we mean associated with the planet Mars, the planet of war and masculine energy. In the compression of Constance to its minimum letters having the same total value (a traditional technique of the Kabbalah), we find Shin, Kaph, and Daleth. Shin represents fire. Shin, Kaph, and Daleth relate to Aries, and have a direct connection to Mars. In addition, the value of Constance relates to various angelic beings or spirits associated with Mars, as the names of these spirits have the same value as Constance. One characteristic associated with the planet Mars that Constance has is loyalty, which is followed by constancy. But we should also expect Constance to be energetic, ambitious, and exceedingly fierce when her anger is roused. Some personalities with a heavy Mars element can be aggressive, but the central presence of Jupiter in this name's compression ensures that Constance maintains a generally optimistic view of the world and displays mainly the positive aspects of the fiery planet.

THE RUNIC INTERPRETATION

ᛇᛋᚨᚾᛏᛟᚲ (Ehwaz, Sowelu, Ansuz, Teiwaz, Sowelu, Nauthiz, Othila, Kano)

Constance is a vamp! She knows just how to talk and how to walk. Things come so easily to Constance, for she has her feet firmly planted on terra firma. She knows it's vital to be financially independent. She works hard and magnetizes opportunities. One might think she is coldhearted, but this is far from the case. Constance is patient, and she is extremely aware of all that is happening around her. She needs to be encouraged to be a bit more humble and to rest now and then . . . alone.

Elements: Air, air, air, air, air, fire, earth/fire, water

THE NUMEROLOGICAL INTERPRETATION

Constance (NV = 4, CV = 1, VV = 3, FL = 3)

Active, ambitious, and assertive are but three adjectives to describe the qualities in this name. Others include communicative, curious, and cultured. Constance is a woman who gives her all to the fulfillment of her dreams and visions. She is aware that it is only through personal perseverance that she may achieve her aims—and she is willing to pay the price to do so. In fact, she enjoys her work and takes pleasure in seeing that her efforts pay off in terms of material comforts and success. An adventurous person, Constance will seek out pastimes that are both educational and challenging.

Cooper

DERIVATION: Of Latin and Saxon origin. Means "barrel" or "cask maker."

PRINCIPAL COLORS: The darker shades of pink, crimson, and red

GEMSTONES AND PRECIOUS METALS: Rubies, garnets

BOTANICALS: Garlic, onion, nettle, broom

UNIQUE SPELLINGS: Cuper, Kooper, Kuper

RELATED TO: Coop, Coops, Coopy

A KABBALISTIC SYNOPSIS
כעפ —KA'APH (Kaph, Ayin, Peh)

If you settle down to chat with Cooper for an hour, you may well find that you don't get anything done for the rest of the day; this guy will talk forever if you let him! The final letter in Cooper's name means "mouth" in Hebrew, and in addition, the overall value of his name can also be associated with this letter, so conversation pretty much rules Cooper's world. This is not a bad thing, since there are many careers that need someone who can communicate confidently. Cooper would do very well in the public relations or marketing world, where such skills are really appreciated. As Cooper is a very thoughtful individual, it is often his wide-ranging ideas that he likes to get across to people. At parties Cooper can always be relied upon to make sure that everyone is enjoying themselves, and he loves to socialize as much as possible. Cooper is a very physical person and values his fitness almost as much as he values his thoughts. He can often be seen working out in the gym or on the track. His one vice is that he can tend toward vanity. The central letter in his name is Ayin, which indicates the strong pull of physical desire in his life, but as a central letter Ayin can sometimes suggest that this desire is somewhat self-directed.

THE RUNIC INTERPRETATION
ᚱᛗᛈᛟᚲ (Raido, Ehwaz, Perth, Othila, Kano)

Benefits and the acquisition of property bless Cooper's name. Cooper was born with not only a silver spoon in his mouth but also the knife and fork! Opportunities come along, and Cooper is very happy in the living room counting all his money while the queen is in the parlor eating tea and honey. Mystery is a vital part of this name, and Cooper may need to dig deep into his soul in order to meet the requirements of living an authentic and satisfying life. Experiencing a kind of psychic death is very likely for Cooper in the first years of his life. With this trauma new energy is released, and Cooper moves and begins a life oriented toward service, love, and fulfillment.

Elements: Water, air, water, earth/fire, water

THE NUMEROLOGICAL INTERPRETATION
Cooper (NV = 9, CV = 1, VV = 8, FL = 3)

Cooper is not afraid to be an individual. He has a very definite agenda, and at the top of his list are the words "I seek to know myself." Cooper is therefore an adventurous person, one who is very much the head of his committee of one. This does not mean that he is unsociable. Cooper likes people, but they have to have some depth and substance in order for him to form a friendship with them. Although Cooper has many idealistic plans, he is very much a practical person at heart. Finances mean a lot to him, and he is not apt to engage in a project unless he is sure of its monetary returns. Proper care and respect of his physical body are also priorities for him.

DERIVATION: English, created by
James Fenimore Cooper in *The
Last of the Mohicans* (1826).
Possibly from the Greek *kore*,
meaning "maiden." In Greek
mythology, a nickname of
Persephone, the goddess of the
underworld. Popular since the
nineteenth century.

PRINCIPAL COLORS: All yellows,
from the palest to the deepest
and most brilliant

GEMSTONES AND PRECIOUS
METALS: Yellow diamonds, topaz,
any other yellow stone

BOTANICALS: Borage, chamomile,
lavender

UNIQUE SPELLINGS: Chora,
Chorah, Corah, Khora, Khorah,
Kora, Korah

RELATED TO: Corabella,
Corabelle, Corable, Coral,
Coralie, Corey†, Cori, Corie,
Corine, Corinna, Correen,
Corrinne, Kora, Korabell, Korina,
Korinne, Koryne, Koryssa

Cora

A KABBALISTIC SYNOPSIS
כערא —KA'ARA (Kaph, Ayin, Resh, Aleph)

Cora will not be seen surfing the Web. She isn't even all that keen on television; she would rather be active. Women with this name will be at their happiest when working with their hands. The name is ruled by K, or Kaph, meaning "hand," immediately followed by Ayin, meaning "eye." Cora loves activities that require attention to detail and a dexterous touch. She will enjoy a range of pastimes, from carpentry to gardening to sculpture. With this hands-on earthy outlook one may suspect a contented and unambitious nature—far from it! There are definite leadership qualities in this name, which reduces to four—the number of the Emperor in the tarot, as well as the number of the elements. If Cora starts a carpentry business, you can guarantee that she'll end up with a string of stores. This combination of manual skills, sensitivity to detail, and intense energy makes an intriguing mix, and as a lover—wow!

THE RUNIC INTERPRETATION
ᚨᚱᛟᚲ (Ansuz, Raido, Othila, Kano)

Make no mistake: Cora may have started out in life miserable and confused, but she is determined to change, and she makes her own luck. The Othila rune of separation made Cora feel isolated and lonely growing up. Kano, the rune of opening, taught her to discard worn-out relationships and people. Cora learned that she never found a job she could keep for more than a few months because she didn't feel she deserved to succeed; she sabotaged her success. Ansuz, the rune of signals, helped Cora rely on her intuition to find love in herself and attract wonderful friends and lovers. The Raido rune carries Cora along on her healing journey to enjoy new experiences and satisfaction. Cora redesigns her life, and it is her masterpiece.

Elements: Air, water, earth/fire, water

THE NUMEROLOGICAL INTERPRETATION
Cora (NV = 1, CV = 3, VV = 7, FL = 3)

The name Cora contains numbers that indicate a person who is not afraid to express herself. In fact, Cora has little choice in the matter! A strong individual with very firm opinions about life, Cora will not compromise herself. She is a person of true integrity and an honest, forthright disposition. Her opinions are not superficial. She has taken the time to educate herself and is constantly seeking more information about life. Self-development is very important to her, and she will not rest until she knows that she has done her very best in every situation.

Corey

A Kabbalistic Synopsis
כערי —KA'ARY (Kaph, Ayin, Resh, Yod)

Things happen when Corey is around, and they don't usually take long! Corey adds up to three hundred, and three is the number of reproduction. The multiplication by a hundred suggests an incredibly fertile nature and also points to the fact that the creativity here revealed is concerned with the material rather than the imaginative or abstract realm. In other words, Corey likes to create things that work—such as new and innovative gadgets—rather than ideas or two-dimensional pieces of art. Three hundred is also the value of the letter Shin, which indicates a considerable reserve of energy. This energy is associated with the power of judgment and rationality, so we can expect Corey's creations to stem from plenty of careful analytical planning. Corey is a very creative person who ideally likes to see his or her own visions come to fruition rather than simply applying his or her skills to the ideas of others. An ideal career for Corey would be something requiring imagination, such as an architect or landscaper. In relationships Corey needs to learn to temper his or her judgmental ways, as patterns cannot be remolded and shaped according to his or her grand design in the same way that a building can!

The Runic Interpretation
ᛇᛗᚱᛟ< (Eihwaz, Ehwaz, Raido, Othila, Kano)

Corey is a high-strung creative type. He or she has problems with perfectionism and procrastination but can call on the Eihwaz rune energy in his or her name to surround himself or herself with supportive people who will do what they can to market his or her work and keep contracts and assignments pouring in while Corey sticks to artistic pursuits. The Eihwaz rune will also help Corey to know his or her strengths and weaknesses, and Corey may find that it's better to do one thing well than to scatter his or her forces. Corey listens to the voice of inspiration, and this is the main reason Corey is so successful and productive. Coreys will go far in life and help thousands with their perceptive eyes.

Elements: Earth/fire, air, water, earth/fire, water

The Numerological Interpretation
Corey (NV = 3, CV = 3, VV = 9, FL = 3)

Expressive is the key word in Corey's name: expressive in his or her emotions and the way he or she communicates them to others, expressive in his or her urge to be creative. Corey is quite a restless person. His or her mind is very alive and is constantly at work. One thing that Corey has to cultivate is an inner sense of peace and stillness. The mind should not be Corey's master; he or she must learn how to master it. Once Corey realizes how to take charge of his or her mind, he or she will find that the creative quality contained within will grow and develop even further.

DERIVATION: Originally an Irish surname, used as a given name since the 1960s. Once a male name, now also used for females.

PRINCIPAL COLORS: All purple hues, from pale violet to deep maroon

GEMSTONES AND PRECIOUS METALS: Garnets

BOTANICALS: Apple, bilberry, lungwort

UNIQUE SPELLINGS: Cori, Correy, Corrie, Corry, Corrye, Cory, Kori, Korrey, Korrie, Korry, Kory

RELATED TO: Cora†, Coralie, Coreienne, Corin, Corina, Corine, Corinn, Corinna, Corinne, Correen, Corrin, Corrina, Corrine, Corrinna, Corrinne, Cory Anne, Cory Lee, Korain, Koreen, Korin, Korrina

DERIVATION: English, both
masculine and feminine. Originally
a Norman surname from the part
of northern France known as
Courtenay. Used as a given name
partly based on the nickname
court nez, from the Old French for
"short nose."

PRINCIPAL COLORS: The full
spectrum of medium tones, also
very bright hues

GEMSTONES AND PRECIOUS
METALS: Sapphires

BOTANICALS: Celandine, sage

UNIQUE SPELLINGS: Corteney,
Corteni, Cortenie, Corteny,
Cortnay, Cortney, Courtenay,
Courteni, Courtenie, Courteny,
Korteni, Kortenie, Korteny,
Kortnay, Kortney, Kourtenay,
Kourteni, Kourtenie, Kourteny

RELATED TO: Coreyt, Cori,
Correy, Corrie, Corry, Corrye,
Cory, Kori, Korrey, Korrie, Korry,
Kory

Courtney

A KABBALISTIC SYNOPSIS
כערטני —KA'ARTNY (Kaph, Ayin, Resh, Teth, Nun, Yod)

As with all names beginning with a combination of Kaph and Ayin, Courtney has a personality in which the powers of observation and reflection are inextricably linked with the desire to make or create. She will probably use this inclination to forge a career in the arts or in education, where her intuition will help her guide her students. In Courtney's case there are some powerful astrological influences from Scorpio and Leo that make her work intensely and with great passion. She will have little time or need for relationships; her work is her life. The negative, somewhat morbid aspects of N, or Nun, in her name combine with the striking force of the serpent of T, or Teth; this may lead Courtney into self-doubt about the validity of her work, so we can expect Courtney to be ruthless in the destruction of any work that does not meet up to her exacting standards. This negativity can become quite self-destructive if not checked. The final Yod is an encouraging sign of positive energy breaking through, but what Courtney really needs, although she won't admit it, is a supportive partner.

THE RUNIC INTERPRETATION
ᛇᛗᚻᛏᚱᚾᛟᚲ (Eihwaz, Ehwaz, Nauthiz, Teiwaz, Raido, Uruz, Othila, Kano)

Courtney is young when she's old and old when she's young. Doors swing wide for Courtney in her late teens, and she exerts her independence with a confidence seldom seen in one so young. The Uruz energy of strength affords Courtney the chance of experiencing many careers in one lifetime. Courtney is quick, creative, and versatile. She enjoys learning and has friends in many parts of the world. She will experience a great deal of change, and change is rarely easy, even for one as strong as Courtney. Change always involves surrender and a passage through the darkness of the unknown. Courtney uses her Teiwaz energy of the warrior to withstand the stress of these maturing passages.

Elements: Earth/fire, air, fire, air, water, earth, earth/fire, water

THE NUMEROLOGICAL INTERPRETATION
Courtney (NV = 4, CV = 1, VV = 3, FL = 3)

An independent attitude is very important for Courtney. She needs to have her own way and not be overly dependent on others. This is a person who can be very assertive and demanding. A perfectionist by nature, Courtney wants to achieve the very best that life has to offer. She is determined and strong by nature, and makes a very loyal friend. Courtney has a need for material security and its comforts. She is generally liked and appreciated for her original wit and intelligent spirit.

Craig

DERIVATION: Scottish and English, from the Gaelic *craeg* or Welsh *craig*, meaning "rock." Originally a surname, first used as a given name in the 1940s. Became immediately popular and spread to English-speaking countries.

PRINCIPAL COLORS: Creamy white, the full range of greens

GEMSTONES AND PRECIOUS METALS: Cat's-eye, moonstones, white pearls

BOTANICALS: Cabbage, chicory, plantain

UNIQUE SPELLINGS: Craigg, Creg, Cregg, Kraig, Kraigg, Kreg, Kregg

RELATED TO: Greg†, Gregg

A KABBALISTIC SYNOPSIS
כראיג —KRAYG (Kaph, Resh, Aleph, Yod, Gimel)

Craig is quite a surprising character. On the surface he seems a solitary figure, reluctant to engage in conversation and likely to spend his weekends tucked away on his own. Yet despite the value of his name equating him with the Hermit from the tarot, he can be highly sociable in the right circumstances. Look at the individual letters of his name and place them on their appropriate paths on the Tree of Life; they reveal that his personality is born in the side known as the Pillar of Severity but is always moving toward the side known as the Pillar of Mercy. Craig is a quiet and practical man who is likely to work in some way with transport, very possibly with car maintenance and repair. Inside this quiet individual is a chatty and warm personality, which the right person will have no trouble finding.

THE RUNIC INTERPRETATION
ᚷᛁᚨᚱᚲ (Gebo, Isa, Ansuz, Raido, Kano)

Craig has the powerful Gebo rune of partnership placed prominently in his name. Gebo implies freedom and wholeness, and may indicate that Craig is quite brilliant at timing his financial moves and positioning himself to rise to power. Craig isn't the most honest man you'll ever meet, though, and he knows how to mold the truth to whatever suits him at the moment; he could enjoy a life in politics. He is dramatic and bold, and given to a kind of intensity that few women can resist. Craig needs to learn the lessons of patience, simplicity, modesty, and sincerity—but he will not learn these lessons easily as long as doing it his way continues to make him powerful.

Elements: Water, earth, air, water, water

THE NUMEROLOGICAL INTERPRETATION
Craig (NV = 2, CV = 1, VV = 1, FL = 3)

Craig is ready to overcome any and all of the obstacles he faces in life. Given the chance, he will rise to the top—and he often creates that chance himself. Not open to compromises of any sort, Craig is his own person. Yet he has a strong romantic nature and a profound need for partnership. Because partnership requires sharing, a real sharing of oneself, many of Craig's life lessons revolve around the issue of how he integrates his strong sense of himself within the structure of his personal relationships.

Crystal

DERIVATION: English, from the common word *crystal*. Created in the nineteenth century, along with several other gemstone names. From the Greek *krystallos*, meaning "ice." Also a Scottish pet form of Christopher.

PRINCIPAL COLORS: Deep blue, purple, and gray; black

GEMSTONES AND PRECIOUS METALS: Black pearls, black diamonds, any other dark stones

BOTANICALS: Shepherd's purse, pilewort, gravel root

UNIQUE SPELLINGS: Christal, Christle, Chrystal, Chrystle, Cristal, Cristol, Crystle, Khristal, Khristle, Khrystal, Khrystle, Kristal, Kristol, Krystal, Krystle

RELATED TO: Christie, Christy, Chrystalla, Kristie, Kristy

A KABBALISTIC SYNOPSIS
כריסטל —KRYSTL (Kaph, Resh, Yod, Samech, Teth, Lamed)

Crystal may have a preoccupation with the religious or spiritual side of life, although she may be drawn more to alternative spirituality. The total value of Crystal is 329. The most significant aspect of this number is its function as a multiple of seven, indicating that Crystal will have a higher-than-average chance of achieving her goals in life. She's a good woman to hook up with if your own earning power is on the slim side, because looking at the multiplier used to arrive at 329, we find that it is forty-seven—a combination of material concerns and success again! In Crystal we have a woman whose spirituality does not interfere with her ability to make money, and it may even be that her beliefs form the basis of her business. The four and the seven produce eleven, which is the number of magic and connects back to the association with ancient religious beliefs that is suggested by the actual letters in her name. Of course, there are plenty of Crystals out there with absolutely no interest in the religious whatsoever; are they perhaps the holders of the wrong name? Not at all. In this Crystal's case we are looking at one strong-minded woman who has her principles or business ethics but is happy to bend or break them for the right deal. Even if Crystal does fit the religious mold, don't expect her to be all sackcloth and ashes; the number eleven has very strong sexual connotations, as it represents two individuals being joined. And if you are ever thus joined with Crystal, it really will be a "magical" experience!

THE RUNIC INTERPRETATION
ᛚᚨᛏᛋᛇᚱᚲ (Laguz, Ansuz, Teiwaz, Sowelu, Eihwaz, Raido, Kano)

Crystal is well named because her thoughts are clear and her speech is articulate. Crystal values honesty and integrity, and goes out of her way to read up on body language and vocal qualities that reveal a liar. Raido, the rune of good communication, combined with Isa for standstill, enhances Crystal's perceptive gifts. The warrior Teiwaz energy, combined with Ansuz for intuition, means Crystal would enjoy a career in forensic criminology, psychiatry, or military intelligence. She'd also be a good teacher or counselor because she has the Laguz rune of flexibility to give her an easy rapport with people. Kano for opening and Sowelu for wholeness add to Crystal's sparkling personality. Crystal is confident and welcomes new opportunities. She attends sweat lodges and near-death-experience groups, and might find a partner there who is "dying" to meet her!

Elements: Water, air, air, air, earth/fire, water, water

THE NUMEROLOGICAL INTERPRETATION
Crystal (NV = 8, CV = 9, VV = 8, FL = 3)

Crystal may easily find herself at home in the business world, as this is a name that points to a feeling of comfort with material things. Crystal is very much in her own element when she holds an executive role, as she is not averse to the responsibilities that such a position brings. Crystal needs to be recognized for what she accomplishes, and enjoys whatever level of success she manages to achieve. This name also reveals a humanitarian side, and Crystal can be counted on to lend her support to the causes in which she believes.

Curtis

A KABBALISTIC SYNOPSIS
כורטיס —KVRTYS (Kaph, Vau, Resh, Teth, Yod, Samech)

There are plenty of unscrupulous people out there just waiting for Curtis to come along so they can exploit his amiable and trusting nature. One equivalent to Curtis is the Hebrew שה, meaning "lamb." Curtis exhibits all the qualities one would expect from such an association: He is eager to try out new activities; is friendly, open, energetic, and athletic, but above all, innocent and one could even say gullible. Luckily for Curtis there are plenty of people who will be charmed by his winning ways. As his friends they will ensure that he steers clear of any trouble. Yet Curtis is by no means weak as a person. Anyone who has seen lambs at play will testify to their boisterous manner, and Curtis can be equally vigorous when he feels attacked. In these situations he can often defuse tension with his quick wit and natural flair for finding the comic in any event.

THE RUNIC INTERPRETATION
ᛋᛁᛏᚱᚢᚲ (Sowelu, Isa, Teiwaz, Raido, Uruz, Kano)

Curtis has the rune Sowelu, meaning "wholeness," at the beginning of his name. Curtis loves giant sequoias and tall buildings because they're the only things that make him feel small. And Sowelu helps Curtis see the big picture; in fact, he thinks big so much that when you meet him he may even *seem* tall! The Teiwaz warrior energy, combined with Uruz for strength, compels Curtis to put large deals together and head straight into global problems like pestilence and weather disaster detection techniques. With Isa for standstill, Curtis is capable of deep concentration and brilliant insights. Raido, the rune of good communication, could mean Curtis has his own news show or makes informative film documentaries. Curtis amasses a large fortune and creates wonderful philanthropic projects.

Elements: Air, earth, air, water, earth, water

THE NUMEROLOGICAL INTERPRETATION
Curtis (NV = 9, CV = 6, VV = 3, FL = 3)

Curtis is a very idealistic name and gives a person a strong sensitivity to others. It is a name that inspires one's poetic and romantic tendencies. When Curtis is in an intimate relationship, he feels he has full reign to express the depth and beauty of the love he carries. Yet he has to be careful not to fall in love with love. Curtis is also capable of sharing his love impersonally; in this respect, he is charitable and giving, ever ready to be of help. He should regularly take some time by himself in order to recoup his energy and reconnect with himself.

DERIVATION: English, from the French *curteis*, meaning "courteous." Originally a surname, it has been commonly used as a given name since the early nineteenth century. Popular in the United States since the 1950s.

PRINCIPAL COLORS: The full gamut of reddish hues, particularly the deepest and richest

GEMSTONES AND PRECIOUS METALS: Deep red garnets and bloodstones

BOTANICALS: Onion, nettle, garlic

UNIQUE SPELLINGS: Curtiss, Kertis, Kertiss, Kurtis, Kurtiss

RELATED TO: Curt, Kurt†

Cynthia

DERIVATION: English, from the Greek *kynthia*, a name of the moon goddess Artemis, who was supposedly born on Mount Kynthos on the island of Delos. Appeared in the great literature of the seventeenth century, including the works of Jonson, Raleigh, and Spenser. Commonly used in the nineteenth century as a slave name. Especially popular in the United States during the 1950s.

PRINCIPAL COLORS: Dark shades of purple and azure

GEMSTONES AND PRECIOUS METALS: Carbuncles, rubies, sapphires

BOTANICALS: Angelica, pilewort, and marsh mallow

UNIQUE SPELLINGS: Cinthea, Cinthia, Cynthea, Cynthya, Sinthia, Synthea, Synthia

RELATED TO: Cindi, Cindie, Cindy†, Cyndi, Cyndie, Cyndy, Hyacinth, Lucinda

A KABBALISTIC SYNOPSIS
סינתי —SYNThYA (Samech, Yod, Nun, Tau; Yod, Aleph)

Cynthia is dominant and authoritative. She manages both her employees and her children with a firm hand, and all of them had better work their buns off—or they'll answer to her. They will also learn that the vast majority of the time Cynthia is right, since her strength is born from a wide and varied experience of life. The initial Samech, meaning "prop," tells us that Cynthia uses her past as a resource to guide her decisions in the present. She effectively sacrifices her midlife—usually the time between thirty and fifty years old—to her family, as shown by the Th, or Tau. However, it is this self-sacrifice that gives her immense amounts of energy for the future and fuels her mind with ideas and plans for when her brood finally flees the nest. If Cynthia hasn't had a family, she will probably retire early, having had a very successful, if somewhat stormy, career. Cynthia is a very cultured woman and may well spend her free time and her retirement traveling. In fact, a footloose Cynthia may even settle in some cultural center like Florence, Rome, or Paris.

THE RUNIC INTERPRETATION
ᚨᛁᚦᚾᛇᛋ (Ansuz, Isa, Thurisaz, Nauthiz, Eihwaz, Sowelu)

The rune Thurisaz, or "gateway," which appears in Cynthia's name, is the door to subconscious motives. And Cynthia knows that one of the best feelings in the world is "finally understanding." She thinks a Ph.D. after her name has more appeal than an Mrs. before it. This is because romance is so illogical, and Cynthia enjoys having her life in order. She is conscientious about having emergency funds, various insurance policies, and whatever else her clearheaded mind tells her to do to keep troubles at bay. Money is important to Cynthia, and she amasses surprising wealth in her lifetime. She enjoys family reunions and outdoor clubs, and she leads a clean and sober life.

Elements: Air, earth, fire, fire, earth/fire, air

THE NUMEROLOGICAL INTERPRETATION
Cynthia (NV = 8, CV = 9, VV = 8, FL = 3)

There is within this name a sense of power and control that radiates into the environment. Cynthia takes charge and gets things done. She is considered very dependable and reliable by her friends and coworkers. Single-minded and focused, Cynthia finds that her goals and reputation are very important to her. She will arrive at an appointment when she says she will and get done what must be done. There is enough personal creative ability in her name to enable her to finalize all her plans and projects. Cynthia has to take care at times not to lose her sense of compassion and to learn to work in ways that support mutual achievements.

Daisy

A KABBALISTIC SYNOPSIS
דאיסי —DAYSY (Daleth, Aleph, Yod, Samech, Yod)

Daisy has a classic Aries temperament; her name can be compressed to the letters Peh and Heh, meaning Mars and Aries, respectively. As an Arian character, Daisy has vast amounts of enthusiasm for any number of different pastimes, careers, and friends but lacks the ability to stick to anything for a considerable length of time. If Daisy is born under Pisces or Scorpio, the effects of these signs will cancel out the minimal attention span possessed by the typical Aries. The individual letters of Daisy's name also emphasize the Aries influence, since as soon as the initial door is opened, there follow a series of energetic letters, punctuated only by the S, or Samech, which represents her need to have some form of secure base (probably her partner or possibly the parental home). The primary aspect of Daisy's nature is her love of talking, from chatting to serious debates.

THE RUNIC INTERPRETATION
ᛈᛋᛁᚨᛞ (Eihwaz, Sowelu, Isa, Ansuz, Dagaz)

The Isa image of her name requires Daisy to experience change, which may cause her to feel an emptiness for a while. Although gentle and kindhearted, Daisy may not be able to rely on the support of her friends. She can use the Isa energy to draw on her inner strengths and to help her move through this difficult time. Daisy finds new opportunities for learning, and betterment comes to her once she grows and changes to survive. And she does! In the end, Daisy emerges with a deep sense of self-reliance and comfort. When the ebbs and flows of life bring her a bump in the road, she is better equipped to navigate the passage because she understands that accepting change is the best strategy.

Elements: Earth/fire, air, earth, air, fire

THE NUMEROLOGICAL INTERPRETATION
Daisy (NV = 4, CV = 5, VV = 8, FL = 4)

No doubt about it: Daisy means *business*. This name is dominated by the numbers four and eight, and indicates a very practical woman. Daisy feels that money, material possessions, and social position are the ways to achieve the personal freedom that is so important to her. She is a hardworking and ambitious individual who may be overly concerned with material success. Dependable, productive, and reliable, Daisy bears a name that connotes loyalty and steadfastness.

DERIVATION: English, from the name of the flower. First appeared as a name in the mid-1800s, and was sometimes used as a pet name for Margaret, since *marguerite* is the French word for "daisy."

PRINCIPAL COLORS: Moderate shades of any color

GEMSTONES AND PRECIOUS METALS: Sapphires

BOTANICALS: Sage, wild spinach, wintergreen

UNIQUE SPELLINGS: Daisey, Daisie, Daizy, Dasey, Dasi, Dasie, Dasy, Daysie, Daysy

RELATED TO: Dahlia, Daia, Dasia

"She was a timid, sensitive girl, looking like her name—Daisy-ish industrious and thorough in her studies: her teachers thought her one of the best students they had ever known. She had very little fire, or denial in her; she responded dutifully to instructions; she gave back what had been given to her. She played the piano without any passionate feeling for the music; but she rendered it honestly with a beautiful rippling touch. And she practised hours at a time."

—FROM *LOOK HOMEWARD, ANGEL* BY THOMAS WOLFE

DERIVATION: English, originally a surname referring to someone who lived near a valley. In the twentieth century, it has become more common as a first name, and is used for both males and females.

PRINCIPAL COLORS: The full spectrum of medium tones

GEMSTONES AND PRECIOUS METALS: Palest to richest sapphire

BOTANICALS:: Wild spinach, Iceland moss, lesser celandine

UNIQUE SPELLINGS: Dail, Daile, Dayl, Dayle

RELATED TO: Dahlia, Daley, Dalia, Daly

〜

"Take a chance! All life is a chance. The man who goes farthest is generally the one who is willing to do and dare."

—DALE CARNEGIE (AUTHOR, PUBLIC SPEAKING INSTRUCTOR)

Dale

A KABBALISTIC SYNOPSIS
דאיל —DAYL (Daleth, Aleph, Yod, Lamed)

Dale has an extremely tempestuous, deceptive nature. He or she can be smiling sweetly one minute, and in an absolute fury the next. Dale's temperamental personality is evidenced by the balance of fire and water energies in this name, creating an explosive mixture. This mix is also positive in that it creates interesting and novel ideas that only Dale would imagine. Dale will make a good ideas person, not just because of the conflicting energies in this name but thanks to the Yod-Lamed combination, which indicates a powerful driving force within Dale and ensures a constant flow of new projects. Indeed, it may well be this intense energy that lies behind his or her frequent outbursts!

THE RUNIC INTERPRETATION
ᛖᛚᚨᛞ (Ehwaz, Laguz, Ansuz, Dagaz)

Dale is a tactful person. Whether a male or female name, the interpretation remains the same. Rather than confront anyone directly, Dale prefers to invite the individual to explain his or her point of view. Dale uses few words and remembers what he hears. People are impressed by Dale's memory and often believe him to be keenly intelligent; Dale notices this and finds it amusing. Dale makes good decisions not because of brilliance, necessarily, but because he meditates and the guidance received is solid and helpful. Dale's patient and tactful nature afford him the skills to negotiate and intervene in crisis situations with finesse and wisdom.

Elements: Air, water, air, fire

THE NUMEROLOGICAL INTERPRETATION
Dale (NV = 4, CV = 7, VV = 6, FL = 4)

Deep within Dale is the urge for harmony and peace. She (or in the case of a male, he) will often express herself through the arts, and takes great pleasure in using her talents and abilities to beautify her environment. Dale is a name that signifies a person of profound caring. She may, however, place too much emphasis on the material side of life and worry unnecessarily about her economic state. The lessons Dale is learning in life have to do with organizing herself and making a friend of time. She has enough creative energy to bring forth into her physical reality the beauty she contains within.

〜

Damien

A Kabbalistic Synopsis
דאמיאן —DAMYAN (Daleth, Aleph, Mem, Yod, Aleph, Nun)

Forget every *Omen* film you have seen: Damien bears absolutely no relation to his devilish namesake. Far from possessing the cold self-confidence expressed by the Antichrist child of film fame, Damien is on the whole a nervous man who is not at all comfortable with power. Damien's name adds up to 756, which contains the letter N, or Nun, in both of its possible numerations. Therefore Damien is a high-strung and deeply emotional individual. Due to his nervous and anxious character, he tends to live a much richer imaginative life than his day-to-day existence might suggest. The combination of solitude and heightened emotional sensitivity, along with an advanced imagination, makes Damien an ideal candidate for the arts, particularly poetry. But remember that each person reacts in many ways to their given nature. In Damien's case it may be that as a defense against his sensitive nature, he consciously portrays a very masculine, almost aggressive side of himself, and if he does write poetry, this will show in his work.

The Runic Interpretation
ᚾᛖᛁᛗᚨᛞ (Nauthiz, Ehwaz, Isa, Mannaz, Ansuz, Dagaz)

Damien has a right-brained view of the world. He is blessed with Mannaz energy, which encourages playfulness and joy as well as focused work. Mannaz allows us to live in the present and enjoy process. While lack of direction is a challenge for Damien, Mannaz energy is available to help him on his way. It may not matter that Damien has difficulty focusing on goals; if he enjoys his work, his mind will come up with the best direction for the next cycle in his long and fruitful life. Travel and higher education are vehicles Damien uses to explore the many possibilities open to him.

Elements: Fire, air, earth, air, air, fire

The Numerological Interpretation
Damien (NV = 1, CV = 4, VV = 6, FL = 4)

Damien is a name that encourages a person to be innovative and creative in his particular line of endeavor. It gives its bearer the courage and forthright determination needed to succeed. Damien is not fond of taking orders from other people, and lessons of cooperation will be part of his encounters in his personal and professional relationships. He has great potential to be successful on the material plane, as he tends to persevere no matter what opposition he may meet along his life path.

DERIVATION: French form of Damian, initially from the Greek name Damianos. Used in the Middle Ages as a church name, and started being used by the general public in the 1950s.

PRINCIPAL COLORS: The full range of yellow hues

GEMSTONES AND PRECIOUS METALS: Citrine, amber, any yellow stones

BOTANICALS: Chamomile, eyebright, Saint-John's-wort

UNIQUE SPELLINGS: Daemian, Daemien, Damean, Dameon, Damian, Damion, Daymian, Daymien

RELATED TO: Damiano, Damiao, Damio, Damont, Demyan

Damon

DERIVATION: English, short form of Damian, which is from the Greek name Damianos, meaning "to tame." The Latinate form, Damianus, is the name of a fifth-century saint who became the patron of physicians. Popular since the 1950s.

PRINCIPAL COLORS: Cream, the palest to the richest shades of green.

GEMSTONES AND PRECIOUS METALS: Jade, moonstones, pearls

BOTANICALS: Cabbage, lettuce, plantain

UNIQUE SPELLINGS: Daeman, Daemen, Dacmin, Daemon, Daemyn, Daman, Damen, Damin, Damyn, Dayman, Daymen, Daymin, Daymon, Daymyn

RELATED TO: Damian, Damiano, Damianos, Damient, Demion

❧

"The race is not always to the swift, nor the battle to the strong—but that's the way to bet."
—DAMON RUNYON (AUTHOR)

A KABBALISTIC SYNOPSIS
דאמון —DAMVN (Daleth, Aleph, Mem, Vau, Nun)

In Damon, both M (or Mem) and N (or Nun) are present, each of which indicates a primacy of emotional concerns. While Mem is suggestive of the womb and therefore positive, Nun is connected to Scorpio and has darker, sometimes morbid, overtones. These two aspects of the emotional state are separated by Vau, symbolic of choosing. Damon has a fairly constant struggle on his hands to keep his feelings in check, and when he fails, he has a tendency to sink into a depressive state. Damon adds to thirteen, the number of change, and it is likely that constant change of home or work enables him to avoid the sort of strong emotional commitments that inevitably get him down. The final resolution of Damon's situation is unclear from his name alone. Whether he is basically content or in a state of depression ultimately depends on his own choice, as indicated by the Vau.

THE RUNIC INTERPRETATION
ᚾᛟᛗᚨᛞ (Nauthiz, Othila, Mannaz, Ansuz, Dagaz)

Though Damon is a derivative of the English Damian, Damon substitutes the Othila energy for Damien's Isa and Ehwaz energy. This creates quite a different energy pattern. While Ehwaz and Isa encourage introspection and meditation, Othila is the rune of separation. Damon will have many material possessions, but at some point in his life, he will face separation and be forced to relinquish something of great importance. This is not an easy test. Damon must be honest and see the situation clearly and with humility. Once he accomplishes this, he comes to know that material objects don't matter and love is really all there is. He must overcome his anger and replace rage with feelings of love and union in order to free his soul.

Elements: Fire, earth/fire, air, air, fire

THE NUMEROLOGICAL INTERPRETATION
Damon (NV = 11, CV = 4, VV = 7, FL = 4)

An unusual man with a strong intuitive sense and a deeply penetrating mind, Damon brings insight and vision into all his relationships. This is a person who likes to go his own way in life and does not easily conform to established codes of behavior. His material ambitions are strong, and he will create his own methods, techniques, and processes in order to accomplish his goals. With a name that focuses on the reflective and contemplative sides to life, Damon has a strong urge to develop a deeper understanding of both himself and others. In this respect, he makes a fascinating friend or partner.

❧

Dan

A KABBALISTIC SYNOPSIS
דאן —DAN (Daleth, Aleph, Nun)

Dan's life is ruled by his emotions, as revealed by the letter N (or Nun), but his is not a depressive personality, thanks to the weight of other factors in his name. Dan is actually a jovial guy who is likely to wonder why people get so depressed when "in a hundred years, no one will care!" Dan is driven by feelings of oneness with his family and, to a lesser degree, his community. This is not a profound or philosophical emotion, but a basic gut feeling of belonging that makes Dan feel good and able to tolerate the problems life brings him without falling into despair. It is the numerical value of Dan's name that has this effect; his name totals fifty-five, a number with occult significance. It has the effect of "grounding" Dan and putting him in touch with the general balance of the world in which he lives.

THE RUNIC INTERPRETATION
ᚾᚨᛞ (Nauthiz, Ansuz, Dagaz)

Dan likes to work with his hands. He can't understand why anyone would want to work indoors. He likes carpentry, painting, and jobs that let him see the splendor of the natural world. Dan likes to sing and tell jokes. He's easily moved to tears when he sees a child in a wheelchair, unable to run and play. Dan does a lot for charities and is good at organizing food distribution and clothing drives. The Dagaz energy in Dan's name gives him a sense of abundance that permeates his very being. People like to be with Dan because he infects them with childlike wonder and faith.

Elements: Fire, air, fire

THE NUMEROLOGICAL INTERPRETATION
Dan (NV = 1, CV = 9, VV = 1, FL = 4)

Dan works very well by himself. He has a strong sense of his own individuality and uses it most productively. He is at his best when he is given a free hand to express his creativity. Dan is a name that bestows the urge to win. Whatever he sets out to accomplish, he will do his utmost to achieve. This is not a superficial person with a vast array of plans; Dan likes to take things one at a time, succeeding step by step as he climbs his personal mountain.

DERIVATION: Short form of Daniel, a Hebrew name meaning "God is my judge." In the Bible, Dan is the name of one of Jacob's twelve sons, whereas Daniel is the name of an Israelite prophet who escapes from a lion's den with the help of God. Today Dan is more commonly found as a nickname for Daniel but is sometimes an independent given name as well.

PRINCIPAL COLORS: Bronze, gold, any yellow tone

GEMSTONES: Amber, topaz, yellow diamonds

HERBS: Borage, lavender, nutmeg, sorrel

UNIQUE SPELLINGS: Dann, Danne, Dayn

RELATED TO: Danek, Danel, Danial, Danielt, Daniele, Danilo, Danny†

DERIVATION: English, a feminine
version of Dan or Daniel.
Originally used as a male first
name, but in the United States
it has consistently been more
common for girls. In Britain Dana
is a fairly common male name.

PRINCIPAL COLORS: Green, white

GEMSTONES AND PRECIOUS
METALS: Moonstones, cat's-eye,
jade

BOTANICALS: Lettuce, colewort,
moonwort, rapeseed

UNIQUE SPELLINGS: Daena,
Daina, Dayna

RELATED TO: Daneen, Danella,
Danette, Daniella, Daniellet,
Danise, Danita, Danna, Dannika,
Danuta

Dana

A' KABBALISTIC SYNOPSIS
דאנא —DANA (Daleth, Aleph, Nun, Aleph)

Dana is a wonderful woman, so languidly sensual she almost pours herself into the room. But Dana is not at all vain; in fact, she is quite unassuming. There is a strong influence of Taurus in Dana's name, which adds to the heavily sensual nature of her sexuality. The presence of Nun indicates that her powerful sexual energy is not confined to trysts with the right long term partner. Though Dana will likely enjoy whatever occupation she chooses, she is not very ambitious, since her sensual nature emphasizes living in the moment. She will be happiest when she finds the right person with whom to share her enormous affection.

THE RUNIC INTERPRETATION
ᚨᚾᚨᛞ (Ansuz, Nauthiz, Ansuz, Dagaz)

Dana is fortunate to have double Ansuz energy in her name. Ansuz is the rune of messages from beyond. Dana can sense others' energy and gathers information to help people without being able to explain how she does it. Dana notices things more subtle than what the average person sees, and feels things in her body, with her mind, and in her head. But having so much empathy for others can be exhausting, and Dana needs plenty of rest. People may seek out Dana, and she can help guide them to the life they want.

Elements: Air, fire, air, fire

THE NUMEROLOGICAL INTERPRETATION
Dana (NV = 11, CV = 9, VV = 2, FL = 4)

Women who have this name look for the new and different. Partnership is very important to Dana. She is very comfortable in relationships and is compassionate and very attentive to her "special other." She will need time alone in order to be in contact with her thoughts and inner processes. Dana appreciates a partner that is supportive of this facet of her nature and will give a great deal in return for this understanding.

Daniel

A Kabbalistic Synopsis
דניאל —DNYAL (Daleth, Nun, Yod, Aleph, Lamed)

Most people are familiar with the biblical story in which Daniel survives being trapped in the lions' den. The bravery Daniel exhibits in this tale is reflected in his name, since Daniel is equivalent to "Madym," Hebrew for the planet Mars. Daniel is not only brave but is at his best when under fire. He likes the fact that people look to him as a protector, and he will probably select a vulnerable partner who likes to feel looked after. In the compression of the name we produce the letters Tzaddi and Heh. Heh represents Aries, a sign associated with Martian force and bravery. This additional association with strength and courage often means we may find Daniel in the armed forces, although his headstrong character may make his path up the ranks somewhat erratic. Tzaddi is associated with the tarot card the Star, which represents divine guidance and protection. In the biblical tale this refers to the many prophetic visions of Daniel; for our Daniel, it suggests a heightened intuition and vivid imagination.

The Runic Interpretation
ᚾᛗᛁᛏᛖᛗ (Laguz, Ehwaz, Isa, Nauthiz, Ansuz, Dagaz)

Daniel is a kind gentleman on all levels. He likes to play music, often with unusual instruments such as the harmonica or spoons, build cars or models, and dress in unusual ways. In other words, Daniel is both creative and mechanical. He has a quick wit and gives nicknames to his many friends. Daniel shares his house with the whole neighborhood and likes to create good memories there for his pals. The Dagaz energy of breakthrough helps Daniel to focus his career direction, which is necessary; Daniel has so many talents that this is difficult for him. However, once Daniel sets his course, he is bound for friends, prosperity, and satisfaction in life on many levels.

Elements: Water, air, earth, fire, air, fire

The Numerological Interpretation
Daniel (NV = 9, CV = 3, VV = 6, FL = 4)

Communicative and willing to please, Daniel is a man with a well-developed sensitivity to others. He has an eager mind and is willing to learn and to acquire knowledge that can be put to practical use. He is patient and kind by nature, and is always ready to listen to those who can benefit from his advice and sympathy. This name contains numbers that contribute to a wide variety of talents and ability. In this respect, Daniel can choose from many professions. If he is centered on one line of endeavor, it has to be a career that promises a great deal of variety, as he is easily bored by routine.

DERIVATION: Biblical, name of a prophet who was an Israelite slave of the Assyrian king Nebuchadnezzar. Daniel's enemies trapped him in a lions' den, but he was able to escape due to God's help. In Hebrew, the name means "God is my judge." Daniel is a popular name throughout all English-speaking countries.

PRINCIPAL COLORS: The full range of red hues, including pink and crimson

GEMSTONES AND PRECIOUS METALS: Garnets, bloodstones, red rubies

BOTANICALS: Broom, garlic, onion, white hellebore

UNIQUE SPELLINGS: Daneal, Danial, Daniol, Danniel, Danyel

RELATED TO: Dant, Danek, Danil, Danilo, Danny†, Deiniol, Donald†

❦

"The courage to imagine the otherwise is our greatest resource, adding color and suspense to all our life."
—DANIEL BOORSTIN (AUTHOR)

Danielle

DERIVATION: French feminine form of Daniel. Primarily used in France during the first half of the twentieth century, but in recent years, it has become increasingly popular throughout English-speaking countries.

PRINCIPAL COLORS: Relatively dark gray and blue tones, black

GEMSTONES AND PRECIOUS METALS: Amethyst, black pearls, richly hued sapphires

BOTANICALS: Angelica, ragwort, celery

UNIQUE SPELLINGS: Daniale, Daniele, Dannielle, Dannyelle, Danyel, Danyele, Danyelle

RELATED TO: Dana†, Danette, Dani, Dania, Danica, Daniela, Danielita, Daniella, Danna

A KABBALISTIC SYNOPSIS

דניאלל —DNYALL (Daleth, Nun, Yod, Aleph, Lamed, Lamed)

Danielle can often come across as placid and demure, but this is merely an outward appearance. Danielle is happy to play the role of a quiet, down-to-earth figure as long as it suits her, but a sensitive person will realize that she has an iron will. When her chosen partner begins to take her for granted, Danielle will transform before his eyes, and it is unlikely that he will make the same mistake twice. Danielle likes to have an active life and enjoys working outdoors in the garden, cutting down trees, or building a shed. Danielle is a wonderfully stimulating lifelong companion for anyone who can match her self-confidence and lust for life.

THE RUNIC INTERPRETATION

ᛗᛚᛚᛗᛁᛏᚨᛞ (Ehwaz, Laguz, Laguz, Ehwaz, Isa, Nauthiz, Ansuz, Dagaz)

Danielle sports the double Laguz energy for flow in her name. Laguz affords Danielle an intuitive and subtle nature. Yet Danielle must be sure her reach doesn't exceed her grasp. If she is willing to set realistic, attainable goals, hers will be a happy life. Laguz is good luck to those who follow the counsel of balance and harmony. Danielle could do well in teaching and writing. She also has the strength and power of all four elements in her name. This is another indication of balance and foretells success in future endeavors for Danielle.

Elements: Air, water, water, air, earth, fire, air, fire

THE NUMEROLOGICAL INTERPRETATION

Danielle (NV = 8, CV = 6, VV = 2, FL = 4)

Danielle likes to be in control of her own destiny. She is very at home when she is in charge of things, and has no problem administrating tasks. Yet she is able to do this with considerable charm and grace. For this reason, people find that they like cooperating with her. Danielle is a name that connotes an ability to handle people with sensitivity and compassion. She knows that her personal success depends on the goodwill of the people with whom she works. She is therefore eager to be cooperative as she strives to achieve her own goals and aspirations.

Danny

A KABBALISTIC SYNOPSIS
דני —DNY (Daleth, Nun, Yod)

See that guy in the background, careful to keep out of the limelight but looking intensely busy as he moves from person to person, phone call to phone call? He is probably a Danny. Danny is a man who makes things happen—for other people, usually. Ideal careers for Danny include promoter, PR man, entertainment manager, or any role that involves spotting the talent possessed by other individuals and bringing it to the public eye—for a good profit, of course. Danny is a likable guy who has a good sense of humor and a generally laid-back attitude toward life. He likes the trappings of success, but the influence of Jupiter ensures that this does not make him grasping or miserly. In fact, Danny gets the most enjoyment in life from seeing people he believes in doing well for themselves. This attitude will apply to his family as well as his colleagues and clients, and his children will have a father who encourages and supports them in any chosen endeavor.

THE RUNIC INTERPRETATION
ᛇᚾᚾᚨᛞ (Eihwaz, Nauthiz, Nauthiz, Ansuz, Dagaz)

Danny is a risk taker. He is the child most likely to climb to the very top of a tree while his pregnant mother fearfully looks on. He shoots pool with gangsters who don't laugh, wipes them out, and then spends the afternoon skydiving—it's just the way he is. But if you have a Danny in your life, don't panic yet: The double Nauthiz energy of constraint, buried deep within the name, saves the day. Danny will eventually confess that his daredevil pranks even have *him* worried! Luckily he has Nauthiz in his name to keep his feet planted firmly on mother earth, where he's nice and safe.

Elements: Earth/fire, fire, fire, air, fire

THE NUMEROLOGICAL INTERPRETATION
Danny (NV = 4, CV = 5, VV = 8, FL = 4)

Danny seeks to create a firm foundation in the material world. A solid and dependable person, Danny lives up to his word. This is a person who seeks to provide well for the people in his life, and is hardworking and honest by nature. People like Danny, especially those who may work for him, as he is very responsible to others when placed in an executive position. Danny has a need for predictable order and an established routine. Once these are in place, he may then feel comfortable in exploring the more adventurous side of his nature.

DERIVATION: English, short form of Daniel, which is a Hebrew name meaning "God is my judge." In the Bible, Daniel is an Israelite prophet who escapes from a lions' den with God's help. During the twentieth century, Danny has been an independent given name as well.

PRINCIPAL COLORS: Medium shades of most colors, electric hues

GEMSTONES AND PRECIOUS METALS: Sapphires

BOTANICALS: Sage, Solomon's seal, medlar

UNIQUE SPELLINGS: Danee, Dannee, Danney, Danni, Dannie

RELATED TO: Dant, Danek, Danial, Danielt, Danielo, Danil, Danilo

"Life is a great big canvas, and you should throw all the paint on it you can."

—DANNY KAYE (ACTOR)

209

DERIVATION: English, probably a
form of the adjective "darling."
Especially common in the
mid-1900s.

PRINCIPAL COLORS: The full
spectrum of very light hues

GEMSTONES AND PRECIOUS
METALS: Platinum, diamonds, any
very pale stone

BOTANICALS: Hazel, oats,
caraway, parsley

UNIQUE SPELLINGS: Darlean,
Darleane, Darleen, Darleene,
Darlein, Darleine

RELATED TO: Darla, Darlena,
Darlenna, Darlynn

Darlene

A KABBALISTIC SYNOPSIS
דעלין —DA'ALYN (Daleth, Ayin, Lamed, Yod, Nun)

We have all probably been sold something we didn't really want by Darlene at some point in
our lives; Darlene could sell burgers to vegetarians or hairbrushes to the bald! Her gift for
producing an extremely convincing sales pitch will be obvious from an early age, when her
parents will find themselves agreeing to all sorts of unsuitable activities without actually
knowing why. Not only can Darlene persuade you of the virtues of the most useless piece of
equipment, but she also possesses an indefatigable spirit. In her name we see the driving force
of the ox goad (Lamed) whipping up the already powerful energy signified by Y, or Yod, into
an even greater source of determination and drive. She will win potential lovers over with
her spirited nature and nonstop verbal fireworks. However, they should be aware that the
final Nun in this name suggests that her ambition and love of selling may stem from an unwillingness to slow down and reflect. It may be that her overactive nature masks a deeper vulnerability, which the right partner will be able to help her overcome.

THE RUNIC INTERPRETATION
ᛗᚺᛗᛚᚱᚨᛞ (Ehwaz, Nauthiz, Ehwaz, Laguz, Raido, Ansuz, Dagaz)

Darlene loves children, and with her considerable writing ability, children's literature is a
good field for her. Raido, the rune of good communication, means Darlene can write convincing plots and lovely dialogue. Darlene also loves animals and is always willing to go out of
her way to rescue any in distress. The Nauthiz energy of constraint in her name helps Darlene identify with the vulnerability of needy members of the animal kingdom. Darlene also
enjoys the mysteries of nature. The rune Ehwaz means Darlene could work and live abroad
while observing children and animals and writing books about their adventures in faraway
lands. Darlene is also well suited to being a vet or running a humane shelter.

Elements: Air, fire, earth, water, water, air, fire

THE NUMEROLOGICAL INTERPRETATION
Darlene (NV = 5, CV = 3, VV = 11, FL = 4)

Not one to sit at home and waste her days, Darlene is adventurous by nature. This is the name
of a woman who is original, intuitive, and extroverted. She loves to travel and make the most
out of her talents and abilities. Darlene is a friend to many people, as she enjoys variety in her
social life and differences in others. Personal freedom is very important to her, and she respects other people who, like herself, enjoy life to its utmost.

Darren

DERIVATION: English, came into use only in the twentieth century. Fairly common from the 1950s on.

PRINCIPAL COLORS: All but the brightest shades of azure

GEMSTONES AND PRECIOUS METALS: Emeralds, turquoise

BOTANICALS: Daffodils, dog rose, walnuts

UNIQUE SPELLINGS: Daren, Darin, Darrin, Darryn, Daryn

RELATED TO: Darrel, Darrylt

A Kabbalistic Synopsis
דארון —DARVN (Daleth, Aleph, Resh, Vau, Nun)

Darren is a torn individual; he has a love of great open spaces and craves a sense of absolute freedom, but has to reconcile this with a pull toward conventional family life and the sense of stability it brings. The central presence of R, or Resh, meaning "head," suggests that Darren will make decisions based on careful thought rather than by following his gut instinct. There are suggestions that Darren is attracted to a cozy home life not because of what it offers him but simply because it removes the anxiety and uncertainty he associates with going it alone. Still, if you have a partner who is a Darren, it would be wise to encourage him to spend time alone once in a while; otherwise, he will come to feel trapped! Darren has hobbies and interests that reflect his love of the unconventional and a long-standing concern with the unexplained. This is indicated by the strong influence of the number eleven in his name.

The Runic Interpretation
ᚾᛖᚱᚱᚨᛞ (Nauthiz, Ehwaz, Raido, Raido, Ansuz, Dagaz)

Darren has solid musical ability. Darren loves sound, and if he isn't playing music or writing lyrics, he's setting up sound equipment or writing music reviews. Darren likes all kinds of music, and probably began drumming four or five months before he was born! He needs parents who will invest in music lessons, several instruments, and good recording equipment for Darren at an early age. Darren will appreciate his opportunities, and the time and money will be well spent. Darren can use his analytical mind to do everything, from designing architecture computer programs to studying vibrational healing. In addition to his love of music he has an appreciation of design and mathematical ability.

Elements: Fire, air, water, water, air, fire

The Numerological Interpretation
Darren (NV = 6, CV = 9, VV = 6, FL = 4)

Darren is a person who is very comfortable at home. It is here that he expresses the depth of his caring for others. Darren's family is very important to him, and he is very responsive to their needs. People flock to Darren because they can count on his generous spirit and compassionate heart. Love is definitely at the foundation of his life. This love expresses itself in his intimate personal relationships, but it is also evident in his community projects. Darren is a person who does not think only about himself. Others are very important to him, and he shows it.

DERIVATION: English, originally the surname of a Norman baronial family. Became a popular first name in the twentieth century.

PRINCIPAL COLORS: All but the brightest shades of azure

GEMSTONES AND PRECIOUS METALS: Emeralds, turquoise

BOTANICALS: Vervain, violets, almonds, walnuts

UNIQUE SPELLINGS: Darell, Daril, Darill, Darol, Daroll, Darrell, Darril, Darrill, Darrol, Darroll, Darryll, Daryl

RELATED TO: Daren, Darren†

Darryl

A Kabbalistic Synopsis

דאריל —DARYL (Daleth, Aleph, Resh, Yod, Lamed)

Darryl is the archetypal businessman; he rushes from one meeting to the next and has his finger in any number of corporate pies. He lives by his wits and relies on his adrenaline and enthusiasm to keep him going through periods of intense activity when others might simply burn out. Mind you, Darryl must remember to unwind, as even he can be subject to stress! One equivalent to his name in Hebrew is "gall," or "bile," which is a symptom of stress and overwork. Yet Darryl is not wholly concerned with commerce; he has a very romantic side, shown by the presence of Virgo and Venus in his name, and he will always find time in his busy schedule for the partner in his life. The letters of his name show an understanding of the need to relax, and he finds his peace at home surrounded by his family, with the door firmly closed against the hectic outside world.

The Runic Interpretation

ᛚᛇᚱᚱᚨᛞ (Laguz, Eihwaz, Raido, Raido, Ansuz, Dagaz)

Darryl is a facilitator. He has deep compassion and a caring nature, and is not thwarted when the accolades he so richly deserves are withheld occasionally. He operates from his core; he isn't critical of outcomes because he has his sights set on high goals. Darryl is able to laugh at himself, and this is the way he stays in the flow of life. He finds humor in everything. He's also modest and knows how to respect confidences and speak modestly. Darryl can go far in almost any field because he likes people and understands how to get things done in a peaceful and open way.

Elements: Water, earth/fire, water, water, air, fire

The Numerological Interpretation

Darryl (NV = 6, CV = 7, VV = 8, FL = 4)

This name bestows an interesting combination of a profoundly logical mind and a deep emotional sensitivity. It is in the integration of these two tendencies that Darryl will face his life's challenges. When the mind and the emotions are truly united, intuition is the result. Darryl has the opportunity to cultivate this higher faculty of consciousness and apply it creatively to his life. Material success and social achievement are very important to Darryl. He enjoys the comforts and sense of security that come with money, but is not willing to compromise his ideals of human harmony for their attainment.

Dave

DERIVATION: A form of the biblical name David, which means "dear one" or "beloved." A common nickname for an extremely popular name among both Christians and Jews.

PRINCIPAL COLORS: The lightest hues in the spectrum

GEMSTONES AND PRECIOUS METALS: Diamonds, silver, platinum

BOTANICALS: Marjoram, parsley, hazel, oats

UNIQUE SPELLING: Dayv

RELATED TO: Daven, Davey, Davidt, Davide, Davidson, Davie, Davis, Davon, Davy

A KABBALISTIC SYNOPSIS
דאיו —DAYV (Daleth, Aleph, Yod, Vau)

Dave likes to be in charge of his world, and chances are he will find himself in a relatively senior position early on in life. People are quite happy to be managed by Dave, as he has an air of professionalism about him that is reassuring to his coworkers. The total value of Dave's name is twenty-one, which can be represented by the letters Kaph and Aleph, meaning "hand" and "oxen," respectively. Taking these two letters together, we can see Dave as a director and organizer who has the drive and commitment to see any project through to a successful conclusion. While Dave is a great organizer, he is not so good at rolling his sleeves up and actually doing the mundane work. The final letters of his name represent fire and air, respectively, which tell us Dave is fired up by his ideas but he likes that others implement them. This approach may cause him some difficulties in his emotional life, since it may translate into a reluctance to do his share in the domestic setting. Dave will have to be very careful not to take undue advantage of a partner who is willing to take on all the responsibility of running a house. However, Dave is great at relating to people, and he can be a great emotional support to his friends and family. With his lively brain, Dave can not only listen to people's problems but usually has a solution to offer as well.

THE RUNIC INTERPRETATION
ᛗᚠᚨᛞ (Ehwaz, Fehu, Ansuz, Dagaz)

Dave secretly believes that each of us has a pivotal moment in his life when luck shines upon us. His strategy, then, is to have a kind of openness and willingness to grasp the brass ring when it appears. Chances that this will happen are very favorable based on Dave's assets, and Dave will indeed have his fondest dreams come true and live out his destiny. Fulfillment and satisfied ambition along with true love are the hallmarks of this name. Yet Dave must curb his lustful tendencies and channel his passion into endeavors in the arts or business, or his lascivious nature could well be a tragic flaw.

Elements: Air, fire, air, fire

THE NUMEROLOGICAL INTERPRETATION
Dave (NV = 5, CV = 8, VV = 6, FL = 4)

The name Dave brings a sense of harmony and peace into a life that is filled with hard work and effort. Success on the material plane is very important to this man. He is one who strives after the fulfillment of his ambitions—but without having to step on other people's toes to reach his own aims in life. Dave has high energy and an eagerness to explore life. He is fun to be around, and people generally find him uplifting, supportive, and stimulating. He has the ability to make friends easily, and enjoys the pleasures of shared companionship. His direct manner could be taken as offensive by some, if it weren't for the fact that he is sincerely concerned about how others feel and is, by nature, a gentleman.

DERIVATION: Biblical, name of the greatest Israelite king. As a boy, David defeated the giant Philistine Goliath with a slingshot. During his reign, he unified the Israelites, expanded their territory, and built the city of Jerusalem. An extremely popular name throughout the twentieth century.

PRINCIPAL COLORS: Any color of medium hue

GEMSTONES AND PRECIOUS METALS: Sapphires

BOTANICALS: Sage, spinach, medlar

UNIQUE SPELLINGS: Daevid, Daved, Davidd, Dayved, Dayvid

RELATED TO: Dai, Davet, Davey, Davis, Davy, Devint

A KABBALISTIC SYNOPSIS
דוד —DVD (Daleth, Vau, Daleth)

David's nature is pictorially displayed by the Hebrew spelling of his name; we see the central character caught between two "doors," uncertain as to which is the right choice. In positive terms this represents David's variety of skills; he is able and willing to turn his hand to a wide range of jobs. It also reflects David's tendency to search for the ideal. For David, the grass is always greener on the other side, and he will often expend much energy trying to get there— only to find that it must have been a trick of the light. Connected to this restlessness is the final significant aspect of his name's design, which relates to the doors as being gateways to the past and the future. David is an excessively nostalgic man who can often reflect on what was at the expense of what is. At the same time he is something of a dreamer who can be too busy planning the next five years to attend to those things requiring immediate attention.

THE RUNIC INTERPRETATION
ᛞᛁᚠᚨᛞ (Dagaz, Isa, Fehu, Ansuz, Dagaz)

David is intelligent and can embrace huge concepts quickly. He is willing to take on large projects in order to make large sums of money. The Fehu rune assures David of considerable financial success, and the double Dagaz energy assures him of many fortunate opportunities. Yet David can become smug if things come too easily for him. It's good for David to be with tactful people who are concept oriented. David has the Isa rune of standstill to teach him the value of spirituality in his life. He needs to slow down and learn to wait. Once he grasps the value of patience, his wonderful dreams come true. He can be a very sweet lover to one who believes he can do no wrong and tells him that constantly. He'll be a strong husband and good provider—once he learns to be patient.

Elements: Fire, earth, fire, air, fire

THE NUMEROLOGICAL INTERPRETATION
David (NV = 4, CV = 3, VV = 1, FL = 4)

David indicates a man who stands with a firm foundation under his feet and an inner sense of purpose in his heart. This is a practical person, one who is more concerned with what is permanent than with what is transient, more involved with the tangible than with the ephemeral. It is important for David to succeed in life, and it is natural for him to create this success for himself. David enjoys friendships and social interaction, but he is fundamentally his own person, a man who finds it necessary to do his own thing in his own way.

Dawn

DERIVATION: English, a direct use of the word meaning "daybreak." Became popular as a first name in the twentieth century.

PRINCIPAL COLORS: Pale to medium blue tones

GEMSTONES AND PRECIOUS METALS: Blue-green and blue turquoise

BOTANICALS: Apricots, vervain, violets, walnuts

UNIQUE SPELLINGS: Daun, Dawne, Dawnn

RELATED TO: Dawna, Dawnetta, Dawnielle, Dawnysia

A Kabbalistic Synopsis

דאון —DAVN (Daleth, Aleph, Vau, Nun)

The name Dawn has associations with both "belly" and "wealth." Dawn is a gourmet for whom good food is one of the best aspects of living the good life. But it is not the only worthwhile aspect; the greater questions in life occupy Dawn's mind a great deal, and there is nothing she likes better than to discuss in detail the purpose of life over a sumptuous dinner. While Dawn will often put her own opinions down as irrelevant or baseless thoughts, it is common for her to possess a high level of understanding of spiritual matters. Those areas of which she does have knowledge she will tend to be silent on, as she firmly believes that it is up to each individual to draw their own conclusions.

The Runic Interpretation

ᚾᚹᚨᛞ (Nauthiz, Wunjo, Ansuz, Dagaz)

Dawn has the delightful energy of joy, represented by the Wunjo rune that appears in the heart of her name. She is a sincere friend who knows the universe returns her trust, and that each lesson life sends us brings both pain and joy. Dawn has learned from past mistakes, and makes necessary changes in her life based on the knowledge she has gained. She carefully considers her actions and words in life and always keeps her viewpoint optimistic. Dawn is willing to extend herself and follow through. She's a happy person because her needs are modest. She knows that as long as she tries, she will experience a sense of well-being and love.

Elements: Fire, earth, air, fire

The Numerological Interpretation

Dawn (NV = 6, CV = 9, VV = 6, FL = 4)

Kindness and a gentle, compassionate attitude characterize the name Dawn. Slow to anger, but quick in her helpful responses to others, Dawn can be relied upon for her loving support. She is a humanitarian at heart and can always find the time to be there when needed. The numbers in this name signify a woman who is attracted to all forms of beauty: art, music, theater, etc. Due to her humanitarian and creative nature, she is best off in a helping or artistic profession, and would make a wonderful teacher of the visual or performing arts. Dawn is also one who carries grace and beauty with her, always adding harmony, balance, and a sense of inclusiveness to her surroundings.

Dean

DERIVATION: English, originally a surname meaning someone who lived in a valley (a *dene* in Old English). Became common after the 1950s.

PRINCIPAL COLORS: All but the brightest shades of blue

GEMSTONES AND PRECIOUS METALS: Emeralds, turquoise

BOTANICALS: Dog rose, violets, almonds, any type of bean

UNIQUE SPELLINGS: Deane, Deen, Deene, Dene

RELATED TO: Dino

A KABBALISTIC SYNOPSIS
דין —DYN (Daleth, Yod, Nun)

Only a fool would cross Dean; this man has a temper that has to be seen to be believed. Dean is not an aggressive or argumentative individual by nature, but he does have deeply held views about what constitutes appropriate behavior. His name is the equivalent of "Justice," which is one of the titles for the fifth sephirah on the Tree of Life. This sephirah is also known as Geburah or "Power," and it refers to the process of destruction (as opposed to creation). This should not be seen as negative, since without destruction or constraints there could be no life. In human terms Dean acts to curtail the behavior of other people, and is ideally suited to some form of enforcement role where a good understanding of and sympathy for long lists of regulations and prohibitions is required. Still, Dean can be quite an overpowering force in social situations. Like a police officer, his presence tends to make people feel guilty even if they have done nothing wrong. However, Dean is perfectly pleasant . . . provided that nobody actually is guilty!

THE RUNIC INTERPRETATION
ᚾᚨᛖᛞ (Nauthiz, Ansuz, Ehwaz, Dagaz)

Dean likes to live in orderly surroundings but doesn't necessarily keep things in order. He is personable, and his voice and manner inspire confidence. Dean utilizes the terminal Nauthiz energy of constraint in his name to become versatile. He is likely to have more than one job and may enjoy working at home. Dean also values his recreation time and enjoys the great outdoors. He is good at sports and may join hiking and biking clubs as a way to meet friends. Potential mates are drawn to Dean because he looks fit and is approachable, but he really doesn't want to settle down—and he lets the lovers in line know that!

Elements: Fire, air, air, fire

THE NUMEROLOGICAL INTERPRETATION
Dean (NV = 6, CV = 9, VV = 6, FL = 4)

There is a profound philosophical and humanitarian nature inherent in this name. Dean is a person who cares about others and does something about it. He is not satisfied just to contemplate how people may lead better lives; he is willing to participate actively in order that social welfare be put into practice. A gentle man with a deep sensitivity to other people's feelings, Dean can be counted upon for his assistance and strength. This name endows a person with an inner sense of fair play and justice for all, as well as the willingness to help bring these qualities into daily life.

Deanna

DERIVATION: English, a variant of Diana. First seen in the twentieth century, and became more common with the rise of Canadian singer/actress Deanna Durbin (b. 1921).

PRINCIPAL COLORS: The full range of violets, from pale bluish purple to deep reddish purple

GEMSTONES AND PRECIOUS METALS: Garnets

BOTANICALS: Apple, barberry, beetroot, lungwort

UNIQUE SPELLINGS: Deeana, Deeanna, Deiana

RELATED TO: Deanne, Dena, Diana†, Diane, Dianna, Dianne

A KABBALISTIC SYNOPSIS
דיינא —DYNA (Daleth, Yod, Nun, Aleph)

The simple addition of an Aleph to the name Dean completely changes the name's significance, as does the change in value of N, or Nun (as it is no longer the final letter in the name). Deanna's name adds up to sixty-five—a great number of power in occult circles, as it combines the energies of the Universe wand and the power of the individual. This means that Deanna's choices in life are usually sensible ones, since she has a natural instinct for going with the flow. By this we are not simply referring to the trends in one office or even one corporation but to the broader trends and fluctuating energies that affect all of us. As we cannot determine the primary direction of the universal current at any given time, it is hard to say what Deanna will do in terms of her career or even how she will approach relationships. However, it is almost certain that she will always land on her feet. There is a possibility, particularly for Scorpio and Aquarian Deannas, that she will pick up on this knack and may explore it further—in which case, she will be well rewarded for her efforts.

THE RUNIC INTERPRETATION
ᚨᚾᚾᚨᛖᛞ (Ansuz, Nauthiz, Nauthiz, Ansuz, Ehwaz, Dagaz)

Deanna needs a bottle of glue to mend all the broken hearts she's left behind! She knows just how to intrigue a lover, and once she knows she has won her lover's affection, she loses interest. Deanna needs to understand that she has a passion for challenges. Once she does, she can accept the double energy of constraint, or Nauthiz, in her name. In fact, Deanna is so conditioned to struggle that it's become comfortable for her. Instead, Deanna should learn to pursue challenges in sports and business, and find a mate to teach her that love can be more than a game of conquest.

Elements: Air, fire, fire, air, air, fire

THE NUMEROLOGICAL INTERPRETATION
Deanna (NV = 3, CV = 5, VV = 7, FL = 4)

Deanna is interested in exploring the numerous ways in which she is able to express herself creatively. She requires variety and change, adventure and excitement. Women named Deanna make for very uplifting and fascinating companions. They always are open to new possibilities and reject routine life patterns. Deanna is therefore easily bored and rather restless by nature. She requires a career that allows her the freedom to be herself, and a relationship that is open to the many possibilities of self-discovery.

DERIVATION: Pet form of Deborah, derived from the Hebrew word for "bee." In ancient times, bees were seen as symbolic of wisdom and industry. Since the 1950s, Debbie has been regularly used as an independent name.

PRINCIPAL COLORS: Deep, rich reds

GEMSTONES AND PRECIOUS METALS: Bloodstones, rubies, garnets

BOTANICALS: Onion, garlic, leeks, pepper

UNIQUE SPELLINGS: Debbi, Debby, Debi, Deby

RELATED TO: Deborah, Debra, Debs, Devora, Devorah

Debbie

A KABBALISTIC SYNOPSIS
דאבי —DABY (Daleth, Aleph, Beth, Yod)

It's hard to believe that anyone could navigate through life as successfully as Debbie does and remain as innocent as she often seems. For those who look a little closer, it is clear that Debbie is not at all naive; instead, she has very good reason for her bright and positive manner. Debbie totals to 17, which is a number of protection and guidance. This number is also the product of the symbol of success when it is linked to the number of luck or good fortune. Debbie combines this fortunate framework with a deep understanding of human nature, as indicated by the Beth in her name, which acts as a balance for the other more energetic letters. Since her real interest lies in people, Debbie's work will most likely revolve around helping others.

THE RUNIC INTERPRETATION
MIBBMⴹ (Ehwaz, Isa, Berkana, Berkana, Ehwaz, Dagaz)

Debbie draws her strength from nature and will probably adore animals. Unlike so many pet owners, she will never abandon a furry friend just because it costs money or is a nuisance once in a while. This, in combination with her strong people skills, would make her a good veterinarian. Debbie cares about feelings more than material possessions, and she is deeply vulnerable. She is honest and tactful, and verbal abuse can make her very upset. Debbie is fortunate to have the double Berkana energy of growth in her name. As she matures, Debbie is careful to protect herself and surround herself with loving, optimistic people. Debbie loves to believe romance really does exist—and yes, she does find her true love.

Elements: Air, earth, air/earth, air/earth, air, fire

THE NUMEROLOGICAL INTERPRETATION
Debbie (NV = 9, CV = 8, VV = 1, FL = 4)

Debbie has a strong sense of inner purpose and a need to express herself individually. However, she will do this in ways that tend to conform to society. She is an individualist, but not a rebel. Social achievement is very important to her as she strives toward the fulfillment of her goals. A person who can be quite generous, Debbie will always make the time to assist others, as she is a woman who cares for other people's success as much as she cares for her own.

Deborah

A KABBALISTIC SYNOPSIS
דאבורה —DABVRH (Daleth, Aleph, Beth, Vau, Resh, Heh)

Deborah's caring side takes priority over all other considerations. Yet Deborah has a tendency to shy away from serious, long-term relationships. This is not because she enjoys a wild single lifestyle but so that she can devote her time to the causes about which she feels so strongly. The compression of her name yields the letter Cheth, meaning "fence" or "enclosure," which indicates her desire to protect the weak and vulnerable. Deborah has a practical nature and is more than happy to roll her sleeves up and get her hands dirty in order to be of assistance. The total of her name is twelve, the number identified with self-sacrifice, and while this adds weight to the view of Deborah as a caring, committed woman, it raises questions as to what it is that drives her to such self-abnegation. Deborah's strong beliefs and dedication make her well suited to a career in civil service or social work.

THE RUNIC INTERPRETATION
ᚺᚨᚱᛟᛒᛗᛇ (Hagalaz, Ansuz, Raido, Othila, Berkana, Ehwaz, Dagaz)

The Raido and Hagalaz runes of journey and disruption give the name Deborah excitement, power, and a love of foreign cultures. While Deborah has goals, she is willing to modify them should something better come her way. When the Hagalaz lessons of chaos come crashing in on her, Deborah is able to shore herself up with the Raido energy of travel, new ideas, and deep-rooted optimism. Deborah learns from challenges, consistently strives for her highest goals, and banishes people from her life who attempt to undermine her strength.

Elements: Water, air, water, earth/fire, air/earth, air, fire

THE NUMEROLOGICAL INTERPRETATION
Deborah (NV = 8, CV = 5, VV = 3, FL = 4)

The numerical value in this name denotes a person for whom worldly achievement is very important. Deborah has an inborn sense of responsibility and a keen sense of structure and order. Yet within her overall plan, she is ever ready to explore the many opportunities that life has to offer. She loves to travel and is open to adventure, but all of her experiences have to fit into her overall vision of what she is seeking to achieve. In this sense, Deborah is not a careless and carefree individual. She always has a sense of purpose in mind and conforms her many activities to this larger goal.

DERIVATION: Hebrew, from the word meaning "bee." In ancient times, bees were seen as symbolic of wisdom and industry. In the Bible, Deborah was a judge and prophetess who helped the Israelites to defeat the Canaanites. Became very popular in the mid-1900s.

PRINCIPAL COLORS: Black, gray, deeply toned azure and purple

GEMSTONES AND PRECIOUS METALS: Amethyst, black pearls, black diamonds, any other very richly toned, dark stones

BOTANICALS: Marsh mallow, gravel root, shepherd's purse

UNIQUE SPELLINGS: Debbora, Debbra, Deberah, Debora, Deborrah, Debra, Debrah

RELATED TO: Debbiet, Debby, Devora, Devorah

DERIVATION: English variant of
the Spanish name Dolores, which
comes from the word for "sorrow."
Both the De- and Do- spellings
are common in the English-
speaking world.

PRINCIPAL COLORS: Pale to
medium blue

GEMSTONES AND PRECIOUS
METALS: Turquoise, emeralds

BOTANICALS: Vervain, violets,
walnuts, almonds

UNIQUE SPELLINGS: Deeloris,
Deloris, Dolores, Doloris,
Dolorris

RELATED TO: Dolly, Dorist, Lolat,
Lolita, Lorit

Delores

A Kabbalistic Synopsis
דלעראס —DLA'ARAS (Daleth, Lamed, Ayin, Resh, Aleph, Samech)

Delores does not have an easy life, although this does not mean that she will be unhappy (still, some signs, such as Gemini, will find it difficult to maintain a cheerful outlook on life). Delores's life changes little from year to year, as exemplified by the total value of her name, which is 365. Fortunately Delores has considerable fire energy, a helpful force that enables her to bear all the responsibilities life will lay at her door. As she grows older, Delores will be a support to an increasing number of people, from friends to children to grandchildren. Many people will be set on their way to success by her efforts, and while she has the time to advise them on a wide variety of problems, she rarely finds the time to consider her own development. Mostly Delores is happy with her lot in life and derives pleasure from the assistance she can give to others. However, there are occasions (indicated by the Ayin in her name) when she wishes that she could break away from others and just pay attention to herself.

The Runic Interpretation
ᛋᛗᚱᛟᛚᛗᛈ (Sowelu, Ehwaz, Raido, Othila, Laguz, Ehwaz, Dagaz)

Always levelheaded, Delores has the energy of all four elements blessing her name. Delores is an idealist who likes camaraderie. She is also a joiner who is likely to belong to several clubs. She will often work till all hours of the night, setting a high standard for her colleagues. Delores is good with people, yet she is amazingly unaware of herself. Delores needs the company of friends who like her just the way she is. Delores has many fans.

Elements: Air, air, water, earth/fire, water, air, fire

The Numerological Interpretation
Delores (NV = 6, CV = 8, VV = 7, FL = 4)

An idealistic person with a strong romantic nature, Delores places personal relationships at the center of her life. This is a name that reveals a woman of deep sensitivity and profound personal magnetism. She uses these qualities to anchor harmony and beauty in her environment, and may be counted on to bring her grace and charm into the lives of all with whom she comes in contact. Material security and life's comforts are also important to her. She has the ability to balance her home and career with ease and artistry.

Denise

A KABBALISTIC SYNOPSIS
דניס —DNYS (Daleth, Nun, Yod, Samech)

Denise is extremely quiet and can often *seem* to be shy and retiring, the sort of person you expect to see working studiously as a clerk or a librarian, complete with sensible tweed suit. In one sense this is a reasonable portrait of Denise, who enjoys a peaceful and restrained working life. However, out of the office, Denise can be quite an animal! Denise has absolutely no desire to settle down and get married; she wants to play the field as long and as often as she can. As far as she is concerned, variety really is the spice of life. Her tendency to close the door on relationships almost as soon as they have started and to begin the next one equally quickly is not just due to her love of sexual variety. More important to Denise is the collection of *experience*, particularly emotional experience. But she is also a woman of discretion; the influence of Scorpio in her name more than ensures that her activities remain her secret.

THE RUNIC INTERPRETATION
ᛖᛋᛁᛏᛖᛉ (Ehwaz, Sowelu, Isa, Nauthiz, Ehwaz, Dagaz)

Denise is capable and, dare we suggest it, a bit self-centered. She has the Isa energy in her name, which makes her comfortable with isolation. She will excel in careers that involve planning, constructing, developing, or building, as well as any positions dependent upon leadership qualities. The double Ehwaz energy in her name belies the fact that Denise's soul's goal is to better her situation in life. Denise demonstrates for us all that there is a direct correlation between the work we do on the inside and how wonderful life is on the outside.

Elements: Air, air, earth, fire, air, fire

THE NUMEROLOGICAL INTERPRETATION
Denise (NV = 2, CV = 1, VV = 1, FL = 4)

Denise has the need to be highly independent while at the same time remaining quite intimate with that special person in her life. She requires a life that reinforces her own individuality. Denise is attracted by life's opportunities and wants to take advantage of them. At the same time, she is very romantic and is constantly seeking perfection in partnership. Denise would be best suited to a relationship with a partner who is as independent as she is so that they both may be supportive of each other.

DERIVATION: French, feminine form of Dennis, which originates from the Greek name Dionysius, the god of wine. Originated during the Middle Ages, and became popular in English-speaking countries during the mid-1900s.

PRINCIPAL COLORS: Pale grassy to rich, dark forest green; white

GEMSTONES AND PRECIOUS METALS: Jade, cream-colored pearls, cat's-eye

BOTANICALS: Cabbage, lettuce, plantain, turnips

UNIQUE SPELLINGS: Daneece, Daneese, Danice, Danise, Danyse, Deneice, Denese, Denice, Denize, Dennise, Denyse

RELATED TO: Deenie, Demmoe, Deni, Denisa, Dionysa

Dennis

A KABBALISTIC SYNOPSIS
דנס —DNS (Daleth, Nun, Samech)

Hardware stores, basement workshops, auto shops: These are all places where you can expect to find Dennis. But even if you locate him in the office of CEO, Dennis still seems reliable and uncomplicated. He is the kind of guy who insists on doing all the repairs in the house. Even if the washing machine is a brand-new model complete with computer chips, he will try to mend it with sticky tape and elastic bands! Despite his simple style of living and his love of the mechanical, Dennis is a complex creature emotionally. In part his reluctance to move beyond the familiar stems from insecurities caused by the presence of N, or Nun, in his name, which manifests itself as a need to feel in control of all aspects of his life. In love Dennis is incredibly supportive and is always there for his partner—as long as he receives the same level of attention in return. However, due to his insecurities, it is unusual for Dennis to open up fully about his own feelings.

THE RUNIC INTERPRETATION
ᛋᛁᚾᚾᛖᛞ (Sowelu, Isa, Nauthiz, Nauthiz, Ehwaz, Dagaz)

Dennis bears the double Nauthiz energy of constraint in his name, and this may sometimes cause him to feel like he is past hope and has been abandoned. The Nauthiz energy of his name fosters the need to act on alternative plans. Doing something different invites in new energy for Dennis, and it all hinges on him taking the first step. Once this breakthrough comes for Dennis, he will have luck beginning new endeavors. As Dennis finds personal freedom from past hurts, his life expands and proceeds with a clear-cut plan for success.

Elements: Air, earth, fire, fire, air, fire

THE NUMEROLOGICAL INTERPRETATION
Dennis (NV = 11, CV = 6, VV = 5, FL = 4)

Dennis requires a career in which there are many changes and opportunities for self-exploration. Dennis has an inborn sense of intuition. He is not logical by nature; his mental processes go beyond the rational. In this respect, he may not be fully understood by most other people. He should therefore cultivate friends who are highly original, inventive, and open to alternative ways of dealing with life.

Derek

DERIVATION: British, originally from the German name Theodoric. Has become fairly common in recent years.

PRINCIPAL COLORS: Pale to deep, rich yellow and green hues

GEMSTONES AND PRECIOUS METALS: Moonstones, pearls, moss agate

BOTANICALS: Blackberry, elder, hops

UNIQUE SPELLINGS: Derec, Deric, Derick, Derik, Derreck, Derrek, Derrick, Deryck, Deryk

RELATED TO: Del, Diederick, Dietrich, Dirk, Theodoric

A KABBALISTIC SYNOPSIS
דארכ —DARK (Daleth, Aleph, Resh, Kaph)

Derek would make the ideal bartender, as he has a wonderful facility for listening to people in a completely unobtrusive manner. Rather than leaping in with advice after a couple of minutes, which is common for most of us, Derek will instead patiently listen and nod encouragingly. Clearly, with his high intelligence and excellent listening skills, Derek also would make a good psychoanalyst. Derek tends not to push himself forward, and so probably would be quite happy working in a low-key middle-management role for a large corporation. Derek's main focus is his family, and once home he really comes alive. There he is the life and soul of the party—a contrast to the quiet demeanor he shows the outside world most of the time.

THE RUNIC INTERPRETATION
ᚲᛖᚱᛖᛞ (Kano, Ehwaz, Raido, Ehwaz, Dagaz)

Derek is emotional, moody, changeable, kind, and sometimes cranky. The double Ehwaz energy of this name tells us that Derek has built a comfortable life for himself. He values his home and may be very successful as a doctor, minister, or restaurant owner. People are willing to support Derek's ideas, and if he chooses big business, he can make a mark for himself there. Derek can use the Ehwaz energy to remember that what is good will come to each of us. As a father, Derek is a wonderful leader because he has the best interests of his family in mind. He anticipates their needs, and they willingly follow.

Elements: Water, air, water, air, fire

THE NUMEROLOGICAL INTERPRETATION
Derek (NV = 7, CV = 6, VV = 1, FL = 4)

The name Derek denotes a man who is introspective and analytical by nature. He has the tendency to search deeply beneath the surface of life's activities in order to uncover their true meaning. Derek is therefore a philosopher at heart. Quite happy when investigating his interests, Derek can be somewhat of a loner. It is not that he avoids intimate contact with others, but just that he prefers intimate contact with his own inner world. In partnerships, he will seek others of a similar disposition.

Desiree

DERIVATION: French, from the
Latin word meaning "desired."
In early Christian times, people
used this name for long-awaited
children; the Puritans used the
name Desire for girls.

PRINCIPAL COLORS: White, any
hue of green

GEMSTONES AND PRECIOUS
METALS: Jade, moonstones,
cat's-eye

BOTANICALS: Cabbage, plantain,
lettuce, willow ash

UNIQUE SPELLINGS: Deseree,
Desirae, Desiray, Desyree

RELATED TO: Desi, Desiderata,
Desira, Desire, Desy

A KABBALISTIC SYNOPSIS
דאסירי —DASYRY (Daleth, Aleph, Samech, Yod, Resh, Yod)

Desiree is unashamedly vain, and for her, the main event of the day is the ritual parade in front of the full-length mirror as she decides what to wear for the day. One thing you can be sure of is that whatever she chooses, it will be designed to stop traffic! While most people with an excessive interest in their own appearance tend to cause ill feeling among their colleagues and acquaintances, Desiree is very popular thanks to the sheer flamboyance of her behavior. Not only does she dress to impress, but Desiree has enormous charisma. She is guaranteed an invitation to every party, and is well worth the amount of attention she demands. Any negative responses she does attract will not bother Desiree in the slightest, as she has great strength of character, indicated by the positioning of the two Yods in her name.

THE RUNIC INTERPRETATION
ᛗᛗᚱᛁᛊᛗᛈ (Ehwaz, Ehwaz, Raido, Isa, Sowelu, Ehwaz, Dagaz)

Desiree has Isa, the symbol of isolation, buried deep within her name, but ironically, many Desirees will start families of their own early on. It is not until she is loaded down with home and family responsibilities that Desiree discovers her need for independence. She may carve out some time for her spirit to grow by joining a class that draws on her creative ability. Desiree is elegant, beautiful, and powerful. With patience and solitude Desiree grows ever stronger and rises to a position of influence in her community.

Elements: Air, air, water, earth, air, air, fire

THE NUMEROLOGICAL INTERPRETATION
Desiree (NV = 11, CV = 5, VV = 6, FL = 4)

Desiree is the name of a woman with very special qualities. She has a heightened sense of perception that allows her to see both the beginning and the end of a situation at the same time. Thus she is truly intuitive, with a strong sense of compassion. Desiree will not conform to most ordinary patterns of life. She will dress the way she wishes, and make friends with very artistic and bohemian people. Her personal freedom is very important to her, and she can change direction very suddenly. Spontaneity is her key word—Desiree thrives on life's surprising adventures.

Devin

DERIVATION: British, from the name of an English county, Devon. Used as a first name primarily in the United States. Its use as a first name has been dated to the early 1960s.

PRINCIPAL COLORS: All shades of red, from light pink to rich, deep rose

GEMSTONES AND PRECIOUS METALS: Red stones, such as rubies and bloodstones

BOTANICALS: Broom, pepper, rape, wormwood

UNIQUE SPELLINGS: Deven, Devinn, Devon, Devonn, Devonne

RELATED TO: David†, Dejuan

A KABBALISTIC SYNOPSIS
דאוין —DAVYN (Daleth, Aleph, Vau, Yod, Nun)

If you have been blessed with the name Devin, now is the time to thank your lucky stars. Devin is a name absolutely bursting with signs of good fortune; at the most basic level, it reduces to ten, which indicates that Devin is lucky in matters of chance. In addition, this name adds up to 721—a combination of the sign of success with the Universe tarot card, which relates to the successful completion of a project or cycle in one's life. The specific nature of these symbols when combined along with the letters in Devin's name suggest that Devin will probably make it big in business. The presence of V, or Vau, indicates that Devin will have a choice of areas in which to operate, and that he will often rely on gut instinct to guide him. Interestingly, a further sign of success is the number 721. Both seven and twenty-one are associated with success, and ten (the result of adding seven, two, and one) is also associated with fortune.

THE RUNIC INTERPRETATION
ᚾᛁᚠᛖᛞ (Nauthiz, Isa, Fehu, Ehwaz, Dagaz)

Devin is fair, balanced, perceptive, and selfless. He can appear weak or vacillating because he takes his time to make decisions and weighs all sides before voicing an opinion. Devin is good in public relations, counseling, and law, as well as in art. He will probably decide what he wants early on in life. He has many hobbies and loves animals, particularly horses. He has Fehu, the rune of possessions, in his name, but chances are that Devin realizes that material possessions hold less appeal for him than self-discipline and a strong will. On the other hand, Devin could also lose the money he has gained with risky investments, due to his sincere desire for more, more, more!

Elements: Fire, earth, fire, air, fire

THE NUMEROLOGICAL INTERPRETATION
Devin (NV = 9, CV = 4, VV = 5, FL = 4)

A complex name with many implications, Devin connotes a multifaceted man. Although Devin may be very concerned about his finances and personal security, he is by nature a generous soul. Hardworking and responsible, he also looks forward to those times when he can leave his routine behind and set forth on some special adventure. Yet such periods have to be structured within a larger, more predictable schedule. It is only then that he feels free enough to enjoy these breaks from his regular life.

DERIVATION: English, of Latin origin, meaning "divine." The Roman goddess of the moon and hunting, whose Greek counterpart was Artemis. Diane, its French form, enjoyed a short-lived popularity in the mid-twentieth century. Princess Diana (1961–1997) gave this name an internationally known face.

PRINCIPAL COLORS: Green, white, cream

GEMSTONES AND PRECIOUS METALS: Moonstones, jade, pearls, cat's-eye

BOTANICALS: Lettuce, cabbage, chicory, plantain

UNIQUE SPELLINGS: Dayanna, Dianna, Dyana, Dyanna

RELATED TO: Danne, Deana, Deane, Dede, Dee, Di, Diahann, Diane, Diann, Dianne, Dyan

Diana

A KABBALISTIC SYNOPSIS
דיאנא —DYANA (Daleth, Yod, Aleph, Nun, Aleph)

It is difficult to think of the name Diana without remembering the late Princess of Wales, although clearly not every Diana can match the princess's achievements. The total value of this name is sixty-six, which is a highly mystical number, since it is the sum of all the numbers from one to eleven added together. And since eleven is the number of magic and mystery, we would expect Diana to possess the potential to have a significant hold over people. Diana's name can also be represented by the two letters Samech and Vau. As Vau relates to the element of air and to thought, while Samech refers to strong support for others, Diana is likely to spend much of her time thinking about the needs of others and, wherever possible, offering her support for those who require some assistance in their life. Diana is strongly associated with the Hanged Man tarot card, which again refers to self-sacrifice for the good of the community as a whole. The two Alephs in her name suggest a considerable level of drive and determination as well as great single-mindedness. However, the two Alephs are separated by the letter Nun, which is associated with emotional pain and distress. This suggests that at times Diana's own personal worries and emotions can get in the way of her achieving her goals in the outside world. But since the Nun is followed by a second Aleph, it is highly likely that Diana will be able to overcome such barriers to her progress.

THE RUNIC INTERPRETATION
ᚨᚾᚨᛁᛞ (Ansuz, Nauthiz, Ansuz, Isa, Dagaz)

Diana has been depicted in art as the huntress, and once she overcomes her childhood shyness, Diana is one fierce opponent. She has a kind of instinctual power that men find irresistible, and in business she has a sense of where to place her arrow so that the deal flies through. Diana has intuition, a retentive mind, and a keen insight into human nature. She is easily embarrassed, and this explains why she is so well organized—some would say *overly* prepared for meetings—and why her grooming is impeccable. As Diana learns to play the fool and laugh at herself, people will warm up to her and appreciate her humility and tolerance.

Elements: Air, fire, air, earth, fire

THE NUMEROLOGICAL INTERPRETATION
Diana (NV = 2, CV = 9, VV = 11, FL = 4)

A romantic and philosophical nature characterizes this name. Diana has a strong need for a poetic life, one filled with visions, ideals, and dreams. She is genuinely concerned and caring in her dealings with people, and possesses an intuitive understanding of their feelings. People tend to come to her with their problems and look to her for her ability to peer into the heart of every issue. Yet Diana has to learn how to deal with and respect her own sensitivity, for every little ripple in her surroundings can create an emotional reaction in her. Relationships are at the center of her life, and her own lovers and partnerships will take up much of her time and effort. Yet Diana is also open to relationships of a more impersonal nature, and will give of herself to the causes that concern her.

Dominic

DERIVATION: English and Irish, from the Latin name Dominicus, which stemmed from the root meaning "lord." During the Middle Ages, Saint Dominic founded the Dominican order of monks.

PRINCIPAL COLORS: Any color of medium hue, particularly gray and blue

GEMSTONES AND PRECIOUS METALS: Sapphires

BOTANICALS: Lesser celandine, wild spinach, wintergreen

UNIQUE SPELLINGS: Domenic, Domenick, Domenik, Dominick, Dominik

RELATED TO: Domenico

A Kabbalistic Synopsis

דעמיניכ —DA'AMYNYK (Daleth, Ayin, Mem, Yod, Nun, Yod, Kaph)

If you want to get Dominic to sign a contract or otherwise agree to any business agreement, simply send along a beautiful messenger with the paperwork and he'll sign anything! Dominic is very much ruled by material considerations and particularly by his own senses, especially sight. Dominic will spend his money on paintings and sumptuous furnishings long before he considers upgrading his culinary intake from takeout and frozen food! His greatest weakness is women, and he will let everything go at the sight of a gorgeously attired female. This can be quite awkward if he is with his current partner at the time, since even her presence may not stop him from flirting outrageously. Ultimately, however, Dominic will find a permanent partner, although he must make the choice—indicated by the reduction of his name's value to the number of the Lovers in tarot—between the lover who looks great and the lover he actually has real emotional feelings for.

The Runic Interpretation

ᚲᛁᚾᛁᛗᛟᛞ (Kano, Isa, Nauthiz, Isa, Mannaz, Othila, Dagaz)

Dominic is like the King of Pentacles: enterprising, skillful, adaptable, confident, and diversified. He is accomplished in the arts, particularly entertainment. The Mannaz energy of the self is in the heart of his name. Dominic needs this rune to learn modesty. Dominic likes to play and to throw money around. Women love him and are attracted to his charisma. Dominic is the Hollywood dandy, and his wit and charm are the stuff movies are made of.

Elements: Water, earth, fire, earth, air, earth/fire, fire

The Numerological Interpretation

Dominic (NV = 4, CV = 7, VV = 6, FL = 4)

Dominic tends to have his feet planted firmly on the ground. This name describes a person who is very connected to life's physical comforts and has the urge to bring material security into his life and the lives of his loved ones. Home and family are very important to Dominic, and he tends to create strong connections with both his birth family and the family he creates around himself. This sense of loyalty and responsibility to others extends to his friendships.

Donald

A KABBALISTIC SYNOPSIS

דענעלד —DA'ANA'ALD (Daleth, Ayin, Nun, Ayin, Lamed, Daleth)

One meaning of Donald in its Hebrew spelling is "blessed"—and if only Donald realized that, he would be a much more relaxed chap than he often is. The predominant influence in Donald's name is that of Capricorn. This suggests a good head for money matters along with a concern for maintaining a comfortable lifestyle—and all of this is likely to be reflected in Donald's own choices, including his career, which will be secure and reasonably well paying. On the other hand there is the central influence of N, or Nun, which causes Donald to be somewhat insecure in his relationships. He may be concerned that he will lose his lover to the outside world, either to his partner's time-consuming interests or even to another man. For this reason Donald tends to be very possessive.

THE RUNIC INTERPRETATION

ᛞᛚᚨᚾᛟᛞ (Dagaz, Laguz, Ansuz, Nauthiz, Othila, Dagaz)

Always ambitious, Donald is apt to pursue advanced degrees for many years. He is clever with words, and jokes around so much that even his best friends don't really know him. Donald likes it that way and may have a secret life. He loves cookies and may need to watch his diet. Donald has a special interest in genealogy, and he gets along well with old people—especially the old ones who love to bake.

Elements: Fire, water, air, fire, earth/fire, fire

THE NUMEROLOGICAL INTERPRETATION

Donald (NV = 5, CV = 7, VV = 7, FL = 4)

Donald wants to know how things work. An inquisitive person with a very analytical mind, Donald is open to a wide world of discovery. This is a person who is easily attracted by psychology and other fields of study that seek to unlock the inner workings of humanity. Never content with the status quo in his own life, Donald is always pushing himself forward toward greater self-knowledge and awareness. He will require certain periods of solitude and a relationship that does not demand constant interaction.

Donna

A KABBALISTIC SYNOPSIS
דענא —DA'ANA (Daleth, Ayin, Nun, Aleph)

Donna is not a woman to be trifled with. She knows her own mind, is not afraid to speak it, and has a refreshingly forthright way of interacting with others. This may occasionally get her into trouble, as she will treat her bosses in the same way that she treats her close family. However, she is a hard worker by nature, and employers are inclined to overlook the odd outburst, since she is a real asset to any company. At home she will be very protective of her closest family members, a factor that is shown by the reduction of the value of her name to eight, standing for Chet, which means "enclosure." There is a powerful Martian element in her name; in this case the energies of the red planet manifest themselves as a capacity for the vigorous defense of her property if she feels under threat. Possessions are very important to Donna. Because of her strong character and forceful nature, Donna will have to be careful not to allow her relationships, particularly those with her children, to develop into a battle of wills.

THE RUNIC INTERPRETATION
ᚨᚾᚾᛟᛞ (Ansuz, Nauthiz, Nauthiz, Othila, Dagaz)

Donna is often the one to get the empty fortune cookie. This is the sort of effect the naughty Nauthiz rune of constraint has on her. But with the Dagaz rune for breakthrough in her name, Donna has a good sense of timing, and she seizes opportunities that come her way. Othila, the rune of separation, teaches Donna that negative friends can drain our reserves and that we need to embrace positive people. Othila prompts Donna to discard old, worn-out ideas as well. Now Donna has so many wonderful things in her life, she doesn't bother with fortune cookies anymore!

Elements: Air, fire, fire, earth/fire, fire

THE NUMEROLOGICAL INTERPRETATION
Donna (NV = 3, CV = 5, VV = 7, FL = 4)

This name bestows an urge for adventure and a need for excitement. Donna also likes to talk a great deal about a great many subjects, and may prefer breadth to depth. But although Donna may appear to be frivolous at times, this is only one aspect of her varied nature. She also has another, more profound facet to her personality. As Donna rapidly moves through life, she is constantly observing people. Her inner nature is seeking and grasping the deeper significance of external events. This is why Donna will often amaze her friends with the profundity of her insights.

DERIVATION: English, from the Italian word *donna*, meaning "lady." In Italian, Donna is not a first name, but a title of respect. Became common as a first name in English-speaking countries in the twentieth century, and was especially popular during the 1950s.

PRINCIPAL COLORS: All shades of purple, including maroon and mauve

GEMSTONES AND PRECIOUS METALS: Garnets, amethyst

BOTANICALS: Cherry, lungwort, mint, strawberry

UNIQUE SPELLINGS: Dahna, Dhana, Dona, Donnah

RELATED TO: Donaleen, Donelda, Donella, Donita, Donnelle, Donnita, Madonna

DERIVATION: English, from the original Greek root *doron*, meaning "gift." The suffix *een* is an Irish diminutive. Entered into popular use after the publication of Edna Lyall's 1894 novel, *Doreen*. Used quite frequently during the early 1900s.

PRINCIPAL COLORS: Gold, the full gamut of yellows and greens

GEMSTONES AND PRECIOUS METALS: Moss agate, pearls, any other white stones

BOTANICALS: Elder, juniper, hops, linseed

UNIQUE SPELLINGS: Doireen, Doirene, Dorean, Doreane, Doreene, Dorene

RELATED TO: Dora, Dorette, Doria, Dorinda, Dorist, Dorothea, Dorothy†, Dory

Doreen

A KABBALISTIC SYNOPSIS
דעריין —DA'ARYN (Daleth, Ayin, Resh, Yod, Nun)

Doreen usually gets her own way. She has a persuasive tongue, and if that fails, she has a broad streak of stubbornness that only the most determined can withstand. Her name can be reduced to twenty-one, which signifies success, but in Doreen's case this success is likely to come from the efforts of others. Doreen is often a great source of comfort, as she offers a happy and humorous personality and an affectionate manner. It is important that any close friend or partner of Doreen realizes that her determined nature and sense of humor are not all there is to Doreen; she is also a deeply emotional woman. The trouble is that her emotions are kept far below the surface and can often be ignored by others.

THE RUNIC INTERPRETATION
ᛏᛖᛖᚱᛟᛞ (Nauthiz, Ehwaz, Ehwaz, Raido, Othila, Dagaz)

Doreen can walk under ladders and still have a great day. With the double female intuition rune, Ehwaz, Doreen has an instinct for avoiding trouble. She has her challenges, having Nauthiz, the rune of constraint, in her name, but Doreen turns trouble on end and sends it whirling back from whence it came! Wonderful opportunities come to Doreen. She can travel or surf the Internet while chance encounters bless her life. Dagaz, the rune of daybreak, could indicate winning the lottery or starting a successful business. Doreen also has Raido, the rune of journey, offering her a concise, articulate style. People enjoy taking Doreen out to lunch; she networks and helps her friends just by weaving suggestions into the mealtime conversation. Doreen leads a rich, and far from boring, existence.

Elements: Fire, air, air, water, earth/fire, fire

THE NUMEROLOGICAL INTERPRETATION
Doreen (NV = 7, CV = 9, VV = 7, FL = 4)

A quiet and profound person, Doreen takes life seriously. She is not fooled by the masks of superficiality that so many people wear. Within this name there is a strong combination of the numbers seven and nine. When linked together, this yields a woman who is compassionate and inclusive. Her philosophical or spiritual beliefs enrich her life, and Doreen lives by these convictions. Sometimes she may appear to be overly cautious, apprehensive, and even reclusive. This is just her way of protecting herself, for at heart, she is a very sensitive person.

Doris

A Kabbalistic Synopsis
דעריס —DA'ARYS (Daleth, Ayin, Resh, Yod, Samech)

The central energy in Doris's personality comes from the sun, as represented by the letter R, or Resh. This solar force produces a cheerful and outgoing woman with the capacity to brighten up any room she walks into. The sun can have a range of effects on a person's character; in Doris's case, it is the fiercer aspect of the sun that is in the ascendancy, thanks to the accompanying effect of Aries in the name. The Arian element can be seen in Doris's ability to more than hold her own in an argument, and in the fact that she can be mobilized into vigorous protest against anything she sees as unjust. The total of Doris's name is 344, which in terms of the tarot associates her with the Emperor and the Empress. The presence of both these cards indicates a passion for the family and Doris's ability to establish a comfortable base for her nearest and dearest, to whom she will be a great source of support.

The Runic Interpretation
ᛋᛁᚱᛟᛗ (Sowelu, Isa, Raido, Othila, Dagaz)

Green lights as far as the eye can see! Doris seems to zoom to the top, and she shouldn't be smug because she has fewer hindrances to detour her than most. Lucky Doris has Othila, the rune of separation, to teach her to make good choices. She probably has a knack for picking stocks and follows her investments with a watchful eye. With Dagaz, the rune of breakthrough, helping Doris, she encounters opportunities that catapult her to success. The Raido rune of journey indicates Doris can travel and is a good communicator. She might enjoy the performing arts or business. Sowelu, the rune of wholeness, paves the way for a healthy family and a satisfying lifestyle. If Doris takes good care of her health and stays rested, she can accomplish more than most.

Elements: Air, earth, water, earth/fire, fire

The Numerological Interpretation
Doris (NV = 11, CV = 5, VV = 6, FL = 4)

Fun-loving and open to life are but two qualities that describe Doris. This is a very individualistic woman who needs a great deal of space for self-discovery. She has a kind disposition and a warmth that radiates around her. This joyful magnetism is quite attractive to others, and Doris will have many friends and admirers. Quick-witted and insightful, Doris enjoys travel. This is a person who can be counted on to give an interesting twist to ordinary life situations and add dynamism to all social situations.

"Think wrongly, if you please, but in all cases think for yourself."
—DORIS LESSING (AUTHOR)

DERIVATION: English, composed of the Greek roots *doron*, meaning "gift," and *theos*, meaning "god." Became common after the sixteenth century throughout all English-speaking countries.

PRINCIPAL COLORS: The full range of blue tones

GEMSTONES AND PRECIOUS METALS: Emeralds, turquoise

BOTANICALS: Vervain, daffodils, walnuts, almonds

UNIQUE SPELLINGS: Dorathy, Dorethy, Dorothee, Dorothey, Dorothi, Dorothie

RELATED TO: Dora, Doreent, Dorete, Dori, Doria, Dorist, Dorothea, Dory, Dosia, Dot, Dottie

❧

"A mother is not a person to lean on but a person to make leaning unnecessary."
—DOROTHY CANFIELD FISHER
(AUTHOR)

A KABBALISTIC SYNOPSIS
דערעתי —DA'ARA'ATHY (Daleth, Ayin, Resh, Ayin, Tau, Yod)

If you were to speak to Dorothy's friends and her colleagues about her, it would be understandable if you came away with the impression that there were two separate people sharing Dorothy's life. It isn't that Dorothy suffers from a split personality or any other similar problem, but that she likes to keep her work and personal life totally separate. It is highly unlikely, for instance, that her friends will come from the office. In fact, she will probably have the same circle of friends she had as a young adult, since she has strong connections to her emotional past that she is reluctant to relinquish. At work Dorothy operates under the energy of Capricorn and is perceived as ambitious, efficient, and potentially ruthless. However, with her friends and family Dorothy enjoys simple conversation and family gatherings; she loves to reminisce about the "good old days." It is probable that the sense of continuity in Dorothy's emotional life provides a sense of stability that enables her to act quite boldly in the workplace.

THE RUNIC INTERPRETATION
ᛇᚦᛟᚱᛟᛞ (Eihwaz, Thurisaz, Othila, Raido, Othila, Dagaz)

Dorothy is imaginative and lighthearted. The double Othila rune of separation offers Dorothy wisdom in the choices she makes. She can try to ignore warning signs in her relationships, such as impulsiveness and gullibility, but she can only make relationships last so long before the lesson of separation and retreat kicks in. It takes a lot of strength to look closely at circumstances and use your free time to become your best self, but this should be Dorothy's goal. Self-love is the way to peace for Dorothy. As Dorothy grows stronger, she appreciates her independence and attracts similar partners. She cultivates fine friends because she's learned to let people earn her trust.

Elements: Earth/fire, fire, earth/fire, water, earth/fire, fire

THE NUMEROLOGICAL INTERPRETATION
Dorothy (NV = 6, CV = 5, VV = 1, FL = 4)

The number values in Dorothy indicate a person who is balanced and harmonious by nature. She is able to communicate this peaceful quality and to see the potential good in every situation. Artistic self-expression is very important to her, as she has a strong need to be her own person. This may sometimes conflict with her urge to be ever present for the needs of family and other loved ones. The integration of this polarity is challenging but will bear abundant fruit.

❧

Doug

A Kabbalistic Synopsis
דוג —DVG (Daleth, Vau, Gimel)

Doug tends to find himself repeatedly pulled in opposite directions in life. On the one hand, he likes to be thoughtful and somewhat philosophical about life, while at the same time he is a man of action who enjoys exploring new experiences and activities. The more contemplative aspect of his personality is shown both by the central letter Vau in his name and by the fact that the final letter Gimel can be related to the tarot card the High Priestess. Doug's dynamic side is indicated most strongly by the association of the total value of his name with the tarot card the Emperor. The Emperor is a very strong character who likes to dominate material concerns. Doug will make an excellent businessman, especially if he is born under Aries, which will counter his tendency to daydream. Doug finds it hard to stay in one relationship for too long, as he is both eager for variety in all aspects of his life and prone to feeling that the grass must be greener elsewhere. However, his dynamic personality means that he tends to leave quite an impression on people, and will never be short of potential partners, however short-lived their involvement may prove to be.

The Runic Interpretation
ᚷᚢᛟᛞ (Gebo, Uruz, Othila, Dagaz)

Doug is likable. He has a light touch with people and simply doesn't criticize or gossip. Guilelessness takes him far in life. Few people grasp that Doug's disposition is grounded in a deep faith and that his strength originates in a union with his higher self. Doug clowns around a lot and understands that often the only way we can love people is to help them relax and see things in a comical light. Doug isn't ambitious, but fortune favors him because people are happy to help him get ahead. When they are around Doug for any time at all, they leave feeling a little better about themselves.

Elements: Water, earth, earth/fire, fire

The Numerological Interpretation
Doug (NV = 2, CV = 11, VV = 9, FL = 4)

This is a name whose numbers evoke a philosophical attitude and a real intuition about people. Doug may not be allied with any particular religion, as his is a way of life that is open and universal in nature. He is definitely a people person, and would benefit tremendously from some form of active participation in a humanitarian organization. In return, the group would profit from Doug's insightful understanding and ability to harmonize dissent. Doug tends to think much more in holistic rather than separatist ways, and is always looking for the fundamental truth underlining events and circumstances. Some people may find him too idealistic, and there is a need for Doug to be able to balance his higher aspirations with practical, everyday life on earth.

DERIVATION: From the name Douglas, of Gaelic origin, meaning "black water." A very popular nickname.

PRINCIPAL COLORS: All shades of white and green

GEMSTONES AND PRECIOUS METALS: Cat's-eye, jade, pearls, moonstones

BOTANICALS: Plantain, lettuce, cabbage, chicory

UNIQUE SPELLINGS: Dug, Dugg, Dugh

RELATED TO: Doogie, Dougal, Dougie, Douglast, Douglass, Dugaid, Dugal

Douglas

A KABBALISTIC SYNOPSIS
דוגלום —DVGLVS (Daleth, Vau, Gimel, Lamed, Vau, Samech)

Douglas is certainly an exciting chap to know, although if you hang around him too long, you may find yourself involved in dangerous, if not downright crazy, activities. Douglas is the sort of guy who does a bungee jump in the morning before breakfast just to set himself up for the real business of the day! To Douglas life is for living, and he feels most alive when faced with a potentially life-threatening situation. While all of his friends are advising Douglas against his next trip, be it mountaineering or white-water rafting, he will view their concerns with quiet amusement. Luckily for Douglas his name reduces to ten, suggesting that not only does he enjoy games of chance but he usually wins. As with most extremely adventurous spirits, there is a deeper reason for his behavior. This is hinted at by the presence of the letter T, or Teth, meaning "serpent," in the compression of his name. At some level in Douglas's personality there are certain self-destructive tendencies; his love of risk-taking is probably an expression of that unconscious instinct.

THE RUNIC INTERPRETATION
ᛋᚨᛚᚷᚢᛟᛞ (Sowelu, Ansuz, Laguz, Gebo, Uruz, Othila, Dagaz)

The Gebo energy in Douglas's name ensures a life of companionship and a close walk with God. Gebo is the rune of partnership. Douglas is a facilitator, with a deeply compassionate and caring nature, who is not thwarted when the accolades he so richly deserves are withheld occasionally. He operates from his own core. He isn't critical of outcomes because he has his sights set on high goals. Douglas is able to allow the other person freedom in a relationship; he's a live-and-let-live sort of chap. He is also modest and knows how to keep his lips zipped. He regards himself in a positive and warm way, and nurtures the child within on many levels.

Elements: Air, air, water, water, earth, earth/fire, fire

THE NUMEROLOGICAL INTERPRETATION
Douglas (NV = 7, CV = 6, VV = 1, FL = 4)

Douglas will embark on many paths of self-development. He may thus find himself attracted to psychology, philosophy, or even some branch of metaphysics. All of these pursuits will open doors to life's mysteries for Douglas—and especially to the mystery of himself. In his personal relationships, Douglas seeks a partner who can be supportive of his profound searching and intellectual interests.

Drew

A Kabbalistic Synopsis
דרע —DRA'A (Daleth, Resh, Ayin)

Drew is first and foremost a thinker who loves to play with concepts and possibilities. Drew is quite mischievous in nature, a trait that does not end with childhood but continues into adulthood. If Drew is a woman, this may come out as coquettishness, whereas a guy named Drew will go for the full-blown practical jokes, which he may well spend days planning. His love of a laugh is an endearing quality, particularly in light of his powerful intellect, which can make many people expect a dour and unapproachable character. If Drew decides to work in the field of higher education, which he or she is more than capable of doing, Drew will be a popular tutor with the students as he/she has an ability to take complex concepts and render them accessible. Male Drews may be less likely to venture into education, as they like the idea of "playing with the big boys" and will aim for a career in business, preferably for a large and prestigious firm. Drew reduces to thirteen, and therein lies the only problem: Drew is like a firefly flitting from one interest to the next, and the only thing that could hold back his career is his inability to commit to a single area of investigation for a reasonable period of time.

The Runic Interpretation
ᛈᛖᚱᛞ (Wunjo, Ehwaz, Raido, Dagaz)

Drew is able to tolerate uncertainty and paradoxes in life. Drew is an extrovert and has a lively, passionate nature. He may be likely to ask a lot of questions, and he needs drama in his life. His artistic nature is always probing for unique solutions and is easily discouraged by negativity and repetition. Drew may be prone to exasperation. He needs help with his finances but will work well with a manager and accountant who keep him in line. Drew has the patience to put up with all these left-brained types. A female Drew will share these traits.

Elements: Earth, air, water, fire

The Numerological Interpretation
Drew (NV = 5, CV = 4, VV = 1, FL = 4)

Men and women named Drew are freedom-loving and expansive. Their high energy level makes them fun to be around, and they usually have many friends. Drew enjoys sharing life's adventures and seeks a partner who is unafraid to explore the many pathways and opportunities that life presents. But Drew is not an entirely carefree soul. People with this name have a decidedly practical side to their nature. They are also career and success oriented, using their ability to be open to a number of creative possibilities to channel their experiences into financial and material rewards.

DERIVATION: Scottish, originally a pet name of Andrew. It has become increasingly common as an independent first name throughout the English-speaking world in recent years. Andrew originally derives from the Greek word *andreas*, meaning "manly," although the name is now used for both sexes.

PRINCIPAL COLORS: The full spectrum of very pale hues

GEMSTONES AND PRECIOUS METALS: Diamonds, platinum, silver

BOTANICALS: Hazel, oats, parsley

UNIQUE SPELLINGS: Drewe, Droo, Drue

RELATED TO: Andreas, Andrew†; Andrea†

DERIVATION: Scottish and English, from the Gaelic name Donnchadh, meaning "brown battle." Became popular in England in the 1950s and 1960s.

PRINCIPAL COLORS: The darker shades of all reddish colors

GEMSTONES AND PRECIOUS METALS: Bloodstones, garnets

BOTANICALS: Broom, nettle, garlic, onion

UNIQUE SPELLINGS: Dunkan, Dunkin

RELATED TO: Dunham, Dunky, Dunley, Dunlop, Dunmore, Dunn, Dunstan

Duncan

A KABBALISTIC SYNOPSIS
דונכן —DVNKN (Daleth, Vau, Nun, Kaph, Nun)

They often say that the quiet ones are the worst, and this expression could have originated with Duncan in mind! On the outside, Duncan can easily come across as a fairly moderate, stable guy, but the reality is enormously different. In fact, Duncan tends to have only one thing on his mind—and it isn't his work! The name Duncan has a total value of 780, which can be compressed by addition to fifteen, the number of the tarot card the Devil. The Devil card indicates that Duncan is dominated by his physical appetites, and as he has quite an impressive personality, he will have plenty of opportunities to indulge those appetites to the fullest. However, Duncan is not entirely at ease with himself, since his name can also be represented by the letter Peh followed by the letter Nun. This can indicate that Duncan has a need to talk through certain deep-seated emotional anxieties, since Peh relates strongly to conversation, while Nun refers to emotional concerns. The existence of two Nuns in his name strengthens this possibility, and their specific position in the name may point to a danger that worries can sometimes overtake him. If Duncan is a Pisces or Virgo, it may take a lot of work to overcome this tendency.

THE RUNIC INTERPRETATION
ᛏᚨᚲᚺᚾᛞ (Nauthiz, Ansuz, Kano, Nauthiz, Uruz, Dagaz)

The double rune of constraint is clearly offset in Duncan's name by clarity, industry, and transformation. The presence of the four elements in this name give it an extra splash of strength and resourcefulness. Duncan can handle a lot of responsibility, and should he get off track early in life because of poor judgment, he will welcome the help it will take to bring him back into the light. Duncan is willful, but he also has the ability to learn from his mistakes. With three fire elements in his name and the rune of strength, Duncan has a flair for taking risks and being persuasive. He can excel in the healing arts or in entrepreneurial endeavors.

Elements: Fire, air, water, fire, earth, fire

THE NUMEROLOGICAL INTERPRETATION
Duncan (NV = 9, CV = 5, VV = 4, FL = 4)

Duncan is a blend of the philosophical and the practical. He definitely possesses much of the spirit of the romantic poet in his nature. Yet the material world means a great deal to him as well, and he will work long hours to achieve the financial stability and security that are also important to him. Duncan is sincere in his affections and tends to be a loyal friend and faithful lover. This name definitely indicates a man who is curious about life and eager for experience. But Duncan does not just go through life superficially in the pursuit of pleasure; he is in search of truth. This is a person who is able to draw out the inner meaning of his experiences and add it to his ever growing understanding of himself and the world around him.

Dustin

DERIVATION: English, originally a Norman surname from the root *thurstan*, meaning "Thor's stone." Has become somewhat common in recent years, particularly due to the popularity of film actor Dustin Hoffman (b.1937).

PRINCIPAL COLORS: The full range of blue hues

GEMSTONES AND PRECIOUS METALS: Emeralds, blue and blue-green turquoise

BOTANICALS: Dog rose, violet, walnuts

UNIQUE SPELLINGS: Dousten, Doustin, Doustyn, Dusten, Dustinn, Dustyn

RELATED TO: Dunstan, Dusty, Thurstan

A KABBALISTIC SYNOPSIS

דוסטין —DVSTYN (Daleth, Vau, Samech, Teth, Yod, Nun)

Dustin is both an attractive and an incredibly frustrating individual. He is always interested in some new project, and his enthusiasm is usually quite infectious. Dustin will often call up his friends in the evening so that he can tell them all about his latest idea, and his ability to hold an audience's attention will mean that the conversation often goes on into the small hours. However, the frustrating element to his character is that despite his initial energy, his ideas rarely, if ever, become realities. His name adds up to 789, which can be seen as the three sephirot immediately above the material plane. In other words, Dustin tends to function in something of a dreamworld and lacks the element of earth, which ensures that something concrete will result from his thoughts. If Dustin can find himself a job where his responsibility is simply to come up with concepts, rather than follow through with them, this characteristic should not cause him any real problems.

THE RUNIC INTERPRETATION

ᚺᛁᛏᛊᚢᛞ (Nauthiz, Isa, Teiwaz, Sowelu, Uruz, Dagaz)

This name is fortunate to have the Teiwaz rune energy of the spiritual warrior contained within it. Dustin demands more of himself than anyone asks of him, and he keeps on trying regardless of the outcome. But however difficult his task is, Dustin is always able to rejuvenate himself and carry on. The Teiwaz rune affords him a great capacity for perseverance. Dustin is modest and has a developed and cultivated emotional range. He can make most people instantly comfortable. He is a traditional and polite gentleman who tries not to push the envelope too severely.

Elements: Fire, earth, air, earth, fire

THE NUMEROLOGICAL INTERPRETATION

Dustin (NV = 6, CV = 3, VV = 3, FL = 4)

Often a person of physical as well as intellectual balance and beauty, Dustin seeks to communicate this sense of harmony into the world around him. This name offers the capacity to be skilled in the arts as well as in some branch of the media. Dustin usually has many friends, as he is loving and caring by nature. There is great tolerance of other people's differences and a tendency toward inclusiveness and open-mindedness. Dustin can be very diplomatic, making it easy for him to have his abundant thoughts, ideas, and opinions universally accepted.

DERIVATION: Spelling variation of
the Irish and English name Duane,
which is originally from the Gaelic
dubh, meaning "dark." Popular
since the mid-twentieth century.

PRINCIPAL COLORS: The
complete gamut of red and
reddish hues, including crimson,
pink, and maroon

GEMSTONES AND PRECIOUS
METALS: Red rubies and
bloodstones

BOTANICALS: Broom, mustard
seed, nettle, onion

UNIQUE SPELLINGS: Dewain,
Dewayne, Duane, Duwain, Dwain,
Dwane

RELATED TO: Dubdara, Dubhan,
Wayne†

Dwayne

A KABBALISTIC SYNOPSIS
דואין —DVAYN (Daleth, Vau, Aleph, Yod, Nun)

Dwayne is decidedly the strong and silent type. Like a battery, he holds all his emotional energy inside, where it circulates and constantly increases in magnitude. The end result is a man with immense reserves of strength who is well suited to high positions of power in the commercial world. Yet his power is based on sheer energy rather than particular skills in management or business strategy. Dwayne is a leader rather than a planner. At home it is Dwayne who rules the roost, and if he has chosen a partner with an equally strong character, he should expect fireworks! One Hebrew equivalent of the value of Dwayne's name is "fullness," and Dwayne certainly enjoys the fruits of his labor. His taste is unlikely to be particularly refined, but what he has he will have in vast quantities. Luckily for his neighbors, despite his reluctance to engage in personal conversation, Dwayne delights in displaying his success and will often have barbecues and invite the whole neighborhood.

THE RUNIC INTERPRETATION
ᛖᚾᛇᚫᚹᛞ (Ehwaz, Nauthiz, Eihwaz, Ansuz, Wunjo, Dagaz)

Dwayne follows his heart, and so he may be a truly marvelous writer. Dwayne uses the Dagaz energy of breakthroughs to transform a simple event, such as a ride on Rollerblades, to a tale of insight and delight. Dwayne has not led an ordinary life, and his eyes and heart are open, ready to record the plight of characters he meets along his path. Dwayne knows that the darkness will pass away and that he will achieve success and prosperity for surviving some tough early lessons. Dwayne is an artist and is not striving to be comfortable; he strives to be *real*. His work is a contribution to our culture.

Elements: Air, fire, earth/fire, air, earth, fire

THE NUMEROLOGICAL INTERPRETATION
Dwayne (NV = 9, CV = 9, VV = 9, FL = 4)

The number nine dominates this name, giving Dwayne a distinct humanitarian orientation. Dwayne is very set on being of help to others. He is often quite selfless, and strives to participate in those groups and organizations that seek to bring positive changes into other people's lives. He may be attracted to one of the helping professions, so that he may use his talents and abilities to be of benefit to those less fortunate than himself. Dwayne has to take care that he is objective and not overcome by his own profound idealism, or else he may become blindly devoted to causes and people that may not be of the most benefit to him.

Dylan

A KABBALISTIC SYNOPSIS
דילון —DYLVN (Daleth, Yod, Lamed, Vau, Nun)

Dylan has a real sense of direction in life, which he will follow with the persistence of a man on a mission. He rarely relaxes from the pursuit of his goal, thanks to the power of the letter L, or Lamed, meaning "ox goad." All of this constant activity can cause Dylan problems, not just in terms of physical exhaustion, but also because of its potential to cause emotional stress. The final N, or Nun, marks Dylan as an emotionally sensitive individual, and it is likely that his goal in life will relate to emotional concerns. Dylan has the capacity to make money from his personal goals, so we can expect to see Dylan working in a creative environment where emotional expression is an integral part of the work. Despite the primacy of emotions in Dylan's psychological makeup, relationships can be a difficult area for him because of his tendency to become totally absorbed in his emotional state.

THE RUNIC INTERPRETATION
ᚾᚨᛚᛇᛞ (Nauthiz, Ansuz, Laguz, Eihwaz, Dagaz)

Dylan has music in his laugh and a way of making you feel better about yourself after you've been with him. Dylan is lucky—that's all there is to it. He picks up a guitar and his fingers have a fluid mind of their own. He walks on the dance floor and people form a circle around him because his body gives the music form. Dylan can make you laugh with the look on his face, and kids love to joke around with him. The Laguz energy of flow in his name gives Dylan a close connection to the lunar or emotional side of his nature, and the world is a better place for it!

Elements: Fire, air, water, earth/fire, fire

THE NUMEROLOGICAL INTERPRETATION
Dylan (NV = 11, CV = 3, VV = 8, FL = 4)

People look up to Dylan for his special intuitive insight. They often call upon him for his ability to peer deeply under the surface of a given situation in order to reveal its deeper truth. Dylan can be quite an inspiration to others. He is careful not to force his views on people but has a great ease in communicating what he sees in ways that are universal in their application. Dylan also seeks worldly success and social recognition, and can easily convert his personal talents and abilities into both.

DERIVATION: Welsh, from a Celtic root meaning "sea." In Welsh lore, Dylan was a legendary sea god. Since the 1950s, it has become increasingly popular outside of Wales due to the fame of Welsh poet Dylan Thomas (1914–1953) and singer Bob Dylan (b.1941).

PRINCIPAL COLORS: White, any shade of green

GEMSTONES AND PRECIOUS METALS: Jade, moonstones, cat's-eye

BOTANICALS: Chicory, lettuce, plantain

UNIQUE SPELLINGS: Dillan, Dillen, Dillon, Dylann, Dylen, Dylin, Dyllen

RELATED TO: Dill, Dilys, Dylis

Ed

A KABBALISTIC SYNOPSIS
אד —AD (Aleph, Daleth)

Ed has a very special name indeed, as its value is five without any reduction needed to arrive at this value. The holder of this name will have a very strong self-image, which he will project clearly and confidently. We can expect Ed to have an inquiring nature. This is further suggested by the initial Aleph, which signifies the element of air. Ed's curiosity is not just a desire for knowledge, but represents a hunger for information about the world that he can actually use in a practical sense. Ed has strong leanings toward management or other positions where he has responsibility for other people. Since he has an almost perfectly balanced character, it is highly unlikely that he will exploit any positions of power that he gains.

THE RUNIC INTERPRETATION
ᛞᛖ (Dagaz, Ehwaz)

Ed uses the power of Dagaz, or breakthrough, and Ehwaz, or movement, to steer his life. Ed understands that the outer self is a mere reflection of the inner self. Ed progresses slowly to build his character and manifest prosperity in his world. The Ehwaz energy is there to help him realize that he needs to share his good fortune with those less fortunate. The Dagaz energy of transformation helps swing wide the doors of change for Ed. It's highly likely that this Dagaz energy requires Ed to move and/or change jobs as well as restructure his lifestyle several times.

Elements: Fire, air

THE NUMEROLOGICAL INTERPRETATION
Ed (NV = 9, CV = 4, VV = 5, FL = 5)

Ed has a very complex disposition. On the surface, he may appear to have a life that is defined by his material concerns and practical circumstances. Yet underneath, there is a powerful urge within him to expand his horizons and search out new dimensions. This may give rise to a certain sense of duality. On the one hand, Ed has the urge to open himself up to different possibilities, while on the other, he feels the need to stay put and deal with what is in front of him. The resolution is to create a career that is stable and yet offers abundant variety.

Edgar

DERIVATION: English, from the Old English roots *ed* and *gar*, which respectively mean "prosperity" and "spear." An old Anglo-Saxon name that predated the Norman Conquest.

PRINCIPAL COLORS: Black, dark gray, the darkest shades of blue and violet

GEMSTONES AND PRECIOUS METALS: Carbuncles, amethyst, any dark-colored stones

BOTANICALS: Angelica, shepherd's purse, ragwort

UNIQUE SPELLINGS: Eddgar, Eddger, Edger, Edgir, Edgyr

RELATED TO: Edt, Edmund, Edwardt, Edwint, Medgar

⤻

"Those who dream by day are cognizant of many things which escape those who dream only by night."
—EDGAR ALLAN POE (AUTHOR)

A KABBALISTIC SYNOPSIS
אדגה —ADGH (Aleph, Daleth, Gimel, Heh)

The song "Rambling Man" could have been written with Edgar in mind. This guy will never settle down if he can possibly avoid it. His work will almost definitely involve travel, and his ideal job would be to act as a tour guide of sorts, especially on a wilderness outing. People find Edgar an intriguing man, and he quite enjoys the air of mystery he carries with him. In fact, there are hints in his name that suggest he is not averse to embellishing the details of his travels from time to time—particularly in female company! Edgar is easily bored by routine; not only does his name contain the letter G, or Gimel, representing exploration, but the total value of his name is thirteen, the number of change. He usually can keep himself amused though, as he is likely to have a number of leisure pursuits that involve a considerable amount of physical exertion. Edgar's biggest problem is romance; he mates easily but loses partners just as easily! While he is happy to exaggerate, Edgar is essentially an honest man who feels obliged to tell people very early on in a relationship that it will never last.

THE RUNIC INTERPRETATION
ᚱᚨᚷᛞᛖ (Raido, Ansuz, Gebo, Dagaz, Ehwaz)

Edgar is blessed with the Raido rune of union in his name. Raido is here to teach us all to value inner guidance. Raido cautions us to wait until we grow into our purpose, and to use the waiting time to remove blocks to psychological progress. Edgar also uses Raido to resist his desire for instant gratification. The message of Raido is to forestall decisions until the way is made clear for "right action." Edgar knows that discipline and self-love are enormous achievements in this life. He is also interested in developing his creativity, and in so doing, he is able to commune with his higher intelligence.

Elements: Water, air, water, fire, air

THE NUMEROLOGICAL INTERPRETATION
Edgar (NV = 8, CV = 2, VV = 6, FL = 5)

Edgar contains the numerological indicators of a person who is very productive. This is a man who knows how to create material comfort both for himself and others. Edgar seeks to wear the best clothes and drive the finest car he can afford. He carries a sense of personal self-worth and exudes authority and achievement. Edgar is also a kind and gentle person, a man for whom home and family are very important. He is capable of sincere personal intimacy, and partnership is central to Edgar's life.

⤻

DERIVATION: English, from the Old
English root *ed*, meaning
"prosperity." A very popular name
from the late nineteenth to the
early twentieth century.

PRINCIPAL COLORS: From pale to
deep golden yellow; shades of
brown

GEMSTONES AND PRECIOUS
METALS: Citrine, topaz, amber

BOTANICALS: Chamomile,
lavender, sorrel, thyme

UNIQUE SPELLINGS: Edithe,
Edyth, Edythe

RELATED TO: Eda, Edie, Editha,
Edytha

Edith

A KABBALISTIC SYNOPSIS
אדית —ADYTh (Aleph, Daleth, Yod, Tau)

Edith is a great believer in fate—not in horoscopes and predictions, but in a greater force of destiny—and she is convinced that all the major events in our lives are to a large extent pre-determined. There will be very few occasions when Edith has cause to resent the hand that the fates have dealt her, as on the whole she is a lucky woman; her name equates with the number ten, which is linked to the Wheel of Fortune in the tarot. However, the presence of the letter Th, or Tau, indicates that she will be close to considerable suffering in her life. This may suggest a career in nursing or emergency services. Edith would certainly be suited to such a profession, since she is very down-to-earth and unflappable. In fact, she is the ideal person to be with in a crisis.

THE RUNIC INTERPRETATION
ᚦᛁᛞᛖ (Thurisaz, Isa, Dagaz, Ehwaz)

Edith loves to solve mysteries and is given to a weird fascination with the macabre. For example, she may belong to a mystery writers club whose members sit around and talk about the smoothest way to do someone in. On the surface Edith appears to be a very normal woman, but her mind is like a chess board, and when she negotiates a contract, she usually gets her way on a large number of issues. Edith uses the Thurisaz, or gateway rune, to examine her actions long before she undertakes any moves.

Elements: Fire, earth, fire, air

THE NUMEROLOGICAL INTERPRETATION
Edith (NV = 1, CV = 5, VV = 5, FL = 5)

Change, variation, and above all, personal freedom characterize this name. Edith has a tremendous need to express herself with versatility and enthusiasm. She has to work to create firm goals and objectives, or else she has the tendency to become scattered and unstable. Edith avoids the routine and the mundane. She looks forward to changing her environment and is an avid traveler. Her basic nature gives her a very independent orientation to life. This has to be balanced with the awareness of personal boundaries, not to limit her but to bring Edith a sense of cohesive focus with which she can achieve success.

Edward

DERIVATION: English and Polish, from Old English roots meaning "wealth" and "guard." The name of eight kings of England since the Norman Conquest.

PRINCIPAL COLORS: The full range of yellow hues, including orange and gold

GEMSTONES AND PRECIOUS METALS: Amber, citrine, yellow diamonds

BOTANICALS: Borage, lavender, Saint-John's-wort

UNIQUE SPELLINGS: Edouard, Eduard, Edwerd, Edwyrd

RELATED TO: Edt, Eddie, Eddy, Edgart, Edlin, Edmund, Edwint, Edwyn

A KABBALISTIC SYNOPSIS
אדואדד —ADVARD (Aleph, Daleth, Vau, Aleph, Resh, Daleth)

A true individual, one usually well respected for his unique outlook and beliefs, Edward is an intelligent man with the capacity to create an entire set of values from within his own mind. His very unusual way of looking at the world can make him shy away from company, and in a few rare cases this may go to the point of reclusiveness. Despite his qualifications, Edward is unlikely to pursue a career in business. The commercial world needs people who can make quick decisions, often with minimal supporting data. Edward finds it very difficult to commit to any line of action until he has all the relevant facts in front of him—and probably a fair bundle of irrelevant facts, too! He then likes to ponder for a long time before finally making a decision. His approach to love is very similar, and this can prove frustrating, to say the least. When a partner asks a simple question of the type that lovers are bound to ask—"Am I looking older?" for example—most spouses know the answer, which is always a resounding "No!" However, Edward will make the terrible mistake of taking a few hours to think it over!

THE RUNIC INTERPRETATION
ᛞᚱᚨᚠᛞᛖ (Dagaz, Raido, Ansuz, Wunjo, Dagaz, Ehwaz)

Edward loves auctions and poking around antiques shops on rainy Sunday afternoons. He loves his family and designs his home with carefully chosen objects that create a comfortable, familiar mood. The Wunjo energy of nourishment assures Edward of a prosperous life filled with many beautiful and carefully acquired possessions. Edward also enjoys the rune Wunjo; it signifies love fulfilled, and he will seldom be disappointed when it comes to romance. Edward appreciates the importance of emotional growth in relationships. He has overcome many obstacles to arrive at a level of harmony and gratitude, and his family benefits from his warmth and caring.

Elements: Fire, water, air, earth, fire, air

THE NUMEROLOGICAL INTERPRETATION
Edward (NV = 1, CV = 8, VV = 11, FL = 5)

Edward is a name that contains a very powerful combination of number values. Edward is highly individualistic, with a strong need to create his world relative to some inner plan. The name also bestows acute powers of observation, giving Edward well-developed intuition about people and life situations. Edward has an inner sense of personal direction, and he carries authority as well as the potential to rise high socially. The numbers indicate a man who is geared for material success and for whom no obstacle is too big to overcome. It is a very strong name!

DERIVATION: English, from Old
English roots meaning "friend"
and "wealth." A popular Anglo-
Saxon name that was revived in the
nineteenth century.

PRINCIPAL COLORS: Yellows, gold,
orange, bronze

GEMSTONES AND PRECIOUS
METALS: Any yellow stone,
including topaz and citrine

BOTANICALS: Chamomile,
eyebright, gentian root

UNIQUE SPELLINGS: Eadwin,
Eadwinn, Edwinn, Edwyn, Ehdwin,
Ehdwinn, Ehdwyn, Ehdwynn

RELATED TO: Ed†, Eddie, Edgart,
Edlin, Edmund, Ned, Neddy, Ted

Edwin

A KABBALISTIC SYNOPSIS
אדוין —ADVYN (Aleph, Daleth, Vau, Yod, Nun)

In Edwin we find a continuation of the searching for a truth of sorts that was so strong in Ed. This name transforms the quest into an almost purely emotional one. To Edwin, the right relationship is more important than any other factor in his life. It is not unusual for Edwin to sacrifice a financial or career opportunity because it will interfere with his love life. Thus he is likely to attract some negative comments from the more competitive men in his social circle for his lack of ambition in the workplace. However, they will be equally envious of his married life, which is likely to be blissfully happy. You will never see Edwin roaming the streets on Christmas Eve trying to get all those presents at the last minute. No, Edwin will have done all this in November and will know exactly what his partner is hoping for. What is more, he will move heaven and earth to try to fulfill all her dreams for her.

THE RUNIC INTERPRETATION
ᚺᛁᛈᛞᛖ (Nauthiz, Isa, Wunjo, Dagaz, Ehwaz)

Edwin is the kind of father children adore. He never raises a hand to them but speaks with calm authority; they willingly follow his lead because he has earned their trust. Edwin defuses tension with a rhyme or a limerick, and the children love his fantastic stories of faraway places and times. Edwin has filled his memory with poems, songs, and bits of poignant verse to delight wee minds and inspire dignity and hope in their fragile hearts. And when the children get out of line, he uses the Isa energy of isolation to find a peaceful place for himself within which to meditate. Edwin is a nester. He could have a lucrative career in interior design or architecture. His rooms are playful, and his colors invite you into a living space that is fresh and safe.

Elements: Fire, earth, earth, fire, air

THE NUMEROLOGICAL INTERPRETATION
Edwin (NV = 1, CV = 9, VV = 1, FL = 5)

Edwin is an individualist. His life lesson will be to develop a clear sense of who he is and how he should direct the flow of his personal creative power. Edwin is evolving toward a conscious awareness of his own potency. The awareness of his power allows him to produce additional opportunities for his success—and as Edwin has a generous and humanitarian facet to his nature, the greater his ability to develop his potential and succeed in life, the more he will want to share.

Eileen

A KABBALISTIC SYNOPSIS
יל׳ין —YLYN (Yod, Lamed, Yod, Nun)

This name sets out all the archetypical qualities of womanhood. Eileen is influenced by Virgo, Libra, and Scorpio, which can be seen as representing three aspects of femininity. In Virgo we have woman as mother and protector, and Eileen will be wonderfully supportive to all her children, who will come to look back on their childhood with a sense of amazement at her reserves of advice and seemingly infinite patience—especially when they themselves have their own little herds driving them crazy! The Scorpio influence in this name represents woman as seductress and mistress of passion. Another aspect of this planetary influence will be a passionate temperament, and woe betide the lover who fools around behind Eileen's back! The central letter of the name is Lamed, and in terms of Eileen's personality, this letter represents the balancing signs of Libra. It is the Libran factor that provides the conciliatory element to her character. Eileen is very skilled in resolving inevitable family arguments through a rational and compromising approach.

THE RUNIC INTERPRETATION
⼊MMⱵⲒM (Nauthiz, Ehwaz, Ehwaz, Laguz, Isa, Ehwaz)

Eileen keeps trying when a lesser soul might fold. She acknowledges her challenges in life as wake-up calls to try harder, and this often means exercising more patience and an impeccable demeanor. Eileen is persevering and strong, and the Laguz energy helps Eileen to relax as events unfold and resist the impulse to try to hurry things along. She withstands times of limitation and discomfort, knowing that growth is most certainly her reward.

Elements: Fire, air, air, water, earth, air

THE NUMEROLOGICAL INTERPRETATION
Eileen (NV = 5, CV = 8, VV = 6, FL = 5)

This name has several noteworthy qualities. Eileen has the ability to channel her energies in ways that transform and improve any situation in which she finds herself. In addition, she has strength of character and a positive sense of her own willpower. Home and family are important to her, and she will use her many talents for other people's comfort and well-being. She may also find that her sense of devotion comes into conflict with her own need for self-expression. She should make sure that she gives herself enough of the latter, so that her urge to serve remains free of resentment.

DERIVATION: Irish, originally from the Irish root Eiglin. Entered England in the late nineteenth century, and subsequently spread to the United States. Especially common during the first half of the twentieth century.

PRINCIPAL COLORS: The full spectrum of very light hues

GEMSTONES AND PRECIOUS METALS: Diamonds, platinum, silver

BOTANICALS: Hazel, parsley, sweet marjoram

UNIQUE SPELLINGS: Aileen, Aylean, Ayleen, Eilean, Eilleen, Ilean, Ileen, Ilene

RELATED TO: Eily, Eleanort, Ellent, Evelynt, Helent, Helenet

DERIVATION: English, originally from the Greek name Helen. In the legend of King Arthur, Elaine was the mother of Sir Galahad. Used in all English-speaking countries, especially in Scotland and Britain. Became very popular in the mid-1900s.

PRINCIPAL COLORS: Gold and golden brown, all shades of yellow

GEMSTONES AND PRECIOUS METALS: Citrine, topaz, yellow diamonds

BOTANICALS: Borage, eyebright, thyme

UNIQUE SPELLINGS: Alaine, Alane, Allayne, Elane, Elayne, Ellaine, Ellayne, Ilaine, Ilane, Illayne

RELATED TO: Alana, Elaina, Elana, Eleanort, Elenat, Ellent, Helent, Helenet

A KABBALISTIC SYNOPSIS
אלאין —ALAYN (Aleph, Lamed, Aleph, Yod, Nun)

Everyone wants to get to know Elaine; she has a naturally vivacious manner and lifts the spirits of any get-together with her highly developed sense of fun. Occasionally, though, her love of amusement can result in somewhat embarrassing or awkward situations, as she lacks the ability to distinguish where the line should be drawn between what's funny and what's hurtful. Elaine loves emotional intrigue, and if you play with her, you are playing with fire. She is an inveterate flirt, but, as with her practical jokes, this can get out of hand; she will sometimes go as far as initiating a relationship simply because of curiosity. If someone gets involved with Elaine without knowing what makes her tick, they are likely to come out of it with their pride dented. However, most people will discover Elaine's nature very soon after meeting her and will be able to have a good time without getting too hurt.

THE RUNIC INTERPRETATION
ᛗᚺᛁᚨᛚᛗ (Ehwaz, Nauthiz, Isa, Ansuz, Laguz, Ehwaz)

Elaine is an artist. Whether her canvas is one of cloth or life, she wields her brush with a decisive stroke directed by a sure and honest heart. In her art Elaine uses the Laguz energy of flow to design her compositions, and incorporates texture and value to excite the eye. Her talent invites the viewer to participate in a walk throughout the composition, and she never lets the viewer lose his way. In the same vein, she lives a rich and varied life, and draws people to her through her sureness and direction. Elaine also may opt for a career outside the arts; her creative nature will give her conversation color, and she can work well in sales or healing areas. Elaine designs her life according to the same principles of honesty, sureness, and variety that inspire others to an appreciation of the wonder and elegance of creation. The four elements in her name give it a rare power.

Elements: Air, fire, earth, air, water, air

THE NUMEROLOGICAL INTERPRETATION
Elaine (NV = 1, CV = 8, VV = 2, FL = 5)

Elaine is basically an independent woman with a strong need to achieve her goals. Yet Elaine is also aware that her path in life depends on the way she interacts with those around her. Although she is precise in her need to have her own area of influence in life, Elaine is definitely not a loner. Her success depends on the harmony of her interchanges with others.

Eleanor

A Kabbalistic Synopsis
אלאנער—ALANA'AR (Aleph, Lamed, Aleph, Nun, Ayin, Resh)

Eleanor is a softy of the first order, and everybody loves her for it. In Hebrew, one meaning of her name is "merciful," and Eleanor always has time for those elements in society that the rest of the world has given up on. She sees the good in the worst of us and can usually explain away the bad. Eleanor has a quick mind and a real understanding of the world in which she lives. If Eleanor has a fault, it is her inability to see that there will always be some individuals who will not respond to any amount of understanding or encouragement to mend their ways.

The Runic Interpretation
ᚱᛟᚾᚨᛖᛚᛖ (Raido, Othila, Nauthiz, Ansuz, Ehwaz, Laguz, Ehwaz)

Eleanor has the Ehwaz rune of movement in her name along with the Raido rune of journeys and the Laguz rune of flow. Eleanor is an activist, and she has a rare genius for sensing the pulse of her society. Preferring to work behind the scenes in a modest way, she is broadminded and spare with her words, and will take a stand when she feels social injustice is running rampant. Eleanor is a way shower, and she detests self-pity in anyone. She keeps the frequency of faith for her followers and works harder than any of them to correct social ills.

Elements: Water, earth/fire, fire, air, air, water, air

The Numerological Interpretation
Eleanor (NV = 7, CV = 8, VV = 8, FL = 5)

The right outlet for her personal ambition is very important to a woman named Eleanor. This is a very practical, down-to-earth person. Eleanor feels at home in the world of business and finance. She has the ability to sustain the responsibilities of an executive position, and is quite able to structure the talents of others into large plans and projects. The name Eleanor also endows a person with a fine analytical and probing mind.

DERIVATION: English, possibly a form of Helen, from the Greek meaning "light" or derived from another Greek root meaning "mercy."

PRINCIPAL COLORS: The full range of green and yellow hues

GEMSTONES AND PRECIOUS METALS: Cat's-eye, moss agate, cream-colored pearls

BOTANICALS: Blackberry, elder, juniper

UNIQUE SPELLINGS: Elenore, Eleonore, Elinor, Elinore, Elleanor, Ellenore, Elleonor, Ellinor, Ellinore

RELATED TO: Aleanor, Alenor, Aleonore, Aline, Eileent, Elainet, Eleanora, Elen, Elenat, Elenora, Eleonora, Elianora, Ellat, Elladine, Elle, Elleanora, Ellent, Ellene, Ellie, Elna, Flnora, Elyn, Enora, Heleanor, Helent, Leanora, Lena, Lenora, Nellt, Nelly, Nora

❧

"Women are like tea bags; put them in hot water and they get stronger."
—ELEANOR ROOSEVELT (FIRST LADY OF THE UNITED STATES, HUMANITARIAN)

Elena

DERIVATION: Italian and Spanish form of Helen. In Greek lore, Helen was the beautiful princess whose seizure by Paris of Troy sparked the Trojan War. This name has spread to English-speaking countries in recent years.

PRINCIPAL COLORS: From the palest to the most brilliant shade of yellow

GEMSTONES AND PRECIOUS METALS: Yellow diamonds, topaz, amber

BOTANICALS: Eyebright, chamomile, sorrel

UNIQUE SPELLINGS: Alaina, Alayna, Alena, Alenna, Elaina, Elayna, Elenna

RELATED TO: Alana, Elainet, Elana, Eleanort, Ellent, Helent

A KABBALISTIC SYNOPSIS
אלאנא —ALANA (Aleph, Lamed, Aleph, Nun, Aleph)

There are individualists, and then there is Elena! You will know when you are in the presence of an Elena simply because she will be like no one else you have ever met. Most names give quite a good indication of personalities, career ideals, and lifestyles, but Elena's uniqueness may be expressed in any number of ways. Elena's name is dominated by Aleph; there are three of them in her name, which is only five letters long. Aleph, being the first letter of the alphabet, is associated with individuality, hence the highly idiosyncratic nature of Elena. However, there are some clues as to how this will show itself in Elena's case. Her name adds up to 83, indicating a rich imagination and the ability to express this imagination in an interesting and creative way. In addition, there are the three Alephs—and three is the number of creation. Therefore, we may expect to find Elena working as a writer or illustrator, probably for some fringe or alternative publication.

THE RUNIC INTERPRETATION
ᚨᚾᛖᛚᛖ (Ansuz, Nauthiz, Ehwaz, Laguz, Ehwaz)

Elena is very intuitive. This insight serves her well. She knows if anyone in her life is doing her wrong—and with antennae like Elena's, it's no wonder that she has a stinger as well! Elena may choose to work with the police on unsolved crimes using her psychic ability. If she does, and you are guilty of a crime, you'd better leave town in a hurry! Elena also might land a great job with the government predicting megatrends for the millennium.

Elements: Air, fire, air, water, air

THE NUMEROLOGICAL INTERPRETATION
Elena (NV = 1, CV = 8, VV = 11, FL = 5)

The name Elena is very powerful. It contains within its letters the possibility to call upon a deep well of inner inspiration to help one succeed in life. Elena is very intuitive and a visionary. She has the distinct ability to see the subtleties that exist in all facets of human relationships. Elena has a strong urge to get ahead, as she is very fond of personal recognition and social achievement. Her challenge is to use her insightfulness wisely, not only for her own benefit but for the welfare of others.

Eli

A Kabbalistic Synopsis
אלי —ALY (Aleph, Lamed, Yod)

Wherever there is trouble you will find Eli, trying his best to make sure that the good triumphs. Eli is a powerful man, physically and in terms of his personality. People are more likely to respect Eli than to be his friend, since he is a man of unusual moral conviction and courage. In many ways Eli is likely to be the closest thing we can find in the modern world to a classical or biblical hero. In Hebrew his name equates to "ram" and "force," and he represents the powerful energies of the warrior who fights for truth—whatever the cost—with boundless enthusiasm and determination. Eli will have extremely passionate views, and this is the one area where he can let himself down. If he feels that his values are being ridiculed or attacked, he often will respond with immediate force and a complete lack of forethought.

The Runic Interpretation
ᛁᛚᛖ (Isa, Laguz, Ehwaz)

Eli is a man who enjoys working with his hands and prefers working outside. If he must work in business, he can channel his talents into mechanical duties, such as industrial design or auto maintenance. He likes building stone walls and making beautiful furniture out of rare woods. He's comfortable in work shoes and casual clothes. The Isa rune of standstill makes Eli a solitary worker. Ehwaz means he could live or work abroad, where Eli would relish the opportunity to learn the old European trade secrets. Laguz, the rune of flow, makes Eli flexible; if he has a well-stocked workshop, that is all he asks. He turns his talents to fashioning whatever designs come his way. Eli will build a business with a following because of his easy disposition and old-fashioned standards of excellence.

Elements: Earth, water, air

The Numerological Interpretation
Eli (NV = 8, CV = 3, VV = 5, FL = 5)

Eli can use his abundant mental abilities for material success. His mind is very active—sometimes too much so. This can easily lead to dissipation and a lack of creative cohesion. Yet when Eli can maintain consistency in his focus and be persistent in his actions, he will find that he can turn his ideas into positive financial returns. Eli craves personal freedom and takes great pleasure in different and stimulating surroundings.

DERIVATION: Biblical, from the Hebrew, meaning "high." The name of the high priest who taught the prophet Samuel. Also the short form of names like Elijah and Elisha. Especially common in the eighteenth and nineteenth centuries.

PRINCIPAL COLORS: Dark blue and purple, black, dark shades of gray

GEMSTONES AND PRECIOUS METALS: Lackluster rubies, richly hued sapphires, any other dark stones

BOTANICALS: Marsh mallow, pilewort, gravel root, shepherd's purse

UNIQUE SPELLINGS: Eeli, Eely, Ely

RELATED TO: Eliast, Elihu, Elijah, Elisha, Elizer

DERIVATION: Greek version of the Hebrew name Elijah, meaning "the Lord is God." Especially popular in the seventeenth century.

PRINCIPAL COLORS: Gold, orange, all shades of yellow

GEMSTONES AND PRECIOUS METALS: Citrine, amber, yellow diamonds

BOTANICALS: Chamomile, lavender, Saint-John's-wort

UNIQUE SPELLINGS: Ellias, Ellyas, Elyas

RELATED TO: Elit, Elie, Elihu, Eliot, Elliot, Ellist, Ely

Elias

A KABBALISTIC SYNOPSIS
אל יאס —ALYAS (Aleph, Lamed, Yod, Aleph, Samech)

Elias is imbued with all the energy we found in Eli, but in Elias this manifests itself in a much more low-key manner. The key word for Elias's personality is "support," as evidenced by the final letter S, or Samech, meaning "prop." Elias will use his own energy to keep those around him going when they have all but lost their will to carry on. For this reason he is ideally suited to working in some kind of coordinating role, probably with the responsibility for ensuring that projects are completed on time and in accordance with all the original specifications. At the back of his mind Elias carries the potential for aggression, and he will probably express this through sporting endeavors. Emotionally he is a good catch; in addition to his ability to provide moral support in all circumstances, the presence of B, or Beth, in his name's compression points to a well-developed understanding of the feelings of others.

THE RUNIC INTERPRETATION
(Sowelu, Ansuz, Isa, Laguz, Ehwaz)

Elias has many of the charming qualities and talents of Eli. Elias may choose to work with his hands, or he may repair and rebuild in a more abstract way, in fields like child psychology or social work. The Ansuz rune of signals gives Elias brilliant insight, and his perception of people is impressive. Sowelu, the rune of wholeness, gives Elias a wonderful emotional balance. His personality is easy, and he develops instant rapport with people. The healing professions are a good vehicle for Elias to express his considerable abilities. Should he choose to work with his hands, he will build a solid business with many repeat customers and many word-of-mouth referrals.

Elements: Air, air, earth, water, air

THE NUMEROLOGICAL INTERPRETATION
Elias (NV = 1, CV = 4, VV = 6, FL = 5)

Elias is the name of a man who is very generous and giving to those he loves. Yet this generosity is very much based on his sense of personal security. He is at his best when he is at home or in other familiar environments. When he finds himself in strange or foreign surroundings, he is closed off from the more sensitive and compassionate sides to his nature. One of the major life challenges for this name is to create a firm sense of personal identity. This will be accomplished more easily through established patterns and a secure environment.

Eliza

A Kabbalistic Synopsis
אליזא —ALYZA (Aleph, Lamed, Yod, Zayin, Aleph)

Eliza has strong connections to the construction industry, due to associations in her name with structures, building, and labor. Her ideal position in this industry is as an overseer of the work. Eliza has a fierce temper and is the lucky owner of one of the sharpest tongues in the business. With these qualities she will have no trouble in getting sufficient work out of a team of laborers. Eliza has the power of Z, or Zayin, meaning "sword" or "armor," to sustain her, and she will be more than able to stand her ground in the face of skepticism about her suitability for any task she chooses to take on.

The Runic Interpretation
ᚨᛉᛁᛚᛗ (Ansuz, Algiz, Isa, Laguz, Ehwaz)

The Algiz rune of protection keeps Eliza in control of her emotions. In the past, she needed other people's help when things were really overwhelming. Now Eliza takes things one day at a time. She keeps things simple and strives for moderation. When she feels like she's getting worked up, she might build a box kite or work on her stamp album. Eliza has learned how to rest, and she makes an effort to add no longer to the burdens of her family and friends.

Elements: Air, air, earth, water, air

The Numerological Interpretation
Eliza (NV = 8, CV = 11, VV = 6, FL = 5)

Eliza is the name of a woman with a great deal of life energy flowing through her spirit, mind, and body. Life will definitely not permit her to be lazy! Career goals are essential to her, and Eliza will feel very comfortable dealing with large issues that test her creative abilities. At heart she is a romantic woman, one who seeks to provide comfort and material security for friends and family alike. Eliza's intuition is one of her greatest gifts, one that she can use along with her natural grace and sense of beauty.

DERIVATION: English, short form of Elizabeth, which is originally from the Hebrew name Elisheba, meaning "oath of God." Commonly used as a nickname since the sixteenth century, and popular as an independent name since the eighteenth century.

PRINCIPAL COLORS: Purple, gray, black, the darker shades of blue

GEMSTONES AND PRECIOUS METALS: Black pearls, black diamonds, sapphires

BOTANICALS: Angelica, marsh mallow, shepherd's purse

UNIQUE SPELLINGS: Alyza, Eliesa, Elighza

RELATED TO: Elisa, Elisabet, Elisabetta, Elise, Elizabeth†, Elizabetta, Elsbeth, Else, Elsie, Elspeth, Ilse, Isabel, Isabelle†, Lis, Lisat, Lisbet, Lise, Lisette, Liz, Liza, Lizzie

Elizabeth

DERIVATION: English, originally from the Hebrew name Elisheba, meaning "oath of God." Found in the Old Testament as the wife of Aaron, and in the New Testament as the mother of John the Baptist. First became popular with the rise of Queen Elizabeth I in the sixteenth century. Has become extremely popular in the twentieth century.

PRINCIPAL COLORS: Gold, the palest to the deepest shades of green and yellow

GEMSTONES AND PRECIOUS METALS: White stones, including pearls and moonstones

BOTANICALS: Elder, hops, juniper

UNIQUE SPELLINGS: Alisabeth, Alizabeth, Elisabeth, Elizahbeth

RELATED TO: Bess, Bessie, Beth†, Bethany, Betsy†, Betty†, Elisa, Elisabet, Elisabetta, Elise, Eliza†, Elizabetta, Elsbeth, Else, Elsie, Elspeth, Ilse, Isabel, Isabelle†, Lis, Lisa†, Lisbet, Lise, Lisette, Liz, Liza, Lizzie

"People are like stained-glass windows. They sparkle and shine when the sun is out, but when the darkness sets in, their true beauty is revealed only if there is a light from within."
—DR. ELIZABETH KÜBLER-ROSS (AUTHOR)

A KABBALISTIC SYNOPSIS
אליזאבית —ALYZABYTh (Aleph, Lamed, Yod, Zayin, Aleph, Beth, Yod, Tau)

If Eliza is likely to be involved with construction, it would be reasonable to expect that Elizabeth has even stronger ties with this field; her name is made by adding the full spelling of Beth, meaning "house," to the end of Eliza. However, the Kabbalah is never straightforward, and like a Buddhist koan or riddle, it is constantly presenting us with paradox after paradox. Elizabeth's name can be reduced to eleven, which is the number of magic, and she is likely to have a long-standing interest—if not an active involvement—in the occult or the unexplained. The house signified by Beth is not a physical house but a representation of Elizabeth's complex worldview. Elizabeth likes to be able to categorize, which may manifest itself as a desire to control. She sees the world in some ways as a jigsaw puzzle that fails to make sense only because the pieces are not quite in the right place. In order to solve the puzzle, she brings a sense of the religious or spiritual. But although Elizabeth likes the world to make sense, she also wants it to retain its soul. The first half of the name, Eliza, refers not to physical construction but to a more mysterious building process: the building of a magical or spiritual understanding. Elizabeth retains Eliza's inner strength and potentially vicious tongue, and these will both stand her in good stead when faced with snide comments and ridicule for her beliefs.

THE RUNIC INTERPRETATION
ᚦᛖᛒᚨᛉᛁᛚᛖ (Thurisaz, Ehwaz, Berkana, Ansuz, Algiz, Isa, Laguz, Ehwaz)

Elizabeth is most fortunate to have Thurisaz, the gateway, in her name, which provides her a place in her mind to gather strength and contemplate hidden aspects of the self. The Algiz energy of protection cautions against emotional extreme, so Elizabeth seeks to remain calm and stable. Elizabeth is aware of her personal power, and for her this equals self-discipline, which is her strongest asset. Elizabeth is probably drawn to politics or the courtroom. She is highly motivated to fight for a cause and is persuasive and heartfelt in her appeals for justice. Elizabeth is not easily intimidated, and when the going gets tough, Elizabeth quadruples her efforts and emerges victorious.

Elements: Fire, air, air/earth, air, earth, water, air

THE NUMEROLOGICAL INTERPRETATION
Elizabeth (NV = 7, CV = 5, VV = 2, FL = 5)

Elizabeth is a name that gives abilities in all mental pursuits. A woman possessed of a wide variety of intellectual interests, Elizabeth has a very introspective side to her nature, and will find no problem spending time alone investigating what beckons to her. At the same time, her relationships are most important to her sense of personal completion. She requires a partner who will be supportive of her more subjective moments and enjoy sharing her urge to travel and explore all of life's many possibilities.

Ella

DERIVATION: English, from the Old German, meaning "all." Brought to Britain by the Normans in the eleventh century. Especially popular in the United States in the 1870s.

PRINCIPAL COLORS: Pale, deep, rich shades of violet and purple

GEMSTONES AND PRECIOUS METALS: Garnets, amethyst

BOTANICALS: Apple, dandelion, lungwort, mint

UNIQUE SPELLINGS: Ela, Elah, Ellah

RELATED TO: Eleanort, Ellent, Elletta, Ellette, Elli, Ellie, Ellina, Elly

A KABBALISTIC SYNOPSIS
אללא —ALLA (Aleph, Lamed, Lamed, Aleph)

Thanks to the phonetics of the Hebrew alphabet, the name Ella takes us back to those names beginning with "Al" that were shown to have a strong connection to religious concerns. Ella is no exception. Her name contains both "AL," meaning "God," and "LA," meaning "nothing." Ella takes her religious beliefs very seriously and is likely to have a firm faith the vast majority of the time. However, there are times when she becomes convinced that there is no God or purpose to this life. The reasons for these lapses in faith are probably connected to her job. One meaning of her name is "healing," and this, along with certain astrological influences in the name, points toward a career in medicine. Such a career will expose Ella to all kinds of depressing and frustrating situations that will provide a constant challenge to her belief in a loving God. In spite of her doubts, she will ultimately remain true to her religion, which will help her to maintain a sense of balance in her stressful job.

THE RUNIC INTERPRETATION
ᚨᛚᛚᛖ (Ansuz, Laguz, Laguz, Ehwaz)

Ella has the vision of an artist. No matter what she chooses to do for a living, she will enrich her experience with her vivid imagination. The double Laguz runes give her musical and artistic ability and a sensitive, flexible personality. Ansuz is the rune of intuition, and helps Ella know just how to strike up a conversation and ingratiate herself with people. She can sit in a car on the Orient Express with people from many nations and varied walks of life—and before the ride ends, she has them sharing her food and singing together. The Ehwaz rune of movement signifies travel and relocating abroad, and strengthens the tendency toward intuitive abilities that are indicated by the double Laguz and Ansuz. Ella is drawn to learning native customs and dances. She enjoys meeting new people, and whether she portrays them somehow in art or not, her experience is all the richer for her warm and sensitive spirit.

Elements: Air, water, water, air

THE NUMEROLOGICAL INTERPRETATION
Ella (NV = 3, CV = 6, VV = 6, FL = 5)

Ella is a very idealistic name and speaks of a woman who is talented in the arts. Beauty is fundamental to her nature, and not only the beauty of her own persona, but beauty in the more figurative sense as well. This is a person who is constantly improving on the quality of her environment, creating surroundings that uplift and please the eye. She is an open communicator and enjoys a wide variety of friends and associates. Ella has to be careful about giving herself too completely to the person she loves, so as not to lose her sense of personal integrity.

DERIVATION: English version of
Helen, the Greek name borne by
the mythological Helen of Troy,
supposedly the most beautiful
woman in the world. Became very
common in the first half of the
twentieth century.

PRINCIPAL COLORS: All shades of
purple, including pale lilac and
deep maroon

GEMSTONES AND PRECIOUS
METALS: Amethyst, garnets

BOTANICALS: Barberry, cherry,
mint, strawberry

UNIQUE SPELLINGS: Elen, Elin,
Ellan, Ellin, Ellon, Ellyn, Elon,
Elyn, Llen

RELATED TO: Elaina, Elainet,
Eleanort, Elenat, Eleni, Ellat,
Ellenor, Elli, Ellie, Helent, Helenet,
Nellt, Nelliet

Ellen

A KABBALISTIC SYNOPSIS
אללון —ALLVN (Aleph, Lamed, Lamed, Vau, Nun)

Ellen really can't lose in life. Wherever she decides to move, she will meet with success, as indicated by the total value of her name, 767, the symbol of choice surrounded by signs of success. Given the dual presence of L, or Lamed, it is unlikely that there will much in the way of choice regarding Ellen's career. Whatever she does, it will have been decided in her mind from an early age; she will then go all out to ensure that she succeeds. With such gritty determination, Ellen can set herself the sort of career goals many people would never dare to consider. The choices that rule Ellen's life are not about alternative directions but about alternative areas of focus in her life; for example, she may have to choose between her emotional needs and her career needs. Thanks to the final Nun in her name, it is probable that the emotional will ultimately win out, but whichever way the cards fall, it will turn out fine.

THE RUNIC INTERPRETATION
ᚾᛖᛚᛚᛖ (Nauthiz, Ehwaz, Laguz, Laguz, Ehwaz)

Ellen is a happy camper. She is likable, but she gives bad advice—and yet, everyone still confides in her! She's warm and well meaning, and she wears fruity colors and makes sure she looks good. The double Laguz runes give her flexibility and artistic talent. The double Ehwaz runes of movement mean Ellen likes to keep fit. She exercises each day and usually sleeps like a baby at night. The Nauthiz rune brings constraint into Ellen's life: She could have a bundle of problems, but you'd never know it! Ellen cultivates a pleasant disposition and cheery nature. She has a chance to live and work abroad. Life improves for Ellen when she stops giving bad advice and learns to follow the advice of people whom she admires.

Elements: Fire, air, water, water, air

THE NUMEROLOGICAL INTERPRETATION
Ellen. (NV = 3, CV = 11, VV = 1, FL = 5)

Ellen is the name of a woman endowed with strong psychic sensitivity. This means that she has a particular insight that allows her to know another person at first glance. No one is a stranger to her, and she can make great use of this special gift. Highly individualistic by nature, Ellen is not satisfied by the normal routines and patterns of everyday life. She has to discover the new and the different. Her sense of her personal identity is very connected to her ability to uncover what is left unseen by most others.

Ellis

DERIVATION: English, originally a surname derived from Elias, the Greek version of the Old Testament name Elijah. The name Elijah, in turn, is from the Hebrew, meaning "the Lord is God."

PRINCIPAL COLORS: Pale shades of purple to the richest shades of violet

GEMSTONES AND PRECIOUS METALS: Amethyst, garnets

BOTANICALS: Apple, cherry, lungwort, mint

UNIQUE SPELLINGS: Elis, Ellys, Elys

RELATED TO: Eliast, Elice, Elie, Elijah, Ellice, Eloi, Eloy, Elyas

A Kabbalistic Synopsis
אלליס —ALLYS (Aleph, Lamed, Lamed, Yod, Samech)

Ellis is not comfortable living in a modern city and will do his best to find himself a home in a much smaller community where he can truly be happy. Once he has found a suitable home, he will set about making himself an integral feature of town life, volunteering for and probably organizing any number of community events. Ellis is not an egotist but longs to feel part of something valuable. He has no desire for recognition as a result of his efforts—one meaning of his name is "humility"—and his fellow citizens will not fail to notice the unassuming way in which he does his part for his community. Another equivalent of his name is Samael. Samael was the original name of the angel who was later associated by the Church with Satan, but does not actually signify anything evil in nature. And in the case of Ellis, it refers to his personal life. Any partner of Ellis will quickly realize that any humble attitude Ellis has in public life ends the minute he gets into the bedroom!

The Runic Interpretation
ᛦᛁᛚᛚᛖ (Sowelu, Isa, Laguz, Laguz, Ehwaz)

Ellis likes to sing and dance away his troubles. The plucky Ehwaz energy of movement makes Ellis tap his feet and makes his endorphins start pumping. With the double Laguz runes of flow, Ellis is really quite talented. He has a warm and flexible nature and a creative mind. Sowelu, the rune of wholeness, enhances Ellis's remarkable creative gifts. He may be drawn to a career in the fine or performing arts, where he will meet with success and accolades. Isa, the rune of standstill, cautions Ellis to seek out his inner wisdom: He must be ever honest and genuine so his art can capture the heart and ring true.

Elements: Air, earth, water, water, air

The Numerological Interpretation
Ellis (NV = 3, CV = 7, VV = 5, FL = 5)

A strong mind that is amazingly adaptable characterizes Ellis. This is a man who requires a great deal of intellectual freedom. He is a perpetual student and tends to spend lots of his time in intense pursuit of his interests. He must be careful not to become involved with so many projects that his nervous system suffers as a result. If he can consolidate his focus and bring a sense of logical order to his avid search for knowledge, he may indeed acquire true wisdom.

DERIVATION: French version of Elizabeth, which comes from the Hebrew word *elisheba*, meaning "God is perfect" or "pledged to God." Entered English-speaking countries in the late nineteenth century.

PRINCIPAL COLORS: The full range of purple hues

GEMSTONES AND PRECIOUS METALS: Garnets, amethyst

BOTANICALS: Bilberry, dandelion, mint, endive

UNIQUE SPELLINGS: Eliese, Elise, Ilise, Ilyse

RELATED TO: Elisa, Elisabeth, Elissa, Elizat, Flizabeth†, Elyssa, Ilysa, Lisat, Lise, Lissa, Liza, Lize

A KABBALISTIC SYNOPSIS
אליש —ALYSh (Aleph, Lamed, Yod, Shin)

Elyse would make the ideal partner for Ellist; she, too, is looking for a smaller living environment. Elyse has a great skill for coming up with ideas, and she has the energy to develop them, as well as the sensitivity to choose projects that will appeal to the whole community. All she needs is someone to take on the project and actually make it happen. Not surprisingly, as her name is equivalent to the three mother letters, Elyse may be far more concerned with having a family than with a career. Her children could not hope for a more understanding or fun parent, whose own enjoyment of this role will communicate itself to her offspring.

THE RUNIC INTERPRETATION
ᛖᛚᛇᛚᛖ (Ehwaz, Sowelu, Eihwaz, Laguz, Ehwaz)

Elyse embraces change. She has an imaginative and flexible nature. The Laguz rune of flow makes her easy to be with, and Elyse has lots of good old friends. The old friends who caused her trouble have drifted away, thanks to the Eihwaz rune of defense. Eihwaz has taught Elyse to be discriminating, and it was a hard lesson for her. She learned to be less gullible and uncover obstacles in her life that blocked her happiness, like procrastination and people-pleasing. The Ehwaz rune for movement gives Elyse a chance to broaden her view of human nature and reside abroad for a time. Sowelu, the rune of wholeness, helps Elyse realize people are just about the same wherever you go.

Elements: Air, air, earth/fire, water, air

THE NUMEROLOGICAL INTERPRETATION
Elyse (NV = 3, CV = 4, VV = 8, FL = 5)

This name indicates a woman who takes great pride in her appearance. She is very health oriented and wants not only to look good but to feel good, too. Clothes and personal adornments matter a great deal to Elyse. She likes to feel wealthy and will work to achieve a measure of financial success in life. Elyse has a strong love of nature and the outdoors, and she may become involved with ecological issues.

Emily

A KABBALISTIC SYNOPSIS
אמילי —AMYLY (Aleph, Mem, Yod, Lamed, Yod)

The name Emily tends to conjure up an image of a frail, and almost ethereal, figure full of emotion and hidden feelings. In a lot of ways, this is an entirely accurate description of Emily. However, it fails to mention her incredibly tenacious nature, signified by the letter Tzaddi, meaning "fishhook," found in the compression of her name. Emily has a plan, and you can be sure she will carry it out—whatever its odds of success. Emily's heightened emotional state can make her difficult to live with, since she is easily hurt. On a higher level she is likely to make creative use of all the feelings that flood her senses, and you may find that your words and actions are being collected, possibly to be published and read by the world!

THE RUNIC INTERPRETATION
ᛇᛚᛁᛗᛖ (Eihwaz, Laguz, Isa, Mannaz, Ehwaz)

Emily uses the Mannaz energy of her name to form a correct relationship with the self. The rune Isa in her name also underlines this quest for authenticity because Isa is the ancient rune symbolizing independence. Emily is devoted and modest. She likes to nest and enjoys the companionship of family and friends. She strives for simplicity and learns to budget her time and energies to this noble end. Emily is courteous and shuns upsetting news in the media, preferring upbeat and humorous stories of human nature to sensationalism. Emily is a very sweet woman.

Elements: Earth/fire, water, earth, air, air

THE NUMEROLOGICAL INTERPRETATION
Emily (NV = 1, CV = 7, VV = 3, FL = 5)

Emily is the name of a woman who can be very strong-willed. Although she has a tremendous need to be assertive, there is an introspective facet of her nature that holds her back. And in fact, this might provide the balance that Emily requires. Emily feels the need to spend long hours investigating life from a more contemplative perspective. It will only be after she has thoroughly investigated taking her next step that she will make the move. This helps her acquire a more global perspective on things and curbs her more impulsive tendencies.

DERIVATION: English, from the Latin name Aemilia, the feminine form of the old Roman family name, Aemilius. Also from Amalia, a feminization of the Goth god-ancestor Amal. One of the most popular names in America and England by the late nineteenth century. Declined in popularity for the majority of the twentieth century, although its usage has dramatically risen since the 1970s.

PRINCIPAL COLORS: All shades of yellow, deep golden brown, orange

GEMSTONES AND PRECIOUS METALS: Citrine and yellow diamonds, yellow stones

BOTANICALS: Lavender, Saint-John's-wort, thyme

UNIQUE SPELLINGS: Ameli, Amelie, Emeli, Emelie, Emely, Emilee, Emileigh, Emiley, Emilie

RELATED TO: Amalie, Amalija, Ameliat, Ammella, Emelina, Emeline, Emelyn, Emera, Emila, Emilia, Emmat, Milica

❧

"Not knowing when the dawn will come, I open every door."
—EMILY DICKINSON (POET)

"I'll walk where my own nature would be leading. It vexes me to choose another guide."
—EMILY BRONTË (AUTHOR)

❧

PRINCIPAL COLORS: The full spectrum of pale hues, especially light gray

GEMSTONES AND PRECIOUS METALS: Pale stones, diamonds, silver

BOTANICALS: Mushrooms, oats, parsley

UNIQUE SPELLINGS: Ema, Emah, Emmah, Emme, Emmeh

RELATED TO: Emmalina, Emmaline, Emmeline, Emmie, Emmila, Emily†

❧

"Emma Woodhouse, handsome, clever, and rich, with a comfortable home and happy disposition, seemed to unite some of the best blessings of existence . . ."
—FROM *EMMA* BY JANE AUSTEN

Emma

A KABBALISTIC SYNOPSIS
אממא —AMMA (Aleph, Mem, Mem, Aleph)

Emma has the same numerical value as Anael, the angel of Venus, and is often regarded as an angel by those who have the luck to come into contact with her. There are few people as kindly as Emma; in the office, she will always try to include others in her successes and smooth out any problems. There are other reasons why Emma has so many close friends—one is that she is often an excellent and prolific cook! But people turn to Emma when they need advice, support, or just a shoulder to cry on. What others appreciate about Emma is not just that she is there for them, but that she is always scrupulously honest. If Emma thinks someone is making a mistake or is being unfair, she will be quite happy to tell them—but always in a way that prevents anyone from taking offense.

THE RUNIC INTERPRETATION
ᚨᛗᛗᛖ (Ansuz, Mannaz, Mannaz, Ehwaz)

Emma likes water and music. She enjoys her dreams and may even record them in a notebook on her bedside table. The double Mannaz energy of the self in Emma's name helps her to learn to become more self-confident. If she feels blocked and she can't get the information she needs from within, she has a cup of tea with an old friend, and this helps her come back to her center. Emma appreciates the value of exercise to help her stay optimistic and focused. Exercise increases her stamina and confidence. Emma is well suited to counseling and social work. Her first and foremost desire is a willingness to become enlightened when needed.

Elements: Air, air, air, air

THE NUMEROLOGICAL INTERPRETATION
Emma (NV = 5, CV = 8, VV = 6, FL = 5)

Idealistically romantic with a strong need to express her dreams and inner aspirations, Emma has the soul of a poet. This is a name that may endow a person with talents in the arts as well as in creative writing. A woman of grace and charm, Emma feels fulfilled when she can bring a deep sense of harmony, beauty, and peace into the lives of the people she loves. Love is central to her life, and thus her personal relationships take on great meaning. Emma's romanticism is complemented by a practical urge for worldly success, and she will find that she needs a professional as well as a domestic life to give her a sense of personal completion.

❧

Enrique

DERIVATION: Spanish form of Henry, which comes from the Old English roots meaning "home" and "ruler."

PRINCIPAL COLORS: Black, gray, purple, darker shades of blue

GEMSTONES AND PRECIOUS METALS: Carbuncles, amethyst, black diamonds

BOTANICALS: Angelica, shepherd's purse, ragwort

UNIQUE SPELLINGS: Enreke, Enreque, Enrikay, Enrike, Inrike, Inrique

RELATED TO: Enric, Enrico, Hank†, Harry†, Hendrik, Henrik, Henry†, Rick†, Ricky

A KABBALISTIC SYNOPSIS

אנריק —ANRYQ (Aleph, Nun, Resh, Yod, Qoph)

Enrique shares the value of his name with the angel of Saturn whose name is Cassiel. Saturn is associated with age, among other things, and therefore the wisdom of experience. Enrique may well have such wisdom, but he is not particularly eager to share it with others. The specific letters in his name show Enrique as connected very strongly with material concerns, and point to a high probability that he will start his own business, the success of which will be his primary goal in life. Any partner of Enrique will have to accept that they take second place after his work. As a result of all the hours of labor and a certain amount of destiny, his business will probably become quite successful. The problem for Enrique is that even after he achieves his initial goals he will still work the same hours in order to try and make his business even more profitable.

THE RUNIC INTERPRETATION

ᛗᚲᛁᚱᛏᛗ (Ehwaz, Kano, Isa, Raido, Nauthiz, Ehwaz)

Enrique is proud to have the torch energy of the rune Kano in his name. Kano may point to an ending of a relationship or a way of life that has become an energy drain. Kano and Isa help Enrique learn to live on his own for a time in order to develop inner stability. During this transition it is tempting to return to familiar ways and people, but this just doesn't work. Enrique often feels discomfort and the loneliness of being misunderstood. This is partially because Enrique can only be happy in relationships that enhance each participant. The presence of all four elements brings great power to the name Enrique.

Elements: Air, water, earth, water, fire, air

THE NUMEROLOGICAL INTERPRETATION

Enrique (NV = 8, CV = 22, VV = 22, FL = 5)

A rare and powerful combination of numbers is contained in this name. Enrique's life is dominated by the master number twenty-two. This is a man who is not comfortable with a life centered on small issues and petty details. Enrique's inner vision of himself demands extraordinary success, abundant financial achievement, and a position of high responsibility in the world. He has the potential to take any idea and turn it into a reality. Only a person with the highest of moral values and the deepest of spiritual commitments can live up to the tremendous potentialities inherent in this name.

Eric

A Kabbalistic Synopsis
אריכ —ARYK (Aleph, Resh, Yod, Kaph)

Eric's name has great significance. His name adds to 231, and in the Tree of Life the third sephirah, Binah, has 231 gates known as the 231 Gates of Wisdom. These gates are accessible only to adepts of the highest levels of development. In terms of Eric and the importance of this fact to his personality, we can expect Eric to be a very thoughtful and deep individual given to much solitary musing. He is not particularly interested in the practicalities of the world; you wouldn't ask Eric to take a look at your broken washing machine, for example. Given the nature of the gates of Binah, it is likely that Eric will be a very understanding father and husband, even if he may lack a certain something when it comes to having fun. Unfortunately for Eric, the value of his name suggests that his inner self will always be searching for some higher truth that is likely to be permanently just beyond his reach.

The Runic Interpretation
ᚲᛁᚱᛗ (Kano, Isa, Raido, Ehwaz)

Eric is a strong Viking name. The Raido energy of the journey figures prominently in Eric, who may be a composer, a philosopher, or an adventurer involved in travel and anthropology. Eric uses the energy of the Raido rune to embrace obstacles and detours, but he may have some difficulty staying with a task because of his restless nature and investigative mind. Eric is at his best when he surrenders his impatience to the will of God and follows his heart. Eric needs time away from his friends to assess where he stands on issues; otherwise he may be too influenced by others' opinions—which is tempting for Eric, but could be detrimental.

Elements: Water, earth, water, air

The Numerological Interpretation
Eric (NV = 8, CV = 3, VV = 5, FL = 5)

Eric is a name that reveals a man with strong intellectual powers. He is also gifted with a healthy dose of personal drive and ambition. Eric will never be bored, as he is inventive and adventurous. Sometimes his innate restlessness works against him, and he can be in too many places at the same time, both physically and mentally. Focus is a quality that he should always endeavor to obtain. If he can maintain constant focus, he is capable of creating financial abundance and social success.

DERIVATION: English, originally from the Old Norse roots *ei*, meaning "ever," and *ríkr*, meaning "ruler." Introduced into Britain by early Scandinavian settlers, and became fairly common in the nineteenth century. Especially common in Sweden.

PRINCIPAL COLORS: Black, dark gray, only the darkest shades of azure

GEMSTONES AND PRECIOUS METALS: Black diamonds, black pearls, rubies

BOTANICALS: Marsh mallow, shepherd's purse, mandrake root

UNIQUE SPELLINGS: Erich, Erick, Erik, Erric, Errick, Errik

RELATED TO: Eirik, Herrick, Rickt, Ricky

Erica

A KABBALISTIC SYNOPSIS
אריכא —ARYKA (Aleph, Resh, Yod, Kaph, Aleph)

Erica is a defiantly jolly person. Even if you run her down, steal her car, and burgle her house, she will still insist that it could have been worse and may even find the bright side in it all! However, in the compression of her name we do see that her infectiously optimistic approach to life also has a serious side to it. In order to progress toward her chosen goals in life, Erica needs to drive herself hard to avoid being distracted by other possibilities that seem interesting. Still, her cheery behavior and outlook keep her on the straight and narrow, and on track to hit her personal targets. If she behaves in a serious or dour manner, she will lose her motivation very quickly. Erica is a very well liked woman for obvious reasons, although she will have to make sure that her jovial nature is not mistaken for a lack of commitment by her boss.

THE RUNIC INTERPRETATION
ᚨᚲᛁᚱᛗ (Ansuz, Kano, Isa, Raido, Ehwaz)

Whether Erica is good at sports or management or the arts, she must follow her joy. She can ease her sporadic loneliness the minute she follows her strengths. This loneliness has nothing to do with being alone or in a crowd. The Isa rune sways Erica into situations where she feels alienated from time to time, but she is blessed to have friends who support her artistic endeavors. The Kano energy of opening helps Erica through these periods of confusion to a better time of clarity and self-awareness.

Elements: Air, water, earth, water, air

THE NUMEROLOGICAL INTERPRETATION
Erica (NV = 9, CV = 3, VV = 6, FL = 5)

This name gives its bearer many gifts. Erica has the ability to be patient and kind, gentle and benevolent. She is humanitarian by nature and can be generous to a fault. She is greatly disturbed when she sees other people in distress and will do all she can to bring harmony into their lives. She is most suited to a profession that is based on healing and service work. Erica is a caregiver, a missionary, a physician, or a therapist. She is never petty and tends to deal much more with the wider, universal life principles that form the core of her spiritual life.

DERIVATION: Feminine form of Eric, an Old Norse name meaning "always ruler." In Latin, the word *erica* means "heather." Originally a Scandinavian name, Erica has become increasingly common in English-speaking countries in the late twentieth century.

PRINCIPAL COLORS: Rose, pale shades of red to deep bloodred

GEMSTONES AND PRECIOUS METALS: Rubies, garnets, bloodstones

BOTANICALS: Onion, garlic, nettle

UNIQUE SPELLINGS: Ereca, Ericka, Erika, Errica, Erricka, Errika

RELATED TO: Era, Eri, Rica, Ricki, Rika

DERIVATION: Gaelic, from the word *eireann*, meaning "western island," and referring to Ireland in particular. Often used in poetry as a name for Ireland, but more popular in the United States than in Ireland.

PRINCIPAL COLORS: The full range of yellow hues, brown, orange

GEMSTONES AND PRECIOUS METALS: Topaz, yellow diamonds, any yellow stone

BOTANICALS: Borage, chamomile, eyebright, saffron

UNIQUE SPELLINGS: Erinn, Errin, Errinn, Erryn, Errynn, Eryn, Erynn

RELATED TO: Erena, Erene, Erenna, Erina, Irina

Erin

A KABBALISTIC SYNOPSIS
אריך —ARYN (Aleph, Resh, Yod, Nun)

Erin is a quiet woman who is happiest with just herself for company—which is not to say that she dislikes people in general or that she is uncomfortable in social circumstances. In fact, everyone is keen to have Erin at their parties. She is a very interesting and knowledgeable character with a variety of developed views on a whole range of subjects. Yet her opinions are generated during all the time she spends musing on her own. While many people with a tendency toward solitude can be somewhat pessimistic, Erin has a positive outlook on life, which is another reason for her popularity. Close friends may try to fix her up with a partner, but Erin is resolutely single. Secretly Erin does not mind this at all; the only thing that really holds her back from embarking on a relationship is her fear that she will never meet someone who can appreciate her particular lifestyle.

THE RUNIC INTERPRETATION
ᚺᛁᚱᛗ (Nauthiz, Isa, Raido, Ehwaz)

Erin inspires courage in her friends. She may be handicapped in some way, or the constraint could be financial or social. In any case, the Nauthiz energy in Erin's name, which is also a constraint, spurs her on to discover her true creative power within. Erin is an artist of the highest sort and is sensitive to the needs of others. She goes all out, and this is one of the ways Erin expresses joy in life. Erin uses the Nauthiz rune to remind her to pay off old debts and to strive for balance in relationships. She overcomes her obstacles by being who she truly is and by believing in herself.

Elements: Fire, earth, water, air

THE NUMEROLOGICAL INTERPRETATION
Erin (NV = 1, CV = 5, VV = 5, FL = 5)

There is no room for restraint in Erin's life. This name is dominated by the numbers five and one, so Erin requires an enormous sense of personal freedom in order to express her distinct individuality. If she is feeling at all limited or restrained, Erin will flee. She is a woman who regards monotony as a living death. An incredible communicator with a strongly developed intellect, Erin requires friends who are as mentally and energetically alive as she is. She is a most fascinating partner in relationships but demands a lover who can sustain a constant enthusiasm for life and has the vital energy to back it up.

Erma

A Kabbalistic Synopsis
אַרמא —ARMA (Aleph, Resh, Mem, Aleph)

There are some people we meet in life who seem to be completely accepting of their lot, and who are content with their position in the world whatever it might be. Erma is one of those people, and despite the lack of any particularly sensational aspect to her personality or lifestyle, she can expect to be the envy of others, particularly as she and her friends get older. It is tempting to look for the unusual and outstanding at the expense of the ordinary; however, there is a lot to be said for the ordinary. It is the everyday individuals who allow the unusual people to actually make their mark in society. Erma is unlikely to have a high-profile career or to be exceptionally creative. Nevertheless, Erma is a balanced, warm, and caring individual, much liked in her own small circle of acquaintances.

The Runic Interpretation
ᚾᛗᚱᛗ (Ansuz, Mannaz, Raido, Ehwaz)

Erma is musical and poetic and intuitive. She knows that she must love herself well in order to love others. For this reason, Erma is a way shower, and many friends and acquaintances follow her advice. Erma will be in the public eye during her lifetime. The Raido energy of the journey gives Erma the opportunity to travel and enjoy new ways of seeing the world. Erma is fond of children, and in her later years she will work as a philanthropist.

Elements: Air, air, water, air

The Numerological Interpretation
Erma (NV = 1, CV = 4, VV = 6, FL = 5)

Blessed with a strong will and a distinct sense of individuality, Erma is best suited to achieving goals in a familiar and predictable environment. This is not a person seeking wild adventures or foreign intrigues. Erma is very content to help provide and sustain a consistent home life with a loving partner by her side. She will be a faithful and loyal companion in return, ever ready to add beauty and grace to the environment. Erma likes to have a sense of control over her life but does not need to control other people. She is happy within the loving embrace of friends and family.

DERIVATION: Spelling variation of the German name Irma, which is from an Old German root meaning "entire." Especially popular in the first half of the twentieth century.

PRINCIPAL COLORS: Gold, orange, the lightest to the most brilliant golden yellow

GEMSTONES AND PRECIOUS METALS: Amber, citrine, yellow diamonds

BOTANICALS: Chamomile, eyebright, borage, sorrel

UNIQUE SPELLINGS: Ermah, Irma, Irmah

RELATED TO: Irmgard, Irmigarde, Irmina, Irmine, Irmtraud

Ernest

DERIVATION: English, from the Old German roots *eornost* and *ernst*, meaning "seriousness" and "vigor." Became quite popular in the late nineteenth and early twentieth century. Oscar Wilde's 1895 play *The Importance of Being Earnest* helped increase the name's fame.

PRINCIPAL COLORS: All shades of red, including pink, rose, and maroon

GEMSTONES AND PRECIOUS METALS: Rubies, deep red bloodstones, garnets

BOTANICALS: Broom, nettle, wormwood

UNIQUE SPELLINGS: Earnest, Earnist, Earrnest, Ernist, Errnest

RELATED TO: Ern, Ernesto, Erniet, Erno, Ernst

A KABBALISTIC SYNOPSIS
ארניסט —ARNYST (Aleph, Resh, Nun, Yod, Samech, Teth)

Ernest really is an earnest individual; it would be difficult to find anyone more sincere in their beliefs than Ernest. The central N, or Nun, in his name is an indication not only of deeply seated emotions but also of a tendency toward secrecy. Ernest has good reason to keep his beliefs to himself and a select circle of friends: One equivalent of his name in Hebrew is "revolution," and there are other pointers in his name that suggest an extremely radical set of political or economic beliefs. Obviously not every Ernest is a card-carrying communist, but Ernest certainly will have some radical views that he will not share with everyone. Ernest's only difficulty in keeping his beliefs to himself is his temper. Although he tries to control himself, there are times when his passion leads him into vigorous and vociferous outbursts, which, if his beliefs really *are* revolutionary, will get him into hot water.

THE RUNIC INTERPRETATION
↑⑀ᛗᚺᚱᛗ (Teiwaz, Sowelu, Ehwaz, Nauthiz, Raido, Ehwaz)

Ernest puts a lot of miles on his car. Ernest enjoys the double Ehwaz runes, symbolizing movement, which make him enjoy staying active. He likes to travel and may even relocate to a foreign country with a prestigious job someday. Ernest was a nerd in high school, and now that he's middle-aged you'd swear he was still in high school! He wears sneakers and cares about looking cool, even though he's put on forty pounds. He likes eating late at night in front of videos of movies from the thirties. He is good at swimming and enjoys getting exercise on his bike and hiking in the mountains. Ernest secretly knows he's got to put more effort into seeming modest.

Elements: Air, air, air, fire, water, air

THE NUMEROLOGICAL INTERPRETATION
Ernest (NV = 9, CV = 8, VV = 1, FL = 5)

Ernest is a name that bestows a strong need for personal attainment. Determined to get ahead and eager for success in life, Ernest will work to reach a higher place in society but is loath to step on anyone else's toes to get there. Once he arrives, Ernest will be a most helpful boss, administrator, or chief. People feel that they can come to Ernest for advice, as he possesses a very kind and humanitarian nature. In his private relationships, Ernest tends to be passionate and emotionally present. He prefers long-lasting monogamous unions over quick flirtations.

Ernestine

DERIVATION: English, feminine form of Ernest, which is from the Germanic root *eornost*, meaning "serious" or "sincere." Popular since the end of the nineteenth century.

PRINCIPAL COLORS: Yellow, gold, bronze, golden brown

GEMSTONES AND PRECIOUS METALS: Amber, citrine, topaz

BOTANICALS: Lavender, sorrel, thyme, cloves

UNIQUE SPELLINGS: Ernastine, Ernastyne, Ernestyne

RELATED TO: Erna, Ernaline, Ernestina, Ernestyna

A KABBALISTIC SYNOPSIS

ארניסטין —ARNYSTYN (Aleph, Resh, Nun, Yod, Samech, Teth, Yod, Nun)

Ernestine has many similarities to Ernest†; she, too, has a whole host of novel ideas all bursting to be articulated. However, Ernestine is not concerned with political issues and would not ordinarily be described as a "revolutionary." Ernestine's main area of interest is in relationships and the interaction between couples. It may well be that Ernestine works as a marriage counselor of some sort, or her actual involvement in emotional behavior may be limited to academic work in this field. Indications in her name show Ernestine as a naturally conservative woman. The key factor for emotional success, according to Ernestine, is a recognition that the couple should function more as a single unit than as two separate individuals. This element of self-sacrifice is very important in Ernestine's own personal life, and is indicated by the heavy influence exerted by the Hanged Man card of the tarot in her name.

THE RUNIC INTERPRETATION

ᛗᚺᛁᛏᛋᛗᚺᚱᛗ (Ehwaz, Nauthiz, Isa, Teiwaz, Sowelu, Ehwaz, Nauthiz, Raido, Ehwaz)

Ernestine travels every chance she gets. She is the perfect match for Ernest, with all the same likes and dislikes. The difference is that Ernestine has the additional triple Ehwaz and double Nauthiz runes in her name, signifying movement and constraint. On the one hand Ernestine has the courage to relocate abroad—and yet, when she does, she could feel like she is living in a house of cards. Her perception of loneliness changes as Ernestine develops her inner child and uses her playfulness to live in the moment. As this growth occurs, Ernestine no longer feels limited by the language and customs of her new home and embraces the new opportunities in this phase of her life.

Elements: Air, fire, earth, air, air, air, fire, water, air

THE NUMEROLOGICAL INTERPRETATION

Ernestine (NV = 1, CV = 22, VV = 6, FL = 5)

The name Ernestine possesses quite a strong combination of numerological influences. The consonant value of twenty-two bestows a personality that is capable of great achievements. This is a person who will not tolerate pettiness either in herself or in others. Ernestine is highly motivated and able to work out her particular creative interests in very expansive ways. The name value of one reveals a person who has to be herself—and only herself—no matter the cost. Ernestine's greatest challenge has to do with channeling her tremendous willpower. She will require a firm spiritual basis in her life in order to bring out her greatest potential.

Ernie

DERIVATION: Italian and Spanish form of Ernest, an English name from the Germanic root meaning "seriousness."

PRINCIPAL COLORS: Light shades of any color

GEMSTONES AND PRECIOUS METALS: Pale, sparkly stones; diamonds, platinum, silver

BOTANICALS: Sweet marjoram, hazel, oats, parsley

UNIQUE SPELLINGS: Erknee, Ernee, Erny

RELATED TO: Earnest, Ernest†, Ernesto

A KABBALISTIC SYNOPSIS
ארני —ARNY (Aleph, Resh, Nun, Yod)

Every town has an Ernie. The career indicators in his name suggest that he will probably have his own small business, which is likely to be a central focus for the community—a bar or food store, for instance. Ernie is always happy to have a chat with his customers and will freely offer his opinion on pretty much every current event and issue, from the latest budget debate to the problem with today's pop music. Ernie's comments tend to have the characteristics of pronouncements from on high, as Ernie will always begin with something along the lines of, "Of course, what they should do . . ." However, Ernie is quite a wise man and has a lot of experience behind him, and it is not unusual for his statements to have a strong element of truth to them. Ernie's worst fault is a lack of tolerance for alternative viewpoints and lifestyles; he defines anything that doesn't fit his version of the American way as misguided at best and positively subversive at worst.

THE RUNIC INTERPRETATION
MIᛏRM (Ehwaz, Isa, Nauthiz, Raido, Ehwaz)

Ernie longs to be happy-go-lucky and free. He travels, but it's more of a responsibility than an adventure. He's always double-checking his reservations, scrutinizing the exchange rates, and making work out of the process of getting around. Yet Ehwaz, the rune of movement, lures him on, which is a new level for Ernie, who spent time as a couch potato years earlier. Now that the Nauthiz rune of limitation phase is well behind him, Ernie is on his way to expand. As he travels, he becomes more familiar with the process and finds himself relaxing and taking it all in stride. A smile comes across his face as he realizes that he *can* do it! With Raido, the rune of journey, to spur him on, Ernie travels the whole wide world and returns home to inspire others to become part of the family of man.

Elements: Air, earth, fire, water, air

THE NUMEROLOGICAL INTERPRETATION
Ernie (NV = 5, CV = 8, VV = 7, FL = 5)

A kind and gentle man, Ernie also possesses a wide range of life interests. Home, family, and familiar friends are very important to him, but so is his sense of personal freedom. He has the need to explore the possibilities of his individuality, but at the same time, he prefers to avoid the conflicts in intimate relationships that too much personal independence sometimes can bring. Ernie has to balance his need to explore his own boundaries with his need to feel connected to others in order to have the peaceful life he requires.

Estelle

DERIVATION: English, an Old French name, originally from the Latin *stella*, meaning "star." Used occasionally in the Middle Ages, and quite popular since the nineteenth century.

PRINCIPAL COLORS: All but the brightest shades of blue

GEMSTONES AND PRECIOUS METALS: Emeralds, turquoise

BOTANICALS: Dog rose, violets, melon, almonds

UNIQUE SPELLINGS: Estel, Estele, Estell

RELATED TO: Astra, Estella, Esthert, Estrella, Estrellita, Stellat, Stelle

A Kabbalistic Synopsis
אסטאל —ASTAL (Aleph, Samech, Teth, Aleph, Lamed)

Estelle has only one direction in life—and that is up, up, and then up some more! The overriding concern in Estelle's life is material gain: She is absolutely determined to make it financially, and she knows exactly what she wants when she gets there. To be fair to Estelle, she will make it perfectly clear to any prospective partner what she expects of them. Estelle also is more than prepared to work for her own goals, and has the capacity to be ruthless in the workplace when it comes to assuring her own promotion.

The Runic Interpretation
ᛗᛚᛚᛗᛏᛋᛗ (Ehwaz, Laguz, Laguz, Ehwaz, Teiwaz, Sowelu, Ehwaz)

Estelle has the gift of a pleasant voice. If she chooses to develop her singing ability, Estelle could join a traveling chorus and visit many nations on tour. The Laguz rune gives Estelle wonderful gifts. Also, the double Ehwaz energy of movement creates a love of culture that prompts Estelle to live and study abroad. She could travel, doing healing work wherever suffering beckons, or simply indulge her interest in travel by taking seminars in universities. Estelle would love a career in the humanities. Her artistic ability is one of her primary strengths. The Teiwaz warrior rune gives Estelle the pluck she needs to take on almost any challenge. Sowelu for wholeness provides healing gifts and a gift of persuasion. Estelle is a citizen of the world, and her legacy is as an artist and healer.

Elements: Air, water, water, air, air, air, air

The Numerological Interpretation
Estelle (NV = 6, CV = 9, VV = 6, FL = 5)

Kindness, humility, and serenity all characterize this name. Estelle is a woman who has a deep love of family. To her, this concept extends outward to encompass the entire human race. She is compassionate, generous, and a humanitarian. Estelle has an inward quality of harmony and grace that will give her the creative edge in any form of design work. Partnership is of major importance to her, and she needs to be with a person who is as inclusive in their life orientation as she is.

DERIVATION: Biblical, the name of a Jewish woman who married the Persian king Ahasuerus. Through her intelligence and cunning, Esther managed to save many of her fellow Jews from the evil plans of the king's adviser, Haman. Esther's success in saving the Jews is celebrated during the Jewish holiday of Purim.

PRINCIPAL COLORS: The full range of purple hues, including pale violet and mauve

GEMSTONES AND PRECIOUS METALS: Garnets

BOTANICALS: Barberry, bilberry, olives, figs

UNIQUE SPELLINGS: Essther, Ester, Esterre, Estir

RELATED TO: Eister, Esta, Eszter, Hester, Ishtar

Esther

A KABBALISTIC SYNOPSIS
אסתה —ASThH (Aleph, Samech, Tau, Heh)

Esther cannot do without suffering: She is drawn to it, like a moth to a flame. This is because Esther is firmly convinced that she can help. If you are involved with Esther, you will have to take a backseat to any charitable cause that stirs her to action—and there will be plenty. Esther's name reduces to sixteen, the number of the Tower in the tarot, a symbol of catastrophic events. The Tower also suggests that the individual will ultimately benefit from any trauma. In Esther's case, her involvement with a range of tragic situations will develop her from someone who is overly interested in her own position as a helper to someone who can act as a genuine source of support for others in a distressed state. The more she is involved, the greater becomes Esther's natural intuition for what it is that people need to feel better.

THE RUNIC INTERPRETATION
ᚱᛖᚦᛊᛖ (Raido, Ehwaz, Thurisaz, Sowelu, Ehwaz)

Esther is always concerned with love, and she uses the Thurisaz rune to learn that love is a gateway. Esther is loyal and understands that love involves tremendous self-discipline and courage. She is willing to reach out to people and risk rejection. Esther has remarkable healing gifts. Esther understands that with tolerance comes the gift of unity. The Sowelu rune of wholeness ensures Esther will progress in her quest toward self-realization. Once Esther understands that she already is perfectly whole and should follow her own special talents, the world will see this wholeness in her as well. Esther's greatest talent is love.

Elements: Water, air, fire, air, air

THE NUMEROLOGICAL INTERPRETATION
Esther (NV = 3, CV = 2, VV = 1, FL = 5)

Esther is blessed with an all-around well-integrated personality. This name indicates a woman who has an unquestioned sense of her own identity. Her connection with herself is so strong that it permits her to extend herself comfortably into other people's lives. Esther is a natural-born communicator and would feel very much at home working in some branch of the media. She is a "people person" who enjoys social interactions and stimulating conversation. Esther likes to cultivate friends with varied intellectual interests, and she is as eager to learn as she is to teach.

Eva

A KABBALISTIC SYNOPSIS
יוא —YVA (Yod, Vau, Aleph)

Do not under any circumstances ask Eva to do anything remotely practical, as you will only come to regret it bitterly! Eva is, in the lingo of the era she best represents, far-out! The primary influence in Eva's name is the sign Aquarius, which is reflected in her love of anything that smacks of an alternative lifestyle. She will still be seen doing the rounds of all the shops selling incense and lava lamps when everyone else her age is drawing their pension. It is her irrepressible nature that makes her such fun to be with; one meaning of her name is "to make joyful." Her name adds up to seventeen, the number of divine guidance and protection. Eva has a sense of this higher force, and this helps her to persist in her nonconformist lifestyle. It is unlikely that she will have a lifetime partner, since this would be too conventional, but anyone who is lucky enough to share her life for even a short while will be left with plenty of colorful memories.

THE RUNIC INTERPRETATION
ᚨᚠᛖ (Ansuz, Fehu, Ehwaz)

Eva is powerful and magical. She can get her way in almost any situation. She is ideally suited for freelance work because the jobs and money come rolling in from unexpected sources. Eva will never lack for money; the problem is there are always a lot of hands out there poised to grab it! Therefore she needs to rely on her intuition and entrust her inheritances and investments to solid, trustworthy individuals. The Ansuz rune in her name can help her choose honest associates.

Elements: Air, fire, air

THE NUMEROLOGICAL INTERPRETATION
Eva (NV = 1, CV = 4, VV = 6, FL = 5)

Eva is a name that indicates a strong and assertive personality. This is someone who definitely wants to make a name for herself in the world. Eva has an energetic nature and is very enthusiastic about her plans and projects. She projects these ideas out into the environment with vitality and verve. Eva is also very enamored of the finer things in life, and works with a determined effort to achieve a secure financial position for herself. Charming and magnetic, Eva is also artistically oriented and is very relaxed when surrounded by beautiful environments.

DERIVATION: Latin version of Eve, the Biblical name of the first woman created by God. The name Eve originally derives from the Hebrew word *havva*, meaning "living." Quite common in English-speaking as well as Spanish-speaking countries.

PRINCIPAL COLORS: Every shade of yellow, bronze, gold, orange

GEMSTONES AND PRECIOUS METALS: Yellow diamonds, topaz, amber

BOTANICALS: Chamomile, eyebright, thyme

UNIQUE SPELLINGS: Evah, Iva, Ivah

RELATED TO: Evet, Evelina, Evelyn, Evette, Evie, Evita, Evonne

Evan

DERIVATION: Welsh variant on the name John. Very popular in Wales since the nineteenth century, but has also become increasingly common in other English-speaking countries in the late twentieth century.

PRINCIPAL COLORS: The complete gamut of blue tones

GEMSTONES AND PRECIOUS METALS: Emeralds, blue and blue-green turquoise

BOTANICALS: Dog rose, violets, almonds, walnuts

UNIQUE SPELLINGS: Evann, Even, Evenn, Evin, Evinn, Ewan, Ewen, Evyn, Evynn

RELATED TO: Evans, Everett†, Ivan†, John†

A KABBALISTIC SYNOPSIS
אואן —AVAN (Aleph, Vau, Aleph, Nun)

Evan has two definite sides to his nature, and the main focus of any personal development he undertakes should be the reconciliation of these two conflicting influences. In the letters of his name we see the presence of both A, or Aleph, relating to matters of the mind and self, and the letter N, or Nun, referring to emotional connections with others. Interestingly, the value of his name equals the value of all the so-called double letters in Hebrew when added together. The double letters are those that represent opposed concepts, such as life and death. We can find the source of the conflict by looking at the reduction of Evan's name, which comes to fifteen—the number of the Devil card in the tarot. Evan has a tendency toward excessive indulgence of his lower appetites at the expense of his emotional responsibilities. This could range from the extreme of sexual infidelity to simple selfishness with the family finances, but in order to increase his happiness Evan needs to learn to control his desires.

THE RUNIC INTERPRETATION
ᚾᚨᚠᛖ (Nauthiz, Ansuz, Fehu, Ehwaz)

Evan is like the Hero in the tarot deck; he is a seeker after knowledge and he plays the fool. The Ansuz rune of signals gives Evan a strong sense of intuition, which he applies to his life and his career. Evan enjoys research. Whether he uses his talents in business or to acquire a Ph.D., he travels the world probing new solutions. The lucky Fehu rune of possessions promises material wealth. The Ehwaz rune for movement suggests that Evan will relocate abroad. He accepts the frustration inherent in research and can put up with delays and obstacles from the Nauthiz rune of constraint. His goal is to bring information and intuition to bear on a problem, and Evan gains untold satisfaction from the aha! experience of finally understanding.

Elements: Fire, air, fire, air

THE NUMEROLOGICAL INTERPRETATION
Evan (NV = 6, CV = 9, VV = 6, FL = 5)

A compassionate man with strong emotions and feelings, Evan can be a devoted father, a faithful husband, and a passionate lover. He is an idealist by nature whose social and/or spiritual beliefs are very much at the core of his being. Generous and self-sacrificing, Evan has to take care that he balances the real with the ideal. Blind devotion is his weak spot; unconditional love is his strength. A humanitarian, Evan will be most comfortable in an occupation that is service oriented.

Eve

A KABBALISTIC SYNOPSIS
י" —YV (Yod, Vau)

We all know the story of the Garden of Eden and how Eve blew it all for a bite of apple! It is primarily for this reason that Eve's name adds up to sixteen (without any reduction needed) and is therefore symbolic of major catastrophe. However, we should remember that sixteen is also connected to the *positive* effects of catastrophe, and therefore we need not regard Eve as a bad apple! In fact, the serpent is actually a symbol of the search for self-mastery and development, and Eve's initial act of disobedience was also the first step toward higher understanding. We can expect from this alone that Eve will be a brave and daring woman. There will be many times in Eve's life when she takes enormous risks that those around her would refuse. However, after some initial suffering, it will invariably turn out that her actions have ultimately benefited her either in her career or her love life. Needless to say Eve is also intensely sexy, since she has the influences of both Taurus and Virgo in her name.

THE RUNIC INTERPRETATION
ᛖᚠᛖ (Ehwaz, Fehu, Ehwaz)

Eve is given many of the same lessons as Eve in the Bible. She is curious and inquisitive, as well as passionate and rebellious. The Fehu rune blesses her with abundance, and Eve needs to guard her money from the hands of unscrupulous people. It's a lifetime goal for Eve to remember to discard old beliefs and shift from old dwelling places that no longer serve her. She expands and grows in wisdom by inviting new challenges into her world. Eve is capable of creating charitable foundations and doing philanthropic work. She excels, and her ideas ignite once she learns to share her blessings with others. Eve's lessons, like those of the biblical Eve, are clear-cut, with promised rewards.

Elements: Air, fire, air

THE NUMEROLOGICAL INTERPRETATION
Eve (NV = 5, CV = 4, VV = 1, FL = 5)

Eve loves adventure! This is a woman who seeks a great deal of variety and creative freedom. But Eve will not want to flit around the world aimlessly; she has her feet firmly planted on the ground. Eve has definite material goals and ambitions, and can use her versatility to achieve her objectives in any of a number of life pursuits. At her core, Eve is an individualist moving from her center outward, radiating enthusiasm and energy wherever she goes.

DERIVATION: English and French, from the biblical name of the first woman created by God. Originally from the Hebrew word *havva*, meaning "living."

PRINCIPAL COLORS: Any light color

GEMSTONES AND PRECIOUS METALS: Pale, shiny stones; diamonds, silver, platinum

BOTANICALS: Caraway seeds, hazel, oats, sweet marjoram

UNIQUE SPELLINGS: Eave, Eeve, Eiv, Eive

RELATED TO: Evat, Eveline, Evelynt, Evette, Evie, Evilina, Evita, Evone

Evelyn

DERIVATION: English, originally from an English surname similar to Avila or Aveline. Initially a male name; became more common as a female name in the late nineteenth century. Especially popular during the early twentieth century.

PRINCIPAL COLORS: Cream, the full range of green hues

GEMSTONES AND PRECIOUS METALS: Moonstones, cat's-eye, jade

BOTANICALS: Cabbage, lettuce, moonwort

UNIQUE SPELLINGS: Evelin, Evelyne, Evelynn

RELATED TO: Evat, Evet, Evelina, Evelyna, Evette, Evie, Evita, Evonne

A KABBALISTIC SYNOPSIS
אואלין —AVALYN (Aleph, Vau, Aleph, Lamed, Yod, Nun)

Evelyn is one of the great unsung heroines of society. She has a variety of talents, including being practical and handy around the house. From changing a fuse to redecorating the entire home, Evelyn is more than capable of the task. In addition, she is blessed with a vivid imagination and has a good eye for the little details that fill out a story and make it live. However, Evelyn voluntarily keeps her own light hidden in order to benefit a greater whole, be it her workplace, community, or family. The presence of the L, or Lamed, is an indication that all her actions and skills are put to the service of one driving aim: As a parent, that aim is to prepare her children for the greatest success in the outside world that they can possibly achieve. Elsewhere, Evelyn uses her direction to build the best possible support network for her friends or colleagues, helping them to achieve their goals.

THE RUNIC INTERPRETATION
ᚾᛇᛚᚠᛖ (Nauthiz, Eihwaz, Laguz, Fehu, Ehwaz)

The Ehwaz rune of movement characterizes this name, along with material wealth. Evelyn has a curious and retentive mind. Her conversation is lively and stimulating, and friends seek out her company because she makes the world come alive for them. Evelyn is flexible and easygoing, but also introspective and restricted either socially, financially, or physically. Evelyn is an overcomer, and she rises to a position of influence on her sheer will and desire. She is not the victim of her passions, and she lives her life in a stable and logical way. She is modest and seeks harmony and justice. She is a self-created woman, and she is outstanding.

Elements: Fire, earth/fire, water, air, fire, air

THE NUMEROLOGICAL INTERPRETATION
Evelyn (NV = 11, CV = 3, VV = 8, FL = 5)

The numerological qualities in this name suggest a woman with a serious mind intent on success. Gifted with a keen perception of human nature, Evelyn is not easily fooled by others. She has her eye on the larger picture and is most comfortable when in an executive role. Evelyn is not one to shirk responsibility; in fact, she is happiest when she has assumed a large creative challenge. She may have to learn how to integrate the coolness of her mind with the warmth of her heart.

Everett

A KABBALISTIC SYNOPSIS

אוראאת —AVARATh (Aleph, Vau, Aleph, Resh, Aleph, Tau)

The first thing that leaps out when you look at Everett's name is that the letter Aleph comes before and after each and every other letter in the name. This tells us two things about Everett. The first is that he is intensely individualistic in everything that he does. Everett is well suited to any kind of creative activity where the individual vision is all-important. The huge influence of Aleph also points to a highly thoughtful man who considers every move in his life extremely carefully. It is unlikely, due to the high level of concern with the self, that Everett will waste much time thinking about wider social issues. Everett's name reduces to fifteen, and clearly there is a danger that, notwithstanding his creative expertise, Everett may well fall into the trap of vanity or conceit, thanks to this potentially excessive interest in himself at the expense of others.

THE RUNIC INTERPRETATION

ᛏᛏᛖᚱᛖᚠᛖ (Teiwaz, Teiwaz, Ehwaz, Raido, Ehwaz, Fehu, Ehwaz)

Everett is destined to be a risk taker who completes many lessons and severs many ties in this lifetime. The Ehwaz energy of his name creates travel opportunities as well as a receptive and open mind. Everett will move often and have friends around the world who value his honesty and personal power. Everett's personal power lies in his self-discipline and his balanced personality. Anger and fear used to rise to the surface and sabotage his success, but Everett has integrated that shadow side of his personality. He's harnessed those emotions in a positive way to motivate himself and to set attainable goals in his life. In this way, Everett overcomes challenges. He'll always have money, creature comforts, and a lifestyle sparkling with humor and pizzazz.

Elements: Air, air, air, water, air, fire, air

THE NUMEROLOGICAL INTERPRETATION

Everett (NV = 5, CV = 8, VV = 6, FL = 5)

Everett is a versatile man who possesses a wide scope of interests. His name bestows the urge to explore many career possibilities and the ability to structure these experiences into nicely balanced packages. A good coordinator with an artistic disposition, Everett has a number of talents he can develop and use. His challenge is not to dissipate his gifts indiscriminately. His success depends upon his ability to focus his energies so that he does not diffuse his creative impulses.

DERIVATION: English, originally from the surname Everard. Has been used as a first name since the early twentieth century.

PRINCIPAL COLORS: The full spectrum of very pale hues

GEMSTONES AND PRECIOUS METALS: Silver, diamonds, platinum

BOTANICALS: Oats, sweet marjoram, parsley

UNIQUE SPELLINGS: Everet, Everit, Everitt, Eviret, Evirit

RELATED TO: Evant, Everard

Fannie

A KABBALISTIC SYNOPSIS
פאני —PhANY (Peh, Aleph, Nun, Yod)

The function of Peh in Fannie's name is to provide her with a strong Martian energy, which means that she can withstand any amount of opposition and still resolutely follow her intended plan of action. It takes an enormous amount of negativity to stop Fannie in her tracks; one equivalence of her name is "robust," and she is physically strong and has an admirably firm resolve. Any employer is happy to have Fannie on staff, as she is always a reliable, hard worker and is rarely, if ever, out due to illness. At home Fannie will be the linchpin of the family, and it will be up to her to hold everything together—a task she can handle with her eyes closed!

THE RUNIC INTERPRETATION
ᛖᛁᚾᚾᚨᚠ (Ehwaz, Isa, Nauthiz, Nauthiz, Ansuz, Fehu)

Fannie loves to primp in front of the mirror and compose love letters. Fannie may find peace and recognition in a modeling career or as an actress if these careers interest her. However, she is challenged by the double Nauthiz rune of constraint in her name, which indicates she has a lot of obstacles to overcome. Rather than whine about this, Fannie just builds a lovely world in her imagination. She will prosper because she has the Fehu rune of possessions at her command. As an added bonus, Fannie is a wild lover and has strong appetites.

Elements: Air, earth, fire, fire, air, fire

THE NUMEROLOGICAL INTERPRETATION
Fannie (NV = 4, CV = 7, VV = 6, FL = 6)

This is a name that depicts a hardworking, determined person. Fannie is practical, reliable, and dependable. Her material possessions and her home are very important to her, and she guards them with care and concern. Fannie likes to be well organized. People see her as being very down-to-earth and can easily confide in her. This is a woman who definitely prefers a stable emotional life with one committed partner. She is sincere in her feelings and loyal in her affections.

❧

Faye

A Kabbalistic Synopsis
פֿאי —PhAY (Peh, Aleph, Yod)

Few people argue with Faye, and those who do are unlikely to do it more than once. Faye has a very quick mind, and is more than capable of using her mental alacrity to come up with stinging and fierce retorts in any verbal dispute. However, Faye is not an argumentative woman by nature; a number of positive energies in her name ensure that her outgoing character is primarily friendly. An ideal career for Faye would be teaching, as she has an excellent speaking voice, and the Aleph of the name shows her to have the ability to use her speaking skills to explain a variety of concepts. Faye's bundles of energy will be of great assistance when dealing with children, as will be her capacity to be stern when it is needed. Faye's biggest fault is her constant desire for absolute precision. She cannot abide vagueness of any kind, which is great in that it makes her a straight talker, but can become frustrating over time.

The Runic Interpretation
ᛗᛇᚨᚠ (Ehwaz, Eihwaz, Ansuz, Fehu)

Faye is blessed with runes representing possessions, signals, and movement. She loves to collect memorabilia and souvenirs from her travels to remote and mysterious lands. She has impeccable taste and an eye for art that will increase in value. Faye is prosperous and probably jets from one residence to another. She is highly intuitive as well, and does brilliantly by investing her money and following her hunches. She is superstitious and amusing, and she dresses in a creative and oddly beautiful way. But most of all, Faye is *quirky*. She hides things in teapots and keeps a little lapdog who eventually inherits most of her money.

Elements: Air, earth/fire, air, fire

The Numerological Interpretation
Faye (NV = 1, CV = 4, VV = 6, FL = 6)

Faye enjoys a good challenge. The harder she has to work for something, the more she enjoys the rewards of her accomplishments. The easy way out for her is definitely not the best. Faye is very goal oriented, whether in her professional life or in her emotional relationships. She can be overly focused on her personal life and will need to find those friendships and life experiences that take her out of herself. Once this is achieved, Faye can become a staunch defender of the underdog, eagerly using her forthright nature to help others in distress.

DERIVATION: English, coined in the nineteenth century, from the French *fée*, meaning "fairy." Also a short form of Faith. Especially popular in the United States in the 1920s.

PRINCIPAL COLORS: All the shades of bronze, gold, golden brown, yellows

GEMSTONES AND PRECIOUS METALS: Topaz, amber, any yellow stone

BOTANICALS: Eyebright, borage, sorrel, thyme

UNIQUE SPELLINGS: Fae, Fay

RELATED TO: Faith, Fayth, Fee

∽

"The only safe ship in a storm is leadership."
—FAYE WATTLETON (AUTHOR, FAMILY PLANNING ADVOCATE)

∽

In the absence of any direct equivalent to the letter *f* in the Hebrew alphabet, the letter Peh is used. Peh can function as either a hard or a soft letter, and as such, is one of the seven "doubles."

Felicia

DERIVATION: Latin, the female version of Felix, meaning "lucky."

PRINCIPAL COLORS: All red hues, including bloodred, pink, and rose

GEMSTONES AND PRECIOUS METALS: Deep red bloodstones, rubies, and garnets

BOTANICALS: Broom, onion, wormwood

UNIQUE SPELLINGS: Faleesha, Falesha, Faleysha, Falicea, Falicia, Falisha, Falycia, Feleysha, Felicea, Felisha, Felycia, Phalicia, Phalycia, Phelecia, Phelycia, Phlycia, Phylecia, Phylesha, Phylisha

RELATED TO: Felice, Felicidad, Felicie, Felicita, Felicity

In the absence of any direct equivalent to the letter *f* in the Hebrew alphabet, the letter Peh is used. Peh can function as either a hard or a soft letter, and as such, is one of the seven "doubles."

A KABBALISTIC SYNOPSIS
פלישא —PhLYShA (Peh, Lamed, Yod, Shin, Aleph)

Felicia's aims in life are not particularly spectacular; she wants a loving partner, an interesting job, and a comfortable family life. Not very much to ask, most of us would agree, but many people have difficulty achieving and maintaining this seemingly simple set of desires. Not so with Felicia, who, even if she does experience, say, divorce or downsizing, will simply dust herself off and carry on with the same determination as before. In name analysis there are letters that describe aspects of life and those that simply point to the manner in which a person approaches their life. In the case of Felicia there is little in the way of description, but her name is packed with fire energy. We may not know in detail what Felicia hopes to achieve in life, but we can be sure that she will be unceasing in her efforts and will move heaven and earth in order to realize her goals.

THE RUNIC INTERPRETATION
ᚾᛁᛋᛁᛚᛖᚠ (Ansuz, Isa, Sowelu, Isa, Laguz, Ehwaz, Fehu)

Felicia has all four elements in her name, which gives her a lot of power. Lucky Felicia can weather any storm. She can spot a con man a mile away. In addition to being strong, Felicia is seductive, and she enjoys the company of powerful and influential people who look out for her. Felicia makes a good mother because she has learned to be modest and nurturing. She is also a hard worker and a loyal friend to those who have earned her respect.

Elements: Air, earth, air, earth, water, air, fire

THE NUMEROLOGICAL INTERPRETATION
Felicia (NV = 9, CV = 3, VV = 6, FL = 6)

There is a soft and gentle energy that comes with this name. Felicia is a woman who is quite spiritually oriented and who holds within her a strong sense of what is right. Felicia is very sensitive to the injustices in the world and will do whatever she can to bring out a deeper humanity in others. Felicia is very aware of other people's situations in life, and would most likely find herself in a service-oriented profession. Psychology, sociology, history, and classical literature will likely be of interest to her.

Felipe

DERIVATION: Spanish version of the Greek name meaning "lover of horses."

PRINCIPAL COLORS: Black, dark gray, very deep shades of azure and violet

GEMSTONES AND PRECIOUS METALS: Amethyst, carbuncles, black pearls, black diamonds

BOTANICALS: Angelica, marsh mallow, pilewort

UNIQUE SPELLINGS: Filip, Fillip

RELATED TO: Filippo, Flip, Lippo, Philip, Pip, Pippo

In the absence of any direct equivalent to the letter *f* in the Hebrew alphabet, the letter Peh is used. Peh can function as either a hard or a soft letter, and as such, is one of the seven "doubles."

A KABBALISTIC SYNOPSIS
פליף —PhLYPh (Peh, Lamed, Yod, Peh)

Oh boy, what a talker! Felipe has the dubious pleasure of having his name begin and end with Ph, or Peh, meaning "mouth." This lets us know that earplugs may be a requirement when spending more than an hour or so in his company. Luckily for Felipe's friends, the remainder of his name suggests an interesting and lively personality, and so if his monologues are long, as they are likely to be, they will probably not be boring at all. In fact, with this name Felipe is ideally suited to working as a radio talk-show host or, at a more ordinary level, as a salesman. It is not just that Felipe enjoys talking; there is a driving force within him to communicate with others. This may stem from a feeling that he can define himself only in relation to the reactions of others, as there are some hints of insecurity in the name.

THE RUNIC INTERPRETATION
ᛗᛈᛁᛚᛗᚠ (Ehwaz, Perth, Isa, Laguz, Ehwaz, Fehu)

Felipe has all four elements in his name—a good sign. He also has charisma and good looks. Felipe may have to pull himself up from humble beginnings. His gift of Vision is considerable, and it will aid him in his quest. Felipe is intuitive, and like all artistic people, he has a sense of the trends in his culture. Felipe is also a Don Juan who is a wonderful cook, and who serenades his sweetheart as the hot chocolate pie and leg of lamb with adobo and garlic scent the air with homey aromas.

Elements: Air, earth, earth, water, air, fire

THE NUMEROLOGICAL INTERPRETATION
Felipe (NV = 8, CV = 7, VV = 1, FL = 6)

Felipe is a name that gives a very strong urge for success. This is a very productive man with abundant drive and great determination. Felipe has to express his own uniqueness to the world. He will most likely do this through his profession, by which he may win position and status. A man with a probing mind, Felipe can cut through the surface layers of any situation. He is capable of organizing his ideas logically, giving new insights and clarity to his perceptions.

PRINCIPAL COLORS: Light gray,
   any very pale color

GEMSTONES AND PRECIOUS
   METALS: Lightly hued stones,
   silver, platinum

BOTANICALS: Sweet marjoram,
   hazel, oats

UNIQUE SPELLINGS: Fernendo,
   Phernando, Phernendo

RELATED TO: Ferdinand, Fernie

❧

In the absence of any direct
equivalent to the letter *f* in the
Hebrew alphabet, the letter Peh is
used. Peh can function as either a
hard or a soft letter, and as such, is
one of the seven "doubles."

Fernando

A KABBALISTIC SYNOPSIS
פארנאנדע —PhARNANDA'A (Peh, Aleph, Resh, Nun, Aleph, Nun, Daleth, Ayin)

Fernando is not one for bright lights and glamour. He is a deep and brooding individual with an intensity that is both attractive and worrying to those who know him well. If Fernando does get married it will be to someone as intensely self-absorbed as himself, and their relationship, while mutually satisfying, is likely to appear dark and gloomy from the outside. On a bad day Fernando can make the sunniest weather seem dull and overcast. When he is not sitting in a darkened room, he will be working in a solitary role, and if he works in a large company, he will make sure that he has his own office. Fernando's outlook on life is not born out of pretension but from a deep understanding of the way of the world. Unfortunately for Fernando, he has a better understanding of the negative aspects of society than the brighter side. He will benefit from any friends who can convince him that there is a sunnier side of the street.

THE RUNIC INTERPRETATION
ᛟᛞᚾᚨᚾᚱᛖᚠ (Othila, Dagaz, Nauthiz, Ansuz, Nauthiz, Raido, Ehwaz, Fehu)

Fernando is proud to sport the double Nauthiz rune of constraint in his name. All the danger and hardships in Fernando's life have made him brave and fiercely strong. Fernando has the runes for movement and journey in his name, along with the lucky Fehu energy to afford him money for his travels. Over the course of his life, Fernando loses a few lovers, but he never forgets any of them. He ends his life with grandchildren who sit by his knee and have him recount his adventures and narrow escapes over and over, the way loving children do.

Elements: Earth/fire, fire, fire, air, fire, water, air, fire

THE NUMEROLOGICAL INTERPRETATION
Fernando (NV = 5, CV = 11, VV = 3, FL = 6)

The odds are all in favor of Fernando leading a most interesting life. A very intuitive man who is aware of the more profound meanings of his experiences and encounters with people, Fernando is closely connected to his own creative spirit. His sensitivity is such that he can often sense the quality of other people's thoughts. He has an inexhaustible urge for personal freedom and will not easily conform to established patterns and dull routines. In his personal life, he will tend to delay committing to one person, preferring instead the excitement of various relationships.

❧

Flora

A Kabbalistic Synopsis
פלערא —PhLA'ARA (Peh, Lamed, Ayin, Resh, Aleph)

With a name that's a direct lifting of the Latin for "flowers," Flora is bright and gentle. Her personality is injected with the fiery energy of Shin, the compression of her name. Flora is a genuinely happy individual who finds it hard to take pressures and responsibilities particularly seriously. If someone tells her their troubles, she is likely to point out to them the trees and the birds and then ask them why on earth they are getting so worked up. Understandably, Flora will meet with mixed reactions to her approach to life. There will be those who dismiss her as unrealistic, and there will be others who appreciate her refreshing optimism and become her friend for life. The latter will certainly be in the majority.

The Runic Interpretation
ᚨᚱᛟᛚᚠ (Ansuz, Raido, Othila, Laguz, Fehu)

Flora's name is built on runes signifying signals, journey, separation, flow, and possessions. Flora may lose her heart many times, but in the end, she will emerge with her true love. She needs a man who is cosmopolitan and well-to-do. Flora appreciates the finer things in life, and wants joy and pretty things to comfort her. She can be fragile and needs tenderness and approval to stay healthy and carry on. Flora will travel a great deal and bring back mementos from foreign lands to hold in her lap on rainy days.

Elements: Air, water, earth/fire, water, fire

The Numerological Interpretation
Flora (NV = 7, CV = 9, VV = 7, FL = 6)

Always in pursuit of additional ways to improve herself, Flora knows there is more to life than just the material world. This name suggests a woman who is reflective, contemplative, and introspective. Flora's consistent focus upon the inner qualities of life contribute to her strength and depth of character. She is always studying and is able to gain a great deal from these efforts. A generous person, Flora can be counted upon to give clear and precise advice. On the surface she is sometimes cool and distant, but she responds easily to others when called upon for her help and guidance.

DERIVATION: English, German, and Scottish, from the Latin *flos*, meaning "flower." The name of a ninth-century saint. Brought to England from Scotland in the eighteenth century, and especially popular in the second half of the nineteenth century.

PRINCIPAL COLORS: Green, gold, any shade of yellow

GEMSTONES AND PRECIOUS METALS: Cat's-eye, moss agate, white pearls

BOTANICALS: Elder, hops, linseed

UNIQUE SPELLINGS: Florah, Phlora, Phlorah

RELATED TO: Fiora, Fiore, Fiori, Fleur, Flo, Flore, Florella, Florencet, Floris, Florise, Florrie, Flossie

‿

In the absence of any direct equivalent to the letter *f* in the Hebrew alphabet, the letter Peh is used. Peh can function as either a hard or a soft letter, and as such, is one of the seven "doubles."

DERIVATION: English and French, originally from the Latin *florens*, meaning "in bloom." The name of a third-century saint. Extremely popular in Britain and the United Sates in the latter half of the nineteenth century.

PRINCIPAL COLORS: The full range of blue hues, except for the brightest azure

GEMSTONES AND PRECIOUS METALS: Emeralds, turquoise

BOTANICALS: Dog rose, vervain, violets

UNIQUE SPELLINGS: Florance, Florince, Florrance, Florynce, Phlorance, Phlorence, Phlorince, Phlorrance, Phlorynce

RELATED TO: Fiora, Fiore, Fiorentain, Fiorentina, Fiorenza, Flo, Flor, Florat, Flore, Florencia, Florentina, Florenza, Floriana, Florina, Florinda, Florry, Flossy, Fora

❧

"I stand at the altar of the murdered men, and while I live, I fight their cause."
—FLORENCE NIGHTINGALE
(NURSE)

❧

In the absence of any direct equivalent to the letter *f* in the Hebrew alphabet, the letter Peh is used. Peh can function as either a hard or a soft letter, and as such, is one of the seven "doubles."

Florence

A KABBALISTIC SYNOPSIS
פלערונס —PhLA'ARVNS (Peh, Lamed, Ayin, Resh, Vau, Nun, Samech)

Florence has a mission in life, and she will not be swayed from it, although she is aware of the difficulties this causes her closest family and will try to make amends in any way that she can. Still, it is unlikely that Florence will get too much flak from her nearest and dearest for the time she spends away from them helping others, since the sincerity of her desire to be of use to society and the fervor with which she works are obvious to all. Florence is particularly concerned about the plight of children and will almost definitely make a career of helping them in some capacity. Thanks to her persuasive manner and winning smile she may well be employed in a fund-raising capacity. Whatever she does she will throw herself into it heart and soul. Her charming personality ensures that she gets immense support for all her good works.

THE RUNIC INTERPRETATION
ᛗᛋᛏᛗᚱᛟᛁᚠ (Ehwaz, Sowelu, Nauthiz, Ehwaz, Raido, Othila, Laguz, Fehu)

Florence is in the fortunate position of having enough money to pursue a career based solely on her interests. With the Ehwaz rune of movement in her name, Florence makes a career of travel. She learns languages and assimilates concepts and gains artistic vision wherever she goes. Florence has a charming sense of humor. If you ask her, she'll gladly demonstrate a native dance for you, right then and there, from start to finish! Florence is a trouper with a big heart. When she hears about a flood or suffering people, she's been known to board a plane and spend several weeks—or even longer—helping the needy. The pain caused by leaving her family and friends comes from the Othila rune for separation and is part of her destiny. Florence finds she has healing gifts.

Elements: Air, air, fire, air, water, earth/fire, water, fire

THE NUMEROLOGICAL INTERPRETATION
Florence (NV = 6, CV = 8, VV = 7, FL = 6)

Florence needs to be present for everyone who needs her. Her name carries the numerological significance of a person who is most sympathetic and understanding. It may therefore be necessary for her to develop a respect for her own emotional boundaries so that she doesn't overly absorb other people's energy. Florence is also aware of her need to establish her own success in life. She may be able to profit from her sensitivity through an education in psychology, philosophy, and other areas of humanistic interest.

❧

Floyd

A Kabbalistic Synopsis
פלעיד —PhLA'AYD (Peh, Lamed, Ayin, Yod, Daleth)

Floyd's name equates to the word "justice" in Hebrew, and this is where his concerns lie. In addition, his name reduces to fourteen, which is the number of Temperance in the tarot. The card Temperance refers to the reconciliation of opposing forces and the creation of unities from disparate elements. We can apply this very neatly to the field of law and may expect to see Floyd as a lawyer with hopes of becoming a judge—a role in which he would excel. As a prosecutor he will be a dangerous opponent; the compression of his name produces the letter Tzaddi, meaning "fishhook," and relates to his ability to stick doggedly to a single line of questioning and not give up until he has landed the required answer.

The Runic Interpretation
ᛗᛇᛟᛚᚠ (Dagaz, Eihwaz, Othila, Laguz, Fehu)

Floyd is most fortunate to have runic energies representing breakthrough, defense, separation, flow, and possessions in his name. However, Floyd's task in life is to distance himself from negative people and limiting opinions in order to progress. As he looks at his outer self, Floyd realizes that the negativity he encounters in life mirrors the negativity within himself. This is a strong and useful insight that helps Floyd to slow down and work on himself. He uses these delays as a time to exercise, clean out his drawers, and create room for the new in his world. In the end, he will achieve material success and invest his money well, based on his considerable intuitive promptings.

Elements: Fire, earth/fire, earth/fire, water, fire

The Numerological Interpretation
Floyd (NV = 8, CV = 4, VV = 4, FL = 6)

The strongest element in this name has to do with Floyd's practical orientation and his focus on material and financial matters. Floyd is aware of limitations and the struggles required to emerge from them. He has a choice: either become limited by the existing structures that surround him, or create structures that support and sustain him. The latter (and the only real choice) is done through the development of self-esteem and the attainment of right mental attitudes. Floyd is a builder by nature. The world he builds outside of himself is a direct reflection of the construction of his inner world.

DERIVATION: English, variation of the Welsh name Lloyd, meaning "gray-haired." Particularly common in the southern United States in the twentieth century.

PRINCIPAL COLORS: Black, violet, the darkest shades of azure and gray

GEMSTONES AND PRECIOUS METALS: Richly shaded sapphires, amethyst, black diamonds

BOTANICALS: Marsh mallow, shepherd's purse, gravel root

UNIQUE SPELLINGS: Floid, Floidd, Floydd

RELATED TO: Lloyd†

In the absence of any direct equivalent to the letter *f* in the Hebrew alphabet, the letter Peh is used. Peh can function as either a hard or a soft letter, and as such, is one of the seven "doubles."

Forrest

DERIVATION: Latin, meaning "woods dweller."

PRINCIPAL COLORS: White, all shades of green

GEMSTONES AND PRECIOUS METALS: Jade, moonstones, pearls

BOTANICALS: Chicory, plantain, colewort

UNIQUE SPELLING: Forest

RELATED TO: Forester, Forrester, Foster

∽

In the absence of any direct equivalent to the letter *f* in the Hebrew alphabet, the letter Peh is used. Peh can function as either a hard or a soft letter, and as such, is one of the seven "doubles."

A KABBALISTIC SYNOPSIS
פעריסט —Pha'ARYST (Peh, Ayin, Kesh, Yod, Samech, Teth)

A wily individual is Forrest, and not one to forget a face, a conversation, or a grudge! His mind is like a camera, and everything he experiences is noted down for possible future use. In business he will probably succeed, if not through knowledge of a specific industry sector then because of everything he knows about his competitors' business, and possibly their personal lives and behavior. An ideal career for Forrest would be to work with one of the intelligence agencies, where he could legitimately employ his skills for covert observation and his knack for recalling the most incriminating portions of any conversation. Not surprisingly, his partners will rarely argue with him unless they are absolutely certain of their facts. Unless Forrest has a strong influence of Scorpio or Capricorn astrologically, it is unlikely that he will be particularly malicious with his talents, as he is on the whole a decent man with a belief in fair play.

THE RUNIC INTERPRETATION
↑∫MRR◊ⴱ (Teiwaz, Sowelu, Ehwaz, Raido, Raido, Othila, Fehu)

Forrest prides himself on his great taste. He frequents the best restaurants, and once he's sniffed the cork, he sends the bottle back with grand flourish. Forrest is a bit like the fine wine he admires, because he, too, mellows with age. In the process, he discards insincere friends in favor of a few who really enjoy his quirks and foibles; Forrest realizes these are friends he has no need to impress. With more appropriate and positive people in his life, Forrest relaxes and takes time to develop his interests in the fine arts and humanities. He writes articles for the local paper and busies himself on historical research and landmarks preservation projects. The double Raido rune of good communication affords Forrest with many opportunities to share his knowledge and love of life.

Elements: Air, air, air, water, water, earth/fire, fire

THE NUMEROLOGICAL INTERPRETATION
Forrest (NV = 2, CV = 9, VV = 11, FL = 6)

Men named Forrest have a very special intuition when it comes to their dealings with others. Partnership oriented by nature, Forrest is very open to sharing. Friends and family have no problem approaching Forrest, as they can expect a sincere helping hand and an insightful response to their needs. Forrest is a safety zone when things get rough, and a focus for security when things are uncertain. A definite humanitarian by nature, Forrest would do well in larger community projects where his inclusive scope of vision could be used most successfully.

∽

Frances

A Kabbalistic Synopsis
פראנסאס —PhRANSAS (Peh, Resh, Aleph, Nun, Samech, Aleph, Samech)

Frances should choose to live where her highly nonconformist approach to life will seem normal and be accepted—but her stubborn streak is likely to make her move right to the middle of the Bible Belt and wait for the inevitable conflict! Frances reduces to eleven, which is the number of magic. Frances is likely to be engaged in the actual practice of the occult arts and sciences rather than, like most people associated with the number eleven, being merely interested in the strange and unexplained. From the initial position of Peh, meaning "mouth," and its relationship to the other letters we can see that Frances is completely open about her activities and, to a certain extent, may delight in any element of notoriety they bring her. Frances will enjoy shocking the more conservative members of her community, but there is absolutely nothing sinister about her activities except in very rare circumstances.

The Runic Interpretation
ᛋᛖᛋᚾᚨᚱᚠ (Sowelu, Ehwaz, Sowelu, Nauthiz, Ansuz, Raido, Fehu)

Frances is like a butterfly made of steel. When she enters a room, people respond to her silliness and spontaneity. She enjoys an audience and finds her simplest comments can make the room burst into laughter. People watch Frances closely because her facial expressions are fleeting and subtle, and they don't want to miss a laugh. People who know her well admire the Sowelu energy of wholeness in Frances, which gives her the emotional stability and the honesty of a genuine comedienne. They probably recognize that she's been through a lot and that much of her humor is based on personal experience. The Nauthiz rune of constraint has taught Frances difficult lessons. Frances has a prosperous life that is rich in money, friends, and love.

Elements: Air, air, air, fire, air, water, fire

The Numerological Interpretation
Frances (NV = 3, CV = 6, VV = 6, FL = 6)

Clear powers of communication and a benevolent attitude are just two of the fine characteristics associated with this name. Frances is a woman who brings kindness and grace into every social situation. She has an innate interest in the world around her, and her friendly disposition makes her a very welcome friend and coworker. Frances's worldview is very open, and her ideas and opinions expand other people's viewpoints tremendously. Home and family are very important to her. She is a faithful partner and very much geared toward long-lasting relationships.

DERIVATION: English, feminine form of Francis, which is from the Latin name Franciscus, meaning "Frenchman." Common since the seventeenth century, and especially popular in the United States around 1900.

PRINCIPAL COLORS: All shades of purple, from pale violet to deep maroon

GEMSTONES AND PRECIOUS METALS: Amethyst, garnets

BOTANICALS: Apple, cherry, bilberry, mint

UNIQUE SPELLINGS: Francis, Francys, Franses, Fransis, Fransys, Phrances, Phrancis, Phrancys, Phransis, Phransys

RELATED TO: Fancie, Fancy, Fanniet, Fanny, Fran, Franceline, Francene, Francesca, Francey, Francie, Francine, Frannie, Franny

~

"I am sure there is Magic in everything, only we have not sense enough to get hold of it and make it do things for us."
—FRANCES HODGSON BURNETT (AUTHOR)

"Apparent failure may hold in its rough shell the germs of a success that will blossom in time, and bear fruit throughout eternity."
—FRANCES ELLEN WATKINS HARPER (POET)

~

In the absence of any direct equivalent to the letter f in the Hebrew alphabet, the letter Peh is used. Peh can function as either a hard or a soft letter, and as such, is one of the seven "doubles."

Francis

DERIVATION: Latin origin, meaning
"free, liberated."

PRINCIPAL COLORS: Any color
with green or yellow tones

GEMSTONES AND PRECIOUS
METALS: Moonstones, cat's-eye,
all white stones

BOTANICALS: Hops, juniper,
blackberries

UNIQUE SPELLINGS: Frances,
Phrances, Phrancis

RELATED TO: Fran, Franciscot,
Frankt, Franny

In the absence of any direct
equivalent to the letter *f* in the
Hebrew alphabet, the letter Peh is
used. Peh can function as either a
hard or a soft letter, and as such, is
one of the seven "doubles."

A KABBALISTIC SYNOPSIS

פראנסיס —PhRANSYS (Peh, Resh,
Aleph, Nun, Samech, Yod, Samech)

Francis always has a spring in his step—although he may well be about to trip, given the Sagittarian clumsiness that his name suggests. If he does stumble, he won't be put out, as Francis sees life as more of a game than anything else. This doesn't mean that he won't take things seriously; he certainly does, and will always play the game to win. However, the difference between Francis and other competitive people is that on the occasions when he loses, Francis will shake it off with a shrug and won't let it spoil his appetite. To match his admirably laid-back approach to the vicissitudes of life, Francis has a great enjoyment of fun. He won't sit and stare at the TV screen over the weekend, but will instead take the family out to visit new and interesting places. Francis treats life like a dog does a bone, and intends to suck every last drop of marrow out of it.

THE RUNIC INTERPRETATION

ᛋᛁᛒᚺᚨᚱᚠ (Sowelu, Isa, Sowelu, Nauthiz, Ansuz, Raido, Fehu)

Francis has the same destiny as his namesake, Frances, with the important exception of the substitution of the Isa energy for the Ehwaz energy. Consequently, the name Francis has less movement in it and more standstill. Whereas Frances is flexible in her thoughts and mobile, Francis is somewhat fixed in his opinions and may be unwilling to move a lot to better his career or surroundings; he is primarily a homebody. Francis is fairly introspective and can be given to religious fanaticism. He needs supportive friends and lots of exercise to maintain a sunny mental outlook. However, Francis is powerful and benefits from having all four elements in his name.

Elements: Air, earth, air, fire, air, water, fire

THE NUMEROLOGICAL INTERPRETATION

Francis (NV = 7, CV = 6, VV = 1, FL = 6)

Francis possesses natural insight into life. This comes from his own efforts at personal reflection and self-study. This is definitely not a superficial person. Francis takes his interests seriously and is ever eager to improve the world. This inner contemplation and investigation into life's meanings lead to a sense of wisdom that other people feel when they are around him. Francis's domestic life is central to his life. Home needs to be an oasis of peace that provides a wonderful atmosphere of comfort and stability.

Francisco

A Kabbalistic Synopsis

פראנסיסכע —PhRANSYSKA'A (Peh, Resh, Aleph, Nun, Samech, Yod, Samech, Kaph, Ayin)

There are many people who would love to have Francisco's lifestyle. Francisco has all of the happy-go-lucky attributes of Francis except that for Francisco, wherever possible, life should be a holiday. The compression of Francisco's name reveals a strong affinity with the sea, and we can expect to see him living and working somewhere along the coast. A love of company and relaxed conversation may well lead Francisco to open up a beach bar or other similar venue. Whatever line of work he chooses, he will make sure that he can pretty much specify his own hours. For many people such a lifestyle could never be more than a pipe dream, but the driving force in Francisco's name indicates that if this is what he wants, he will almost definitely achieve it.

The Runic Interpretation

ᛟᚲᛋᛁᚲᛏᚨᚱᚠ (Othila, Kano, Sowelu, Isa, Kano, Nauthiz, Ansuz, Raido, Fehu)

Francisco is humorous and strong like his namesake, Francis. The additional runes in his name lend him open-mindedness and the ability to be discriminating. Francisco had a challenging childhood and it taught him to be wise about the ways of the world. He works well in sales or in fields such as detective work and law, which require him to be sophisticated about people and circumstances. Francisco has the Raido rune of good communication and he loves words. He has a dry sense of humor and slips a pun in now and then to ambush a potentially volatile situation with an unexpected giggle. Francisco's ability to avert hostility is one of his most endearing qualities. He is a peacemaker and a born arbitrator because he has deep reserves of patience.

Elements: Earth/fire, water, air, earth, water, fire, air, water, fire

The Numerological Interpretation

Francisco (NV = 8, CV = 9, VV = 8, FL = 6)

An ambitious man with a powerful urge for success, Francisco is dedicated to making his mark in the world. He has a sense of self-confidence that radiates power and control. Francisco likes to take charge and get things done, and is considered very dependable by his friends and associates. He has to take care that his material concerns do not so completely dominate his life that he becomes overly concerned with his social standing and professional status. Balance comes to him through his humanitarian side, which is also indicated within the numbers in his name.

DERIVATION: Latin and Spanish origin, meaning "free."

PRINCIPAL COLORS: Gold, the full range of yellow and green hues

GEMSTONES AND PRECIOUS METALS: Cat's-eye, moss agate, pearls

BOTANICALS: Elder, hops, linseed

UNIQUE SPELLING: Phrancisco

RELATED TO: Francesco, Francis†, Frank†

In the absence of any direct equivalent to the letter f in the Hebrew alphabet, the letter Peh is used. Peh can function as either a hard or a soft letter, and as such, is one of the seven "doubles."

DERIVATION: Latin and Germanic origin, meaning "spear" or "Frenchman."

PRINCIPAL COLORS: Any very pale hue, particularly light shades of gray

GEMSTONES AND PRECIOUS METALS: Silver, platinum, diamonds

BOTANICALS: Hazel, parsley, oats

UNIQUE SPELLING: Phrank

RELATED TO: Francist, Franciscot

In the absence of any direct equivalent to the letter *f* in the Hebrew alphabet, the letter Peh is used. Peh can function as either a hard or a soft letter, and as such, is one of the seven "doubles."

A KABBALISTIC SYNOPSIS
פראנכ —PhRANK (Peh, Resh, Aleph, Nun, Kaph)

Frank is in need of a very supportive partner who has the strength of character to make sure that he takes a rest every now and then; otherwise, he is likely to burn out. There is little doubt that Frank will do well careerwise, as he is prepared to work absurdly long hours in order to progress up the corporate ladder—and climb that ladder he will, potentially right to the top. While he is an amiable chap by nature and always warm and welcoming to friends and family, Frank can be exceptionally ruthless when it comes to work. What few people will ever realize is that this aggressive approach to his working life is driven by deep-seated anxieties. His name reduces to eighteen, which represents the moon and is associated with a variety of insecurities. In Frank's case, it is a fear of failure and of losing pace with new developments that drives him on. Having made a life of his work, he has strong anxieties about what his life would become if he ever found himself without it.

THE RUNIC INTERPRETATION
ᚲᚾᚨᚱᚠ (Kano, Nauthiz, Ansuz, Raido, Fehu)

Frank has the runic energies of opening, constraint, signals, journey, and possessions in his name. Just as the water and fire elements in Frank's name are in opposition, there is also tension between the Nauthiz energy of constraint and the Kano energy of opening. As Frank moves beyond early limitations to prosperity, he arrives at a place of ease, and the desire to go ahead and share his bounty overwhelms him. It is at this point that the Kano, or opening, energy kicks in, and Frank finds a higher spiritual path at last. It is only by delving into his own anger and fear that Frank is able to finally embrace them and forge ahead to a greater sense of humility and oneness, which he demonstrates as generosity.

Elements: Water, fire, air, water, fire

THE NUMEROLOGICAL INTERPRETATION
Frank (NV = 5, CV = 22, VV = 1, FL = 6)

Frank can be just that—frank! This name indicates a man who is not afraid to state his opinions or beliefs. He does this not so much as a way to dominate others but to bring greater understanding to his environment. Frank usually has a point to make and will not rest until he does so. He feels a sense of purpose within himself and prefers to deal with the larger issues in life rather than getting bogged down in petty issues and small details. Frank makes a very fine teacher and is at his best when showing others ways in which their lives may be improved.

Fred

A Kabbalistic Synopsis
פראד —PhRAD (Peh, Resh, Aleph, Daleth)

Fred is an absolutely regular guy and is proud of the fact that there are no surprises in his personality. A solid, down-to-earth man, Fred has no time for anything remotely out of the ordinary and probably considers activities such as name analysis to be completely ridiculous. In spite of his preference for the safe and familiar, Fred is not a boring individual. He is likely to have a strong interest in the history of his local community and have a whole range of physical leisure pursuits. Fred can recount any number of stories relating to the good old days and can do so in an appealing way. Fred's family may wish that he could be more broad-minded from time to time, but they will appreciate the fact he can always be relied upon to provide financial and fatherly support to the family.

The Runic Interpretation
ᛞᛖᚱᚠ (Dagaz, Ehwaz, Raido, Fehu)

Fred could be an art buyer or international businessman. He acquires money through his own efforts and has a restless nature that leads him to obtain new homes in different parts of the country. He probably lives and earns money abroad for part of the year. Fred is blessed by the breakthrough rune, which ensures joy and transformation on a spiritual level. The change comes after he overcomes his old habits. When he is no longer seeking love or accolades, and desires only to serve, his life turns around and he is able to appreciate what he has. From this point on, Fred's gratitude is overwhelming. Fred is also curious and broad-minded.

Elements: Fire, air, water, fire

The Numerological Interpretation
Fred (NV = 6, CV = 1, VV = 5, FL = 6)

Fred projects himself into his environment with enthusiasm and high energy. His name endows him with an avid curiosity and a need to explore all of his many interests. Home is very important to him, and he will want to make sure that what he does brings positive results to friends and family. In this respect, Fred is an unselfish person who really cares about others. He is well liked and respected, and will find that people will be as open in helping him as he is in lending his advice and goodwill to others.

DERIVATION: Short form of Frederick, from the Old German for "peaceful ruler."

PRINCIPAL COLORS: All but the brightest shades of azure

GEMSTONES AND PRECIOUS METALS: Emeralds, blue and blue-green turquoise

BOTANICALS: Vervain, violets, walnuts, almonds

UNIQUE SPELLING: Phred

RELATED TO: Alfredt, Freddie, Frederick†

⌒

In the absence of any direct equivalent to the letter *f* in the Hebrew alphabet, the letter Peh is used. Peh can function as either a hard or a soft letter, and as such, is one of the seven "doubles."

⌒

Frederick

A KABBALISTIC SYNOPSIS

פראדריכ —PhRADRYK (Peh, Resh, Aleph, Daleth, Resh, Yod, Kaph)

If you need to get something done in a hurry, ask a Frederick to help out. Here is a man who above all else knows how to get things done; stuff happens when Frederick is around! The initial Peh in his name indicates his ability to organize, and when combined with the letter Heh and the final Kaph, the name shows a strong capacity for ensuring that work gets completed on time. Frederick has a natural air of authority and commands respect wherever he goes. If his career is going well, as it should, then his home life will be happy. If his business ventures fail, then unfortunately, it tends to affect his family negatively. As his career success is almost guaranteed, it is safe to say that his wife and children will regard him as a warm and generous man. One fault Frederick does have is that he can be too authoritarian from time to time, particularly as his children get to an age when they begin to question his attitudes.

THE RUNIC INTERPRETATION

ᚲᛁᚱᛖᛞᛖᚱᚠ (Kano, Isa, Raido, Ehwaz, Dagaz, Ehwaz, Raido, Fehu)

Frederick expands on the blissful energies of Fred and adds the double Ehwaz energy of movement, the Kano energy of opening, the Isa of isolation, and the double Raido energy of the journey. Frederick will be twice as broad-minded, flexible, and curious as Fred, who shares these same traits. Both men achieve breakthroughs that set them on a high spiritual path. One could say with assurance that Frederick is an evolved seeker. He has the power of all four elements to strengthen him in his quest.

Elements: Water, earth, water, air, fire, air, water, fire

THE NUMEROLOGICAL INTERPRETATION

Frederick (NV = 7, CV = 6, VV = 1, FL = 6)

An ethical man with a deep sense of right and wrong, Frederick is a philosopher at heart. The numerological contents of his name suggest a person of profound thoughts and a loving disposition. Frederick is attracted by beauty and is therefore a lover of art, music, and fine writing. He may find that he has a certain talent in one or more of these areas himself. Frederick enjoys taking long walks and spending a certain amount of his time with his books and thoughts. He will appreciate a partner who is supportive of his sensitivity and need for personal space.

⁓

Gabriel

A KABBALISTIC SYNOPSIS
גבריאל —GBRYAL (Gimel, Beth, Resh, Yod, Aleph, Lamed)

One expects someone who shares their name with one of the most well-known of angels to have a strong character and an impressive personality. In Gabriel our expectations are more than satisfied. Many people are aware that Gabriel functions as the messenger of God, but fewer are aware of Gabriel's role as the Archangel of the West and his angelic representation of the element of water. We can rightly expect the mortal holder of this name to be a man with great understanding of emotional matters. Gabriel is probably employed in a very senior advisory capacity in a profession that is wholly concerned with emotional behavior, such as clinical psychiatry. While Gabriel is deeply sensitive to emotional situations, he is not in any way indulgent of weakness; angels have the capacity to be stern and judgmental, and the human version of Gabriel is no different. Gabriel will have no difficulty in revealing some harsh home truths to people who consult him.

THE RUNIC INTERPRETATION
ᛚᛖᛁᛉᛒᚨᚷ (Laguz, Ehwaz, Isa, Raido, Berkana, Ansuz, Gebo)

Gabriel is affected by the Gebo rune of partnership, along with runes signifying flow, movement, isolation, journey, growth, and signals. It's certain that Gabriel will be tested at some point during his life, and will pass his spiritual challenges with flying colors. His highest partnership is with God. Gabriel will most assuredly have a loving mate as well. When Gabriel stops striving and appreciates what has been given to him, he learns to find peace and satisfaction in simplicity.

Elements: Water, air, earth, water, air/earth, air, water

THE NUMEROLOGICAL INTERPRETATION
Gabriel (NV = 9, CV = 3, VV = 6, FL = 7)

Gabriel is a name that contains a strong spiritual vibration. It indicates a man of deep beliefs with a profound sense of universal harmony. He knows a great deal about correct human behavior and strives to bring this understanding into his personal relationships. He is a lover and romantic by nature. Many of his life lessons will come as a result of his emotional involvements—lessons that he is able to share with others. The heart is definitely at the center of Gabriel's life.

DERIVATION: Biblical, from the Hebrew, meaning "man of God." Archangel who announces to Mary that she is pregnant with the Christ child. Regularly used as a given name in the English-speaking world.

PRINCIPAL COLORS: Pink, crimson, maroon, any shade of red

GEMSTONES AND PRECIOUS METALS: Bloodstones, red rubies, garnets

BOTANICALS: Garlic, onion, wormwood

UNIQUE SPELLINGS: Gabrial, Gabriall, Gabrieel, Gabriell, Gabryal, Gabryall, Gabryel, Gabryell

RELATED TO: Gabe, Gabi, Gábor, Gaby, Gay

"He who awaits much can expect little."
—GABRIEL GARCÍA MÁRQUEZ (AUTHOR)

DERIVATION: Feminine form of the biblical name Gabriel, one of the archangels, meaning "man of God." Common in English-speaking countries for almost a century.

PRINCIPAL COLORS: Purple, black, the darker shades of gray and blue

GEMSTONES AND PRECIOUS METALS: Sapphires as well as other dark stones, such as black pearls, black diamonds, carbuncles, and amethyst

BOTANICALS: Angelica, shepherd's purse, marsh mallow

UNIQUE SPELLINGS: Gabriele, Gabriell, Gabryelle

RELATED TO: Gabbe, Gabbie, Gabby, Gabi, Gabriela, Gabriella, Gabryella, Gaby, Gavra

Gabrielle

A KABBALISTIC SYNOPSIS

גבריאל —GBRYAL (Gimel, Beth, Resh, Yod, Aleph, Lamed)

Gabrielle is a feminine version of Gabriel†, which in turn is an anglicized version of the Hebrew GBRYAL. The name Gabrielle has the same value as the Hebrew for "myrrh," which hints at Gabrielle's interest in matters spiritual. Thus she is likely to be drawn to a mystical field of knowledge. Gabrielle is much more of a thinker than a doer in life, but her thoughts are extremely interesting and are likely to take her into relatively uncharted waters in terms of ideas about who we are and why we are here. However, her name also has a reduced value that associates her with the tarot card Force. This tells us that while Gabrielle may come across as a dreamer, she has an inner core that is as strong as iron. Any ideas she has will be subject to considerable challenge, for Gabrielle is not the sort of person who falls for every trend; she is looking for something of genuine value. In her relationships Gabrielle is a very giving person, although if she is born under the sign of Scorpio, she may make excessive demands on herself, as well as on others, when it comes to emotional commitment. People warm to Gabrielle very easily and respect her ideas; also, when it comes to looking for a serious relationship, Gabrielle will be very likely to find the partner of her dreams.

THE RUNIC INTERPRETATION

ᛚᛖᛇᚱᛒᚨᚷ (Laguz, Ehwaz, Eihwaz, Raido, Berkana, Ansuz, Gebo)

Four elements in a name is always a most fortunate aspect, implying strength and energy. Gabrielle has a kind of high-minded love and patience that is the glue in relationships. She's a tolerant woman, but don't expect her to compromise her values or she will ease on down the road in her own quiet way—and it will be a waste of energy to try to find her. Gabrielle's the kind of lover that people appreciate better once they've lost her. She could be an herbalist or a fashion designer. Gabrielle also works with the spirit in art or healing, or combines the two for a unique alchemy all of her own devising.

Elements: Water, air, earth/fire, water, air/earth, air, water

THE NUMEROLOGICAL INTERPRETATION

Gabrielle (NV = 8, CV = 6, VV = 2, FL = 7)

The world of the arts will play an important part in Gabrielle's life. This is a name that denotes a love of beauty and a definite orientation to sensuous refinement. Gabrielle is very attracted by beautiful objects and by the money that can purchase them. The development and expression of her creativity is central to her life mission. Gabrielle tends to bring harmony into her environment. She is a very peace-loving person who can work wonders in calming others and mediating problems. Her home is of great significance to her, but she has to be careful not to compromise herself in order to maintain peace in her domestic environment. If Gabrielle speaks and supports her own truth, a more beautiful reality will follow.

Gail

DERIVATION: English, shortened form of the biblical name Abigail, from the Hebrew, meaning "father of exaltation." Commonly used as a given name since the middle of the twentieth century.

PRINCIPAL COLORS: The full range of greens, cream

GEMSTONES AND PRECIOUS METALS: Cat's-eye, moonstones, jade

BOTANICALS: Chicory, plantain

UNIQUE SPELLINGS: Gael, Gaille, Gale, Gayl, Gayle

RELATED TO: Abigail†, Gaila, Gala, Galia, Galina, Gay, Gayle†, Gayleen, Gaylene

A KABBALISTIC SYNOPSIS
גאיל —GAYL (Gimel, Aleph, Yod, Lamed)

Gail is a comfortable woman who is completely ruled by the element of earth. Her existence revolves around her personal life. Gail loves to be close to her family and is unlikely to move far away from her hometown. Whenever she can, Gail will be arranging family get-togethers and reunions. To Gail, occasions such as Christmas and Thanksgiving are the overall framework on which the rest of life hangs. While Gail always has her heart in the right place, her outlook can nevertheless cause certain problems. Gail needs to learn that friends, colleagues, and even some family members may not share her vision of the ideal family situation.

THE RUNIC INTERPRETATION
ᚾᛁᚨᚷ (Laguz, Isa, Ansuz, Gebo)

Gail is a romantic. She needs to utilize the Gebo rune of partnership in her name and be discriminating in her choice of a husband. In particular, Gail needs to learn to let her partner have his own ideas and differing opinions. This accomplished, theirs can be a union with easy empathy and mental stimulation. The strong sympathy between the two results in romantic fulfillment on a permanent basis, which they achieve more effortlessly than many other people. Gail uses the Isa energy of isolation to have quiet times by herself as well.

Elements: Water, earth, air, water

THE NUMEROLOGICAL INTERPRETATION
Gail (NV = 2, CV = 1, VV = 1, FL = 7)

A strong sense of individuality and a powerful way of expressing herself are but some of the many facets inherent in this name. Gail will use her innate sense of herself to be of help to others. She is very other-oriented, and she is a peacemaker. She works well when she has to mediate between two opposing forces. Gail is also effective when working in a group, as she is as clear about her own beliefs as she is about other people's points of view.

PRINCIPAL COLORS: Black, gray, dark azure and purple hues

GEMSTONES AND PRECIOUS METALS: Black diamonds, amethyst, sapphires

BOTANICALS: Angelica, marsh mallow

UNIQUE SPELLINGS: Garet, Garett, Garit, Garret, Garrit, Garritt

RELATED TO: Gareth, Garry, Garth, Garyt, Geraldt, Gerard, Gerhard, Gerlach, Gerrard, Gerrit, Gerritt

Garrett

A KABBALISTIC SYNOPSIS

גאראט —GARAT (Gimel, Aleph, Resh, Aleph, Teth)

Garrett positively radiates good feelings. He is like a beacon of happiness, and as a result people find it very difficult to feel blue when he is around. Garrett has quite a unique and sometimes mischievous sense of humor, which is another reason why depression doesn't stand much of a chance when he is present. While he can have great fun when the time is right, Garrett also knows when to be serious, and would never let his love of a good time get in the way of a career opportunity. Garrett will need to work in an environment where he has plenty of contact with the public and his colleagues, as he loves to meet and speak with people. An ideal role for Garrett would be as a trainer in some large corporation; his sense of humor would certainly lighten the load for the trainees at difficult times in the course.

THE RUNIC INTERPRETATION

↑↑MRRRX (Teiwaz, Teiwaz, Ehwaz, Raido, Raido, Ansuz, Gebo)

Garrett looks danger in the eye. He is apt to be a reporter for a major news magazine or a photojournalist of high repute. Garrett has double Raido runes for good communication, as well as the double Teiwaz warrior runes, which give him strength. He can handle courtroom drama and investigate stories that would make a weaker man fold. Garrett is good with kids and especially talented with troubled youth. He may do volunteer work with difficult populations or choose a career in psychiatry or social work. Garrett has a way of explaining things that speaks to his audience. He can create rapport with his body language and mimic the speech cadences of those lucky enough to appreciate his healing presence.

Elements: Air, air, air, water, water, air, water

THE NUMEROLOGICAL INTERPRETATION

Garrett (NV = 8, CV = 11, VV = 6, FL = 7)

Garrett is a name that gives courage and stamina. This is a man who is constantly formulating new goals for himself and has the determination and drive to succeed. Yet his success is not just centered on his own achievements; Garrett tends to be very community or group oriented. What he seeks for himself is part of a larger whole within which many people may benefit. A sentimental man with a great love of home and family, Garrett will be hard at work bringing betterment into the lives of those close to him and to people in general.

Gary

A Kabbalistic Synopsis
גארי —GARY (Gimel, Aleph, Resh, Yod)

One equivalent of Gary should be "smooth"! Of course it isn't, and it's doubtful if the ancient Hebrew people who studied the Kabbalah had to deal with too many Gary equivalents, since his loves are likely to be fast cars, fashion, and romance! The effect of the travel element as represented by G, or Gimel, in Gary's name translates as a desire to travel socially. A career for Gary is simply a means to ensure that he can keep up with all the latest gadgets and lifestyles. Permanent relationships are not on Gary's agenda; he is looking for a good time without any invasion of his personal space. Potential partners are likely to be attracted to Gary as he combines his opulent manner with a vibrant and sociable personality. However, Gary does need to watch that he doesn't get so caught up in what is found in the pages of glossy magazines that he forgets about real life.

The Runic Interpretation
ᛇᚱᚨᚷ (Eihwaz, Raido, Ansuz, Gebo)

Gary will travel far and wide before he meets a woman he can call his own. When this lucky day arrives, Gary isn't sure he can remain true to only one. Until Gary gets his act together and focuses on commitment in his relationships and his career, he will continue to flounder from job to job and girlfriend to girlfriend in search of peace. The inward journey begins when Gary begins to wonder how he's let so many opportunities slip through his fingers and the nagging doubt creeps in that here he is without much to show for all his efforts. In the end Gary emerges victorious because he has the four elements represented in his name.

Elements: Earth/fire, water, air, water

The Numerological Interpretation
Gary (NV = 6, CV = 7, VV = 8, FL = 7)

Gary is a man who seeks peace and harmony both at home and in the workplace. It is important to him to be surrounded by people who are cooperative rather than competitive, people who can work together for the actualization of mutual aims and ideals. This is a dedicated man, one who has very specific aspirations. A deep thinker, Gary will need some time alone to pursue his intellectual interests.

DERIVATION: English, originally a surname. Probably derived from a Norman name related to the Old German *gar*, meaning "spear." Became popular in the 1930s as a given name almost entirely due to the influence of the American actor Gary Cooper. Very popular in many English-speaking countries from the 1950s to the 1970s.

PRINCIPAL COLORS: Virtually any shade of azure

GEMSTONES AND PRECIOUS METALS: Emeralds, turquoise

BOTANICALS: Dog rose, melon, walnuts

UNIQUE SPELLINGS: Garey, Garie, Garrey, Garrie, Garry

RELATED TO: Gareth, Garett, Garrettt, Geraldt, Gerard, Gerlach, Gerritt

DERIVATION: English, shortened form of the biblical name Abigail, from the Hebrew, meaning "father of exaltation." Commonly used as a given name since the middle of the twentieth century.

PRINCIPAL COLORS: Dark blue, gray, and purple tones, also black

GEMSTONES AND PRECIOUS METALS: Carbuncles, amethyst, rubies

BOTANICALS: Angelica, shepherd's purse, gravel root

UNIQUE SPELLINGS: Gael, Gail, Gaille, Gale, Gayl

RELATED TO: Gailt, Gaila, Gala, Galia, Galina, Gay, Gayleen, Gaylene

Gayle

A KABBALISTIC SYNOPSIS
גאיהל —GAYHL (Gimel, Aleph, Yod, Heh, Lamed)

Gayle is a true matriarch, and will prove herself to be the ruler of the roost, whether she is in the home or the office. She enjoys the challenge of taking control and making others happy. Gayle will do her best to satisfy her mate and will have a thoroughly good time in the process. However, her name equates to the "Qlipphoth," or negative side of the sephirah Geburah. This means "severity," or suggests that she can become unreasonably angry and has the potential for vicious behavior if not treated as she sees fit.

THE RUNIC INTERPRETATION
ᛗᛚᛇᚨᚷ (Ehwaz, Laguz, Eihwaz, Ansuz, Gebo)

Gayle has the Eihwaz rune of defense in her name. She dates one scoundrel after another and loses money and time in the process. Fortunately the Gebo rune saves the day. Eventually Gayle calls on her Ansuz intuition and tries dating nice guys for a change. The experiment proves to be a success, and Gayle is happy in love at last. She has the Laguz energy of flow to thank for helping her make the necessary changes in her life. As Gayle matures, she transmutes her need for partnership to her need for a more spiritual life. Gayle is able to find joy and satisfaction in life because she has the power of all four elements in her name.

Elements: Air, water, earth/fire, air, water

THE NUMEROLOGICAL INTERPRETATION
Gayle (NV = 5, CV = 1, VV = 4, FL = 7)

People named Gayle are self-assured and openly curious about life. This self-confidence gives them the courage to venture forth when others are more likely to hold back. Finances are important to Gayle. She is therefore dedicated to being successful in her chosen career. This profession should give stability but not stagnancy. In their personal lives, people named Gayle prefer a committed but creative relationship. Gayle needs personal freedom and variety in order to feel whole and complete, and must have a partner who is the same.

Gene

DERIVATION: English, shortened form of Eugene, from the Old French form of the Greek *eugenios*, meaning "noble." Commonly used as a given name in the United States.

PRINCIPAL COLORS: Colors of medium shade

GEMSTONES AND PRECIOUS METALS: From pale to very deeply toned sapphires

BOTANICALS: Celandine, sage, wintergreen

UNIQUE SPELLINGS: Gean, Geen, Geene, Jeen, Jeene

RELATED TO: Eugene

A KABBALISTIC SYNOPSIS
יהן —YHN (Yod, Heh, Nun)

If you think that you know Gene, you are probably mistaken. However, if you really *do* know Gene well, then you are an extremely privileged individual. Gene is possibly the most secretive name in this book. Not only does his name mean "secret" when analyzed through the kabbalistic art of gematria, but his name has a very powerful Scorpio element to it, and Scorpio is the most secretive of all the signs. Gene is not some depressive recluse, though. His name begins with the creative force of Y, or Yod, which suggests that his dislike and suspicion of the outside world will not prevent him from achieving a reasonable level of career success. Emotionally Gene is certainly a challenge to any potential partner, but if you manage to penetrate his defensive wall, you will find a complex and intense personality well worth waiting for. Gene can also be very understanding of his partner's concerns and insecurities, thanks to his own experience with having been hurt.

THE RUNIC INTERPRETATION
ᛗᚾᛗᚷ (Ehwaz, Nauthiz, Ehwaz, Gebo)

Gene is fortunate to have the rune energies of movement, constraint, defense, and partnership in his name. One day Gene realizes that his so-called friends are so busy with their own pain that they do very little to encourage or support him. To put an end to this, Gene opens his big brown eyes to see who's really there for him, and who is interested only in themselves. If a friend is self-absorbed and negative, Gene sends him packing. The Gebo energy of partnership ensures that Gene will learn from his mistakes, and draw in new friends and lovers that will nurture and support him. Then Gene will begin to find true joy in living.

Elements: Air, fire, air, water

THE NUMEROLOGICAL INTERPRETATION
Gene (NV = 4, CV = 3, VV = 1, FL = 7)

Hardworking and dedicated describe two of the most important facets of Gene's personality. This name indicates a man who is very communicative and friendly. He will often make others laugh with his wit and fine sense of humor. His career will be at the center of his life, as he is very focused on the physical manifestation of his creative efforts. Gene is well organized and usually very logical. He prefers what is predictable to what is spontaneous or surprising. Money is important to him, and he usually has a number of ways in which he takes pleasure earning it.

PRINCIPAL COLORS: Moderately toned colors

GEMSTONES AND PRECIOUS METALS: Sapphires

BOTANICALS: Celandine, medlar, spinach

UNIQUE SPELLINGS: Genaveave, Genaveeve, Genavive, Geneveave, Geneveeve, Genevive, Geniveave, Geniveeve, Genivive, Genoveave, Genoveeve, Genovive, Genyveave, Genyveeve, Genyvive, Jenaveave, Jenaveeve, Jenavive, Jeneveave, Jeneveeve, Jenevive, Jeniveave, Jeniveeve, Jenivive, Jenoveave, Jenoveeve, Jenovive, Jenyveave, Jenyveeve, Jenyvive

RELATED TO: Gena, Genette, Geneva, Genista, Genna, Genoveffa, Ginevra, Jean†, Jeane, Jeanette†, Jeanie, Jeanne

Genevieve

A KABBALISTIC SYNOPSIS
יאנויו —YANVYV (Yod, Aleph, Nun, Vau, Yod, Vau)

Genevieve is a vision of sweetness. She is deeply attractive and has an air of innocence in her personality to match. Genevieve will have no shortage of mates trying to win her affections, but she will not allow herself to be exploited—she is not as innocent as she appears. Genevieve has a natural intuition about people that compensates for any lack of worldly wisdom. Her name has associations with both the Empress and the High Priestess in the tarot, and any partner who is lucky enough to be involved with her will find a woman who is enormously affectionate and loving and who possesses a deep understanding of all emotional matters as well.

THE RUNIC INTERPRETATION
ᛗᚠᛗᚠᛗᚾᛗᚷ (Ehwaz, Fehu, Ehwaz, Fehu, Ehwaz, Nauthiz, Ehwaz, Gebo)

Genevieve has the quadruple rune energy of Ehwaz, or movement, in her name. Ehwaz brings lessons of transition and flexibility into Genevieve's life. She will surely get to move and see various countries and experience different cultures and works of art. Genevieve thrives on the excitement of travel. She may learn foreign languages and become an accomplished gourmet cook. She could own a restaurant or travel agency someday, or be a foreign ambassador. Best of all, the Ehwaz energy prompts Genevieve to share all the good fortune that comes her way.

Elements: Air, fire, air, fire, air, fire, air, water

THE NUMEROLOGICAL INTERPRETATION
Genevieve (NV = 4, CV = 2, VV = 11, FL = 7)

Gifted with an especially strong intuition, Genevieve is a woman who will do everything possible to be of help and assistance. Her friends come from all walks of life. Her name indicates that she is a person free of prejudice. She cannot be bothered with petty thoughts that separate people, for she is a uniting force and a peacemaker at heart. Genevieve tends to be very demanding of herself and is a perfectionist. Honest, determined, and sincere, she expects others to be the same. As not all people can live up to the high standards she has for herself, she will occasionally be disappointed.

Geoffrey

A KABBALISTIC SYNOPSIS
יאפרי —YAPhRY (Yod, Aleph, Peh, Resh, Yod)

If you were to place bets on who would make a complete success of their life and career, then Geoffrey would be a very good choice. An intelligent and refined man, Geoffrey is entirely at ease in any company, whether it be in a bar in the run-down part of town or the boardroom of a multinational corporation. Geoffrey always makes his success appear effortless, as if it has been achieved almost incidentally to the rest of his life. His manner is best described as languid, which conceals the powerhouse of energy that drives him. Geoffrey is geometrically equivalent to the Hebrew "ASh," meaning "fire" and representing a huge reserve of personal energy. However, it also equates to "candlestick," thereby pointing to the fine control that Geoffrey exercises over this emotional reserve.

THE RUNIC INTERPRETATION
ᛇᛇᚱᚠᚠᛟᛖᚷ (Eihwaz, Eihwaz, Raido, Fehu, Fehu, Othila, Ehwaz, Gebo)

Geoffrey has the double Fehu energy of possessions in his name and may even enjoy being a millionaire someday. After choosing a slew of inappropriate mates, Geoffrey will find his true love, who is a good match for him because she shares his love of philanthropy. Together they help a lot of less fortunate people. The Eihwaz energy of this name may lead Geoffrey into some dangerous situations, but he is protected by the Gebo rune of partnership, ensuring that guardian angels will be with him on his travels to help the needy.

Elements: Earth/fire, air, water, fire, fire, earth/fire, air, water

THE NUMEROLOGICAL INTERPRETATION
Geoffrey (NV = 6, CV = 1, VV = 5, FL = 7)

Bearing a name that bestows an artistic temperament, Geoffrey would do well to experiment with painting, sculpture, music, or writing. It is important for him to express his individuality, and the arts are the most natural outlets for him. This is a man who will enjoy traveling, especially with his chosen partner. He is a romantic and prefers to concentrate his emotional energy on one primary relationship. A peaceful and nurturing home life is essential to him, and he will do all he can to create a comfortable environment for himself and those closest to him.

DERIVATION: English, of uncertain meaning. Possibly from the Germanic *gawia*, meaning "territory," and *walah*, meaning "stranger." Also possibly from the Germanic *frithu*, meaning "peace." Particularly popular in England and France in the later Middle Ages.

PRINCIPAL COLORS: All but the brightest shades of blue

GEMSTONES AND PRECIOUS METALS: Emeralds, blue and blue-green turquoise

BOTANICALS: Vervain, violets, walnuts

UNIQUE SPELLINGS: Geoffery, Geoffry, Geofrey, Jefery, Jefferey, Jeffery, Jeffree, Jeffrie, Jeffry

RELATED TO: Geoff, Godfrey, Jeff†, Jefferies, Jefferson, Jeffrey†

In the absence of any direct equivalent to the letter *f* in the Hebrew alphabet, the letter Peh is used. Peh can function as either a hard or a soft letter, and as such, is one of the seven "doubles."

DERIVATION: English, from the Greek *georgos*, meaning "farmer." The name of several saints, including the patron saint of England, who was martyred in the fourth century and is identified with his legendary fight with a dragon. Made popular by the first king of England named George, in the eighteenth century.

PRINCIPAL COLORS: The full range of violet and purple hues

GEMSTONES AND PRECIOUS METALS: Garnets, amethyst

BOTANICALS: Apple, bilberry, dandelion, mint

UNIQUE SPELLING: Jeorge

RELATED TO: Geordie, Georgie, Jorget

∽

"A life spent making mistakes is not only more honorable, but more useful than a life spent doing nothing."
—GEORGE BERNARD SHAW (PLAYWRIGHT)

"Don't tell people how to do things. Tell them what to do and let them surprise you with their results."
—GEORGE S. PATTON (GENERAL, U.S. ARMY)

A KABBALISTIC SYNOPSIS
יערי —YA'ARY (Yod, Ayin, Resh, Yod)

George has no fantastic dreams of fame or riches. His main desire in life is to provide for his family while maintaining enough time for his own personal interests. The need for personal space is shown by the Y, or Yod, at both ends of his name. In this context they function as their literal meaning, which is "palm," and we are given an image of a man with arms outstretched against the outside world in order to keep it from enveloping him completely. (Note: The letter Y in Hebrew represents both the Y and J sounds, hence its use here rather than Gimel.) George is a hard worker and a small spender; his main gratification comes from his family's appreciation of his efforts. While he is willing to work very long hours for his dependents, it is important that he have a job that allows him some free time, both mentally and physically. If not, he will find that his desire for some space slowly develops into almost paranoiac fears of the outside world closing in on him.

THE RUNIC INTERPRETATION
ᛖᚷᚱᛟᛖᚷ (Ehwaz, Gebo, Raido, Othila, Ehwaz, Gebo)

George has the double Ehwaz energy of movement combined with the double Gebo energy of partnership in his name. George may well work for an international dating service or perform weddings and marriage counseling. This type of work suits him, since he is extremely easygoing and gets along with people from all walks of life. He also could be drawn to the ministry or a career in international relations. A marriage partner who can share in the joys of life is of utmost importance to George. He is perceptive and will only give his heart to a woman who is mature and developed in her own right. He is drawn to intelligent, professional types.

Elements: Air, water, water, earth/fire, air, water

THE NUMEROLOGICAL INTERPRETATION
George (NV = 3, CV = 5, VV = 7, FL = 7)

There are two distinct facets to the name George. A communicator with a wide range of friends and interests, George can be counted upon to add his intelligent comments to any gathering. He thrives on mental stimulation and is eager to share what he knows or has recently discovered with friends and associates. On the other hand, he has the tendency to be reclusive and enjoys spending long hours alone. There are times when he absolutely seeks out an upbeat party with loud music, while on other days, only peace and quiet will do.

∽

Georgia

DERIVATION: English, feminine form of George. From the Greek *georgos*, meaning "farmer." Name of a fifth-century saint who lived near Clermont in the Auvergne.

PRINCIPAL COLORS: Black, gray, the darkest shades of blue and purple

GEMSTONES AND PRECIOUS METALS: Black diamonds, black pearls, any other dark stone

BOTANICALS: Marsh mallow, pilewort

UNIQUE SPELLING: Georgya

RELATED TO: Georgana, Georgeana, Georgeanne, Georgeina, Georgena, Georgenia, Georgette, Georgiana, Georgianna, Georgie, Georgina

A KABBALISTIC SYNOPSIS
יעריא —YA'ARYA (Yod, Ayin, Resh, Yod, Aleph)

Georgia is driven by a desire to help all those around her—whether they need help or not! Although her name can be reduced to twelve, the Hanged Man, it is Georgia who benefits most from her self-sacrifice. It is highly likely that Georgia has had a reasonably well-heeled upbringing, and her need to do good works may well stem from unresolved feelings of guilt. The effect of her privileged background is likely to show in other areas, too. For instance, the letter derived from the compression of her name is Tzaddi, meaning "fishhook"—indicating that once Georgia decides what she wants, she will not give up until she gets it. This applies as much to her emotional life as to her material environment; if Georgia wants you, there's no point fighting it!

THE RUNIC INTERPRETATION
ᚨᛁᚷᚱᛟᛗᛇ (Ansuz, Isa, Gebo, Raido, Othila, Ehwaz, Gebo)

Georgia has the power of all four elements in her name. The double Gebo energy of partnership ensures that Georgia will spend time on her soul and its development, and will be happiest when she is working as a humanitarian. She is likely to marry because partnership is important to her. She and her partner may not have the greatest romance, but they are loyal and work well together for a common cause, and beyond all else, they are best friends. Georgia is idealistic and very spiritual. Her needs in this world are few, and her heart is big.

Elements: Air, earth, water, water, earth/fire, air, water

THE NUMEROLOGICAL INTERPRETATION
Georgia (NV = 8, CV = 5, VV = 3, FL = 7)

Georgia will find that her extensive social contacts can help her achieve her professional objectives. This name indicates a person who thrives on the excitement of success. Georgia has definite goals and intends to reach them. She enjoys the pleasures of the material world and looks forward to sharing these experiences with energetic and vivacious friends. Georgia has stamina, control, and courage. The integration of her spiritual life into her material success can only take her higher. Georgia requires a partner who is as creative and strong willed as herself. A person of little ambition would not last long in her life.

Gerald

DERIVATION: English and Irish, from the Old German *gar*, meaning "spear," and *wald*, meaning "rule." Brought to Britain by the Normans, but disappeared in England by the end of the thirteenth century. Remained in use in Ireland, and reemerged in England in the nineteenth century.

PRINCIPAL COLORS: White, from pale to deep forest green

GEMSTONES AND PRECIOUS METALS: Moonstones, pearls

BOTANICALS: Chicory, cabbage, lettuce

UNIQUE SPELLINGS: Gerold, Gerrald, Gerrold, Jerald, Jerold, Jerrald, Jerrold

RELATED TO: Garrard, Garrat, Garrett†, Ged, Geraldo, Gerard, Gerardo, Gerhard, Gerrit, Gerry†, Giraldo, Jed, Jerry†

A KABBALISTIC SYNOPSIS
יארולד —YARVLD (Yod, Aleph, Resh, Vau, Lamed, Daleth)

At the age of eighty-five you will still see Gerald strutting his stuff on the dance floor; Gerald is, in terms of kabbalistic name analysis, literally an "evergreen" individual. For most of his life Gerald appears to be quite normal, with the possible exception that he will have naturally more ambition and drive than his contemporaries. He may not hit the top of his chosen field, but he will certainly do very well for himself and his family. Family is very important to Gerald, and he will get on well with all of his children, having almost a sixth sense as to their likely directions in life. In old age Gerald really hits his stride. While his friends are starting to slow down and take it easy, Gerald will be just embarking on a whole series of new pursuits. Gerald's retirement will be the most exciting and dynamic period of his entire life.

THE RUNIC INTERPRETATION
ᛞᛚᚨᚱᛖᚷ (Dagaz, Laguz, Ansuz, Raido, Ehwaz, Gebo)

Gerald feels he is on the planet to help those less fortunate than himself. His family members sometimes approach him for money, and Gerald opens his pockets wide. He is generous to a fault and he likes it that way. Gerald is highly intuitive and gets answers to his prayers. Some may think him a mystic. Gerald's needs are modest, and he is wise beyond his years. Recognized early on for his generosity and peace, he knows that we are all one and he follows the dictates of his heart. Sometimes he incurs personal hardship, but that is of little concern to Gerald.

Elements: Fire, water, air, water, air, water

THE NUMEROLOGICAL INTERPRETATION
Gerald (NV = 11, CV = 5, VV = 6, FL = 7)

Gerald is a very gifted man whose intuition is matched by his kindness. This is a person with a generous disposition who feels the need to spend some of his time in service to others. People find Gerald very easy to approach, as he usually has a friendly word, an open smile, and some genuine advice to offer. His home life is at the center of his heart, and he makes a fine husband, a dedicated father, and a very stimulating lover. He has to take care that his social and romantic ideals are not beyond the reach of fulfillment or else he may find himself frequently disappointed.

Geraldine

DERIVATION: English, feminine form of Gerald, from the Old German *gar*, meaning "spear," and *wald*, meaning "rule." Invented in the sixteenth century by the Earl of Surrey, who wrote love poems addressed to "the fair Geraldine," actually named Lady Elizabeth Fitzgerald.

PRINCIPAL COLORS: All shades of purple, from pale violet to deep maroon

GEMSTONES AND PRECIOUS METALS: Garnets, amethyst

BOTANICALS: Cherry, barberry, lungwort

UNIQUE SPELLINGS: Geraldean, Geraldeen, Geraldene, Jeraldean, Jeraldeen, Jeraldene

RELATED TO: Deena, Dina, Geri, Gerry†, Jeri

A KABBALISTIC SYNOPSIS

יארולדין —YARVLDYN (Yod, Aleph, Resh, Vau, Lamed, Daleth, Yod, Nun)

If you're looking for Geraldine, the chances are you will find her in church—and not just on Sundays! The total value of Geraldine's name is 961, which is the third power of thirty-one. Thirty-one is the value of one of the main mystical names of God, so we should not be surprised at the importance of religion in Geraldine's life. When we multiply a number in Kabbalah, we associate it with an increase in the power of the meaning of that number, so many people might assume that Geraldine is a pious and dogmatic lady. However, since each number has its own significance and the meaning of three is related to growth and creativity, Geraldine has a vibrant and refreshing approach to her faith, and may well work with the church. If she does she will be ideally placed to find new ways of presenting religion to the local youth in the hope of attracting them to her chosen religion.

THE RUNIC INTERPRETATION

ᛖᚾᛁᛞᛚᚨᚱᛖᚷ (Ehwaz, Nauthiz, Isa, Dagaz, Laguz, Ansuz, Raido, Ehwaz, Gebo)

Geraldine has the four elements in her name, and this gives her tremendous personal power. This power manifests itself in her character as discipline, leadership, vision, and an ability to produce money when needed. With all these fine traits it is no surprise that Geraldine attracts the company of strong and successful individuals. Geraldine may or may not be interested in marriage. She is interested in her own happiness, fulfillment, and spirituality, which are of supreme importance in her life.

Elements: Air, fire, earth, fire, water, air, water, air, water

THE NUMEROLOGICAL INTERPRETATION

Geraldine (NV = 3, CV = 1, VV = 2, FL = 7)

Openly communicative and easy to please, Geraldine is a woman who makes friends easily. People appreciate the wide variety of her interests and her informative and pleasant manner. Geraldine moves very freely in most social settings, helping others to feel at ease and generally spreading goodwill in group situations. Geraldine is equally comfortable by herself. She definitely has her own agenda but is not the type of person to feel lonely when alone. Geraldine shares freely in her personal relationships and makes a very supportive partner.

DERIVATION: English, both
masculine and feminine.
Shortened form of Gerald,
Gerard, or Geraldine. Related to
the Old German *gar*, meaning
"spear."

PRINCIPAL COLORS: Pale to the
most brilliant yellow, also bronze,
orange, gold

GEMSTONES AND PRECIOUS
METALS: Topaz, amber, citrine

BOTANICALS: Lavender,
chamomile, nutmeg, saffron

UNIQUE SPELLINGS: Jerry†; Geri,
Gerie, Gerri, Gerrie, Gery, Jeri,
Jerie, Jerri, Jerrie, Jery

RELATED TO: Garrard, Garrat,
Garrett†, Geraldt, Gerard,
Gerrald, Gerrold, Jerald, Jerold;
Geralda, Geraldinet, Geralyn,
Geralynn, Gerilyn, Gerrilyn,
Jerilene

Gerry

A KABBALISTIC SYNOPSIS
יארי —YARY (Yod, Aleph, Resh, Yod)

There is no distinction in Hebrew between Gerry and Jerry, so for the purposes of kabbalistic analysis, these names have the same meaning. (Readers should therefore refer to the entry for Jerry, as well as to what follows below.) The central core of Gerry's name suggests a person who enjoys and is skilled at making ideas become reality—particularly ideas that originally relate to some practical concern. Over time Gerry will gain more confidence in his or her abilities in his or her chosen field, and what began as a youthful enthusiasm marked by the initial Yod develops into mature skill and expertise. This development is reflected in the value of the name, which represents a person in a position of recognized authority within a given area. Similarly, Gerry's home life will gradually become more contented as Gerry becomes less urgent in his or her desire to succeed.

THE RUNIC INTERPRETATION
ᛇᚱᚱᛖᚷ (Eihwaz, Raido, Raido, Ehwaz, Gebo)

Gerry seems to thrive when helping in a difficult situation. He or she is never content to sit back when people are suffering. Gerry may choose to work in a disaster patrol or as a paramedic. Gerry's cool, calm personality relaxes those he or she comes in contact with. Double Raido, the rune of good communication, helps Gerry take a leadership role and delegate tasks in a clean, concise manner. In addition to high-risk careers, Gerry could also turn his or her talents to teaching, counseling, lobbying, or negotiating. He or she will be in demand as a powerful advocate. Because Gerry has wellsprings of patience, he or she can see two sides of every situation, and restore order and harmony and avert catastrophe. With the four elements gracing this name, Gerry is powerful.

Elements: Earth/fire, water, water, air, water

THE NUMEROLOGICAL INTERPRETATION
Gerry (NV = 1, CV = 7, VV = 3, FL = 7)

Gerry is a very aware person. Gerry knows who he or she is and is intent on continuous self-development. Taking the necessary time to reflect on his or her actions is part of this process. Gerry is neither superficial nor flighty. In relationships, Gerry prefers a partner with drive and purpose. His or her orientation is definitely toward monogamy, and Gerry is not the type to move from one person to another. Gerry has a number of intellectual interests and is often found with a book close at hand.

Gertrude

A Kabbalistic Synopsis

גורטרעד—GVRTRA'AD (Gimel, Vau, Resh, Teth, Resh, Ayin, Daleth)

More than anything Gertrude wants to understand the world around her, and in turn understand herself much more clearly. There are definite indications in her name that she will have a very comfortable lifestyle; the two Rs, or Reshes, in her name are associated, in part, with the enjoyment of good fortune. In addition her name totals to fifteen, indicating that she gets a lot of satisfaction from indulging her desire for luxury. However, at a deeper level Gertrude wants everyone else to enjoy these finer things with her and share her happiness. It is likely that at a later stage in life Gertrude will actively set about trying to alleviate some of the suffering in the world, not just by doing charity work but by actually opening up her home and possessions to those less fortunate than herself. She may even use her wealth to set up some kind of refuge or other center.

The Runic Interpretation

ᛖᛞᚢᚱᛏᚱᛖᚷ (Ehwaz, Dagaz, Uruz, Raido, Teiwaz, Raido, Ehwaz, Gebo)

Gertrude is successful and influential because she has the four elements in her name. Gertrude is also fortunate to have the double Raido energy and the double Ehwaz energies of journey and movement in her name. Gertrude will probably marry, and her husband will enjoy travel as much as she does. The Uruz rune of strength adds stability to their marriage even though they may be separated for months at a time. The Dagaz energy of breakthroughs makes Gertrude a good mate because she is happy and independent. Gertrude has found peace within herself.

Elements: Air, fire, earth, water, air, water, air, water

The Numerological Interpretation

Gertrude (NV = 7, CV = 3, VV = 4, FL = 7)

This name is usually associated with a woman of substance; Gertrude is a deep thinker who is always aware of the consequences of her actions. She tends to be responsible, dependable, and hardworking. A woman with a strong intellect and a determined attitude, Gertrude is often wise beyond her years. This is a person who can spend a great deal of time by herself. Romantic idealism is not her style, and although she appreciates warm and intelligent companionship, her focus is much more on how people can support one another in practical ways than on "falling in love with love."

DERIVATION: Dutch, English, and German, from Germanic roots meaning "spear strength." The name of a seventeenth-century saint and a thirteenth-century mystic. Especially popular in many English-speaking countries around 1900.

PRINCIPAL COLORS: Black, dark gray, deep purple and azure hues

GEMSTONES AND PRECIOUS METALS: Amethyst, lackluster rubies, black pearls

BOTANICALS: Shepherd's purse, ragwort, mandrake root

UNIQUE SPELLINGS: Gertraud, Gertrood, Gertrud

RELATED TO: Geltruda, Gerda, Gert, Gerta, Gerti, Gertie, Gertruda, Trude, Trudi, Trudie, Trudy

"Everybody gets so much information all day long that they lose their common sense."
—GERTRUDE STEIN (AUTHOR)

DERIVATION: Italian and English, mainly a shortened form of Georgina or Regina. Used independently since the 1920s. Also a shortened form of the Italian Luigina.

PRINCIPAL COLORS: Blues, grays

GEMSTONES AND PRECIOUS METALS: Sapphires

BOTANICALS: Celandine, Iceland moss, sage

UNIQUE SPELLINGS: Geena, Gena, Jeana, Jeena, Jena, Jina

RELATED TO: Geenie, Geeny, Georgina, Giorgina, Jeanie, Jeany, Regina†

A KABBALISTIC SYNOPSIS
אנ׳ —YNA (Yod, Nun, Aleph)

When people talk about the guy and gal Fridays, they are referring to people like Gina, who are always very handy members of any team. Gina avoids the limelight and is happy to work out of the public view. A kabbalistic analysis of her name produces the letters Samech and Aleph, which demonstrate her preference for being a support or "prop" to an idea or project rather than an active leader. The reason for this approach to life is indicated by the N, or Nun, which points to both secrecy and a certain amount of emotional insecurity. Gina's favorite way to relax is by eating good food, and she could be considered to be quite a gastronome. In fact, if you want to coax Gina out of her shell, the best way would be to take her to a fancy restaurant and let her have her pick of the menu.

THE RUNIC INTERPRETATION
ᚨᚾᛁᚷ (Ansuz, Nauthiz, Isa, Gebo)

Gina has the runes for signals, constraint, standstill, and partnership in her name. Gina knows that hard times can be overcome by hard work and a good attitude. Once Gina learns to set goals for herself and not give up until her goals are realized, she conquers the saboteur in her own head. This frees Gina to bring new people into her life, including a wonderful mate to share her joys and sorrows. Gina uses the Nauthiz rune of constraint to end the sadness in her life. She learns to enjoy her own company, and with this newfound peace she attracts the man of her dreams.

Elements: Air, fire, earth, water

THE NUMEROLOGICAL INTERPRETATION
Gina (NV = 4, CV = 3, VV = 1, FL = 7)

Gina is developing a clear sense of who she is and how to use her creative powers with the greatest efficiency. This is a woman who wants to be able to follow her own path and seeks neither to be dependent on others nor to be involved with dependent people. In this respect, she is attracted to partners who also have a strong connection to their own inner being and can use their abilities in practical ways. Gina is able to use logic and reason toward pragmatic ends and enjoys creating a positive sense of order in her surroundings.

Glen

DERIVATION: Scottish and English, from the Gaelic *gleann*, meaning "valley." Probably once a surname, it appeared as a given name in the early nineteenth century. Popular in the 1970s, but less so today.

PRINCIPAL COLORS: The full range of green tones, white, off-white

GEMSTONES AND PRECIOUS METALS: Pearls, cat's-eye

BOTANICALS: Cabbage, plantain, moonwort

UNIQUE SPELLING: Glenn

RELATED TO: Glendower, Glennt, Glenton, Glentworth, Glenvil, Glenville

A KABBALISTIC SYNOPSIS
גלאן —GLAN (Gimel, Lamed, Aleph, Nun)

Glen is one of life's loners. If he could act out any movie fantasy he wished, Glen would probably pick a Western—preferably one that originally starred Clint Eastwood as a high plains drifter! Glen craves adventure in his life, and roaming the country is, in one sense, a way of inviting things to happen. The initial Gimel, when connected with the driving ox goad of Lamed, shows us a man who feels very uncomfortable in anything but a temporary home. Luckily for Glen he has a good deal of common sense, which helps him to find the sort of work that allows him to travel while still keeping him fed and clothed. Glen's name can be reduced to fourteen, which is the Temperance card in the tarot, suggesting a positive balancing of conflicting energies within his personality. In Glen's case this refers to the conflict he may experience between his love of freedom and travel, and his desire for a long-term emotional commitment.

THE RUNIC INTERPRETATION
ᚾᛖᛚᚷ (Nauthiz, Ehwaz, Laguz, Gebo)

Glen has the runic energies of constraint, movement, flow, and partnership in his name. The Nauthiz rune of constraint gives us the opportunity to learn lessons we need in order to advance to deeper levels of trust and faith. Glen faces challenges in relationships because he is rigid and fixed. The Ehwaz rune of movement affords Glen the opportunity to move his home and to travel a lot in life until he finds his right place. People have right places, too, where they can grow and learn and where the energies in the earth support their unfoldment. Glen finally attracts the perfect mate and realizes his dreams.

Elements: Fire, air, water, water

THE NUMEROLOGICAL INTERPRETATION
Glen (NV = 11, CV = 6, VV = 5, FL = 7)

Glen is a name that will give a person the opportunity to come in contact with many people in ways that serve and are helpful to them. A peaceful person with a wide range of talents, Glen uses his abilities to bring a sense of greater cooperation between people. He is thus very effective in group situations where interpersonal interactions are so very important. A peaceful and stable home life is essential to his sense of well-being, and he will seek a partner who will be equally open to the many people who are likely to pass in and out of their home's doors.

DERIVATION: Scottish and English, alternate spelling of Glen. From the Gaelic *gleann*, meaning "valley." Probably once a surname, it appeared as a given name in the early nineteenth century. Commonly used since the 1930s.

PRINCIPAL COLORS: All yellow and green hues

GEMSTONES AND PRECIOUS METALS: Moonstones, moss agate, white pearls

BOTANICALS: Blackberry, linseed, elder

UNIQUE SPELLING: Glen

RELATED TO: Glent, Glendower, Glenton, Glentworth, Glenvil, Glenville

Glenn

A KABBALISTIC SYNOPSIS
גלאנן —GLANN (Gimel, Lamed, Aleph, Nun, Nun)

The letter Nun is associated with strong emotions, and it has a connection to the astrological sign Scorpio, which can indicate depressive and solitary tendencies. Glenn has this letter occurring twice in his name, and we might expect him to be terribly woeful as a result. However, Glenn is on the whole a cheerful and decidedly laid-back guy. This is largely because his name's value reduces to nineteen, which is the number of the tarot card the Sun. The Sun is a card that suggests a cheerful and intelligent personality. In Glenn's case he has an intellectual interest in the nature of emotion; he may even be a psychologist. He himself is an emotional man, but he has an upbeat outlook on life rather than a depressed one. He likes to act on the spur of the moment and will often take his family off on surprise trips; the letter Gimel tells us that he has a love of travel. His family, if he has one, or his friends will be able to turn to him for advice on all sorts of matters, and he has a knack for finding ways of opening the doors of opportunity for people that initially appear to be locked.

THE RUNIC INTERPRETATION
ᚺᚺᛗᛚᚷ (Nauthiz, Nauthiz, Ehwaz, Laguz, Gebo)

Glenn sports the double Nauthiz energy of constraint. Constraint confers a painful lesson, no doubt about that. Glenn does everything right and more than what is needed, and yet he still gets called on the carpet for phony, trumped-up charges. This happens time and time again. Lessons repeat themselves until we get them right. The lesson for Glenn is self-love. When there are no fish to be had, a smart fisherman gets busy sewing up the loose ends in his fishing net. The same is true for the Nauthiz lesson: Once Glenn corrects errors in his attitudes, things right themselves. All that is needed is for Glenn to take a look at who he is on the inside and express himself from his heart.

Elements: Fire, fire, air, water, water

THE NUMEROLOGICAL INTERPRETATION
Glenn (NV = 7, CV = 2, VV = 5, FL = 7)

Glenn's mind needs to explore, and he will do this through travel, business, and education. He is one to take encouragement from life in order to evolve his natural abilities and talents into greater and more varied forms of self-expression. There is a distinct urge suggested in this name for freedom from routines and stultifying habit patterns. Glenn is a man who takes a great deal of pleasure in his many adventures and who loves to share his fun with others. Togetherness is very important to him, and whether or not he is in an intimate relationship, he will do his best to lend a sense of harmony to his surroundings.

Gloria

DERIVATION: English, from the Latin *gloria*, meaning "glory." Perhaps first used as a given name by George Bernard Shaw in *You Never Can Tell* (1898). Especially popular in the United States in the 1920s.

PRINCIPAL COLORS: Deeply toned azure, black, dark shades of gray and purple

GEMSTONES AND PRECIOUS METALS: Dark sapphires, black pearls, black diamonds

BOTANICALS: Pilewort, shepherd's purse, angelica

UNIQUE SPELLINGS: Gloriah, Glorria, Glorriah, Glorya

RELATED TO: Glory, Lorie, Lory

A KABBALISTIC SYNOPSIS

לעריא —GLA'ARYA (Gimel, Lamed, Ayin, Resh, Yod, Aleph)

As a child Gloria may be drawn to the wilderness, initially due to the sense of excitement and the element of danger that can be found in the great outdoors. By the time she reaches adulthood this desire is driven by an urge to protect the flora and fauna found in the wild. Her name is the equivalent of Metatron, who is one of the guardian angels of the sphere of Earth, or Malkuth, and it is this connection that is reflected in her desire to preserve the life and diversity of the planet. It takes a very strong character to be able to cope with the loneliness and isolation of the wilderness environment, and Gloria has this great strength of character. It is evidenced by the presence of the letter Shin in the compression of her name, and also by the value of her name, which associates her with the tarot card Strength. Gloria has the capacity to withstand any amount of isolation and work in pursuit of her aims. Of course, not every Gloria will live in the great outdoors, but there are still plenty of ways in which she can express her concern for the environment. An urban Gloria may be involved in a recycling project or even in lobbying for stricter antipollution laws.

THE RUNIC INTERPRETATION

ᚨᛁᚱᛟᛚᚷ (Ansuz, Isa, Raido, Othila, Laguz, Gebo)

Gloria has the four power elements of completion in her name. Gloria is powerful, and she knows it! She uses the runes representing signals, defense, journey, separation, flow, and partnership in her name to further her on her soul journey. The Ansuz and Laguz runes heighten Gloria's intuition and help her identify the dishonest culprit every time. The Raido rune ensures Gloria a life of travel and an openness to new ideas. The Gebo rune helps Gloria find the mate for her journey through life and points the way to the loving soul within.

Elements: Air, earth, water, earth/fire, water, water

THE NUMEROLOGICAL INTERPRETATION

Gloria (NV = 8, CV = 1, VV = 7, FL = 7)

The name Gloria suggests a very strong-willed person. Not one to sit back and let life pass her by, Gloria is out there making things happen. After she has accomplished her immediate goal, she will find a quiet spot to reflect on what has taken place and plan her next step. She is thus a woman with a natural rhythm, one that permits her to balance the very assertive part of her nature with her more contemplative side. Gloria is a passionate woman, one who requires a partner who is very stimulating and equally eager for worldly success.

Gordon

DERIVATION: Scottish and English, from a Scottish surname and place-name, of uncertain origin. Very popular in Scotland since the beginning of the twentieth century, and has gained popularity in other English-speaking countries.

PRINCIPAL COLORS: Bronze, gold, all shades of yellow

GEMSTONES AND PRECIOUS METALS: Topaz, yellow diamonds, any yellow stone

BOTANICALS: Borage, sorrel, gentian root

UNIQUE SPELLINGS: Gordan, Gorden, Gordyn

RELATED TO: Gordey, Gordie, Gordy

A KABBALISTIC SYNOPSIS

גערדון —GA'ARDVN (Gimel, Ayin, Resh, Daleth, Vau, Nun)

Gordon is a unique individual whose personality will stand out in any crowd. This difference from the norm is indicated by the fact that the total value of Gordon's name is 983, which is a prime number. A large part of Gordon's individuality relates to his talents, which are likely to be in the area of creative writing. The presence of Gimel and Ayin suggests that a focus of his writing will be travel, or if not specifically related to travel, his writing will cover a very wide range of subjects and character types. There is another unique aspect to Gordon's personality that relates to his emotional makeup. But since we find N, or Nun, as the final letter in this name, it is likely that only his partner—if anyone—will ever find out the exact nature of this particular mystery. However, from the reduction of his name's value we get a clue: Gordon is likely to be unusually concerned with the opinions and attitudes of others, and will rarely reveal his true self when in the company of any other than his very closest friends.

THE RUNIC INTERPRETATION

↑◇ᛝᛉ◇✕ (Nauthiz, Othila, Dagaz, Raido, Othila, Gebo)

Gordon is an intellectual and an artist. But he needs firm boundaries growing up because he is rebellious and imaginative, and is different from a lot of other children. He may feel already grown-up as a child, and if he feels an authority figure is weak, he will go for the jugular. He often tries to even the score. With maturity comes modesty and humility. If this is the path for Gordon, he can use the double Othila rune in his name to separate from his bad habits and meditate on oneness. This level of consciousness is extremely healing for Gordon, who has a reputation for being selfish and somewhat tactless.

Elements: Fire, earth/fire, fire, water, earth/fire, water

THE NUMEROLOGICAL INTERPRETATION

Gordon (NV = 1, CV = 7, VV = 3, FL = 7)

Gordon is the name of a very independent and individualistic man. He is quite happy to go his own way and to do things at his own pace. Not a person whom one can easily get to know, Gordon can be a bit shy or reclusive. He enjoys people, but usually his friendships are limited to those who share his interests. Gordon is seeking to perfect certain talents within himself and to use his time and energy efficiently. He needs a partner who is an intellectual equal as well as a person who has special projects of their own.

Grace

A Kabbalistic Synopsis
גראיס —GRAYS (Gimel, Resh, Aleph, Yod, Samech)

The letter Gimel means "camel" and represents travel in all its forms. In Grace this letter represents the most radical form of travel, that of exploration. Given the limited number of undiscovered places left in the world, it is quite possible that this exploration will take place undersea, or that Grace may even be involved with the space program! One Hebraic equivalent of the name Grace is the word "paths," so it is possible Grace will have a role in the establishment of new routes in already-mapped territories for trade or vacation purposes. Of course, not everybody called Grace will be an explorer in the literal sense. However, all Graces will have an exploratory personality, daring, inventive, and always ready to take on the next challenge.

The Runic Interpretation
ᛖᛋᚨᚱᚷ (Ehwaz, Sowelu, Ansuz, Raido, Gebo)

Grace has runic energies signifying movement, wholeness, signals, journey, and partnership. She needs to travel and try on different points of view before she arrives at a sense of wholeness. The Ansuz rune of signals helps her become more intuitive, and as she seeks balance in her personality, her limiting thought patterns are modified and Grace comes into balance. In time Grace arrives at a state of well-being and joy. She no longer lives according to the opinions of others but seeks her own higher counsel.

Elements: Air, air, air, water, water

The Numerological Interpretation
Grace (NV = 7, CV = 1, VV = 6, FL = 7)

Sometimes a name depicts a quality of being that is totally supported by the numbers. This is indeed the case with the name Grace. A woman of deep feelings, Grace is capable of creating a harmonious and beautiful environment. Grace has a need to shine in her own right and usually does so when she is either at home or with close friends. She likes what is intimate and familiar, and has the ability to make total strangers feel welcome in her presence. Her family is at the center of her life, and she is also fond of animals and pets.

DERIVATION: English, Irish, and Scottish, from the common word *grace*, derived from the Latin *gratia*. It was used commonly as a given name in the seventeenth century by the Puritans. Very popular in the United States from the end of the nineteenth century to the 1920s.

PRINCIPAL COLORS: Gold, any yellow or green tone

GEMSTONES AND PRECIOUS METALS: Moss agate, moonstones

BOTANICALS: Hops, linseed, elder

UNIQUE SPELLINGS: Graece, Graice, Grayce

RELATED TO: Gracey, Gracie

Grant

DERIVATION: Scottish and English, originally a Scottish surname. From the French *grand*, meaning "tall, large." Commonly used as a first name in the United States due to the influence of Ulysses S. Grant.

PRINCIPAL COLORS: The full range of azure hues

GEMSTONES AND PRECIOUS METALS: Turquoise, emeralds

BOTANICALS: Dog rose, almonds, walnuts, violets

UNIQUE SPELLINGS: Grante, Grantt

RELATED TO: Grantley, Granville

A KABBALISTIC SYNOPSIS
גראנט —GRANT (Gimel, Resh, Aleph, Nun, Teth)

Grant's name can be interpreted in two different ways: one mundane, the other esoteric. In everyday terms Grant is a man with a deep understanding of human psychology, particularly in the realm of desire. It is likely that Grant will not pursue this skill professionally but rather will use it for his own personal advantage. From an esoteric perspective, Grant's name has the value eleven, and consequently Grant is strongly connected to the occult. Given the context of his name, it is highly likely that Grant will be an active practitioner of some magical art, and he is particularly suited to Tantric or sexual magic practices. It is interesting to note that perhaps the most interesting practitioner of sexual magic in our times is Kenneth Grant.

THE RUNIC INTERPRETATION
↑ᚺᚾᚱᚷ (Teiwaz, Nauthiz, Ansuz, Raido, Gebo)

Grant uses the runic energies symbolizing warrior, constraint, signals, journey, and partnership in his name to lead a life of remarkable courage and perseverance. Grant is eager to improve himself so that he is in top physical condition, and he is disciplined in his eating habits, conduct, and thought. In order to accomplish this difficult task, Grant learns early on that he must turn to a higher power for his strength. The Gebo rune of partnership points out that Grant is able to make contact with this power, which guides him lovingly on his journey toward perfection.

Elements: Air, fire, air, water, water

THE NUMEROLOGICAL INTERPRETATION
Grant (NV = 6, CV = 5, VV = 1, FL = 7)

Handsome in appearance, soft-spoken and charming, Grant is a man most people find very attractive. His name reveals a combination of numbers that bestow a great deal of personal magnetism and appeal. As much as he likes to please other people, Grant is not a man to compromise his own desires. He has a distinct sense of himself. This is a person who has no difficulty balancing his needs and desires with the needs and desires of others.

Greg

DERIVATION: English and Scottish, short form of Gregory or Gregor. From the Greek *gregoros*, meaning "watchful." Popular as an independent name since the 1950s.

PRINCIPAL COLORS: Pale to bright yellow, orange and golden russet shades

GEMSTONES AND PRECIOUS METALS: Citrine, topaz

BOTANICALS: Eyebright, lavender, sorrel

UNIQUE SPELLINGS: Gregg, Grehg, Grehgg

RELATED TO: Gregor, Gregory†, Greig

A Kabbalistic Synopsis
גראג —GRAG (Gimel, Resh, Aleph, Gimel)

Greg returns us to the travel bug theme associated with the letter Gimel. However, we are not dealing with literal physical journeying. Greg could be aptly described as a mental traveler. He is a collector of any amount of mental trivia. His bookcases will be stacked with collections of curious and little-known facts. In addition, Greg has a strong analytical intellect and can cope with a whole range of complex concepts. One meaning of Greg's name is "melt" or "fuse," and what is special about Greg's mind is his ability to take a set of disparate concepts and forge links between them in order to construct a new and coherent whole. Greg's insatiable curiosity makes him an interesting guy to know; a chat with Greg is never going to be dull, even if, at times, a little hard to follow! His love of all manner of information about the world gives Greg a real sense of wonder at the complexity of creation, a wonder that lasts throughout his life and imbues him with an unshakable optimism.

The Runic Interpretation
XMRX (Gebo, Ehwaz, Raido, Gebo)

Greg has the double Gebo energy of partnership, as well as the runes of movement and journey, in his name. Greg is apt to be a principal in an international partnership that requires him to be fluent in several languages and enables him to travel frequently. On a spiritual level the double partnership rune means that Greg is like a cat with nine lives: He can narrowly escape disaster. If you ask him, chances are good that he will recount the grisly tale of an accident that he survived when most others did not fare as well. Greg is protected.

Elements: water, air, water, water

The Numerological Interpretation
Greg (NV = 1, CV = 5, VV = 5, FL = 7)

The name Greg shouts personal freedom. Not one to be tied down to anyone or anything, Greg is very energetic, forthright, direct, and vivacious. He is usually very enthusiastic about his plans and projects, of which there are many. He has to be careful about being too self-centered, and must remember that other people also have goals and opinions that are at least equal in importance to his own. On the other hand, Greg is very inspirational by nature, making people think, "If Greg can do it, so can I." Well, Greg can do it, and he does!

Gregory

DERIVATION: English and Scottish, from the Greek *gregoros*, meaning "watchful." Very common during the Roman Empire, but declined between the sixteenth and eighteenth centuries. Reemerged strongly with the popularity of the actor Gregory Peck.

PRINCIPAL COLORS: The full spectrum of very lightly shaded hues

GEMSTONES AND PRECIOUS METALS: Silver, diamonds

BOTANICALS: Hazel, caraway, oats

UNIQUE SPELLING: Greggory

RELATED TO: Gregi, Gregg, Gregor, Greig, Grigor

A KABBALISTIC SYNOPSIS

גראגורי —GRAGVRY (Gimel, Resh, Aleph, Gimel, Vau, Resh, Yod)

Gregory would make an ideal priest, especially in terms of a priest's pastoral responsibilities. Gregory has a very wise head, even when it is on relatively young shoulders. From early adulthood onward he will be the first port of call for all those who know him whenever they have a problem or dilemma. Gregory gets a lot of satisfaction from helping others, particularly if the problem is related to some kind of moral confusion. In the compression of his name we reveal the letters Tau, Kaph, and Gimel, which indicate Gregory's view of his role in life and society. Those who are suffering come to him at some crossroads in their life, and he provides a practical and sensitive solution, shown by the letter Kaph, which then enables them to continue on life's journey with renewed vigor and hope. With such a talent Gregory is clearly destined for some kind of socially useful career.

THE RUNIC INTERPRETATION

ᛇᚱᛟᚷᛖᚱᚷ (Eihwaz, Raido, Othila, Gebo, Ehwaz, Raido, Gebo)

Gregory has all the blessings of Greg in his name, with the important addition of the power of the four elements. Gregory is strong, and his name reveals much effort on his part to overcome difficult challenges. The runes in this name represent defense, journey, separation, movement, journey, and partnership. The double rune of journey signifies that Gregory needs to practice tact and good communication skills. If he does not do this, his relationships will be severely damaged, as the double partnership rune indicates. Poor Gregory will get dumped frequently and abruptly until he learns the value of modesty and humility. The lessons will be worth the pain, however, for Gregory will emerge more loving as a result of changing.

Elements: Earth/fire, water, earth/fire, water, air, water, water

THE NUMEROLOGICAL INTERPRETATION

Gregory (NV = 5, CV = 5, VV = 9, FL = 7)

Gregory is refreshingly free of personal repression and is usually ready and eager to try something new. One of his best qualities is that he can see the potential joy that life has to offer. He is also a very compassionate and generous person, always willing to share his sense of inner bounty with others. This positive life attitude makes Gregory fun to be around, as people find him naturally uplifting and stimulating.

Gretchen

DERIVATION: German, pet form of Margaret, from the Greek *margaron*, meaning "pearl." Commonly used as an independent name since the end of the nineteenth century.

PRINCIPAL COLORS: Black, the deepest shades of gray, violet, and blue

GEMSTONES AND PRECIOUS METALS: Carbuncles, lackluster rubies, sapphires

BOTANICALS: Angelica, ragwort, mandrake root, shepherd's purse

UNIQUE SPELLINGS: Gretchin, Grettchen, Grettchin

RELATED TO: Greeta, Greta, Gretel, Grethel, Margarett

A KABBALISTIC SYNOPSIS

גראחון —GRAChVN (Gimel, Resh, Aleph, Cheth, Vau, Nun)

In many ways Gretchen comes across as a regular person, unsurprising in her living habits, choice of partner, and choice of friends. Friends are likely to comment on her excellence as a mother. She manages to be immensely protective of her children, and often of her friends and lovers. At the same time, she allows the people in her life a very real sense of freedom. A close analysis of her name reveals an affinity for the sort of issues that would normally be of interest only to intelligence agencies. Gretchen has a deep and natural instinct for security considerations, and is likely to be blessed with an uncanny knack for both constructing and deciphering code. If she doesn't end up working for a security agency, she could also have a profitable career as a computer programmer.

THE RUNIC INTERPRETATION

ᚾᛖᚺᛋᛏᛖᛗᚱᚷ (Nauthiz, Ehwaz, Hagalaz, Sowelu, Teiwaz, Ehwaz, Raido, Gebo)

Gretchen sports the runes signifying constraint, movement, disruption, wholeness, warrior, journey, and partnership. The double Ehwaz energy in Gretchen's name means she will experience much travel and change her residence often. She will also experience several value systems in life, and will be equally comfortable with both her wealthy and poor friends. Early on it will be important to her to find someone to support her and help her through the difficulties life will surely present her. Her mate helps her survive these lessons, meant not to destroy her, but to purify her.

Elements: Fire, air, water, air, air, air, water, water

THE NUMEROLOGICAL INTERPRETATION

Gretchen (NV = 8, CV = 7, VV = 1, FL = 7)

Gretchen is not afraid to prove herself to the world. In fact, that is one of her greatest pleasures. People think of her as being a very productive person, and they are quite right. Gretchen knows how to create material comfort for herself. She likes to make a good appearance and seems to have a certain aura of success around her; at least, she is heading in that direction!

DERIVATION: Spanish form of
William, from the German roots
meaning "will, desire" and "helmet,
protection."

PRINCIPAL COLORS: Electric
hues, such as azure

GEMSTONES AND PRECIOUS
METALS: Sapphires

BOTANICALS: Celandine,
Solomon's seal, spinach

UNIQUE SPELLING: Guiyermo

RELATED TO: Guillaume, Liam,
William†

Guillermo

A KABBALISTIC SYNOPSIS

גוילרמע —GVYLRMA'A (Gimel, Vau,
Yod, Lamed, Resh, Mem, Ayin)

Oh dear! Guillermo, as bizarre as it may seem, is a direct equivalent of ShTN, which is the Hebraic form of Satan! On the positive side, it is only relatively recently that Satan has had such negative connotations when one looks at how long the name has been in use by one culture or another. The real meaning of Satan, and by gematric correspondence of Guillermo, refers to a personality that possesses great charisma and energy with a razor-sharp intellect to boot. There you go—not such a bad name after all!

THE RUNIC INTERPRETATION

ᛟᛗᚱᛖᛚᛚᛇᚷ (Othila, Mannaz, Raido,
Ehwaz, Laguz, Laguz, Eihwaz, Gebo)

The double Laguz energy of flow equips Guillermo with outstanding intuition, which enables him to withstand the dangerous and painful lessons he must endure in this life. Guillermo will relinquish lovers and home before he learns not to trust so freely. It is imperative for Guillermo to toughen up in order to carry out the leadership lessons his karma requires of him. But Guillermo is powerful because he has the energy of the four elements in his name, and he will triumph in the end.

Elements: Earth/fire, air, water, air,
water, water, earth/fire, water

THE NUMEROLOGICAL INTERPRETATION

Guillermo (NV = 4, CV = 8, VV = 5, FL = 7)

This is a name associated with status and success—and Guillermo is willing to work for it! The major numerological indications in this name indicate a man who is very concerned with finances and career. Material things mean a great deal to Guillermo, and their importance may be overemphasized. Looking good is of major concern to him, and he has to be careful not to spend more money than he may be able to afford. People find Guillermo magnetic, dependable, responsible, and determined. A passionate lover, Guillermo has an intensely emotional nature, and he seeks a partner who is of a similar nature.

Gus

DERIVATION: English, Scottish, and Irish, a short form of *augustus*, from the Latin, meaning "worthy of respect." May also be a short form of Angus and Gustave.

PRINCIPAL COLORS: Cream, the full range of green hues

GEMSTONES AND PRECIOUS METALS: Moonstones, cat's-eye

BOTANICALS: Chicory, plantain, rapeseed

UNIQUE SPELLINGS: Guhs, Guhss, Guss

RELATED TO: Angus, Augustus, Gustaf, Gustaff, Gustav, Gustave, Gustavus

A Kabbalistic Synopsis
סוג —GVS (Gimel, Vau, Samech)

Gus is an interesting character. The indications in his name are that he will be a physically well-built man of considerable strength, and there is a strong likelihood that he will work in the building trade. Gus likes the odd drink and is very fond of his food—although quantity is by far more important than quality. It is a rare weekend indeed that doesn't find Gus in the local sports bar with his mates enjoying a beer and the game. Yet in contrast to this macho image, Gus's name has very definite associations with birth and children. As far as the kids are concerned, Gus is a new man in every sense of the word—much to the delight of his wife. Gus is not only happy in the kitchen or playing with his children, but is equally at home with a dirty diaper or a crying baby, and will often send his wife out with her friends while he baby-sits.

The Runic Interpretation
ᛋᚢᚷ (Sowelu, Uruz, Gebo)

Gus is fortunate to have the runes signifying wholeness, strength, and partnership in his name. His deep faith heals his sense of inadequacy, and he draws in the woman of his dreams. Gus shows her his strength and keeps her best interests at heart. She grows to trust him and gladly relinquishes her power to his dependable leadership skills. In this way, Gus claims authority as the head of his household without bullying or demanding tactics. His partner surrenders, gladly knowing that the final outcome of decisions concerning them will always benefit her. He is a born leader and part of his talent is in his well-modulated tone of voice, which inspires a sense of order and trust in his colleagues.

Elements: Air, earth, water

The Numerological Interpretation
Gus (NV = 11, CV = 8, VV = 3, FL = 7)

Bearing a name that gives a man a certain magical twist, Gus is a highly productive person. Yet the purpose of his productivity is not so much to fill his own pockets, but to use this abundance of energy and resources for the welfare of many others. A friendly and very communicative man, Gus works well with large numbers of people. He is great at making connections and distributing reliable information. Gus tends to be sincere in his affections and faithful to his partner.

Guy

A KABBALISTIC SYNOPSIS
גוי —GVY (Gimel, Vau, Yod)

If your name isn't Guy and you're reading this description out of curiosity, you may wish to move on to the next name or prepare for some serious envy. If you are a Guy—congratulations! Your name is immensely lucky and is associated with good fortune throughout. Kabbalistically, Guy becomes ten—the number attributed to luck, fortune, and material wealth. You are not likely to meet a poor Guy, and if you do, his amazing luck will soon have him back on his feet. Guy is likely to work in a field associated with money, such as stockbroking. Not surprisingly, with all this good luck and cash flowing in his direction, Guy has an easygoing and optimistic temperament. The indications in his name are that he is likely to be fit and well put together. Combine his good luck with his appealing personality and his likely wealth, and you can expect Guy to have a busy love life as well!

THE RUNIC INTERPRETATION
ᛇᚢᚷ (Eihwaz, Uruz, Gebo)

Guy is elegant of stature and refined in manner. He benefits by the strength of the Uruz rune and the Gebo rune of partnership. Before Guy has a relationship that leads to commitment, he may go through some painful separations. He may even resort to begging and manipulative tactics—to no avail. He despairs of ever finding a mate who will endure his personality. Fortunately, this painful walk helps Guy learn to wait until self-reliance becomes a deeply ingrained habit. It is only then that Guy is given his true love. Guy is very strong and grounded, due to the Eihwaz and Uruz runes in his name.

Elements: Earth/fire, earth, water

THE NUMEROLOGICAL INTERPRETATION
Guy (NV = 8, CV = 7, VV = 1, FL = 7)

Guy likes to be number one. This name reveals a man who has a strong drive to achieve status in the world. It is not difficult for Guy to reach his lofty goals; he definitely has the numbers for success! A person at ease with himself, Guy has no problem turning his ideas into money. Guy tends to be quite intelligent and is interested in several intellectual pursuits. These pursuits may preoccupy him at times, turning Guy inward and revealing the more introspective side to his nature.

Gwen

A KABBALISTIC SYNOPSIS
גואן —GVAN (Gimel, Vau, Aleph, Nun)

It is amazing that Gwen finds time for a career when her love life is such an emotional roller coaster. She is unusually fickle and falls in and out of love with ease. But when she does fall in love, she does so wholeheartedly, picturing a future and children together. And when she falls out, she does so suddenly and often with only the slightest indication of trouble. Despite this unique approach to love, Gwen will ultimately find her mate, who is likely one who refused to let himself be dumped. The initial Gimel in Gwen's name points to a love of travel, and ideally she will work in an environment that involves a considerable degree of movement from place to place. With her excellent interpersonal skills, she may well succeed in a sales role, as she can convince people to buy almost anything. Gwen rarely unwinds completely, as even when she is enjoying time for herself, she likes to be engaged in some active pursuit, especially cycling or swimming.

THE RUNIC INTERPRETATION
ᚾᛖᚹᚷ (Nauthiz, Ehwaz, Wunjo, Gebo)

Gwen uses the runes representing constraint, movement, possessions, and partnership to enhance her life. Gwen is dramatic and extroverted. A career in the theater is well suited to this imaginative and talented woman. The Nauthiz energy cautions that Gwen will have challenges on an emotional, financial, or physical level to overcome before she is allowed to rise to power in her career. The spiritual path is difficult, but Gwen reaps the rewards and spends the rest of her life traveling with a partner she adores and feeling more authentic and whole each day.

Elements: Fire, air, earth, water

THE NUMEROLOGICAL INTERPRETATION
Gwen (NV = 4, CV = 3, VV = 1, FL = 7)

Gwen is the name of a woman who is very versatile. It is quite important to Gwen that she perfect her highly individual talents and abilities. Material success and economic security mean a great deal to her. Gwen always has a plan in her bright mind and is determined to succeed with it. She is attracted to partners who are very practical in their orientation to life. She is good at business, especially when she can be in contact with the public.

DERIVATION: English and Welsh, short form of Gwendolen, which is from the Welsh roots *gwen*, meaning "white, fair," and *dolen*, meaning "bow." An ancient Welsh name, Gwendolen was revived in the late nineteenth century, possibly due to the influence of George Eliot's novel *Daniel Deronda*.

PRINCIPAL COLORS: Moderately toned hues

GEMSTONES AND PRECIOUS METALS: Sapphires

BOTANICALS: Sage, spinach, medlar

UNIQUE SPELLINGS: Guen, Guenne, Gwenn, Gwenne

RELATED TO: Gwendolyn, Gwenette, Gwenna, Gwenni, Gwyn, Gwyneth, Gwynna, Gwynne, Wendi, Wendie, Wendy†, Win, Winnie, Wynne

Hank

DERIVATION: English, short form of Henry, which is from the Germanic roots *haim*, meaning "home," and *ríc*, meaning "power." Popular as a nickname, and occasionally used independently.

PRINCIPAL COLORS: All yellow and greenish hues, also gold

GEMSTONES AND PRECIOUS METALS: Cat's-eye, cream-colored pearls, moss agate

BOTANICALS: Blackberry, hops, juniper

UNIQUE SPELLINGS: Hanck, Hankk

RELATED TO: Enrique†, Hal, Harry†, Heindrick, Heindrik, Heinrick, Henri, Henrik, Henry†

A KABBALISTIC SYNOPSIS
האנכ —HANK (Heh, Aleph, Nun, Kaph)

The letter H, or Heh, is astrologically ruled by Aries, and we can expect to find Arian characteristics in all names beginning with this letter. Hank is no exception. He is a headstrong man who will often rush into a course of action in a moment of heightened passion without considering any of the possible outcomes. Fortunately for Hank, the lucky number seven looms large in his name, and it will take a pretty huge error on his part before he causes himself any real problems. Hank's name has various associations with concepts of servitude, so, unfortunately for Hank, he really will have to push for any promotion. However, there are equally strong indications that his marriage will be blissfully happy. Hank is not really concerned with work as such; he dreams of success as an entertainer. While there are no real signs of any major career successes, Hank will apply himself with great dedication to his chosen talent, and may become a star simply through hard work and determination.

THE RUNIC INTERPRETATION
ᚲᚾᚨᚺ (Kano, Nauthiz, Ansuz, Hagalaz)

While it's certainly true that obstacles and chaos arrive on a fairly regular basis for Hank, there is good news, too. Hank is fortunate that obstacles arrive in tandem with opportunities, and chaos, from Hagalaz, arrives on the arm of Ansuz, the rune of problem-solving ability. Because Hank is resourceful and receptive to new ideas, people, and solutions, he is more likely than most to learn from his challenges and make adversity his ally. Hank has an excellent sense of timing. People say Hank is a doer and will accomplish a lot in this lifetime. He's fairly impatient and tactless, but people admire his honesty and take-charge attitude. With perseverance Hank can rise quickly to the top. Challenges for Hank at this point involve cultivating his spiritual development.

Elements: Water, fire, air, water

THE NUMEROLOGICAL INTERPRETATION
Hank (NV = 7, CV = 6, VV = 1, FL = 8)

Hank tends to be an honest and ethical person. His name indicates a man who lives by his principles. A deep thinker with a penchant for periods of introspection and solitude, Hank has ideas that, if properly developed, could be of significant help to society. The numbers in this name also indicate a man for whom home and family are very important. Hank is very responsible in his personal relationships and tends to be loyal and faithful to his partner.

Hannah

A KABBALISTIC SYNOPSIS
האנא —HANA (Heh, Aleph, Nun, Aleph)

Hannah is an impressive woman, and even those who disagree with her will find it hard not to respect her for her behavior and the way in which she presents her arguments. Hannah tends to split the world into black and white with very little gray in between. She is not afraid to voice her opinions, and may well be involved with a range of protest movements and pressure groups. The value of Hannah's name can be reduced to twelve, which indicates she is a great believer in sacrifices for a higher good. One meaning of Hannah is "destruction," which may seem to be a negative association; however, Hannah is not concerned with destruction for its own sake. Rather, Hannah is interested in destroying that which is outmoded and unjust. Having destroyed something, Hannah will have a new and, in her view, more equitable structure to put in its place.

THE RUNIC INTERPRETATION
ᚺᚨᚾᛏᚨᚺ (Hagalaz, Ansuz, Nauthiz, Nauthiz, Ansuz, Hagalaz)

Hannah is a name with spiraling energy. The double Hagalaz runes of disruptions, the double Ansuz runes of signals, and the double Nauthiz runes of constraint make this a fascinating name to interpret. The runes suggest that Hannah may have physical problems. Physical, mental, or emotional challenges are the soul's way of teaching the hardest of all human lessons: the lessons of waiting and patience. Hannah should be encouraged to pray and to detach from problems in her family that may overwhelm her. She must surround herself with peaceful healers who can teach her much about her higher calling. She must honor her path by spreading love in order to ease the challenges that face her.

Elements: Water, air, fire, fire, air, water

THE NUMEROLOGICAL INTERPRETATION
Hannah (NV = 1, CV = 8, VV = 2, FL = 8)

Hannah is very aware of her own special uniqueness. She will take full advantage of her talents, and accomplish much through the directed use of her abilities. Leadership qualities are strong in this name, and contribute to a personality that enables her to take charge and accomplish what needs to be done. Hannah can be very ambitious, as success in the world means a great deal to her. A woman of considerable grace and charm, Hannah usually finds it very easy to locate people who will be supportive of her many plans and projects.

DERIVATION: Hebrew, meaning "grace." Found in the Old Testament, as the mother of the prophet Samuel. Especially popular among the Puritans.

PRINCIPAL COLORS: Orange, gold, every shade of yellow and bronze

GEMSTONES AND PRECIOUS METALS: Citrine, yellow diamonds, any yellow stones

BOTANICALS: Borage, lavender, eyebright

UNIQUE SPELLINGS: Hana, Hanah, Hanna

RELATED TO: Annt, Annat, Annet, Annettet, Johanna

"Obstacles are those frightful things you see when you take your eyes off the goal."
—HANNAH MORE (AUTHOR)

"In my life's chain of events nothing was accidental. Everything happened according to an inner need."
—HANNAH SENESH (HOLOCAUST AUTHOR)

Harold

DERIVATION: English, from the Old English *here*, meaning "army," and *weald*, meaning "ruler." A similar Scandinavian name, Harald, was introduced to Britain by Norse settlers before the Norman Conquest. Especially popular in all English-speaking countries around 1900.

PRINCIPAL COLORS: Any medium-toned color

GEMSTONES AND PRECIOUS METALS: Sapphires

BOTANICALS: Medlar, Iceland moss, sage

UNIQUE SPELLINGS: Harald, Haraldd, Haroldd, Harrald, Harraldd, Harrold, Harroldd

RELATED TO: Araldo, Aroldo, Garald, Garold, Hal, Harry†, Herold, Herrick, Herrold

❧

"The roots of true achievement lie in the will to become the best that you can become."

—HAROLD TAYLOR (ARCHAEOLOGIST)

A KABBALISTIC SYNOPSIS
הארולד —HARVLD (Heh, Aleph, Resh, Vau, Lamed, Daleth)

Having a name that reduces to twelve suggests a person with a capacity for self-sacrifice, and the individual letters that produce this value allow us to be specific about the exact nature of Harold's altruism. Politically, Harold is ambivalent and will have a limited interest in current affairs. However, Harold will have an abiding interest in matters concerning the soul. He is rarely religious in the conventional sense, but instead seeks out a variety of beliefs to examine and consider. Unfortunately he has the youthful enthusiasm of an Aries and will find it hard to distinguish between the plausible, the possible, and the completely ridiculous. Harold's dream is to somehow find some valuable core to unite these belief systems, so that he can share his findings with the rest of the world. Unfortunately this is unlikely to happen. This valuable core may be as mundane as the ideal way to structure his family, but it will be no less important to Harold for that. His family, especially his kids, if he has any, will love him for his wonderful imagination. Another factor is his patience, which also makes him very attractive to potential partners. He is a great listener and is unusually sympathetic to all manner of problems.

THE RUNIC INTERPRETATION
ᛞᛚᛟᚱᚨᚺ (Dagaz, Laguz, Othila, Raido, Ansuz, Hagalaz)

Harold has many energies to use in this lifetime. He sees the painful side of human suffering, and may be a rescue worker or hospice caregiver. He does this job well because he has the Laguz rune of flow and the Ansuz rune for signals in his name as protection, a kind of inner, intuitive radar scanning for danger and security. The Othila rune of separation hints at losses in love and money and at career obstacles. Fortunately, Harold can counteract some of this negativity with the runes of Laguz, Ansuz, and Raido. Harold will have a good sense of timing, and know in his heart when to reposition his chances of success by relocating.

Elements: Fire, water, earth/fire, water, air, water

THE NUMEROLOGICAL INTERPRETATION
Harold (NV = 3, CV = 5, VV = 7, FL = 8)

Variety of creative expression characterizes this name. Harold is a man of many interests. He possesses a quick mind and a curious intellect. Ever eager to acquire new knowledge, Harold is traveling about more often than he is at his home or office. Although he has many friends and companions, he is as likely to be found in a library as he is at a party, or he may be taking an interesting voyage whose main purpose is for him to attend an educational seminar. Harold has a definite serious side to his nature. Nonetheless people enjoy Harold; he always has something of interest and importance to contribute to any group setting.

❧

Harriet

A KABBALISTIC SYNOPSIS

הארית —HARYAT (Heh, Aleph, Resh, Yod, Aleph, Teth)

No wonder she's always smiling: Harriet has an extreme case of Arian good luck! Her name is ruled by Jupiter, and his benevolent influence can be found in most aspects of her daily life. Not only that, her name reduces to ten, connecting her to the Wheel of Fortune in the tarot. People warm to Harriet easily, and not just because she is usually so cheerful. Harriet has a very understanding air, which is more matched by the usefulness of her advice to those who discuss issues of concern with her. There is a strong indication in her name that she will have more than the average number of children, a situation she will be quite happy with, as she is drawn to family life. The advisory role she occupies in relation to her friends and colleagues will set her in good stead for all the problems and questions that her children will present to her.

THE RUNIC INTERPRETATION

ᛏᛖᛁᚱᚱᚨᚺ (Teiwaz, Ehwaz, Isa, Raido, Raido, Ansuz, Hagalaz)

Harriet must overcome the Hagalaz energy of disruptions. Much like the Tower card in the tarot deck, Hagalaz stands for chaos. The painful journey of the double Raido rune can cause loss of faith in oneself or in one's world. When Harriet is past hope, her health can break down. Poor health is an important warning for Harriet, who must claim the solitude promised by the Isa rune—to be still and relax in order to heal. Harriet needs a break to get her perspective back. The Teiwaz energy of the warrior indicates that Harriet will grow even stronger from this period of solitude and shine as an example of a person who operates from strength, focus, and integrity.

Elements: Air, air, earth, water, water, air, water

THE NUMEROLOGICAL INTERPRETATION

Harriet (NV = 7, CV = 1, VV = 6, FL = 8)

A serious student of life, Harriet will work hard to perfect her special areas of interest. This name denotes a woman of considerable self-assurance. She does not mind taking on a challenge and fighting for what she believes. At heart, this is a very peace-loving and kind individual, but Harriet can easily exhibit an assertive attitude in her day-to-day dealings with the world around her. In her personal relationships, Harriet seeks a partner of strong mental abilities who can complement her own need to discover some of the deeper meanings of the universe in which we live.

DERIVATION: English, feminine form of Henry, originally from the Germanic roots *haim*, meaning "home," and *ric*, meaning "power." Coined in the seventeenth century, and quite popular in England in the early nineteenth century.

PRINCIPAL COLORS: Pale to bright yellow, light to deep green

GEMSTONES AND PRECIOUS METALS: Moss agate, pearls, any white stones

BOTANICALS: Blackberry, elder, linseed

UNIQUE SPELLINGS: Hariet, Hariett, Hariette, Hariot, Hariott, Harriett, Harriette, Harriot, Harriott

RELATED TO: Harrietta, Hatsie, Hatsy, Hattiet, Hatty, Henrieta, Henrietta, Henrika, Henryetta, Hetti, Hettie

Harry

A KABBALISTIC SYNOPSIS
הארי —HARY (Heh, Aleph, Resh, Yod)

Harry is a man of many minds who is highly intelligent and philosophical in outlook. Harry's character is such that he will try to take on a whole conceptual system in one go, and then effectively live through that set of values until, at some point, they fail him. This is both inevitable and, to a certain degree, traumatic for him. Harry will be in a semidepressive state until he finds a new set of ideas to adopt. While many people would find it hard, if not impossible, to deal with this approach to life, it is very beneficial to Harry and enables him to grow in wisdom. Harry's home life can be somewhat strained unless he has a partner with similar abilities and interests. Having said that, Harry will be able to turn even a negative relationship into a positive learning experience. If he does find the right partner, they are likely to avoid company, as most people will not follow their favorite areas of conversation.

THE RUNIC INTERPRETATION
ᛇᚱᚱᚨᚺ (Eihwaz, Raido, Raido, Ansuz, Hagalaz)

Harry is challenged by the Hagalaz rune of disruptions. He could lose money and social status in this lifetime. But so what? Harry is not materialistic. He is gullible and poetic and one of the most charming and loving men you can imagine. He may work as a veterinarian or serve in a spiritual capacity in any of a thousand ways. Harry may not be able to afford luxury trips in this lifetime. He'll tell you, on a rare sad day, that he always wished he could visit the Canary Islands. His family has remarked that Harry is probably dreaming of lemon yellows and clear blues and the jewel-like colors of a real canary when he thinks of the place. That's just like Harry, who has a lovely, romantic view of life.

Elements: Earth/fire, water, water, air, water

THE NUMEROLOGICAL INTERPRETATION
Harry (NV = 7, CV = 8, VV = 8, FL = 8)

The number eight dominates this name. This tells us that Harry has a great deal of willpower and stamina when it comes to achieving his goals. He has little problem spending many hours a day at his profession, working very intensely toward the fulfillment of his ambitions. Harry is much more comfortable in relationships in which he has the giving hand, for it is not as easy for him to be on the receiving end of things. A responsible person, Harry may sometimes feel weighed down by all that he has created. He would do well to investigate the more spiritual side to life, as this would be a natural balance to his more materialistic leanings.

❧

Harvey

A Kabbalistic Synopsis

הארוי —HARVY (Heh, Aleph, Resh, Vau, Yod)

Harvey is a calm, quiet individual, not at all keen on the busy pace of city life. He feels a real need to commune with nature. There are indications in Harvey's name of an affinity for high technology, and when combined with the high intelligence possessed by Harvey, this strongly suggests an interest in, if not employment within, the field of computing. Harvey's name adds up to 222, so he is ruled by issues of duality and union, the symbolic significance of the number two. Here is a clear example of the sort of duality that will concern Harvey. On the one hand he loves the rustically simple—and on the other, he has a brain that is always chasing the latest developments in technology. But the number two is also connected to the High Priestess, so we can expect Harvey to have sufficient understanding to deal satisfactorily with these conflicts.

The Runic Interpretation

ᛇᛒᚱᚨᚺ (Eihwaz, Berkana, Raido, Ansuz, Hagalaz)

Harvey is bound to make it through the challenges of his youth with a few physical scars and an impressive understanding of human nature. Chaos runs through his early life, and Harvey develops a kind of hypervigilance to assess the moods of those around him. Even during the hard times indicated by Hagalaz, the rune of disruption, Harvey believes that God has a plan for his life. The Berkana rune confirms that Harvey's trust is rewarded. Berkana (growth) combined with Ansuz (signals) and Eihwaz (defense) indicate that Harvey is protected and guided by help from beyond. Harvey loves travel, and the Raido rune of journeys suggests that Harvey will have the enjoyment of comfortable vacations in years to come.

Elements: Earth/fire, air/earth, water, air, water

The Numerological Interpretation

Harvey (NV = 7, CV = 3, VV = 4, FL = 8)

A practical philosopher and a man who can find rapid solutions to life's questions is a typical Harvey. This is a man who requires and enjoys long periods of solitude; it is then that he may enter his private world of ideas and ponder the issues that confront him. But Harvey is also very at home with other people and enjoys a lively debate and interesting dinner conversation. He likes to share his ideas and find useful ways to utilize what he has discovered. This name makes for an excellent teacher, scientist, or researcher.

DERIVATION: English form of the French name Hervé. From the Celtic root *haer*, meaning "strong" or "ardent." Entered Britain during the Norman Conquest. Especially popular in Britain in the 1970s.

PRINCIPAL COLORS: All colors of yellow or green tone, gold

GEMSTONES AND PRECIOUS METALS: Moonstones, pearls

BOTANICALS: Linseed, mushrooms, elder

UNIQUE SPELLINGS: Haervey, Harvee, Harvie, Harvy

RELATED TO: Harv, Harve, Herve, Hervey

DERIVATION: English, pet form of
Harriet, the feminine form of
Henry. Henry, in turn, is from the
Germanic roots *haim*, meaning
"home," and *ríc*, meaning "power."
Hattie is mainly a nickname, but
has been used independently,
especially at the end of the
nineteenth century.

PRINCIPAL COLORS: The
complete range of red hues,
particularly deep, rich reds

GEMSTONES AND PRECIOUS
METALS. Rubies, bloodstones

BOTANICALS: Garlic, wormwood

UNIQUE SPELLINGS: Hattey,
Hatti, Hatty

RELATED TO: Harriett, Harrietta,
Hatsie, Hatsy, Henrieta,
Henrietta, Henrika, Henryetta,
Hetti, Hettie

Hattie

A KABBALISTIC SYNOPSIS
הָאטי —HATY (Heh, Aleph, Teth, Yod)

One kabbalistic equivalent of Hattie is "to break," and Hattie has a real talent for destruction.
However, Hattie is not a violent woman, nor is she is some sort of nihilist. Hattie's talent lies
in seeing when something, such as a product, has reached the end of its useful life. While it
may not seem pleasant, the development of new ideas and products is dependent on the ter-
mination of old ones, and it is here that Hattie's talent comes in. Anyone who has been in a
relationship with Hattie will testify that she is a caring and fun person to be with. She has a
very strong Martian influence in her name; consequently, she can have a fiery temper when
riled.

THE RUNIC INTERPRETATION
ᛗᛁᛏᛏᚨᚺ (Ehwaz, Isa, Teiwaz, Teiwaz, Ansuz, Hagalaz)

Hattie isn't afraid of authority figures. She never felt disillusioned about her parents because
she knew from the start they were fallible, and forgave them their shortcomings. Hattie has
trouble ahead, and the Hagalaz rune warns of disruptions. Hattie also has the double Teiwaz
configuration, which is the energy of the warrior. Hattie should consider studying the martial arts because she needs self-discipline and courage. She can use the masculine energy of
Teiwaz to give her confidence and strength. Hattie will endure the tests ahead, and others
will look to her for encouragement.

Elements: Air, earth, air, air, air, water

THE NUMEROLOGICAL INTERPRETATION
Hattie (NV = 9, CV = 3, VV = 6, FL = 8)

This name belongs to a generous and charitable woman. Hattie is an inspiration to others
who can be open to the spiritual message that she carries. This message is simple: "Do unto
others as you would have them do unto you." The Golden Rule is Hattie's guide to life, and
she embodies its simple teaching. One of Hattie's life lessons is detachment. She needs to
learn she is not responsible for other people's happiness, nor can she protect them from their
own weaknesses. Hattie would be most comfortable in a profession that is service oriented.

Heather

DERIVATION: English, from the plant name. Started to be used as a first name in the late 1800s, and has become one of the most popular botanical names ever.

PRINCIPAL COLORS: All white and green shades

GEMSTONES AND PRECIOUS METALS: Moonstones, pearls, jade

BOTANICALS: Cabbage, plantain

UNIQUE SPELLINGS: Heatherre, Heathir, Heathyr, Heathyrre, Hether, Hethir

RELATED TO: Heath, Hetha

A KABBALISTIC SYNOPSIS
האתר —HAThR (Heh, Aleph, Tau, Resh)

Heather has her eyes fixed firmly on the big picture, and can often be found churning through all the serious items in a quality newspaper. Heather's name means "turtledove," and this is an appropriate connection, given her overriding concern with global social ills. The strong position of Tau, meaning "cross," in her name points to the fact that in reading about the suffering of others, Heather can almost feel the pain they are experiencing. This acute sensitivity to the needs of others is also noticeable in her relationships. Heather's partners are likely to be surprised by how she always seems to know exactly how they are feeling. Her partner will need to be equally sensitive, as the concern she has for others takes its toll on her own emotional state.

THE RUNIC INTERPRETATION
ᚱᛖᚦᚨᛖᚺ (Raido, Ehwaz, Thurisaz, Ansuz, Ehwaz, Hagalaz)

Heather can thank the tough lessons of disruption contained in the Hagalaz rune for prompting her to improve her life. The double Ehwaz runes of movement and the Raido rune of journey promise Heather will have a chance to move and explore new places. On a spiritual level Heather communicates with higher realms of consciousness. Heather is probably very energetic and able to make things happen. She is undoubtedly magical, for she is able to create money when she needs it, as well as call on protection out of the blue. Heather is living on the edge, and she likes it fine that way.

Elements: Water, air, fire, air, air, water

THE NUMEROLOGICAL INTERPRETATION
Heather (NV = 2, CV = 9, VV = 11, FL = 8)

Heather is the name of a woman with considerable intuitive gifts. She knows people instantly and has an immediate understanding of their possibilities and problems. In this respect, Heather would make an excellent personal counselor, psychologist, or astrologer. Not only can she relate to people individually but she also has the capacity to see those patterns of human relationships that are common to us all. Heather's gifts are many, her compassion is wide-reaching, and her personal magnetism is strong. People adore her, and with good reason!

DERIVATION: Greek, from the word meaning "holding fast." Name of the heroic Trojan soldier who was killed during the Trojan War by the Greek fighter Achilles.

PRINCIPAL COLORS: Electric hues

GEMSTONES AND PRECIOUS METALS: Sapphires

BOTANICALS: Lesser celandine, wintergreen

UNIQUE SPELLINGS: Hecctor, Hocktor, Hecktore, Hecter, Hectore

RELATED TO: Heckie, Heitor

A KABBALISTIC SYNOPSIS
האכתער —HAKTA'AR (Heh, Aleph, Kaph, Teth, Ayin, Resh)

This guy has so much excess energy, he could run an electricity-generating station off the surplus! It is amazing how much pure fire energy is packed into what tends to be a fairly small and slightly built individual. In addition to the Aries influence of the initial Heh, we have a direct connection to the tarot card Strength, while the compression of the name produces Shin, meaning "fire." Hector will probably make a great athlete, and with his inclination toward a sinewy rather than a muscular and solid frame, he should excel at running, particularly over long distances. If he misses out on sport, he will be at home in any high-pressure work environment. If he is born under Capricorn, nothing will be able to halt his continuing rise in the business world. His lover will probably have a difficult job keeping up and may worry about his possible escapades with others, although in reality she has no need to worry, as Hector is a deeply loyal husband.

THE RUNIC INTERPRETATION
ᚱᛟᛏᚲᛖᚺ (Raido, Othila, Teiwaz, Kano, Ehwaz, Hagalaz)

Hector has challenges to overcome. He may face bitter disappointments early in his childhood. Separations are indicated by the Othila rune, and disruptions are signified by the Hagalaz. The Teiwaz rune helps Hector call on strength he didn't know he had to help him through these emotional times. The Ehwaz and Kano runes show us that Hector will land on his feet. He will enjoy journeys as a young adult. Undoubtedly he will be singled out from the crowd and maybe awarded some money to further his studies or develop his talents. Hector will vow that his children will have a better start in life than he did, and he will help his parents in their old age because he has a big heart.

Elements: Water, earth/fire, air, water, air, water

THE NUMEROLOGICAL INTERPRETATION
Hector (NV = 6, CV = 11, VV = 22, FL = 8)

Hector contains both of the master numbers: eleven and twenty-two! His potential to make an important contribution to life is therefore very strongly indicated. Can Hector live up to this destiny? He will find that the more he thinks about others and dedicates his professional talents and abilities to the welfare of humanity, the happier his life will be. If he is at all egocentric or emotionally selfish, he will find that his desires will lead to frustration. Hector's success in life is assured as long as he rises up to the possibilities of his potential; the numbers in his name certainly give him an advantage.

Heidi

A KABBALISTIC SYNOPSIS
הידי —HYDY (Heh, Yod, Daleth, Yod)

Heidi sees life as something of a theme park, and the big bonus is that you don't even have to pay to get in! Many people have tried to get Heidi to take life more seriously, and they all fail. Their job is not made any easier by the fact that she always seems to get by and actually enjoys her life a whole lot more than those who are busy trying to reform her. If someone really does threaten Heidi's freedom to live her life in the way she wishes, she has the capacity to turn on them quickly, and can strike like a cobra without any warning. However, most people have a great time with Heidi even if they can't quite keep up with the pace! Her family has no problem with the way she lives her life, and they respect her wishes. She has a good relationship with all her family members, with whom she shares a mutual understanding and openness.

THE RUNIC INTERPRETATION
ᛁᛞᛁᛇᚺ (Isa, Dagaz, Isa, Eihwaz, Hagalaz)

Heidi is sensitive and introspective and more than a little bit secretive. The Isa rune of standstill creates opportunities for introspection, and Heidi develops a rich fantasy life in childhood. The Eihwaz rune of defense is a warning that Heidi may need to rally her reserves of courage and reach out for support at some point in her life. The Hagalaz energy of disruption teaches Heidi that dwelling in the past won't serve her. She uses the Dagaz energy of breakthrough to do something different and start a new way of life. Success comes to Heidi once she starts fresh, after being inspired by a new idea, and proceeds in a focused direction that uses her considerable talents.

Elements: Earth, fire, earth, earth/fire, water

THE NUMEROLOGICAL INTERPRETATION
Heidi (NV = 8, CV = 3, VV = 5, FL = 8)

Heidi possesses a sparkling personality, an active and curious mind, and a vivaciousness that is most appealing. She is very firm about what she seeks to achieve in life. This is a woman with considerable ambition and the will to back it up. She wants to be recognized for her talents and is definitely enamored of life's finer things. Heidi will work hard for success, but she also wants to make sure that she has a good time in the process.

DERIVATION: German-Swiss, originally a pet form of Adelaide, which comes from the Old German root meaning "nobility." Johanna Spyri's 1881 children's classic *Heidi* dramatically increased this name's popularity in both German- and English-speaking countries.

PRINCIPAL COLORS: Black, dark gray, the deepest shades of azure and purple

GEMSTONES AND PRECIOUS METALS: Black pearls, amethyst, carbuncles

BOTANICALS: Angelica, gravel root, celery

UNIQUE SPELLINGS: Heidee, Heidie, Heidy, Heydee, Heydi, Heydie, Hydee

RELATED TO: Ada, Addy, Adela, Adelaide, Hedda, Hedia, Hedy, Heida, Heidelinde, Hetta

DERIVATION: Greek, from the root *helenos*, meaning "bright" or "shining." Name borne by the mythological Helen of Troy, the most beautiful woman in the world, who was known to have "the face that launched a thousand ships." Her kidnapping supposedly spawned the Trojan War. A popular name throughout the ages and around the world. Other famous Helens have included the blind and deaf writer Helen Keller (1880–1968).

PRINCIPAL COLORS: Black, gray, dark violet, blue

GEMSTONES AND PRECIOUS METALS: Rubies, sapphires, black diamonds

BOTANICALS: Spinach, sage, ragwort

UNIQUE SPELLINGS: Helin, Hellen, Hellin, Hellyn, Helyn

RELATED TO: Elainet, Elana, Eleanort, Elenat, Ellent, Halina, Helena, Helenet, Ilana, Ilene, Ilona, Lena, Nellt, Nelly

❦

"If you rest, you rust."
— HELEN HAYES (ACTRESS)

Helen

A KABBALISTIC SYNOPSIS
האלן —HALN (Heh, Aleph, Lamed, Nun)

Helen is a driven woman, for deeply hidden, emotional reasons that she only half understands herself. She has a driving passion for material gain, although she is not greedy, and will be more than generous with her small circle of close friends if she achieves her financial goals. Indications in this name suggest that Helen feels trapped very easily and is extremely uncomfortable unless she has a variety of options open to her. Wealth, or at least a surplus of money, is one way of ensuring that lifestyle choices are available for her to select from. Obviously this element of instability—feeling trapped—will affect both her career and her relationships. In career terms, a number of job moves may be advantageous. In love she is likely to prove fickle until she finds a man who can provide the empathetic ear that she needs in order to work through her fears.

THE RUNIC INTERPRETATION
ᚺᛖᛚᛖᚾ (Nauthiz, Ehwaz, Laguz, Ehwaz, Hagalaz)

Helen is a versatile and accomplished woman. Unfortunately the disruptive energy of Hagalaz suggests that she may face the loss of family members and grieve for years. Helen is very sure to know constraint because the double Ehwaz energy warns her against poor money management and counsels her to guard her independence and freedom. The Laguz blessing of flow and the double Ehwaz energies of movement assure us that gentle Helen will go far in the healing arts. But whatever career she chooses, she can accomplish wonders.

Elements: Fire, air, water, air, water

THE NUMEROLOGICAL INTERPRETATION
Helen (NV = 8, CV = 7, VV = 1, FL = 8)

Helen is a name that exudes self-confidence. This lady naturally aspires to a position of authority and, when so placed, radiates a sense of power and control. Helen likes to take charge. She easily assumes responsibility and can be most single-minded and focused. Helen arrives at appointments when she says she will, and expects others to act likewise. Her organizational skills are such that she is fully capable of managing her time so that things run as smoothly as possible both for herself and for the other people in her life as well.

❦

Helene

A Kabbalistic Synopsis
האלאן —HALAN (Heh, Aleph, Lamed, Aleph, Nun)

There is an old Saxon saying that a person's life is no more than the flight of a bird from one end of the Great Hall to the other, beginning and ending in darkness with a brief but intense blaze of light in the middle. This is exactly the way Helene lives her life: in one blaze of glory. Life with Helene is hectic, to say the least, but most people would agree that it is well worth the rush. The value of Helene's name is framed at each end by a seven, which suggests that her approach will yield her the successes she is looking for. The central three in her name's number points to a creative personality, although given her need for fast living, it is likely that this refers to popular culture rather than any so-called high-art endeavors. Even if her attempts to live off her creativity fail her, she will not allow herself any time to look back and regret, as she is always charging forward to the next challenging experience.

The Runic Interpretation
ᛗᚺᛗᛁᛗᚺ (Ehwaz, Nauthiz, Ehwaz, Laguz, Ehwaz, Hagalaz)

Helene has the advantages and painful challenges of Helen's name. Helene is especially vulnerable to handsome men with soulful eyes who need someone to understand them and subsidize their expensive habits. She emerges from these experiences embittered and cynical for a time, until she realizes these limiting attitudes are only hurting herself. Once she leaves the past behind and makes new friends, the second half of her life is better and better. Once on track, Helene is unstoppable.

Elements: Air, fire, air, water, air, water

The Numerological Interpretation
Helene (NV = 4, CV = 7, VV = 6, FL = 8)

Considerable creative talents are inherent in this name. Helene would do well working in the arts or in some associated career that allows her to contribute beauty and greater understanding to her surroundings. It is very important to Helene that people treat each other well. Correct human relations are vital to her view of success. Financial well-being is important to her as well, and she will use a great deal of concerted energy to ensure both her own and her loved ones' economic security.

DERIVATION: The German form of the Greek name Helene, the feminine form of the name Helenos, meaning "shining one." Helena has always been a typical variant of Helen.

PRINCIPAL COLORS: Moderately toned hues, grays, blues

GEMSTONES AND PRECIOUS METALS: Sapphires

BOTANICALS: Sage, lesser celandine

UNIQUE SPELLINGS: Helean, Heleane, Heleen, Helleen, Helleene, Hellene

RELATED TO: Ailene, Eileen†, Elaina, Elaine†, Eleanor†, Elinor, Ella†, Ellen†, Ellie, Ellyn, Helen†, Helena, Hellen, Hellenor, Ilene, Ilona, Jelena

Henry

DERIVATION: English, from the German root *haim* and *ríc*, meaning "home" and "power." Entered Britain during the Norman Conquest in the eleventh century, where it was pronounced as "Harry." The royal name of eight British kings.

PRINCIPAL COLORS: The full range of green and yellow tones

GEMSTONES AND PRECIOUS METALS: Cat's-eye, pearls

BOTANICALS: Juniper, blackberry

UNIQUE SPELLINGS: Henri, Henrie, Hennrie, Hennry

RELATED TO: Enrico, Enrique†, Hal, Hank†, Harry†, Heinrik, Heinz, Hendrick, Henning

❧

"There cannot be a crisis next week. My schedule is already full."
—HENRY KISSINGER (DIPLOMAT, POLITICAL SCIENTIST)

"The man who goes alone can start today; but he who travels with another must wait till that other is ready."
—HENRY DAVID THOREAU (AUTHOR)

A KABBALISTIC SYNOPSIS
הנרי —HNRY (Heh, Nun, Resh, Yod)

Henry is a complex name that suggests a conflict within the personality. Henry is a very creative guy, full of new and exciting ideas. He is no pie-in-the-sky dreamer, though; he wants to put these ideas into *action*. The biggest obstacle Henry faces is his own self-doubt. Having developed an idea, he is likely to lack the confidence to carry it through. Henry is a character whose creativity comes from his intellect, and so he is unlikely to be particularly artistic. If he is unable to overcome his lack of confidence, a career as an architect or planner generally will enable him to realize his visions without having to carry them out himself.

THE RUNIC INTERPRETATION
ᛇᚱᚾᛖᚺ (Eihwaz, Raido, Nauthiz, Ehwaz, Hagalaz)

Henry just can't get it right. He has a quick temper that alienates many people and causes him to feel sorry for himself. The Nauthiz energy of constraint, coupled with Hagalaz for disruptions, can make a strong man weep, and Henry is such a tearful bloke. Fortunately, the Raido rune of journey kicks in and pushes him out of town to begin a new life. Ehwaz, the rune for movement, keeps Henry traveling in high style. He feels better than ever these days. The tears are all wiped away, and a smile is there to stay!

Elements: Earth/fire, water, fire, air, water

THE NUMEROLOGICAL INTERPRETATION
Henry (NV = 7, CV = 22, VV = 3, FL = 8)

This name reveals a soft-spoken man with a profound urge to investigate life, who will be very comfortable in a career that is scientific or philosophic in its orientation. Henry is a person who is very methodical. He prefers to handle all of life's situations a step at a time. He is particularly at ease when dealing with the material world, and can shape and form his environment to suit himself. If his orientation is more humanitarian and collective in nature, Henry can use his talents to organize the resources necessary to help many people.

❧

Herb

A Kabbalistic Synopsis
הורב —HVRB (Heh, Vau, Resh, Beth)

You might not expect it from a name like Herb, which suggests a high degree of nonconformity at first glance, but Herb is all set to become a top-level manager. As Herb is likely to have very close ties to his hometown, it may well be that his rise to the top is a gradual one, achieved after years of working at the local firm. Many would find the thought of working for twenty years in the same company pretty unappealing, but one of Herb's main traits is a deep-seated loyalty. This loyalty expresses itself in his relationships as well. He tends to make lifelong friendships, and when he marries, it will be for life; he is not one to stray from the marriage bed. As he is loyal himself, he will reward loyalty in others when he is in a position to do so. This reciprocal approach will be most noticeable in the workplace.

The Runic Interpretation
ᛒᚱᛖᚺ (Berkana, Raido, Ehwaz, Hagalaz)

Herb is on the road a lot. He's just a travelin' kind of man. With Raido for journey and Ehwaz for movement, Herb finds it hard to sit still. He not only visits new places, but he could even pack up his family and relocate; Herb just can't help it. He loves travel so much, it might be a good idea for him to pursue a career that pays some of the plane fare! Hagalaz for disruption and Berkana for growth give Herb a strangely comfortable feeling as he's loading up the rental truck. Hagalaz, the rune of disruption, describes the upheaval of frequent changes of residence and lifestyle. Fortunately the beneficent Berkana rune of growth makes change easy. Berkana blesses Herb with an uncanny ability to nest quickly and expand his circle of friends in every new neighborhood. As Herb unloads his belongings once again, he has a smile in his heart: He has the runic powers to move his family to new horizons and still enjoy every minute of the process.

Elements: Air/earth, water, air, water

The Numerological Interpretation
Herb (NV = 6, CV = 1, VV = 5, FL = 8)

Herb is a defender of people less fortunate than himself. His name contains the numerological indications of a charitable man who is a person of strength and dignity. Herb has a strong sense of his own individuality and will work diligently to perfect his special gifts. People are attracted to him because he radiates a sense of comfort and support. Parents rely equally on his kindly nature and his strength. Perhaps this is because his strength is derived from his kindness.

DERIVATION: English, short form of Herbert, which is from the Germanic roots *heri*, meaning "army," and *berht*, meaning "bright." Among English-speaking countries, most popular in the United States.

PRINCIPAL COLORS: All but the brightest of azures

GEMSTONES AND PRECIOUS METALS: Turquoise, emeralds

BOTANICALS: Apricots, vervain, walnuts, almonds

UNIQUE SPELLING: Herbb

RELATED TO: Harbert, Herbert†, Herbie, Heriberto

↜

"Telling the future by looking at the past assumes that conditions remain constant. This is like driving a car by looking in the rearview mirror."
—HERB BRODY (AUTHOR)

Herbert

A KABBALISTIC SYNOPSIS

הורבארט —HVRBART (Heh, Vau, Resh, Beth, Aleph, Resh, Teth)

Herbert is a very shrewd man, and an excellent tactician in business; this is the result of many years of experience and his own good instincts. He has a habit of running over past transactions in his mind until he has worked out all of the causes that led to the final outcome and, more important, the points at which the outcome could have been altered. There is a strong solar influence in Herbert's name, which gives him both an amiable and outgoing nature as well as an air of power. Herbert certainly has ambition, although on the whole he is not prepared to play dirty to get where he wants, as he has a strong personal code of honor. However, the final Teth, meaning "serpent," is a sign that if necessary, he is more than capable of a defensive strike against any person or group who tries to play foul themselves.

THE RUNIC INTERPRETATION

ᛏᚱᛖᛒᛒᚱᛖᚺ (Teiwaz, Raido, Ehwaz, Berkana, Raido, Ehwaz, Hagalaz)

Herbert has a lot in common with Herb: Both would love to quit their day jobs and travel with a road show. Neither can seem to stay in one place for very long. Herbert has the double Ehwaz energy for movement and the double Raido energy for journey. The Raido energy also fosters good communication. Maybe Herbert could be a foreign language instructor. He also loves to pilot his family to exotic places. With the Berkana rune for growth, family is terribly important to Herbert.

Elements: Air, water, air, air/earth, water, air, water

THE NUMEROLOGICAL INTERPRETATION

Herbert (NV = 4, CV = 3, VV = 1, FL = 8)

Reliable, honest, and appreciative of hard work, Herbert is a dedicated man, one who can remain content with that one special person for his entire life. He also appreciates an occupation that is predictable. He likes to know how much money he is going to earn each month, and he relies upon life's consistencies to give him a sense of security. Herbert is endowed with a healthy intellect, and will take great pleasure in reading, continuous education (especially in his field), and travel.

∽

Herman

A Kabbalistic Synopsis

הורמאן —HVRMAN (Heh, Vau, Resh, Mem, Aleph, Nun)

Herman is everybody's dream Dad: he always finds time to listen to his kids, and when they are younger, to join in their games. He is also a practical enough man to make the sorts of things a lot of dads have to purchase: Go-carts, dollhouses, you name it; Herman will find the wood and build it if his children want one. Unfortunately his easy way with children is mirrored by a lack of confidence when dealing with fellow adults. In career terms this may cause him a number of setbacks. However, with a supportive family, as he will almost definitely have, he will be able to build on these incidents and overcome his problem. The total value of Herman's name can be reduced to sixteen, which, while it indicates a number of traumatic incidents in his life, also suggests that Herman will benefit in some way from each catastrophe.

The Runic Interpretation

ᚺᛖᛗᚨᚱᛖᚺ (Nauthiz, Ansuz, Mannaz, Raido, Ehwaz, Hagalaz)

Herman is cursed with the Hagalaz rune of disruption and the rune of necessity in his name, which spells Trouble with a capital T—although the Mannaz rune says that he will have people to help him. Herman goes through life feeling a little beat up, and he may feel bad about himself because of this. His mom was a complainer, and Herman does a bit of that himself. It's uncomfortable to witness, but lately he's stopped sulking, and seems to have a secret that keeps him feeling delicious inside. It's a wonderful sight to behold.

Elements: Fire, air, air, water, air, water

The Numerological Interpretation

Herman (NV = 5, CV = 8, VV = 6, FL = 8)

Herman enjoys good company and fine entertainment. He likes variety in life, but he is not frivolous. Herman tends to be devoted to the people he loves, and family means a great deal to him. He is establishment oriented, and will work with patience and perseverance to achieve his goals. But Herman is far from being a workaholic; he likes life's pleasures too much for that! He works hard to reach a place of financial abundance and security—because achieving these enables him to play equally hard.

DERIVATION: English spelling of the German name Hermann, which is from the roots *heri*, meaning "army," and *man*, meaning "man." Brought to Britain by the Normans in the eleventh century. Especially popular in the United States in the second half of the nineteenth century.

PRINCIPAL COLORS: Virtually any color, as long as it is a very light shade

GEMSTONES AND PRECIOUS METALS: Platinum, silver, shiny stones

BOTANICALS: Hazel, sweet marjoram, parsley

UNIQUE SPELLINGS: Hermann, Hermin, Herminn, Hermon, Hermonn, Hermyn, Hermynn

RELATED TO: Armand, Armand†, Ermanno, Ermano, Harman, Harmon, Hermie

⁓

"We cannot live only for ourselves. A thousand fibers connect us with our fellow men; and among those fibers, as sympathetic threads, our actions run as causes, and they come back to us as effects."

—HERMAN MELVILLE (AUTHOR)

DERIVATION: English, from the Latin *hilaris*, meaning "cheerful." A common male name until the seventeenth century, when it faded from use. Became popular once again in the 1890s, but as a female name. Very common in the 1950s and 1960s.

PRINCIPAL COLORS: Grays, azure, electric hues

GEMSTONES AND PRECIOUS METALS: Sapphires

BOTANICALS: Celandine, wintergreen, Solomon's seal

UNIQUE SPELLINGS: Hilarey, Hilari, Hilarie, Hilary, Hilerey, Hileri, Hilerie, Hilery, Hillarey, Hillari, Hillarie, Hillerey, Hilleri, Hillerie, Hillery

RELATED TO: Hilaria, Hilario, Hilarion, Hilliary

A KABBALISTIC SYNOPSIS
הילארי —HYLARY (Heh, Yod, Lamed, Aleph, Resh, Yod)

You can always trust Hillary; she is scrupulously honest in every way. Hillary is one of those rare people who will actually go back to a shop if she gets home and discovers that she has been undercharged. Unlike some, Hillary does not use her own moral code as an excuse to berate everyone else for their lax behavior. Another key attribute of Hillary is her tolerance of other people, her ability to live and let live. She is honest and decent, so she tends to meet with honesty and friendship in return. The only problem Hillary really has is that she will force herself to be pleasant even to those people she isn't really keen on. This can lead to a dangerous buildup of repressed anger.

THE RUNIC INTERPRETATION
ᛇᚱᚨᛚᛚᛁᚺ (Eihwaz, Raido, Ansuz, Laguz, Laguz, Isa, Hagalaz)

Hillary faces disruption, suggested by the Hagalaz rune in her name. The double Laguz rune of flow provides her with a good sense of timing. Her Eihwaz rune cautions her to rally her defenses and not automatically trust those who are close to her. The Ansuz rune of signals heightens her insight to her advantage. Hillary can use the Isa energy of separation and the Raido energy of journey to travel and distance herself from concerns on the home front. She is sure to wander far and wide, but she can become just about whatever she sets her mind to being.

Elements: Earth/fire, water, air, water, water, earth, water

THE NUMEROLOGICAL INTERPRETATION
Hillary (NV = 4, CV = 5, VV = 8, FL = 8)

A highly disciplined and focused woman, Hillary takes herself and life very seriously, and is decidedly practical in her life orientation. The physical world is more important to her than the metaphysical. Hillary wants to tackle the problems of this life, not the next! She is most attracted to the outdoors, and will tend to be involved in ecological issues.

Holly

A Kabbalistic Synopsis
הֶעְלִי —HA'ALY (Heh, Ayin, Lamed, Yod)

Holly is often physically petite, but she has a strong will and an equally forceful voice. Thankfully, Holly is rarely moved to anger, for she has the capacity to really raise the roof when she is genuinely enraged. In fact, Holly possesses the archetypal Arian trait of being permanently convinced that everything will work out right in the end. As is usually the case, Holly will find that events have a knack of producing the results that you expect them to, and with her bright outlook on the world she will rarely have cause to feel blue. Holly is usually the center of attention at parties, thanks largely to her vivacious nature. She usually gets more than her fair share of romantic attention as well.

The Runic Interpretation
ᛇᛚᛚᛟᚺ (Eihwaz, Laguz, Laguz, Othila, Hagalaz)

Holly has a life of extremes. The Othila rune of separation, combined with the Hagalaz rune of disruption, means Holly learns to survive by her wits as a child. She may be an orphan, or she may leave home at an early age to improve her life. The Eihwaz rune of defense shows that Holly isn't prepared for the challenges and dangers that punctuate her flight to freedom, and she may encounter some obstacles in her life that are insurmountable. The double Laguz rune of this name is a treasure for Holly during this period of her life. Holly's guides surround her and whisper reassuring words of advice to her that protect her against enormous odds. Later, Holly finds herself in a better place with kind associates and friends.

Elements: Earth/fire, water, water, earth/fire, water

The Numerological Interpretation
Holly (NV = 9, CV = 5, VV = 4, FL = 8)

Holly believes that in order to have personal freedom, she has to live up to her responsibilities. This is the name of a balanced individual, a woman who is definitely not a conformist and yet knows that part of winning the game involves playing by its rules. Holly has a developed sense of compassion and understanding. She can be relied upon for her sincere advice and warm acceptance of others. In relationships, she is most suited to a career-oriented partner who also has the inclination to be genuinely unselfish and caring.

DERIVATION: English, from the plant name. Began to be used as a first name at the beginning of the twentieth century, and used most often for babies born during the December holiday season.

PRINCIPAL COLORS: The palest to the richest of reds, maroon, crimson

GEMSTONES AND PRECIOUS METALS: Rubies, garnets, bloodstones

BOTANICALS: Broom, wormwood, onion

UNIQUE SPELLINGS: Hollee, Holley, Holli, Hollie

RELATED TO: Holla, Hollena

DERIVATION: English; from the name of the Greek epic poet who wrote *The Iliad* and *The Odyssey*. Possibly from the Greek *homeros*, meaning "pledge." Common in Britain in the nineteenth century.

PRINCIPAL COLORS: The full spectrum of very pale hues

GEMSTONES AND PRECIOUS METALS: Silver, diamonds, any other very pale stone

BOTANICALS: Hazel, oats, sea kale

UNIQUE SPELLINGS: Hohmer, Hohmir, Hohmyr, Homir, Homyr

RELATED TO: Holmer, Holmes, Homeros, Homerus, Omero

A KABBALISTIC SYNOPSIS
העמאר —HA'AMAR (Heh, Ayin, Mem, Aleph, Resh)

Depending on your cultural background, Homer is either the first great poet of Western civilization or Bart's long-suffering dad! This illustrates that one can expect to find little obvious connection between any one Homer and another. Partly this is due to a strong desire in Homer to belong. Homer will tend to satisfy this need to feel a part of something bigger than himself by looking at his local community and emulating what seem to be the primary interests and values of the other residents. This chameleon-like quality is another, but less well-known, trait of people born under Aries. Consequently there are at least as many different Homer types as there are types of neighborhoods. What does unite every Homer is an intense loyalty and desire to protect his family against threats, often both real and imagined.

THE RUNIC INTERPRETATION
ᚱᛖᛗᛟᚺ (Raido, Ehwaz, Mannaz, Othila, Hagalaz)

Homer has one adventure after another and travels extensively in his long life. The Hagalaz rune of disruption sets the stage early on for a bumpy ride. The Othila rune of separation joins Raido for journey, along with the Ehwaz rune of movement, in Homer's name. His travels take Homer to other worlds and realms of consciousness that he may not remember until later in life. The spiritual meaning of Homer's name is indicated by the Mannaz rune for the self. It is because Homer is intelligent and sensitive, loves life, and survives by his strong will that his faith grows deeper daily. Homer has a lot to teach us all.

Elements: Water, air, air, earth/fire, water

THE NUMEROLOGICAL INTERPRETATION
Homer (NV = 5, CV = 3, VV = 11, FL = 8)

An intuitive man with many talents, Homer can be a wise friend and an inspirational companion. This name contains a very special combination of numbers that reveals a definite spiritual inclination. More humanitarian than monkish, Homer is most comfortable when functioning in an educational capacity. He therefore makes an excellent teacher, writer, or spokesperson. This name suggests a tendency to be more comfortable in impersonal relationships than in intimate, personal ones. For this reason, Homer chooses his partners very carefully.

Hope

A Kabbalistic Synopsis
העפ —HA'APh (Heh, Ayin, Peh)

Hope's name is in itself a description of her personality. The central Ayin displays her concern with the world around her, although its position next to the letter Heh may suggest that Hope tends to feel somehow cut off from those people with whom she is concerned. The use of gematria produces words connected with both the natural world and with protection. It could possibly be that Hope's concerns are more based in ecology than humanity. But wherever her hope lies, the final Peh in her name, meaning "mouth," demonstrates her ability to voice her opinions clearly and powerfully. Hope can also expect to meet with a reasonable amount of success in her efforts, as she has a knack for reading situations to her benefit. Her enthusiasm for her cause will also prove effective in attracting more support.

The Runic Interpretation
ᛖᛈᛟᚺ (Ehwaz, Perth, Othila, Hagalaz)

Hope brings order out of confusion. Before she is able to do this for others, however, she must do it for herself. Hope has the Ehwaz rune of movement, Perth of initiation, Othila of separation, and Hagalaz for disruption. Perth counsels that the old ways must end, and Hope cannot afford to focus on outcomes. She must remove herself from the chaos in a step-by-step fashion. The Ehwaz rune will lift Hope out of herself to find a new mate; a new home and unexpected gains come from this transition. Hope knows there is no such thing as security. She lives in the moment, grateful for a renewal of spirit, opportunity, and hope.

Elements: Air, water, earth/fire, water

The Numerological Interpretation
Hope (NV = 8, CV = 6, VV = 11, FL = 8)

Faith and charity definitely go along with this name. Hope has a deep need to bring a sense of peaceful coexistence into all of her relationships. She tends to be very understanding of others and is a natural mediator. Hope is courageous when faced with difficult moral issues, and stands firm in her beliefs. She has a spiritual orientation, which allows her to be of comfort to others in distress. Yet this is not a lady with her head and heart in the clouds. Hope knows that she has to make a practical contribution to life, and sets to work with great determination in order to do so.

DERIVATION: English. Especially common among the Puritans, and has been the most popular of the three names deriving from the cardinal virtues: faith, hope, and charity.

PRINCIPAL COLORS: Very deeply toned azure, dark purple and gray, black

GEMSTONES AND PRECIOUS METALS: Carbuncles, black pearls, rubies

BOTANICALS: Shepherd's purse, pilewort, ragwort

UNIQUE SPELLING: Hoepe

RELATED TO: Esperance, Esperanza (the French and Spanish translations of Hope)

Howard

A KABBALISTIC SYNOPSIS
העורד —HA'AVRD (Heh, Ayin, Vau, Resh, Daleth)

Howard is a very private person. Although he is a cheerful man, he likes his own space and is reluctant to let too many people in. However, in compressing the name Howard, we produce Resh, Chet, and Heh; these letters indicate that while Howard feels a need to put a wall of sorts around his private life, he still likes to be able to look out at the world. The yearning for privacy may well come from his career, which is likely to be well paid but will involve lots of fairly stressful public contact. Howard certainly gets a kick out of enjoying the fruits of his labor, and is generous, too, but it is with his family and very close friends only that he wants to do his enjoying! Even with his family there will be occasions when he needs some time alone, and he will probably have a room of his own where he can go and be by himself.

THE RUNIC INTERPRETATION
ᛞᚱᚨᚹᛟᚺ (Dagaz, Raido, Ansuz, Wunjo, Othila, Hagalaz)

Howard likes to move. He could enjoy living on a houseboat or in a recreational vehicle or mobile home. He might need to maintain a mobile lifestyle because of his career path or vice versa. Howard could be a traveling veterinarian or craft fair vendor. He needs change, and while others might find the challenges of relocating disruptive, Howard thrives on the thrill of uncharted territory to conquer! Dagaz, the rune of breakthrough, along with Wunjo, the rune of joy, describes Howard as a nomad who understands his home is within his heart. Howard finds joy wherever he goes. This is because Howard understands that his warm, engaging personality is a manifestation of his inner joyful spirit. Howard projects this Wunjo rune for joy into his outer world to create favorable experiences.

Elements: Fire, water, air, earth, earth/fire, water

THE NUMEROLOGICAL INTERPRETATION
Howard (NV = 6, CV = 8, VV = 7, FL = 8)

Howard needs a peaceful and beautiful environment in order to function at his best. His name indicates a man who tends to be somewhat reserved, one who speaks only when it is necessary to do so, but when he does, he usually says something quite profound. A philosopher and teacher at heart, Howard is most at ease when sharing ideas and advice that serve to uplift and improve other people's lives. He is a perfectionist by nature and is constantly trying to better his life. Howard loves very deeply, and he tends toward committed and monogamous relationships.

❧

Hugh

DERIVATION: German, from the word meaning "mind" and "thought." Entered Britain during the Norman Conquest, and became extremely popular during the Middle Ages.

PRINCIPAL COLORS: Black, gray, dark shades of violet and blue

GEMSTONES AND PRECIOUS METALS: Lackluster rubies, deep sapphires, other dark stones

BOTANICALS: Marsh mallow, mandrake root, shepherd's purse

UNIQUE SPELLINGS: Hew, Hewe, Huw

RELATED TO: Hewson, Hudson, Huegues, Hughes, Hughie, Hugot, Ugo

A KABBALISTIC SYNOPSIS
היע —HYA'A (Heh, Yod, Ayin)

The Hebrew spelling of Hugh seems particularly strange, so it is worth pointing out that the letter Ayin, while represented in English as A'A, has among its possible phonetic readings the "oo" sound as well as the "aa" sound one would expect. Accepting, then, the spelling of Hugh as it is, we find that it is equivalent to the word Boaz. Boaz is one of the pillars in the Temple of Solomon and is connected to the sephirah Hod. In layman's terms this means that Hugh is an intellectual and a rationalist. He is likely to be involved in one of the hard sciences, as there are strong earth energies in the name. Hugh is also a great talker, and it may be that this leads him into lecturing, or it may even be that his career is based around his voice. Whatever he does, Hugh will carry it out with considerable panache.

THE RUNIC INTERPRETATION
ᚺᚷᚢᚺ (Hagalaz, Gebo, Uruz, Hagalaz)

Hugh thrives on danger and chaos, and may pursue a high-risk career. Hugh makes an outstanding venture capitalist, air traffic controller, emergency room professional, or litigator. The possibility exists that some Hughs could choose a life as a military strategist or even a terrorist in some capacity. Hugh could have a tendency to gamble because the pressure of high stakes and impending disaster provides an edge of tension Hugh thoroughly enjoys. As a family man, Hugh can be a bit selfish and poker-faced. He needs to develop his meditative skills and learn to value peace and harmony. Gebo will help him do this. Hugh can achieve emotional intimacy if he is able to value personal development as a worthwhile goal.

Elements: Water, water, earth, water

THE NUMEROLOGICAL INTERPRETATION
Hugh (NV = 8, CV = 5, VV = 3, FL = 8)

The expression "There are many ways to skin a cat" is most apt for Hugh. This is a man who has definite and fixed objectives in life but who is also quite versatile. Hugh knows that there are any number of alternatives available to help him achieve his goals, and he intends to explore them all. Besides, it's more fun that way, and Hugh enjoys having a good time. Nonetheless, Hugh is capable of perseverance and has a most determined nature. It may take him a bit longer to get places, but he will always arrive in style.

Hugo

A KABBALISTIC SYNOPSIS
היעגע —HYA'AGA'A (Heh, Yod, Ayin, Gimel, Ayin)

Hugo has little time for relationships, as he is far too busy with his work. To Hugo, work is more than just a means to an end; it is a vocation and, quite possibly, the defining feature of his personality. The strong impact of Capricorn in his name tells us that Hugo not only likes his job but stands a better chance than most of being successful at it. The double Ayin also points to a real love of watching the world; it is likely that Hugo's considerable business acumen is partly the result of his close observation of other people's behavior. The ideal line of business for Hugo would be travel or some other industry connected to leisure. The problem that Hugo will face in later life is that he will have amassed a considerable amount of money and property but may well have nobody to share it with. Once he retires, Hugo will start looking around for someone to share his life.

THE RUNIC INTERPRETATION
ᛟᚷᚢᚺ (Othila, Gebo, Uruz, Hagalaz)

Hugo can counteract the disruptive energy of Hagalaz and the Othila separation energy in his name, for the Uruz rune of strength and the Gebo rune of partnership are there to save the day. Hugo is the kind of man who needs a good mate to make life friendlier. Once he finds her, she is attracted to his John Wayne personality. He's seen trouble, and he's looked it in the eye. He's rugged and manly, and she swoons when he picks her up off the bar stool. He swishes her around the dance floor, and the faces of her smiling friends become a blur as she falls deeply in love. There are many separations between the two of them because of travel and business, but Hugo and his love do ride into the sunset together.

Elements: Earth/fire, water, earth, water

THE NUMEROLOGICAL INTERPRETATION
Hugo (NV = 6, CV = 6, VV = 9, FL = 8)

Home and family are especially important to this man. Hugo's name carries a very peaceful vibration, and he is most comfortable when surrounded by what is emotionally familiar. Hugo can carry this sense of comfort into all of his relationships, and is known by his friends as a man with a kind heart. Charitable by nature, Hugo can be counted upon to help others in need. He will be well suited to a career in one of the healing professions or in one of the arts. Beauty is also a healing tool, and men named Hugo may be attracted to painting, acting, or music.

Ian

A Kabbalistic Synopsis

יאן —YAN (Yod, Aleph, Nun)

In common with all names beginning with Y, or Yod, Ian has a higher than average amount of energy. However, the energy represented by Yod is very specific. In the mystical tetragrammaton, Yod is the initial flame or spark of creation; thus, Yod is the energy of beginning, which is very different from the energy of sustaining or completing. Ian is capable of coming up with new ideas on an almost daily basis. Unfortunately, these ideas rarely progress, as once Ian has been hit by inspiration, he begins to doubt the wisdom or feasibility of the idea. This self-doubt is not a rational process of analysis but stems from a lack of self-confidence. If Ian teams up with a partner who can boost his confidence sufficiently, the world is his oyster! Ideally his business partner will also be an emotional partner, as Ian does not like to share his ideas with just anybody and may well exclude his wife from his work activities unless she is actively involved.

The Runic Interpretation

ᚾᚨᛁ (Nauthiz, Ansuz, Isa)

Ian's name is composed of Nauthiz, the rune of constraint; Ansuz, signals; and Isa, standstill. It's going to be very difficult to get Ian to the altar. Ian always cries at weddings, especially his own. He thinks of himself as a confirmed bachelor. But Mama always said that those are the men who fall the hardest. Ian loves deeply but doesn't feel he can breathe in a close relationship. The lucky partner who can win Ian's heart is happy, free, and spontaneous. Ian needs a mate who is lighthearted and tons of fun. When he finds a partner whom he has to chase to get, he'll parachute to the wedding if need be.

Elements: Fire, air, earth

The Numerological Interpretation

Ian (NV = 6, CV = 5, VV = 1, FL = 9)

People enjoy Ian's company because he is genuinely interested in others. This name indicates a love of good company and an eager mind capable of learning and storing a great deal of knowledge. Ian is a sensual man, one who is usually quite in touch with his feelings. He therefore makes for a very romantic partner, one who enjoys the adventure of personal relationships. Travel is also important to Ian, who is an avid collector both of experiences and of the lovely objects that he brings home from his many journeys.

DERIVATION: Scottish version of John, which stems from the Hebrew word meaning "God is gracious." Spread from Scotland to become popular in all English-speaking countries during the twentieth century.

PRINCIPAL COLORS: All shades of blue with the exception of the electric tones

GEMSTONES AND PRECIOUS METALS: Emeralds, blue and blue-green turquoise

BOTANICALS: Dog rose, vervain, daffodils

UNIQUE SPELLINGS: Ean, Eann, Iain, Iann

RELATED TO: Evan†, Hans, Ivan†, Iwan, Jack†, Jan†, John†, Juan†, Sean†, Shawn†

"Love is never what we looked for and always takes us by surprise."
—IAN SHOALES (PERSONA OF MERLE KESSLER, AUTHOR-COLUMNIST)

341

DERIVATION: Pet form of names ending in "ina," such as Christina and Martina. From the Latin suffix *ina*, which transforms male names into female ones. Used independently since the nineteenth century.

PRINCIPAL COLORS: All but the brightest shades of blue

GEMSTONES AND PRECIOUS METALS: Turquoise, emeralds

BOTANICALS: Violets, almonds, walnuts

UNIQUE SPELLINGS: Eena, Ena, Inna

RELATED TO: Andrewina, Bettina, Christina†, Georgina, Martina, Regina†

A KABBALISTIC SYNOPSIS

ינה —YNH (Yod, Nun, Heh)

They say that money attracts money, but so does Ina. Not only does the value of her name reduce to the symbol of success, but one equivalent of her name under kabbalistic analysis is "wealth." Whatever level of wealth Ina achieves, she will derive far more pleasure from spending it than from earning or merely hoarding it. If Ina is greedy in any way, it relates to her love of all forms of consumption; from shopping to eating, Ina can't get enough of it. In principle there is nothing necessarily wrong with such a perspective on life. However, in Ina's case, the core of her personality is represented by N, or Nun. We must therefore suspect that this excessive consumption masks a deeper emotional need. Since her name suggests that Ina will triumph in life, it is probable that this one problem will be resolved and that she will be able to continue to enjoy her money without any negative feelings.

THE RUNIC INTERPRETATION

ᚨᚾᛁ (Ansuz, Nauthiz, Isa)

The Nauthiz rune of constraint urges that Ina work on mending, restoring, and creating balance in her life. Ina welcomes the Isa energy of standstill to go within herself and create order and harmony on a cellular level. As Ina takes the time and effort to love herself with care and consideration, her relationships in the outer world will change for the better as well. The emotional abusers who thwart her efforts and undermine her confidence will witness her leaving. Ina is on her way.

Elements: Air, fire, earth

THE NUMEROLOGICAL INTERPRETATION

Ina (NV = 6, CV = 5, VV = 1, FL = 9)

Ina is especially fond of people. She enjoys a good party and is known to be a very amiable hostess. Ina will be interested in making sure that her home is beautiful and that people feel welcomed and comfortable there. Her name reveals a great love of family. Ina tends to be a very caring partner and a devoted mother. She will feel very comfortable in a child's world, and knows how to communicate with both her own and other people's kids. Ina would also do well working in the arts, as she is a sensuous woman who is attracted by beauty in all of its many forms.

Inez

A Kabbalistic Synopsis
יִנאַז —YNAZ (Yod, Nun, Aleph, Zayin)

Inez has a brain that most people can only dream about. She is wise rather than intelligent, in that her intellectual concerns are related more to philosophical questions than scientific issues. There is a price to this wisdom, which is reflected in the word "pity," one of the gematric equivalents of this name. By understanding the world so completely, Inez is exposed to all of its pain and suffering. Due to the effect of N, or Nun, it is the negative aspects of the world and society that preoccupy her. While lesser minds might convince themselves that all problems can be solved, Inez understands that there must be suffering in order to have the possibility of joy. Inez's tendency to suffer depression can be alleviated to a degree by her friends, who will be able to stress all the good things about life.

The Runic Interpretation
ᛉᛖᚾᛁ (Algiz, Ehwaz, Nauthiz, Isa)

Inez is considered by many to be a terrific individual. Inez is independent, honest, and kind. The Isa rune of standstill makes Inez comfortable with solitary pursuits. Because she can appreciate being alone, Inez has a lot to offer in relationships; she is neither clingy nor dependent. Inez has the Nauthiz rune of constraint in her name, which means she has grown from the challenges and limitations on a social or economic level in her life. Inez appreciates freedom and gladly seizes the Ehwaz rune of power or movement, which allows her to be very open-minded. Inez grows spiritually and emotionally, and has strength of character and independence.

Elements: Air, air, fire, earth

The Numerological Interpretation
Inez (NV = 9, CV = 4, VV = 5, FL = 9)

The romantic who bears this name would like to flee the cares and responsibilities of the ordinary world and move to some exotic outpost in a remote corner of the earth. But Inez's more dominant practical nature just won't let her do this. Inez requires a great deal of variety and personal freedom in her life—at least, after work and during her vacation time! While on the job Inez is a very hardworking person who is determined to achieve her practical goals in life. Inez appreciates a partner who shares her need to break from life's routine and do something very special.

DERIVATION: Spanish form of Agnes, which is originally from the Greek *hagnos*, meaning "pure, holy."

PRINCIPAL COLORS: The complete range of red hues, from pink to deep rose

GEMSTONES AND PRECIOUS METALS: Rich red bloodstones, rubies, garnets

BOTANICALS: Broom, garlic, wormwood

UNIQUE SPELLINGS: Eenes, Eenez, Ines

RELATED TO: Agnes†

"You amuse me with your 'flukes.' As if they left anything to chance! I tell you they've thought it all out. Down to the last detail. Nothing was left to chance. This room was all set for us."
—INEZ IN *NO EXIT* BY JEAN-PAUL SARTRE

DERIVATION: Greek, from the word
eirene, meaning "peace." The
name of a Greek goddess who
represented peace, it was very
common during the Roman
Empire. Became very popular in
English-speaking countries during
the nineteenth century.

PRINCIPAL COLORS: All but the
brightest shades of azure

GEMSTONES AND PRECIOUS
METALS: Emeralds, turquoise

BOTANICALS. Dog rose, vervain,
apricots

UNIQUE SPELLINGS: Eireen,
Eirene, Ireen, Irine, Iryne

RELATED TO: Arina, Irena, Irenie,
Irina, Rena, Renie

Irene

A KABBALISTIC SYNOPSIS
ירין —YRYN (Yod, Resh, Yod, Nun)

Irene would make an excellent counselor, as she is likely to have been through a variety of tough circumstances herself. Her name begins very positively: The initial Yod tells us that she is a person with immense energy and initiative, while the Resh (the sun) tells us that her enthusiasm doesn't wane once the initial spark has burned out. However, the final half of her name is dominated by self-doubt and insecurity due to the presence of the letter Nun. Irene is likely to be the sort of person who abandons a piece of work when it is all but completed because of a sudden lack of confidence. There is hope in the second Yod, though, which indicates a further boost of energy that may be sufficient to get Irene through her anxiety. If it is, she will be more than willing to use her own experiences to benefit others.

THE RUNIC INTERPRETATION
MᚺMᚱI (Ehwaz, Nauthiz, Ehwaz, Raido, Isa)

Irene's name combines the double Ehwaz energy of movement and the Raido rune of journey, so she will live in many places. Nauthiz, the rune of constraint, and Isa, the rune of standstill, suggest that Irene will need to motivate herself. She knows that she must make her own luck. The lessons of constraint paralyze her briefly, until she figures out that by hopping on a plane or changing her address, she can begin again. It's that easy. Irene succeeds because she is willing to look at her behaviors and make a change here and there to position herself for success. Irene could travel and have friends around the world. She's powerful as well; this is suggested by the presence of the four elements in her name.

Elements: Air, fire, air, water, earth

THE NUMEROLOGICAL INTERPRETATION
Irene (NV = 6, CV = 5, VV = 1, FL = 9)

Irene enjoys a very convivial name. She is most content when she is among friends. She loves to chat and makes a very stimulating conversationalist. Her interests are many, and she will therefore have a wide range of associates. Irene has a strong need to express her individuality, and she will use any special talent she may have to be of help; fundamentally, she is an unselfish person. Irene has to take care not to spread herself too thin, however, as she may have a tendency to dissipate her energy by attempting to do too many things simultaneously.

Iris

A Kabbalistic Synopsis
ירים —YRYS (Yod, Resh, Yod, Samech)

There is no room for any lack of self-confidence in Iris; she is supremely confident in herself and in her abilities. To be fair, it isn't arrogant of her to feel this way; she has lots of energy, a good brain, and every right to feel good about herself. It should be no surprise that the value of her name links Iris to the Wheel of Fortune card. To fail with the hand of cards that Iris has been dealt would require considerable effort! While Iris is likely to be successful in whatever field she chooses for her career, her name makes her especially suited for areas such as journalism or politics. Nobody will begrudge Iris her success; it is the result of much hard work, and the final Samech suggests that she is happy to offer a leg up or a helping hand to any struggling new talent. In fact, Iris quite enjoys the role of talent scout.

The Runic Interpretation
ᛋᛁᚱᛁ (Sowelu, Isa, Raido, Isa)

Always watchful, Iris has the double Isa energy of standstill in her name. Iris sets her goals and records her progress, and the Raido energy of her name allows her to engage in fascinating communications along the way. Iris will learn to interact with people from all walks of life easily, since she is comfortable with who she is. She enjoys the process of her day-to-day existence and uses Isa energy to guard her time wisely. Over the years, she is escorted into the Sowelu realm of wholeness and can teach others how to achieve the peace she has earned.

Elements: Air, earth, water, earth

The Numerological Interpretation
Iris (NV = 1, CV = 1, VV = 9, FL = 9)

Like the flower that bears her name, Iris stands very erect and then blooms. This name is dominated by the numbers one and nine. The strong qualities of leadership, courage, fortitude, initiative, and drive are all associated with the number one. Iris is very much her own person and is keen to use her pioneering spirit to demonstrate her talents and abilities. But she is not really egocentric; the number nine sees to that. At heart, Iris is a charitable and humanitarian soul, a woman who will not hesitate to make many personal sacrifices when it comes to being of service.

DERIVATION: Greek, from the word meaning "rainbow." The name of a minor goddess who served as a messenger to the gods, as well as the name of a common flower. Started being used as a first name at the turn of the twentieth century.

PRINCIPAL COLORS: Orange, golden russet, the full gamut of yellows and golds

GEMSTONES AND PRECIOUS METALS: Yellow diamonds, amber, topaz

BOTANICALS: Borage, sorrel, lavender

UNIQUE SPELLINGS: Eiris, Eirys, Eyris, Irys

RELATED TO: Irisa, Risa

Irma

DERIVATION: German, pet form of names such as Irmgarde and Irmtraud. From the Old German *irmin*, meaning "entire." Used in the English-speaking world since the end of the nineteenth century.

PRINCIPAL COLORS: The palest shades of any color

GEMSTONES AND PRECIOUS METALS: Diamonds, silver

BOTANICALS: Hazel, parsley, mushrooms

UNIQUE SPELLINGS: Erma, Ermah, Ermma, Ermmah, Irmah, Irmma, Irmmah

RELATED TO: Irmgard, Irmgarde, Irmina, Irmine, Irmtraud

A KABBALISTIC SYNOPSIS
ירמא —YRMA (Yod, Resh, Mem, Aleph)

Work and career are all very well, but in Irma's world they are simply a backdrop to the real issue of life: relationships. Irma is a loving person and is quite sexual by nature. Her name reduces to eight, and strongly suggests that Irma will usually find her mate, and be able to extract from him all that she wants and needs. Irma is actively searching for Mr. Right but certainly intends to enjoy kissing the frogs along the way. While she may be seen as outrageous by some, Irma is a popular woman. She has a quick wit and will have a hilarious one-liner ready at just the right moment. Irma will always make sure she is gainfully employed and, when in the workplace, can push herself really hard.

THE RUNIC INTERPRETATION
ᚨᛗᚱᛁ (Ansuz, Mannaz, Raido, Isa)

Irma uses the Isa energy of standstill intermittently throughout her life when she needs to kick off her shoes and rest. The Mannaz energy of the self requires that Irma cultivate a thoughtful nature. Irma would agree with the adage that the unexamined life is not worth living. She can benefit by keeping a journal and learning the art of breathing and meditation. This boosts her creative vision. The Ansuz energy of signals makes Irma creative. Irma uses the Raido energy of journey to explore her world as well as her inner sanctum of emotions, which are inspired by love and nothing less. Irma sees the world with the eyes of an artist.

Elements: Air, air, water, earth

THE NUMEROLOGICAL INTERPRETATION
Irma (NV = 5, CV = 4, VV = 1, FL = 9)

This is a name that gives a woman a firm foundation of self-assurance upon which to base her life. Irma stands on solid ground. It is because of her sense of inner purpose that she can move outward from her center without losing herself. Irma has a need for exploration and adventure, yet she must always come back to home base. You can imagine Irma like a daisy: All the individual petals radiate outward, but they also remain attached to the flower's round core at its center.

Irv

A KABBALISTIC SYNOPSIS
יִרוּ —YRV (Yod, Resh, Vau)

Irv is the consummate professional: always technically up-to-date, excellent with clients, and a good manager as well. Needless to say, Irv will have a good career and is likely to breeze from promotion to promotion. Success can be very seductive, and as emotions do not figure strongly in his name, Irv needs to ensure that he leaves time for his family and also for his own outside interests. If Irv follows his excellent instincts, as indicated by the tarot associations of the final V, or Vau, he has every chance of getting to the very pinnacle of his profession. With his boundless enthusiasm and vision, Irv will be a good choice for any business looking for someone to lead them into the next century.

THE RUNIC INTERPRETATION
ᚠᚱᛁ (Fehu, Raido, Isa)

Irv has Fehu, the rune for possessions, in his name. Irv will always have money. But with the Isa rune for standstill, the problem is Irv will *always* have money. Get it? In other words, he tends to be a tightwad. Irv has the Raido rune for journey—but all that means, in his case, is that he travels on foot a lot to save bus fare! We all have our weaknesses, and actually Irv has many talents as well. Irv could be a fiscal analyst with a radio program or syndicated newspaper column all his own. Raido affords Irv the considerable ability to communicate effectively. Irv is intelligent and thinks in terms of concepts. He can teach or consult as a corporate adviser. He conveys large ideas with an economy of words.

Elements: Fire, water, earth

THE NUMEROLOGICAL INTERPRETATION
Irv (NV = 4, CV = 4, VV = 9, FL = 9)

The presence of only fours and nines in this name tells us something special about Irv. This is a man known to be very work oriented. He has a distinct tendency to be rather conservative, both politically and in his personal appearance. Irv does not like to show off. He is a quiet and honest man who prefers the simple pleasures in life and is not particularly spontaneous about showing affection: This is the energy of the fours at work. The nines add another dimension to his life. Their influence is revealed by Irv's spiritual nature, specifically his humanitarian gestures and his kind and generous character.

DERIVATION: English and Scottish, pet form of Irving, which is from Old English roots meaning "sea friend."

PRINCIPAL COLORS: Any medium-toned color

GEMSTONES AND PRECIOUS METALS: Sapphires

BOTANICALS: Sage, wild spinach, Iceland moss

UNIQUE SPELLINGS: Earv, Earve, Erv, Irve

RELATED TO: Earvin, Earving, Irvin, Irvine, Irving†

DERIVATION: English and Scottish, originally a Scottish surname and place-name, from Old English roots meaning "sea friend." Commonly used as a first name since the mid-nineteenth century.

PRINCIPAL COLORS: Any yellow or green hue, bright gold

GEMSTONES AND PRECIOUS METALS: Pearls, moss agate, any cream-colored stone

BOTANICALS: Blackberry, elder, grapes

UNIQUE SPELLINGS: Earving, Earvyng, Erving, Ervyng, Irvyng

RELATED TO: Earvin, Erv, Irvt, Irvin, Irvine

Irving

A KABBALISTIC SYNOPSIS
ירוינג —YRVYNG (Yod, Resh, Vau, Yod, Nun, Gimel)

Although he begins with all the good prospects of Irv, it is unlikely that Irving will reach the upper echelons of his chosen career. This does not, of course, mean that he won't be as happy or even happier than Irv; the presence of Nun in Irving's name shows that Irving is just as focused on his family's happiness and well-being as on his career. Irving is the sort of guy who will leave the office early on Friday to take his family off for the weekend and enjoy some of the money he has been earning. Irving's name has strong associations with the moon, which makes him particularly prone to stress. Given the pressurized nature of his work, it is essential for his health that Irving know when to relax, and for him a trip is an ideal way to achieve this.

THE RUNIC INTERPRETATION
ᛜᛁᚠᚱᛁ (Inguz, Isa, Fehu, Raido, Isa)

Irving has a lot in common with the frugal Irv—with an important difference. The double Isa rune for standstill, combined with the Inguz rune for fertility, suggests that Irving enjoys long periods of gestation. His ideas come slowly, but when they arrive, look out, world! Irving is a gifted musician, and he has the talent to amass a fortune. He will have a following around the world. His creative endeavors permit him the luxury of travel, as indicated by the Raido rune. If Irving is not living up to the potential of his name, this could also mean that Irving journeys simply to collect things off the curb so he can stuff his apartment with other people's junk. Irving's likely to produce a big family, but he will have to be careful not to treat them like objects.

Elements: Water, earth, fire, water, earth

THE NUMEROLOGICAL INTERPRETATION
Irving (NV = 7, CV = 7, VV = 9, FL = 9)

The presence of two sevens and two nines tells us much about the energy contained within Irving's name. This is a man who may not be particularly talkative. Irving's mode of communication is much more internal. He is a very analytical man who takes life seriously, will enjoy periods of solitude, and may find it necessary to get away from the world once in a while. Irving's temperament is both introspective and philosophical. The sevens make Irving a contemplative person. His nines bestow a sincere caring about the ills of the world and an urge to make a contribution toward the betterment of humanity.

Isaac

A Kabbalistic Synopsis
יסעכ —YSA'AK (Yod, Samech, Ayin, Kaph)

The story of Isaac in the Bible is that he was offered as a sacrifice to Abraham's God. As with all biblical names, Isaac has a meaning that is relevant to the story in which he plays a part. In the letter Ayin we even see a hidden association with the goat, which was ultimately substituted for Isaac! As we might expect, Isaac is an altruistic man always willing to do a favor for someone—even if it is going to make his own life more difficult. While this is an admirable trait, Isaac needs to avoid being exploited by others who will be promoted on the back of his hard work. At home Isaac is a sensitive and supportive husband. He can combine this sensitivity with an energetic manner, which allows him to pull his weight around the house and, once the chores are over, in the bedroom!

The Runic Interpretation
ᚲᚨᚨᛋᛁ (Kano, Ansuz, Ansuz, Sowelu, Isa)

Isaac is signified by the double Ansuz rune for signals. While the runes in this name, through the energies of Kano (for opening) and Isa (for standstill) make his a hopeful name, Isaac may well be one of those brooding, melancholy types who see the world in sepia tones. Isaac may feel thwarted by a lack of friends and heavy family responsibilities; during these blue periods he can avail himself of the sun's energy in Sowelu. The Sowelu rune ensures that Isaac will gain control over his heavy emotions, but he will have to make an effort to take care of himself. The somber life Isaac endures originates in his attitude and his belief system. Isaac can turn his attitude around with prayer and the support of good counselors. The Kano rune says Isaac will experience a leap of faith and know gratitude and joy at long last.

Elements: Water, air, air, air, earth

The Numerological Interpretation
Isaac (NV = 6, CV = 4, VV = 11, FL = 9)

With a name containing profound numerological significance, Isaac will have keen insight into the deeper nature of humanity. This is a very kind, gentle, and loving man, one who gives freely of himself to others. Isaac has a distinct spiritual affinity with life, allowing him to see behind people's masks and into their hearts. He is also hardworking and dedicated to his beliefs. He will find himself very comfortable in the role of adviser or counselor, and make a fine teacher or psychologist. Isaac is also quite home oriented and a devoted family man.

DERIVATION: Hebrew, from the word meaning "laughter." In the Old Testament, the name of the son of Abraham and Sarah. Their son was so named because the elderly Sarah laughed with joy when she heard that, at long last, she would bear a child. Well-known Isaacs have included the scientist Isaac Newton (1642–1727) and the Yiddish writer Isaac Bashevis Singer (1904–1991).

PRINCIPAL COLORS: All shades of azure, except for the brightest blue

GEMSTONES AND PRECIOUS METALS: Emeralds, blue or blue-green turquoise

BOTANICALS: Dog rose, vervain, violets

UNIQUE SPELLINGS: Aizik, Isaak, Isac, Isack, Isak, Isic, Izak, Izik

RELATED TO: Ike, Ikey, Yitzhak, Zach, Zacharyt, Zack

Isabelle

DERIVATION: French form of Isabel, which is the Spanish version of Elizabeth, meaning "oath of God" or "God is perfection." Most common from the late nineteenth century on, and especially popular during the 1950s.

PRINCIPAL COLORS: Pale, grassy to rich, forest green, also white

GEMSTONES AND PRECIOUS METALS: Jade, moonstones

BOTANICALS: Cabbage, lettuce, turnips

UNIQUE SPELLINGS: Isabel, Isabell, Isobel, Isobell, Isobelle, Izabel, Izabell, Izabelle, Izobel, Izobell, Izobelle

RELATED TO: Bel, Bell, Bella, Belle, Bellita, Isa, Isabela, Isabella, Issie, Issy, Izabela, Izabella, Izzie, Izzy

〜

"A nomad I will remain for life, in love with distant and uncharted places."
—ISABELLE EBERHARDT (AUTHOR)

A KABBALISTIC SYNOPSIS

יסאבאל —YSABAL (Yod, Samech, Aleph, Beth, Aleph, Lamed)

Isabelle looks as though butter wouldn't melt in her mouth—but we all know how deceptive looks can be! In the workplace, Isabelle will be the boss, even if that isn't her official position. Her name adds up to five, which, among other things, points to an accepted air of authority, and it is unlikely that Isabelle will have to push very hard to have her dominant position accepted. The value of Isabelle's name is equal to the full spelling of the letter Tzaddi, which demonstrates her tenacious nature. This determined streak will win Isabelle respect both in the workplace and at home. At work and with her family, Isabelle will quickly show that if she is thwarted, she can react quite explosively!

THE RUNIC INTERPRETATION

ᛗᛖᛚᛚᛗᛒᚨᛋᛁ (Ehwaz, Laguz, Laguz, Ehwaz, Berkana, Ansuz, Sowelu, Isa)

Lovely Isabelle will have many different homes and many rich experiences in her life, as shown by the Ehwaz rune for movement. The double Laguz rune indicates considerable artistic talent. Isabelle will feel fairly isolated while she is rearing her large family. To stave off her loneliness, she will seek the companionship of positive friends and return to school or work to keep her mind stimulated and hopeful. The children will benefit by having a mother who is in touch with the world and excited about life. The Ansuz rune hints at Isabelle's intuitive ability. The Sowelu rune of wholeness says Isabelle will have a comfortable and secure existence.

Elements: Air, water, water, air, air/earth, air, air, earth

THE NUMEROLOGICAL INTERPRETATION

Isabelle (NV = 11, CV = 9, VV = 2, FL = 9)

This is a woman who must do something out of the ordinary with her life. Isabelle is a name that confers the urge to move out into the larger society and create networks of communication between herself and others. She has the potential to be highly intuitive, and will work very devotedly to make people aware of the more subtle aspects of life that unite rather than separate us. Isabelle is a peacemaker who works for the common good. However, she must take care not to get so involved with her ideals that she loses her practical footing.

〜

Israel

A Kabbalistic Synopsis
יסראיל —YSRAYL (Yod, Samech, Resh, Aleph, Yod, Lamed)

It is unlikely that you will find Israel on the shop floor of a factory; this is not surprising, given that he shares his name with the nation of Judaism. Israel is a born leader. His ability to handle authority is emphasized by the fact that his name reduces to the value of the Hierophant or High Priest card in the tarot. As a manager, Israel could be described as firm but fair. He is happy to expend vast amounts of energy on employees who are prepared to work hard. By the same token, the final Lamed indicates Israel's willingness to be a stern taskmaster with those who fail to put in the requisite effort. While this is a fine approach at work, there is a danger that Israel will take his disciplinarian attitudes home with him. On the positive side, Israel will always encourage his children to strive for excellence in their work and their interests.

The Runic Interpretation
ᛚᛗᚨᚱᛋᛁ (Laguz, Ehwaz, Ansuz, Raido, Sowelu, Isa)

Flow, movement, signals, journey, wholeness, and standstill exemplify the name Israel. Israel is a spiritual being. He will emerge from a time of doubt to realize that the seed of his new self is delicately sheathed in the casings of his former self, and he will find a career in which he can express his true nature. Who he really is has been there all along! This is a revelation for Israel and helps him become whole at last. The Ehwaz rune hints that Israel will have a chance to own property in different countries and travel extensively to study and learn about foreign cultures.

Elements: Water, air, air, water, air, earth

The Numerological Interpretation
Israel (NV = 1, CV = 4, VV = 6, FL = 9)

A distinct sense of personal identity characterizes this name. Israel is a very devoted man, a person keenly aware of other people's suffering. He is a leader by nature and is not afraid to put forth ideas and concepts that, because of their very originality, may meet with some resistance from others. Highly creative and dedicated to making a success out of his life, Israel has no problem extending his workdays beyond normal limits in order to accomplish his goals.

DERIVATION: Biblical, from the Hebrew word meaning "wrestling with the Lord." In the Old Testament, this was the name given to Jacob after he had wrestled with an angel. Jacob's descendants were called the children of Israel, from which came the name given to the Jewish state founded in 1948. Especially popular as a Puritan name.

PRINCIPAL COLORS: Gold, bronze, orange, brown, pale to brilliant yellow

GEMSTONES AND PRECIOUS METALS: Citrine, topaz

BOTANICALS: Borage, chamomile, eyebright

UNIQUE SPELLINGS: Israell, Izrael, Izraell

RELATED TO: Iser, Issur, Issy, Jacobt, Yisrael

DERIVATION: Russian version of John, which comes from the Hebrew word meaning "God is gracious." Started to be used in the English-speaking world in the twentieth century.

PRINCIPAL COLORS: The complete range of yellow and gold hues, golden brown

GEMSTONES AND PRECIOUS METALS: Amber and yellow diamonds

BOTANICALS: Sorrel, thyme, lavender

UNIQUE SPELLINGS: Ivann, Iven, Ivin, Ivinn, Ivyn

RELATED TO: Evan†, Ian†, Jack†, Johann, John†, Juan†, Sean†, Shawn†, Vanek, Zane

Ivan

A KABBALISTIC SYNOPSIS
יואן —YVAN (Yod, Vau, Aleph, Nun)

Ivan is a dreamer first and foremost, and despite the energy created by the initial Yod, Ivan has little desire for any sort of career. He can often appear somewhat listless, but this is simply because all the frenzied emotional activity going on inside his mind is invisible. Above all, Ivan is searching for some form of emotional home and a sense of community. He is uncomfortable being the dominant one in any relationship, and is looking for a partner with a strong and possibly authoritarian personality. Nostalgia plays a big part in Ivan's life, and he has a tendency to romanticize his childhood, primarily his parents' relationship. In certain cases, particularly if Ivan is born under Cancer, this can lead to an impossible desire to re-create a mythical past with his own partner.

THE RUNIC INTERPRETATION
ᚾᚨᚠᛁ (Nauthiz, Ansuz, Fehu, Isa)

Ivan's inventive mind might be misdirected, but there's always hope. Ivan uses his runic powers of constraint, signals, possessions, and standstill for either positive or negative results in life. Parents may call him Ivan the Terrible. In fact, he's a naughty kid; teachers are always giving him "time-out" in a corner of the classroom. Ivan likes to grab pencils and take things from his teacher's desk. When the milk money is missing, a sulking Ivan digs deep in his pocket to fork it over. As an adult, Ivan usually learns to restrain his impulses. If Ivan fails to get his act together, however, the standstill lesson of the runes in his name can be learned in a maximum security time-out. However, Ivan can also be a good listener, and because of hardships he will endure, he may become very good at managing money or possessions.

Elements: Fire, air, fire, earth

THE NUMEROLOGICAL INTERPRETATION
Ivan (NV = 1, CV = 9, VV = 1, FL = 9)

Ivan is an adventurous person, ready to express himself in a most distinct manner. He is not afraid to create new paths, either for himself or for others to follow. In fact, Ivan enjoys the challenge of his own spontaneity. The nines in his name give Ivan the gift of a humanitarian viewpoint. He therefore acts not just for his own personal success; rather, his goals are connected to some larger issue that will benefit many.

Jack

A Kabbalistic Synopsis
יאכ —YAK (Yod, Aleph, Kaph)

Jack's name adds up to thirty-one, the same total as one of the mystical names of God. Although Jack is not particularly religious, he is possessed by an intense fervor. It is politics that draws Jack in. He firmly believes that even in an age of multinational corporations, the right political leadership can still change the world for the better. In purely personal terms this makes Jack an optimistic man, and he can be highly motivating as a friend or, for that matter, as a father. When those he cares for feel that they have been beaten by some challenge, Jack has the capacity to get them to climb back on the horse so that they speak up and give it another go. The combination of the Yod and Aleph mark Jack out as an individualist; it is unlikely that he will simply follow one of the existing main parties. Far more likely—given Jack's nature—is that he will construct his own political viewpoint and theories. Jack is consequently likely to be drawn to fringe activist groups where he has a chance of seeing his own ideas adopted. This may not be directly political, but could be some unusual or off-the-wall hobby that he enjoys. Jack is always an interesting, if lively, addition to any party!

The Runic Interpretation
ᚲᚲᚨᛃ (Kano, Kano, Ansuz, Jera)

Jack is an artist in any arena of life. He could own his own advertising agency and exhibit his paintings in a local gallery. Or he could be a brilliant healer. Jack may feel melancholy at times, which often accompanies the creative personality. But when he is positive and productive, he can lift the spirits of those around him on a profound level. Jack is a good friend and a fierce opponent. He will risk everything, including his very life if necessary, for a cause he upholds. He is generous to a fault and must learn to pace his activities; the double Kano gives Jack these characteristics. A period of rest allows him to revitalize his creativity.

Elements: Water, water, air, earth

The Numerological Interpretation
Jack (NV = 7, CV = 6, VV = 1, FL = 1)

Jack is constantly striving for self-improvement. He is also somewhat of an idealist, and it is very important for him to manifest his beliefs through his work and personal relationships. Sometimes Jack can go to extremes, and he must take care that his own convictions do not blind him to other people's opinions. The danger here is that such behavior will lead Jack to becoming too exclusive and judgmental. Jack appreciates intelligence and depth, for he is definitely not a superficial person. Jack needs a partner who will both support and challenge him in his urge to achieve his personal best.

DERIVATION: English, a pet form of John that has now become an independent name. First used during the Middle Ages, and started appearing as a given name during the mid-nineteenth century.

PRINCIPAL COLORS: Maroon, pink, deep, rich shades of red

GEMSTONES AND PRECIOUS METALS: Bloodstones, deep red rubies

BOTANICALS: Nettle, garlic, onion

UNIQUE SPELLINGS: Jac, Jak

RELATED TO: Iant, Ivant, Jackiet, Jackson, Jacques, Jant, Janek, Jock, Johan, Johnt, Juant, Seant, Shawnt

"I would rather be ashes than dust! I would rather that my spark should burn out in a brilliant blaze than it should be stifled by dry-rot. I would rather be a superb meteor, every atom of me in magnificent glow, than a sleepy and permanent planet. The proper function of man is to live, not to exist. I shall not waste my days in trying to prolong them. I shall use my time."

—JACK LONDON (AUTHOR)

DERIVATION: Diminutive form of
Jacqueline or Jaclyn, which are of
French origin. Started to be used
as an independent name in the
twentieth century.

PRINCIPAL COLORS: All shades of
purple, from pale, bluish violet to
deep maroon

GEMSTONES AND PRECIOUS
METALS: Garnets, amethyst

BOTANICALS: Apple, bilberry,
lungwort, pineapple

UNIQUE SPELLINGS: Jackee,
Jackey, Jacki, Jacky, Jacquee,
Jacquey, Jacqui, Jacquie

RELATED TO: Jacklyn, Jaclyn,
Jacquelina, Jacquelinet,
Jacquelyn, Jacquetta

Jackie

A KABBALISTIC SYNOPSIS
יאכי —YAKY (Yod, Aleph, Kaph, Yod)

While the value of her name associates her with the tarot's Hierophant, Jackie has far more in common with the Empress when one analyses the gematria of her name. The Hierophant usually refers to very authoritative and potentially strict people, while the Empress relates to abundance and fortune, along with feelings usually regarded as maternal. Jackie wants it all: the career, the marriage, the children, and a nice, comfortable lifestyle. Thanks to the double influence of Y, or Yod, she has every chance of achieving all these aims. Out of all the items on her wish list, Jackie most wants to have children, and it is likely that she will have at least three. Jackie is a very attractive woman and has a definite aura of raw passion, which attracts men in the way that a lightbulb attracts moths. Jackie will be very careful to select the right guy, particularly in terms of having children, which she sees as part of her spiritual link to the divine. The Hierophant card can be seen as referring to Jackie's concern for the next generation; she wants to ensure that they are brought up and educated in the correct manner.

THE RUNIC INTERPRETATION
ᛗᛁᚲᚲᚨᛜ (Ehwaz, Isa, Kano, Kano, Ansuz, Jera)

Jackie is always well put together and well coiffed. She has a taste for the glamorous in everything—clothes, cars, people—both for her own enjoyment and for the effect they have on others. Jackie tends to be crafty, sometimes even deceitful, and has a real mischievous streak. But she is always charming and adaptable. Jackie can go with the flow and knows where it's going.

Elements: Air, earth, water, water, air, earth

THE NUMEROLOGICAL INTERPRETATION
Jackie (NV = 3, CV = 6, VV = 6, FL = 1)

People are very attracted to Jackies, as this is a name that bestows a lively intelligence and a compassionate nature. Women with this name are very much at ease with others. They always have something good to say and tend to see the positive side to life. Sometimes people named Jackie are too empathetic, not knowing where their feelings end and other people's begin. This may lead to complications in personal relationships, as the boundaries of individual emotional responsibilities may be obscured. Jackie is an artist at heart, and enjoys expressing her many talents through music, painting, and writing.

Jacob

DERIVATION: English and Dutch form of the Hebrew name Yaakov.

PRINCIPAL COLORS: Electric colors

GEMSTONES AND PRECIOUS METALS: The palest to the richest of sapphires

BOTANICALS: Celandine, medlar, wintergreen

UNIQUE SPELLINGS: Jacub, Jakob, Jakub

RELATED TO: Cob, Cobb, Cobby, Giacobo, Giacomo, Giacopo, Hamish, Iacopo, Iacovo, Iago, Iakob, Iakobos, Iakov, Jaco, Jacobo, Jackt, Jacko, Jacky, Jacques, Jacquet, Jago, Jaimet, Jaket, Jakie, Jakov, Jamest, Jamesie, Jamey, Jamiet, Jamsey, Jayt, Jayme, Jimt, Jimmie, Seamus, Shamus, Yakov

A KABBALISTIC SYNOPSIS
יאכעב —YAKA'AB (Yod, Aleph, Kaph, Ayin, Beth)

If at all possible, Jacob will arrange his career so that he can work from home. The final B, or Beth, in his name indicates a strong bond with the family, while the value of his name suggests an urge to be there for his immediate relatives. It is not that Jacob is paranoid about the things that could happen to his family in his absence; rather, he very much enjoys the feeling of being a protective figure for them. Jacob has an excellent eye for detail and a knack for working with his hands, so a career in design might suit him. Jacob's name adds up to four, the number of the elements, which also represents material concerns. It is very likely that Jacob will provide his family not only with strong emotional support but with exceptional financial support as well.

THE RUNIC INTERPRETATION
ᛒᛟᚲᚨᛃ (Berkana, Othila, Kano, Ansuz, Jera)

Jacob will break with the past as a young man in his twenties. He will realize that he needs to follow his dream. A few years later he can return to his family with his new identity and direction firmly rooted. The family will need to readjust because they will be meeting the real Jacob for the first time. Jacob follows his intuition and experiences a rebirth, signified by the Berkana rune, on many levels. As his heart opens, he is able to accept family and friends and look for the best he can find in them. When Jacob's need for approval is finally laid to rest, he enjoys the harvesttime, signified by the Jera rune. Jacob's lessons are of the highest order.

Elements: Air/earth, earth/fire, water, air, earth

THE NUMEROLOGICAL INTERPRETATION
Jacob (NV = 4, CV = 6, VV = 7, FL = 1)

A man dedicated to his home and career, Jacob is faithful and determined. His parents will be a strong influence on him, and he is very loyal to all of his loved ones. This name indicates a man who is practical, as money and financial stability are very important to him. Jacob is not a lazy man, and he will do what is necessary to increase his economic status and material security. Quiet, thoughtful, sensitive, and reserved, Jacob has an inner strength that is admired by those who know him. However, Jacob may not be the most optimistic of people, and this trait is complicated by his imagination, which is very strong. He can conceive of the worst and may have to learn to worry less and relax more.

PRINCIPAL COLORS: The complete spectrum of yellow and green hues

GEMSTONES AND PRECIOUS METALS. Cat's-eye, cream-colored pearls, white stones

BOTANICALS: Elder, hops, linseed

UNIQUE SPELLINGS: Jacklin, Jacklyn, Jaclyn, Jaclynne, Jacquelin, Jacquelyn, Jacquelyne, Jacquelynne, Jacquilen, Jacquiline, Jacquilyn, Jaquelin, Jaqueline, Jaquelyn

RELATED TO: Jacki, Jackiet, Jacoline, Jacqui, Jaquetta

Jacqueline

A KABBALISTIC SYNOPSIS

יאכולין —YAKVLYN (Yod, Aleph, Kaph, Vau, Lamed, Yod, Nun)

When looking at any name, one usually finds a combination of positive and negative factors in the analysis. However, in Jacqueline's case there are only positive factors. Jacqueline's name adds to 777, a number with a whole variety of occult functions and meanings. In terms of name analysis, we can note that this name's value is made up entirely of symbols of success. From this we can tell that in love and money, home and career, Jacqueline can expect to have great triumphs. Whatever Jacqueline happens to be doing, she does it with a sense of urgency. As a result, she always meets her deadlines and seems to be ahead of herself at work and at home.

THE RUNIC INTERPRETATION

ᛗᚾᛁᛚᛛᚲᚱᛜ (Ehwaz, Nauthiz, Isa, Laguz, Uruz, Kano, Kano, Ansuz, Jera)

The double Ansuz rune for signals refers to Jacqueline's strong intuition. Ansuz, combined with the Nauthiz rune of constraint, affords Jacqueline a creative disposition, marked by bouts of melancholy that cycle into joy and an outpouring of sensitive artistic expression; this pattern is signified by the Jera rune for harvest, or cycles. Given a brilliant agent and a financial platform, Jacqueline can do what she enjoys her whole life. Jacqueline needs a lot of exercise, and positive friends around to cushion her moments of self-doubt.

Elements: Air, fire, earth, water, earth, water, water, air, earth

THE NUMEROLOGICAL INTERPRETATION

Jacqueline (NV = 7, CV = 2, VV = 5, FL = 1)

Jacqueline is a woman whose depth of character and inner strength radiate into the world around her. Her name gives her true talent for many kinds of creative expressions. She has a natural inclination toward philosophy and literature, poetry and art. Jacqueline is endowed with a profound sense of fair play and a sensitivity to other people's needs. This allows her to establish conditions of cooperation between people, and she promotes those plans and projects that can be of mutual benefit to all. Her basic life challenge is a penchant for too much idealism. She sometimes overestimates other people's capabilities, then becomes disappointed when they fall short of her expectations.

Jaime

A KABBALISTIC SYNOPSIS
יאים —YAYM (Yod, Aleph, Yod, Mem)

Jaime's routine revolves around his love life, which is likely to be as busy as Times Square—and may potentially involve as many people as tourists that visit there. In the case of a female Jaime, she is likely to be an incorrigible flirt and enjoy the attentions of a whole range of admirers. Luckily Jaime has considerable energy, which enables him (or her) to cope with the rigors of being a party animal while holding down a reasonably challenging job. However, it is unlikely that Jaime will ever achieve his maximum career potential, as his mind has a tendency to wander to his next romantic engagement. If Jaime is a woman, the tendency to daydream may have more to do with future plans for her career or her general direction in life than with purely romantic scenarios. There is a definite downside to Jaime's approach to relationships: Despite a genuine desire to find real and lasting emotional fulfillment, Jaime will never get there until he alters his fickle, short-term treatment of his partners. Jaime the woman does not really have this problem, as she will give the impression of any genuine interest only to those who sincerely interest her. In their leisure time, both genders of Jaimes enjoy sports, whether spectators or participants.

THE RUNIC INTERPRETATION
ᛗᛗᛁᚨ◇ (Ehwaz, Mannaz, Isa, Ansuz, Jera)

Jaime is impressionable, and con artists spot Jaime from the air. The fact that Jaime has all sorts of kitchen gadgets—none of them useful—should warn her against gullibility. Luckily for Jaime, the Ansuz rune gives her the insight to stop negative habits. The Mannaz rune says Jaime will become the helmsman of the soul. Finally, the Jera rune for harvest promises that Jaime will enjoy a rich and prosperous life. But this can happen only when Jaime's big, trusting eyes take on a faint squint of skepticism. Males named Jaime will have similar experiences.

Elements: Air, air, earth, air, earth

THE NUMEROLOGICAL INTERPRETATION
Jaime (NV = 11, CV = 5, VV = 6, FL = 1)

The numbers in this name reveal a person with a considerably developed intuition. Jaime is a man or woman with a big heart and a generous disposition. His or her view of life extends beyond the immediacy of personal desires and physical needs. This is a person with a spiritual outlook on life that is integrated into all of their relationships. This spirituality is not constrained within the doctrines of any one religion or belief system. Jaime respects all faiths and the cultures that birthed them. Jaime needs a partner who can share this humanitarian orientation and who is willing to work as a team toward the betterment of society.

DERIVATION: Spanish version of James. Used in Spanish-speaking countries as a name for males. In English-speaking countries, particularly Canada, it is a common way to spell the female name Jamie.

PRINCIPAL COLORS: The complete gamut of green hues, creamy white

GEMSTONES AND PRECIOUS METALS: Jade, moonstones, moss agate

BOTANICALS: Chicory, lettuce, moonwort

UNIQUE SPELLINGS: Jaimee, Jaimey, Jaimi, Jamee, Jami, Jamie, Jayme, Jaymee, Jaymi

RELATED TO: James†, Jim†, Jimmy; Jamesina, Jamila

Jake

DERIVATION: English, variant of Jack and Jacob. Sometimes used as a nickname for Jacob, but has become increasingly common as an independent name in recent years.

PRINCIPAL COLORS: The full spectrum of reds, from light pink to deep crimson

GEMSTONES AND PRECIOUS METALS: Bloodstones, garnets

BOTANICALS: Broom, garlic, nettle

UNIQUE SPELLINGS: Jaike, Jayke

RELATED TO: Jack†, Jackson, Jacob†, Jacques, Jakie, Jakob, Jay†

A KABBALISTIC SYNOPSIS
יאיכ —YAYK (Yod, Aleph, Yod, Kaph)

The bright lights and bustle of city life are not for Jake; he is much happier in a little wooden house in the country. If he does live in town, he will want a decidedly quiet part of the city and will ensure that his apartment is full of references to greener environments—even if he has to make do with a window box and a goldfish! Jake has a yearning for power and position, but finds the harsh and cutthroat world of big business deeply unattractive. Consequently, if he can make it happen, Jake would rather be a big fish in a small pond than run the risk of drowning without trace in the major leagues of business. Jake certainly has the courage to make the leap into a small, backwoods community, and once there, he has a number of practical skills that will be most useful to a small and self-sufficient town. An urban Jake will still get involved in community action groups of some kind. In his family life Jake has to be in charge, but he has a calm manner about him and is not at all oppressive in his leadership of the family.

THE RUNIC INTERPRETATION
ᛖᚲᚨᛇ (Ehwaz, Kano, Ansuz, Jera)

Running, fumbling, always late, Jake has the Ehwaz energy for movement. It's lucky he's fast, because he spends his life beating the clock. But at some point the Kano energy of opening will come to his rescue; maybe Jake will take a time management seminar. Afterward he's prompt more of the time, and when he's not, Jake vows to do better—and does. Jake is more organized and relaxed now, and he has the time to arrive early once in a while and soak up some inspiration. Jera, the harvest rune, ensures that Jake is doing okay.

Elements: Air, water, air, earth

THE NUMEROLOGICAL INTERPRETATION
Jake (NV = 9, CV = 3, VV = 6, FL = 1)

A sympathetic man who has a pronounced sense of honesty and goodwill, Jake can be an inspiration to his friends and loved ones. This is a name that brings out the peacemaker. Jake is therefore very adept at mediating disputes, as he can dig deep into any conflict and find the points of resolution. This is a man who understands others with a greater depth than he is understood with. Jake is always in search of helpful information that he can share with his friends and associates. He enjoys creating situations that allow people to interconnect their mutual talents and abilities. Professionally, Jake will also do well as a teacher, counselor, or community service worker.

James

DERIVATION: Latin, alternate form of the Hebrew name Jacob, meaning "one who takes by the heel." Became very popular after James Stuart became king of England in 1603, and has since been extremely common in all English-speaking countries.

PRINCIPAL COLORS: All shades of violet, from light purple to deep maroon

GEMSTONES AND PRECIOUS METALS: Garnets, amethyst

BOTANICALS: Apple, cherry, dandelion, strawberry

UNIQUE SPELLINGS: Jaimes, Jamez, Jaymes

RELATED TO: Jacob†, Jacques, Jaimet, Jamell, Jameson, Jamie†, Jim†, Jimmy

A KABBALISTIC SYNOPSIS
יאימס —YAYMS (Yod, Aleph, Yod, Mem, Samech)

The guy still making appointments with his career adviser at the age of thirty could very easily be James. Despite having the capacity for long hours of work along with a good head on his shoulders, James will not commit to a specific career path until very late in life. There is a real danger that if James fails to cut his ties with his parents in any meaningful sense, he may well still be living at home at thirty, which will seriously hamper his attempts at self-definition or independence. Ultimately James will come to a decision about the direction he should be taking in life and catch up with his peers. However, in the case of a Piscean or Cancerian James, it may take a push from a close friend or relative.

THE RUNIC INTERPRETATION
ᛋᛖᛗᚨᛇ (Sowelu, Ehwaz, Mannaz, Ansuz, Jera)

Always ambitious, James is drawn to items that reflect material wealth and status, although he may not feel inclined to work toward them. James comes a long way as he matures. The Sowelu rune of wholeness takes him to a high level of responsibility, and the Mannaz rune for self teaches James to stop blaming others for the weakness residing within himself. Ansuz, the energy of signals, provides a sense of intuition for James. He begins to understand that the outer world is but a reflection of the inner. James can enjoy a career in business or finance because he has good common sense and a strong analytical mind. The harvest rune, Jera, assures James of success on every level.

Elements: Air, air, air, air, earth

"Know from whence you came. If you know whence you came, there are absolutely no limitations to where you can go."
—JAMES BALDWIN (AUTHOR)

THE NUMEROLOGICAL INTERPRETATION
James (NV = 3, CV = 6, VV = 6, FL = 1)

Creativity is central to James's life. Even if he is not an artist by profession, he is one by temperament. He must be surrounded by beauty, as he has a highly developed sense of aesthetics. James is fair in all of his relationships and is a born diplomat. Although he is fundamentally a peace-loving individual, he is not responsible for his friends' happiness. In this respect, James should take care not to shoulder burdens that other people may have to carry themselves. James will want a committed and emotionally supportive personal relationship. He is much more geared toward faithfulness and loyalty in partnership, and seeks the same in the choice of his loved one.

DERIVATION: Scottish, a diminutive
of James. Since the 1960s,
has often been used as an
independent female name as well.

PRINCIPAL COLORS: The full
range of greens, from pale to
deep, rich shades, also cream

GEMSTONES AND PRECIOUS
METALS: Jade, moonstones,
pearls

BOTANICALS: Plantain, moonwort,
colewort

UNIQUE SPELLINGS: Jaimet,
Jaimey, Jamee, Jayme, Jaymee,
Jaymie

RELATED TO: Jamest, Jameson,
Jimt, Jimmy; Jamela, Jamesina,
Jamille

Jamie

A KABBALISTIC SYNOPSIS
יאימי —YAYMY (Yod, Aleph, Yod, Mem, Yod)

With the fiery energy of Yod in every second letter, Jamies are like human fireballs: Once they start, there is no stopping them. Not only is Jamie filled to the brim with enthusiastic dynamism, this name reduces to eight, indicating a forceful and resilient personality. You have as much chance of slowing down a runaway train as you do of stopping Jamie. Jamie is as energetic at home as at work, and will keep any partner more than happy despite the long hours he or she is likely to spend in the office. The one thing that Jamie should remember is that eventually all fireworks explode, and everyone needs to remember to take time out to recharge their batteries.

THE RUNIC INTERPRETATION
ᛗᛁᛗᚨᛇ (Ehwaz, Isa, Mannaz, Ansuz, Jera)

Blessing, benefits, and opportunities rain down on Jamie. He has the Jera rune for harvest, and he will most assuredly reap the rewards of his efforts. The Mannaz rune for self gives Jamie a good strong inner beacon of light to direct him in his endeavors. Jamie has a lot of interests and can easily carry out about five projects simultaneously. This would frazzle most mere mortals, but Jamie actually is happy with this work style. Jamie gets bored easily, and he's a bit greedy. He wants to do it *all*. He needs to learn that he can, and that he has the time he needs to complete each project with satisfaction, enjoying the process as much as the product. A female Jamie will share this same high energy and good fortune.

Elements: Air, earth, air, air, earth

THE NUMEROLOGICAL INTERPRETATION
Jamie (NV = 11, CV = 5, VV = 6, FL = 1)

Although people named Jamie are usually very much involved with their spiritual development, they are not necessarily linked to any of the orthodox religions. Theirs is a path that is fundamentally connected to the underlying unifying spirit that is at the core of all belief systems and creeds. Jamie is a name associated with men and women who are extremely sensitive to other people and naturally find themselves in the helping professions. They also work well in those community and social projects in which group cooperation is essential to success. Jamie is ever seeking a path of personal expansion and is never content with a life based on routine. These are people who look for (and find!) the adventurous in life.

Jan

DERIVATION: Scandinavian version of John, pronounced "Yan." Often used as a feminine name, both independently and as a nickname for Janet.

PRINCIPAL COLORS: All varieties of green and yellow hues, gold

GEMSTONES AND PRECIOUS METALS: Cat's-eye, moss agate, any other cream-colored stone

BOTANICALS: Blackberry, juniper, mushrooms

UNIQUE SPELLINGS: Jann, Yan

RELATED TO: Ian†, Ivan†, Johann, John†, Johnny, Jon; Jana, Janet†, Janelle, Janette, Janice†, Janine, Janne

A KABBALISTIC SYNOPSIS

יאן —YAN (Yod, Aleph, Nun)

Jan seems to be something of a contradiction: someone whose name begins with the spark of creativity represented by the letter Y, or Yod, yet a person who keeps to him or herself in the office and has little in the way of a social life. In fact, it is quite common for Jans to live alone all their lives. However, when we realize that the value of this name reduces to nine, things begin to make sense. Nine is the number of the Hermit in the tarot, and symbolizes both wisdom and the search for enlightenment. Jan is a seeker after truth, and it is to this end that all his or her energies are directed. While Jan has every chance of success in his or her quest, Jan will have to overcome self-doubt and anxiety if he or she is to really find the ultimate answer he or she seeks.

THE RUNIC INTERPRETATION

ᚾᚨᛃ (Nauthiz, Ansuz, Jera)

Jan is fortified with the Nauthiz rune of defense, the Ansuz rune of signals, and the Jera rune of harvest. The Nauthiz rune keeps Jan's heart in a strong state of repair, and Jan likes it that way. Cuddles and kisses and promises of enduring love exude from Jan, and many a trusting lover has swooned under Jan's spell. Jan is a heartbreaker. Uncommon finesse and fancy footwork typify Jan's retreat. Jan is so stealthy, many a jilted lover awakens from the enchantment a decade down the road! Still, better to have loved and lost than never to have met Jan at all. . . . Jan leaves his or her lover without bitterness or guile, but with a tender memory inspired by the magic of the Jera rune of harvest at work in Jan's life.

Elements: Fire, air, earth

THE NUMEROLOGICAL INTERPRETATION

Jan (NV = 7, CV = 6, VV = 1, FL = 1)

Jan pays a great deal of attention to the expression of his or her own individual form of creativity. Such a person is very concerned with the development of his or her own talents, and will find ways to distinguish him- or herself from others. Gifted with a keen perception and an active mind, Jan tries to use his or her energy to uplift and educate. Jan is not selfish with what he or she knows, and is not shy about bringing improvements and opportunities to his or her particular area of professional interest. Jan may have to do a bit of work in his or her relationships, as his or her self-interest has to align with his or her partner's needs and wishes in order for a successful union to take place.

Jane

A KABBALISTIC SYNOPSIS
יאין —YAYN (Yod, Aleph, Yod, Nun)

You can spot Jane in any office usually rushing with coffee in one hand, notepad in the other, and pen between her teeth toward her desk and her phone, which never stops ringing! In spite of being one of the busiest people in the office, Jane always finds time to unwind. For such a committed and serious worker, Jane is, unexpectedly, a confirmed flirt. An ideal way for her to relax and relieve her stress is to socialize or joke around with her buddies. At home, Jane loves to be peaceful and sit by the fire, probably while watching an old romantic film.

THE RUNIC INTERPRETATION
ᛖᚾᚨᛃ (Ehwaz, Nauthiz, Ansuz, Jera)

Jane uses the Nauthiz rune of defense to stay healthy. With the signals rune of Ansuz there to guide Jane, she has keen insight into healing and self-defense. The Ehwaz rune of movement takes Jane on the road, and she may lecture and write books. The Jera rune of joy indicates that Jan is a success at staying fit and happy, and people respect and appreciate her opinions far and wide.

Elements: Air, fire, air, earth

THE NUMEROLOGICAL INTERPRETATION
Jane (NV = 3, CV = 6, VV = 6, FL = 1)

Kindness and understanding characterize the name Jane. This is a woman who takes other people's problems to heart. She is genuinely concerned about their welfare and will do everything she can to alleviate discomfort and pain. Jane wants to bring harmony and peace into her surroundings, the most important of which is her home. She is decidedly oriented toward a long-lasting relationship, and makes a very dedicated partner and parent. In addition, she has a very active mind, and will always be found with a good book close at hand.

Janet

A KABBALISTIC SYNOPSIS
יאנאם —YANAT (Yod, Aleph, Nun, Aleph, Teth)

Watch out for Janet. If you work with her—if you're simply a friend, you are safe!—Janet is going to make it to the top and doesn't really mind how she gets there. Her motto could be Malcolm X's: "by any means necessary." The influence of Scorpio ensures that no one will know the details of her current career strategy. Janet is not averse to floating a few red herrings just to make sure that nobody knows what her plans are. The final Teth indicates that anyone who does challenge her will be dealt with swiftly and ruthlessly. Her friends are another matter entirely; Janet will stick by them whatever the situation, and is more than happy to use her skills to protect them or simply to sit down and have a really good chat with them.

THE RUNIC INTERPRETATION
↑ᛗᚻᚨ◇ (Teiwaz, Ehwaz, Nauthiz, Ansuz, Jera)

Janet features the important addition of the Teiwaz energy of the warrior to the name Jane. Teiwaz heightens Janet's involvement with the cause of healthy, loving, and peaceful coexistence. Janet may well be involved with her favorite causes on a global level, and she is willing to lobby in Washington for her beliefs. Janet is an idealist with the Teiwaz energy of the zealot. She must guard against hasty or ill-timed strategies in her quest for a better quality of life for all.

Elements: Air, air, fire, air, earth

THE NUMEROLOGICAL INTERPRETATION
Janet (NV = 5, CV = 8, VV = 6, FL = 1)

Janet can be refreshingly free from personal repression. Her name opens her up to anything that is new. She is curious, keen to learn, and very adaptable. Janet has the ability to see the potential joy in everything that life has to offer. She accumulates her experiences as if they were a collection of shells, finding the pearl in every one of them. Janet also likes to wear pearls! This is a woman who appreciates elegance and sets her goals on worldly success and achievement. However, she has to take care that she does not become obsessed by material desires and sensual pleasures.

DERIVATION: English, diminutive of Jane. Primarily a Scottish name in the nineteenth century, and became common in other English-speaking countries during the twentieth century. Especially popular during the 1950s.

PRINCIPAL COLORS: The full spectrum of pale hues

GEMSTONES AND PRECIOUS METALS: Platinum, diamonds

BOTANICALS: Hazel, marjoram, mushrooms

UNIQUE SPELLINGS: Janit, Jannet, Jannit, Jannitt

RELATED TO: Jan†, Jana, Janet†, Janetta, Janette, Janice†, Janine, Jean†, Jeanette†, Jenetta, Jennetta, Joan†

DERIVATION: English, a derivative of Jane, which is originally from Hebrew roots meaning "The Lord has been gracious." Coined at the turn of the nineteenth century, and commonly used since the 1930s.

PRINCIPAL COLORS: All but the brightest shades of blue

GEMSTONES AND PRECIOUS METALS: Turquoise, emeralds

BOTANICALS: Vervain, violets, walnuts, apricots

UNIQUE SPELLINGS: Janis, Janiss, Jannice, Jannis, Janniss, Jannyce, Janyce

RELATED TO: Jant, Jana, Janet, Janett, Jani, Jania, Janica, Janie, Janine, Janna, Jannel, Jannelle, Janni, Janny, Jany, Jayne

❧

"Asserting yourself while respecting others is a very good way to win respect yourself."
—JANICE LAROUCHE (AUTHOR)

Janice

A KABBALISTIC SYNOPSIS
יאניס —YANYS (Yod, Aleph, Nun, Yod, Samech)

Janice is a deeply creative woman, and with the force of fire behind her, she has a good chance of becoming a successful artist. The central N, or Nun, suggests that her work will be mainly concerned with emotional behavior, possibly in its negative and obsessive forms. Whatever the focus, Janice's art will strike a chord with its audience and is likely to be powerful and almost overwhelming in its intensity. As the value of her name has associations with both the Hierophant card in tarot and with a Hebrew name of God, her creations may well contain religious or spiritual messages and themes. Janice not only wants success for herself but is deeply committed to helping others practice in similarly artistic areas.

THE RUNIC INTERPRETATION
ᛗᛋᛁᛏᚨᛜ (Ehwaz, Sowelu, Isa, Nauthiz, Ansuz, Jera)

Janice loves humanity. The runes for wholeness (Sowelu) and harvest (Jera) foster a nurturing spirit in Janice. The Nauthiz rune of constraint makes her especially sensitive to the needs of others. Janice can be a little gullible at times, but the Isa rune of standstill can help her to overcome this problem. Janice finds that if she takes time to walk or rest—or does anything to clear her head—intuition provides her with a true picture of her circumstances. Janice has a lovely, childlike trust, one worth preserving.

Elements: Air, air, earth, fire, air, earth

THE NUMEROLOGICAL INTERPRETATION
Janice (NV = 6, CV = 9, VV = 6, FL = 1)

People tend to see Janice as balanced and beautiful, both in body and mind. She is able to communicate this sense of harmony to the world around her, and strives to look at life with an optimistic perspective. Janice wants to believe in people; she tends to emphasize their positive characteristics and underestimate their faults. This is a name that denotes sympathy and understanding, and indicates a woman with depth of character who is capable of easily accepting other people's differences. Prejudice of any kind is anathema to her, and she will do everything possible to foster better human relations. Among Janice's other special gifts are grace and gentility.

❧

Jared

A KABBALISTIC SYNOPSIS
יאראד —YARAD (Yod, Aleph, Resh, Aleph, Daleth)

You will always get a smile from Jared, no matter what the circumstances. Even when every-one else is stressed to the point of breaking, Jared will be as cheery as ever, doing his best to convince his fellow workers that problems aren't as bad as they seem. This bright outlook on life is quite infectious, so Jared usually has a wide circle of friends. His sunny disposition also means Jared will be very good with children, except when it comes to discipline. Then he will tend to shy away from them. Jared is a sincerely religious man, and believes that his opti-mistic attitude is a possible doorway to a higher level of understanding of his faith. It may be that his religious beliefs are the reason for his positive determination even in the face of im-possible odds.

THE RUNIC INTERPRETATION
ᛗᛖᚱᚨᛟ (Dagaz, Ehwaz, Raido, Ansuz, Jera)

Jared might start out his career as an underachiever. He lacks focus and confidence initially, and becomes frustrated by his economic circumstances and the pressures of survival. Dagaz and Jera, the runes for breakthrough and harvest, suggest that help arrives in the nick of time for eager Jared. Advice from positive role models catapults Jared into pursuing his dreams. Jared has good communication skills and a strong intuitive ability. As a family member, he is sensitive, empathetic, and a born peacemaker. He loves to travel and will most certainly live and work abroad for extended periods of time during his long and productive career. Jared may get off to a slow start, but once he is launched, he appreciates the benefits of a rich and rewarding life.

Elements: Fire, air, water, air, earth

THE NUMEROLOGICAL INTERPRETATION
Jared (NV = 11, CV = 5, VV = 6, FL = 1)

Jared can be quite an inspiration to others. Although he may be opinionated, Jared doesn't force his ideas upon anyone. He reflects the depth of his inner strength just by being himself. His life goals are usually more concerned with collective interests than with just the purely personal. Jared is community and group oriented, and he can be a gifted communicator. He may tend to seek a wide variety of relationships rather than commit himself to one particular person too early in life. He has to be cautious about spreading himself too thin and becoming involved in personality issues between other people that don't involve him.

DERIVATION: Hebrew, from the word meaning "to descend." Found in the Old Testament as the name of one of Adam's descendants. Popular among the Puritans, and surged in popularity in English-speaking countries during the 1960s.

PRINCIPAL COLORS: The complete range of green hues, creamy white

GEMSTONES AND PRECIOUS METALS: Jade, moonstones, cat's-eye

BOTANICALS: Plantain, chicory, lettuce

UNIQUE SPELLINGS: Jarad, Jarid, Jarod, Jarrad, Jarred, Jarrod, Jerad

RELATED TO: Gerald†, Jerrold, Jerry†

Jasmine

DERIVATION: English, from the flower name. Originally from the Persian root *yasmin*. First became common at the end of the nineteenth century.

PRINCIPAL COLORS: Black, the deepest shades of azure, purple, and gray

GEMSTONES AND PRECIOUS METALS: Sapphires, rubies, black diamonds

BOTANICALS: Angelica, shepherd's purse

UNIQUE SPELLINGS: Jasmin, Jasmyn, Jasmyne, Jazmine

RELATED TO: Yasmin, Yasmina, Yasmine

A KABBALISTIC SYNOPSIS
יאסמין —YASMYN (Yod, Aleph, Samech, Mem, Yod, Nun)

All of Jasmine's energy goes into communication. She can talk or write her way out of or into anything she wants. But Jasmine may come across as almost manic due to her tendency to talk twice as fast as anyone else; this is mainly because the ideas she is expressing are being generated at an equally fast rate. If she doesn't want to make a living from writing or some form of journalism, she will probably work as part of a creative team. Jasmine has all the qualities of a high-level ideas person. The total value of her name is a prime number, so her ideas, like her personality, tend to be unique and off-the-wall. Still, she is instinctively in touch with the mood of the times, so her concepts, however way-out they may be, will resonate with the person on the street.

THE RUNIC INTERPRETATION
ᛗᚾᛁᛗᛊᚱᚨ◇ (Ehwaz, Nauthiz, Isa, Mannaz, Sowelu, Ansuz, Jera)

Jasmine loves to cook. She has perfect technique and a sense of flavors, even if she never had any formal cooking lessons. Jasmine used to hide under her grandmother's kitchen table and listen as her aunts discussed their favorite dishes; it's easy to see why the Jera rune for harvest is in her name. The Sowelu rune of wholeness gives Jasmine a balanced outlook on life. Jasmine is basically a happy person, and she tries to make every day a feast in her world.

Elements: Air, fire, earth, air, air, air, earth

THE NUMEROLOGICAL INTERPRETATION
Jasmine (NV = 8, CV = 11, VV = 6, FL = 1)

As her name suggests, Jasmine is an exotic woman with tremendous personal magnetism. She has an air of mystery about her that is part of her allure, but this same gift may also act like a veil that keeps others from getting too close. People who do take the time to cultivate Jasmine's friendship are well rewarded. A woman who can be a truly loving friend and a devoted companion, she has a definite psychic sensibility and often knows people intimately from their very first meeting. Jasmine may hold many secrets within herself, but people can have no secrets from her.

Jason

A Kabbalistic Synopsis

יאיסון —YAYSVN (Yod, Aleph, Yod, Samech, Vau, Nun)

Jason is well liked, mainly because he is totally up-front. There are no hidden agendas with Jason. If Jason likes you as a friend but also finds you a useful business contact, he will tell you so. In fact, Jason is so straightforward that he may even tell people when they are being useful but not really his friend! The power of Leo is prevalent in his name, which assures him a good level of success in his life while also indicating a forceful and charismatic personality. Interestingly, the value of Jason's name reduces to twenty-two, the number of the Fool in the tarot; this symbolizes innocence, enthusiasm, and often naïveté. In Jason's case we should see this symbol in its position at the end of the tarot cycle, where it indicates the enlightened position of the so-called Wise Fool.

The Runic Interpretation

ᛏᛟᛊᚨᛜ (Nauthiz, Othila, Sowelu, Ansuz, Jera)

Jason has the Othila rune of separation in his name. He has lots of friends, but he really loves it when they all go home and he can be alone. He values his private time because he feels truly free then. The Ansuz rune of signals, or intuition, urges him to use his inventive mind for new ideas. Jason is a creative man, and he can turn his talents toward business, science, or art, and make wonderful and unique contributions. The Jera rune for harvest hints that there are accolades in store for Jason.

Elements: Fire, earth/fire, air, air, earth

The Numerological Interpretation

Jason (NV = 5, CV = 7, VV = 7, FL = 1)

Jason is a very insightful person with a wealth of knowledge about people and their personalities. One of the most important things in life to him is his own urge to know himself. In this respect, Jason is a very reflective and introspective human being. He is also loyal and tends to keep his friendships intact, although he may disappear every now and then, as he has a real need for solitude. When he does emerge from his self-imposed exiles (which can be taken in some very interesting parts of the world!), he will come forth with fresh insights about life and enthusiastically share them with others.

DERIVATION: Greek, created by biblical translators as a version of the Hebrew name Joshua. A figure in the New Testament, and also a legendary hero in Greek mythology. Popular among the Puritans, and has been extremely common during the late twentieth century.

PRINCIPAL COLORS: The very palest shades of any color

GEMSTONES AND PRECIOUS METALS: Diamonds and silver, any shiny stone

BOTANICALS: Hazel, sweet marjoram, parsley

UNIQUE SPELLINGS: Jaisen, Jaison, Jasen, Jasin, Jasyn, Jaysen, Jaysin, Jayson

RELATED TO: Jase, Jay†, Joshua†

Javier

DERIVATION: Spanish version of Xavier, which originally comes from the Basque word meaning "new house." Saint Francis Xavier was a sixteenth-century Jesuit missionary, and his name subsequently was used as a first name.

PRINCIPAL COLORS: From pale to deep, rich greens; white

GEMSTONES AND PRECIOUS METALS: Jade, pearls, moonstones

BOTANICALS: Cabbage, colewort, moonwort

UNIQUE SPELLINGS: Havier, Javierre

RELATED TO: Xavier, Xever, Zavier

A KABBALISTIC SYNOPSIS
יאויה —YAVYH (Yod, Aleph, Vau, Yod, Heh)

The total value of Javier's name is thirty-two, which is the total number of paths on the Tree of Life. Mystically this number is of great significance and is suggestive of wide-ranging occult understanding and experience. In terms of character types we should expect Javier to be a very knowledgeable man, especially in the area of philosophy or theology. This same understanding also makes him an excellent manager, particularly in the area of human resources. Javier will make an ideal personnel officer. In his own relationships Javier will have a fruitful and satisfying emotional life. Although arguments will occur, as they do in any relationship, Javier's understanding nature will keep their impact to a minimum. Few people will expect Javier to be as understanding as he is, since he is incredibly energetic, always dashing from one place to the next. But Javier makes mental connections just as quickly; he doesn't need long to get to the bottom of any situation.

THE RUNIC INTERPRETATION
ᚱᛖᛁᚠᚨ◇ (Raido, Ehwaz, Isa, Fehu, Ansuz, Jera)

Javier is absolutely brilliant without any help from anyone. He is a heavy hitter. He is the type of guy who can graduate from college at fifteen, and the president will pay him to skip grad school and head up the CIA. Actually, the CIA is the perfect place for Javier, who is more than a little sneaky.

Elements: Water, air, earth, fire, air, earth

THE NUMEROLOGICAL INTERPRETATION
Javier (NV = 11, CV = 5, VV = 6, FL = 1)

The numbers in this name reveal an active man, one who takes great pleasure in his uniqueness and needs a lot of freedom. Javier is adventurous in both his career and his relationships. At heart, he is a definite romantic, and a partner to share his life is essential to him. But he is not one to commit prematurely to a permanent partnership. Javier has a very broad perspective on life and will expect his beloved to be equally independent and open-minded. Too much nervous energy may present a challenge for Javier, who will need to pay attention to how he channels it or else he may find himself quite scattered.

Jay

A Kabbalistic Synopsis
יאי —YAY (Yod, Aleph, Yod)

Don't bother him with details; this guy doesn't want to know. Just tell him where to sign and leave it at that. Jay is a finisher; he can tie up and settle any project or contract quickly. This skill is indicated by the value of his name, which, because twenty-one is associated with the Universe card in the tarot, is connected to ideas of completion and success. Jay has considerable ambition, and in order to find the position that really suits him, he will need to use all his fiery energy to ensure his rise to a position of seniority. When he isn't working, Jay tends to relax by undertaking a creative hobby, particularly if it involves some practical skill. He is also a family man and likes to spend as much time as possible with his kids, who do him as much good as he does them.

The Runic Interpretation
ᛇᚨᛃ (Eihwaz, Ansuz, Jera)

Jay has Jera, the harvest rune, combined with Ansuz, the signals rune, in his lucky name. When Ansuz is present in a name, it offers intuition as well as blessings, benefits, and opportunities. Jay is the kind of man who runs into old friends on the street and turns these chance encounters into great advantages. Jay feels lucky because unexpected opportunities come his way, and the Jera rune of harvest brings joy and patience along with the opportunities. Jay understands that it takes time and effort to reap the rewards of his labors, but he's willing to wait because the outcome is beneficial. Jay has an inventive mind that works well in terms of developing fresh ideas.

Elements: Earth/fire, air, earth

The Numerological Interpretation
Jay (NV = 9, CV = 1, VV = 8, FL = 1)

Jay is an ambitious person, a man of clear goals and distinct objectives with a strongly philosophical orientation to life. Jay possesses a fundamentally humanitarian nature and a strong urge to use his talents and abilities for others as well as for himself. He has to make sure that the ground underneath his feet can support the weight of his creativity, however. Jay prefers fewer and deeper relationships to a wide range of more superficial associations.

DERIVATION: Latin, from the root *gaius*, meaning "gay." Used both as an independent name and as a nickname for longer names beginning with the letter J.

PRINCIPAL COLORS: The full range of reds, from pink to rich crimson, particularly the deeper shades of red

GEMSTONES AND PRECIOUS METALS: Bloodstones, rubies

BOTANICALS: Onion, garlic, wormwood

UNIQUE SPELLINGS: J, Jae, Jaye, Jey

RELATED TO: Jacob†, Jason†, Jeyes

DERIVATION: English and Scottish, derived from the Latin name Johanna, the female form of John. Originally a primarily Scottish name. Became common in other English-speaking countries in the early twentieth century.

PRINCIPAL COLORS: All violet shades, from pale lilac to deep, rich purple and maroon

GEMSTONES AND PRECIOUS METALS: Garnets, amethyst

BOTANICALS: Apple, dandelion, lungwort

UNIQUE SPELLINGS: Jeane, Jeanne, Jeen, Jeene

RELATED TO: Genie, Gina†, Janet, Janine, Janett, Jeana, Jeanelle, Jeanette†, Jeanie, Jeanine, Jennetta, Joanna†, Johanna

Jean

A KABBALISTIC SYNOPSIS
יהן —YHN (Yod, Heh, Nun)

The central letter in Jean's name is H, or Heh, meaning "window," which tells us she is concerned with other people and how they live their lives. The final N, or Nun, further indicates it is their *feelings* that most interest her. There are no suggestions in Jean's name of any counseling or advisory tendencies, so her interest relates purely to observation, either for her own personal reasons or, possibly, to gather evidence for a writing project or academic research. Jean's own emotional life is unlikely to be particularly settled. She has some deep-seated emotional anxieties and insecurities, which are bound to affect any relationship she has and may even propel her interest in other people. For someone so centered around feelings, Jean is surprisingly upbeat and outgoing. On the surface she is quite a live wire and always ready for fun. It is only when people know her closely that her inner nature becomes clearer.

THE RUNIC INTERPRETATION
ᚾᚨᛖᛃ (Nauthiz, Ansuz, Ehwaz, Jera)

Jean has the runes for constraint, signals, movement, and harvest in her name. Jean may have moved around a lot, changing schools and making new friends, as a child. Above all, Jean wants love and security in her life. Jean is intuitive and a peacemaker. She uses the Ansuz rune of signals to anticipate challenges for her family and keep everyone on an even keel. She requires a strong level of kindness and gentility in her home. The Jera rune for harvest ensures that Jean will succeed in having a warm home life as well as the blessings, benefits, and opportunities that come from kind and loving friends.

Elements: Fire, air, air, earth

THE NUMEROLOGICAL INTERPRETATION
Jean (NV = 3, CV = 6, W = 6 FL = 1)

Beauty and artistry characterize women named Jean. These are individuals who have a strong sense of aesthetics and whose surroundings have to reflect their sense of harmony and grace. Jean is an active name, bestowing a keen wit and a bright intelligence. It also gives to its bearers a profound need to acquire knowledge, along with the creative skills that they need to enhance and enrich their environment. The numbers in this name bestow a strong romantic and sentimental nature. Jean is very easily enamored and adores sharing fine food and candlelight with that very special friend.

Jeanette

A KABBALISTIC SYNOPSIS

ינאת —YNATh (Yod, Nun, Aleph, Tau)

Everybody could use a friend called Jeanette. She is the sort of person who is always willing to put her life on hold for other people. If you need a ride to the airport, a loan, or pretty much anything else, Jeanette is the person to see. Her name totals to 461, a prime number, so unfortunately for the rest of us she is pretty unique. You won't easily find many people as generous as Jeanette. The compression of her name produces Tau, Samech, and Aleph, which tells us that by putting herself last and supporting those around her, Jeanette is able to fulfill her own sense of personal identity. There are a few Jeanettes in whom this altruistic attitude to life has a slightly sour edge. This is the person at work who insists that everyone else go to the office Christmas party while she minds the phones. She will then remind all her colleagues for the next month or so how generous she was to volunteer!

THE RUNIC INTERPRETATION

ᛗᛏᛏᛗᛁᚾᛗ◇ (Ehwaz, Teiwaz, Teiwaz, Ehwaz, Nauthiz, Ansuz, Ehwaz, Jera)

Jeanette has many of the nurturing qualities of Jean with the additional Nauthiz and double Teiwaz runes to toughen her up. Nauthiz brings difficult lessons of constraint, delays, and limitation. Teiwaz offers the warrior energy of patience, discrimination, and knowledge. The triple Ehwaz rune of movement indicates new dwelling places and transitions. Jeanette can use these strengths to better understand herself and others. She can work as a psychologist, social worker, or healer. She might also pursue a career in law and create programs for reform on a global level. Jeanette is strong and wise, and a positive influence in any setting.

Elements: Air, air, air, air, fire, air, air, earth

THE NUMEROLOGICAL INTERPRETATION

Jeanette (NV = 8, CV = 1, VV = 7, FL = 1)

Jeanette is very success oriented and tries to do everything possible to make her mark on the world. This is a woman who has strong willpower and will not hesitate to use it. Career-minded and practical, Jeanette is respected as a no-nonsense, do-what-must-be-done kind of person. Her name's numbers also reveal a highly analytical nature, one that is capable of perceiving the real importance of any issue. Jeanette is happiest when she is the most productive. She also likes to look good and will pay a lot of attention to her personal appearance and health. Sensitivity to other people's emotions is a quality that she may need to develop further.

DERIVATION: French, diminutive form of Jeanne or Jean. Originally most popular in Scotland, and spread to the English-speaking world in the twentieth century.

PRINCIPAL COLORS: Dark shades of blue and gray, black

GEMSTONES AND PRECIOUS METALS: Carbuncles, black diamonds, black pearls

BOTANICALS: Marsh mallow, shepherd's purse

UNIQUE SPELLINGS: Jeanete, Jeannette, Jenett, Jenette, Jennette

RELATED TO: Janet†, Janett†, Janine, Jean†, Jeana, Jeanie, Jeanine, Jeannetta, Jeannine, Joanna†

"As a woman I can't go to war, and I refuse to send anyone else."
—JEANETTE RANKIN (FIRST WOMAN ELECTED TO THE HOUSE OF REPRESENTATIVES)

Jeff

DERIVATION: English. Originally a short form of the Old German Jeffrey or the Old English Jefferson. Now a common independent name, especially in the United States.

PRINCIPAL COLORS: The richer shades of pink, crimson, and reddish purple

GEMSTONES AND PRECIOUS METALS: Rubies, bloodstones, garnets

BOTANICALS: Garlic, onions, nettle, broom

UNIQUE SPELLING: Geoff

RELATED TO: Geoffrey†, Geoffry, Godfrey, Jefery, Jefferson, Jeffrey†, Jeffy, Jefry, Jeoffroi

❧

In the absence of any direct equivalent to the letter *f* in the Hebrew alphabet, the letter Peh is used. Peh can function as either a hard or a soft letter, and as such, is one of the seven "doubles."

A KABBALISTIC SYNOPSIS
יאפ —YAPh (Yod, Aleph, Peh)

Jeff really likes to live the high life. His name has the same total value as the Hebrew word for "manna," and manna was the food from heaven eaten by the Hebrew people during their time in the wilderness. Indeed, Jeff is likely to be able to afford the finer things in life, as the total value of his name when reduced can be associated with the Wheel of Fortune card in the tarot; this points to Jeff as being a naturally lucky individual. They usually say "lucky in love, unlucky in money," but this is not so in Jeff's case. He is likely to be lucky in money, and when it comes to love he has a natural charm and offers winning conversation. Jeff is a dedicated partner, and when he finds his ideal soul mate he is very unlikely to look elsewhere again. Jeff's only problem is that he can have an extremely fiery temper, which is made worse by its unpredictability. However, as fiery as it is, it does not usually last long, and Jeff is never a man to bear a grudge—no matter what he might say in the midst of his anger.

THE RUNIC INTERPRETATION
ᚠᛗᛜ (Fehu, Ehwaz, Jera)

Jeff has the ability to stay the course in pursuit of his goal. Whether in love or in his career, Jeff is determined and focused. He is patient, and the indication in his name is that he will reap a bountiful harvest in all areas of his life. Hopefully, once his goal is achieved, Jeff will blast out of his comfort zone; whether it's the challenge of learning a new language and traveling, or taking up some form of art, Jeff needs to open his mind to other cultures and diverse approaches to living. With his patience and self-discipline, he can excel at whatever he chooses.

Elements: Fire, air, earth

THE NUMEROLOGICAL INTERPRETATION
Jeff (NV = 9, CV = 4, VV = 5, FL = 1)

The numbers in Jeff denote a person who takes the practical affairs of life very seriously. He has a need to be responsible in his profession and fulfill his obligations. Although Jeff can be quite happy among his friends, he is basically a quiet person, one who has a deep introspective side to his nature. He is cautious and tends to think things through to their logical conclusions. Jeff is an active man, but his activities are primarily geared to creating security for himself and his loved ones. Although he seeks to establish a firm financial foundation in life, Jeff is not a selfish man. His full name value is nine, indicating that Jeff uses his understanding and know-how for other people's benefit, not just his own.

❧

Jeffrey

A KABBALISTIC SYNOPSIS
יאפרי —YAPhRY (Yod, Aleph, Peh, Resh, Yod)

You will never see Jeffrey waiting around for an opportunity to be handed to him on a plate; he is a go-getter. Make no mistake: Jeffrey is likely to leave his competitors stranded and dumbfounded in his wake! In the compression of Jeffrey's name we have both the sustaining energy of Shin and the pragmatic characteristics of Aleph. Jeffrey is the kind of guy who can not only generate ideas but has the will to make them happen; this combination may well make him a considerable amount of money. The central letter in the name is P, or Peh, meaning "mouth," so we can rest assured that Jeffrey will have no trouble in marketing his ideas. It also indicates, within the context of other aspects of his name, that Jeffrey has a garrulous nature and loves to socialize. This is an excellent way for Jeffrey to make those all important business contacts.

THE RUNIC INTERPRETATION
ᛖᛖᚱᚠᚠᛖ◇ (Ehwaz, Ehwaz, Raido, Fehu, Fehu, Ehwaz, Jera)

Jeffrey has the power of all four elements in his name, a sign of balance and good fortune. The double Fehu rune of possessions makes Jeffrey a prosperous individual. The Raido rune, of journeys, Ehwaz, of movement, and Jera, of harvest, influence this name. Jeffrey's career will involve travel, and he may also live many different places with his family. The Eihwaz rune shows that Jeffrey is an astute guard of his fortune. He struggles to increase his net worth each year and he succeeds. The harvest rune ensures that Jeffrey could leave a vast estate to his family and friends, and donate large sums to charity as well.

Elements: Air, air, water, fire, fire, air, earth

THE NUMEROLOGICAL INTERPRETATION
Jeffrey (NV = 3, CV = 22, VV = 8, FL = 1)

A man gifted in many disciplines, Jeffrey's name value of three indicates the ability to achieve success in more than one area in life. It gives him an active mind and body plus many communications skills. In addition, this name reveals a combination of the number for the attainment of wealth, eight, along with the number that indicates mastery over matter, twenty-two. The latter is especially significant, as it indicates that Jeffrey is a bit of a magician when it comes to dealing with the practicalities of life. He has a definite way with money, and if spiritually developed, he will seek to create economic channels that can distribute life's abundance where it is most needed.

DERIVATION: English, alternate spelling of the Old German name Geoffrey, meaning "peace." Common during the Middle Ages, then became rare until the late nineteenth century. Jeffrey is the more common spelling in the United States, whereas Geoffrey is popular in Britain.

PRINCIPAL COLORS: The lightest to the deepest shades of violet

GEMSTONES AND PRECIOUS METALS: Garnets, amethyst

BOTANICALS: Cherry, barberry, mint

UNIQUE SPELLINGS: Geoffrey†, Jeafrey, Jefferey, Jeffery, Jeffree, Jeffry, Jefree

RELATED TO: Geoff, Godfrey, Jeff†, Jefferson

In the absence of any direct equivalent to the letter *f* in the Hebrew alphabet, the letter Peh is used. Peh can function as either a hard or a soft letter, and as such, is one of the seven "doubles."

Jennifer

DERIVATION: Welsh, the modern form of Guinevere. Comes from roots meaning "white" and "smooth." Became extremely common in the early twentieth century, and is still one of the most popular female names today.

PRINCIPAL COLORS: From light pink to the deepest of reds, crimson, rose

GEMSTONES AND PRECIOUS METALS: Garnets, red rubies

BOTANICALS: Broom, garlic, nettle

UNIQUE SPELLINGS: Genifer, Gennifer, Genyfer, Jenefer, Jenifer, Jeniffer, Jenniffer, Jennyfer, Jenyfer

RELATED TO: Genna, Guinevere, Jen, Jenn, Jenna, Jenni, Jennica, Jennie, Jenny†

❧

In the absence of any direct equivalent to the letter *f* in the Hebrew alphabet, the letter Peh is used. Peh can function as either a hard or a soft letter, and as such, is one of the seven "doubles."

A KABBALISTIC SYNOPSIS

יאניפור —YANYPhVR (Yod, Aleph, Nun, Yod, Peh, Vau, Resh)

Jennifer will waste no time in letting you know if you don't come up to scratch in any way. Jennifer's name reduces to fifteen, which indicates her love of luxury and material goods. She loves to receive gifts and values them highly, probably because of her need to be reassured fairly constantly that she is wanted and appreciated. At work, Jennifer flounders when she doesn't get enough feedback or compensation, yet she is too proud and fiery to actually ask overtly for this level of reassurance; demanding tokens of affection is as close as she can get.

THE RUNIC INTERPRETATION

ᚱᛖᚠᛁᛏᛏᛖᛃ (Raido, Ehwaz, Fehu, Isa, Nauthiz, Nauthiz, Ehwaz, Jera)

Jennifer is charming and witty. The double Ehwaz energy of movement gives her a lively mind as well as the opportunity to experience life in many parts of the world. The Raido rune of journey underlines Jennifer's curiosity and willingness to hop on the next plane. She needs to fight against the Isa rune of standstill and the double Nauthiz rune of constraint, which can interrupt her plans and cause delays and cancellations. The double Nauthiz rune could make Jennifer a bit manipulative. She is the type who can charm her way around either a supervisor or an assistant. Jennifer enjoys the special power of having all four of the elements in her name.

Elements: Water, air, fire, earth, fire, fire, air, earth

THE NUMEROLOGICAL INTERPRETATION

Jennifer (NV = 9, CV = 8, VV = 1, FL = 1)

Jennifer is a name containing a very interesting blend of numerical influences. There is a strong idealistic orientation to life indicated in this name, one that stimulates the romantic inside of Jennifer. This is a person who has a need to express beauty, not only through her physical appearance but through her actions as well. Jennifer also has a very potent personal will and is decidedly goal oriented in terms of achieving her practical aims and ambitions. Thus in Jennifer we have a woman who has both a poetic as well as a decidedly pragmatic temperament.

❧

Jenny

DERIVATION: English, pet form of Jennifer, which is originally from Welsh roots meaning "white" and "smooth." Used as an independent name since the nineteenth century.

PRINCIPAL COLORS: The full spectrum of light shades

GEMSTONES AND PRECIOUS METALS: Silver, platinum, diamonds

BOTANICALS: Sweet marjoram, oats, parsnips

UNIQUE SPELLINGS: Jenee, Jeney, Jeni, Jenie, Jennee, Jenney, Jenni, Jennie, Jeny

RELATED TO: Jen, Jena, Jenn, Jennica, Jennifer†, Jenniver

A KABBALISTIC SYNOPSIS
יאני —YANY (Yod, Aleph, Nun, Yod)

When it comes to strong women, you have to go a long way to get tougher than Jenny, who could give a she-lion a good run for her money on a bad day. As well as having powerful connections to the Strength card in tarot, her name begins and ends with letters directly related to creative energy. Jenny is the type who can blow up at you in a moment, and who can equally quickly decide that you're a great person! This can be very confusing for those around her, since the people who, in Jenny's opinion, are either great or awful often shift places with disturbing speed! Her name suggests that as she grows in experience she will gradually develop her understanding of people, even to the extent that she may be more perceptive than most about the personalities of others. It is likely that she will somehow put this knowledge to good commercial use.

THE RUNIC INTERPRETATION
ᛇᚾᚾᛖᛃ (Eihwaz, Nauthiz, Nauthiz, Ehwaz, Jera)

It's not always easy to maintain, but Jenny has a positive attitude. With the double Nauthiz energy of constraint, she needs assistance sometimes, but the universe supports her, much to the amazement of family and friends. When Jenny asks for help, she is so trusting and positive that the Jera rune for harvest kicks in and her answer from above always comes. Jenny can play the lottery, and will often reap a harvest of cash.

Elements: Earth/fire, fire, fire, air, earth

THE NUMEROLOGICAL INTERPRETATION
Jenny (NV = 5, CV = 11, VV = 3, FL = 1)

This is a name that denotes a friendly, gregarious, and cheerful woman. Jenny loves people and has a talent for communicating her affections with ease. Jenny also possesses a quick wit and a highly active mind. She loves to travel, which appeals to her natural sense of adventure. Intuitive by nature, Jenny has an instantaneous understanding of others. Her communicative talents may lead her toward teaching or other forms of public service, which may play an important part in her life. Jenny tends to have a wide variety of friends. She gets along well with all sorts of people and finds an immediate rapport with strangers. Her basic life challenges have to do with setting clear priorities and establishing self-discipline.

DERIVATION: Biblical, from the Hebrew root meaning "appointed by God." Name of a great Hebrew prophet, whose prophesies are recorded in the Book of Jeremiah and the Book of Lamentations (found in the Old Testament). Fairly common name among the Puritans; in recent years, Jeremy has been a popular variant.

PRINCIPAL COLORS: Pale to moderately shaded azure

GEMSTONES AND PRECIOUS METALS: Turquoise, emeralds

BOTANICALS: Dog rose, violets, walnuts

UNIQUE SPELLINGS: Jeremaea, Jeremia, Jeremyah, Jerremiah

RELATED TO: Jem, Jeremy†, Jerome†, Jerry†

❧

"Just because you can't see the air doesn't keep you from breathing. And just because you can't see God doesn't keep you from believing."
—JEREMIAH BIGGS IN *THE PREACHER'S WIFE* (1996)

A KABBALISTIC SYNOPSIS

יארמיאה —YARMYAH (Yod, Aleph, Resh, Mem, Yod, Aleph, Heh)

Jeremiah is a man with a mission, one from which he cannot be swayed or diverted. It is highly probable that his mission, in the traditional sense of the word, will be driven by a deep religious conviction. If Jeremiah's activities aren't all that spiritual, he still will make it sound as if he's on a religious quest—even if it's a matter of ensuring that various packages arrive at their chosen destination! On the whole, though, Jeremiah is a spiritual man and is likely to see himself as a spiritual warrior. To Jeremiah his faith is a war cry rather than a solitary matter for personal contemplation. Mind you, Jeremiah is no hell-and-high-water preacher. He has a great and sincere sympathy for his fellow human beings. His real aim in life is to offer as much support of whatever nature to as many people as he possibly can.

THE RUNIC INTERPRETATION

ᚺᚨᛁᛗᛗᚱᛗ◇ (Hagalaz, Ansuz, Isa, Mannaz, Ehwaz, Raido, Ehwaz, Jera)

Jeremiah is going to end up okay. He'll enjoy the accolades he earns from the fruits of his labors and may be invited to travel and live all over the world; the double Ehwaz rune promises this. His early years will test him with delays and insecurity, but Jeremiah will learn a lot about himself in the process. When circumstances are unbearable, it's always helpful to summon the Ansuz energy of signals and go within oneself to make improvements, which will surely be reflected in one's outer experience soon.

Elements: Water, air, earth, air, air, water, air, earth

THE NUMEROLOGICAL INTERPRETATION

Jeremiah (NV = 6, CV = 22, VV = 2, FL = 1)

A compassionate and poetic man, Jeremiah is a harmonizing agent in any social situation in which he participates. Usually gifted in the arts, he has many avenues for creative self-expression. This is emphasized by the consonant value of twenty-two, which tells us that Jeremiah is quite capable of bringing his ideas to fruition. Jeremiah is a name that also instills an unselfish and humanitarian orientation to life. In addition to his potential talent in the arts, Jeremiah will be called to a profession that serves and helps people. Romantic and sensual, Jeremiah finds that his personal relationships are extremely important to him, and he will tend to enter a committed partnership early in life.

❧

Jeremy

A KABBALISTIC SYNOPSIS

יארמי —YARMY (Yod, Aleph, Resh, Mem, Yod)

There is one thing Jeremy values above all else, and that is honesty. On the whole Jeremy likes to think of himself as a trusting sort, and usually he is. Unfortunately, from time to time that trust is exploited, and there is nothing that disillusions Jeremy more than having his good nature taken for granted. You can bet that in Jeremy's relationships both parties will have to have a genuine faith in each other. If his loved one does go astray, Jeremy will be able to forgive— but only if his mate is immediately up-front about everything that has occurred. Otherwise, the relationship will be over. Jeremy's name reduces to the number of the Hermit in the tarot, and he is a deeply serious man. While he can be very supportive of those he trusts and has a kind nature, he is not renowned for his cheery disposition.

THE RUNIC INTERPRETATION

ᛇᛘᛖᚱᛖᛃ (Eihwaz, Mannaz, Ehwaz, Raido, Ehwaz, Jera)

Jeremy is characterized by the double Ehwaz energy of movement; Jeremy just can't sit still. He's the type to put his house on the market the first week he moves in. Jeremy has the Raido rune for travel, and this only adds to his wanderlust. The Eihwaz rune power of defense allows Jeremy to develop aggressive and assertive abilities. Jeremy could work as an outstandingly successful judge or litigator. He is a good troubleshooter in the corporate arena, and would thrive as a freelance consultant. On a spiritual level, Jeremy makes an exciting lover and a warm, engaging father. No one is ever bored around Jeremy. As a healer or therapist, he would give his whole heart to his work. He also could lobby the government for the rights of the oppressed and disadvantaged. As long as Jeremy is permitted flexibility and variety, he will enjoy success.

Elements: Earth/fire, air, air, water, air, earth

THE NUMEROLOGICAL INTERPRETATION

Jeremy (NV = 4, CV = 5, VV = 8, FL = 1)

Hardworking and practical, Jeremy has determination and drive. This is a person who feels perfectly at home when dealing with material issues. He could have a career in a financial profession. Personal security, as well as a sense of social stature and achievement, is important to him. A perpetual student, Jeremy has an avid intellectual curiosity. Jeremy never tires of exploring all the many opportunities for success that come his way. His life can only be more enhanced if he incorporates some sort of spiritual discipline into his routine.

DERIVATION: English version of the biblical name Jeremiah, which comes from the Hebrew root meaning "appointed by God." Found in the New Testament. Until the early nineteenth century, the Jeremiah version was more common. Since that time, however, Jeremy has been increasing in popularity.

PRINCIPAL COLORS: Moderate shades of any color

GEMSTONES AND PRECIOUS METALS: Sapphires

BOTANICALS: Sage, wild spinach, medlar

UNIQUE SPELLINGS: Jeramy, Jereme, Jeremey, Jeremi, Jeremie, Jerimy

RELATED TO: Jem, Jeremiah†, Jeromet, Jerrard, Jerry†

~

"People who have nothing to do are quickly tired of their own company."
—JEREMY COLLIER
(ENGLISH CLERGYMAN)

Jermaine

A KABBALISTIC SYNOPSIS

יארמאין —YARMAYN (Yod, Aleph, Resh, Mem, Aleph, Yod, Nun)

For Jermaine, all roads lead to *home*. Crucial to Jermaine's sense of well-being is a feeling of emotional wholeness, and his family connections are an important part of this aspect of Jermaine's life. No matter how far he travels, he will always have a deep attachment to his hometown, and he is likely to be closer than usual with his family. Jermaine will make regular visits, not just to his parents but to all his uncles, aunts, and cousins. Equally significant is his partner, and Jermaine is one of the most affectionate partners that one could hope for—although his mate may still feel at times that she is competing with the rest of his relatives for his attention! In addition, where Cancerian Jermaines are concerned, his love of closeness may begin to cause his partner to feel somewhat smothered or trapped. Jermaine is a good listener, so this problem should not prove insurmountable.

THE RUNIC INTERPRETATION

ᛖᚾᛁᛋᚨᛗᚱᛖᛃ (Ehwaz, Nauthiz, Isa, Ansuz, Mannaz, Raido, Ehwaz, Jera)

Jermaine sports the double Ehwaz energy of movement and Raido for journeys. Raido is a rune signifying good communication, and Ehwaz promises the opportunity to relocate abroad. But the Isa energy of standstill and the Nauthiz rune of constraint create a tension here. Isa offers Jermaine a chance for introspection and rest, and Nauthiz teaches him to be resourceful concerning problem-solving strategies. Still, Nauthiz sets up blockages and limitations in mental, emotional, and financial arenas. Jermaine uses the Ansuz energy to intuit a way out of such constraints, and the Jera rune for harvest hints that Jermaine emerges victorious. As the initial rune energy in the name, Jera sets a tone for the whole name as one of productivity, accomplishment, and pride in accomplishment. The Ansuz rune helps Jermaine with answers to prayers and the gift of perceptive friends, who guide him in life. Jermaine uses the Mannaz energy of the self to clear out emotional blocks and live in harmony. As they struggle to improve their lives, others see Jermaine as an inspirational leader and supportive friend. Jermaine is blessed with the powers of the four elements in his name.

Elements: Air, fire, earth, air, air, water, air, earth

THE NUMEROLOGICAL INTERPRETATION

Jermaine (NV = 4, CV = 2, VV = 2, FL = 1)

It is important for Jermaine to have his life well organized and under control. He likes things to be predictable and dependable. This is a name that contains a very down-to-earth quality, one that gives Jermaine an easy and casual air. He tends to be unpretentious and at ease with himself. Jermaine is a very sociable person, one who likes warm and friendly interpersonal relationships. He cannot abide intolerance and prejudice of any kind, and tries to share his sense of acceptance with others.

Jerome

DERIVATION: English, from the Greek root *hieros*, meaning "holy," and *onoma*, meaning "name." The name of a fourth-century saint who translated the Bible into Latin. Common in the sixteenth and nineteenth centuries.

PRINCIPAL COLORS: From pale, bluish purple to deep violet and maroon

GEMSTONES AND PRECIOUS METALS: Garnets, amethyst

BOTANICALS: Barberry, bilberry, mint

UNIQUE SPELLINGS: Geroam, Gerome, Jeroam

RELATED TO: Geronimo, Gerri, Gerry†, Hierome, Icronim, Jeremiah†, Jeremy†, Jerri, Jerry†

A KABBALISTIC SYNOPSIS

יארעם —YARA'AM (Yod, Aleph, Resh, Ayin, Mem)

If you've ever sat next to a guy on a train or a plane and he has talked nonstop throughout the journey, he may well have been a Jerome! If you find that, despite the seemingly endless monologue, you're not at all bored, then the character alongside you is almost definitely a Jerome. His name adds up to 881, thereby containing both possible values of the Hebrew letter Peh along with the Aleph, which usually ensures that his chat, while incessant, is never dull. The presence of the Ayin indicates that he has a keen eye for observation and this no doubt helps add interest to his narratives. Jerome also has the advantage of being irrepressibly cheerful, a feature that rubs off on those around him after a short exposure to his humorous observations on life. As most women love a man who can make them laugh, Jerome should have plenty to be cheerful about when it comes to relationships.

THE RUNIC INTERPRETATION

ᛖᛗᛟᚱᛖᛃ (Ehwaz, Mannaz, Othila, Raido, Ehwaz, Jera)

Jerome works with the runes of separation, movement, and journey to strike out on his own at an early age, and he is happy as can be with his nomadic life. He is the type who will enjoy peddling his wares at craft fairs and sleeping in a trailer at night while raising his kids on granola and gyros. Jerome is never in one place long enough to make enemies; he gets by on his charm and keeps the engine runnin' clean.

Elements: Air, air, earth/fire, water, air, earth

THE NUMEROLOGICAL INTERPRETATION

Jerome (NV = 3, CV = 5, VV = 7, FL = 1)

Men with this name find that they have an incessant inner drive toward continuous self-exploration. This can lead to an overly egocentric and introspective nature. It is true that Jerome seeks to create more and better intellectual tools in order to enhance his communicative abilities, but real communication involves the heart as well as the mind. Once Jerome integrates and balances the two within himself, he will have achieved a major step in his growth. In partnership, he requires a lover who is free-spirited and intellectually stimulating. Jerome insists that he will never, ever be bored (or boring!).

DERIVATION: English, short version of several names beginning with "Jer," or an alternate spelling for Gerry. A common nickname for Jeremy, Jeremiah, Jerrold, and Jerrard.

PRINCIPAL COLORS: Electric colors, any hue of medium tone

GEMSTONES AND PRECIOUS METALS: From pale to rich sapphires

BOTANICALS: Celandine, spinach, Iceland moss

UNIQUE SPELLINGS: Gerrie, Gerry, Gery, Jerri, Jerrie, Jery

RELATED TO: Gerald†, Gerard, Gerrold, Gerry†, Jeremiah†, Jeremy¹, Jerrard, Jerrold

A KABBALISTIC SYNOPSIS
יארי —YARY (Yod, Aleph, Resh, Yod)

There is no distinction in Hebrew between Jerry and Gerry, so for the purposes of kabbalistic analysis, these names have the same meaning. (Readers should therefore refer to the entry for Gerry, as well as to what follows below.) The double Yod represents a process of self-development in Jerry. The first Yod gives Jerry the initiative to look at his life and consider whether he has made the right choices. The final Yod represents Jerry as full of renewed vigor, having made those changes that he feels are right for him and actively reviewing the effects of those changes. Jerry has a disarmingly amiable way of looking at the world, which may seem foolish to those around him but also ensures him a good many friends. There is a possibility that Jerry will be abnormally picky about the cleanliness and tidiness of his home; this excessive concern for an almost sterile level of hygiene is a Virgoan attribute, highlighted by Jerry's name.

THE RUNIC INTERPRETATION
ᛇᚱᚱᛖᛃ (Eihwaz, Raido, Raido, Ehwaz, Jera)

Jerry is an outstanding communicator. At home, he is blessed with negotiating skills and a diplomatic tongue, and family members appreciate all he does to keep the peace. In business, Jerry is in demand either as a spokesman or as a speechwriter behind the scenes. He could choose a career in journalism, because the ability to travel and make large sums of money is in his name. Whether Jerry uses words or photography or another art form to express his ideas, it's certain that he will receive recognition and praise for his simplicity and style. The Eihwaz rune of defense gives Jerry strong persuasive talents, and he could be a successful politician or litigator. Jera is the initial consonant rune and is the powerful rune of harvest. Jerry works for everything he accomplishes, and he appreciates the rewards of his efforts. Jera delivers satisfaction financially and in all areas of his personal life, bringing love and joy into Jerry's future.

Elements: Earth/fire, water, water, air, earth

THE NUMEROLOGICAL INTERPRETATION
Jerry (NV = 4, CV = 1, VV = 3, FL = 1)

Jerry is determined to succeed in life. This name contains a large dose of personal will-power. Jerry is very capable of structuring and coordinating the many facets of his life. He is intellectually curious but not overly adventurous. He tends to avoid circumstances that can upset his plans and projects. It would be very healthy for him to cultivate a special interest that can take him out of himself, as a bit of self-absorption can be a problem. Jerry is genuinely concerned about the material welfare of his loved ones, and makes a dedicated business associate, life partner, and parent.

Jesse

DERIVATION: English, from a Hebrew root meaning "the Lord exists." In the Old Testament, the name of the father of King David. Commonly used since the eighteenth century.

PRINCIPAL COLORS: Any moderately shaded hues

GEMSTONES AND PRECIOUS METALS: Sapphires

BOTANICALS: Lesser celandine, sage

UNIQUE SPELLINGS: Jessee, Jessey, Jessie†

RELATED TO: Jes, Jess

A KABBALISTIC SYNOPSIS
יאסה —YASH (Yod, Aleph, Samech, Heh)

If you have a business that is flagging, you should really call a Jesse to help you out—and rest assured, he will come along, brimming with new ideas. Jesse likes to see himself as something of a troubleshooter. He may have no desire for a long-term or permanent post anywhere but prefers to travel from company to company solving particular problems. The units that make up the total value of Jesse's name are suggestive not only of a love of change but also of a propensity for success and achievement followed by a change of direction. This is suggested by the fact that the full value of his name is seventy-six: The seventy refers to success, while the six, which comes after success, implies that Jesse will review his position and move on. Jesse is very stable emotionally, and this is what enables him to live with such upheaval and uncertainty in his professional life. Of course, Jesse's partner will have to be as flexible and instinctively nomadic as he is for their relationship to work well.

THE RUNIC INTERPRETATION
ᛖᛋᛋᛖᛃ (Ehwaz, Sowelu, Sowelu, Ehwaz, Jera)

Jesse uses the double Ehwaz energy of movement along with the Sowelu energy of wholeness and combines them with the Jera energy of harvest. What a fortunate name! Jesse has many admirers. He's able to make each one of us feel special and unforgettable with his perceptive comments and well-timed compliments. Jesse has the money to travel, and he is cosmopolitan in his worldview. Jesse enjoys life and entertains his pals with ready wit and easy charm because he loves himself. People feel good when they're with Jesse.

Elements: Air, air, air, air, earth

THE NUMEROLOGICAL INTERPRETATION
Jesse (NV = 4, CV = 3, VV = 1, FL = 1)

This is a name that instills a passion to express oneself creatively. Jesse develops a clear sense of who he is and how he may distinguish himself. He tends to be very pragmatic and keeps a firm eye on the financial dynamics of life. Career and money are therefore of utmost importance to him, and he has no problem spending long hours in pursuit of his aims and goals. Jesse can be very orderly, structured, and tidy. He tends to avoid waste and needless spending. Sometimes these traits may be extravagances in their own right, as Jesse can go overboard in his concern for his financial condition.

DERIVATION: English, originally
from the biblical name Jesca,
found in Genesis 11:29. The
first use of Jessica occurs in
Shakespeare's *The Merchant of
Venice*, published circa 1596. In the
late twentieth century, it became
extremely common in all English-
speaking countries, particularly
the United States.

PRINCIPAL COLORS: The full
range of violet hues

GEMSTONES AND PRECIOUS
METALS. Garnets

BOTANICALS: Dandelion,
lungwort, mint, strawberry

UNIQUE SPELLINGS: Jesaca,
Jesica, Jesicah, Jessaca, Jesseca,
Jessicah

RELATED TO: Jesca, Jess, Jessa,
Jessalin, Jessi, Jessiet, Jessy

Jessica

A KABBALISTIC SYNOPSIS

יאסיכא —YASYKA (Yod, Aleph, Samech, Yod, Kaph, Aleph)

Jessica is a real Trojan. There are few people who can work as hard and as consistently as she does, and certainly few who toil as willingly. Although Jessica enjoys work, she is not a masochist or some stern puritan type—far from it; Jessica knows very well how to have a good time. She just derives satisfaction from seeing a job well done. This attitude reveals something of the perfectionist in her makeup, which is all well and good in the workplace but will cause more than its fair share of disagreements at home. Despite her sometimes excessive attention to detail, Jessica is a well-liked woman, not the least because she is completely trustworthy and reliable. It is likely that this reliability will ensure Jessica a post with some level of responsibility; the more responsibility Jessica has, the happier she will be in life.

THE RUNIC INTERPRETATION

ᚨᚲᛁᛋᛋᛗᛟ (Ansuz, Kano, Isa, Sowelu, Sowelu, Ehwaz, Jera)

Jessica supports the energy of Jesse† with the additional Isa energy of standstill, the Kano energy of opening, and the Ansuz energy of signals. Jessica cultivates people with a positive viewpoint. She senses positive energy when she enters a room. It's as if on a subconscious level she takes the emotional temperature of everyone there. Jessica would rather be alone than with angry and conflicted people. She is always clear and receptive to new ideas and new experiences. Jessica is highly intuitive, and her gifts keep her safe and happy.

Elements: Air, water, earth, air, air, air, earth

THE NUMEROLOGICAL INTERPRETATION

Jessica (NV = 3, CV = 6, VV = 6, FL = 1)

This is a name that brings a distinct sense of grace and charm to its bearer. Jessica is blessed with an innate sense of beauty and natural balance. She is very sensitive and takes offense easily herself, so she is careful not to hurt other people's feelings. This emotional sensitivity extends itself into her environment; Jessica is always seeking to enrich her surroundings with colors and objects that bring joy to the eye of the beholder. Her home is very important to her, as are her family and loved ones. She makes a dedicated partner, a supportive parent, and a loyal friend. She has to take care that empathy does not lead to self-compromise, however. One of her most important life lessons has to do with the correct assessment of emotional boundaries.

Jessie

DERIVATION: Scottish and English, a short form of Jessica. In Scotland, sometimes used as a nickname for Janet.

PRINCIPAL COLORS: Electric colors

GEMSTONES AND PRECIOUS METALS: Sapphires

BOTANICALS: Sage, Solomon's seal

UNIQUE SPELLINGS: Jesset, Jessey, Jessi, Jessy

RELATED TO: Jess, Jessa, Jessalyn, Jessicat

A KABBALISTIC SYNOPSIS
יאסי —YASY (Yod, Aleph, Samech, Yod)

You are most likely to see Jessie at a stadium or a running track. There are very strong physical connections in Jessie's name, which indicate a love of all sporting activities. The total value of Jessie's name is eighty-one, and from this we can deduce that her connection with sport is likely to be supportive rather than active. She is not likely to be on the team; instead, she will be the trainer or coach. In addition there are suggestions that Jessie has a very powerful voice, and that she achieves success through the use of effective communication. The presence of Samech emphasizes her ability to be supportive to others. Jessie has a down-to-earth attitude about relationships and is a loving and warm mate. The only area where problems may arise is Jessie's commitment to her weekend games. It is probable, however, that Jessie will marry a similarly sporting type who will understand her obsession.

THE RUNIC INTERPRETATION
ᛗᛁᛋᛋᛗ◇ (Ehwaz, Isa, Sowelu, Sowelu, Ehwaz, Jera)

Jessie makes a habit of seeming really normal and well adjusted. In truth, she really *is* well adjusted! She has the double Sowelu runes for wholeness in her name. She seems like Snow White sometimes; birds are comfortable enough to land on her shoulders, and babies stop their crying when she speaks their name. Jessie is a healer, and her peacefulness and soothing nature make her welcome wherever she goes.

Elements: Air, earth, air, air, air, earth

THE NUMEROLOGICAL INTERPRETATION
Jessie (NV = 4, CV = 3, VV = 1, FL = 1)

This name reveals a woman who is a storehouse of information, one who is eager to acquire any ideas and bits of information that can be of practical use. There is, however, a tendency toward mental clutter, so Jessie will have to learn what to keep and what to toss out from her "mental encyclopedia." Jessie is quite sociable and very open to friendship. She is at heart a woman with a clear need to make something of her life, and will not waste valuable time on frivolities. Jessie is thus quite involved with the career facets of her life, and getting ahead means a great deal to her. In this respect, she requires an ambitious partner, one who is not afraid to struggle alongside her toward their mutual success.

DERIVATION: Hebrew, meaning "the Lord is salvation." A variant of the earlier Hebrew name Joshua. Especially common in Spanish-speaking countries.

PRINCIPAL COLORS: From pale, grassy to rich, forest green; white

GEMSTONES AND PRECIOUS METALS: Jade, white pearls, cat's-eye

BOTANICALS: Cabbage, lettuce, colewort

UNIQUE SPELLINGS: Hesus, Jeesus, Jezus

RELATED TO: Hosea, Joshua†, Jozua, Yehoshua

Jesus

A KABBALISTIC SYNOPSIS
יאסוס —YASVS (Yod, Aleph, Samech, Vau, Samech)

This is a name that yields any number of kabbalistic interpretations for obvious reasons. Even if we remove the overwhelming religious connotations of the name and consider it purely in terms of a standard analysis, Jesus yields some impressive results. You can guarantee that Jesus will have a strong and forceful character. He will rarely resort to anger, as the double presence of the letter Samech suggests that he is supportive rather than confrontational. Jesus' name reduces to eleven, which is the number of all things magical; this may refer to an interest in the occult or the arena of paranormal activity. Whatever Jesus' interests, he will be a driven man and will ensure that he is as knowledgeable as anyone can be in any field that interests him. Jesus can surprise us as well. His outward manner tends to be calm and relaxed, yet his underlying energy is apparent to all who come into contact with him.

THE RUNIC INTERPRETATION
ᛋᚢᛋᛖᛃ (Sowelu, Uruz, Sowelu, Ehwaz, Jera)

What a lucky name! Jesus has the double Sowelu runes for wholeness. He also supports the Uruz energy of strength and the Jera rune for harvest. The double Sowelu energy, as in the name Jessie, is an indicator of the ability to love. This ability and the capacity for self-love define the good mental health Jesus has. Jesus also has the strength rune, which provides depth of character and the capacity to persevere against all odds. Uruz is a rune of transformation; it indicates an ending to worn-out relationships and old ways of being. Uruz implies a death within the self and rebirth accompanied by greater strength; this process is part of the perpetual cycle of renewal.

Elements: Air, earth, air, air, earth

THE NUMEROLOGICAL INTERPRETATION
Jesus (NV = 11, CV = 3, VV = 8, FL = 1)

As one can easily imagine, the numerological significance of the name Jesus contains a very high spiritual potency. This name adds up to a master number, eleven. Men called Jesus have the potential to be quite intuitive and psychic. They are capable of experiencing life with a penetrating depth and clarity that gives them amazing insight into others. People therefore look to Jesus for aid and advice, counsel and support. Jesus can be inspirational to those around him, as he has a potent source of inner strength. He is also a visionary, tending to be idealistic about his beliefs. Jesus is a highly emotive communicator by nature, and will be active in sharing his worldview and personal opinions.

Jill

DERIVATION: English, short form of Gillian, which originally stems from the Latin name Julius. Popular before the seventeenth century, then declined, and has been in resurgence since the early twentieth century.

PRINCIPAL COLORS: The full range of yellow, gold, and green hues

GEMSTONES AND PRECIOUS METALS: Cat's-eye, pearls, moss agate

BOTANICALS: Blackberry, elder, hops

UNIQUE SPELLINGS: Jil, Jille, Jyl, Jyll, Jylle

RELATED TO: Gillian, Jilian, Jilleen, Jillian, Jilliana, Jillie, Jilly

A KABBALISTIC SYNOPSIS
לי —YL (Yod, Lamed)

If you want to keep something a secret, don't go near Jill! Jill will sniff out any hidden business in no time at all, and this skill makes her an ideal detective. Luckily, Jill is not the type to gossip, and anything that she finds out will remain with her. Jill's ability to pick up on everything that's going on in any given environment, be it home or the workplace, stems from her acute sensitivity to detail. Understandably this is both a bonus and a drawback in any close relationships she has. The value of Jill is forty—the value of the material world multiplied by four, or the number of elements multiplied by the number of the earth. In other words, Jill is completely tied up with material concerns; her chief priority in life will be career advancement rather than personal development. To her, promotion is personal development.

THE RUNIC INTERPRETATION
ᛚᛚᛁ◇ (Laguz, Laguz, Isa, Jera)

Jill is able to enjoy the double Laguz rune of flow along with the Isa rune for standstill and the Jera rune for harvest. Psychic ability and the ability to prophesy are fundamental to this name. The Isa rune indicates a need for rest and times of meditation. Jill stays in balance by serving and by listening. The Jera rune of harvest assures Jill that the good deeds she does behind the scenes never go unnoticed by the powers that be. She will enjoy prosperity and love in years ahead.

Elements: Water, water, earth, earth

THE NUMEROLOGICAL INTERPRETATION
Jill (NV = 7, CV = 7, VV = 9, FL = 1)

Jill is rather reserved and introspective by nature. She has a need for solitude as well as an urge to explore the more philosophical and spiritual facets of life. These aspects of her nature may lead her to do a great deal of research. It is easy to find Jill behind a book, attending a seminar, or teaching a class. She is very much at home in academic surroundings and enjoys education opportunities. Jill is naturally inclined to look beneath the surface of superficial realities in order to uncover some of life's mysteries.

DERIVATION: English, short form of James, which is an English version of Jacob. Occasionally used as a given name.

PRINCIPAL COLORS: The palest shade of any color

GEMSTONES AND PRECIOUS METALS: Diamonds, silver, any other stone that sparkles

BOTANICALS: Oats, parsley, caraway seeds

UNIQUE SPELLINGS: Jimm, Iiym

RELATED TO: Jaime†, James†, Jameson, Jamie†, Jimi, Jimmy

❧

"Let's just say I was testing the bounds of society. I was just curious."
—JIM MORRISON (MUSICIAN)

Jim

A KABBALISTIC SYNOPSIS
םי —YM (Yod, Mem)

Jim may come across as somewhat surly to those who aren't used to his ways—but really, Jim doesn't have a nasty bone in his body. He is a deep and profoundly caring individual, one who is simply not given to expressing his feelings publicly. This reluctance to communicate may well be connected to the unusual intensity with which Jim feels; if he is a Scorpio, not only will he be more passionate than most of us could ever manage even for a day, he will also be as silent as the grave! If you are close to a Jim, you will see that in private the fiery energies of this name mingle with the watery element of the final M, or Mem, to produce a wonderfully protective and caring partner. In his most intimate relationships, Jim likes to be in control—which is fine if he has a partner who takes a similar view.

THE RUNIC INTERPRETATION
ᛗᛁᛃ (Mannaz, Isa, Jera)

Jim is a live-and-let-live kind of fellow. The Mannaz rune of self gives Jim a sense of confidence and focus that helps him find success in life. He needs to feel that he is *heard*. As a child he might have felt overlooked. His childhood also lacked some of the lighthearted joy he would have appreciated. So, as a man, Jim relishes sports and technological gadgets, wonderful automobiles and hobby equipment. He loves to play, and he *needs* to play in an effort to make up for his somewhat overly responsible childhood. The Isa rune of standstill suggests that Jim is a loner and possibly an introvert. He requires time to relax and gather his reserves of energy. He likes to work as hard as he plays. Jera, the fortunate rune of harvest, intimates that Jim will enjoy status, wealth, and honor in this lifetime.

Elements: Air, earth, earth

THE NUMEROLOGICAL INTERPRETATION
Jim (NV = 5, CV = 5, VV = 9, FL = 1)

Jim has no tolerance for personal restrictions. This name reveals a man who is an avid explorer of life, an adventurer by nature and temperament. Jim's inner drives are characterized by the urge to expand his horizons, and he will stretch his talents and abilities to their limits. An unselfish and optimistic person, Jim likes to share his life with others and enjoys good company. In relationships, he prefers to be open to a number of possibilities, preferring a variety of romantic partners to early marriage. He has to take care to spend some time integrating his many experiences so that in the ocean of external possibilities he doesn't lose contact with his inner self.

❧

Joan

A Kabbalistic Synopsis

יען —YA'AN (Yod, Ayin, Nun)

There are very strong associations with water in the name Joan, not the least because of the final N, or Nun, meaning "fish." One can find various equivalents to the value of this name that connect it to the sea and to the coast generally. If Joan does not live by the sea already, it is certainly her ambition to move to the coast—although she is unlikely to be attracted to tourist traps, and is more at home in an isolated environment. In earlier days, Joan would have made a great lighthouse keeper. In today's world, the sea influences in her name would suit her to a job with the Coast Guard. The centrality of the Ayin in Joan's name indicates a very observant individual, and also suggests that she is physically resilient and strong-minded. Any man who gets involved with Joan will have a rewarding time if he has the strength of character to match hers.

The Runic Interpretation

ᚾᚨᛟᛃ (Nauthiz, Ansuz, Othila, Jera)

Joan learns that when she really enjoys what she is doing, things work out well for her. She has the Nauthiz rune for constraint, Ansuz for signals, Othila for separation, and Jera for harvest in her name. A Nauthiz-Othila rune combination indicates restraint and separation. These lessons of limitation foster her independence and flexibility. The Ansuz rune of signals helps Joan's intuitive nature to develop, and Jera for harvest brings success to Joan at all levels. Joan is so capable, she can be a success in many careers. She just needs to follow her heart because she will excel at what she enjoys best.

Elements: Fire, air, earth/fire, earth

The Numerological Interpretation

Joan (NV = 4, CV = 6, VV = 7, FL = 1)

A woman who requires balance and order in her life, Joan tends to be tidy, neat, and sometimes even a bit *too* fastidious! Personal appearance means a great deal to her, but she will tend to dress more practically than ostentatiously. She is not given to false airs about herself, nor is she self-dramatizing. Joan is a kind woman who is dedicated to family harmony and human cooperation. She also likes her quiet moments—times when she can be alone to think and nurture her inner life. Joan may not be the most forthcoming of people, but she can always be relied upon to give her best to any situation. She is a loyal friend and caring partner.

DERIVATION: English, one of the female forms of the Hebrew name John, which means "the Lord is gracious." One of the most prominent name bearers is Joan of Arc (1412–1431), the French "maid of Orléans" who believed she was guided by the voices of the saints. She led the French army in the siege of Orléans, and was burned at the stake at age eighteen or nineteen. She was canonized in 1920.

PRINCIPAL COLORS: The full spectrum of moderately shaded hues

GEMSTONES AND PRECIOUS METALS: Sapphires

BOTANICALS: Sage, spinach, medlar

UNIQUE SPELLINGS: Joane, Jone

RELATED TO: Janet, Jeant, Joanie, Jo Ann, Joannat, Joannet, Johana, Joni, Juanitat

DERIVATION: Latin form of the
Greek name *Ioanna*, originally from
Hebrew roots meaning "the Lord
has been gracious." Regularly
used in the Middle Ages in many
parts of Europe, and became
extremely popular in the 1950s.

PRINCIPAL COLORS: The palest to
the most brilliant shades of yellow
and brown, also gold

GEMSTONES AND PRECIOUS
METALS: Citrine, topaz, yellow
diamonds

BOTANICALS: Chamomile,
lavender, Saint-John's-wort

UNIQUE SPELLINGS: Joana,
Johanna, Johannah

RELATED TO: Jo, Joann, Jo Ann,
Joannet, Jo Anne, Juanitat

Joanna

A KABBALISTIC SYNOPSIS
יעאנא —YA'AANA (Yod, Ayin, Aleph, Nun, Aleph)

Those who are wise are careful when they are around Joanna, as she is one of the most intuitive people you are likely to meet. The average Joanna is so empathetic that she picks up feelings like a radio receiver. This can sometimes prove confusing for her if she is not aware of her abilities. Like many people with latent sensitivities, Joanna is also a highly emotional person. On the whole this is a positive aspect of her personality, but with certain astrological influences—that of Libra, for example—this can lead to a somewhat self-indulgent temperament. If she becomes fully conscious of her emotional sensitivity, Joanna probably will use this skill in some professional capacity, such as counseling.

THE RUNIC INTERPRETATION
ᚨᚾᚾᚨᛟᛃ (Ansuz, Nauthiz, Nauthiz, Ansuz, Othila, Jera)

The harvest rune combined with the strong signal energies in this name will help Joanna overcome her troubles. She used to complain a lot, but now she pays more attention to the words she speaks. She remains positive and hopeful and is a good influence on her friends. Joanna could have a great career working with the public because of her sunny disposition. She has the Jera rune of harvest to bring her satisfying and loving times ahead.

Elements: Air, fire, fire, air, earth/fire, earth

THE NUMEROLOGICAL INTERPRETATION
Joanna (NV = 5, CV = 6, VV = 8, FL = 1)

Joanna tends to be a peace-loving, gracious person. She is a caring woman who reaches out with creativity to bring her sense of inner harmony into her surroundings. She is careful about her environment, and ecologically oriented—a woman not given to wasting her resources on any level. She both needs and enjoys her home life but does not want to feel limited by domesticity. A career is very important to her.

Joanne

A Kabbalistic Synopsis

יעאן —YA'AAN (Yod, Ayin, Aleph, Nun)

Joanne has the same highly emotional nature as Joanna, with whom she shares a major section of her name. However, far from being a delicate, frail woman, Joanne is as tough as they come. You will never see Joanne crying or asking friends for advice about an emotional dilemma. Instead it is likely that Joanne will strive to be seen as almost hard-hearted. This front masks a vulnerable and potentially insecure person who more than anything needs positive emotional attention and support in order to feel genuinely fulfilled in life. The reduction of her name's value to sixteen, the number of the Tower of Destruction in the tarot, may indicate that she will cause herself personal trauma if she persists in hiding her feelings. There also are strong suggestions in her name of a generally successful life, so we may reasonably expect that she will meet the man she can finally trust with her emotions.

THE RUNIC INTERPRETATION

ᛗᚾᚾᚨᛟᛃ (Ehwaz, Nauthiz, Nauthiz, Ansuz, Othila, Jera)

Joanne is challenged by the double Nauthiz runes of constraint. As a child Joanne may have felt overlooked or disempowered on some level; perhaps she stood in the shadow of a busy parent or older, more outgoing sibling. For whatever reason, Joanne learned to be resilient and self-contained. Her inner resourcefulness helped her become independent and somewhat stoic concerning the vicissitudes of life. Othila, the rune of separation, further emphasizes the pragmatic and self-sufficient side of Joanne. The Ansuz rune of intuition makes Joanne a good listener, and she has an innate ability to empathize with people from various walks of life. Most important, Joanne is blessed with the Jera rune of harvest, implying that life for Joanne is full and rich with dreams realized and adversities well integrated into the overall pattern of her life.

Elements: Air, fire, fire, air, earth/fire, earth

THE NUMEROLOGICAL INTERPRETATION

Joanne (NV = 5, CV = 11, VV = 3, FL = 1)

Joanne has the potential to lead a most interesting life. She is quite intuitive and perceptive, and will have interests in people and places quite different from her own family origins. Joanne is a natural-born traveler who will continue to stay in touch and network with friends while she is on the road. Her attitude toward people is very inclusive. She knows that there are many races but only one human family. She respects all the different religions and belief systems in the world because she also sees their essential unity. Joanne is attracted to a partner who can be supportive of her expansive and tolerant views and has a wide range of intellectual interests.

DERIVATION: French, from the Latin name Johanna, which is a feminine form of John. Especially common during the 1950s.

PRINCIPAL COLORS: The full spectrum of lightly toned hues

GEMSTONES AND PRECIOUS METALS: Silver, platinum

BOTANICALS: Hazel, marjoram, parsnips

UNIQUE SPELLINGS: Joann, Jo Ann, Jo-Ann, Jo-Anne, Joeanne

RELATED TO: Janet†, Jean†, Jeanie, Jo, Joant†, Joanie, Joanna†, Jona, Juanita†

Jocelyn

DERIVATION: English, from the Old German, of uncertain origin. Brought to Britain by the Normans in the eleventh century. A male name in the Middle Ages, but revived as a girl's name in the twentieth century.

PRINCIPAL COLORS: Light to very deep shades of purple, maroon, mauve

GEMSTONES AND PRECIOUS METALS: Garnets, amethyst

BOTANICALS: Cherry, dandelion, mint, lungwort

UNIQUE SPELLINGS: Jocelin, Joscelin, Joscelyn, Joselyn, Josselyn, Josslyn

RELATED TO: Joceline, Josaline, Josceline, Joseline, Josline, Jossline, Joycet

A KABBALISTIC SYNOPSIS

יעסילין —YA'ASYLYN (Yod, Ayin, Samech, Yod, Lamed, Yod, Nun)

Possessed of a highly infectious love of life, Jocelyn brings joy to any environment. The prevalence of the letter Yod suggests a very energetic person positively brimming over with enthusiasm. Jocelyn will succeed in business largely through her oral communication skills, which are excellent. Sales is one ideal area for Jocelyn; she has the ability to get potential customers hooked on any product simply by talking. This ability is shown in the compression of her name, which yields the letters Peh, meaning "mouth," and Tzaddi, meaning "fishhook." At home Jocelyn is more affected by the final N, or Nun, in her name and is likely to want to leave the activity at the office, preferring to spend her evenings relaxing, probably with a good book. Jocelyn's partner will be happy to hear that she will still reserve plenty of energy and enthusiasm for the bedroom!

THE RUNIC INTERPRETATION

ᛏᛁᛚᛗᛋᛟᛇ (Nauthiz, Eihwaz, Laguz, Ehwaz, Sowelu, Othila, Jera)

Jocelyn learns that she must rely on her own judgment and believe in her talents because she is unusually gifted in many areas. The Nauthiz rune of constraint combined with Othila for separation teach Jocelyn to go her own way and find her freedom. Jocelyn uses silence to relax and get ideas. Sowelu for wholeness and Jera for harvest ensure Jocelyn will have a rich and fascinating mind. Jocelyn is a good conversationalist and has a wry sense of humor.

Elements: Fire, earth/fire, water, air, air, earth/fire, earth

THE NUMEROLOGICAL INTERPRETATION

Jocelyn (NV = 3, CV = 3, VV = 9, FL = 1)

Jocelyn has something to say about any life situation that she encounters. Generally curious and inquisitive by nature, she will eagerly investigate any set of circumstances that strikes her interest. Jocelyn has a genuinely friendly disposition and a heart that is open to helping others. People feel uplifted in her presence, as she has a fine sense of humor and a well-developed wit. Jocelyn has to take care not to monopolize a conversation by talking too much. She also has to avoid gossip and attachment to petty issues.

Jodie

A KABBALISTIC SYNOPSIS
יעדיה —YA'ADYH (Yod, Ayin, Daleth, Yod, Heh)

Employers like to hang on to Jodie, and if they treat her well, there is every chance that they will succeed, as she is immensely loyal. Most of Jodie's decisions in life are made on the basis of a strong sense of duty or obligation; it is rare that she will determine a course of action simply because it makes her happy. One effect of this trait is that she will often find opportunities for her friends. The presence of Daleth in her name suggests she has a capacity for opening doors in other people's lives. The value of her name is ninety-nine, so we can expect Jodie to have a good mind that is wiser than it is clever. This wisdom originates in part from her interest in the outside world and the lives of those around her. From time to time Jodie may experience depressive phases, which are usually the result of some conflict between work and home or her family commitments and the needs of her partner. They are rarely directly related to her own direction in life.

THE RUNIC INTERPRETATION
MIⱵ◇◇ (Ehwaz, Isa, Dagaz, Othila, Jera)

Jodie needed to carve out an identity at a tender age. Whether Jodie chose sports or languages, it's fairly certain that as an adult she has numerous opportunities to use her athletic prowess in a social setting such as sailing or tennis. Jodie has a good head for business, and money comes her way because Jodie is independent and entrepreneurial. The Dagaz rune of breakthrough could insinuate a healing of childhood wounds. Jodie is fortunate to have the Jera rune for harvest prominent in her name. This promises good luck in terms of wealth, and a bountiful life on all levels. See also the runic interpretation for Jody.

Elements: Air, earth, fire, earth/fire, earth

THE NUMEROLOGICAL INTERPRETATION
Jodie (NV = 7, CV = 5, VV = 2, FL = 1)

Jodie possesses a natural insight into life that comes to her as a result of her consistent personal reflection. She is very philosophical by nature and has the capacity to understand historical cycles and wide-reaching social issues. Jodie can derive a lot of benefit from higher education. She has the ability to apply what she knows to the practical issues of life, and her advice can be very down-to-earth. In her own special way, Jodie is a free spirit. Although intimacy in a relationship is very important to her, there is a special place within her that cannot be touched. It is here that she finds her inner strength and personal fortitude.

DERIVATION: English, pet form of Judith, which is from the Hebrew *yehudith*, meaning "Jewess." Extremely popular in the United States, Canada, and Australia in the second half of the twentieth century. The film actress Jodie Foster is a popular name bearer.

PRINCIPAL COLORS: Light to deep shades of yellow and green

GEMSTONES AND PRECIOUS METALS: Moss agate, white pearls, moonstones

BOTANICALS: Juniper, linseed

UNIQUE SPELLINGS: Jodee, Jodey, Jodi, Jody

RELATED TO: Joan†, Jody†, Jude, Judie, Judith†, Judy†

DERIVATION: English, possibly a
pet form of Judith or Jude. Has
been a popular female name since
the 1960s, and is occasionally
used for males as well.

PRINCIPAL COLORS: Any shade
of red, from pink to deep rose

GEMSTONES AND PRECIOUS
METALS: Bloodstones, garnets

BOTANICALS: Garlic, wormwood

UNIQUE SPELLINGS: Joady,
Jodee, Jodey, Jodi, Jodie

RELATED TO: Joseph†, Jude;
Joan†, Jodie†, Judie, Judith†,
Judy†

Jody

A KABBALISTIC SYNOPSIS
יעדי —YA'ADY (Yod, Ayin, Daleth, Yod)

If Jody is going to open doors for anyone it will be for him or herself—or possibly for the senior manager who can give that next promotion! It isn't that Jody is cold or ruthless; he or she simply has a lot of self-confidence and the ability and the energy to go far. If possible, Jody will do this without treading on anybody else's ambitions. In fact, Jody has the energy and confidence to do very well if he or she sets up a business alone. Emotionally Jody is one of the few people in life who really has got it together; he or she is rarely depressed, and when things go wrong in life, Jody is able to move on to the next challenge without harboring resentments or doubts about his or her own abilities. Nor surprisingly, with this cheerful approach to the world Jody has many friends who admire Jody's go-getting manner.

THE RUNIC INTERPRETATION
ᛇᛞᛟᛃ (Eihwaz, Dagaz, Othila, Jera)

Jody can be a male or female name, and the following interpretation holds true for both. Plus, since the "ie" and "y" endings (for Jodie and Jody) are both signified by the Eihwaz rune of defense, the interpretations are identical for both spellings. The athletic prowess signaled in both these names can also be recognized as indicating a competitive edge in business. Jody can be a shrewd businessperson who will be successful in whatever he or she decides to take on.

Elements: Earth/fire, fire, earth/fire, earth

THE NUMEROLOGICAL INTERPRETATION
Jody (NV = 9, CV = 5, VV = 4, FL = 1)

This is a name of numerological complexity, one that results in a most interesting personality. Jody is broad and inclusive in his or her viewpoints. Jody is inspired by poetry and philosophy, and can be quite the romantic idealist. Yet there is another side to Jody's nature that is quite distinct from this dreamier person: Jody is also a pragmatist, especially when it comes to finances and career. Jody may thus spend a lot of his or her time and energy working to balance and integrate these two sides of his or her nature. The achievement of this integration will count as a major personal success. Jody will also be involved in some form of volunteer charity work, as the humanitarian part of Jody's personality also needs to be expressed.

Joe

DERIVATION: English, short form of the biblical name Joseph. Sometimes given as an independent name.

PRINCIPAL COLORS: The full spectrum of mauve through violet

GEMSTONES AND PRECIOUS METALS: Garnets and amethyst

BOTANICALS: Cherry, strawberry, apple, dandelion, mint

UNIQUE SPELLING: Jo

RELATED TO: Giuseppe, Jodie†, Jody†, Joey, José†, Josef, Joseph†, Jozef, Pepe, Peppi, Pino, Seppi, Yousef

A Kabbalistic Synopsis
יעה —YA'AH (Yod, Ayin, Heh)

Joe is a very straightforward guy; with Joe, what you see really *is* what you get! Joe is quite happy about this, and prides himself on the fact that he is a regular guy in a world seemingly full of endlessly complex individuals. He is a popular man, and is likely to be most at home in a relatively small community where he will know everyone in the local bar and will probably be a mainstay of the town's social scene. The final letter in Joe's name is Heh, which means "window" in Hebrew; consequently, we can expect Joe to be interested in the world around him. Due to Heh's connection with the letter it follows—Ayin, which refers to physical appetites—it may well be that Joe is not only an avid partygoer himself but likes to watch other people enjoying themselves as well. Joe likes to lead a very active life. The initial Yod in his name lets us know that Joe is full of energy and enthusiasm, while the total value of his name is associated with the tarot card Death, which indicates a need for a change in lifestyle. Thanks to his interest in the outside world, Joe may well be suited to working in the travel industry. Joe is likely to get married relatively early in life. Being a very stable, down-to-earth guy, he is sometimes overly keen to get established in a stable relationship. While Joe may not be the most romantic man in the world, he will certainly be loyal and dependable.

The Runic Interpretation
◇◇ (Othila, Jera)

Joe has both boots planted firmly on the big blue marble in space. And special boots they are, because Joe is different! Music is one of his main interests, and he composes songs in his head and enjoys his time alone. He isn't a slave to social conventions, and could leave his lovers a bit bemused with his ability to offer every one of them their freedom. Joe has a strong sense of adventure and hopes to learn more about ancient cultures, with a focus on unlocking ancient subtle mysteries. The harvest is an appropriate image for this name, and Joe is sure to reap special rewards from his rich imagination and unique point of view.

Elements: Earth/fire, earth

The Numerological Interpretation
Joe (NV = 3, CV = 1, VV = 11, FL = 1)

This is a very independent and assertive man, one who is totally ready to overcome any of the odds in life by himself if necessary. Joe is usually quite ambitious and is definitely success oriented. The numbers in this name indicate that Joe is quite communicative and always has something to say about any life situation. He is curious and inquisitive, a person who takes great pleasure in exploring all the many opportunities that come his way to improve himself. Joe knows how to move freely in and out of most social settings, helping others feel at ease and generally spreading harmony in group situations. His interests are quite varied—too varied, at times. Joe has to take care that he does not scatter his mental energy and wind up involved in too many projects at the same time.

DERIVATION: Hebrew, meaning
"Jehovah is the Lord." The name
of a prophet in the Old Testament,
and also the name of one of King
David's men. Especially popular in
recent years.

PRINCIPAL COLORS: Pale sky to
deep midnight blue

GEMSTONES AND PRECIOUS
METALS: Blue and blue-green
turquoise

BOTANICALS: Dog rose, vervain,
melon

UNIQUE SPELLINGS: Joal, Jole

RELATED TO: Joe†, Joey, Joseph†

Joel

A KABBALISTIC SYNOPSIS
יעאל —YA'AAL (Yod, Ayin, Aleph, Lamed)

Oh boy! This man intends to make an impact on the world in a big way—and may well do so. His name totals to 111—all ones—so we have somebody who is completely individual in personality, bursting with ideas and spilling over with self-confidence. Not only that, but the final letter in his name (L, or Lamed, meaning "ox goad"), suggests that he will stop at nothing to achieve his goals in life. Joel is also quite charming, and while you are gasping at what is almost blatant arrogance in his conviction that he will succeed, you cannot help but like the man. His powerful charismatic personality means that people do tend to listen to him—increasing his chances of proving himself right.

THE RUNIC INTERPRETATION
ᛚᛖᛟᛃ (Laguz, Ehwaz, Othila, Jera)

Joel is easygoing and thoughtful. The Laguz rune of flow suggests musical talent, and a creative and inventive mind. Othila, the rune of separation, prompts Joel to stand outside the middle road and think for himself. This tendency to be original can cause him to feel alienated and lonely at times, but it's a small price to pay for freedom in the long run. Ehwaz, the rune of movement, implies that Joel has talent on the dance floor. He has a flexible mind and a good sense of timing in life in general. Ehwaz always holds out the hope that whomever it blesses will be given the opportunity to relocate abroad, and Joel would love nothing better! He welcomes fresh ideas and new sights and sounds. Joel has an artistic temperament, and functions best when he has lots of enrichment and exposure to new ways of seeing the world. He can be a bit moody, and variety helps him feel balanced and hopeful.

Elements: Water, air, earth/fire, earth

THE NUMEROLOGICAL INTERPRETATION
Joel (NV = 6, CV = 4, VV = 11, FL = 1)

An artistic nature and a sense of harmony characterize this name. Joel has the need to communicate his talents and abilities to the world and has the potential to develop this orientation toward beauty into a number of creative avenues of self-expression. This can be in music, art, or writing and may even be carried into the business world. Joel's practical side is very much in evidence within the numbers of this name. Career and success oriented, Joel wishes to be in a position to enjoy the many beautiful objects that come with financial abundance. His life will bring him a wide range of friends and associates.

John

DERIVATION: English, from the Hebrew name Johanan, meaning "God is gracious." Found in the New Testament as the name of John the Baptist. The name of many saints and popes, and also a common royal name. Has been one of the most common male names in all English-speaking countries.

PRINCIPAL COLORS: Cream, the full range of greens

GEMSTONES AND PRECIOUS METALS: Jade, pearls, cat's-eye

BOTANICALS: Cabbage, rapeseed, willow ash

UNIQUE SPELLINGS: Gian, Johnn, Jon, Jonn

RELATED TO: Evan†, Giovanni, Hans, Ian†, Ivan†, Jack†, Jan, Jock, Johannes, Johnathan, Johnnie, Johnny, Johnson, Jonathan†, Juan†, Sean†, Shawn†, Yan, Zane

❧

"I can't understand why people are frightened of new ideas. I'm frightened of the old ones."
—JOHN CAGE (COMPOSER)

A KABBALISTIC SYNOPSIS
יען —YA'AN (Yod, Ayin, Nun)

On the surface John seems to be a regular guy—a good guy, friendly and helpful, but not particularly outstanding in any way. Where many people might argue against such a label, John is more than happy to be regarded as supremely normal. He can see the value of being a supportive husband or loving dad. He also sees the value of being a hard worker who is also loyal to his company. Those who know John well may see something of his hidden depths. He tends to have quite unusual taste, evident from the way he furnishes his house and even the books that he buys. John often has an interest in the bizarre, and is almost definitely a fan of believe-it-or-not-type publications—although he prefers his coworkers be unaware of this interest.

THE RUNIC INTERPRETATION
ᚾᚺᛟᛃ (Nauthiz, Hagalaz, Othila, Jera)

John is a loving soul. He always has time for someone who just needs to talk. John has the Nauthiz rune for constraint and Hagalaz rune for disruptions. Unfortunately, this combination brings limitations and disappointments. Fortunately, John has the Othila rune of separation. He learns to be independent early in life, and he learns to think for himself. When troubles come, John realizes that a positive attitude is the best antidote. He keeps his mind filled with hope and dreams—and it works! The Jera rune for harvest lets us know that John reaps rewards for his perseverance.

Elements: Fire, water, earth/fire, earth

THE NUMEROLOGICAL INTERPRETATION
John (NV = 11, CV = 5, VV = 6, FL = 1)

John's name instills in him an intuitive capacity to look behind surface appearances into the true value of things. He is thus possessed of a special kind of vision, one that allows him a deep understanding of human nature and the world in which he lives. John seeks to be of service to others. It is important to him that other people in his life be happy, and he does whatever he can in order to bring a sense of joy into his relationships. John's romantic side is quite prominent, and he is very open to a number of adventures in this respect. John is a man who likes to be on the move.

❧

Jonathan

DERIVATION: Hebrew, meaning "gift of God." Found in the Old Testament as the best friend of King David, and the son of King Saul. Became very popular as a name during the seventeenth century, and has been on the rise since the mid-twentieth century.

PRINCIPAL COLORS: White, all shades of green

GEMSTONES AND PRECIOUS METALS: Cat's-eye, moonstones

BOTANICALS: Chicory, plantain, moonwort

UNIQUE SPELLINGS: Johnathan, Johnathon, Jonathann, Jonathen, Jonathin, Jonathon, Jonothan, Jonothen, Jonothon

RELATED TO: Hans, Ian†, Ivan†, John†, Johnny, Jon, Jonny, Juan†, Sean†, Shawn†

❧

"Nothing is impossible. Some things are just less likely than others."
—JONATHAN WINTERS (ACTOR)

A KABBALISTIC SYNOPSIS
יענאתן —YA'ANAThN (Yod, Ayin, Nun, Aleph, Tau, Nun)

Jonathan is quite a strange guy. In almost direct contrast to John, he faces the world with an image that is at least unusual and can often be quite bizarre. Jonathan is the sort of man who is drawn to obscure religious or political groups; older Jonathans may still be clinging to the hippie values of their youth. Jonathan certainly knows how to have a good time—and no one's parties are quite like his! On a more serious note, Jonathan is intensely loyal; he tends to commit emotionally quite late in life, but once he does, he will stand by his lover through any amount of trouble or hardship. As a friend Jonathan is equally reliable, and no matter how much help he offers, Jonathan will never ask for anything in return. Sometimes, especially in the case of Piscean Jonathans, he can be something of a magnet for lame ducks, but this is not really a problem, as Jonathan gets immense satisfaction from helping to ease the suffering of others.

THE RUNIC INTERPRETATION
ᚾᚨᚦᚨᚾᛟᛃ (Nauthiz, Ansuz, Thurisaz, Ansuz, Nauthiz, Othila, Jera)

Jonathan likes to feel free and unimpeded. It's not easy, with double Nauthiz in his name for constraint. The double Ansuz rune of signals is combined with Thurisaz for gateway, Othila for separation, and Jera for harvest. Jonathan can accomplish wonders in careers such as film, broadcasting, science, and the law. He has a keen intuitive ability and longs for freedom. He excels at finding new ways of looking at things. Jonathan has a strong, analytical mind and this carries him far in the world, as the Jera rune for harvest promises. The Thurisaz rune of gateway hints that wonderful opportunities await Jonathan.

Elements: Fire, air, fire, air, fire, earth/fire, earth

THE NUMEROLOGICAL INTERPRETATION
Jonathan (NV = 11, CV = 3, VV = 8, FL = 1)

The name value of eleven, combined with the consonant value of three, constitutes a very special gift. It allows Jonathan to sense the quality of other people's thoughts and feelings, and it contributes to his ability to read other people's characters easily. He is a communicator by nature, and may find writing and speaking are suitable outlets for this facet of his personality. Psychology and the metaphysical sciences can be very appealing to him as well. Jonathan is interested in the relationship between the energies of life and the forms that they take. He is creative and can easily produce an abundance of life's necessities.

❧

Jordan

A KABBALISTIC SYNOPSIS
יערדון —YA'ARDVN (Yod, Ayin, Resh, Daleth, Vau, Nun)

Here is a man who will go to almost any lengths to achieve his ambitions. Jordan is a real fighter. The initial Yod gives him that burst of energy to get started, but what maintains his drive toward his goals is the central letter Resh, which represents the less intense but persistent energy of the sun. A lot of driven people can be pretty glum and antisocial; they have their dream and everything else is subordinate to it. Not Jordan: He is a laid-back, cheerful guy who manages to have fun without once forgetting about his long-term plans. As any partner of Jordan's will agree, this man is a damn good catch. He's funny, he's fit, he's usually good-looking, and he always pays his own way! What's more, Jordan is a highly sensitive individual—an aspect of his personality that is shown by the combination of Vau and Nun in his name.

THE RUNIC INTERPRETATION
ᛏᚨᛞᚱᛟᛃ (Nauthiz, Ansuz, Dagaz, Raido, Othila, Jera)

Jordan has resourcefulness, intuition, power, and compassion with the blessings of the four elements in his name. While it's true that Nauthiz, the rune of limitation, is around to dull the joy, Jordan is a pro at averting disaster. With the powerful Dagaz rune of breakthrough in his name, Jordan occasionally turns adversity into opportunity. Many advantages come along, and Jordan has the presence of mind not to let them slip by. The Raido rune of good communication helps him go far in business. He could excel in sales or research, and would enjoy biotechnology. The Ansuz rune of signals is represented in strong communication skills and an unusually persuasive style. Jordan enjoys people from all walks of life, and his optimistic attitude gives him a deep appreciation of all that life has to offer. The Jera rune for harvest helps Jordan realize his dreams in a wonderful way.

Elements: Fire, air, fire, water, earth/fire, earth

THE NUMEROLOGICAL INTERPRETATION
Jordan (NV = 8, CV = 1, VV = 7, FL = 1)

Jordan is success oriented and quite ambitious in his chosen field of endeavor. This is a name that indicates a strong personal will and a definite need to achieve. Social status is important to Jordan, and he will use all of his abundant vitality toward conquering the challenges that face him as he moves from one level to another. He has to be careful of a tendency toward egocentricity, as he is apt to put his personal goals first and may have to work at being considerate of others. Jordan will require a lot of time by himself. He is introspective and needs this time to assess what has taken place in his life so that he may slowly structure his future course.

DERIVATION: Hebrew, from the name of the Jordan River, which comes from the Hebrew word *yardan*, meaning "to descend." A common surname during the Middle Ages.

PRINCIPAL COLORS: Deep azure, rich violet, dark gray, black

GEMSTONES AND PRECIOUS METALS: Carbuncles, dull rubies, black pearls

BOTANICALS: Angelica, marsh mallow

UNIQUE SPELLINGS: Jordaan, Jorden, Jordenn, Jordin, Jordon, Jordyn, Jourdan

RELATED TO: Giordano, Jared†, Joord, Jordi, Jory, Jourdain, Judd

DERIVATION: Spanish version of George, which originally stems from the Greek word *georgos*, meaning "farmer" or "husbandman."

PRINCIPAL COLORS: Orange, gold, the full spectrum of yellow and bronze hues

GEMSTONES AND PRECIOUS METALS: Citrine, amber, any yellow stone

BOTANICALS: Eyebright, sorrel

UNIQUE SPELLINGS: Jorhe, Jorje

RELATED TO: Georget, Georgie, Giorgio, Igor, Jorg, Jorgen, Jori

❧

"I have always imagined that Paradise will be a kind of library."
—JORGE LUIS BORGES (AUTHOR)

A Kabbalistic Synopsis
יערהי —YA'ARHY (Yod, Ayin, Resh, Heh, Yod)

You will not meet many people as interesting as Jorge. Even the way his name appears in Hebrew is a conversation piece—especially if you forget that Y in Hebrew is also J! Aquarius is the main influence on Jorge's personality, and this means that he is unconventional in a dreamy, philosophical kind of way. Jorge can think at some length about issues that never enter most people's heads at all. Other aspects of his name suggest that Jorge is a great conversationalist, not the least because of his willingness to break the ice with strangers and his ability to pick topics far from the expected spectrum of subjects. Jorge is a man you would like to sit with at a coffee bar and while away a few hours just listening to him talk. In many cases Jorge has an air of mystery about him, which attracts people's attention even if they're not really sure why it is they want to spend time with him.

The Runic Interpretation
ᛗᚷᚱᛟᛃ (Ehwaz, Gebo, Raido, Othila, Jera)

Jorge has a wonderful sense of humor that is only marred by his occasional sarcasm and propensity for practical jokes. Jorge has the runes for partnership and separation in his name, which could imply that he is probably the kind of so-called confirmed bachelor that usually falls the hardest. Jorge has the Jera rune for harvest, and once he settles down with the right partner, Jorge will be quite content. He is a good, clear communicator and his peace-loving nature makes him a good mate. Jorge needs time alone and requires a study or workshop, if at all possible, to call his own. Retaining his individuality within the partnership keeps Jorge a balanced and fulfilled man.

Elements: Air, fire, water, earth/fire, earth

The Numerological Interpretation
Jorge (NV = 1, CV = 8, VV = 11, FL = 1)

A man with a broad point of view and multiple aspirations, Jorge is aiming for the top in whatever career he chooses. Jorge is not afraid of life and thrives on the adventure of achieving success. This is a name that bestows personal authority along with a commanding nature and the urge to dominate one's environment. Jorge will seek a partnership with a person who is supportive of his far-reaching ambitions. If spiritually developed, the name Jorge can indicate a man who will use his fiery vitality for the betterment of humanity. He is forthright and believes in himself and the causes he espouses. His challenge in life is to keep his emotional nature balanced with the pragmatic realities of everyday living.

José

DERIVATION: Spanish form of Joseph, which stems from the Hebrew root meaning "Jehovah adds." Joseph is found in the Old Testament as the twelfth son of Jacob, and in the New Testament as the husband of the Virgin Mary.

PRINCIPAL COLORS: Moderate shades of any color

GEMSTONES AND PRECIOUS METALS: Sapphires

BOTANICALS: Celandine, sage

UNIQUE SPELLINGS: Hose, Josay, Josey

RELATED TO: Che, Giuseppe, Joe†, Joey, Josef, Joseph†, Jozef, Pepe, Yosef

A KABBALISTIC SYNOPSIS
העסאי —HA'ASAY (Heh, Ayin, Samech, Aleph, Yod)

A name like José gives us a choice in pronunciation, and in this analysis, the Spanish pronunciation is used. José is very bright and rarely sits still long enough for you to get a close look at him, but if you do get a chance, he is likely to have lean features and an intense expression. José watches everything, and it is through his ever open window on the world (represented by the initial H, or Heh) that he understands his own personality. Quite often, José will be a nervous individual, although this may be in the sense of nervous energy rather than anxiousness. Whatever José takes on as a task or career, it will not be long before he is an old hand at it, since one of his main skills is an ability to learn very quickly—an ability no doubt aided by his excellent talent for keen observation.

THE RUNIC INTERPRETATION
Mᛋᛜ◇ (Ehwaz, Sowelu, Othila, Jera)

José is watchful. The Othila rune of separation gives José a good sense of timing. He is eager to discard the old, and this is true of his relationships as well as his ideas. José has a quick mind and embraces new concepts with a depth of understanding that is truly unusual. His detail-oriented mind strives for balance in the company of artists and comedians. José enjoys living, and the harvest rune implies that he'll be fortunate in a career that uses his talents of observation.

Elements: Air, air, earth/fire, earth

THE NUMEROLOGICAL INTERPRETATION
José (NV = 4, CV = 2, VV = 11, FL = 1)

Men named José are usually very focused on their personal relationships and find themselves continually involved in intimate relations with others. José will have a naturally compassionate nature as well as a deep respect for his home and community. He is well aware of the material necessities of life and is very dedicated to working toward his financial success. He also possesses a strong spiritual orientation, one that allows him to think and act for the betterment of other people's welfare as well as his own. This is a man of faith, drive, and determination. However, he has to be careful of disillusionment when he comes in contact with people who may not be as honest in their intentions as he is.

> "Effort is only effort when it begins to hurt."
> —JOSÉ ORTEGA Y GASSET (AUTHOR)

DERIVATION: Hebrew, meaning
"Jehovah adds." The name of
Jacob's twelfth son in the Old
Testament, and of the Virgin
Mary's husband in the New
Testament.

PRINCIPAL COLORS: The full
range of russet and yellow shades,
orange

GEMSTONES AND PRECIOUS
METALS: Amber, topaz, yellow
diamonds

BOTANICALS: Borage, Saint-
John's-wort, eyebright

UNIQUE SPELLINGS: Josef,
Joseff, Josif, Josiff, Josiph,
Josyf, Josyff, Josyph

RELATED TO: Che, Giuseppe,
Joet, Joey, José†, Josef, Jozef,
Pepe, Yosef, Yusuf

~

"When you follow your bliss . . .
doors will open where you would not
have thought there would be doors;
and where there wouldn't be a door
for anyone else."
—JOSEPH CAMPBELL (AUTHOR)

Joseph

A KABBALISTIC SYNOPSIS
יוסאף —YVSAPh (Yod, Vau, Samech, Aleph, Peh)

See that man with peanut butter on his tie, a Barbie in his pocket, and a wallet thick with kids' pictures? You are probably looking at a Joseph. He may look like he's just crawled through a kindergarten, but he is a deeply thoughtful man. Children are the most important thing in Joseph's life, and his name has strong kabbalistic associations with fatherhood. One equivalent of the value of his name is "lingam," which is the phallus and the prime symbol of fertility. There are also very definite indications that Joseph gets great pleasure out of the creative side of his fatherhood role. At work Joseph is keen to take on responsibilities and makes a firm but sympathetic manager. He is not obsessively ambitious but will make sure that he gradually rises within his chosen profession. As he comes across as innately trustworthy, he will have no problem in achieving a level of seniority over time.

THE RUNIC INTERPRETATION
ᚺᚲᛗᛋᛟ◇ (Hagalaz, Perth, Ehwaz, Sowelu, Othila, Jera)

Joseph is a child of love, and dearly loved he is. However, the Hagalaz rune of disruption will carry challenging lessons for Joseph. Joseph could lose friends and leave homes in his youth because his family travels a good deal. This could cause disruption, and separation from some of those he cares about. On the positive side the many changes in Joseph's life teach him self-reliance and good social skills. He learns a lot about people by being exposed to various attitudes and situations. The Jera rune for harvest keeps Joseph hopeful, and his optimism ensures delightful experiences in his life. Joseph is strong because he has the four elements in his name.

Elements: Water, water, air, air, earth/fire, earth

THE NUMEROLOGICAL INTERPRETATION
Joseph (NV = 1, CV = 8, VV = 11, FL = 1)

There is no challenge too great for Joseph. This is a name with a very powerful combination of numbers, one that gives insight, vision, and intuition. Joseph gives people the impression that he is very independent—and this is very true. He has an inner conviction about how he lives his life, and will not compromise himself. Joseph has to take care to be emotionally, as well as mentally, sensitive to others. He will need the cooperation of friends, coworkers, and loved ones in order to fulfill his many projects. He should always strive to be in touch with his heart and not use his mind as the only tool to take him through life.

~

Josephine

A Kabbalistic Synopsis

יוסאפין —YVSAPhYN (Yod, Vau, Samech, Peh, Yod, Nun)

Josephine is the female version of Joseph† . . . so Josephine must be a real mother figure, right? Wrong! You're more likely to see Josephine in the company head office than in the maternity ward. Some people have a natural charm, and Josephine has charm in spades. A persuasive tongue and a convincing expression are all she needs to get right to the top. The position of the letter Samech in her name indicates that she relies an awful lot on luck, and the power of her personality, to get her through. In most situations there's a good chance that she will succeed with this approach. Josephine's only real problem is that she can sometimes hanker for a deeper relationship. It may come later than for most, but ultimately, Josephine will find an ideal mate.

The Runic Interpretation

ᛗᚾᛁᚺᚨᛗᛉᛟᛜ (Ehwaz, Nauthiz, Isa, Hagalaz, Perth, Ehwaz, Sowelu, Othila, Jera)

Josephine has many of the affectionate qualities of Joseph and many of the challenges as well. The additional runes lend standstill, constraint, and double movement energies to Josephine's name. Josephine could have a life of travel and many residences. The movement rune can have psychological implications as well, and in Josephine's case this means that she has a quick and flexible mind with lots of insight. Josephine is witty and sophisticated. The initiation rune, Perth, means she will experience many unexpected gains. Life is never boring for Josephine, whose social skills win her prestige, power, and genuine friends along the way.

Elements: Air, fire, earth, water, water, air, air, earth/fire, earth

The Numerological Interpretation

Josephine (NV = 11, CV = 22, VV = 7, FL = 1)

Can a person live up to the numbers of this name? Josephine is one of the very few names that contains the two master numbers: eleven and twenty-two. Josephine's higher potential is thus enormous! She is a woman who has both creative potency and deep compassion. Josephine can create a utopian vision for human welfare as well as put her enormous potential to work for its concrete manifestation. When this name expresses itself on a more mundane level, eleven becomes two and twenty-two becomes four. If Josephine is living a more routine life, the expansive indications of her name are definitely lessened. The two and four produce a hardworking woman, one very devoted to her partner and to the creation of a financially secure life. It is her spiritual life that will bring her to the doors of the "double digits."

DERIVATION: French version of Joseph, which originally derives from the Hebrew meaning "Jehovah adds." The name of Napoleon Bonaparte's first wife. Became fashionable during the nineteenth century.

PRINCIPAL COLORS: Pale to deep, rich shades of green, also white

GEMSTONES AND PRECIOUS METALS: Jade, moonstones, pearls

BOTANICALS: Plantain, colewort, moonwort

UNIQUE SPELLINGS: Josefeen, Josefene, Josefine, Josefyne, Josepheene, Josephene, Josephyne, Josiphene, Josiphine, Josiphyne, Josyphene

RELATED TO: Fifi, Fina, Jo, Jolene, Josefa, Josefina, Josephina, Josetta, Josie

"One never learns by success. Success is the plateau that one rests upon to take breath and look down from upon the straight and difficult path, but one does not climb upon a plateau."

—JOSEPHINE PRESTON PEABODY (AUTHOR)

PRINCIPAL COLORS: The full range of green hues, creamy white

GEMSTONES AND PRECIOUS METALS: Moonstones, cat's eye

BOTANICALS: Lettuce, cabbage, colewort

UNIQUE SPELLINGS: Joshooa, Joshuah

RELATED TO: Hosea, Josh, Joshy, Josua, Oshea, Yehoshua

Joshua

A KABBALISTIC SYNOPSIS
יעשוה —YA'AShVH (Yod, Ayin, Shin, Vau, Heh)

They say the Mounties always get their man; well, Joshua would make a great Mountie! The compression of his name contains letters meaning both "tooth" and "fishhook"—clear indications of his dogged persistence. Without a doubt, if Joshua sets his heart on a partner or house or even a job, he will keep on going until he gets it. Interestingly, the value of his name reduces to thirteen, the number of the Death card in tarot, symbolic of change. In some areas of life Joshua is the first to agree that change is good—but when it comes to relationships, he is as solid as a rock. Thinking of rocks, it is quite rare to see a thin Joshua; he usually likes to work out—even body build—as he certainly loves a challenge and enjoys the immediacy of physical activity and sports.

THE RUNIC INTERPRETATION
ᚨᚢᚺᛊᛟᛇ (Ansuz, Uruz, Hagalaz, Sowelu, Othila, Jera)

Joshua truly loves his life and all that it brings him. He uses the force of the Ansuz, Uruz, and Sowelu runes to remind himself of who he really is, and to consider his true nature. Joshua may need to learn how to release stress, and yoga and meditation may help him to relax. His life has plenty of tense moments, and the Hagalaz and Othila runes may bring painful lessons for Joshua. But the Jera rune of harvest lets Joshua know he has nothing to fear from any of his challenges.

Elements: Air, earth, water, air, earth/fire, earth

THE NUMEROLOGICAL INTERPRETATION
Joshua (NV = 2, CV = 1, VV = 1, FL = 1)

Joshua may find that he is torn between his need to be his own person and his need to be in a very intimate relationship. Perhaps he can have both total independence and the love of his life at the same time; anything is possible when there is enough love. In any event, he will be put to the test until both sides of his nature—his need to be free and his need to be loved—are "happily married." Joshua has a very intense personal drive. He has to be creative, and his creations have to reflect his personal urges. Ideas cannot be given to him; they must rise up from his own interior resources. He is also a very romantic man, one who has a caring disposition and deep feelings.

Joy

A KABBALISTIC SYNOPSIS
יעי —YA'AY (Yod, Ayin, Yod)

Joy by name and joy by nature—she is popular with everyone, and hasn't got a malicious bone in her body or a nasty thought in her head. Joy isn't passive or saintly, though; her thoroughly kind personality doesn't mean that she can't enjoy herself! The presence of a Yod at both ends of her name tells us that she has energy to spare. With a zestful attitude, Joy sucks every last good moment out of life that she can, and involves as many other people in the fun as possible. The strong influence of the number nine on her name indicates a definite sense of duty in her life, and we are likely to meet Joy in some public service–based job or another, bringing her own special touch of happiness to the whole workplace.

THE RUNIC INTERPRETATION
↑◇◇ (Eihwaz, Othila, Jera)

It's interesting to note that the name Joy does not contain the Wunjo rune for joy! But when Joy feels safe and secure, she surely ascends to these blissful heights. Once she learns not to bemoan the experiences that advance her and free her from limitations, Joy feels at ease. Joy's security is implied by the Eihwaz rune of defense. Joy can be tactful and assertive, and it takes a lot to ruffle her confident demeanor. The Othila rune of separation intimates that circumstances in her family life could have necessitated that Joy carve out an identity independent of her role within the family. She could have felt misunderstood as a child. When confusion no longer has the upper hand in Joy's life, she is able to gain perspective on who she is and where she intends to steer the sailboat of her soul. It is at this point that Joy becomes a picture of vitality in mind, body, and spirit.

Elements: Earth/fire, earth/fire, earth

THE NUMEROLOGICAL INTERPRETATION
Joy (NV = 5, CV = 1, VV = 4, FL = 1)

As her name indicates, Joy is an expansive and optimistic person, one who needs to be free to enjoy life. She cannot be in a relationship with a domineering partner, or one who is overly emotionally dependent on her. Joy needs room to fly. It is in this way only that she will stay connected to her nest. Joy accumulates life experiences in much the same manner a butterfly collector gathers her specimens. The result of Joy's collection is that it gives her an outlook on life that is quite a bit more inclusive than many other people's. Joy is a visionary who is able to see the possibilities for her own creativity, and then sets out to crystallize that vision into a practical reality.

DERIVATION: English, from the common noun. First used as a name during the Middle Ages, and fairly popular among the Puritans. Especially common during the 1950s.

PRINCIPAL COLORS: The full spectrum of pale hues

GEMSTONES AND PRECIOUS METALS: Silver, platinum, diamonds

BOTANICALS: Sweet marjoram, oats, mushrooms

UNIQUE SPELLINGS: Joi, Joiye, Joye

RELATED TO: Jo, Joie, Joya, Joyann, Joyanna, Joycet

"I believe poets have to be inside their poems somewhere, or the poem won't work."

—JOY HARJO (POET)

DERIVATION: English, originally
from a Norman male name that was
used by a seventh-century Breton
saint. During the seventeenth and
eighteenth centuries, Joyce began
to be used as a female name.
Especially popular during the
early twentieth century.

PRINCIPAL COLORS: Electric
colors, moderately shaded hues

GEMSTONES AND PRECIOUS
METALS: Sapphires

BOTANICALS: Sage, wild spinach

UNIQUE SPELLINGS: Joice, Joise,
Joisse, Joyse

RELATED TO: Joy†, Joya, Joycela,
Joycelyn, Joycie

Joyce

A KABBALISTIC SYNOPSIS
יעים —YA'AYS (Yod, Ayin, Yod, Samech)

Mountains, lakes, and other rural settings hold a special attraction for Joyce. Her favorite leisure activity is walking—not the half-hour stroll that most might enjoy after dinner, but the real deal, with hiking boots and a backpack. Under kabbalistic analysis we find that "walking shoe" is a numerical equivalent of Joyce's name, while the Ayin in her name suggests the mountain goat, with whom she shares an agile surefootedness in the most challenging terrain. Joyce is also a real family woman who loves to be with her children, especially on occasions that allow for festive gatherings with all the food, fun, and games that accompany such events. Joyce can afford quite luxurious holiday celebrations, as she has an acute feel for business and, in most cases, accumulates a reasonable amount of property over what is usually a long lifetime.

THE RUNIC INTERPRETATION
ᛗᛋᛇᛟᛃ (Ehwaz, Sowelu, Eihwaz, Othila, Jera)

Joyce has many of the strengths and fears of her namesake, Joy, but Joyce's name adds the additional powers of the runes for movement and wholeness. Joyce makes an effort to live in the present, and she is able to delight in all that she encounters when her vision is clear and her mind and body are at ease. Over her lifetime, though, Joyce has many changes of residence, which is potentially disruptive on every level. On the other hand, these many moves also make Joyce independent and self-sufficient. Joyce learns to answer to herself and sidestep the trap of seeking other people's approval. Joyce finds wholeness in part by realizing that loneliness comes from denying our true selves. Therefore, Joyce develops her talents, disciplines her mind to experience the moment, and finds much in her life to savor.

Elements: Air, air, earth/fire, earth/fire, earth

THE NUMEROLOGICAL INTERPRETATION
Joyce (NV = 4, CV = 4, VV = 9, FL = 1)

Joyce is a person who likes a sense of order and permanence. She strives to make sure that her own material needs and those of her loved ones are suitably taken care of, and tries not to do anything that may threaten her stability. Most of Joyce's decisions are made with a view as to their practical outcome. She will appreciate a position in life that has a steady rise in pay as well as rank, and will be attracted to partners who possess an honest and determined attitude and who are as hardworking as she is. Joyce should work to free herself from the worry that can come when one is too preoccupied with money.

Juan

A Kabbalistic Synopsis
יואן —YVAN (Yod, Vau, Aleph, Nun)

Juan is a spectacular lover. His name's value reduces to fifteen, which lets us know that he is likely to submit to his physical appetites pretty much whenever he feels like it. Any partner needs to keep a sharp eye—and a tight leash—on this one! What's more, there is a high influence of the number seven in his name, so we know that for the most part, Juan succeeds in his endeavors. Juan is not just a lothario, though; he has an extremely romantic nature and likes to woo his partners with great care and sensitivity. Indeed, he is often in love with each and every lover—even if only for a short time!

The Runic Interpretation
ᚾᚨᚢᛃ (Nauthiz, Ansuz, Uruz, Jera)

The Nauthiz rune of constraint will help Juan budget his time wisely and keep his finances in order. Having the Ansuz rune of signals gives Juan the upper hand in negotiations, since it makes him perceptive and intuitive. He knows just when to go forward with his demands, and when to remain silent. Uruz, or the rune of strength, gives Juan the appropriate personality for business dealings because he can keep his expression neutral—even when he wants to yell "Yippee!" from the bottom of his toes.

Elements: Fire, air, earth, earth

The Numerological Interpretation
Juan (NV = 1, CV = 6, VV = 4, FL = 1)

Juan has a definite love of beauty that extends to his choice of partners as well as to his need to be surrounded by the finer things in life. He likes nothing better than to share fine food, good music, and a quiet evening at home with the person he loves. Juan needs and will work for a sense of financial security, and would choose a career that assures his material comfort. Focusing on his mental and intellectual development will help him to balance an emotional nature that is often overstimulated.

DERIVATION: Spanish version of John, which originally derives from the Hebrew word *yohanan*, meaning "God is gracious."

PRINCIPAL COLORS: The most pale to the most brilliant yellow, also orange, gold, and bronze

GEMSTONES AND PRECIOUS METALS: Citrine, yellow diamonds

BOTANICALS: Borage, chamomile, sorrel

UNIQUE SPELLINGS: Juann, Wan, Wann

RELATED TO: Gian, Giovanni, Hans, Iant, Ivant, Jackt, Jant, Johannes, Johnt, Johnny, Jon, Juanito, Seant, Shawnt, Yan, Zane

DERIVATION
DERIVATION: Spanish version of Joan, which was an English version of the Latin name Johanna. Entered the United States at the beginning of the twentieth century.

PRINCIPAL COLORS: Any color of medium tone

GEMSTONES AND PRECIOUS METALS: Sapphires

BOTANICALS: Celandine, sage

UNIQUE SPELLINGS: Juaneeta, Juaneta, Juanyta, Waneeta, Waneta, Wanita, Wanyta

RELATED TO: Joan†, Joanie, Joanna†, Joanne†, Joni, Juana, Nita

Juanita

A KABBALISTIC SYNOPSIS

יועניטא —YVANYTA (Yod, Vau, Ayin, Nun, Yod, Teth, Aleph)

They say that the exception proves the rule—and in Juanita, we have exactly that. The beauty of kabbalistic analysis is that a single letter makes a world of difference to the meaning of a name. However, in the case of Juanita we have almost an exact female replica of Juan†, her male counterpart. To give some idea of the sexual power exuded by this lioness, her name equates to the Hebrew for "a live coal"! Juanita is likely to settle down with one partner sooner or later, and once she does, she will feel passionate about her partner for the rest of her life. Children are definitely in the cards for her, and they will bring her much happiness; she will make an excellent mother who encourages her children to express themselves freely. Both creative and artistic, Juanita is well suited to a career—perhaps in a museum or gallery—that will make use of her own talents and her appreciation of beauty and the sensuous world.

THE RUNIC INTERPRETATION

ᚨᛏᛁᚾᚨᚢᛃ (Ansuz, Teiwaz, Isa, Nauthiz, Ansuz, Uruz, Jera)

Juanita has the standstill and constraint runes in her name, and this is a problem. She knows what it is to have an idea she loves discarded by people in positions of authority. Luckily, the Teiwaz, or warrior rune, comes to her rescue, as does the Uruz rune of strength during these potentially disappointing times. No one really knows when Juanita feels discouraged because she picks herself up with lightning speed. The double signals rune (Ansuz) of intuition brings forth new ideas, and Juanita is considered by many to be an unusually self-reliant and capable woman for this reason. Jera, the rune of harvest, helps Juanita feel capable and successful.

Elements: Air, air, earth, fire, air, earth, earth

THE NUMEROLOGICAL INTERPRETATION

Juanita (NV = 4, CV = 8, VV = 5, FL = 1)

Juanita has a flair for the dramatic, which she expresses through her choice of clothing and in the way she presents herself to others. Juanita lives to enjoy her life. Material objects and social status are important to her. However, she is also a hard worker who is determined to be a success both professionally and personally. Juanita has long-range plans and strives to achieve her many aims and goals with steadfast determination. She should take care that her desirous nature does not dominate her life, as it can overwhelm her better judgment.

Judith

A Kabbalistic Synopsis
יודית —YVDYTh (Yod, Vau, Daleth, Yod, Tau)

Judith deserves a medal for her hard work and reliability. She packs it in, working full-time, sitting on the school board, and having hobbies on the side. While few people comment on it, what Judith does is quite remarkable and requires an incredible level of resilience and the sort of management skill it takes to run a major corporation. The instinctual drives of basic humanity drive Judith's behavior, and as a result, if she has kids, she may feel compelled to stay at home and look after them—a role that will likely fulfill her as much as continuing with her career would. This may befuddle her friends, but it will make Judith happy—which is what she wants most.

The Runic Interpretation
ᚦᛁᛞᚢ◇ (Thurisaz, Isa, Dagaz, Uruz, Jera)

Gateways are indicated by the Thurisaz rune in Judith's name. Judith will encounter many opportunities to relinquish the past and take the fork in the road that points to greater expansion and self-expression. Othila, the rune of separation, further emphasizes this life direction for Judith. Change isn't easy for any of us, and it can be a lonely walk at times. There's a bit of the proverbial hermit in Judith, though, and she actually craves solitude and prefers to stay far from the crowd. Dagaz, for breakthrough, implies that Judith will be richly rewarded by her struggle to retain her individuality and nonconformist endeavors. Uruz, the rune of strength and determination, further emphasizes Judith's independent style. All will be well as Judith forges her unique path; the delightful Jera rune for harvest signifies bounty and satisfaction in life for our courageous Judith!

Elements: Fire, earth, fire, earth, earth

The Numerological Interpretation
Judith (NV = 9, CV = 6, VV = 3, FL = 1)

The name Judith bestows compassion and a humanitarian disposition. She is an idealist by nature, and a very generous woman who seeks to bring other people happiness as much as she works to secure her own. That said, she can become very disappointed when people fall short of her expectations. Therefore, it is very important for her to hold on to her aspirations but also to live in the minute. She must learn to accept people for who and what they are, not for how they could or should be. Judith is strong in her convictions and dedicated to the causes that occupy a great deal of her time and energy. Gifted with an intense intellectual curiosity, Judith seeks mental stimulation as well as romance in her choice of partners.

DERIVATION: Biblical, from the Hebrew meaning "woman from Judea" or "Jewish." Name of Esau's wife in the Old Testament, and of a Jewish heroine in the Apocrypha.

PRINCIPAL COLORS: Deep, rich reds, also pink and maroon

GEMSTONES AND PRECIOUS METALS: Rubies, garnets

BOTANICALS: Garlic, broom, wormwood

UNIQUE SPELLINGS: Judeth, Judithe, Judyth, Judythe, Juedith

RELATED TO: Jodi, Jodie†, Jody†, Judi, Judie, Judita, Juditha, Judy†, Jutta

"It is harder to stay where you are than to get out."
—JUDITH ROSSNER (AUTHOR)

Judy

DERIVATION: English, pet form of Judith, which stems from the Hebrew meaning "woman from Judea" or "Jewish." Sometimes used as an independent name.

PRINCIPAL COLORS: All but the brightest shades of blue

GEMSTONES AND PRECIOUS METALS: Turquoise, emeralds

BOTANICALS: Dog rose, violets, walnuts

UNIQUE SPELLINGS: Judee, Judi, Judie, Judye, Juedy

RELATED TO: Jitta, Jodi, Jodie†, Jody†, Judita, Judith†, Juditha

"What you will do matters. All you need is to do it."
—JUDY GRAHN (POET)

A KABBALISTIC SYNOPSIS
יודי —YVDY (Yod, Vau, Daleth, Yod)

Judy is after the bright lights and glamour. The Th, or Tau, representing suffering and self-sacrifice, which we have in Judith, is missing from Judy, leaving her with huge amounts of energy and more than her fair share of confidence. The combination of the Vau and Daleth in Judy's name suggests a choice in her life between two routes. In her case, one route is a profitable but safe career, very possibly in the travel industry. The other route is high risk, with Judy perhaps trying to make it one way or another on the stage. But each Judy will have to come to her own decision on which route to take. The value of Judy's name is thirty, relating directly to a path on the Tree of Life ruled by the sun. Consequently, whether she makes it or not, Judy will rarely let life get her down, and is excellent at cheering up all those around her.

THE RUNIC INTERPRETATION
ᛇᛞᛟᚢᛃ (Eihwaz, Dagaz, Uruz, Jera)

Judy boasts the runes for defense, breakthrough, strength, and harvest in her name. Judy knows the best defense is a good offense, and the verbal Eihwaz rune gives Judy the skills she needs to defend herself. She takes whatever thrust is hurled her way and sends it zinging back at her adversary! The Uruz rune of strength assists in this process. The breakthrough rune implies that Judy will reach a time in her life when she is recognized for her talents as a negotiator. Judith can use her skills as a powerful peacemaker in labor disputes and conflict resolution tasks. The Jera rune for harvest shines on her career, bringing her success and recognition.

Elements: Earth/fire, fire, earth, earth

THE NUMEROLOGICAL INTERPRETATION
Judy (NV = 6, CV = 6, VV = 1, FL = 1)

Music, theater, painting, and design work naturally appeal to Judy, if not professionally then certainly as a dedicated pastime. This is a woman who wants to aid and uplift other people. She is very sympathetic and aware of the underdog in any social situation. Judy is not one to sit back and let things happen. She is actively engaged all the time in what matters most to her: social harmony and goodwill. Her family is at the center of her life, and it may be difficult for her to allow her children or other loved ones the space to fall on their faces. She tends to pick them up before they have the chance to discover where they tripped!

Julia

A Kabbalistic Synopsis
יוליא —YVLYA (Yod, Vau, Lamed, Yod, Aleph)

The key element in Julia's name is the central letter, the L, or Lamed, which suggests a highly driven nature, which is quite often due to an unshakable feeling of obligation to a particular course of action. In Julia the function of the Lamed is explained by the value of her name, which reduces to twelve, the number of the Hanged Man tarot card. Julia always puts others before herself and somehow feels duty-bound to do this. Her friends will try to persuade her that while her altruism is respectable and valued, one need not devote one's whole life to the pursuit of other people's happiness. Julia is highly individualistic, and the strength of her personality normally will be sufficient to ensure that she does indeed save some time for her own interests. Emotionally Julia will have a very rich life, since she has a natural tendency to attract a wide circle of reliable friends. And chances are she will have a marriage that many of us can only dream about.

The Runic Interpretation
ᚨᛁᛚᚢᛃ (Ansuz, Isa, Laguz, Uruz, Jera)

Julia soars through life with the signals, standstill, flow, strength, and harvest runes in her lucky name. She is intuitive and patient and, as it says in the Bible, "bears all things and endures all things." Julia values light, food, warmth, comfort, energy, joy, and love. She uses the Laguz rune to know the invigoration of courage, the expansiveness of hope, and the poignancy of appreciation. However, Julia needs to learn to let go of her guilt over having such a great life! It's better for her to value what she has, develop her talents to the hilt, and enjoy her blessings.

Elements: Air, earth, water, earth, earth

The Numerological Interpretation
Julia (NV = 8, CV = 4, VV = 4, FL = 1)

Career and finances are the two areas that will be of most interest to Julia. She is very aware of the economic circumstances of life. Julia wants the best and is willing to do whatever it takes to achieve her goals in life. She is not spontaneous or adventurous, and much prefers predictability. Julia is loyal, dependable, and hardworking. She is sensuous, loves beautiful things, and tends to take very good care of her health and general physical appearance. Her life can reach its higher potential through education of a philosophical or spiritual nature.

DERIVATION: Latin, the feminine form of Julius, a Roman family name. Name borne by several early saints. Largely disappeared during the Middle Ages, then reappeared during the eighteenth century.

PRINCIPAL COLORS: Black, the deepest shades of blue, purple, and gray

GEMSTONES AND PRECIOUS METALS: Rich sapphires, carbuncles, black pearls

BOTANICALS: Angelica, ragwort, pilewort

UNIQUE SPELLINGS: Giulia, Giulya, Jiulia, Joolia, Juelia, Julea, Julya

RELATED TO: Julee, Julianna, Julianne, Juliet, Julienne, Juliet, Juliette, Julina, Julita, Julyanna

"Life itself is the proper binge."
—JULIA CHILD
(CULINARY ARTIST)

Julian

DERIVATION: English, from the Latin family name Julius. The name of several early saints, and of the Roman emperor Julian. Especially common in Britain.

PRINCIPAL COLORS: Electric colors, moderately shaded hues

GEMSTONES AND PRECIOUS METALS: Pale to rich sapphires

BOTANICALS: Sage, spinach, Iceland moss

UNIQUE SPELLINGS: Giulian, Jiulian, Juelian, Julien, Julion, Julyan

RELATED TO: Giulio, Jules, Julianus, Juliot, Juliust

A KABBALISTIC SYNOPSIS
יוליאן —YVLYAN (Yod, Vau, Lamed, Yod, Aleph, Nun)

If Julian were an animal, he would be a lion, and not just any lion either; he would undoubtedly be the leader of the pack. Even on the weekend when he's casually dressed and doing the weekly shopping with his family, he gives off a definite aura of leadership. Julian possesses a rare combination of charisma and skill. As a young man he may well have got into his fair share of scrapes, but never anything terrible. As he gets older his energy is directed more constructively, and Julian has the ability to take an idea and build up a thriving business on the basis of it. Leo rules Julian, and his name is associated with עואל or A'AVAL, a spirit connected to Leo. With all this natural power it is not surprising that Julian is sexually voracious, and his biggest problem in life may be keeping his oversize libido in check. Thankfully, Julian is very emotional and takes commitment seriously.

THE RUNIC INTERPRETATION
(Nauthiz, Ansuz, Isa, Laguz, Uruz, Jera)

Julian knows he is articulate and bright and can push to get things done his way. But this is not usually the best course of action for him; he will find being insistent limits his progress. Instead, Julian needs to use the standstill rune to slow down and consider that once he is in harmony with his true nature, he will find balance and satisfaction in his life. Julian learns this lesson by first learning to say no to offers that would pull him from his true path. Julian can use the heightened intuitive abilities of the Laguz rune to sense situations ahead of time and harmonize them. The Jera rune assures Julian of success at all levels. Julian has the power of all four elements in his name.

Elements: Fire, air, earth, water, earth, earth

THE NUMEROLOGICAL INTERPRETATION
Julian (NV = 4, CV = 9, VV = 4, FL = 1)

Julian is attracted to structure and order. He tends to be a neat person, and his material possessions mean a great deal to him. He has to take care not to accumulate money just for the sake of psychological security. His true success in life will result from the way he circulates his resources and the nature of the value he places on his own truth. The consonant value of nine in his name gives Julian the potential ability to develop a real economic philosophy, one that permits the integration of his ideas and aspirations into the forms of his material life. This is a man who is very self-disciplined and appreciates other well-mannered and respectful people.

Julie

A KABBALISTIC SYNOPSIS
יולי —YVLY (Yod, Vau, Lamed, Yod)

From time to time as you're walking down the street you will pass someone you cannot help but watch in admiration until they are out of view. It's not their sexual attraction, but their innate beauty that draws you in. Julie's name is directly equivalent to the Hebrew for "beautiful." In addition, Julie's name adds up to fifty-six, a powerful combination of the energies of success and the power of the individual will. As a result, Julie is likely to achieve most of her goals in life with relative ease, and has a great personality as well as a great physique. Julie is also likely to possess a high degree of intuition, and has a good knack for picking up what others are thinking.

THE RUNIC INTERPRETATION
ᛗᛁᛚᚢᛃ (Ehwaz, Isa, Laguz, Uruz, Jera)

Julie loves feeling spontaneous and free. She is a risk taker who always lands on her feet. Ehwaz gives her freedom of movement, and Isa gives her power to take stock of her situation. Laguz for flow and Uruz for strength make Julie a persuasive individual. She is confident and flexible. Since Laguz represents the lunar nature, Julie is clear about her emotions and a good communicator. She will do well in a profession that deals with the public, either in business or the performing arts. Whatever career she chooses, Julie will succeed because she is blessed by the Jera rune for harvest in her name.

Elements: Air, earth, water, earth, earth

THE NUMEROLOGICAL INTERPRETATION
Julie (NV = 3, CV = 4, VV = 8, FL = 1)

Julie has a lively intelligence and a fast wit. She is generally inquisitive and is open to investigating any situation that appeals to her. There is one qualification, however; Julie is very practical, and she will want to know that her involvement in a relationship or a job opportunity has the potential to provide material rewards. She has definite long-range plans and is not resistant to putting in long hours in order to achieve her visions. Julie expects loyalty and honesty in her relationships, and is very capable of offering these same qualities in return.

DERIVATION: French version of Julia, which originally derives from the Latin family name Julius. Entered English-speaking countries in the 1920s, and has steadily increased in popularity since then.

PRINCIPAL COLORS: All shades of purple, including maroon and pale violet

GEMSTONES AND PRECIOUS METALS: Garnets, amethyst

BOTANICALS: Apple, barberry, mint, lungwort

UNIQUE SPELLINGS: Jeulie, Jewelie, Joolie, Juelie, Julee, Juley, Juli, July

RELATED TO: Giulia, Juliat, Julianna, Julianne, Julie-Anne, Julienne, Juliet, Julietta, Juliette, Julina, Julita

"Some people regard discipline as a chore. For me, it is a kind of order that sets me free to fly."
—JULIE ANDREWS (ACTRESS)

"You have to set new goals every day."
—JULIE KRONE (ATHLETE)

Julio

DERIVATION: Spanish version of the Latin name Julius, which was originally a Roman family name. Julius was the name used by Gaius Julius Caesar, as well as by several Roman popes.

PRINCIPAL COLORS: Medium shades of any color, especially grays and blues

GEMSTONES AND PRECIOUS METALS: Sapphires

BOTANICALS: Celandine, spinach

UNIQUE SPELLINGS: Hoolio, Huleo, Hulio, Hulyo, Juleo, Julyo

RELATED TO: Giulio, Jules, Juliant, Julien, Juliust

A KABBALISTIC SYNOPSIS
יליע —YVLYA'A (Yod, Vau, Lamed, Yod, Ayin)

Not many people get to know Julio that well, but that's not for lack of trying. Julio is a very sociable guy and loves to mix, particularly at big parties where he can perform at his extroverted best. He is the heart and soul of any occasion. Most people assume that this is what makes Julio tick, but it is in fact only a minor interest. The strongest influences in Julio's name suggest an affinity for nature and wildlife. In the way that the Kabbalah sometimes can be surprisingly specific, Julio is associated primarily with horses; if he has a small frame, he may even have a career as a professional jockey. To the very few individuals that Julio gets really close to, he is a deeply sensitive man with a great store of instinctive wisdom. Animals tend to respond well to Julio, and he gets a great deal of satisfaction from this natural bonding.

THE RUNIC INTERPRETATION
♢Iᛁᛙᚼ (Othila, Isa, Laguz, Uruz, Hagalaz)

Julio has the runes for separation, standstill, flow, strength, and disruption in his name. But Julio is self-reliant and resourceful, and he is fortunate, in a way, to have had so many challenges in his life. Julio may be denied many things in early childhood, but once he achieves them on his own, he appreciates them more deeply than someone who never struggled. The Uruz rune gives Julio the perseverance he needs to cultivate a sense of discernment, and he has a reputation as a good judge of character. He resists the temptation to run from challenges, and refuses to make his life containable and predictable. This is one of the miracles that helps shape Julio into a whole person.

Elements: Earth/fire, earth, water, earth, water

THE NUMEROLOGICAL INTERPRETATION
Julio (NV = 4, CV = 4, VV = 9, FL = 1)

People look at Julio as being very down-to-earth. He is respected for his loyalty and steadfastness. On the surface this is true, as Julio is very dedicated to making a living and providing a firm financial basis for himself and his loved ones. Yet underneath his pragmatic exterior is the heart of a poet and the soul of a romantic. Julio is always imagining a better world in his mind, while with his hands he is creating the best out of the present opportunities his life has to offer. Progress for him will be gradual, but what he accomplishes has the tendency to become permanent, a basis from which future growth is possible.

Julius

A Kabbalistic Synopsis
יוליוס —YVLYVS (Yod, Vau, Lamed, Yod, Vau, Samech)

Julius has a simple goal in life: He wants to change the world! To Julius there is nothing as exciting or fulfilling as politics. He has very firm beliefs, which he will passionately expound upon to anyone who will listen, and Julius has the necessary strength of character to maintain a role in the cutthroat world of Washington, D.C. Julius has room in his heart for the whole country, even the whole world, in terms of his beliefs, but he is unlikely to have time for a deep personal relationship until fairly late in life; this is a sacrifice he is more than willing to make. The value of his name reduces to five, which indicates that he will indeed achieve a position of some authority and will also be regarded as an honest and moral individual. The biggest conflict in Julius's life is not between relationships and politics but between his desire for actual power and the purely academic interest he has in the nature of power itself. On the one side he wants to get involved and get his hands dirty, while on the other he likes being able to remain objective and analyze what is going on. He finds it difficult to achieve both objectivity and active involvement at the same time.

The Runic Interpretation
ᛋᚢᛁᛚᚢᛃ (Sowelu, Uruz, Isa, Laguz, Uruz, Jera)

Being strong has many benefits. Physical strength implies fortitude and endurance. Emotional strength implies good mental health and the ability to negotiate and communicate clearly and effectively. The double Uruz runes in Julius's name give him all of these strengths. He also benefits from Isa, or standstill, which makes him contemplative and introspective at times. The Laguz rune of flow further emphasizes Julius's good mental outlook. He is a well-meaning man, and the Sowelu rune of wholeness further strengthens this marvelous trait. Jera, the rune of harvest, suggests that Julius will reap rich rewards in life.

Elements: Air, earth, earth, water, earth, earth

The Numerological Interpretation
Julius (NV = 11, CV = 5, VV = 6, FL = 1)

Community and public service work call very strongly to Julius. The numbers in this name indicate a connection to things new and original. Julius is very much at home in a profession that allows him to reach the public. He has a definite message that he would like to communicate, and the charm, personal magnetism, and intelligence to do so. His goals and aspirations are humanitarian in their direction—definitely geared for the benefit of the many rather than the profit of the few.

DERIVATION: Latin, from the Roman family name Julius. Most prominently borne by Gaius Julius Caesar, the Roman conqueror, and also the name of two popes.

PRINCIPAL COLORS: All shades of green, white

GEMSTONES AND PRECIOUS METALS: Jade, cat's-eye, white pearls

BOTANICALS: Cabbage, chicory, colewort

UNIQUE SPELLINGS: Giulius, Jeulius, Juleus, Julyus

RELATED TO: Giulio, Jules, Juliant, Julien, Juliot

↩

"The foolish man seeks happiness in the distance; the wise grows it under his feet."
—JULIUS ROBERT OPPENHEIMER (SCIENTIST)

PRINCIPAL COLORS: The palest tones of any color

GEMSTONES AND PRECIOUS METALS: Silver, diamonds, any other very pale stone

BOTANICALS. Hazel, oats

UNIQUE SPELLINGS: Joon, Joone

RELATED TO: Juna, Junella, Junelle, Junette, Junia, Junina, Junine

June

A KABBALISTIC SYNOPSIS
יוהן —YVHN (Yod, Vau, Heh, Nun)

As you might expect with such a name, June is indeed full of the joys of spring. The more depressing aspects of life—particularly issues of global proportion—tend to pass her by, as her focus is strictly on the personal and local. You will likely see June at the town fair or helping out at the school. She is one of life's volunteers and always arrives with a smile and a joke. But family issues are very serious to June; the planetary influences in her name make her extremely protective of her children, and she firmly believes that the primary duty of a married couple is to take care of the generation that will come after them. If anyone dares to upset her kids, they will soon learn that June has a side that is as fierce as her usual mood is friendly. Sometimes, especially if June is a Leo or Aries woman, there will be a conflict between her desire to be at the center of family life and her wish for a career in her own right. You may find June working in the teaching profession as a means of resolving this dilemma.

THE RUNIC INTERPRETATION
Mᚺᚢᛜ (Ehwaz, Nauthiz, Uruz, Jera)

June is stable and constant. The runes for June are movement, constraint, strength, and harvest, respectively. June uses the Uruz rune to help her through the challenging times she is likely to encounter, as indicated by Nauthiz in her name. June realizes when darkness covers the sky, the sun will return again. When challenges come, her life is still intact. June's mind is quick and alert, and she has learned to appreciate her adversities as strengthening experiences. June is stoic. She is aware of her feelings, but not ruled by them—and this is her special strength.

Elements: Air, fire, earth, earth

THE NUMEROLOGICAL INTERPRETATION
June (NV = 5, CV = 6, VV = 8, FL = 1)

Most people tend to accept only those ideas that are relevant to their own lives—not June! This name reveals a woman who is very intellectually expansive and eager to explore life's many opportunities. This gives her inner strength, and poise as well as compassion. Although June requires a sense of personal freedom, she is not a loner. A positive domestic life is vital to her sense of well-being, and she will place a great deal of importance on her family life.

Justin

DERIVATION: English, from the Latin name Justinus, which was used by many early saints. Especially common in Ireland during most of the twentieth century, and has been increasingly common in the United States in recent years.

PRINCIPAL COLORS: The palest to the deepest shades of purple, violet, mauve, and maroon

GEMSTONES AND PRECIOUS METALS: Garnets, amethyst

BOTANICALS: Apple, bilberry, mint

UNIQUE SPELLINGS: Jusstin, Justen, Justenn, Justinn, Justyn

RELATED TO: Giusto, Justinius, Justino, Justo, Justus

A KABBALISTIC SYNOPSIS

יוסטין —YVSTYN (Yod, Vau, Samech, Teth, Yod, Nun)

To most people Justin is one of the good guys. In his relationships he offers constant moral support to any of his partner's endeavors, and he can be hugely reassuring in the bad times. He is also more sensitive than most to the deeper emotional needs of his partner. In the workplace Justin is ideally positioned in operations, as he is skilled in making the right choices about exactly how to translate any requirement into action, and has the ability to motivate his staff and coworkers well. This aptitude is emphasized by the letter Samech, meaning "prop," which refers to his reliable and supportive tendencies. However, the letter Teth means "serpent" and overwhelms the former aspect of his personality, making two sides to Justin's character. If anyone attempts to thwart Justin either at home or at work, he will not rest until he has well and truly paid them back for their transgression. Justin will always have the advantage in such situations, as he is fairly inscrutable; you only know he's mad with you when it's far too late to retreat!

THE RUNIC INTERPRETATION

ᚺᛁᛏᛊᚢᛜ (Nauthiz, Isa, Teiwaz, Sowelu, Uruz, Jera)

The runes of constraint and standstill have shaped Justin's life. He is a champion of the underdog and never ceases to be amazed by people's endurance. Justin is anxious to help others and hopes, with true sincerity, that everyone will one day be free to celebrate life and know firsthand the opportunities life provides for love, as well as experience the bliss of solitude.

Elements: Fire, earth, air, air, earth, earth

THE NUMEROLOGICAL INTERPRETATION

Justin (NV = 3, CV = 9, VV = 3, FL = 1)

People find Justin intellectually stimulating. Justin is happiest when reading, researching, and communicating. He has a wide variety of interests—sometimes too many—and he can be overactive mentally. He may have nervous energy in abundance, and should take care not to dissipate himself by being in too many places at once. When mature, Justin will have anchored himself at his center, allowing him to go far afield but find his way home again. Justin is quite comfortable in most social settings and usually has no problem ingratiating himself with people from all different social backgrounds.

DERIVATION: English, variation of Cara, from the Italian *cara*, meaning "beloved," or the Gaelic *cara*, meaning "friend." Quite popular since the 1970s.

PRINCIPAL COLORS: Hues of medium shading, electric colors

GEMSTONES AND PRECIOUS METALS: Sapphires

BOTANICALS: Celandine, sage, medlar

UNIQUE SPELLINGS: Cara, Carra, Carrah, Karra, Karrah

RELATED TO: Careen, Carey, Caridad, Carina, Carolt, Carolynt, Karent

Kara

A KABBALISTIC SYNOPSIS
כאר —KARA (Kaph, Aleph, Resh, Aleph)

If you need a hand with the local Thanksgiving parade, bring in Kara. She not only has a strong artistic and creative bent, but is also highly skilled when it comes to anything manual or craft-based. With Kara on your side, you can be sure you'll have the best float in the parade! Professionally Kara will do her best to avoid the standard nine-to-five routine, and will try to make her living utilizing her creative talents, very possibly by selling sculpture, as her primary skill lies in her hands. However, if she cannot make a go of it as an artist, she will take on a more normal job and will be content to pursue her real love in the evenings and on weekends. The influence of Resh, meaning "sun," ensures that Kara maintains a sunny and cheerful outlook on life whatever the circumstances. Kara certainly makes an interesting friend or partner. Although she will never admit to it, Kara is quite an intellectual and can talk knowledgeably about a whole range of subjects.

THE RUNIC INTERPRETATION
ᚨᚱᚨᚲ (Ansuz, Raido, Ansuz, Kano)

Kara is a mother to the world. She is very idealistic and avoids people she feels she can't trust. This woman has the double Ansuz rune in her name for signals, and as a result, she is observant, perceptive, and intuitive. The Ansuz rune implies family solidarity and nurturing ability. The Kano rune brings to Kara opening, or mental clarity, which facilitates harmony and good communication. The Raido rune of journey also assists with clarity of speech. Kara is a well-meaning family member, friend, and nurturing humanitarian. She will succeed in health care or other related fields.

Elements: Air, water, air, water

THE NUMEROLOGICAL INTERPRETATION
Kara (NV = 4, CV = 11, VV = 2, FL = 2)

Kara is very mindful of her need to create bonds that link people together for their greater good. This is a woman who is dedicated to working with other people for the benefit of society. Kara seeks to foster a sense of unity among all people—no matter what their differences in ideology or background. Kara's partner has to be very supportive and hardworking, a person equally dedicated to the creation of social harmony. Kara knows that one must eat to survive. Her work therefore has a decidedly practical approach and application.

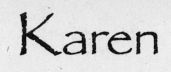

Karen

DERIVATION: Danish form of Katherine and Katarina. Brought to the United States by Danish settlers in the 1930s, and became immensely popular in the 1950s and 1960s.

PRINCIPAL COLORS: Blues and grays, moderately shaded hues

GEMSTONES AND PRECIOUS METALS: Sapphires

BOTANICALS: Lesser celandine, Iceland moss

UNIQUE SPELLINGS: Cairn, Caren, Carin, Caron, Caronne, Carren, Carrin, Caryn, Karan, Karin, Karon, Karyn

RELATED TO: Carina, Catharine, Catherine†, Cathryn, Karena, Karina, Katarina, Kate†, Katerina, Katharine, Katherine†, Kathleen†, Kathryn†, Kathy†, Katie†, Katrina†, Kay†, Kitty†

A KABBALISTIC SYNOPSIS
כאראן —KARAN (Kaph, Aleph, Resh, Aleph, Nun)

A cheery, laid-back manner conceals the considerable ambition that motivates Karen to achieve great things in the workplace. While her colleagues will appreciate her easy manner and relaxed approach to work, her bosses will recognize the fact that her projects are always completed on a timely basis and notice her willingness to stay late to ensure that everything goes smoothly. Karen has a very innovative personality, which translates into a good use of initiative in the office and a highly individual lifestyle outside of work. Karen is very definitely a night person—not only because she likes to party, but also because it is usually in the middle of the night that she thinks up new ideas. Earth is a strong influence on Karen's personality, and it is usual for her to have her feet planted firmly on the ground when it comes to her material security. Mind you, her concern for financial stability can go right out the window when she finds the right partner, as it won't matter what he can provide as long as she loves him.

THE RUNIC INTERPRETATION
ᚾᛖᚱᚨᚲ (Nauthiz, Ehwaz, Raido, Ansuz, Kano)

Karen has a strong character. The Kano energy of opening gives her mental clarity and a flexible and quick mind. The Ansuz rune of signals makes Karen perceptive and intuitive. The Ehwaz energy of movement, combined with the Raido energy of journey and good communication, give Karen many travel opportunities. She also has a nonjudgmental nature and a willingness to try out new ideas and to grow. The Nauthiz rune of constraint opposes this expansive nature and can sabotage some of Karen's plans. So sometimes Karen feels like she has to try a little harder than the next one to get ahead—but succeed she will.

Elements: Fire, air, water, air, water

THE NUMEROLOGICAL INTERPRETATION
Karen (NV = 4, CV = 7, VV = 6, FL = 2)

Karen may be found hard at work developing her mental capacities. She is intelligent and analytical, with the ability to think through a situation to its natural conclusion. Karen is profound in her understanding about life and has a compassionate and peace-loving heart. Her name also describes a woman with great creative potential. She will be attracted to the arts, especially to music and writing. Although very kind to other people, Karen also needs to spend time by herself. Those who love her will respect her requirement for privacy, as you never know what she will come up with when she emerges from her periods of solitude.

DERIVATION: German and
Scandinavian form of Charles.
From the Old English *ceorl*,
meaning "man, husbandman." The
name of seven Austrian emperors
and the root of the Polish, Czech,
and Hungarian words for
"emperor."

PRINCIPAL COLORS: From pale to
deep azure

GEMSTONES AND PRECIOUS
METALS: Turquoise, emeralds

BOTANICALS: Violets, vervain,
almonds

UNIQUE SPELLINGS: Caarle, Carl,
Carle, Kaarle, Karle

RELATED TO: Carlt, Carlo,
Carlost, Carlton, Charlest,
Charley, Charliet, Charlton, Chaz,
Chuck, Kaarle, Karel, Karol,
Károly, Séarlas, Siarl

❧

"Being on the tightrope is living;
everything else is waiting."
—KARL WALLENDA (ACROBAT)

Karl

A KABBALISTIC SYNOPSIS
כארל —KARL (Kaph, Aleph, Resh, Lamed)

It is unlikely that Karl is reading this book, as he will regard name analysis as a load of hocus-pocus. In Karl's world things aren't really to be trusted unless they come with tangible proof. Karl may well be employed as an engineer, for instance; he simply has no time for speculative ideas and projects. However, Karl is not unemotional; in fact, he is a very good husband and loving partner. He will make sure that the person in his life is well looked after, and one thing is certain: They will have all the latest gadgets! One thing everyone appreciates about Karl is his great sense of humor. He can take any number of jokes made at his expense. In addition, he is a master of practical jokes himself—a skill no doubt helped by his instinct for all things mechanical.

THE RUNIC INTERPRETATION
ᛚᚱᚨᚲ (Laguz, Raido, Ansuz, Kano)

Karl has an artistic temperament, which prepares him for work in a number of fields requiring intuition, creativity, and originality. Karl has the runes of flow, journey, signals, and openings in his name. The runes of flow and journey imply musical and literary ability. By the same token, the runes for signals and openings suggest intuition and clarity of thought and expression. Karl is the negotiator in the family because he is sensitive and able to appreciate various points of view. His succinct use of language helps him quell disagreements and arbitrate from a standpoint of solicitude. Karl makes a wonderful artist or lawyer, and can work well in sales and management because he is optimistic and able to solve problems. He advocates a win-win situation for all involved, and this makes him popular and sought after as both a professional and a friend.

Elements: Water, water, air, water

THE NUMEROLOGICAL INTERPRETATION
Karl (NV = 6, CV = 5, VV = 1, FL = 2)

Most people know Karl to be a loving man who expresses compassion and sympathy in his relationships. Karl can accept what other people have to say without their having to qualify themselves. He is therefore very tolerant of other people's individuality, and he wishes to be treated the same way by others. He has to take care that his open attitude does not turn into gullibility. Karl is indeed a very individualistic soul, a man who finds it imperative to walk his own path through life. Although his home life is very important to him (for he is a caring and romantic man), he will also need frequent periods to explore life on his own.

❧

Kate

DERIVATION: English, short form of Katherine, associated with the Greek adjective *katharos*, meaning "pure." Consistently popular since the Middle Ages.

PRINCIPAL COLORS: The palest to the brightest yellow and bronze, also orange, gold

GEMSTONES AND PRECIOUS METALS: Citrine, topaz, amber

BOTANICALS: Borage, eyebright, sorrel

UNIQUE SPELLINGS: Cate, Cayte, Kayte

RELATED TO: Caitlin, Caitriona, Catarine, Cateline, Cathaleen, Catharin, Catharina, Catherina, Catherleen, Cathie, Cathleen, Cathrene, Cathy†, Catrin, Catrina, Catrine, Catriona, Karen†, Karin, Katarina, Katerina, Katey, Katharine, Katheleen, Katheline, Kathereen, Katherinet†, Katherina, Kathie, Kathileen, Kathleen†, Kathlyn, Kathlynn, Kathrene, Kathryn†, Kathy†, Katie†, Katina, Katleen, Katrena, Katrina†, Katriona, Katryna, Kattrina, Katy, Kayt†, Kitty†, Treena, Trina

A Kabbalistic Synopsis
כאיט —KAYT (Kaph, Aleph, Yod, Teth)

You will never see Kate relying on her partner for financial or material support. Kate is a truly independent woman who doesn't like to feel that she owes anyone anything. The initial K, or Kaph, makes it clear that, from a practical point of view, Kate is quite capable of looking after herself. She is happy to roll up her sleeves and get her hands dirty with plumbing and decorating. Careerwise, Kate will perform well in a competitive environment and actually enjoys this type of pressurized workplace. The summation of her name is forty, which suggests that Kate is very fond of her creature comforts. In addition, she likes to have things in her house "just so," and knows another person might make this more difficult to maintain. Kate is not easily won over, but should one succeed in doing so, it will be worth the effort!

The Runic Interpretation
ᛖᛏᚨᚲ (Ehwaz, Teiwaz, Ansuz, Kano)

Kate uses the runes representing movement, warrior, signals, and opening (respectively) to move to ever greater levels of awareness. With the warrior rune figuring so prominently in her name, Kate is a natural leader. She may use Kano to clear her consciousness and calm her emotions. Kate is capable of patience and good mental health. Her family and colleagues rely on her compassionate judgment, and Kate counsels friends in a tender, easy manner. Kate will move several times in her journey toward self-realization. With each transition, she grows more self-reliant and confident.

Elements: Air, air, air, water

The Numerological Interpretation
Kate (NV = 1, CV = 4, VV = 6, FL = 2)

Kate has strong inner convictions that give her self-confidence and an iron will. She is highly individualistic by nature, and has no trouble expressing her thoughts, ideas, and viewpoints. Yet her name does not indicate a person who is extremely egocentric. Kate is definitely her own person, but there is plenty of room in her life for others. She is a woman who requires a very intimate, romantic, and loving personal relationship. Her domestic life is at the core of her being, and her family is a very important part of who she is. Kate will look to the arts as another potential outlet for the expression of her creative energies.

"If you are all wrapped up in yourself, you are overdressed."
—KATE HALVERSON (AUTHOR)

"To be one woman, truly, wholly, is to be all women. Tend one garden and you will birth worlds."
—KATE BRAVERMAN (AUTHOR)

DERIVATION: English, originally from the Greek *aikaterina*, of unknown meaning. Spelled Katerina by the Romans, who associated it with the Greek *katharos*, meaning "pure." The name of several saints, one of whom was martyred at Alexandria in 307.

PRINCIPAL COLORS: All yellow and russet hues, orange

GEMSTONES AND PRECIOUS METALS: Topaz, yellow diamonds

BOTANICALS: Chamomile, lavender, thyme

UNIQUE SPELLINGS: Catharin, Catherinet, Catheryn, Cathrene, Cathrine, Cathryn, Katharine, Kathereen, Katheryn, Katheryne, Kathrene, Kathrine, Kathrynt, Kathryne, Kathyrine

RELATED TO: Caitlin, Caitriona, Catarine, Cateline, Cathaleen, Catharina, Catherina, Catherinet, Catherleen, Cathie, Cathleen, Cathyt, Catrin, Catrina, Catrine, Catriona, Karent, Karin, Katarina, Katet, Katerina, Katey, Katheleen, Katheline, Katherina, Kathie, Kathileen, Kathleent, Kathlyn, Kathlynn, Kathrynt, Kathyt, Katiet, Katina, Katleen, Katrena, Katrinat, Katriona, Katryna, Kattrina, Katy, Kayt, Kittyt, Treena, Trina

"Regret is an appalling waste of energy; you can't build on it."
—KATHERINE MANSFIELD
(AUTHOR)

A KABBALISTIC SYNOPSIS

כאתארין —KAThARYN (Kaph, Aleph, Tau, Aleph, Resh, Yod, Nun)

In Hebrew there is no difference between C and K; consequently, individuals with the name Catherine and Katherine are of the same basic personality type as far as kabbalistic analysis is concerned. Katherine, like Catherine, has definite artistic leanings and will show a strong pull toward the spiritual in the way in which she expresses herself. Katherine is deeply emotional and will be even more focused on forging a perfect relationship than on her art. When it comes to kids, Katherine will sacrifice her own desire to work professionally in an expressive medium if it will benefit the children. The letter Tau in her name indicates her capacity for self-sacrifice under the right circumstances. Katherine is not just artistic in the standard sense of the word, but is wonderfully inventive when it comes to family celebrations. You can bet that her parties are the most imaginative in the whole neighborhood. (See also Catherine.)

THE RUNIC INTERPRETATION

ᛖᚾᛁᚱᛖᚦᚨᚲ (Ehwaz, Nauthiz, Isa, Raido, Ehwaz, Thurisaz, Ansuz, Kano)

Katherine is even stronger emotionally than Kate. But Katherine's challenges are tougher, due to the Nauthiz rune of constraint in her name. The Isa rune will slow Katherine down so she can meditate and relax—but Isa can also cause project delays and cancellations. The Thurisaz rune for gateway means Katherine is able to release memories and keep herself emotionally clear. She is wonderfully able to live in the moment. Thurisaz is also a motivator and a protector. The four elements are in Katherine's name, giving her power, and Katherine can benefit many as a healer.

Elements: Air, fire, earth, water, air, fire, air, water

THE NUMEROLOGICAL INTERPRETATION

Katherine (NV = 1, CV = 8, VV = 2, FL = 2)

This is a no-nonsense woman! Katherine is intent on making her mark in life. She is quite enthusiastic about what she does, and pursues her aims to their successful conclusion. In the process, if she does not like what is going on around her or if something displeases her, she is not one to hide her feelings about it. This name gives Katherine a very energetic, self-protective disposition. She can give the impression that she is domineering, but it is usually just herself that she is trying to control. Organized and tidy in both her appearance and demeanor, Katherine is also loyal and faithful in her personal relationships.

Kathleen

A Kabbalistic Synopsis
כאתלין —KAThLYN (Kaph, Aleph, Tau, Lamed, Yod, Nun)

You won't meet many women with a stronger character than Kathleen; she is capable of taking on any challenge, no matter how daunting. In most cases Kathleen will have a physical strength to match her willpower. As you would expect from a name that represents a nation like Ireland, Kathleen has a great store of homespun wisdom. Many is the time when her friends and relatives will turn to her for advice on a whole range of personal issues, and she will always be happy to offer what help she can.

The Runic Interpretation
ᚾᛖᛖᛚᚦᚨᚲ (Nauthiz, Ehwaz, Ehwaz, Laguz, Thurisaz, Ansuz, Kano)

Kathleen needs to feel free as a bird, and so the constraint of the Nauthiz rune drives her to a point of agitation at times. Help is at hand; Kathleen has the gateway rune to offer her choices and the knowledge that she wants to be creative and free. The Laguz rune of flow offers her just this opportunity. When Kathleen really enjoys what she is doing, it shows. The runes of signals and opening help Kathleen spend her time pursuing artistic endeavors. The double Ehwaz rune frees her to move, and indicates she has strong feminine intuition.

Elements: Fire, air, air, water, fire, air, water

The Numerological Interpretation
Kathleen (NV = 4, CV = 2, VV = 11, FL = 2)

People mean a great deal to Kathleen. She works hard at being a responsible friend to those with whom she lives and works. This is a name that bestows a caring disposition, and its numbers indicate a person who is both dedicated and loyal. Kathleen is well suited to act as an intermediary. She has the ability to see both sides of any situation and is fair and just in her viewpoints. Her ambitions are not exclusively personal, and she will give a great deal of herself to social and community projects. Kathleen is a practical person, one who is concerned with ecology and the conservation of energy. Environmental concerns may be of considerable interest to her.

DERIVATION: Irish and English, anglicized form of the Gaelic Caitlin, a form of Catherine. Related to the Greek adjective *katharos*, meaning "pure." Extremely popular in the United States in the 1950s.

PRINCIPAL COLORS: Any hue of medium shade

GEMSTONES AND PRECIOUS METALS: Sapphires

BOTANICALS: Sage, Solomon's seal

UNIQUE SPELLINGS: Cathaleen, Cathleen, Cathleene, Cathlene, Katheleen, Katheline, Kathileen, Kathleene, Kathlene

RELATED TO: Caitlin, Caitriona, Catarine, Cateline, Catharin, Catharina, Catharine, Catherina, Catherinet, Catherleen, Cathie, Cathrene, Cathryn, Cathyt, Catrin, Catrina, Catrine, Catriona, Karent, Karin, Katarina, Katerina, Katey, Katharine, Kathereen, Katherina, Katherinet, Kathie, Kathlyn, Kathlynn, Kathrene, Kathrynt, Kathyt, Katiet, Katina, Katleen, Katrena, Katrinat, Katriona, Katryna, Kattrina, Katy, Kayt, Kittyt, Treena, Trina

"Life is easier than you'd think; all that is necessary is to accept the impossible, do without the indispensable, and bear the intolerable."
—KATHLEEN NORRIS (AUTHOR)

Kathryn

DERIVATION: American form of Katherine. Originally from the Greek *aikaterina*, of unknown meaning. Spelled Katerina by the Romans, who associated it with the Greek *katharos*, meaning "pure." In the United States, Kathryn is the most common spelling of this name.

PRINCIPAL COLORS: Gold, the full range of green and yellow hues

GEMSTONES AND PRECIOUS METALS: Moonstones, pearls, moss agate

BOTANICALS: Juniper, linseed, hops

UNIQUE SPELLINGS: Catharin, Catherine, Catheryn, Cathrene, Cathrine, Cathryn, Katharine, Kathereen, Katherine, Katheryn, Katheryne, Kathrene, Kathrine, Kathryne, Kathyrine

RELATED TO: Caitlin, Caitriona, Catarine, Cateline, Cathaleen, Catharina, Caterina, Catherinet, Catherleen, Cathie, Cathleen, Cathy†, Catrin, Catrina, Catrine, Catriona, Karen†, Karin, Katarina, Kate†, Katerina, Katey, Katheleen, Katheline, Katherina, Katherine†, Kathie, Kathileen, Kathleen†, Kathlyn, Kathlynn, Kathy†, Katie†, Katina, Katleen, Katrena, Katrina†, Katriona, Katryna, Kattrina, Katy, Kay†, Kitty†, Treena, Trina

A KABBALISTIC SYNOPSIS
כאתרין —KAThRYN (Kaph, Aleph, Tau, Resh, Yod, Nun)

You will hear Kathryn long before you see her, as she has a voice that carries for miles and she is very fond of using it! This doesn't mean that she spends her time shouting; far from it. Kathryn has a natural sense of rhythm and a good ear for tone, so she would make a great singer. She is unlikely to be found singing the blues, though; Kathryn has an optimistic outlook on life, which she will need if she does try to break into show business. If she is not on-stage, you may find it difficult to locate Kathryn, since she likes to spend much of her time outdoors. Emotionally, Kathryn is surprisingly well balanced and is not given to extreme feelings. Once she has found a lover, she will be perfectly honest with him or her, and it is likely that a long and comfortable relationship will follow.

THE RUNIC INTERPRETATION
ᚾᛇᚱᚦᚨᚲ (Nauthiz, Eihwaz, Raido, Thurisaz, Ansuz, Kano)

Kathryn enjoys wonderful communication skills offered her by the Raido rune of journey. Clear communication is a by-product of her good, clear thinking. Kathryn knows that she can benefit by meditation, and the insight she garners from the silence helps her keep her life in balance. The standstill Isa rune supports her in her efforts. The Raido rune also affords Kathryn many opportunities to travel and expand her appreciation of the world and its peoples.

Elements: Fire, earth/fire, water, fire, air, water

THE NUMEROLOGICAL INTERPRETATION
Kathryn (NV = 7, CV = 8, VV = 8, FL = 2)

Kathryn tends to be emotionally mature and seeks stability and material security in her personal relationships and choice of partners. She is much more a pragmatist than an idealist and is quite ambitious by nature. This name bestows an orientation toward health. In its most apparent sense, it means that she is careful about her diet and appreciates the benefits that come from leading a natural lifestyle, one with lots of exercise and outdoor activity. On a wider level, health for Kathryn also means a clean environment.

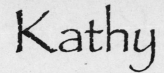

Kathy

A KABBALISTIC SYNOPSIS

כאתי —KAThY (Kaph, Aleph, Tau, Yod)

Like Katherine, Kathy shares her meaning with Cathy since, in the language of the Kabbalah, they are essentially the same name. Kathy is the ultimate materialist. One aspect of Kathy's personality that may surprise you is her relationship with children: Kathy loves kids. A great way for her to unwind is to spend a few hours outdoors or indulging her childlike nature—the side of her that never really gets exposed to her peers. To adults Kathy is always sensible and pragmatic. Although serious in outward appearance, in intimate relations Kathy is passionate and playful. (See also Cathy.)

THE RUNIC INTERPRETATION

ᛇᚦᚨᚲ (Eihwaz, Thurisaz, Ansuz, Kano)

Kathy is full of fun. She has the runes of movement, gateway, signals, and opening in her name. Kathy has plenty of romance in her life. She keeps ten partners dangling at a time, and she charms every one of them. Kathy's so intuitive that she knows which one is going to call when the phone rings. Kathy will probably marry late in life because she's having too much fun to slow down, but once she does, she'll be devoted. Her charm and easy manner make her well suited to careers in sales or politics.

Elements: Earth/fire, fire, air, water

THE NUMEROLOGICAL INTERPRETATION

Kathy (NV = 11, CV = 3, VV = 8, FL = 2)

Kathy will tend to have a wide range of social contacts. She enjoys her friendships and cultivates people from all different backgrounds and walks of life. People are very fond of her, and she adds enthusiasm and intelligent conversation to all social situations. Kathy is very quick on the uptake and displays a good sense of humor and a witty disposition. But all is not play and frivolity where she is concerned; Kathy has a distinct need to participate in those projects that speak to social and community issues. Her choice of work may lead her into some field related to communication, where she can be instrumental as a networker.

DERIVATION: English, short form of Katherine. Originally from the Greek *aikaterina*, of unknown meaning. Associated with the Greek *katharos*, meaning "pure." Commonly used as an independent name since the 1950s.

PRINCIPAL COLORS: All shades of green and white

GEMSTONES AND PRECIOUS METALS: Jade, pearls

BOTANICALS: Colewort, cabbage, plantain

UNIQUE SPELLINGS: Cathi, Cathie, Cathy, Kathi, Kathie

RELATED TO: Caitlin, Caitriona, Catarine, Cateline, Cathaleen, Catharin, Catharina, Catherina, Catherinet, Catherleen, Catheryn, Cathleen, Cathrene, Cathrine, Cathryn, Cathyt, Catrin, Catrina, Catrine, Catriona, Karent, Karin, Katarina, Katet, Katerina, Katey, Katharine, Katheleen, Katheline, Kathereen, Katherina, Katherinet, Katheryn, Katheryne, Kathileen, Kathleent, Kathlyn, Kathlynn, Kathrene, Kathrine, Kathrynt, Kathryne, Kathyrine, Katiet, Katina, Katleen, Katrena, Katrinat, Katriona, Katryna, Kattrina, Katy, Kayt, Kittyt

---

DERIVATION: English, pet form of Kate, a short form of Katherine or Kathleen. Associated with the Greek adjective *katharos*, meaning "pure." Used as an independent name since the mid-nineteenth century.

PRINCIPAL COLORS: The full range of brown and yellow hues, orange, gold

GEMSTONES AND PRECIOUS METALS: Citrine, amber, yellow diamonds

BOTANICALS: Chamomile, lavender, Saint-John's-wort

UNIQUE SPELLINGS: Catey, Cati, Catie, Caty, Katey, Kati, Katy

RELATED TO: Caitlin, Caitriona, Catarine, Cateline, Cathaleen, Catharina, Catherina, Catherine†, Catherleen, Cathie, Cathleen, Cathrene, Cathryn, Cathy†, Catrin, Catrina, Catrine, Catriona, Karen†, Karin, Katarina, Kate†, Katerina, Katharine, Katheleen, Katheline, Kathereen, Katherina, Katherine†, Kathie, Kathileen, Kathleen†, Kathlyn, Kathlynn, Kathrene, Kathryn†, Kathy†, Katina, Katleen, Katrena, Katrina†, Katriona, Katryna, Kattrina, Kay†, Kitty†, Treena, Trina

A KABBALISTIC SYNOPSIS
כאיטי —KAYTY (Kaph, Aleph, Yod, Teth, Yod)

Katie is a woman who feels most at home when she's wearing white—not a wedding dress, but a lab coat! The world of science has a lot to gain from Katie's presence; she has a remarkable mind, and has the ability to untangle seemingly unsolvable problems. As a child she probably spent more time taking her toys apart than actually playing with them. This interest in what makes things function will stay with her throughout her life. Even though Katie is likely to earn a reasonable amount of money from her work, she is not one for luxuries. In fact, she is the sort of person who will give very generously to charity on a regular basis, and is only really concerned that she has the basics in life. Katie could never be described as someone who fits into other people's expectations. She may be the classically objective scientist at work, but at home she is usually fond of some very traditional pursuits; you are more likely to catch her with an embroidery needle than a joystick.

THE RUNIC INTERPRETATION
ᛖᛁᚦᚨᚲ (Ehwaz, Isa, Thurisaz, Ansuz, Kano)

Katie has the same energies as Kathy. She is not at all gullible, and she has trained herself to protect herself. She is very strong. The Ansuz rune of signals points to the fact that Katie is insightful and flexible in her outlook. Openings happen because the Kano rune brings with it chance encounters and unexpected good fortune. Katie has the mettle to live by her wits.

Elements: Air, earth, fire, air, water

THE NUMEROLOGICAL INTERPRETATION
Katie (NV = 1, CV = 4, VV = 6, FL = 2)

The practical considerations of life mean a great deal to Katie. She is apt to choose a profession that allows for financial security and job stability. In this respect, she would do well in some branch of financial management. Katie has a strong urge to express her individuality in ways that bring harmony and abundance into other people's lives. Family and home mean a great deal to her, and she is generous with those whom she loves. Katie likes to look good and tends to dress modestly but with care. Although she is closely tied to her family, she will also seek to create private interests of her own. These hobbies and activities will most likely take her into the world of the arts, as she is inspired by beauty in all its forms.

Katrina

DERIVATION: Modern form of Catriona and Katarina. Related to the Greek adjective *katharos*, meaning "pure."

PRINCIPAL COLORS: The full gamut of green hues, cream

GEMSTONES AND PRECIOUS METALS: Jade, moonstones

BOTANICALS: Chicory, cabbage, lettuce

UNIQUE SPELLINGS: Catreena, Catrina, Katreena, Katrena, Katryna, Kattrina

RELATED TO: Caitlin, Caitriona, Catarine, Cateline, Cathaleen, Catharina, Catherina, Catherine†, Catherleen, Cathie, Cathleen, Cathrene, Cathryn, Cathy†, Catrin, Catrina, Catrine, Catriona, Karen†, Karin, Katarina, Kate†, Katerina, Katey, Katharine, Katheleen, Katheline, Kathereen, Katherina, Katherine†, Kathie, Kathileen, Kathleen†, Kathlyn, Kathlynn, Kathrene, Kathryn†, Kathy†, Katie†, Katina, Katleen, Katriona, Katy, Kay†, Kitty†, Treena, Trina

A KABBALISTIC SYNOPSIS

כאטרינא —KATRYNA (Kaph, Aleph, Teth, Resh, Yod, Nun, Aleph)

Katrina seemingly would be perfect in the role of fashion model. The dual energies of the sun, represented by Resh, and fire, represented by Yod, at the center of her name let us know that her charismatic character is immediately obvious to all who see her, even from a distance. Many men make the mistake of treating her like a helpless little girl, thinking that beauty is equivalent to naïveté. However, Katrina has a range of practical skills and is very resourceful and worldly. She has a wickedly sarcastic tongue when she wants to, and any man who attempts to patronize her will come away with his pride more than a little stung. With the right partner she is more than ready to melt—but only the right partner will ever find this out.

THE RUNIC INTERPRETATION

ᚨᚾᛁᚱᛏᚨᚲ (Ansuz, Nauthiz, Isa, Raido, Teiwaz, Ansuz, Kano)

Katrina has the double Ansuz rune of signals, and she is always looking for signs to guide her direction. The Nauthiz rune in her name provides lessons of constraint for Katrina, and Isa offers isolation. These are difficult lessons she undergoes, and Katrina must exercise restraint so as not to wallow in self-pity when things don't go her way. As she develops patience, she learns to wait for an understanding of her situation or an issue to arrive.

Elements: Air, fire, earth, water, air, air, water

THE NUMEROLOGICAL INTERPRETATION

Katrina (NV = 2, CV = 9, VV = 11, FL = 2)

Katrina is very compassionate and understanding. When her friends need someone to talk to or a strong supportive hand, they know that they can approach Katrina for help. She, in turn, has to be careful not to be overly sensitive and lose her sense of personal boundaries. Her emotional nature can sometimes be too responsive, and it may overwhelm her. Katrina would do well in one of the helping professions, such as psychology or social work, so that she may structure her urge to be of service around her career. Katrina would derive a great deal of benefit from working with groups of people. She has a sense about other people's talents and an instinct about who would work best with whom. She therefore makes a very good social coordinator.

Kay

A KABBALISTIC SYNOPSIS
כאי —KAY (Kaph, Aleph, Yod)

The value of Kay's name is thirty-one, which is equivalent to אל, one of the main kabbalistic names of God. Kay herself is likely to be fairly religious in quite a conservative way. She attends church regularly, and celebrates all religious holidays with quite a solemn and serious attitude. However, her real religious beliefs are likely to be expressed through her work. It is possible that Kay will be a minister of religion, but it is even more likely that she will devote her life to helping those less fortunate than herself. Her favorite activities will probably involve areas such as carpentry, construction, and other pursuits traditionally considered to be exclusively male. Kay has no problem with making money, although she tends to be a saver rather than a spender.

THE RUNIC INTERPRETATION
ᛇᚨᚲ (Eihwaz, Ansuz, Kano)

Kay is an old-fashioned clear thinker, and she can thank the Kano rune of opening for this attribute. Kano, for opening, combined with Ansuz, for signals or intuition, is a powerful mix. Kay can do just about anything she sets her mind to. She is a quick learner, with a steel-trap memory and good people skills. Kay is the kind of person who remembers names, dates, and figures. People may think she's even a bit more intelligent than she actually is, because her memory is so fantastic. Kay is easy to get along with because she isn't carrying around emotional baggage. She strives for harmony in relationships and is modest and kind.

Elements: Earth/fire, air, water

THE NUMEROLOGICAL INTERPRETATION
Kay (NV = 1, CV = 2, VV = 8, FL = 2)

Kay has a distinct sense of her own individuality, and will never compromise herself in this respect. In fact, she projects herself with great vitality into life, as she is unafraid of the challenges that await. But she is also aware of the importance of balance and structure in terms of the larger social circumstances in which we live. Kay is attracted by people and attractive to them. She is never long without an intimate partner. In order for her unions to be successful, Kay requires a companion who is also of a highly independent nature.

Keith

A KABBALISTIC SYNOPSIS
כית —KYTh (Kaph, Yod, Tau)

Any partner of Keith's is extremely lucky. You could spend your whole life looking, and you would never find a man as devoted as Keith. He lives for his partner; indeed, he is driven by the desire to ensure the happiness of those close to him. This aspect of his character is due to the major significance of the initial and final letters of his name. Not only can Keith be incredibly affectionate and utterly loyal, but he will put his practical skills to use as well; if you want a conservatory or a new patio, Keith will be only too happy to build you one. Workwise, Keith will never be a millionaire; he is happy simply to have a regular secure job, one that he can leave behind once the day is over. This means that big material declarations of love are out, but then when you have someone like Keith, material luxuries aren't so important.

THE RUNIC INTERPRETATION
ᚦᛁᛇᚲ (Thurisaz, Isa, Eihwaz, Kano)

Keith has the runic configuration of gateway, defense, and opening, and will therefore make a good trial lawyer, investigator, or detective. He could also be a scientific researcher or troubleshooter. Keith has the gateway rune to teach him to slow down and consider all the evidence before formulating a decision. Gateway also helps him learn patience and perseverance. Eihwaz and Isa also teach patience, because Keith learns not to push when he encounters resistance and obstacles in his path. He has learned that a delay in a situation like this can make all the difference in the outcome. The Kano rune lends clarity and truth to any situation.

Elements: Fire, earth, earth/fire, water

THE NUMEROLOGICAL INTERPRETATION
Keith (NV = 8, CV = 3, VV = 5, FL = 2)

Keith possesses a wide range of talents and interests. He is a person who is seldom bored, as he is able to invent opportunities for his creative self-expression. With a name that is motivated by the urge for social and professional achievement, Keith likes the finer things in life and is determined to get them. Although he seeks a career with job security and sound financial benefits, Keith must also have variety and personal freedom in his work. He will prefer a job that permits him to travel and meet people, as he is a sociable man, one who takes great pleasure from interacting intellectually with others. Keith can be so mentally and physically active that he may minimize the importance of the heart and the necessity of staying in contact with his feelings.

DERIVATION: English and Scottish, from a Scottish surname. Of uncertain origin, but possibly from a Celtic word meaning "wood." Commonly used since the nineteenth century, and especially popular in the United States in the 1960s.

PRINCIPAL COLORS: Deep, rich azure, purple, and gray shades, also black

GEMSTONES AND PRECIOUS METALS: Carbuncles, sapphires, black diamonds

BOTANICALS: Shepherd's purse, ragwort, mandrake root

UNIQUE SPELLINGS: Keath, Keeth, Keethe

RELATED TO: Kenneth†

Kelly

DERIVATION: English, both masculine and feminine. From the Gaelic name Ceallach, meaning "the warlike one." Extremely popular in the United States in the 1970s.

PRINCIPAL COLORS: From pale to deep, rich green; white

GEMSTONES AND PRECIOUS METALS: Green jade, white pearls, moonstones

BOTANICALS: Cabbage, colewort, moonwort

UNIQUE SPELLINGS: Kelley, Kelli, Kellie

RELATED TO: Kaylee, Kayley, Kealey, Kealy, Keelie, Keely, Keighley, Keiley, Keilly, Keily, Kelda, Kieley, Kieli, Kiley, Kleday, Kylee, Kylie

A KABBALISTIC SYNOPSIS
כללי —KLLY (Kaph, Lamed, Lamed, Yod)

Kelly is a thinker more than a feeler, and is comfortable that way. A person named Kelly is happiest when surrounded by the trappings of intellectual activity, like books and computers. He or she will definitely have an area in the house that's just for thinking, and is likely to work as a teacher or a researcher. Recognition is important to Kelly. The immense drive Kelly has to achieve intellectually is partially fueled by this desire to be recognized. Kellys can best achieve this by using their excellent communication skills, which are represented by Peh, meaning "mouth," which the name Kelly is equivalent to in value. Never afraid of new ideas, Kelly is refreshing company and a stimulating coworker. In relationships, though, Kelly must learn to resist the urge to dominate.

THE RUNIC INTERPRETATION
ᛇᛚᛚᛖᚲ (Eihwaz, Laguz, Laguz, Ehwaz, Kano)

Male or female, Kelly learns valuable lessons from the powers in this name. Kelly is musical, and her mind is artistic and creative in any of a number of areas. She has that Laguz strength to suggest she has good use of her right brain, which gives her the ability to make unexpected associations and inventive leaps. She has a delightful sense of humor and likes to express herself, both in the way she dresses and in the way she decorates her home. Kelly is probably one of those artists who is very neat and proper-looking on the outside, but when you open her portfolio, her work is more imaginative than that of most other artists.

Elements: Earth/fire, water, water, air, water

THE NUMEROLOGICAL INTERPRETATION
Kelly (NV = 11, CV = 8, VV = 3, FL = 2)

Men and women named Kelly can be quite an inspiration to their friends, family, and coworkers. Their own inner strength is reflected in what they do and how they do it. Determined and strong-willed, these are people who have the potential to combine a bright intellect and a clear, intuitive sensibility. Kellys have both insight and precision—tools that they can apply to the large projects they enjoy undertaking. Kelly requires a partner who is community minded and unafraid of success. Kelly has a long distance to go in life, and is intent upon getting there.

Kelsey

DERIVATION: English, from the Old English surname Ceolsige, composed of *ceol*, meaning "ship," and *sige*, meaning "victory." Both masculine and feminine.

PRINCIPAL COLORS: The full spectrum of very pale hues

GEMSTONES AND PRECIOUS METALS: Silver, platinum

BOTANICALS: Hazel, sweet marjoram, mushrooms

UNIQUE SPELLINGS: Kelci, Kelcie, Kelcy, Kelsi, Kelsie, Kelsy

RELATED TO: Keely, Kelly†, Kelsa

A KABBALISTIC SYNOPSIS
כאלסי —KALSY (Kaph, Aleph, Lamed, Samech, Yod)

You have to be quick to catch Kelsey, who is a real bundle of energy and loves to be constantly on the move. It may be that he or she uses athleticism professionally; the influences in the name suggest great suppleness, as well as agility and speed. If Kelsey is male he will be inclined more toward agility-based sports rather than those emphasizing strength. Although all Kelseys adore a fast lifestyle, they do not really push themselves toward their goals, and often need a partner or friend to cajole them into taking the next step. It's not that Kelsey lacks confidence; it has more to do with the fact that Kelsey is fairly laid-back and doesn't really hunger for success. Kelsey gets a real kick out of seeing others do well for themselves, and with this relaxed approach Kelsey may well make an ideal coach or trainer.

THE RUNIC INTERPRETATION
ᛇᛖᛋᛚᛖᚲ (Eihwaz, Ehwaz, Sowelu, Laguz, Ehwaz, Kano)

Kelsey can be a male or female name, and the meaning is just the same for either sex. Kelsey is fortunate to have the runes of defense, wholeness, flow, movement, and opening, respectively, in his or her name. Kelsey is capable of behaving assertively or aggressively, depending on what the situation warrants, and is good at negotiating contracts. Because of the Eihwaz rune in this name, Kelsey feels confident and willing to hold to a hard line. The Laguz rune gives Kelsey an intuitive edge with people. The Sowelu rune hints that Kelsey gains a great deal of personal satisfaction from life. Kelseys will move and reside in many different places before they finally settle down. But everywhere they go, people welcome them.

Elements: Earth/fire, air, air, water, air, water

THE NUMEROLOGICAL INTERPRETATION
Kelsey (NV = 5, CV = 6, VV = 8, FL = 2)

An enthusiasm for life and a high energy level make Kelsey a great deal of fun to be around. The numerological significance of this name urges Kelsey toward significant friendships, and signals a need for the freedom to explore many different ways of self-expression. Kelsey enjoys travel and is adventurous by nature. Kelsey is not a loner, however, and would much prefer to be accompanied by a loving and exciting partner. When the journey is over, Kelsey will return home, bringing along some of the beautiful objects acquired along the way. Beautifying the environment is a great pleasure for Kelsey.

Ken

DERIVATION: English, pet form of Kenneth, an anglicized form of the Gaelic names Cinaed and Cainnech, meaning "born of fire" and "handsome one," respectively.

PRINCIPAL COLORS: All shades of violet, from pale bluish purple to dark, rich purple

GEMSTONES AND PRECIOUS METALS: Garnets, amethyst

BOTANICALS: Apple, cherry, strawberry

UNIQUE SPELLING: Kenn

RELATED TO: Kendall, Kendrick, Kenelm, Kennard, Kennedy, Kenneth†, Kenny, Kent†, Kenton, Kenward, Kenway, Kenyon

❧

"People who produce good results feel good about themselves."
—KEN BLANCHARD (AUTHOR)

A KABBALISTIC SYNOPSIS
כאן —KAN (Kaph, Aleph, Nun)

Ken really likes to be at the center of things; he doesn't have to be personally involved, but he has to know exactly what is going on in any given situation. Ken is the kind of guy who seems to be the chairman of every committee in the neighborhood. It is very possible that his desire to sit at the center of things—like a spider watching every line of his web for the slightest twitch—stems from a sense of insecurity and a fear of being excluded; this may well be the significance of the final Nun in his name. On the whole, Ken makes a great organizer and chairperson. The initial Kaph ensures that he takes a pragmatic approach to situations. Ken also has the capacity to make people feel at ease when he takes control of a situation, and usually he gets it right.

THE RUNIC INTERPRETATION
ᚾᛖᚲ (Nauthiz, Ehwaz, Kano)

When a name has opposing energies in it, such as constraint and opening, we can assume the bearer of the name in question has done a lot of work to change the direction of his life. The name Ken is a perfect example. Ken has runes for constraint, defense, and opening in his name. He clearly begins life with the Nauthiz rune of constraint bogging him down with negativity. However, the Kano rune of opening points to the time of transition in which Ken examines his beliefs, sets about to alter them, and invites prosperity into his life.

Elements: Fire, air, water

THE NUMEROLOGICAL INTERPRETATION
Ken (NV = 3, CV = 7, VV = 5, FL = 2)

Ken has a keen intellect and a great curiosity about life. His inner creative drive is supported and nourished by his ability to open up to the constantly new opportunities that present themselves to him. Ken evolves his natural abilities into greater and more varied forms of expression. He is a man for whom freedom of choice is most important—and Ken likes to choose! He tends to have a number of relationships rather than to select a permanent partner early in life. Ken seeks the excitement that a variety of life experiences offer and, if at all possible, will choose a career that does not bind him to a chair.

❧

Kendra

A Kabbalistic Synopsis

כאנדרא —KANDRA (Kaph, Aleph, Nun, Daleth, Resh, Aleph)

If you're thinking of changing your name, you could do a lot worse than opting for Kendra. Kendra's name adds up to 276, which when compressed indicates a natural cheerfulness that allows Kendra to mix easily with any number of people and provides a wider-than-usual horizon of lifestyle choices. In addition, the name reduces to fifteen, showing Kendra's enjoyment of the so-called simple pleasures: sex, good food, good wine—the list goes on! Kendra has a deeply happy marriage and is very balanced emotionally. This levelheadedness allows her to indulge in any number of minor vices without any lasting ill effects. If Kendra has any problems in life it will probably be that with her hectic social life and large number of friends to spend time with, it is difficult to find enough hours in the day!

The Runic Interpretation

ᚨᚱᛞᚾᛖᚲ (Ansuz, Raido, Dagaz, Nauthiz, Ehwaz, Kano)

Kendra is sure to go far in business. She has the intuition of the Ansuz rune (signals) to guide her. Her receptivity to new endeavors is indicated by the Kano rune of opening. The Nauthiz rune of constraint gives her plenty of practice in overcoming sales resistance. Once the Dagaz rune of breakthrough comes into play, Kendra goes to a higher level of achievement. The Raido rune of journey and good communication afford Kendra a chance to travel and possibly work in sales. The Ehwaz rune of movement indicates that Kendra could make a lot of money by relocating to a foreign country. Because of her faithfulness and perseverance, Kendra is sure to succeed.

Elements: Air, water, fire, fire, air, water

The Numerological Interpretation

Kendra (NV = 8, CV = 2, VV = 6, FL = 2)

This name is associated with a strong urge to create harmony and prosperity. Kendra is capable of making a number of positive connections among people that allow for an increase in mutual creative potential. She may thus act as an intermediary who can bring benefit to all concerned. Kendra is a woman who is very much involved with her career and is most comfortable in a profession that is geared toward the media or the arts. Kendra knows instinctively how the various social and interpersonal pieces of a creative puzzle fit together into a larger picture.

DERIVATION: English, feminine form of Kendrick. Of uncertain origin, but possibly from Old Celtic roots meaning "high summit." May also be a blend of Kenneth and Alexandra. Especially popular in the United States in the late 1940s.

PRINCIPAL COLORS: Dark gray, black, deep shades of azure and violet

GEMSTONES AND PRECIOUS METALS: Lackluster rubies, sapphires, black pearls

BOTANICALS: Marsh mallow, angelica

UNIQUE SPELLINGS: Kendrah, Khendra, Khendrah

RELATED TO: Alexandra†, Sandra†

∽

"There is no reason for any individual to have a computer in his home."
—KENNETH H. OLSON (PRESIDENT OF DEC, CONVENTION OF THE WORLD FUTURE SOCIETY, 1977)

Kenneth

A KABBALISTIC SYNOPSIS
כאננת —KANNTh (Kaph, Aleph, Nun, Nun, Tau)

Kenneth likes a quiet life and usually lives in a close-knit community, preferably as far away from any major city as possible. One reason for this is Kenneth's mistrust of modern technology. He is much happier with less technologically advanced possessions and is quite capable of making much of his own household equipment. In fact, it is very likely that Kenneth's profession will be related in some way to traditional crafts. He is exceptionally skilled with his hands and has the patience required to make a success of such a business. Kenneth will be at his happiest when he is fully integrated into a little enclave of friends and has a wife and a bunch of kids. If people try to take advantage of Kenneth's simple and straightforward manner, they will be in for a shock. On the whole Kenneth is an extremely good-natured man—but he also has a very strong will, and doesn't take kindly to anyone trying to take him for a fool.

THE RUNIC INTERPRETATION
ᛑᛖᚻᚻᛖᚲ (Thurisaz, Ehwaz, Nauthiz, Nauthiz, Ehwaz, Kano)

Kenneth is confronted with the double rune for constraint and the double rune for movement. Obviously, Kenneth has far to go! He needs to understand that all the stress of living in new places for short periods of time is just part of his earthly lesson. The universe is organized so that we continually grow, and we grow by facing challenges every day. We grow by embracing struggles and learning from them. Kenneth reaches the Thurisaz rune of gateway, and he will do so by being open to his feelings and experiencing new adventures on the way.

Elements: Air, water, fire, fire, air, water

THE NUMEROLOGICAL INTERPRETATION
Kenneth (NV = 5, CV = 22, VV = 1, FL = 2)

Kenneth is a self-starter, a man who is able to find the energy to bring his plans and projects to fruition through his profound vision and self-confidence. This name bestows a highly individualistic nature, one that will not be compromised by social or peer pressures. This demonstrates his strength of character and bestows upon Kenneth a strong will and an urge to succeed in life. Kenneth may need to cultivate patience and tolerance, as not everyone in his environment has the same level of self-assurance as he does. If his talents and will are misdirected, there is a tendency toward a lack of compassion and the urge to be socially manipulative.

∽

Kent

A Kabbalistic Synopsis

כאנט —KANT (Kaph, Aleph, Nun, Teth)

Kent's biggest asset is his mouth. His name adds to eighty, the value of Peh, which means "mouth." Thanks to the practical associations of the letter Kaph, we can envisage Kent using his communication skills in some kind of training context, and his sharp sense of humor will be of great use to him in this role. Kent is definitely a ladies' man and is skilled in seduction. Despite his love of all things sensual, Kent is trustworthy, and would never dream of cheating on an existing partner. Not all is sweetness and light, though. The final letter in his name means "serpent," and serves to remind us that Kent can use his communication skills to become highly critical if he is pushed to it. In fact, when angry, Kent is an extremely formidable opponent.

The Runic Interpretation

↑ᚺᛗᚲ (Teiwaz, Nauthiz, Ehwaz, Kano)

Kent moves—perhaps from one country to another—but not as frequently as Kenneth. Kent must learn to be adaptable and flexible in his dealings with people and events. There is no such thing as security, and this is one of Kent's lessons. Once Kent learns to nurture himself by keeping his nails well groomed and his clothing in good repair, he begins to understand that the body is indeed a temple. As long as Kent is comfortable within his soul, he always has a home, and a friend within.

Elements: Air, fire, air, water

The Numerological Interpretation

Kent (NV = 5, CV = 9, VV = 5, FL = 2)

This name suggests a very mercurial nature, making Kent quick-witted and very changeable. This is a man who requires constant activity, variety, and excitement in life. He is eager for new experiences and is always in search of adventure. Kent makes an excellent salesman, advertising executive, or promoter of special projects, as he has a gift with words and is a born communicator. Kent may have to cultivate greater sincerity in his relationships, as there is a tendency with this name to be fickle or superficial. He will do well to cultivate the humanitarian and service facets of his personality, as these characteristics appear in his name, and their expression can only add to his success in life.

DERIVATION: English, originally a surname denoting someone from the county of Kent. Of uncertain origin, but most likely from a Celtic root meaning "border." Particularly common in the 1930s and 1940s.

PRINCIPAL COLORS: The full spectrum of pale shades

GEMSTONES AND PRECIOUS METALS: Diamonds, silver, platinum

BOTANICALS: Marjoram, oats, parsley

UNIQUE SPELLINGS: Kehnt, Kehnte, Kehntt, Kente, Kentt

RELATED TO: Kent, Kendall, Kendrick, Kenelm, Kennard, Kennedy, Kenneth, Kenny, Kenton, Kenward, Kenway, Kenyon

Kerry

DERIVATION: English, from the county in southwestern Ireland. Used for both boys and girls.

PRINCIPAL COLORS: All but the brightest shades of azure

GEMSTONES AND PRECIOUS METALS: Emeralds, blue and blue-green turquoise

BOTANICALS: Vervain, melon, apricots

UNIQUE SPELLINGS: Kehri, Kehrie, Kehrri, Kehrrie, Kehry, Keri, Kerie, Kerri, Kerrie, Kery

RELATED TO: Cari, Carriet, Cary, Kerr, Kerstin

A KABBALISTIC SYNOPSIS
כאררי —KARRY (Kaph, Aleph, Resh, Resh, Yod)

Resh means "sun" and usually indicates a sunny, jovial character. With two Reshes in her name, we can rightly expect Kerry to be positively glowing with contentment. Resh also points to a keen sense of humor, and Kerry certainly knows how to have a laugh; if she were offered a dream date, Robin Williams would be her choice hands down over Richard Gere or Tom Cruise! As sun worshipers go, you can't beat Kerry, who feels naked without a good tan. Kerry may well find herself working the comedy circuit as a comedienne. People warm to her pretty much immediately, and any partner will have to accept that they are dating not just Kerry but a whole group of her friends. All this fun doesn't mean that Kerry is a slacker; she is capable of working long and hard. It's not what motivates her in life, but she is well aware of the value of a good reference. A man named Kerry will share this same sunny demeanor, good work ethic, and love of life.

THE RUNIC INTERPRETATION
ᛇᚱᚱᛖᚲ (Eihwaz, Raido, Raido, Ehwaz, Kano)

Kerry is a pilgrim on his journey. The double Raido rune indicates much movement and travel in Kerry's life. He must embrace these changes, for with them come the growth and experiences he needs to grow. As he progresses, the difficulty of his challenges increases. Kerry uses the Kano energy of opening to welcome these journeys in his life. The Ehwaz rune of movement ensures that Kerry advances in all his varied experiences. Women named Kerry will face similar challenges and reap similar rewards.

Elements: Earth/fire, water, water, air, water

THE NUMEROLOGICAL INTERPRETATION
Kerry (NV = 5, CV = 2, VV = 3, FL = 2)

A charming man with a vivacious smile, Kerry likes people, and they admire him in return. Kerry is filled with curiosity and has an active intellect to match. He is usually taking some course or workshop to widen his understanding about life. When in social situations, Kerry can be relied upon to stimulate the conversation, as he always has some interesting comment to make on almost any subject. Kerry can be fussy about details; he likes being tidy, and his personal environment has to be peaceful and harmonious. Females named Kerry will be similarly neat and are equally charming and curious. Having such an organized home is a balance to Kerry's external life, which tends to be very changeable and unpredictable. Personal relationships are very important to Kerry, and he or she always seems to have a loving partner—if not always the same one!

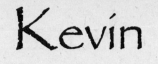

Kevin

A Kabbalistic Synopsis
כאוין —KAVYN (Kaph, Aleph, Vau, Yod, Nun)

Whatever you do, never try to tie Kevin down; there is no surer way to guarantee that you will never see him again. Kevin has very itchy feet and is best suited to jobs that require a considerable amount of travel—preferably where traveling is itself the job. Otherwise, he is likely to go through as many jobs in a year as the rest of us do in a lifetime! The central letter in Kevin's name is V, or Vau, which, among other things, represents the element of choice in life; he sees the world around him as full of possibilities, and he wants to experience as many of them as he can. Kevin's parents can rest easy, though; there is a very practical streak running through Kevin, which means that his various travels aren't likely to result in financial or personal disaster—although as he loves excitement, he may at times come close!

The Runic Interpretation
ᚾᛁᚠᛖᚲ (Nauthiz, Isa, Fehu, Ehwaz, Kano)

The Irish say "May the road rise up to meet you," and blessings, benefits, and opportunities surely will greet Kevin. The movement and possessions runes of his name hint that Kevin will overcome obstacles early in his life. The runes of constraint and standstill place Kevin in limited circumstances as a young man. Whether these constraints are financial, emotional, physical, or otherwise is not the point; constraint feels the same in whatever form it manifests itself. After a time, Kevin will overcome these hardships and will have financial security and opportunities.

Elements: Fire, earth, fire, air, water

The Numerological Interpretation
Kevin (NV = 7, CV = 11, VV = 5, FL = 2)

There is a distinct urge for scientific or philosophical inquiry inherent in this name. Kevin is a deep thinker, a man who has the need to uncover the hidden meanings in both himself and in the world around him. Kevin is inclined to spend a great deal of his time pursuing some form of self-discovery. His analytical nature is such that he may see his life as an onion, and he keeps peeling away its layers in order to discover its core significance. Kevin may find himself involved with his church and community, as he is very much concerned with large social and moral issues. An intuitive and perceptive person, Kevin is quite aware of other people's needs, and strives to create a personal outlet that allows him to be of service.

DERIVATION: Irish and English, from the Gaelic name Caomhin, meaning "handsome, beloved." The name of a seventh-century saint who is one of the patrons of Dublin. Especially popular in the United States in the mid-1960s.

PRINCIPAL COLORS: The full range of green and yellow hues

GEMSTONES AND PRECIOUS METALS: Moonstones, white pearls, moss agate

BOTANICALS: Blackberry, elder, juniper

UNIQUE SPELLINGS: Kehvin, Kehvyn, Kevyn

RELATED TO: Kevan, Keverne

DERIVATION: English, pet form of Kimberley. Kimberley is a town in South Africa, named after a certain Lord Kimberley, whose name was derived from the name of a town in England. Made popular by Edna Ferber's *Showboat* in 1926.

PRINCIPAL COLORS: From light to medium azure

GEMSTONES AND PRECIOUS METALS: Emeralds, turquoise

BOTANICALS: Dog rose, vervain, walnuts

UNIQUE SPELLINGS: Khim, Khimm, Khym, Khymm, Kihm, Kihmm, Kimm, Kyhm, Kyhmm, Kym

RELATED TO: Kimba, Kimba Lee, Kimber, Kimberley, Kimberly†, Kimberlyn, Kimbley, Kimmie, Kimmy

❧

"If you want to live on the edge of life, you need to be flexible."
—KIM NOVAK (ACTRESS)

A KABBALISTIC SYNOPSIS
כים —KYM (Kaph, Yod, Mem)

The value of Kim is seventy—in other words, the number of success multiplied by the symbol of fortune. Lucky Kim! Many people dream of absolute success, but few have the knack to achieve it. Kim, on the other hand, is both pragmatic and idealistic, which means that people named Kim have big ideas and yet keep their feet close enough to the ground to make them a reality. While it is true that Kim can be ruthless and driven in the pursuit of his or her goals, Kim will make many friends along the way who will not be forgotten once Kim has finally made it to the top. But loved ones are the only people who will get Kim's absolute and total support in all that they do; love and loyalty run deep and wide for Kim.

THE RUNIC INTERPRETATION
ᛗᚨᚲ (Mannaz, Ansuz, Kano)

The energies of the name apply to both the male and female Kim. Kim understands that a reputation is a precious commodity, and will do well in business because Kim treats others with courtesy. The Mannaz energy of the self urges Kim to dress carefully, although Kim is not vain. The fact is, people notice how others dress, and it's a reflection of self-respect to dress well; Kim knows enough to put the best foot forward. The Ansuz rune of signals provides Kim with a good sense of timing, and the Kano rune for opening characterizes Kim as flexible and broad-minded. Kim travels through life on a spiritual path, using the gift of introspection to move forward.

Elements: Air, air, water

THE NUMEROLOGICAL INTERPRETATION
Kim (NV = 6, CV = 6, VV = 9, FL = 2)

Poetry, grace, charm, and beauty are all evoked by the numbers in this name. Kim is a kind and gentle person who is most at ease when surrounded by art, music, and people who appreciate him or her. Probably the most important factor in Kim's life is home and family. This need for domestic harmony extends out into the larger human family as well, as Kim can often be seen at work in some humanitarian enterprise. A very balanced person, Kim is modest in his or her tastes and easy to please. Kim has an inherent sense of personal responsibility in all things. Kim's conscious unwillingness to insult anyone or hurt their feelings may cause the suppression of emotion at times. Kim may be learning the lesson that expressing the inner truth is a right and a necessity.

❧

Kimberly

A Kabbalistic Synopsis
כימבלי —KYMBLY (Kaph, Yod, Mem, Beth, Lamed, Yod)

As a young adult, Kimberly sits late into the night with a textbook or a microscope for company while the rest of her pals are out partying. Kimberly is likely to be interested in science, particularly science as it relates to the earth. In fact, there are definite suggestions that she will be drawn to ecological causes, and may even devote her career to such passions. Kimberly also has a real feel for history and is very interested in the history of society and the role of women. The presence of the letter Beth, which is associated with the archetypal woman figure, and its surrounding letters indicate that she may even become prominent as a powerful speaker on causes relating to women's rights.

The Runic Interpretation
ᛇᛚᚱᛗᛒᛗᛁᚲ (Eihwaz, Laguz, Raido, Ehwaz, Berkana, Mannaz, Isa, Kano)

Kimberly is positive and optimistic. Defense, flow, journey, movement, growth, self, standstill, and opening are represented in this name. Like Kim!, Kimberly is on a spiritual path. Kimberly evaluates people and circumstances with an open heart. She is a good judge of character, and assertive when challenged. Kimberly is compassionate; at the same time, she is discerning, and not easily manipulated by people or circumstances. Over the course of her life, she will have some difficult lessons, as indicated by the Eihwaz energy of defense. Darkness likes to snuff out the light, and Kimberly must be on guard against negative energy. Kimberly can make rapid progress on her spiritual path because of her willingness to explore the trials and tribulations of relinquishment, patience, and release. Kimberly simplifies her life, and her soul expands in the greater space she affords it.

Elements: Earth/fire, water, water, air, air/earth, air, earth, water

The Numerological Interpretation
Kimberly (NV = 5, CV = 2, VV = 3, FL = 2)

Kimberly has a life that is filled with change and surprise. This is good, as she is not the type of person who is attracted to routine. Kimberly needs the excitement of a wide range of social contacts. Although she is definitely not a rebel, Kimberly is also not afraid to try something new. Relationships mean a great deal to her, and she will never be at a loss for company, either in terms of friendships or on a more intimate level. Her challenge will never have to do with lack of anything. On the contrary, she must learn how to discriminate wisely so that she may use her physical and emotional resources wisely.

DERIVATION: English. Kimberley is a town in South Africa, named after a certain Lord Kimberley, whose name was derived from the name of a town in England. Used for both boys and girls, but became more common as a girl's name in the 1940s, and became one of the most popular female names in the United States during the 1960s and 1970s.

PRINCIPAL COLORS: All very pale hues

GEMSTONES AND PRECIOUS METALS: Platinum, diamonds

BOTANICALS: Hazel, oats

UNIQUE SPELLINGS: Kimberlee, Kimberlei, Kimberley, Kimberli, Kimberlie, Kymberley, Kymberly

RELATED TO: Kim!, Kimarie, Kimba, Kimba Lee, Kimber, Kimberlyn, Kimbley, Kimette, Kimiko, Kimmie, Kimmy

DERIVATION: Scottish and English, from a northern English and Scottish surname for someone who lived near a church. Became popular partially due to the influence of the actor Kirk Douglas (b. 1916).

PRINCIPAL COLORS: Any moderately shaded hues

GEMSTONES AND PRECIOUS METALS: Sapphires

BOTANICALS: Celandine, spinach

UNIQUE SPELLINGS: Curk, Kerk, Kurk

RELATED TO: Kirby

Kirk

A KABBALISTIC SYNOPSIS
כירכ —KYRK (Kaph, Yod, Resh, Kaph)

Kirk's name begins and ends with K, or Kaph, meaning "hand," and lets us know that Kirk is never happier than when he's up to his ears in wood shavings and motor oil. Although his business may be small, it will assuredly do well, and will more than keep Kirk in hammers and nails, or whatever the stuff of his handiwork. Anyone who decides that they are going to pay him late will soon find out that Kirk has quite a temper on him; his name adds to 250, which is a direct multiple of the magical number of Mars—the planet of warfare. You should also remember that while he does enjoy a good joke, Kirk is inclined to lose his sense of humor if the joke is made at his expense!

THE RUNIC INTERPRETATION
ᚲᚱᛁᚲ (Kano, Raido, Isa, Kano)

Kirk is a welcoming spirit. The double rune for opening and the runes for journey and standstill lend a spiritual orientation to Kirk's name. Kirk uses the Isa rune to slow down his activities and widen the space he creates in life for select friends and the process of prayer, order, cleansing, and simplicity. Kirk is willing to relinquish conventional paths to success. The Kano rune with its powerful double energy means Kirk achieves a remarkable level of clarity, and this is a direct correspondence to his ability to love and heal. The double Kano can also mean that Kirk may be very artistic and creative as well.

Elements: Water, water, earth, water

THE NUMEROLOGICAL INTERPRETATION
Kirk (NV = 4, CV = 4, VV = 9, FL = 2)

It is important for Kirk to pay close attention to the material world, as that is where many of his life lessons are to be learned. This is a very practical name, one that promises success to its bearer if he observes the rules and regulations that govern our social interactions. This is one person who will be rewarded by conforming to what is expected of him (and what he expects from himself). Kirk does best when expressing himself through an orderly and well-structured life. This does not mean that he should be miserly or engage in excessive self-denial. It does mean that hard work and discipline will pay off for him, while wantonness and extremes of any kind will not.

Kitty

A Kabbalistic Synopsis
כיטטי —KYTTY (Kaph, Yod, Teth, Teth, Yod)

From time to time one finds a wonderfully appropriate connection between the literal meaning of a name and its kabbalistic significance. Kitty is just such a name. We all know how cats can scratch and hiss when annoyed; well, most noticeable in Kitty's name are the two Teths, meaning "serpent," right in the middle. This says "beware" in letters six feet tall. Interestingly, her name is also largely ruled by Leo, who is, of course, a very large cat. People will find that Kitty has quite a domineering character and likes to play with people's perceptions of her. However, there is no nastiness intended by this unless perhaps you have annoyed her in some way. At a deeper level, Kitty's outward brashness is a means by which she conceals her emotions, as in reality she is much more sensitive than most people to any form of emotional rejection.

The Runic Interpretation
ᛇᛏᛏᛁᚲ (Eihwaz, Teiwaz, Teiwaz, Isa, Kano)

The double warrior rune makes Kitty aware, discriminating, and persevering. If you're going to lie, don't let Kitty hear you—Kitty won't tolerate a liar. She is a golden advocate but woe be it unto you if you have Kitty for your adversary. She can smell a phony at a hundred paces, and she'll gun 'em down with targeted comments that stun. Kitty invites challenges, and no problem is untenable for her. Kitty needs to focus on process as much as outcomes. She can benefit from yoga and art and a variety of disciplines that help her relax.

Elements: Earth/fire, air, air, earth, water

The Numerological Interpretation
Kitty (NV = 4, CV = 6, VV = 7, FL = 2)

A charming and talented person by nature, Kitty is very attracted to beauty in all its many permutations and forms. Music is especially appealing to her, and she enjoys hearing it at all times of the day. Kitty is attached to her home and family; they are held deeply in her heart. She has been very profoundly affected by her childhood, carrying its rewards and its wounds with her throughout her adult years. She is especially aware of her need to establish harmony in her domestic life, but has to take care not to compromise herself in her personal relationships for the sake of temporary peace. Kitty is concerned with money issues, and devotes a lot of her time and energy toward maintaining a secure financial footing for herself and her loved ones.

DERIVATION: English, pet form of Katherine and Kathleen, associated with the Greek *katharos*, meaning "pure." Went out of fashion in the sixteenth century, but reemerged in the eighteenth century and became quite popular in the 1930s.

PRINCIPAL COLORS: Electric colors, colors of medium shade

GEMSTONES AND PRECIOUS METALS: Pale to deeply toned sapphires

BOTANICALS: Sage, medlar, Iceland moss

UNIQUE SPELLINGS: Khiti, Khitie, Khitti, Khittie, Khitty, Kiti, Kitie, Kitti, Kittie

RELATED TO: Caitlin, Caitriona, Catarine, Cateline, Cathaleen, Catharina, Catherina, Catherine†, Catherleen, Cathie, Cathleen, Cathrene, Cathryn, Cathy†, Catrin, Catrina, Catrine, Catriona, Karen†, Karin, Katarina, Kate†, Katerina, Katey, Katharine, Katheleen, Katheline, Kathereen, Katherina, Katherine†, Kathie, Kathleen†, Kathlyn, Kathlynn, Kathrene, Kathryn†, Kathy†, Katie†, Katina, Katleen, Katrena, Katrina†, Katriona, Katryna, Kattrina, Katy, Kay†, Treena, Trina

DERIVATION: Czech, Estonian, and Latvian form of Christina or Christine, ultimately from the Greek *christos*, meaning "anointed." Popular in the United States since the mid-1960s.

PRINCIPAL COLORS: The full range of azure hues

GEMSTONES AND PRECIOUS METALS: Turquoise, emeralds

BOTANICALS: Dog rose, violets, daffodils

UNIQUE SPELLINGS: Christa, Chrysta, Crista, Crysta, Khrista, Khrysta, Krysta

RELATED TO: Christina†, Christine†, Kirsten, Kirsti, Kirstyn, Kristen†, Kristie, Kristina†, Kristine, Kristy, Kyrsty

A KABBALISTIC SYNOPSIS

כרסטא —KRYSTA (Kaph, Resh, Yod, Samech, Teth, Aleph)

The value of Krista's name is associated with the tarot card Judgment, and Krista is very well suited to a career in law. Thanks to the combination of Teth and Samech, she is able to cut to the truth of the matter, and has the capacity to unnerve her opponents without appearing in any way flustered herself. While she can be quite brutal in the workplace, be it in a courtroom or some other type of office, Krista is decidedly laid-back in her approach to life outside of work, and likes to relax about the house in old jeans, doing nothing very much at all. Krista is an idealistic woman, and this idealism very often drives her initial choice of career. Even once Krista has experienced a cold dose of reality, she will retain an idealism that is very refreshing to those who know and live alongside her in an increasingly cynical world.

THE RUNIC INTERPRETATION

ᚨᛏᛊᛁᚱᚲ (Ansuz, Teiwaz, Sowelu, Isa, Raido, Kano)

Lovely Krista mellows with age. Krista begins life thinking of her future as a superhighway to the stars. As she matures and uses the calming Isa energy to reconsider her goals, she comes around to the point of view that life is more of a meandering country road. She shies away from people who hold fear-based opinions and are rigid in their outlook. The runes promise to validate her accomplishments, and Krista has the capacity to achieve a remarkable state of wholeness and balance in her life.

Elements: Air, air, air, earth, water, water

THE NUMEROLOGICAL INTERPRETATION

Krista (NV = 6, CV = 5, VV = 1, FL = 2)

Krista enjoys being of service, as she finds that she is most herself when contributing to the welfare of others. She has a deep respect for the sanctity of her home, and tends to do all she can to bring beauty and peace into her domestic environment. Krista has a sense of fair play as well, and is fundamentally an honest and generous woman, a soothing presence in times of conflict. Although she will enjoy traveling and seeing the world, Krista's motto is "There's no place like home." She will do well in a profession that helps other people fulfill their potential and accomplish their dreams.

Kristen

DERIVATION: Shortened form of Kristina or Kristine. Ultimately from the Greek *christos*, meaning "anointed." Popularly used in English-speaking countries since 1960.

PRINCIPAL COLORS: Pale to deep, rich blue

GEMSTONES AND PRECIOUS METALS: Blue and blue-green turquoise, emeralds

BOTANICALS: Vervain, almonds, violets

UNIQUE SPELLINGS: Christin, Christyn, Chrystin, Chrystyn, Cristin, Cristyn, Crystin, Crystyn, Kristin, Kristyn, Krystin, Krystyn

RELATED TO: Christina†, Christine†, Khristina, Khristine, Kirsten, Kirstie, Kirsty, Kirstyn, Krista†, Kristina†, Kristine, Kristie, Kristy, Kyrsty

A KABBALISTIC SYNOPSIS

כריסטאן —KRYSTAN (Kaph, Resh, Yod, Samech, Teth, Aleph, Nun)

There are the lucky, the very lucky, and then there is Kristen! Her name has a value of one thousand, which is the number of good fortune multiplied by itself not just once but twice. If Kristen can't win, nobody can. It has to be said that Kristen deserves all the good luck that she gets, as she is a completely honest woman with firmly held principles; she sticks by them, whatever the cost. Material good fortune will not bring Kristen the happiness she seeks; she is an emotionally centered woman who imagines and values the notion of an ideal partner. She is a deeply sensual individual, so her daydreams are usually pretty interesting!

THE RUNIC INTERPRETATION

ᚻᛗᛏᛋᛁᚱᚲ (Nauthiz, Ehwaz, Teiwaz, Sowelu, Isa, Raido, Kano)

Kristen is a seeker. The runic energies signify constraint, movement, warrior, wholeness, standstill, journey, and opening in her name. Kristen knows she has many mountains to climb. She succeeds in having a satisfying life because she learns how to experience her feelings and then get past them. The wounds of the past scar her soul, but she heals and goes on to integrate these negative experiences so that they don't block her on an emotional level. Kristen seems to understand the relationship of body, mind, and spirit. The Sowelu rune indicates Kristen will arrive at a state of clarity and productivity.

Elements: Fire, air, air, air, earth, water, water

THE NUMEROLOGICAL INTERPRETATION

Kristen (NV = 6, CV = 1, VV = 5, FL = 2)

The numbers in this name reveal a woman with many facets to her personality. Kristen's most important concern is for the well-being of her family. She is a gracious person and makes a very supportive partner and a devoted mother. But she is definitely no pushover. Kristen has a firmly rooted sense of herself. She is a self-starter and is not afraid to live up to the challenges that are put before her or those that she creates for herself. Kristen enjoys the feeling of personal freedom, but would tend not to do anything that would threaten the harmony of her domestic life. Her natural sense of balance will give her the potential to integrate her personal interests with those of her family. Emotional conflicts may come about if she is unsuccessful in accomplishing this alignment.

DERIVATION: Swedish form of Christina, an abbreviated form of the Latin Christiana. Ultimately from the Greek *christos*, meaning "anointed." Common in English-speaking countries since the early 1950s.

PRINCIPAL COLORS: The complete range of green hues, also white and cream

GEMSTONES AND PRECIOUS METALS: Jade, pearls, moonstones

BOTANICALS: Chicory, colewort, rapeseed

UNIQUE SPELLINGS: Christina, Chrystina, Chrystyna, Cristina, Crystina, Crystyna, Khristina, Khrystina, Khrystyna, Krystina, Krystyna

RELATED TO: Christina†, Christine†, Khristine, Kirsten, Kirstie, Kirsty, Kirstyn, Krista†, Kristen†, Kristie, Kristine, Kristy, Kyrsty

Kristina

A KABBALISTIC SYNOPSIS

כריסטינא —KRYSTYNA (Kaph, Resh, Yod, Samech, Teth, Yod, Nun, Aleph)

Kristina is a born salesperson; she has so much confidence that she could carry it with her in its own separate valise! She loves to talk, and is extremely skilled at demonstrating the wonderful qualities of the dullest product in such a way that you absolutely have to have it. Kristina enjoys socializing and probably keeps a fairly hectic schedule; when she parties, she parties with a capital P. When Kristina ultimately finds the right partner, she will be inseparable from him. Any partner will appreciate her affectionate manner, but at the same time they would be advised to look out for a verbal assault if she gets annoyed. Such incidents, though, should be few and far between, as Kristina is very careful to pick the right partner.

THE RUNIC INTERPRETATION

ᚨᚾᛁᛏᛋᛁᚱᚲ (Ansuz, Nauthiz, Isa, Teiwaz, Sowelu, Isa, Raido, Kano)

Kristina is blessed with the power of the four elements in her name. She is like Kristen, but with the additional Isa energy, Kristina is more reclusive and inclined toward solitary pursuits. She may be an artist or spiritual teacher. The additional Ansuz rune in her name makes Kristina very intuitive. She could well be a healer or yoga teacher. Kristina is strong and clear and intent on the truth. She can be a tough taskmaster, and she needs to learn to lighten up. She is especially hard on herself. She will benefit if she stays close to the arts and makes friends who give her a good laugh each day.

Elements: Air, fire, earth, air, air, earth, water, water

THE NUMEROLOGICAL INTERPRETATION

Kristina (NV = 2, CV = 1, VV = 1, FL = 2)

This name contains a strong and equal mix of two numbers. The one bestows the urge to be oneself at all times and under all circumstances. Kristina has a distinct sense of her own uniqueness, and will express this singularity through all of her many creative endeavors. She wants others to appreciate her uniqueness as well, and works at putting her personal stamp on everything that she does. The two, however, provides a far more social vibration that reveals Kristina's need to be involved with many cooperative projects that require engaging many others in the process. Kristina may find success in life through using her strong will and sense of self in battling for justice and fair play. She makes an excellent lawyer, arbitrator, or personnel officer.

Kurt

DERIVATION: German, short form of Konrad, from Germanic roots meaning "bold counsel." Commonly used as an independent name since the 1950s.

PRINCIPAL COLORS: All green and yellow hues, gold

GEMSTONES AND PRECIOUS METALS: Moonstones, cat's-eye, creamy white pearls

BOTANICALS: Elder, blackberry, juniper

UNIQUE SPELLINGS: Curt, Curtt, Kert, Kertt, Kurtt

RELATED TO: Connort, Conrad, Curtist, Konrad

A KABBALISTIC SYNOPSIS
כורט —KVRT (Kaph, Vau, Resh, Teth)

Kurt is as solid and dependable as they come. Kurt is an asset to any business, thanks to his loyalty, willingness to work, and general enthusiasm for the job, no matter what it involves. Kurt tends to be extremely fit; his temperament, and belief in order and discipline, suggest that he might enjoy a career in the military. Kurt is not an overly tolerant man—although you wouldn't say that to his face! However, he also can be extremely kind. One thing that Kurt really does hate is to see people unhappy, particularly children. Kurt is always there to offer assistance to pretty much anyone who is going through a genuinely bad time. Not surprisingly, sport is a driving passion in Kurt's life, and he will probably actively participate in a whole range of different games.

THE RUNIC INTERPRETATION
↑RⱮↀ (Teiwaz, Raido, Uruz, Kano)

To look at his name, Kurt has all the markings of success. The warrior and strength runes foster his entrepreneurial nature. He is assertive, courageous, and bold. The Raido rune gives Kurt outstanding communication skills. He can manage people and projects because he speaks clearly and people know what he expects of them. He may be challenged by people who lack ambition or organizational skills, and they could find him somewhat overbearing. He can cut through verbiage and save time organizing large projects. Kano is the fortunate rune of opening. Kano blesses Kurt's life with an abundance of opportunities, and Kurt has all the requisite skills in place to tackle almost anything and take it to the top.

Elements: Air, water, earth, water

THE NUMEROLOGICAL INTERPRETATION
Kurt (NV = 7, CV = 4, VV = 3, FL = 2)

The mind is Kurt's fundamental tool for success. In this respect, Kurt can always be found with a book near at hand. He is a perpetual student and teacher who takes great pleasure in serious discussions and debates. Although he does have a love of knowledge for knowledge's sake, this is also a very pragmatic name. Kurt will therefore be perpetually training his mind and adding to his storehouse of information for career and social advancement. This strong mental emphasis is an indication that Kurt may have to cultivate a more sensitive and compassionate emotional nature, so as not to allow the dominating nature of his mind to block out the reality of his feelings.

DERIVATION: English, from the
Scottish surname meaning "a
strait, narrow piece of land."
Introduced in the United States in
the late 1940s. Can be used for
both boys and girls.

PRINCIPAL COLORS: Black, gray;
very deep, rich shades of blue and
violet

GEMSTONES AND PRECIOUS
METALS: Sapphires, carbuncles,
black pearls

BOTANICALS: Angelica, shepherd's
purse, marsh mallow

UNIQUE SPELLING: Kile

RELATED TO: Kiley, Kyly

Kyle

A KABBALISTIC SYNOPSIS
כיאל —KYAL (Kaph, Yod, Aleph, Lamed)

Kyle is unlikely ever to run a business, but this doesn't mean that his chance to make vast amounts of money is out of reach. Kyle is likely to make a tidy profit by acting as a consultant or troubleshooter for others. Such a career satisfies both a desire for a professional challenge and Kyle's need to attain a reasonable level of financial security. Money is very important to Kyle, as it is a way of validating his choices in life. In the case of a female Kyle, the money that she makes is also important as a way of guaranteeing her independence in a relationship. Although Kyle can be very decisive in the workplace, there is a tendency to a high level of self-doubt that is alleviated only by the visible and tangible trappings of success. Kyle needn't worry, though; all the indications in the name point to an enviable upward slope in career prospects over the years. Kyle loves to shower gifts on a loved one, which goes a long way toward making up for the fact that Kyle finds it difficult to be emotionally expressive. A Kyle who is a woman is just as keen to express herself through objects rather than words, but is also likely to expect similar behavior in return.

THE RUNIC INTERPRETATION
ᛖᛚᛇᚲ (Ehwaz, Laguz, Eihwaz, Kano)

Kyle is the kind of chap who wins the heart of many a comely admirer with his amenable nature. Kyle enchants his lover, who will learn to see things through his eyes. His perspective demands a leap to a creative and magical realm; it's a world inhabited by glimpses at architecture and snippets of information about ancient cultures. Kyle inspires eloquence in his partner, and more. Even the most brilliant career type will spend the lunch hour selecting yarns with just the right feel to knit a sweater for Kyle. He's used to such demonstrations and is always most gracious and appreciative. Female Kyles will experience the same level of appreciation and devotion.

Elements: Air, water, earth/fire, water

THE NUMEROLOGICAL INTERPRETATION
Kyle (NV = 8, CV = 5, VV = 3, FL = 2)

There is a great deal of perseverance and stamina that comes with the numbers in this name. Kyle is a person who can easily find the willpower to back up his or her talents and abilities. Bent on being a success, Kyle enjoys the material rewards that come with an established professional life. People are very attracted to Kyle, who is vivacious and candid in speech and actions. Kyle must learn a great deal about values. On a superficial level, this has to do with financial values, but on a deeper level, Kyle is dealing with human values. In essence, she or he is learning how to value herself or himself. Kyle will definitely have a multitude of experiences in life, as one of many goals for Kyle is to avoid boredom at all costs.

Lance

DERIVATION: English, from the Germanic name Lanzo, with the first element, "lan," meaning "land, territory." Associated with the Old French *lance*, the weapon. May also be a shortened form of Lancelot. Quite popular in the United States in the 1940s and 1950s.

PRINCIPAL COLORS: The darkest shades of azure, violet, and gray, also black

GEMSTONES AND PRECIOUS METALS: Rich sapphires, rubies, carbuncles

BOTANICALS: Shepherd's purse, pilewort, ragwort

UNIQUE SPELLINGS: Lanz, Laynce, Laynz

RELATED TO: Lancelet, Lancelot, Lancelott, Launce, Launcelet

A KABBALISTIC SYNOPSIS
לאנס —LANS (Lamed, Aleph, Nun, Samech)

Most people have an underlying desire to feel part of some wider group, but not Lance. He is an absolute individual, and is more than happy to be that way. In Lance this difference from the norm tends to include a rejection of the modern concept of leisure; he is unlikely to have a TV in the house and can't really understand, for example, why people go to the gym to get fit and then pay someone else to do their gardening. Lance has a love of the countryside and an instinctive feel for nature. The overriding pull toward all things rustic is shown by the Hebrew equivalences to his name, one of which is אמיע or AMYA'A, meaning "oaken." In keeping with his otherwise traditional outlook on life, Lance hopes to have a large family, and if he does, his children will be very happy to be with him—especially if they're romping on that farm that's at the heart of all his dreams.

THE RUNIC INTERPRETATION
ᛗᛋᚺᚨᛚ (Ehwaz, Sowelu, Nauthiz, Ansuz, Laguz)

Lance feels like music runs all through him. He has the runes of movement, wholeness, constraint, signals, and flow in his name. Lance is a musician at heart, and he has other talents as well. He truly appreciates beauty and genuinely enjoys the company of a delightful partner, or a few. Lance often feels the familiar surge of friendship turn the corner into love, which is okay by him; Lance is a consummate lover. He's so comfortable in the rhythms of his life, he's able to shrug off the brief encounters with jealousy or conflict that life brings.

Elements: Air, air, fire, air, water

THE NUMEROLOGICAL INTERPRETATION
Lance (NV = 8, CV = 11, VV = 6, FL = 3)

Lance is a name that comes with an abundance of creative possibilities. In addition, this is a man who has the fortitude to withstand the pressures of success. Lance is aware of the wider social issues in life. He is a man of broad interests with a considerable depth of understanding that reaches deep below the surface of events. Lance seeks a career that will allow him to communicate with a large number of people. He has a strong inner sense of morality and seeks to bring justice and equanimity to the situations in his life. Sometimes he may be too lofty and abstract in his concepts, making him appear detached and uninvolved. Lance may have to work a bit on the personal or the emotional level, as networking with a lot of people may be easier for him than being intimate with men and women one at a time.

Larry

A KABBALISTIC SYNOPSIS
לאררי —LARRY (Lamed, Aleph, Resh, Resh, Yod)

If you need to relax or de-stress, a visit with Larry will do you a world of good. Larry seems to have found the secret of getting through life without letting all of its trials disturb him in any significant way. Larry's name reduces to nine, which is representative of wisdom. In part, Larry's laid-back approach to life stems from his deep understanding of the things that really matter. Although people are very fond of Larry, he is rarely seen at parties or social functions, as on the whole Larry is a quiet man who prefers company in small numbers (although it is possible, in the case of a Larry born under Leo or Aries, that he will be happy to mix and socialize with larger groups). He is always cheerful, however, and may come across as something of an extrovert when you encounter him alone. Despite his relaxed approach to all he encounters in life, Larry is a very determined man, and will ensure that he achieves any personal goal he sets himself; he just won't allow himself to get too frustrated along the way.

THE RUNIC INTERPRETATION
ᛇᚱᚱᚨᛚ (Eihwaz, Raido, Raido, Ansuz, Laguz)

Travel, anyone? Larry is first in line. He might be a songwriter or be involved in almost any area of the performing arts. Then again, Larry may travel as a professional businessman. He is so multitalented, he may even have more than one career. But one thing's for sure: Larry is on the go. Not only does he travel, but he may relocate to foreign countries several times in his life. Larry has the artistic nature of the Laguz rune. The Ansuz rune gives Larry better intuition than the average person, and the wonderful ability to take what life sends his way and enhance it.

Elements: Earth/fire, water, water, air, water

THE NUMEROLOGICAL INTERPRETATION
Larry (NV = 11, CV = 3, VV = 8, FL = 3)

Larry is intellectually open and capable of consistently adding to his knowledge and understanding of life. People respect him for his tolerance, lack of prejudice, and support of various social causes. Larry has no problem being called upon to act in an executive capacity. He takes his social responsibilities seriously, and can easily structure and coordinate other people's talents and resources. Larry also likes to handle money, and enjoys the prospect of creating opportunities for financial growth and expansion.

Latoya

A KABBALISTIC SYNOPSIS
לאטעיא —LATA'AYA (Lamed, Aleph, Teth, Ayin, Yod, Aleph)

Latoya is a spirited woman. Her decidedly youthful zest for life is unlikely ever to leave her. Whatever Latoya does careerwise, it will have to allow for some level of personal creativity. Responsibility and authority are not nearly as important to her as having the space to develop her own ideas. Sometimes her enthusiasm for herself can lead her to be quite spiteful to those around her, even when they are not actually trying to thwart her in any way. However, Latoya will always apologize afterward. Despite all her efforts, in most cases Latoya will feel dissatisfied with results that most people would be happy to achieve. In her own mind, if she isn't at the absolute top of the heap, she has failed. A strong circle of supportive friends should be able to make her see that in fact she already is a success.

THE RUNIC INTERPRETATION
ᚨᛖᛟᛏᚨᛚ (Ansuz, Eihwaz, Othila, Teiwaz, Ansuz, Laguz)

Latoya is a very outstanding woman, and the double Ansuz rune for signals in this name make Latoya insightful and armed with the dignity and steel will of a ram. She is musical, with the Laguz rune powerfully positioned in her name. She is a fierce opponent and a zealous fighter for the cause. Latoya would make a great advocate. A law degree would be a powerful tool in Latoya's hands; she would see it as her license to do good, which would really please her.

Elements: Air, earth/fire, earth/fire, air, air, water

THE NUMEROLOGICAL INTERPRETATION
Latoya (NV = 11, CV = 5, VV = 6, FL = 3)

This is a woman who can reach large numbers of people. Latoya possesses a special magnetism. There is a great need for personal freedom and a distinct urge for rebelliousness suggested by this name. One of the qualities that it will be important for her to develop is self-discipline. Latoya needs to structure and direct the wide variety of talents that she possesses. Home and family will be of major importance in her life, but she will have a difficult time being constrained by traditional family values.

DERIVATION: Of unknown origin and meaning. Possibly a simplified form of Latonya.

PRINCIPAL COLORS: The full range of green hues, white, off-white

GEMSTONES AND PRECIOUS METALS: Moonstones, cat's-eye, pearls

BOTANICALS: Chicory, cabbage, moonwort

UNIQUE SPELLINGS: Latoia, Latoiah, Latoyah

RELATED TO: Laonsya, Lasonia, Latanya, Latonya, Latoyla

Laura

DERIVATION: Italian, Spanish, and English, feminine form of the Latin *laurus*, meaning "bay laurel." Saint Laura was a ninth-century Spanish nun who died in a cauldron of molten lead. Also the name of Petrarch's beloved in his famous sonnets. Very popular in the early 1980s.

PRINCIPAL COLORS: The deepest, richest shades of azure, violet, and gray, also black

GEMSTONES AND PRECIOUS METALS: Black pearls, black diamonds, rich sapphires

BOTANICALS: Angelica, marsh mallow, pilewort

UNIQUE SPELLINGS: Lara, Larah, Laurah, Lora, Lorah

RELATED TO: Laureen, Laurel, Laurent, Laurena, Laurene, Lauretta, Laurette, Lauri, Lauriane, Lauriet, Laurina, Laury, Loraine, Loree, Loreen, Lorit, Lorraine†, Lorrie, Lorry, Lory

A KABBALISTIC SYNOPSIS
לאורא —LAVRA (Lamed, Aleph, Vau, Resh, Aleph)

Laura's absolute priority in life is her family, primarily her children. The compression of her name reveals the powerful drive to protect them from any harm or possible upset. Now, of course most parents feel this way about their kids, but with Laura we have someone who goes to unusual lengths to ensure her children's safety and happiness. In addition, Laura is incredibly innovative, always thinking up approaches and challenges within the context of her life. Laura is a very intuitive individual, and it is not unusual for her to have "feelings" about what is the right course of action in any given situation. She loves change, and the family will probably move a lot more than most, although it will all be organized with absolute precision by Laura.

THE RUNIC INTERPRETATION
ᚨᚱᚢᚨᛚ (Ansuz, Raido, Uruz, Ansuz, Laguz)

Laura is deeply affected by the Laguz rune of flow, which figures prominently in her name and indicates that Laura is always willing to try something new. The Laguz energy of the moon makes her sensitive and emotional. Laura has the double Ansuz power of signals, which makes her intuitive and flexible in her approach to life. Ansuz gives Laura a good sense of timing. The Raido rune of good communication and journey will provide Laura with wonderful chance encounters and blessings that enhance her personally and help advance her career.

Elements: Air, water, earth, air, water

THE NUMEROLOGICAL INTERPRETATION
Laura (NV = 7, CV = 2, VV = 5, FL = 3)

Laura will benefit tremendously from the further development of her mental and intellectual faculties. She has a great deal of intellectual potential, and important life benefits will result from the discipline she imposes on herself to study. This is a name that holds a lot of creative promise, but in order to achieve its full potential, Laura needs to engage in a certain amount of introspection. Laura is a person who wants to bring harmony into her social situations. It is easy for her to see both sides of every situation, so it is important for her to know where she stands on the issues in question. Laura can be so easygoing that it may be difficult for her to solidify her own perspective. Laura tends to be neat and modest in her physical appearance, preferring to blend in rather than to stand out. Her strength comes from her honesty; her weakness, from indecisiveness.

Lauren

DERIVATION: English, diminutive form of Laura, or a feminine version of Laurence. Became popular due to the influence of the film actress Lauren Bacall (b. 1924).

PRINCIPAL COLORS: Dark blue and purple hues, black, gray

GEMSTONES AND PRECIOUS METALS: Carbuncles, rubies, black diamonds

BOTANICALS: Marsh mallow, ragwort, shepherd's purse

UNIQUE SPELLINGS: Laurin, Lauron, Lauryn, Loren, Lorin, Loron, Loryn

RELATED TO: Laura†, Laureen, Laurel, Laurena, Laurene, Lauretta, Laurette, Lauri, Lauriane, Lauriet, Laurina, Laury, Loraine, Loree, Loreen, Lorit, Lorraine†, Lorrie, Lorry, Lory

A KABBALISTIC SYNOPSIS
לאורון —LAVRVN (Lamed, Aleph, Vau, Resh, Vau, Nun)

Lauren has a strong sense of being driven in life, probably by feelings of duty. Emotionally Lauren is fiercely loyal, but she will always tell a loved one if he is in the wrong. In public, though, she would never let her partner down, and she expects the same consideration in return. Lauren is a top performer, but she needs to avoid her tendency to put in too many hours. She is demanding both of herself and her associates. Honesty is of paramount importance to Lauren in all her dealings with people, and she never forgets a thing! If Lauren has had an overly strict childhood, not only will she remember, she will get even—and then some!

THE RUNIC INTERPRETATION
ᚾᛖᚱᚢᚨᛚ (Nauthiz, Ehwaz, Raido, Uruz, Ansuz, Lagaz)

Lauren is blessed with the power of the four elements in her name. Her runes stand for constraint, movement, journey, strength, signals, and flow. Lauren knows it takes tremendous strength (Uruz) and courage to stand strong when people are urging you to do something. Lauren has *patience*. She awaits Ansuz, or the signal rune, and during this resting time she gains insight into her situation. The Nauthiz rune of constraint is a strong energy that causes delays and limitation. The Ehwaz rune of movement and the Raido energy of journey insinuate that Lauren surmounts all of her difficulties eventually, and moves ahead with a sense of purpose and direction.

Elements: Fire, air, water, earth, air, water

THE NUMEROLOGICAL INTERPRETATION
Lauren (NV = 8, CV = 8, VV = 9, FL = 3)

Lauren can take hold of chaotic situations and create order. She is eager to prove her capabilities, and looks forward to large projects where she may assert her responsible nature. Personal appearance means a great deal to her, and she has no problem at all wearing expensive but tasteful clothes. Lauren is not a show-off, though; she doesn't have to be. She has an inner sense of what is appropriate in every social situation, and acts accordingly. She must have a partner who is ambitious and dynamic, as she is very intolerant of laziness.

Laurie

DERIVATION: English, originally a pet form of the male name Laurence, which is ultimately from the Latin *laurus*, meaning "laurel." In the twentieth century, it has become much more common as a female name, and is often used independently. Especially common during the 1960s.

PRINCIPAL COLORS: All shades of violet, including mauve and lilac

GEMSTONES AND PRECIOUS METALS: Amethyst, garnets

BOTANICALS: Apple, lungwort, mint, strawberry

UNIQUE SPELLINGS: Lauree, Lauri, Loree, Lorey, Lori, Lorie, Lorri, Lorry, Lory

RELATED TO: Laura†, Laurent†, Laurena, Laurette, Laurina, Lorena, Loretta†, Lorit†

A KABBALISTIC SYNOPSIS
לערוי —LA'AVRY (Lamed, Ayin, Resh, Vau, Resh, Yod)

You can spot a Laurie by her commanding presence, which can be completely out of proportion to her physical stature, as Laurie is often small or slight. Any position of power will suit Laurie, although business is more attractive to her than politics, thanks to the influence of Capricorn in this name. Laurie has a fierce temper, and quite often seems to be bristling and about to castigate somebody or other. However, her temper only actually breaks when there is a valid reason for it to do so. With those who are prepared to work well and hard, Laurie can be very supportive. At home there is no question that Laurie is in charge, but she is by no means unfair or selfish in the way she organizes the family routine. In fact, Laurie has a strong sense of duty to those who are in some way dependent on her.

THE RUNIC INTERPRETATION
MIRNAΓ (Ehwaz, Isa, Raido, Uruz, Ansuz, Laguz)

Laurie is confident in the knowledge that the runes signifying movement, standstill, journey, strength, signals, and flow can assist her. Laurie ventures forth undeterred by the fear she encounters in life. She reasons that since we're all going to die and we know it, we carry around a lot of terror on a deep level. Laurie, on the other hand, is courageous because she knows she won't run out of time or disappear. She understands life to be a continuum. Whether she's right or not, this is a belief that sustains Laurie. Since there is no rush, Laurie takes her time and generously extends herself to the family of man. She enjoys doing service work.

Elements: Air, earth, water, earth, air, water

THE NUMEROLOGICAL INTERPRETATION
Laurie (NV = 3, CV = 3, VV = 9, FL = 3)

This is a name that is dominated by the number three. Laurie is therefore very sociable, charming, and witty. She knows how to converse with anyone, and puts people immediately at their ease. Laurie stands out at the center of any group of people. She is vivacious and alive with intelligence. She may have a gift with languages, as her mind tends to absorb new concepts easily. In addition, Laurie loves to talk. The vowel value of nine in her name adds depth, compassion, and sensitivity. Laurie is at heart a kind person with a generous spirit. She will be most at ease in a career that allows her to use her communication gifts to entertain, educate, and uplift.

Lawrence

A KABBALISTIC SYNOPSIS

לאוראנס —LAVRANS (Lamed, Aleph, Vau, Resh, Aleph, Nun, Samech)

Lawrence likes the good things in life, and has the driving force and commitment (evidenced by the influence of the letters Shin and Cheth in the compression of his name) to ensure that he is able to enjoy them. Lawrence is able to combine a demanding approach to staff and family with a genuine good humor, which means that people are usually happy to work with him—even when he requires them to go that extra mile. At home he likes to relax and has very discriminating taste, so he is more likely to savor a good wine and conversation than to munch popcorn in front of the tube. Lawrence has a good understanding of what makes people tick, and gets a lot of satisfaction from his own generosity, as he likes to give people gifts that they really want.

THE RUNIC INTERPRETATION

ᛗᛋᛏᛗᚱᛈᚨᛚ (Ehwaz, Sowelu, Nauthiz, Ehwaz, Raido, Wunjo, Ansuz, Laguz)

Lawrence surmounts difficulties with courage and steadfastness. The runes of constraint and defense are challenges, which Lawrence overcomes with his intuition (Ansuz) and a good mental outlook (signified by Sowelu). The outcome for him is terrific. Lawrence gets to travel and possibly live abroad. He enjoys prosperity and feels balanced and flexible. Where the Wunjo energy of joy is present, we can always assume a happy outcome. This is the name's legacy.

Elements: Air, air, fire, air, water, earth, air, water

THE NUMEROLOGICAL INTERPRETATION

Lawrence (NV = 9, CV = 2, VV = 7, FL = 3)

Lawrence can be very idealistic in his attitude to life. His is a name that adds a definite contemplative facet to his personality and a need to spend many hours alone in reflective thought. Lawrence pushes himself to acquire greater intellectual tools; he wants to unlock and uncover. He would do well in a teaching capacity, either in the sciences or the humanities. Lawrence is a modest man, unassuming and basically quiet. It takes a while for him to open emotionally, and he does so then only to a select few. Yet beneath his sometimes introverted exterior is a great depth of human understanding.

DERIVATION: English, anglicized spelling of Laurence, from a French form of the Latin name Laurentius, meaning "man from Laurentium." Laurentium was a town in Latium, possibly getting its name from the Latin *laurus*, meaning "laurel." Brought to Britain with the Norman Conquest.

PRINCIPAL COLORS: Pink to deep red shades, crimson, rose

GEMSTONES AND PRECIOUS METALS: Bloodstones, rubies, garnets

BOTANICALS: Broom, nettle, wormwood

UNIQUE SPELLINGS: Laurence, Laurince, Lawrince, Lorince

RELATED TO: Larry†, Lars, Laurent, Lawson, Lawton, Lenz, Lorenzo

PRINCIPAL COLORS: Gray, black, dark shades of blue and purple

GEMSTONES AND PRECIOUS METALS: Lackluster rubies, black pearls, sapphires

BOTANICALS: Marsh mallow, pilewort, mandrake root

UNIQUE SPELLINGS: Lea, Leea, Leeah, Lhea, Lheea, Lheeah, Lhia, Lhiah, Lia, Liah

RELATED TO: Leanne, Leda, Leet, Leight, Liane, Lianne

Leah

A KABBALISTIC SYNOPSIS
ליאה —LYAH (Lamed, Yod, Aleph, Heh)

First and foremost, Leah is a lover; all other aspects of her life are secondary to this. In Hebrew, her name's value is equivalent to a phrase meaning "concubine" or "female slave." However, this does not mean that Leah will slavishly follow her partner around. Instead, it should be taken as an indication that Leah arranges her life to suit her relationships—and this is, of course, as gratifying to her as to her partner. Emotional connections are hugely important to Leah, but she still ensures that she has time for herself. Leah is not the passive type, and is unlikely to sit around all day waiting for her mate to come home. The initial letter, Lamed, is an indication of the considerable drive and energy Leah has to accomplish things according to her own agenda. A lover she most certainly is, but a doormat? Never.

THE RUNIC INTERPRETATION
ᚺᚨᛖᛚ (Hagalaz, Ansuz, Ehwaz, Laguz)

Leah knows the runes for disruption, signals, movement and flow will bring challenges in life, but she can use the Hagalaz rune of lessons to overcome the challenges that they bring about. As trouble presents itself, Leah knows it's important to experience it, integrate it, and move forward. If she can move forward alongside a pleasing partner, so much the better. Leah is willing to move and relocate and face whatever situation arises on her path. She has learned the important lesson that where we live makes little difference because our destiny is inside us.

Elements: Water, air, air, water

THE NUMEROLOGICAL INTERPRETATION
Leah (NV = 8, CV = 11, VV = 6, FL = 3)

This is a lady who functions on many levels simultaneously. Her name contains a very special combination of energies that yields both grace and charm, as well as willpower and independence. Leah has amazing strength of character, and is a person who is capable of communicating with large numbers of people in a very intimate one-on-one fashion. People are fascinated by her, as she exudes an air of mystery and gives one the sense that no matter how well you know her and no matter how much of herself she may reveal, there is still so much more to uncover. If spiritually centered, Leah will use her gifts in a service capacity. If materially centered, she will find she has a great talent for attaining power and money.

Lee

DERIVATION: English, originally a surname with the Old English root *leah*, meaning "clearing" or "meadow." Commonly used for both boys and girls. Especially popular in the southern United States, where it is sometimes used to honor Robert E. Lee, the Confederate general (1807–1870).

PRINCIPAL COLORS: The full spectrum of moderately shaded hues

GEMSTONES AND PRECIOUS METALS: Sapphires

BOTANICALS: Sage, spinach, medlar

UNIQUE SPELLINGS: Lea, Leigh, Lhea, Lhee, Lheigh

RELATED TO: Layton, Leander, Leight, Leighton, Lelandt, Leot, Leont, Leonardt, Lest, Leaht, Leandra, Lia, Liane, Lianne

A KABBALISTIC SYNOPSIS
לי —LY (Lamed, Yod)

The name Lee can be a male or female name. Lee has a name just about as short as is possible—but that does not mean it has a minimal meaning. The minimal number of letters in the name serves to emphasize the power of the letters that are included. Both letters, Lamed and Yod, are connected with ideas of energy and motivation, creativity and commitment. Consequently, Lee is an energetic personality unlikely to be tied down by the monotony of a repetitive job. Unfortunately for Lee, there are no stabilizing influences in the name, which means that Lee may be inclined to dash from project to project, and needs a steadier head to ensure that work is approached in a productive manner. Emotionally Lee will take longer than the majority to settle down, but in most cases Lee has an extremely good time getting there! Even in middle age Lee will have a name for being somewhat wild and rebellious—and it has to be said that Lee enjoys a certain amount of notoriety.

THE RUNIC INTERPRETATION
ᛗᛗᛚ (Ehwaz, Ehwaz, Laguz)

Lee has the runes of movement and wholeness in this name. Lee has the double Ehwaz energy and raw courage to boot. He or she can have a successful career in a dangerous field, such as bomb detection, rescue work, or even politics. Lees have what it takes to survive and bring others to safety, and are equally fortunate to have the Laguz rune for flow in their name. The Laguz energy is intuitive, flexible, and emotional. Lee can depend on opinions and hunches. This name is one in a million!

Elements: Air, air, water

THE NUMEROLOGICAL INTERPRETATION
Lee (NV = 4, CV = 3, VV = 1, FL = 3)

Lee is very much an individual who approaches life with gusto and verve, but who needs to establish a stable foundation for him- or herself. Often preoccupied with financial matters, Lee has a very powerful personality. It is important for Lees to prove their self-worth and to anchor themselves firmly in the world. Only after this is accomplished can Lee allow the more fanciful parts of his or her nature to flourish. Lee needs to be free to be independent. Although Lees have a definite preference for longevity in partnerships, they will not wish to be dominated by a lover.

Leigh

DERIVATION: English, variant spelling of Lee, which is derived from a surname with the Old English root *leah*, meaning "clearing" or "meadow."

PRINCIPAL COLORS: The full spectrum of lightly shaded hues

GEMSTONES AND PRECIOUS METALS: Silver, platinum

BOTANICALS: Hazel, sweet marjoram, oats

UNIQUE SPELLINGS: Lea, Lee, Lhea, Lhee, Lheigh

RELATED TO: Ashley†, Leah†, Leandra, Lee†, Leighanne, Leona†, Lia, Liane, Lianne

❧

"Affection, like melancholy, magnifies trifles; but the magnifying of the one is like looking through a telescope at heavenly objects; that of the other, like enlarging monsters with a microscope."

—LEIGH HUNT
(BUSINESSPERSON)

A KABBALISTIC SYNOPSIS
ליה —LYH (Lamed, Yod, Heh)

Leigh is quite a solitary figure, often to be found in libraries or sitting quietly tapping away at a computer keyboard. Leigh is equivalent to the Hebrew for "mind," and it is through mental ability that Leigh progresses in the world. There is a heavy Saturnine influence in the name, which can make Leigh prone to melancholia, and in extreme cases, it can even cause a depressive nature in general. However, this influence can be countered by the inspiring energy of the central Yod and the positive drive toward new intellectual insight. Leigh will always weigh and balance all her options before making a decision, which has the dual effect of ensuring good judgment most of the time, along with the danger that Leigh will act too hesitantly to embark on any course of action at all. When it comes to emotions, though, Leigh has no such problems and is the type who will fall head-over-heels in love at first sight.

THE RUNIC INTERPRETATION
ᚺᚷᛁᛖᛚ (Hagalaz, Gebo, Isa, Ehwaz, Laguz)

Change comes naturally to Leigh. Her name is signified by the runes for disruption, partnership, standstill, movement, and flow. Leigh meets disappointments in life with equanimity once she realizes that her experience is her choice. Once Leigh forgoes blaming people for her problems and accepts that she creates her own reality, she will have the tool she needs to fight the onslaughts of the mighty Hagalaz rune. Leigh is going to need to rely on the partnership and close associations implied by the Gebo rune for support in times of turmoil. She will emerge stronger and wiser at the end of her eventful life, having learned lessons of patience and flexibility that serve her well always.

Elements: Water, water, earth, air, water

THE NUMEROLOGICAL INTERPRETATION
Leigh (NV = 5, CV = 9, VV = 5, FL = 3)

Change is the constant in Leigh's life. She is a person who has the ability to create a multitude of opportunities. Full of surprises, Leigh makes a point of asserting her unpredictability. She must remain unfettered and detached. Her personality requires adventure and a continuous flow of interesting encounters with people. Leigh naturally loves to travel—the more exotic the destination, the better. Yet she is much less of a rebel than she is an experimenter. She doesn't want to overthrow social convention; she merely wants to enjoy herself. Leigh has the willingness and the courage to release old patterns and structures that inhibit her creativity. Her orientation is very universal, and she makes friends easily with people from all different walks of life.

❧

Leland

DERIVATION: English, originally a surname from a local name for someone who lived near a patch of fallow land. From the Middle English root *lay* or *ley*, meaning "fallow." Also the name of a town in Mississippi. Particularly common in the United States in the 1940s.

PRINCIPAL COLORS: Pale bluish purple to deep violet hues

GEMSTONES AND PRECIOUS METALS: Amethyst, garnets

BOTANICALS: Bilberry, dandelion, beetroot

UNIQUE SPELLINGS: Leeland, Leighland, Leyland

RELATED TO: Layton, Leander, Leet, Leighton

A KABBALISTIC SYNOPSIS
לילענד —LYLAND (Lamed, Yod, Lamed, Aleph, Nun, Daleth)

In Leland we have the relatively rare union of intellectual insight and practical know-how—a union that may well make Leland a considerable amount of money. The first half of Leland's name acts almost like a booster rocket, consisting as it does of the inspirational energy of Yod surrounded by the sustaining energy represented by Lamed. This tells us that Leland is never far from his next idea, and that he has the capacity to push those ideas forward. In emotional terms, it marks Leland as impulsive and somewhat rash in his actions. The final part of Leland's name refers to an ability to implement projects, and the final letter D, or Daleth, meaning "door," is suggestive of the probable positive outcomes of Leland's undertakings. In terms of Leland's love life, it indicates that while his approach may be wild and erratic, once he finds his partner, he knows how to make sure she'll stick around.

THE RUNIC INTERPRETATION
ᛞᚾᚨᛚᛖᛚ (Dagaz, Nauthiz, Ansuz, Laguz, Ehwaz, Laguz)

Leland is a pioneer. With the breakthrough rune, Dagaz, offsetting the Nauthiz power of constraint, we know Leland is flexible and insightful. He has the courage to discard worn-out relationships as well as question authority and worn-out attitudes. Leland sets trends and moves on. The double Laguz energy could make him a popular figure in the performing arts. He will always do well in the public eye because he is controversial and ahead of his time, and he works to keep it that way. Leland believes the only constant is change. One can't help admiring the way Leland lives in the moment, for it keeps him young.

Elements: Fire, fire, air, water, air, water

THE NUMEROLOGICAL INTERPRETATION
Leland (NV = 3, CV = 6, VV = 6, FL = 3)

Although Leland can be found enjoying himself in many different social situations, he is basically a home-oriented man, one who will want to secure a permanent relationship at an early age. His name gives him a sense of honor and fair play. A just and balanced person, Leland brings a sense of moral integrity into his social contacts. He is very connected to the arts, and finds that music and painting bring him inspiration and relaxation. Writing is another creative outlet for him, and he would do well in a career that allows him freedom to express his ideas.

DERIVATION: English, Scottish, Dutch, German, and Scandinavian, pet form of several names ending in "lena" or "lina," such as Helena and Marlena. Commonly used as an independent name since the 1860s. Gained popularity in the United States due to the influence of the singer Lena Horne (b. 1917).

PRINCIPAL COLORS: All very pale colors

GEMSTONES AND PRECIOUS METALS: Diamonds, silver, any pale stone

BOTANICALS: Sweet marjoram, oats, parsley

UNIQUE SPELLINGS: Leena, Leenah, Lheena, Lhina, Lina

RELATED TO: Lenda, Lene, Leni, Lenna

෨

"You have to be taught to be second class; you're not born that way."
—LENA HORNE (MUSICIAN)

A KABBALISTIC SYNOPSIS
לינא —LYNA (Lamed, Yod, Nun, Aleph)

If Lena says something is going to happen, you had better believe it—because come hell or high water, she will make sure that it does. The compression of Lena's name produces the letters Tzaddi, meaning "fishhook," and Aleph, meaning "ox." This combination shows both an irresistible determination to succeed and the basic ability to undertake long hours of hard and boring work in order to get a result. Lena can be pretty severe when angry, a tendency indicated by the fact that the value of her name has strong associations with the sphere on the Tree of Life associated with all qualities of severity known as Geburah. However, this association also ensures that her anger is nearly always justified. There is another much softer side to Lena that craves love and attention, and she is prepared to be more than normally affectionate in return. The astrological influences on her behavior really determine which side Lena is most likely to present to the world.

THE RUNIC INTERPRETATION
ᚨᚾᛖᛚ (Ansuz, Nauthiz, Ehwaz, Laguz)

Lena designs her life according to her own agenda, and she loves it! Ansuz, the signals rune, starts off this name, and it offers Lena a good sense of timing and powerful insight. Lena may be stuck with a poverty mentality early in life, but the Laguz rune gives Lena the flexibility she requires to overcome this rough start later in her life. With some effort, Lena can cultivate a new consciousness. The Ehwaz rune of movement indicates that Lena will indeed prosper.

Elements: Air, fire, air, water

THE NUMEROLOGICAL INTERPRETATION
Lena (NV = 5, CV = 8, VV = 6, FL = 3)

Physical beauty and material security are very important to Lena. She is an active woman whose name bestows a great deal of talent in artistic pursuits. She has a great eye, and will work hard to make her home environment a peaceful and uplifting place for friends and loved ones alike. Lena is endowed with a great deal of personal charm, which brings her into contact with many people who are very happy to befriend her and support her in her various plans and projects. She is a sensual woman whose choice in partners will reflect her need for the exploration of life's many pleasures. Lena's relationships are the school from which she will learn (and perhaps teach!) her most profound life lessons.

෨

Leo

A Kabbalistic Synopsis
ליע —LYA'A (Lamed, Yod, Ayin)

With a name like Leo we have very definite expectations about the personality behind the name, whether they stem from astrology or simply the common knowledge that Leo is the Latin name for "lion." A kabbalistic analysis confirms this mental picture of Leo. He is indeed likely to be a decidedly proud individual, a trait that is usually obvious simply from the way he carries himself. It becomes much more apparent after one has spent some time in his company. A dominant figure, Leo has good reason for his pride, as he has a good head for business as well as a wily understanding of human interaction. The surprise in Leo is the association of the name's value with the Hanged Man card in tarot. This card refers to self-sacrifice and altruism, and while it may not fit our image of a Leo, he is indeed greatly motivated to do his bit for society.

The Runic Interpretation
ᛟᛖᛚ (Othila, Ehwaz, Laguz)

Leo is an overcomer. It isn't easy to change habits or belief systems that are instilled in childhood but are serving a detrimental purpose in one's adult life. However, Leo does this; the Othila rune empowers Leo to separate from his past, and the Ehwaz rune allows him to move away from bad habits. The discipline involved in this process is substantial, and the Laguz rune helps Leo relax into this healing process. Leo could do very well as a counselor or business adviser.

Elements: Earth/fire, air, water

The Numerological Interpretation
Leo (NV = 5, CV = 3, VV = 11, FL = 3)

Leo is very perceptive when it comes to dealing with others. He has an inner awareness of how people act in various social situations, and is a person who can deal very effectively with all sorts of individuals. People enjoy Leo. His name gives him an expansive and open intellect, as well as a very curious disposition. Leo has no problem at all uncovering the most intimate details about other people without intimidating or alienating them. Leo is an attractive and charming man who finds it very easy to circulate in society. He is generous and open, but must not be taken in by flattery.

DERIVATION: English, from the Latin *leo* and Greek *leon*, meaning "lion." The name of thirteen popes and several early Christian saints.

PRINCIPAL COLORS: The full spectrum of pale hues

GEMSTONES AND PRECIOUS METALS: Diamonds, silver, platinum

BOTANICALS: Oats, parsley, sea kale

UNIQUE SPELLINGS: Leeoh, Leigho, Leighoh, Leoh

RELATED TO: Lee†, Leodegar, Leon†, Leonard†, Leonardo, Leone, Leontios, Lion, Lyon

DERIVATION: English, German, and Gaelic form of Leo, from the Latin *leo* and Greek *leon*, meaning "lion." One of the top thirty names in the United States by the 1870s.

PRINCIPAL COLORS: All the shades of yellow, also any gold or brown hues

GEMSTONES AND PRECIOUS METALS: Citrine, topaz, amber

BOTANICALS: Lavender, eyebright, chamomile

UNIQUE SPELLINGS: Leahn, Leeahn, Leeon, Leighon

RELATED TO: Leet, Len, Leot, Leonardt, Leontios, Lion, Lonny, Lyon

❧

"The free man is he who does not fear to go to the end of his thought."
—LEON BLUM (FRENCH SOCIALIST AND WRITER)

A KABBALISTIC SYNOPSIS
ליען —LYA'AN (Lamed, Yod, Ayin, Nun)

Perhaps the best known Leon is Leon Trotsky, leader of the Red Army and Lenin's favorite comrade in the early days of the Russian Revolution. This individual certainly illustrates one of Leon's primary characteristics: a driving passion and a desire to persuade others of the benefit of his beliefs and values. While this famous Leon took this to an extreme, you can often see Leons as preachers or minor politicians; Leon is usually too attached to his own personal principles to rise to any great heights in politics. His passion carries over into his personal life, and the influence of the final Nun here suggests that his affairs will be few but deeply intense. Leon is pretty much incapable of a safe and comfortable relationship; his romances will be riddled with dramatic declarations of love and equally dramatic fights. However, anything less would probably bore him to tears!

THE RUNIC INTERPRETATION
ᛏᛟᛗᛚ (Nauthiz, Othila, Ehwaz, Laguz)

Leon has a good sense of design, rhythm, and composition. The Laguz rune gives Leon considerable artistic ability. He is emotional and sensitive. The Othila rune of separation adds another artistic quality to Leon's disposition. He enjoys simplicity and imbues his work with heartfelt integrity. Should Leon work in a field other than the arts, it is advisable for him to stay in touch with art in his free time because it nurtures his spirit. The Nauthiz energy of constraint can set up obstacles for Leon. He must work with the Laguz energy of flow to keep the channels of his creativity open in order to maintain his emotional balance.

Elements: Fire, earth/fire, air, water

THE NUMEROLOGICAL INTERPRETATION
Leon (NV = 8, CV = 8, VV = 11, FL = 3)

A born executive and moneymaker, Leon is blessed with highly developed organizational skills. He has the tendency to focus his talents on the material plane, and is very much at ease when involved with highly complex, long-range goals and plans. Leon is very intuitive and adept at perceiving which people in his environment are the most suitable to assist him in his plans. He seeks his own financial security but is also very happy when those associated with him also reap the benefits of their mutual efforts. He may find himself challenged in his personal relationships, as emotional intimacy does not come easily to him.

❧

Leona

DERIVATION: English and German, Latinate feminine form of Leon. From the Latin *leo* and Greek *leon*, meaning "lion." Commonly used since the 1940s.

PRINCIPAL COLORS: The full range of green hues, white

GEMSTONES AND PRECIOUS METALS: Jade, moonstones, pearls

BOTANICALS: Chicory, plantain, colewort

UNIQUE SPELLINGS: Leeohna, Leeona, Leeonha, Leighohna, Leighona, Leighonha

RELATED TO: Leight, Leoline, Leone, Leonia, Leonicia, Leonie, Leonin, Leontine

A KABBALISTIC SYNOPSIS

ליענא —LYA'ANA (Lamed, Yod, Ayin, Nun, Aleph)

You will find Leona working in the most depressing of places, and yet she will always maintain an optimistic view of the world, resolutely committed to the belief that if enough people chip in—even in a small way—the world can change for the better. Leona has it in her to carry all the world's problems on her shoulders, and it will be up to her many friends to make sure that she doesn't do this. She is likely to work with troubled and forgotten people, such as the homeless, but even Leona can give support to only so many people without losing herself in the process. Leona is very observant and notices all the little details in any given scene; this is useful in her work and is likely to have an effect on her chosen hobbies. Pastimes such as painting or poetry will have a distinct appeal to her.

THE RUNIC INTERPRETATION

ᚨᚾᛟᛗᛚ (Ansuz, Nauthiz, Othila, Ehwaz, Laguz)

Manipulators and con artists spot Leona and move right in for the kill. With experience, and probably major losses of time and money, Leona learns to be less gullible. Othila, the rune of separation, teaches her to discard worn-out relationships and judge people by actions, not by words. As she learns these invaluable lessons, Leona will feel limited and confused, as indicated by the Nauthiz rune of constraint. By surrounding herself with open, flexible, creative people, Leona gains her strength. She is musical and intuitive, with an easy, adaptable nature. The key to Leona's happiness hinges on her ability to populate her world with people as kind as herself. Leona is fortunate to have the power of the four elements in her name.

Elements: Air, fire, earth/fire, air, water

THE NUMEROLOGICAL INTERPRETATION

Leona (NV = 11, CV = 8, VV = 3, FL = 3)

Gifted is the word for Leona! This is a woman with the strength, stamina, and perseverance to achieve a great deal of success in her chosen career. Her name gives her the ability to interact very easily with others. She is both charming and convincing. People find Leona very magnetic and are eager to participate in actualizing her visions. Challenges come into Leona's personal life when her ambition overcomes her compassion. This could be balanced by using some of her abundant energy for charitable and volunteer community service.

DERIVATION: English, from an Old
French name of Germanic origin,
meaning "strong as a lion."
Introduced into Britain by the
Normans, but not common until
the eighteenth century.

PRINCIPAL COLORS: All but the
brightest shades of blue

GEMSTONES AND PRECIOUS
METALS: Blue and blue-green
turquoise, emeralds

BOTANICALS: Vervain, walnuts,
almonds

UNIQUE SPELLINGS: Lenard,
Lenhard, Lennard, Lennerd,
Lennhard, Leonhard

RELATED TO: Leet, Len, Lennie,
Lenny, Leot, Leont, Leonardo,
Leonid, Leonidas, Leonides,
Lonnard, Lonny

Leonard

A KABBALISTIC SYNOPSIS
לאנארד —LANARD (Lamed, Aleph, Nun, Aleph, Resh, Daleth)

Most of us find that from time to time, we get so stressed that we really find it hard to keep going. Leonard is one of those rare people who will probably never experience such feelings. He is so balanced and mentally stable that those who know him may find themselves wondering what keeps Leonard on such an even keel! He will use this strong inner balance to advance in his career. He is often driven to help people who are going through emotional difficulties, and may well work as a psychiatrist or counselor—a job for which he is ideally suited. His own love life is of great importance to Leonard, and he is the sort of man who will still be romantic many years after the wedding day. His wife would certainly testify to the fact that despite being remarkably balanced, he is anything but boring.

THE RUNIC INTERPRETATION
ᛞᚱᚨᚾᛟᛗᛚ (Dagaz, Raido, Ansuz, Nauthiz, Othila, Ehwaz, Lagaz)

Leonard may find that he has difficulty living in the present and responding spontaneously. Leonard can use the runes to help him integrate his negative emotions that prevent him from enjoying his life as it unfolds, and to clear his mind of old baggage. He comes to realize that our beliefs create our world. The Dagaz rune of breakthrough and Othila rune of separation hint that Leonard will succeed in freeing himself from a limiting belief system. As he chooses new friends and embraces a more positive view of the future, life will open up for Leonard. Leonard could have ample opportunity to try out residences in various parts of the world, but he will maintain his emotional makeup, which travels with him in his heart.

Elements: Fire, water, air, fire, earth/fire, air, water

THE NUMEROLOGICAL INTERPRETATION
Leonard (NV = 6, CV = 3, VV = 3, FL = 3)

A man who is very sensitive to the needs of others, Leonard has a generous disposition and a kind nature. Home and family are very important to him, as are the lives of his friends. These he has in abundance, as he is a gifted communicator sincerely interested in other people's activities. He has a broad outlook on life and is usually well educated. Leonard can be counted on to bring harmony to any social conflict. He is able to bring a quality of joy into his relationships, and makes a very devoted (and entertaining) partner and parent.

Leroy

DERIVATION: English, from the Old French, meaning "the king." Especially popular in the United States in the late nineteenth century.

PRINCIPAL COLORS: The full range of purple hues

GEMSTONES AND PRECIOUS METALS: Amethyst, garnets

BOTANICALS: Apple, cherry, bilberry

UNIQUE SPELLINGS: Leeroi, Leeroy, Leroi, Le'Roy, Le Roy

RELATED TO: Delroy, Elroy, Leet, Royt, Royden, Roydon, Royston

∽

"Be glad of life because it gives you the chance."
—LEROY VAN DYKE (MUSICIAN)

A KABBALISTIC SYNOPSIS
לרעי —LYRA'AY (Lamed, Resh, Ayin, Yod)

Leroy is a confirmed idealist, so he doesn't get depressed about the things that he wants to change; he is convinced that change will come in time. In spite of this, Leroy isn't merely an idle dreamer. He has considerable practical skills that he is prepared to use to try to further his aims and goals for society. Leroy commands a considerable amount of respect in his community due to his untiring willingness to pitch in. He rarely talks about his own achievements and is quick to give credit to others. In relationships, Leroy's partner comes first, and Leroy makes an excellent listener. However, at times his innate sensitivity can begin to grate, and he should bear in mind that no one has to be virtuous all of the time. As they say: A little misbehavior goes a long way.

THE RUNIC INTERPRETATION
ᛇᛟᚱᛖᛚ (Eihwaz, Othila, Raido, Ehwaz, Laguz)

Leroy is a frequent flier. He has the double travel energy of Ehwaz for movement and Raido for journey. The Eihwaz rune of defense could mean that Leroy travels to dangerous places. This might be the case if he is a journalist, diplomat, or a member of the armed services. The Othila rune of separation accounts for all the emotional adjustments Leroy's life requires as he works and lives abroad. Throughout his travels, Leroy has courage and perseverance. The Laguz rune of flow ensures that Leroy enjoys his life, because he is flexible and imaginative by nature, and his curiosity is further engaged by foreign sights and sounds.

Elements: Earth/fire, earth/fire, water, air, water

THE NUMEROLOGICAL INTERPRETATION
Leroy (NV = 3, CV = 3, VV = 9, FL = 3)

This is a warm and friendly man, one who usually has something nice to say about everyone. People are naturally attracted to Leroy, as they know they can depend on his goodwill and kind gestures. The numbers in his name give Leroy many opportunities to use his communicative skills. He would make a great teacher, as young people find his open mind very refreshing and stimulating. Leroy would also be good in advertising, public relations, and sales. He tends to have a number of personal relationships, as he has a broad range of interests and may prefer to explore them with various partners.

∽

DERIVATION: English, short form
of the Scottish surname Leslie,
derived from the lands of Lesslyn
in Aberdeenshire.

PRINCIPAL COLORS: The full
range of red hues, particularly the
deep, rich shades

GEMSTONES AND PRECIOUS
METALS: Bloodstones, rubies,
garnets

BOTANICALS: Broom, garlic, onion

UNIQUE SPELLINGS: Lehs,
Less, Lez

RELATED TO: Leicester, Leslee,
Lesley, Leslie†, Lesly, Lester†,
Lezly

Les

A KABBALISTIC SYNOPSIS
לאז —LAZ (Lamed, Aleph, Zayin)

There are few true innocents, but Les comes very close. He is honest and sincere and expects to find the same qualities in others. No matter how many times he overestimates people, he does not change his basic attitude. However, negative experiences will lead him to become more reclusive than he would be otherwise—and he is already something of a loner by nature. Les is at his best when working with machinery or possibly computers, as they can be trusted to act as instructed and therefore hold no unpleasant surprises. Les will have quite a wide circle of friends outside the workplace, and they will tend to be people he has known for a number of years. Interestingly, Les's naive attitude toward people does not tend to hinder his career development, as it will be natural for him to be the top person in his field of expertise.

THE RUNIC INTERPRETATION
(Sowelu, Ehwaz, Laguz)

Les has a wonderful signature. His name stands for wholeness, movement, and flow—a great combination. Les is prosperous and could travel throughout his lifetime. He is artistic and sensitive, and so the wonderful sights and experiences of his frequent excursions nourish his soul. Les is drawn to music and festivals; concerts and midnight cabaret will be familiar entries on his social calendar. The possibility exists that Les might not physically travel. If this is the case, he will travel vicariously through books and conversations with sophisticated acquaintances. Les has a flexible mind and is open to people from all walks of life. He understands that everyone has a story to tell, and he feels he can learn from people in all stations of life.

Elements: Air, air, water

THE NUMEROLOGICAL INTERPRETATION
Les (NV = 9, CV = 4, VV = 5, FL = 3)

Les has to work on integrating his urge for personal freedom and travel with his need for financial security and a down-to-earth, stable lifestyle. He should therefore look for a career that allows him a steady income while at the same time does not tie him to his desk. This name is also indicative of a man who would do well cultivating a strong inner belief system—a practical philosophy, religion, or creed that supports his actions. External success for him is based on a solid foundation of faith.

Leslie

A KABBALISTIC SYNOPSIS
לאזלי —LAZLY (Lamed, Aleph, Zayin, Lamed, Yod)

The value of Leslie's name adds up to seventy-eight, a number that has wide-ranging mystical associations. It suggests a very broad-based individual, and since this name can be given to both men and women, this seems particularly appropriate. Leslie has a whole range of influences and interests, and is as happy at the football field as at the local library. The variety of experiences that Leslie faces makes for a very interesting conversationalist; Leslie is more than happy to be the center of attention and is likely to have a full social life. Although Leslie will have a considerable understanding of the world, aspects to this name suggest that boredom is often a problem due to a fairly short attention span. This often affects Leslie's performance at work. Determined to do well, Leslie will often take the quickest route to recognition.

THE RUNIC INTERPRETATION
ᛗᛁᛚᛋᛗᛚ (Ehwaz, Isa, Laguz, Sowelu, Ehwaz, Laguz)

The double energy of flow makes Leslie receptive to feelings. Leslie has a tendency to succumb to the urge to blame others. Leslies will become clearheaded and well balanced when they stop submerging their feelings, although they may have to take a slow path for a while to heal themselves. However, given time to study life, Leslie can experience tremendous personal growth, and will find life transformed on all levels. Ehwaz and Isa offer learning and growth with slow but steady progress.

Elements: Air, earth, water, air, air, water

THE NUMEROLOGICAL INTERPRETATION
Leslie (NV = 8, CV = 7, VV = 1, FL = 3)

The urge to succeed at one's chosen career dominates the indications of this name. Leslie has an extremely analytical and powerful mind, one that he/she uses in very practical ways. Leslie has drive, determination, and perseverance. Never one to avoid a challenge, Leslie has an eye on a big prize, and will do all that is necessary to obtain it. This is a person who earns the respect of friends and associates through personal effort and a sense of inner authority, although it may be necessary to temper some of these characteristics in order to be equally successful on emotional levels. Self-discipline is not one of Leslie's virtues, and he/she can become easily distracted by the excitement of social activities or the promise of new relationships.

DERIVATION: Scottish and English, originally a Scottish surname derived from the lands of Lesslyn in Aberdeenshire. Of unknown meaning, but possibly from the Gaelic *leas cuilinn*, meaning "garden of hollies." Made popular by the British film actor Leslie Howard (1893–1943), who appeared in *Gone with the Wind* (1939). Used for both boys and girls.

PRINCIPAL COLORS: Dark blue, violet, and gray hues; black

GEMSTONES AND PRECIOUS METALS: Amethyst, carbuncles, dull rubies

BOTANICALS: Angelica, marsh mallow

UNIQUE SPELLINGS: Leslea, Leslee, Lesley, Lesli, Lesly, Leslye, Lesslie, Lezly

RELATED TO: Leet, Leicester, Lest, Lesley, Lestert; Leight

"I think it's the end of progress if you stand still and think of what you've done in the past. I keep on."
—LESLIE CARON (ACTRESS)

DERIVATION: English, the phonetic form of the English place-name Leicester. Originally a surname, but commonly used as a first name since the 1840s.

PRINCIPAL COLORS: The full range of yellow and green hues

GEMSTONES AND PRECIOUS METALS: Moonstones, pearls, cat's-eye

BOTANICALS: Blackberry, elder

UNIQUE SPELLINGS: Lehster, Lehstir, Lehstyr, Lestir, Lestyr

RELATED TO: Leicester, Lest†, Lesley, Lesliet

A KABBALISTIC SYNOPSIS
לאסטור —LASTVR (Lamed, Aleph, Samech, Teth, Vau, Resh)

It's not often that you find a name that defines the ideal job for its holder as clearly as Lester does. Lester was born to be a critic of some persuasion. The platform for this calling might be a contemporary medium such as television, but most probably will involve more traditional art forms, such as literature or music. This name's value features Vau, indicating a creative combination of the powers of objective judgment and taste or intuition. If Lester is not a critic, he will certainly be working in an environment where those skills are paramount. Outside of the office, Lester is a generally cheerful man, with a strong commitment to his family. However, Lester does have a very short fuse and can switch from being happy to furious with very little warning.

THE RUNIC INTERPRETATION
ᚱᛖᛏᛊᛖᛚ (Raido, Ehwaz, Teiwaz, Sowelu, Ehwaz, Laguz)

The double rune of movement, or Ehwaz, is emphasized in Lester's name by appearing twice. Lester will strive for security—and yet he will move many times in his life. When Lester begins to understand that he must embrace a journey of self-healing, he will enjoy his reality. He will experience a new sense of well-being and recover a love of himself he may have lost. As is always the case, his self-love makes him better able to love the outside world, as indicated by Sowelu, the rune that represents wholeness. The Teiwaz warrior rune implies that Lester has the courage and discipline to reach out to people from all walks of life and make meaningful connections wherever he goes. Lester understands that having friends on a global level enriches his life tremendously.

Elements: Water, air, air, air, air, water

THE NUMEROLOGICAL INTERPRETATION
Lester (NV = 7, CV = 6, VV = 1, FL = 3)

Lester has a private world that few people may understand, although he is a compassionate man, one who seeks peace and harmony in all of his relationships. Lester is also a deep thinker, a man with a strong urge to come in contact with the fundamental truths in life. Education is important to him, as he is eager to expand his knowledge and add to his skills. As a critical thinker, Lester may do well as a scientist or psychologist. Home and family are important to him, but he will need a partner who understands his need for solitude and private space.

Leticia

DERIVATION: English, from the Latin *laetitia*, meaning "gladness." The English medieval form of the name was Lettice.

PRINCIPAL COLORS: All very lightly shaded hues

GEMSTONES AND PRECIOUS METALS: Platinum, diamonds, silver

BOTANICALS: Hazel, oats, sweet marjoram

UNIQUE SPELLINGS: Laetitia, Laetizia, Latisha, Letisha, Letitia, Letizia, Lettitia

RELATED TO: Latashia, Latia, Leda, Leta, Letha, Letice, Letta, Lettice, Lettie, Letty, Tish, Tisha

A KABBALISTIC SYNOPSIS

לאטישיא —LATYShYA (Lamed, Aleph, Teth, Yod, Shin, Yod, Aleph)

Leticia is ruled by the planet Saturn and can consequently come across as quite depressed and taciturn by nature. However, Saturn is also associated with ideas of family tradition and duty, so we can expect Leticia to be deeply loyal to all of those close to her. One Hebrew equivalent of Leticia is "foundations," and Leticia is best suited to a career role where she is involved in getting projects off the ground, as she can provide the initial burst of energy needed in such circumstances. Leticia may even find herself involved in the construction industry. One of her best skills is the ability to motivate others, and in spite of her sometimes somber manner, she almost always can convince people of the value of new schemes. Leticia really comes alive in her relationships, both emotionally and physically.

THE RUNIC INTERPRETATION

ᚾᛁᛋᛁᛏᛖᛚ (Ansuz, Isa, Sowelu, Isa, Teiwaz, Ehwaz, Laguz)

The double Isa rune of standstill in Leticia's name opposes the Ehwaz rune for movement. Leticia may move about in life, each location farther from the last. Leticia realizes that she can use the Sowelu rune of wholeness to stop rejecting herself and begin the path to self-love and self-acceptance. Rather than searching for oneness in the outer world, Leticia must learn first to love herself. She needs to accept that the love she perceives as coming from another is really just a reflection of her own inner love.

Elements: Air, earth, air, earth, air, air, water

THE NUMEROLOGICAL INTERPRETATION

Leticia (NV = 5, CV = 8, VV = 6, FL = 3)

Leticia moves through life with an open attitude. She wants to acquire all the necessary experiences that will help her achieve her goals, but she is neither careless nor indiscriminate about her choices in this respect. She has a plan in mind at all times. Life is a chess board for her, and she wants to be the queen. Leticia is a name that gives grace, charm, and kindness. People will want to be of help to her, and Leticia will return their support and generosity in kind. She must take care that she is not swayed in her decisions by people who are promising on the surface but who may not live up to their words.

DERIVATION: English, Welsh, Scottish, and Irish. Generally, the common English form of the French name Louis, which is derived from Germanic elements meaning "fame" and "warrior." In Wales, a simplified form of Llewellyn; in Scotland, a variation of Ludovic; and in Ireland, an anglicized form of the Gaelic Laoiseach and Lughaidh. Made famous by the English author Lewis Carroll, well known for his classic work *Alice in Wonderland*.

PRINCIPAL COLORS: The full spectrum of very pale hues

GEMSTONES AND PRECIOUS METALS: Silver, platinum, any shiny stones

BOTANICALS: Oats, parsley, caraway

UNIQUE SPELLINGS: Lewes, Louis

RELATED TO: Lew, Lewie, Lou, Louie, Louist

A KABBALISTIC SYNOPSIS
לעוים —LA'AVYS (Lamed, Ayin, Vau, Yod, Samech)

If you're in a jam, speak to Lewis, as not only is he an excellent listener but he will also be able to give you some good advice. Lewis is drawn to the role of adviser. He particularly enjoys the ability to ease people's worries, and may well forge a career for himself in a profession where advice plays a major role. He has a deep sense of justice, and this affinity for the law may lead him to the legal profession. He is innately supportive and tries to help others in a number of ways. When Lewis relaxes, he likes to get away from it all, and is very fond of rugged outdoor activities.

THE RUNIC INTERPRETATION
ᛋᛁᛈᛗᛚ (Sowelu, Isa, Wunjo, Ehwaz, Laguz)

Lewis is a great humanitarian. Lewis is also a rock of stability. He enjoys his own company and can be alone for extended periods of time without a sense of deprivation. Lewis uses the rune of standstill to rest and rejuvenate, for he gives a lot to both his career and his friends. People enjoy his company because they feel they have his undivided attention. Lewis can live in the moment and has wonderful powers of concentration. He needs to be careful about the emotion of jealousy, because it never occurs to him that people can be petty in that way. The Laguz rune signifies an easygoing temperament. The Wunjo rune for joy shows that Lewis is a winner.

Elements: Air, earth, earth, air, water

THE NUMEROLOGICAL INTERPRETATION
Lewis (NV = 7, CV = 6, VV = 1, FL = 3)

Lewis is a man who is inspired by his ideals and who can obtain great strength through his religious or philosophical beliefs. But faith is not enough; Lewis needs to apply what he feels inside in ways that are helpful on practical levels. Lewis wants to know the truth about life and share what he has learned with others. Teaching and counseling are fine outlets for Lewis. This name stimulates the emotional nature as well as the intellectual. Lewis is very open to a committed relationship as well as to having a family. He enjoys the comforts of a familiar environment and is attracted to music and the arts.

Lillian

A Kabbalistic Synopsis
ליליאן —LYLYAN (Lamed, Yod, Lamed, Yod, Aleph, Nun)

People often meet Lillian on trains, usually when the seat next to her is the only one left. If they do end up sitting next to her, they can forget about reading that book or finishing up that report for the office; Lillian will talk to just about anyone, and it often doesn't matter whether they are particularly interested or not. With Lillian you don't just get idle chitchat, you'll probably come away knowing every last detail of her life—particularly her emotional state, which tends to vary from tragic to very tragic. It may come as a surprise, then, to learn that Lillian's partner will consider himself to be deeply happy in their relationship. This is because, in spite of her tendency for melodrama, Lillian is an intensely interesting woman who has views and knowledge about the most out-of-the-way things. In addition, she has a deeply creative streak, and her partner is likely to forgive any histrionics thanks to the fact that she produces some brilliant pieces of art—and can do this only by behaving in the way she does.

The Runic Interpretation
ᚾᚨᛁᛚᛚᛁᛚ (Nauthiz, Ansuz, Isa, Laguz, Laguz, Isa, Laguz)

It's usually a struggle on a financial level to be an artist like Lillian. She has the Nauthiz rune of constraint in her name. It takes deep faith to follow a dream, and it's not easy to live when there is no steady paycheck. But Lillian knows all this and has the courage of the double Isa rune to patiently wait for her dreams to become reality. The Ansuz rune hints that Lillian is on the right track. She may be happy being involved with the performing arts. The triple Laguz energy of flow in her name signifies that Lillian has what it takes to enjoy her creative life to the utmost. Lillian is also very intuitive.

Elements: Fire, air, earth, water, water, earth, water

The Numerological Interpretation
Lillian (NV = 6, CV = 5, VV = 1, FL = 3)

Lillian is happiest when her domestic life is secure. It is natural for her to use her home and family as her foundation, moving in and out of this intimate circle relative to her other activities. And there are many of these! Lillian is a very active person, with a strong need to express herself and expand her horizons. This she would most naturally tend to do through education. Lillian is a name that connotes a woman who is a perpetual student. Lillian is also a good teacher. She takes great pleasure in sharing what she knows, and in encouraging her friends and associates to continue opening themselves to life's possibilities. Her numbers reveal that she would do well to cultivate patience, as she has a habit of moving too quickly for her own good.

DERIVATION: English, variant spelling of Lilian, a name of uncertain origin. First recorded in the late sixteenth century, possibly as a form of Elizabeth. Also a derivative of the flower name lily. Particularly popular in the United States from the 1890s to 1930s.

PRINCIPAL COLORS: From pale to medium azure tones

GEMSTONES AND PRECIOUS METALS: Emeralds, turquoise

BOTANICALS: Dog rose, vervain, walnuts

UNIQUE SPELLINGS: Lilian, Lilien, Lillyan, Lilyan, Lylian, Lylien, Lyllian, Lyllyan, Lylyan, Lylyen

RELATED TO: Lilia, Lilian, Liliana, Lilith, Lilla, Lilli, Lillia, Lillianna, Lillianne, Lillias, Lillie, Lilyt, Lilly

DERIVATION: English, from the Latin word for the flower of that name, lilium. A symbol of purity in Christian imagery. Not popular since the turn of the century.

PRINCIPAL COLORS: Medium shades such as blues and grays

GEMSTONES AND PRECIOUS METALS: Sapphires

BOTANICALS: Sage, wild spinach, lesser celandine

UNIQUE SPELLINGS: Lili, Lilie, Lilley, Lillie, Lilly

RELATED TO: Lil, Lila, Lilac, Lilas, Lilia, Lilias, Lilibet, Lilith, Lilliant, Lillianne

Lily

A KABBALISTIC SYNOPSIS
לילי —LYLY (Lamed, Yod, Lamed, Yod)

Everyone wants to be Lily's best friend. Not only is Lily an absolute hoot go out with, since she has an excellent sense of humor, but she is also one of the most efficient people you could wish to meet. If you're moving house and getting into a mess, just give Lily a call and she will sort you out in no time! Like Joey, Lily has the enormous energy that comes from having the letter Yod twice in a name. However, as the letter Lamed makes a double appearance in Lily, she has considerably better skills when it comes to directing that energy in a controlled manner. Lily's name adds up to eighty, which is the same value as the Hebrew letter Peh, meaning "mouth." Consequently Lily is an excellent conversationalist and loves to talk. Mind you, she doesn't just chatter pointlessly; whatever Lily says is usually well worth listening to. Whoever she has a relationship with had better be prepared to let her wear the trousers, as Lily always knows exactly what she wants to do and how she wants to do it—and Lily is not someone you want to argue with too often! Interestingly, if we split Lily's name into two equal parts of a Lamed and a Yod, we get a value that is equivalent to the letter Mem. The letter Mem represents maternal and nurturing feelings, so we can see that although Lily is a very dominant character, she is also a well-meaning and fiercely protective woman. She will make an excellent mother and businesswoman.

THE RUNIC INTERPRETATION
ᛇᛚᛁᛚ (Eihwaz, Laguz, Isa, Laguz)

Lily is in her own world—and why not? Any teacher who criticizes this gentle sprite for daydreaming should be advised that highly creative children require such escape time to stay in balance! Lily loves to dance in front of the mirror for hours on end. She plans movies in her head, and as an adult Lily is able to use her flexible and perceptive insight to her advantage. Lily needs to dance and sing and float through life, with her keen inner eye directed by the muses, who are her most reliable companions.

Elements: Earth/fire, water, earth, water

THE NUMEROLOGICAL INTERPRETATION
Lily (NV = 4, CV = 6, VV = 7, FL = 3)

A romantic and artistic spirit dominates this name. Lily is greatly stimulated by music and enjoys working to the sounds of her favorite tunes. This is a woman who is also in touch with nature. Lily has a side to her that is reflective and introspective. She can spend many happy hours working in a garden or roaming through mountainous or forested areas. Although Lily lives in a world that is greatly inspired by beauty, she is a balanced individual, one who realizes that having her feet firmly planted on the earth is essential to her well-being. She tends to respect her body, dresses well, and strives to maintain a healthful diet. Her domestic life is important to her. She is family oriented and does quite well interacting with children.

Linda

DERIVATION: English, of uncertain origin. First recorded in the nineteenth century. Possibly a shortened form of Belinda, or an adoption of the Spanish word *linda*, meaning "pretty." May also be derived from several Germanic female names ending in "lind," meaning "snake." Extremely popular in the twentieth century.

PRINCIPAL COLORS: Electric hues, any color of medium shade

GEMSTONES AND PRECIOUS METALS: Sapphires

BOTANICALS: Sage, spinach, wintergreen

UNIQUE SPELLINGS: Lhinda, Lhindah, Lhynda, Lhyndah, Lindah, Lynda, Lyndah

RELATED TO: Lin, Lindee, Lindey, Lindi, Lindie, Lindy, Linn, Lyn, Lynde, Lyndy, Lynnt, Lynndie, Lynne, Melinda†

A KABBALISTIC SYNOPSIS
לינדא —LYNDA (Lamed, Yod, Nun, Daleth, Aleph)

Linda certainly doesn't need any man to look after her, for she is extremely brave and can tackle any challenge head-on. This courageous attitude is due to the strong influence of Mars, the planet of war, in her name. Linda has a love of travel—particularly if it involves unusual modes of transport or places that are off the beaten track. Water holds a special appeal for Linda as well, and if she happens to be born under Pisces or Scorpio, there is a very strong chance that she will work in some connection with water. It is easy to assume from Linda's surface behavior that she is emotionally tough, when in fact Linda is an extremely sensitive woman. Linda can take any amount of physical hardship but tends to go to pieces when she feels emotionally insecure, and any partner will need to take this into account.

THE RUNIC INTERPRETATION
(Ansuz, Dagaz, Nauthiz, Isa, Laguz)

Linda carries a portable heaven within. When the hard obstacles come along, Linda knows that her ability to trust her faith is her greatest joy. The breakthrough rune lets Linda believe in the process, and the signals rune prompts her to surrender her anxiety. Linda is determined to simplify her life and detoxify her body and her thoughts in order to walk in closer accord with harmony and love. Challenges and constraints present themselves, but Linda is well prepared to meet all with equanimity.

Elements: Air, fire, fire, earth, water

THE NUMEROLOGICAL INTERPRETATION
Linda (NV = 4, CV = 3, VV = 1, FL = 3)

Linda works hard at establishing herself through her chosen profession. Material stability and financial security are very important to her. Linda likes having her life well organized and under control. Her name gives her the ability to mix well with others. She is a good conversationalist and is concerned about what people have to say. Linda is admired for her dependability, thoughtfulness, and good intentions. She will be most happy with a partner who is a good provider and who is definitely geared to long-range commitments in relationships.

Lindsey

DERIVATION: Scottish and English, the surname of a certain Sir Walter de Lindesay, who brought the name to Scotland from Lindsey in Lincolnshire in the eleventh century. Of uncertain meaning, but from the Old English, possibly meaning "island of serpents" or "island of linden trees." Used as both a masculine and feminine name.

PRINCIPAL COLORS: The full gamut of green and yellow hues

GEMSTONES AND PRECIOUS METALS: Moss agate, white pearls

BOTANICALS: Hops, juniper, blackberry

UNIQUE SPELLINGS: Lindsay, Lindsaye, Lindsea, Lindsie, Lindsy, Lindzi, Lindzy, Linsay, Linsey, Linzey, Linzi, Linzie, Lyndsay, Lyndsey, Lyndsy, Lynsay, Lynsey, Lynsie

RELATED TO: Lin, Lindee, Lindey, Lindi, Lindie, Lindy, Linn, Lyn, Lynde, Lyndy, Lynnt, Lynndie, Lynne

A Kabbalistic Synopsis

 לינדסי —LYNDSY (Lamed, Yod, Nun, Daleth, Samech, Yod)

When we look at other Hebrew words with the same value—a process known as analyzing gematric equivalences—we find that the words "brains" and "science" have the same value as Lindsey. This strongly suggests that Lindsey will be working in a laboratory of some sort or other and, given her intelligence, working at a senior level. Other aspects of this name also point toward medical science. Working in medicine satisfies Lindsey's desire to offer support to others, as he or she will be helping to advance the treatments that are available to people. While at work, Lindsey is decidedly objective and manages not to let the sometimes depressing side of medicine affect him or her. At home, though, Lindsey is very much a feelings-based person. Lindsey doesn't really go in for long intellectual debates around the dinner table, but instead likes to switch off and just enjoy the company of friends and family.

The Runic Interpretation

ᛇᛖᛊᛞᚾᛁᛚ (Eihwaz, Ehwaz, Sowelu, Dagaz, Nauthiz, Isa, Lagaz)

Lindsey has the raw courage it takes to start a business of his or her own, go for a Ph.D., or train for the Olympics. The runes of breakthrough (Dagaz) and defense (Nauthiz) have tested Lindsey's courage, and Lindsey has emerged from times of pain and confusion victorious. The Isa rune of standstill will create a welcome break at some point in Lindsey's life, giving him or her a chance to experience the many possibilities his or her future holds. No longer in a survival mode, Lindsey forges ahead with a dream that he or she has transmuted into a focused goal. With the Sowelu rune in this name, Lindsey has the capacity to feel focused and complete.

Elements: Earth/fire, air, air, fire, fire, earth, water

The Numerological Interpretation

Lindsey (NV = 7, CV = 4, VV = 3, FL = 3)

The name Lindsey endows one with a strong intellect and a genuine curiosity about life. This is a person who loves to communicate, but his or her interchanges with others have to have some deeper goal or meaning; Lindsey is not prone to small talk and avoids gossip. Lindsey wants to investigate life and is happiest when surrounded by intelligent friends. Mental stimulation is vital in his or her personal life, and he or she only will choose a partner who is at least an intellectual equal. Lindsey has a strong practical side to his or her nature, too, and is well suited for a career that involves public relations, education, or scientific research.

Lionel

DERIVATION: English, from the Old French name Léon, meaning "lion," or from the Latin *leonellus*, meaning "little lion." Especially common in the 1920s and 1930s.

PRINCIPAL COLORS: The full spectrum of moderately toned hues

GEMSTONES AND PRECIOUS METALS: Sapphires

BOTANICALS: Celandine, wild spinach

UNIQUE SPELLINGS: Lianel, Lianyl, Linel, Lionyl, Lylet

RELATED TO: Leet, Leot, Linus, Lionello

A KABBALISTIC SYNOPSIS
ליענאל —LYA'ANAL (Lamed, Yod, Ayin, Nun, Aleph, Lamed)

Very few people will know it—as he tends to be a quiet character—but Lionel has an incredibly vivid imagination. The central letter in his name, A'A or Ayin, meaning "eye," suggests his highly observant nature. Lionel takes the reality confronting him and turns it into something far more exciting in his mind's eye. If he has the confidence, Lionel could probably carve out a living for himself as a published writer—although in many ways Lionel likes the fact that his imagination occupies his own private space. It is important for Lionel to remember to rest, as he has a tendency to burn the candle at both ends. In addition, the fact that the letter Lamed both begins and ends his name indicates a susceptibility to stress, and he may well feel pressured to work excessively hard.

THE RUNIC INTERPRETATION
ᚱᛁᛟᚾᛖᛚ (Laguz, Ehwaz, Nauthiz, Othila, Isa, Laguz)

Lionel has the rune of separation marking his name. Lionel will undoubtedly inherit property or acquire it on his own. This is signaled by the Othila rune, which could also mean that Lionel might benefit from strong family traits. While land ownership is an attribute of the Othila rune, this rune also requires the ability to relinquish something of importance. For example, Lionel may have to let go of something familiar in order to gain his reward. The Laguz energy in this name could steer Lionel toward music, languages, or any of the performing arts. He will face challenges and delays because the Nauthiz rune is present to offer lessons, and lessons take time to be absorbed. Lionel has good humor on his side and patience, which is offered by the Isa rune of standstill. In the end, Lionel will triumph over his challenges.

Elements: Water, air, fire, earth/fire, earth, water

THE NUMEROLOGICAL INTERPRETATION
Lionel (NV = 4, CV = 11, VV = 2, FL = 3)

Lionel tends to use his keen intuition and insight for very practical purposes. Lionel likes to know that there is a certain predictability to his life and that his foundation is secure. He is open to the new and the unusual, but he will not allow these interests to greatly upset his routine. He is a natural economist, developing theories for the right use of resources. He is also good at organizing other people's activities, and can readily see how component parts fit together into a more harmonious whole. Lionel is a sensuous man who enjoys the comforts of life, and is pleased when he can share these with his loved ones.

Lisa

A KABBALISTIC SYNOPSIS
ליסא —LYSA (Lamed, Yod, Samech, Aleph)

Lisa can make men feel very uncomfortable—a skill of which she is well aware and that she enjoys immensely. Lisa is attractive in her self-confidence. Her best feature is likely to be her eyes, which suggest that Lisa knows exactly what you're thinking about. Indeed, Lisa has a good understanding of what makes people tick, as she is an excellent listener. Her friends will often seek her out when they have a dilemma that they can't resolve alone. Lisa herself is rarely in this position, since she has a very decisive nature. While her strong personality may put some people off, there are plenty of prospective partners who will appreciate a woman who knows her own mind.

THE RUNIC INTERPRETATION
(Ansuz, Sowelu, Isa, Laguz)

Lisa is patient, thanks to the Isa rune of standstill, and she can focus with great concentration on highly detailed work. She could be an accomplished editor, conductor, writer, painter of miniatures, or succeed in any number of careers that reward a detail-oriented personality. Lisa has the Ansuz rune for signals, which means she is intuitive and perceptive. She can read between the lines. To some, Lisa can seem too skeptical and negative; this is just her attempt to avoid gullibility. Once Lisa trusts, she can be warm and vulnerable. The Laguz rune of flow makes her an original thinker. Lisa is a superb student of human nature.

Elements: Air, air, earth, water

THE NUMEROLOGICAL INTERPRETATION
Lisa (NV = 5, CV = 4, VV = 1, FL = 3)

Lisa leads a very busy life, as her world is one of constantly shifting circumstances. The numbers in this name speak of a highly individualistic person, a woman who has a definite sense of herself and who has very definite practical goals and plans. Finances mean a great deal to her, and she will use her multifaceted personality to acquire the material objects she needs and desires. Lisa must have an exciting partner, one who is also financially secure or who at least shows financial promise.

Lloyd

A Kabbalistic Synopsis
לליעד —LLA'AYD (Lamed, Lamed, Ayin, Yod, Daleth)

If you want to get Lloyd excited, show him a suitcase full of money! The driving passion in Lloyd's life is the desire to accumulate wealth. Lloyd doesn't just want to be comfortable; he wants to be wealthy. The presence of two Lameds at the start of his name indicates a highly unusual level of determination to succeed. However, Lloyd is very easily bored and is unlikely to make his mark by gradually building up a business. Thus he would rather try to achieve his goals by a series of moneymaking schemes that he has dreamed up. There is nothing wrong with ambition, of course, but Lloyd does need to be careful not to focus on cash at the expense of his relationships. Even Lloyd needs to have a bit of fun from time to time.

The Runic Interpretation
ᛞᛇᛟᛚᛚ (Dagaz, Eihwaz, Othila, Laguz, Laguz)

Lloyd hears music most of us miss. Blessed with the double Laguz rune of flow, this affords him intuitive ability and great creative gifts, particularly in music. The Laguz rune is symbolized by water, the moon, and the emotions. Lloyd would feel perfectly at peace living by the sea. Ask him if he is a night person; he'll probably tell you he feels like he's more awake at night, and more productive. Lloyd needs to take this into account when he plans his career, because a 9 A.M. desk job could be hard on him. The Eihwaz and Othila runes, signifying defense and separation, respectively, point to challenges for Lloyd. He could feel alienated for a time. When he learns to avoid peer pressure, Lloyd experiences the Dagaz energy of breakthrough and his life takes off.

Elements: Fire, earth/fire, earth/fire, water, water

The Numerological Interpretation
Lloyd (NV = 4, CV = 9, VV = 4, FL = 3)

This is a well-organized and structured man who uses these character traits to achieve his place in the world. Lloyd enjoys establishing patterns and routines that work. He is a pragmatist of the first order. This is wonderful when it comes to anchoring his plans and projects, but may not be so useful when it comes to adjusting to the surprising circumstances that always enter our lives. Lloyd is definitely not spontaneous, and he avoids people whose actions are unpredictable. People feel confident when in a business or personal relationship with Lloyd, as they know he can be counted on to fulfill his promises and keep his word.

DERIVATION: English, originally a Welsh surname, from the root *llwyd*, meaning "gray" or "holy." Very popular in the United States during the 1940s, probably due to the influence of the actor Lloyd Bridges (1913–1998).

PRINCIPAL COLORS: The full spectrum of very pale hues

GEMSTONES AND PRECIOUS METALS: Diamonds, silver; any pale, shiny stones

BOTANICALS: Oats, caraway, sweet marjoram

UNIQUE SPELLINGS: Lloid, Lloydd, Loid, Loidd, Loyd, Loydd

RELATED TO: Floyd

"The men who try to do something and fail are infinitely better than those who try nothing and succeed."
— LLOYD JONES (MUSICIAN)

DERIVATION: From the New Testament, the name of Timothy's grandmother. Of unknown origin and meaning, though thought to be a Greek name. Especially popular in the United States in the beginning of the twentieth century.

PRINCIPAL COLORS: Pale to brilliant yellow and russet shades, orange, gold

GEMSTONES AND PRECIOUS METALS: Citrine, topaz, yellow diamonds

BOTANICALS: Lavender, thyme, sorrel

UNIQUE SPELLINGS: Lohis, Lohys, Loiss, Lowis, Lowiss, Loys

RELATED TO: Eloisa, Louisa, Louise†

Lois

A KABBALISTIC SYNOPSIS
לעיס —LA'AYS (Lamed, Ayin, Yod, Samech)

Interestingly, the real meaning of Lois has more than a few connections to that famous Lois: Superman's good friend, Lois Lane. When the name's value is compressed, the two letters Qoph and Ayin add up to 170. When analyzed, these two letters indicate a combination of a keen mind and a good eye for detail—skills ideally suited to journalism. Lois has a strong sense of civic duty as well, and is likely to be very public-spirited, and always ready to support a good cause. Lois is a very up-front woman and has loads of confidence; it will usually be she who makes the first move in any relationship, and she will get very few rejections.

THE RUNIC INTERPRETATION
(Sowelu, Isa, Othila, Laguz)

A sense of purpose and talent waiting to be expressed characterize Lois's personality. The Laguz rune of flow offers creative gifts, and the Isa rune of standstill provides Lois with the patience to bring these gifts into reality. The Othila rune of separation is a great benefit to Lois because it helps her discard old, worn-out relationships and keep her mind eager to grow and try out new ideas. A sense of complacency may be all right for the average person, but for an artist, it's dangerous. Lois is unwilling to be bound by old traditions or authority. Slowly, the rune of wholeness will reveal a career for Lois in which she can express her considerable talents and abilities.

Elements: Air, earth, earth/fire, water

THE NUMEROLOGICAL INTERPRETATION
Lois (NV = 1, CV = 4, VV = 6, FL = 1)

Lois likes to put her personal stamp on everything that she does. She walks through life with a sense of assurance and self-confidence. The numbers in her name point to a woman who is balanced and graceful. She is proud of her physical appearance and takes care of her health. Money is important to her, and she will make sure that she has found a career that allows her a great deal of upward mobility. Lois tends to be traditional when it comes to romance, and is most comfortable in a committed relationship.

Lola

A KABBALISTIC SYNOPSIS
לעל —LA'ALA (Lamed, Ayin, Lamed, Aleph)

Lola has the capacity to make the simplest gesture seem immensely sexual. She is also extremely comfortable with the power that she holds over her admirers. Lola will usually settle down at a relatively early age with someone who appreciates her personality as much as her physical impact. Although she flirts with abandon, Lola will remain totally faithful to her partner. Although there is little that Lola won't try at least once, she is quite a homebody in private. Children are high on her agenda, and she will make a great mother who fills all her children with a firm belief in their abilities and value.

THE RUNIC INTERPRETATION
ᚨᛚᛟᛚ (Ansuz, Laguz, Othila, Laguz)

A double Laguz rune is always a fortunate signifier in a name. Laguz encourages deep cleansing and provides order for each of us. It also offers creative gifts in abundance. The Ansuz energy of signals indicates that Lola assumes a variety of lifestyles to suit her different audiences. Lola could find satisfaction in the performing arts because the Laguz energy gives her emotional depth. Othila, the rune of separation, makes Lola independent, open-minded, and very intuitive. She could enjoy choreographing, composing, directing, painting, or all of the above. Chances are good that Lola will meet with success in all of her artistic endeavors.

Elements: Air, water, earth/fire, water

THE NUMEROLOGICAL INTERPRETATION
Lola (NV = 4, CV = 6, VV = 7, FL = 3)

A romantic at heart and a poet by temperament, Lola is a woman who appreciates beauty in all its forms. She will therefore be attracted by the arts and make sure that her home is pleasing to the senses. Lola doesn't just want to go to a museum or an art gallery to be surrounded by beauty; she wants to own some herself. A hard worker, Lola seeks a partner who is both emotionally sensitive and materially secure. Lola's numbers also point to a woman who needs a peaceful and balanced environment in order to do her best work. She is less a seeker of excitement than a seeker of truth.

DERIVATION: Spanish and English, a shortened form of Dolores, from the Spanish word meaning "sorrows." Made popular partially due to the influence of Lola Montez (1818–1861), the Irish dancer and mistress of Louis I of Bavaria.

PRINCIPAL COLORS: Electric colors, any color of medium tone

GEMSTONES AND PRECIOUS METALS: Pale and deep, rich sapphires

BOTANICALS: Lesser celandine, sage, medlar

UNIQUE SPELLINGS: Lohla, Lohlah, Lohlla, Lowla, Lowlah

RELATED TO: Delora, Delorcita, Delorest, Deloria, Dolorita, Lolita, Loly

DERIVATION: English, of uncertain origin. Possibly an anglicized form of the Spanish name Alonzo or a variation of the name Lenny. Quite popular in the United States in the 1980s.

PRINCIPAL COLORS: All but the most brilliant shades of blue

GEMSTONES AND PRECIOUS METALS: Turquoise, emeralds

BOTANICALS: Violets, vervain, daffodils

UNIQUE SPELLINGS: Lahnie, Lahnnie, Lahnny, Lahny, Lonny

RELATED TO: Alonso, Alonzo†, Lennie, Lenny, Leonard†, Lon, Lonny, Lonzo; Loni

A KABBALISTIC SYNOPSIS
לעני —LA'ANY (Lamed, Ayin, Nun, Yod)

Lonnie's name is closely associated with symbols of success, which suggests that Lonnie will lead a relatively untroubled life, free from any major worries or concerns. In Lonnie's case, the desired success is not so much financial as it is emotional. Lonnie has a real urge to build a perfect family, and he or she has every chance of doing so. While it may not be Lonnie's major focus, it is probable that Lonnie will also do very well financially. Lonnie is happy to sacrifice a great deal of time for his or her children. What little time Lonnie allows for his or her own interests is often spent preparing a gourmet meal or handcrafting a piece of furniture—hobbies that bring pleasure to others as much as to Lonnie. However, the energetic letter Y, or Yod, which comes at the end of this name suggests a new lease on life in retirement, when Lonnie will reap the many rewards earned by being so unselfish.

THE RUNIC INTERPRETATION
ᛖᛁᚾᚾᛟᛚ (Ehwaz, Isa, Nauthiz, Nauthiz, Othila, Laguz)

The double Nauthiz rune of constraint characterizes this name. Constraint brings lessons of resourcefulness, positive attitudes, resiliency, and perseverance. This name also offers the Othila rune of separation and the Laguz rune of flow. Lonnie is independent and capable of original thinking. People named Lonnie can think their way through difficult problems and employ considerable intuitive powers provided by the Laguz energy of this name. This resourcefulness will give Lonnie a strategy for confronting any limitations and turning them into advantages.

Elements: Air, earth, fire, fire, earth/fire, water

THE NUMEROLOGICAL INTERPRETATION
Lonnie (NV = 6, CV = 4, VV = 2, FL = 3)

Supportive in relationships, adaptable and gentle, Lonnie bears a name that bestows charm, grace, and kindness. A peace-loving and healing nature is also an important component of Lonnie's personality. He or she works very well as a go-between, a mediator, and a harmonizer between opposing factions. Lonnie is good at these activities because of his or her own inner balance. Lonnie never wishes to hurt anyone's feelings—but must take care, then, not to compromise his or her own truth. Lonnie would work well in any career in the healing professions. Lonnie would also make a fine teacher for young people.

Loren

DERIVATION: English, short form of the German Lorenz or the Spanish and Italian Lorenzo, ultimately from the Latin *laurentius*, meaning "from Laurentium," a city in Latium. May also be a variant spelling of Lauren.

PRINCIPAL COLORS: All yellow and bronze shades, from the palest to the brightest

GEMSTONES AND PRECIOUS METALS: Yellow diamonds, amber

BOTANICALS: Eyebright, borage, Saint-John's-wort

UNIQUE SPELLINGS: Laurin, Lorin, Lorren, Lorrin

RELATED TO: Lawrence‖, Lorenz, Lorenzo†

A Kabbalistic Synopsis

לערֿאן —LA'ARAN (Lamed, Ayin, Resh, Aleph, Nun)

It's hard to pin down someone as individual as Loren. He is resolutely determined not to fit into any recognizable category or pigeonhole. This means that we can say more about his innate nature than we can about the exact way he will live his life. Loren is one of the most cheerful people you could wish to meet. In part, this is due to his refusal to buy into the nine-to-five routine, but it also comes from a naturally friendly character. He is absolutely a free spirit, and will attract many friends who are of a similar age but who may be mired in much more standard working lives. To them, Loren is like a breath of fresh air. The only thing that ever bothers Loren is a worry that people will assume that he doesn't take life seriously because of his unconventional lifestyle.

The Runic Interpretation

ᚺᛖᚱᛟᛚ (Nauthiz, Ehwaz, Raido, Othila, Laguz)

Loren likes to be on the go. The Raido rune for good communication and journey, coupled with Nauthiz for constraint and Othila for separation, give Loren a deep-rooted desire for freedom as well as a strong sense of himself. Loren knows what he wants in life, but he makes others aware of his wishes in a gracious way. Loren is probably athletic or at least knows that he feels wonderful when he is exercising regularly. The Ehwaz rune of movement adds to Loren's stamina and imagination, and gives him the urge to live in foreign countries and see the world. Laguz, the rune of flow, could mean that Loren is drawn to water and favors swimming as his sport. The rune of flow inclines him to music and dance as well.

Elements: Fire, air, water, earth/fire, water

The Numerological Interpretation

Loren (NV = 1, CV = 8, VV = 11, FL = 3)

Powerful is the best word to describe this name. Loren has a sense of his own potency and does not hesitate to use it. He is ambitious and clear about his goals in life. He has the potential to develop his intuition to a very advanced degree, allowing him to see another person's true nature with great precision and accuracy. Loren seeks to develop all of his potential and is possessed of a good deal of willpower. He is energized and ready to go—and he goes! It is important for him to develop patience and tolerance for those who may move at a slower pace but who may have a lot to teach and offer him.

DERIVATION: Italian and Spanish
form of Laurence, ultimately from
the Latin *laurentius*, meaning
"from Laurentium," a city in
Latium.

PRINCIPAL COLORS: Pale to
medium and rich blue

GEMSTONES AND PRECIOUS
METALS: Emeralds, blue and
blue-green turquoise

BOTANICALS: Dog rose, daffodils,
almonds

UNIQUE SPELLINGS: Laurenso,
Laurenzo, Lorenso

RELATED TO: Laurence,
Lawrence†, Lorent†, Lorenz, Renzo

Lorenzo

A KABBALISTIC SYNOPSIS

לער’אנזע —LA'ARANZA'A (Lamed, Ayin,
Resh, Aleph, Nun, Zayin, Ayin)

Lorenzo is one of the few genuinely good guys in the world. Most people in this world act primarily in their own interest and may then spare some time and energy for others—not so Lorenzo. Thus it is quite appropriate that, when kabbalistically analyzed, his name has connections to a number of angelic beings, given Lorenzo's wholly altruistic attitude to life. When we use compression on his name we get the letters Tau, Kaph, and Cheth. The Tau tells us that Lorenzo believes in self-sacrifice for the greater good, so he is likely to do a lot of volunteer work. The Kaph indicates that in spite of his high principles he is essentially a practical man. The final Cheth means "fence" or "enclosure," and shows that the prime motivator in Lorenzo's selfless life is a desire to protect people.

THE RUNIC INTERPRETATION

ᛟᛉᚾᛖᚱᛟᛚ (Othila, Algiz, Nauthiz, Ehwaz, Raido, Othila, Laguz)

Guardian angels encircle Lorenzo like a scene in a Florentine painting. Algiz, the rune of protection, ensures Lorenzo a stable personality. The impulsiveness or extreme high and low moods that most people experience when they are faced with major changes are buffered in Lorenzo's life. The Laguz rune of flow adds subtlety and charm to his personality; this helps him cope with life's ups and downs. The Nauthiz rune of constraint sets up limitations and challenges for Lorenzo, which he surmounts. Lorenzo is always able to rise to the occasion. Unsentimental and capable of discarding worn-out opinions and relationships, Lorenzo gets his strength and decisiveness from the double Othila configuration in his name. The Ehwaz rune of movement and the Raido rune for journey mean Lorenzo will travel and relocate with relish several times in his life.

Elements: Earth/fire, air, fire, air, water, earth/fire, water

THE NUMEROLOGICAL INTERPRETATION

Lorenzo (NV = 6, CV = 7, VV = 8, FL = 3)

This is a name that has "lover" written all over it! But what does Lorenzo love? The name value of six points to home, family, and a settled emotional life. It also means that Lorenzo has a love of beauty that connects him to painting, music, finely prepared food, and beautiful people. The vowel value of eight gives him a love of success, financial abundance, and material objects. Finally, the consonant value of seven gives Lorenzo a love of philosophy. Perhaps it will be through the latter that he comes to understand the deeper meaning behind all his other "loves."

Loretta

A KABBALISTIC SYNOPSIS
לער'אטטא —LA'ARATTA (Lamed, Ayin, Resh, Aleph, Teth, Teth, Aleph)

If Loretta's family saw her at work they would be amazed . . . as would her colleagues if they could be a fly on the wall in her home. In the office Loretta is happy-go-lucky and is always ready to help a coworker in times of trouble. She is ambitious, but she will get her promotions through commitment and hard work rather than through office politics. At home it is a very different story. In the evenings, Loretta has a tendency to unleash pent-up resentment and residual bad feelings from her job. The dual appearance of Teth, meaning "serpent," in her name indicates that Loretta can be spiteful when she wants to be, and the family will soon learn that in the first hour after she gets home it is best to stay out of her way. On the positive side, her ability to be herself at home means that her family will get the benefit of Loretta at her most relaxed, when she is great fun to be with.

THE RUNIC INTERPRETATION
ᚨᛏᛏᛖᚱᛟᛚ (Ansuz, Teiwaz, Teiwaz, Ehwaz, Raido, Othila, Laguz)

Patient and discriminating, Loretta is strong and self-contained. The double Teiwaz rune of warrior in this name is associated with masculine energy and the sun. Loretta prefers to be active and considers herself broad-minded and fair. She can laugh at herself and at the foibles of the human condition. The Ansuz rune of signals indicates that Loretta is intuitive and she trusts her inner sense of timing when there's a decision to be made. The Laguz rune of flow shows that Loretta is musical and artistic and could enjoy a career in the fine arts or law. She might also be interested or involved in sports.

Elements: Air, air, air, air, water, earth/fire, water

THE NUMEROLOGICAL INTERPRETATION
Loretta (NV = 1, CV = 7, VV = 3, FL = 3)

There is little doubt that Loretta is a unique individual. Her name gives her a strong need to express herself in ways that establish her sense of her own "I am" in no uncertain terms. Yet, interestingly enough, Loretta is not an egotist. Her sense of self is connected with a wider view of the world, one that leads her down a life path filled with opportunities for philosophical and spiritual investigation. She is a person who loves her friends and is always present to share both good and bad times. Loretta also enjoys periods of solitude, especially those spent with a good book in hand.

DERIVATION: English, variant spelling of Lauretta, ultimately from the Latin male name Laurus, meaning "laurel."

PRINCIPAL COLORS: The full range of yellow hues, also gold, bronze, orange

GEMSTONES AND PRECIOUS METALS: Citrine, topaz, yellow diamonds

BOTANICALS: Chamomile, eyebright, thyme

UNIQUE SPELLINGS: Laurettah, Lorehta, Lorehtta, Lorettah, Lorrehta

RELATED TO: Laura†, Laureen, Laurel, Laurent†, Lauretta, Laurette, Lauriane, Loreen, Lorena, Lorene, Lorenza, Lorette, Lorinda, Lorine, Lorita, Lorna, Lorraine†

DERIVATION: English, variant spelling of Laurie. From the Latin male name Laurus, meaning "laurel." Extremely popular in the United States in the 1960s.

PRINCIPAL COLORS: All shades of red, especially the dark, rich tones

GEMSTONES AND PRECIOUS METALS: Deep red bloodstones, rubies

BOTANICALS: Nettle, onion, wormwood

UNIQUE SPELLINGS: Lauri, Laurie, Lorey, Lorie, Lorri, Lorry

RELATED TO: Delores†, Laura†, Laureen, Laurel, Laurent†, Lauretta, Lauriane, Loreen, Lorena, Lorene, Lorenza, Loretta†, Lorette, Lorinda, Lorine, Lorita, Lorna, Lorraine†

A KABBALISTIC SYNOPSIS
לערי —LA'ARY (Lamed, Ayin, Resh, Yod)

Competition is Lori's middle name. This is great in terms of career advancement, but it can be a real pain for her family when all they want is a relaxed game and it becomes an Olympic competition! It has to be said, though, that Lori is not just a good loser; she also has a great sense of humor. She is not afraid to laugh at herself for her excessive zeal and determined approach to life. However, you can be sure that her kids will always have the most fancy costumes come Halloween. In other respects Lori is very down-to-earth, and even when Lori's career has really taken off, there is not a hint of snobbery in anything that Lori does or says.

THE RUNIC INTERPRETATION
ᛁᚱᛟᛚ (Isa, Raido, Othila, Laguz)

Editing, writing, music, or other careers involving scrutiny and timing suit Lori's talents. Never one to give up easily, Lori can handle tasks that would make a weaker soul fold. Lori has Isa for standstill in her name, signifying her need to spend time alone and her great facility with details. The powerful Laguz rune of flow is associated with the moon or an emotional, lunar nature. This positioning indicates that Lori's emotions are near the surface, and she laughs and cries easily. The lunar nature responds well to music, which soothes and delights Lori on a deeper level than it does most people. Lori is able to benefit by the Othila rune of separation, which allows her to keep her life free of extraneous detail. She'll travel (the Raido rune urges her on) to see the world, but in a streamlined fashion.

Elements: Earth, water, earth/fire, water

THE NUMEROLOGICAL INTERPRETATION
Lori (NV = 9, CV = 3, VV = 6, FL = 3)

Lori is a sympathetic and compassionate woman, very much given over to assisting others in distress. Her name indicates that she is very well suited to one of the helping professions, such as counselor, healer, or teacher. Lori is possessed by an idealistic and romantic spirit. This leads her into a number of profound, emotionally charged relationships. She needs to take an objective view about other people's needs so that she does not lose herself while trying to be of service to others. Lori's attachment to her mother and to mothering are central aspects of her life. Even if she does not have any children, she will offer a caring and maternal attitude to friends and strangers alike. Because of this, she also needs to be aware of her own emotional boundaries.

Lorraine

A KABBALISTIC SYNOPSIS

לעראין —LA'ARAYN (Lamed, Ayin, Resh, Aleph, Yod, Nun)

Lorraine is quite an unassuming woman who is more than happy to stay in the background, especially at work. She is a proficient and dedicated worker, but she has seen too many people lose their families through career-related stress to go chasing after that great promotion. To Lorraine, family is everything, and she sees her role as the glue that holds the family together. It might not be a very modern outlook, but it is hers, and she is more than happy with the resulting lifestyle. It has to be said that Lorraine makes sure that she does have some time for herself, and is not one to make a martyr of herself. She loves to socialize and is likely to have a wide circle of friends who will become more and more important to her as the children grow up.

THE RUNIC INTERPRETATION

 MᚺIᚨᚱᚱ♈ᚾ (Ehwaz, Nauthiz, Isa, Ansuz, Raido, Raido, Othila, Laguz)

Listening is the most important part of conversation to Lorraine. She is a good communicator and has a natural counseling ability. People can't wait to phone her at the end of a frenzied day. The Othila rune for separation, along with the Laguz rune of flow, helps her keep her conversational style clear and flowing. The Nauthiz rune brings constraint and assumes that Lorraine is patient and will try to help people solve their problems. The intuition of Ansuz helps Lorraine overcome limitations. She has sophisticated perspectives, and the Ehwaz rune for movement spurs her on to explore the world and live abroad, or to look inward and learn more about herself.

Elements: Air, fire, earth, air, water, water, earth/fire, water

THE NUMEROLOGICAL INTERPRETATION

Lorraine (NV = 11, CV = 8, VV = 3, FL = 3)

Lorraine's numbers indicate a strong sense of personal drive and practical ambition. Lorraine's name value is a master number, eleven. She may thus find that her vocation can become her avocation. If this is the case, Lorraine may well work in some community affairs or public service program in order to advance the welfare of a large number of people. No matter what the form of her profession, Lorraine will want to reach out to people, as communication is very essential to the expression of her true nature.

DERIVATION: English and Scottish, from a surname denoting someone from the province of Lorraine in eastern France. Lorraine, in turn, is derived from the Latin *lotharingia*, meaning "territory of the people of Lothar." Especially popular in the United States in the 1940s.

PRINCIPAL COLORS: White, pale to bright and deep green

GEMSTONES AND PRECIOUS METALS: Jade, moonstones, pearls

BOTANICALS: Chicory, cucumber, plantain

UNIQUE SPELLINGS: Laraine, Laurraine, Lorain, Loraine, Lorane, Lorayne, Lorrane, Lorrayne

RELATED TO: Laurat, Laureen, Laurel, Laurent, Lauretta, Lauriane, Loreen, Lorena, Lorene, Lorenza, Lorettat, Lorette, Lorit, Lorinda, Lorina, Lorine, Lorita; Lorna

DERIVATION: French, from the Germanic elements *hlud*, meaning "fame," and *wig*, meaning "warrior." The name of eighteen kings of France from the eighth century on. Especially common in the United States in the beginning of the twentieth century.

PRINCIPAL COLORS: The full spectrum of moderately shaded hues

GEMSTONES AND PRECIOUS METALS: Sapphires

BOTANICALS: Celandine, sage, wintergreen

UNIQUE SPELLINGS: Lewes, Lewist

RELATED TO: Lew, Lewie, Lou, Louie

A KABBALISTIC SYNOPSIS
לוים —LVYS (Lamed, Vau, Yod, Samech)

Louis has immense drive to do something important with his life. The only problem? He can't decide what it is that he is going to do. Louis is terminally indecisive and really needs a push before he will take decisive action on anything. This is a real shame, as Louis is without doubt an intelligent and talented individual. He need not get too depressed, though; Louis is very good in relationships, and provides masses of moral support to his partner in whatever it is that they want to do. He can then rely on his partner to give him the push—or possibly, the kick!—that he needs to get himself motivated and committed to one particular goal. Once he has this direction, the sky is the limit.

THE RUNIC INTERPRETATION
ᛋᛁᚢᛟᛚ (Sowelu, Isa, Uruz, Othila, Laguz)

Being emotionally strong is such a help . . . and luckily, Louis is positively affected by the Sowelu rune for wholeness and the Uruz rune for strength. Louis probably keeps physically strong by lifting weights or practicing the martial arts or some other form of body building. Louis has a strong sense of identity as well, and the Othila rune for separation gives him an ability to discard relationships that can become codependent or a big energy drain for him. Louis has a generous nature, and when he overextends himself, the Isa rune of isolation is there to help him rejuvenate and rest. Handsome Louis the heartbreaker needs to shore himself up now and then. The Laguz rune of flow helps him keep his emotions in balance.

Elements: Air, earth, earth, earth/fire, water

THE NUMEROLOGICAL INTERPRETATION
Louis (NV = 4, CV = 4, VV = 9, FL = 3)

Louis is well organized mentally, with a physical dexterity to match. This name is well suited to a man who can combine head and hand to make a success of himself in the world. Louis is stable and efficient, loyal and steadfast, with a nature that people come to depend upon. Louis plays by the rules. He enjoys creating routines and habit patterns that he knows will work for him. He has to take care that these same structures that work out so positively in the short run do not inhibit his growth and possibilities for future expansion. Louis always has to be prepared to let go and release what is no longer a proper tool for his growth.

Louise

DERIVATION: French and English, feminine form of Louis, which is from the Germanic elements *hlud*, meaning "fame," and *wig*, meaning "warrior." Very popular in the United States at the end of the nineteenth century.

PRINCIPAL COLORS: Light pink to deep, rich and brilliant reds

GEMSTONES AND PRECIOUS METALS: Garnets, rubies

BOTANICALS: Borage, garlic, wormwood, pepper

UNIQUE SPELLINGS: Loise, Loyise, Luise

RELATED TO: Aloisa, Aloysia, Eloisa, Eloise, Heloisa, Heloise, Loist, Louisa, Louisetta, Louisette, Louisiane, Lu, Ludovica, Luisa, Lula, Lulita

A Kabbalistic Synopsis
לויז —LVYZ (Lamed, Vau, Yod, Zayin)

Life for Louise is an emotional journey. There is a strong desire to feel complete, and most of her life is spent in search of this ideal state of being. This doesn't mean that she is a depressed individual; far from it. Louise has large numbers of friends, and her greatest pleasure in life is making new friends and forging new and varied relationships. When Louise does find her perfect match, she will not be able to contain herself, and her usually cheerful demeanor will be transformed into an absolutely radiant appearance. Louise is ideally suited to work that is focused on assisting people, and the satisfaction she gets from her work is far more important to her than career advancement. Louise loves a peaceful home environment, and one of her favorite ways to relax is to putter about in her carefully tended garden.

The Runic Interpretation
ᛗᛋᛁᚾᛟᛚ (Ehwaz, Sowelu, Isa, Uruz, Othila, Lagaz)

Louise is private, and while she enjoys conversation, she really values her time alone. Louise might enjoy knitting or collecting treasures from around the world. The Sowelu rune of wholeness combined with Uruz for strength is a great combination, indicating depth of character and perseverance. Louise has the Ehwaz rune of movement, and will live in foreign lands and travel when anyone suggests it! Laguz for flow signifies that Louise can establish a nice and easy rapport with people, who will always enjoy spending time with Louise.

Elements: Air, air, earth, earth, earth/fire, water

The Numerological Interpretation
Louise (NV = 9, CV = 4, VV = 5, FL = 3)

Louise has a name that is very connected to manifesting her ideals in physical form. This means looking for the perfect partner, the perfect profession, and the perfect pattern for success. Louise can be a perfectionist. She may enjoy design work or any other profession that allows her to improve upon ideas or concepts until they meet her expectations. Louise will encounter a lot of opportunities for friendship and material reward in her life. She has a very active mind, and a vivid intelligence. As such, she is given to making many changes in life. Such shifts and movements also alter her ideal of perfection. But in the meantime, Louise would do well to learn how to live in and accept each moment as perfection in itself.

"Love is the great miracle cure. Loving ourselves works miracles in our lives."

—LOUISE HAY (AUTHOR)

Lowell

DERIVATION: English, from the Old French, meaning "young wolf." Made popular by the New England poet Robert Lowell (1917–1977).

PRINCIPAL COLORS: From lightly shaded to brilliant yellow and green, gold

GEMSTONES AND PRECIOUS METALS: Moonstones, pearls, Cat's-eye

BOTANICALS: Elder, hops, juniper

UNIQUE SPELLINGS: Loel, Loell, Lohwel, Lohwell, Lowel

RELATED TO: Lovel, Lovell

❧

"Do a little more each day than you think you possibly can."
—LOWELL THOMAS (AUTHOR)

A KABBALISTIC SYNOPSIS
לעואל —LA'AVAL (Lamed, Ayin, Vau, Aleph, Lamed)

The average life has never appealed to Lowell. The thought of a reasonably good job in an office that offers security and a pension fills him with horror. To Lowell, the world of commerce and business is far too pressurized for anyone to truly be themselves and remain within it. He is an extremely sensitive man who has a tendency to absorb the atmosphere around him. Consequently, it is more important to him than most that he work in a situation that complements his own personality and values. His sensitivity, intuition, and skill as a wordsmith make him an excellent poet, and it may well be that he follows his talent with the intention of making a name as a writer. Lowell is not at all interested in casual relationships, and will not become involved with anyone unless he thinks it has the potential to become serious.

THE RUNIC INTERPRETATION
ᚾᚾᛗᛈᛟᚾ (Laguz, Laguz, Ehwaz, Wunjo, Othila, Laguz)

Wunjo, the rune of joy, offers Lowell positive energy. When it combines in Lowell's name with the triple Laguz energy of flow, it blesses him with material gain or a sense of well-being or emotional freedom, as well as a love of rhythm and a love of music. Lowell can enjoy a career in the performing arts. If his bent is scientific, he could use these talents as a systems engineer or in chaos physics or any number of mathematical applications. Lowell is flexible, calm, and soothing to be around.

Elements: Water, water, air, earth, earth/fire, water

THE NUMEROLOGICAL INTERPRETATION
Lowell (NV = 9, CV = 9, VV = 7, FL = 3)

Lowell is a name that expresses generosity, benevolence, and patience. He is a man who naturally seeks to help other people grow and develop. Lowell is most naturally able to accomplish this through the sharing of his deep perceptions of life, and he makes an excellent teacher, scientist, or writer. This is a person who understands the ebb and flow of life and is aware of the cyclic rhythm within which we all live. Lowell is given to long periods of contemplation and solitude, and would thus seek a partner who is rather independent by nature. The challenging side to this name has to do with Lowell's propensity to go to extremes to promote his ideals and beliefs. He thus has to guard against a tendency to be too self-righteous.

❧

Lucas

A Kabbalistic Synopsis
לוכאס —LVKAS (Lamed, Vau, Kaph, Aleph, Samech)

If Lucas has just gambled away a week's salary, rather than fall into a dark depression about it, he is more likely to be convinced that if he just gives it one more try he will get it all back. Lucas is incorrigibly optimistic; it seems nothing will bring him down. This is largely a good thing, but as in the example above, he can be led into making some less-than-sensible decisions. Workwise, Lucas is not looking to make a big name for himself, although he enjoys the camaraderie of the workplace. The influences of his name suggest that a job related to infrastructure, such as highway management, would suit Lucas. His partner will have a lot of fun being with Lucas, as he certainly knows how to lift people out of the doldrums and can be a wonderful listener when he needs to be.

The Runic Interpretation
ᛋᚨᚲᚢᛚ (Sowelu, Ansuz, Kano, Uruz, Laguz)

Lucas might feel comfortable in a job involving water such as underwater photography. The Laguz rune of flow of his name indicates this. The Uruz rune gives Lucas strength, and the Kano rune provides his receptive nature. The Ansuz rune suggests good intuitive ability, and the Sowelu signifies wholeness. Lucas could benefit from some boundaries and deadlines, for he could easily become a procrastinator. He values his freedom but is most productive when answering to outside accountability. Lucas has an original mind, and the Uruz energy of strength ensures good stamina and balance in all areas.

Elements: Air, air, water, earth, water

The Numerological Interpretation
Lucas (NV = 11, CV = 7, VV = 4, FL = 3)

There are several gifts associated with this name, but first and foremost is the gift of intuition. When developed, Lucas has a special insight into life that permits him to feel an instantaneous bond with all people. This leaves him free of prejudice and gives him a universal and inclusive sense about life. Lucas also possesses an investigative mind, one that seeks to perceive beyond superficiality to see the inner truth standing behind life's outer events and circumstances. Lucas requires a profession that allows him space for his explorations, and he would do well as a scientist, teacher, or economist. He could receive a great deal of benefit working with professional or special-interest groups and organizations, as he enjoys sharing information with like-minded men and women.

DERIVATION: English, a form of Luke, from the Latin name Lucanus, meaning "man from Lucania," a region of southern Italy. Used almost exclusively as a surname until the 1930s.

PRINCIPAL COLORS: Any green hue, white, cream

GEMSTONES AND PRECIOUS METALS: Moonstones, pearls

BOTANICALS: Colewort, moonwort, lettuce

UNIQUE SPELLINGS: Loocas, Lookas, Loukas, Lukas

RELATED TO: Luc, Lucian, Lucien, Lucio, Lucius, Luck, Lucky, Luke†

DERIVATION: French form of Lucilla, which is the Latin form of Lucia. Ultimately derived from the Latin *lux*, meaning "light." Quite popular in the 1950s and 1960s, probably due to the influence of the comedienne Lucille Ball (1911–1989).

PRINCIPAL COLORS: The full range of greens and whites, including cream

GEMSTONES AND PRECIOUS METALS: Jade, moonstones, Cat's-eye

BOTANICALS: Chicory, plantain

UNIQUE SPELLINGS: Lewcile, Lewseal, Lucile, Luseal

RELATED TO: Luce, Lucetta, Lucette, Luci, Lucía, Luciana, Lucida, Lucie, Lucienne, Lucila, Lucilia, Lucilla, Lucina, Lucinda, Lucine, Lucita, Lucy†, Luz†

A KABBALISTIC SYNOPSIS
לוסיאל —LVSYAL (Lamed, Vau, Samech, Yod, Aleph, Lamed)

Interestingly, Lucille shares the same name value with Lowell†. As has been explained elsewhere, in Kabbalah, names that share the same numerical value are connected in terms of their meaning. Lucille is as unconventional as Lowell, and is equally unwilling to submit herself to the mainstream. However, in her case, she has considerably more willpower and strength of character. Lucille is not what you could describe as sensitive; she tends to be blatantly outrageous and delights in her own nonconformity. She will probably be involved in the arts, but her extroverted nature and driving energy make her more suited to the role of agent or promoter than artist. Lucille likes to have fun, and any partner will have to have plenty of stamina if they're going to keep up with her hectic lifestyle. Lucille doesn't have much time for romantic declarations; she will demonstrate her feelings through her actions.

THE RUNIC INTERPRETATION
ᛖᛚᛚᛁᛋᚢᛚ (Ehwaz, Laguz, Laguz, Isa, Sowelu, Uruz, Laguz)

Take Lucille on a long walk by the sea on a moonlit evening and she will be your valentine! The powerful Laguz rune brings with it emotional sensitivity and an appreciation of inspiration. And the triple Laguz energy is always the mark of a gifted dancer, mathematician, or musician. Mystery and subtlety captivate Lucille. She enjoys concerts and theater, and could enjoy a career in the performing arts. Lucille gives from her heart, and the Isa rune is there to encourage Lucille to save some energy for herself. Lucille is optimistic, healthy, and blessed with all the benefits that befit the Uruz rune of strength.

Elements: Air, water, water, earth, air, earth, water

THE NUMEROLOGICAL INTERPRETATION
Lucille (NV = 11, CV = 3, VV = 8, FL = 3)

Lucille is likely to handle the strong mental energy of the master number eleven in her name in one of two ways. If gifted with the expanded vision of this number, she will want to contribute to some form of social welfare and participate in community work and public service. But if communicating with large numbers of people is not her orientation, she will use her intuitive understanding of others in more personal and practical realms, working at uniting and harmonizing with people on a one-to-one level. Lucille is a "people person"; her friends are very important her. She can be relied upon for her loyalty, support, and caring. It may be easier for her to feel intimate with friends than with her family or her life partner.

Lucy

DERIVATION: English form of Lucia, ultimately derived from the Latin *lux*, meaning "light." Often associated with Lucy Stone (1818–1893), the American reformer and advocate of women's rights.

PRINCIPAL COLORS: The full gamut of green and yellow hues

GEMSTONES AND PRECIOUS METALS: White pearls, moonstones, moss agate

BOTANICALS: Blackberry, juniper, linseed

UNIQUE SPELLINGS: Luci, Lucie

RELATED TO: Luce, Lucetta, Lucette, Lucia, Luciana, Lucida, Lucie, Lucila, Lucilla, Lucillet, Lucinda, Lucita, Luz!

A KABBALISTIC SYNOPSIS

לוסי —LVSY (Lamed, Vau, Samech, Yod)

Lucy is going to be a successful woman, and nothing will stand in her way. She is not particularly pushy but simply has the force of destiny behind her, making a high level of achievement inevitable. The compression of her name reveals her to be both witty and naturally understanding of complex problems. Lucy is able to find solutions to seemingly intractable difficulties, and makes an excellent ideas person in any business. She is incredibly enthusiastic, and her excitement is often infectious. If you are taking Lucy out on a date, you should avoid the obvious. Rather than taking her to dinner, try taking her on a boat trip or to a comedy show. She will appreciate your originality.

THE RUNIC INTERPRETATION

(Eihwaz, Sowelu, Uruz, Laguz)

Happy-go-lucky Lucy: the Uruz rune gives her strength and fortitude physically, spiritually, mentally, and emotionally. Laguz brings her benefits in romance. But before she settles on Mr. Right, Lucy needs to expand her vision of herself and seize some of her Sowelu energy for wholeness. She is capable but so deeply frightened of success! The Eihwaz energy of defense makes Lucy sabotage her own valiant efforts at times. Once she understands that the Eihwaz rune in her name can be used to guard her from negativity, she will be on her way to a generous and productive life.

Elements: Earth/fire, air, earth, water

THE NUMEROLOGICAL INTERPRETATION

Lucy (NV = 7, CV = 6, VV = 1, FL = 3)

There is a definite kindness associated with this name. Lucy is a charming woman who enjoys bringing happiness into other people's lives. Her home and family are very much at the center of her daily life, and her career focus is balanced and tempered by the needs of her loved ones. Lucy has a strong urge to individualize her own nature and looks for ways in which she can be creatively self-expressive. She may easily find this in the arts, as she is attracted to beauty in her life. She may work in one of the healing professions, where she can use her compassion and understanding of others.

487

DERIVATION: English, from the Greek name Loukas, meaning "from Lucania," a region of southern Italy. In the New Testament, Saint Luke the Evangelist is the author of one of the four Gospels and the Acts of the Apostles.

PRINCIPAL COLORS: All hues of medium tone, electric colors

GEMSTONES AND PRECIOUS METALS: Sapphires

BOTANICALS: Sage, spinach, Solomon's seal

UNIQUE SPELLINGS: Looke, Luc

RELATED TO: Lucas†, Lucian, Lucien, Lucio, Lucius, Luck, Lucky, Lukas

Luke

A KABBALISTIC SYNOPSIS
לוכ —LVK (Lamed, Vau, Kaph)

The value of Luke's name is fifty-six, which is a very powerful number and is made by the multiplication of the number seven, representing success, and the number eight, representing strength of character. Luke is pretty much guaranteed a good life thanks to these forces in the value of his name. However, Luke is not really interested in material success. In fact, he may turn down the chance for monetary wealth in favor of a work environment that he finds more enjoyable and sociable. Luke loves to party and so will his partner; it is a prerequisite for Luke in a relationship. This love of a good time will not mellow as Luke gets older. He will probably be—quite literally—the oldest swinger in town! Luke does have a serious side, and he takes his emotional loyalties very seriously. If you are a friend of Luke's, you can be sure that he will never let you down.

THE RUNIC INTERPRETATION
MKΠΓ (Ehwaz, Kano, Uruz, Laguz)

Always interested in the finer things life has to offer, Luke sometimes finds himself just a tiny bit overdrawn at the bank. His credit cards carry generous balances to be paid off as well. What's a tasteful and sophisticated gent to do? Stay home now and then . . . but one reason Luke gets overextended is that he loves to travel and live in remote places. He prefers an interesting and varied life to one of predictability and security. The Uruz rune gives him the strength to withstand strange foods and weather conditions. The Kano rune of opening helps Luke empathize with the people he meets in his travels. He learns languages and customs and makes himself right at home with the headhunters of Papua New Guinea or Timbuktu. The Laguz rune of flow gives him an interest in foreign music and dance, so that someday he can come home and possibly earn a living based on what he has learned on his many adventures.

Elements: Air, water, earth, water

THE NUMEROLOGICAL INTERPRETATION
Luke (NV = 4, CV = 5, VV = 8, FL = 3)

Luke is a name that carries a strong practical vibration. Luke's physical possessions are important to him, and he takes care to preserve what he has worked so hard to achieve. He likes to look good and keep up his physical appearance and health. There is an expansive side to his nature, but he tends to ignore it, preferring instead to funnel his experiences into avenues that solidify his position in life. Luke looks for reliability and loyalty in all of his relationships and prefers to be in control. Unless he is linked with a very submissive partner, this characteristic can certainly bring some potential conflict into his relationships.

Luther

DERIVATION: English, originally a German surname from the elements *lúit*, meaning "people," and *heri*, meaning "army." Often used to honor the Protestant reformer and theologian Martin Luther (1483–1546).

PRINCIPAL COLORS: All shades of violet, from mauve through deep maroon

GEMSTONES AND PRECIOUS METALS: Garnets, amethyst

BOTANICALS: Bilberry, strawberry, mint

UNIQUE SPELLINGS: Loother, Loothur, Luthur

RELATED TO: Lotario, Lothair, Lothar, Lothario, Lutero

A KABBALISTIC SYNOPSIS
לותר —LVThR (Lamed, Vau, Tau, Resh)

Luther is not an easy man to talk to; he is friendly enough, but his topics of conversation tend to be depressing. Luther is a deeply philosophical individual whose particular interests tend to be fairly metaphysical in nature. He is concerned about the relationship between the individual and the cosmos or the divine, if such a thing exists. It is probable that he is employed in some academic capacity, and that it is his job to think about such things. However, Luther is also concerned at a very personal level about the amount of suffering in the world, and spends a lot of time trying to understand why it exists and what can be done to alleviate it. His partner will have to get used to this side of his nature but will probably not mind, as Luther is an immensely understanding lover and will do his utmost to ensure the happiness of his partner. Those people who know Luther in a social capacity will also tell you that once he has got his philosophical meanderings out of the way, he is as happy as the next person to have a drink, a good laugh, and a good gossip!

THE RUNIC INTERPRETATION
ᚱᛖᚦᚢᛚ (Raido, Ehwaz, Thurisaz, Uruz, Laguz)

Talent and charm describe Luther's attributes. Dancing comes easily to Luther, who has the Uruz rune of strength, Ehwaz for movement, Raido for journey, and Laguz for flow. Where can Luther go with all these talents? The Thurisaz rune of gateway teaches Luther that he can go in any number of directions and express his gifts; he needs only focus and dedication. Luther also needs a bit more self-confidence, and this will come as he matures and realizes how fortunate he is to have so many blessings in life. Chances are good fortune will shine on Luther.

Elements: Water, air, fire, earth, water

THE NUMEROLOGICAL INTERPRETATION
Luther (NV = 3, CV = 22, VV = 8, FL = 3)

This is one of the rare names that carries the energy of the master number twenty-two. As such, Luther is certain to undertake large projects. He is very open to those challenges in life that meet his demanding need for establishing himself firmly and prominently in the world. Luther wants his influence to be seen and felt by a large group of people. The number eight is also an important component of this name, and when combined with twenty-two, you certainly have a master builder. Luke is therefore very enterprising, with a keen eye for opportunities that advance his plans and projects. He is a very charismatic and magnetic man who can wield a lot of influence over others.

DERIVATION: Spanish, from the
common word meaning "light."
Another title of the Virgin Mary,
who is called Santa María de Luz.

PRINCIPAL COLORS: The full
spectrum of very pale hues

GEMSTONES AND PRECIOUS
METALS: Silver, diamonds

BOTANICALS: Hazel, sweet
marjoram, oats

UNIQUE SPELLING: Luce

RELATED TO: Luce, Lucetta,
Lucette, Lucía, Luciana, Lucida,
Lucie, Lucila, Lucilla, Lucillet,
Lucinda, Lucita, Lucy†

Luz

A KABBALISTIC SYNOPSIS
לוז —LVZ (Lamed, Vau, Zayin)

One kabbalistic equivalent of Luz is the word "rejoice," and Luz is a great lover of celebration. If possible, Luz would have Christmas every day. This love of joyful events may lead Luz into a career such as conference organizing, party management, or possibly night club management. The presence of the letter Zayin, meaning "sword" or "armor," lets us know that despite an enjoyment of parties and fun, Luz is not in any way naive or gullible. Luz will make sure that whatever venture she is involved in succeeds and that she gets her fair share of the rewards. With her family, Luz is great, and her children will have the most wonderful birthdays and holidays one could imagine. Luz retains a girlish sense of humor and can relate directly to children in an impressive way. Young at heart, she is more than likely also to spend time with the children of the neighborhood, and is the first to volunteer for any local children's events.

THE RUNIC INTERPRETATION
↑ᚢᛚ (Algiz, Uruz, Laguz)

Protection, strength, and flow characterize this name. Luz leaves a mark. She is hyperaware and, frankly, doesn't have the patience for pretenders and liars. Luz can spot a man of courage and conviction when he is still several blocks away. She also knows when danger lurks, and the Laguz energy of flow makes her particularly insightful about people and their vulnerabilities. Luz is gentle with the weak and a fierce opponent to the arrogant. She has good mental health and is well balanced, and she expects those close to her to share these same virtues. Luz is brave enough to realize that we see the world as we are.

Elements: Air, earth, water

THE NUMEROLOGICAL INTERPRETATION
Luz (NV = 5, CV = 11, VV = 3, FL = 3)

Personal freedom and independence are two of the most important characteristics found in this name. Luz is unafraid to enter into new and challenging situations. She thrives on change and movement and loves to travel. People enjoy her presence in their lives, as Luz is very vivacious and entertaining. She also has an interesting and expansive personality, one that is upbeat and optimistic. The master number eleven in her name gives her the potential to do a great deal of networking. Should she not live up to the higher nature of eleven, Luz will find that she dissipates her mental resources on more frivolous conversations. In any event, Luz is a woman with a high degree of nervous energy.

Lydia

A Kabbalistic Synopsis
לידיא —LYDYA (Lamed, Yod, Daleth, Yod, Aleph)

Lydia shares the value of her name with the secret name of the bottom level, or sephirah, on the Tree of Life, which represents the material, everyday world. This shared association means that Lydia is a very down-to-earth woman who is concerned with the practicalities of life rather than ideals or daydreams. This does not make her cynical, though; she has a great sensitivity to the suffering and needs of others. Lydia possesses great energy, as indicated by the two Ys, or Yods, in her name. She uses this energy to bring some brightness into the world of those who have little happiness. She is likely to work as a counselor or in social work, and will gain much satisfaction from seeing clients able to stand on their own two feet again. Lydia's name also means "the bride," and she has a hidden romantic nature that surfaces only when she is with her lover. At such moments, she is also prone to daydreamimg and frivolity.

The Runic Interpretation
ᚨᛁᛞᛇᛚ (Ansuz, Isa, Dagaz, Eihwaz, Laguz)

Where oh where is sweet Lydia? She's down by the seaside sifting sand. . . . Lydia needs time alone to reflect on the events and dreams in her life, and she can become physically ill if she has too hectic a schedule without a break. Lydia can work under pressure, if necessary, but she prefers not to. Lydia also profits by the Dagaz rune for breakthrough, Ansuz for signals, and Laguz for flow. These runes indicate that Lydia is vigilant, insightful, and receptive to trends and currents within her culture. Lydia could enjoy a career in fashion, advertising, or research.

Elements: Air, earth, fire, earth/fire, water

The Numerological Interpretation
Lydia (NV = 6, CV = 7, VV = 8, FL = 3)

Lydia is kind and generous. She is eager to please and is often found in the position of peace-maker. People will come to Lydia for advice and counsel, as she not only has a sympathetic ear but an inner wisdom as well. Her professional life is important to her. She may be most comfortable as a psychologist, teacher, or healer. It is important for Lydia to interact with others. She enjoys people, and they trust her.

DERIVATION: English, from the Greek, meaning "woman from Lydia," a region of Asia Minor. In the Bible, the name of a woman who was converted by Saint Paul. Especially popular in the eighteenth and nineteenth centuries.

PRINCIPAL COLORS: All but the brightest shades of blue

GEMSTONES AND PRECIOUS METALS: Blue and blue-green turquoise, emeralds

BOTANICALS: Dog rose, daffodils, vervain

UNIQUE SPELLINGS: Lidia, Lidya, Lydiah, Lydya

RELATED TO: Leda, Lida, Lidija, Lydie

⟿

"You find yourself refreshed in the presence of cheerful people. Why not make an honest effort to confer that pleasure on others? Half the battle is gained if you never allow yourself to say anything gloomy."
—LYDIA M. CHILD (AUTHOR, ABOLITIONIST)

DERIVATION: English and Scottish, originally a surname that denoted someone who came *de l'isle,* meaning "from the island." Commonly used as a first name in the United States since the 1930s.

PRINCIPAL COLORS: The full range of red hues, from pink to rich crimson

GEMSTONES AND PRECIOUS METALS: Bloodstones, rubies

BOTANICALS: Broom, garlic, nettle

UNIQUE SPELLINGS: Lile, Lisle, Lyall, Lyell, Lysle

RELATED TO: Lionel†

A KABBALISTIC SYNOPSIS
ליאל —LYAL (Lamed, Yod, Aleph, Lamed)

Holidays are little more than an extra quiet day at the office for Lyle. He is such a hard worker that he rarely takes one day off. This is great for his bank balance—assuming he gets overtime—but not much fun for his family. Ironically, the main reason that Lyle puts in so many hours is so that he can provide the best for his family. He feels an enormous pressure to do this, possibly from a sense of duty instilled in him as a child. The planet Saturn has an important influence on Lyle's name, which makes him worldly-wise but also quite a serious and somber man. However, the central position of the Yod and Aleph indicate that Lyle contains a lot of energy and a highly individual personality. All he is waiting for is the right person to unlock it.

THE RUNIC INTERPRETATION
ᛗᛚᛇᛚ (Ehwaz, Laguz, Eihwaz, Laguz)

Lyle can move. He hears the beat and his feet start to tap. Music goes into his body on a cellular level, a result of the double Laguz rune of flow. Just as a rest between notes makes each sound more distinct, Lyle needs to stop between projects and empty his mind, to allow fresh ideas to flow in an orderly and not overwhelming fashion. Ehwaz for movement appears in a prominent place in Lyle's name, and it promises that Lyle will have a chance to live in a foreign land some day. As long as he can dance and have time to himself, Lyle can make any spot his home.

Elements: Air, water, earth/fire, water

THE NUMEROLOGICAL INTERPRETATION
Lyle (NV = 9, CV = 6, VV = 3, FL = 3)

This is a name that carries a great deal of humanitarianism and compassion in its numbers. Lyle is mission oriented and is always responsible in his dealings with others. He is very aware of human weakness and never stands in judgment of people. Instead, he is there to help, counsel, and assist. Lyle has a deep sense of the spiritual and is devoted to his moral and philosophical principles. This is not a man who seeks superficial relationships. He is capable of real intimacy and tenderness. He desires a committed partnership and will be very discriminating in his choice of a loved one.

Lynette

A Kabbalistic Synopsis
ליגאט —LYNAT (Lamed, Yod, Nun, Aleph, Teth)

If you want to cheer up Lynette, take her to the biggest shopping mall and let her shop till she drops! The value of Lynette's name is one hundred, which is connected to the mystical number for the material world. It indicates a love of all things material, and a preference for things over thoughts. However, Lynette is not necessarily shallow; she simply sees life as a process of accumulation. The more things one has, the better one is doing in life. For Lynette this is not a bad way to approach the world, and the indications in Lynette's name are that she will do very well for herself. Interestingly, though, Lynette has a very traditional view of relationships, and will expect to be wooed and treated with respect before she will consider dating anybody. However, the most romantic wooer is not necessarily the one who will give Lynette the most enjoyable time in the long term. In fact, from a practical point of view the most unromantic of lovers can make the most reliable of partners for Lynette.

The Runic Interpretation
ᛗᛏᛏᛗᚺᛁᛚ
(Ehwaz, Teiwaz, Teiwaz, Ehwaz, Nauthiz, Eihwaz, Laguz)

Being drawn to a cause greater than the daily dramas of her own life has great appeal for Lynette. The double Teiwaz warrior runes keep Lynette idealistic and involved with world issues. Part of Lynette's motivation comes from a desire to see and learn about various cultures and people. With the double Ehwaz rune, Lynette may visit different continents and get her wish. She might also be more famous or better known in a foreign land than in her home country. Lynette has the power of the four elements in her name.

Elements: Air, air, air, air, fire, earth/fire, water

The Numerological Interpretation
Lynette (NV = 11, CV = 3, VV = 8, FL = 3)

The numbers in this name bode well for financial success. Whether or not it is achieved has to do with the way Lynette focuses her energy. These numbers reveal a very active mind and a vivid imagination. Sometimes these factors combine to give Lynette more energy than she can handle. However, Lynette does have an ability to structure and organize her life. In fact, she may be well suited to an executive position. On a personal level, she has a magnetic personality and a broad circle of friends. Relationships abound. To achieve success in an intimate partnership, Lynette has to be very clear about what she is seeking. Otherwise, she may have a tendency to move through a lot of potential partners.

DERIVATION: English, from a Welsh name meaning "idol." Made popular by the English poet Alfred Lord Tennyson in his "Idylls of the King." Also a derivative of Lynn, with the French diminutive suffix "ette."

PRINCIPAL COLORS: The full gamut of green shades, white

GEMSTONES AND PRECIOUS METALS: Jade, pearls

BOTANICALS: Chicory, cabbage, plantain

UNIQUE SPELLINGS: Linette, Linnett, Linnette, Lynnett

RELATED TO: Lin, Linell, Linn, Linnell, Lyn, Lyndel, Lyndell, Lynell, Lynelle, Lynn†, Lynna, Lynne, Lynnelle

DERIVATION: English, a shortened form of Linda, which is probably from the Spanish word meaning "pretty." Very popular in the twentieth century.

PRINCIPAL COLORS: Pale to deep, rich green; cream, white

GEMSTONES AND PRECIOUS METALS: Jade, cat's-eye

BOTANICALS: Chicory, cucumber, plantain

UNIQUE SPELLINGS: Lin, Linn, Lyn, Lynne

RELATED TO: Linda†, Linell, Linnell, Lyndel, Lyndell, Lynell, Lynelle, Lynette†, Lynna, Lynnelle, Melinda†

A KABBALISTIC SYNOPSIS
לינן —LYNN (Lamed, Yod, Nun, Nun)

You will never forget your first meeting with Lynn. She has an almost ethereal appearance and may come across as delicate or frail. Her natural shyness accentuates this impression, but in fact, although she may be shy, Lynn also has a supreme inner strength and is not frail at all. Lynn is an intensely emotional woman, which means that she feels things passionately, although she is often reluctant to speak about her feelings. She may be silent on a matter for months; then, when it becomes too much for her to hold in, she will expound on her feelings dramatically. This behavior stems from the influence of Scorpio in her name. She certainly knows how to keep a secret—another Scorpio trait—and for this reason makes an excellent friend.

THE RUNIC INTERPRETATION
ᚾᚾᛇᛚ (Nauthiz, Nauthiz, Eihwaz, Laguz)

Lynn is used to misfortune with the double Nauthiz rune of constraint in her name, but she comes to understand that setbacks in life can become beneficial. Nauthiz teaches us to value the lessons of adversity. Eihwaz, or defense, is just what the doctor ordered in this case, and this rune teaches Lynn to avert limitation and defeat. The Laguz rune of flow affords her one of the most prized characteristics of the millennium, and that is flexibility. Lynn will surely serve as an example in the years ahead. Her good sense of humor helps her to turn her problems into amusing stories for her many friends who love her dearly.

Elements: Fire, fire, earth/fire, water

THE NUMEROLOGICAL INTERPRETATION
Lynn (NV = 11, CV = 4, VV = 7, FL = 3)

An active mind and a profoundly insightful understanding of people give Lynn a lot of advantages in life. This name allows a person to combine an idealistic nature with a practical focus. Lynn can use these dual talents most effectively in a professional capacity, as Lynn takes her responsibilities seriously and is dedicated to the projects before her. She would do well in a career that is involved with communications and/or public service. Lynn is not a fickle person; she offers loyalty and faithfulness to her partner and expects nothing less in return. She can be very useful in coordinating and organizing group or community projects. Lynn has a very nice way of dealing with people, and no one that she meets is seen as a stranger.

Mack

A Kabbalistic Synopsis
מאח —MACh (Mem, Aleph, Cheth)

Mack doesn't really come of age until he has a family of his own—but from then on, he is a changed man. Until that point Mack likes to lead a classic bachelor life. He has his own seat in the bar and never misses a ball game. In short, he is generally a laid-back, easygoing guy with little sense of responsibility. However, once he is married Mack becomes one of the most protective men you could hope to meet. His family will always come first—especially his children, who as they get older may have to point out to him that they no longer need quite so much looking after! Mack is likely to have a very happy life, as his desires are simple and reasonable, and he is more than able to generate his own happiness. Careerwise, Mack will probably be content with any job that is regular and secure and gives him plenty of time to spend with his family.

The Runic Interpretation
ᚲᚲᚨᛗ (Kano, Kano, Ansuz, Mannaz)

Dispelling confusion is one of Mack's numerous talents; he's fortunate to have the double Kano runes of opening in his name, which provide clarity. For many of us, it's easier to give than to receive—but not Mack! Kano affords Mack a sterling sense of entitlement and the ability to receive blessings, benefits, and opportunities graciously. Chance encounters that prove fortuitous are one of the golden gifts of the Ansuz rune. Mack is aware of this, and he is able to seize opportunities that come his way on a regular basis. The Mannaz rune of self gives Mack the strength of character to rework limiting situations in such a way that positive outcomes ensue.

Elements: Water, water, air, air

The Numerological Interpretation
Mack (NV = 1, CV = 9, VV = 1, FL = 4)

Mack is a very energetic name, one that possesses inner strength and considerable fortitude. This is a man who is firm and direct. Mack can inspire others with his enthusiasm for life and his sense of personal direction. People tend to see him as a natural leader. Mack may not be so interested in telling others what to do, but he certainly likes to rule his own life and resists taking orders. He is therefore most suited to being self-employed or to working at a job where he is given authority over his own work. Diplomacy and group work may be challenging for him, as he is a rather independent person.

DERIVATION: Gaelic, from the root meaning "son of." Often a nickname for longer names beginning with "Mac."

PRINCIPAL COLORS: All shades of yellow and brown, also gold, orange

GEMSTONES AND PRECIOUS METALS: Topaz, amber, yellow diamonds

BOTANICALS: Lavender, sorrel, thyme

UNIQUE SPELLING: Mac

RELATED TO: Macallister, Macardle, Macdonald, Macdougal, Mackenzie, Mackey, Malcolmt

DERIVATION: French and English, derived from the New Testament figure Saint Mary Magdalene. After the Middle Ages, the *g* was dropped from the name.

PRINCIPAL COLORS: Deep, rich reds, also pink

GEMSTONES AND PRECIOUS METALS: Bloodstones, garnets

BOTANICALS: Broom, onion, nettle

UNIQUE SPELLINGS: Madalenne, Madalin, Madaline, Madalinne, Madalyn, Maddaline, Maddeline, Maddelyn, Maddelyne, Maddilin, Maddiline, Maddilyn, Maddilyne, Maddylen, Maddylin, Madeleine, Madelen, Madelin, Madelinne, Madelyn, Madelynne, Madilin, Madilyn, Madylen, Madylin

RELATED TO: Madalaina, Madalena, Maddie, Maddy, Madelayne, Madella, Madge, Magda, Magdalena, Magdalene, Marlena, Marlene†, Maud

Madeline

A KABBALISTIC SYNOPSIS

מאדאלין —MADALYN (Mem, Aleph, Daleth, Aleph, Lamed, Yod, Nun)

It is impossible to be bored when you're in Madeline's company. Her name is ruled by Jupiter, a planet whose influences are wholly benevolent, since they are connected to good fortune, joviality, and social cheer. Blessed with a warm and sensitive emotional nature, Madeline uses her sense of humor to make others feel relaxed and at home. Whatever professional field Madeline enters she will be well liked and respected for her exceptional skill in handling clients. The name also suggests that she has a capacity for teaching, though this may be in an informal context; for example, she may help out colleagues when they get stuck. Madeline also has some deeply personal ambitions relating to her creative abilities, and these will keep her occupied throughout her working life and well into her retirement. Madeline is destined to have a very full life.

THE RUNIC INTERPRETATION

ᛗᚾᛁᛚᛗᛞᚨᛗ (Ehwaz, Nauthiz, Isa, Laguz, Ehwaz, Dagaz, Ansuz, Mannaz)

Growth and changing locations characterize Madeline's name, which has the double Ehwaz rune of movement and progress. Mannaz or the rune of the self, combined with Ehwaz, suggest that Madeline will appreciate all the experiences inherent in the changes life brings her. Laguz, the rune of flow, enables peaceful Madeline to adapt quite well to her transitions, frequent moves, and adjustments in life. The Isa rune shows that Madeline seeks solitude as a way to slow down and balance her energy. Ansuz for signals and Dagaz for breakthrough indicate that lovely Madeline sails through life using her intuition to resolve problems and surmount challenges with great aplomb!

Elements: Air, fire, earth, water, air, fire, air, air

THE NUMEROLOGICAL INTERPRETATION

Madeline (NV = 9, CV = 7, VV = 2, FL = 4)

Madeline is idealistic. Her name inspires romance and poetry, and adds a touch of beauty to all her forms of self-expression. When people are in a relationship with Madeline, they experience the love she shares with them as something very deep and personal. Her success in life comes more from the development of her inner character than from external achievement. This does not negate her ability to make it in the world; it just indicates that she is a very sensitive woman, one whose real sense of value comes more from who she is than from what she owns. It is important for Madeline not to lose sight of her own standards and to remain somewhat detached, for other people may not always live up to her high expectations of them.

Mae

DERIVATION: English, spelling variation of May, which is a pet form of Mary and Margaret, and associated with the other month names, April and June. Became quite popular in the 1920s.

PRINCIPAL COLORS: The palest to the brightest, richest yellow and bronze shades

GEMSTONES AND PRECIOUS METALS: Citrine, yellow diamonds

BOTANICALS: Borage, eyebright, Saint-John's-wort

UNIQUE SPELLINGS: May, Maye, Meigh

RELATED TO: Maia, Margarett, Maryt, Mayt, Maya

A KABBALISTIC SYNOPSIS

מאהי —MAHY (Mem, Aleph, Heh, Yod)

First and foremost Mae enjoys emotional connections to people. She thrives on making new friends and acquaintances. Mae has a keen interest in the way other people live their lives, and her wide circle of friends is one way in which she provides herself with a window on the world. Mae has a very easy air when in public, and possesses an almost intuitive understanding of others and how they feel. The value of her name reduces to twelve, which is the number of the tarot card the Hanged Man. As a result we can expect Mae to have an altruistic nature. Mae is always willing to help people out and put her own interests on hold in the process.

THE RUNIC INTERPRETATION

ᛗᚨᛗ (Ehwaz, Ansuz, Mannaz)

How we treat ourselves is how we treat others, and our view of the world is also a projection of self. Therefore, as Mae can tell you, one of the keys to happiness lies in having a healthy relationship to the self. Mannaz, or self, figures prominently in Mae's name. The air elements afford her good communication skills, and Mae just might take this to an extreme; she loves the sound of her own voice. That's okay because what she has to say is valuable, even if she does tend to make a long story even longer. Ansuz for signals signifies that Mae operates with a good sense of intuition. The Ehwaz rune of movement blesses Mae with voyages, or an inner ability to grow and change.

Elements: Air, air, air

THE NUMEROLOGICAL INTERPRETATION

Mae (NV = 1, CV = 4, VV = 6, FL = 4)

Mae is a very forthright and goal-oriented person. She is a determined woman who is clear about her intentions and follows through with a distinct sense of personal responsibility. The vowel value of six indicates that she is very aware of other people's feelings and seeks cooperation and harmony whenever possible. Mae is certainly self-motivated, but not so much so that she runs over people. On the contrary, she does all that she can to include and embrace. But if such support is not forthcoming, she goes ahead with what she has to do, aims her arrow at its target, and fires away!

DERIVATION: English, short form
of Margaret. Sometimes used as
a full name, which was especially
common during the late nineteenth
century. Extremely popular in
Scotland.

PRINCIPAL COLORS: Pale to
moderately shaded azure

GEMSTONES AND PRECIOUS
METALS: Turquoise, emeralds

BOTANICALS: Violets, vervain,
almonds, walnuts

UNIQUE SPELLINGS: Maggey,
Maggi, Maggy, Magi, Magy

RELATED TO: Mag, Magda,
Magnilda, Magnolia, Maiga,
Margaret†, Margareta, Margarita†,
Margery, Margie, Margo,
Marguerite†, Meg, Megan†, Meggie

〜

"There must be a goal at every stage
of life! There must be a goal!"
—MAGGIE KUHN (AUTHOR)

Maggie

A KABBALISTIC SYNOPSIS
מאגי —MAGY (Mem, Aleph, Gimel, Yod)

If you meet Maggie at a party and you're hoping to get away at a reasonable hour or even before daylight, don't under any circumstances bring up politics as a subject. Maggie is a principled woman, and her concerns relate to actual issues and events rather than hypothetical situations. She is unlikely to go out and demonstrate at marches, but she will join in more restrained activity to support her cause. Unusually for someone with such firm political commitments, Maggie is also highly talented creatively. Although she is not likely to make a career out of it, she will have minor exhibitions or shows in her name. It is her other interests, rather than a lack of talent, that prevent her from taking this further. Her career is going to be in one of the professions, particularly law, and within the law she is ideally suited to practicing as a defense lawyer. Work will take up a lot of her time, but she gets a great deal of satisfaction from it.

THE RUNIC INTERPRETATION
MIXXᚠᛗ (Ehwaz, Isa, Gebo, Gebo, Ansuz, Mannaz)

Codependency is a drag, and Maggie could fall into dysfunctional relationships in the wink of an eye with the double Gebo rune aspecting her name. True, Gebo is the rune of partnership, but Maggie must remember that we can't live and breathe for our partner. The Mannaz rune of self ensures ego strength, and this is precisely what is needed. The Ansuz rune of signals supplies Maggie with the common sense to follow her hunches and pursue her dreams. Letting go of the need to rescue or change anyone and keeping one's own needs foremost is the key to dealing with the double Gebo configuration.

Elements: Air, earth, water, water, air, air

THE NUMEROLOGICAL INTERPRETATION
Maggie (NV = 6, CV = 9, VV = 6, FL = 4)

Anyone who knows Maggie thinks of her as a loving and caring woman. The combination of her name numbers speaks clearly about the sincerity of her sympathy, compassion, and good intentions. Maggie has a great deal of tolerance for others and is devoid of prejudice. She is very diplomatic with people and has the ability to see all sides of a given situation. She often feels compelled to come up with a balanced solution to any disagreement. Maggie has to make sure that she does not give away her power by overextending herself.

〜

Malcolm

A Kabbalistic Synopsis

מאלכום —MALKVM (Mem, Aleph, Lamed, Kaph, Vau, Mem)

If you're looking for Malcolm, the best place to start is in a restaurant, as Malcolm has a great love of food. Malcolm has a vigorous nature and is very quick to put any plans into action. This is shown by the presence of the letters Lamed and Kaph in his name. Malcolm is usually driven to succeed out of a desire to live up to some icon or other, such as his father or some other male relative. This touchstone is often self-created, and this drive to accomplish can sometimes make him difficult to work with. Malcolm can be extremely demanding. However, he is a very loving man and has the greatest respect for those he works with. Thus others quickly forget his flares of temper.

The Runic Interpretation

ᛗᛚᛟᚲᛚᚨᛗ (Mannaz, Laguz, Othila, Kano, Laguz, Ansuz, Mannaz)

Self-confidence is great to have, but Malcolm can be a little overbearing with his gestures of self-importance. Othila, or the rune of separation, shows that Malcolm could lose friends because of this. The double Mannaz rune of self could indicate that Malcolm needs a big dose of humility and patience. Fortunately, the double Laguz rune of flow, which signifies flexibility, and the Ansuz rune of signals or intuition promise that Malcolm will probably catch on to the hints his friends whisper about his egotistical nature. The Kano rune of opening intimates that Malcolm will be receptive to changing his style with people, and may learn that charm involves letting the person you're talking to feel they have your undivided attention.

Elements: Air, water, earth/fire, water, water, air, air

The Numerological Interpretation

Malcolm (NV = 6, CV = 8, VV = 7, FL = 4)

A man who seeks tangible rewards for his efforts, Malcolm is very involved with creating material success. He has a strong attraction to beauty and needs to have an aesthetically pleasing environment in which to live and work. Malcolm appreciates quality—the best clothes, the nicest restaurants, a great car. Malcolm should be aware of his tendency toward self-indulgence, and needs to develop his ability to rationalize and qualify his desirous nature. As he is a gentleman, he tends to achieve his objectives more through tact and charm than through aggressive self-promotion. Physical attractiveness and a sense of style are important to Malcolm when he is selecting a partner.

DERIVATION: Scottish and English, traditionally a royal name in Scotland. The name of the Scottish prince who became king after Macbeth killed his father, Duncan. Today, the name is often associated with civil rights leader Malcolm X.

PRINCIPAL COLORS: All but the most brilliant of blues

GEMSTONES AND PRECIOUS METALS: Blue and blue-green turquoise, emeralds

BOTANICALS: Dog rose, walnuts, apricot

UNIQUE SPELLINGS: Malcom, Malcum, Malkolm, Malkom, Malkum

RELATED TO: Mackt, Malcolum

"The future belongs to those who prepare for it today."
—MALCOLM X
(CIVIL RIGHTS LEADER)

"By the time we've made it, we've had it."
—MALCOLM FORBES
(BUSINESSPERSON)

DERIVATION: Spanish, from the Hebrew name Emanuel, meaning "God is with us." Manuel is much more common than Emanuel or Emmanuel, particularly in the United States.

PRINCIPAL COLORS: Any shade of violet, from pale, bluish purple to deep, rich purple

GEMSTONES AND PRECIOUS METALS: Amethyst, garnets

BOTANICALS: Cherry, barberry, mint

UNIQUE SPELLINGS: Manuele, Manuell, Manuwel, Manyuel

RELATED TO: Emanuel, Emmanuel, Manny

Manuel

A KABBALISTIC SYNOPSIS
מאנואל —MANVAL (Mem, Aleph, Nun, Vau, Aleph, Lamed)

Dramatic is one word that adequately sums up Manuel. Whatever Manuel is feeling, everyone around him will know it. He is a very expressive man with what can best be described as a Latin temperament—so if he is mad, it is usually advisable to duck! Manuel can be equally passionate in love, and has a knack for knowing just what to say to make his prospective partner melt. His name is ruled by the sign Aquarius, which makes him something of a dreamer, and he is often attracted to some pretty unusual pastimes and practices, although they rarely hold his interest more than a month or so. Against this Aquarian nonconformity is another side to his nature that is extremely practical: He is a very handy guy to have around the house. It is highly likely that his work will have a manual basis to it, and he is particularly suited to work involving repairs and maintenance.

THE RUNIC INTERPRETATION
ᛚᛖᚢᚾᚨᛗ (Laguz, Ehwaz, Uruz, Nauthiz, Ansuz, Mannaz)

Stronger than any obstacle that crosses his path, Manuel stays his course and triumphs. The Nauthiz rune represents constraint and limitations, but the Uruz rune for strength in this name compensates for this. The Mannaz rune of self along with the Ansuz rune of intuition suggests that Manuel has the strength to feel his way through even the most difficult problems. Laguz, or flow, affords Manuel musical as well as mathematical ability and a flexible nature. Ehwaz, or movement, indicates that Manuel will be adaptable. Manuel has rich and rewarding adventures because he is optimistic and spontaneous. He also has the blessing of having all four elements in his name.

Elements: Water, air, earth, fire, air, air

THE NUMEROLOGICAL INTERPRETATION
Manuel (NV = 3, CV = 3, VV = 9, FL = 4)

Manuel is a sociable person, one who contains a storehouse of ideas about many different subjects. He is talkative, gregarious, and makes a very interesting friend or partner. Manuel has no problem approaching people, and is a great asset in social situations, as he adds considerably to any conversation. He has a playful side to his nature as well, making him fun to be around. There is, however, a tendency to be superficial and indecisive. He may lack a sense of priorities, and needs to check himself occasionally to keep in touch with his true direction.

Marcia

A Kabbalistic Synopsis
מארסיא —MARSYA (Mem, Aleph, Resh, Samech, Yod, Aleph)

Everyone is cheerful when Marcia is around! Marcia's home life tends to be warm and supportive, and she can always rely on her partner to cheer her up on the rare occasions that she is feeling down. Thanks to her secure home environment, Marcia is able to offer her support to all those people she meets who have problems of their own. And as she is probably working in some kind of government office dealing with the public, it is extremely likely that Marcia will meet all kinds of needy people. As well as having a sunny personality, Marcia has the energy to do whatever is needed to make things right for others. If necessary, she will go to all lengths to help someone out. The only thing that ever really troubles Marcia is when she has to decide whether to continue at work to help out her clients, or to go home to be with her family, who need her just as much.

The Runic Interpretation
ᚨᛁᛋᚱᚨᛗ (Ansuz, Isa, Sowelu, Raido, Ansuz, Mannaz)

By the end of her life, Marcia can say she knows who she is and she likes who she has become. The Mannaz rune of self means Marcia faces the painful task of integrating her emotions. Later in life, she remembers how this felt when she counsels others through challenging times. The Isa rune of standstill affords Marcia the solitary time she needs for soul-searching, and Marcia does her homework with care. The Raido rune of journey could mean travel, but in Marcia's case it most certainly goes to another level and implies inward journeys of self-discovery. The Ansuz rune blesses Marcia with the intuition she needs to examine her feelings. Sowelu for wholeness suggests that Marcia is balanced and expressive, and could enjoy counseling or social work as a career.

Elements: Air, earth, air, water, air, air

The Numerological Interpretation
Marcia (NV = 9, CV = 7, VV = 11, FL = 4)

Marcia tends to look at the big picture in life. She is philosophical by nature and seeks to be well educated. Marcia is more involved with life principles than small issues, and avoids petty disputes whenever possible. People will benefit greatly from her objectivity, as she has an uncanny knack for being able to see the true essentials of any situation. Yet she has to be careful not to overutilize her mental and objective skills, as she can deny her own emotions and negate her feelings, making more intimate relationships challenging. Marcia requires a partner of high intelligence with a wide range of intellectual interests.

DERIVATION: Latin, from the Roman name Marcus, which originally derived from the name for the Roman god of war, Mars. Especially popular during the mid-twentieth century.

PRINCIPAL COLORS: All red hues, especially the deepest ones

GEMSTONES AND PRECIOUS METALS: Rubies, garnets

BOTANICALS: Broom, onion

UNIQUE SPELLINGS: Marciah, Marsha, Marshah, Martia

RELATED TO: Marcella, Marcelle, Marci, Marcie, Marcille, Marcita, Marshat

"The possibilities are unlimited as long as you are true to your life's purpose."
—MARCIA WIEDER (AUTHOR)

DERIVATION: Italian form of Mark, which ultimately derives from the name of the Roman god of war, Mars. A well-known name bearer is Marco Polo (1254–1324), explorer of the Far East.

PRINCIPAL COLORS: The full spectrum of lightly shaded hues

GEMSTONES AND PRECIOUS METALS: Silver, platinum

BOTANICALS: Hazel, oats, parsley

UNIQUE SPELLINGS: Marcoe, Marku, Markoe

RELATED TO: Marc, Marcel, Marcos, Marcus†, Mariot, Mariont, Marius, Markt

A KABBALISTIC SYNOPSIS
מארכע — MARCA'A (Mem, Aleph, Resh, Kaph, Ayin)

Marco is a religious man who has a definite faith in the God he was brought up to believe in by his family. However, this belief is the result of family tradition rather than personal discovery, and it doesn't stop Marco from behaving in ways that those of his faith would be unlikely to smile on! Marco is a rogue; he is not a criminal as such (although if Marco is born under Gemini, the chances of actual crime do tend to increase), but he is inclined to bend the law as far as it will stretch. In spite of these antics, he is a very lovable guy and has a real loyalty to his friends and family. His sense of humor tends to be on the cruel side but is no less funny for that, and people often laugh at Marco's jokes in spite of themselves. He will probably make a reasonable amount of money from any number of business interests of varying legality. However, as far as the IRS is concerned, he struggles along, barely making ends meet!

THE RUNIC INTERPRETATION
◇<ʀᚨᛗ (Othila, Kano, Raido, Ansuz, Mannaz)

The Raido rune of journey figures prominently in Marco's name. Voyages and travel await Marco. He keeps his passport in his pocket and scans the paper for airline discounts. Marco would enjoy a job as a courier or photojournalist, or any occupation that lets him stay in motion. Marco is independent as well. This is indicated by the appearance of the Mannaz rune for self strengthening his name. Marco can withstand separation and feels at home just about anywhere. He is a friend to the world, and people gravitate to Marco. The Kano rune of opening hints that Marco has a warm and sunny disposition. Ansuz, the rune of signals, shows that Marco runs on his intuition and has good social skills.

Elements: Earth/fire, water, water, air, air

THE NUMEROLOGICAL INTERPRETATION
Marco (NV = 5, CV = 7, VV = 7, FL = 4)

Marco is very involved with self-development. He is ever seeking to enlarge the scope of his understanding and is frequently at work developing new concepts and ideas in order to ensure the success of the creative projects with which he is involved. Marco makes friends easily. He has high energy and a joyful attitude. He tends to see the positive side to most situations, and freely offers his help and assistance when called upon. Yet Marco has to be aware of the importance of the emotional side of life as well, for not everything is either a concept or a theory. People will ask him to share more of himself as an intimate friend, and not just act as a detached source of information.

Marcus

DERIVATION: Roman, after the name for the Roman war god, Mars. Very common during the Roman era, and has resurged in popularity during the late twentieth century.

PRINCIPAL COLORS: The full range of purple hues

GEMSTONES AND PRECIOUS METALS: Garnets, amethyst

BOTANICALS: Dandelion, strawberry, mint

UNIQUE SPELLINGS: Markis, Markus

RELATED TO: Marc, Marcot, Mariano, Mariot, Mariont, Marius, Markt, Marko, Marshallt, Martint, Martyt

A KABBALISTIC SYNOPSIS

מעכס —MA'AKS (Mem, Ayin, Kaph, Samech)

Marcus needs to surround himself with friends—good friends. He has the capacity to be a happy, balanced person, if only he would realize it. Marcus in kabbalistic terms represents both the mundane solidity of the material world and the tendency to cling to all of our fantasies as if they were realities. In terms of personality this can produce something of a Walter Mitty figure. If he isn't careful, Marcus can become very disenchanted with the everyday world. This is where good friends can help. A really good friend will point out the pie in the sky for what it is, but will also help Marcus to see that the workaday world does have plenty to offer. Chances are good that Marcus will have such people around him, as he has an affable nature with others and is very empathic. All is not doom and gloom for Marcus, though; there is a strong Jovian current in this name, which has graced many respected ancients. If the holder of the name can leave behind the imaginary and seize the reality, there will be little to stand in his way.

"How ridiculous and unrealistic is the man who is astonished at anything that happens in life."
—MARCUS AURELIUS (AUTHOR)

THE RUNIC INTERPRETATION

ᛋᚢᚲᚱᚨᛗ (Sowelu, Uruz, Kano, Raido, Ansuz, Mannaz)

A born leader, Marcus knows deep inside that bullying others is not the answer—quite the contrary. A natural leader like Marcus is so aware of the needs of his charges that he acts in their best interests. People follow him because Marcus inspires their trust. The Sowelu rune of wholeness reveals that Marcus loves himself and is able to love others. Uruz gives Marcus strength. The Ansuz rune signifies considerable intuition. Raido blesses Marcus with travel opportunities and the capacity for introspection and communication. Mannaz, the rune of the self, means that Marcus has good self-respect and the golden ability to draw out the strengths in others.

"If you have no confidence in self, you are twice defeated in the race of life. With confidence, you have won even before you have started."
—MARCUS GARVEY (ACTIVIST)

Elements: Air, earth, water, water, air, air

THE NUMEROLOGICAL INTERPRETATION

Marcus (NV = 3, CV = 8, VV = 4, FL = 4)

One of the most important life lessons contained in this name is the need to create structure and order. This is a name that teaches a person about self-discipline. Marcus has to learn to recognize the correct personal and social boundaries and then work within them. Once he has properly assessed these, Marcus can accept greater responsibility for himself and construct his pathway to success. Habit patterns can either restrict or enhance a person's efficiency, and Marcus is working to establish patterns that can benefit him in the future. His name value of three gives him just the right amount of flexibility so that he can adjust his routines to avoid stagnation and thus attract more opportunities into his life.

Margaret

DERIVATION: English, from the Greek word *margaron*, meaning "pearl." An extremely common female name since the Middle Ages. Many saints have been named Margaret, as have many royal figures, including Margaret Tudor of Scotland (1489–1541) and Queen Margarita of Denmark and Norway (b. 1935). Most common in Scotland, but extremely popular in all English-speaking countries. Another prominent name bearer is the first female prime minister of Britain, Margaret Thatcher (b. 1925).

PRINCIPAL COLORS: Light to dark shades of green, white

GEMSTONES AND PRECIOUS METALS: Jade, cat's-eye

BOTANICALS: Chicory, lettuce, moonwort

UNIQUE SPELLINGS: Maergaret, Margarete, Margarett, Margarette, Margarit, Margarite, Margaryt, Margeret, Margret, Margrett, Margrette, Margrit, Margritte

RELATED TO: Gret, Greta, Gretchen†, Gretel, Maggie†, Maisie, Margaretta, Margarita†, Margaux, Marge, Margery, Margie, Margo, Margot, Marguerita, Marguerite†, Marjorie†, Markita, Meg, Megan†, Meggie, Peg, Peggy†, Rita†

"Until you've lost your reputation, you never realize what a burden it was."

—MARGARET MITCHELL (AUTHOR)

"Often people attempt to live their lives backwards; they try to have more things, or more money, in order to do more of what they want, so they will appear happier. The way it actually works is the reverse. You must first be who you really are, then do what you need to do, in order to have what you want."

—MARGARET YOUNG (AUTHOR)

A KABBALISTIC SYNOPSIS

מארגאראט —MARGARAT (Mem, Aleph, Resh, Gimel, Aleph, Resh, Aleph, Teth)

Many people go to Margaret for advice not only because of her friendly and receptive nature but because of the practicality of her comments. Margaret may be a very friendly woman, but she has no time for wishy-washy talk about feelings and what-if scenarios. No, if you ask Margaret for her opinion, you will get a very clear statement laying out a definite course of action. More often than not her advice is well worth taking. Margaret also has a rare gift for objectivity. This can have its drawbacks, though, in that she will tell her friends certain truths that most people would be too tactful to mention. On the whole her behavior is driven by a very real concern for the well-being of others. For herself Margaret would love to travel, possibly as a solo explorer of all the places she dreams about visiting.

THE RUNIC INTERPRETATION

ᛏᛗᚱᛉᚷᚱᛉᛗ (Teiwaz, Ehwaz, Raido, Ansuz, Gebo, Raido, Ansuz, Mannaz)

Margaret is a chameleon, and friends are always amazed at her versatility and finesse. The double Ansuz rune promises psychic ability. Another double runic configuration of journey or Raido shows that Margaret is fascinated by different peoples of the world and travels extensively, to her great delight. The Ehwaz rune of movement, combined with the double Raido rune of journey, states that Margaret may reside abroad. Although Margaret is independent and self-reliant, she never lacks for a date on Saturday night. Gebo, the rune of partnerships, is there in her name to help her keep friends and lovers in close proximity. The Mannaz rune of self indicates that Margaret is able to love herself and others because she loves the world.

Elements: Air, air, water, air, water, water, air, air

THE NUMEROLOGICAL INTERPRETATION

Margaret (NV = 11, CV = 4, VV = 7, FL = 4)

Margaret may find that she has a more profound understanding of others than most people do. She is a very intuitive and intelligent woman, one whose depth and clarity intrigue people. Her name also carries a very practical facet to its vibration. Margaret will find it natural to direct her intuition toward the achievement of some professional goal. She is well suited for a career that involves organization and communication, and has a natural aptitude for community and social work, avenues that allow her to utilize her long-range vision. Margaret tends toward the traditional in her romantic involvements and seeks a committed relationship.

Margarita

DERIVATION: Spanish form of Margaret, which initially derives from the Greek word *margaron*, meaning "pearl." Used in both Spanish-speaking and English-speaking countries.

PRINCIPAL COLORS: Pale to deep, rich shades of yellow and green

GEMSTONES AND PRECIOUS METALS: Pearls, moonstones, any white stones

BOTANICALS: Blackberry, elder, linseed

UNIQUE SPELLINGS: Margareta, Margaretha, Margaryta, Margeretha, Margerita, Margeryta, Margherita, Margireta, Marguerita

RELATED TO: Gret, Greta, Gretchen†, Marga, Margaret†, Margaretta, Margaux, Marge, Margery, Margie, Margita, Margo, Margot, Margueritet, Marjoriet, May†, Meg, Megan†, Meggie, Meta, Peg, Peggy†, Rita†

A KABBALISTIC SYNOPSIS

מארגאריטא —MARGARYTA (Mem, Aleph, Resh, Gimel, Aleph, Resh, Yod, Teth, Aleph)

As far as Margarita is concerned there is no mystery to the meaning of life. The purpose of existence is simply to cram in as much enjoyment as possible. Margarita especially enjoys sensuous pleasures—beautiful objects, beautiful people, lovingly prepared foods, long vacations in exotic locales. The positioning of the letter Resh, meaning "sun," suggests that holidays are of great importance to her, and in truth, Margarita will go without a number of things in order to ensure her two weeks in the sun. The letter Teth, meaning "serpent," and its combination with the letter Yod indicate that Margarita has a very forceful nature and can drive or goad people into action when needed. For this reason, along with her generally motivating outlook on life, Margarita makes an excellent staff manager.

THE RUNIC INTERPRETATION

ᚨᛏᛁᚱᚨᚷᚱᚨᛗ (Ansuz, Teiwaz, Isa, Raido, Ansuz, Gebo, Raido, Ansuz, Mannaz)

With all the talents and finesse of the name Margaret, Margarita is blessed with the additional terminal Ansuz rune. This is a remarkable triple Ansuz configuration. The result of adding the third Ansuz rune of signals increases Margarita's psychic gifts. She could be a medium or a prophet or a brilliant inventor. She may even win the Nobel prize! With the triple Ansuz rune in her name, Margarita can anticipate surprises and opportunities and even a few upsets on her path. Circumstances will align themselves in unexpected configurations. It could be a bumpy ride, but one thing is certain: Margarita will never be bored.

Elements: Air, air, earth, water, air, water, water, air, air

THE NUMEROLOGICAL INTERPRETATION

Margarita (NV = 7, CV = 4, VV = 3, FL = 4)

This name gives a person the ability to easily distinguish right from wrong. Margarita has an inner sense of ethics and morality. She is an honest woman who needs to have friends and associates who are not afraid to tell the truth. Margarita finds strength in solitude and is confident in her own understanding of life. She enjoys increasing her intellectual knowledge and learns new techniques quite easily. Eager to share what she has learned, Margarita is generous with her information. However, she tends to keep her innermost feelings to herself, making it difficult for others to be in touch with her emotionally. She can be a bit self-protective, but when she gives her heart, it is with sincerity and purpose.

Marguerite

DERIVATION: French form of Margaret, which originally derives from the Greek word *margaron*, meaning "pearl." Also the French word for "daisy." Especially common in the United States during the mid-twentieth century.

PRINCIPAL COLORS: Pink to deep, rich crimson shades

GEMSTONES AND PRECIOUS METALS: Bloodstones, rubies

BOTANICALS: Onion, wormwood

UNIQUE SPELLINGS: Margarete, Margarite, Margaritte, Margaryte, Margerete, Margeryte, Margherite, Margirite, Margiryte

RELATED TO: Gret, Greta, Gretchen†, Marga, Margaret†, Margarita†, Margaux, Marge, Margery, Margie, Margita, Margo, Margot, Marjorie†, Meg, Megan†, Meggie, Meta, Peg, Peggy†, Rita†

"Genius is the gold in the mine; talent is the miner that works and brings it out."

—LADY MARGUERITE POWER BLESSINGTON (AUTHOR)

"Tears may be dried up, but the heart—never."

—MARGUERITE DE VALOIS (QUEEN OF FRANCE, CONSORT OF NAVARRE)

A KABBALISTIC SYNOPSIS

מארגאריט —MARGARYT (Mem, Aleph, Resh, Gimel, Aleph, Resh, Yod, Teth)

Marguerite is wonderfully generous. She gives her time as well as her money. Unlike many people, she will often offer help without being asked. Occasionally, of course, this may produce a negative reaction, as some people might view her as interfering. Marguerite will be quick to apologize in such cases, and is not one to bear a grudge or take comments to heart. Her family life tends to be warm and loving, although she will need to make sure that she keeps some time reserved for her family and, of course, for herself. Marguerite has a very earthy nature and views the world with a good, if sometimes coarse, sense of humor. Marguerite loves down-and-dirty leisure activities, such as climbing, hiking, camping, or gardening. She also loves a good laugh.

THE RUNIC INTERPRETATION

ᛗᛏᛁᚱᛗᚢᚷᚱᛅᛗᛗ (Ehwaz, Teiwaz, Isa, Raido, Ehwaz, Uruz, Gebo, Raido, Ansuz, Mannaz)

A gradual emergence into new attitudes and relationships, and the opportunity to live in different places characterize Marguerite's name. The double Ehwaz rune of movement means that gradual change molds Marguerite's outlook on life. She may go on for advanced degrees and even teach in a university. The Raido rune emphasizes her love of travel. Uruz and Mannaz signify strength, and the Mannaz rune of self combined with the independence of Teiwaz, the warrior rune, means that Marguerite has the courage to endure many transitions. The Isa rune of standstill balances out her need to be on the go, and helps Marguerite derive great satisfaction from silence and meditation. The Gebo rune for partnership ensures a committed relationship for Marguerite. On top of these positive traits, Marguerite is blessed with the power of the four elements in her name, which signifies balance, wholeness, and satisfaction.

Elements: Air, air, earth, water, air, earth, water, water, air, air

THE NUMEROLOGICAL INTERPRETATION

Marguerite (NV = 9, CV = 4, VV = 5, FL = 4)

Two predominant influences are present in this name. Marguerite has a strong inner urge to expand her potential. This gives her a love of freedom and independence. Yet Marguerite also has a profound need for stability and financial security. She can struggle frequently with the tension this duality in her name creates. If she acts too independently, she loses her security; if she maintains the consistency of a routine, she compromises her freedom. Her objective, therefore, is the integration of these two sides of her nature. Once that is accomplished, tension will give way to abundance.

Maria

A Kabbalistic Synopsis
מאריא —MARYA (Mem, Aleph, Resh, Yod, Aleph)

Maria has a strong sensual side to her nature, one that matches her good looks. This often makes her a sought-after woman. Maria possesses a natural wisdom and is regarded as being wise about the world. She is more than happy to offer her opinion on any matter, particularly if the topic of conversation relates to emotional or romantic problems. A passionate nature makes Maria fiery, so she also can be extremely jealous. If she thinks you are making a play for her partner, you can expect to be burned—and she will waste no time in telling you to keep well away! Her appreciation for affairs of the heart and all manner of emotional intrigue can lead her to be something of a gossip. There is never any malicious intent in what she says—unless, of course, you have made the mistake of arousing her jealousy.

The Runic Interpretation
ᚨᛁᚱᚨᛗ (Ansuz, Isa, Raido, Ansuz, Mannaz)

Surprising coincidences and unexpected happenings typify Maria's life because her name possesses the double Ansuz rune of signals. This rune makes Maria superstitious and intuitive. She follows her hunches, and people say she has good luck. Maria knows better. What other people call luck, Maria knows she earns by paying attention to body language, handwriting, global trends, and tendencies in human nature. The Isa rune of standstill gives Maria the patience to pause and think. The Mannaz rune of self indicates good self-knowledge, and the Raido rune of journey shows that Maria has a great understanding of herself and others. She is a humanitarian and loves deeply.

Elements: Air, earth, water, air, air

The Numerological Interpretation
Maria (NV = 6, CV = 4, VV = 11, FL = 4)

Bearing a name filled with the power of grace and compassion, Maria is an emotional woman. Her task is to express her feelings without compromising her sense of personal integrity. Maria's family will definitely dominate her choices. She is inclusive and generous, and she associates her own needs with the needs of the people around her. In this respect, Maria has to be careful of codependent behavior. She has to remember that she is responsible for her own emotional nourishment and must respect the strength of her own individuality. Beauty, charm, and personal magnetism are also closely associated with this name.

DERIVATION: Latin form of Mary, which was the New Testament version of the Hebrew name Miriam. As the name of the Virgin Mary, the mother of Jesus, Mary has been the most enduring of all female Christian names. The name Maria was originally more popular in Spain, Italy, and Portugal, but entered the English-speaking world in the nineteenth century. Now, it is common throughout Europe, North America, and South America.

PRINCIPAL COLORS: All but the brightest of blues

GEMSTONES AND PRECIOUS METALS: Emeralds, turquoise

BOTANICALS: Vervain, daffodils, walnuts

UNIQUE SPELLINGS: Marea, Mareea, Mariea, Marya

RELATED TO: Maire, Mara, Maren, Mari, Mariah, Mariannet, Mariet, Mariel, Mariella, Marielle, Marietta, Marika, Marilee, Marilynt, Marisa, Marissat, Maryt, Maura, Maureent, Mayt, Mimi, Minniet, Miriamt, Mitzi, Moira, Mollyt, Murielt, Myrat

Marianne

DERIVATION: French, a combination of the names Marie and Anne. Marie is the French version of the English name Mary, and Anne is the French version of the Hebrew name Hanna.

PRINCIPAL COLORS: Pale lilac to deep purple and rich violet

GEMSTONES AND PRECIOUS METALS: Garnets, amethyst

BOTANICALS: Strawberry, mint, lungwort

UNIQUE SPELLINGS: Mariane, Mariann, Maryann, Mary Ann, Mary-Ann, Maryanne, Mary Anne, Mary-Anne

RELATED TO: Ann†, Anna†, Anne†, Annemarie, Annette†, Hanna, Hannah†, Mara, Mare, Maria†, Mariah, Marian, Mariana, Marianna, Maribel, Mariet†, Mariel, Mariella, Marielle, Marietta, Marigold, Marika, Marilyn†, Marissa†, Marla, Mary†, Mary Ann†, Maura, May†, Miriam†, Moira, Molly†, Muriel†

꙳

"To experience love in ourselves and others, is the meaning of life. Meaning does not lie in things. Meaning lies in us."

—MARIANNE WILLIAMSON (AUTHOR)

"Your thorns are the best part of you."

—MARIANNE MOORE (POET)

A KABBALISTIC SYNOPSIS

מאריאן —MARYAN (Mem, Aleph, Resh, Yod, Aleph, Nun)

Marianne's life seems to be beset by a series of traumatic events. Her name's value reduces to sixteen, which is the number of the Tower card in tarot and represents catastrophic life events. However, these events are fated, and ultimately are for the benefit of the individual who has to endure them. So, although Marianne may have a tough time of it in early adulthood, her experiences will prove invaluable to her in later life. One thing Marianne doesn't need to learn is the importance of hard work and commitment. She is an immensely diligent worker and is always willing to stay late or work at home in order to get the job done. This commitment to her career, which may well be in the field of communications, will guarantee her success and promotion in the long run; all the late nights will have been worth it. Emotionally Marianne has a tendency to shy away from serious relationships because she has a fear of rejection. A very emotionally giving woman, Marianne simply needs a partner who is prepared to give her sufficient reassurance that the relationship will last.

THE RUNIC INTERPRETATION

ᛖᚾᚾᚨᛁᚱᚨᛗ (Ehwaz, Nauthiz, Nauthiz, Ansuz, Isa, Raido, Ansuz, Mannaz)

Marianne can return anyone's serve with power and precision. For every problem the double Nauthiz runes of constraint lob her way, Marianne grows ever stronger. Life is unpredictable and the floor collapses out from under her at times, but Marianne always lands on her feet. Marianne uses the Isa rune of standstill to think and formulate her opinions in an articulate and clear fashion. She agrees that the unexamined life is not worth living, and Marianne's capacity for self-examination helps her stay balanced and ride the winds of change. She has the four elements blessing her name.

Elements: Air, fire, fire, air, earth, water, air, air

THE NUMEROLOGICAL INTERPRETATION

Marianne (NV = 3, CV = 5, VV = 7, FL = 4)

Marianne is a woman who values life experiences. In fact, she is a collector of them. Her wide social resources give her ample opportunity to move out into the world to learn, share, seek, and find. Marianne's friendships are many, as she is curious about people and lifestyles other than her own. This expansive nature is complemented by an introspective and contemplative facet to her personality. After a period of social interchange, Marianne will pull back and retreat into her own space. She will then assess and analyze her experiences in order to understand the deeper meanings of these encounters and situations.

꙳

Marie

A KABBALISTIC SYNOPSIS
מארהי —MARHY (Mem, Aleph, Resh, Heh, Yod)

You will never hear Marie complain that she is bored; she barely has time in the day to stop and eat! Marie likes to squeeze every last drop of enjoyment out of life and is a great person to be with, although most people prefer her in small doses. Paradoxically, the most significant and stable feature of Marie's life is change. From her job to her lifestyle to her country of residence and her partners, Marie changes everything—sometimes with quite startling rapidity. She has a real interest in world cultures, so extensive travel is definitely in the cards for Marie. She may well decide to work her way round the world, picking up a variety of temporary jobs as she goes. The total value of her name suggests that she will eventually settle down, but that might not be until she has turned sixty!

THE RUNIC INTERPRETATION
MIRAM (Ehwaz, Isa, Raido, Ansuz, Mannaz)

Making a home on uncharted waters gives life a thrill beyond compare for Marie. The Mannaz rune of self offers Marie a clear identity and inner reserves of faith and optimism. Isa, the rune of standstill, indicates that Marie welcomes stillness and enjoys studying foreign languages and history. She likes to be by herself and actually requires a good deal of time alone to feel rested and orderly. The Ehwaz rune of movement, combined with Raido for journey, signifies travel, good communications, and numerous transitions and adjustments ahead for Marie.

Elements: Air, earth, water, air, air

THE NUMEROLOGICAL INTERPRETATION
Marie (NV = 1, CV = 4, VV = 6, FL = 4)

Marie is sensitive, with a deep desire for peace and cooperation. She is also her own individual with a very personal agenda. She is very fond of children and is naturally inclined to be nurturing and emotionally caring. It is important for her to create a beautiful home environment, and she is skilled in doing so. Her name value is one—the number that stands for "I am me and no one else!" Marie has to assert and prove her sense of singularity in the world. Her challenge consists in the alignment of her responsibility to herself with the responsibility she feels for others.

DERIVATION: French form of Mary, which was the New Testament form of the Hebrew name Miriam. Very common in both English-speaking and French-speaking countries. Frequently used in compounds with other names.

PRINCIPAL COLORS: Very light to deep, rich shades of yellow and brown, also orange

GEMSTONES AND PRECIOUS METALS: Topaz, amber

BOTANICALS: Chamomile, sorrel, thyme

UNIQUE SPELLINGS: Maree, Marey, Marye

RELATED TO: Maire, Mara, Maren, Mari, Mariat, Mariah, Marianna, Mariannet, Mariel, Mariella, Marielle, Marietta, Marika, Marilee, Marilynt, Marisa, Marissat, Maryt, Maura, Maureent, Mayt, Mia, Mimi, Minniet, Miriamt, Mitzi, Moira, Mollyt, Murielt, Myrat

◖

"Nothing in life is to be feared, it is only to be understood."
—MARIE CURIE (SCIENTIST)

"True friendship is never serene."
—MARIE DE RABUTIN-CHANTAL (AUTHOR)

◖

Marilyn

DERIVATION: English, either a diminutive of Mary or a combination of the names Mary and Ellen. Very common in the United States during the first half of the twentieth century, spurred by such famous name bearers as 1920s musical star Marilyn Miller and 1950s film star Marilyn Monroe.

PRINCIPAL COLORS: Cream, the full gamut of green hues

GEMSTONES AND PRECIOUS METALS: Jade, moonstones

BOTANICALS: Chicory, cabbage, lettuce

UNIQUE SPELLINGS: Maralen, Maralin, Maralyn, Maralynne, Marelin, Marelyn, Marelynne, Marilen, Marilenne, Marilin, Marilynne, Marrelyn, Marrelynne, Marrilyn, Marrilynne, Marylin, Marylinn, Marylyn, Marylynne

RELATED TO: Ellen†, Mara, Mare, Maria†, Mariah, Marian, Mariana, Marianna, Marianne†, Maribel, Marie†, Mariel, Mariella, Marielle, Marietta, Marigold, Marika, Marissa†, Marla, Mary†, Maura, May†, Miriam†, Moira, Molly†, Muriel†

❧

"Ever notice that 'what the hell' is always the right decision?"
—MARILYN MONROE (ACTRESS)

"A good idea will keep you awake during the morning, but a great idea will keep you awake during the night."
—MARILYN VOS SAVANT (AUTHOR)

A KABBALISTIC SYNOPSIS
מארילין —MARYLYN (Mem, Aleph, Resh, Yod, Lamed, Yod, Nun)

How can one discuss the name Marilyn without considering Marilyn Monroe? Such an icon is impossible to ignore, and as with other famous owners of certain names, we see a definite relationship between the meaning of the name and her life. Marilyn is a woman who is driven to succeed in life. The final position of the letter Nun suggests that her energy is directed at a desire for emotional acceptance or fulfillment of some kind. Although the Nun can indicate a tendency toward keeping her feelings to herself, there are other indicators that show Marilyn to be quite extroverted in her behavior. The value of her name reduces to nineteen, which is the number of the Sun card in the tarot, another indicator of her jovial outward appearance. Marilyn gets on very well with a range of people. She is a good listener, and is genuinely interested in how other people are feeling and in hearing about their life and interests.

THE RUNIC INTERPRETATION
ᚾᛁᛚᛁᚱᚨᛗ (Nauthiz, Isa, Laguz, Isa, Raido, Ansuz, Mannaz)

Stillness and silence weave through Marilyn's life and help keep her balanced. The Laguz rune of flow indicates musical ability and flexibility, along with an appreciation of uncertainty, mystery, and incongruity. True, the Nauthiz rune of constraints figures prominently in Marilyn's name, but Marilyn understands that challenges help us grow more than comfort and complacency. The Raido rune of journey signifies spiritual attainment and the capacity to communicate her faith in meaningful ways to many. Marilyn knows she's fortunate to have the power of the four elements gracing her name.

Elements: Fire, earth, water, earth, water, air, air

THE NUMEROLOGICAL INTERPRETATION
Marilyn (NV = 11, CV = 3, VV = 8, FL = 4)

The combination of an eleven name value and an eight vowel value is very potent. It gives Marilyn the potential to create and accomplish much. The power in this name comes from the ability to organize and structure one's projects with precision and ease. The name Marilyn also endows an individual with charisma, magnetism, and physical attractiveness. At the very least, Marilyn knows how to enhance her personal appearance to make the most out of her physical attributes. Ambition, individualism, and rebelliousness run high in this name. As such, many people can view Marilyn as being a bit eccentric. Nervous tension may also be a factor, and Marilyn may display a distinct tendency to scatter her energy on numerous impractical causes.

❧

Mario

DERIVATION: Italian, from the Latin name Marius, which originally dates from the name of the Roman god of war, Mars. Extremely common in Italy, Spain, and Portugal.

PRINCIPAL COLORS: All colors of green tone, also cream, white

GEMSTONES AND PRECIOUS METALS: Moonstones, pearls, cat's-eye

BOTANICALS: Plantain, turnips, willow ash

UNIQUE SPELLINGS: Mareo, Marioe, Marioh, Marreo, Marrio, Marryoh, Maryo

RELATED TO: Marc, Marcot, Marcust, Mariont, Marius, Markt

A KABBALISTIC SYNOPSIS

מאריע —MARYA'A (Mem, Aleph, Resh, Yod, Ayin)

Mario seems to have an angle on *everything*. You wouldn't go to Mario to discuss anything deep or philosophical, but if you want business or legal advice, Mario is definitely the man to talk to. Not surprisingly, Mario usually does very well for himself financially; he has both the knowledge and the drive to succeed, and also has the capacity to compete quite aggressively when it is needed. Mario's biggest weakness is luxury. He has to have all the trappings of success, and this may lead him into problems if he tries to run before he can walk in terms of spending. His relationships, although often quite stormy—Mario has a roving eye—are often a lot of fun.

THE RUNIC INTERPRETATION

◇IRﷲ (Othila, Isa, Raido, Ansuz, Mannaz)

Sensitivity has two sides because the sensitive person appreciates the valleys and heights of the human condition and at the same time frequently feels alienated and out of step. Mario has the Isa rune of standstill urging him to draw apart and gather together his reserves of strength. The Othila rune of separation emphasizes his need to stand alone at times. Intuitive by nature and strong, as indicated by Ansuz and Mannaz, Mario is able to enjoy and value his sensitive nature. The Raido rune of journey promises the ability to communicate insights and also to travel and inspire others. Mario is versatile and precise, with much to offer humanity.

Elements: Earth/fire, earth, water, air, air

THE NUMEROLOGICAL INTERPRETATION

Mario (NV = 11, CV = 4, VV = 7, FL = 4)

Mario combines a powerful mind with a strong will. He is a serious and sometimes aloof person who can easily create a sense of distance between himself and others. There is a giant game of chess going on inside of him, and he keeps his strategy to himself. If he is a more spiritually oriented man, Mario will use his talents toward goals that are involved with social welfare and community development. He is a brilliant addition to any collective effort, as he is capable of seeing and resolving many facets of a project simultaneously.

DERIVATION: French diminutive
of Marie, which stems from the
English name Mary. During the
Middle Ages, it was spelled more
commonly as Marian. Since the
nineteenth century, however, the
Marion spelling has been equally
common. This spelling is more
popular as a male name.

PRINCIPAL COLORS: Gold, the full
range of green and yellow hues

GEMSTONES AND PRECIOUS
METALS: Pearls, moss agate

BOTANICALS: Elder, juniper,
linseed

UNIQUE SPELLINGS: Mareon,
Mareonn, Marian, Marien,
Marionn, Maryan, Maryen,
Maryin, Maryon, Maryonn

RELATED TO: Marc, Marcot,
Marcust, Mariot, Marius, Markt

Marion

A KABBALISTIC SYNOPSIS
מאריון —MARYVN (Mem, Aleph, Resh, Yod, Vau, Nun)

People will either love or loathe Marion. To some people, Marion's apparent lack of concern for his own happiness is overly altruistic, and they find it too selfless. However, the vast majority of people will regard Marion as a genuinely nice individual and envy his ability to get on so well with life's various trials and tribulations. Marion has a natural instinct with children. He understands how their minds work, particularly younger kids, and he would make an excellent kindergarten teacher. He is able to suspend his adult view of the world and really enter into the imagination of youngsters. This trait is often very appealing to potential partners, who may be quite surprised by the fact that Marion is also very astute. He has an agile and witty mind capable of discussing quite complex academic issues.

THE RUNIC INTERPRETATION
ᛏᛟᛁᚱᚨᛗ (Nauthiz, Othila, Isa, Raido, Ansuz, Mannaz)

Mannaz, or the rune of self, combined with Ansuz, or signals, indicates that Marion integrates emotions and relies on intuition to strengthen his identity. The Othila rune of separation requires that Marion become independent and self-reliant, and with Isa for standstill in the name, Marion is sure to accomplish this. The Raido rune of journey offers the chance for Marion to lighten up and travel. Raido also means good communication, and Marion can articulate his insights and inspire others. With Nauthiz, the rune of constraint and limitation, vexing some of his plans, Marion develops a unique set of coping mechanisms and is willing to share this knowledge with the world.

Elements: Fire, earth/fire, earth, water, air, air

THE NUMEROLOGICAL INTERPRETATION
Marion (NV = 7, CV = 9, VV = 7, FL = 4)

This is a name very well suited to the study of metaphysics, philosophy, astrology, and even numerology! Marion is definitely a man with a profoundly introspective and contemplative nature. He looks more deeply into life than most other people. For this reason, Marion is often found in one of the healing and serving professions. He makes an excellent psychologist or counselor, teacher or physician. People find Marion fascinating but may have a difficult time communicating with him on his own level. He always seems to know something that he is not saying, and his eyes easily express his inner wisdom. One only has to look.

Marissa

DERIVATION: English, variation on the Latin name Maris, meaning "of the sea." Found primarily during the twentieth century.

PRINCIPAL COLORS: The darkest shades of azure, violet, and gray, also black

GEMSTONES AND PRECIOUS METALS: Sapphires, rubies, carbuncles

BOTANICALS: Angelica, mandrake root, pilewort

UNIQUE SPELLINGS: Marisa, Marisah, Marissah, Marysa, Maryssa

RELATED TO: Maire, Mara, Maren, Mari, Mariat, Mariah, Marianna, Mariannet, Mariet, Mariel, Mariella, Marielle, Marika, Marilee, Marilynt, Maris, Marise, Marisha, Marisol, Maryt, Maura, Mayt, Merisa, Merissa, Miriamt, Moira, Morisa, Morissa

A KABBALISTIC SYNOPSIS

מאריססא —MARYSSA (Mem, Aleph, Resh, Yod, Samech, Samech, Aleph)

Marissa has no time for the fripperies of ladylike fashions and behavior. Her name has a strong Sagittarian influence, and one result of this is that she likes to be out in the world doing stuff rather than sitting in front of a makeup mirror. She has a real love of the outdoors, and probably spends her free time horseback riding or possibly even hunting. However, the extent of her involvement in country pursuits depends a lot on where she was raised. If she is a native New Yorker, for instance, she is not likely to be fly-fishing on the weekends, and will settle for a jog in Central Park instead. Marissa is an instantly likable woman, one who really does want to help other people out. Unfortunately she is often quite clumsy, so it's best not to ask her to help you move anything easily breakable or particularly valuable!

THE RUNIC INTERPRETATION

ᛗᛋᛋᛁᚱᚨᛗ (Ansuz, Sowelu, Sowelu, Isa, Raido, Ansuz, Mannaz)

Marissa doesn't always get what she wants just when she wants it. She may have to rethink things first and do some work on herself before she can accomplish her goals or clearly express herself. This process is typical of a double Sowelu configuration. The Sowelu rune of wholeness promises success on all levels—eventually. The double Ansuz rune for signals ensures Marissa has the courage to rely on her faith and intuition. Isa, the rune of standstill, makes Marissa crave solitude and meditative practices such as exercise and breathing techniques. The Mannaz rune of self points to the process of emotional clearing that keeps Marissa in balance. The Raido rune of journey gives Marissa a chance to travel and draw on her inner reserves, which are solid.

Elements: Air, air, air, earth, water, air, air

THE NUMEROLOGICAL INTERPRETATION

Marissa (NV = 8, CV = 6, VV = 11, FL = 4)

If we combine sensuality, physical beauty, and magnetic attractiveness, we are describing some of the characteristics associated with this name. Marissa possesses exceptional allure and is always surrounded by admirers. Therefore she must use discretion in her choice of partners, as her own intensely desirous nature may get the best of her, and her need to be emotionally supportive of others may dominate over her better judgment. Marissa has an artistic flair, and will find it easy and pleasurable to enhance the physical beauty of any environment. She also has a love of family and tends to partner early in life.

Marjorie

A KABBALISTIC SYNOPSIS

מארייורי —MARYVRY (Mem, Aleph, Resh, Yod, Vau, Resh, Yod)

Next time you buy a lottery ticket, get Marjorie to choose the numbers or pick up the ticket. She is an inordinately lucky woman, and her fortune has a tendency to rub off on those who are around her. Her name's value reduces to seventeen, the number of the tarot card the Star, which denotes not only good fortune but also a strongly optimistic outlook on life. Her cheerful nature is further emphasized by the presence of the letter R, or Resh, meaning "sun," which appears twice in her name. In many ways Marjorie is like a favorite aunt figure; she always has a gift for everyone who visits her, and seems to remember everything about you, even if you've been introduced only once. She is likely to be as lucky in love as in other aspects of her life, and her home is, on the whole, a jolly place to be.

THE RUNIC INTERPRETATION

ᛖᚱᛟᛃᚱᚨᛗ (Ehwaz, Raido, Othila, Jera, Raido, Ansuz, Mannaz)

Jera, the rune of harvest, blesses the name Marjorie. Although she must undergo shifts in friendships, and some loss of idealism because of the Othila rune of separation, Marjorie emerges victorious. The Mannaz rune of self combined with Ansuz for signals indicates that Marjorie has a high opinion of herself and focuses on the positive. She relies on her intuition rather than listening to the limiting—and frequently negative—opinions of the outside world. Marjorie is faced with changes of residence and lots of travel with the double Raido rune of journey in her name. No matter where she is, she is able to look out for herself and avert danger.

Elements: Air, water, earth/fire, earth, water, air, air

THE NUMEROLOGICAL INTERPRETATION

Marjorie (NV = 8, CV = 5, VV = 3, FL = 4)

Marjorie likes to look on the bright side of life and is an entertaining friend and partner. She thrives on change and stimulating social circumstances. But there is also a serious side to her nature, and Marjorie has a definite practical streak as well. Marjorie is ambitious and has a need to achieve prominence in life. She will leave home at an early age to seek her career path. Her easy way with people, well-developed sense of humor, and personal attractiveness make it simple for her to get the support she needs in order to move toward success.

Mark

A KABBALISTIC SYNOPSIS
מארכ —MARK (Mem, Aleph, Resh, Kaph)

Mark is a serious fellow and will almost definitely receive his graduate degree. He is most suited to work with at least some practical aspect to it, so engineering would be an ideal field for Mark to consider. On the whole, Mark is happy in any career where he can "get his hands dirty" at least some of the time. He will not enjoy a job that keeps him tied to a desk away from where all the action is; he likes to have a hands-on role. He has the ability to be quite inventive, especially if he has been born under Aries or Aquarius, and in such cases, he may well be responsible for designing new projects or products. It is quite difficult to get to know Mark, as he has a very quiet and sometimes withdrawn personality, but if you manage to find a topic of conversation close to his heart, he will really open up and reveal a lively and interesting side of himself that not many will see.

THE RUNIC INTERPRETATION
ᚲᚱᚨᛗ (Kano, Raido, Ansuz, Mannaz)

Positive and balanced, Mark enjoys spontaneity. The Ansuz rune of signals gives him his remarkably insightful nature and helps him with problem solving in his career. Mark is blessed with the Raido rune for journey and good communication. Curious and adventurous, he will travel frequently and extensively, much to his satisfaction. The Kano rune of opening points to Mark's ability to set goals and remain focused on them.

Elements: Water, water, air, air

THE NUMEROLOGICAL INTERPRETATION
Mark (NV = 7, CV = 6, VV = 1, FL = 4)

The philosopher combines with the sensualist in this name. Mark is very individualistic. Although he requires a lot of alone time to plan and organize his life, he is not a loner. His emotional needs are strong, and he is most comfortable with a partner by his side. Family is important to him, and he requires a firm home base in order to feel psychologically secure. He has to take care not to assume that other people understand his motivations, and may need to work at his ability to share himself more intimately with others.

DERIVATION: English, from the Latin name Marcus, which originally derives from the name of the Roman god of war, Mars. In the Old Testament, Saint Mark the Evangelist is the author of the second gospel. Especially popular in the United States during the 1950s.

PRINCIPAL COLORS: The palest to the deepest shades of yellow and green

GEMSTONES AND PRECIOUS METALS: Pearls, moss agate

BOTANICALS: Hops, blackberry, linseed

UNIQUE SPELLINGS: Marc, Marck, Markk

RELATED TO: Marco†, Marcus†, Mario†, Marion†, Marius, Marko, Markus, Martin†, Marty†

"I've imagined great victories, and I've imagined great races. The races are better."
—MARK HELPRIN (AUTHOR)

"All things are possible to him that believeth." —MARK 9:23

515

DERIVATION: German, blended
    form of the New Testament name
    Mary Magdalene. Made famous
    by German screen actress Marlene
    Dietrich in the early twentieth
    century, and extremely popular in
    the 1940s and 1950s.

PRINCIPAL COLORS: All the very
    lightly shaded colors

GEMSTONES AND PRECIOUS
    METALS: Diamonds, silver, any
    shiny stones

BOTANICALS: Hazel, oats,
    mushrooms

UNIQUE SPELLINGS: Marleen,
    Marleene, Marline

RELATED TO: Magdaline, Marla,
    Marlana, Marlane, Marlee,
    Marlena, Marlo, Marlynne, Marna,
    Mary†

❧

"It is the friends you can call up at
4 A.M. that matter."
—MARLENE DIETRICH (ACTRESS)

A KABBALISTIC SYNOPSIS

מארליהן —MARLYHN (Mem, Aleph, Resh, Lamed, Yod, Heh, Nun)

Marlene will talk to anyone and everyone about anything. However, it is important to say that she is not a gossip in that she doesn't discuss other people or their problems behind their backs; rather, she talks about a range of topics. Marlene tends to be a very bright woman with strong analytical skills who would be well suited to any job that involves making sense of complex regulations. She is likely to find herself in a position of authority at a relatively young age, and is more than up to the challenges that this position will bring. Her only problem is that she can be somewhat pedantic at times, but mostly she is a very lively and interesting person to know.

THE RUNIC INTERPRETATION

ᛖᚾᛖᛚᚱᚨᛗ (Ehwaz, Nauthiz, Ehwaz, Laguz, Raido, Ansuz, Mannaz)

Always ready for a laugh, Marlene is blessed by the company of good friends. The double Ehwaz energy of movement combined with the Raido rune of journey could give Marlene the privilege of living abroad and traveling often. The importunate Nauthiz rune of constraint is a challenge for Marlene, but she deals with its limitations by summoning the intuitive energy in her name to feel and think her way around these obstacles. Laguz, the rune of flow, helps Marlene maintain her calm demeanor; few people will ever guess the extent of the challenges Marlene overcomes. Mannaz, the rune of self, provides strength of character and fortitude. Capable Marlene derives a great deal of satisfaction from having friends around the world.

Elements: Air, fire, air, water, water, air, air

THE NUMEROLOGICAL INTERPRETATION

Marlene (NV = 5, CV = 3, VV = 11, FL = 4)

Not one enamored with rules and regulations, Marlene is decidedly a free spirit. The numbers in her name suggest a woman who is eager for life's many journeys. What is not offered to her at home, she will create, and her travel agent can be one of her best friends! Marlene is never satisfied with the status quo. There are always limits to be challenged, boundaries to be broken, and new territories to be explored, conquered, and cultivated. Although fully endowed with an abundance of vital energy, Marlene has to take care not to lose her sense of purpose within the whirlwind of her many activities. She should spend some time alone so that she may integrate her experiences and draw out their essential meanings.

❧

Marsha

A KABBALISTIC SYNOPSIS
מאראש —MARShA (Mem, Aleph, Resh, Shin, Aleph)

Marsha is a wonderfully creative woman with a whole set of artistic skills at her disposal. She may be interested in creating folk art or engaging in other handicrafts such as embroidery or blanket making. However, she is equally capable in more modern media such as photography or even graphic design. Her house is probably very simply but tastefully decorated. Marsha is a very decisive woman who also has very good judgment. You can rely on her decisions to be sound. In love Marsha is especially discriminating, and will not go out with a date until she knows a considerable amount about his background and interests.

THE RUNIC INTERPRETATION
ᚨᚺᛋᚱᚨᛗ (Ansuz, Hagalaz, Sowelu, Raido, Ansuz, Mannaz)

Hagalaz, the rune of disruption, is a breeder of chaos and confusion. Fortunately, the double Ansuz runes of signals help Marsha intuit her way through a few rough spots in life while still feeling dearly loved and keenly protected. Marsha handles the vicissitudes of life with a philosophical style, which comes from the ego strength contained in her name afforded by the Mannaz rune of self. Raido, the rune of journey, promises Marsha the thrill of travel and also good communication skills. Marsha is capable and willing to ask for advice when she needs to. Because some disruptions over the course of her life threaten to unseat her, Marsha is wise to seek good counsel at such times. The Sowelu rune of wholeness hints that when all is said and done, Marsha is her own best advocate.

Elements: Air, water, air, water, air, air

THE NUMEROLOGICAL INTERPRETATION
Marsha (NV = 6, CV = 22, VV = 2, FL = 4)

Marsha is one of the rare names containing the master number twenty-two. Her powers to manifest her inner reality in the external world are thus heightened—so much so that it is vitally important for her to be clear and distinct about her goals. The three other important numbers in this name are six, two, and four. All of these digits contribute to a strong emotional nature. The six is an especially powerful influence in this respect, and tells us that Marsha possesses poise and balance—characteristics that balance a name with such potency. The six will give Marsha artistic ability as well, and Marsha is a natural for a career in the arts, as the twenty-two tends to bring its bearer into contact with large numbers of people.

DERIVATION: English, alternate spelling of the Latin name Marcia, which originally derives from the name of the Roman war god, Mars. The Marcia spelling is the more common form in the United States.

PRINCIPAL COLORS: Light to medium blue

GEMSTONES AND PRECIOUS METALS: Blue and blue-green turquoise, emeralds

BOTANICALS: Dog rose, walnuts, almonds

UNIQUE SPELLINGS: Marcea, Marcia, Marciah, Marrcia, Marshah, Martia

RELATED TO: Marcelia, Marcella, Marcene, Marci, Marciat, Marcie, Marcilynn, Marcy, Marshella, Marshita

❧

"To find in ourselves what makes life worth living is risky business, for it means that once we know we must seek it. It also means that without it life will be valueless."
—MARSHA SINETAR (AUTHOR)

DERIVATION: English, originally
from a French surname that
denoted someone who worked as
a horse keeper. Used as a first
name since the nineteenth
century.

PRINCIPAL COLORS: Mauve to
deep purple hues

GEMSTONES AND PRECIOUS
METALS: Garnets, amethyst

BOTANICALS: Barberry, mint,
thyme

UNIQUE SPELLINGS: Marcial,
Marschal, Marschall, Marshal,
Marshell, Martial, Martiall

RELATED TO: Marcel, Marcellus,
Marcus†, Marius, Marsh, Martin†

Marshall

A KABBALISTIC SYNOPSIS

מארשאל —MARShAL (Mem, Aleph, Resh, Shin, Aleph, Lamed)

Success is of prime importance to Marshall. The Lamed in his name is an indication of his drive and ambition, while the letter Shin emphasizes the fiery enthusiasm with which he will pursue his goals. This overwhelming desire to achieve often makes Marshall a very impatient man, and this can lead him to make some rash and unwise business decisions when he is first starting out. On the positive side, he has the ability to learn from his mistakes and isn't one to dwell on opportunities that he may have missed. For Marshall the direction is always onward and upward. He has a good deal of common sense and an interest in practical or mechanical matters, so a career in heavy industry, particularly manufacturing of some kind, will suit him well—although it is unlikely that he will spend much time, if any, on the shop floor. Marshall's driving energy has certain compensations for his romantic partner. In addition to the money that he is likely to bring home, he is also an exciting and energetic lover!

THE RUNIC INTERPRETATION

ᛗᚨᚾᛋᚱᚨᛗ (Laguz, Laguz, Ansuz, Hagalaz, Sowelu, Raido, Ansuz, Mannaz)

Having a double Laguz runic configuration gives Marshall an ace up his sleeve when he is challenged by the naughty Hagalaz rune of disruption in this name. Chaos is a form of negativity, and Marshall needs all the help he can muster to avert disaster. Luck is with him, though. Marshall can summon the strength of inner reserves indicated by the Mannaz rune of self, and the double Laguz rune of flow affords him flexibility. He can also draw strength from the doubly powerful Ansuz runes, which give him good intuition. Blessed Sowelu, the rune of wholeness, also helps to save the day and brings Marshall order, satisfaction, and fulfillment.

Elements: Water, water, air, water, air, water, air, air

THE NUMEROLOGICAL INTERPRETATION

Marshall (NV = 3, CV = 1, VV = 2, FL = 4)

Marshall has an innate ability to recognize how individuals of differing backgrounds and talents can use their gifts for mutual benefit. He sees the deeper connections between people and is able to transform their differences into creative unity. Marshall doesn't lose his sense of himself in his relationships. His name carries a very strong consonant value of one, giving Marshall a distinct awareness of his own identity. He tends to walk through life with confidence, and enjoys one-on-one competitive sports. Marshall requires a partner who doesn't mind sharing him with friends and associates.

Martha

A Kabbalistic Synopsis
מארתא —MARThA (Mem, Aleph, Resh, Tau, Aleph)

If you encounter a Martha in your life, the key thing to remember is: Be sensitive. Martha is ruled by emotion rather than rationality. She is usually fairly insecure, and can be deeply stung by comments that most would shrug off, although she may hide her upset. The presence of the letter Tau, and the fact that the value of her name can be reduced to the number of the Hanged Man tarot card, indicates a willingness to try to help others cope with the pain in their lives. Martha gets a great deal of pleasure from being able to do this. Martha loves kids and will make a great mother; her children will bring her immense pleasure. She would do well in socially active or service-oriented careers, perhaps as a nurse or caretaker.

The Runic Interpretation
ᚨᚦᚱᚨᛗ (Ansuz, Thurisaz, Raido, Ansuz, Mannaz)

Thurisaz, the rune of gateway, always indicates receptivity, curiosity, and opportunities. Martha uses the gateway rune to welcome opportunities and transitions. Martha looks for meaning in the small as well as the large events in her life. The Raido rune of journey presents itself strongly in Martha's name, and beckons her to travel and tell others about her experiences. Martha can communicate with others by using images, music, writing, film, or any creative medium of expression; it all comes effortlessly to Martha. With Mannaz, the rune of self, in her name, Martha works hard to know herself and it shows, because her friends adore her.

Elements: Air, fire, water, air, air

The Numerological Interpretation
Martha (NV = 7, CV = 5, VV = 2, FL = 4)

Martha is a woman of many skills. This is a name that indicates a high degree of mental and physical dexterity. Martha is also a bit of a perfectionist, ever seeking to improve her own and other people's lives. Intellectually gifted, she is very at home in a school or library. A natural-born teacher, Martha is very keen on exploring a variety of ideas and interests. Many things appeal to her, and perhaps that is her greatest challenge. It may be difficult for her to prioritize, and she has to take care not to dissipate her energy. Martha is devoted to her close friends and tends to cultivate these relationships over long periods of time.

DERIVATION: Aramaic, meaning "lady" or "mistress." Found in the New Testament as the name of the sister of Lazarus and Mary, who serves Jesus when he visits their house. Also, the name of the first first lady of the United States, Martha Washington. Especially common during the first half of the twentieth century.

PRINCIPAL COLORS: The full spectrum of green and yellow hues

GEMSTONES AND PRECIOUS METALS: Cat's-eye, pearls, any white stones

BOTANICALS: Elder, juniper, linseed

UNIQUE SPELLINGS: Marrtha, Marthah

RELATED TO: Maret, Mart, Marta, Martella, Martelle, Marthe, Marthena, Marti, Martie, Martina, Marty, Matti, Mattie

"Practice means to perform, over and over again in the face of all obstacles, some act of vision, of faith, of desire. Practice is a means of inviting the perfection desired."
—MARTHA GRAHAM (DANCER-CHOREOGRAPHER)

"Hyperactivity is not a major fault in anyone."
—MARTHA STEWART (AUTHOR, DESIGN CONSULTANT)

*"Hatred paralyzes life; love
  releases it.
Hatred confuses life; love
  harmonizes it.
Hatred darkens life; love illumines it."*
    —MARTIN LUTHER KING JR.
       (CIVIL RIGHTS LEADER)

Martin

A KABBALISTIC SYNOPSIS

מארטין —MARTYN (Mem, Aleph, Resh, Teth, Yod, Nun)

For all of his days, Martin will remain an avid campaigner for the things in which he strongly believes, and that is usually a fairly lengthy list of causes. People are often surprised when they discover this side of Martin's personality, as in general Martin comes across as a mild-mannered and quiet individual. However, the letter Teth, meaning "serpent," in his name suggests that Martin can be vigorous, to say the least, when it comes to organizing a protest or demonstration. Martin always has a kind word for people and is usually a cheerful chap even when he is down on his luck. For this reason he has good relationships with his friends and his partner. His loyalty and commitment add to the special bond he is able to form with a whole range of individuals.

THE RUNIC INTERPRETATION

ᚺᛁᛏᚱᚨᛗ (Nauthiz, Isa, Teiwaz, Raido, Ansuz, Mannaz)

With the troublesome rune of constraint, Nauthiz, figuring prominently in his name, Martin is fortunate to have the powers of Teiwaz, the warrior, and Mannaz, the self, to gird up his faith and fortitude. The Isa rune of standstill cautions Martin to keep his own counsel at times in order to acquire perspective on the events of his busy and productive days. The Raido rune of journey gives Martin a chance to exit when the going gets tough and rejuvenate his health. Travel opportunities abound in Martin's life. The transitions indicated by the Raido rune are smooth for Martin because he can rely on his intuition and the blessing of the Ansuz rune of signals to guide his way.

Elements: Fire, earth, air, water, air, air

THE NUMEROLOGICAL INTERPRETATION

Martin (NV = 3, CV = 2, VV = 1, FL = 4)

Straightforward and direct in speech and manner, Martin is an uncomplicated man. He likes to go right to the heart of any matter and not create extra work for himself. Martin enjoys the company of people, but he has no problem spending time alone. He doesn't get too many of these opportunities for solitude, however, as he is an active person with a number of friends. The consonant value of two focuses him on relationships, and he finds himself constantly involved with others. He has a natural understanding of people and may often be called upon to act as a counselor. He does well in any profession that involves communication or instruction.

Marty

A Kabbalistic Synopsis

מארטי —MARTY (Mem, Aleph, Resh, Teth, Yod)

Simply by losing a letter in the Hebrew spelling of a name we change the personality quite dramatically. Marty shares with Martin a strong value and belief system, but he is not likely to pronounce his worldview from a soapbox in the park. To Marty life is too much fun to spend a whole bunch of time protesting about the things that are wrong in the world. Marty would rather do his bit by spreading some happiness around. Marty is a supportive friend, though, and he knows how to be serious when the situation calls for it. A career in teaching would suit Marty very well, as would any job where Marty is able to define a reasonable portion of what he actually does. In other words, Marty likes to be master of his own destiny. He also possesses quite a rare gift in that he seems to understand what makes teenagers tick! However, as a teacher, he will have to watch his sense of humor, which at times can edge toward being slightly too cruel.

The Runic Interpretation

ᛇᛏᚱᚨᛗ (Eihwaz, Teiwaz, Raido, Ansuz, Mannaz)

Love abounds for our Marty. The Mannaz rune of self promises love of self and the capacity to love others with depth and imagination. Marty has the Teiwaz rune to give him the courage to defend principles he upholds, and the Ansuz rune of signals to intuit others' hidden agendas. Marty has superlative social skills, and this takes him far in life. He prospers because he is honest and a clear communicator and he inspires trust. The Eihwaz rune of defense cancels out any tendencies in Marty to be gullible or victimized. He is perceptive and astute.

Elements: Earth/fire, air, water, air, air

The Numerological Interpretation

Marty (NV = 5, CV = 6, VV = 8, FL = 4)

Marty tends to be down-to-earth, one not given over to philosophical speculation or abstract theories. He expresses himself most easily in physical ways. He enjoys sports and makes an effort to keep himself healthy and active. Marty is attracted by beauty and may have a gift for sculpture or painting. He is an emotional man, and his home and family are important motivations for him. In essence, this name suggests a balanced and integrated life—quite an advantage in a world in which chaos is no stranger. Since his foundation is so intact, Marty may wish to pay more attention to his spiritual nature, as there are many gifts waiting for him behind this door.

DERIVATION: English, short form of Martin, which originally derives from the name of the Roman god of war, Mars. Especially common during the mid-twentieth century, and sometimes found as an independent given name.

PRINCIPAL COLORS: Any very lightly shaded hue

GEMSTONES AND PRECIOUS METALS: Platinum, silver, diamonds

BOTANICALS: Hazel, oats, sweet marjoram

UNIQUE SPELLINGS: Martee, Martey, Marti, Martie

RELATED TO: Maarten, Marc, Marcel, Marcellus, Marcus†, Marius, Marshall†, Marten, Martin†, Martino, Martinus, Martyn, Morton

"Every day is a good day to be alive, whether the sun's shining or not."
—MARTY ROBBINS (MUSICIAN)

Marvin

DERIVATION: English, from the Old Welsh names Merfyn and Mervyn. First seen in the United States during the nineteenth century, and especially popular in the first half of the twentieth century.

PRINCIPAL COLORS: The full spectrum of pale hues

GEMSTONES AND PRECIOUS METALS: Silver, platinum

BOTANICALS: Parsley, sea kale, mushrooms

UNIQUE SPELLINGS: Maervin, Marrvin, Marven, Marvenn, Marvinn, Marvyn, Marvynn

RELATED TO: Marv, Marvy, Marwin, Merv, Mervin, Mervyn, Merwyn, Murvynn

A KABBALISTIC SYNOPSIS

מארויין —MARVYN (Mem, Aleph, Resh, Vau, Yod, Nun)

The value of the name Marvin reduces to twenty-one, the number of the Universe card in the tarot, which indicates success in life and the achievement of one's ambitions. In general Marvin has plenty to be cheerful about. His primary skill lies not in coming up with new ideas but in making sure that things actually get done on time. He is what you could call a "finisher." He has a great talent for putting people at their ease, and is the ideal man to send out to woo clients. And Marvin will no doubt use his wooing abilities in his personal life as well as in his work environment!

THE RUNIC INTERPRETATION

ᛏᛁᚠᚱᚨᛗ (Nauthiz, Isa, Fehu, Raido, Ansuz, Mannaz)

Marvin will live a rich life of abundance and have the opportunity to see the world. The Fehu rune of possessions gives Marvin prosperity and many creative ideas. The Raido rune of journey lets him travel to his heart's content. Mannaz for self combined with Ansuz for signals gives Marvin a strong and insightful personality. The Isa rune encourages the introspective side of Marvin's sensitive nature. The Nauthiz energy of constraint means limitations come his way, but Marvin is rich and resourceful and has the capacity to surmount difficulties. He appreciates his wealth and is grateful for the good life he leads.

Elements: Fire, earth, fire, water, air, air

THE NUMEROLOGICAL INTERPRETATION

Marvin (NV = 5, CV = 22, VV = 1, FL = 4)

Marvin is going to focus his life on big accomplishments and is capable of an incredible amount of creative output. He has practical know-how combined with vision and insight. His name indicates a highly independent person, a man who expects a great deal from himself. Marvin is charismatic, attractive, and magnetic. People are usually quite willing to lend him their support and follow his lead. But where is he *going*? What is the focus of his life's direction? Marvin must cultivate a clear sense of his own goals. His ambitions may be too big for his capabilities, however, and failure will be the natural result. Education, self-discipline, and a focused spiritual life are essential to a man of such potential.

Mary

A KABBALISTIC SYNOPSIS

מארי —MARY (Mem, Aleph, Resh, Yod)

Mary has obvious historical associations with Mary the mother of Jesus, and her name's meaning in Christian cultures has taken on aspects of this association. However, in kabbalistic analysis, we may well be reminded of that other famous biblical Mary: Mary Magdalene. Mary is very protective and will do anything to ensure the safety and well-being of her family, particularly her children. At work she is able to handle promotions confidently and take on considerable responsibility; she also has the energy to run her own business successfully if she wants to do so. Mary has a very strong, forceful character, which is indicated by the fact that her name reduces to eight, the number of the Strength card in the tarot. She is also very sexual, and can be as demanding of her lovers as she is of her staff.

THE RUNIC INTERPRETATION

ᛇᚱᚨᛗ (Eihwaz, Raido, Ansuz, Mannaz)

Always listening and quietly forming opinions, Mary is nobody's fool. The Eihwaz energy of defense makes Mary perceptive and careful in her dealings with people. She may not appear wise or sophisticated, but under that great smile and pleasant demeanor is a woman who knows how to wait for her moment of glory. The Ansuz energy enhances her intuitive gifts. Mannaz for self gives Mary her strong sense of who she is and her high standards of personal integrity. The Raido rune makes Mary a clear communicator and student of human nature. Mary loves to travel, and with Raido in her name, Mary is sure to be a frequent flier.

Elements: Earth/fire, water, air, air

THE NUMEROLOGICAL INTERPRETATION

Mary (NV = 3, CV = 4, VV = 8, FL = 4)

This is the name of a woman who is very preoccupied with her physical environment. Her material well-being is very important to her, and she is not totally secure unless she knows she has the means to pay her bills and support her loved ones. On a personal level, Mary may be quite health-conscious and concerned with her finances. Professionally, Mary may be very interested in planetary ecology and the general state of the health of humanity. If that is the case, Mary will choose a profession that responds to these concerns. She is well suited to the healing professions or a career that involves the distribution of food and other economic resources.

DERIVATION: English, the New Testament form of the Hebrew name Miriam, which is of uncertain origin. The most popular of all female Christian names, being the name of the Virgin Mary, the mother of Jesus Christ. Before the Middle Ages, the name Mary was considered too sacred to be used, but throughout the medieval period, Mary became increasingly common in every country in Europe. Since this time, many common variations on the name Mary have emerged as well.

PRINCIPAL COLORS: Pale bluish purple to deep, rich shades of violet

GEMSTONES AND PRECIOUS METALS: Amethyst, garnets

BOTANICALS: Apple, cherry, mint

UNIQUE SPELLINGS: Mairee, Mairey, Mairy, Marey

RELATED TO: Maire, Mara, Maren, Mari, Mariat, Mariah, Marianna, Mariannet, Mariet, Mariel, Mariella, Marielle, Marietta, Marika, Marilee, Marilynt, Marisa, Marissat, Maura, Maureent, Mayt, Mia, Mimi, Minniet, Miriamt, Mitzi, Moira, Mollyt, Murielt, Myrat, Polly

523

DERIVATION: English, one of the most common compound names. The name Mary derives from the Hebrew name Miriam; the name Ann derives from the Hebrew name Hannah. Mary Ann became a popular name in the eighteenth century, and was especially common during the 1950s and 1960s in the United States.

PRINCIPAL COLORS: Any color, as long as it is lightly shaded

GEMSTONES AND PRECIOUS METALS: Platinum, diamonds

BOTANICALS: Oats, parsley, hazel

UNIQUE SPELLINGS: Mariane, Mariann, Marianne, Maryann, Mary-Ann, Maryanne, Mary Anne, Mary-Anne

RELATED TO: Ann†, Anna†, Anne†, Annemarie, Annette†, Hanna, Hannah†, Mara, Mare, Maria†, Mariah, Marian, Mariana, Marianna, Marianne†, Maribel, Marie†, Mariel, Mariella, Marielle, Marietta, Marigold, Marika, Marilyn†, Marissa†, Marla, Mary†, Maura, May†, Miriam†, Moira, Molly†, Muriel†

A KABBALISTIC SYNOPSIS

מאריאנן —MARYANN (Mem, Aleph, Resh, Yod, Aleph, Nun, Nun)

Mary Ann loves to play games. She is a real sport who is always ready to have fun, and who is fond of all forms of athletic activity. Needless to say, Mary Ann is usually an extremely fit woman. Her success in races is also in part due to her natural good fortune; she is likely to be a relatively wealthy lady whose wealth may come more from happy circumstance than from hard work and long hours. Mary Ann has a double N, or Nun, ending to her name, and her name begins with Mem; both letters are associated with the emotions. Thus Mary Ann is a very emotive woman, and she is far more likely to be concerned with her family life and her relationships than with her career. In fact, if she has children, which in her case is more than likely, she actually will be very happy to stay at home with the kids rather than work for a company.

THE RUNIC INTERPRETATION

ᛇᚱᚨᛗᚾᚾᚨ (Eihwaz, Raido, Ansuz, Mannaz, Nauthiz, Nauthiz, Ansuz)

Mary Ann has all the capabilities and opportunities contained in the name Mary, but the additional ending creates some problems for Mary Ann. The double Nauthiz energy of constraint is a double whammy; Mary Ann will know firsthand what limitations, delays, and disappointments are all about. Fortunately, Mary Ann has the double Ansuz runes of signals to save the day. With every lemon, Mary Ann makes lemonade. She is highly intuitive, and knows which doors open to new opportunities and offset some of the obstacles wrought by the Nauthiz power in her name. Mary Ann has tough lessons to learn, but by meeting these challenges she becomes stronger, and she learns a lot about self-reliance and faith.

Elements: Earth/fire, water, air, air, fire, fire, air

THE NUMEROLOGICAL INTERPRETATION

Mary Ann (NV = 5, CV = 5, VV = 9, FL = 4)

Mary Ann finds that there is no end to things that have to be accomplished. This name reveals a very busy woman, one who struggles to keep up with herself. Her challenge is to coordinate head and hand so that she does not splinter herself off into too many directions. Mary Ann has a tremendous need to explore the limits of her creativity. Once she reaches this boundary, she pushes it out a little farther. Her motto is "I see the goal, I reach that goal, and then I see another." Her vowel value of nine tells us that there is an unselfish and humanitarian side to her nature as well. Mary Ann is not preoccupied with herself. Whatever else she may be doing, Mary Ann will make the time to give of herself in some form of service work.

Matt

DERIVATION: English, short form of Matthew, which derives from the Hebrew meaning "gift of God." Occasionally given as an independent name.

PRINCIPAL COLORS: The full range of red hues, particularly the deepest shades

GEMSTONES AND PRECIOUS METALS: Bloodstones, garnets

BOTANICALS: Garlic, nettle, wormwood

UNIQUE SPELLINGS: Maht, Mat

RELATED TO: Mateo, Matheson, Matheu, Mathew, Mathias, Matias, Mats, Matteas, Matthewf, Matthias, Mattias, Mattieu, Matty, Matz, Mayhew

A KABBALISTIC SYNOPSIS

מאטט —MATT (Mem, Aleph, Teth, Teth)

It's very difficult to get Matt to slow down, as he loves his work so much. In most cases Matt will run his own company; if not, he makes an excellent salesman. He has a very charming manner, one which he is quite happy to employ in order to close a deal. Matt is a shrewd man who will always find a way to make a buck—and probably considerably more than a buck! The double presence of the letter Teth at the end of his name lets us know that he is a difficult competitor to beat and he is not above using dirty tricks in order to win. And Matt will remember his losses; he is bound to find some way to get even for them even if it takes him a while. Surprisingly Matt is quite calm and relaxed at home, and may well let his partner take the dominant role in the relationship.

THE RUNIC INTERPRETATION

↑↑ᚾᛗ (Teiwaz, Teiwaz, Ansuz, Mannaz)

If you ever need a brave scout to go ahead of the party and sense if danger or opportunity lies ahead, send Matt. He is a born leader. His bravery is remarkable. Matt is wonderfully discriminating, and he has all the self-esteem he needs to stand by his hunches. Matt is patience personified. He has the double Teiwaz energy of the warrior in his name, along with the energy of the Ansuz rune, which makes him highly intuitive. He can rely on himself to make the most of almost any situation.

Elements: Air, air, air, air

THE NUMEROLOGICAL INTERPRETATION

Matt (NV = 9, CV = 8, VV = 1, FL = 4)

Matt has to prove himself. He regularly takes on challenges and hopes to surpass his previous accomplishments. He works to create awareness of issues that affect everyone, including people from all walks of life. Very often he is involved in some project that benefits others. Although Matt can be very occupied with making a name for himself in the world, he is a generous man. The vowel value of one gives him courage and strength enough to fight, while the name value of nine tells us that these fights can be in defense of human rights. Matt is a passionate man whose relationships are intensely emotional and sensual.

Matthew

A KABBALISTIC SYNOPSIS
מאתוה —MAThVH (Mem, Aleph, Tau, Vau, Heh)

Matthew is a man of high principles indeed, and they are often, but not always, principles originating from a very religious personality. This does not mean that Matthew is self-righteously pious—not at all. Matthew firmly believes that his values are right and will win out eventually, a belief that gives him a very optimistic air and makes him full of hope for the future. Even those who disagree with his beliefs cannot fault Matthew for the way in which he puts them into action. The letter Heh, meaning "window," which completes his name, tells us that he is always looking out at the outside world, while other elements of his name indicate that Matthew is very concerned with the needy and neglected in society. He is likely to do a lot of work for others without asking for any reward or recognition.

THE RUNIC INTERPRETATION
ᛗᛏᛞᚾᛖᛜ (Wunjo, Ehwaz, Thurisaz, Teiwaz, Ansuz, Mannaz)

Matthew isn't the brave warrior that Matt surely is; Matthew has his own set of attributes. The Thurisaz rune of gateway is in this name, which offers Matthew the ability to wait for opportunities and also the ability to release emotional issues from the past. The Ehwaz energy brings in movement, along with the possibility of travel to exotic lands. The Wunjo rune of joy is the best rune of all, and it colors the outcome of all of Matthew's lessons. Wunjo signifies the end of a period of testing and tribulation. The new energy brings blessings, benefits, opportunities, and an enhanced sense of well-being.

Elements: Earth, air, fire, air, air, air

THE NUMEROLOGICAL INTERPRETATION
Matthew (NV = 9, CV = 7, VV = 11, FL = 4)

Matthew will seek out educational opportunities that enhance his spiritual attunement to life. Once this is accomplished, he will move out into the public sphere to take up some very interesting communicative projects. His ability to reach people and affect their lives in a positive manner is very dependent upon his inner growth. If he is not inclined toward a more spiritual path, Matthew will find that his analytical mind will dominate his life. His interests will then be much more intellectual, and his personality more self-absorbed.

Maureen

DERIVATION: Irish form of Maire, a variant of Mary. Entered into use during the late 1800s, and most popular in the United States during the mid-twentieth century.

PRINCIPAL COLORS: The full spectrum of very pale hues

GEMSTONES AND PRECIOUS METALS: Silver, diamonds

BOTANICALS: Sweet marjoram, oats, hazel

UNIQUE SPELLINGS: Maureene, Maureine, Maurene, Maurine, Mauryne, Moreen, Morene, Morreen

RELATED TO: Maire, Maria†, Mariet†, Mary†, Maura, Maurena, Maurise, Maurita, Mo, Moira, Mora, Moria, Molly†

A KABBALISTIC SYNOPSIS

מערין —MA'ARYN (Mem, Ayin, Resh, Yod, Nun)

Whenever you hear laughter in the office, there is a good chance that Maureen is involved. She is a real joker who will go to quite elaborate lengths at times in order to play her practical pranks on people. Out of work she is equally cheerful, bubbly, and extroverted—especially when you meet her at a party. However, beneath this happy-go-lucky exterior is a very sensitive woman who wants a long-term relationship with a partner who will treat her seriously. Her outgoing nature attracts large numbers of potential dates, and anyone worth their salt will very quickly recognize what a gem they have in Maureen. Maureen is very proud of her house, and is keen to show it off to her friends, so any permanent partner will have to learn where everything goes—fast!

THE RUNIC INTERPRETATION

ᚾᛇᚱᚢᚨᛗ (Nauthiz, Eihwaz, Raido, Uruz, Ansuz, Mannaz)

Maureen can have it all but not because it's handed to her on a silver platter. Indeed, she needs to venture out on her own to carve out a new identity independent of her family. But no one with an Ansuz-Mannaz combination fails to find out who they are and where they are going; Ansuz offers intuition, and Mannaz contributes a strong sense of self. The Nauthiz rune of constraint tells us that Maureen has some limitations to overcome, and she needs to be not always so trusting in her dealings with people. The Uruz energy of strength allows Maureen to use effectively the Raido energy of journey. She will have inner journeys of the soul as well as blissful vacations. While traveling hither and yon, Maureen will love every adventure that comes her way.

Elements: Fire, earth/fire, water, earth, air, air

THE NUMEROLOGICAL INTERPRETATION

Maureen (NV = 5, CV = 9, VV = 5, FL = 4)

Maureen tends to have a smile on her face and an optimistic attitude in her heart. She is never down for too long and is a source of inspiration and uplift to those around her. Maureen is a name that instills an avid curiosity about life. Maureen is open to widening her horizons and pushing other people to surpass their own limitations. She makes an excellent teacher, especially to people who have some sort of disability. Maureen likes to eat and have a good time, and has to watch a tendency toward overindulgence. Although she is attracted to the idea of partnership, she needs to be with a lover or spouse who does not suppress her natural exuberance and love of freedom.

Maurice

DERIVATION: Roman, from the Latin name Mauritius, meaning "Moorish, dark-skinned." Entered Britain during the Norman Conquest, and especially popular in the United States during the late nineteenth century.

PRINCIPAL COLORS: Any color of yellow, green, or gold tone

GEMSTONES AND PRECIOUS METALS: Moss agate, moonstones

BOTANICALS: Elder, blackberry

UNIQUE SPELLINGS: Maurece, Maureese, Maurese, Maurise, Mauryce, Morece, Moreese, Morice, Morrece, Morrice, Morryce

RELATED TO: Mauricio, Maury, Moet, Moritz, Morrell, Morrist, Morry, Moss

❧

"There must be more to life than having everything."
—MAURICE SENDAK
(ILLUSTRATOR)

"Remember that happiness is as contagious as gloom. It should be the first duty of those who are happy to let others know of their gladness."
—MAURICE MAETERLINCK
(AUTHOR)

A KABBALISTIC SYNOPSIS
מערים —MA'ARYS (Mem, Ayin, Resh, Yod, Samech)

Maurice is not destined to have an easy life. Among the kabbalistic equivalencies of his name are Hebrew words meaning "difficulty," "narrowness," and "pain." But in fact, there will be many rewards for Maurice, even if his life is tough. The difficult and narrow path that Maurice treads on the way to achieving his goals in life is so narrow because of the restrictions that Maurice places on himself. Another kabbalistic equivalence of Maurice is a Hebrew name for God, and this is, of course, a very positive sign. While Maurice will find it more difficult than most to achieve the things he wants, once he has done so, he will derive much more pleasure from his achievements than others.

THE RUNIC INTERPRETATION
ᛗᛋᛁᚱᚾᚨᛗ (Ehwaz, Sowelu, Isa, Raido, Uruz, Ansuz, Mannaz)

Maurice is gently cared for and has good mental health. He has the Sowelu rune of wholeness in his name, combined with Mannaz for self and Uruz for strength. Ansuz, the rune for signals, indicates that Maurice has good intuition. He also has the Isa rune of standstill, which causes him to be a bit moody and introspective at times. When he is like this, he just needs to work it out on his own; eventually he'll come around. The Raido rune for journey provides good communication skills, so whatever is bothering Maurice is bound to come out eventually. Raido also means travel, and Maurice keeps his suitcase packed in anticipation of his many journeys.

Elements: Air, air, earth, water, earth, air, air

THE NUMEROLOGICAL INTERPRETATION
Maurice (NV = 7, CV = 7, VV = 9, FL = 4)

The urge to develop one's intellect dominates the energy of this name. Maurice is a natural-born researcher. He tends to be scientifically oriented or, at the very least, quite logical and rational in his approach to life. Maurice has a very disciplined mind, allowing him to think through a situation and come up with some very interesting conclusions. He is occupied with world events and is a keen observer of politics and the media. Maurice requires a lot of privacy and is not what one would call a "party person." He much prefers intimate dinners at home with a few well-chosen friends. He usually selects his companions because of their intelligence and similar views.

❧

Max

A KABBALISTIC SYNOPSIS

מאחס —MAChS (Mem, Aleph, Cheth, Samech)

Max is a deeply suspicious man. If you're having an affair when you're dating Max, your chances of getting away with it are pretty near zero! As Max is a very practical man, he is aware that often his jealous attitude is unwarranted; still, it does cause him some difficulties in his relationships. At work Max is ideally suited to heading up research and development departments for the reason that he knows how to keep things quiet. To those people Max trusts, he is a very loyal and supportive friend. There will not be many such people in his life, but those close to him will remain his friends for a considerable length of time.

THE RUNIC INTERPRETATION

ᛋᚲᚨᛗ (Sowelu and Kano, Ansuz, Mannaz)

Max is approachable and comfortable with people and with himself. This is no accident: Max has the ego strength of Mannaz for self in his name. This power, when combined with the Ansuz rune for signals, tells us Max has a highly intuitive nature. The Kano rune of opening provides Max with clarity and the ability to give and receive love. Furthermore, Max is blessed with the Sowelu energy of wholeness, which gives him a feeling of self-realization. Max is nonjudgmental because he can accept himself for who he is and others for who they are becoming. Max is fortunate to have such an easy rapport with others.

Elements: Air and water, air, air

THE NUMEROLOGICAL INTERPRETATION

Max (NV = 2, CV = 1, VV = 1, FL = 4)

Max has a great deal of appeal and will find that people want to be a part of his life. He has a caring disposition and highly developed feelings. When his friends need someone to talk to, they come to Max, as he is very empathetic. Relationships are very important in his life, and Max seeks to build strong and stable connections to other people. At the same time, this name denotes a very individualistic and independent person. Max loves his friends but is not dependent upon them. He does very well by himself, having learned from an early age how to make the most out of his talents and abilities and enjoy his time alone.

DERIVATION: English, short form of Maximilian, which is ultimately from the Latin name Maximus, meaning "greatest." Also a common nickname for Maxwell, which derives from a Scottish place-name. Max is fairly common as an independent given name as well.

PRINCIPAL COLORS: All shades of green, white

GEMSTONES AND PRECIOUS METALS: Jade, moonstones, white pearls

BOTANICALS: Chicory, colewort, moonwort

UNIQUE SPELLINGS: Macks, Macs, Maks, Maxx

RELATED TO: Mac, Mackt, Maxie, Maxim, Maxime, Maximilian, Maximillian, Maximo, Maxwell, Maxy

In the absence of any direct equivalent to the letter *x* in the runic alphabet, the runes Sowelu and Kano are used in conjunction.

Maxine

DERIVATION: English, female form of the male name Max, which derives from the Latin name Maximus, meaning "greatest." First appeared during the 1930s, and was especially popular during the mid-twentieth century.

PRINCIPAL COLORS: The full range of purple hues, from pale lilac to deep maroon

GEMSTONES AND PRECIOUS METALS: Amethyst, garnets

BOTANICALS: Cherry, dandelion, strawberry

UNIQUE SPELLINGS: Maxeane, Maxeen, Maxeene, Maxene, Maxyne

RELATED TO: Massima, Maxena, Maxi, Maxie, Maxina, Maxy

❧

In the absence of any direct equivalent to the letter *x* in the runic alphabet, the runes Sowelu and Kano are used in conjunction.

A KABBALISTIC SYNOPSIS

מאחסין —MAChSYN (Mem, Aleph, Cheth, Samech, Yod, Nun)

Maxine is driven by a desire to protect others. The positioning of the letter Cheth next to the letter Samech tells us that not only does she want to assist those who are having emotional difficulties, but that she has the strength of character to make a career of offering genuinely reliable support to clients until they feel better. The value of Maxine's name is 819, and the initial eight again refers to the letter Cheth and the desire to put a protective wall around others. The reduction of 819 is 18, which is related to the Moon card in the tarot, which deals with all manner of emotional concerns and insecurities. Maxine tends to be full of confidence in her own abilities, and likes to have a lively and physically challenging set of leisure interests to contrast with what is likely to be the emotionally draining work of her week.

THE RUNIC INTERPRETATION

ᛗᚾᛁᛋᚲᚨᛗ (Ehwaz, Nauthiz, Isa, Sowelu and Kano, Ansuz, Mannaz)

Will the real Maxine please stand up? Maxine can be many people, and she is quite a good actress. She will excel in sales positions because of her ability to transmute. Sometimes Maxine is shy and introverted when the Isa energy for standstill and the Ehwaz energy keep her hidden away. At other times—when the Nauthiz rune of constraint forces her to deal with conflicts and limitations—she is confrontational. Maxine uses the Ansuz rune of signals to her advantage, to sense whom she needs to be for any given situation. The Kano rune of opening encourages Maxine to move ahead with concentrated effort when she wants to. The Sowelu energy of wholeness integrates all these traits into one powerful woman!

Elements: Air, fire, earth, air and water, air, air

THE NUMEROLOGICAL INTERPRETATION

Maxine (NV = 3, CV = 6, VV = 6, FL = 4)

A very romantic woman, Maxine has a big heart and a very generous disposition. This is one of her greatest gifts as well as one of her most profound challenges. Maxine has to learn to take care of herself; she is so sensitive to other people's emotional needs that it is very difficult for her to say no. Maxine yields too easily under emotional pressure, yet it is precisely the depth of her emotional nature that endows her with her special gifts. She is attracted to music and the arts, and can easily find herself in a profession that involves these areas. Maxine is usually in love and must take care to balance her heart with her head.

❧

May

A Kabbalistic Synopsis
מאי —MAY (Mem, Aleph, Yod)

In terms of traditional Western beliefs, May is a very important and joyous month of the year—hence the May queen, the May fairs, and of course, the potent fertility rite of maypole dancing. The name May is kabbalistically equivalent to the Hebrew word meaning "devoured," this hints at the self-indulgence and feasting associated with the May festival. May herself loves to celebrate; if there's a party, she will be there, and if not, she'll have her own. It is impossible to be glum when May is around; her own sense of joy is just too infectious. She has a real feel for all things natural and can often grow plants in gardens that anyone else would have given up on. May doesn't really change her outlook or her behavior as she gets older. Even when she is well into late middle age, she will have a certain youthful energy about her.

The Runic Interpretation
ᛇᚨᛗ (Eihwaz, Ansuz, Mannaz)

It takes a lot to fool May. Mannaz figures prominently in her name, and Mannaz offers May a good sense of who she is and what she stands for. May values honesty, and should friends ever lie to her, they may as well give up on their relationships with her because May will never trust them again. The Ansuz rune of signals gives May such good intuition that she can rely on a built-in lie detector. The Eihwaz energy of defense affords May an ability to snake past obstacles. May curbs her escapist tendencies and looks problems in the eye. She has good control over her emotions and isn't compromised by the extreme highs and lows that weaken so many.

Elements: Earth/fire, air, air

The Numerological Interpretation
May (NV = 3, CV = 4, VV = 8, FL = 4)

May is apt to focus on the practical affairs of life and is therefore very attuned to the successful completion of her daily responsibilities. She aims to earn enough money to buy the best possible food, clothing, and cars, as well as to fulfill her other material needs and desires. It is through the accumulation of these outward proofs of her self-worth that May identifies herself in the world. She tends to be cautious and doesn't like to leave anything to chance. May wants to live in an assured, secure environment.

DERIVATION: English, pet form of Margaret or Mary, and also used as an independent name. Of the common month names—April, May, and June—May was the first to become popular, and was extremely common during the early twentieth century.

PRINCIPAL COLORS: All shades of violet, from the palest to the richest purple

GEMSTONES AND PRECIOUS METALS: Amethyst, garnets

UNIQUE SPELLINGS: Mae, Mai, Maye, Mei, Mey

BOTANICALS: Apple, cherry, bilberry

RELATED TO: Mae†, Maia, Margaret†, Mari, Maria†, Marianne†, Marie†, Marilyn†, Marissa†, Mary†, Mary Ann†, Maya, Maybelle, Mayella, Mia, Mya

DERIVATION: Welsh, pet form of
Margaret, which ultimately derives
from the Greek word *margaron*,
meaning "pearl." Now exists as an
independent name, and has been
increasingly common in the United
States during the twentieth
century.

PRINCIPAL COLORS: Moderately
shaded hues, electric colors

GEMSTONES AND PRECIOUS
METALS: Sapphires

BOTANICALS: Celandine, sage,
medlar

UNIQUE SPELLINGS: Meagan,
Meaghan, Megann, Megen,
Meghan, Meghann, Meghanne

RELATED TO: Mag, Maggie†,
Margaret†, Margarita†, Margie,
Margo, Margot, Marguerite†, Meg,
Meggi, Meggie, Meggy, Peg,
Peggy†

Megan

A KABBALISTIC SYNOPSIS
מאגון —MAGVN (Mem, Aleph, Gimel, Vau, Nun)

Megan is a good traditional Welsh name, and one gets a sense that she is a strong-willed woman who knows her own mind and is happy to share it with others—and she does this quite vigorously indeed if they disagree with her! Megan is well known for her hospitality. Her name has the letter Gimel as its central focus, which means a love of travel, and given its position in her name, the love of travel is going to have a considerable impact on Megan's lifestyle as a whole. Whether she ends up jetting around the world or living out of a suitcase as a holiday courier, she will always keep in touch with her friends; the ties of friendship are very strong for Megan, no matter how far away the friend may be living.

THE RUNIC INTERPRETATION
ᚾᚨᚷᛖᛗ (Nauthiz, Ansuz, Gebo, Ehwaz, Mannaz)

Megan enjoys company and is rarely alone, thanks to the combination of Mannaz (self) and Gebo (partnership) in her name. Mannaz is also the rune for connecting with others, and Megan seems to gather energy from the people closest to her in her life. When she is separated from her friends, she uses the Ehwaz energy of movement and travels to visit them. The Ansuz rune of signals provides the intuitive capabilities Megan needs to survive her many trips to exotic lands and will help her should she decide to set up house in a foreign country. This process of relocation can be problematic, as indicated by the Nauthiz rune, but Megan is strong and capable of tolerating any confusion that a move may bring. Living in foreign lands is exciting and actually less stressful for Megan than living securely in a boring environment.

Elements: Fire, air, water, air, air

THE NUMEROLOGICAL INTERPRETATION
Megan (NV = 4, CV = 7, VV = 6, FL = 4)

Megan is a very complex woman whose name connects her to many paths and streams. She has a sincere love of nature and a sense of connection to the beauty inherent in the outdoors. She is also a hard worker who definitely earns her free time, and she is likely to spend this at a national park or in some other natural setting. In addition to her love of nature, Megan enjoys cultivating intellectual pursuits. She can be counted on to present new ideas that can be of great benefit to her company. She is a team player and finds it very easy to work cooperatively. Megan likes to dress well, but not ostentatiously. This is a woman of poise, grace, and balance.

Mel

A Kabbalistic Synopsis
מאל —MAL (Mem, Aleph, Lamed)

Mel, whether male or female, is definitely a cool customer, so you should never play poker with Mel unless you're very confident of your hand. Mel will outbluff the rest of the party like a pro. Mel is very business minded and is determined to climb right to the top of the corporate ladder. For relaxation, Mel loves any form of demanding physical activity, especially if there is an element of competition involved. Because of Mel's competitive nature, relationships with Mel can be a little shaky—especially if Mel's partner likes a very close and sharing relationship; the sex, though, will probably be as intense as Mel certainly is.

The Runic Interpretation
ᛗᛖᚺ (Laguz, Ehwaz, Mannaz)

A star is born! Mel could achieve satisfaction in the performing arts or in a travel-related field. The Laguz rune of flow offers Mel dancing ability, musical ability, and a flexible and focused mind. The Ehwaz rune for movement makes it hard for Mel to sit still for long; Mel loves to experience the joys of travel. The Mannaz rune of self shows Mel what it is to be self-reliant and self-assured. Mel really likes him or herself, and Mel's self-confidence attracts friends no matter what part of the globe he or she visits.

Elements: Water, air, air

The Numerological Interpretation
Mel (NV = 3, CV = 7, VV = 5, FL = 4)

Mel has a scientific approach to life. His analytical mind is definitely where he has major gifts. Mel can cut through the surface layers of a given problem and find its resolution. He has a broad range of interests and never ceases educating himself. Mel responds intellectually to his surroundings, and may have to learn how to cultivate his emotional nature in order to deepen his level of intimacy in his personal relationships. Mel needs time alone to organize his ideas and prioritize his activities. He knows that without a sense of clear priorities he is liable to be pulled in a number of directions simultaneously. The same holds true for a female Mel.

DERIVATION: English, originally
from the Greek adjective *melas*,
meaning "dark" or "black." Two
early Roman saints were named
Melania, and the name entered
into popular use in Britain during
the seventeenth century. The
name dramatically increased in
popularity, becoming especially
popular in the United States
during the late twentieth century.

PRINCIPAL COLORS: The full
spectrum of very lightly shaded
hues

GEMSTONES AND PRECIOUS
METALS: Silver, platinum

BOTANICALS: Oats, parsley

UNIQUE SPELLINGS: Melanee,
Melaney, Melany, Melenie,
Melinie, Meliny, Mellani, Mellanie,
Mellannie, Mellany, Mellenie,
Melleny, Melliney, Melliny,
Melloney, Mellonie, Mellony,
Melony

RELATED TO: Melt, Melantha,
Mellaine, Mellane, Mellie

Melanie

A KABBALISTIC SYNOPSIS

מאלוני —MALVNY (Mem, Aleph, Lamed, Vau, Nun, Yod)

Melanie's name reduces to eleven, the number of magic and the supernatural. It is actually quite likely that Melanie will have some natural, although latent, psychic ability. If Melanie is aware of this, she will investigate it thoroughly and welcome it as a gift. A career in alternative therapy would be ideal for Melanie. She is something of a dreamer, and probably would not last long in the cutthroat world of business. Besides, Melanie also has too much of an independent Aquarian spirit to be tied down by a regular routine. Melanie will attract many admirers, but she is not easily won over. As a real romantic, Melanie must be properly wooed and flattered before she will consider looking at anyone seriously.

THE RUNIC INTERPRETATION

ᛗᛁᚺᚾᛗᛗᛗ (Ehwaz, Isa, Nauthiz, Ansuz, Laguz, Ehwaz, Mannaz)

Melanie loves change, and the Laguz rune of flow assists Melanie in maintaining an open and flexible point of view. The combination of Ehwaz and Isa give her balance. Melanie can be strong because she is intuitive and has a good sense of her own identity due to the Ansuz rune of signals and the Mannaz rune of self. Travel increases Melanie's confidence and makes her enthusiastic about further adventures.

Elements: Air, earth, fire, air, water, air, air

THE NUMEROLOGICAL INTERPRETATION

Melanie (NV = 5, CV = 3, VV = 2, FL = 4)

Life is filled with many variations and possibilities, and Melanie likes to explore as many of them as time permits. This is a well-rounded woman with many insightful thoughts that she is eager to share with others. She is a virtual walking encyclopedia with an abundant supply of facts and figures at her fingertips. Melanie is very sociable, well liked, and attractive. She is clever, witty, and given to practical jokes. Her playful nature makes her fun to be around, and she usually has a number of friends and associates that want to be in her company.

Melinda

A KABBALISTIC SYNOPSIS
מאלינדא —MALYNDA (Mem, Aleph, Lamed, Yod, Nun, Daleth, Aleph)

Melinda is a very intelligent woman; she's the sort who can work out everyone's share of the restaurant bill without going near a calculator or even a pencil and paper. But despite her exceedingly agile mind, Melinda has no desire to work in academic circles. Instead she intends to use her brainpower to generate something more interesting to her than ideas: money! Melinda has the additional advantage of being very lucky; the total value of her name is associated with the Fortune card in the tarot and consequently is an indication of good fortune. Her ambition has no limits, although her concern is strictly with the gain of material wealth rather than any position of superiority or power. Once she gets her hands on a reasonable amount of money, Melinda will be very generous and will not forget the friends she makes on the way up.

THE RUNIC INTERPRETATION
ᚨᛞᚾᛁᛚᛖᛗᚨ (Ansuz, Dagaz, Nauthiz, Isa, Laguz, Ehwaz, Mannaz)

Melinda is happiest when she is on the go. She loves to travel, except when she has to overcome some constraints in her life indicated by the Nauthiz rune. During these periods, Melinda's problems could make her isolate herself from others. This is indicated by the Isa rune of solitude in her name. The Ansuz rune of signals points to Melinda's ability to correctly intuit situations. The Dagaz rune of gateway lets us know that Melinda has the patience to wait when circumstances warrant it. The Laguz rune of flow is beneficial when Melinda needs to change something about herself. The Mannaz rune of self signifies that Melinda is willing to strive for self-improvement and that she enjoys her life.

Elements: Air, fire, fire, earth, water, air, air

THE NUMEROLOGICAL INTERPRETATION
Melinda (NV = 4, CV = 7, VV = 6, FL = 4)

Melinda makes sure that her material needs and those of her family and loved ones are secure. She is not one to do anything so unusual or unreasonable that it throws off her daily routine. Melinda focuses a lot of her attention on being well organized and having her life under control. She is thus very efficient and reliable. She is attracted to people who are more spontaneous and daring, but although she will cultivate them as friends, she seeks a partner who is pragmatic and down-to-earth. It may be difficult for her to break loose from the responsibilities that she has created. It is good for her to find a hobby or develop an interest that expands her beyond the boundaries that she makes for herself.

DERIVATION: English, composed of the Latin root *mel*, meaning "honey," and the popular female name ending, "inda." First coined in the eighteenth century, when other names ending in "inda" (such as Belinda and Dorinda) were very common. Its usage became widespread during the nineteenth century.

PRINCIPAL COLORS: The full spectrum of moderately shaded tones

GEMSTONES AND PRECIOUS METALS: Sapphires

BOTANICALS: Lesser celandine, wintergreen, Iceland moss

UNIQUE SPELLINGS: Malinda, Mallinda, Mallynda, Mallyndah, Malynda, Melindah, Mellinda, Melynda, Melyndah, Milinda

RELATED TO: Lin, Linda†, Lindy, Linnie, Lynn†, Lynne, Mailie, Mandy, Mel†, Melina, Melinde, Meline, Mella

DERIVATION: Greek, meaning "bee." A common name in ancient Greece. Became popular in English-speaking countries in the late twentieth century, particularly during the 1970s.

PRINCIPAL COLORS: From pale to medium azure shades

GEMSTONES AND PRECIOUS METALS: Turquoise, emeralds

BOTANICALS: Daffodils, dog rose, violets

UNIQUE SPELLINGS: Malisa, Malissa, Malysa, Malyssa, Melisa, Melysa, Melyssa, Milissa, M'lissa

RELATED TO: Lissa, Mel†, Melise, Melisse, Melita, Mellie, Melosa, Millicent, Millie†, Missa, Missy, Misty†

Melissa

A KABBALISTIC SYNOPSIS

מאליסטעא —MALYSSA (Mem, Aleph, Lamed, Yod, Samech, Samech, Aleph)

You won't meet many women more quintessentially feminine than Melissa. As a result, many people feel immediately protective of her and try to tell her how to run her life. Generally Melissa will be too impressionable to tell them to leave her alone, so it may be up to someone who really understands her to get rid of those who are interfering. Melissa is wonderfully idealistic and charmingly innocent. When Melissa tells people how the world could be if we all behaved decently, the most hardened cynic will be impressed by her conviction. Friends are very important to Melissa and will continue to be even after she settles down with a partner, so any lover of Melissa's will have to be willing to share her with other people.

THE RUNIC INTERPRETATION

ᚨᛋᛋᛁᛚᛗᛗᚨ (Ansuz, Sowelu, Sowelu, Isa, Laguz, Ehwaz, Mannaz)

The double Sowelu rune of wholeness could lead one to ask, "How can anything be *doubly* whole?" The answer is that Melissa is whole, and she encourages wholeness in others. Melissa understands that she can use the Mannaz rune of self and the Isa rune of isolation to help her clear out her head and to create balance in her life. Once Melissa feels she is a whole person, she spreads this soothing wholeness and balance out to other people. The Ansuz rune gives Melissa wonderful intuition. The Laguz rune provides her with flexibility, and Ehwaz, the rune of movement, allows Melissa to kick up her heels and travel if she so chooses.

Elements: Air, air, air, earth, water, air, air

THE NUMEROLOGICAL INTERPRETATION

Melissa (NV = 6, CV = 9, VV = 6, FL = 4)

Melissa has a balanced view of life and is able to communicate this sense of harmony to the world around her. This can be through music, writing, or art, all of which may reflect her natural creative tendencies. Melissa is genuinely loving and caring. She is a very sympathetic and compassionate woman who is very tolerant of other people's differences. She is also very diplomatic and avoids hurting other people's feelings at all costs. This characteristic can sometimes lead her into being very self-compromising, as Melissa prefers to say yes whenever possible. Melissa may have to learn to be more in touch with her own feelings and needs, and to express them clearly to others in her life.

Melody

A KABBALISTIC SYNOPSIS

מאלעדי —MALA'ADY (Mem, Aleph, Lamed, Ayin, Daleth, Yod)

As her name might indicate, Melody is a very creative individual. When we compress her name, we find that this creativity stems from her head rather than her heart. In other words, her creativity is quite carefully directed. Melody loves to look at the world going about its business, and gets most of her inspiration by observing other people's lives rather than talking about her own experiences. Melody is not a highly strung artistic type living in a tiny apartment waiting for the world to see the value of her work; Melody intends to make money and will tailor her output accordingly.

THE RUNIC INTERPRETATION

ᛃᛞᛟᛚᛖᛗ (Eihwaz, Dagaz, Othila, Laguz, Ehwaz, Mannaz)

Good-bye and good-bye again! Melody is off on another wonderful excursion to faraway places, and this time she's going to stay and live there for a while. Melody has a good strong sense of self, which comes from the Mannaz rune in her name. The Ansuz rune allows her to intuit the needs of others, and Othila, the rune of separation, gives her the strength to discard worn-out relationships. The Laguz rune of flow gives Melody the flexibility to withstand the gateways or new beginnings in her life. There surely will be many fresh starts because Melody is guided by Dagaz energy. Eihwaz, the rune of defense, gives Melody the strength to see other people's motives and protect herself accordingly.

Elements: Earth/fire, fire, earth/fire, water, air, air

THE NUMEROLOGICAL INTERPRETATION

Melody (NV = 2, CV = 11, VV = 9, FL = 4)

It is easy for Melody to understand people. She has insight, intuition, and a clear intellect. Other people come to her for her wisdom, and she may easily find herself drawn into one of the helping professions, perhaps teaching. Relationships are essential to her life, as she is a natural-born communicator and likes to exchange opinions and views. If she is living up to the highest potential of the eleven vibration contained in her name, Melody will find herself at work in the media. She has some profound messages to share, and the more people who can hear her, the better.

DERIVATION: English, from the common noun, which originally derives from the Greek word *melodía*, meaning "singing of songs." Became widespread as a first name in the mid-twentieth century.

PRINCIPAL COLORS: Pale, grassy to deep forest green, also white

GEMSTONES AND PRECIOUS METALS: Jade, cat's-eye

BOTANICALS: Chicory, lettuce, cabbage

UNIQUE SPELLINGS: Mellodey, Mellodi, Mellodie, Mellody, Melodee, Melodey, Melodi, Melodie

RELATED TO: Melt, Mela, Meli, Mella, Melli, Melodia

Melvin

A KABBALISTIC SYNOPSIS
מאלוין —MALVYN (Mem, Aleph, Lamed, Vau, Yod, Nun)

If communication is the key to a great relationship, we should all find ourselves a Melvin and live happily ever after! Melvin not only knows how to keep a listener interested and how to get his point across clearly, succinctly, and with style, but he also understands what other people find interesting and want to talk about. He also has a gift that is rare in a good talker—which is that he listens carefully to others instead of just waiting for his next opportunity to talk. Melvin loves life and is always incredibly enthusiastic no matter what he is doing. Melvin has the knack of making the most mundane tasks interesting for himself. He has a deeper side, too; his name reduces to twenty-two, the number of the Fool card in the tarot. The Fool card is associated with spirituality, and it is likely that Melvin spends a lot of his time pondering the great questions of life.

THE RUNIC INTERPRETATION
ᚾᛁᚠᛚᛖᛗ (Nauthiz, Isa, Fehu, Laguz, Ehwaz, Mannaz)

Not everyone is capable of uprooting and relocating to a foreign country, but Melvin can because he thrives on change. The Laguz rune gives him flexibility, the Mannaz rune in his name provides ego strength, and the Ehwaz rune offers Melvin the chance to relocate. The challenge of obstacles and adjustments—such as a transcontinental move—are indicated by the troublemaking Nauthiz rune of constraint. One strategy that Melvin can use to combat the limitation of Nauthiz is to employ the Isa rune of standstill in his name. Just by stepping back and pacing his moves, Melvin is able to quickly restore order in his life. The Fehu rune promises Melvin wealth and material possessions.

Elements: Fire, earth, fire, water, air, air

THE NUMEROLOGICAL INTERPRETATION
Melvin (NV = 3, CV = 7, VV = 5, FL = 4)

Melvin has a wide range of interests. People come away from being with him feeling informed. Melvin likes to read and study, and may always be found with an open book or two around. Actually, he can be so full of information about everything (and everyone!) that he is very much like a walking book himself. Melvin has a fine sense of humor and thoroughly enjoys putting a smile on people's faces.

Mercedes

A KABBALISTIC SYNOPSIS

מארסאידס —MARSAYDS (Mem, Aleph, Resh, Samech, Aleph, Yod, Daleth, Samech)

The high importance of the number three in the numerical construction of this name suggests the importance of children and motherhood to Mercedes. But Mercedes doesn't want to spend all day at home cleaning and cooking; she likes to be able to travel, and has a very independent streak. Her natural vigor and zest for life are very appealing, and her kids will love her for the fact that she has no inhibitions about joining in the most raucous, energetic games in public.

THE RUNIC INTERPRETATION

 SMᛞMᛋRMᛗ (Sowelu, Ehwaz, Dagaz, Ehwaz, Sowelu, Raido, Ehwaz, Mannaz)

Mercedes is a very genuine person. She has the good fortune to have the double Sowelu energy of wholeness in her name. The triple configuration of the Ehwaz rune points to movement and abundant travel opportunities. Mercedes loves all the adventure this provides! The Dagaz rune of gateway gives Mercedes an incredible sense of timing in life. Mannaz, the rune of self, gives Mercedes good self-esteem. She communicates well, and is liked by friends and associates. Raido also indicates journeys, so Mercedes is gone more than she's home, and she likes it that way.

Elements: Air, air, fire, air, air, water, air, air

THE NUMEROLOGICAL INTERPRETATION

Mercedes (NV = 9, CV = 3, VV = 6, FL = 4)

Mercedes is a very compassionate person. This name bestows a caring disposition, one that expresses itself as the need to do something concrete about the difficulties people have in life. Mercedes may easily become a nurse or physician. She is drawn to being of service, and no matter what the form of her profession, she carries this attitude with her. Her high ideals and urge for truth are so strong that she may find herself easily disappointed or disillusioned. Not all people can live up to Mercedes's standards of unselfishness, and this is one more thing that she may have to learn to accept.

DERIVATION: Spanish, from one of the names of the Virgin Mary, María de las Mercedes. Originally from the Latin word *mercedes*, meaning "ransom." Since in Christian theology, Christ's sacrifice is considered a ransom on behalf of the sins of mankind, the word *mercedes* began to mean "mercy" or "grace."

PRINCIPAL COLORS: The full range of red hues, particularly the deeper shades

GEMSTONES AND PRECIOUS METALS: Garnets, rubies

BOTANICALS: Broom, garlic, wormwood

UNIQUE SPELLINGS: Mercedies, Mercedys, Mersaydes, Mersedes, Mersedies, Mersedys

RELATED TO: Merced, Merche, Merci, Mercia, Mercy, Sadi, Sadiet, Sady

Meredith

DERIVATION: Old Welsh, meaning "lord" or "chief." Originally a male name, and is still used as such in Wales. In other English-speaking countries, however, it is used primarily for females.

PRINCIPAL COLORS: The palest to the richest, brightest yellow and bronze hues, orange

GEMSTONES AND PRECIOUS METALS: Citrine, topaz, yellow diamonds

BOTANICALS: Borage, sorrel, thyme

UNIQUE SPELLINGS: Meradith, Meredeth, Meredithe, Meredyth, Meredythe, Merideth, Meridith, Meridyth, Meridythe, Merradeth, Merradithe, Merredith, Merrideth, Merridith, Merridythe, Merrydith, Merydeth, Merydith

RELATED TO: Mer, Mera, Meri, Merri, Merridie, Merry

A KABBALISTIC SYNOPSIS

מאראדית —MARADYTh (Mem, Aleph, Resh, Aleph, Daleth, Yod, Tau)

The total value of Meredith's name is 656. The name begins and ends with the number six, associated with the gift of intuition. Meredith is not consciously aware of any such gift, but will usually follow her gut when making a decision—even if it seems to conflict with what her head might be saying at the time! On most occasions this is the sensible thing to do, as her instinct is rarely wrong. Meredith's name is also associated with the tarot card the Star, signifying a protected destiny or something akin to a charmed life. When Meredith does screw up, it is usually in spectacular style, and yet she always manages to work her way out of trouble. Meredith has a very evenly balanced temperament and is slow to anger, which means that she can thrive in high-pressure work environments without having to worry about stress or burnout.

THE RUNIC INTERPRETATION

ᚦᛁᛞᛖᚱᛖᛗ (Thurisaz, Isa, Dagaz, Ehwaz, Raido, Ehwaz, Mannaz)

Thurisaz, the gateway rune, suggests that Meredith takes responsibility for problems whether they occur in her own life or in the world at large. The standstill Isa rune offers Meredith the opportunity to meditate on what changes she can make to improve the quality of her life and others'. The Dagaz rune of breakthrough explains that Meredith will make the necessary changes to build a successful and rewarding life; nothing can keep Meredith down for long! The double Ehwaz energy of movement foretells of opportunities to travel and live abroad. The Raido rune of journey underlines Meredith's chances to travel. The Mannaz energy of self tells us that Meredith has the courage and strength to seize opportunities and make the best of her circumstances with grace and charm.

Elements: Fire, earth, fire, air, water, air, air

THE NUMEROLOGICAL INTERPRETATION

Meredith (NV = 1, CV = 9, VV = 1, FL = 4)

A highly individualistic and assertive woman, Meredith easily projects her inner thoughts, opinions, and viewpoints out into society. This is the name of a woman who has to be seen and heard. She has a fiery nature and a determined will. Meredith is possessed of an inner conviction about herself and the world; she doesn't censor her opinions. If there is something she is doing that she truly likes, she does not hesitate to express herself with the full force of the enthusiasm she feels. Meredith has good intentions and a kind spirit, but she can come into conflict with others who see her as egocentric.

Michael

A Kabbalistic Synopsis
מיחאל —MYChAL (Mem, Yod, Cheth, Aleph, Lamed)

Michael is a really good guy to have on your side and an absolute nightmare to have against you! When Michael gets annoyed, he can get quite riled up, but he does not direct his anger at other people unless they actually start in with him. The ideal career for Michael would be in the armed forces or the police; he tends to have a deep sense of loyalty to his family and to his country. Michael has a more sensitive side, and if you saw him with a baby, you would be amazed. This gentle side is often expressed as a love of animals, and Michael will be a sucker for any injured animal that finds itself in his garden. Michael may not be overtly intellectual, but he is an honest and sincere individual.

The Runic Interpretation
ᛚᛗᚨᚺᚲᛁᛗ (Laguz, Ehwaz, Ansuz, Hagalaz, Kano, Isa, Mannaz)

The one thing Michael wants above all else is *harmony*. The Laguz rune of flow makes his wish come true—that is, until the Hagalaz rune of disruption arrives on the scene to ruin everything. It's time then for him to withdraw and assess the situation by calling on the Isa rune for standstill. Michael is intuitive and flexible, and will do what he can to maintain order in his life. Mannaz, the rune of self, gives Michael the necessary resources to do this. With Kano, the rune of opening, in his name, Michael has many opportunities come his way from out of the blue, and this suits him just fine.

Elements: Water, air, air, water, water, earth, air

The Numerological Interpretation
Michael (NV = 1, CV = 22, VV = 6, FL = 4)

The numerological indications of Michael contain a very positive combination of influences that bestow tremendous possibilities—but everything depends on the nature of Michael's spiritual direction. If Michael is awakened to the life of his soul, he can do great things to bring harmony and uplift into the world. When twenty-two combines with one, as it does in this name, the results endow a person with a clarity of will and a sense of individual mission that is oriented to the betterment of humanity. It gives the bearer of this name the courage to overcome any obstacle in order to follow the dictates of one's "inner guidance system." The more "average" Michael will find that he, too, needs to bring harmony and peace into the world around him, and he will tend to do this through his daily contacts with people.

DERIVATION: Greek form of a biblical name meaning "Who is like God?" Found in the New Testament as the name of the archangel who is Satan's adversary. Popular during the Middle Ages, it declined during the early 1800s, then rose tremendously in popularity during the twentieth century. Among the most popular male names in the United States.

PRINCIPAL COLORS: All but the brightest shades of blue

GEMSTONES AND PRECIOUS METALS: Turquoise, emeralds

BOTANICALS: Vervain, violets, walnuts

UNIQUE SPELLINGS: Meichael, Meichal, Micheal, Micol, Mikael, Mikel, Mikol, Mikul, Mikull, Mikyl, Mychael, Mychal, Mykel, Mykol, Mykul, Mykull

RELATED TO: Micah, Michal, Michel, Mick, Mickey, Miguel†, Mike, Mikey, Mikhail, Mikkel, Mikko, Mischa, Mitch, Mitchell†

"Love one another and you will be happy. It's as simple and as difficult as that."

—MICHAEL LEUNIG (AUTHOR)

Michelle

A KABBALISTIC SYNOPSIS
מישאל —MYShAL (Mem, Yod, Shin, Aleph, Lamed)

Michelle is incredibly spirited. You will probably see her helping out in a volunteer organization day after day; she is willing to work extra hours to aid pretty much anybody who has a genuine need. Although Michelle likes to help others because she passionately believes that it is right to do so, she would never allow herself to be exploited or pushed around. Michelle is very energetic and always manages to find time in her day to do the things that appeal to her. The TV is rarely on in her house, as Michelle likes to pass her free time in more strenuous ways; a good place to start looking for her on her day off would be the local gym or swimming pool. Another of Michelle's great loves is usually the theater, and anyone wanting to impress her should consider getting tickets for the two of them.

THE RUNIC INTERPRETATION
ᛗᛚᛚᛗᚺᚲᛁᛗ (Ehwaz, Laguz, Laguz, Ehwaz, Hagalaz, Kano, Isa, Mannaz)

The double Laguz energy of flow in Michelle's name suggests flexibility and musical talent. The double Ehwaz energy of movement indicates that Michelle can dance and likes to keep active. The Hagalaz rune brings her some trouble and disruption, as well as some challenging life lessons. The Kano rune of opening indicates that Michelle will have clarity and a sense of entitlement when it comes to giving and receiving love. The Isa rune of standstill symbolizes Michelle's introspective nature. The Mannaz rune for self indicates that Michelle will enjoy self-respect and great strength of character.

Elements: Air, water, water, air, water, water, earth, air

THE NUMEROLOGICAL INTERPRETATION
Michelle (NV = 4, CV = 3, VV = 1, FL = 4)

Michelle has a great urge for individualization. She is developing a clear sense of who she is through the expression of her personal creative talents. The most important thing to Michelle is to find a secure place where she may fit into life. She needs her own special niche, a central point from which she may move outward into the world. She anchors herself in her career, but her sense of who she is usually comes from her efforts to understand herself subjectively, rather than from looking at what she does for her job.

Miguel

DERIVATION: Spanish form of Michael, which comes from the Hebrew root meaning "Who is like God?" Used more commonly in the United States than in other English-speaking countries.

PRINCIPAL COLORS: The full spectrum of moderately shaded hues

GEMSTONES AND PRECIOUS METALS: Sapphires

BOTANICALS: Sage, wintergreen, medlar

UNIQUE SPELLINGS: Migell, Miggel, Miggell

RELATED TO: Micah, Michael†, Michal, Michel, Mick, Mickey, Mike, Mikey, Mikhail, Mikkel, Mikko, Mischa, Mitch, Mitchell†

A KABBALISTIC SYNOPSIS
מיגואל —MYGVAL (Mem, Yod, Gimel, Vau, Aleph, Lamed)

Don't get into an argument with Miguel unless you are prepared to concede complete defeat in whatever subject is being debated; Miguel's name has the same value as the Hebrew letter Tzaddi, meaning "fishhook." The implication is that once Miguel has "hooked" you, he will never let go. Tenacity is Miguel's middle name, and this is immediately obvious in his relationships. He is the type of guy who will relentlessly ask and ask a preferred date to go out with him until she finally gives in. He does have a sparkling wit and is a lively talker, so it is probable that having succumbed to his persistence, any date will be pleasantly surprised at how enjoyable the evening proves to be. Passionate he may be, but Miguel is rarely faithful forever; he is far too excitable for that. The one consistency in his life is his search for the right job. The real focus in Miguel's life is his career, and he will travel anywhere, consider anything, if he thinks it will take him nearer to his ultimate career goals.

THE RUNIC INTERPRETATION
ᛚᛖᚢᚷᛁᛗ (Laguz, Ehwaz, Uruz, Gebo, Isa, Mannaz)

Miguel is strong and independent, and above all, he wants to retain his identity within a relationship. This analysis is based on the runic configuration in Miguel's name of Uruz for strength along with the Mannaz rune of self-reliance and the Isa rune of introspection. Since the Ehwaz energy promises travel and homes abroad, the flexibility afforded by the Laguz rune of flow comes in handy. The Gebo rune promises union with a mate, yet cautions Miguel and his lover to remain independent and self-reliant so that freedom and joy can remain alive in the relationship.

Elements: Water, air, earth, water, earth, air

THE NUMEROLOGICAL INTERPRETATION
Miguel (NV = 4, CV = 5, VV = 8, FL = 4)

One of the most important lessons contained in the numbers of this name concerns the proper use of money and material objects. Miguel is aware of social status and is very conscious about who holds the power in every situation. He is a man who finds himself very much at home in the world of business and enterprise, and can be counted upon to give all of himself to his plans and projects. It is important for him to own, possess, and enjoy that which he can touch with his hands. This attitude may extend into his personal life, where he can be jealous and possessive in his relationships. This is a sure way to lose the object of one's affection, so Miguel's test in life is to learn to trust.

Mildred

A KABBALISTIC SYNOPSIS
מילדראד —MYLDRAD (Mem, Yod, Lamed, Daleth, Resh, Aleph, Daleth)

There are two distinct sides to Mildred's personality, and the side that you get to see depends very much on the context in which you know her. If you are a very close friend, a partner, or a family member, you see the intense Mildred. This is a woman who is overflowing with feelings and incredibly passionate. Yet those who work with Mildred would never suspect this of her: In the office, she is a very bright and breezy individual who seems content to take life as it comes. She rarely, if ever, expresses any deep feelings about any work issue. The presence of two Ds, or Daleths, meaning "door," in her name indicates that not only will she promote her own career but she will be very happy to try to open doors for others. Mildred is certainly popular at work, even if they don't know her as well as they might think.

THE RUNIC INTERPRETATION
ᛞᛖᚱᛞᛚᛁᛗ (Dagaz, Ehwaz, Raido, Dagaz, Laguz, Isa, Mannaz)

The double Dagaz energy of breakthrough characterizes Mildred's name. She may find herself attracted to a new lifestyle or career path she hadn't counted on—at least not consciously. Her personal breakthrough involves trying something new and risking almost everything in the process. This rune calls forth spontaneity and faith. The Ehwaz rune of movement and the Raido rune of journey portend a huge amount of travel for Mildred. The Laguz rune of flow means Mildred can accept this challenge. The Mannaz rune of self inspires Mildred to learn about her feelings and integrate them into her personality with ease.

Elements: Fire, air, water, fire, water, earth, air

THE NUMEROLOGICAL INTERPRETATION
Mildred (NV = 11, CV = 6, VV = 5, FL = 4)

Mildred's concern for her family may extend outward into society in general, for she is a very compassionate person. Domestic harmony is one of her top priorities, and with a name value of eleven, Mildred's urge for peace includes all people. Friendship and good relationships with others are her goals in life. She carries an aura of poise and is gracious to everyone. Mildred will do well working in any career that involves community welfare. Her partner has to be an equal, a person who shares her goals and supports her efforts at achieving them.

❧

Millie

DERIVATION: English, a pet form of Mildred or Millicent. Often given as an independent name, and especially popular during the early twentieth century.

PRINCIPAL COLORS: From light to medium shades of azure

GEMSTONES AND PRECIOUS METALS: Blue and blue-green turquoise, emeralds

BOTANICALS: Vervain, violets, walnuts

UNIQUE SPELLINGS: Milee, Mili, Millee, Milli, Milly, Mily

RELATED TO: Amelia†, Camilla, Emily†, Milana, Mildred†, Milena, Milla, Millicent

A KABBALISTIC SYNOPSIS
מיללי —MYLLY (Mem, Yod, Lamed, Lamed, Yod)

Do you know a Millie? If you do and you consider yourself her friend, simply say two words to her: "Slow down!" Of course, you will probably have to run alongside her as you say this, since Millie doesn't usually stop for conversation. Millie has a name that is full of letters associated with drive, energy, and ambition. This is all very well, but there is little in her name that indicates a capacity to take some time out to smell the roses. Consequently, Millie faces a higher-than-usual risk of burnout in her career. She is so full of potential and obvious ability that it would be a great shame if this were to happen. Apart from success, the one thing Millie craves is a feeling of certainty that she is loved by one special individual. If her partner can give her that security, she will be willing to take his advice even when it means slowing down. As she has a basically warm and caring nature, Millie should have little difficulty in finding just such a person.

THE RUNIC INTERPRETATION
ᛗᛁᛚᛚᛁᛖ (Ehwaz, Isa, Laguz, Laguz, Isa, Mannaz)

Flexibility and clarity are important character assets for the millennium. Millie has the double Laguz powers of flow offering these assets in abundance. The Isa energy of standstill encourages Millie to stay calm and composed during the vicissitudes of life. Mannaz, the rune of self, gives Millie a confident personality that is resilient and balanced. Most important, the Ehwaz rune of movement encourages exploration and travel. Millie is curious and open-minded, and gravitates to people of other cultures.

Elements: Air, earth, water, water, earth, air

THE NUMEROLOGICAL INTERPRETATION
Millie (NV = 6, CV = 1, VV = 5, FL = 4)

Millie knows that she has to stand on her own two feet and be her own person. Yet she is very sensitive and can be overly emotional. Her challenge is to maintain her poise and self-assurance even when surrounded by people who have a lot of problems. She is aware of the needs of her friends and family, and will do everything within her power to assist and support them. Millie has the capacity to balance her own personal integrity with her desire to be present when called upon, and she needs to make sure that she does this.

DERIVATION: English, pet form of Wilhelmina, which is from the Old German roots *will*, meaning "desire" and *helm*, meaning "helmet." Became popular in the 1850s, and was especially common in Britain and the United States in the 1870s.

PRINCIPAL COLORS: The full range of yellow and russet hues, also gold and orange

GEMSTONES AND PRECIOUS METALS: Topaz and yellow diamonds

BOTANICALS: Lavender, Saint-John's-wort, thyme

UNIQUE SPELLINGS: Minnee, Minney, Minni, Minny

RELATED TO: Mary†, Min, Minette, Minna, Minne, Wilhelmina

❧

"God has a plan for all of us, but He expects us to do our share of the work."

—MINNIE PEARL (COMEDIENNE)

Minnie

A KABBALISTIC SYNOPSIS
מינני —MYNNY (Mem, Yod, Nun, Nun, Yod)

In certain respects Minnie is similar to Millie†; she is equally committed to her career and very desirous of success. However, she lacks the insatiable ambition and totally goal-centered approach of Millie. In Minnie we see the letter L, or Lamed, replaced by N, or Nun, which relates to strong emotional feelings. Due to the association with Scorpio, these feelings can often be negative in nature, and so Minnie is very reluctant to discuss them with others. In some cases Minnie can be quite depressed until she finds a friend in whom she can confide. Inevitably Minnie's fears are unfounded; they stem from irrational insecurity and feelings of inadequacy. With the right friend Minnie will see that her concerns are mere illusions, and she will be able to enjoy life to the fullest. One Hebrew equivalent of her name means "to embrace," and a Minnie rid of her insecurities is a very tactile and loving woman.

THE RUNIC INTERPRETATION
ᛗᛁᚾᚾᛁᛗ (Ehwaz, Isa, Nauthiz, Nauthiz, Isa, Mannaz)

Hold on to your hat, Minnie; you've got a bumpy ride ahead! The double Nauthiz runes of limitation and constraint in your name are here to teach you challenging lessons. Nauthiz represents Jung's concept of the shadow side of life that sabotages our best-laid plans and attracts misfortune to us. Once Minnie calls upon Isa, the rune of standstill, she will find she hungers for silence and emotional clarity. Minnie will understand that she must use the Mannaz rune of self to sort out just what misfortune she creates and what energy she draws into her life from the people around her.

Elements: Air, earth, fire, fire, earth, air

THE NUMEROLOGICAL INTERPRETATION
Minnie (NV = 1, CV = 5, VV = 5, FL = 4)

An expansive nature with an ability to express herself in a number of different ways characterizes Minnie. The name gives adaptability and flexibility. She can accomplish almost anything if given the time and space to do so. Minnie demands a great deal of personal freedom. She hates being tied down and fettered by responsibilities that are not the direct result of her own actions. Minnie is intent on enjoying a life that is full of excitement and opportunity. She can make the most out of the least and is able to find a smile even in the most challenging of circumstances. This is a woman with great resilience and gusto.

❧

Miriam

A Kabbalistic Synopsis
מירים —MYRYAM (Mem, Yod, Resh, Yod, Aleph, Mem)

The man who marries Miriam had better love the pitter-patter of tiny feet! Miriam loves kids, and if she had the money to support them, she would have a whole herd of little ones running about the place. Her name is equivalent to the Hebrew for "fecundity," or "fertility"—which means not only will she have plenty of children but she is also likely to have a strong creative urge or leaning toward the arts. Miriam is always cheery and seems like a ray of sunshine whenever she enters a room or joins in a conversation. Although she is very concerned with the needs of others and is keen to offer her support, she does so without being overwhelmed by the seriousness of the situation, and as a result never loses her happy demeanor.

The Runic Interpretation
ᛗᚨᛁᚱᛁᛗ (Mannaz, Ansuz, Isa, Raido, Isa, Mannaz)

Know thyself: This is the motto for Miriam, who has the double Mannaz rune of self in her name. Mannaz teaches us to live in the moment and enjoy the process of creation rather than only the product. The Ansuz rune of signals helps Miriam be intuitive and aware. Double Isa for standstill beckons Miriam to meditate. The Raido rune for journey applies to her journey back to the self. In terms of career, Miriam would enjoy counseling and hypnotherapy as well as healing work and the performing arts in just about any capacity. Creating artwork is wonderful for Miriam, as it helps her learn to live in the present and feel free and spontaneous.

Elements: Air, air, earth, water, earth, air

The Numerological Interpretation
Miriam (NV = 9, CV = 8, VV = 1, FL = 4)

Miriam likes being in control. She is highly structured and organized. Her name gives her the power to see life unfolding several steps at a time. Miriam uses this vision to plan her days and is hardly ever caught off guard. Independent and strong-willed, Miriam has her eye on the prize and has no problem taking her time to achieve her aims in life. Although she has a strong sense of her own being, she is not an egotist. A lot of Miriam's effort and a great deal of her time are spent finding ways to help other people. She may not be the most emotionally open person, but her feelings are deep and true.

DERIVATION: Biblical, found in the Old Testament as the name of Moses' sister, who rescued Moses from the river and raised him in the pharaoh's home. The root form of the New Testament name Mary. Especially common during the early twentieth century.

PRINCIPAL COLORS: Light pink to the deepest shade of crimson red

GEMSTONES AND PRECIOUS METALS: Bloodstones, garnets

BOTANICALS: Garlic, onion, wormwood

UNIQUE SPELLINGS: Meariam, Meeriam, Meiriam, Miream, Miriem, Mirream, Mirriam, Miryam, Miryem

RELATED TO: Marah, Maria†, Mariamm, Marie†, Mary†, Mimi, Mira, Miram, Miri, Mirian, Mirra, Mitzi, Myra†

"We must not make war on each other while, in our vulnerability, we try to create something new."
—MIRIAM SCHAPIRO (ARTIST)

Misty

A KABBALISTIC SYNOPSIS
מיסטי —MYSTY (Mem, Yod, Samech, Teth, Yod)

When everyone else is down on the beach or living it up in the local nightclub, Misty will be busily typing away at her keyboard surrounded by serious-looking books. Misty is the consummate intellectual; she loves to think and ponder in the way most of us love to spend the day boating or shopping. For Misty, deep, reasoned thought is both her job and her leisure activity. Misty does have quite an impulsive nature, though, and can often defy the stereotype of the staid intellectual with her sometimes outrageous behavior. Her high energy also shows in the way she works—from inspiration followed by research, rather than the other way around. The combination of the letters Teth and Yod at the end of her name tells us that she is a capable woman when it comes to defending her viewpoint, and Misty will argue with great vigor until she has gotten her argument across.

THE RUNIC INTERPRETATION
ᛇᛏᛋᛁᛗ (Eihwaz, Teiwaz, Sowelu, Isa, Mannaz)

Our home is always inside of us and has little to do with our physical dwelling place. So Misty makes her home wherever she is—which could be almost anywhere! Misty needs to use the Isa rune of standstill to quiet her thoughts and retain her composure in new and potentially frightening circumstances. The Teiwaz energy of the warrior strengthens Misty and keeps her brave and reasonable. The Mannaz rune for self indicates that Misty thrives on her travels and voyages, and returns more self-reliant as a result of being on her own. The Sowelu rune of wholeness promises that Misty will integrate her experiences in a positive way. She can get on with her life with confidence and real pleasure.

Elements: Earth/fire, air, air, earth, air

THE NUMEROLOGICAL INTERPRETATION
Misty (NV = 5, CV = 7, VV = 7, FL = 4)

This is a woman who appreciates precision. Misty is very analytical by nature, preferring to think things out very carefully before committing herself. She does not avoid responsibility but is just very discriminating about which responsibilities she will take upon her shoulders. Misty spends a lot of her time in pursuit of higher education. She wants to acquire those tools, methods, and processes that will enhance her personal arsenal of talents. Misty likes to be prepared for any eventuality, and she usually is.

Mitchell

DERIVATION: English, a variant form of Michael. Commonly used since the mid-nineteenth century and especially popular in the United States during the 1950s.

PRINCIPAL COLORS: Pale to brilliant yellow and brown

GEMSTONES AND PRECIOUS METALS: Citrine, amber, topaz

BOTANICALS: Sorrel, eyebright, thyme

UNIQUE SPELLINGS: Mitchel, Mitchil, Mitchill, Mitchyl, Mitchyll, Mytchell

RELATED TO: Michael†, Mick, Mickey, Miguel†, Mihail, Mike, Mikhail, Mikkel, Misha, Mitch

A Kabbalistic Synopsis

מיטחאל —MYTChAL (Mem, Yod, Teth, Cheth, Aleph, Lamed)

One of the Hebrew equivalences for the value of Mitchell's name is "hide," and this word indicates Mitchell's secretive nature. He is a very reserved character who reveals very little about himself unless he has to; he operates on a strictly need-to-know basis! There are very strong associations with food in Mitchell's name, and it is possible that he may not simply like his food a great deal but may actually work in the catering industry. Of course, if Mitchell is a chef he will make sure that his own recipes stay absolutely secret! To his few friends Mitchell is a wonderful guy, generous, humorous, and totally loyal. To others he is a quiet and deeply intriguing man who can become very angry when annoyed and has a very sharp tongue for those who offend him.

The Runic Interpretation

ᛚᛚᛖᚺᛋᛏᛁᛗ (Laguz, Laguz, Ehwaz, Hagalaz, Sowelu, Teiwaz, Isa, Mannaz)

Any nonsense represented by the Hagalaz rune of disruption in his name can be quickly squelched by powerful Mitchell. The Teiwaz rune of the warrior will not tolerate chaos for long. When events get out of control, Mitchell uses the double Laguz rune of flow and flexibility to ride out the storm. Isa, the rune of standstill, has an added calming effect. The Mannaz rune of self teaches Mitchell that he can take charge of any situation. Ehwaz, the rune of movement, lifts him up and away to adventures abroad. Mitchell will have an international reputation one day, with acquaintances around the world.

Elements: Water, water, air, water, air, air, earth, air

The Numerological Interpretation

Mitchell (NV = 1, CV = 5, VV = 5, FL = 4)

What is not openly given to Mitchell by his large number of friends and associates, Mitchell will create for himself. He is not a shy person and has no problem carving out his own path in life. You could say that Mitchell is a lucky man, as life allows him many chances to improve himself. If one thing fails, two other possibilities will come to take its place. Mitchell does not like to feel suppressed or limited, and so it may be difficult for him to commit himself to one career or one relationship. People who know Mitchell well give him plenty of space to be himself.

Moe

DERIVATION: English, short form of Maurice. A common nickname, but not frequently used independently.

PRINCIPAL COLORS: Pale to medium shades of azure

GEMSTONES AND PRECIOUS METALS: Emeralds, turquoise

BOTANICALS: Dog rose, almonds, apricots

UNIQUE SPELLINGS: Mo, Moh, Mow

RELATED TO: Maurice†

A KABBALISTIC SYNOPSIS
מע —MA'A (Mem, Ayin)

It is often the case that the simplest things turn out to be the most complex in the end. The name Moe is typical of this. As the Hebrew letter Ayin (A'A) represents, among other things, the long "o" sound, Moe's name consists of only two letters when transliterated for analysis. Yet these two letters symbolize a clash between Moe's purely emotional drives—including his love of close family life—with the ambition and business acumen he possesses as shown by the letter Ayin. Moe has to tread a tightrope between these two drives in his personality. If he works too late at the office, not only does his family mind but he gets pretty upset about it, too. The positive emotional influences make Moe a good manager and an excellent motivator. His family life is very rewarding, and his sense of spontaneity and fun means that his family—particularly his kids—never know what he is going to surprise them with next.

THE RUNIC INTERPRETATION
ᛗᛟᛗ (Ehwaz, Othila, Mannaz)

Moe is out to prove himself, and in order to express his dreams, he needs to move far away from home for a spell. The Othila rune of separation helps him discard limiting belief systems and start fresh with a new vision of the goals he wants to realize. The Mannaz rune of self promises to sustain Moe in his attempts to gain personal power. Moe knows the value of discipline and goal setting. Moe uses his family experiences to grow as he matures.

Elements: Air, earth/fire, air

THE NUMEROLOGICAL INTERPRETATION
Moe (NV = 6, CV = 4, VV = 11, FL = 4)

Moe is a nice guy. He tries to avoid conflicts with other people and in fact works to harmonize any opposition or difficulties in his immediate environment. This is a name that belongs to a man dedicated to his friends, family, and career. A most reliable individual, Moe can be counted on to keep his word and fulfill his responsibilities in life. His vowel value is eleven, and when this number appears in a name, it indicates a special gift. In Moe's case this has to do with the sudden inspirational impulses that rise up within him. He uses these insights to reveal to people things that they do not see in themselves. In this respect, Moe can act as a highly polished mirror.

Molly

A Kabbalistic Synopsis
מעלי —MA'ALY (Mem, Ayin, Lamed, Yod)

Molly is a fiercely independent woman who loves to achieve. This is commendable, but she also needs to learn to ask for help when she really needs it. Her free spirit is also in evidence when we look at her favorite pastimes. Molly loves to walk—to go on not just rambles but full-blown hikes; one equivalence of the value of her name is "walking shoes." When she is out walking, Molly loves to ponder all manner of issues, although she is less inclined to enter into any discussion about the things that interest her. Despite her ability to enjoy life alone, she does have a romantic side, as a glance at her bookshelves would reveal. However, her innate practicality means that she does not get caught up in any unrealistic daydreams for herself. Only when she has definitely decided that she has met the right partner will she give any inkling of her affections.

The Runic Interpretation
ᛇᛚᛚᛟᛗ (Eihwaz, Laguz, Laguz, Othila, Mannaz)

Molly is confident and innovative. She could start her own business or go on to acquire a Ph.D. Molly has the double Laguz rune of flow in her name, which gives her musical and mathematical ability as well as a flexible mind. The Othila rune of separation affords Molly the wonderful capacity to break with the past and grow beyond limiting belief systems or relationships that waste her valuable time. The Mannaz energy of self combined with the Eihwaz rune of defense proves that Molly can assert herself, and she's skeptical and alert to opportunities and pitfalls in deals and in relationships. Once you lie to Molly you're done for.

Elements: Earth/fire, water, water, earth/fire, air

The Numerological Interpretation
Molly (NV = 5, CV = 1, VV = 4, FL = 4)

Patience is one of the most important characteristics that Molly needs to incorporate into her life. Molly is a very active woman with a tremendous need to express herself. Her many ideals tend to move like a circle of arrows out from the same central point. She has a strong center that she identifies with, but she projects her thoughts too much and too often. Such intense self-expression requires time to see where the arrows of actions land and a certain amount of patience to wait for their return. Molly has a number of creative gifts. The study of astrology or numerology may be most helpful to her, as these disciplines deal with cycles and can give Molly a greater sense of wholeness.

DERIVATION: English, originally a pet form of Mary, which originally stems from the Hebrew name Miriam. Now commonly used as an independent name.

PRINCIPAL COLORS: The palest shade of any color

GEMSTONES AND PRECIOUS METALS: Diamonds, silver, platinum

BOTANICALS: Hazel, oats, parsley

UNIQUE SPELLINGS: Moli, Molli, Mollee, Molley, Mollie

RELATED TO: Malia, Mallie, Maria†, Mariet, Mary†, Maureen†, Moll, Poll, Polly

DERIVATION: Irish and English, from the Irish word *muadh*, meaning "noble." Occasionally a pet form of Monica. Originated during the nineteenth century, and increased in popularity during the early twentieth century.

PRINCIPAL COLORS: The full range of yellow and green shades, also gold

GEMSTONES AND PRECIOUS METALS: Any white stone, moonstones, moss agate

BOTANICALS: Elder, juniper, blackberry

UNIQUE SPELLINGS: Moana, Moena, Monah

RELATED TO: Moina, Monica†, Monique†

Mona

A KABBALISTIC SYNOPSIS
מענא —MA'ANA (Mem, Ayin, Nun, Aleph)

Mona has what you might call a quirky personality, and people tend to admire and respect her for her refusal to be restricted by normal conventions and expectations. Her eccentricity is often appealing to potential partners who are looking for someone with a decidedly unique personality. Mona hates being tied down to any one place, and will try to settle in a career that involves both regular travel and the possibility of relocation, even to other countries. The presence of the letter Ayin in her name tells us that there are influences of Capricorn in her character. From this we can expect that no matter what sort of lifestyle Mona chooses, she will ensure that she is financially well set. Mona is not in any way pretentious, and another popular side to her character is her ability to laugh at herself. She also has a good supply of one-liners, which she is happy to use on other people. If you work with Mona, you had better be able to take a joke.

THE RUNIC INTERPRETATION
ᚨᚾᛟᛗ (Ansuz, Nauthiz, Othila, Mannaz)

Mona dances to her own drummer. The Othila rune of separation and the Nauthiz rune of constraint mean that Mona has to break away from her past for a while until she carves out a life for herself. The Mannaz energy of self keeps Mona in balance and searching for the ability to live in the moment. Mona could do well in sales or in the hotel and resort industry. The Ansuz rune of signals gives her a good sense of timing, and she is good at closing deals based on her intuition. Once Mona launches herself, she will prosper and gain a great deal of satisfaction from her career.

Elements: Air, fire, earth/fire, air

THE NUMEROLOGICAL INTERPRETATION
Mona (NV = 7, CV = 9, VV = 7, FL = 4)

Peace of mind is attained through self-knowledge. This urge toward greater self-understanding is at the core of the name Mona. Mona is basically a quiet, understated woman, one with a retiring and contemplative disposition. She is much happier at a symphony than at a rock concert, much more content with one special person than with a room full of people, no matter how interesting they may be. Education is the key to her success, and Mona can often be found at lectures, workshops, and seminars. She may even be teaching them, as it is important for her to express and share her search for knowledge with others.

Monica

A Kabbalistic Synopsis
מעניכא —MA'ANYKA (Mem, Ayin, Nun, Yod, Kaph, Aleph)

Monica can often be misunderstood by those around her, particularly her female friends and coworkers. She spends a great deal of her time talking about herself, especially her looks and her relationships. Often this can be seen as a sign of vanity or attention-seeking. If Monica has been born under the sign of Cancer or Pisces, this is less likely, as she will be more inclined to be asking for advice or reassurance on an equally regular basis. What Monica really wants is approval, and she tries to achieve this by verbally showing everyone what a nice, popular, and well-turned-out individual she is. Once people realize that this is the cause of her self-references, they look at her in a different light. Monica is usually quite a lucky person, so she should have no trouble finding herself a sensitive partner who will understand and reassure her in the way that she needs.

The Runic Interpretation
ᚨᚲᛁᛏᛟᛗ (Ansuz, Kano, Isa, Nauthiz, Othila, Mannaz)

Monica is unaccustomed to spontaneity and freedom. The Nauthiz rune of constraint and the Isa rune of standstill keep her fairly isolated. The good news is that Othila, the rune of separation, stimulates Monica's imagination and fills her with the urge to break away from safety and security and live it up! The Mannaz rune of self suggests that Monica needs to learn to live in the moment and stop being so watchful. The Kano rune for opening helps Monica eventually to write her own agenda for emancipation from these limitations. The Ansuz rune of signals gives lucky Monica great insight, which helps her to find direction. In the end, she emerges confident and free as a bird.

Elements: Air, water, earth, fire, earth/fire, air

The Numerological Interpretation
Monica (NV = 1, CV = 3, VV = 7, FL = 4)

Vivacious and alive, Monica bears a name that bestows a warm personality and a happy smile. She is very at ease in group situations and enjoys interesting conversations. But this is not the only facet of her complex nature; Monica also enjoys spending time alone. It is important for her to reflect on her life circumstances. She doesn't like to make mistakes, and wants to assure herself that she has learned from her experiences. Monica is magnetic and attractive, and will find that she is sought after as a lover and partner. She enjoys this attention, and will respond in kind if it feels right to her. After all, love is also an education!

DERIVATION: English, of uncertain origin. Possibly from the Latin word *monere*, meaning "to advise" or "to warn." The name was first established by Saint Monica (332–387), the mother of Saint Augustine. Since Saint Monica and Saint Augustine were from Carthage, the name may be of Phoenician origin.

PRINCIPAL COLORS: All shades of yellow and bronze, also orange

GEMSTONES AND PRECIOUS METALS: Citrine, topaz

BOTANICALS: Thyme, sorrel, borage

UNIQUE SPELLINGS: Manica, Manika, Mannica, Mannicka, Mannika, Moneca, Moneka, Monicah, Monicka, Monika, Monikah, Monneca, Monnecka, Monnica, Monnicka

RELATED TO: Manka, Mica, Mique, Monat, Monca, Monie, Moniquet

Monique

DERIVATION: French version of
Monica, an English name of
uncertain origin. Has been
common in English-speaking as
well as French-speaking countries
since the 1950s.

PRINCIPAL COLORS: Electric
colors, any color of moderate
tone

GEMSTONES AND PRECIOUS
METALS: Sapphires

BOTANICALS: Lesser celandine,
medlar

UNIQUE SPELLINGS: Maunike,
Moanike, Monike

RELATED TO: Mica, Mique, Monat,
Monicat, Monika

A KABBALISTIC SYNOPSIS

מעניק —MA'ANYQ (Mem, Ayin, Nun, Yod, Qoph)

Those who know Monique respect her enormously and often find themselves telling her their innermost worries. Monique is an unusually wise woman, both in matters of the emotions and in more practical matters such as family finances. She has a combination of inherited common sense and a strongly rational mind, which makes her well qualified for any form of advisory work. In her relationships, though, Monique tends to throw caution to the wind and trust her emotions. Careerwise, Monique should do very well, not only because of her considerable ability and intelligence but also due to her very personable nature, which helps her to progress. The only problem Monique does face is that she may lose her drive to succeed from time to time when her attention is caught by more contemplative matters.

THE RUNIC INTERPRETATION

ᛗᚾᚲᛁᛏᚢᛈᛗ (Ehwaz, Uruz, Kano, Isa, Nauthiz, Othila, Mannaz)

Living in the present is wonderful, and Monique is one of the few who can achieve this. The Mannaz rune of self teaches her how to enjoy each moment as it unfolds. The Othila rune of separation helps Monique make a break from the hurts of her past. The Nauthiz rune of constraint gives her a strong desire for freedom and authenticity. The Ehwaz rune of movement lets her know that she is a citizen of the world. The Kano rune of opening provides her with a good clear vision of her goals and dreams, and with the inspiration necessary to make those dreams a reality. Uruz provides her with strength.

Elements: Air, earth, water, earth, fire, earth/fire, air

THE NUMEROLOGICAL INTERPRETATION

Monique (NV = 4, CV = 8, VV = 5, FL = 4)

Put Monique next to a jewelry box and a closet full of fine clothing, and you will find a very contented woman. This name raises one's level of sensuousness. Monique is very aware of life as experienced through her five senses, and takes great pleasure in the sight, sound, taste, smell, and touch of it. Her life tests involve learning to discriminate when applying her personal magnetism. Specifically, Monique can attract a lot of money into her life. But her real sense of security will come from her ability to pierce through the veils of illusion that cloak fortune and form. Once this is accomplished, a wiser and richer Monique will emerge.

Morgan

A Kabbalistic Synopsis
מערגון —MA'ARGVN (Mem, Ayin, Resh, Gimel, Vau, Nun)

The name Morgan can be used for both men and women, which is just as well, since it means that the good fortune associated with this name can benefit both sexes. Morgan really does have the potential to have it all. There is a definite ability to do well in business, either as an employee climbing up the ranks or as a self-made individual running his or her own company. In addition Morgan recognizes the importance of having a good time. A considerable amount of spare time and money will be spent in pursuit of wine, women (or men), and song. Morgan loves to travel in style and enjoys soaking up different cultures. With the influences in this name there is no reason why he or she shouldn't be able to do just that. However, good fortune and a comfortable lifestyle are not enough for Morgan. What really drives this individual is a desire for emotional fulfillment, and Morgan has a definite belief that one day an ideal partner will arrive for him or her. Until this day comes, Morgan won't entertain the thought of serious emotional commitment.

The Runic Interpretation
ᚾᚨᚷᚱᛟᛗ (Nauthiz, Ansuz, Gebo, Raido, Othila, Mannaz)

Morgan has many friends who wish her well. The Gebo rune of partnership ensures that Morgan will have a companion to share life's joys and sorrows. The Othila rune of separation suggests that Morgan will need to break away from her past in order to live life authentically. The Ansuz rune enhances Morgan's intuition, and the Mannaz rune strengthens her sense of who she is. Nauthiz, the rune of constraint, stifles Morgan a bit until she eventually overcomes these limitations by educating herself about the ways of the world. When the day is done, she has a mate to share her triumphs and to lend her a shoulder to cry on until the sun comes out again. Men named Morgan will be similarly well loved.

Elements: Fire, air, water, water, earth/fire, air

The Numerological Interpretation
Morgan (NV = 5, CV = 7, VV = 7, FL = 4)

The numerological significance of this name centers upon Morgan's intellectual abilities, of which there are many. He tends to have a fine mind, easily given over to clear logic and precision. Morgan can do well working in computer science, where the structuring and analysis of data are very important. He may also have a particular gift for research, especially of the technical kind. Women named Morgan will be equally gifted intellectually. Morgan doesn't mind spending time alone in pursuit of his particular interests; in fact, he looks forward to it. His life challenge is found on the emotional level. Since Morgan is so mentally polarized, the bearer of this name may suppress or deny his feelings.

DERIVATION: Welsh from the Old Welsh name Morcant, meaning "great" or "circle." Originally a male name, but has become increasingly common as a female name, especially in the United States during the late twentieth century.

PRINCIPAL COLORS: The full spectrum of lightly toned hues

GEMSTONES AND PRECIOUS METALS: Diamonds, silver

BOTANICALS: Oats, mushrooms, hazel

UNIQUE SPELLINGS: Morgann, Morgen, Morgin, Morginn, Morgyn, Morgynn

RELATED TO: Morgance; Morgana, Morganica, Morganne

Morris

A KABBALISTIC SYNOPSIS
מערריס —MA'ARRYS (Mem, Ayin, Resh, Resh, Yod, Samech)

The truest saying in the world—as far as Morris is concerned—is that "a change is as good as a rest." Morris cannot stand routine. It drives him wild with boredom, and any employer would do well to ensure that Morris is given a whole range of responsibilities to keep him occupied. When he is motivated, Morris is an excellent worker—but when he's bored, he can simply sit and stare at the wall. The entertainment industry would be a good place for Morris to work. The letter Resh, meaning "sun," which represents a jolly outlook on life, appears twice in his name. And in fact, it may sometimes seem to people that Morris is incapable of taking anything seriously. However, Morris does have a very serious and thoughtful side to his character, but this is an aspect of his personality that he likes to keep to himself and his partner.

THE RUNIC INTERPRETATION
ᛋᛁᚱᚱᛟᛗ (Sowelu, Isa, Raido, Raido, Othila, Mannaz)

The double Raido energy of journey keeps Morris hopping. He vacations every few months and loves to explore uncharted waters. The Raido water elements keep Morris returning to the sea. When he can't get to the beach, he turns to music for relaxation and inspiration. The runes for standstill and separation make it easy for Morris to pack his bags and fly away at a moment's notice. The Mannaz energy of self makes Morris a bit selfish, and this is the one way he's learned to get his needs met. The Sowelu rune of wholeness encourages Morris to consider the needs of others, too, and when he keeps that in mind, he becomes a good team player. The rune for standstill, Isa, can indicate stagnation or boredom. When Isa is accompanied, as it is here, by the rune for separation or departure, Othila, it's easy to conclude that Morris could be very impulsive.

Elements: Air, earth, water, water, earth/fire, air

THE NUMEROLOGICAL INTERPRETATION
Morris (NV = 11, CV = 5, VV = 6, FL = 4)

Morris can be quite an inspiration to the people around him. He is not one to try to change people's minds or force his opinions on them. His understanding about life comes from within himself, and people who are perceptive enough realize that Morris has a special gift. Morris is no doubt aware of his sensitivity, but may have to wait until he is older and more mature in order to make practical use of it. Until then, he may be somewhat of an idealist with more dreams than he has necessary tools to create something concrete out of his vision and insight.

∽

Muriel

A Kabbalistic Synopsis
מוריאל —MVRYAL (Mem, Vau, Resh, Yod, Aleph, Lamed)

Fools rush in where angels fear to tread, and unfortunately so does Muriel. Anyone who knows her will be quick to point out the many and varied occasions when her rash behavior has gotten her into a scrape. Muriel has a very fiery nature and tends to act before thinking. Luckily for Muriel, her name's value reduces to seventeen, which is the number of the Star card in the tarot. The Star symbolizes fortune, particularly in the context of protection. In other words, while Muriel may be quicker than most to get into difficult situations, she always manages to find a positive way out. Muriel will need to have a good job, as she has a love affair with shopping, especially at expensive stores. This may be an even bigger issue for her than for other shopaholics, thanks to her tendency to buy on impulse. Muriel is very popular, and if she does manage to make it big, she will be exceptionally generous with her friends.

The Runic Interpretation
ᛚᛖᛁᚱᚢᛗ (Laguz, Ehwaz, Isa, Raido, Uruz, Mannaz)

Muriel is strong-willed and capable, and she can choose almost any career and make a success of it. The Uruz rune of strength in combination with the Mannaz rune of self assures Muriel will have fortitude and perseverance. Always willing to change directions when opportunity presents itself, Muriel finds a way to get ahead in life. Ansuz, the rune of change, helps her intuit her situation and make a move when the timing is perfect. The Isa rune of standstill teaches Muriel the value of silence. Laguz keeps Muriel flexible and nonjudgmental. The Ehwaz rune signifies movement, and in combination with Raido for journey, ensures that Muriel will travel far and wide.

Elements: Water, air, earth, water, earth, air

The Numerological Interpretation
Muriel (NV = 6, CV = 7, VV = 8, FL = 4)

With her open and honest personality, Muriel is a pleasure to have as a friend. Her name contains the numbers of a woman who is generous of heart, unpretentious, and caring. Muriel is most comfortable in intimate settings with trusted friends and her special partner. She is very home oriented. Her door can be open, but not always. Muriel is aware that her boundaries can be crossed, and she has a degree of self-protection built into her nature. Taken to an extreme, this can make her mistrustful and give her the urge to close that door behind her. A person as emotionally sensitive as Muriel has to be able to balance a respect for her own limitations with the rest of her giving nature.

DERIVATION: Irish, from the word *muirgheal*, meaning "sea-bright." Very popular during the Middle Ages, then declined, only to rise in popularity during the late nineteenth and early twentieth centuries.

PRINCIPAL COLORS: All but the brightest shades of blue

GEMSTONES AND PRECIOUS METALS: Blue and blue-green turquoise

BOTANICALS: Vervain, daffodils, walnuts

UNIQUE SPELLINGS: Muiriel, Muiriele, Muirielle, Murial, Muriale, Muriall, Muriell, Murielle, Muryal, Muryelle

RELATED TO: Maria†, Marie†, Mary†, Merial, Meriel, Merrelle, Merriol, Merryl, Meryl, Muri, Muriella

"In time of crisis, we summon up our strength. Then, if we are lucky, we are able to call every resource, every forgotten image that can leap to our quickening, every memory that can make us know our power. And this luck is more than it seems to be: it depends on the long preparation of the self to be used."
— MURIEL RUKEYSER (POET)

Myra

A KABBALISTIC SYNOPSIS
מירא —MYRA (Mem, Yod, Resh, Aleph)

When you see Myra you are likely to be looking at a facade. Myra rarely, if ever, shows her true feelings or personality to the outside world. Even her partner will spend a considerable amount of time in the dark where his lover's feelings are concerned. This excessively private nature will be exacerbated if the Myra in question is also a Scorpio. On the whole, though, Myra comes across as jolly and easygoing. This is good in that it makes her a very easy person to work with. However, underneath Myra is often deeply insecure, and she worries a great deal about how others really feel about her. In spite of her worries, Myra is a very energetic character who can be incredibly innovative when it comes to thinking up new ways of doing things or, for that matter, sparking up a relationship that has become dull and lifeless. The one true aspect of Myra's personality that all will see is her strength of character and forceful demeanor when she is put on the defensive.

THE RUNIC INTERPRETATION
ᚨᚱᛇᛗ (Ansuz, Raido, Eihwaz, Mannaz)

Myra is intuitive and perceptive. The rune for Ansuz, or signals, in her name gives her a capacity to sense the moods of her colleagues and friends. It's as if she takes everyone's emotional temperature when she enters a room and knows just how to handle them to bring out the best in them. The Mannaz rune of self gives Myra a good, strong ability to love and care for herself. Raido signifies good communication, and Myra is a skillful negotiator on the home and business front. Myra is versatile, and will enjoy work that takes advantage of her talents with language and her impressive social skills.

Elements: Air, water, earth/fire, air

THE NUMEROLOGICAL INTERPRETATION
Myra (NV = 3, CV = 4, VV = 8, FL = 4)

Myra is physically strong and a very determined individual. She is more traditional than rebellious. This is a woman who is very comfortable working at a management- or executive-level job. She likes to create order around herself, and is at ease when advising other people on how to increase their productivity and efficiency. When not at work, Myra prefers to be in a natural setting. Hiking, camping, and climbing are very good recreational outlets for her. She is definitely geared for a committed and responsible relationship.

Myron

A Kabbalistic Synopsis

מירון —MYRVN (Mem, Yod, Resh, Vau, Nun)

Myron would make an excellent lawyer, and he has the drive and energy to succeed and prosper in this career. Myron's name has a value that can be reduced to twenty, the number of the tarot card known as Judgment. Myron certainly has plenty of good judgment, and in addition to his ability to rationally analyze any given set of information, he has the gift of common sense as well. Myron will be highly respected by his peers, as he has a dedication to truth and honesty above all other considerations. Myron has a keen eye for the opposite sex—so much so that it can interfere with his work from time to time! He can almost instantly become besotted with someone and spend his workday planning how best to treat her to a romantic surprise.

The Runic Interpretation

ᚾᛟᚱᛇᛗ (Nauthiz, Othila, Raido, Eihwaz, Mannaz)

With the runes for both constraint and separation contained in Myron's name, he will face many challenges early on. The Mannaz rune says Myron can enjoy his own company because he knows who he is and he likes himself. Myron would make a good editor or writer. The Raido rune of journey promises travel opportunities and a good ability with words. He could also handle a high-stress position such as air traffic controller. Because he is patient and has a good mind for details, Myron might also make a fine accountant. Myron can succeed in a variety of jobs because he has the power of the four elements in his name.

Elements: Fire, earth/fire, water, earth/fire, air

The Numerological Interpretation

Myron (NV = 4, CV = 9, VV = 4, FL = 4)

The tangible, the useful, and the practical attract Myron. He enjoys being involved in the creation of form. In this respect, it is natural to find him working as a craftsman, shaping wood, clay, or other building materials. He needs to see the results of his efforts, whether they come in the shape of a new set of cabinets he has built or as a check he receives each week in a salary envelope. Myron is connected to the earth and enjoys the touch and feel of things. He is an honest and dependable man, one who can be called upon for help and advice. He tends to be a responsible, but sometimes strict, parent. Myron makes many demands upon himself that he is willing to fulfill, and passes this same attitude on to his children or to his subordinates in the workplace.

DERIVATION: English, from a Greek root meaning "fragrant oil." Especially common among early Christians because it was associated with the gift of myrrh given to Christ by one of the Three Kings. Very popular in the United States in the 1940s.

PRINCIPAL COLORS: The full spectrum of moderately shaded hues

GEMSTONES AND PRECIOUS METALS: Pale to deep, rich sapphires

BOTANICALS: Lesser celandine, wild spinach

UNIQUE SPELLINGS: Miron, Myran, Myren, Myrin, Myryn

RELATED TO: Ron

DERIVATION: French, an
elaboration of Nadia, which is
ultimately from a Russian word
meaning "hope." Commonly used
in English-speaking countries
since the 1890s.

PRINCIPAL COLORS: Pale to deep,
rich shades of green; cream

GEMSTONES AND PRECIOUS
METALS: Jade, cat's-eye, pearls

BOTANICALS: Chicory, plantain,
colewort

UNIQUE SPELLINGS: Nadeen,
Nadene, Naydeen, Naydene,
Nadyne, Naydyne

RELATED TO: Nada, Nadege,
Nadena, Nadezhda, Nadia,
Nadina, Nadiya, Nadja, Nady,
Nadya, Nadyenka, Nadyna,
Nadzia, Naida, Nata, Natka

❧

"If I had my life to live over again, I'd
dare to make more mistakes next
time."

—NADINE STAIR (AUTHOR)

Nadine

A KABBALISTIC SYNOPSIS
נאידיהן —NAYDYHN (Nun, Aleph, Yod, Daleth, Yod, Heh, Nun)

The value of Nadine's name is 770. In certain occult circles this is a number of great importance. This does not necessarily mean Nadine will be involved in any practices of a mystical nature, but the energies of that particular number and its significance will affect her personality. Nadine is a genuinely honest woman, a rare find in this day and age. She is uncomfortable with even the smallest lie. You would never see her taking even a pen home from the office. Nadine has a wide circle of friends, and while she can be somewhat serious, those who know her really appreciate her generosity of spirit and loyalty. She is always ready to listen when someone has a problem. Nadine is quite a handy woman, and she gets a real kick out of repairing things herself. She may even follow this activity as a profession; she certainly has the skill to make a go of it.

THE RUNIC INTERPRETATION
ᛗᚾᛁᛞᚫᚾ (Ehwaz, Nauthiz, Isa, Dagaz, Ansuz, Nauthiz)

Once the music starts Nadine can't help herself; she just starts tapping her feet. The Ehwaz rune for movement gives her rhythm and a deep love of music. The double Nauthiz rune in this name inflicts some limitations, which could be financial or emotional. However, Nadine has absolutely no intention of putting up with these constraints, and she changes her situation with determination and vigor. The Isa rune in this name suggests Nadine should spend some time alone healing and figuring out her goals and career direction. Once Nadine accomplishes this, with the help of her good intuition (Ansuz), nothing can slow her down. The Dagaz rune for breakthrough helps Nadine transform her future.

Elements: Air, fire, earth, fire, air, fire

THE NUMEROLOGICAL INTERPRETATION
Nadine (NV = 11, CV = 5, VV = 6, FL = 5)

Nadine has a sincere need to be of help and service. She is a very sympathetic woman who is emotionally sensitive and responsive to people in difficulty. Nadine has the potential to develop true intuition, but sometimes it is difficult for her to cope with her emotions. She needs to balance her emotional sensitivity with the development of her mind. It is only when the mind and the heart combine that her larger gift will unfold. Working with groups of people can be of great benefit to her. She will feel much more comfortable in these social settings once she has integrated her emotional nature and become more objective about her own strong feelings.

❧

Nancy

A Kabbalistic Synopsis
נאנסי —NANSY (Nun, Aleph, Nun, Samech, Yod)

Nancy very rarely thinks about anything; she feels instead. If you ask her opinion on the most dry and factual matter, her response will be based entirely on her emotional response to the issue. One result of this is that she is hopelessly impractical. Nancy's friends know that while Nancy may be deeply emotional and have a tendency toward dreaminess, she is full of exciting ideas. She simply needs someone more pragmatic to take charge of them. Nancy will never be short of male admirers.

The Runic Interpretation
ᛇᛋᚾᚨᚾ (Eihwaz, Sowelu, Nauthiz, Ansuz, Nauthiz)

Nancy surmounts the obstacles in her life with patience and the benefit of time, which always provides a healing influence. The Ansuz rune of signals shows Nancy how to use her intuition to get along with people as well as when to move ahead in business and when to retreat. Eihwaz is the rune of defense, and it gives Nancy a natural sense of self-protection that also extends to others. The Sowelu rune is a blessing, indicating that Nancy will learn to achieve wholeness in her life. Nancy will choose a career such as scientific research or teaching that makes use of her considerable gift of patience.

Elements: Earth/fire, air, fire, air, fire

The Numerological Interpretation
Nancy (NV = 3, CV = 4, VV = 8, FL = 5)

The achievement of success and social standing is very important to Nancy. It is equally important that writing and speaking be central parts of Nancy's chosen field. She might be a professor or a diplomat. On the surface Nancy is charming and an easy mixer, but let there be no doubt: Nancy has a very potent will. She is determined and can be very set in her ways. This stubbornness and internal inflexibility can be problematic for her. Many of Nancy's life lessons come through tests surrounding the proper use of her will.

DERIVATION: English, a pet form of Ann or Anne, from the Hebrew name Hannah, meaning "grace." Especially popular in the United States between 1920 and 1960.

PRINCIPAL COLORS: All shades of purple, from pale lilac to rich violet

GEMSTONES AND PRECIOUS METALS: Amethyst, garnets

BOTANICALS: Apple, bilberry, lungwort

UNIQUE SPELLINGS: Nainsi, Nancee, Nanci, Nancie, Nancsi, Nanncey, Nanncy, Nansee, Nansey

RELATED TO: Ann†, Anna†, Annet, Annie, Hannah†, Nan, Nance, Nanice, Nannie, Nanny

"Doubt yourself and you doubt everything you see. Judge yourself and you see judges everywhere. But if you listen to the sound of your own voice, you can rise above doubt and judgment. And you can see forever."
—NANCY KERRIGAN (ATHLETE)

Naomi

DERIVATION: Biblical name meaning "pleasantness" in Hebrew. In the Bible, the name of the wise mother-in-law of Ruth. Commonly used in English-speaking countries since the eighteenth century.

PRINCIPAL COLORS: Light to deep, rich yellow and green

GEMSTONES AND PRECIOUS METALS: Moonstones, pearls

BOTANICALS: Elder, blackberry, juniper

UNIQUE SPELLINGS: Naomie, Naomy, Nayomi, Nayomie, Nayomy

RELATED TO: Naoma, Naomia, Navit, Noami, Noemi, Noemie

↬

"Complacency is a far more dangerous attitude than outrage."
—NAOMI LITTLEBEAR
(MUSICIAN)

A KABBALISTIC SYNOPSIS
נאיעמי —NAYA'AMY (Nun, Aleph, Yod, Ayin, Mem, Yod)

In ancient times a woman with this name could have made a promising warrior queen. Naomi is tough with a capital T, and is more than happy to demonstrate it in order to get her own way. Naomi can sometimes be regarded as vain by those around her, and in a sense this is true. However, when you are good-looking, intelligent, and courageous in any situation, you probably have good cause to be quite pleased with yourself! While she is certainly gutsy, Naomi doesn't go out of her way to create confrontation; in fact, she would far rather sit down and discuss things calmly and rationally. The central number in the value of her name indicates that along with everything else, she has the gift of gab, and Naomi will usually be able to talk people around to her way of viewing things. In relationships Naomi likes her partner to be as strong as she is.

THE RUNIC INTERPRETATION
ᛁᛗᛟᚨᚾ (Isa, Mannaz, Othila, Ansuz, Nauthiz)

Naomi is capable of making sweeping gestures that help her discard old ways and build a better world for herself. The Nauthiz rune of constraint confirms some lack and limitations in her life, but Naomi will set out to change this situation. She may be somewhat blunt at times, but what counts is that she can use the Othila rune of separation to discard circumstances that no longer serve her. The Mannaz rune of self could mean Naomi is selfish. But maybe Naomi is putting her needs first because nobody has done this for her in the past. The Isa rune of standstill affords Naomi time to heal and reflect on things that don't go well.

Elements: Earth, air, earth/fire, air, fire

THE NUMEROLOGICAL INTERPRETATION
Naomi (NV = 7, CV = 9, VV = 7, FL = 5)

Naomi is very concerned with ethics and morality. She is a natural-born student of history, and does well either as a teacher or as a lawyer or judge. It is important for Naomi to be able to separate truth from fiction, good from evil. Naomi wants to live correctly, and expects others to be true to themselves as well. She may be a perfectionist and, if so, is liable to be disappointed when her expectations fall short of her results. Naomi is a very intelligent woman. She will want to be surrounded by interesting friends. Naomi is the type of person who will never stop educating herself and others.

↬

Natalie

A KABBALISTIC SYNOPSIS

נאתאלי —NAThALY (Nun, Aleph, Tau, Aleph, Lamed, Yod)

If anyone deserves a medal for commitment to a cause, it is Natalie: She is a tireless fighter for all that she feels is right. The value of her name has associations with the letter Tzaddi, meaning "fishhook," and this tells us that she will never let go of a prospect until she feels that her work has been successful. Other influences in her name suggest that she is likely to be drawn to quite controversial issues and is also very likely to be active in the women's movement to some degree or other. Despite her altruism, Natalie is quite a hedonist; her name's value reduces to fifteen, which is the number of the Devil card in the tarot. This card tells us that Natalie is a lover of luxury and that she will spend a good portion of her time and money pampering herself in whatever way she prefers. She is likely to enjoy physical exercise, so she may well splurge on dues at an exclusive health club.

THE RUNIC INTERPRETATION

ᛖᛁᛚᚨᛏᚨᚾ (Ehwaz, Isa, Laguz, Ansuz, Teiwaz, Ansuz, Nauthiz)

Natalie is particularly receptive during conversations with learned people and during coincidental meetings. No one ever taught this to Natalie; she is a naturally good listener, and she has a double Ansuz runic configuration in her name, blessing her with exceptional intuition. The Laguz rune of flow keeps Natalie open to new experiences. She will have some difficult lessons to absorb involving limitations and obstacles because Nauthiz is present in a prominent position in this name. With the runes Ehwaz (growth), Isa (patience), and Teiwaz (warrior) in her name, Natalie has the ability to look these troubles in the eye and wave good-bye.

Elements: Air, earth, water, air, air, air, fire

THE NUMEROLOGICAL INTERPRETATION

Natalie (NV = 8, CV = 1, VV = 7, FL = 5)

"I dare you!" is Natalie's motto. This is a woman of stamina and courage, a person who stands up bravely to life's many challenges. She has a very clear idea of who she is, and is never pleased to hear the word *no*. Natalie is her own authority figure and is willing to attain her goals by her own efforts. She wants to be recognized for something special, and will cultivate her interests until she has devised a very original method of self-expression. Some people may find it difficult to get along with her; after all, Natalie is not the most obliging or compromising of people. But she is a loyal, steadfast friend and has profound affection for the people closest to her.

DERIVATION: French form of the Russian name Natalya, from the Latin *natalis*, meaning "birthday," especially Christ's birthday. Very common in France and in the English-speaking world.

PRINCIPAL COLORS: Black, dark gray, very deep shades of azure and violet

GEMSTONES AND PRECIOUS METALS: Carbuncles, rubies, amethyst

BOTANICALS: Angelica, pilewort

UNIQUE SPELLINGS: Natalee, Natelie, Nathalie, Natilie, Nattailie, Nattalee, Nattalie, Nattelie, Nattilie

RELATED TO: Nat, Nata, Natala, Natalene, Natalia, Nataline, Natalja, Natalya, Natashat, Nathalia, Natividad, Nattie, Nettie, Tasha

"It is my hope that you will listen with new ears, for there is something different here that you may notice. I think they call it attitude."
—NATALIE COLE (MUSICIAN)

Natasha

DERIVATION: Russian, a pet form of Natalya, which is from the Latin *natalís*, meaning "birthday," especially Christ's birthday.

PRINCIPAL COLORS: The palest to the brightest yellow, also brown

GEMSTONES AND PRECIOUS METALS: Topaz, yellow diamonds

BOTANICALS: Lavender, eyebright, thyme

UNIQUE SPELLINGS: Natacha, Natachah, Natascha, Nataschah, Natashah

RELATED TO: Nastaliya, Nastalya, Nat, Nata, Natala, Natalia, Nataliet, Natalja, Natalya, Natashenka, Nathalia, Nathalie, Natividad, Tasha

A KABBALISTIC SYNOPSIS

אשאטאנ —NATASHA (Nun, Aleph, Teth, Aleph, Shin, Aleph)

The prevalence of the letter A, or Aleph, in this name indicates that Natasha is, above all else, a thinker. Aleph means "oxen" and relates to practical concerns. The letter Aleph is also associated with the element of air, which is concerned with mental processes. Natasha may well be an academic, as her ideas often tend to be more abstract rather than related to actual concerns in industry and business. In addition she enjoys being a radical and living somewhat on the outside or at the edge of mainstream society. A job in academia would allow Natasha an offbeat lifestyle without endangering her finances. Natasha is canny when it comes to money matters. While she may be off-the-wall in many other ways, no one will question her ability and willingness to work hard. Her love life often takes second place to her work life.

THE RUNIC INTERPRETATION

ᚾᚺᛊᚨᛏᚨᚾ (Ansuz, Hagalaz, Sowelu, Ansuz, Teiwaz, Ansuz, Nauthiz)

The triple Ansuz configuration in Natasha's name makes her positively psychic. She can use these talents as an inventor, strategist, troubleshooter, or detective, or as a welcome boost to her skills in any job. Unfortunately, Natasha's name also features the dreadful whammy of the Hagalaz rune for disruption and Nauthiz for constraint. Bad as this is (for it suggests danger, which could involve car accidents, bankruptcy, or illness), Natasha's considerable intuition is there to warn her of trouble. The Teiwaz warrior rune makes her brave and stable in the face of calamity, and the Sowelu rune gives her a sense of wholeness. When all is said and done, Natasha comes through her personal fire walk with amazing wisdom.

Elements: Air, water, air, air, air, air, fire

THE NUMEROLOGICAL INTERPRETATION

Natasha (NV = 1, CV = 7, VV = 3, FL = 5)

Natasha is a natural-born leader. It is not so much that she seeks others to follow in her fiery wake, as much as she prefers to lead herself down the path of life and not be led. Natasha wants the freedom to make her own discoveries, recover from her own mistakes, and take credit for her own successes. She seeks a very passionate lover, a person with a fiery will and no lack of courage. Unless her partner displays these characteristics, it will be very difficult for her to sustain a long-lasting relationship. Natasha is not the most tolerant of women, and she definitely will not abide laziness in others. One of her lessons in life has to do with compassion and its development, as not everyone is as assertive as she is.

Nate

DERIVATION: Pet form of Nathaniel and Nathan, from the Hebrew, meaning "he [God] has given."

PRINCIPAL COLORS: Moderately shaded hues of any color, also electric colors

GEMSTONES AND PRECIOUS METALS: Sapphires

BOTANICALS: Sage, celandine, wintergreen

UNIQUE SPELLINGS: Nayt, Nayte, Neight

RELATED TO: Nat, Nataniel, Nathant, Nathanial, Nathanielt, Thaniel

A Kabbalistic Synopsis
נאים —NAYT (Nun, Aleph, Yod, Teth)

If you ever decide to try rock climbing, you could do a lot worse than ask Nate to come along. Nate's name adds up to seventy, the value of the letter Ayin, which is connected to the sign Capricorn and the qualities of the mountain goat. Physically Nate is usually of quite a slight build, but he is enormously agile and surefooted. In addition, Nate is one of the bravest men you could meet—the sort who goes white-water rafting for relaxation. Nate would never be comfortable in an urban setting, and would probably cut something of a Crocodile Dundee figure if he ever lived in a city. His values are traditional, to say the least, although he is by no means a puritan and can enjoy a good time as much as the next man. Nate is often a loner, and if he does ever settle down or marry, it will be relatively late in life. Even then he will still need his own space on a regular basis.

The Runic Interpretation
ᛖᛏᚨᚾ (Ehwaz, Teiwaz, Ansuz, Nauthiz)

People admire Nate because he lives out their secret fantasy in real life. Nate will reside abroad and travel all around the world, as indicated by the Ehwaz energy of movement. Courageous and bold, Nate takes advantage of the lessons of the Teiwaz warrior rune to live spontaneously and take risks. The Ansuz rune for signals gives Nate strong insight into people and circumstances and is a protective influence for Nate. The Nauthiz rune of constraint alludes to obstacles and distractions that can throw Nate off course, and he needs to treat these disruptions as significant, because focus and order are required for his journey.

Elements: Air, air, air, fire

The Numerological Interpretation
Nate (NV = 4, CV = 7, VV = 6, FL = 5)

Nate needs to see the tangible returns on his investments in life. He enjoys reading and studying, but he is much more of a practical man than an idealistic one. Personal and financial security are important facets of his life, but he is not obsessive about his possessions or social status. He tends to be a well-balanced individual, one with a kind and sincere disposition. Nate likes the outdoors and feels very close to nature. Partnership for him means a relationship in which both parties are standing side by side in solid and trusting companionship.

Nathan

DERIVATION: Biblical name meaning "he [God] has given" in Hebrew. In the Bible, the name of one of King David's sons, and the name of a prophet who reproached King David for arranging the death of Uriah the Hittite. Popular since the eighteenth century.

PRINCIPAL COLORS: The full spectrum of medium-toned hues, also electric colors

GEMSTONES AND PRECIOUS METALS: Sapphires

BOTANICALS: Iceland moss, medlar, sage

UNIQUE SPELLINGS: Nathen, Nathin, Nathyn, Naythan, Naythen, Naythin

RELATED TO: Nat, Natanael, Nate†, Nathaneal, Nathanial, Nathaniel†, Thaniel

❧

"I only regret that I have but one life to lose for my country."
—NATHAN HALE (PATRIOT)

A KABBALISTIC SYNOPSIS
נאתאן —NATHAN (Nun, Aleph, Tau, Aleph, Nun)

Nathan would get on very well with Nate, and they may even be neighbors, as there is no way you could get Nathan to happily leave the countryside. The ideal role for Nathan is farming, as he has a natural connection to the rhythm of the land. While he is not particularly religious, he does have a real sense of wonder when it comes to the power and beauty of nature. Nathan has a great store of natural common sense, and is often on hand to give advice to his friends and neighbors. Thanks to his friendly nature and wisdom he is likely to play a reasonably large part in the civic affairs of his hometown. In fact, he may even find himself entering local politics, although he has no wish to make a big career out of it. Home life is immensely important to Nathan, and he will make a wonderfully caring father and husband. If anything, he is likely to dote on his kids too much.

THE RUNIC INTERPRETATION
ᛏᚾᚦᚨᛏ (Nauthiz, Ansuz, Thurisaz, Ansuz, Nauthiz)

Nathan swerves around obstacles like a downhill skier. The double Ansuz rune affords Nathan the intuition he requires to circumvent obstacles and problems. And this is fortunate for poor Nathan, who will have a chance to test out his coping mechanisms on a daily basis due to the unfortunate double Nauthiz rune energies in his name, which symbolize constraint. Overcoming this constraint teaches Nathan never to settle for second best but rather to aim for the highest life has to offer, and to plan ahead. If Nathan is patient, the hard times will pass. The Thurisaz rune of gateway lets Nathan let go of anger and hurts from the past so that he can get on with his life in a productive and positive fashion.

Elements: Fire, air, fire, air, fire

THE NUMEROLOGICAL INTERPRETATION
Nathan (NV = 4, CV = 2, VV = 2, FL = 5)

This is a name that describes a very peaceful man. Nathan is rather modest, both in his appearance and demeanor. He does not care to call attention to himself, preferring to take a supportive role in life rather than a dominating one. Nathan likes to work behind the scenes, organizing other people's efforts in order to create the most harmonious results possible. He is a natural-born moderator, go-between, and mediator. Personal relationships are very important in his life, as Nathan is a confirmed romantic. Nathan seeks a monogamous and committed relationship, one that continues to grow and develop, bringing additional emotional security into his life.

❧

Nathaniel

A Kabbalistic Synopsis

נאתאניאל —NATHANYAL (Nun, Aleph, Tau, Aleph, Nun, Yod, Aleph, Lamed)

If you want to get something done and the deadline was yesterday, ask Nathaniel to take care of it. He is brimming with energy, and he will work any length of time necessary. With incredible gusto he manages to finish in half a day what it takes the rest of us two days plus overtime to deal with. In addition, he has a natural eye for detail, so although he works at high speed, there is unlikely to be much need for correction of his work once it is completed. Although he has more than enough ability, Nathaniel is quite reluctant to accept promotions. This, in part, relates to a deep-seated feeling that success comes only with a considerable amount of suffering. Thus Nathaniel will feel entitled to the corner office only when he has done his stint at the bottom. Nathaniel feels very protective toward his family, but can sometimes be too overbearing and disciplining. He needs a partner with a more laid-back and less earnest approach to life in order to mellow him out a little.

The Runic Interpretation

ᛚᛖᛁᛋᚨᚦᚨᛏ (Laguz, Ehwaz, Isa, Nauthiz, Ansuz, Thurisaz, Ansuz, Nauthiz)

The same strengths and weaknesses in the name Nathan apply to Nathaniel, but the runes of Isa, Ehwaz, and Laguz offer additional influences. Isa is the rune of standstill, and it encourages Nathaniel to seek silence when he needs to restore his energy and gain perspective on the events of his life. The Ehwaz rune of movement suggests that Nathaniel may choose to travel and reside abroad. If he selects this option, the Laguz energy of flow is at hand to keep Nathaniel flexible and open-minded during all his experiences so he can maximize the benefits of his adventures.

Elements: Water, air, earth, fire, air, fire, air, fire

The Numerological Interpretation

Nathaniel (NV = 3, CV = 5, VV = 7, FL = 5)

The numbers in this name reveal a person whose emphasis is on intellectual pursuits and development. Nathaniel has an inborn curiosity about life that he tends to nourish through interesting friends, frequent travel, and continuous education. This is a man with distinct interests and the ability to continually expand his understanding of life. However, Nathaniel may be somewhat challenged in personal relationships, when a more emotional approach is demanded of him. Thus the integration of his feelings with the broad scope of his intellect will be a major life lesson for Nathaniel.

DERIVATION: English form of Nathan, meaning "he [God] has given" in Hebrew. Popular among the Puritans, and common ever since.

PRINCIPAL COLORS: All shades of purple, from pale violet to deep maroon

GEMSTONES AND PRECIOUS METALS: Amethyst, garnets

BOTANICALS: Apple, bilberry, strawberry

UNIQUE SPELLINGS: Nathaneal, Nathanial, Nathanyal, Nathanyel, Nethaniel, Nethanyel

RELATED TO: Nat, Natanael, Nataniel, Natet, Nathant, Nathen, Thaniel

"Reason and emotion are not antagonists. What seems like a struggle is a struggle between two opposing ideas or values, one of which, automatic and unconscious, manifests itself in the form of a feeling."
—NATHANIEL BRANDON
(AUTHOR)

DERIVATION: Irish, Scottish, and English, anglicized form of the Gaelic name Niall, probably meaning "champion." Popular in Ireland during the Middle Ages, but now popular all over the English-speaking world.

PRINCIPAL COLORS: All colors of medium tone

GEMSTONES AND PRECIOUS METALS: Sapphires

BOTANICALS: Sage, spinach

UNIQUE SPELLINGS: Neal, Neale, Neall, Nealle, Neel, Neile, Neill, Neille, Niel

RELATED TO: Nealon, Neils, Nels, Nelson, Nial, Niall, Niles

༆

"That's one small step for man, one giant leap for mankind."
—NEIL ARMSTRONG (ASTRONAUT)

"If you choose not to decide—you still have made a choice!"
—NEIL PEART (MUSICIAN)

A KABBALISTIC SYNOPSIS
ניאל —NYAL (Nun, Yod, Aleph, Lamed)

The wheel of fortune always seems to turn in Neil's favor, and he has a knack for landing on his feet almost all the time. If Neil was being mugged, you could almost guarantee that the assailant's gun would jam or the blade would be too dull or the mugger would suddenly suffer a massive stroke in the act of robbing him. Unfortunately, Neil would then immediately lose his wallet anyway, as he is one of the most forgetful people ever! People often tell Neil that he is not making enough of the many opportunities that come his way. This is not due to his lack of ability but rather to his sense of uncertainty about himself. In reality his worries are without any basis; people like Neil. He is a modest and polite guy with absolutely no pretensions. He is always ready to sit and chat with people even when he is busy himself (although he may well have forgotten that he is busy!). All Neil needs to give him that push up the corporate ladder is a supportive partner who can persuade him to believe in himself. Once that happens, the sky's the limit!

THE RUNIC INTERPRETATION
ᚾᛖᛁᛚ (Laguz, Isa, Ehwaz, Nauthiz)

Neil is one who will judge people by their actions and not their words. The Isa rune of standstill helps Neil tolerate solitude and even crave the peace it brings him. The Laguz rune of flow keeps Neil open-minded and flexible. Nauthiz, the rune of constraint, suggests that Neil may live away from family and friends. Whatever troubles he may face, Neil learns to confront problems as they arise and to patiently await the outcome.

Elements: Water, earth, air, fire

THE NUMEROLOGICAL INTERPRETATION
Neil (NV = 4, CV = 8, VV = 5, FL = 5)

There is no doubt about it: Neil has the urge for professional and financial success. This is a planner, a man who tends to structure every move he makes. Neil doesn't like to leave anything to chance, and is definitely a person who has to be in control. Trust, faith, and an understanding of the more cyclic nature of life will be very important (and sometimes difficult) lessons for him to learn. Neil is a man dedicated to his plans and projects. He enjoys team efforts, especially when he's the team's captain! A sensuous person, Neil enjoys fine dining, comfortable surroundings, and passionate relationships.

༆

Nell

DERIVATION: English, pet form of Eleanor, Ellen, Helen, and other such names. Possibly related to a Greek word meaning "light." Used as a given name since the seventeenth century.

PRINCIPAL COLORS: Pale to bright greens and yellows, also gold

GEMSTONES AND PRECIOUS METALS: Pearls, moonstones, any white stone

BOTANICALS: Elder, linseed, blackberry

UNIQUE SPELLINGS: Nehl, Nel, Nelle

RELATED TO: Eleanor†, Elena†, Ella†, Ellen†, Ellie, Helen†, Helena, Helene†, Leanor, Nelia, Nella, Nelley, Nelliet, Nelly

A KABBALISTIC SYNOPSIS
נאלל —NALL (Nun, Aleph, Lamed, Lamed)

Nell is one of the sexiest names going, and Nell knows it! Her name's value—111—is a number made up entirely of ones, which shows that not only is Nell unique, she is also fiercely independent. Nell may enjoy the company of partners, but that doesn't mean that she will ever let herself become dependent on their company. She will make her own way in life, and whatever she does, it will be done with style and panache. Nell knows how to make a big entrance, and loves any kind of drama in life. Her biggest concern should be controlling her passionate nature, since she has a tendency to let her heart rule her head. Sometimes this can mean a tough time at work, as Nell may fail to bite her tongue and may violently disagree with her boss. But Nell is not one to be put off by setbacks in life, and as soon as she is down, she picks herself right back up again.

THE RUNIC INTERPRETATION
↑MM↑ (Laguz, Laguz, Ehwaz, Nauthiz)

Nell is given easily to tears. She cries at the movies even when they're comedies. Her sensitive and emotional nature is combined with a strong maternal disposition; home and family are important to her. As a mother, Nell feels fulfilled. Nell probably is actively involved in charity work. Her lunar nature creates a longing in her heart for union and merging. The Ehwaz rune for movement insinuates that Nell will love travel and living in foreign countries. The Nauthiz rune of constraint places limitations in her life. Although this is annoying, Nell uses these situations to her advantage. Her credo is "A setback is nothing but a setup for a comeback!"

Elements: Water, water, air, fire

THE NUMEROLOGICAL INTERPRETATION
Nell (NV = 7, CV = 11, VV = 5, FL = 5)

Nell contains a very fascinating numerological combination. When seven is found with eleven as primary name factors, it suggests a person with special gifts. Nell is very intuitive and is able to see behind and beyond the material superficialities of life. This natural gift, plus an introspective nature, may easily lead Nell to a study of metaphysics or some other philosophical investigations. She is a serious-minded woman, sincere in her urge to be of help to her family and community. The fives in her name only enlarge her perspective and desire to know, share, and give. An important lesson for her has to do with establishing clear priorities and boundaries; otherwise, she can easily dissipate her energy.

DERIVATION: English, pet form of Eleanor, Ellen, Helen, and other such names. Possibly related to a Greek word meaning "light." Especially popular from the 1860s to the 1930s.

PRINCIPAL COLORS: Pale bluish purple to deep shades of violet

GEMSTONES AND PRECIOUS METALS: Amethyst, garnets

BOTANICALS: Strawberry, mint, lungwort

UNIQUE SPELLINGS: Neli, Nelley, Nelli, Nelly

RELATED TO: Eleanort, Elenat, Ellat, Ellent, Elliet, Helent, Helena, Helenet, Leanor, Nelia, Nellt, Nella

A KABBALISTIC SYNOPSIS
נאללי —NALLY (Nun, Aleph, Lamed, Lamed, Yod)

Life for Nellie is very much tied up in family traditions, and she will probably be the first girl in her class to find a partner and settle down. The thought of running around with a whole host of different dates horrifies her; she isn't a prude, but she knows what is right for her. While her attitude may not suit many people in today's world, Nellie is likely to be very happy in her relationship for a good many years, even though it will have started at a relatively young age. Nellie has a very wise head on her shoulders and is successful at earning a good living. She is concerned with material comforts and often measures her success in life by her material wealth. This focus on things rather than ideas or emotions is shown by the value of her name, which reduces to four, a number that is associated with objects rather than concepts.

THE RUNIC INTERPRETATION
ᛖᛁᛚᛚᛖᚾ (Ehwaz, Isa, Laguz, Laguz, Ehwaz, Nauthiz)

Nellie has the same opportunities and challenges as Nell. Ehwaz and Isa offer opportunities for growth and patience. Nellie knows that manipulative people usually give themselves away if you listen to what they say. She refuses to be a gullible victim, and would rather discard a relationship than settle for friends who are dishonest. The extra Ehwaz rune of movement, combined with the double water element, makes her more free-spirited than Nell, and indicates that she is willing to keep moving on until she finds what she's looking for.

Elements: Air, earth, water, water, air, fire

THE NUMEROLOGICAL INTERPRETATION
Nellie (NV = 3, CV = 11, VV = 1, FL = 5)

Nellie is a name associated with a woman with a great deal of vivacity and vitality. Nellie can easily be the center of attention, but this is due more to her natural fiery disposition than to her craving for social approval. People like to listen to Nellie, as her advice is quite accurate and perceptive. She is definitely socially oriented, and is a natural for any profession dealing with communications, public relations, and advertising. However, Nellie is not the most patient person, and may have little tolerance for people who are not as quick on the uptake as she can be.

Nelson

A KABBALISTIC SYNOPSIS
נאלסען —NALSA'AN (Nun, Aleph, Lamed, Samech, Ayin, Nun)

When one thinks of Nelson, one is reminded of two particularly famous Nelsons separated by hundreds of years but sharing one common characteristic: heroism. Those two individuals are Admiral Nelson of the British navy and Nelson Mandela. If we look closely at the name Nelson, we can see that great courage and determination are its key characteristics. The L, or Lamed, suggests a very active personality, and because of its position in the name, it suggests an individual in vigorous pursuit of that which they believe to be right. Nelson is a man of strong principles who has a deep sense of duty. In a less grand sense this means that he can be relied upon by his family to look after them in times of trouble, and that he is a valuable and hardworking member of any team in the workplace. It will be no surprise, though, if Nelson goes on to greater things than the standard nine-to-five job.

THE RUNIC INTERPRETATION
ᛏᛟᛋᛚᛖᛏ (Nauthiz, Othila, Sowelu, Laguz, Ehwaz, Nauthiz)

Nelson is adaptable and confident. Laguz, the rune of flow, helps Nelson be flexible, easy-going, and accepting. The Othila rune helps him discard the debris of false opinions, insincere friends, and worn-out thinking. The Ehwaz rune for movement signifies that Nelson will choose a foreign country to make his home for a time. Ehwaz can also signify new attitudes. Having a double Nauthiz configuration in his name means that Nelson will endure constraint and that he must overcome lack and limitation. Nelson can enjoy a career in international business, foreign languages, or political science. He most assuredly will, because Nelson has the blessing of Sowelu for wholeness in his life.

Elements: Fire, earth/fire, air, water, air, fire

THE NUMEROLOGICAL INTERPRETATION
Nelson (NV = 7, CV = 5, VV = 11, FL = 5)

This is a very philosophical person, a man with a depth of understanding and an expansive worldview. Even if not well educated, Nelson will have a comprehension of other people that may come from beyond his personal experience. His understanding comes from a hidden source within himself, the treasure chest within his heart. Nelson is the name of a teacher who has the need to pass on what he has acquired. His life lessons have to do with the more practical issues of life; Nelson may not be particularly good with money management, and should seek a partner in whom these qualities are more developed than in himself.

DERIVATION: English, originally a surname meaning "son of Neil." Used as a given name. Linked to the British admiral Viscount Horatio Nelson (1758–1805), who defeated the French and Spanish at the Battle of Trafalgar in 1805.

PRINCIPAL COLORS: The full range of yellow and green hues, gold

GEMSTONES AND PRECIOUS METALS: White pearls, cat's-eye

BOTANICALS: Blackberry, elder, hops

UNIQUE SPELLINGS: Nehllsohn, Nehllson, Nehlsohn, Nehlson, Nehlsson, Nellsohn, Nellson, Nelsohn, Nelsson

RELATED TO: Nealson, Neilt, Neils, Nels, Niles, Nils, Nilson, Nilsson

"Our deepest fear is not that we are inadequate. Our deepest fear is that we are powerful beyond measure. It is our Light, not our Darkness, that most frightens us."
—NELSON MANDELA (LEADER OF THE AFRICAN NATIONAL CONGRESS, PRESIDENT OF SOUTH AFRICA)

Nicholas

A KABBALISTIC SYNOPSIS

ניכאלוס —NYKALA'AS (Nun, Yod, Kaph, Aleph, Lamed, Ayin, Samech)

If you go out for a night on the town with Nicholas, you shouldn't expect to be back until morning! In fact, you may be gone for quite a few days and nights, as Nicholas is something of a wild individual. Nicholas will never descend into a wholly dissolute lifestyle, though. He may know better than most how to have an outrageously good time, but he also intends to do well for himself careerwise, and won't let his taste for pleasure get in the way. Nicholas rarely relaxes in any real sense. He is always doing something, and this immense energy is shown by the letters Yod and Lamed in his name. However active and hedonistic he may be, Nicholas always has time for others. His name's value reduces to twelve, which is the number of the Hanged Man card in the tarot, and indicates a person who is willing to sacrifice his own needs for others.

THE RUNIC INTERPRETATION

ᛋᚨᛚᛟᚺᚲᛁᛏ (Sowelu, Ansuz, Laguz, Othila, Hagalaz, Kano, Isa, Nauthiz)

With the benefit of Sowelu in his name representing wholeness, Nicholas will find satisfaction and happiness in life. The runes can tell him what it takes to get there: Nicholas can incorporate solitude from Isa, intuition from Ansuz, flexibility from Laguz, and release from Othila. Once Nicholas has let go of anger and hurt, he can build a solid life. The Hagalaz rune of disruption, combined with Nauthiz for constraint, afford Nicholas many wake-up calls along the way. Once he comes into his own, Nicholas could do well in the performing arts or business.

Elements: Air, air, water, earth/fire, water, water, earth, fire

THE NUMEROLOGICAL INTERPRETATION

Nicholas (NV = 1, CV = 2, VV = 8, FL = 5)

Nicholas likes challenges—the bigger, the better. He always has a goal in mind and structures his life accordingly. Although Nicholas needs to make it on his own, he is not a loner. Intimate relationships are very important to him, both in terms of his emotional needs as well as for another, more important reason. It will be through his relationships that Nicholas learns how to share himself and begins to merge more consciously into the larger collective called "life."

❧

Nicole

DERIVATION: French, feminine form of Nicholas†, from the Greek roots *nike* and *laos*, meaning "victory" and "people," respectively. Especially popular in the United States in the 1970s.

PRINCIPAL COLORS: The full spectrum of moderately shaded hues

GEMSTONES AND PRECIOUS METALS: Sapphires

BOTANICALS: Sage, Iceland moss, Solomon's seal

UNIQUE SPELLINGS: Nichol, Nichole, Nicholle, Nickol, Nickole, Nicol, Nicolle

RELATED TO: Colette, Cosetta, Cosette, Nichelle, Nichola, Nicholette, Nicia, Nicki, Nicola, Nicolea, Nicolene, Nicolette, Nicolie, Nicolina, Nicoline, Nicolla, Nicolle, Nikki, Nikola, Nikoleta, Nikolia

A KABBALISTIC SYNOPSIS
ניכעהל —NYKA'AHL (Nun, Yod, Kaph, Ayin, Heh, Lamed)

The key word in describing Nicole's character is *balance*. The reduced value of her name is fourteen, which connects her to the tarot card Temperance. The Temperance card suggests a calm nature as well as somebody who can take conflicting opinions or people and bring them together. This talent makes Nicole particularly suited to any job that involves mediation; thus her job could range from international relations to certain aspects of police work. Nicole is particularly blessed, as she tends to have an unusually reassuring and calming voice. Not surprisingly, she is a big hit with kids, although if she has children herself, it may well be later in life. Nicole is very ambitious, but not in the usual way. Rather than lusting after money, power, or position, more than anything Nicole longs for understanding—which is, of course, a never-ending search.

THE RUNIC INTERPRETATION
ᛖᛚᛟᚲᛁᚾ (Ehwaz, Laguz, Othila, Kano, Isa, Nauthiz)

Nicole might want to set her alarm a little earlier so she can start her day with deep breathing. The Isa rune for meditation and the Kano rune for clearing figure prominently in Nicole's name. Nicole's like a finely tuned race car that is gorgeous but needs a lot of maintenance to run at top performance. The Nauthiz rune of constraint could present problems with fatigue or constraint in any form. Fortunately, the Laguz rune of flow gives Nicole an optimistic nature, and she can roll with the punches. The Ehwaz rune of movement means Nicole requires a lot of exercise and might excel at sports. She'll travel, too, as this appeals to her spontaneous nature.

Elements: Air, water, earth/fire, water, earth, fire

THE NUMEROLOGICAL INTERPRETATION
Nicole (NV = 4, CV = 11, VV = 2, FL = 5)

The name Nicole reveals an artistic temperament and indicates a woman with a highly individualistic flair. Nicole seeks to express herself in her own unique way, but in such a manner that she garners wide social appeal. She is a woman who avoids clashes and conflicts, a person who is much more at home in peaceful rather than chaotic circumstances. Art for Nicole is not just for "art's sake." Nicole is very interested in earning a good living at her craft. She appreciates beauty, enjoys dressing in fine clothes, and will appreciate both the sensuous and the sexual elements in her relationships.

DERIVATION: Russian, pet form of Antonina, Annina, Ann, or related names. Related to *nina*, Spanish word for "girl." Gained popularity in the 1970s.

PRINCIPAL COLORS: The full gamut of green shades, also creamy white

GEMSTONES AND PRECIOUS METALS: Jade, pearls

BOTANICALS: Chicory, rapeseed, moonwort

UNIQUE SPELLINGS: Neena, Neenah, Neenna, Nena, Nenah, Ninah

RELATED TO: Ann†, Anna†, Anne†, Annina, Anninka, Antonina, Janina, Ninacska, Nineta, Ninete, Ninetta, Ninette, Ninian, Ninnette, Ninochka, Ninon, Ninotchka

A KABBALISTIC SYNOPSIS
נינא —NYNA (Nun, Yod, Nun, Aleph)

No one would ever describe Nina as calm. She is a great person . . . but she also can be an absolute nightmare. This is because in this very short name, we have the letter Nun appearing twice. This letter is all about heightened emotional states, and you can pretty much guarantee that at any time of the day Nina will be in one heightened state or another! When she is in a good mood she is in a great mood—but if she is down, she plunges into a black hole of absolute despair. Nina can be quite solitary, especially if she is born under Capricorn. Usually her preference for solitude comes from her strong business ambition. Her desire to get to the top of her chosen career means that she will often work late at the office rather than hang out in the bar with the rest of the gang. When she does decide to join in and is in the mood for a good time, she parties with gusto.

THE RUNIC INTERPRETATION
ᚨᚾᛁᚾ (Ansuz, Nauthiz, Isa, Nauthiz)

Nina needs to restock her life regularly with good friends, opinions, and endeavors. The double Nauthiz rune of constraint says that Nina will benefit from setting boundaries and exercising restraint. This might apply to her finances or to her tendency to want it all now. Patience is worth cultivating, and the Isa rune affords Nina the lessons of introspection and solitude as she orders her life. The Ansuz rune for signals blesses Nina with good common sense and a built-in feeling for timing. Nina can use music and dance to express herself beautifully.

Elements: Air, fire, earth, fire

THE NUMEROLOGICAL INTERPRETATION
Nina (NV = 2, CV = 1, VV = 1, FL = 5)

A woman who carries herself with confidence and strength of character, Nina is both capable and caring. She has the ability to integrate her highly independent and forthright nature with her need to live harmoniously with other people. Nina is able to accomplish this in such a way that friends and coworkers are eager to seek her out for her guidance and leadership. This name bestows the gifts of courage and honesty. Nina is unafraid to approach new challenges, and she marches forward into life with an open and brave heart.

Noah

A Kabbalistic Synopsis
נעאה —NAʾAAH (Nun, Ayin, Aleph, Heh)

This guy is one of life's survivors. Noah can tolerate conditions in his life that would make most of us just give up. In fact, it often seems that Noah actually thrives in difficult situations. This characteristic makes Noah ideal for any career that contains a strong element of risk or exposure to the elements. Given the original holder of the name (the biblical ark builder), we can easily see Noah as a lifeboat man or deep-sea fisherman. Noah is very interested in other people and likes to have many friends—none of whom are necessarily intimate friends but all of whom are well liked and regularly visited. If you want to spend some time with Noah, you usually have to book him early, as he enjoys a very busy social life. Morality is very important to Noah, and he is a very principled man—although if he has a strong Virgoan influence in his horoscope, he can come off as something of a moralist to other people.

The Runic Interpretation
ᚺᚨᛟᚾ (Hagalaz, Ansuz, Othila, Nauthiz)

Noah has days when he feels like building the ark just so he can escape! With the lessons of Hagalaz bringing disruption, the rune Nauthiz causing constraint, and the Othila rune bringing separation, this man has challenges to face. Luckily, the lovely Ansuz rune heightens his intuition, sensitizing him to the signals sent by his environment and the people he encounters. Slowly, when he masters the art of optimism and positive thinking, Noah learns patience and the value of release. He can then move ahead with large plans for his life. Noah will excel in dangerous occupations, and he needs to keep himself in good health, for much is required of him in this lifetime.

Elements: Water, air, earth/fire, fire

The Numerological Interpretation
Noah (NV = 11, CV = 4, VV = 7, FL = 5)

A profound thinker with a love for education, Noah has the capacity to envision and carry out very long-range plans. He is well organized, orderly, and pays a lot of attention to details. More likely than not, Noah will reach some level of distinction among his peers. He is highly inspired, a man who seems to know some inner secret about life. His personal challenges come through intimate relationships, as he may be more inclined to pursue an intellectual or spiritual life rather than concern himself with emotional issues and personal feelings.

DERIVATION: Hebrew, of uncertain meaning, but possibly meaning "rest" or "wandering." In the Bible, the name of the man who built the ark. Commonly used as a given name since the seventeenth century.

PRINCIPAL COLORS: The complete range of green hues, also white

GEMSTONES AND PRECIOUS METALS: Pearls, moonstones

BOTANICALS: Plantain, lettuce, colewort

UNIQUE SPELLINGS: Noa, Noé, Noha

RELATED TO: Noach, Noak

Noel

DERIVATION: The French word for Christmas, from the Latin *natalis*, meaning "birthday." Both masculine and feminine.

PRINCIPAL COLORS: Pale to deep and brilliant shades of yellow and brown, also orange

GEMSTONES AND PRECIOUS METALS: Citrine, topaz, amber

BOTANICALS: Borage, eyebright, lavender

UNIQUE SPELLINGS: Nole, Noll, Nowel, Nowell

RELATED TO: Noela, Noeleen, Noelene, Noeline, Noella, Noelle, Noelleen, Noelynn, Noweleen

A KABBALISTIC SYNOPSIS
נעאל —NA'AAL (Nun, Ayin, Aleph, Lamed)

If you are married to a Noel, don't ever go out without telling your partner where and with whom you are going; Noel is intensely jealous, and will suspect the worst immediately. This will be the case whether Noel is a man or a woman. On the positive side, Noel is an extraordinarily attentive partner and lover. If you treat Noel right, you will want for nothing in every aspect of your life. When Noel finds the right partner, there is no changing his or her mind, and on the whole Noel will settle down much earlier than any of Noel's friends. Noel can be demanding of any staff under his or her management. To be fair, Noel is equally demanding of him- or herself. You will never see a female Noel looking scruffy; she will be immaculately dressed at all times. In a similar vein, all male Noels will ensure that they maintain the peak of physical fitness throughout their usually long lives.

THE RUNIC INTERPRETATION
ᛚᛖᛟᚾ (Laguz, Ehwaz, Othila, Nauthiz)

Noel has the Nauthiz lesson of constraint, and must learn to reassess plans and move with deliberation and caution. The Laguz rune allows Noel to swerve from one situation to the next without undue stress during transitions. This makes it easy to see how Noel can enjoy living abroad and traveling much more than the average person—opportunities hinted at by the delightful Ehwaz rune of movement. The Othila rune gives Noel the ability to edit out ideas that are redundant. Noel is spontaneous and can live in the moment, and this makes him or her creative and fun to know.

Elements: Water, air, earth/fire, fire

THE NUMEROLOGICAL INTERPRETATION
Noel (NV = 1, CV = 8, VV = 11, FL = 5)

There is a great deal of ambition contained in the name. Noel has a lot of self-confidence in his or her ability to achieve goals, and is undaunted by obstacles. Challenges to his or her sense of personal direction only further stimulate this urge to succeed. Noel has fine organizational skills and is at ease when assessing the complexities of large projects. Noels seem to know where all the details in a situation belong, and they look at life through a wide-angle lens. It will be important for Noels to cultivate humor and lightheartedness, as they have the tendency to take life too seriously.

Nora

A Kabbalistic Synopsis

נערא —NA'ARA (Nun, Ayin, Resh, Aleph)

Busy, busy, busy: Nora is always running around doing something. She seems to have enough jobs for a whole family rather than a single individual! She is an extremely hard worker, and is always happy to take on the most difficult task that needs doing—although not always out of pure kindness. Nora intends to succeed in her career. This ability to work hard and the desire for business achievement are shown by the letters Ayin and Resh in her name. The association of the letter Resh with the sun also suggests that Nora is a generally cheerful person despite her heavy workload. When Nora does make a decision, she tends to go with her gut instinct and is very often right in her choices. Although she herself would probably scoff at the suggestion, she is very intuitive, and this is indicated by the fact that the value of her name reduces to six, a number associated with such powers.

The Runic Interpretation

ᚨᚱᛟᚾ (Ansuz, Raido, Othila, Nauthiz)

Nora is romantic and imaginative. She can easily envision herself in bygone days, and history comes alive for her. Nora is also interested in what the future holds, and is quick to anticipate trends in fashion and music. The Othila rune makes Nora streamlined; she is quick to eliminate nonessentials from her life. She enjoys cars with sleek lines and elegant simplicity. When Nora travels, she keeps her baggage to a minimum and engineers a manageable itinerary. The Nauthiz rune of constraint teaches Nora to order and restore facets of her life that have troubled her and to overcome limiting attitudes and beliefs.

Elements: Air, water, earth/fire, fire

The Numerological Interpretation

Nora (NV = 3, CV = 5, VV = 7, FL = 5)

This is a name that marks a strong intellect. Nora enjoys reading, communicating, and writing. She is most happy when surrounded by intelligent people with whom she may engage in lively discussions about the things that interest her. She requires an occupation that allows her the personal freedom to expand her creative talents. She is very bored by routine, and will rebel against a job that offers no intellectual stimulation. One of her life challenges has to do with consistency. Nora's mind can be overactive, creating a lot of nervous energy. Physical exercise will be a most helpful tool to help her relax.

DERIVATION: English, Irish, Scottish, and Scandinavian, pet form of Eleanor, Leonora, Honora, and other such names. Possibly related to a Greek word meaning "light." The name of the heroine of Henrik Ibsen's play *A Doll's House.*

PRINCIPAL COLORS: All shades of violet, from the palest to the richest

GEMSTONES AND PRECIOUS METALS: Garnets, amethyst

BOTANICALS: Apple, lungwort, dandelion

UNIQUE SPELLINGS: Nohra, Nohrah, Norah, Norra, Norrah

RELATED TO: Eleanor, Eleanora, Honora, Leonor, Leonora, Noreen, Norina, Norine

DERIVATION: Italian and English,
from the Latin *norma*, meaning
"standard, model." Apparently
invented by Felice Romani in the
libretto for the Bellini opera
entitled *Norma* (first performed
in 1831). Sometimes considered a
feminine form of Norman. Very
popular in the 1920s.

PRINCIPAL COLORS: Gold, any
green or yellow hues

GEMSTONES AND PRECIOUS
METALS: Moonstones, pearls

BOTANICALS: Blackberry, hops,
juniper

UNIQUE SPELLINGS: Narumah,
Naurma, Normah

RELATED TO: Normi, Normie

Norma

A KABBALISTIC SYNOPSIS
נערמא —NA'ARMA (Nun, Ayin, Resh, Mem, Aleph)

They don't come much more traditional than Norma. If Norma lives in a big city, she is not likely to be happy, as she will be constantly annoyed and frustrated by the intrusions of the modern world and modern values. No, Norma is much happier in some out-of-the-way village, preferably one where cable TV and microwave meals have so far failed to penetrate. This attitude doesn't make Norma dull; in fact, she is a very lively woman and needs to be physically fit to keep up with her preferred lifestyle, which often involves a high degree of self-sufficiency. Norma does love to chat, though, and will put down whatever she is working on if there is an opportunity for a good talk. Best of all, Norma likes great big family get-togethers. She will put as much effort into a single Thanksgiving meal as most people do to an entire year's worth of cooking.

THE RUNIC INTERPRETATION
ᚨᛗᚱᛟᚾ (Ansuz, Mannaz, Raido, Othila, Nauthiz)

Norma makes a good teacher or entrepreneur. She is original, humorous, and nurturing. She laughs at the problems in life, and we all love her for getting us to laugh, too—even at ourselves. The Mannaz rune of self gives Norma the humility to be the brunt of everyone's good jokes. Othila, the rune of separation, gives her an economy of words, and Norma enjoys reading and writing. Norma likes to stay vigorous because she gives so much to people all day long. So she learns to guard her energy. The Ansuz rune means her intuition is strong, and the Raido rune provides good communication skills, which she will use to tell funny stories about her escapades.

Elements: Air, air, water, earth/fire, fire

THE NUMEROLOGICAL INTERPRETATION
Norma (NV = 7, CV = 9, VV = 7, FL = 5)

Norma has a profound and a serious side to her personality. She is intent on resolving complex issues with her very analytical mind, and is naturally drawn to the world of science and technology. If Norma's spiritual side is developed, her interests will tend to be more metaphysical than physical. This name gives Norma a natural aptitude for psychology and for the exploration of the more hidden sides to human nature. A rather shy person, Norma prefers intimate evenings at home with a special companion to bright lights and parties.

Norman

A KABBALISTIC SYNOPSIS
נערמאן —NA'ARMAN (Nun, Ayin, Resh, Mem, Aleph, Nun)

Norman doesn't usually have a lot to say for himself. He is a quiet guy, largely because of his shyness. If he is also born under Cancer, this shyness may be quite serious in terms of its impact on his life. However, in most cases, all Norman needs is the right friends to bring him out of himself. Norman is acutely aware of emotional issues, and has a genuine understanding of a whole range of personal problems, not the least because he himself is likely to have grown up with a whole range of personal anxieties and insecurities. Norman has a great sense of humor. This often starts as a cover for his shyness, but over time he develops this humor to a fine art and may even make a career out of his comedy. As a partner, Norman is sensitive and understanding; he will make a great dad, but he also needs to try not to worry too much about those who depend on him. When he does let go, Norman can be very fun to be around.

THE RUNIC INTERPRETATION
ᚾᚨᛗᚱᛟᚾ (Nauthiz, Ansuz, Mannaz, Raido, Othila, Nauthiz)

Norman is compassionate and kind. He has considerable artistic ability, and may be torn between work as a healer, minister, counselor, or teacher and work in the fine or performing arts. Luckily for him, it's entirely possible for Norman to juggle a few careers simultaneously. However, Norman has the double Nauthiz runes to clobber him if he isn't careful. He must use limitation and constraint, combined with some time alone, to simplify his life and replenish his reserves. The Ansuz rune of intuition gives Norman a good sense of when his health or finances are winding down. Ocean voyages and traveling frequently are favorable for Norman, and he is one person who can appreciate every minute of his journeys.

Elements: Fire, air, air, water, earth/fire, fire

THE NUMEROLOGICAL INTERPRETATION
Norman (NV = 3, CV = 5, VV = 7, FL = 5)

Norman is a living reference library. This is a man of facts, figures, data, and information on a wide variety of subject matter. He is much more of a generalist than a specialist, and is well suited to a career as a computer programmer, research analyst, or travel agent. Norman is a lively conversationalist with a witty sense of humor and an appreciation for a good turn of phrase. But he is also very content to take time alone to read and study. Life is his laboratory, and Norman enjoys experimenting with the opportunities that he encounters along his way.

DERIVATION: English, from the Old English *nord*, meaning "north," and *man*, meaning "man." Common in the Middle Ages prior to the Norman invasion, but died out after the fourteenth century. Became popular once again in the nineteenth century, and saw immense popularity in the 1920s.

PRINCIPAL COLORS: All violet hues, from the palest to the deepest shades of purple

GEMSTONES AND PRECIOUS METALS: Amethyst, garnets

BOTANICALS: Dandelion, mint, endive

UNIQUE SPELLINGS: Normen, Normin, Normyn

RELATED TO: Norm, Normand, Norris

〜

"What is all wisdom save a collection of platitudes? But the man who orders his life according to their teachings cannot go far wrong."
—NORMAN DOUGLAS (AUTHOR)

〜

Olga

DERIVATION: Russian form of Helga. From a Nordic name meaning "holy." Brought to Russia in the ninth century by Scandinavian settlers. Appeared in the English-speaking world in the late nineteenth century.

PRINCIPAL COLORS: Deep shades of azure, gray, and violet, also black

GEMSTONES AND PRECIOUS METALS: Carbuncles, sapphires, amethyst

BOTANICALS: Angelica, pilewort, shepherd's purse

UNIQUE SPELLINGS: Ohlga, Ohlgah, Olgah

RELATED TO: Elga, Helga, Ola, Olenka, Olia

A KABBALISTIC SYNOPSIS
עלגא —A'ALGA (Ayin, Lamed, Gimel, Aleph)

People don't often mess with Olga. If they do, it won't take long for them to realize what a terrible mistake they have made, as Olga is a remarkably strong woman, both mentally and physically. The value of her name reduces to five, which is the number of the Hierophant in the tarot and consequently suggests a person with considerable authority. We can expect to see Olga in some position of power in society, and it is likely that she will hold public office rather than owning a successful business. Olga has a very dominant personality, and you have to be both tough and willing to work very hard in order to do well as part of her staff. However, Olga is never slow in recognizing real talent, and is always happy to reward those who deserve it. A relationship with Olga will never be dull—but if you're the type who likes to be in charge, you had better be prepared for some pretty stormy scenes!

THE RUNIC INTERPRETATION
ᚨᚷᛚᛟ (Ansuz, Gebo, Laguz, Othila)

The Gebo rune of partnership signifies lessons in relationships. For Olga, this suggests she will never be alone for long, and once she finds a mate, she will be flexible enough to accept the other person into her life. Olga values her independence, and one reason her relationships are fulfilling is that she knows she can stand alone when she has to and even like it. The Ansuz rune gives Olga good intuitive skills, and she knows when to advance and when to retreat. Othila, the rune of separation, teaches Olga to make her own life rich and full, and this ensures that her conversations with her partner are always interesting and varied. The rune of separation could also indicate a temporary parting of the ways, but one thing is sure: Olga will have a companion throughout her life.

Elements: Air, water, water, earth/fire

THE NUMEROLOGICAL INTERPRETATION
Olga (NV = 8, CV = 1, VV = 7, FL = 6)

The numbers in this name denote a woman with stature and a high degree of personal dignity. Olga has a refined personality and appreciates a sense of style in others. She is in touch with the more subtle nuances of interpersonal relations, and nothing passes her unnoticed. Olga is very attracted by money and success. She is ambitious and quite concerned with her personal level of achievement. She may find that she has to guard against envy, jealousy, and the tendency to gossip. One of her greatest life lessons has to do with learning how to distinguish between the impulses of her desirous nature and the love in her heart.

Oliver

DERIVATION: English, of uncertain origin. Possibly related to the Latin *olivarius*, meaning "olive tree." First used in the French epic entitled *Benét's Chanson de Roland*, where Oliver (French Olivier) was Roland's friend and one of Charlemagne's retainers.

PRINCIPAL COLORS: All shades of red, especially the richest

GEMSTONES AND PRECIOUS METALS: Bloodstones, red rubies

BOTANICALS: Broom, nettle, wormwood

UNIQUE SPELLINGS: Olivor, Olliver, Ollivor

RELATED TO: Noll, Olley, Ollie, Oliverio, Olivero, Olivier, Oliviero

> "I find the great thing in this world is not so much where we stand, as in what direction we are moving—we must sail sometimes with the wind and sometimes against it—but we must sail, and not drift, nor lie at anchor."
> —OLIVER WENDELL HOLMES (POET AND JURIST)

A KABBALISTIC SYNOPSIS
עליוה —A'ALYVH (Ayin, Lamed, Yod, Vau, Heh)

Oliver is a man of mental rather than physical agility. He will never be mistaken for an Olympic athlete, but this will never bother him; he will always be able to deal with any physical threat by using his sharp verbal wit. Oliver is a freethinker and sticks firmly to his belief that it's okay to march to his own drum. Working for other people does not really suit Oliver, who is likely to have his own company or work independently in an academic setting. Comfort is important to Oliver, as is shown by the fact that his name's value reduces to four, a number associated with material concerns. The full total of his name is 121, and the fact that his name's value begins and ends in one is a further sign of his independence.

THE RUNIC INTERPRETATION
RMFIᛚᛟ (Raido, Ehwaz, Fehu, Isa, Laguz, Othila)

Oliver is the type who accumulates precious possessions, and he needs to be careful not to treat his friends as objects. The Fehu rune for possessions ensures Oliver prosperity on every level, and Oliver's generosity is noteworthy. The Laguz rune of flow gives Oliver a good sense of when to make an aggressive investment and when to secure his money for slow growth. Intuitive by nature, Oliver is good with investment strategies, and positions himself in business like a moving player on a chessboard. Having the Othila rune for separation in his name means Oliver regularly makes changes in his personal life. Raido indicates journeys, Ehwaz suggests relocation, and Isa cautions that Oliver needs more time to rest. Oliver is a powerful man with all four of the elements represented in his name.

Elements: Water, air, fire, earth, water, earth/fire

THE NUMEROLOGICAL INTERPRETATION
Oliver (NV = 9, CV = 7, VV = 2, FL = 6)

Oliver is a student of human nature with a strong philosophical facet to his personality. This is a gentle soul who loves to find peace and harmony in all of his relationships. Oliver is concerned about people and has a strong humanitarian orientation. He may easily find himself drawn to one of the helping professions, and will be a naturally gifted doctor, therapist, or teacher. His relationships tend to be few but very profound. Oliver avoids superficial social gatherings, much preferring solitude.

Olivia

DERIVATION: English, first appeared in Shakespeare's *Twelfth Night* in 1599. Possibly a feminine form of Oliver. Became quite popular in the eighteenth century and has remained widely used.

PRINCIPAL COLORS: The palest shades of any color

GEMSTONES AND PRECIOUS METALS: Silver, platinum

BOTANICALS: Hazel, sweet marjoram

UNIQUE SPELLINGS: Oliviah, Olivya, Olyvia, Olyvyva

RELATED TO: Liv, Liva, Livia, Livvie, Livvy, Olia, Oliva, Olive, Olivet, Olivette, Olivine, Olva

❧

O! when mine eyes did see Olivia first,
Methought she purg'd the air of pestilence.
That instant was I turn'd into a hart,
And my desires, like fell and cruel hounds,
E'er since pursue me.
FROM *TWELFTH NIGHT* (I, i) BY WILLIAM SHAKESPEARE

A KABBALISTIC SYNOPSIS
עליויא —A'ALYVYA (Ayin, Lamed, Yod, Vau, Yod, Aleph)

The world is full of wonderful possibilities for Olivia, thanks to her persistently optimistic outlook on life and her powerful imagination. No matter how uninspiring her current situation, Olivia can always imagine herself in a few years' time as having hit the big time. Along with a strong imagination, Olivia has a real taste for fashion, and her ideal career may involve her sense of style. While fashion is a difficult area to break into, Olivia has a lucky streak, which is suggested by the repeated occurrence of seven, the number of success, in the letters and total value of her name. Emotionally Olivia is a very passionate woman and will have several intense relationships. Her only problem in this regard is a tendency to rush things into a more serious stage before her partner is really ready.

THE RUNIC INTERPRETATION
ᚨᛁᚠᛁᛚᛟ (Ansuz, Isa, Fehu, Isa, Laguz, Othila)

Olivia has her head in the clouds, which is a problem for most people when practical considerations arise, such as the phone bill. Not for Olivia, however; her needs are minimal, and at the same time, she attracts money. Olivia's financial security gives her a firm platform in life so that she can just be herself. Fehu signifies possessions, ambition satisfied, and romantic and materialistic rewards. The double Isa configuration will emphasize the introspective side of her nature. Othila for separation suggests that Olivia is creative and has a good eye for simplicity. The Ansuz rune of signals means that Olivia is sensitive to messages sent to her by people and her environment. She may be an artist with spiritual leanings. The important Laguz rune of flow inclines Olivia to moonlight and mystery and romance in all its glory. Olivia is also powerful, as she has all four elements in her name.

Elements: Air, earth, fire, earth, water, earth/fire

THE NUMEROLOGICAL INTERPRETATION
Olivia (NV = 5, CV = 7, VV = 7, FL = 6)

Self-development and the refinement of intellectual capacities are two of the major interests inherent in this name. Olivia sincerely works to better herself. This may extend into her financial condition, but money is not one of her main concerns. Olivia is much more involved with the hidden and the mysterious. She is seeking to join her intellect and her intuition. She will do this through both the physical sciences and more metaphysical investigations. Astrology could be a very helpful study for her, as it combines these two interests.

❧

Oscar

A Kabbalistic Synopsis
עסכא —A'ASKA (Ayin, Samech, Kaph, Aleph)

A fine, upstanding member of the community, always ready to take on some civic duty, Oscar is a genuinely nice guy. One kabbalistic equivalence of his name is a Hebrew phrase meaning "to stand upright." This sums up the dominant feature of Oscar's personality: He is an honest, responsible, and honorable man. Oscar is usually happy with his lot, and he has enormous dignity and self-confidence. His own contented nature makes him a great mediator for people who are going through tough times, particularly in their relationships. A seemingly contrasting equivalence of this name is "jealous," and emotionally this is Oscar's only obstacle: He is incurably jealous. This is unlikely to spoil his relationships, though, as most people are prepared to accept at least one failing in their partner.

The Runic Interpretation
ᚱᚨᚲᛋᛟ (Raido, Ansuz, Kano, Sowelu, Othila)

"Clarity of thought and economy of word" is Oscar's motto. The Othila rune for separation, combined with Kano for opening, implies a desire for simplicity and clear intent. Oscar seems happy-go-lucky on the outside, for only his closest friends are permitted to glimpse the exacting, sensitive, and self-critical side to this sweet man's nature. Ansuz, the rune of signals, suggests Oscar has the ability to develop an instant rapport with people. The Raido rune of journey blesses Oscar with opportunities to travel and with considerable literary talents. Sowelu, the rune of wholeness, indicates Oscar's capacity for success.

Elements: Water, air, water, air, earth/fire

The Numerological Interpretation
Oscar (NV = 11, CV = 4, VV = 7, FL = 6)

Oscar gets bored easily and displays a constant urge to find new dimensions to life. Yet he is not totally free to fly off and wander through the bazaars of Morroco or the mountains of the Americas. His name reveals a distinct practical preoccupation with the financial factors of daily life. If he integrates these two tendencies correctly, Oscar will be able to work hard during most of the year and still be able to enjoy those special journeys to the fascinating parts of the world that attract him. Oscar needs to cultivate balance and inner harmony, so that his nervous restlessness may be channeled into his creative self-expression.

DERIVATION: English and Irish, from Old English roots meaning "divine spear." Especially popular in the United States in the 1870s.

PRINCIPAL COLORS: The full gamut of green hues, white

GEMSTONES AND PRECIOUS METALS: Jade, moonstones, pearls

BOTANICALS: Chicory, plantain, colewort

UNIQUE SPELLINGS: Ahskar, Ahsker, Oskar, Osker

RELATED TO: Ossie, Ozzy

"The effect of one upright individual is incalculable."
—OSCAR ARIAS (NOBEL PEACE PRIZE WINNER)

Owen

DERIVATION: Welsh, of uncertain origin. Possibly from the Latin name Eugenius, meaning "well-born." Popular outside of Wales since the eighteenth century.

PRINCIPAL COLORS: Any violet shade, from pale lilac to rich purple

GEMSTONES AND PRECIOUS METALS: Amethyst, garnets

BOTANICALS: Dandelion, lungwort, mint

UNIQUE SPELLINGS: Ohwin, Ohwinne, Ohwyn, Owin, Owinne, Owyn

RELATED TO: Ewen, Owain

A KABBALISTIC SYNOPSIS
עון —A'AVN (Ayin, Vau, Nun)

Owen is going straight to the top, and he doesn't really care how he gets there. In his personal life Owen is quite a sensitive guy, but put him in a suit, stick a briefcase and a cell phone in his hands, and he is transformed into the most competitive, unscrupulous man you could wish to meet! To Owen the cut and thrust of business is something of a game. When he happily trounces a corporate opponent, he sees it on the same level as if he had just won a game of squash. This is why he is prepared to do pretty much anything to win; he never really looks at some of the more serious consequences of his actions. Once he has made his fortune— which he will—Owen will be happy to settle down. At this point there are indications that Owen will become a much more contemplative man and will start to look for deeper satisfactions than money alone.

THE RUNIC INTERPRETATION
ᚾᛖᚹᛟ (Nauthiz, Ehwaz, Wunjo, Othila)

Owen is a citizen of the world and he just loves it. Owen is fortunate to have the Wunjo rune for joy in his name. Wunjo implies that Owen will have all his needs met, and that he knows enough to be grateful and happy about this. The Nauthiz rune of constraint points to limitations and obstacles Owen has to overcome. However, most of his long and generous life is spent transitioning from one opportunity to the next. Owen may build an international empire or enjoy a satisfying career in the public eye. With Ehwaz in his name, it is possible that Owen will relocate often and could spend much of his life traveling.

Elements: Fire, air, earth, earth/fire

THE NUMEROLOGICAL INTERPRETATION
Owen (NV = 3, CV = 5, VV = 7, FL = 6)

An attractive man who offers both his smile and his friendship freely, Owen is kind and gregarious. He cultivates a wide circle of friends and associates, and tends to have the freedom to leave his current surroundings at any time. Owen likes to change his physical appearance, and does not wear the same clothes or have the same hairstyle year after year. He is not particularly attracted to settling down to a committed relationship—at least, not in his youth! Even when Owen is a more mature person, he will require a partner who supports his urge for independent travel and periods of solitude.

Pablo

A KABBALISTIC SYNOPSIS
פאבלע —PABLA'A (Peh, Aleph, Beth, Lamed, Ayin)

This man is definitely an athlete. Not only is he likely to be strong and well built, but the arrangement of letters in his name suggests that he may well be fleet of foot. However, Pablo isn't inclined to take up physical activities professionally; he'll more likely be happy playing a few games of baseball with his friends or joining the local running club. All this leisure activity will have to work in around his many other commitments, though, as Pablo is a man with many causes. His willingness to take a stand on issues he cares about is shown both by the initial Peh, or P, in his name, and particularly by his name's association with kabalistic symbols representing self-sacrifice and altruism. Pablo may have his own strong views, but he will never try to force them on anyone else. He is also excellent with kids and enjoys their company immensely. If Pablo doesn't have any children himself, he will be very happy as a favorite uncle.

THE RUNIC INTERPRETATION
◇ᚱᛒᚾᚷ (Othila, Laguz, Berkana, Ansuz, Perth)

Pablo explores many aspects of his rich personality by changing careers often and making friends with people of various walks of life. Each experience demands that he draw on his hidden resources and put them to work. The Perth rune signifies initiation, and when combined with Othila, the rune of separation, it suggests radical change in Pablo's life. Because this fortunate configuration is accompanied by the Berkana rune of growth, it means Pablo makes changes for the better that enrich his life. The Laguz rune of flow indicates flexibility and artistic talents. Laguz combined with Perth and Ansuz is a very powerful combination, signifying Pablo's faith and vision.

Elements: Earth/fire, water, air/earth, air, water

THE NUMEROLOGICAL INTERPRETATION
Pablo (NV = 1, CV = 3, VV = 7, FL = 7)

An original in many senses of the word, Pablo likes to carve his own path through life. This name bestows artistic creativity, a strong will, and an active mind. Pablo has a pioneering spirit and is eager to prove himself against the backdrop of new life experiences. However, he is not the most cooperative person. He much prefers to contribute his special talents to a group endeavor in his own way than to conform to peer pressure. In romance, Pablo tends to be very sensuous but not always completely faithful. So enjoy Pablo while you can; he will not promise you tomorrow, but you will surely have a great time with him today!

DERIVATION: Spanish form of Paul, from the Latin *paulus*, meaning "small."

PRINCIPAL COLORS: Pale to bright yellow and russet tones, orange

GEMSTONES AND PRECIOUS METALS: Citrine, topaz

BOTANICALS: Lavender, eyebright

UNIQUE SPELLINGS: Pabloh, Pablow, Pahblo, Pahbloh, Pahblow

RELATED TO: Paavo, Paolo, Pault, Paulie, Paulus, Pauly, Pavel

∽

"I am always doing that which I can not do, in order that I may learn how to do it."
—PABLO PICASSO (ARTIST)

∽

Pamela

DERIVATION: English, created in the sixteenth century by the poet Sir Philip Sidney. It is unknown what influenced Sidney in the invention of this name, although it may be from Greek roots meaning "all honey." Especially popular in all English-speaking countries in the 1950s and 1960s.

PRINCIPAL COLORS: All shades of purple, from the palest to the brightest and richest

GEMSTONES AND PRECIOUS METALS: Amethyst, garnets

BOTANICALS: Bilberry, barberry, mint

UNIQUE SPELLINGS: Pamala, Pamalla, Pamella, Pamilla, Pammela

RELATED TO: Pam, Pamelia, Pammie, Pammy

A KABBALISTIC SYNOPSIS
פאמלא —PAMLA (Peh, Aleph, Mem, Lamed, Aleph)

In her relationships as in her working life, Pamela likes to call the shots, and there are very few people who are willing to argue with her on that score. Her name adds up to 152, which gives Pamela a complex personality. Because this number reduces to eight, it indicates Pamela has a forceful personality and strength of character. Other elements in Pamela's name tell us that her forceful side is apt to allow her to get into situations that she would rather not be in, and often she acts rashly only to later feel regret and embarrassment over her behavior. Balancing out Pamela's strong will is her deeply emotional nature, as indicated by the fifty and the two in her name. Despite her strength of will, Pamela longs for a meaningful relationship, and will probably find the right person who has the strength of character to make a suitable partner. While the number two relates to positive feelings of affection and nurturing instincts, the number fifty can indicate negative emotions. In Pamela's case, this tends to be an excessive concern with other people's opinions of her.

THE RUNIC INTERPRETATION
ᚨᛚᛖᛗᚨᛈ (Ansuz, Laguz, Ehwaz, Mannaz, Ansuz, Perth)

Pamela has a very mutable personality because of the double Ansuz rune for signals. She can change her mood or approach in a twinkling of an eye. This gift is hers because the intuitive Ansuz rune combines with Laguz for flow and Perth for initiation in her name. The Perth rune signifies a radical severance with her past. Mannaz, the rune of the self, signifies that Pamela undergoes many changes with this particular runic combination. The Ehwaz rune of movement speeds up this transmutation. Pamela is a free spirit, and fortunately the Ehwaz rune affords her ample chances to travel.

Elements: Air, water, air, air, air, water

THE NUMEROLOGICAL INTERPRETATION
Pamela (NV = 3, CV = 5, VV = 7, FL = 7)

How can you restrain a person with boundless curiosity and enthusiasm for life? Pamela is just such a person. Pamela's name gives her the urge to be herself at all times, to follow her whims and wishes, and to share her vivid and dramatic personality with all her many friends. She is a fluent conversationalist and may have a gift for foreign languages. Pamela knows that she was put on this earth to learn, and she does so through continuously educating herself. Friendships are very important to her, and she tends to find it easy to bond with others regardless of their social background.

Pat

A Kabbalistic Synopsis
פאט —PAT (Peh, Aleph, Teth)

Whether Pat is male or female, one thing is certain: Pat will certainly be intelligent. It may even be the case that Pat works professionally as an academic or in some similar career area. The total value of Pat's name is ninety, which is the same value as the letter Qoph, which means "back of head," and indicates a concern with things of a cerebral nature. Mind you, Pat is not a quiet introvert—far from it. Pat loves to chat with a wide social circle and may even occasionally be prone to be something of a gossip, although rarely a malicious one. The fact that Pat's name ends with the letter Teth, meaning "serpent," lets us know that this individual can strike out at any threat when necessary. However, given Pat's generally thoughtful nature, it is not likely that Pat is a particularly vindictive person. In Pat's case, emotional relationships are always likely to take second place to career. This is not so much because Pat is excessively ambitious but is more related to Pat's overwhelming interest in and commitment to his or her particular field of work. Of course, if Pat finds someone with the same interests, they may spend many happy evenings working together in the lab on their latest development, which to Pat would be bliss!

The Runic Interpretation
↑ᚾᛈ (Teiwaz, Ansuz, Perth)

At the end of each day, Pats recount events and wonder how they could have been more patient and kind. These unrelenting standards can cause a lot of nervous problems later in life, and Pats need to be as patient with themselves as they are with everyone else. For some reason, Pat is quite lucky. Male or female, Pat amazes friends at games of chance and possesses a sense of intuition that allows occasional flamboyance and jubilation. Perhaps Pat needs more opportunities to walk on the wild side.

Elements: Air, air, water

The Numerological Interpretation
Pat (NV = 1, CV = 9, VV = 1, FL = 7)

The numbers of this name definitely reveal men and women who are highly individualistic. People named Pat are definitely ready to fight their own battles and make their own way through life. They also have an inner conviction about the way they want to live, and refuse to compromise themselves because other people may disagree with them. Men and women named Pat are generally very enthusiastic, and like nothing better than to encourage others to get on with their own agendas and make the best of themselves, too. At times, Pats can appear self-centered and so attached to their personal convictions that they are closed to any outside influence. Pats can also give the impression of being too domineering or aggressive, even though it is only their own lives over which they demand control.

DERIVATION: English, short for the Latin name Patricius and its female equivalent, Patricia, both of which mean "noble."

PRINCIPAL COLORS: The darkest to the lightest shades of bronze and yellow

GEMSTONES AND PRECIOUS METALS: Yellowish stones such as topaz and amber

BOTANICALS: Lavender, chamomile, borage, sorrel

UNIQUE SPELLING: Patt

RELATED TO: Paddie, Paddy, Patric, Patricio, Patrick†, Patrik, Pats, Patton; Patrice, Patricia†, Patti, Pattie, Patty†, Tricia, Trish

Patricia

DERIVATION: English, feminine form of Patrick, from the Latin name Patricius, meaning "noble." The name of a seventh-century nun who became the patron saint of Naples. Very popular in the United States in the middle of the twentieth century.

PRINCIPAL COLORS: The full spectrum of very pale hues

GEMSTONES AND PRECIOUS METALS: Silver, platinum, diamonds

BOTANICALS: Hazel, parsley, oats

UNIQUE SPELLINGS: Patrisha, Petricia, Petrisha, Pitricia, Pitrisha

RELATED TO: Patt, Patreece, Patrizia, Patsy, Pattie, Patty†, Tricia, Trish, Trisha

A KABBALISTIC SYNOPSIS

פאטרישא — PATRYShA (Peh, Aleph, Teth, Resh, Yod, Shin, Aleph)

Patricia has always been about sixty years old—even as a child she happily played the matriarch. Everyone loves Patricia because she is such a character; she has a tendency to treat everybody as if they were her child or, as she gets older, her grandchild. Patricia will quite happily tell a boss that they need to get a new suit, change their diet, or even find a new partner. Interestingly, there is something about the way Patricia says these things that makes us all listen to her advice without a murmur of protest. Patricia has enormous reserves of energy and is likely to be engaged in a wide range of work—as a professional, a volunteer, and a homemaker. Money will not be an overwhelming concern for Patricia. Not only is she a very hard worker, but she also has a deeply practical nature and a great head for figures, matched by her sharp eye for a bargain.

THE RUNIC INTERPRETATION

ᚪᛁᛋᛁᚱᛏᚪᛈ (Ansuz, Isa, Sowelu, Isa, Raido, Teiwaz, Ansuz, Perth)

Long walks by herself keep Patricia happy. The double Ansuz rune of intuition combines beautifully with the double Isa rune of standstill in this name. Patricia changes a lot as she matures, and the Perth rune of initiation suggests that at some point Patricia breaks free of the past, and this is a great relief to her. The Teiwaz warrior energy gives Patricia clarity and courage. The Raido energy of journey emphasizes clear communication and travel opportunities. It can also refer to the inner journey of prayer, self-healing, and the union of worldly and heavenly forces. Patricia may become slightly more sociable as she matures, but she will always need to balance the time she spends with others with her own solitary pursuits. The Sowelu rune of wholeness will ultimately help Patricia realize that what she is striving to become is what she already is.

Elements: Air, earth, air, earth, water, air, air, water

THE NUMEROLOGICAL INTERPRETATION

Patricia (NV = 5, CV = 3, VV = 2, FL = 7)

If you have a product or idea you would like to market, you might want to give this project to Patricia. She is an excellent mixer, and can be very persuasive when it comes to convincing other people of her beliefs and opinions. She genuinely likes people and has an inner wish to be of service. Patricia has a plethora of small skills; she is a virtual toolbox, in fact, and is a natural-born mender. Whether it is repairing a broken faucet or a broken heart, if Patricia doesn't know how to fix it herself, she certainly has a friend with the required aptitude.

Patrick

A KABBALISTIC SYNOPSIS

פאטריכ —PATRYK (Peh, Aleph, Teth, Resh, Yod, Kaph)

You won't find Patrick being enticed by the bright lights of the big city. No way—Patrick is a country boy through and through. The compression of his name produces the letters Shin and Kaph, which between them indicate a man with a real drive and lust for life and a good deal of practical ability. In fact, Patrick is most suited to a career as a craftsman; he would be excellent at making and restoring fine furniture or renovating old cars. The important element to any job Patrick chooses is that it not be situated in an office, and that it allow him to use his manual skills to their best effect. Money isn't particularly important to Patrick but tradition usually is, and he may well spend all his life in his hometown. This wouldn't suit many people, but Patrick finds all the variety he wants in his familiar environment and doesn't much feel the need to seek out new sights and sounds elsewhere. If all this seems a little dull, you should attend one of Patrick's holiday parties sometime!

THE RUNIC INTERPRETATION

ᚲᚲᛁᚱᛏᚨᚲ (Kano, Kano, Isa, Raido, Teiwaz, Ansuz, Perth)

Firmly closing the door on the past makes the window of new opportunities pop right open. The Perth rune of initiation causes a radical severance of some kind with the past. Ansuz, the rune of intuition, helps Patrick keep his balance during this transformation. Isa, the rune of standstill, cautions him not to fight the changes he is enduring. The Teiwaz energy of the warrior gives Patrick the stamina and the vision he needs to set new goals and forge ahead. Once Patrick has charted a new path for himself, the world will warmly support this change in him. Kano, the rune of opening, offers Patrick clarity and focus. The Raido rune helps Patrick explore new lifestyles and discuss his adventures in a persuasive and informative manner that helps others on their own journeys.

Elements: Water, water, earth, water, air, air, water

THE NUMEROLOGICAL INTERPRETATION

Patrick (NV = 5, CV = 4, VV = 1, FL = 7)

The numerological significance of this name includes qualities of leadership and drive. At times Patrick can be too stubborn for his own good, but he is determined and will not compromise himself. He is a proud man who does not easily accept help from others. Intensely sensuous, Patrick has no trouble attracting partners into his life. He is challenged, however, by commitments that require him to be deeply emotional and responsive. Thus Patrick may eventually alienate the person with whom he wishes to be the closest. Once he learns to trust the open heart, this problem will fade away.

DERIVATION: English and Irish, from the Latin name Patricius, meaning "noble." The name of the patron saint of Ireland, who did missionary work in Ireland in the fifth century. The name spread beyond Ireland in the eighteenth century.

PRINCIPAL COLORS: All but the brightest shades of azure

GEMSTONES AND PRECIOUS METALS: Turquoise, emeralds

BOTANICALS: Dog rose, vervain, daffodils

UNIQUE SPELLINGS: Patric, Patrik, Patryck, Patryk

RELATED TO: Paddy, Padraig, Padriac, Patt, Patrizio, Patrizius, Patton

"Is life so dear, or peace so sweet, as to be purchased at the price of chains or slavery? Forbid it, Almighty God! I know not what course others may take but as for me; give me liberty or give me death!"
—PATRICK HENRY (PATRIOT)

589

DERIVATION: English and Irish, pet
form of Patrick, from the Latin
name Patricius, meaning "noble."

PRINCIPAL COLORS: The full
gamut of yellow and bronze hues,
also orange

GEMSTONES AND PRECIOUS
METALS: Topaz, yellow diamonds

BOTANICALS: Lavender, Saint-
John's-wort

UNIQUE SPELLINGS: Patti, Pattie

RELATED TO: Patt, Patreece,
Patriciat

Patty

A KABBALISTIC SYNOPSIS
פאטטי —PATTY (Peh, Aleph, Teth, Teth, Yod)

The central element of Patty's name is the double appearance of the letter T, or Teth, meaning "serpent." Now, while this can refer to a certain element of spite in her character, it can also be taken as a sign of her physical grace and sensuality. It should also be said that any capacity for unpleasantness is usually only a reaction on Patty's part to someone else's bad behavior. While she can be "too hot to handle" at times, her quick-witted nature and natural attractiveness mean that she is never short of prospective partners. The initial Peh in her name suggests that she may use her ability to cut to the quick in an entertaining way; Patty may even be a satirist of some sort. The value of her name reduces to ten, which is the number of the Wheel of Fortune card in the tarot. This ensures Patty a generally happy and lucky life, although Patty's own talents are sufficient to guarantee that.

THE RUNIC INTERPRETATION
ᛇᛏᛏᚨᛈ (Eihwaz, Teiwaz, Teiwaz, Ansuz, Perth)

Masculine energy is associated with the Teiwaz rune, and the double Teiwaz rune in Patty's name is an unusual configuration that affords rare courage, strength, and conquest. Patty could use these talents in dangerous jobs like espionage, police work, or a career in the military. Patty has nerves of steel and a nose for danger, with the Ansuz rune of intuition appearing in her name. The Perth rune indicates that part of Patty's strength comes from conquering herself. She is focused and dedicated to an idea or a cause, and she will give it her all. The Eihwaz rune of defense tells us that part of Patty's power comes from knowing where the enemy lurks.

Elements: Earth/fire, air, air, air, water

THE NUMEROLOGICAL INTERPRETATION
Patty (NV = 1, CV = 11, VV = 8, FL = 7)

A fascinating woman with a ready smile, Patty is a friend to everyone who needs her. Yet her name reveals that she is not manipulated by other people's emotional requirements. She is basically a very independent and unique person with a deep understanding of human nature. No matter what demands are made on her, Patty has a distinct sense of her own path. She has had to go through a number of challenging experiences in order to strengthen her own identity, and she has learned her lessons well.

Paul

A Kabbalistic Synopsis
פעול —PA'AVL (Peh, Ayin, Vau, Lamed)

Paul's name reduces to fifteen, a number that is associated with the Devil card in the tarot. However, this doesn't indicate anything remotely sinister about Paul; it merely suggests that Paul has a love of luxury and a higher-than-average level of interest in the so-called baser appetites! However, Paul is a complicated man because alongside this propensity for self-indulgence is a great concern with morality—both his own, and morality in general. In some cases (especially in any Paul born under Pisces), this may lead to a number of guilt feelings with which he will need to cope. However, for the most part, Paul is able to see that his lifestyle is not necessarily immoral—unless he chooses to see it that way.

The Runic Interpretation
ᛚᚢᚨᛈ (Laguz, Uruz, Ansuz, Perth)

Counseling comes easily to Paul because he is genuinely sympathetic to the needs of others and has a sincere desire to heal. The Perth rune of initiation means that Paul perseveres on his journey to put his life in balance. This task is hard work, but Uruz, the rune of strength, is at hand, giving Paul the fortitude he needs to endure the healing process—and giving him physical strength as well. Laguz, the rune of flexibility, helps Paul during the transition. Ansuz, the rune of intuition, grows ever stronger, as Paul is able to see himself clearly and those around him benefit from his insights. Paul is stable and kind, and patient with those who are still searching for peace.

Elements: Water, earth, air, water

The Numerological Interpretation
Paul (NV = 5, CV = 1, VV = 4, FL = 7)

Organization is the key to Paul's success. This is a man who has a knack for being able to prioritize, structure, and consolidate his plans and projects. Paul's name gives him the urge to be tidy without being excessively compulsive. He is a man who needs an orderly space for his abundant creativity, and he makes sure that he has it. Paul seeks to cultivate inner space as well, so he avoids cluttering his mind and feelings with the unessential. The potential in his name gives him a very special gift: practical discrimination.

DERIVATION: English, French, and German form of the Latin family name Paulus, meaning "small." The name of the saint who cofounded the Christian Church and was beheaded in Rome in the first century. Became quite popular in English-speaking countries in the 1920s.

PRINCIPAL COLORS: Pale shades of any color

GEMSTONES AND PRECIOUS METALS: Diamonds, platinum, any pale stones

BOTANICALS: Hazel, parsley, parsnips

UNIQUE SPELLINGS: Pall, Pawel, Pawl

RELATED TO: Paavo, Pablot, Palie, Paolo, Paulus, Pauly, Pavel

DERIVATION: English and German, feminine form of Paul, which is from the Latin family name Paulus, meaning "small." Extremely popular in the United States in the 1950s and 1960s.

PRINCIPAL COLORS: Pale to medium shades of blue

GEMSTONES AND PRECIOUS METALS: Blue and blue-green turquoise, emeralds

BOTANICALS: Dog rose, walnuts, almonds

UNIQUE SPELLINGS: Palla, Paulah, Pawela, Pawelah, Pawla, Pawlah

RELATED TO: Paola, Pauletta, Paulette, Paulina, Paulinet, Pollie, Polly

❧

"My mother told me stories all the time. . . . And in all of those stories she told me who I was, who I was supposed to be, whom I came from, and who would follow me. In this way, she taught me the meaning of the words she said, that all life is a circle and everything has a place within it."

—PAULA GUNN ALLEN
(NATIVE AMERICAN AUTHOR)

Paula

A KABBALISTIC SYNOPSIS
פּערלא —PA'ARI A (Peh, Ayin, Resh, Lamed, Aleph)

Paula is the ideal person to have around in a crisis, since she is permanently confident that everything will turn out fine—and chances are that if she is around, everything will indeed turn out fine! Her name has a value that equates to the Star card in the tarot, and the Star card is a sign of protection and guidance. Paula is a cheerful woman who loves to enjoy a joke, even to the point where she can sometimes fail to see the need to be serious about certain things. The final A, or Aleph, in her name connects her to the element of air, which is associated with thought—although in Paula's case, her thoughts are as often daydreams as they are plans of action.

THE RUNIC INTERPRETATION
ᚨᛚᚢᚨᛈ (Ansuz, Laguz, Uruz, Ansuz, Perth)

The many healing attributes of the name Paul apply to the name Paula as well. Paula benefits from the additional Ansuz rune in her name, which further strengthens her intuitive nature. The Ansuz rune is linked with the air element and inclines Paula to be verbal and articulate. This rune also reveals that there are no coincidences. Paula often reviews the events of the day and considers what conversations and chance encounters might signify on a deeper level in her life. Paula is attuned to subtleties and looks for meaning in the coincidences she sees in nature. She is a deeply caring person, and her nurturing ways are soothing and kind.

Elements: Air, water, earth, air, water

THE NUMEROLOGICAL INTERPRETATION
Paula (NV = 6, CV = 1, VV = 5, FL = 7)

Paula has the need to establish a cohesive center from which she may radiate her various creative expressions. She will find that working at home can be an appealing scenario. Paula is a woman who can easily balance her family life with her professional interests. She has a distinct love of music and the arts, and is also a natural-born arranger. Paula likes to be in control of her life, and she tends to dominate her marriage or partnership. But she also knows how to give of herself, and is basically an unselfish and open person.

❧

Pauline

A Kabbalistic Synopsis
פעולין —PAVLYN (Peh, Aleph, Vau, Lamed, Yod, Nun)

Don't try to get a word in when you're around Pauline; it's absolutely hopeless. Not only does Pauline's name begin with the letter Peh, meaning "mouth," but her name's value begins with eight hundred, which is the value of Peh multiplied by ten—hence the nonstop conversation. On the whole, nobody minds Pauline's talkative ways, but if Pauline is a Virgo, there is a danger that the talking could turn into complaining. The final six in the total value of her name suggests that she has an intuitive nature, which makes her a good and understanding friend to have around when you're feeling low; Pauline will know just how to cheer you up. If she wishes, Pauline has the drive and the ability to do well for herself financially, although she is often more interested in friendship and socializing than in making money.

The Runic Interpretation
ᛗᚺᛁᛏᛚᚾᚨᚲ (Ehwaz, Nauthiz, Isa, Laguz, Uruz, Ansuz, Perth)

Pauline could go through a difficult transition and face loneliness and isolation. However, the adjustment she must undergo will make her more self-reliant and sophisticated. The Laguz rune in this name helps Pauline become more easygoing and flexible. Uruz, the rune of strength, gives Pauline the fortitude she needs to succeed. The Perth rune for initiation promises change on a deep level. Pauline might find herself assimilated into a foreign culture, and the challenge could prove invigorating for this adventurous soul. Pauline is powerful, with all four of the elements in her name.

Elements: Air, fire, earth, water, earth, air, water

The Numerological Interpretation
Pauline (NV = 6, CV = 6, VV = 9, FL = 7)

When you think of violin music and lovely bouquets of flowers, think of Pauline: Her heart is the foundation of her entire nature. This is a woman who takes other people's problems to herself—sometimes too much so. Pauline is very protective and nurturing, but she has to respect her own emotional boundaries. She does well as a teacher, therapist, doctor, or other form of caregiver.

DERIVATION: French form of Paulina, ultimately from the Latin family name Paulus, meaning "small." Brought to the English-speaking world in the nineteenth century. Especially popular in the United States at the end of the nineteenth century.

PRINCIPAL COLORS: All but the most brilliant of azure hues

GEMSTONES AND PRECIOUS METALS: Turquoise, emeralds

BOTANICALS: Violets, almonds, daffodils

UNIQUE SPELLINGS: Pauleen, Paulene, Paulyne, Pawleen, Pawlene, Pawline, Pawlyne

RELATED TO: Paola, Paulat, Paule, Pauletta, Paulette, Paulie, Paulina, Polly

DERIVATION: English, from the
common word for the jewel.
Coined in the nineteenth century,
along with other gemstone names,
such as Opal and Amber. May be
considered an English form of
Margaret, which means "pearl" in
Greek.

PRINCIPAL COLORS: The full
spectrum of very pale hues

GEMSTONES AND PRECIOUS
METALS: Diamonds, silver, any
shiny stone

BOTANICALS: Sweet marjoram,
parsley

UNIQUE SPELLINGS: Pearle, Perl,
Perle, Purl, Purle

RELATED TO: Margaret†, Pearie,
Pearla, Pearleen, Pearlena,
Pearlette, Pearley, Pearlie,
Pearline, Pearly, Perla, Perline,
Perlita, Perly, Purly

Pearl

A KABBALISTIC SYNOPSIS
פארל —PARL (Peh, Aleph, Resh, Lamed)

The value of Pearl's name is 311, which reduces to five and indicates that she has an air of authority about her that is immediately recognizable. The number five is also associated with religious duty, and thanks to other elements in her name, it is likely that Pearl is a very spiritually oriented woman. However, as the value of her name ends with eleven, the number of mystery and magic, it is unlikely that her religious feelings are restricted to a weekly visit to church. She is more likely to want to share her intensely spiritual inclinations with the world. On rare occasions (usually in the case of Pearls who are born under Leo), this can manifest itself as pious sermonizing, but in most cases it is just a sharing of her happiness in her beliefs. One kabbalistic equivalence of Pearl's name is "west," which indicates a love of water.

THE RUNIC INTERPRETATION
ᛚᚱᚨᛖᛉ (Laguz, Raido, Ansuz, Ehwaz, Perth)

Deep tones and haunting rhythms inspire Pearl, who has a wonderful feel for music. Laguz, the rune of flow, enhances her musical acumen and provides emotional flexibility, too. Laguz combined with Ansuz, the rune for signals, gives Pearl considerable insight and sensitivity. But Pearl could be a bit compulsive, because Perth, the rune of initiation, may prompt her to extremes. Perth clears suppressed energies, and this process can feel like an emotional teeter-totter until balance occurs. Ehwaz, for movement, and Raido, for journey, signify motion. When Pearl dances, she can draw a crowd.

Elements: Water, water, air, air, water

THE NUMEROLOGICAL INTERPRETATION
Pearl (NV = 7, CV = 1, VV = 6, FL = 7)

Pearl has an inner dignity that radiates out into her environment. She is a woman with a strong inner life, one to which few people are privy. Pearl can give the impression that she is an independent loner, but this is only partially true. At heart, Pearl is a very tender and romantic woman, one who is aware of her specialness and vulnerability. Anyone seeking to be intimate with Pearl must exhibit patience and persistence to win her trust. It is certainly worth the effort to do so.

Pedro

DERIVATION: Spanish form of Peter, ultimately from the Greek *petros*, meaning "stone."

PRINCIPAL COLORS: Any moderately shaded color

GEMSTONES AND PRECIOUS METALS: Sapphires

BOTANICALS: Celandine, sage, medlar

UNIQUE SPELLINGS: Paydro, Paydroh, Pedroh

RELATED TO: Pearce, Peder, Petert, Piero, Pierre, Pieter, Pietro, Piotr

A KABBALISTIC SYNOPSIS
פאדרע —PADRA'A (Peh, Aleph, Daleth, Resh, Ayin)

Pedro is always on the lookout for a new opportunity to make some money. He has the ability to get a good job with a large corporation, but as he hates to feel tied down, he prefers to be self-employed. Consequently, Pedro has to take a very opportunistic approach to life. The reduction of the value of his name gives us thirteen, which is the number of the Death card in the tarot. This doesn't mean that Pedro can look forward to an early exit from life, but simply that he has a love of change, and unlike most people, he is not really looking to settle down into a particular lifestyle. Pedro loves to party, so it's just as well he never stays anywhere too long; instead of cleaning up in the morning, he just moves on!

THE RUNIC INTERPRETATION
ᛟᚱᛞᛖᛈ (Othila, Raido, Dagaz, Ehwaz, Perth)

The Perth rune brings about a psychological or spiritual transformation that requires one to relinquish attachments and start again, if need be. This process brings Pedro prosperity and growth. The Dagaz rune of breakthrough indicates that Pedro will emerge from his enormous transition feeling empowered and integrated. The Raido rune of journey encompasses not only travel but also good, clear communication. Pedro may well go on to teach others the benefits of starting over and the dangers inherent in an unexamined life. The Ehwaz rune is there for playtime; Pedro enjoys life.

Elements: Earth/fire, water, fire, air, water

THE NUMEROLOGICAL INTERPRETATION
Pedro (NV = 3, CV = 1, VV = 11, FL = 7)

This name reveals a very strong will and an uncompromising urge to be oneself, no matter what it costs in time and energy. The question is, in which direction is Pedro moving? If he is a man who is developing his higher nature, Pedro will use his will and drive, his uniqueness and special gifts, for the benefit of the community in which he lives. If he is a man who is attached to his lower nature, Pedro will apply his strong ego to get what he wants out of his personal relationships, regardless of the results. The choice is his.

Peggy

DERIVATION: English, pet form of Margaret, which is from the Greek *margaron*, meaning "pearl." Used independently since the eighteenth century, and quite popular at the beginning of the twentieth century.

PRINCIPAL COLORS: Light to medium shades of azure

GEMSTONES AND PRECIOUS METALS: Turquoise, emeralds

BOTANICALS: Dog rose, apricots

UNIQUE SPELLINGS: Peggey, Peggi, Peggie, Pehggey, Pehggie, Pehggy

RELATED TO: Maggie†, Margaret†, Meg, Megan†, Meggi, Meggie, Meggy, Meghan, Peg, Pegeen

"Some of us just go along . . . until that marvelous day people stop intimidating us—or should I say we refuse to let them intimidate us?"
—PEGGY LEE (MUSICIAN)

A KABBALISTIC SYNOPSIS
פאגגי —PAGGY (Peh, Aleph, Gimel, Gimel, Yod)

Peggy is a doer rather than a talker. Although her name begins with the Hebrew letter meaning "mouth," it is immediately followed by a letter associated both with thoughts and with practical action. Peggy has a very creative personality and may be either a writer or a painter, although she will not necessarily pursue this as a full-time career. Peggy has a strong element of common sense in her personality, and will always make sure that she can pay the rent before she takes off with her easel and brushes! The letter Gimel, featured twice in her name, is the letter G in English and means "camel." It represents a love of travel, and by appearing twice it suggests that if Peggy doesn't live on the road, she certainly spends a good deal of time on it—literally or figuratively. Despite her wandering ways, it is likely that Peggy will have a steady and long-lasting marriage with someone equally unfettered.

THE RUNIC INTERPRETATION
↑XX M↑ (Eihwaz, Gebo, Gebo, Ehwaz, Perth)

With the four elemental powers in her name, Peggy can succeed on all levels. With a double Gebo rune combination in her name, Peggy has partnership on her mind, but she needs a partner who affords her freedom and understanding. The Ehwaz rune of movement makes her a lover of travel and music. Eihwaz, the rune of defense, combined with Perth, the rune of initiation, mean Peggy will not tolerate anyone who is dictatorial, narrow-minded, or bigoted. Peggy is creative and can do well as a writer or performing artist. She is attractive to others and naturally charming.

Elements: Earth/fire, water, water, air, water

THE NUMEROLOGICAL INTERPRETATION
Peggy (NV = 6, CV = 3, VV = 3, FL = 7)

This is a woman that people naturally like. Peggy has a warm, open, kindly disposition. She is eager to hear what other people have to say and really knows how to listen. A multifaceted woman, Peggy has many hobbies and interests. She is endowed with a natural aptitude for communications and does well in the study of language arts, including poetry, writing, drama, and even the mastery of foreign or cyber tongues. Peggy is romantic but not at all flighty. Her ideal is to be the center of a warm and healthy family unit, and she is very willing to give whatever is needed to create this vision.

Penelope

A Kabbalistic Synopsis
פאנאלעפי —PANALA'APY (Peh, Aleph, Nun, Aleph, Lamed, Ayin, Peh, Yod)

One kabbalistic equivalence of Penelope is the Hebrew word "BKSh," meaning "lamb." Penelope certainly suits this association: she will still be young in spirit even when she can get around only with a walking stick! Penelope can always be relied upon to liven up the day with her quirky sense of humor and bright demeanor. She is a joy to have in any work environment. Penelope can sometimes run into difficulties in relationships. When her partner is thinking about getting serious, she is likely to still just want to have fun. When Penelope does decide to settle down, however, she will derive peace and happiness from it. Her house will be a gathering place, and the site of wonderful parties any time there's a good excuse for a celebration. Penelope can be naive at times, but it is unusual for anyone to be able to take advantage of this since she is surrounded by so many good friends.

The Runic Interpretation
ᛗᛖᛟᛚᛗᛁᛗᛖ (Ehwaz, Perth, Othila, Laguz, Ehwaz, Nauthiz, Ehwaz, Perth)

This name features the double Ehwaz rune of transition combined with the double Perth rune of transformation. Penelope may have to go to great lengths to break with the past and find herself. Othila, the rune of separation, further emphasizes Penelope's transition and break with her earlier ties. The Nauthiz rune of constraint helps Penelope overcome limitations, and the Laguz rune of flow keeps her flexible and resilient in the face of any obstacle. Don't worry about Penelope, though, for in the end she carves out a wonderful life for herself because of her optimism and luck. Becoming a counselor or social worker, psychologist or healer, would befit Penelope's talents. Penelope is also exceptionally powerful because her name features all four elements.

Elements: Air, water, earth/fire, water, air, fire, air, water

The Numerological Interpretation
Penelope (NV = 7, CV = 22, VV = 3, FL = 7)

This name has the very rare combination of seven and twenty-two as three of its prime indicators. As such, Penelope is not a superficial woman; she is a deep thinker, an introspective person with a fundamental desire to accomplish something of merit for herself and others. Whatever her age, she knows more than her years and is possessed of a penetrating understanding of the "human condition." When we include the vowel value of three, we see that Penelope is gifted with diplomacy and the ability to be quite successful in the resolution of interpersonal conflicts.

DERIVATION: English, from the Greek root *pene*, meaning "bobbin," part of the equipment for weaving. In Homer's *Odyssey*, Penelope was the steadfastly loyal wife of the Greek soldier Odysseus, who was forced to wander for twenty years before returning to her. Especially common in the mid-twentieth century.

PRINCIPAL COLORS: All the various yellow and green hues, also gold

GEMSTONES AND PRECIOUS METALS: Moonstones, moss agate, any cream-colored stone

BOTANICALS: Blackberry, linseed, elder

UNIQUE SPELLINGS: Penelopea, Penelopee, Penelopi, Penelopie, Penelopy, Penelopye, Penilope, Pennelope, Pennelopi, Pennelopie

RELATED TO: Penelopa, Penina, Penna, Penni, Pennie, Penny†

Penny

DERIVATION: English, diminutive form of Penelope, from the Greek, meaning "bobbin." Also connected to the Greek *penelops*, meaning "duck." Used as an independent name since the 1930s, and quite popular in the mid–1940s.

PRINCIPAL COLORS: Pale to deep shades of green, white

GEMSTONES AND PRECIOUS METALS: Jade, pearls

BOTANICALS: Cabbage, plantain, moonwort

UNIQUE SPELLINGS: Pehnee, Pehnnee, Pehnney, Pehnni, Pehnnie, Pehnny, Penee, Pennee, Penney, Penni, Pennie

RELATED TO: Pen, Penelopa, Penelopet, Penina, Penna

A KABBALISTIC SYNOPSIS
פאננ‍י —PANNY (Peh, Aleph, Nun, Nun, Yod)

Penny is a worrier. She will worry about everything, from whether she will get to work on time to matters of international diplomacy. The main cause of Penny's problem is that she is a deeply intelligent woman but she thinks too much about irrelevant things. If she can find herself a thoroughly engrossing and mentally challenging career or leisure activity, she will find that she spends much more time enjoying life and a lot less time worrying about it. On the positive side, Penny is a genuinely friendly woman and will gather a good circle of pals about her who will be able to lessen her insecurities. Penny is a very affectionate woman by nature, and any partner will be lucky to have her as a soul mate—but they will need to make sure that they give her the right level of emotional support.

THE RUNIC INTERPRETATION
ᛇᚾᚾᛖᛈ (Eihwaz, Nauthiz, Nauthiz, Ehwaz, Perth)

Penny knows that beauty is power, so she keeps herself looking glamorous. Being born anew is the message of Perth. The double Nauthiz runes point to constraint, and the Ehwaz rune of movement signifies freedom to move and relocate. This helps neutralize some of the double Nauthiz energy that is limiting Penny. Penny can be tough when she needs to be, and she is willing to walk away rather than compromise for a cause she holds dear. Penny will be a good teacher or philanthropist, but she'd much prefer arguing in a courtroom. Penny is powerful with the four elements in her name.

Elements: Earth/fire, fire, fire, air, water

THE NUMEROLOGICAL INTERPRETATION
Penny (NV = 11, CV = 8, VV = 3, FL = 7)

There is no mountain so high that Penny will not attempt to climb it. Penny has a powerful combination of numbers in her name that indicates a woman of substance and ambition. This is a lady who will reach a pinnacle of success in life, and from this place, she can help many others to grow. Her name gives her the ability to share power unselfishly. Penny is a person who wants to use whatever influence she may have achieved for her community's benefits. Penny will do well to educate herself in sociology, history, economics, and psychology.

Perry

A KABBALISTIC SYNOPSIS

פאררי —PARRY (Peh, Aleph, Resh, Resh, Yod)

The central portion of Perry's name is occupied by two Rs or, in Hebrew, the letter Resh, which means "sun." This tells us that Perry is a jolly fellow. Perry can always see the funny side of any situation, even when others around him can't. Perry's presence is welcome when friends need cheering up—but not so much so when, in the middle of a business meeting, he finds something highly amusing while the rest of the attendees are trying to discuss important issues. The value of Perry's name reduces to fourteen, which indicates a balanced nature. In Perry's character this balance is struck by his willingness to suffer in order to help out others—thus adding a little gravity to his generally lighthearted view of the world.

THE RUNIC INTERPRETATION

ᛇᚱᚱᛖᚦ (Eihwaz, Raido, Raido, Ehwaz, Perth)

Perry is a travelin' man; nothing can keep him in one place for long. Double Raido combined with Eihwaz for defense and Ehwaz for movement could point to a career in foreign affairs. The Eihwaz rune means Perry can take care of himself and do the other person in if the occasion arises. The Perth rune of initiation keeps Perry free of entanglements, which harmonizes with the adventures in Perry's life.

Elements: Earth/fire, water, water, air, water

THE NUMEROLOGICAL INTERPRETATION

Perry (NV = 1, CV = 7, VV = 3, FL = 7)

Although Perry can be a very informative and entertaining communicator, the numbers in this name indicate a man who can also be a loner. Perry has a need to establish his own identity in the world. He is very much involved with processes that individualize his particular life. He is often found engaging in some form of self-education: attending seminars and courses, or simply reading a variety of books meant to enlighten. Perry is much more a leader than a follower, and likes the feeling of being in control of his own destiny.

DERIVATION: Common nickname
for the name Peter, from the
Greek *petros*, meaning "rock" or
"stone." Occasionally given as
independent name.

PRINCIPAL COLORS: The full
spectrum of yellow and bronze,
including orange and gold

GEMSTONES AND PRECIOUS
METALS: Topaz, yellow
diamonds, citrine

BOTANICALS: Saint-John's-wort,
sorrel, borage, chamomile

UNIQUE SPELLING: Peet

RELATED TO: Peadar, Pearce,
Pedro†, Perry†, Peter†, Petey,
Pierce, Piero, Pierre, Pierro, Piet,
Pietro, Pyotr

Pete

A KABBALISTIC SYNOPSIS
פיהט —PYHT (Peh, Yod, Heh, Teth)

In Pete we find an example of the letter Teth tending to work in its negative aspect, as an instigator of argument and, sometimes, unpleasantness. This does not mean that Pete is an unpleasant guy but that he doesn't know when to let go of an issue. Thus Pete would make an excellent prosecutor and an absolutely awful negotiator! Pete's name adds up to 104, the same as the value of the letter Tzaddi when spelled in full. Pete has a very strong connection to Tzaddi, and as this letter means "fishhook" and has the same value as the Hebrew word for "quarrel," we have an image of a man who hooks into a situation and will then refuse to move an inch if challenged. The value of Pete's name can be reduced to five and is associated with the letter Heh and the tarot card the Emperor. These connections suggest that Pete is indeed ideally suited to any role that sees him in charge of large numbers of people and responsible for significant decisions. In reducing the letters of his Hebrew name to the minimum, we reveal the two letters Qoph and Daleth. As Qoph is associated with thoughts and means "head" and Daleth means "door," we may expect Pete to be somewhat nostalgic or even sentimental. This softer side to his nature will enhance his appeal in any relationship.

THE RUNIC INTERPRETATION
ᛗᛏᛗᛇ (Ehwaz, Teiwaz, Ehwaz, Perth)

Pete is apt to surprise his family by relocating to the other side of the world and taking a highly dangerous job! New dwelling places, new attitudes, and expanding knowledge hold a special appeal for Pete. He probably knows several languages. On a deeper level, he may feel somewhat emotionally depleted. With that in mind, Pete finds his penchant for change and the accompanying rush of emotion actually help him feel he is living life to the fullest, because he requires strong emotions to enable him to feel his feelings.

Elements: Air, air, air, water

THE NUMEROLOGICAL INTERPRETATION
Pete (NV = 1, CV = 9, VV = 1, FL = 7)

Vibrationally, the numbers in Pete are very connected to those in the name Pat†, and as such, both names have many traits in common. The major difference—and it is a significant one—is that Pete is a name dominated by the vowel *e*, a letter with the energy of the number five. This adds the element of expansion to Pete's life path. It impresses on Pete the urge for freedom, and brings him into contact with experiences gained through travel, as well as through an abundance of relationships of all types. Pete will not be satisfied with the status quo in life, and is happiest when exploring new opportunities for his growth and development. He knows that he has a number of latent talents and abilities, and seeks out those people and places that can enhance his understanding of life.

Peter

A KABBALISTIC SYNOPSIS
פיטא —PYTA (Peh, Yod, Teth, Aleph)

Having a value of one hundred, Peter's name is associated with material wealth in a big way. Peter is likely to make his money through skill and hard work rather than by luck or good fortune. He is particularly suited to industries that are in some way connected to the spoken or written word, such as journalism or publishing. As well as being extremely well heeled, Peter is blessed with high intelligence. There are many people who make their way in business on the basis of gut instinct, but Peter prefers to use his admirable analytical skills to make his personal fortune grow. A cultured man, Peter will invest heavily in his own education and will continue to have a real thirst for knowledge well into his old age. Peter's only negative trait is his vengeful streak; if he is slighted either in business or in his relationships, he will carry the desire for revenge any number of years until he finally gets satisfaction.

THE RUNIC INTERPRETATION
ᚱᛖᛏᛖᛈ (Raido, Ehwaz, Teiwaz, Ehwaz, Perth)

Since Peter's name contains both air and water elements, he develops a rapport with people easily and has a good, chatty conversational style. He's fun on the dance floor because of the Ehwaz rune of movement in his name. Teiwaz, the warrior rune, makes Peter bold and self-assured and able to love deeply. Peter can be very tender. Raido, the rune of journey, combined with Perth, the rune of initiation, signifies that Peter voyages to great heights of brilliance and calls attention to himself by his remarkable achievements.

Elements: Water, air, air, air, water

THE NUMEROLOGICAL INTERPRETATION
Peter (NV = 1, CV = 9, VV = 1, FL = 7)

Many men named Peter feel that they have a special mission in life—and they are right. Two words dominate the vibrations of this name, and these are "I am." Peter has a distinct sense of himself, his own uniqueness, and his own identity. But with what is he identifying? The answer to this question will determine Peter's destiny and the fulfillment of his mission. If his "I am" is the desires of his lower self, then Peter will be a very egocentric and self-centered human being. If his identification with "I am" is more spiritual and transcendental in nature, then Peter will be a very inspirational man, one to whom many will look for guidance and support.

DERIVATION: English, German, and Scandinavian, from the Greek *petros*, meaning "stone." The name of one of Christ's Apostles, regarded as a cofounder of the Christian Church. Became popular in the United States around 1930.

PRINCIPAL COLORS: Orange, gold, any yellow or bronze hue

GEMSTONES AND PRECIOUS METALS: Citrine, topaz

BOTANICALS: Borage, eyebright

UNIQUE SPELLINGS: Peeter, Peetir, Peetyr, Petir, Petyr, Pieter, Pietyr

RELATED TO: Peadar, Pearce, Pedro†, Perry†, Pete†, Petey, Pierce, Piero, Pierre, Pierro, Piet, Pietro, Pyotr

DERIVATION: English, pet form of Philip, from the Greek root *phílein* meaning "to love," and *híppos* meaning "horse." Has been occasionally used as an independent name since the late nineteenth century.

PRINCIPAL COLORS: The full range of red hues, particularly the richest

GEMSTONES AND PRECIOUS METALS: Bloodstones, garnets

BOTANICALS: Garlic, broom, wormwood

UNIQUE SPELLINGS: Fil, Fill, Fyl, Fyll, Phill, Phyl, Phyll

RELATED TO: Felipe†, Filippo, Phelps, Philip, Philipp, Philippe, Phillip†, Phillips, Pippo

A KABBALISTIC SYNOPSIS
פיל —PhYL (Peh, Yod, Lamed)

You can always rely on Phil, and for this reason he is a well-liked friend and a highly valued employee. He has no real ambition to speak of other than to be settled in a stable, comfortable family life. While this is an unassuming goal, any partner will have the benefit of being the absolute center of Phil's life. The only time this becomes a problem is when Phil gets possessive, which he does from time to time. Every so often a Phil will come along who takes his virtues of honesty and fidelity very seriously, and he may well take up a more spiritual vocation. The number 120, which is the value of his name, has strong symbolic associations in the Western mystery tradition, and it has associations with the virtues of honesty, duty, and unconditional love for one's neighbor.

THE RUNIC INTERPRETATION
ᛚᛁᚺᛈ (Laguz, Isa, Hagalaz, Perth)

Phil is an intuitive, responsive mate. He brings his partner coffee in the morning and keeps his critical nature under lock and key. The Laguz rune of flow provides him with flexibility and an inclination toward the performing arts. Generosity, warmth, and passion are the gifts of the Perth rune of initiation. Perth requires that Phil let go of everything in order to discover who he really is, and at this point he will align himself with love. The Hagalaz and Isa runes instigate disruptions, isolation, and obstacles that require further soul-searching. The process is fruitful, though, and Phil emerges with real leadership ability and a sensitive way of managing people that serves him well in his career.

Elements: Water, earth, water, water

THE NUMEROLOGICAL INTERPRETATION
Phil (NV = 9, CV = 9, VV = 9, FL = 7)

The number nine strongly dominates this name, indicating that Phil is a perfectionist and idealist of the first order. This is a very humanitarian man, one who expects the best from people. He is truthful and has a hard time understanding how a person could be otherwise. Until he brings a more practical outlook into his life, Phil may find himself very disappointed in other people's conduct. A charitable and compassionate man, he does well in group situations where the fundamental link between members is philosophical or spiritual.

Phillip

DERIVATION: English, from the Greek root *philein*, meaning "to love," and *hippos*, meaning "horse." The name of one of Christ's Apostles. Particularly popular among early Christians.

PRINCIPAL COLORS: The palest to the brightest shades of yellow and bronze, also orange

GEMSTONES AND PRECIOUS METALS: Citrine, yellow diamonds

BOTANICALS: Eyebright, Saint-John's-wort

UNIQUE SPELLINGS: Filip, Fillyp, Filyp, Fylip, Fyllip, Fyllyp, Fylyp, Philip, Philipp, Phillyp, Philyp, Phylip, Phyllip, Phyllyp, Phylyp

RELATED TO: Felipe, Filippo, Phelps, Philt, Philippe, Phillips, Pippo

A Kabbalistic Synopsis
פיליף —PHYLYP (Peh, Yod, Lamed, Yod, Peh)

If you have spent a long time in the company of a Phillip, you will understand when we say that he is relentlessly cheerful, for there are times in life when we actually want people to feel as weighty or blue as we do! Unfortunately, Phillip rarely hits such a low emotional state, and this can be frustrating for those around him. Phillip has energy to spare and is an excellent choice in the workplace if you are looking for someone to act as a "finisher" and ensure that projects are completed. One worry for Phillip is that the middle of his name contains the letter Yod twice and the letter Lamed, which together represent energy and drive. The danger is that by approaching everything like a speeding train, Phillip may ultimately burn out. However, his jovial outlook should help prevent him from suffering from the stress that would strike other people working at the same rate.

The Runic Interpretation
ᛩᛁᛚᛚᛁᚺᛩ (Perth, Isa, Laguz, Laguz, Isa, Hagalaz, Perth)

Phillip has all the strengths and weaknesses of Phil—only more so. The double Isa rune stresses standstill and Phillip's need to meditate and reflect on life. He can enjoy work requiring enormous powers of concentration, for he has tremendous analytical ability and patience. The double Perth rune indicates that nothing less will do for Phillip than a full severance with his past. Phillip therefore might join an ashram or the foreign legion or do something radical at some point in his life. The double Laguz rune of flow means Phillip will experience shifts in relationships and in the direction of his career. Hagalaz, the rune of disruption, indicates that some of these transitions will be painful and chaotic, but Phillip will emerge victorious and happy to have security and focus at last.

Elements: Water, earth, water, water, earth, water, water

The Numerological Interpretation
Phillip (NV = 1, CV = 1, VV = 9, FL = 7)

The name Phillip indicates a crusader, a man who can be very self-sacrificing in order to promote or defend his ideals. This is a passionate person with a profound sense of self-confidence. He is so strongly connected to his future visions and goals that he may trip over the rock in front of his feet! Because of this, Phillip would do well to choose a partner who is of a more practical nature, one who can create a solid foundation for Phillip's long-range plans. Phillip should have no problem attracting people into his life who will be willing to support him.

DERIVATION: English and German, from the Greek *phullís*, meaning "foliage." The name of a character in Greek mythology who turned into an almond tree after her death. Commonly used since the eighteenth century, and especially popular in the 1920s.

PRINCIPAL COLORS: The complete range of green hues, creamy white

GEMSTONES AND PRECIOUS METALS: Jade, moonstones

BOTANICALS: Chicory, colewort, plantain

UNIQUE SPELLINGS: Filis, Fillys, Filys, Fylis, Fyllis, Fyllys, Fylys, Philis, Phillys, Philys, Phylis, Phylliss, Phyllys, Phylys

RELATED TO: Felipa, Fillida, Phillie, Phillipa, Phillipina, Phillyda, Phyllida, Pippa, Pippy

Phyllis

A KABBALISTIC SYNOPSIS
פילים —PHYLYS (Peh, Yod, Lamed, Yod, Samech)

Phyllis is an intellectual through and through, and her overwhelming desire to spend hours in deep and complex thought or poring over books means that she makes an ideal academic. However, if she also likes the idea of commercial success, she would do well in law or publishing, and Capricorn Phyllises should give these options serious consideration. Phyllis is never content merely to follow others and must find her own way in life and in her profession. To her credit, while she will never be good at taking advice, she is always happy to admit when she has made a mistake. Phyllis has a strong social conscience and will spend a good deal of her limited free time doing some form of volunteer work. She gets a big kick out of helping people, and this side of her personality is shown by the final S in her name, which is Samech in Hebrew and means "prop" or "support."

THE RUNIC INTERPRETATION
ϟІГГ⋊ΗΚ (Sowelu, Isa, Laguz, Laguz, Eihwaz, Hagalaz, Perth)

Chaos and transformation are indicated by the Hagalaz and Perth runes. It's only through faith and a generous dose of humor that any of us emerge intact from such difficult passages in life. Isa, the rune of standstill, affords Phyllis the time she needs to slow down and reflect on her progress. As she is licking the stamp to mail off yet another résumé, she may wonder where all this change is leading her. The double Laguz rune of flexibility helps her keep her spirits hopeful. The Sowelu rune of wholeness promises that Phyllis will emerge from this change with a new identity and rewarding existence—and she deserves it.

Elements: Air, earth, water, water, earth/fire, water, water

THE NUMEROLOGICAL INTERPRETATION
Phyllis (NV = 5, CV = 7, VV = 7, FL = 7)

Phyllis is interested in separating right from wrong. She is a very moral and ethical person who seeks to discover the truth at the heart of every situation. Phyllis would therefore make an excellent psychologist, scientist, or laboratory worker. Sometimes, however, she looks too deeply and can become suspicious without firm reason. It is important for her to not become overly absorbed either in herself or in life's less important issues. Nevertheless, Phyllis is able to be very self-sufficient, and finds great support within herself in her moments of solitude and introspection.

Preston

A Kabbalistic Synopsis
פראסטון —PRASTVN (Peh, Resh, Aleph, Samech, Teth, Vau, Nun)

If there is anyone who hates to see a glum face, it is Preston. A natural comic, Preston will always manage to raise a smile in all but the most depressed of people; his voice in itself is often inherently amusing. Preston's genuine good nature and willingness to offer his services for the greater good mean that he may well be found doing volunteer or career work at a local hospital or children's home. Preston himself is fairly insecure, as shown by the final letter Nun in his name, and this is accentuated by the fact that the letter Teth in his name, which is associated with spite, is in his case turned against himself. This all sounds far too much like the stereotypical sad clown, but there is a bright side. Thanks to his highly emotional nature Preston responds very quickly to anyone who expresses any affection toward him, and he can lose his self-doubt with the help of supportive friends.

The Runic Interpretation
ᚾᛟᛏᛊᛖᛗᚱᛈ (Nauthiz, Othila, Teiwaz, Sowelu, Ehwaz, Raido, Perth)

Constraint, separation, and transformation are reflected in the name Preston. Teiwaz, the warrior rune, shores Preston up for this bumpy ride. Ehwaz, the rune of movement, and Raido, the rune of journey, suggest that Preston may travel and live in foreign countries. Raido also signifies good communication and honesty. Preston can anticipate prosperity and a career that incorporates his love of travel and promotes friendliness toward humanity. Sowelu, the rune of wholeness, is a blessing, promising that Preston will be a conduit for a higher will to act through him. Sowelu infuses Preston with energy and vitality and a clear head with which to navigate life's challenges.

Elements: Fire, earth/fire, air, air, air, water, water

The Numerological Interpretation
Preston (NV = 8, CV = 6, VV = 11, FL = 7)

Preston is a name that indicates a strong-willed individual, a person of stamina and drive. He is very determined to achieve financial and social success and is prepared to do whatever is required of him to reach his lofty goals. This is a man who does very well under pressure, but he is not a workaholic; he is much too balanced within himself to go to extremes. Preston will definitely put in a fifty-hour workweek, but then he will spend his free time relaxing and pursuing his special interests. These usually are involved with the arts, as this man enjoys museums, theater, or other cultural activities.

DERIVATION: English, originally a surname, from the Old English *preost*, meaning "priest," and *tun*, meaning "estate." Used as a given name since the 1860s.

PRINCIPAL COLORS: The richest shades of azure, purple, and gray, also black

GEMSTONES AND PRECIOUS METALS: Carbuncles, sapphires, amethyst

BOTANICALS: Angelica, marsh mallow

UNIQUE SPELLINGS: Prestan, Presten, Prestin, Prestyn

RELATED TO: Presleigh, Presley, Priestley, Priestly

❧

"The world basically and fundamentally is constituted on the basis of harmony. Everything works in cooperation with something else."
—PRESTON BRADLEY (MUSICIAN)

DERIVATION: New Testament name, from the Roman family name Priscus, from a Latin root meaning "ancient." Especially popular among the Puritans in the seventeenth century.

PRINCIPAL COLORS: Pink to the deepest shades of red, crimson

GEMSTONES AND PRECIOUS METALS: Rubies, garnets

BOTANICALS: Broom, garlic, onion

UNIQUE SPELLINGS: Priscella, Priscila, Prisilla, Pryscila, Prysila, Prysilla

RELATED TO: Cilla, Cillie, Pris, Prisca, Prissie, Prissy

Priscilla

A KABBALISTIC SYNOPSIS

פריסילא —PRYSYI A (Peh, Resh, Yod, Samech, Yod, Lamed, Aleph)

The keynote in Priscilla's life is change; if her activities remain the same for long, she quickly begins to feel trapped and bored. Priscilla is attracted to anything with an element of the unusual or with a relatively high risk factor. You will find Priscilla bungee jumping or sky-diving . . . and loving every minute of it. Her attraction to risk, combined with a sincere wish to help others, may lead her to careers in police work, firefighting, or even the armed forces. The final two letters in her name, when transliterated into Hebrew, are Lamed and Aleph, which when combined translate as "nothing." Priscilla has moments in her life when she gets deeply depressed about the apparent pointlessness of her life; such times are rare, though, and it may be that they function in part to suggest times when it is important to settle down.

THE RUNIC INTERPRETATION

ᚨᚱᚱᛁᛊᛁᚱᛈ (Ansuz, Laguz, Laguz, Isa, Sowelu, Isa, Raido, Perth)

Perth's prominent position suggests Priscilla might change her name or her attitudes over the course of her life. The Ansuz rune steps up Priscilla's intuitive ability. Being musical and flexible is second nature to Priscilla; she has the Laguz energy to provide her with additional talents in the performing arts. Quiet time and the company of calm associates are of paramount importance to Priscilla, who eschews the limelight. This is indicated by the double Isa rune of standstill, which dominates her name. The Raido rune promises introspection and outward journeys, and implies the journey of the self to self-actualization and union. Sowelu, the rune of wholeness, provides Priscilla with abundant energy and self-knowledge.

Elements: Air, water, water, earth, air, earth, water, water

THE NUMEROLOGICAL INTERPRETATION

Priscilla (NV = 9, CV = 8, VV = 1, FL = 7)

This is a woman who carries herself with authority. From a very early age, Priscilla holds a vision of herself and her possible achievements. She is endowed with determination and drive as well as the necessary willpower to face life's many challenges. Although her personal ambitions may dominate her life, Priscilla is not an egocentric person; part of the challenges she takes on has to do with helping people less fortunate than herself. She is a compassionate woman, one with very wide and unprejudiced views of life who easily earns people's admiration and respect.

Rachel

A KABBALISTIC SYNOPSIS
ראיחל —RAYChL (Resh, Aleph, Yod, Cheth, Lamed)

This woman will really knock you off your feet, given her forceful character. Rachel is sexual to her core and couldn't disguise it from the rest of the world even if she wanted to. As she would quite rightly point out in her matter-of-fact way, she is not to blame for her effect on others. Rachel has numerous friends, and a night out with Rachel is an event not to be missed—or for that matter, repeated more than once every couple of months! Rachel avoids serious relationships, although surprisingly this has more to do with irrational fears that her partner may be disloyal than with a desire to stay single forever—although Rachel will have a great time as long as she stays that way.

THE RUNIC INTERPRETATION
ᛚᛖᚺᛋᚨᚱ (Laguz, Ehwaz, Hagalaz, Sowelu, Ansuz, Raido)

In today's emancipated society, it's not unusual for a person to be full of flexibility and a willingness to travel and live abroad. Raido and Ehwaz indicate that Rachel will do just that. Ansuz, the rune of intuition, helps Rachel gain her bearings on foreign turf. Hagalaz, the rune of disruption, is along for the ride to provoke a mishap or two. It's at just such times that the Laguz rune of flow comes to the fore to save the day, and Rachel remains flexible through it all. Sowelu, the rune of wholeness, blesses Rachel's life with energy and vitality and an abiding sense of satisfaction and accomplishment.

Elements: Water, air, water, air, air, water

THE NUMEROLOGICAL INTERPRETATION
Rachel (NV = 11, CV = 5, VV = 6, FL = 9)

Insightful, intuitive, and intelligent are three adjectives that best characterize Rachel. An easy communicator who moves very fluidly between people of all different social levels and backgrounds, Rachel has a real curiosity about life. Rachel is a person who understands community issues and can garner the necessary support to get things done. She works well with large groups of people and is able to unify diverse interests toward a single goal. Rachel has to take care that she doesn't splinter herself into too many pieces. She is a woman who has a high degree of nervous energy and has a hard time sitting still.

DERIVATION: English, French, and German, from the Old Testament, meaning "ewe" in Hebrew. In the Bible, the name of Jacob's beloved wife, who gave birth to Joseph and Benjamin. Used by Puritans in the seventeenth century, but not extremely popular until the 1960s and 1970s.

PRINCIPAL COLORS: Cream, white, the full gamut of green hues

GEMSTONES AND PRECIOUS METALS: Moonstones, cat's-eye

BOTANICALS: Chicory, lettuce, colewort

UNIQUE SPELLINGS: Rachael, Racheal, Rachil, Raychael, Raycheal, Raychel, Raychil

RELATED TO: Chell, Chella, Rach, Rache, Rachele, Rachelle, Rae, Rahel, Rahil, Rakel, Raquelt, Raquela, Raquelinda, Raquelita, Raquelle, Rashell, Rauquella, Ray, Raychelle, Shell, Shelley, Shellie, Shellyt

DERIVATION: English, French, and German, from Hebrew roots meaning "God has healed." Raphael is the name of an archangel who appears in the apocryphal tale of Tobias. Especially popular in the nineteenth century.

PRINCIPAL COLORS: Pale to deep, rich shades of yellow and green

GEMSTONES AND PRECIOUS METALS: Moonstones, moss agate

BOTANICALS: Elder, blackberry

UNIQUE SPELLINGS: Rafayal, Rafayel, Raphael, Raphaell, Raphayal, Raphayel

RELATED TO: Rafe, Rafel, Rafello, Raffaelo

⟆

In the absence of any direct equivalent to the letter *f* in the Hebrew alphabet, the letter Peh is used. Peh can function as either a hard or a soft letter, and as such, is one of the seven "doubles."

Rafael

A KABBALISTIC SYNOPSIS
ראפאיל —RAPhAYL (Resh, Aleph, Peh, Aleph, Yod, Lamed)

Rafael has a very prodigious name. Its Hebrew equivalent is Raphael, one of the better-known archangels in the Judeo-Christian tradition. In the kabbalistic tradition Raphael is the Archangel of the East and is associated with the element of air and all aspects of the mind. Consequently Rafael is something of a dreamer in life and is often regarded as having his head in the clouds. In fact, he often has a wisdom and understanding of the truly important things in life that pass many by as they pursue other, more material goals. The value of Rafael's name is 322. The three hundred represents the energy and drive that Rafael possesses, and that makes him such an interesting person to spend time with. The twenty-two is associated with the Fool card in the tarot. Like Rafael, the fool is a very complex character, simultaneously innocent and knowledgeable.

THE RUNIC INTERPRETATION
ᚱᛖᚨᚠᚨᚱ (Laguz, Ehwaz, Ansuz, Fehu, Ansuz, Raido)

Decoding people, situations, and the environment is one of the intuitive talents of sensitive Rafael. The double Ansuz rune of signals cautions Rafael to be alert during exchanges with people more learned and experienced than himself. Rafael has a patient way of listening and making the other person know he really is being heard. He also feels that nothing is an accident, and he pays attention to the so-called coincidences in his life. Laguz keeps him flexible, and Fehu indicates that he will be prosperous. The Ehwaz rune of movement combined with Laguz could indicate dancing and musical talent. Ehwaz combined with Raido signifies travel. Ehwaz can also mean a change of attitude, and Raido can also signify the inner spiritual journey.

Elements: Water, air, air, fire, air, water

THE NUMEROLOGICAL INTERPRETATION
Rafael (NV = 7, CV = 9, VV = 7, FL = 9)

The name is totally dominated by sevens and nines. Rafael is therefore an introspective man, one who has a profound philosophy of life and a strong inner faith that carries him far. This is an individual who believes in people and can be quite idealistic in his interpersonal relationships. Rafael is much more comfortable with small groups of intimate friends than with large groups of relative strangers. He must have a peaceful setting in which to do his work, and he has no problem at all spending long hours by himself. Naturally inclined to be a minister, teacher, or healer, this is a man who does well as a humanitarian or spiritual worker.

⟆

Ralph

A Kabbalistic Synopsis
ראלף —RALPh (Resh, Aleph, Lamed, Peh)

If Ralph is also an Aries, he may well be the most pedantic man you have ever met! Ralph has an almost obsessive eye for detail, and you can be sure that he will find the defects in just about everything—if there are any to be found. While this can be intensely irritating in some situations, there are some professions where such an ability is a very definite asset. For example, law requires a very keen mind and a close understanding of every procedure that needs to be followed. Those who work closely with Ralph will have the utmost respect for him, as he can be deeply creative when it comes to juggling ideas or concepts. Ralph loves to discuss his ideas and opinions and is a lively conversationalist, although he can sometimes dominate the discussion. In relationships Ralph has problems relating to the fact that his partner may hold different views from himself, but to his credit, he is willing to be steered toward a more tolerant frame of mind.

The Runic Interpretation
ᚺᛈᛚᚨᚱ (Hagalaz, Perth, Laguz, Ansuz, Raido)

Who minds a bit of disruption and transformation if everything turns out fine in the end? Not Ralph. He has the Laguz rune of flow to keep him flexible through the shifts in friendships, jobs, houses, and even his own heart. He's a champ. Highly intuitive and given to moments of brilliant insight, Ralph perseveres against all odds. He just whistles a happy tune and no one ever knows he's trying to cheer himself on! Raido, the rune of journey, indicates that Ralph navigates this voyage of the soul with great aplomb. Patience and escapism in the form of excursions and voyages are Ralph's reward for hard lessons won.

Elements: Water, water, water, air, water

The Numerological Interpretation
Ralph (NV = 1, CV = 9, VV = 1, FL = 9)

Ralph has the need to project his inner thoughts, opinions, and viewpoints. If he doesn't like what is going on or someone displeases him, he does not hide his irritation or displeasure (although some people would prefer it if he did). Ralph's personality is very forthright and energetic. He has an inner conviction about the way he lives and avoids self-censorship. He is also prepared to defend the underdog with the same vehemence and passion that he uses to promote and assert himself.

DERIVATION: English, a form of the Germanic name Radulf, from Old English roots meaning "wolf" and "counsel." Very common from the sixteenth century to the eighteenth century.

PRINCIPAL COLORS: The palest to the most brilliant shades of yellow, also brown, orange

GEMSTONES AND PRECIOUS METALS: Amber, yellow diamonds

BOTANICALS: Borage, thyme, gentian root

UNIQUE SPELLINGS: Raalf, Raalff, Raalph, Ralf, Ralff

RELATED TO: Rafe, Raff, Rault, Rolf, Rolph

"I start with the premise that the function of leadership is to produce more leaders, not more followers."
—RALPH NADER (PUBLIC ADVOCATE)

Ramiro

A KABBALISTIC SYNOPSIS
ראמירע —RAMYRA'A (Resh, Aleph, Mem, Yod, Resh, Ayin)

Ramiro is a complicated guy who combines a very forceful and charismatic personality with a deeply sensitive and caring nature. He is wonderfully encouraging, making him an ideal parent or manager. In general, Ramiro is the kind of guy who is able to get results without making people feel put-upon or overworked. Ramiro's natural warmth and cheery disposition mean that he is very popular and is never short of invitations. Once he is among friends, Ramiro has a great time. Ramiro is always the first to break the ice in any social situation, and his self-confidence is such that he will happily get up and dance when everyone else is still sitting down thinking about the possibility. Ramiro's weak area in life is in working with his hands; even hanging a picture can be a real challenge to Ramiro!

THE RUNIC INTERPRETATION
ᛟᚱᛁᛗᚨᚱ (Othila, Raido, Isa, Mannaz, Ansuz, Raido)

Modesty is a valuable attribute of the Mannaz rune, and it serves Ramiro well. The double Raido rune of journey keeps Ramiro traveling and sharing his talents and inspiration wherever he ventures. Ramiro is a clear communicator, and the Isa rune of standstill helps him write with focus and style. Othila, the rune of separation, gives Ramiro's writing brevity and insight. Ansuz, the rune of signals, helps strengthen Ramiro's intuition and may give him some added skill in writing plots and dialogue. Whether he chooses a career in writing or an unrelated field, Ramiro's understanding of human nature and the foibles of the human experience enrich his life and imbue him with compassion and tolerance for his fellow man.

Elements: Earth/fire, water, earth, air, air, water

THE NUMEROLOGICAL INTERPRETATION
Ramiro (NV = 11, CV = 22, VV = 7, FL = 9)

Ramiro contains a very rare and potentially powerful combination of numbers. It is one of the few names that has both master numbers—eleven and twenty-two—as prime signifiers. The question is, can Ramiro the man live up to Ramiro the name? A great deal depends upon Ramiro's level of consciousness and the focus of his spiritual development. People will easily do what Ramiro tells them, as he possesses incredible magnetism. His ambitions are great, and he has the drive and determination to match. But if he directs all of his energy toward self-gratification, the tendency is for him to be manipulative and abusive. If he uses the power in this name for higher purposes, he will find himself loved, respected, and greatly enriched on all levels.

Ramón

A Kabbalistic Synopsis

ראמען —RAMA'AN (Resh, Aleph, Mem, Ayin, Nun)

The value of Ramón's name is 1011 . . . and with all those ones in his name we can expect Ramón to be a unique character. One is the number of individuality and self-expression. As Ramón's name is dominated by this number, it is difficult to say with confidence exactly how he will behave; there are few people quirkier than Ramón. It is likely that Ramón will have an interest in the unusual or the unexplained. Luck plays a big part in his life, and more often than not it is good luck, since his name has associations with the Fortune card in the tarot. Good fortune will be especially useful to Ramón in his relationships, since he sometimes has difficulty considering other people's feelings, which may cause a certain amount of strife.

The Runic Interpretation

ᚾᛟᛗᚨᚱ (Nauthiz, Othila, Mannaz, Ansuz, Raido)

Adaptability is one of Ramón's many gifts. The Ansuz rune of signals gives Ramón an inward sense of timing, while the Othila rune of separation calls for patience. Ramón is able to seize opportunity wherever he finds it, even if it means shifting his direction. He can work in government or in social service agencies because he handles stress extremely well. The Nauthiz rune of constraint indicates that even in a less-than-ideal environment, Ramón functions efficiently. The Raido rune of journey gives Ramón an ability to explain things simply and clearly.

Elements: Fire, earth/fire, air, air, water

The Numerological Interpretation

Ramón (NV = 7, CV = 9, VV = 7, FL = 9)

Ramón is endowed with a depth of perception about other people that comes from his constant personal reflections. When taken to extremes, this can indicate a very self-absorbed nature, one that easily leads to a sense of alienation and isolation. Yet when balanced with faith and trust, Ramón's natural sensitivity allows him to focus on the inner qualities of life, creating a man of deep compassion and understanding. When someone needs an answer to a perplexing issue, they look to Ramón to offer some good advice—advice that he offers with a generous heart.

DERIVATION: Spanish form of Raymond, which is from Old German roots meaning "counsel protection." Usage influenced by the 1920s silent-movie star, Ramón Novarro.

PRINCIPAL COLORS: All the shades of green and yellow, also gold

GEMSTONES AND PRECIOUS METALS: Moonstones, pearls

BOTANICALS: Juniper, linseed

UNIQUE SPELLINGS: Rahmon, Ramoan, Ramone

RELATED TO: Raemond, Raimundo, Ramond, Ray†, Raymond†, Raymundo

DERIVATION: Spanish, feminine form of Ramón, which is from Old German roots meaning "counsel protection." Widely known as the main character of several popular children's books by Beverly Cleary.

PRINCIPAL COLORS: Black, gray, dark azure and violet

GEMSTONES AND PRECIOUS METALS: Black pearls, black diamonds, rubies

BOTANICALS: Angelica, shepherd's purse, pilewort

UNIQUE SPELLINGS: Rahmona, Ramonna, Romona

RELATED TO: Monat, Ramonda, Ramonde, Romonda, Romonde

Ramona

A KABBALISTIC SYNOPSIS
ראמענא —RAMA'ANA (Resh, Aleph, Mem, Ayin, Nun, Aleph)

Ramona is likely to have an exceptionally well-paying job, although she is unlikely actually to be in business by herself. This woman is no pushover: Ramona is not just a hard worker, but she is also highly perceptive and can sniff out a wooden nickel at twenty paces. Politically she tends to be conservative, and this conservatism extends to her emotional life. She will most likely have only a few relationships before settling down. A strong sense of duty affects Ramona's behavior in many ways, and she will probably be a regular giver to charity.

THE RUNIC INTERPRETATION
ᚨᚾᛟᛗᚨᚱ (Ansuz, Nauthiz, Othila, Mannaz, Ansuz, Raido)

Ramona understands that when life changes, people need to be tolerant of each other. However, the Othila rune of separation states that Ramona will discard relationships that are dysfunctional, if she is satisfied that she has tried her best to renegotiate them and the friendship has failed. The Mannaz rune of the self signifies that Ramona is loving and self-confident. Ramona would be wise to work as one who nurtures in any number of capacities. The double Ansuz rune of signals symbolizes heightened intuition and a positive kind of opportunism. Travel is indicated by the Raido rune of journey. Ramona could teach in an international school or work in foreign affairs. She is at home wherever there are people with open hearts.

Elements: Air, fire, earth/fire, air, air, water

THE NUMEROLOGICAL INTERPRETATION
Ramona (NV = 8, CV = 9, VV = 8, FL = 9)

Ramona's name gives her the power to manifest what is required for her comfort and well-being. This is a woman who enjoys the niceties of life and intends to have them. Ramona likes to wear fine clothes and eat at fine restaurants. She enjoys the company of men and women who have achieved a certain degree of status and position in the world. Respected by other people for her self-confidence and sense of personal control, Ramona is also a very emotionally sensitive person, whose help, financial and otherwise, can often be solicited for a charitable cause.

Randall

DERIVATION: English, a medieval form of Randolf, from Old English roots meaning "shield-wolf." Increased in popularity in the late twentieth century.

PRINCIPAL COLORS: Black, the deepest shades of blue, purple, and gray

GEMSTONES AND PRECIOUS METALS: Carbuncles, black pearls

BOTANICALS: Ragwort, shepherd's purse

UNIQUE SPELLINGS: Randal, Randel, Randell, Randle

RELATED TO: Randolf, Randolph†, Randy†

A KABBALISTIC SYNOPSIS

ראנדאל —RANDAL (Resh, Aleph, Nun, Daleth, Aleph, Lamed)

Randall is a rash man, to say the least. He will rush into any number of situations when it would have been wiser to wait. The position of the letter Nun in his name strongly suggests that Randall allows his emotions to govern the changes in his life, even when they relate to nonemotional matters like career choices. There will probably be more than one occasion when Randall leaves a perfectly good job because someone in the workplace has upset or offended him. However, the signs are that Randall has the energy and drive to find new opportunities with little delay, and the central D, or Daleth, meaning "door," in his name indicates that it will never be long before a bright new start becomes available to him. Randall will have a very close relationship with his mate, and they are likely to share everything about each other's lives, spending long evenings sitting and enjoying the chance to chat with each other about everything and nothing.

THE RUNIC INTERPRETATION

ᛚᛚᚨᛞᚾᚨᚱ (Laguz, Laguz, Ansuz, Dagaz, Nauthiz, Ansuz, Raido)

Randall knows how to go with the flow. He has the double Laguz runic configuration, making him flexible and tolerant. Intuition is another one of his strengths. Randall knows how to anticipate trends, and moves when the time is right. Because Randall is patient, he can also retreat when indicated. Randall may be a procrastinator due to the Nauthiz rune of constraint in this name, but he works well under pressure. With Raido for journey, and Dagaz for breakthroughs, Randall travels often, and his inventive mind offers fresh insights and images of what he sees that he can share with others through photography and other fine arts.

Elements: Water, water, air, fire, fire, air, water

THE NUMEROLOGICAL INTERPRETATION

Randall (NV = 8, CV = 6, VV = 2, FL = 9)

Randall is very connected to beauty and the arts. He is the kind of man for whom a well-designed house and office are absolutely essential elements of life. Randall tends to dress well and has a good eye for color and combinations of textures. He tends to be very charming, and is equally at home in the presence of men or women and admired by both. He does very well in the role of peacemaker, as he is diplomatic and has no problem resolving complex business or personal issues. Randall is also aware of the possibilities that life has to offer, and he finds it easy to take advantage of them. He is a man who can go far if he is not fooled by the outer forms and trappings of life.

Randolph

DERIVATION: English, from Old English roots meaning "shield-wolf." Not very common in the eighteenth century, but more popular in modern times.

PRINCIPAL COLORS: Gold, all the various green and yellow hues

GEMSTONES AND PRECIOUS METALS: Pearls, moss agate, any white stone

BOTANICALS: Elder, hops, linseed

UNIQUE SPELLINGS: Randalf, Randalph, Randolf

RELATED TO: Randal, Randall†, Randel, Randell, Randle, Randy†

A KABBALISTIC SYNOPSIS

ראנדעלפ —RANDA'ALPh (Resh, Aleph, Nun, Daleth, Ayin, Lamed, Peh)

Don't ever crack a joke at Randolph's expense; not only will he be unable to see its humor, but he may well make sure that you regret having teased him at some later date. And with the powerful energies in his name, there is every chance that Randolph will be in a position of sufficient authority to make really sure that you wish you hadn't said a word to him. Not that Randolph is an unpleasant man—he isn't—but he is deeply serious about himself and his future. Randolph is a man with a mission, and he will work all hours of the day and night in order to achieve his goals. As a result, there is a danger that he may severely overwork himself. He needs a strong partner who can persuade him to stop and rest now and then. With those close to him, Randolph is no longer the authoritative figure he is in the office. He is, instead, a genuinely decent man who will listen to those he really cares about when they offer him advice.

THE RUNIC INTERPRETATION

ᚺᛈᛚᛟᛞᚾᚨᚱ (Hagalaz, Perth, Laguz, Othila, Dagaz, Nauthiz, Ansuz, Raido)

Lessons of constraint present obstacles for Randolph and give him a cosmic pinch to change in a hurry. As he matures and considers other value and belief systems, Randolph challenges his childhood values. He discards worn-out friendships and attitudes that no longer serve him well by using the Othila rune of separation to clip his ties to the past. The powerful Hagalaz rune of disruption is responsible for so much chaos that Randolph surrenders to the forces of change. Fortunately he is a flexible and broad-minded man, and the Dagaz rune of breakthrough implies that Randolph achieves prosperity and success. He's resourceful and can excel in sales, marketing, research, or fields involving problem-solving ability. Randolph may encounter opportunities to travel. He designs his life in a creative and empowering manner.

Elements: Water, water, water, earth/fire, fire, fire, air, water

THE NUMEROLOGICAL INTERPRETATION

Randolph (NV = 7, CV = 9, VV = 7, FL = 9)

Randolph is like the ocean: He alternates between highs and lows. When Randolph is feeling low, he is quiet and withdrawn. When high, he generously shares his inner gifts with those around him. Randolph is both intelligent and sensitive. He enjoys the pursuit of knowledge and has quite an extensive library. But Randolph never buries himself in his books so that he closes himself off from friends and family. It is true that he is not always available, preferring a certain degree of solitude. But Randolph is certainly aware of other people's needs, and can be depended upon for support and comfort.

Randy

A Kabbalistic Synopsis

ראנדי —RANDY (Resh, Aleph, Nun, Daleth, Yod)

The value of Randy's name reduces to thirteen, which is, of course, the number of change and may indeed relate to a tendency to have more than the average number of partners. However, other aspects of this name suggest someone with a strong sense of loyalty, and so the focus on change is more likely to relate to career changes or geographical moves rather than to a promiscuous nature. In fact, Randy tends to have a very serious attitude toward relationships. He is the sort of person who will carefully analyze every aspect of his union to make sure that it is working.

The Runic Interpretation

ᛇᛞᚾᚨᚱ (Eihwaz, Dagaz, Nauthiz, Ansuz, Raido)

Randy regularly averts disaster. The Eihwaz rune of defense helps him to know just how to anticipate trouble, and it gives Randy an assertive personality. With Nauthiz, the rune of constraint, Randy can act just a tad stubborn—and even spoiled—at times. He enjoys the company of many friends, but only one or two really will know how insecure Randy feels on occasion. The Dagaz rune of breakthrough portends prosperity and riches as Randy's reward for learning to rely on his faith. Randy is powerful, with the energy of the four elements in his name.

Elements: Earth/fire, fire, fire, air, water

The Numerological Interpretation

Randy (NV = 8, CV = 9, VV = 8, FL = 9)

This name evokes a need for achievement. Randy perseveres in his career and has the ability to spend intensive hours in the pursuit of success. A man of polished organizational skills, Randy is very good at finding a place for everything and making sure that everything and everyone is in its proper place. Yet Randy is not a dictator; he knows that he has to keep an open and compassionate ear so that he may be able to obtain the cooperation he requires. This is a man who cares about his health and physical appearance, and he rates physical beauty as very important in his choice of lovers or partners.

DERIVATION: English, diminutive form of Randolph or Randall, which are both from Old English roots meaning "shield-wolf." More common in the United States than in Britain, where the word carries lewd connotations.

PRINCIPAL COLORS: Dark azure, purple, and gray hues, also black

GEMSTONES AND PRECIOUS METALS: Rubies, rich sapphires

BOTANICALS: Angelica, pilewort, mandrake root

UNIQUE SPELLINGS: Randey, Randi, Randie

RELATED TO: Randal, Randall†, Randel, Randell, Randle, Randolf, Randolph†

Raquel

A KABBALISTIC SYNOPSIS
ראקאל —RAQAL (Resh, Aleph, Qoph, Aleph, Lamed)

If we compress the value of Raquel's name, we find that the first letter is Shin. The letter Shin relates to the element of fire, and tells us that once Raquel finds her true calling in life, there will be literally no stopping her as she shoots her way to the top. If Raquel is an Aries, the results may be even more astonishing. Raquel, like most fire types, is full of optimism and tends to look forward, rather than dwelling on past successes or failures. Raquel always wants to be moving on to the next challenge. The letters Aleph and Qoph in her name indicate that she is full of exciting ideas, and that she has the mental agility to turn those ideas into viable projects. No one will ever regret getting emotionally involved with Raquel; even if it only lasts a short while, it will be an experience that they will never forget.

THE RUNIC INTERPRETATION
ᛚᛖᚢᚲᚨᚱ (Laguz, Ehwaz, Uruz, Kano, Ansuz, Raido)

Raquel is strong and coordinated and probably enjoys swimming, boating, and waterskiing. She's good at sports, and loves the camaraderie of competitive sports, in addition to more solitary pursuits. If sports is not her love, Raquel may be drawn to dancing and participation in musical performances. The Laguz rune of flow helps Raquel keep her life in balance. Ehwaz, the rune of movement, affords Raquel the opportunity to relocate after much travel, indicated by the Raido rune of journey. Ansuz is responsible for Raquel's intuition, and Kano, the rune of opening, gives Raquel a chance to help others by looking at their problems through her clear viewpoint. Uruz, the rune of strength, means Raquel will grow into a position of leadership, and she can endure stress because her mind, body, and spirit are blessed with stamina and fortitude.

Elements: Water, air, earth, water, air, water

THE NUMEROLOGICAL INTERPRETATION
Raquel (NV = 11, CV = 2, VV = 9, FL = 9)

Raquel is very intuitive and psychically perceptive; however, she is not as easily understood by others. She experiences the realities of life with a penetrating depth and a clarity that intrigues people. Raquel can be quite an inspiration to those in her environment. She has definite ideas and opinions, but she doesn't force her views on anyone else. Instead, she is flexible and permissive, allowing people just to be themselves. This tolerant outlook is in keeping with Raquel's own need for personal freedom. Sometimes Raquel's friends see her as a bit eccentric. She is certainly unpredictable, and not the easiest person to pin down.

Raul

DERIVATION: Spanish form of Ralph, which is a form of the Germanic name Radulf, from Old English roots meaning "wolf" and "counsel."

PRINCIPAL COLORS: Pale to rich green, light to deep yellow, gold

GEMSTONES AND PRECIOUS METALS: Moonstones, pearls

BOTANICALS: Blackberry, juniper, mushrooms

UNIQUE SPELLINGS: Rahool, Rahul, Rahwul, Raool, Raoul

RELATED TO: Rafe, Raff, Ralf, Ralph†, Rolf, Rolph

A Kabbalistic Synopsis
ראול —RAVL (Resh, Aleph, Vau, Lamed)

Raul is a calm man, and this is usually the first thing that anyone notices about him. He gives the impression of being completely unflappable, no matter what the crisis. For this reason he is ideally suited to take on positions of high responsibility, especially where there is a need to boost the morale of those working with him. The value of Raul's name tells us that he is headed for success in his work life. His decisions can always be relied upon, as he has a decidedly judicious way of weighing all the possibilities. Outside of the office this all goes right out the window, and Raul becomes a deeply passionate and emotional guy who will make his partner feel like the most important person in the world. He loves romantic surprises, and will still be keeping the sense of romance alive in his relationship as the decades pass by.

The Runic Interpretation
ᛚᚢᚨᚱ (Laguz, Uruz, Ansuz, Raido)

Raul enjoys watching his money grow. He senses trends in the market and has an innate feeling for when to advance and when to retreat. People watch Raul on the dance floor, too, because he seems to know just which way to go. Raido, the rune of journey, means Raul will be dancing to faraway rhythms during the many voyages and travels of his life. The Uruz rune of strength blesses Raul with the physical stamina and emotional strength to endure many changes in his life. Raul is emotional and sentimental about all living things. He could be a vegetarian or an advocate for animal rights. And he probably has at least one pet on whom he dotes!

Elements: Water, earth, air, water

The Numerological Interpretation
Raul (NV = 7, CV = 3, VV = 4, FL = 9)

Raul probably needs to become more self-disciplined if he is to fulfill his practical responsibilities. The establishment of positive habits and the creation of helpful routines will not only aid him in directing the expression of his creativity, but also will be essential to his success. He will need to fight the desire to flit about from relationship to relationship. Raul achieves his goals through dedication and loyalty both to his own principles and to the needs of others.

DERIVATION: English, pet form of Raymond, which is from Old German roots meaning "counsel protection." Very popular in the United States at the beginning of the twentieth century.

PRINCIPAL COLORS: Black, all the deep shades of blue, gray, and violet

GEMSTONES AND PRECIOUS METALS: Lackluster rubies, carbuncles, amethyst

BOTANICALS: Angelica, pilewort, shepherd's purse

UNIQUE SPELLINGS: Rae, Rai, Raigh, Raye

RELATED TO: Raimund, Raimundo, Ramón†, Ramond, Raymond†, Raymondo

❧

"Don't think. Thinking is the enemy of creativity. It's self-conscious, and anything self-conscious is lousy. You can't try to do things. You simply must do things."
—RAY BRADBURY (AUTHOR)

"The quality of a leader is reflected in the standards they set for themselves."
—RAY KROC (FOUNDER OF McDONALD'S)

Ray

A KABBALISTIC SYNOPSIS
ראי —RAY (Resh, Aleph, Yod)

To many people Ray comes across as something of a dull man who spends the vast majority of his time working. He has a real drive to provide his family with the best of everything, and he is prepared to work seven days a week to ensure that this occurs. However, his family also wants to see him from time to time, so he often has to be firmly told to come home. Ray will throw his energies into building up his own company, and this will consume much of his time, leaving precious few hours for leisure. However, Ray has a plan: by working so hard now, he will have more time for himself later in life, when it will be his turn to sit back and smell the roses. When he does relax, Ray prefers more cerebral pursuits like chess rather than physical activity, although he may well have a taste for sailing and other water-based pursuits.

THE RUNIC INTERPRETATION
ᛇᚨᚱ (Eihwaz, Ansuz, Raido)

The Ansuz and Raido runes are potent and invigorating. Ansuz is the rune of signals, which makes Ray intuitive and perceptive. The ability to understand people and communicate clearly will mean that Ray can succeed in any number of careers. The Raido rune emphasizes concise language and purity of thought. Ray loves travel, and Raido gives him the chance to travel throughout his life and to prosper from his many trips.

Elements: Earth/fire, air, water

THE NUMEROLOGICAL INTERPRETATION
Ray (NV = 8, CV = 9, VV = 8, FL = 9)

Ray is less involved with abstract theories and more preoccupied with the practical realities of life. Ray likes to see the tangible proof of his efforts. He is very fond of money and beautiful objects. A sensuous man, he will choose a lover or partner with whom he can enjoy life's pleasures. Ray likes the outdoors and is attracted by sports and physical exercise. When spiritually developed, Ray will find his strong connection to the material plane expresses itself in a very humanitarian way. He will then work to help people financially, creating products and projects that foster material security and well-being in the world.

❧

Raymond

A Kabbalistic Synopsis

ראימונד —RAYMVND (Resh, Aleph, Yod, Mem, Vau, Nun, Daleth)

You won't often see Raymond having a laugh and a joke in the local bar, except perhaps at Christmas or some other special occasion. He is quite a loner, and by choice will spend his weekends out trekking or camping in the countryside with just the sounds of nature for company. Part of this desire for peace and solitude stems from the fact that his work life is usually extremely hectic. He has a very good head for figures, and with his substantial capacity for hard work and his strong ambition, Raymond will probably have a high-powered career, possibly in finance. Raymond will pursue all his goals vigorously. He is a natural competitor and always plays to win—which can be awkward when he's just playing the kids at Monopoly! In most ways, his family life is a happy one. Raymond really appreciates the security and friendliness of a home environment after the harsh world of business.

The Runic Interpretation

ᛞᚾᛟᛗᛇᚨᚱ (Dagaz, Nauthiz, Othila, Mannaz, Eihwaz, Ansuz, Raido)

Raymond has all the good fortune of Ray with the additional runes signifying self, separation, constraint, and breakthrough. Raymond may need to learn patience. Once Raymond stops leading from a sense of self-importance, he learns to surrender his will, edit his responses to others, and become more watchful. Raymond may have had a bad temper as a child, but he mellows with age and experience. He can enjoy a good career in jobs requiring policy-making skills; he could even become a judge, referee, or school superintendent someday.

Elements: Fire, fire, earth/fire, air, earth/fire, air, water

The Numerological Interpretation

Raymond (NV = 9, CV = 22, VV = 5, FL = 9)

A deeply philosophical man, Raymond is very connected to his spiritual beliefs. He draws inspiration from teachers, books, and other sources that serve to support his quest for a deeper initiation into life's mysteries. Raymond is capable of an incredible amount of creative output during his life. He is high-powered and has a lot of energy to share in group projects. Yet he is more of a contributor and organizer than a joiner. This is a charismatic man whose personal magnetism easily attracts other people into his sphere of influence.

DERIVATION: English and French, from Old German roots meaning "counsel protection." Brought to England by the Normans in the eleventh century. Became less popular over the years, but was revived in the middle of the nineteenth century.

PRINCIPAL COLORS: The full gamut of red hues, from pink to rich crimson

GEMSTONES AND PRECIOUS METALS: Rubies, garnets, bloodstones

BOTANICALS: Broom, wormwood, rapeseed

UNIQUE SPELLINGS: Raemond, Raemund, Raimond, Raimund, Ramond, Raymund, Raymunde

RELATED TO: Rae, Rai, Raigh, Raimondo, Raimundo, Ramón†, Ramone, Ray†, Raymondo, Raymundo

DERIVATION: Biblical, of uncertain
meaning, but possibly meaning
"joined" in Hebrew. In the Bible,
the name of the wife of Isaac,
mother of Jacob and Esau.
Commonly used from the
sixteenth century to the
nineteenth century, when it
faded from usage. Became
popular again in the United
States in the 1930s.

PRINCIPAL COLORS: Gold,
orange, the full range of russet
and yellow hues

GEMSTONES AND PRECIOUS
METALS: Topaz, amber, any other
yellow stone

BOTANICALS: Chamomile,
eyebright, sorrel

UNIQUE SPELLINGS: Rebbecca,
Rebeca, Rebecah, Rebecka,
Rebeckah, Rebeka, Rebekah,
Rebekka, Rebekkah

RELATED TO: Becca, Becka,
Beckie, Becky, Reba, Rebbie,
Ree, Reeba, Riva, Rivah, Rivi,
Rivkah, Rivy

Rebecca

A KABBALISTIC SYNOPSIS

ראבאחה —RABAChH (Resh, Aleph, Beth, Aleph, Cheth, Heh)

You'll always be glad you spent some time with Rebecca, for her name adds up to 217. The two hundred refers to the letter Resh, meaning "sun," and sums up Rebecca's general demeanor and manner. Rebecca is like a spring morning: She never seems to be down or to notice any of the negative aspects of life, as she is too busy enjoying all the fun there is to be had. The seventeen in the value of her name refers to the tarot card the Star, which is a symbol of protection and hope. This manifests itself in Rebecca's life and personality in that she is a permanent optimist. In her case, her optimism is usually well founded, since things always seem to turn out fine when she is around. A kabbalistic equivalent of her name is the Hebrew for "food," and Rebecca does indeed love to eat and to cook. Rebecca has a real sweet tooth and is never happier than when making some wickedly decadent dessert; in fact, she may well make a profession out of her culinary skills.

THE RUNIC INTERPRETATION

ᚨᚲᚲᛖᛒᛖᚱ (Ansuz, Kano, Kano, Ehwaz, Berkana, Ehwaz, Raido)

Through the double rune of Kano, or opening, Rebecca finds her success by networking with people. Kano requires seriousness and concentration, and implies a sense of entitlement. Rebecca enjoys working with people and helping them to aid one another and share their ideas. In the past, Rebecca was a cheerful giver; now she is a gracious recipient. In love, Rebecca is no longer willing to settle for a mate she tolerates; she sets her sights on a fabulous catch. In business, Rebecca can keep a straight face when she asks for a whopping raise, for she knows she deserves it. Rebecca could live abroad and use her considerable nurturing instincts to raise a family. She could also help nurture a wonderful new idea and develop it so it assumes a life of its own.

Elements: Air, water, water, air, air/earth, air, water

THE NUMEROLOGICAL INTERPRETATION

Rebecca (NV = 1, CV = 8, VV = 11, FL = 9)

Unique is the best word to describe Rebecca. This is a name that connotes a highly independent woman, a person who appreciates surprises and is often very surprising herself. Rebecca is very drawn to the spiritual side of life, but is not necessarily at home in any of the established orthodox religions. Instead, she may draw her spiritual inspiration from her own contact with the divine force inside of herself. She has a very universal nature and can easily find herself linked to people from all paths and backgrounds.

Regina

A KABBALISTIC SYNOPSIS
ראגינא —RAGYNA (Resh, Aleph, Gimel, Yod, Nun, Aleph)

With a name like Regina, you would expect a personality with at least some connection to royalty. In fact, the only real connection is the fact that Regina, like most members of the aristocracy, can be extremely aloof and haughty. However, in Regina's case, this is not really due to feelings of superiority but is instead her way of coping with feelings of insecurity and inadequacy—feelings that are indicated by the presence of the letter Nun in her name. Luckily, the letter Nun is followed by the letter Aleph, which, among other things, relates to practicality; the meaning of Aleph is suggested by the very earthy and useful "ox." Regina's innate common sense will eventually enable her to see that her self-doubt is unnecessary. Regina loves to travel, but she prefers to travel light. Often she will leave town with only her two feet for transportation.

THE RUNIC INTERPRETATION
ᚨᚾᛁᚷᛖᚱ (Ansuz, Nauthiz, Isa, Gebo, Ehwaz, Raido)

Gebo, the rune of partnership, means Regina is always searching for the ideal mate. Until Regina figures out who she really wants and, more to the point, who she really *is*, she won't recognize him even when the perfect partner comes along. However, the Gebo rune hints that the right one *will* come along. The Isa rune of isolation dictates that Regina learn to be self-reliant and totally independent so that her union can be strong. The Ansuz rune of intuition guides Regina throughout life Ehwaz and Raido point to relocation abroad, and Nauthiz cautions that these transitions will be somewhat constraining in Regina's mind. Regina is blessed with the powers of the four elements in her name.

Elements: Air, fire, earth, water, air, water

THE NUMEROLOGICAL INTERPRETATION
Regina (NV = 9, CV = 3, VV = 6, FL = 9)

A woman of poise and gentle dignity, Regina has a kind word for everyone. She much prefers to give people a great deal of latitude and avoids being judgmental. Regina will volunteer her time to worthy causes, especially where children and family are concerned. She cares about education and is involved in the distribution of information that helps other people's lives. Regina has to be aware of her own idealism, as she sometimes avoids accepting the truth when its reality is too harsh for her sensibilities.

DERIVATION: English, from the Latin word meaning "queen." The name of an early saint, celebrated as a virgin martyr. Commonly used since the Victorian era.

PRINCIPAL COLORS: All the various shades of red and pink

GEMSTONES AND PRECIOUS METALS: Rich bloodstones, rubies

BOTANICALS: Garlic, nettle, white hellebore

UNIQUE SPELLINGS: Ragena, Ragina, Rajeena, Rajena, Rejeena

RELATED TO: Geena, Gena, Gina†, Jeena, Jena, Raina, Regan, Regine, Reina, Reine, Rina

Reginald

A KABBALISTIC SYNOPSIS

ראגינאלד —RAGYNALD (Resh, Aleph, Gimel, Yod, Nun, Aleph, Lamed, Daleth)

Reginald is a deeply judgmental individual, although he would probably refer to himself as discriminating. Reginald always has an opinion about everything, especially if it relates to an aspect of the law. His views are often seen as harsh, but at the same time he is a wonderful and generous friend to those whom he respects and likes. In career terms, Reginald is a deeply determined man, and his commitment to his goals more than makes up for the fact that he is unlikely to excel in any particular field. His ability to persist doggedly at any task is shown by the presence of the letter Tzaddi in the value of his name. The letter Tzaddi means "fish-hook" and refers to Reginald's capacity to hang on through thick and thin.

THE RUNIC INTERPRETATION

ᛞᛚᚨᚾᛁᎶᛖᚺᚱ (Dagaz, Laguz, Ansuz, Nauthiz, Isa, Gebo, Ehwaz, Raido)

Reginald has opportunities and challenges identical to Regina's†. He also has the added rune powers of Laguz (flow) and Dagaz (breakthrough). The Laguz rune offers Reginald flexibility and offsets some of the sense of constraint he may feel because of the Nauthiz rune in his name. Dagaz blesses a life with prosperity and wonderful achievements, and so Reginald will achieve much in politics and various arenas where he is in the public eye, including international affairs or business. Much of Reginald's success hinges on his finding the perfect mate, the pursuit of which could make or break him on an emotional level. Reginald needs a partner who can let him take the bows. Reginald is blessed with the powers of the four elements in his name.

Elements: Fire, water, air, fire, earth, water, air, water

THE NUMEROLOGICAL INTERPRETATION

Reginald (NV = 7, CV = 1, VV = 6, FL = 9)

Reginald can be somewhat aloof and distant. The numbers in this name give a tendency toward intellectual self-absorption, so that Reginald is comfortable only when surrounded by people who think and believe as he does. His way out of this isolation is also found in his name. The vowel value of six opens him up to good relationships with family and brings out the lover in him. A sensitive and patient partner can do wonders to help Reginald express the deep emotions that are also a part of his nature.

Rene

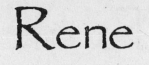

DERIVATION: English and French, from the Late Latin name Renatus, meaning "reborn." Especially popular among seventeenth century Puritans.

PRINCIPAL COLORS: All but the brightest shades of blue

GEMSTONES AND PRECIOUS METALS: Turquoise, emeralds

BOTANICALS: Dog rose, daffodils, vervain

UNIQUE SPELLINGS: Renae, Renay, René

RELATED TO: Renell, Renelle, Renie, Rennie, Renny

ᔕ

"I think, therefore I am."
—RENÉ DESCARTES (PHILOSOPHER)

A KABBALISTIC SYNOPSIS
ראהן —RAHN (Resh, Aleph, Heh, Nun)

The value of Rene's name reduces to fifteen, the number of the Devil card in the tarot, which refers to the pursuit of one's personal pleasures. In Rene's case this may refer to his enjoyment of food and drink. Rene is a gastronome par excellence, and he will happily spend large sums of money on a single meal if it's at the right restaurant. Emotionally Rene is a very generous person who has a great concern for others. He can be quite intuitive at times, and would make an excellent counselor or therapist. Rene likes to relax in style, and will spend as much of the summer as possible lazing on a beach, getting up only to sample more of the local cuisine.

THE RUNIC INTERPRETATION
MᛀMR (Ehwaz, Nauthiz, Ehwaz, Raido)

With the Nauthiz rune of constraint in his name, Rene is accustomed to delays, cancellations, and setbacks. Since Rene travels habitually and could live abroad for extended periods of time, it's easy to see that he is going to need to learn modesty and patience in the face of adversity. The double Ehwaz rune of movement signifies transitions in career, relationships, and upward mobility. The highest lesson that Rene needs to learn is to share the bounty. Raido brings clear communication, and for Rene, self-knowledge and the power to broaden his worldview.

Elements: Air, fire, air, water

THE NUMEROLOGICAL INTERPRETATION
Rene (NV = 6, CV = 5, VV = 1, FL = 9)

Rene is a partnership-oriented man with a strong love of home, family, and an intimate circle of friends. He mixes well in society and is fond of hosting dinners and parties. He may even have an office in the home. A man of many talents and interests, Rene enjoys new challenges and bright opportunities. Rene achieves a comfortable balance in life between his own needs and his relationships with others. He has a way of promoting himself without being self-absorbed.

ᔕ

DERIVATION: English and French, alternate spelling of Rene. From the Late Latin name Renatus, meaning "reborn." Especially popular among seventeenth-century Puritans.

PRINCIPAL COLORS: Pale to deep, rich green hues, also cream

GEMSTONES AND PRECIOUS METALS: Pearls, cat's-eye

BOTANICALS: Chicory, cabbage, melon

UNIQUE SPELLINGS: Renae, Renay, René

RELATED TO: Renata, Renell, Renelle, Renie, Rennie, Renny

Renee

A Kabbalistic Synopsis

ראנאי —RANAY (Resh, Aleph, Nun, Aleph, Yod)

The value of Renee's name reduces to ten, and we can therefore expect her to be a lucky individual. Renee is rarely alone; not only is she a very sociable person who loves to meet with friends, she also depends on an ongoing relationship in her life in order to feel happy and secure. This desire to always have a partner may cause her some problems if she hooks up with the wrong sort. With her natural good fortune, however, it is likely that Renee will find the right lover without too much trouble. Renee is a sensitive soul who needs a lot of emotional support, but it is rewarding to be her friend, as she is always quick to show her appreciation to her loved ones.

The Runic Interpretation

ᛖᛖᚾᛖᚱ (Ehwaz, Ehwaz, Nauthiz, Ehwaz, Raido)

Renee has the same lessons and opportunities as her namesake, Rene†. Yet Renee has no use for gullibility; people sense that she can take care of herself. Renee is attracted to whatever she can do to become self-reliant and responsible. She understands how to manage money and how to seek good counsel. She tries to be tolerant of people who are helpless and dependent, but most of the time they really annoy her. Renee has the power to avert blockages and defeat, and when things do go amiss, Renee bounces back with tremendous resilience. With the triple Ehwaz rune in her name, Renee is more than likely to be intuitive and receptive, and will attract others into her life who will help her grow emotionally and spiritually.

Elements: Air, air, fire, air, water

The Numerological Interpretation

Renee (NV = 11, CV = 5, VV = 6, FL = 9)

Renee is a name that gives a woman a definite flair for the dramatic. She loves adornment and is fond of unusual clothing and mixtures of color. Her home is an extension of herself, and it is usually a lively place, filled with lots of interesting and eclectic objects and people. Renee has to be free. She is not a woman who enjoys habits and routines. Travel is important to her, and she is an avid collector. Renee is at her best when she has a cause to defend, and will work hard to support the right for all people to express their particular beliefs and lifestyles.

Rex

DERIVATION: English, from the Latin *rex*, meaning "king." Most commonly used in the twentieth century.

PRINCIPAL COLORS: White, all shades of green

GEMSTONES AND PRECIOUS METALS: Jade, moonstones

BOTANICALS: Plantain, colewort, willow ash

UNIQUE SPELLINGS: Recks, Reks

RELATED TO: Reginal, Reginaldt

In the absence of any direct equivalent to the letter *x* in the runic alphabet, the runes Sowelu and Kano are used in conjunction.

A Kabbalistic Synopsis
רָאחס —RAChS (Resh, Aleph, Cheth, Samech)

With the name Rex's obvious kingly overtones, we expect Rex to be a pretty imposing figure. In fact, Rex's demeanor *is* usually suitably regal and dignified. As his name reduces to seventeen, the number of protection, Rex will have a safe and secure life. He is exposed to far less trouble and difficulty than most of us, a fact that makes him much more relaxed and laid-back than those of us who have to struggle for everything we get. Rex is a very popular man, and this is partially due to his very protective nature; he always tries to ensure that his friends and family are well looked after. This desire to look after people is indicated by the letter Cheth in his name, which means "fence" or "enclosure" and refers to instincts of self-defense and protection.

The Runic Interpretation
ᛋᚲᛖᚱ (Sowelu and Kano, Ehwaz, Raido)

Rex is a live-and-let-live kind of guy. He is sophisticated and lets people know the boundaries of their relationship with him at the outset. Rex is a clear thinker, and he is articulate as well because he has the Raido rune of communication in his name. With each new experience, Rex realizes that people are really pretty much the same everywhere. Rex is confident and has a light touch with people; they feel comfortable around him because he appears to be unflappable. He isn't really, though. He's easily upset when he spills something on his tie or when his shirts are late from the cleaners. He values good grooming and likes to make a good first impression. Kano, the rune of opening, signifies that Rex will find success, and opportunities come his way to help him achieve his goals.

Elements: Air and water, air, water

The Numerological Interpretation
Rex (NV = 11, CV = 6, VV = 5, FL = 9)

This name indicates a man who is unique in every aspect. Rex has an aesthetic sensibility all his own and is perfectly suited for a career in the media and in the arts. He also does well when working in community service programs where he has the space and the place to express his liberal points of view. This is not the most practical man; he is one who tends to be neither tidy nor particularly given over to the detailed management of his finances. He will rely on a more pragmatic partner for these important facets of life.

DERIVATION: English, a blend of
Rhoda and Rhona. Understood
to be a Welsh name from the roots
rhon, meaning "lance" and *da*,
meaning "good."

PRINCIPAL COLORS: Pale to
medium shades of azure

GEMSTONES AND PRECIOUS
METALS: Emeralds, blue or blue-
green turquoise

BOTANICALS: Violets, apricots,
walnuts

UNIQUE SPELLINGS: Rhondah,
Rhonnda, Rhonndah, Ronda,
Rondah, Ronnda

RELATED TO: Rhoda, Rhona,
Roana, Rona, Roni, Ronni, Ronnie

Rhonda

A KABBALISTIC SYNOPSIS
רענדא —RA'ANDA (Resh, Ayin, Nun, Daleth, Aleph)

Don't annoy this woman, not ever, or you will live to regret it. Rhonda can be surprisingly aggressive. She tends to be quite small physically, but don't let her size fool you; she can reduce grown men to tears with her vicious tongue. Her fiery temperament is suggested by the numerical value of her name, which is 325. The three hundred refers to the letter Shin, which represents the element of fire, while the number twenty-five is the mystical number of Mars, the planet of war and masculine aggression. Undoubtedly Rhonda will be a self-made businesswoman, as she has considerable ambition as well as skill and tenacity; this should guarantee her a good and lengthy career. Rhonda is more than just energy and drive, though; she also has a very tender side, of which only her few close friends will be aware. In addition, when she has a moment to herself she can be quite a daydreamer—just don't ever tell her that you know this about her.

THE RUNIC INTERPRETATION
ᚨᛞᚾᛟᚺᚱ (Ansuz, Dagaz, Nauthiz, Othila, Hagalaz, Raido)

Rhonda is attached to yesterday. The Hagalaz rune of disruption combined with Nauthiz rune for constraint could mean that growing up was difficult for Rhonda and left painful memories. Fortunately Othila, the rune of separation, is at hand to help Rhonda distance herself from her past. Ansuz provides the gifts of intuition and good timing. The Raido rune for journey and good communication provides writing ability and a critical flair that helps Rhonda in her artistic pursuits. The Dagaz rune of breakthrough enhances Rhonda's faith, and she emerges with a peaceful attitude and is able to dream dreams and set attainable goals for her future.

Elements: Air, fire, fire, earth/fire, water, water

THE NUMEROLOGICAL INTERPRETATION
Rhonda (NV = 6, CV = 8, VV = 7, FL = 9)

Rhonda is a romantic woman whose personal relationships take up a great deal of her time and energy. Yet she has to be careful not to build her world around someone else, as that may unbalance her potential to achieve success in her own right. Rhonda has a strong will and a fine, perceptive intelligence. Her emotional nature is her driving force, but when she matures, her passion leads to compassion, and romance comes to be redefined as right human relations. This does not mean that Rhonda will not achieve her romantic goals; it just means that there is more than romance waiting for her in life.

Ricardo

A Kabbalistic Synopsis
ריכאַרדע —RYKARDA'A (Resh, Yod, Kaph, Aleph, Resh, Daleth, Ayin)

This man positively radiates authority and power, and so Ricardo is immediately noticed when he enters a crowded room. His physical presence provides him with the sort of image that enables Ricardo to achieve a level of responsibility and authority within an organization. Ricardo is a highly gifted man intellectually, and thanks to additional influences in his name, he may well take up medicine or possibly law as a profession. Unlike some people in high positions, Ricardo is completely unaffected by his success and treats all those around him with the utmost respect and decency. In his leisure time Ricardo loves to relax by puttering about his home working with bits of wood or on other forms of handiwork. His simple enjoyment of making or renovating something acts as a great stress reliever for him.

The Runic Interpretation
ᛟᛞᚱᚲᛁᚱ (Othila, Dagaz, Raido, Kano, Isa, Raido)

Few people would ever guess that Ricardo could change so radically over the course of his life, but once he is on his own, gaining recognition for his artistic talents, the accolades he receives boost his confidence. The Isa rune of standstill encourages Ricardo to love silence and seek time to read and reflect. Double Raido, the rune of good communication, blesses Ricardo with fabulous verbal skills. Kano, the rune of opening, hints that Ricardo will have some significant lucky breaks in his career. And Ricardo likes getting paid handsomely for doing what he thoroughly enjoys. Othila, the rune of separation, gives Ricardo a certain economy of words and wonderful editing skills. Dagaz for breakthrough indicates that Ricardo emerges from his transition successful and satisfied.

Elements: Earth/fire, fire, water, water, earth, water

The Numerological Interpretation
Ricardo (NV = 5, CV = 7, VV = 7, FL = 9)

Ricardo is aware that life contains a buried treasure, and he is looking for a way to find it. Ricardo is quite intelligent, but he may be very mentally undisciplined at times. He tends to move quickly from one field of study or particular interest to another. Ever seeking to expand and express his potential, he is never satisfied with the status quo, nor should he be. One of his greatest gifts is his lack of complacency; Ricardo is definitely not a lazy man. If Ricardo is consistent in his search, he will find that the buried treasure he seeks lies within himself.

DERIVATION: Spanish and Portuguese form of Richard, which is from the Germanic roots *ric*, meaning "power," and *hard*, meaning "strong." Commonly used in English-speaking countries since the end of the nineteenth century.

PRINCIPAL COLORS: The full spectrum of very pale shades

GEMSTONES AND PRECIOUS METALS: Silver, platinum, diamonds

BOTANICALS: Hazel, oats, parsley

UNIQUE SPELLINGS: Riccardo, Rickardo, Rikardo, Rikkardo

RELATED TO: Dick, Dickie, Dicky, Rich, Richard†, Richardo, Richart, Richie, Rick†, Rickard, Rickey, Rickie, Ricky, Riocard

DERIVATION: English, French, German, and Czech, from the Germanic roots *ríc*, meaning "power," and *hard*, meaning "strong." The name of three kings of England, including Richard I (1157–99), who gained the nickname "Lionheart." Popular in England since the Norman Conquest, and now common in all English-speaking countries.

PRINCIPAL COLORS: The full gamut of yellow, green, and gold hues

GEMSTONES AND PRECIOUS METALS: Moonstones, pearls, cat's-eye

BOTANICALS: Elder, juniper, hops

UNIQUE SPELLINGS: Richerd, Ritchard, Ritcherd, Ritchyrd, Ritshard, Ritsherd

RELATED TO: Dick, Dickie, Dicky, Ricardo†, Rich, Richardo, Richart, Richie, Rick†, Rickard, Rickey, Rickie, Ricky, Riocard

Richard

A KABBALISTIC SYNOPSIS
רידאחיר —RYChARD (Resh, Yod, Cheth, Aleph, Resh, Daleth)

People are often confused by Richard's behavior, as he is something of a contradiction. On the one hand, he is a jolly fellow who loves nothing better than to sit down with a drink and watch his favorite comedy on television. This element of his personality is shown by the existence of two Rs in his name, R being Resh in Hebrew, meaning "sun" and indicating a jovial outlook on life. At the same time, Richard is quite a solitary man who often takes off by himself to think about life and the universe. Many people assume wrongly that such a philosophical person must have a melancholy personality; in fact, most of Richard's musings are of an extremely cheerful nature. The reclusive aspect of this name is hinted at by the fact that the value of Richard reduces to nine, which is the number of the Hermit card in the tarot.

THE RUNIC INTERPRETATION
ᛗᚱᚨᚺᛊᛁᚱ (Dagaz, Raido, Ansuz, Hagalaz, Sowelu, Isa, Raido)

Richard can be a complainer, but he's so lovable that friends overlook his pickiness and try their best to comfort him. He's just a sensitive romantic, and the vicissitudes of modern-day life wear him down at times. The Hagalaz rune of disruption is responsible for Richard's intolerance. Isa, the rune of standstill, counsels rest and moderation, which will help keep Richard from getting cranky. Richard's intuition is good, and he can move up to a better lifestyle, as signified by the Ansuz and Dagaz runes for signals and breakthrough. Richard will bask in the changes he has created and find pleasure and ease in his new life; the Sowelu rune of wholeness assures this. Richard is also blessed with the powers of the four elements in his name.

Elements: Fire, water, air, water, air, earth, water

THE NUMEROLOGICAL INTERPRETATION
Richard (NV = 7, CV = 6, VV = 1, FL = 9)

Complexity of character, an introspective nature, and a need to express beauty are all characteristics contained in this name. Richard is a richly endowed individual, a person filled with intellectual possibilities and an abundance of creative potential. Much of his success depends on his ability to synthesize, to put all of his parts together and integrate the varied facets of himself into a potent whole. The consonant value of six in Richard's name can be most helpful in this respect. It is the number that gives balance, harmony, and the love of a well-designed life.

Rick

DERIVATION: English, pet form of Richard, Frederick, or Derrick. Related to the Old German root meaning "ruler." Not commonly used in Britain, but quite popular in the United States.

PRINCIPAL COLORS: Light gray, the palest shades of any color

GEMSTONES AND PRECIOUS METALS: Silver, diamonds, any very pale stone

BOTANICALS: Hazel, sweet marjoram, sea kale

UNIQUE SPELLINGS: Rihck, Rihk, Rik

RELATED TO: Derek†, Derrick, Dick, Dickie, Dicky, Enrique†, Eric†, Fred†, Frederick†, Ricardo†, Rich, Richard†, Rickey, Ricky

A KABBALISTIC SYNOPSIS
ריך —RYK (Resh, Yod, Kaph)

Rick's biggest problem with money is not getting it but holding on to it. He usually has a reasonably good managerial job, or he may even run his own small business. His name reflects the influence of the letter Kaph, which indicates an attraction to all things practical. In his home life, Rick is very comfortable in a traditional family environment; two kids, a house, and a couple of pets. He usually has the ability to make the rest of his family feel as generally content as himself, and he seems untouched by the stresses that depress others from time to time. There is a strong influence of Jupiter in the name, which goes a long way toward explaining Rick's well-balanced and generally optimistic attitude to life. Rick has quite a forceful character, which makes it very difficult for anyone to resist the influences of his good nature.

THE RUNIC INTERPRETATION
ᚲᚲᛁᚱ (Kano, Kano, Isa, Raido)

Rick has emerged from hard lessons, and he feels good about himself and ready to receive the blessings life has for him. His career takes giant leaps after a time of stagnation. His thinking process becomes clearer, and people remark that he has found true happiness and has a new twinkle in his eyes. Rick is happy thanks to Kano, the rune of opening, appearing twice in his name. Maintaining balance is half the battle in life, and Rick uses the Isa rune to meditate and slow down and regroup. The Raido rune of journey gives Rick a wonderful ability with words, which is useful in his career. Raido also works with Kano to enhance personal relationships. Rick is artistic and sensitive and will go far in his life.

Elements: Water, water, earth, water

THE NUMEROLOGICAL INTERPRETATION
Rick (NV = 5, CV = 5, VV = 9, FL = 9)

Rick is a very flexible man, one who is capable of changing directions at a moment's notice. His name also endows him with a love of variety and the fluidity to take advantage of the many opportunities that come his way. Rick has a very optimistic nature. He can never be down for too long, and can be counted upon to buoy the moods of his friends and loved ones. Yet many of these same characteristics can work to his detriment if he is not focused. Rick's versatility can lead to his becoming a jack of all trades, and his easy adaptability can become a way of avoiding responsibility.

Rita

DERIVATION: English and Scandinavian, originally a pet form of Margarita, a Spanish name meaning "daisy." Used independently since the end of the nineteenth century.

PRINCIPAL COLORS: Pale to deep, rich shades of violet

GEMSTONES AND PRECIOUS METALS: Garnets, amethyst

BOTANICALS: Lungwort, mint

UNIQUE SPELLINGS: Reeta, Reetah, Reita, Reitah, Rheeta, Rheetah

RELATED TO: Margaret†, Margarita†, Marguerite†

❧

"Lead me not into temptation; I can find the way myself."
—RITA MAE BROWN (AUTHOR)

A KABBALISTIC SYNOPSIS
ריטא —RYTA (Resh, Yod, Teth, Aleph)

Rita is chock-full of fire. From the first letter of her name, which is associated with the sun, to the last, associated with Aries, this is a name literally bursting with energy. The value of the name equates Rita with a journey. Given her energy, she is well suited to travel, and this will probably figure in any career she chooses. Rita is a popular and attractive woman. With her confidence, a career in film or television would be ideal. One note of caution, though: T, or Teth, means "serpent," and this manifests itself in Rita as a capacity for sarcasm. Most of the time this does not arise, but like the cobra, once disturbed the serpent will strike—and Rita rarely misses.

THE RUNIC INTERPRETATION
ᚱᛁᛏᚨ (Ansuz, Teiwaz, Isa, Raido)

Having double air elements in her name makes Rita very verbal. The earth element keeps her practical. Ansuz, the rune of intuition, helps Rita to survive some of her more impulsive moves. The Teiwaz warrior energy gives Rita so much courage that she often ventures beyond her safety zone, and yet she still lands on her feet. Isa, the rune of standstill, cautions Rita to rest and keep herself fit for the exciting adventures ahead. Having Raido, the rune of journey, in her name means Rita will communicate her needs effectively and ask for help when she needs it. Rita is an exciting friend to have, but she needs to exercise caution; she has a tendency to feel more vitally alive when her safety is in danger, and she could well become addicted to the adrenaline rush that accompanies her rash actions.

Elements: Air, air, earth, water

THE NUMEROLOGICAL INTERPRETATION
Rita (NV = 3, CV = 11, VV = 1, FL = 9)

Rita is a natural-born dancer. Just watch the way she moves through a room, her feet never seeming to touch the ground! People enjoy her presence and seek her out for all types of social functions. Rita has a way with people and is quite comfortable with unfamiliar faces and large groups. She is very socially oriented and likes to organize people into mutually beneficial plans and projects. Rita's name lacks those numbers that endow a person with practicality, however. She needs to learn how to deal with money and finances as well as the other more pragmatic issues of life.

❧

Rob

A Kabbalistic Synopsis
רעב —RA'AB (Resh, Ayin, Beth)

Rob is a deeply sensitive guy who builds very close bonds with his small circle of friends. If you are in that select group, then you should consider yourself very lucky; Rob is one of the most loyal people you could hope to meet. He does have one problem, though, which is his tendency to rush headlong into new ventures without taking the time to think through the consequences. This is particularly pronounced in the case of those born under the sign of Aries. In his marriage (and it is almost certain that Rob will be married), he is a very affectionate man, although he can also be somewhat staid and may need encouragement in order to keep his relationship interesting.

The Runic Interpretation
ᛒᛟᚱ (Berkana, Othila, Raido)

Rob has a gentle energy; he is the type who may talk to his plants. Blessed by the Berkana rune of growth, Rob is able to nurture living things with his love. He derives keen satisfaction when the fruits of his labor (children, projects, ideas, and flower beds) unfold and blossom in all their glory. Othila, the rune of separation, cautions Rob to weed his garden occasionally and discard worn-out ideas and relationships on a regular basis. As Rob prunes his thinking, he develops a reputation as a controlled and well-meaning gentleman. Rob needs to take time to cultivate his mind because he needs art and beauty as much as oxygen.

Elements: Air/earth, earth/fire, water

The Numerological Interpretation
Rob (NV = 8, CV = 11, VV = 6, FL = 9)

Unless his ambitions get the better of him, Rob is a very balanced individual, a man who has an amazing talent for turning his visions into reality. He is a talented man, one who finds great joy in the achievement of his goals, of which there are many. Rob has highly developed organizational skills, too. He can easily think in categories, and is quite capable of arranging his life and all of its details into neat compartments. Business and financial success are important to him, but he is also very much the romantic and is never without a partner for too long.

DERIVATION: English and Scottish, pet form of Robert, which is from the Germanic roots *hrod*, meaning "fame," and *berht*, meaning "bright." The name of the Scottish outlaw Rob Roy (1671–1734).

PRINCIPAL COLORS: Black, rich, dark shades of azure, violet, and gray

GEMSTONES AND PRECIOUS METALS: Carbuncles, amethyst, black pearls

BOTANICALS: Angelica, shepherd's purse

UNIQUE SPELLINGS: Rahb, Rahbb, Robb

RELATED TO: Bob†, Bobbie, Bobby, Robbie, Robbin, Robbins, Robert†, Roberto†, Robertson, Robin†, Robinson, Roby

PRINCIPAL COLORS: Pale to rich shades of blue

GEMSTONES AND PRECIOUS METALS: Turquoise, emeralds

BOTANICALS: Vervain, dog rose

UNIQUE SPELLINGS: Rahbert, Rahbbert, Robbert, Robbertt, Robertt

RELATED TO: Bert, Bertie, Bob†, Bobby, Riobard, Rob†, Robbie, Robby, Roberto†, Robin†, Robinson, Rupert, Ruperto

∽

"There are those who look at things the way they are, and ask why. I dream of things that never were, and ask why not?"

—ROBERT F. KENNEDY (POLITICIAN)

Robert

A KABBALISTIC SYNOPSIS
רברת —RBRTh (Resh, Beth, Resh, Tau)

Robert is incredibly logical. He has analyzed the world around him from a very early age, and is likely to be noticed as a budding scientist before he even reaches high school. He has a down-to-earth nature, though, which prevents him from coming across as too remote. Indeed, Robert has a great love of the comforts and trappings of home. He would be ideally suited to a career that requires the ability to think quickly and rationally. A Robert born under one of the earth signs, particularly Virgo, is sitting especially pretty with regard to his name, since Virgo is not only associated with affairs of the heart but also with the practical nature of the good scientist. Robert is more than capable of forming emotional attachments, but it will take him a long time to get really intimate with anyone.

THE RUNIC INTERPRETATION
↑RMBⓍR (Teiwaz, Raido, Ehwaz, Berkana, Othila, Raido)

Robert is happy out on the tennis court making his opponent run. Robert has the appealing qualities of Rob, with the addition of the runes Teiwaz (warrior), Raido (journey), and Ehwaz (movement). Robert can be manipulative, but as long as he channels these tendencies into sports he will excel at them. This same drive, perseverance, and ambition can help him in business as well. The Teiwaz rune makes him a fierce and ruthless competitor. Raido, the rune of good communication, helps Robert quickly gain an overview of the game and brilliantly formulate a clear strategy for success. The Raido rune also gives him the ability to think and communicate clearly, and this is reflected in his game. He's good at sales, teaching, or finance.

Elements: Air, water, air, air/earth, earth/fire, water

THE NUMEROLOGICAL INTERPRETATION
Robert (NV = 6, CV = 22, VV = 11, FL = 9)

This is a very common name with a very uncommon numerological content. Both master numbers, eleven and twenty-two, are present in this name. Few Roberts will live up to this significance, but those who are in full possession of the energy of this name will find that their life is geared for great success. This is a person who can command huge enterprises, create wonderful inventions for the world, lead political parties to success, or be a teacher for a hungry humanity. The majority of men named Robert are kind and well-intentioned and share the need for a close family life.

∽

Roberta

A KABBALISTIC SYNOPSIS

רעבאראטא —RA'ABARTA (Resh, Ayin, Beth, Aleph, Resh, Teth, Aleph)

Roberta is an absolute lover of luxury. This is shown by the fact that the value of her name reduces to fifteen, the number of the Devil card in the tarot. In order to discover exactly what form of luxury she most prefers, we can refer to the full value of her name, which is 483, which again reveals that Roberta's interest lies more in material goods than in other indulgences. In addition, the final number of Roberta's name is the number of the Empress in the tarot, which is associated with abundance and fortune. Roberta loves to surround herself with gorgeous and expensive things but is far from greedy; she loves to give things to her close friends as well. Roberta can cope with almost any kind of emotional upset, but is genuinely devastated if she is ever without money. This should not really be a problem for her, though, as she is a very hardworking and determined person who will no doubt be able to provide herself with all the material comforts she enjoys.

THE RUNIC INTERPRETATION

ᚨᛏᚱᛗᛒᛟᚱ (Ansuz, Teiwaz, Raido, Ehwaz, Berkana, Othila, Raido)

Roberta has all the competitive edge that we see in Robert's runic configuration with the addition of Ansuz, the rune of signals. If Roberta chooses to compete, she might like chess or any game involving strategy rather than physical strength. Ansuz is the rune of signals, and Roberta has wonderful insights about people and an uncanny ability to anticipate her opponent's next ten moves. Roberta is always finding significance in seemingly unrelated occurrences. She may have a temper, but if she can channel it into aggressive action, she will be able to learn ways to manage her stress level and feel more in control and in balance.

Elements: Air, air, water, air, air/earth, earth/fire, water

THE NUMEROLOGICAL INTERPRETATION

Roberta (NV = 7, CV = 22, VV = 3, FL = 9)

Roberta is an investigator by nature and does well as a psychologist, scientist, or laboratory researcher. She tends to be honest and direct in her dealings with people, and is attracted neither by the masks people wear nor by frills and glamour. Many people find Roberta hard to understand but her complexity resides in her basic simplicity: She is after truth. Roberta tends to be sincere and faithful in personal relationships. Her close friends and lovers are few, but they are true to Roberta. Her relationships tend to be long-lasting and are deeply meaningful.

DERIVATION: English, feminine form of Robert, which is from the Germanic roots *hrod*, meaning "fame" and *berht*, meaning "bright." First used in the 1870s. Especially popular in the United States in the 1950s.

PRINCIPAL COLORS: Gold tones, the full range of green and yellow hues

GEMSTONES AND PRECIOUS METALS: Moonstones, white pearls

BOTANICALS: Elder, blackberry, linseed

UNIQUE SPELLINGS: Rabertah, Rahberta, Rahbertah, Robberta, Robertah, Robertta

RELATED TO: Berta, Berti, Bertie, Bobbette, Bobbi, Bobbie, Robbi, Robbie, Robena, Robenia, Robertain, Robertena, Robint, Robina, Robyn, Rupetta

DERIVATION: Spanish and Italian
form of Robert, which is from the
Germanic roots *hrod*, meaning
"fame" and *berht*, meaning
"bright."

PRINCIPAL COLORS: Pale shades
of lilac to deep violet

GEMSTONES AND PRECIOUS
METALS: Amethyst, garnets

BOTANICALS: Mint, dandelion,
endive

UNIQUE SPELLINGS: Rahbberto,
Rahberto, Robberto, Robbertto,
Robertto

RELATED TO: Bert, Bertie, Bob†,
Bobbie, Bobby, Riobard, Rob†,
Robbie, Robby, Robert†, Robin†,
Robinson, Rupert, Ruperto

❧

"The moment avoiding failure becomes your motivation, you're down
the path of inactivity. You stumble
only if you're moving."
—ROBERTO GOIZUETA
(BUSINESSPERSON)

Roberto

A KABBALISTIC SYNOPSIS
רעבבארטע —RA'ABARTA'A (Resh, Ayin,
Beth, Aleph, Resh, Teth, Ayin)

Roberto is an entrepreneur par excellence; he can make money on the most unlikely
schemes. His success is due to a combination of absolute dedication to the pursuit of profit
and an innate knack for knowing what other people want. He can be difficult to work with,
though, since he expects everyone else to share his vision and have the same level of commitment he does. Roberto just loves to compete, and he will be an avid sports player and specta-
tor in the small amount of time he allows himself. As for relationships, Roberto is often not
the marrying kind. He likes to live in the fast lane and, as such, has little time for permanent
relationships—but if there is a person out there who shares his drive and zest for a high-speed
lifestyle, he may just give in!

THE RUNIC INTERPRETATION
ᛟᛏᚱᛗᛒᛟᚱ (Othila, Teiwaz, Raido, Ehwaz, Berkana, Othila, Raido)

Roberto has all the advantages of Robert's runic configuration with the addition of the
Othila rune of separation. Roberto is aggressive and manipulative and a fierce opponent who
relishes a challenge. Yet the double Othila rune power gives Roberto a tendency to retreat.
Roberto makes a good sprinter or hit-and-run baseball player. He could also be a stuntman.
He isn't bound by fear, and he is willing to make radical moves to reposition himself. He can
withstand danger and challenges that could make a lesser soul fold. Roberto is happy to be a
nonconformist who is well paid for living an exciting life.

Elements: Earth/fire, air, water, air, air/earth, earth/fire, water

THE NUMEROLOGICAL INTERPRETATION
Roberto (NV = 3, CV = 22, VV = 8, FL = 9)

Roberto has a metaphysical perspective on life. He is fascinated by the process through which
ideas take form. He is an attractive man, one with a very magnetic personality. It is easy for
him to gather together the people and the resources he needs to realize his visions. Roberto is
a very sensuous man, one who enjoys the pleasures of life. The choice of a spiritual direction
will yield wonderful results for him and balance a nature that could otherwise become very
egocentric.

Robin

A Kabbalistic Synopsis
רעבין —RA'ABYN (Resh, Ayin, Beth, Yod, Nun)

If you need someone with brains to help you out of a jam, Robin's your person. In the world of comic books he may have been only a superhero sidekick, but in real life Robin is quite capable of shining in his or her own right. Intelligent and witty, Robin has the capacity to find loopholes in any situation, no matter how intractable it seems, and is consequently an ideal business adviser. Emotionally Robin is looking for someone to share the fun things in life. Robins can be deadly serious in the workplace, but when they get home, they like to relax.

The Runic Interpretation
↑|BⵙR (Nauthiz, Isa, Berkana, Othila, Raido)

Robin has all the assets of the name Rob with the additional energies of Nauthiz for constraint and Isa for standstill. Robin could be a man or woman who loves children but may have none of their own. Robin enjoys plants and animals, too, and will gravitate to environments where people and ideas are free to bloom. Robin is gentle and might have success illustrating children's books or writing TV scripts and songs for kids. Men named Robin will also excel in teaching or the performing arts, because Robins are happiest when they feel close to love and life.

Elements: Fire, earth, air/earth, earth/fire, water

The Numerological Interpretation
Robin (NV = 4, CV = 7, VV = 6, FL = 9)

Robins are very dedicated to their plans and projects. Hardworking and determined, people named Robin will not let up until they have completed their tasks or fulfilled their responsibilities. Robin is a name usually connected with highly creative individuals such as writers, artists, and artisans. Men and women called Robin are quite financially oriented. They have a very strong need for security and may overemphasize the financial aspect of things in their general dealings in life.

DERIVATION: English, originally a pet form of Robert, from Germanic roots meaning "bright fame." By the middle of the twentieth century, often associated with the bird. Both masculine and feminine.

PRINCIPAL COLORS: Gray, azure, the full spectrum of moderately shaded hues

GEMSTONES AND PRECIOUS METALS: Sapphires

BOTANICALS: Celandine, sage

UNIQUE SPELLINGS: Robben, Robbin, Robbyn, Roben, Robyn

RELATED TO: Rob†, Robby, Robert†, Roberto†; Robbi, Robena, Robenia, Roberta†, Robina, Robinette, Robinia

Rod

DERIVATION: English, short form of Roderick, from the German, meaning "renowned ruler." Popular as a nickname, but an uncommon given name.

PRINCIPAL COLORS: The palest to the most brilliant yellow and bronze hues

GEMSTONES AND PRECIOUS METALS: Citrine, amber, yellow diamonds

BOTANICALS: Lavender, borage, eyebright

UNIQUE SPELLINGS: Rahd, Rahdd, Rodd

RELATED TO: Broderick, Roddie, Roddy, Roderich, Roderick†, Rodney†, Rodrigo, Rodrik, Rodrique, Rurik

&

"Once I thought ideas were exceptions not the rule. That is not so. Ideas are so plentiful that they ride by on air. You've only to reach out and snatch one."
—ROD McKUEN (POET)

A KABBALISTIC SYNOPSIS
רעד —RA'AD (Resh, Ayin, Daleth)

Rod has one abiding interest in life: sex. He has a lifestyle that would defeat most people, as he likes to spend his evenings out and about rather than at home in front of the television. Rod is completely turned off by the idea of a regular nine-to-five job and longs for a career with an element of excitement. Rod's ideal job would be working as a circus entertainer, stuntman, or motor car racer, although he may never do any of these crazy things. He has a wide circle of fairly casual friends and is well known for his excesses, which can sometimes be quite outrageous. Not surprisingly Rod gets himself into a number of scrapes, but his natural good luck means that on the whole he is able to extricate himself from any problematic situation without too much difficulty.

THE RUNIC INTERPRETATION
ᛞᛟᚱ (Dagaz, Othila, Raido)

Sometimes it's two steps forward and one step back; that swervy backstep is what makes Rod a success. Thanks to Raido, the runic power of good communication, Rod is goal oriented and headed to the top. Dagaz, the rune of breakthrough, means that life is unpredictable for Rod, and many careers and opportunities will surface that suit Rod's considerable abilities. Dagaz brings transformation and major achievements and prosperity. The important Othila rune of separation is what puts Rod over the top. He uses Othila to become more truly who he is, by taking time to step back and reflect on his desires and by carefully considering what makes life worthwhile for him.

Elements: Fire, earth/fire, water

THE NUMEROLOGICAL INTERPRETATION
Rod (NV = 1, CV = 4, VV = 6, FL = 9)

The name Rod belongs to a strong-willed man, one who takes the initiative in life. Rod enjoys being innovative and setting the pace for others to follow. He likes nothing better than to introduce a new system, investigate a new project, or promote a new idea. Yet he is most comfortable when all of these interests can be integrated into an existing routine or career. Rod likes to have the security of a job, one with long-lasting potential. Although he is definitely his own person, family and the companionship of coworkers or business partners also means a great deal to him.

&

Roderick

DERIVATION: English, from the Germanic roots *hrod*, meaning "fame," and *ríc*, meaning "power." First brought to Britain by settlers from Scandinavia. Made popular by Sir Walter Scott in *The Vision of Don Roderick* (1811).

PRINCIPAL COLORS: White, the full range of green hues

GEMSTONES AND PRECIOUS METALS: Jade, moonstones

BOTANICALS: Chicory, colewort, moonwort

UNIQUE SPELLINGS: Rodderick, Roddrick, Roderic, Roderyck, Roderyk, Rodrick, Rodrik, Rodryck, Rodryk

RELATED TO: Broderick, Brodrick, Rodt, Rodd, Roddie, Roddy, Roderigo, Rodney†, Rodrigo, Rurik

A Kabbalistic Synopsis

רעדאריכ —RA'ADARYK (Resh, Ayin, Daleth, Aleph, Resh, Yod, Kaph)

Roderick absolutely adores tradition and firmly believes in the good old days. This doesn't mean that he refuses to use computers or drive a car, but he probably isn't too keen on television. Roderick's yearning is for old-fashioned values. He is likely to run his own business or possibly own a sizable company, and he will impose his particular management style with great vigor. In the home as in the workplace, Roderick can be stern, but he is also a very loving husband and father. In fact, in the privacy of his own home, he can actually be laid-back. Roderick may earn a considerable amount of money, but he still likes to make things for himself. If he has children, he will get great pleasure out of making them treasures rather than buying them.

The Runic Interpretation

ᚲᚲᛁᚱᛗᛖᛞᛟᚱ (Kano, Kano, Isa, Raido, Ehwaz, Dagaz, Othila, Raido)

Roderick has his eyes on the stars, just like Rod. But Roderick also has the additional runes of Ehwaz (movement), Raido (journey), Isa (standstill), and Kano (opening). Roderick has discovered the hard way that he learns more by listening. He'll prosper and many opportunities will come his way, because he has Ehwaz and Dagaz to bless him from above. Roderick's greatest strength is the double Raido energy of good, clear communication. He makes a living by listening and making sense out of other people's thoughts—and that's not easy.

Elements: Water, water, earth, water, air, fire, earth/fire, water

The Numerological interpretation

Roderick (NV = 11, CV = 9, VV = 2, FL = 9)

Independent and spontaneous, Roderick has a name that indicates a rather surprising person. Roderick avoids a predictable life and is not happy at a career that demands a set schedule and fixed routine. He is a very intuitive man with a profound understanding about people; there is no one that Roderick meets who is a stranger to him. He knows how to befriend nearly everyone and support others. His sensitivity allows him to look below the surface and understand the true nature of another person. A kind man with distinctly humanitarian instincts, Roderick does well in professions that have some form of political or social orientation.

Rodney

DERIVATION: English, originally a surname, probably derived from a place-name. Of uncertain origin, possibly meaning "island near a clearing." Used independently since the eighteenth century, but only popular since the mid-nineteenth century.

PRINCIPAL COLORS: Any red hue, particularly the deep, rich shades

GEMSTONES AND PRECIOUS METALS: Bloodstones, garnets

BOTANICALS: Nettle, rape, onion

UNIQUE SPELLINGS: Roddnee, Roddney, Roddnie, Rodnee, Rodnie

RELATED TO: Rodt, Rodd, Roddie, Roderickt, Rodman

A KABBALISTIC SYNOPSIS
רעדני —RA'ADNY (Resh, Ayin, Daleth, Nun, Yod)

The value of the name Rodney is 334, and the three hundred indicates that Rodney has a fiery temper and is a passionate man—especially given the three that immediately follows it. On its own the three represents a creative personality, and Rodney is likely to excel in at least one area of the visual arts. The four indicates an appreciation of the material comforts in life and lets us know that Rodney intends to make money from his talents. He may well consider a career in design rather than pure artistic expression as a means to provide himself with a livelihood. The reduction of his name's value equates to ten, which is the number of the Wheel of Fortune card and suggests that Rodney is a lucky man. This gives him a better than average chance of being discovered as an artist if he should choose to carve out a career based on his creative ability.

THE RUNIC INTERPRETATION
↑M↑ᛉᛟᚱ (Eihwaz, Ehwaz, Nauthiz, Dagaz, Othila, Raido)

Rodney has Rod's success formula and the benefit of the additional runes signifying Nauthiz for constraint and Eihwaz for defense. Rodney knows that dangerous jobs are moneymakers, and that suits him just fine because he wants to retire early. The Nauthiz rune makes him intolerant of limitations in terms of finance, relationships, or living conditions. Rodney travels first-class, and his lovers benefit from his gourmet tastes. He gives his partners a lot of freedom, but he requires freedom in return. Eihwaz, the rune of defense, offers Rodney courage and nerves of steel, and he has the muscle to avert disaster. It's sometimes frightening to be a passenger in Rodney's car, because he takes risks and assumes everyone loves excitement as much as he does.

Elements: Earth/fire, air, fire, fire, earth/fire, water

THE NUMEROLOGICAL INTERPRETATION
Rodney (NV = 9, CV = 9, VV = 9, FL = 9)

This is a name that totally embodies the energy of the number nine, making Rodney quite sensitive to social oppression. He will structure his life so that he can respond in some humanitarian way to help others. Rodney may write pamphlets about his favorite causes, create documentaries, or express his sympathies through a variety of other channels. As the number nine is so very pronounced, some men named Rodney may express this number as its opposite extreme. In this case, Rodney may be too much of an idealist, an armchair philosopher who makes many comments about the world's ills and does nothing about them in any practical sense.

Roger

A KABBALISTIC SYNOPSIS
רעויר —RA'AYVR (Resh, Ayin, Yod, Vau, Resh)

The water is Roger's first love, and when it comes to relaxing, he really enjoys messing about on a river or ocean. Ultimately Roger would like to buy his own full-size yacht, and he may well end up with a sufficiently good income to purchase one. Prudence or caution is one of Roger's key characteristics. Emotionally, Roger is not a man who needs much in the way of support. He is, on the whole, a self-sufficient fellow. He is, however, extremely sensitive to other people's needs. The whole of Roger's name is contained within the two letter Rs, or Resh in Hebrew. Since the letter Resh is associated with a cheery, jovial outlook on life, there is a hint here that Roger suppresses all his deepest feelings underneath a veneer of false cheer. In reality, he does want someone to share these intimate feelings with him.

THE RUNIC INTERPRETATION
ᚱᛖᚷᛟᚱ (Raido, Ehwaz, Gebo, Othila, Raido)

That handsome devil Roger takes the Othila rune of separation literally. But why can't he stay committed in his relationships, since he has the solemn Gebo rune of partnership in his name? Could it be that partnership doesn't necessarily mean one-and-only-one partnership? The double Raido rune of clear communication means that when the candle flame has dimmed for Roger, he knows how to say "Next!" Roger is a hopeless romantic who heads for the hills when reality sets in. He could, however, stay with one partner longer if he has plenty of breathing space.

Elements: Water, air, water, earth/fire, water

THE NUMEROLOGICAL INTERPRETATION
Roger (NV = 9, CV = 7, VV = 11, FL = 9)

Psychic sensitivity is very pronounced in this name. This doesn't necessarily mean that Roger will have his own 900 number, but it does indicate that Roger will be tempted by psychology or even metaphysics. A generous man with a charitable disposition, Roger is open to volunteering his time and energy for community pursuits. He needs to be able to feel like an active and productive member of society. If he is held back at all, it is by his underestimation of his self-worth and a tendency to think of himself as generally misunderstood.

DERIVATION: English and French, from the Germanic roots *hrod*, meaning "fame," and *gar*, meaning "spear." Brought to Britain by the Normans in the eleventh century. Particularly popular in the United States in the first half of the twentieth century.

PRINCIPAL COLORS: Pink to deep shades of crimson

GEMSTONES AND PRECIOUS METALS: Rubies, garnets

BOTANICALS: Garlic, mustard seed, wormwood

UNIQUE SPELLINGS: Rahger, Rahjer, Rajer, Rodger, Rojer

RELATED TO: Rodge, Rog, Rogerio, Rogers, Rogiero, Ruggerio, Rutger

"It is not the place, nor the condition, but the mind alone that can make anyone happy or miserable."
—ROGER L'ESTRANGE (PHILOSOPHER)

DERIVATION: English and Scottish, from the Old Norse roots *regín*, meaning "decision," and *valdr*, meaning "ruler." Short form of Ronald.

PRINCIPAL COLORS: The full spectrum of both green and white

GEMSTONES AND PRECIOUS METALS: Cat's-eye, moonstones, jade

BOTANICALS: Cabbage, chicory, lettuce, plantain

UNIQUE SPELLINGS: Rahn, Ronn

RELATED TO: Ranald, Ronald†, Ronan, Ronit, Ronnie, Ronny

Ron

A KABBALISTIC SYNOPSIS
רען —RA'AN (Resh, Ayin, Nun)

Having a barbecue? Planning a party? If you are, make sure you have Ron on hand to help you out. Ron really is the life and soul of the party, and will make sure that everyone has a good time. This is shown both by the initial letter of his name, Resh, which is associated with the tarot card the Sun and refers to a bright, optimistic individual, and also by the letter Ayin, which suggests an indulgence in fun and good times. The total value of Ron's name is 320, which can be represented by the two letters Shin and Kaph. Shin is associated with the energy of life itself, but also with judgment and decision making. Kaph means "palm" and is often associated with practical skills. Consequently, we should not be surprised if Ron works as a skilled craftsman or possibly as an engineer of some kind. Certainly he should be able to get the barbecue going without too much trouble! Ron tends to be a big man physically but is not at all aggressive in his manner. In fact, when it comes to relationships, he will be very successful with those women who are looking for a man who can play the part of a big teddy bear. If you are married to Ron, you already know that you have one of the most solid, reliable chaps you could hope for in life.

THE RUNIC INTERPRETATION
ᚾᛟᚱ (Nauthiz, Othila, Raido)

It would take a motion detector to get this guy down the aisle. Ron needs his freedom so much, he travels with an assumed name and rents apartments without a lease. No one knows how Ron has stayed single so long, but it is a matter of sanity for him. Actually he is a likable guy who is tolerant, and he offers his friends their privacy and all the freedom he so desperately requires.

Elements: Fire, earth/fire, water

THE NUMEROLOGICAL INTERPRETATION
Ron (NV = 11, CV = 6, VV = 5, FL = 9)

The combination of numerical influences in this name indicates a very intuitive man, one who experiences life with a penetrating depth and clarity that intrigues people. Ron's nature is very complex, and he may not be easily understood upon first meeting. It takes time to get to know Ron, but it is well worth the effort. Ron is very comfortable when he is out in the world interacting and communicating with as many people as possible. Ron may participate in social activism, engaging in those pursuits and causes that seek to bring about improvements for humanity. He is very idealistic, a man more involved with tomorrow than today. Ron is romantic and home-loving, but not particularly practical. Ron would do well choosing a life partner who enjoys the more financial side to life and is willing to take care of this important facet of the relationship.

Ronald

DERIVATION: English and Scottish, from the Old Norse roots *regin*, meaning "decision," and *valdr*, meaning "ruler." Originally used in northern England and Scotland, now popular throughout the English-speaking world.

PRINCIPAL COLORS: All the various bronze and yellow hues, also gold, orange

GEMSTONES AND PRECIOUS METALS: Citrine, amber

BOTANICALS: Chamomile, eyebright, thyme

UNIQUE SPELLINGS: Rahnald, Ranald

RELATED TO: Reginald†, Ront, Ronney, Ronnie, Ronny, Ronson

A KABBALISTIC SYNOPSIS
רעננולד —RA'ANVLD (Resh, Ayin, Nun, Vau, Lamed, Daleth)

The value of Ronald's name is 360, which is equal to the number of degrees in a circle. Since geometric shapes and symbols are significant in the Kabbalah, we can see this as indicative of a well-rounded personality; the balance of letters in his name reflects the elements fairly equally. Ronald is a very cheerful man who is completely at ease with his emotions; he's quite capable of expressing his feelings. Ronald has a very strong career drive, which is shown by the presence of the letter L, or Lamed, meaning "ox goad." When he is in the workplace you will never see any signs of emotional weakness from Ronald, as he wants to portray himself as an objective and efficient individual.

THE RUNIC INTERPRETATION
ᛞᛚᚨᚾᛟᚱ (Dagaz, Laguz, Ansuz, Nauthiz, Othila, Raido)

Many careers and activities attract warm, gregarious Ronald. He has the Raido rune for good communication in his name, so a career in the fine or performing arts will appeal to Ronald. Then again, the Laguz rune of flow gives him flexibility and a real talent for music or dance and a variety of sports. The Othila rune of separation combined with Nauthiz for constraint means that Ronald can discard extraneous details in his life and will not hesitate to do so; he values his freedom and abhors anything that holds him back. Having Dagaz for breakthrough means that Ronald is free to prosper and opportunities will come his way. Ronald seems to attract money, and will probably have multiple careers in his lifetime because he thrives on work.

Elements: Fire, water, air, fire, earth/fire, water

THE NUMEROLOGICAL INTERPRETATION
Ronald (NV = 1, CV = 3, VV = 7, FL = 9)

Friendly and gregarious, easygoing and direct, Ronald has no problem being successful in society. People are a pathway to his goals, and he knows how to work cooperatively with them. Ronald has to shine as an individual. He wants to be on top and be a prominent figure in whatever career or profession he chooses. Ronald is very keen on self-development. He doesn't believe that just because he occupies a space on this planet he should be instantaneously recognized. He is patient and willing to do the necessary work to earn the place in life that he seeks.

Rosa

A KABBALISTIC SYNOPSIS
רעסא —RA'ASA (Resh, Ayin, Samech, Aleph)

Rosa is an incredibly energetic woman; when she is rushing for an early meeting, she could put a sprinter to shame. Success is very important to Rosa, and people don't often argue with her, especially when she is working toward one of her typically tight deadlines; Rosa is a dangerous woman to annoy when she is busy. Rosa is something of a political radical. Her radicalism may be either to the right or the left; the main thing with Rosa is her desire to be unique. In the case of a Rosa born as a Gemini, this urge toward uniqueness may cause her to behave in almost self-contradictory ways. For the most part, Rosa is an intriguing woman not easily figured out. She is more than usually private when it comes to matters of personal principle.

THE RUNIC INTERPRETATION
ᚨᛋᛟᚱ (Ansuz, Sowelu, Othila, Raido)

Rosa is special. She has the same configuration as the fetching Rose, but will travel less and have more intuitive talents. The Ansuz rune of signals keeps Rosa's nose twitching like a rabbit's. She notices the wind, the flight of the birds, currents in the water, and weather patterns. Rosa also notices license plates and number sequences on street signs and menus. In fact, Rosa wears herself out reading the abundant messages of the universe! The fast track is not for Rosa, as she's on overload just going for a walk. It's good that Rosa is so talented, for freelance work suits her just fine. She anticipates trends in fashion and finance, and makes a good income with her big inner radar screen.

Elements: Air, air, earth/fire, water

THE NUMEROLOGICAL INTERPRETATION
Rosa (NV = 8, CV = 1, VV = 7, FL = 9)

Rosa is an ambitious person who means *business*! In fact, she will probably own a business or, at the very least, aspire to be in that position. Determined, strong-willed, and with plenty of muscle and drive, Rosa is not afraid of obstacles. Nor does she avoid the challenges that come up in life; she is here to prove herself, and is proud of her record of achievements. Rosa is an independent woman, with plenty of practical know-how. If there is a flaw in her character, it can be that she tries too hard and doesn't know when to leave well enough alone.

Rosalie

DERIVATION: French form of the Italian name Rosalia, from the Latin *rosa*, meaning "rose." The name of a twelfth-century saint who became the patron of Palermo. Commonly used since the 1850s.

PRINCIPAL COLORS: Gold, the full range of green and yellow hues

GEMSTONES AND PRECIOUS METALS: Moonstones, pearls, cat's-eye

BOTANICALS: Elder, juniper, blackberry

UNIQUE SPELLINGS: Rosalee, Rosaley, Roselie, Rozalee, Rozaley, Rozalie, Rozelie

RELATED TO: Rasia, Rosa†, Rosalba, Rosaleen, Rosalia, Rosalin, Rosalind, Rosaline, Rosalyne, Rosanna, Rosannah, Roset, Roseanne†, Roselina, Rosella, Rosemary†, Rosetta, Rosette, Rosita, Roslyn, Rozalia, Rozella

A Kabbalistic Synopsis

רעסאלי —RA'ASALY (Resh, Ayin, Samech, Aleph, Lamed, Yod)

Rosalie is a very business-minded woman. She has a slow and steady approach to her career, but will ensure that over time she builds up quite a sizable income. She is also very canny when it comes to looking after the money she has made, and you can be sure that it will all be wisely invested. The value of her name reduces to eleven, which is a number associated with magic and mystery. There is a strong possibility that Rosalie will be interested in the strange and unusual. Her completely offbeat interests engage her as an ideal way to relax after a hard day at the office. Emotionally, Rosalie is intensely loyal to her partner and is not the sort who could happily marry again if the relationship went wrong. However, with her caring and attentive nature, it is unlikely that she need worry about this happening.

The Runic Interpretation

ᛖᛁᛚᚨᛋᛟᚱ (Ehwaz, Isa, Laguz, Ansuz, Sowelu, Othila, Raido)

Rosalie may travel quite a bit, as indicated by the Ehwaz and Raido runes in her name. She has stars in her eyes when she sets out, and she could be in for a rude awakening when she has to forgo the comforts of home or familiar places. Othila, the rune of separation, dictates a time of prolonged homesickness and an almost physical longing for the past. But Rosalie has the wonderful Ansuz and Laguz combination to heighten her creativity and intuition as well as help her envision a better tomorrow. Sowelu, the rune of wholeness, assures Rosalie that all will right itself in the end, and she will have a rich and rewarding life.

Elements: Air, earth, water, air, air, earth/fire, water

The Numerological Interpretation

Rosalie (NV = 7, CV = 4, VV = 3, FL = 9)

The numerological combination in this name points to a person who is very keen on developing additional tools for her creative self-expression. Rosalie is a pragmatist, a woman who is very in touch with her own talents and abilities. She is also a perfectionist, a characteristic that gives her the tendency to be quite critical of herself. Nonetheless, Rosalie is here to make the best out of who she is, and has the willpower to do it. She is especially fond of the right use of language and can be drawn to one of the communications fields. Rosalie is at home anywhere there is the possibility of an intelligent and useful exchange of ideas.

DERIVATION: English, from the
Latin *rosa*, meaning "rose." During
the Middle Ages, a short form
of several names of Germanic
origin with first elements like *hros*,
meaning "horse," or *hrod*, meaning
"fame." Especially popular during
the nineteenth century.

PRINCIPAL COLORS: All the
shades of violet, from pale mauve
to rich, dark purple

GEMSTONES AND PRECIOUS
METALS: Amethyst, garnets

BOTANICALS: Lungwort, mint,
apple, bilberry

UNIQUE SPELLINGS: Rohz, Rows,
Rowz, Roze

RELATED TO: Rasia, Rosa†,
Rosalba, Rosaleen, Rosalia,
Rosaliet, Rosalin, Rosalind,
Rosaline, Rosalyne, Rosanna,
Rosannah, Roseannet, Roselina,
Rosella, Rosemary†, Rosetta,
Rosette, Rosita, Roslyn, Rozalia,
Rozella

Rose

A KABBALISTIC SYNOPSIS
רֹאהס —RA'AHS (Resh, Ayin, Heh, Samech)

Traditionally the name Rose is associated with images of purity and romantic love, though a kabbalistic analysis reveals a far more complex personality. For starters, there are strong suggestions in the name that Rose is a wild-hearted woman who likes to have a really good time. So Rose may decide to wait quite some number of years before settling into a permanent and committed relationship. Another aspect to Rose's nature is that she can tend to feel lonely, although she has many friends and has no reason to feel alone in the world. However, the effect of the letter Lamed in the compression of her name can be to drive Rose away from socializing and into a more solitary lifestyle. Rose's friends must work to persuade her to stay fully engaged in her relationships.

THE RUNIC INTERPRETATION
ᛗᛋᛟᚱ (Ehwaz, Sowelu, Othila, Raido)

Some people just have a lot going for them, and Rose is one of them. She's very attractive, and she sails high above pettiness and gossip. The Othila rune of separation saves her from the slings of jealousy, and she blithely goes her own way, with confidence and quiet ambition. Raido, the rune of good communication, hints that Rose has a good mind under what's probably a fabulous head of hair. Her clear mind is reflected in her speech. Sowelu, the rune of wholeness, protects Rose and keeps her optimistic and self-directed. Ehwaz, the rune of movement, says she could be a wonderful partner on the dance floor.

Elements: Air, air, earth/fire, water

THE NUMEROLOGICAL INTERPRETATION
Rose (NV = 3, CV = 1, VV = 11, FL = 9)

Rose's life path will lead her to the development of new ways of thinking and communicating. Rose is ever on the alert to find those opportunities to use her abundant, active intelligence. Rose is very bright, talkative, and alive. She knows she is a unique individual, and means to prove it through her specialized interests and activities. Sometimes Rose can be too analytical and judgmental. She needs to put her mental faculties in perspective, and know that the mind, which serves to interpret life, is not life itself.

Roseanne

DERIVATION: English, a combination of the name Rose, from the flower, and Anne, from the Hebrew word for "grace." Coined in the eighteenth century.

A Kabbalistic Synopsis

רעהסאן —RA'AHSAN (Resh, Ayin, Heh, Samech, Aleph, Nun)

Roseanne is a very popular woman at work, as she is always ready to give people advice on their personal problems, and the advice is usually well worth having. Very often Roseanne acts as a mediator between people who are having interpersonal difficulties, and it may be that she decides to make a profession out of this skill by becoming a full-time adviser or marriage counselor. Ironically, Roseanne herself can have more than her fair share of emotional difficulties, which usually stem from insecurities about her popularity with others. Roseanne will have a successful and lasting relationship that is fully capable of surviving all the ups and downs.

PRINCIPAL COLORS: Golden brown, orange, the full gamut of brown and yellow hues

GEMSTONES AND PRECIOUS METALS: Amber, topaz

BOTANICALS: Lavender, eyebright, Saint-John's-wort

UNIQUE SPELLINGS: Rosanne, Roseane, Roseann, Roseayn, Rosseane, Rosseann, Rosseayn, Rozane, Rozann, Rozanne, Rozayn

RELATED TO: Ana, Annt, Annat, Annabel, Annabella, Annabelle, Annet, Annelise, Annetta, Annette, Annie, Annika, Anya, Nan, Nana, Nancyt, Nani, Rasia, Rosat, Rosalba, Rosalia, Rosaliet, Rosalin, Rosalind, Rosaline, Rosanna, Rosannah, Roset, Roseanna, Rosehannah, Roselina, Rosemaryt, Rosetta, Rosette, Rosita, Roslyn, Rozaeanna, Rozanna, Rozella

The Runic Interpretation

ᛗᚺᚺᚾᛗᛊᛟᚱ (Ehwaz, Nauthiz, Nauthiz, Ansuz, Ehwaz, Sowelu, Othila, Raido)

Roseanne has all the fabulous attributes of Rose. The additional rune of Ansuz for signals makes her highly intuitive and good at positioning herself socially. The double Ehwaz configuration may allude to many years abroad in a work-related capacity that Roseanne will really enjoy. The double Nauthiz rune of constraint suggests Roseanne will need restraint when dealing with authority figures and opponents. Nauthiz also cautions Roseanne to take time to order her busy life. Roseanne needs to clean her closets and unscramble her busy schedule in order to restore balance in her life and still have time for fun with friends and long walks in sunshine.

Elements: Air, fire, fire, air, air, air, earth/fire, water

The Numerological Interpretation

Roseanne (NV = 1, CV = 2, VV = 8, FL = 9)

The powerful individuality, coupled with ambition and drive, characterizes this name. Roseanne is a woman for whom intimate relationships are very important. In this respect, she is a person with two distinct tendencies. Roseanne seeks cooperation, peace, and harmony not only in her own partnerships but also within the relationships of everyone near to her. She is definitely a matchmaker and a mediator. Yet Roseanne has a very strong ego and needs to be right all the time. Her name value is one, and that's exactly what she wants to be: number one. The integration of her assertive and receptive sides is therefore one of her primary challenges in life.

Rosemary

DERIVATION: English, from the name of the herb, which is from the Latin root *ros marinus*, meaning "sea dew." Coined in the nineteenth century. Also a combination of Rose and Mary. Especially popular in the 1940s and 1950s.

PRINCIPAL COLORS: Pale to medium shades of blue

GEMSTONES AND PRECIOUS METALS: Emeralds, blue and blue-green turquoise

BOTANICALS: Vervain, violets, walnuts

UNIQUE SPELLINGS: Rosemaree, Rosemarey, Rosemari, Rozemarey, Rozmaree, Rozmary

RELATED TO: Maire, Mara, Mari, Mariat, Mariah, Mariannet, Mariet, Maryt, Maura, Miriamt, Moira, Rasia, Romy, Rosat, Rosalba, Rosalia, Rosaliet, Rosalin, Rosalind, Rosaline, Rosanna, Rosannah, Roset, Roseannet, Roselina, Rosemaria, Rosemarie, Rosetta, Rosette, Rosita, Roslyn, Rozella

A KABBALISTIC SYNOPSIS

רעהסמארי —RA'AHSMARY (Resh, Ayin, Heh, Samech, Mem, Aleph, Resh, Yod)

The best way to describe Rosemary is as irrepressible. She always has a happy word for everyone, and even when she is facing difficulties in her own personal life, she will do her best to bring some sunshine to work with her. The benefit to this approach to life is that, in general, it makes people very fond of Rosemary. Whenever she needs a favor or just someone to talk to, there is usually a whole host of people for her, ready to lend a hand. The second half of her name, the "Mary" part, tells us that she is very maternal. Traditionally, this indicates that she will have a very good relationship with children. However, we shouldn't assume that Rosemary will have children of her own. The overall influence of the name Mary is that it makes Rosemary protective and concerned for the fate of children in general. She may, for instance, work as a nanny or a teacher.

THE RUNIC INTERPRETATION

ᛇᚱᚨᛗᛖᛋᛟᚱ (Eihwaz, Raido, Ansuz, Mannaz, Ehwaz, Sowelu, Othila, Raido)

Rosemary is fetching, like Rose, and perceptive, like Rosa. In addition, she has the runes of Mannaz for self, Raido for journey, and Eihwaz for defense. Rosemary will see much of the world, and this travel will no doubt involve her career. Rosemary's gift for witty conversation and her talent for unscrambling her thoughts and those of others is a considerable help in life. Versatile and mature from an unusually early age, Rosemary can assert herself with a calm breezy style and get what she wants most of the time.

Elements: Earth/fire, water, air, air, air, air, earth/fire, water

THE NUMEROLOGICAL INTERPRETATION

Rosemary (NV = 6, CV = 5, VV = 1, FL = 9)

Rosemary is very focused on the development and refinement of her creative skills. She is a woman with a natural attraction to the arts, graphics, and interior design. Rosemary has many interests and is a person who is bored by routine. She needs to express herself openly and freely, and she does so through a wide variety of social and professional contacts. When Rosemary gets upset, it is usually because she feels that she is not living up to her own expectations. She is a perfectionist in relationships, and knows immediately whenever there is an imbalance in her intimate contacts with people.

Ross

A Kabbalistic Synopsis
רעסס —RA'ASS (Resh, Ayin, Samech, Samech)

Ross is, above all, great fun to be with. He is the sort of person who really wants to suck the marrow out of life and ensure that he has really lived and not simply existed. This often leads him to do things that those around him regard as completely mad. Ross will be the first to bungee jump, or go trekking across the desert on his own, or to try out any number of risky and life-threatening activities. Ross is no macho man, though; he has no desire to use his exploits to show off. In fact, Ross comes across as a very modest and unassuming individual. He may be a bit wild in his spare time, but Ross is totally reliable as a friend or as an employee; the S, or Samech, at the end of his name, which means "prop" or "support," lets us know that when people need him, Ross will be there for them.

The Runic Interpretation
ᛋᛋᛟᚱ (Sowelu, Sowelu, Othila, Raido)

Encouraging and kind, Ross stands apart from the crowd. Whether he serves as a minister or crisis counselor, Ross is able to endure the painful side of life and intervene to help people through tragedies. Ross is calm and loving. He works overtime to follow his heart, and he touches many lives with his unselfish devotion to humanity. The double Sowelu rune of wholeness is a most auspicious mark signifying high mindfulness and strength. Othila, the rune of separation, offers Ross the ability to be tenacious for causes he believes in and not be swayed by the crowd. Raido, the rune of journey, gives Ross a simple and modest personality and the ability to communicate clearly and develop an instant rapport with people.

Elements: Air, air, earth/fire, water

The Numerological Interpretation
Ross (NV = 8, CV = 11, VV = 6, FL = 9)

Physical comfort is very important to Ross. He is most likely involved in an industry or a profession that focuses on making life easier and more comfortable. Ross has a special gift for marketing and can formulate innovative marketing strategies for just about anything. Ross cultivates personal friendships, but he also knows that strong relationships are good for business and he is a businessman first. Ross is not a petty person; he pays attention to the big picture and is prepared to put in years, if needed, to see his projects grow.

DERIVATION: Scottish and English, from a Scottish surname. Of uncertain meaning, but possibly from a Gaelic root meaning "headland." Commonly used since the 1840s.

PRINCIPAL COLORS: Black, and dark gray, the deepest shades of azure and violet

GEMSTONES AND PRECIOUS METALS: Sapphires, black diamonds, amethyst

BOTANICALS: Shepherd's purse, marsh mallow, ragwort

UNIQUE SPELLING: Rosse

RELATED TO: Roscoe, Rossell, Roswell

DERIVATION: English and French, the Latin form of a Persian name, meaning "dawn." The name of the Persian wife of Alexander the Great. More common in the United States than in other English-speaking countries.

PRINCIPAL COLORS: The lightest to the brightest shades of yellow or brown, also gold

GEMSTONES AND PRECIOUS METALS: Topaz, yellow diamonds

BOTANICALS: Borage, lavender, thyme

UNIQUE SPELLINGS: Roksane, Roksann, Roksanne, Roxane, Roxann

RELATED TO: Roxana, Roxanna, Roxene, Ruxey, Roxianne, Roxie, Roxine, Roxy

In the absence of any direct equivalent to the letter *x* in the runic alphabet, the runes Sowelu and Kano are used in conjunction.

A KABBALISTIC SYNOPSIS

רעחסאן —RA'AChSAN (Resh, Ayin, Cheth, Samech, Aleph, Nun)

The value of Roxanne's name reduces to twenty, which is the number of the Judgment card in the tarot and is suggestive of someone with discriminating taste and a good head for the law. The central letter in her name is Cheth, meaning "fence" or "enclosure," and it relates to ideas of protection and self-defense. Emotionally Roxanne is a very passionate woman, and if you get involved with her, you had better prepare yourself for a very intense and sometimes stormy relationship. If she really likes you, you may as well forget any thoughts of ever seeing anyone else, since once she sets her heart on something (or someone), she has a knack of making sure that she gets it (or them).

THE RUNIC INTERPRETATION

ᛖᚾᚾᚨᛊᚲᛟᚱ (Ehwaz, Nauthiz, Nauthiz, Ansuz, Sowelu and Kano, Othila, Raido)

Politics and law hold a special interest for Roxanne, who is articulate and persuasive. The double Nauthiz rune of constraint gives her compassion for the troubled. Ehwaz, the rune of movement, gives her opportunities to travel and possibly live in many different places. Sowelu, the rune of wholeness, helps Roxanne maximize her potential, and Kano brings her money and opportunities. Roxanne is unsentimental and has no difficulty casting off negative relationships; the Othila rune of separation accounts for this. Ansuz, the rune of intuition, helps Roxanne know when to press her point and when to let things slide. With Raido, the rune of good communication, appearing in her name, Roxanne makes a mighty opponent and a comforting ally.

Elements: Air, fire, fire, air, air and water, earth/fire, water

THE NUMEROLOGICAL INTERPRETATION

Roxanne (NV = 1, CV = 7, VV = 3, FL = 9)

Roxanne's success comes from her ability to tap into her own power source and, through her various interests and endeavors, radiate her creative urges out into life. The professions that are the most natural for her include teaching, writing, and any branch of computer technology. In her personal life, Roxanne has to be certain that the energy flow between herself and her partner circulates in equal measure between them. She should make sure that she is not giving her love, power, and support to a person who is not emotionally mature enough to receive and return these qualities in kind.

Roy

DERIVATION: Irish and Scottish, from the Gaelic *ruadh*, meaning "red." Especially popular in the United States around 1900.

PRINCIPAL COLORS: Medium shades of any color, electric colors

GEMSTONES AND PRECIOUS METALS: Sapphires

BOTANICALS: Celandine, sage, Iceland moss

UNIQUE SPELLING: Roi

RELATED TO: Elroy, Leroy†, Royal, Royce, Royden, Roydon, Roystan, Royston

A KABBALISTIC SYNOPSIS
רעי —RA'AY (Resh, Ayin, Yod)

Roy loves to have a really good chat—and sometimes there is a problem convincing him that you really do have to leave at some point in the next day or so! This abundantly verbal nature can cause Roy a few problems at work; his stories are usually both interesting and amusing, so once he starts, there is a danger that the entire office will put down their pens and listen to him. Mind you, when he does get down to business, Roy is a quick and efficient worker. He has a keen eye for any opportunities that other people may have missed, and he is certainly a valuable member of any team. Out of work Roy likes to be quite physically active. This is partly thanks to the influence of the letter Ayin in his name, which represents the character of the mountain goat. We should not be surprised, then, if Roy spends his weekends rock climbing. The strong presence of the planet Venus in the energy of his name makes Roy a very loving man, and any partner will never need to remind him to be attentive.

THE RUNIC INTERPRETATION
ᛇᛟᚱ (Eihwaz, Othila, Raido)

Apologies are one thing Roy handles with great finesse, and Roy will need to apologize often. His naturally self-centered nature may occasionally cause ripples of resentment to sweep over those near and dear. But once Roy sees the error of his ways, with some tactful counsel, he truly is sorry. Roy always gets a second chance because he's charming and there's something so delightfully vulnerable about him that people are willing, in the end, to see his best side. The Othila rune of separation means that Roy is different, and he thrives on his uniqueness. Raido, the rune of journey, has blessed Roy with the gift of gab. The Eihwaz rune of defense means that Roy can field criticism and land on his feet every time.

Elements: Earth/fire, earth/fire, water

THE NUMEROLOGICAL INTERPRETATION
Roy (NV = 4, CV = 9, VV = 4, FL = 9)

The numbers in this name indicate a possible interest in those professions that deal with business, politics, economics, and any type of administrative work. Roy is very much involved with bringing order and structure to his environment. He also has a genuine interest in other people's welfare. Roy knows that his and his coworkers' best interests are served when he designs the model or the outer form of any plan or project. Roy likes stability, whether in his financial dealings or in her personal relationships. He is neither a flirt nor a philanderer. When he gives his word or his promise, it is given with sincerity and a real sense of commitment.

Ruben

DERIVATION: Alternate spelling of Reuben. A biblical name, from the Hebrew, meaning "behold a son." In the Bible, the name of one of the twelve sons of Jacob and, therefore, the name of one of the twelve tribes of Israel. Commonly used since the eighteenth century.

PRINCIPAL COLORS: All but the brightest shades of blue

GEMSTONES AND PRECIOUS METALS: Emeralds, turquoise

BOTANICALS: Vervain, dog rose, daffodils

UNIQUE SPELLINGS: Reuban, Reuben, Reubin, Ruban, Rubin

RELATED TO: Reven, Rouvin, Rube

A KABBALISTIC SYNOPSIS
רובן —RVBN (Resh, Vau, Beth, Nun)

There is a positive fate in store for the holder of this name. The value of the name Ruben reduces to seventeen, which indicates that this guy is likely to have a relatively trouble-free life; the number seventeen is a symbol of protection. One suspects that Ruben is aware of his generally lucky prognosis, and Ruben's lack of any real problems has a calming effect on him. He is regarded as an extremely tranquil man. Not only does he have a balanced temperament, but Ruben is also a very wise individual. He has a level of understanding about human nature that would take most people years of experience and psychological training to attain. Ruben tends to know exactly how to handle people whatever their personality type. From a work point of view, this makes him an excellent manager. Clearly, this trait is of great assistance in ensuring that his relationships are trouble-free, too.

THE RUNIC INTERPRETATION
ᚾᛖᛒᚢᚱ (Nauthiz, Ehwaz, Berkana, Uruz, Raido)

Ruben likes to extend himself in a nurturing way to plants, babies, wildlife, and every living creature he encounters. The Nauthiz rune of constraint implies that this lifestyle weighs Ruben down with responsibility, but that's just fine. Berkana, the rune of growth and nurturing, is the cause of all his care and concern. Uruz, the rune of strength, makes Ruben firm and reliable. Raido, the rune of good communication, hints that Ruben has a book lurking inside him.

Elements: Fire, air, air/earth, earth, water

THE NUMEROLOGICAL INTERPRETATION
Ruben (NV = 6, CV = 7, VV = 8, FL = 9)

Ruben may be especially gifted in working with shapes and colors. This gift is not limited to physical objects, as Ruben may also be able to envision the structure of a musical composition, a piece of art, or the patterns of behavior inherent in human relationships. In essence, this name combines an attunement to the abstract with a direct contact to the physical world. This gives Ruben quite a high degree of creative potential. On a slightly more negative note, Ruben may be prone to procrastination, waste, perfectionism, and idealism.

Ruby

DERIVATION: English, from the word for the gemstone, ultimately from the Latin *rubeus*, meaning "red." Coined along with other gemstone names in the nineteenth century. Especially common in the mid-twentieth century.

PRINCIPAL COLORS: Pale bluish purple to deep, rich shades of violet

GEMSTONES AND PRECIOUS METALS: Amethyst, garnets

BOTANICALS: Lungwort, cherry, wheat

UNIQUE SPELLINGS: Roobey, Roobi, Roobie, Rooby, Rubey, Rubi, Rubie

RELATED TO: Rubetta, Rubia, Rubinia

A KABBALISTIC SYNOPSIS
רובי —RVBY (Resh, Vau, Beth, Yod)

Ruby is unusual, unique, popular, and sometimes a little wacky! She has the oddest sense of humor imaginable, and yet she so obviously enjoys finding things funny that people are amused right along with her. Her behavior may sometimes provoke criticism from more stuffy individuals, but there is never any malice in what Ruby does; she simply loves to flout convention. For someone as off-the-wall as Ruby, it may seem surprising to hear that her family is extremely important to her, but it is, and she will love spending holidays with her parents and relatives. In fact, although she would never admit it, Ruby loves to be part of the traditional, and would be quite upset if everyone else decided to throw convention out the window.

THE RUNIC INTERPRETATION
ᛃᛒᚢᚱ (Eihwaz, Berkana, Uruz, Raido)

Ruby is hard to pin down because the minute she falls in love, she bolts like a deer in the headlights. She may even run off to live in remote and exotic enclaves of the world for years at a time! The Berkana rune of growth makes her a nurturer, though, so chances are good Ruby will have a family of her own someday. The Uruz rune of strength gives her the patience and fortitude Ruby will need to put down roots. Eihwaz, the rune of defense, will give Ruby a forthright style and voice of authority. Raido blesses Ruby with good communication skills so she can share stories and tales of her escapist adventures.

Elements: Earth/fire, air/earth, earth, water

THE NUMEROLOGICAL INTERPRETATION
Ruby (NV = 3, CV = 11, VV = 1, FL = 9)

A woman who needs to be out in the world promoting her ideas and causes, Ruby does well in group settings. This is a name that stimulates the mind and sharpens one's communication skills. Ruby has a vivacious personality. She is like a flashing light activating the world around her. An innovator and original thinker, Ruby seems to be always one step ahead of others. Her social vision is broad, and she thinks of herself as being very much in the "now" of things. Ruby is not attracted to relationships that fetter her urge to explore and contribute to life.

Rudolph

A KABBALISTIC SYNOPSIS

רודעלפ —RVDA'AL Ph (Resh, Vau, Daleth, Ayin, Lamed, Peh)

Rudolph's name reduces to fifteen, and consequently we can say that Rudolph is a person who likes the luxuries of life—food, drink, and festivities. Rudolph is likely to be a very creative individual, and the presence of the letter Peh, meaning "mouth," at the end of his name suggests that his main skill lies in self-expression through the written or spoken word. Although he loves to indulge himself, Rudolph has a very strong social conscience and will devote a large chunk of his own free time—and probably his finances—to helping out those who are less well off than himself.

THE RUNIC INTERPRETATION

ᚺᚲᛟᛞᚢᚱ (Hagalaz, Perth, Othila, Dagaz, Uruz, Raido)

Rudolph likes to be thought of as a proper person who behaves in such a fashion that his associates will never ridicule him. Yet the Perth rune of emotional or spiritual transformation means that at some point in time, Rudolph chooses to turn his back on his old ways, in a kind of Othila separation of sorts, and go out on a limb and become someone new. This decision may bring him a degree of notoriety. At one point, Rudolph will incur the disruptions of the Hagalaz rune. Uruz, the rune of strength, is there to guide him through this rough spot. Raido, the rune of good communication, hints that Rudolph might just turn his difficulties into a book or song one day. With Dagaz blessing his name, the resulting song is sure to sell a million copies and make lucky Rudolph rich, and his life a joy to behold.

Elements: Water, water, earth/fire, fire, earth, water

THE NUMEROLOGICAL INTERPRETATION

Rudolph (NV = 4, CV = 4, VV = 9, FL = 9)

Rudolph is concerned with financial stability and economic security. He much prefers a steady income and a career with long-lasting potential to being self-employed. Rudolph likes a predictable life, and he seeks out a partner who is also geared to the accumulation of material comforts. People can rely on Rudolph's words and deeds. Truthful and dependable, honest and concerned, Rudolph makes a very solid citizen, but he is prone to apprehension when things do not go as planned. Rudolph's challenge is to develop faith and flexibility.

Rudy

A Kabbalistic Synopsis
רודי —RVDY (Resh, Vau, Daleth, Yod)

Rudy is a very analytical individual; his name's value reduces to twenty—the number of Judgment in the tarot. It is also the number associated with the letter Vau, which refers to thoughts, and with the element of air and all intellectual processes. While he may be extremely logical when he needs to be, Rudy tends to see the best in people and in situations. If you have a cloud in your life, you can always rely on Rudy to point out the silver lining. Rudy has a real love affair with nature, and is always amazed by its beauty and its ability to manage itself. In his personal relationships Rudy is a particularly warm individual. He couldn't ever be described as incredibly exciting or seriously romantic, but he is genuinely caring and affectionate to the special people in his life.

The Runic Interpretation
ᛇᛞᚢᚱ (Eihwaz, Dagaz, Uruz, Raido)

Rudy has the riches and fame, strength and clarity of personality in common with Rudolph, but the additional Eihwaz rune makes him all the more defensive. Still, Rudy can hold his own with bullies. He knows how to smoothly sidestep disaster. He just makes a suggestion, but the long-lasting cold look in his eye can make a big man shudder. When delays are blocking his path, Rudy knows just how to wait, and he can sense when it's time to proceed. He gets a lot accomplished by being decisive rather than just being busy, and he can stand being inconvenienced when it leads to a good outcome. Rudy always has money because he knows throwing a little money on problems sometimes makes them resolve themselves. Rudy can turn any situation to his advantage.

Elements: Earth/fire, earth, fire, water

The Numerological Interpretation
Rudy (NV = 5, CV = 4, VV = 1, FL = 9)

Rudy likes to reach out and expand his horizons. His name affirms that he has already established a firm base of operations within himself. He is therefore in search of those life experiences that allow him to further widen his established perspective. Rudy is not so much interested in going beyond the bounds of convention; instead, his desire is to challenge his own sense of limitation. He allows himself to take risks in order to experiment with the opportunities of life, but he is not a rebel by nature. Rather, Rudy is an individualist with an open mind.

DERIVATION: Pet form of Rudolph, which is a Latinized form of the Germanic name Hrodwulf, from the roots *hrod*, meaning "fame," and *wulf*, meaning "wolf." Used independently, although more common as a nickname.

PRINCIPAL COLORS: The full spectrum of very lightly shaded hues

GEMSTONES AND PRECIOUS METALS: Diamonds, platinum

BOTANICALS: Hazel, oats, sweet marjoram

UNIQUE SPELLINGS: Roodey, Roodi, Roodie, Roody, Rudey, Rudi, Rudie

RELATED TO: Dolph, Rodolfo, Rodolphe, Rolf, Rolfe, Rudolfo, Rudolpht, Rudolphus

Rufus

DERIVATION: English, from the Latin *rufus*, meaning "red-haired." Commonly used as a given name since the nineteenth century.

PRINCIPAL COLORS: Electric hues

GEMSTONES AND PRECIOUS METALS: Pale to richly hued sapphires

BOTANICALS: Lesser celandine, medlar

UNIQUE SPELLINGS: Ruffis, Ruffous, Ruffus, Rufis, Rufous

RELATED TO: Rufford, Ruford

᳐

In the absence of any direct equivalent to the letter *f* in the Hebrew alphabet, the letter Peh is used. Peh can function as either a hard or a soft letter, and as such, is one of the seven "doubles."

A KABBALISTIC SYNOPSIS
רופוס —RVPhVS (Resh, Vau, Peh, Vau, Samech)

This guy never seems to take a break from talking, and his nonstop patter makes him an ideal salesman or product demonstrator. The central Peh, which refers to his ability to talk with skill and at length, is surrounded by the letter V, or Vau, which refers to thoughts. This arrangement suggests that Rufus tends to talk off the top of his head—and this can get him into trouble. Rufus is the kind of guy who will go out after work to a game or to a bar and not think to let his partner know where he is because he does things so much on the spur of the moment. Ironically, he is an excellent organizer when it comes to the workplace or to helping other people organize their time more effectively; he just needs to listen to his own advice.

THE RUNIC INTERPRETATION
ᛋᚢᚠᚢᚱ (Sowelu, Uruz, Fehu, Uruz, Raido)

Rufus is blessed with positive and supportive runes promising satisfaction and happiness. Still, he knows that he must remain watchful and alert to stay strong; strength is the lesson of the double Uruz rune in his name. Uruz also implies terminations and uncertainty, which means Rufus may need to retreat for a while and reposition himself a few times over the course of his life. Raido, the rune of good communication, helps Rufus be articulate through all these changes. Fehu is there to bless Rufus with an abundance of riches, either spiritual or material. Sowelu, the wonderful rune of wholeness, indicates that Rufus will feel self-confident and motivated to work in any number of careers. Rufus likes to save money, and will never waste it or throw it away carelessly.

Elements: Air, earth, fire, earth, water

THE NUMEROLOGICAL INTERPRETATION
Rufus (NV = 4, CV = 7, VV = 6, FL = 9)

Rufus is easily attracted by philosophical and scientific concepts and ideas. He is a man who wants to understand how things are put together, and is a natural-born analyzer of systems and structures. Rufus has the ability to transform the vague and the abstract into practical and useful ideas. He is therefore very geared to a career as an engineer, technician, mechanic, or scientist. Home and family are very important to Rufus's sense of psychological well-being. He tends to commit to a long-lasting relationship early in life, and he is neither fickle nor insincere in his affections.

᳐

Russ

A Kabbalistic Synopsis
רוסס —RVSS (Resh, Vau, Samech, Samech)

Russ is a complicated guy. He can be very interesting to spend time with, although he can also get quite intense if you choose to discuss a topic about which he has strong feelings. He may not rest until he has successfully converted you to his point of view. Russ is highly intelligent, and could specialize in a whole range of fields. This in itself is sometimes a problem, as the central Vau, which is connected to the tarot card the Lovers, is a sign of difficult choices; it suggests that Russ is not always good at making firm decisions and sticking to them. In the value of his name the number four is central, and along with other elements of his name, this tells us that Rufus likes to do well for himself financially. However, he needs a strong partner to help him make firm decisions about how exactly he is going to set about achieving his goals.

The Runic Interpretation
ᛊᛊᚢᚱ (Sowelu, Sowelu, Uruz, Raido)

Russ is a rugged individualist who can buck the crowd and take off on paths unknown. He would make a perfect cowboy. Russ has the double Sowelu configuration, and he's a lucky devil; he knows that he has to be himself, and he knows who that is. Russ is honest and forthright, but he can also be stubborn and compulsive. He'll fight for a cause and he'll love deeply. Still, if he marries, he'll probably be away from home a lot. Russ needs to work on communicating clearly, and he will be happiest with a partner who can read between the lines. Freedom is Russ's oxygen, and he doesn't know how to slow down and rest; this is indicated by the Raido rune in this name. Uruz, the rune of strength, suggests Russ needs to pay attention to his body to stay at peak performance, which is the level at which Russ feels most at home. Anyone with a double Sowelu in their name should take good care of themselves but not be *too* careful, as they might have a tendency toward hypochondria.

Elements: Air, air, earth, water

The Numerological Interpretation
Russ (NV = 5, CV = 11, VV = 3, FL = 9)

Russ will experience the urge to move beyond the conventional concepts of what a person "should" and "must" do in life. It is highly likely that he left home at a relatively young age, as Russ has a restless nature combined with an inclusive perspective on life. He may find that his original family structure or social background is too limiting for his psychological comfort. Russ is searching for whatever makes life more stimulating, dynamic, and expansive. He is courageous as well as curious.

DERIVATION: English, short form of Russel, which is from an Old French nickname describing someone with red hair or a red face.

PRINCIPAL COLORS: Any color, as long as it is lightly shaded

GEMSTONES AND PRECIOUS METALS: Silver, platinum

BOTANICALS: Hazel, parsley, caraway seeds

UNIQUE SPELLING: Rus

RELATED TO: Roussel, Ruskin, Russel, Russellt, Rusty

A KABBALISTIC SYNOPSIS

רוססאל —RVSSAL (Resh, Vau, Samech, Samech, Aleph, Lamed)

Russell has a perfectly good brain and is highly intelligent, but without the purposeful channeling of his considerable energies, he might find himself devoting the vast majority of his brainpower to thinking about physical pleasures! Still, Russell is a very honest man, and he would never attempt to deceive anyone about his intentions. His honesty is indicated by the final two letters of his name, Aleph and Lamed, which, when combined, form one of the Hebrew equivalents of God. In terms of name analysis, this suggests an individual who is essentially honest and well-meaning in his treatment of others. Russell is a fierce competitor, which makes for a good businessman, especially if he focuses on an area where competition is high; Russell stands a better chance than most of staying the course and making some money.

THE RUNIC INTERPRETATION

ᚱᚢᛊᛇᛖᛚᛚ (Laguz, Laguz, Ehwaz, Sowelu, Sowelu, Uruz, Raido)

Russell has the sharpest of tongues when provoked. He may never show this side of his nature, but when he wants to call it forth, it's quite a shock. The Uruz rune of strength means Russell will undergo a change of direction. Raido, the rune of journey, keeps Russell articulate and expressive during this ordeal. In the end, Russell will use his considerable talents to great avail. The double Laguz energy of flow assures that opportunities come along at a steady rate. The double Sowelu configuration promises Russell wholeness and satisfaction. He will have the opportunity to show the world his vision.

Elements: Water, water, air, air, air, earth, water

THE NUMEROLOGICAL INTERPRETATION

Russell (NV = 7, CV = 8, VV = 8, FL = 9)

Money, social position, and material comforts are very important to Russell. His tests and challenges in life will revolve around the way he expresses his desirous nature. Russell can be very egocentric, and he can misuse his abundant magnetism and charisma in ways that can be quite manipulative. However, if he uses his profound understanding of the material world to bring financial benefits to many, his rewards will be very ample, in terms of both his pocket and his heart. Banking, investing, big industry, and the management end of the entertainment world are all natural outlets for Russell's talents.

Ruth

A Kabbalistic Synopsis
רות —RVTh (Resh, Vau, Tau)

Ruth is a very interesting name. It begins in the warmth of Resh, which means "sun" and suggests a happy, outgoing person who loves company and socializing with her friends. Her name ends in Tau, which has double the value of Resh and is almost its opposite in that it refers to suffering and self-sacrifice. However, this does not necessarily make for a negative influence on Ruth's name. It merely shows us that Ruth is a deeply altruistic woman who can dedicate a significant amount of her time to working for the benefits of others while still having a generally optimistic and cheerful outlook on life. The central letter V or Vau is a hint at a potential moral dilemma for Ruth between her urge to go out and enjoy herself and her sense of duty to those who rely on her for support. In fact, with the amount of energy Ruth puts into other people's lives, she more than deserves her nights out!

The Runic Interpretation
ᚦᚢᚱ (Thurisaz, Uruz, Raido)

Ruth can make almost any calamity into a comedy; she knows how to laugh. Ordinarily Thurisaz, the gateway rune, implies inaction, but here, where it is accompanied by Uruz, the rune of strength, Thurisaz represents growth and progress and hope at the end of the tunnel. Ruth will be tested in her life, and the testing time could go on for years, but growth is possible throughout this process. Ruth emerges as a new woman, strong and confident and sure of herself and her faith. Ruth is in touch with her inner strength and wisdom, and can initiate her own healing. Thurisaz indicates a thorn that can get under your skin and poke at you until you take action—and for Ruth, the thorn is very protective.

Elements: Fire, earth, water

The Numerological Interpretation
Ruth (NV = 4, CV = 1, VV = 3, FL = 9)

Ruth has a sense of personal security that comes from having won a long series of battles she has waged to prove herself in the world. Having achieved this, she now has a realistic grip on what it takes to succeed. If she is too young at this point in her life for the above process to have taken place, this is what awaits her. The results of her struggles will pay off, if she uses her natural determination and persistence. Ruth has a very flexible intellect, one that allows her to speak about anything to anyone. She is a much more serious person than she demonstrates socially; when mixing with others, she tends to be open and eager for friendship.

DERIVATION: Biblical name from the Hebrew, possibly meaning "friend." Often associated with the archaic word *ruth*, meaning "compassion" or "pity," but this word is not related to the name. Most popular in English-speaking countries during the early twentieth century.

PRINCIPAL COLORS: The full spectrum of medium-toned hues

GEMSTONES AND PRECIOUS METALS: Sapphires

BOTANICALS: Celandine, Solomon's seal, medlar

UNIQUE SPELLINGS: Rooth, Roothe, Ruthe

RELATED TO: Ruthann, Ruthanna, Ruthanne, Ruthi, Ruthina, Ruthie, Ruthine, Ruthy

"Our way is not soft grass, it's a mountain path with lots of rocks. But it goes upward, forward, toward the sun."
—RUTH WESTHEIMER (SEX THERAPIST, AUTHOR)

DERIVATION: English, Irish, and Australian, from the Gaelic surname Riain, possibly from the root rí, meaning "king." Used as a first name in the United States since the 1940s.

PRINCIPAL COLORS: Any moderately toned hue, electric colors

GEMSTONES AND PRECIOUS METALS: Sapphires

BOTANICALS: Sage, spinach, Iceland moss

UNIQUE SPELLINGS: Rían, Ryon, Ryun

RELATED TO: Briant, Bryan, Rine, Ryne

A KABBALISTIC SYNOPSIS

ריאן —RYAN (Resh, Yod, Aleph, Nun)

You have to be very careful with Ryan, as he is one of these people who seems to have two totally separate and completely unpredictable personalities. One day he will chat with you about all manner of subjects quite happily and come across as a sensitive, interested, easygoing kind of guy. However, pick a bad day, and Ryan will treat you with almost total contempt, and any questions you may have will be regarded as the most stupid you could possibly ask. This high-strung nature doesn't put people off, though, because Ryan's good days keep people in his life. In addition, Ryan has a deeply passionate nature that people pick up on and are attracted to. Ryan will have no shortage of partners, although he is likely to be very cautious about finally settling down with any one person.

THE RUNIC INTERPRETATION

ᚾᚨᛇᚱ (Nauthiz, Ansuz, Eihwaz, Raido)

Ryan has the power of the four elements blessing his name. Although he doesn't have the rune of wholeness in his name, the elemental configuration of Ryan provides the same balance. Nauthiz, the rune of constraint, teaches him to be cautious and observant and stay his course during times of uncertainty. The Ansuz rune steps up Ryan's intuitive abilities. People come to Ryan for advice because he gives wise counsel. Eihwaz, the rune of defense, keeps Ryan conscientious, and he is able to head off difficulties with ease—although Ryan doesn't like anything to come easy, even love. Raido, the rune of good communication, encourages travel and graces Ryan with keen powers of observation and the ability to hold people's attention with a good story.

Elements: Fire, air, earth/fire, water

THE NUMEROLOGICAL INTERPRETATION

Ryan (NV = 4, CV = 5, VV = 8, FL = 9)

This name reveals a personality that is adaptable. It gives Ryan an easy disposition and an urge to experiment with life in order to acquire new talents and perfect his own innate abilities. But Ryan is neither a gadabout nor a dilettante. He possesses an inner strength and an ambitious drive that are noticed only by those closest to him. Ryan always has a plan and a goal. He may appear to be carefree, but he is not careless. A sensual man with a need for intense, passionate relationships, Ryan is never alone for too long a period of time.

Sabrina

A Kabbalistic Synopsis

סבּרינא —SBRYNA (Samech, Aleph, Beth, Resh, Yod, Nun, Aleph)

This woman brightens up anyone's day. She is an absolute vision of loveliness, inside and out. While there are plenty of attractive people who become vain and focused entirely on their appearance, Sabrina does not have this problem at all. The central letter in her name is R, or Resh, which means "sun," and it indicates that she has a warm and friendly nature. The two threes at the beginning and the end of her name's value refer to the Empress in the tarot and, among other things, an abundance of feminine charms. The compression of her name reveals K, or Kaph, which tells us that Sabrina is also an extremely practical person.

The Runic Interpretation

ᚨᚾᛁᚱᛒᚨᛋ (Ansuz, Nauthiz, Isa, Raido, Berkana, Ansuz, Sowelu)

The double Ansuz rune of intuition means that Sabrina has what it takes to be an internationally known medium. She may crack obscure computer codes, work as a private investigator, or write books on future trends. She has the fortunate rune Sowelu in her name for wholeness. Berkana, the rune of growth, makes Sabrina nurturing and supportive. Raido makes her articulate. The Nauthiz rune of constraint fosters resourcefulness in Sabrina, and she is able to solve mysteries and counsel people on life's most intricate and hidden concerns.

Elements: Air, fire, earth, water, air/earth, air, air

The Numerological Interpretation

Sabrina (NV = 1, CV = 8, VV = 11, FL = 1)

Sabrina is not preoccupied with the petty issues of life and is a woman of firm ambition. She wants to be recognized and leave an imprint on history. Sabrina can accomplish this by having a career in the media or even in politics. This is a unique person with special talents— talents that want to be noticed! Her challenge is to keep her ego in balance. She will require a certain social diplomacy if she is to reach her goals.

DERIVATION: English, from the Latin name for the Severn River in England. In Celtic legend, Sabrina was the illegitimate daughter of a Welsh king and was drowned in the Severn River on the orders of the king's wife. The name has become increasingly common in United States during the late twentieth century.

PRINCIPAL COLORS: Light to very deep shades of yellow and brown, orange and gold

GEMSTONES AND PRECIOUS METALS: Citrine, amber, topaz

BOTANICALS: Borage, chamomile, sorrel

UNIQUE SPELLINGS: Sabbrina, Sabreena, Sabrena, Sabrinah, Sabryna, Sabrynah, Sebrina

RELATED TO: Bina, Brina, Sabbi, Sabby, Sabia, Sabina, Sabine, Sabrinna, Savina, Sebina

DERIVATION: English, originally a pet form of Sarah, which comes from the Hebrew word meaning "princess." Began to be used as an independent given name in the eighteenth century, and was especially popular in the United States during the first half of the twentieth century.

PRINCIPAL COLORS: White, the full range of green hues

GEMSTONES AND PRECIOUS METALS: Moonstones, cat's-eye, pearls

BOTANICALS: Colewort, chicory, plantain

UNIQUE SPELLINGS: Saidee, Saydee

RELATED TO: Mercedes†, Sada, Sadah, Sadelle, Sally†, Sarah†, Sydell, Sydella, Sydelle

A KABBALISTIC SYNOPSIS
סאידי —SAYDY (Samech, Aleph, Yod, Daleth, Yod)

If Sadie doesn't have a job as an anchorperson on television or as an actress, it will be a waste. The compression of her name produces the letters Peh and Heh. In addition, the value of her name is equivalent to the full Hebrew spelling of the letter Peh, which means "mouth." In other words, Sadie's name is very much tied up with the ideas of speaking and performing, and the presence of the letter Heh in the name's compression suggests an enjoyment of performing in public. In the full spelling of this name the letter Yod appears twice; Yod represents the element of fire in its purest or most potent form, and consequently we know that Sadie has vast amounts of drive and energy. Sadie has the ability to achieve any goal or ambition she sets her heart on.

THE RUNIC INTERPRETATION
ᛗᛁᛞᚨᛋ (Ehwaz, Isa, Dagaz, Ansuz, Sowelu)

Clever, intelligent, and logical, Sadie is naturally intuitive as well, thanks to the Ansuz rune. Dagaz, the rune of breakthrough, blesses Sadie with money and influence. But Sadie has to learn not to be too trusting. Sadie can hold her own in an argument, and knows just when to bring her point home in order to win the sympathy of her audience. The Sowelu rune of wholeness gives Sadie a lot of luck in love. Her life is rewarding, and people respond to Sadie's warmth and kindness.

Elements: Air, earth, fire, air, air

THE NUMEROLOGICAL INTERPRETATION
Sadie (NV = 1, CV = 9, VV = 1, FL = 1)

Highly competitive, with a resolute and determined nature, Sadie sets out in life to prove herself—and she does! She is more concerned with opening new doors than following a path that has already been laid out. Innovative and unique, Sadie has an eye for new opportunities, and is much more suited to being self-employed than to working for others. She requires a partner that can be very supportive of her independence and particular creative talents, and he should be an individual who is far more domesticated than she is.

Sally

A KABBALISTIC SYNOPSIS

סאללי —SALLY (Samech, Aleph, Lamed, Lamed, Yod)

If you know a Sally, then put a day aside next week and take her out for a special treat, because if anyone deserves a little spoiling, Sally does. The letter L, or Lamed, means "ox goad," and this letter appears twice in Sally's name. The Lamed not only indicates a high level of determination and commitment but often suggests that the person has a stronger than average sense of duty or obligation. In Sally's case, we have someone who devotes most of her free time to friends and family. Mind you, Sally still has plenty of her own interests. She is far from being a passive woman, and she will usually achieve a good level of responsibility in her career. She also will have a strong and lasting partnership with her lover.

THE RUNIC INTERPRETATION

ᛇᛚᛚᚨᛋ (Eihwaz, Laguz, Laguz, Ansuz, Sowelu)

Sally possesses a fertile mind that is always busy. The double Laguz rune of flow makes Sally unusually inventive, creative, and flexible. Sally is not one to tolerate unpleasantness for long, and with the Eihwaz rune of defense in her name, she won't have to. Eihwaz helps her finesse difficult situations. In addition, Sally has the Ansuz rune of intuition to help her tune in to brilliant strategies and unusual approaches to problem solving. Sally can make you laugh and fall in love with her—and that's all part of her plan. But it's best not to give your heart to Sally unless you're a bit of a magician yourself!

Elements: Earth/fire, water, water, air, air

THE NUMEROLOGICAL INTERPRETATION

Sally (NV = 6, CV = 7, VV = 8, FL = 1)

Sally is a very caring woman. It is important to her that people be well nourished and looked after properly. In this respect, Sally will spend a great deal of her time in intimate surroundings bonding with her friends and loved ones. Her career is also important to her, as Sally enjoys the niceties of life. If she has to make a choice, however, she will choose family over independence, love over ambition, and commitment over too much personal freedom.

DERIVATION: English, originally a pet form of Sarah, a Hebrew name meaning "princess." Popular as an independent name during both the eighteenth century and the twentieth century.

PRINCIPAL COLORS: Pale and moderate shades of blue

GEMSTONES AND PRECIOUS METALS: Turquoise, emeralds

BOTANICALS: Vervain, dog rose, apricots

UNIQUE SPELLINGS: Sali, Sallee, Salley, Salli, Sallie, Saly

RELATED TO: Salianne, Salla, Salletta, Sallette, Sallyann, Sara, Sarah

"I'm Sally, and I'm going to be a star."
— TALLY ATWATER IN *UP CLOSE AND PERSONAL* (1996)

Salvatore

DERIVATION: Italian, from the Latin word *salvator*, meaning "savior." Common in southern Italy, and was especially popular in the United States during the mid-twentieth century.

PRINCIPAL COLORS: The full spectrum of very pale hues

GEMSTONES AND PRECIOUS METALS: Diamonds, silver, any stone that sparkles

BOTANICALS: Hazel, oats, sweet marjoram

UNIQUE SPELLINGS: Salvador, Salvadore, Salvator, Salvedor, Salvedore, Salvetor, Salvetore, Salvidor, Salvidore, Salvitor, Salvitore

RELATED TO: Sal, Sauveur, Sauvuer, Xavier, Zavier

A KABBALISTIC SYNOPSIS

סאלואטער —SALVATA'AR (Samech, Aleph, Lamed, Vau, Aleph, Teth, Ayin, Resh)

The value of Salvatore's name is 376, which immediately tells us that we are dealing with an impressive individual. One Hebrew equivalent of his name is "dominator," and so we can expect to see Salvatore in positions of power and responsibility. The presence of the letter Ayin, along with influences of the astrological sign Capricorn in his name, suggest that a career in business is more likely for Salvatore than politics or law. Salvatore will pursue his career with absolute ambition, and nobody will be able to stand in the way of his upward progression. However, another Hebrew equivalent of the value of his name is "peace," and Salvatore is not the type to promote himself at the expense of another. His rise will be the result of genuine hard work and ability, rather than due to any office politicking. Emotionally, Salvatore is a very supportive man. He is excellent with children, and has the ability to tap into his own "inner child" when he plays with them.

THE RUNIC INTERPRETATION

ᛗᚱᛟᛏᚨᚠᛚᚨᛊ (Ehwaz, Raido, Othila, Teiwaz, Ansuz, Fehu, Laguz, Ansuz, Sowelu)

As with all complex personalities, Salvatore has his share of rich resources. On the one hand, he loves to live abroad and recount tales of his adventures to anyone he meets. On the other hand, Salvatore is capable of being alone and restricts his circle of intimate friends to those people who are positive and optimistic. He has an analytical mind that can create unique solutions to problems using numbers and research. Salvatore could enjoy being an inventor, a troubleshooter, or a scientific researcher. He could also find satisfaction as an electrician or in other fields related to general contracting. Salvatore is good with languages, and he can create an easy rapport with strangers. The Teiwaz warrior rune gives him courage and energy, and he has a vitality that many envy. His temper is quick to ignite, but as Salvatore matures, he learns to take deep breaths and carefully consider what he says before speaking. This is one example of how Salvatore achieves a sense of balance and wholeness in his life. He is considered by many to be a confident, compassionate, and energetic gentleman. The Sowelu rune of wholeness indicates that Salvatore unites the various aspects of his personality into a focused and productive demeanor.

Elements: Air, water, earth/fire, air, air, fire, water, air, air

THE NUMEROLOGICAL INTERPRETATION

Salvatore (NV = 5, CV = 1, VV = 4, FL = 1)

Salvatore does not like to feel that he is hemmed in or tied down. He has a very adventurous nature, and he seeks to explore life to its fullest. At the same time, he needs the personal security that comes from a firm financial footing. He can thus fluctuate between working for stability and rebelling against the commitments that such a solid foundation requires. Salvatore is best suited for a career that allows him to travel and takes him away periodically from home and office. He needs to acquire patience both with himself and with life in general.

Samantha

A KABBALISTIC SYNOPSIS

אתנאמסס —SAMANThA (Samech, Aleph, Mem, Aleph, Nun, Tau, Aleph)

From looking at the Hebrew presentation of this name, the letter Aleph obviously dominates Samantha's entire personality. The letter Aleph relates to thoughts and ideas, and suggests that Samantha is forever coming up with new concepts in the workplace. She will be best suited to a role in a creative environment where Samantha can really let her mind wander freely. Samantha has an infectious enthusiasm that often persuades other people to give her ideas more serious consideration. Emotionally, Samantha is less confident; there is a strong influence of Scorpio in her name, which can make her somewhat melancholic as well as quite secretive about her real feelings. This need not be a problem, as anyone who is interested in her and willing to listen to her properly will soon win her trust. Once in a relationship, Samantha is a very affectionate and loving partner, which is suggested in part by the letter Th, or Tau, in her name.

THE RUNIC INTERPRETATION

ᚨᚦᚾᚨᛗᚨᛊ (Ansuz, Thurisaz, Nauthiz, Ansuz, Mannaz, Ansuz, Sowelu)

While other girls are thinking about what to buy at the mall, Samantha is likely to be fretting about global warming and concerns related to humanity's survival. The triple Ansuz configuration of signals means Samantha has invisible antennae that sense trends for the future; however, the Nauthiz rune of constraint keeps her from expressing some of her best insights. Once Mannaz, the rune of self, teaches Samantha to surrender her prideful nature, she is more willing to take risks and share her intuition for the benefit of humanity. Opportunities occur that increase her realm of influence, as indicated by the Thurisaz rune in her name. As more people listen to her, Samantha feels deeply validated. The Sowelu rune promises that Samantha will feel productive, generous, and whole.

Elements: Air, fire, fire, air, air, air, air

THE NUMEROLOGICAL INTERPRETATION

Samantha (NV = 5, CV = 2, VV = 3, FL = 1)

Samantha is naturally geared to connecting with others as well as forging new relationships between people. Therefore, she is gifted in social situations and quite receptive to other people's needs. She has an instinct for being able to see the relationship between cause and effect. This helps her understand how to resolve conflicts. Samantha does well in life in a position that requires her to be a mediator, agent, or go-between.

DERIVATION: English, probably the feminine form of Samuel, a Hebrew name meaning "told by God" or "name of God." Originally most common in the southern states of America. Has increased dramatically in popularity in English-speaking countries from the 1960s onward.

PRINCIPAL COLORS: The lightest shades of any color, especially pale gray

GEMSTONES AND PRECIOUS METALS: Diamonds, silver, platinum

BOTANICALS: Marjoram, parsley, parsnips

UNIQUE SPELLINGS: Samentha, Sammantha, Semanntha, Semanta, Simantha, Simmantha, Symanntha, Symantha

RELATED TO: Samala, Samara, Samella, Sammi, Samuela

Samuel

DERIVATION: Biblical, from the Hebrew name Shemuel, meaning "told by God" or "name of God." As told in the Old Testament, Samuel was a prophet of the eleventh century B.C.E. who anointed both Saul and David as kings. The name was especially popular among the Puritans.

PRINCIPAL COLORS: Black, dark gray, the deepest shades of blue and purple

GEMSTONES AND PRECIOUS METALS: Amethyst, carbuncles, any other dark stone

BOTANICALS: Shepherd's purse, ragwort, pilewort

UNIQUE SPELLINGS: Sammuel, Samuell, Samyul, Samyull

RELATED TO: Sam, Sammy, Samuele, Samuello, Shem

A KABBALISTIC SYNOPSIS
סאמואל —SAMVAL (Samech, Aleph, Mem, Vau, Aleph, Lamed)

Samuel is a very earnest man with deeply held principles and beliefs. It is likely that one of his main concerns will be the environment, and he may even make a career out of his willingness to take action against what he perceives to be wrong and unjust in the world. Samuel has quite an imposing and authoritative manner, which can make other people somewhat wary of him. Most of the time, however, Samuel is a pussycat with his friends and family—though he *is* an absolute tiger when it comes to championing his particular causes. One equivalent of his name is "he shall smite," and anyone planning to oppose Samuel should take heed of this phrase before they decide to challenge him.

THE RUNIC INTERPRETATION
ᛚᛖᚢᛘᚨᛋ (Laguz, Ehwaz, Uruz, Mannaz, Ansuz, Sowelu)

Baby Samuel comes into the world to welcoming arms. His early childhood nurturing is probably responsible for Samuel's good mental health. This is indicated by the Sowelu rune for wholeness in his name. As he matures, his many-faceted emotions give him a wide range of friends and much success in the arts. The Laguz rune of flow indicates a strong, flexible mind, one that is moved deeply by the logic and mystery of music. Ansuz, the rune of signals, makes Samuel aware of cadences and sequences in his life. Uruz, the rune of strength, portends a heartrending journey through the dark side of life. Samuel emerges, shaken, but all the wiser. Once the Ehwaz energy of movement arrives, Samuel will kick up his heels and act daring, bold, and reckless on his vacations. He may even decide to live and love abroad for a while.

Elements: Water, air, earth, air, air, air

THE NUMEROLOGICAL INTERPRETATION
Samuel (NV = 8, CV = 8, VV = 9, FL = 1)

Samuel is a natural for a career in the business world. He has the ability to concentrate on creating investment possibilities. He will find that life will bring him opportunities to market objects and services to the general public. Samuel knows how to structure other people's resources, and how to integrate his own talents and abilities within a larger group situation. His challenge in life will be to realize that the physical world is but one facet of a larger reality, one that requires he also develop his emotional sensibilities.

Sandra

DERIVATION: English, the short form of Alessandra, which is the Italian version of Alexandra. First used in the United States during the first half of the twentieth century, and was especially popular during the 1950s.

PRINCIPAL COLORS: The full range of purple shades, including mauve and rich violet

GEMSTONES AND PRECIOUS METALS: Amethyst, garnets

BOTANICALS: Barberry, mint, lungwort

UNIQUE SPELLINGS: Sandrah, Sanndra

RELATED TO: Alessandra, Alexandra†, Kendra†, Sahndra, Sandi, Sandrea, Sandria, Sandrina, Sandy†, Saundra, Sohndra, Sondra, Zandra

A KABBALISTIC SYNOPSIS

סאנדרא —SANDRA (Samech, Aleph, Nun, Daleth, Resh, Aleph)

If you like to bet occasionally, Sandra is a good person to know. Her name reduces to ten, which is the number of the tarot card the Wheel of Fortune, and it relates to general good luck—particularly in situations where the outcome is due to fate rather than action. Sandra herself is unlikely to be a gambling woman. Her name in Hebrew is equivalent to the word for "worship," so we can expect her to be a fairly religious individual. Mind you, this doesn't mean that Sandra doesn't know how to cut loose. Sandra has quite a fiery temperament, and she loves all sorts of sports, especially when she has a good chance of winning. If Sandra is born under Aries, she will enjoy all games in general and have a very fun outlook on life. Sandra is a thoughtful woman, and will ensure that she is spending enough time on her important relationships. Her loved ones are very lucky to have her.

THE RUNIC INTERPRETATION

ᚨᚱᛞᚾᚨᛋ (Ansuz, Raido, Dagaz, Nauthiz, Ansuz, Sowelu)

Sandra can seem a bit frivolous to the unobservant. But in reality, her sometimes scatter-brained demeanor is a ruse to cover up her ambitious and calculating nature. Sandra has a double Ansuz rune configuration in her name; she may not do things logically, but she'll land on her feet every time because her intuition is reliable. Nauthiz, the rune of constraint, has been a hard taskmaster, and Sandra has learned to look out for herself, no matter what. The Raido rune of travel and good communication means Sandra effectively networks wherever she goes in order to promote her abilities. Dagaz promises at least one walk on the dark side for Sandra, who will show real compassion for human suffering, having had a taste of it herself. Sandra vowed long ago to improve her life, and with Sowelu, the rune of wholeness, figuring prominently in her name, she is likely to get her wish.

Elements: Air, water, fire, fire, air, air

THE NUMEROLOGICAL INTERPRETATION

Sandra (NV = 3, CV = 1, VV = 2, FL = 1)

This is a woman who combines her need to be strongly assertive with a need to create inter-personal harmony. Sandra has a distinct sense about who she is and what she needs, and she is not shy about expressing herself. Yet this is not the name of an egotistical person. Rather, it tells us that Sandra has a keen interest in fostering harmony with her friends, associates, and loved ones. Balance is the key to her success in life, and Sandra's name gives her a natural instinct for moderation and sharing.

Sandy

A Kabbalstic Synopsis
סאנדי —SANDY (Samech, Aleph, Nun, Daleth, Yod)

Sandy is a name that can be held by either a man or a woman, but in this case, there is very little difference between genders in terms of the name's chief characteristics. If Sandy is a woman, the tomboy in her will pop up all her life. She loves to get dirty and throw female convention to the wind. In the case of a man with the name Sandy, the central presence of the letter Nun will make him far more emotionally sensitive than the average guy— even though he is still likely to spend two-thirds of his day under the hood of a car! Although Sandy loves to tinker with machinery, he or she has a great respect for education, and will make sure that whatever skills he or she has are properly honed and specialized through training—a fact that also reflects Sandy's tendency toward perfectionism. When not working, Sandy likes to be out on the town and is always the first to crack a joke or pull a stunt, thanks to a love of humor in all its forms.

The Runic Interpretation
ᛇᛞᚾᚨᛊ (Eihwaz, Dagaz, Nauthiz, Ansuz, Sowelu)

Tactful and gracious, Sandy, male or female, could work in politics or in any administrative position that requires patience, diplomacy, and a healthy tolerance of hypocrisy. Nauthiz, the rune of constraint, shows that Sandy is resourceful and disinclined to take no for an answer. Sandy's generous to a fault and responsive to compliments and kindness. One wonders why anyone would ever want to hurt Sandy, but the Dagaz rune of breakthroughs explains that someone does, and this experience leaves its painful marks on Sandy's heart. Fortunately, the Eihwaz rune of defense helps her or him set boundaries, and Sandy emerges from the soulful journey wiser for the experience. The Ansuz rune of intuition helps Sandy find his or her way, and Sowelu, the rune of wholeness, promises triumph in the end.

Elements: Earth/fire, fire, fire, air, air

The Numerologial Interpretation
Sandy (NV = 9, CV = 1, VV = 8, FL = 1)

Sandy can easily find him or herself in the role of a teacher. Sandys have a tremendous interest in communicating. Their own interests will take them into studies that are philosophical and metaphysical in nature. Sandy doesn't avoid challenges, whether personal or social. Sandy confronts a problem head-on, and then looks for the inner reason for the discord. Sandy is not out for personal victory but is more concerned with finding a resolution that can be of benefit to all. Sandy will have to be careful that idealism doesn't overcome practicality.

Santiago

DERIVATION: Spanish, from the root name Iago, an early form of James. This name is often given to invoke the guidance and protection of Saint James, the patron saint of Spain.

PRINCIPAL COLORS: Very light shades of any color

GEMSTONES AND PRECIOUS METALS: Diamonds, platinum

BOTANICALS: Oats, parsley, sea kale

UNIQUE SPELLINGS: Sanntiago, Santeago, Santiaggo, Santiagoe, Santieago, Santyago, Santyagoe

RELATED TO: Diego, Diogo, Iago, Jago, Jamest, Santos

A KABBALISTIC SYNOPSIS

סאנטיאעגע —SANTYA'AGA'A (Samech, Aleph, Nun, Teth, Yod, Ayin, Gimel, Ayin)

Santiago's name is split into two definite sections—one that represents his personal and emotional life, and another that refers to the way he operates in terms of his career. This fact in itself tells us about his nature, in that it suggests Santiago likes to organize his life into separate little chunks. It is unlikely that he will socialize at work; instead he will have a separate group of friends outside work. Santiago is a very jealous man, which is shown by the letter Teth, meaning "serpent," in his name, and this jealousy makes him very passionate and possessive. It is comes from insecurity and may be reduced if he is born under the sign of Leo or if he has a very reassuring and understanding partner. The two Ayins in his name indicate a real head for business and a driving ambition. At the office, Santiago will stop at nothing to make sure that he has a successful and highly profitable career.

THE RUNIC INTERPRETATION

ᛟᚷᚨᛁᛏᚾᚨᛊ (Othila, Gebo, Ansuz, Isa, Teiwaz, Nauthiz, Ansuz, Sowelu)

The rune Sowelu in this name indicates Santiago is a whole person, and as such, he will make a fine mate. Gebo, the rune of partnership, foretells that indeed he will find his true love, and double Ansuz, the rune of intuition, helps him select just the right person. With a ring on his finger, Santiago no longer needs to weather the tides of fate alone. Nauthiz, the rune of constraint, has some heavy lessons concerning limitations and obstacles in store for Santiago. Othila, the rune of separation, tells us that Santiago has the resiliency to bounce back from disappointments and discard limitations. Isa, the rune of standstill, makes Santiago inclined to go within to seek his answers. The Teiwaz energy explains that Santiago has the courage and stamina to maintain a relationship for life and prosper in love.

Elements: Earth/fire, water, air, earth, air, fire, air, air

THE NUMEROLOGICAL INTERPRETATION

Santiago (NV = 5, CV = 6, VV = 8, FL = 1)

Santiago's spiritual orientation is very important to him. One of the most obvious gifts of this name is the ability to harmonize the practical necessities of life with a more profound reason for living, and Santiago will be drawn to a path that helps him keep this integration intact. He is also artistically inclined, and works hard to refine his creative skills and talents. A man of strong emotional sensibilities, Santiago holds his lover or life partner very dear. He has an easy rapport with children and young people in general, and makes a fine teacher, sports coach, or counselor.

DERIVATION: Hebrew, meaning "princess." In the Old Testament, Sarah is the wife of Abraham and the mother of Isaac. First became a common name in English-speaking countries during the sixteenth century.

PRINCIPAL COLORS: Creamy white, every shade of green

GEMSTONES AND PRECIOUS METALS: Jade, moonstones, pearls

BOTANICALS: Chicory, lettuce, colewort

UNIQUE SPELLINGS: Saira, Sairah, Sara, Sarra, Sarrah

RELATED TO: Sadiet, Sallyt, Sara, Sareen, Sari, Sarina, Sarita, Shara, Zara

❧

"Tact is, after all, a kind of mind reading."
—SARAH ORNE JEWETT (AUTHOR)

Sarah

A KABBALISTIC SYNOPSIS
סאראה —SARAH (Samech, Aleph, Resh, Aleph, Heh)

Sarah is a very deceptive woman in that her public persona has very little to do with the Sarah that her partner will know and love. In the workplace, Sarah is cheerful and easygoing and likes to chat with all of her colleagues; still, she is practical enough to know when to get back to her work. There are career aims in Sarah's life, but they are not hugely important or grandiose; most of all, Sarah just wants a relaxing and stress-free life. She is often regarded as quite shy by her coworkers, and she rarely joins in any of their more raucous antics either at work or on nights out. However, when she is at home she is quite different! One equivalent of her name is "forbidden," and it is the very forbidden nature of sex that attracts her to it when she is at home—and any partner of Sarah's benefits from this dynamic.

THE RUNIC INTERPRETATION
ᚺᚨᚱᚨᛋ (Hagalaz, Ansuz, Raido, Ansuz, Sowelu)

One wonders that Sarah isn't driving a better car by now. It may not occur to folks who know and love her that Sarah wouldn't dream of calling attention to herself this way. The double Ansuz runes for signals makes Sarah intuitive and accommodating. She's so compatible that she has many friends and serves the needs of others, even if they can never return the kindness. The Raido rune of travel and good communication means Sarah can teach others. Hagalaz, the rune of disruptions, follows her like a dark shadow throughout her life, but most people will never notice. What people do see is the blessing of Sowelu, the rune of wholeness, on Sarah's life, and her consequent sweetness and light.

Elements: Water, air, water, air, air

THE NUMEROLOGICAL INTERPRETATION
Sarah (NV = 11, CV = 9, VV = 2, FL = 1)

A woman who is strongly inspired by her sense of social idealism, Sarah can be readily found working as a political activist, social worker, or teacher. She wants to know that her life has purpose and meaning and that she is out doing something in the world to make positive changes in people's lives. People respond well to her, even if they do not agree with her political agenda. Group work will be a major facet of her life, and Sarah may have to temper her strong opinions so that they conform to the group's best interests. She definitely requires a partner who shares her sociological and humanitarian interests.

❧

Scott

A Kabbalistic Synopsis
סכעת —SKA'ATh (Samech, Kaph, Ayin, Tau)

There is only one ideal trait for Scott, and that is all-around mechanical genius. He has an instinct for all matters practical, from fixing the car to putting up the guttering to laying down walls. Luckily for Scott, he also gets great pleasure out of his work, especially when it involves building something new from scratch; Scott is incredibly good with his hands. He has a very generous nature and will do anything to help people out. This makes him very popular in his hometown, which is likely to be a fairly small community. Scott's only problem is that he may sometimes be too generous and often refuses to charge people for the work he does for them.

The Runic Interpretation
↑↑◊<5 (Teiwaz, Teiwaz, Othila, Kano, Sowelu)

The double Teiwaz warrior rune fills Scott with masculine energy and an urge toward conquest. Like any remarkable warrior in history, Scott is a thinker and brilliant strategist. Othila, the rune of separation, gives warrior Scott the winning edge. Othila teaches him about separation and the need to align himself with the right principles, rather than follow the dictates of the crowd. His winning smile and physical prowess attract the attention of oh-so-willing followers. Scott is further blessed with Kano, the rune of opening, which brings him money and opportunities from all directions. People want to follow Scott because he has their best interests in mind and he is strong.

Elements: Air, air, earth/fire, water, air

The Numerological Interpretation
Scott (NV = 5, CV = 8, VV = 6, FL = 1)

"If it works, use it!" says Scott. This is a very practical man who likes to get on with life and make things happen. He has a personality that is both efficient as well as experimental. Scott does not mind reaching outside the accepted behavioral boundaries of his circle of friends; in fact, that is one of his more admirable traits. However, he is not seeking to create confrontational challenges with the people in his environment. He is much too much of a peaceful person for such activities. Scott just knows that there is more to life than what meets the eye, and his eyes are open to all of life's potential and possibilities.

DERIVATION: Scottish and English, originally a surname meaning "Scotsman." First used as a given name in the 1930s and 1940s, and has become especially common in the United States in recent years.

PRINCIPAL COLORS: Pale gray, any other very pale color

GEMSTONES AND PRECIOUS METALS: Platinum, silver

BOTANICALS: Sweet marjoram, parsley, hazel

UNIQUE SPELLINGS: Scot, Skot, Skott

RELATED TO: Scottie, Scotto, Scotty

"Remember there's no such thing as a small act of kindness. Every act creates a ripple with no logical end."
—SCOTT ADAMS (AUTHOR, CREATOR OF DILBERT COMIC STRIP)

DERIVATION: Irish version of John, which originally derives from the Hebrew name Johanan, meaning "God is gracious." Became widespread in all English-speaking countries during the twentieth century.

PRINCIPAL COLORS: The palest to the richest shades of purple

GEMSTONES AND PRECIOUS METALS: Amethyst, garnets

BOTANICALS: Beetroot, lungwort, strawberry

UNIQUE SPELLINGS: Shaughn, Shaun, Shaune, Shawn, Shawne

RELATED TO: Evant, Giovanni, Hans, Iant, Ivant, Jan, Johan, Johannes, Johnt, Shanet, Shawnt

A KABBALISTIC SYNOPSIS
סאון —SAVN (Samech, Aleph, Vau, Nun)

Sean is likely to be a winner in every sense of the word. The value of his name both begins and ends with the number seven, which is a mystical number of success in a whole range of cultures and societies. In addition, the reduction of the value of his name produces twenty, which tells us that Sean has excellent judgment; when it comes to business, Sean can generally be relied upon to make the right decision. Sean has a very close relationship with his family, and may well wait considerably longer than most before leaving the parental home. There is sometimes a danger, particularly with those born under the sign of Cancer, that Seans may place too much emphasis on their terrific childhood at the expense of emotionally moving on to the next stage in their life. However, with the amount of money Sean could one day make, there will be no shortage of potential partners ready to show him what he has been missing as an adult.

THE RUNIC INTERPRETATION
ᚾᚨᛖᛋ (Nauthiz, Ansuz, Ehwaz, Sowelu)

Sean is impulsive and playful. He comes home after work and dumps travel brochures on the table and says, "Where do you want to go? Just choose a place." He means it, too. Sean's a clown and he's never going to be a bore. However, he is deeply vulnerable to sadness, limitation, and ennui because of the Nauthiz rune of constraint in his name. Ehwaz, the rune of movement, means Sean has to feel life is fresh and interesting. Ansuz, the rune of signals, assures that Sean knows when to stay and when to go. With the Sowelu rune of wholeness blessing his name, Sean leads a full and generous life.

Elements: Fire, air, air, air

THE NUMEROLOGICAL INTERPRETATION
Sean (NV = 3, CV = 6, VV = 6, FL = 1)

Sean is attracted by beauty and he also seeks to create it. This is a man who is very aware of his personal appearance, and he enjoys wearing stylish clothing. Sean is emotionally sensitive and caring, a person who can easily perceive the inner talents and abilities that reside in other people. Friends trust him and have confidence in his vision and insight. Sean makes an excellent counselor or teacher, in addition to being a natural-born artist. He is a perfectionist, however, and may find that he walks through life with a distinct sense of "divine discontent."

Sergio

A Kabbalistic Synopsis
סאריע —SARYO (Samech, Aleph, Resh, Yod, Ayin)

This guy could charm the birds right out of the trees if he wanted; he is smoothness personified. He has an instinct for knowing what will and what won't work with each potential partner he meets. This is not some con, though; Sergio has a genuine love for women, and a real understanding of them, too. His name's value is equivalent to the value of all the so-called Hebrew mother letters added together, so he has a real sense of how the feminine personality operates. Yet Sergio is not all romance and moonlight; he has a hard-nosed approach to business, and the final Ayin in his name, along with the central number four in the value of his name, tells us that he will do well for himself financially as well as in his many relationships.

The Runic Interpretation
ᛟᛁᚷᚱᛖᛋ (Othila, Isa, Gebo, Raido, Ehwaz, Sowelu)

Sergio longs for his love from afar. This sense of longing permeates Sergio's life like the guitar chords of a classic love song. Othila, the rune of separation, combined with Isa, the rune of isolation, causes Sergio's estrangement, while the Gebo rune of partnership makes Sergio one of those people who truly requires a mate to feel whole. Luckily, Sowelu, the rune of wholeness, saves Sergio from playing out some kind of melancholy desperation scene. Once Sergio finds wholeness within himself, the chances are good that he will be reunited with his lost love. Ehwaz denotes much movement and growth, which Sergio requires before his journey's end.

Elements: Earth/fire, earth, water, water, air, air

The Numerological Interpretation
Sergio (NV = 1, CV = 8, VV = 2, FL = 1)

A magnetic man with a great deal of sex appeal, Sergio is never at a loss for companionship. He is a person who takes great pride in his appearance and dresses for success (or at least to impress). Sergio has a warm, outgoing disposition and enjoys life's pleasures. Money and financial security are very important to him, and he usually has no problem harnessing his talents in order to earn what he requires. Sergio may, however, be too involved with himself and his personal status. If the charitable side of his nature is developed, he will be able to balance his urge for personal satisfaction with a healthy sense of sharing.

DERIVATION: Italian, from the Roman clan name Sergius. The name of a pope and several saints. Found most often in the United States during the twentieth century.

PRINCIPAL COLORS: Orange, gold, the full range of bronze and yellow hues

GEMSTONES AND PRECIOUS METALS: Citrine, amber, yellow diamonds

BOTANICALS: Chamomile, sorrel, Saint-John's-wort

UNIQUE SPELLINGS: Sergeo, Sergyo, Serjeo, Serjio, Sirgio, Sirgyo, Syrgeo, Syrgio

RELATED TO: Serge, Sergei, Sergey, Sergios, Serguei

Seth

DERIVATION: Biblical, from a Hebrew word meaning "appointed" or "set." In the Bible, the name of Adam's third son, who was born after Cain murdered Abel. Especially common among the Puritans, and has shown a resurgence in popularity in the United States in recent years.

PRINCIPAL COLORS: The full range of yellow and green hues

GEMSTONES AND PRECIOUS METALS: Moonstones, moss agate

BOTANICALS: Elder, blackberry, juniper

UNIQUE SPELLINGS: Seath, Sehth, Sethe

RELATED TO: Seathan

A Kabbalistic Synopsis
סאת —SATh (Samech, Aleph, Tau)

You'll not often see Seth in the city, as he is definitely a man of the countryside. He feels uncomfortable when surrounded by buildings, cars, or crowds of people, but he loves to be on a quiet homestead with his dog and his family. To many people, the sort of life that Seth enjoys would be cripplingly dull—no clubs or fancy restaurants here—but Seth never tires of the endlessly changing and wonderful world of nature where he lives. In fact, Seth is quite a spiritual man, and it is in the wonders of nature that he finds God. His family all love him, as he is one of the warmest men you could wish to meet. He will be unlikely to ever make vast amounts of money, but that doesn't really appeal to him anyway, as anything he needs he can grow, raise, or make.

The Runic Interpretation
ᚦᛖᛋ (Thurisaz, Ehwaz, Sowelu)

Seth may be highly evolved one moment and find himself totally unraveling the next. When Seth loses control, Thurisaz, the gateway rune, is requesting that Seth slow down and try not to let his reach exceed his grasp. When Seth tries to function beyond his level of understanding, his intent is misguided. Instead, Seth needs to emerge into higher levels gently. The Ehwaz rune of movement gives Seth the opportunity to live and learn among peoples of the world. Yet the Sowelu rune of wholeness shows Seth that the love he seeks is inside him all along.

Elements: Fire, air, air

The Numerological Interpretation
Seth (NV = 7, CV = 11, VV = 5, FL = 1)

Seth has an insatiable urge to know. His avid intellectual curiosity will lead him into many interesting experiences. This is not a man to sit back and let life pass him by—at least not without understanding what it *is* that's passing! Education is therefore a very important factor in his life, and Seth will be a perpetual student even after the days of his formal education are over. He is a traveler by nature, and so will be drawn to far-off and exotic places. Yet Seth also finds that a trip to a nearby park can be as interesting as a trek through Asia.

Shane

A Kabbalistic Synopsis
שאין —ShAYN (Shin, Aleph, Yod, Nun)

Shane is bursting with energy. The initial Shin, or Sh, in his name relates to the element of fire, and because of its position, it inflames everything that Shane does and thinks. Shane has a creative personality, and he may well attempt to make a profession out of this talent. The ideal format for Shane is the written word; his only problem then will be in maintaining his efforts. Shane has absolutely no problem coming up with ideas, as indicated by the letter Aleph, but he may find it difficult to stick with something once he starts working on it. The final Nun of this name marks Shane as an emotionally sensitive man, which is great as far as his creative expression is concerned. However, he is very vulnerable to emotional hurt, and problems in relationships will affect him far more than the average individual.

The Runic Interpretation
ᛖᚾᚨᚺᛊ (Ehwaz, Nauthiz, Ansuz, Hagalaz, Sowelu)

Shane keeps his mind dusted and his home orderly. The troublemakers, Nauthiz for constraint and Hagalaz for disruption, in this name are always pulling the rug out from under Shane. Shane knows that he just has to accept this, because he can't put a stop to it. So to help himself feel that there is at least *something* he can control, he keeps his environment organized, orderly, and harmonious. This is a brilliant strategy and actually keeps negativity at bay. When discord does swoop into his life, Shane can rely on his routines and order to comfort him with a framework of security. The Ansuz rune makes him intuitive, and Ehwaz lets him travel and live abroad, which he handles with great equanimity. Sowelu, the rune of wholeness, means Shane stays sane through it all.

Elements: Air, fire, air, water, air

The Numerological Interpretation
Shane (NV = 11, CV = 5, VV = 6, FL = 1)

Community service work is a very natural outlet for Shane, and he is also quite at home in a career associated with communications and/or the media. This is a man who has to be actively involved with people, and he is especially geared toward the creation of beautiful environments that enhance the quality of life. If he is more spiritually inclined, Shane will find himself at work expanding people's consciousness. This can be done as a metaphysical counselor, religious minister, or healer. No matter what his profession, Shane is a man with a mission.

DERIVATION: English and Irish, variant form of Sean, which ultimately derives from John. Reflects the Northern Irish pronunciation of the name. The name Shane increased dramatically in popularity in 1953, when the film *Shane* was released. Especially common in Britain.

PRINCIPAL COLORS: From pale, grassy to rich, forest green

GEMSTONES AND PRECIOUS METALS: Jade, pearls

BOTANICALS: Moonwort, plantain, rapeseed

UNIQUE SPELLINGS: Shaene, Shain, Shaine, Shayn, Shayne

RELATED TO: Evant, Giovanni, Hans, Iant, Ivant, Jan, Johan, Johannes, Johnt, Seant, Shaun, Shawnt

DERIVATION: Irish Gaelic, from the
   Celtic river name meaning "old" or
   "ancient." Began to be used as a
   first name in the twentieth century,
   most commonly in the United
   States. Occasionally found as
   a male name.

PRINCIPAL COLORS: Electric
   colors, and any color of medium
   shade

GEMSTONES AND PRECIOUS
   METALS: Sapphires

BOTANICALS: Celandine, sage,
   medlar

UNIQUE SPELLINGS: Shanan,
   Shanann, Shanen, Shanenn,
   Shanin, Shaninn, Shannan,
   Shannen, Shanon, Shanonn

RELATED TO: Shaina, Shan,
   Shana, Shanay, Shani, Shanita,
   Shanna, Shannah, Shannel,
   Shannie, Shayna

Shannon

A KABBALISTIC SYNOPSIS
שאננון —ShANNVN (Shin, Aleph, Nun, Nun, Vau, Nun)

The letter Nun appears three times in this name—which, by all rights, should make Shannon pretty close to a nervous wreck! However, thanks to the initial letter Shin, this influence is weakened to a degree. Still, Shannon does need to be surrounded by supportive and loving individuals in order to feel good about herself and the world around her. Another positive influence in her name is the final letter, which compresses to Zayin, meaning "sword." This letter tells us that Shannon has the capacity to do battle, even when she is feeling down. Thanks to her appealing personality and her genuine kindness, Shannon will have plenty of strong friendships and should not be overly troubled by her emotional insecurities.

THE RUNIC INTERPRETATION
↑◊↑↑ᚨᚺϟ (Nauthiz, Othila, Nauthiz, Nauthiz, Ansuz, Hagalaz, Sowelu)

Shannon has the challenges of Shane† but to a much greater degree. The triple Nauthiz rune of constraint in this name could suggest pronounced physical, mental, or emotional challenges. It could also manifest itself as imprisonment, financial decline, or other unusual problems. With mighty Hagalaz, the rune of disruption, there to further flavor the stew by causing events totally beyond Shannon's control, Shannon needs a strategy, or more realistically, a lifelong program for averting disaster. The Othila rune of separation could mean the friends Shannon relies on in a pinch fail to come through for her. Her family might be there for her, but if not, Ansuz, the rune of intuition, is there to comfort Shannon by allowing her to gain deeper insight and inner guidance. The Sowelu rune of wholeness counsels Shannon that the answers she seeks are within and can emerge through her dreams, chance encounters, and meditations. After much upheaval, Shannon will find her way, thanks to Sowelu, the rune of wholeness, and the powers of the four elements that bless her name.

Elements: Fire, earth/fire, fire, fire, air, water, air

THE NUMEROLOGICAL INTERPRETATION
Shannon (NV = 4, CV = 6, VV = 7, FL = 1)

Shannon is very happy when she is out and about in nature. She may even decide to seek a profession that is connected with the ecological movement. She is very aware of nutrition and diet, and is careful about her physical health. A practical person with a genuine concern about day-to-day life, Shannon is quite close to her family. She is much more concerned about what is of permanent worth than with the fleeting and transient.

Sharon

A KABBALISTIC SYNOPSIS
שארון —ShARVN (Shin, Aleph, Resh, Vau, Nun)

Sharon is a name with mystical significance in the kabbalistic and Western mystery tradition. The value of her name reduces to seventeen, which refers to the tarot card, the Star, the symbol of protection and hope. Sharon will breeze through life with very little in the way of major setbacks or crises, thanks to this protective influence. She will not become self-satisfied as a result of this, though; instead, she will try to use her good fortune as a way of helping those whose lives have been less lucky than her own. Of course, one can be kind and still be extremely competitive, and this certainly applies to Sharon. Sharon loves to compete, and the fact that one Hebrew equivalent of her name is "the first" suggests that quite often she does rather well for herself.

THE RUNIC INTERPRETATION
↑◇ᚱ᛭ᚺᛯ (Nauthiz, Othila, Raido, Ansuz, Hagalaz, Sowelu)

Sharon is a poser. She's a born actress and may gravitate to psychology, modeling, writing, or drama. She is fascinated by the many selves in each of us. Nauthiz and Hagalaz promise a bumpy ride, but Sharon is determined to learn from the challenges of adversity. She uses the Othila rune of separation to discard no longer fruitful friendships and unproductive attitudes and behaviors. In the process, she learns to lighten up and laugh at her clumsiness. Sharon draws in the sun with the power of Sowelu in her name, and she deeply appreciates the power of optimism to bring good luck. Raido, the rune of good communication, inclines Sharon to express herself, and she may find success in the performing arts where posing pays money.

Elements: Fire, earth/fire, water, air, water, air

THE NUMEROLOGICAL INTERPRETATION
Sharon (NV = 3, CV = 5, VV = 7, FL = 1)

This is one lady who enjoys making the most out of her talents and abilities. Sharon has a strong sense of self-worth, a quality that has taken her many years to develop. She enjoys shaping her potential into useful tools with which to express herself. Sharon is also good with physical tools as well, and such objects as pens, brushes, calculators, and musical instruments can frequently be found in her hands. With all of this equipment available to her, Sharon has to take care not to disperse her energy too broadly.

DERIVATION: English, from the biblical place-name. In Hebrew, the word *sharon* means "the plain." Sharon is found in the Old Testament as the name of a plain between Jaffa and Mount Carmel. In the Song of Songs, a beautiful shepherdess from this plain is described as "the rose of Sharon." Especially common in the United States during the 1950s.

PRINCIPAL COLORS: All shades of violet, from pale bluish purple through deep maroon

GEMSTONES AND PRECIOUS METALS: Garnets, amethyst

BOTANICALS: Mint, beetroot, cherry

UNIQUE SPELLINGS: Sharan, Sharann, Sharanne, Sharen, Sharenn, Sharenne, Sharin, Sharinn, Sharinne, Sharran, Sharren, Sharrin, Sharron, Sharryn, Sharyn, Sharynn, Sharynne

RELATED TO: Shara, Shari, Sharla, Sharolyn, Sharona, Sharonda, Sharone, Sheronne, Sherri, Sherry†

❧

"Instead of directing my energy negatively to dwell on the strain, I keep it focused positively on the gain."
—SHARON PRATT KELLY (POLITICIAN)

DERIVATION: English, a common variant of the Irish name Sean, which originally derives from the Hebrew name Johanan, meaning "God is gracious." This spelling is especially common in the United States.

PRINCIPAL COLORS: The full gamut of green hues, also white

GEMSTONES AND PRECIOUS METALS: Moonstones, cat's-eye

BOTANICALS: Colewort, lettuce, cabbage

UNIQUE SPELLINGS: Sean, Shaun, Shaune, Shawne

RELATED TO: Evan†, Giovanni, Hans, Ian†, Ivan†, Jan, Johan, Johannes, John†, Sean†, Shaun

A KABBALISTIC SYNOPSIS

שאון —ShAVN (Shin, Aleph, Vau, Nun)

Shawn has some very firm guiding principles and beliefs about life, which he sticks to rigidly no matter what the situation. His main belief is that life is all about having the best time you can for as much of the time as possible. Consequently, Shawn is not that concerned about his career direction. His only real concern is the amount of money he can earn and how quickly he can earn it! His name's value reduces to fifteen, which is the Devil card in the tarot. This lets us know that Shawn believes in self-indulgence. The final Nun in his name may suggest that all this hedonism is a means to avoid having a serious relationship that could result in Shawn being emotionally hurt. This is particularly likely if Shawn is an Aries or a Scorpio.

THE RUNIC INTERPRETATION

ᚾᚹᚨᚺᛊ (Nauthiz, Wunjo, Ansuz, Hagalaz, Sowelu)

Shawn can make you laugh. The Hagalaz rune for disruption and the Nauthiz rune of constraint have so severe a presence in his life that Shawn just takes his comic material from the many upsets and adventures in his own life. The Ansuz rune of inspiration and intuition, along with Wunjo for joy, make us love Shawn and hope he never changes.

Elements: Fire, earth, air, water, air

THE NUMEROLOGICAL INTERPRETATION

Shawn (NV = 11, CV = 5, VV = 6, FL = 1)

One of the gifts of this name is intuition. Shawn knows about people and can see beyond the projected masks and screens that so many of us create to protect ourselves. Shawn doesn't judge; he just looks at and understands what he sees, and is willing to share what he knows with others. This he can do most naturally through joining one of the service professions. It is important for Shawn to stay in touch with his own emotions, as it is sometimes difficult for him to separate his own feelings from those of the people around him.

Sheila

DERIVATION: English version of the Irish Gaelic name Síle, which originally derives from the Latin name Cecilia, meaning "blind." Especially popular during the mid-twentieth century. In Australian slang, *sheila* is the term for a girl or woman.

PRINCIPAL COLORS: The full gamut of red hues, particularly the richest tones

GEMSTONES AND PRECIOUS METALS: Rubies, garnets

BOTANICALS: Nettle, broom, onion

UNIQUE SPELLINGS: Sheala, Shealah, Sheela, Sheelah, Sheilah, Sheilla, Shela, Shelia, Shiela, Shielah

RELATED TO: Ceciliat, Celiat, Celya, Sasilia, Seelia, Seelie, Shelah, Shelley, Shelli, Shellie, Shellyt, Síle

A KABBALISTIC SYNOPSIS
שׁילא —ShYLA (Shin, Yod, Lamed, Aleph)

It is very difficult to say much about Sheila's personality, mainly because she never stops moving long enough for anyone to actually find out what she is really like. In Sheila's name, we have every letter associated with energy and speed of action. Her name begins with Shin, which tells us Sheila has drive, along with a potentially fiery personality. This letter is followed by Yod, again associated with the element of fire. We know now that it is not a good idea to annoy Sheila, as she has the capacity to get into an outstanding rage when she wants to. Given all her drive, taking into account the letter Lamed in her name, we should not be surprised to find Sheila at the top of her chosen profession, and still rising. If you work with Sheila, you will have to learn to get up to her speed.

THE RUNIC INTERPRETATION
ᚨᛚᛁᛖᚺᛋ (Ansuz, Laguz, Isa, Ehwaz, Hagalaz, Sowelu)

Hagalaz means "hailstorm," and Sheila will know what a stinging experience really feels like. With Laguz for flow and artistic gifts, and Ansuz for intuition, Sheila could be drawn to a career in the arts. The confusion in her life arising from Hagalaz could occur because it's difficult to make a living in the arts. With Isa, the rune of standstill, in her name, Sheila could face a stream of bills and commitments that conflict with her other projects. If this happens, Sheila needs to restore order in her life. With Ehwaz in her name, for movement, and Sowelu, for wholeness, Sheila will probably do just that and find the peace she needs to truly create.

Elements: Air, water, earth, air, water, air

THE NUMEROLOGICAL INTERPRETATION
Sheila (NV = 9, CV = 3, VV = 6, FL = 1)

Sheila is compassionate, understanding, and selfless. She is often involved with other people's welfare, helping them to grow through her support and caring. Her experience of life has a great deal to do with synthesis, inclusivity, and universality. Sheila feels a strong connection with the ebb and flow of life, and has the potential to develop a very great gift: loving detachment. When this occurs, Sheila finds that she is free from any form of obsessive desire and can focus much more on the pure joy that is in her heart.

PRINCIPAL COLORS: Pale gray, all other lightly shaded colors

GEMSTONES AND PRECIOUS METALS: Diamonds, silver, platinum

BOTANICALS: Hazel, oats, sweet marjoram

UNIQUE SPELLINGS: Shelden, Sheldin, Sheldyn, Shellden, Shelldin, Shelldon

RELATED TO: Shel, Shelbey, Shelby, Shelton

❧

"All of the significant battles are waged within the self."
—SHELDON KOPP (AUTHOR)

Sheldon

A KABBALISTIC SYNOPSIS
שאלדון —ShALDVN (Shin, Aleph, Lamed, Daleth, Vau, Nun)

Sheldon finds it very difficult to settle down in any one place for too long. His name reduces to thirteen, the number of the Death card in the tarot. Now, this card very rarely means literal death, but rather suggests major change. Sheldon loves change, and he also has a passion for travel. As to career, whatever Sheldon decides is the right career for him, you can bet that he will doggedly pursue it until he finds success. This facet of Sheldon's character is found when his name is compressed to reveal the letters Shin, Tzaddi, and Aleph. The Tzaddi indicates that Sheldon will never let go of a plan or goal once he has set his heart on it.

THE RUNIC INTERPRETATION
ᛏᛟᛞᛚᛖᚺᛋ (Nauthiz, Othila, Dagaz, Laguz, Ehwaz, Hagalaz, Sowelu)

When his sweetie pulls the covers up around him, Sheldon doesn't feel soothed, he feels smothered. The Hagalaz rune of disruption brings events into Sheldon's life that are beyond his control. Sheldon feels entrapped by circumstances, and with the Nauthiz rune of constraint also in his name, Sheldon values freedom above all else. On the brighter side, the Dagaz rune of breakthrough promises opportunities and prosperity. Laguz, the rune of flow, keeps Sheldon flexible and spontaneous. The Ehwaz rune of movement lets him choose to move abroad if that helps him feel less oppressed. Othila, the rune of separation, means that Sheldon can't stay in any one place too long—and if he can't find peace, Sheldon won't be staying with any one partner too long either.

Elements: Fire, earth/fire, fire, water, air, water, air

THE NUMEROLOGICAL INTERPRETATION
Sheldon (NV = 5, CV = 3, VV = 11, FL = 1)

Sheldon was the type of child who always asked questions. This intellectual curiosity only increases with the years, and Sheldon continues to read, study, and examine life in order to satisfy his innate curiosity. He enjoys writing, sketching, and listening to different types of music. Much more of a generalist than a specialist, he may prefer breadth of experience to depth. The challenge here is for him to avoid becoming superficial and overly mentally polarized. Too much intellectualization of life and relationships will not allow a love of emotional intimacy to develop, and this may block out some of the joys of relationships.

❧

Shelly

A Kabbalistic Synopsis
שאללי —ShALLY (Shin, Aleph, Lamed, Lamed, Yod)

Shelly is a natural artist, and even if she does not end up displaying canvases in some up-market gallery in New York, she will incorporate her artistic talents into her life in one way or another. Shelly is a deeply imaginative woman with a refreshing outlook in this cynical day and age. Unlike many of us, Shelly still has ideals, and although she may tend to be rather dreamy, she has her heart well and truly in the right place. Her imaginative nature and non-materialistic viewpoint may well gravitate to the unusual and the unexplained in life. If you ever spend some time with Shelly, you are guaranteed an interesting and unique experience.

The Runic Interpretation
ᛇᛚᛚᛖᚺᛋ (Eihwaz, Laguz, Laguz, Ehwaz, Hagalaz, Sowelu)

Shelly needs to pick up and go. The Ehwaz rune of movement in this name states that Shelly will live and work far from her initial home. Eihwaz, the rune of defense, combined with Hagalaz, the rune of disruption, could mean that Shelly fights in a battle or endures repeated emotional crises, living in a war zone of confusion for a time. The double Laguz runes of flow and flexibility save Shelly and help her survive. Fortunately, lovely Sowelu is there in Shelly's name to provide a deep-rooted sense of wholeness. Yes, Shelly will find peace and security after all.

Elements: Earth/fire, water, water, air, water, air

The Numerological Interpretation
Shelly (NV = 9, CV = 6, VV = 3, FL = 1)

There is a definite humanitarian facet to Shelly's life. Her name bestows qualities of empathy and compassion. This allows her to accept other people's opinions and lifestyles without fear or judgment. She may not feel or think as others do, but she is clear that we are one human family. Shelly is a romantic and an idealist who is quite sensitive to music and poetry. When people are in a relationship with her, they experience the love she has to offer as something very deep, sincere, and beautiful, but Shelly has to take care not to fall in love with love.

DERIVATION: English, place-name referring to a "meadow on a ledge." First used as a male name during the nineteenth century; during the mid-twentieth century, it became much more common as a female name. Also a common nickname for names ending in "chelle," such as Michelle and Rochelle.

PRINCIPAL COLORS: All shades of red, from light pink through rich crimson

GEMSTONES AND PRECIOUS METALS: Bloodstones, rubies

BOTANICALS: Garlic, wormwood

UNIQUE SPELLINGS: Sheli, Shelie, Shelley, Shelli, Shellie, Shely

RELATED TO: Michelle†, Rachel†, Rochelle, Sheila†, Shella, Shellah, Shirley†

DERIVATION: English, originally a
medieval surname, from the Old
English roots *sceara*, meaning
"shears," and *mann*, meaning
"man."

PRINCIPAL COLORS: All but the
brightest shades of azure

GEMSTONES AND PRECIOUS
METALS: Blue or blue-green
turquoise

BOTANICALS: Violets, vervain,
almonds

UNIQUE SPELLINGS: Scherman,
Schermann, Shermann

RELATED TO: Sherwin, Sherwood

Sherman

A KABBALISTIC SYNOPSIS
שארמון —ShARMVN (Shin, Aleph, Resh, Mem, Vau, Nun)

Because of the famous general and the tank that bears this name, you may expect Sherman to be the ultimate warrior. However, this may not be the case. The name Sherman has very strong influences of Virgo and does point toward a highly emotional character. Still, being warmhearted, caring, and sensitive are very good qualities for a leader, since they prevent him from becoming dictatorial or unfeeling. There is no question about the energy possessed by Sherman; not only does the initial Shin show this, but the final seven in his name's value also points to Sherman's drive and determination. Interestingly, the number seven is the value of the letter Zayin, which means "sword" or "armor"—so maybe Sherman is a pretty good name for a tank after all.

THE RUNIC INTERPRETATION
ᚾᚨᛗᚱᛖᚺᛋ (Nauthiz, Ansuz, Mannaz, Raido, Ehwaz, Hagalaz, Sowelu)

Sherman is attracted to partners that share his strong sense of duty. The Hagalaz rune of disruption and Nauthiz rune of constraint keep Sherman struggling to stay level for a time. At this moment, a partner could provide comfort and help as a bridge out of the confusion. However, Mannaz, the rune of self, makes it hard for Sherman to share his joys and hassles with another person. Ansuz, the rune of intuition, helps Sherman find the career that suits him best. Sometimes, if truth be known, Sherman is more comfortable at work than at home with his partner; pillow talk is Greek to Sherman. Raido, the rune of good communication, doesn't help him as it might in this regard. Living abroad and falling in love with a foreigner appeals to Sherman, and with Ehwaz, the rune of movement, Sherman will probably get his wish.

Elements: Fire, air, air, water, air, water, air

THE NUMEROLOGICAL INTERPRETATION
Sherman (NV = 6, CV = 9, VV = 6, FL = 1)

Sherman is a well-intentioned visionary. It is much easier for him to look on the bright and positive side of things than the dark and gloomy. Although this makes for a very buoyant and uplifting personality, Sherman has to be careful not to deceive himself about people. He does tend to project what he wants to see rather than seeing the reality at hand. Practicality is not his strong suit, but his caring and compassionate nature, and his strong sense of loyalty, compensate for this shortcoming. Still, Sherman might be well advised to make sure that he has a good lawyer and accountant to take care of the more pragmatic facets of his life.

Sherry

DERIVATION: English, variant form of the French *cherie*, meaning "dear one." Also a common variant on Cheryl, Sheryl, and Sharon. Especially popular during the mid-twentieth century.

PRINCIPAL COLORS: Mauve through the deep, rich violet hues

GEMSTONES AND PRECIOUS METALS: Garnets, amethyst

BOTANICALS: Apple, mint, lungwort, strawberry

UNIQUE SPELLINGS: Cherie, Sheree, Sherie, Sherree, Sherrey, Sherri, Sherrie, Sherrye, Sherye

RELATED TO: Cher, Cherie, Cherylt, Sharee, Shareen, Shari, Sharina, Sharita, Sharont, Shary, Sherida, Sheridan, Sherilyn, Sherita, Sherryn, Sherylt

A KABBALISTIC SYNOPSIS
שאררי —SHARRY (Shin, Aleph, Resh, Resh, Yod)

Sherry's name is a happy one. In fact, if you were looking for someone to personify the holiday spirit, you couldn't do much better than Sherry. There are many indications of fun in this name, some more subtle than others. The most obvious is the double Resh, which also tells us that Sherry has a genuinely friendly and generous nature. While she knows how to have a great time, Sherry also has a very serious side, and is in fact a very wise individual, particularly when it comes to affairs of the heart. Sherry will give very good advice to anyone who wants it. Her own marriage is likely to be a warm and cozy one that all her friends admire or envy.

THE RUNIC INTERPRETATION
ᛇᚱᚱᛗᚺᛊ (Eihwaz, Raido, Raido, Ehwaz, Hagalaz, Sowelu)

Equivocation and vacillation keep Sherry swinging like a pendulum. Eihwaz, the rune of defense, makes Sherry ever watchful, and she is so aware of the opposite side of any argument that it paralyzes her. With Hagalaz, the rune of disruptions at hand, Sherry feels overwhelmed and out of control much of the time. The double Raido rune for travel and good communication means Sherry can find comfort during these tempestuous times by confiding in a friend or counselor and journalizing her life in a diary. Ehwaz for movement will give her a chance to escape and find the time to integrate her emotions, thereby experiencing the sense of wholeness Sowelu offers her.

Elements: Earth/fire, water, water, air, water, air

THE NUMEROLOGICAL INTERPRETATION
Sherry (NV = 3, CV = 9, VV = 3, FL = 1)

This name bestows an active and creative imagination. Sherry is very playful and enjoys life to its fullest. Her enthusiasm is catching, and people find that they respond very easily to her childlike wonder and appreciation for life. Sherry always brings a new and interesting idea to explore when she meets up with friends. She can be counted on to be a stimulating influence at home and at work. Sherry believes in circulation; she knows that stagnancy in any form is anathema to growth, and she wants everything and everyone to grow.

Sheryl

DERIVATION: English, alternate spelling of Cheryl, a name that developed from the nineteenth-century name Cherry. Especially popular during the mid-twentieth century.

PRINCIPAL COLORS: Pale through moderate shades of blue

GEMSTONES AND PRECIOUS METALS: Emeralds, turquoise

BOTANICALS: Dog rose, walnuts, daffodils

UNIQUE SPELLINGS: Cheril, Cherril, Cherryl, Cheryl, Cheryll, Cherylle, Sheril, Sherill, Sherril, Sherrill, Sherryl, Sheryll, Sherylle

RELATED TO: Charlotte†, Cherilyn, Cherrie, Cherry, Cheryl†, Shari, Sherilyn, Sherri, Sherrie, Sherry†

A KABBALISTIC SYNOPSIS
שאריל —ShARYL (Shin, Aleph, Resh, Yod, Lamed)

The final letter of Sheryl's name is L, or Lamed, which tells us that Sheryl is a woman with a definite goal in mind and the determination to ensure that she achieves it. It is worth noting that the value of her name is the equivalent of "Israel" in Hebrew. Like this nation, Sheryl is fiercely independent and will stick to her own beliefs and principles in the face of any amount of opposition. Sheryl has a very practical side to her character, too. Although her career is likely to be focused on her intellectual abilities, Sheryl is more than happy to roll up her sleeves and get dirty when the situation calls for hands on labor.

THE RUNIC INTERPRETATION
↑RↁMↁ (Laguz, Isa, Raido, Ehwaz, Hagalaz, Sowelu)

When cheerful, Sheryl makes up her mind to move to a foreign country; her friends aren't surprised. Sheryl is a sprite, and her whimsy is contagious. The Ehwaz rune of movement means she will live in Brigadoon or on the moon if it suits her fancy. She's a powerful artist, with Laguz, the rune of flow, figuring prominently in her name. With or without suitcases, Sheryl can go wherever her imagination will carry her. The nasty Hagalaz rune of disruption means her life is filled with events beyond her control, but Sheryl stays in balance by escaping into the garden of her art, where she is always welcome. Isa means she can tolerate isolation, and Raido, the rune of good communication, blesses her with rich, expressive gifts that allow her to experience the wholeness brought about by Sowelu.

Elements: Water, earth, water, air, water, air

THE NUMEROLOGICAL INTERPRETATION
Sheryl (NV = 6, CV = 3, VV = 3, FL = 1)

Sheryl is very aware of her social and familial responsibilities. She takes her personal relationships seriously and honors the commitments she makes to people. Born with a bright and cheery disposition, Sheryl is not given over to depression or pessimistic thinking. She is a balanced person and finds it very easy to create a harmonious environment both privately and professionally. Instrumental in creating positive group interaction, Sheryl is a natural-born intermediary when it comes to unifying various people and their seemingly conflicting opinions and ideas.

Shirley

A KABBALISTIC SYNOPSIS
שורלי —ShVRLY (Shin, Vau, Resh, Lamed, Yod)

Shirley is an incurable romantic and likes nothing better than to curl up with a big fat romance novel. But you would never guess this from her behavior in the workplace. With Shirley, the watchword is "efficiency," and anyone on her team had better be willing to put in a good day's work if they want to last. Material comfort is very important to Shirley, and she wants to achieve it on her own terms. Consequently she is hungry for promotion at work, and she will do whatever is necessary to ensure that she is first in line for a pay raise. This doesn't mean that she is a sour individual; Shirley can have a good laugh with her colleagues and her staff, but she expects people to give their all when it is time to get down to business. On the whole, people are happy to do so, as Shirley is a very good manager and motivator.

THE RUNIC INTERPRETATION
ᛇᛖᛚᚱᛁᚺᛋ (Eihwaz, Ehwaz, Laguz, Raido, Isa, Hagalaz, Sowelu)

Shirley thrives on danger and the unpredictable. She grew up with it, so it's weirdly familiar. Not one to share her heart easily, Shirley enjoys the Isa rune of standstill, which counsels her to be alone. Hagalaz, the rune of disruptions, keeps things melodramatic and chaotic, which Shirley finds interesting. The Raido rune of good communication could give Shirley the talent she needs to successfully write about her soap opera lifestyle for great financial remuneration. With Sowelu for wholeness, Shirley could construct a good plot line. Laguz, the rune of flow and flexibility, blesses her artistic endeavors and helps her roll with the disruptions that trip her up in a crazy but predictable fashion. Eihwaz, the rune of defense, further inclines Shirley to isolate herself and be cautious in love.

Elements: Earth/fire, air, water, water, earth, water, air

THE NUMEROLOGICAL INTERPRETATION
Shirley (NV = 6, CV = 3, VV = 3, FL = 1)

Movement and the urge to create out of movement characterize this name. Shirley has an inner sense of rhythm and communicates easily with words and gestures. She is naturally attracted to music and loves to dance. But her sense of balance and harmony also extends into her human relationships: Shirley is a fair and honest person, and she expects the same from others, especially from her partner. She has high expectations of people in general. It is only natural therefore that Shirley may become disappointed when people do not live up to her vision of their higher possibilities.

DERIVATION: English, originally a place-name meaning "bright clearing," from the Old English roots *scír*, meaning "bright" and *leah*, meaning "clearing." Became especially popular during the 1930s and 1940s due to the widespread fame of child film star Shirley Temple (b. 1928).

PRINCIPAL COLORS: All but the brightest of azures

GEMSTONES AND PRECIOUS METALS: Turquoise, emeralds

BOTANICALS: Vervain, dog rose

UNIQUE SPELLINGS: Sherlee, Sherley, Sherli, Sherlie, Sherly, Shirlee, Shirli, Shirlie, Shirly, Shurlee, Shurley, Shurli, Shurlie, Shurly

RELATED TO: Shirl, Shirla, Shirleen, Shirleena, Shirlene, Shirena

Sidney

DERIVATION: English, originally a surname from a Norman baronial family. Became increasingly common as a first name during the nineteenth century.

PRINCIPAL COLORS: Electric colors

GEMSTONES AND PRECIOUS METALS: From pale to deeply toned sapphires

BOTANICALS: Lesser celandine, medlar, Solomon's seal

UNIQUE SPELLINGS: Cydnee, Cydney, Cydnie, Cydny, Sidnee, Sidni, Sidnie, Sidny, Sydney, Sydni, Sydnie, Sydny

RELATED TO: Cid, Cyd, Sid, Sidonia, Sidonie, Sidony, Syd, Sydney†

A KABBALISTIC SYNOPSIS
סידני —SYDNY (Samech, Yod, Daleth, Nun, Yod)

Everyone loves Sidney. He is always ready to do his bit for the community, and is often seen in the local café having a laugh and a joke with his neighbors. Sidney likes to feel that he's part of something and is very well suited to life in a small town. He particularly enjoys throwing his efforts behind all the big social events, such as the Thanksgiving day parade. The compression of Sidney's name produces the letters Qoph, Kaph, and Daleth. As shown by the letter Qoph, Sidney has a quick mind, which he likes to use in a practical manner. The practical aspect is indicated by the letter Kaph, while the letter Daleth suggests that Sidney enjoys designing and making things that people can use to simplify their lives or to give themselves more enjoyment.

THE RUNIC INTERPRETATION
ᛃᛗᚺᛝᛁᛊ (Eihwaz, Ehwaz, Nauthiz, Dagaz, Isa, Sowelu)

Sidney follows a lot of rules, poor guy. The Eihwaz rune of defense confuses Sidney into thinking the whole world lives by strict imperatives to avert disaster. But once Sidney realizes that, in fact, sometimes rules were made to be broken, he begins to evolve. With the Nauthiz rune of constraint, he'll try to sort out the old thinking of childhood and substitute attitudes that support his life. Dagaz, the rune of breakthrough, promises money and opportunities. The Sowelu rune hints that Sidney is able to discard worn-out belief systems that no longer serve him and find satisfaction and wholeness.

Elements: Earth/fire, air, fire, fire, earth, air

THE NUMEROLOGICAL INTERPRETATION
Sidney (NV = 4, CV = 1, VV = 3, FL = 1)

Sidney offers the people in his life security, stability, and consistency. This name reveals a man who is hard at work building a foundation for his future growth and expansion. More concerned with the practical issues of life than with the theoretical, he has a vested interest in his economic well-being. Sidney is a very individualistic person, one who is more suited to self-employment than to work under someone else's direction. He is quite disciplined, making sure he stays on track so as not to waste time and energy.

Simon

A Kabbalistic Synopsis

סימון —SYMVN (Samech, Yod, Mem, Vau, Nun)

Simon's life revolves around his emotions and the emotions of others. Although he is an intelligent man, as shown by the presence of the letter Qoph in the compression of his name, Simon tends to feel rather than think. The reduction of the value of his name produces the number thirteen. In Simon's case, this does not refer so much to a love of change in his own life as a desire to create positive change in the lives of other people. The letter M, or Mem, is representative of positive caring—emotions often regarded as maternal, but ones that really express a desire to protect and nurture. Simon would make an excellent priest or some form of counselor, as he has the patience and genuine interest in others to make a worthwhile contribution to their lives.

The Runic Interpretation

ᚾᛟᛗᛁᛋ (Nauthiz, Othila, Mannaz, Isa, Sowelu)

Mannaz, rune of the self, inclines Simon to introspection. But Simon needs to learn that love of self is only a first step toward the bigger picture—namely, love of his fellow man. Isa, the rune of standstill, could bring these revelations forward if Simon heeds their counsel and adopts a more humanitarian approach to living. Othila, the rune of separation, urges Simon to let go of his childish ways and let others into his life. Nauthiz, the rune of constraint, warns that Simon might just be too busy with his own self-involvement to heed the warning. But Sowelu, the rune of wholeness, is overhead all the time, waiting, just waiting, for Simon to evolve.

Elements: Fire, earth/fire, air, earth, air

The Numerological Interpretation

Simon (NV = 7, CV = 1, VV = 6, FL = 1)

Solitude may be a very important factor in Simon's life. This is a man who has a deep and penetrating mind, and he requires time for study, contemplation, and introspection. He is happiest when at home, and should consider devoting a special room in his house to his hobbies and special interests. Simon is not given to group activities, and much prefers to keep his circle of friends small and intimate. He has to take care that his natural inclination to spend time alone does not isolate him from his family. His domestic life is a vital part of his sense of psychological well-being, and his presence will be missed by his loved ones.

DERIVATION: English version of the Old Testament name Simeon. In the Bible, Simon is the name of several New Testament figures, most notably the Apostle Simon Peter. Common throughout the Middle Ages, the name became especially popular in the early twentieth century.

PRINCIPAL COLORS: Gold, the full range of green and yellow hues

GEMSTONES AND PRECIOUS METALS: Pearls, moss agate, any other white stone

BOTANICALS: Hops, linseed, juniper

UNIQUE SPELLINGS: Siemon, Simen, Simin, Simonn, Syemon, Symon

RELATED TO: Shimon, Si, Simeon, Simien, Simmons, Simpson, Sy

Sonia

DERIVATION: Russian, short-form of Sophia, which originally derives from the Greek word for wisdom. Has been a popular first name since the early twentieth century.

PRINCIPAL COLORS: The full spectrum of moderately toned hues, also electric colors

GEMSTONES AND PRECIOUS METALS: Sapphires

BOTANICALS: Sage, wild spinach, Iceland moss

UNIQUE SPELLINGS: Soniah, Sonja, Sonnia, Sonnja, Sonnya, Sonya, Sonyah

RELATED TO: Sofia, Sonni, Sonnie, Sonny, Sophiat, Sophie

A KABBALISTIC SYNOPSIS
סעניא —SA'ANYA (Samech, Ayin, Nun, Yod, Aleph)

The value of Sonia's name reduces to eleven, which is traditionally a number associated with all things magical and mysterious in nature. However, it can also be seen as a number that merely refers to a secretive nature, and this may be the case with Sonia. Emotionally, Sonia finds it very difficult to open up to other people, a fact that is further hinted at by the presence of the letter Nun in her name. In addition, the value of her name is equivalent to the value of the Hebrew word "box" or "chest." This may refer to the way in which she stores away her deepest feelings, or it may possibly refer to her tendency to save rather than spend. The Ayin in her name tells us that she has a good head for business and will probably make a reasonable amount of money. Sonia is naturally cautious and is not the sort to go in for a glamorous lifestyle. Rather, she will save her money and use it when there is something in life that she really wants.

THE RUNIC INTERPRETATION
ᚾᛁᛏᛟᛋ (Ansuz, Isa, Nauthiz, Othila, Sowelu)

Make no mistake: Sonia lands on her feet every time. True, she has Nauthiz, the rune of constraint, placing obstacles in her path. But when it gets to the final hour, something always rescues her. Could it be the Ansuz rune? Ansuz is the rune of signals, and Sonia keeps her antennae up for opportunities along the way. Sonia has Othila, the rune of separation, in her name, too, and so she knows how to discard people and ideas that hold her down. Othila also teaches her to be optimistic, and with Isa, the rune of standstill, also on hand, Sonia knows how to go within and center herself. Sowelu, the rune of wholeness, is prominently positioned in her name as well. Sowelu teaches Sonia to let love work its magic.

Elements: Air, earth, fire, earth/fire, air

THE NUMEROLOGICAL INTERPRETATION
Sonia (NV = 4, CV = 6, VV = 7, FL = 1)

Sonia has a distinct interest in science, technology, and philosophy, but she is a pragmatic person with her feet on the ground. She is interested in how things can be useful in her day-to-day life experience. Her spiritual life is not based on faith, but on the concrete application of spiritual ideals and principles within the context of her personal relationships. Sonia expects people to behave properly and treat themselves and her with dignity and respect.

Sophia

A Kabbalistic Synopsis

סעפיא —SA'APhYA (Samech, Ayin, Peh, Yod, Aleph)

When you think of Sophia, the woman who most springs to mind is Sophia Loren. However, while Sophia may well be an extraordinarily attractive woman, this is not a key feature of her name. It is interesting to note that the name Sophia has a very important place in a form of mysticism known as gnosticism. The key aspect of Sophia's name is the combination of the Ayin and the Peh, which suggests Sophia's ability to make a considerable amount of money from her skills as a communicator. Sophia could have a career as a journalist or a performer. The reduction of the value of her name produces the number five, which relates to religion, particularly traditional, organized religion. So we should not be surprised if Sophia is devoutly religious.

The Runic Interpretation

ᚨᛁᚺᛈᛟᛋ (Ansuz, Isa, Hagalaz, Perth, Othila, Sowelu)

Sophia often thinks trouble has finally left her doorstep—and that's just when it arrives in a new form. The Perth rune of transformation, or secrets revealed, and Hagalaz for disruptions, combined with Othila for separation, give Sophia something to feel sorry about. Fortunately, she learns to toughen up and stop saying "What next?" She can find optimism, but Sophia is careful of what she says and thinks. Ansuz, the rune of intuition, teaches Sophia to trust her own judgment. Sowelu, the rune of wholeness, lets Sophia know that she is resourceful and a survivor, and when she's ready, she just might let others know how she handles it all so well.

Elements: Air, earth, water, water, earth/fire, air

The Numerological Interpretation

Sophia (NV = 5, CV = 7, VV = 7, FL = 1)

Sophia has a lot of questions, and she spends a great deal of her time trying to get them answered. She is very much involved in either finding a creed by which she can live or promoting a belief system for the benefit of others. Sophia is a freedom-loving woman who requires time alone to foster her independent spirit. She desires intimate relationships, but within the context of these relationships, she needs to have time and space to herself. Sophia is neither superficial nor flighty, and she seeks a partner who is also interested in life's deeper issues.

DERIVATION: English, from the Greek word for wisdom. First became a popular name in the seventeenth and eighteenth centuries in England. In Britain and France, the French version, Sophie, is more common. In the United States, however, Sophia is more prevalent. The name increased in popularity in the mid-twentieth century with the rise of the Italian actress Sophia Loren.

PRINCIPAL COLORS: Pale to medium shades of blue

GEMSTONES AND PRECIOUS METALS: Turquoise, emeralds

BOTANICALS: Dog rose, daffodils, walnuts, almonds

UNIQUE SPELLINGS: Soefia, Sofea, Sofia, Sofiah, Sofya, Suphea, Sophiah, Sophya

RELATED TO: Sofey, Sofie, Soniat, Sonja, Sonnie, Sonya, Sophie, Sophy, Zofi, Zofia

"Mistakes are part of the dues one pays for a full life."
—SOPHIA LOREN (ACTRESS)

DERIVATION: English, originally
a surname referring to someone
who dispensed food and drink
at a manor house. During the
twentieth century, it has increased
in popularity as a first name,
aided by the rise of the popular
American film actor Spencer Tracy
(1900–1967).

PRINCIPAL COLORS: Black, gray,
deeply toned azure and purple

GEMSTONES AND PRECIOUS
METALS: Carbuncles, black
diamonds, amethyst

BOTANICALS: Angelica, pilewort,
marsh mallow

UNIQUE SPELLINGS: Spencere,
Spencir, Spencyr, Spenser,
Spensir, Spensyr

RELATED TO: Spen, Spence

Spencer

A KABBALISTIC SYNOPSIS

אסנאפס —SPANSA (Samech, Peh, Aleph, Nun, Samech, Aleph)

Spencer is a decidedly emotional man who is only too happy to wear his heart on his sleeve. Spencer is a wonderfully sensitive individual who will make someone an ideal partner. He is always ready to listen to his lover's personal feelings, and is able to express himself fully as well. Spencer is an excellent boss and is ideal in any career that requires a significant amount of personnel management. In addition to being a very supportive manager, he is always ready to have a good time. A naturally generous man, he is likely to take his staff out on the town on a fairly regular basis.

THE RUNIC INTERPRETATION

ᚱᛖᛋᚾᛖᛈᛋ (Raido, Ehwaz, Sowelu, Nauthiz, Ehwaz, Perth, Sowelu)

What does Spencer have that others lack? Good mental health, for starters! Spencer stands head and shoulders above most of the rest of the world. He's truly blessed with double Sowelu, the rune of wholeness, in his name. True, he has the constraint of Nauthiz to deal with, but we all have our load to bear. The double Ehwaz runes of movement give Spencer a chance to share his sunny disposition with others on foreign shores. Spencer can excel with people and under pressure. Social work, construction, interior design, and the mental health fields are good career opportunities for Spencer. He could also enjoy working in the health care industry. The Perth rune offers growth or change on a spiritual or emotional level. This means that Spencer becomes more spiritual or accepting of contradictions and ambiguities.

Elements: Water, air, air, fire, air, water, air

THE NUMEROLOGICAL INTERPRETATION

Spencer (NV = 8, CV = 7, VV = 1, FL = 1)

The name Spencer contains a very strong urge for personal power. This is a man who absolutely has to be his own boss. He is also very adept at being in charge of large organizations, for it is easy for him to coordinate many people's efforts into a cohesive whole. Spencer seeks personal recognition and abundant financial returns on his investments of time and energy. He will not be satisfied with a little corner of the world, no matter how safe and secure. Spencer is a very sensuous man, and he will choose a partner with whom he can enjoy life's many pleasures.

Stacy

DERIVATION: English, originally a male name. First used for girls as a nickname for Anastasia. Since the 1970s, it has been especially popular as a female name in the United States.

PRINCIPAL COLORS: Any very pale color

GEMSTONES AND PRECIOUS METALS: Diamonds, platinum

BOTANICALS: Hazel, parsley, mushrooms

UNIQUE SPELLINGS: Stacee, Stacey, Staci, Stacie, Staecy, Staicy, Staisy, Stasey, Stasi, Stasie, Stasy

RELATED TO: Anastasia, Stace, Stacia, Stasia, Tasia

A Kabbalistic Synopsis

סטאיסי —STAYSY (Samech, Teth, Aleph, Yod, Samech, Yod)

The value of Stacy's name comes to 150. One hundred is the value of the letter Qoph, which represents intelligence, while fifty is the value of the letter Nun, which is associated with matters of the heart. Because of Stacy's name's value, we can discern that Stacy is a well-balanced woman who is ruled by a combination of brains and feeling. One slight problem in her character is that she sometimes finds it difficult to act in a decisive manner because she is too expert at seeing both sides of any situation. This is suggested by the fact that the value of her name reduces to six, the number related to choice making. When it comes to her friends, Stacy is extremely protective, as is shown by the presence of the letter Teth, which means "serpent." In its position next to the letter Samech, Teth also indicates that Stacy will defend those whom she feels close to with extreme loyalty and vigor.

The Runic Interpretation

ᛇᛋᚨᛏᛋ (Eihwaz, Sowelu, Ansuz, Teiwaz, Sowelu)

Like Spencer, Stacy is blessed by the double Sowelu rune of wholeness. With Teiwaz, the rune of the warrior, making her brave *and* well adjusted, Stacy also has Eihwaz, the rune of defense, in her name—and this makes her one unusual and strong person. Ansuz, the rune of signals, gives Stacy excellent intuition. Stacy really should do something important with her life, like redesign the IRS or be an emissary to other galaxies. Stacy is a happy camper and a fearless opponent, and we like to stay on her good side.

Elements: Earth/fire, air, air, air, air

The Numerological Interpretation

Stacy (NV = 5, CV = 6, VV = 8, FL = 1)

Stacy has a very good sense of structure and knows how to coordinate many details into a harmonious whole. She is an asset to any organization, and will work very diligently to reach a place of executive prominence. Home is as important, if not more important, to her than her professional life, yet Stacy still wants to be out in the world, as she has a real need to express herself creatively. One of her main tasks in life is to balance her domestic life with her career. Stacy is helped in this respect by her consonant value of six, which gives her a good chance of resolving this conflict successfully.

DERIVATION: English, short form of Stanley, which is from the Old English roots *stan*, meaning "stone," and *leah*, meaning "clearing." Not a common given name, but very popular as a nickname.

PRINCIPAL COLORS: Any shade of red, especially the deepest

GEMSTONES AND PRECIOUS METALS: Bloodstones, garnets, rubies

BOTANICALS: Garlic, wormwood, rapeseed

UNIQUE SPELLINGS: Stann, Stanne

RELATED TO: Stanislas, Stanislaus, Stanley†, Stannard, Stansilaw, Stanton

Stan

A KABBALISTIC SYNOPSIS
סטאן —STAN (Samech, Teth, Aleph, Nun)

He may not be the most impressive guy in the neighborhood, and there is no great likelihood that he will ever make vast amounts of money, but Stan is one of the nicest guys you could wish to meet. His name's value is 120, which has very strong connections to all sorts of positive moral qualities. Stan is a deeply honest man who finds it difficult to tell even the whitest of lies; he is also a very hard worker, and despite the fact that he may not be the brightest tool in the box, he is a very valuable asset to any company that has the good sense to hire him. Because he is a loyal man in addition to all his other qualities, he will probably stay with the same company as long as there is work for him to do. Stan's biggest love is his family, and he wants to have plenty of free time in his life so that he can make the most of their company.

THE RUNIC INTERPRETATION
ᚾᚨᛏᛊ (Nauthiz, Ansuz, Teiwaz, Sowelu)

Stan demands to make a difference in the world. The Teiwaz rune of the warrior gives him courage and natural leadership ability. He also relies on Ansuz, the rune of signals, which enhances his intuition. His insight into people and issues is impressive: Nauthiz, the rune of limitation, sensitizes Stan to the suffering among us. Stan insists that things can change, and with a great attitude like that, Stan will make sure it happens. The Sowelu rune of wholeness says Stan has vision and an uncanny ability to think in terms of concepts that encompass the whole picture, while those around him squint at their pinhole visions of an issue.

Elements: Fire, air, air, air

THE NUMEROLOGICAL INTERPRETATION
Stan (NV = 9, CV = 8, VV = 1, FL = 1)

Stan is a person who takes the initiative to tackle bold challenges and big projects. He also has the stamina to see them through to their conclusion. This name indicates a man with a storehouse of understanding. This depth of knowledge allows him to deal with situations of which he has no prior knowledge. The numbers in his name give Stan another gift: an understanding of cycles. He is in touch with the ebbs and flows of life. This helps him tremendously to complete his projects, as he has an instinct about when to start, pause, expand, and contract.

Stanley

DERIVATION: English, originally a surname and place-name. From the Old English roots *stan*, meaning "stone," and *leah*, meaning "clearing." Has been used as a first name since the eighteenth century. Became increasingly common in the 1870s with the fame of explorer Sir Henry Stanley, who set out to find Dr. Livingstone.

PRINCIPAL COLORS: Virtually every shade of azure

GEMSTONES AND PRECIOUS METALS: Blue and blue-green turquoise, emeralds

BOTANICALS: Dog rose, walnuts, vervain

UNIQUE SPELLINGS: Stanlee, Stanlie, Stanly, Stannley

RELATED TO: Stant, Standish, Stanford, Stanmore, Stanton, Stanway, Stanwick

A KABBALISTIC SYNOPSIS

סטאנלי —STANLY (Samech, Teth, Aleph, Nun, Lamed, Yod)

Stanley is destined for success in a big way. His name's numerical value reduces to the number seven, which tells us that he will achieve most, if not all, of his major goals in life. In addition, when we look at the compression of his name, the first letter is Qoph, which indicates that Stanley has a good head on his shoulders. The presence of the letter Lamed lets us know that in Stanley we are dealing with a man who has a fierce ambition to do well. Stanley will work incredibly long hours in order to achieve this. However, Stanley is not the office snake waiting to snatch the position of someone higher up. In fact, Stanley is very good at pushing forward his colleagues for promotion. This willingness to help others stems to a large degree from Stanley's desire to impress others, a feature that is also noticeable in the way that he conducts his personal relationships.

THE RUNIC INTERPRETATION

ᛇᛖᛚᚾᚨᛏᛋ (Eihwaz, Ehwaz, Laguz, Nauthiz, Ansuz, Teiwaz, Sowelu)

Stanley shares many of Stan's idealistic qualities, but the additional Eihwaz rune of defense teaches Stanley how to avert disaster. The Nauthiz rune of constraint makes Stanley hard to pin down. Laguz, the rune of flexibility, combined with Ansuz and Ehwaz, makes Stanley intuitive and adaptable—so adaptable, in fact, that Stanley can hold his own with gangsters and priests, presidents and hooligans. Bravery and nerves of steel are Stanley's hallmarks, thanks to the Teiwaz warrior rune energy. Stanley is additionally blessed with the power of having the four elements in his name.

Elements: Earth/fire, air, water, fire, air, air, air

THE NUMEROLOGICAL INTERPRETATION

Stanley (NV = 6, CV = 11, VV = 4, FL = 1)

Stanley knows when to be intimate with another person and when to give him or her some space. He is very much involved with relationships, both on personal and professional levels. Stanley's inner sense of diplomacy is quite a helpful tool, too, as he is a man who tends to be very active in group work. A practical person who has a real need for economic security, Stanley prefers to follow a familiar rather than a more bohemian track through life. His travels tend to be much more internal than external, although he is always open to sharing with others what he has discovered about himself.

Stella

DERIVATION: English, from the Latin word *stella*, meaning "star." First used as a given name in the sixteenth century when Sir Philip Sidney wrote a famous series of love sonnets, "Astrophel to Stella," in which he referred to himself as Astrophel and to his lady as Stella. Stella became a common name during the eighteenth and nineteenth centuries.

PRINCIPAL COLORS: All but the brightest shades of blue

GEMSTONES AND PRECIOUS METALS: Turquoise, emeralds

BOTANICALS: Violets, daffodils, dog rose

UNIQUE SPELLINGS: Stela, Stelah, Stellah

RELATED TO: Estella, Estellet, Estrella, Star, Stel, Stelle

A KABBALISTIC SYNOPSIS

סטאללא —STALLA (Samech, Teth, Aleph, Lamed, Lamed, Aleph)

You can often see Stella in the park or sitting by the river; she may be reading, but she is just as likely to be simply sitting there, deep in thought. This may sound as though Stella is something of a recluse, but this is not the case at all. Stella is a very popular woman, and loves to go out; in fact, she can be quite a party animal. The thing with Stella is that she also needs her own personal space, and there are few things she prefers to spending some quiet reflective time by herself after a hectic week. The value of her name, when looked at in letter form, reveals two Lameds surrounded on each side by a letter Aleph. This tells us that Stella's thoughts and ideas, as represented by the Aleph, are held very passionately, as shown by the Lamed, which is suggestive of a strong, driving force. Stella is equally passionate in her relationships, and her enjoyment of expressing her passionate feelings may well require some soundproofing of the bedroom walls if she is an apartment dweller!

THE RUNIC INTERPRETATION

ᚨᛚᛚᛖᛏᛋ (Ansuz, Laguz, Laguz, Ehwaz, Teiwaz, Sowelu)

Stella rides on the famous streetcar named Desire. The double Laguz rune of artistic gifts and flexibility makes Stella a glamorous escapist and a dreamer. Teiwaz, the warrior rune, makes Stella feel brave and important in a world of her making. Stella is a star loved by all. The Ehwaz rune of movement suggests that romantic Stella will spin beautiful scenarios in her mind and genuinely appreciate her life.

Elements: Air, water, water, air, air, air

THE NUMEROLOGICAL INTERPRETATION

Stella (NV = 6, CV = 9, VV = 6, FL = 1)

Stella is deeply emotional—sometimes too much so. She requires continuous stimulation and romantic contact. While Stella should express her profoundly sensitive nature, it is not healthy for her to do this outside of her intimate relationships. Stella needs a canvas and paints, a tub of wet clay, or a ream of paper always at hand. If she does not establish and maintain a personal creative outlet, Stella will put too much pressure on her loved ones. Her name certainly gives her the possibility, as well as the potential, to develop latent artistic talents.

Stephanie

A KABBALISTIC SYNOPSIS

יאנאפאטס —STAPhANY (Samech, Teth, Aleph, Peh, Aleph, Nun, Yod)

As soon as you meet Stephanie, you just know you are in for some fun. She tends to have sparkling eyes and a bubbly personality, which makes Stephanie an instant hit with everyone. She loves to chatter, and she usually does so in a very enthusiastic and excitable way, as if she must get her words out before she bursts from having to keep them in! Stephanie is not ideally suited to an office job but is better off in a job that makes use of her outgoing personality and taste for the glamorous side of life. The value of her name is 211. The initial two in this number relates to the High Priestess card in the tarot, and in broad terms this could be regarded as showing a higher than usual level of women's intuition. The final eleven in her name reveals an attraction to the mysterious and bizarre aspects of life.

THE RUNIC INTERPRETATION

ᛗᛁᛏᚾᚺᛈᛗᛏᛋ (Ehwaz, Isa, Nauthiz, Ansuz, Hagalaz, Perth, Ehwaz, Teiwaz, Sowelu)

Stephanie wakes up in the morning with a smile and a confident toss of her head. The Sowelu rune makes Stephanie feel whole. Teiwaz gives her the courage of a warrior, and Ansuz, the intuition of a radar screen. Perth affords transformation on many levels. Hagalaz offers disruptions, and Nauthiz, constraint, but Stephanie is superwoman, and it's all in a day's work; confident Stephanie can handle most anything. Stephanie is blessed with the power of the four elements in her name.

Elements: Air, earth, fire, air, water, water, air, air, air

THE NUMEROLOGICAL INTERPRETATION

Stephanie (NV = 7, CV = 5, VV = 2, FL = 1)

This name is associated with the need for constant activity and intellectual stimulation. Stephanie is a resourceful woman, one who is quite adaptable and eager for new adventures. She is constantly at work processing her many life experiences, and is quite content to travel by herself or at the very least, spend time alone. Stephanie is gifted in speech and may have an aptitude for foreign languages. She certainly loves to be involved with interesting friends, and has a wide circle from which to choose. A woman who tends to be refined and sport a definite interest in the arts, Stephanie is charming and magnetically attractive.

DERIVATION: French version of Stephen, which derives from the Greek name Stephanos, meaning "crown." First used in English-speaking countries in the 1920s, and has steadily increased in popularity since then.

PRINCIPAL COLORS: The full range of yellow and green colors, also gold

GEMSTONES AND PRECIOUS METALS: Pearls, moonstones

BOTANICALS: Elder, juniper, blackberry

UNIQUE SPELLINGS: Stefanee, Stefani, Stefanie, Stefannie, Steffaney, Steffani, Steffanie, Steffany, Stephane, Stephanee, Stephaney, Stephani, Stephannie, Stephany, Stephne

RELATED TO: Stef, Steffi, Steffie, Steph, Stephana, Stephania, Stephie, Stevena, Stevey, Stevie

Stephen

DERIVATION: English, from the Greek name Stephanos meaning "crown." Found in the New Testament as the name of the first Christian martyr. Has been popular in English-speaking countries since the Norman Conquest in the twelfth century. Especially popular during the mid-twentieth century. In the United States, the alternate spelling, Steven, has become increasingly popular.

PRINCIPAL COLORS: Pale to medium-rich shades of blue

GEMSTONES AND PRECIOUS METALS: Turquoise, emeralds

BOTANICALS: Violets, vervain, apricots

UNIQUE SPELLINGS: Stephin, Stephyn, Steven†, Stevin, Stevyn

RELATED TO: Esteban, Esteve, Etienne, Steaphan, Stef, Stefan, Stefano, Stephan, Stevet, Stevenson, Stevie

❧

"My goal is simple. It is complete understanding of the universe, why it is as it is and why it exists at all."
—STEPHEN HAWKING (PHYSICIST)

A KABBALISTIC SYNOPSIS
סטאפון —STAPhVN (Samech, Teth, Aleph, Peh, Vau, Nun)

Stephen is a man who doesn't feel particularly comfortable when he is working for someone else. He is at his happiest when he is in charge of his own affairs. He certainly has the gift of gab, which makes him a terrific deal closer, for he has the ability to persuade the reluctant party to part with their cash after hearing just a few of his carefully chosen words. One Hebrew equivalent of the value of his name is the phrase "they of the world." This phrase refers to Stephen's wisdom, and to the fact that he truly is a man of the world. In spite of his sophisticated nature, Stephen can be challenging when it comes to relationships. It's not that he is emotionally cold or refuses to listen, but simply that he can be a deeply insecure man, which makes him extremely possessive. However, with all that he has going for him, Stephen can attract a partner who is able to deal with these obstacles.

THE RUNIC INTERPRETATION
ᚾᛖᚺᛈᛖᛏᛋ (Nauthiz, Ehwaz, Hagalaz, Perth, Ehwaz, Teiwaz, Sowelu)

With the Perth rune for transformations, Hagalaz bringing disruptions, and Nauthiz for constraint, Stephen is bound to have nagging worries. Luckily, there are many willing arms outstretched to comfort him. The double Ehwaz rune of movement means Stephen can escape into music and dance his blues away. Ehwaz also lures him to live in or visit exotic places and travel. Another cheery note is the manly Teiwaz rune, which makes Stephen feel like a twentieth-century Tarzan. Mighty Teiwaz is the warrior rune, and with all the confusion in his life, Stephen is entitled to pound his chest now and then. But he does so just to let off some steam.

Elements: Fire, air, water, water, air, air, air

THE NUMEROLOGICAL INTERPRETATION
Stephen (NV = 6, CV = 5, VV = 1, FL = 1)

Stephen is a fascinating friend and a very exciting partner. He has a natural sense of grace and seems to glide through a room. He has poise, charm, and magnetism to boot. Stephen is also very self-assertive, and he has a strong need to express his talents and abilities. Although an intimate relationship is important to him, it cannot be with a person who is emotionally dependent and needy. Stephen wants to be free to move through life. He is delighted to have a companion with whom he can share his experiences, but he definitely does not want to be tethered down.

❧

Steve

A Kabbalistic Synopsis
סטיו —STYV (Samech, Teth, Yod, Vau)

If Steve isn't a counselor or working in some other caring profession, he may well be missing out on his true vocation in life. Steve is very adept at understanding other people's problems and is always willing to listen. His name begins with the letter Samech, which means "prop" in Hebrew and should be taken as an indication of his willingness to be a moral and emotional support for others. The central Yod in his name lets us know that Steve is a very active person. Indeed, his name is associated with the Death card in the tarot, which actually refers to a number of changes in the individual's life. Steve would make an ideal catch for anyone looking for an affectionate and supportive partner. The final Vau in his name also suggests that he is a thoughtful person as well as being emotionally attentive. However, Steve also likes to be heard, and anyone who settles down with him will need to make sure that they do give him a chance to speak as well as listen.

The Runic Interpretation
ᛗᚠᛗᛏᛋ (Ehwaz, Fehu, Ehwaz, Teiwaz, Sowelu)

Somewhere along the line Steve decided he preferred animals to the human kingdom. Steve is an animal rights activist and works with vets to help furry patients. His favorite book is *Doctor Doolittle*, and one of these days Steve may find some friends in the human sphere who are accepting, loyal, and kind—but if that never happens, he still has a lot of animal friends who treat him with love and devotion.

Elements: Air, fire, air, air, air

The Numerological Interpretation
Steve (NV = 8, CV = 7, VV = 1, FL = 1)

An ambitious man, one who is very concerned about his social and financial place in the world, Steve is out to achieve big things in life. He may find himself drawn into the business arena at an early age, for he is a person who is naturally inclined to set his goals and then keep after them until he has accomplished his results. Steve has to take care that his focus on achievement does not deny him the pleasures of being emotionally intimate with friends and lovers. There are many opportunities for relationships, both business and personal, as Steve is a magnetic name. Steve is quite potent, full of sexual energy. Important lessons in life come to Steve through the need to be in touch with his more subtle feelings.

DERIVATION: English, short for the Greek Stephanos, meaning "crown," and its English version, Steven.

PRINCIPAL COLORS: Dark colors, such as black, purple, and dark blue

GEMSTONES AND PRECIOUS METALS: Rich sapphires, any other dark stones

BOTANICALS: Marsh mallow, angelica, shepherd's purse

UNIQUE SPELLING: Steeve

RELATED TO: Esteban, Esteve, Etienne, Steaphan, Stef, Stefan, Stefano, Stephan, Stephent, Stevent, Stevenson, Stevie

DERIVATION: English, alternate
spelling of Stephen, which derives
from the Greek name Stephanos,
meaning "crown." This spelling has
become increasingly popular in
the United States in recent years.

PRINCIPAL COLORS: Medium-rich
shades of any color

GEMSTONES AND PRECIOUS
METALS: Sapphires

BOTANICALS: Sage, spinach,
Iceland moss

UNIQUE SPELLINGS: Stephen†,
Stephin, Stephyn, Stevin, Stevyn

RELATED TO: Esteban, Esteve,
Etienne, Steaphan, Stef, Stefan,
Stefano, Stephan, Steve†,
Stevenson, Stevie

Steven

A KABBALISTIC SYNOPSIS
סטאואן —STAVAN (Samech, Teth, Aleph, Vau, Aleph, Nun)

This is one lucky man we are dealing with here! Not only does Steven's name have a value that ends in the number seven—a decidedly potent symbol of worldly achievement—but the value of his name also reduces to ten, the number of the Wheel of Fortune card in the tarot. The Wheel of Fortune card tells us that when it comes to matters of pure chance, Steven has an advantage over the rest of us, since he appears to be genetically lucky. If Steven is not a gambling man, there is a good chance that he will be employed in a field where matters of chance play a big role, such as stockbroking. Steven maintains a very close relationship with his parents throughout his adult life, and it is to his parents that he is most likely to turn when in need of advice. One thing he will need to learn when he gets into a committed relationship is that his first port of call should always be his partner.

THE RUNIC INTERPRETATION
ᚾᛖᚠᛖᛗᛏᛊ (Nauthiz, Ehwaz, Fehu, Ehwaz, Teiwaz, Sowelu)

Steven has it all over the alternatively spelled Stephen; he needn't expect any of the difficult transformations or disruptions that Stephen has to look forward to. No, Steven has the all-important Fehu, the rune of money and possessions, so let the good times roll. Teiwaz, the warrior rune, brings a battle cry to his lips from time to time, but it's usually more of a good-natured whoop than a holler.

Elements: Fire, air, fire, air, air, air

THE NUMEROLOGICAL INTERPRETATION
Steven (NV = 4, CV = 3, VV = 1, FL = 1)

Steven seeks to take control of his own life and perfect himself by learning from the challenges he encounters along his way. He feels most comfortable, however, when he knows that he has a firm home base from which to operate. He will therefore spend the first portion of his life securing his foundation and anchoring his talents and abilities. Thus armed and prepared, Steven sets off to widen his horizons and broaden his perspectives. He requires a relationship that is emotionally stable and able to support his urge for enterprise.

Stewart

A Kabbalistic Synopsis

סטוערט —STVA'ART (Samech, Teth, Vau, Ayin, Resh, Teth)

Stewart is something of a contradictory creature. On the one hand, he has a name that is permeated throughout with the energies of the star sign Leo. This makes Stewart a born leader and a charismatic individual whom people usually like and admire; in fact, they are even willing to take orders from him. This is Stewart's public side, and it is one that usually guarantees him a lot of respect from his colleagues and peers. The other side of Stewart's character is indicated by the fact that the value of his name reduces to twelve, the number of the Hanged Man in the tarot. This tarot card refers to Stewart's tendency toward self-sacrifice; he is someone who nearly always puts others before himself. This aspect of his personality relates mainly to how he treats his partner, in that he is willing to do absolutely anything to ensure her happiness.

The Runic Interpretation

ᛏᚱᚨᚹᛗᛏᛊ (Teiwaz, Raido, Ansuz, Wunjo, Ehwaz, Teiwaz, Sowelu)

Stewart has double Teiwaz, the warrior rune of courage; blessed Sowelu, the rune of wholeness; and Wunjo, the rune of joy! Stewart knows how to express all the enthusiasm generated by this fortunate combination of runes because he also has Raido, the rune of good communication, on his team. Ansuz, for signals, is there to let Stewart know how to be patient and wait for the right opportunities to unfold. Stewart will see the world, and he may conduct some sort of international business. Ehwaz is there to allow him to move and relocate if he so chooses, and reap the benefits when the spirit moves him.

Elements: Air, water, air, earth, air, air, air

The Numerological Interpretation

Stewart (NV = 7, CV = 5, VV = 11, FL = 1)

Stewart has a gift for amassing huge quantities of data, categorizing them, and correctly analyzing the results. He is perfectly suited for the world of computer technology. In addition, he has the type of mind that can convert abstract facts and figures into practical applications. Thus, he is also very well suited to all types of community and social science work. Stewart will need to find balance in his life through his intimate relationships. It will be very important for him to develop his emotions and feelings and not to live exclusively in his mind.

DERIVATION: English, alternate spelling of Stuart, which comes from the Old English root *stigweard*, meaning "steward" or "keeper of the household." Especially popular in the United States during the mid-twentieth century.

PRINCIPAL COLORS: Pale to deeply toned yellow and green, gold

GEMSTONES AND PRECIOUS METALS: Pearls, cat's-eye, any other white stone

BOTANICALS: Blackberry, hops, juniper, linseed

UNIQUE SPELLINGS: Stewert, Stewirt, Stewurt, Stewyrt, Stuart†, Stuert

RELATED TO: Stew, Steward, Stu, Stuey

DERIVATION: English, from the Old English root *stigweard*, meaning "steward" or "keeper of the household." The Stuarts were the ruling house in England from 1371 to 1714. Especially popular in the United States in the mid-twentieth century.

PRINCIPAL COLORS: Light pink to the richest shades of red

GEMSTONES AND PRECIOUS METALS: Garnets, red rubies

BOTANICALS: Nettle, wormwood

UNIQUE SPELLINGS: Stewartt, Stewert, Stewirt, Stewurt, Stewyrt, Stuert

RELATED TO: Stew, Steward, Stu, Stuey

A KABBALISTIC SYNOPSIS
סטוארט —STVART (Samech, Teth, Vau, Aleph, Resh, Teth)

Never give Stuart your expensive crystal glasses to hold if he comes to your house—not unless you're hoping to replace them, as Stuart is an incredibly clumsy man. If he was born under the sign of Sagittarius, then this tendency will be even worse. The value of his name reduces to sixteen, which is the number of the House of God card, or the Tower, in the tarot, which refers to major catastrophes in life. However, Stuart is not really prone to any major catastrophes, but to many minor ones. His only real problem is his temper, which is indicated by the double occurrence of the letter Teth in his name. There is a danger that Stuart's quick temper may, from time to time, put him in some fairly awkward situations, especially if he loses his temper in the workplace. People will make a lot of allowances for this trait, since everyone knows that what Stuart really wants is to do the right thing. Those around him recognize Stuart's good heart, and learn to see behind the minor catastrophes that seem to plague him.

THE RUNIC INTERPRETATION
↑ᚱᚨᚢ↑ᛊ (Teiwaz, Raido, Ansuz, Uruz, Teiwaz, Sowelu)

Stuart has many of the same blessings as Stewart, but his name substitutes the rune of Uruz strength for the Wunjo rune of joy. Not that Stuart isn't happy—he's quietly happy, in a self-contained way. Stuart likes manly touches about him, like leather and the rugged outdoors. Old bound books fill his home, along with an esoteric collection of music and old snapshots from years ago he just can't discard for sentimental reasons. Stuart loves deeply. The Uruz energy, combined with Teiwaz warrior strength, could mean that Stuart risks his life in his profession. If he's injured, he makes a joke of it, and is modest about his adventures. Stuart is especially brave because he has faith in life, and he is willing to skip the applause in order to quietly follow his mission.

Elements: Air, water, air, earth, air, air

THE NUMEROLOGICAL INTERPRETATION
Stuart (NV = 9, CV = 5, VV = 4, FL = 1)

This is a name that bestows the potential for a very broad capacity to love. Stuart is a compassionate man, a person who can relate to everyone's feelings. People can sense his convictions and are easily inspired by his words and deeds. Stuart is not a man with his head in the clouds; he has a very practical side to his nature, and his need to be of service is coupled with a very down-to-earth assessment of his own and other people's physical requirements and circumstances.

Sue

DERIVATION: English, common
short form of a number of names
beginning with "Su," including
Susan, Suzanne, and Susanna.
Recently, it has sometimes been
used as an independent given
name.

PRINCIPAL COLORS: The full
range of red hues, especially the
deepest shades

GEMSTONES AND PRECIOUS
METALS: Bloodstones, garnets

BOTANICALS: Garlic, onion, nettle

UNIQUE SPELLINGS: Soo, Su

RELATED TO: Suellen, Susant,
Susannat, Susannah, Susanne,
Susiet, Suzanna, Suzannet,
Suzette, Suzy

A KABBALISTIC SYNOPSIS
סוה —SVH (Samech, Vau, Heh)

Sue is the sort to end up with her own thriving company, one that could become tops in its industry. Her name totals to seventy-one, and the seventy is associated with the letter Ayin, which, among other things, relates to business success. In particular, seventy relates to the entrepreneurial skills that one needs to set oneself up to do well. In addition, the reduction of seventy-one gives us eight, which is a number indicative of willpower and strength of character. Sue is certainly a force to be reckoned with, and she is not afraid to make this fact clear to everyone she deals with. Emotionally she has a tendency to be independent, and she hates to feel trapped into any sort of commitment. Sue is likely to be very happy in her relationships, but is seeking a partner who can be a friend more than one who will spark any grand romantic passion.

THE RUNIC INTERPRETATION
ᛖᚢᛋ (Ehwaz, Uruz, Sowelu)

There's a good chance Sue speaks assertively, even from the earliest age. Sowelu, the rune of wholeness, gives Sue the kind of good mental health most people would pay money to attain. The Uruz rune of strength enables Sue to be stable and calm; nothing daunts her. She's able to live happily, and goes almost anywhere, as indicated by the Ehwaz rune of movement. It takes a lot to make Sue crumble.

Elements: Air, earth, air

THE NUMEROLOGICAL INTERPRETATION
Sue (NV = 9, CV = 1, VV = 8, FL = 1)

An enterprising and forward-moving woman, Sue finds it difficult to feel complacent about life. This is an active person, one who refuses to inhibit her own urges for success. Sue's appearance means a great deal to her, and she will not hesitate to spend a lot of money on clothing or fitness. Sue's ambitions are quite strong, yet she is not so caught up in her own drive to succeed that she loses sight of others. This is a person who staunchly comes to people's defense. She has a generous disposition, and when called upon, will use whatever influence she may have to be of service.

DERIVATION: English version of Susannah, which comes from the Hebrew root "shoshan," meaning "lily." Popular during the eighteenth century, then declined and experienced a great resurgence in the mid-twentieth century.

PRINCIPAL COLORS: The palest to the richest of greens, also white

GEMSTONES AND PRECIOUS METALS: Jade, moonstones

BOTANICALS: Chicory, colewort, plantain, moonwort

UNIQUE SPELLINGS: Soosan, Soozan, Suesan, Suesen, Suesin, Suezin, Suezyn, Susen, Susin, Susyn, Suzan, Suzin, Suzyn

RELATED TO: Shoshana, Shoshanah, Shoshanna, Shoshannah, Shushana, Suet, Susana, Susanah, Susanetta, Susann, Susannat, Susannah, Susanne, Susette, Susiet, Suzaette, Suzana, Suzanna, Suzannah, Suzannet, Suzette

Susan

A KABBALISTIC SYNOPSIS
סוסאן —SVSAN (Samech, Vau, Samech, Aleph, Nun)

Quite simply, Susan is a lovely woman. She is warmhearted and finds it very hard to see anything but the good in everyone she meets. Even if she has a bad experience with an individual, she is likely to attribute it to a simple misunderstanding. While most of us would find it difficult to maintain this reasonable viewpoint, it does indeed have its benefits for Susan; she is rarely stressed out, and has none of the bitterness that affects most people's lives to some degree or other. Susan may be laid-back, but she is far from boring, as the reduction of the value of her name reveals; the number fifteen relates to the Devil card in the tarot, and in Susan's case, her particular vices are pleasures of a physical nature.

THE RUNIC INTERPRETATION
ᚾᚨᛋᚢᛋ (Nauthiz, Ansuz, Sowelu, Uruz, Sowelu)

The double Sowelu configuration for wholeness means Susan shares Sue's extraordinary mental health, and doubly so. Susan may not live in funky places like Sue, but with Uruz in her name to brace her, she shares Sue's strength and bravery. The addition of Nauthiz for constraint and Ansuz for intuition tells us that Susan has an innate sense of what the future holds. She has had her fair share of limiting circumstances, and as a result, she values freedom and expansiveness more than most people, who take it all for granted. Susan enjoys attention and is a bit of a people pleaser, when it comes right down to it. But she'd blush if you mentioned that to her.

Elements: Fire, air, air, earth, air

THE NUMEROLOGICAL INTERPRETATION
Susan (NV = 11, CV = 7, VV = 4, FL = 1)

Susan is a name that possesses some very spiritual qualities. Susan can be quite intuitive and, at times, even amazingly psychic. Susan seems to experience life's realities with a penetrating depth and clarity that fascinates people. Very often, she will find that her intentions are not fully understood by others. She can be detached and impersonal, but this doesn't mean that she is uncaring. Susan just has an inner voice that she may listen to more than the outer, physical voices around her. She should look for a partner who is a bit more down-to-earth to help bring out her more practical nature.

Susanna

A Kabbalistic Synopsis

סוסאננא —SVSANNA (Samech, Vau, Samech, Aleph, Nun, Nun, Aleph)

The central features in Susanna's name are the two letters Samech and Nun. The letter Samech means "prop" or "support," and relates to Susanna's generally supportive nature. Susanna will help people out whenever she can, although the presence of the letter Vau between the two Samechs hints that Susanna has a certain level of anxiety. And Susanna has reason to fear, because she may be taken for a ride by an apparently deserving case that occupies her attention. The other key letter, the Nun, tells us that Susanna has a tendency for melancholy as well as emotional insecurity. However, this is tempered by the fact that between the first and second Nun is an Aleph, showing that Susanna is capable of rationalizing her emotional feelings of inadequacy. She is so emotionally cognizant, in fact, that she may find herself in a therapist's or adviser's role for others.

The Runic Interpretation

ᚨᚾᚾᚨᛊᚢᛊ (Ansuz, Nauthiz, Nauthiz, Ansuz, Sowelu, Uruz, Sowelu)

Nauthiz, the rune of constraint, appears not once but twice in Susanna's name. Nauthiz creates limitations and roadblocks. Luckily, Uruz, the rune of strength, is around to keep Susanna resilient and patient in the face of these obstacles. While it's true that Susanna has more than her share of challenges, she remains undaunted through it all. The double Ansuz rune of signals provides Susanna with keen insight and a brilliant sense of timing. Susanna knows how to stretch the grocery money and when to splurge on a hot tip in the stock market. The double Sowelu runes of wholeness bring emotional stability and an optimistic and confident mental outlook for lucky Susanna.

Elements: Air, fire, fire, air, air, earth, air

The Numerological Interpretation

Susanna (NV = 8, CV = 3, VV = 5, FL = 1)

A woman who is often at the center of a group of interesting friends and associates, Susanna is magnetic, charming, and attractive. She pays careful attention to her body, exercises, and strives to monitor her diet. Susanna is an avid reader, and her home is filled with all sorts of books. Easy with words and fluid in her conversation, Susanna has a gift for writing and communicating. She has the ability to coordinate people, and is blessed by an aptitude for channeling other people's support for her own abundant plans and projects.

DERIVATION: Biblical, from the Hebrew root *shoshan* meaning "lily." In the Bible, Susannah appears in both the Old and New Testaments, although it is spelled without the *h* in the New Testament. Most commonly associated with the Apocryphal story of Susannah who was falsely accused of adultery but ultimately found innocent. Very popular from the sixteenth century to the eighteenth century.

PRINCIPAL COLORS: Black, gray, dark shades of azure and purple

GEMSTONES AND PRECIOUS METALS: Any dark stone, including black pearls and black diamonds

BOTANICALS: Angelica, shepherd's purse, gravel root

UNIQUE SPELLINGS: Soosana, Soosanna, Suesanna, Susana, Susannah, Suzanna, Suzannah

RELATED TO: Shoshana, Shoshanah, Shoshanna, Shoshannah, Shushana, Suet, Susant, Susanetta, Susann, Susanne, Susette, Susiet, Suzaette, Suzannet, Suze, Suzette, Suzie, Suzy

DERIVATION: English, common
pet form of names beginning
with "Su," such as Susan and
Suzanne. Occasionally used
as an independent given name.

PRINCIPAL COLORS: Any yellow or
bronze hue, also gold, orange

GEMSTONES AND PRECIOUS
METALS: Amber, topaz, yellow
diamonds

BOTANICALS: Chamomile,
lavender, borage

UNIQUE SPELLINGS: Susee,
Susey, Susi, Susy, Suzee, Suzey,
Suzi, Suzie, Suzy

RELATED TO: Sue†, Susan†,
Susana, Susanah, Susann,
Susanna†, Susannah, Susanne,
Susette, Suzaette, Suzana,
Suzanna, Suzannah, Suzanne†,
Suzette

Susie

A KABBALISTIC SYNOPSIS
סוזי —SVZY (Samech, Vau, Zayin, Yod)

Susie is a real live wire, and she will not have any intention of settling down until she is full into the path of her life; even then, she may need some convincing. The compression of her name produces the two letters Peh, meaning "mouth," and Daleth, meaning "door." This suggests that Susie uses her voice as a means to get doors to open for her—or, in other words, the key to her success lies in the use of her voice. In many cases, these letters simply indicate a very persuasive manner. Susie has a great number of friends, not just because she loves to party but because she can be very selfless when it comes to those she cares about. Friends know that whenever they have a problem of any nature, they can come to her for a shoulder to cry on and find her door always open.

THE RUNIC INTERPRETATION
ᛗᛁᛊᚢᛊ (Ehwaz, Isa, Sowelu, Uruz, Sowelu)

Susie doesn't demand love. Instead, she can give and receive love freely because of the double Sowelu rune of wholeness in her name. Susie needs a career that enhances compassion. Counseling and the healing arts or philanthropy work will serve her well. The Uruz rune of strength means Susie could nurse the critically ill, or work with those with special needs in a balanced and kind way. However, Susie needs to contrast the service work in her life with activities that make her laugh and play. Whether it's tickets to the opera or Rollerblading like a kid, Susie needs to feel exhilarated and joyful. Ehwaz and Isa teach Susie patience and how to keep herself feeling hopeful and optimistic. Susie has a lot to offer humanity.

Elements: Air, earth, air, earth, air

THE NUMEROLOGICAL INTERPRETATION
Susie (NV = 1, CV = 2, VV = 8, FL = 1)

Susie is an optimistic person who is unafraid to be herself. She has a plenitude of creative ideas and the courage to experiment. Relationships are very important to her, and she is sought after by friends and lovers alike. Susie brings joy into all her associations, and she can be counted on to raise the level of laughter in any group situation. Susie can take it very personally if people do not respond to her in the way she expects them to, so she has to learn detachment and to not expect instantaneous recognition and approval.

Suzanne

DERIVATION: French version of Susan. Used in English-speaking countries since the early twentieth century, particularly in the United States. Especially common in the mid-twentieth century.

PRINCIPAL COLORS: The full range of yellow and russet tones, orange

GEMSTONES AND PRECIOUS METALS: Citrine, topaz

BOTANICALS: Lavender, Saint-John's-wort, eyebright

UNIQUE SPELLINGS: Susann, Susanne, Suzan, Suzane, Suzann, Suzzane, Suzzanne

RELATED TO: Shoshana, Shoshanah, Shoshanna, Shoshannah, Shushana, Suet, Susant, Susana, Susanah, Susanetta, Susannat, Susannah, Susette, Susiet, Suzaette, Suzana, Suzanna, Suzannah, Suzette

A KABBALISTIC SYNOPSIS

סוזאן —SVZAN (Samech, Vau, Zayin, Aleph, Nun)

Unlike Susie, Suzanne tends to be too serious to spend most of her formative years larking about. Suzanne wants to make a way for herself, and the central letter Zayin in her name, meaning "sword," suggests that she has the natural vigor to ensure that she will make a real go of it. Suzanne has an excellent mind, and the central letter Kaph in the compression of her name relates to practical matters; thus Suzanne's ideal career will involve taking original ideas and plans and turning them into actual products or salable services. However, Suzanne is not all brain and no heart. In fact, her almost total focus on her career may well be born out of a fear of romantic rejection rather than out of an indifference to relationships. She need not worry, though; many people find success a highly attractive quality, and Suzanne will certainly be successful!

THE RUNIC INTERPRETATION

ᛖᚾᚾᚨᛉᚢᛋ (Ehwaz, Nauthiz, Nauthiz, Ansuz, Algiz, Uruz, Sowelu)

Suzanne doesn't scream or break things anymore. Early on, the double Nauthiz combination of constraint made Suzanne feel like she was trapped. Later on, though, she looks at it as a call to freedom and independence and tries not to feel victimized. The calming Algiz rune of protection helps Suzanne control her emotions and subdue her fiery temper. Uruz, the rune of strength, teaches Suzanne to walk away from a fight and to expand her reserves of tolerance. Sowelu, the rune of wholeness, blesses Suzanne with self-assurance. Suzanne will find a career that suits her temperament, and once she does, it may well lead her to the best times of her life.

Elements: Air, fire, fire, air, air, earth, air

THE NUMEROLOGICAL INTERPRETATION

Suzanne (NV = 1, CV = 1, VV = 9, FL = 1)

The numbers in this name indicate a woman who is the driving force behind any project with which she is involved. Suzanne is a go-getter, an initiator, and a highly individualistic woman. She is also a very kind person with a very charitable heart. If she has to modify any aspect of her nature, it is her tendency to begin too many projects at the same time while leaving the completion of their details to others. Suzanne has no problem moving out on her own into uncharted territory; in fact, she appreciates the challenge!

Sydney

DERIVATION: English, alternate spelling of Sidney, which originally derives from a Norman baronial surname. Became increasingly common during the nineteenth century, and is sometimes used as a female name.

PRINCIPAL COLORS: Any shade of green or white

GEMSTONES AND PRECIOUS METALS: Jade, cat's-eye

BOTANICALS: Chicory, lettuce, moonwort

UNIQUE SPELLINGS: Cydnee, Cydney, Cydnie, Cydny, Sidnee, Sidney, Sidni, Sidnie, Sidny, Sydni, Sydnie, Sydny

RELATED TO: Cid, Cyd, Sid, Sidney†; Sidonia, Sidonie, Sidony, Syd

A KABBALISTIC SYNOPSIS
סידני —SYDNY (Samech, Yod, Daleth, Nun, Yod)

As happens from time to time in Hebrew transliterations of a name, the difference between Sidney and Sydney does not exist in Hebrew, as both use the letter Yod for the I or Y sound. However, this gives us the chance to have an in-depth look at the name. This name suggests a very helpful individual who loves to get involved with his local community and is a very popular figure around town. When we look at the value of this name, we get an idea of why Sydney is so helpful: The name adds up to 130, which can be represented by the two letters Qoph and Lamed. Qoph refers to intelligence, so we know that Sydney is a man with loads of ideas stacked up in his mind; he's just waiting for a chance to act on them. The letter Lamed indicates a driven nature, a feeling that things must be done and that people are relying on one to make sure that they happen. Consequently, Sydney has a great sense of duty toward his fellow townsfolk and feels obliged to pitch in. This doesn't mean that he doesn't enjoy it, though; he gets great pleasure out of being so indispensable.

THE RUNIC INTERPRETATION
ᛇᛗᚾᛞᛇᛋ (Eihwaz, Ehwaz, Nauthiz, Dagaz, Eihwaz, Sowelu)

Nauthiz, the rune of constraint, will impose some limiting situations on Sydney, be they social, financial, geographic, or physical. What matters is that constraint is uncomfortable. However, Eihwaz, the rune of defense, gives Sydney some escape valves, and daydreaming is Sydney's favorite coping mechanism. Dagaz, the rune of breakthrough, foretells achievement and prosperity in the end, while Sowelu, the rune of wholeness, indicates that Sydney leads a rich and satisfying life in the real world, after all.

Elements: Earth/fire, air, fire, fire, earth/fire, air

THE NUMEROLOGICAL INTERPRETATION
Sydney (NV = 2, CV = 1, VV = 1, FL = 1)

Sydney's ability to handle people is one of his finest talents. He is definitely a born diplomat. Although he never loses sight of his own direction in life, Sydney has a way of harmonizing other people's interests with his own. He is a very innovative man who tends to dress in his own fashion. An independent person with lots of initiative, Sydney is never lazy or bored, and he remains free to be himself. Sydney always has time for friends, who know that they can come to him for a little extra boost of fiery inspiration.

Sylvester

A KABBALISTIC SYNOPSIS

סילואסמא —SYLVASTA (Samech, Yod, Lamed, Vau, Aleph, Samech, Teth, Aleph)

Here we have a man whose ambition knows no limits and who has the capacity to achieve great things in his life. The value of his name is 177, and the two sevens at the end of this number are themselves a strong pointer toward material success. When we look at the letters these numbers represent, we find that the seventy is Ayin, which suggests a real knack for commercial achievements, while the seven is the value of Zayin, the Hebrew letter meaning "sword," which suggests that Sylvester is a fighter who is quite willing to battle in order to achieve his goals. It isn't all work and no play for Sylvester, though; he does enjoy his luxury, as is shown by the fact that the value of his name reduces to fifteen. In particular, Sylvester likes the cultured side of life, and if he has the money, he will spend it on original artwork, fine wine, and the like.

THE RUNIC INTERPRETATION

ᚱᛖᛏᛋᛖᚠᛚᛇᛋ (Raido, Ehwaz, Teiwaz, Sowelu, Ehwaz, Fehu, Laguz, Eihwaz, Sowelu)

The double Sowelu runes of wholeness bless this name. Sowelu energy rises above everything to assure Sylvester a generous and productive life. Double Ehwaz means lucky Sylvester could live and work abroad in several locations during his career. Raido, the rune of good communication, could mean that Sylvester will share his experience in any number of ways. Fehu, the rune of possessions, means Sylvester will have the money to accumulate many treasures. The warrior Teiwaz rune, combined with Isa for standstill, means Sylvester is a man of his word who can stand up against the crowd if need be. Laguz, the rune of flexibility, offers Sylvester musical ability and an appreciation of the mysteries of life. Sylvester has the power of the four elements in his name.

Elements: Water, air, air, air, air, fire, water, earth/fire, air

THE NUMEROLOGICAL INTERPRETATION

Sylvester (NV = 1, CV = 2, VV = 8, FL = 1)

Sylvester seems to be in a constant process of self-discovery, and he has two primary vehicles for this exploration. The first is through his relationships, which are many. Sylvester likes looking into the mirror of other people's eyes—but at times he has to learn to see what is actually reflected. Sylvester does not like to see any of his own imperfections, and when they are pointed out, he may deny they exist. The second is through his creative ambitions, which are also many. Sylvester is very much the businessman. He has the ability to carve out his life several steps in advance, and he enjoys the strategies involved in creating and climbing his own ladder of achievement.

DERIVATION: English, from the Latin root *silva*, meaning "forest." Name of many early saints and popes. Has been used in English-speaking countries since the Middle Ages. Current film star Sylvester Stallone has increased the name's popularity in recent years.

PRINCIPAL COLORS: Light to deep, rich shades of bronze and yellow

GEMSTONES AND PRECIOUS METALS: Topaz, yellow diamonds

BOTANICALS: Eyebright, sorrel, thyme

UNIQUE SPELLINGS: Silvester, Silvestir, Silvestirre, Silvestyr, Silvestyrre, Sylvestir, Sylvestyr

RELATED TO: Silvestre

Sylvia

DERIVATION: English, from the Italian name Silvia, which derives from the Latin root *silva*, meaning "forest." In Roman mythology, Rhea Silvia was the nature goddess who mothered Romulus and Remus, the founders of Rome. Entered into widespread use in the mid-nineteenth century.

PRINCIPAL COLORS: All shades of gold, green, and yellow

GEMSTONES AND PRECIOUS METALS: Pearls, moss agate, moonstones

BOTANICALS: Elder, blackberry, linseed

UNIQUE SPELLINGS: Sillvia, Silvea, Silvia, Silviah, Silvya, Syllvea, Syllvia, Sylvea, Sylviah, Sylvya

RELATED TO: Silva, Silvie, Sylva, Sylvanna, Sylvetta, Sylvette, Sylvie, Sylvina, Sylvine, Zilvia, Zylvia

❧

"Love has the quality of informing almost everything—even one's work."
—SYLVIA ASHTON-WARNER
(EDUCATOR)

A KABBALISTIC SYNOPSIS
סילויא —SYLVYA (Samech, Yod, Lamed, Vau, Yod, Aleph)

Sylvia is highly intelligent and might find herself going to work in an academic setting. Her intellectual capabilities are focused on areas of thought, such as philosophy or other abstract ideas, rather than on the application of science. Consequently, her extremely good brain doesn't automatically guarantee her a great career in the private sector. However, as an archivist or a researcher in a university Sylvia can make quite a name for herself. Since the number seventeen features prominently in the numerical version of her name, we can assume that Sylvia's life will be relatively trouble-free, and she may also find it easier than most to achieve the things in life that she desires. In addition to her analytical intelligence, Sylvia is also what is best referred to as wise; in other words, she has a good understanding of the world as opposed to simply a good knowledge of it.

THE RUNIC INTERPRETATION
ᚨᛁᚠᛚᛇᛋ (Ansuz, Isa, Fehu, Laguz, Eihwaz, Sowelu)

Sylvia knows what she's looking for in romance, and will have success in affairs of the heart. Laguz, the rune of flow, expands her romantic nature by adding a love of music and talent in the performing arts. Fehu, the rune of possessions, assures Sylvia opportunities and the financial security so helpful to artists. Sylvia's deep appreciation of time spent alone comes from the Isa rune of standstill. The Ansuz rune accounts for Sylvia's love of prophecy and her insightful nature. Best of all, Sowelu radiates wholeness and contributes to Sylvia's well-balanced personality. On top of all these blessings, Sylvia has the power of the four elements in her name.

Elements: Air, earth, fire, water, earth/fire, air

THE NUMEROLOGICAL INTERPRETATION
Sylvia (NV = 7, CV = 8, VV = 8, FL = 1)

Sylvia seeks to gradually gain power and position in life. She does not separate her career from the rest of her life; her career tends to be at its center. Social recognition by her seniors and peers, as well as the financial returns from her work, are very important to Sylvia. Sylvia wants to be in a place of executive responsibility, and feels most comfortable when she is able to control and structure the creative potential in her world. In time, ambition will give way to compassion and control will yield to love. If such is already the case, Sylvia will be using her amazing willpower for the benefit of others as well as herself.

❧

Tamara

A Kabbalistic Synopsis

טאמערא —TAMA'ARA (Teth, Aleph, Mem, Ayin, Resh, Aleph)

If you are ever out with Tamara at a restaurant for the evening, it's probably a good idea to order for the both of you, or you could be there till the next morning! Tamara is a deeply indecisive woman. The value of her name reduces to six, which is the number of the Lovers in the tarot. This is a card that, despite its name, is concerned with difficult choices in life rather than romance. While Tamara may take a while to make up her mind, she does have a large bounty of energy, and once she has settled on a plan of action (or accepts one given to her), she will work like a demon until it is finished. Emotionally, Tamara is looking for a permanent relationship. She is hoping for a truly close and intimate partner who wants to spend as much time as possible with her; she is not inclined toward long-distance relationships.

The Runic Interpretation

ᚨᚱᚨᛗᚨᛏ (Ansuz, Raido, Ansuz, Mannaz, Ansuz, Teiwaz)

Tamara just knows tomorrow will be a better day. And when Tamara knows something, her family and friends sit up and take notice, because she's usually on the money. The unusual triple Ansuz rune of signals heightens Tamara's intuition, sense of timing, and rapport with people. Teiwaz, the warrior rune, also appears in this name in combination with Mannaz, the rune of self. Tamara is hopeful and confident, and while she may not be rich, money always comes her way when she most needs it. She is connected to her logic and her intuition, and feels integrated and empowered. Raido, the rune of good communication, graces Tamara with clearheaded, articulate speech.

Elements: Air, water, air, air, air, air

The Numerological Interpretation

Tamara (NV = 9, CV = 6, VV = 3, FL = 2)

Tamara is very involved in the development of tools, methods, processes, and techniques that allow her to be ready for any eventuality. Tamara is an avid learner, a person who is always cultivating her skills. Her home and family are very important, and she will use many of her acquired gifts to support the people closest to her. She is a very caring, highly emotive, and sensitive person.

DERIVATION: Russian, originally from the Hebrew name Tamar, meaning "palm tree." Found in the Old Testament as the name of several personages. Before the twentieth century, Tamar was the more common version; now Tamara is much more popular.

PRINCIPAL COLORS: All shades of red, from the palest pink to the deepest rose

GEMSTONES AND PRECIOUS METALS: Bloodstones, garnets

BOTANICALS: Broom, wormwood, white hellebore

UNIQUE SPELLINGS: Tamarah, Tamera, Tammara, Tammera

RELATED TO: Tama, Tamah, Tamar, Tamey, Tami, Tamie, Tamma, Tammee, Tammey, Tammi, Tammie, Tammy†, Tamy, Thamar, Thamara

DERIVATION: English, the short
form of Tamara, which derives
from the Hebrew for "palm
tree." Sometimes used as an
independent name, especially
during the 1950s and 1960s.

PRINCIPAL COLORS: The full
range of red hues, particularly the
deep, rich shades

GEMSTONES AND PRECIOUS
METALS: Garnets, rubies

BOTANICALS: Nettle, garlic,
wormwood

UNIQUE SPELLINGS: Tami,
Tammee, Tammey, Tammi, Tamy

RELATED TO: Tama, Tamar,
Tamara†, Tamera, Tamika,
Tammara, Tammera, Thamara,
Thamarra

Tammy

A KABBALISTIC SYNOPSIS
טאממי —TAMMY (Teth, Aleph, Mem, Mem, Yod)

No one could ever accuse Tammy of being anything other than diligent and committed! One Hebrew equivalent of Tammy's name's value is the word "exertion," and Tammy will exert herself to the point of exhaustion if the job at hand requires it—especially if she is helping out a friend. The letter Mem, which relates to all positive emotion, is featured twice in this name, and it's clear that friendship and affection are all-important to Tammy. She is an absolute sucker for old black-and-white tearjerkers, and will watch them whenever they come on television. If she has children, Tammy will make an excellent mother. Her kids will feel decidedly special, and never have any doubt as to their importance in their mother's busy life. The only danger is that Tammy may love them almost too much, and make their lives so easy and pleasant that they never want to strike out on their own.

THE RUNIC INTERPRETATION
ᛇᛗᛗᚨᛏ (Eihwaz, Mannaz, Mannaz, Ansuz, Teiwaz)

Tammy is deeply fascinated by metaphysics and psychology or the study of the soul. After all, Tammy has the double Mannaz power of self in her name. Tammy seeks balance and seems concerned with finding the middle ground between self-aggrandizement and modesty. Teiwaz, the warrior rune, gives her the strength to take a backseat and carry on when her needs are overlooked. Ansuz, the rune of intuition, combined with Eihwaz, the rune of defense, give Tammy a sensitive and compassionate approach toward people and the ebbs and flows of life. With the double Mannaz, Tammy is very connected to others.

Elements: Earth/fire, air, air, air, air

THE NUMEROLOGICAL INTERPRETATION
Tammy (NV = 9, CV = 1, VV = 8, FL = 2)

A wide-reaching sensitivity combines with a strongly ambitious nature in this name. Tammy is one who is very much connected to her own drives and her needs to make her mark on the world. Yet she is also concerned with outward appearances and what society has to say about her. Compassionate and sympathetic, Tammy is very responsive to the weak and the suffering. If she combines all of the aspects of her name correctly, Tammy will find that she can be useful in group activities, especially organizing funds for community and social purposes.

Tanya

A Kabbalistic Synopsis
טאניא —TANYA (Teth, Aleph, Nun, Yod, Aleph)

You have to be very careful when you are around Tanya, as she is a highly sensitive woman who can be easily upset. This is suggested by the positioning of the letter Nun in her name, which reflects the negative side of our emotions in the same way that Mem refers to the more positive side of our feelings. Tanya has a tendency to feel down about herself, which makes her vulnerable to the slightest comment. One way she deals with this is to become snappy and defensive—which is hinted at by the initial Teth in her name, meaning "serpent." On the positive side, this name adds up to seventy-one, which brings Tanya luck in terms of her career prospects. In addition, the final Aleph in her name can be seen as suggesting that over time, Tanya has the capacity to become comfortable with herself as an individual, probably as a result of career success.

The Runic Interpretation
ᚨᛇᚾᚨᛏ (Ansuz, Eihwaz, Nauthiz, Ansuz, Teiwaz)

No one with Nauthiz, the rune of constraint; Teiwaz, the warrior rune; and Eihwaz, the rune of defense ends up being unable to defend themselves, least of all Tanya. With the double Ansuz rune of insight gracing this mighty configuration, Tanya really can go far in life. If she cares to, she can sense trouble and avert disaster. When push comes to shove, Tanya knows how her opponent is going to react. Nauthiz, positioned at the heart of her name, hints that Tanya may experience limitation in finances or another area of her life. Tanya has her challenges to overcome, but she also has all the tools it takes to care for herself.

Elements: Air, earth/fire, fire, air, air

The Numerological Interpretation
Tanya (NV = 7, CV = 7, VV = 9, FL = 2)

Tanya's name gives her the gift of insight into the underlying causes and meanings of life's outer events. She is very curious by nature, and likes to investigate the happenings around her. However, she does have a tendency to gossip and should avoid social intrigues. Tanya can use her fine perceptions of reality to become a counselor or a teacher. Other areas of interest that will call to her are science, laboratory research, and hospital work.

DERIVATION: Russian, the abbreviated version of Tatiana, which derives from the Latin family name Tatianus. Has become a common independent given name, particularly in the English-speaking world. Tatiana is still also found, but much less frequently.

PRINCIPAL COLORS: The full gamut of green and yellow hues, also gold

GEMSTONES AND PRECIOUS METALS: White pearls, cat's-eye, any other white stone

BOTANICALS: Elder, juniper, linseed

UNIQUE SPELLINGS: Tahnya, Tania, Taniah, Tanja, Tannia, Tohnya, Tonya, Tonyah

RELATED TO: Tahnee, Tana, Tani, Tanita, Tarnia, Tatiana, Tonya†

Tara

DERIVATION: Irish, from the word for "hill." The name of a place in Ireland, as well as the name of Scarlett O'Hara's estate in Margaret Mitchell's *Gone with the Wind*. After the success of this film, Tara became a popular first name in the United States.

PRINCIPAL COLORS: Electric colors, the full spectrum of moderately shaded hues

GEMSTONES AND PRECIOUS METALS: Sapphires

BOTANICALS: Lesser celandine, medlar, sage

UNIQUE SPELLINGS: Tarah, Tarra, Tarrah

RELATED TO: Tarena, Tarina, Tarinne, Tarry, Taryn, Taryna

A KABBALISTIC SYNOPSIS
טערא —TA'ARA (Teth, Ayin, Resh, Aleph)

Tara would be a natural host on a morning news show; she has the ability to talk endlessly in a bright and cheerful way. Tara also has the benefit of being naturally lucky; this is indicated by the fact that the value of her name reduces to ten, the number of the Wheel of Fortune card in the tarot. While Tara is a jolly woman, there is a very serious side to her personality as well, in that she will make sure that she is financially secure. Tara will also make the most of her money when it comes time to invest it. Emotionally, Tara has more interest in friendship and fun than in a long-term relationship, but ultimately she is likely to settle down once she finds someone with the right sense of humor.

THE RUNIC INTERPRETATION
ᚨᚱᚨᛏ (Ansuz, Raido, Ansuz, Teiwaz)

Tara believes there are no coincidences in life. And she is so intuitive that she feels constrained by rules and regulations. Her finances might be a big mess, but Tara has the double Ansuz rune of intuition to help her find an accountant who can help her sort things out. Raido, the rune of good communication, means Tara could enjoy making a living in either the arts or another creative field. But don't be fooled into thinking Tara is spacy; Teiwaz, the warrior rune, gives Tara the courage to stand apart from the crowd and live by her talents.

Elements: Air, water, air, air

THE NUMEROLOGICAL INTERPRETATION
Tara (NV = 4, CV = 11, VV = 2, FL = 2)

The numbers in this name present a very interesting and somewhat challenging combination of personality characteristics. The name value of four indicates that Tara has a keen interest in her physical world, so that financial security and material possessions are core issues in her life. The consonant value of eleven points to issues that are more abstract, and deals more with community and collective well-being. The first-letter value of two is a harmonizing influence, and a point of balance and relationship. If able to put all these features together, Tara will use her awareness of life's practical realities to do community service, thereby anchoring her place in the world.

Taylor

DERIVATION: English, originally a surname referring to someone who worked as a tailor. Has become increasingly common as a first name for both males and females.

PRINCIPAL COLORS: The full range of yellow and brown hues, gold

GEMSTONES AND PRECIOUS METALS: Citrine, yellow diamonds

BOTANICALS: Chamomile, sorrel, eyebright

UNIQUE SPELLINGS: Tailer, Tailir, Tailor, Tailyr, Taler, Talyr, Talyrre, Tayler, Taylerre, Taylir

RELATED TO: Talia, Talita, Tallie, Tally, Talya

A Kabbalistic Synopsis
טאילער —TAYLA'AR (Teth, Aleph, Yod, Lamed, Ayin, Resh)

Taylor cuts a very imposing figure. The value of this name reduces to five, which traditionally suggests religious authority but can be taken as a sign of great personal stature and presence. On the whole, though, Taylor is a traditional person who firmly believes in the values of a solid family life and marriage. The combination of the letters Lamed and Ayin mean that Taylor, whether a man or a woman, can be quite unnerving to work with, thanks to Taylor's powerful and authoritative manner. Taylor will ensure that all work is done exactly on time and with maximum effectiveness. Occasionally, Taylor can be something of a tyrant, especially if born under the signs Capricorn or Scorpio, but most people have the utmost respect for Taylor, as he or she always produces the goods. At home Taylor is a more relaxed person, but he or she still insists on ruling the roost.

The Runic Interpretation
ᚱᛟᛚᛇᚨᛏ (Raido, Othila, Laguz, Eihwaz, Ansuz, Teiwaz)

Whether male or female, Taylor is low-maintenance. Taylor has Laguz, the rune of flow, to keep him or her flexible and easygoing. The Eihwaz rune of defense doesn't make Taylor a bully or a fighter—quite the opposite. Taylor values peace and detests violence. Teiwaz, the warrior rune, gives Taylor firsthand experience with self-defense, and Taylor can avert disaster simply by looking it in the eye. Raido, the rune of good communication, makes Taylor a masterful negotiator, or a brilliant arbitrator who prefers conciliation to aggressive tactics. Ansuz, the rune of intuition, combined with Othila for separation, tells us that Taylor is insightful and can separate the wheat from the chaff when assessing people.

Elements: Water, earth/fire, water, earth/fire, air, air

The Numerological Interpretation
Taylor (NV = 1, CV = 5, VV = 5, FL = 2)

The name Taylor indicates fluctuation, variation, and change. This is a most versatile individual, one who is quickly bored with habits and routines. Taylor enjoys the consistency of life's inconstancy, and seeks to widen his or her horizons at every turn of the wheel. But this cannot be done by sitting at a desk; Taylor has to be out and about challenging the world. A very friendly man or woman, Taylor is open to many different kinds of relationships. What will be important for Taylor is to establish an inner purpose so that he or she may learn how to be more specific in choosing activities.

Ted

DERIVATION: English, the short form of Edward or Theodore. Since the nineteenth century, Ted has sometimes been used as an independent name as well.

PRINCIPAL COLORS: White, off-white, the full range of green hues

GEMSTONES AND PRECIOUS METALS: Jade, moonstones, pearls

BOTANICALS: Chicory, plantain, cucumber

UNIQUE SPELLING: Tedd

RELATED TO: Edt, Eddie, Edwardt, Teddie, Teddy, Tedmund, Theo, Theodore

A KABBALISTIC SYNOPSIS
טאד —TAD (Teth, Aleph, Daleth)

It is almost impossible to dislike Ted. He is a wonderfully down-to-earth man with absolutely no false airs about him, despite the fact that he probably has a very good job and is considerably better off than the average person. Ted hates to see arguments, whether in the home or at the office, and the value of his name, which is fourteen, indicates his preference for calm and tranquillity. In fact, the Temperance card in the tarot, which has a value of fourteen, is not just a symbol of calm but also refers to an ability to take two conflicting sides and bring them into harmony, so a career in arbitration may be ideal for Ted. Ted's family thinks the world of him, and he makes sure that they know how he feels about them, even though his career is likely to require a significant amount of traveling away from home.

THE RUNIC INTERPRETATION
ᛞᛖᛏ (Dagaz, Ehwaz, Teiwaz)

Ted may need the companionship of a tolerant partner to help him lighten up and invite spontaneity and joy into his world. Teiwaz, the warrior rune, makes Ted feel like life is a battle. He thinks he needs to be ever vigilant. Ted checks the air in his tires, and when he does get a flat, he goes on the warpath. Fortunately for Ted, Dagaz, the rune of breakthrough, saves the day. Dagaz teaches Ted that as he develops faith in himself to handle the ups and downs of life, he can relinquish control and learn to take risks.

Elements: Fire, air, air

THE NUMEROLOGICAL INTERPRETATION
Ted (NV = 11, CV = 6, VV = 5, FL = 2)

Ted is a born communicator, and it is important to him to spread his message far and wide. What he has to discover is what messages he is seeking to share. There can be a tendency to be too general and diversified in his interests, leading to the dissipation of his vitality. Ted enjoys the challenges inherent in sports. He likes to have a good time in life, and takes his pleasures seriously. Even with all of his activities, Ted is basically a family man. He enjoys being close to his loved ones, and finds that a beautiful and peaceful home is essential to his well-being.

Terence

DERIVATION: English, originally from the Latin clan name Terentius. Became common in English-speaking countries in the late nineteenth century, and was especially popular during the 1950s.

PRINCIPAL COLORS: Gold, the full range of green and yellow hues

GEMSTONES AND PRECIOUS METALS: Pearls, moonstones, moss agate

BOTANICALS: Hops, blackberry, juniper

UNIQUE SPELLINGS: Terance, Terince, Terrance, Terrence, Terrince, Terrynce, Terynce

RELATED TO: Tarrance, Terencio, Terrell, Terrey, Terry†

A Kabbalistic Synopsis

טארונס —TARVNS (Teth, Aleph, Resh, Vau, Nun, Samech)

There are many positive aspects to Terence's character and only one drawback—Terence is emotional. The letter Nun in his name tells us that he can be melancholic and withdrawn from time to time, and by virtue of its position in his name immediately following the letter Vau, we can tell that much of Terence's emotional anxiety stems from spending an excessive amount of time worrying about the possible outcomes of various actions or situations. The net result of this is that he tends to use other people as a support in life and is reluctant to decide things on his own. On the very positive side Terence is a friendly and genuine guy who people find very easy to talk to about all sorts of private matters. He will never be short of friends thanks to the warmth of his character and the fact that when he's in the mood, he has a decidedly quirky but hilarious sense of humor.

The Runic Interpretation

ᛖᛋᚾᛖᚱᛖᛏ (Ehwaz, Sowelu, Nauthiz, Ehwaz, Raido, Ehwaz, Teiwaz)

Terence is a poor loser. He was the kind of kid who punched his opponent in the nose and had to write "I will be a good sport" a hundred times after school. Terence has the triple Ehwaz rune for movement in his name. He loves competitive sports, and the Teiwaz warrior rune may incline him to football or wrestling. The Raido rune of journey makes him love travel and appreciate good communication. His clear thinking helps him out in sports or business or life in general. The Nauthiz rune of constraint makes Terence a fierce opponent who is aggressive and lives to win. The Sowelu rune of wholeness puts Terence in the big leagues in the military or sports or business, and nothing less will do.

Elements: Air, air, fire, air, water, air, air

The Numerological Interpretation

Terence (NV = 7, CV = 1, VV = 6, FL = 2)

A curious man of very specific intellectual interests, Terence may specialize in an area that attracts few professionals. This makes him frequently called upon to give his expert and educated opinions. He is a natural-born researcher and is quite happy spending a great deal of time by himself among his books and computers. These he prefers to keep at home rather than at an outside office or library. Terence is quite happy in his small and private world, as it opens him up to a much larger universe.

Terri

A KABBALISTIC SYNOPSIS
טארי —TARY (Teth, Aleph, Resh, Yod)

When you look at Terri, you can imagine her still strutting her stuff when she's seventy! This woman just loves to go out, and there is rarely a night when she willingly stays in and puts her feet up in front of the television. Mind you, not any old party will suffice for Terri; one equivalent of her name in Hebrew is "elegant," and this sums up her taste in social events. Terri is sophisticated and she knows it. If she was born under the astrological sign Gemini, she can sometimes be a bit of a snob about this and act with an unbecoming arrogance. But on the whole, Terri doesn't make an issue out of things, and she is always at ease at the most glittering of events.

THE RUNIC INTERPRETATION
ᛁᚱᚱᛗᛏ (Isa, Raido, Raido, Ehwaz, Teiwaz)

The double Raido rune of good communication is responsible for Terri's love of language. It's lucky Terri has the Ehwaz rune of movement in her name; she will use her language acumen with great satisfaction when she travels. Raido is the rune of journey, and Terri will travel her whole life, either literally or vicariously through language and literature. Isa, the rune of standstill, makes Terri at ease with the isolation long hours of study require. Teiwaz, the warrior rune, gives Terri the inquisitiveness and courage it takes to relish adventure, and because Terri invites excitement, it comes her way.

Elements: Earth, water, water, air, air

THE NUMEROLOGICAL INTERPRETATION
Terri (NV = 7, CV = 2, VV = 5, FL = 2)

Terri does well in a career that has to do with public relations, advertising, or marketing. She is very gifted in circulating information between people, and works well as a messenger, go-between, or agent of any kind. Terri is happy in the company of friends, but she also requires time alone to think and process her experiences. Concerned about fair play, Terri tends to be very up-front and honest in her dealings with friends and lovers, and she expects the same from them in return.

Terry

A Kabbalistic Synopsis
טאררי —TARRY (Teth, Aleph, Resh, Resh, Yod)

Terry is extremely perky; the letter R, or Resh, is associated with a general feeling of well-being and optimism. The compression of Terry's name gives us the letters Tau and Kaph. This tells us that Terrys are very generous and kindhearted people who are prepared to suffer considerable hardship in order to help those they care about prosper. The letter Kaph means "hand," and suggests that Terry will be highly skilled in all manner of practical roles. Other influences in this name suggest that Terry is more than just a handyperson; he or she may well be a craftsperson held in high regard by those who know his or her work.

The Runic Interpretation
ᛇᚱᚱᛗᛏ (Eihwaz, Raido, Raido, Ehwaz, Teiwaz)

Terry can kill with a word. There are times when Terry verbally slashes a foe and even over-steps the boundaries of good taste and human kindness. The double Raido rune of good communication is found in this name. So Terry can enhance and heal others with his or her powers of persuasion, and most of the time does. It's the Eihwaz rune of defense acting over-time that makes Terry occasionally resort to razor sharp words that sting in the memory. Tei-waz, the warrior rune, with its masculine energy, makes Terry assertive, aggressive, and a tad obnoxious sometimes. Fortunately Ehwaz, the rune of movement, is on hand to incline Terry to exercise and sports as a way to funnel the energy that spurs him or her on. Terry has the opportunity to live abroad, and since the Raido rune of communication makes Terry good with languages, he or she picks up foreign tongues quicker than most.

Elements: Earth/fire, water, water, air, air

The Numerological Interpretation
Terry (NV = 5, CV = 2, VV = 3, FL = 2)

Always up on the latest trends in fashion and music, Terry is very avant-garde. This is a name that indicates a sociable person, one who is quick on the uptake, open, and friendly. Terry likes to entertain and be entertained; boredom is definitely his or her least favorite state of mind. There are so many things that attract Terry that he or she has a hard time sitting still. Travel is more than a hobby with Terry; it is a *passion*. Understandably, Terry does well in any profession that is connected to fun and leisure. Terry would make a great travel agent or concierge, and has an aptitude for show business.

DERIVATION: A nickname used by both males and females. For males, Terry is usually the short form of Terence; for women, it is commonly a short version of Theresa. In both cases, it is sometimes used as an independent name as well. Especially common during the mid-twentieth century.

PRINCIPAL COLORS: The full spectrum of very pale hues, especially light gray tones

GEMSTONES AND PRECIOUS METALS: Diamonds, silver

BOTANICALS: Hazel, sweet marjoram, parsley

UNIQUE SPELLINGS: Teree, Terey, Teri, Terree, Terrey, Terri, Terrie

RELATED TO: Ter, Terencet, Terrell, Terrill; Tera, Teresa, Terese, Teressa, Terra, Territ, Tess, Tessa, Tessie, Theresat, Therese, Tracie, Tracy, Tresa

Thelma

DERIVATION: English, first coined by the novelist Marie Corelli for the name of the heroine in her 1887 novel *Thelma*. Possibly based on the Greek word *thelema*, meaning "wish" or "act of will." Especially common in the early twentieth century.

PRINCIPAL COLORS: Pale gray, light shades of any other color

GEMSTONES AND PRECIOUS METALS: Silver, platinum, diamonds

BOTANICALS: Parsley, oats, mushrooms

UNIQUE SPELLINGS: Thellma, Thelmah

RELATED TO: Selma, Velma†

"You said you 'n' me was gonna get out of town and for once just really let our hair down. Well darlin', look out 'cause my hair is comin' down!"
—THELMA DICKINSON IN *THELMA AND LOUISE* (1991)

A KABBALISTIC SYNOPSIS
תאלמא —ThALMA (Tau, Aleph, Lamed, Mem, Aleph)

Thankfully, not every Thelma is quite as reckless as the character of the same name from the film *Thelma and Louise*, although interestingly Thelma's name's value does reduce to thirteen, which suggests that Thelma has a real taste for change and adventure in her life. Thelma is a very well liked woman, not the least because she will always stop what she is doing in order to help out a friend, no matter how small or trivial their problem might seem. Her house is always a popular drop-in center for anyone in the area when they need coffee and a chat. Her partner will be a lucky individual indeed, as Thelma thrives on affection, and she will both give and receive love warmly and frequently.

THE RUNIC INTERPRETATION
ᚨᛗᛚᛖᚺᛏ (Ansuz, Mannaz, Laguz, Ehwaz, Hagalaz, Teiwaz)

Thelma has the Hagalaz rune, portent of disruptions, upheavals, and delays, in her name. Thelma needs to try ten times harder than most when she's in a cycle of chaos, but with Laguz, the easygoing rune of flow, keeping her flexible, Thelma will muster the patience to persevere. Teiwaz, the warrior rune, gives Thelma the courage to redesign her plans to accommodate changes. Ansuz, the rune of intuition, makes Thelma well equipped to avert trouble whenever possible. Mannaz, the rune of the self, teaches Thelma to step aside and let things fall into place without pushing.

Elements: Air, air, water, air, water, air

THE NUMEROLOGICAL INTERPRETATION
Thelma (NV = 5, CV = 8, VV = 6, FL = 2)

Thelma has many talents and interests, but she is also keenly aware of the importance of correctly organizing her life. This name gives her an innate sense of harmony, and Thelma is quite able to coordinate the professional and personal facets of her life. Thelma loves nature and is especially fond of flowers and plants. She does well working in gardens, and may find a natural aptitude for working with the various properties of herbs and plants. Thelma tends to partner early in life, and she needs to be with a person who can be supportive of her need for both home and career.

Theresa

A Kabbalistic Synopsis

תאריסא —ThARYSA (Tau, Aleph, Resh, Yod, Samech, Aleph)

We can expect to see Theresa's selflessness reflected in everything she does. The initial letter Th, or Tau, refers to Theresa's willingness to always put others first, while the presence of the Resh in her name tells us that she performs all of her kindly acts with a cheerful and outgoing manner rather than with a solemn sense of duty. In addition, the value of her name contains the number six hundred, which is the value of the letter Mem when placed at the end of a word. The letter Mem refers to all positive emotional feelings and, in particular, to what would traditionally be regarded as maternal instincts, such as the desire to protect and nurture the weak and the young.

The Runic Interpretation

ᚨᛋᛖᚱᛖᚺᛏ (Ansuz, Sowelu, Ehwaz, Raido, Ehwaz, Hagalaz, Teiwaz)

Nothing could be sadder than the look on Theresa's face when she's used up her frequent-flier miles. With double Ehwaz, the rune of movement, in her name, Theresa likes to keep her feet in motion. Whether she channels this energy into dance, exercise, sports, or flying, it's all the same. Still, Theresa absolutely delights in frequent changes of scene. Ansuz, the rune of signals, and Teiwaz, the warrior rune, let Theresa make travel connections on time, every time. Raido, the rune of journey, takes her to far-off places, either by foot or by imagining her journeys and writing them down. If Theresa writes, she'll enjoy success. Sowelu blesses her life with a sense of wholeness, so when Hagalaz, the menacing rune of disruptions, comes along to cause chaos, Theresa is ready.

Elements: Air, air, air, water, air, water, air

The Numerological Interpretation

Theresa (NV = 4, CV = 2, VV = 11, FL = 2)

Theresa is a name that combines the ability to think abstractly with good common sense. This is a lady who can see far into the future but is also able to keep her feet firmly planted on the path in front of her. People gravitate to Theresa for advice, as she has the courage and the objectivity to tell people the truth as she sees it. Theresa is able to coordinate and structure the activities around her, and she can be very instrumental in harmonizing group efforts. Theresa enjoys working with large groups of people as well as with more intimate groups.

DERIVATION: English, of uncertain derivation. Possibly from the name of the Greek island Thera. First used in Spain and Portugal, and was made famous by Saint Theresa of Avila in the sixteenth century.

PRINCIPAL COLORS: Electric colors, medium shades of any color, blues, grays

GEMSTONES AND PRECIOUS METALS: Sapphires

BOTANICALS: Sage, spinach, medlar

UNIQUE SPELLINGS: Taresa, Tarisa, Tarysa, Tereesa, Teresa, Terisa, Terresa, Terysa, Thereesa, Therisa, Therresa

RELATED TO: Tera, Terese, Teresia, Teri, Terra, Territ, Terrie, Terryt, Tess, Tessa, Tessi, Tessie, Therese, Theresita, Tracie, Tracyt, Tresa, Tressa

"Kind words can be short and easy to speak, but their echoes are truly endless."

—MOTHER TERESA
(HUMANITARIAN)

DERIVATION: English, found in the New Testament as one of Christ's Apostles. Originally from the Aramaic word meaning "twin." Became very common during the Middle Ages, and has been used much since then.

PRINCIPAL COLORS: The full spectrum of moderately shaded hues

GEMSTONES AND PRECIOUS METALS: Sapphires

BOTANICALS: Celandine, Iceland moss

UNIQUE SPELLINGS: Tamas, Tamis, Tamiss, Thomass, Thomis, Thomys, Tomis, Tommis, Tomys, Tomyss

RELATED TO: Thom, Thomason, Thompson, Thomson, Tom†, Tomas, Tomaso, Tomasso, Tomie, Tomkin, Tomlin, Tommey, Tommie, Tommy, Tomson

❧

"To invent, you need a good imagination and a pile of junk."
—THOMAS ALVA EDISON
(INVENTOR)

A KABBALISTIC SYNOPSIS

תעמאס —ThA'AMAS (Tau, Ayin, Mem, Aleph, Samech)

The value of Thomas's name is thirteen, which indicates a desire for change but, in the context of other influences in the name, could also be seen as suggestive of someone whose own beliefs and principles are quite changeable. This can be very positive in that it makes Thomas more open-minded. Thomas will be a successful man, thanks to the influence of the letter Ayin. Despite a doubting nature, Thomas is a warm and genuinely caring guy, as shown by the central M, or Mem, in his name.

THE RUNIC INTERPRETATION

ᛋᚨᛗᛟᚺᛏ (Sowelu, Ansuz, Mannaz, Othila, Hagalaz, Teiwaz)

Thomas has learned, thanks to the Hagalaz rune of disruptions, how to turn adversity to his advantage. The Othila rune of separation lets him detach from a chaotic situation. Thomas just leaves the room or changes his state of mind until he relaxes and can deal with the dilemma. Teiwaz, the warrior rune, combines nicely with Ansuz, the rune of signals, in this name to make Thomas intuitive, brave, watchful, and observant. Mannaz, the rune of self, makes Thomas humble and patient. Sowelu makes him whole. All in all, Thomas has the fortitude to excel in business, politics, or scientific research. Thomas could be a great scientist, and he will derive much satisfaction from his work.

Elements: Air, air, air, earth/fire, water, air

THE NUMEROLOGICAL INTERPRETATION

Thomas (NV = 11, CV = 4, VV = 7, FL = 2)

A man with great inner reserves of both energy and knowledge, Thomas does not display his true nature easily. It takes a while to get to know this complex man, as Thomas is by no means particularly self-revealing. Thomas is slow to trust others, but when he does finally offer his friendship, it is sincere and profound. This is a man who cares a great deal about social issues and is not egocentric by nature, although he will support his favorite causes and have definite political opinions and beliefs. Not the most confident about expressing his personal emotions, Thomas needs a partner who is perceptive to his changing moods and very patient with his periodic silences.

❧

Tiffany

A Kabbalistic Synopsis

טיפאני —TYPhANY (Teth, Yod, Peh, Aleph, Nun, Yod)

Everyone leans on Tiffany. She is a very sweet woman with a completely noncynical view of the world. Her almost naive take on life means that she is a great friend to have when you're feeling down, since she will always find the silver lining in any cloud that may be hanging over you. Tiffany is a good talker, too, which is indicated by the presence of the letter Peh, meaning "mouth." This is right next to the Aleph in her name, and suggests that Tiffany loves to discuss her ideas. This trait will make her an ideal candidate for a job on any creative team where good ideas are at a premium. Tiffany is enthusiastic in almost everything she does, and is able to carry others along with her in her willingness to do the work. However, she can sometimes be less than practical, so she does need someone more down-to-earth around to circumvent her most harebrained schemes.

The Runic Interpretation

ᛇᚾᚨᚠᚠᛁᛏ (Eihwaz, Nauthiz, Ansuz, Fehu, Fehu, Isa, Teiwaz)

Tiffany will be able to afford shopping at Tiffany's, the famous jewelry store that shares her name. Double Fehu, the rune of possessions, represents dreams coming true and love fulfilled. Fehu is the money stone. Still, the Nauthiz rune of constraint could indicate that Tiffany is feeling pinched by changes in her life. Isa, the rune of standstill, could indicate loneliness. With Ansuz, the rune of signals, combining with Teiwaz for warrior strength, Tiffany is likely to correct this situation with deep reserves of pluck! Ansuz boosts her intuition, and Tiffany can anticipate trends in fashion and finance and keep her fortunes growing so that she can build a castle to the stars.

Elements: Earth/fire, fire, air, fire, fire, earth, air

The Numerological Interpretation

Tiffany (NV = 9, CV = 1, VV = 8, FL = 2)

Tiffany is one who is very comfortable with success. She finds it difficult to compromise, and it is absolutely essential for her to have a career that is reflective of her true nature. Only a profession that allows her a lot of opportunity to stretch her mental muscles will do. Tiffany likes to influence her surroundings and, if given enough latitude, will come up with some very far-reaching concepts and ideas. In terms of her emotional life, Tiffany tends to be quite idealistic about the people she loves. She avoids admitting other people's shortcomings, and tends to look much more closely at their talents and virtues.

DERIVATION: English, from the Greek name Theophania, meaning "epiphany" or "manifestation of God." Originally used for girls born on the feast of the Epiphany (January 6), but then fell out of use. Has become extremely popular in the late twentieth century, probably due to the fame of the New York jewelry store, as well as the 1961 film *Breakfast at Tiffany's*.

PRINCIPAL COLORS: Light pink to the deepest shades of red

GEMSTONES AND PRECIOUS METALS: Bloodstones, garnets, rubies

BOTANICALS: Garlic, wormwood

UNIQUE SPELLINGS: Tifaney, Tifani, Tifany, Tiffaney, Tiffani, Tiffanie, Tiffeney, Tiffeni, Tiffenie, Tiffeny, Tiphaney, Tiphani, Tiphanie, Tiphany, Tyfaney, Tyffani, Tyffanie, Tyffany

RELATED TO: Theophania, Theophanie, Tiff, Tiffie

In the absence of any direct equivalent to the letter *f* in the Hebrew alphabet, the letter Peh is used. Peh can function as either a hard or a soft letter, and as such, is one of the seven "doubles."

DERIVATION: English, pet form of Timothy, which is from the Greek roots *time*, meaning "honor," and *theos*, meaning "god." Especially popular in the 1950s and 1960s.

PRINCIPAL COLORS: All but the brightest shades of blue

GEMSTONES AND PRECIOUS METALS: Emeralds, blue and blue-green turquoise

BOTANICALS: Dog rose, violets, almonds

UNIQUE SPELLINGS: Timm, Tym, Tymm

RELATED TO: Timmi, Timmie, Timmy, Timo, Timofei, Timofeo, Timofey, Timon, Timoteo, Timotheo, Timotheus, Timothy†

A KABBALISTIC SYNOPSIS

טים —TYM (Teth, Yod, Mem)

One Hebrew equivalent of the value of Tim's name is "wall." This refers to Tim's reliability: He is solid in the sense that very little upsets or fazes him, and this makes Tim a good man to have around in a crisis. He will also have a generally high output of work. In Tim's name, we have the opposition of the Mem, which represents Tim's loyalty and generosity of spirit, with the letter Teth, which tells us Tim can have a definite sting if necessary. As the value of his name reduces to fourteen, a number of balance and harmony, Tim is usually calm, but if anyone tries to exploit this or, even worse, upsets a member of his family, the venomous energy of the serpent letter Teth will come to the fore! People will no longer make the mistake of taking Tim's generally laid-back and balanced approach for granted.

THE RUNIC INTERPRETATION

ᛗᛁᛏ (Mannaz, Isa, Teiwaz)

Tim has big, wide shoulders to cry on. He's strong as a warrior, with Teiwaz on guard to offer him emotional strength, or what some people call "patience." It's a rare and fine quality. Isa, the rune of standstill, means that Tim will enjoy solitary pursuits. He has his computer, his books, and his sports. Tim likes to jog and swim and may even play a round of golf when he's feeling sociable. Mannaz, the rune of self, has air as its essence, and it makes Tim flexible. This is a man who values his freedom, and he will give his partner a lot of freedom as well. History, theater, teaching, and counseling would suit Tim. He might also enjoy physical work, such as construction.

Elements: Air, earth, air

THE NUMEROLOGICAL INTERPRETATION

Tim (NV = 6, CV = 6, VV = 9, FL = 2)

A kind and compassionate man, Tim is always ready to be of assistance when called upon. Tim tries to avoid conflict at all costs. He is very much against hurting anyone's feelings, and has to take care that he doesn't emotionally injure or compromise himself in the process. Careers that are appropriate for him are found in any field of healing, especially psychology, counseling, or teaching. The arts are another area where Tim may express his sensitivities creatively.

Timothy

A KABBALISTIC SYNOPSIS
טימתי —TYMThY (Teth, Yod, Mem, Tau, Yod)

Timothy is a bright light. The value of his name reduces to nineteen, which is the number of the Sun card in the tarot. But the Sun card should not be confused with the meaning of the letter Resh, which translates as "sun." While both refer to positive, outgoing individuals, the number nineteen and the Sun card have a more intellectual focus, in that they also refer to someone with a very active and creative brain. As many of the letters in this name relate to either the sign Virgo or the planet Venus, it is unlikely that Timothy will use his intelligence in the area of the hard sciences; Timothy is more likely to be attracted to areas connected to the human emotions. He may be a writer or possibly even a psychiatrist. Timothy's home life will be a lot of fun, as he is full of energy and is always ready to go and play ball or otherwise lark about when he gets home from work.

THE RUNIC INTERPRETATION
ᛇᛚᛟᛗᛁᛏ (Eihwaz, Thurisaz, Othila, Mannaz, Isa, Teiwaz)

Timothy has all the traits of the name Tim, with additional runes for separation, strength, gateway, and defense. Timothy is more resilient and even, if it's possible, a bit more independent than Tim. He might like team sports, for example, and choose soccer over golf. Timothy could enjoy the intrigues of business and flourish in law, contracting, or police work. He can handle aggressive people because he is a great sparring partner. Thurisaz, the gateway rune, means Timothy will face crossroads in his life. The Eihwaz rune of defense helps him avert disaster at these times and choose the right direction.

Elements: Earth/fire, fire, earth/fire, air, earth, air

THE NUMEROLOGICAL INTERPRETATION
Timothy (NV = 11, CV = 7, VV = 22, FL = 2)

This is a highly capable individual, a man whose scope of vision can extend far beyond his own boundaries. The numbers in this name certainly empower him with the ability to realize his visions and dreams. The degree to which Timothy is able to do this has a great deal to do with his level of consciousness. If his orientation is purely personal rather than focused on higher goals for the common good, the master numbers eleven and twenty-two would reduce to two and four. Timothy will then be far more concerned with relationships in his immediate environment and his financial security than with any more altruistic goals. If Timothy is able to function fully on the level of these master numbers, his frame of reference is quite humanitarian and easily extends to the interests of his community, nation, and the world.

DERIVATION: English, from the Greek roots *time*, meaning "honor," and *theos*, meaning "god." In the New Testament, Saint Timothy was a companion of Saint Paul. Started to become a common name in the eighteenth century, and increased in popularity from that point on.

PRINCIPAL COLORS: White, the full range of green hues

GEMSTONES AND PRECIOUS METALS: Moonstones, jade, white pearls

BOTANICALS: Cabbage, lettuce, moonwort

UNIQUE SPELLINGS: Timmothey, Timmothy, Timothey, Timothie, Tymmothy, Tymothy

RELATED TO: Timt, Timmi, Timmie, Timmy, Timo, Timofei, Timofeo, Timofey, Timon, Timoteo, Timotheo, Timotheus

෴

"If you don't like what you are doing, you can always pick up your needle and move to another groove."
—TIMOTHY LEARY (PSYCHOLOGIST, AUTHOR)

Tina

A KABBALISTIC SYNOPSIS
טינא —TYNA (Teth, Yod, Nun, Aleph)

Tina is someone you want to keep on your good side, as she can be a very vengeful enemy; the letter Teth in her name is linked to the letter Yod, a symbol of fiery energy. The result of this combination is that if Tina feels slighted in any way by someone, she will hold on to that grudge as long as it takes until she can get revenge. There is some indication, through the letter Nun in her name, that Tina is sometimes struck by feelings of emotional insecurity. This is best dealt with by appealing to her common sense and pointing out that she does indeed have a number of good friends! The final Aleph suggests that Tina is very good at taking advice, if it is given in an intelligent and rational way rather than an emotional manner. The value of her name reduces to seven, which is a sure sign of a generally successful life, so it is unlikely that Tina will have much cause to be particularly vengeful toward anyone—lucky for the rest of us!

THE RUNIC INTERPRETATION
ᚨᚾᛁᛏ (Ansuz, Nauthiz, Isa, Teiwaz)

Tina says she could never understand how people can fall in love at first sight. She takes time to pledge her heart, and that's perfectly understandable and very sensible; the Nauthiz rune of constraint has taught Tina that it's better not to make a mistake than to try to undo one. Tina's practical nature suits her for a career in medicine, accounting, law, or finance. The Isa rune of standstill gives Tina the ability to hold her ground and wait; thus she is not easily fooled or manipulated. Teiwaz, the warrior rune, helps her defend herself and keep a poker face. Ansuz, the rune of signals, keeps Tina on the alert. When she does find someone to love, Tina will be loyal and true.

Elements: Air, fire, earth, air

THE NUMEROLOGICAL INTERPRETATION
Tina (NV = 8, CV = 7, VV = 1, FL = 2)

The life path evoked by this name is focused on achievement. This aspiration is backed up by Tina's boundless energy and enthusiasm for life. She knows how to market her creative abilities and is steadfast in her determination for success. This is a very supportive woman who is capable not only of organizing her own efforts but of structuring other people's talents and energies as well. Tina has a fine mind, one that is capable of sweeping through a great deal of data in order to get to the heart of any issue.

❧

Todd

DERIVATION: English, originally from the surname meaning "fox" or "fox hunter." Used most often in the twentieth century and was especially common in the 1970s.

PRINCIPAL COLORS: The palest to the deepest shades of green and yellow

GEMSTONES AND PRECIOUS METALS: Moonstones, moss agate

BOTANICALS: Elder, blackberry, hops

UNIQUE SPELLINGS: Tod, Todde

RELATED TO: Teodor, Teodore, Todor

A KABBALISTIC SYNOPSIS
טעדד —TA'ADD (Teth, Ayin, Daleth, Daleth)

Todd loves to do business—the riskier, the better—and he likes to think of himself as a wheeler-dealer rather than as a straightforward businessman. If he is born under Gemini, there is danger that he may move from operating at the boundary of the law—and bending it every *so* often—to a situation where he is operating completely on the other side of that boundary! The double presence of the letter Daleth, meaning "door," at the end of his name lets us know that Todd is always on the lookout for a new opportunity to make a fast buck. While he may act slightly dodgy, and some of his business associates may be found in the corners and the shadows, there is no malice in Todd at all. On a personal level, he is an immensely friendly guy who is great fun to be with, as well as someone who is exceedingly generous.

THE RUNIC INTERPRETATION
⋈⋈◊↑ (Dagaz, Dagaz, Othila, Teiwaz)

Todd can take on different personalities, and he could have a fascinating career, since he is a master of disguise. This might involve a change of names or even adopting a whole new identity. Todd would be safer, however, simply going into politics, sales, or acting. The double Dagaz rune signifies that Todd truly changes several times in his real life. Othila, the rune of separation, means Todd leaves his old habits or ways behind. Teiwaz, the warrior rune, implies that the transformations in his life are hard won. A lesser man would fold in the process, but not Todd.

Elements: Fire, fire, earth/fire, air

THE NUMEROLOGICAL INTERPRETATION
Todd (NV = 7, CV = 1, VV = 6, FL = 2)

This is a man who not only is undeterred by adversity, but is spurred on to even greater achievement as a result of such challenges. Todd has a very profound belief in himself, and his confidence is totally connected to his spiritual or philosophical views. He is an introspective and sensitive person, one who will spend long hours studying the most profound material. A complex individual who can work on many projects simultaneously, Todd is here to do his best at all times. When he does relax, his hobbies will serve to develop his interests in music and art.

DERIVATION: English, short form of Thomas, which is originally from the Aramaic word meaning "twin." Used independently since the eighteenth century, and very popular in the 1870s.

PRINCIPAL COLORS: The palest mauve to the deepest shade of violet

GEMSTONES AND PRECIOUS METALS: Amethyst, garnets

BOTANICALS: Cherry, barberry, lungwort

UNIQUE SPELLINGS: Tahm, Tahmm, Thom, Thomm, Tomm

RELATED TO: Tamas, Thomast, Thomason, Thompson, Thomson, Tomas, Tomaso, Tomasso, Tomie, Tomkin, Tomlin, Tommey, Tommie, Tommy, Tomson

❧

"I had to help Muff. Not helpin' him woulda been wrong."
—TOM SAWYER IN *TOM AND HUCK* BY MARK TWAIN

"Humanity has advanced, when it has advanced, not because it has been sober, responsible, and cautious, but because it has been playful, rebellious, and immature."
—TOM ROBBINS (AUTHOR)

A KABBALISTIC SYNOPSIS
טעם —TA'AM (Teth, Ayin, Mem)

Tom is a great guy and is particularly popular with kids. If he doesn't have any of his own, he may well work as a teacher or a child care worker. His main appeal with children is his wonderful imagination, which unlike that of many adults, is as fresh and unencumbered as a child's! Tom's innocent enjoyment of the world is indicated by the fact that his name's value reduces to twenty-two, which is the number of the Fool card in the tarot. The Fool is a very complex card, but in terms of name analysis it suggests a creative and optimistic person whose only real problem is being too ready to believe that everything will turn out fine. Consequently, devastation may follow on the few occasions when it doesn't. Tom may possibly make a career for himself as an entertainer. He certainly has the charisma that is needed, as well as a good ability to laugh at himself.

THE RUNIC INTERPRETATION
ᛗᛟᛏ (Mannaz, Othila, Teiwaz)

With the Othila rune of separation in his name, Tom will seem different from the beginning. Mannaz teaches us about love for our fellow man, and Tom has the heart of a humanitarian. Being able to see the big picture is one of the attributes of the Mannaz rune of the self. Tom may become an idealist working for a global cause, or he might go into biotechnology or open a health food store. With the Teiwaz warrior energy, Tom might funnel his vision of a better tomorrow into helping erase poverty or ignorance. Whatever path he chooses, he's able to elicit followers because people are attracted to Tom's sincerity.

Elements: Air, earth/fire, air

THE NUMEROLOGICAL INTERPRETATION
Tom (NV = 3, CV = 6, VV = 6, FL = 2)

Children are important to Tom. He is a man who can identify with their imaginative world and their innocence. Tom is always working to improve his creative potential, and this goal carries over into his interactions with the people in his environment. This is why it is easy to see that Tom makes a wonderful teacher or guidance counselor. He is very good with his hands, and can be most productive in work that requires a fine sense of manual dexterity, patience, and calm. His family is the center of his life, and it is easy for him to establish a loving and cooperative relationship with the right partner.

❧

Toni

DERIVATION: English, often a pet form of Antonia, which derives from the Roman family name Antonius. Sometimes used as an independent name as well.

PRINCIPAL COLORS: Medium shades of any color, also electric hues

GEMSTONES AND PRECIOUS METALS: Sapphires

BOTANICALS: Celandine, sage, Solomon's seal

UNIQUE SPELLINGS: Tonee, Toney, Tonie, Tony†

RELATED TO: Antoinette†, Antonella, Antonia†, Antonina, Tonia, Tonja, Tonya†

A KABBALISTIC SYNOPSIS
טעני —TA'ANY (Teth, Ayin, Nun, Yod)

You just can't pin this girl down! Ask her what her job is on Monday, and ask again on Friday, and by then Toni may well have a different answer. A career is not really important to Toni, as she is much more interested in having fun. Although we have Ayin as the central letter, which is usually associated with business success, in Toni's case it is much more the physical aspects of the letter that are important. Ayin also refers to the mountain goat, and we can often find Toni indulging in rigorous outdoor sports such as rock climbing or hang gliding. Toni is something of a firecracker and is not renowned for her fidelity in relationships. She likes brief but exciting experiences, and relationships that last only as long as the excitement remains. If she can meet someone with as much dynamic energy as herself, Toni might consider settling down.

THE RUNIC INTERPRETATION
ᛁᚾᛟᛏ (Isa, Nauthiz, Othila, Teiwaz)

Toni is always flattered when people say she's brave. The Teiwaz warrior rune figures prominently in her name, affording her great courage, which she will need. Toni has the Nauthiz rune of constraint to teach her the harsh realities of false friends, money limitations, delays, disappointments, and disruptions. These experiences may be related to her career since Toni is well suited to work as a social worker, fund-raiser, or wildlife conservationist. Othila, the rune of separation, teaches Toni that many problems are best handled by nonaction. When she goes off on her own and reenvisions her situation, things shift into place. Patience and nonaction require faith and courage, and that's why Toni really is brave.

Elements: Earth, fire, earth/fire, air

THE NUMEROLOGICAL INTERPRETATION
Toni (NV = 4, CV = 7, VV = 6, FL = 2)

Toni has a flair for the dramatic and may well find herself in some branch of show business, either as a career or as a hobby. Her emotional life is very vibrant. Toni is a romantic person easily won over by a gentle word said at the right time in the right place. She works hard to take care of the people she loves, and is gracious, kind, and considerate. Toni needs to remember to spend some time each day by herself, in order to analyze the many emotional impressions she absorbs from her surroundings. If she can balance her feelings with her mind, she will obtain one of the greatest gifts inherent in her name.

DERIVATION: English, common short form of Anthony or Antony, which stem from the Roman family name Antonius. Has been given frequently as an independent first name since the early twentieth century. Occasionally used as a nickname for girls, although the more common feminine spelling is Toni.

PRINCIPAL COLORS: The complete range of greenish hues, also white

GEMSTONES AND PRECIOUS METALS: Cat's-eye, white pearls, jade

BOTANICALS: Plantain, lettuce, willow ash

UNIQUE SPELLING: Toney

RELATED TO: Anthony†, Antoine, Anton, Antonello, Antonino, Antonio†, Antony

A Kabbalistic Synopsis
טעהני —TA'AHNY (Teth, Ayin, Heh, Nun, Yod)

Tony is likely to enjoy his sport, and he is certainly an extremely competitive guy. He will do his utmost to win at anything he puts his hand to, although Tony is very principled and will not allow himself to succeed through any unfair means, as this would ruin the entire process of competing for him. The value of this name comes to 144; the double appearance of the number four lets us know that Tony is a fairly materialistic individual who would not like to be without his creature comforts. The insertion of the letter Heh into his name not only gives Tony a more directed sense of energy than Toni† (thanks to the Aries influence that the letter Heh brings), but also suggests a real interest in other people. Tony will almost definitely enjoy working in a role where he manages a large number of employees.

The Runic Interpretation
ᛇᚾᛟᛏ (Eihwaz, Nauthiz, Othila, Teiwaz)

Tony has the Eihwaz rune of defense, and this makes Tony tackle a problem head-on. Tony uses his warrior energy to avert disaster in a proactive way. He believes in setting his house in order. He's very neat because it's one aspect of his life he can control. Tony may choose a career in politics, law, banking, sports, performing arts, or medicine. He has some healing ability, and is enthusiastic about erasing as much of the Nauthiz constraint in the world as he possibly can by taking charge and seizing the moment.

Elements: Earth/fire, fire, earth/fire, air

The Numerological Interpretation
Tony (NV = 11, CV = 7, VV = 4, FL = 2)

Tony is able to find many alternative approaches to the challenges of daily life. He is aware of day-to-day practical considerations, which are important to him, but he is not limited by habitual patterns of response. He is experimental and willing to look beyond conventional ways of dealing with things. Tony is very just, a man who stands for equal opportunity for all. In an executive role, he can be counted on to deal fairly with his employees. This is a man who is easy to approach, and although his response may not be immediate, when he does answer, he is often correct.

Tonya

DERIVATION: English, short version of Antonia. Now commonly used as an independent first name.

PRINCIPAL COLORS: The full range of purple hues, from the palest lilac to the deepest violet

GEMSTONES AND PRECIOUS METALS: Garnets, amethyst

BOTANICALS: Lungwort, mint, apple

UNIQUE SPELLINGS: Tania, Taniah, Tanya, Tanyah, Tonea, Tonia, Toniah, Tonja, Tonyah

RELATED TO: Antoinette†, Antonia†, Antonie, Antonina, Tanya†, Tonee, Toni†, Tonie, Tony†

A Kabbalistic Synopsis

טעניא —TA'ANYA (Teth, Ayin, Nun, Yod, Aleph)

When you're with Tonya, you know you're in the presence of someone with enormous charisma. She can hold a conversation with a whole roomful of people and have them all listening with interest. The value of her name is equivalent to the Hebrew word "kings." What this equivalence points to is an innate atmosphere of power that seems to follow Tonya around, so that people are immediately impressed by her. As the compression of her name produces letters that refer exclusively to intelligence and emotional warmth, we should not expect this authoritative personality to mean that Tonya is in any way arrogant or pushy. On the whole, people are only too happy to go along with Tonya's ideas, which in the main are perfectly good. Tonya sometimes has a difficult time in relationships, as she doesn't really want to wear the trousers all the time and is looking for someone with an even more dominant personality than she has—quite a tall order!

The Runic Interpretation

ᚨᛇᚾᛟᛏ (Ansuz, Eihwaz, Nauthiz, Othila, Teiwaz)

Tonya is likely to place career ahead of love; she has so much she wants to do. She wants to travel, start her own business, save the dolphins, and play the piano in recital in a foreign country, for starters; the Nauthiz rune of constraint has limited her enough! Now that she's on her own, she wants to be free. Othila, the rune of separation, could mean that Tonya falls for partners at a distance and likes seeing them at her convenience. Eihwaz, the rune of defense, has really done a number on Tonya, and she may be too watchful. Ansuz, the rune of signals, gives Tonya wonderful intuition, and she knows that she must follow her dreams because she has important things to do in life. The Teiwaz warrior energy makes Tonya bright and talented and brave.

Elements: Air, earth/fire, fire, earth/fire, air

The Numerological Interpretation

Tonya (NV = 4, CV = 6, VV = 7, FL = 2)

This is an individual who has a clear sense of personal and social responsibility. Tonya can be counted on to do her part in any group situation. She takes her job, family, and friends seriously, and is neither flighty nor frivolous in her relationships. Tonya also expects others to give 100 percent of themselves, and will be disappointed with anything less. Her life lessons have to do with freeing herself from her sometimes too high expectations and developing a loving sense of detachment. Tonya works very well in any branch of education, from classroom teacher to designer of educational models and programs.

DERIVATION: English, originally a surname, then became a male name. It soon became more common for females, and was considered a pet form of Theresa or Teresa. Especially popular during the mid-twentieth century.

PRINCIPAL COLORS: The full spectrum of moderately shaded hues

GEMSTONES AND PRECIOUS METALS: Sapphires

BOTANICALS: Sage, spinach, medlar

UNIQUE SPELLINGS: Tracee, Tracey, Traci, Tracie

RELATED TO: Teresa, Terese, Territ, Terryt, Tess, Tessa, Tessie, Theresal, Tresa, Tressa

Tracy

A KABBALISTIC SYNOPSIS
טראיסי —TRAYSY (Teth, Resh, Aleph, Yod, Samech, Yod)

In many ways, Tracy is the classic girl next door. She is friendly, warm, and outgoing without being too outrageous. She does have enormous energy, as indicated by the double appearance of the letter Yod in her name. Between these two letters is the letter Samech, which refers to support, and in Tracy's case, this suggests that her energy is only maintained if she has sufficient moral support. It may be that this support comes from Tracy's family or from her long-term partner, but as long as she is getting love from somewhere, the world is her oyster. The value of her name is 280, which expresses the more domestic side of Tracy's nature. It points to someone with a bright manner and demeanor who loves to spend time with her closest friends and relatives just catching up on old times and having a relaxed, cheerful evening.

THE RUNIC INTERPRETATION
ᛇᛋᚨᚱᛏ (Eihwaz, Sowelu, Ansuz, Raido, Teiwaz)

Tracy loves to be outdoors. Gardening, landscape painting, or camping are just her cup of tea. The sounds of nature appeal to the intuitive Ansuz rune in Tracy. Tracy listens to the birds communicate with each other and the world around her. Eihwaz, the rune of defense, combined with Teiwaz, the warrior rune, means that Tracy well might be involved in ecological programs to save the environment, lobbying, or politics. Tracy is a good communicator and persuasive fund-raiser. Sowelu in her name, for wholeness, means Tracy functions at a high level of excellence. Give a project to Tracy, and she will always go that extra mile because she has high integrity.

Elements: Earth/fire, air, air, water, air

THE NUMEROLOGICAL INTERPRETATION
Tracy (NV = 5, CV = 6, VV = 8, FL = 2)

Tracy is a vivacious conversationalist, a woman who enjoys the intellectual and emotional stimulation found at dinners, parties, and other social events. Many of these gatherings she will organize and host herself, as her home is the pivotal aspect of her life. A great deal of her interests revolve around her domestic scene, which has to be very aesthetically pleasing. Tracy takes pride in her surroundings, as well as in her physical appearance. She wants people to think well of her, and aims to please whomever she encounters. However, Tracy must be careful of becoming too attached to superficialities.

Travis

A Kabbalistic Synopsis
טראויס —TRAVYS (Teth, Resh, Aleph, Vau, Yod, Samech)

Travis seems to have an unavoidable tendency to get himself into all manner of difficulties and scrapes simply because of a lack of foresight. Partly this is due to being almost too optimistic about life in general; Travis never really expects a less-than-sensible action to have a negative outcome. This name's value reduces to sixteen, and consequently points us in the direction of the Tower card, which is a symbol of catastrophe. However, the Tower is not a completely negative symbol, as it usually suggests that whatever the crisis, there can be a positive ultimate outcome. The best advice to give Travis when he is in the midst of an inevitably thorny problem is to simply ride it out and wait for the eventual benefit to appear. Travis will make a great partner, as he longs for a committed relationship with the right person. When he does find that person, he will be the most loyal, appreciative lover one could hope to find.

The Runic Interpretation
ᛋᛁᚠᚨᚱᛏ (Sowelu, Isa, Fehu, Ansuz, Raido, Teiwaz)

Travis feels overwhelmed at times by responsibilities. He yearns to be more spontaneous and loose. Fehu, the rune of possessions, boosts Travis's income potential considerably, and this opens doors for him. Raido, the rune of journey, is there to lure him to travel. By redesigning his schedule and getting up an hour earlier in the morning just to sit by the window, Travis feels inspired, and he begins to take charge of his creativity. It's all a state of mind. Sowelu, the rune of wholeness, gives Travis a sense of abundance, whether he's inventing or filming or researching or acting. Once Travis connects to the creative side of his soul, he feels free as a bird on a wire.

Elements: Air, earth, fire, air, water, air

The Numerological Interpretation
Travis (NV = 8, CV = 7, VV = 1, FL = 2)

Travis carries himself with aplomb and great self-assurance. He feels very at ease with the responsibilities that come with money and social position. He dresses well and keeps his body trim and healthy. Travis garners recognition for his perseverance, stamina, and determination. He is a team player in business, and although he requires some direct control over his work, he has no problem integrating his efforts with those of the other people in his company.

DERIVATION: English, originally from the surname, which denoted someone who collected tolls. Most common in the United States, especially during the twentieth century.

PRINCIPAL COLORS: Black, gray, the richest shades of blue and purple

GEMSTONES AND PRECIOUS METALS: Carbuncles, lackluster rubies, black pearls

BOTANICALS: Angelica, ragwort, gravel root

UNIQUE SPELLINGS: Travess, Traviss, Travys, Travyss

RELATED TO: Trav, Traver, Trevar, Trever, Trevort

DERIVATION: Welsh and English, from the common Welsh place-name Trefor, which means "great homestead." Especially popular in the twentieth century.

PRINCIPAL COLORS: Very dark hues, including gray, azure, violet, and black

GEMSTONES AND PRECIOUS METALS: Any dark stone, including black pearls and black diamonds

BOTANICALS: Marsh mallow, mandrake root

UNIQUE SPELLINGS: Trever, Trevir, Trewer, Trewir, Trevvor, Trevvyr, Trevyr

RELATED TO: Trav, Traver, Travers, Travis!, Trefor, Trev

Trevor

A KABBALISTIC SYNOPSIS
טראוער —TRAVA'AR (Teth, Resh, Aleph, Vau, Ayin, Resh)

If there is one expression that Trevor hates, it is probably "good guys finish last." Trevor really, really wants to be big in business. His ultimate dream is to have his own plush office with a brass nameplate. But although Trevor's name has the influence of both the letter Ayin and the letter Teth, which lends the mean streak necessary to a corporate ladder climber, Trevor never quite makes it much past senior manager level. The reason for this is actually a happy one. Thanks to the very strong influence of the letter Resh and the astrological sign of Taurus in his name, Trevor is simply too good at heart to get right to the top. He has a genuinely jolly temperament, and a definite need to be liked more than respected or obeyed. In addition, the influence of Taurus means that Trevor is very committed to his family life. He is just not prepared to put in the suicidal hours that are required to really reach the skies in the corporate world.

THE RUNIC INTERPRETATION
ᚱᛟᚠᛖᚱᛏ (Raido, Othila, Fehu, Ehwaz, Raido, Teiwaz)

Trevor has a way with words; the double Raido rune of communication prominently positioned in his name is the tip-off. He also has the Teiwaz rune of the warrior, and this could make Trevor a public speaker or an advertising executive. Ehwaz, the rune of movement, draws Trevor toward journalism or playwriting. He will work and possibly even live abroad, and he will always be able to say just the right thing in any of several languages. If he's analytical by nature, law is a good career choice for him. Trevor likes to relax on the weekends with a big mug of coffee and a crossword puzzle, which he does in ink. Fehu, the rune of possessions, assures Trevor is well-off and sophisticated, and he has a funny sense of humor to boot.

Elements: Water, earth/fire, fire, air, water, air

THE NUMEROLOGICAL INTERPRETATION
Trevor (NV = 8, CV = 6, VV = 11, FL = 2)

A unique individual with a mind of his own, Trevor can be counted on for his spontaneity. He has a very special sense of humor, one characterized by a nonconformist view of life. Trevor makes a very faithful friend and a passionate lover. He takes his relationships very seriously and prefers to have a few friends for life rather than a great number of superficial acquaintances. Trevor is also very close to his family and makes sure to include them in his major life decisions. In essence, this name denotes a kind and considerate man, one who is open and available to others.

Troy

DERIVATION: English, usually associated with the ancient city of Troy, where the Trojan Wars were fought. Also used as a place-name in the United States. Has become an increasingly popular first name from the 1950s on.

PRINCIPAL COLORS: Pale to medium shades of blue

GEMSTONES AND PRECIOUS METALS: Turquoise, emeralds

BOTANICALS: Dog rose, violets, apricots

UNIQUE SPELLINGS: Troi, Troye

RELATED TO: Torr, Torrence, Torrey, Torrin, Trey

A KABBALISTIC SYNOPSIS
טראוי —TRAVY (Teth, Resh, Aleph, Vau, Yod)

Notwithstanding its considerable historical significance, Troy is actually a pretty good name to have. For a start, it reduces to ten and indicates that Troy is likely to be a fairly lucky individual. He is certainly well liked, having both a cheerful disposition and a very intuitive side to his nature that enables him to act as an understanding friend. In his own relationships, though, Troy can have something of a roving eye, even if this tendency doesn't usually amount to much. The central number in the value of this name is eighty, which refers to the letter Peh, meaning "mouth." The value following eighty is nine, the value of the letter Teth, which can refer to aggression, but if there is a warlike side to Troy, it is purely a verbal one. Troy is also an energetic guy, as shown by the final Yod in his name, and so he may possibly be professionally employed in some sports-related area.

THE RUNIC INTERPRETATION
ᛇᛟᚱᛏ (Eihwaz, Othila, Raido, Teiwaz)

Troy is drawn to intrigue. He enjoys science and the mysteries of nature. Whether Troy works in criminal justice or something else, he has a quick, analytical mind. He enjoys puzzles and mysteries and is the best in the family at guessing who done it. Competitive sports such as wrestling and football also appeal to Troy. He's a good shot, and his sure eye suits him for golf and baseball. With the warrior rune in his name combined with the rune of defense, Troy is protective and brave.

Elements: Earth/fire, earth/fire, water, air

THE NUMEROLOGICAL INTERPRETATION
Troy (NV = 6, CV = 11, VV = 4, FL = 2)

Troy has a highly developed artistic sensibility that is uniquely his own. He is definitely at home with people who are more avant-garde than conformist. A deeply emotional man, Troy is very much the romantic. This extends beyond his sexual life into every facet of his being. He sees the romance in spring, feels the romance in a song, tastes the romance in a sip of wine. But Troy is not a total idealist. He wants to sell his paintings, publish his books, and find a collector for his sculpture. He wants to be able to afford his romanticism!

Trudy

A KABBALISTIC SYNOPSIS
טרודי —TRVDY (Teth, Resh, Vau, Daleth, Yod)

Trudy is sometimes too kind for her own good; friends are of great importance to her, and she will do all that is within her power to help them out. She is a woman who possesses a great deal of natural understanding; this is indicated by the central letter Vau in her name. The presence of the letter Daleth suggests that Trudy will put a lot of time and energy into trying to create all sorts of opportunities for those close to her, but she needs to make sure that she puts the same amount of effort into ensuring her own happiness in life. Careerwise, Trudy has the capacity to make a good salary, probably in a consulting capacity, but she needs to make sure that she isn't so generous that she puts someone else forward to receive the credit that she deserves.

THE RUNIC INTERPRETATION
ᛇᛞᚢᚱᛏ (Eihwaz, Dagaz, Uruz, Raido, Teiwaz)

Trudy has nerves of steel and great reserves of patience. She is stable and calm and gets along with everyone. It's not easy, but she extends herself to difficult people and treats everyone with courtesy and respect. Yet Trudy has to be careful she doesn't hold her emotions inside and so develop health problems. With the warrior rune, combined with the rune of defense and Uruz for strength in her name, Trudy is perfectly suited to the military, social work, child psychology, or high-risk occupations. Dagaz, the rune of breakthrough, offers Trudy opportunities that seem to come her way out of the blue. Raido, the rune of journey, makes Trudy a good communicator. She loves to travel and rather enjoys visiting dangerous places in the world. Trudy is powerful, with the attributes of all four elements in her name.

Elements: Earth/fire, fire, earth, water, air

THE NUMEROLOGICAL INTERPRETATION
Trudy (NV = 7, CV = 6, VV = 1, FL = 2)

A devotional attitude to life characterizes this name. Trudy is a very faithful person and can be counted on to hold her friends' secrets, exceed her boss's expectations at work, and be faithful to her partner. She is one who is able to offer support and strength in times of need. Trudy likes to collect things, and the nooks and corners of her home are filled with special objects. They do not have to be expensive, but they always have some special sentimental value for this very kind person.

Tyler

DERIVATION: English, originally from the surname used for someone who tiles roofs. Primarily a twentieth-century name, and has become more common in recent years.

PRINCIPAL COLORS: The deepest shades of blue, violet, gray, and black

GEMSTONES AND PRECIOUS METALS: Carbuncles, sapphires, any other dark stones

BOTANICALS: Angelica, pilewort

UNIQUE SPELLINGS: Tieler, Tilar, Tiler, Tilerr, Tilyr, Tyeler, Tylar, Tylerr, Tylir, Tylyr

RELATED TO: Ty, Tynan, Tyson

A KABBALISTIC SYNOPSIS
טילא —TYLA (Teth, Yod, Lamed, Aleph)

If you need some good advice, you could do a lot worse than ask Tyler for his or her opinion, which Tyler will be more than happy to give you. The only time that this might not be such a good idea is if Tyler has been born under Scorpio. Then Tyler may have a rather jaundiced view of the world, which leads Tyler to maker rather negative assumptions about the outcome of any given event. The central letter in this name is the L, or Lamed, which lets us know that Tyler is a very committed individual. The driving passion is likely to be politics; he or she is often found hanging out in radical meeting places, and is more attracted to the fringes of mainstream party activities rather than to the solid center ground. Tyler's emotional life is best described as intense. Tyler will fall in love at the drop of a hat and can sometimes blow it by expecting a similar response on the part of his or her intended, who is more than a little taken aback at Tyler's sudden protestations of undying love when they have only just met.

THE RUNIC INTERPRETATION
ᚱᛖᚾᛇᛏ (Raido, Ehwaz, Laguz, Eihwaz, Teiwaz)

Whether this is a male or female name, the interpretation is the same. Tyler is the strong, silent type and has a literary, romantic nature. Brave, easygoing, and flexible, Tyler is the kind of person who can calm a crying child or help his or her partner through a difficult situation by being a good listener. Yet Tyler really doesn't like crises, and will try to avoid them. Tyler will take the burned cookie on the plate and not complain because self-aggrandizement is not on Tyler's agenda. Tyler's used to being overlooked, and he or she is truly humble. This is not to imply that Tyler is a martyr; Tyler has the Teiwaz warrior energy to call on when asserting oneself is necessary. People rarely notice when Tyler corrects them because Tyler does it in a laid-back style that is courteous and clear but not at all confrontational. Tyler is someone who makes you feel loved.

Elements: Water, air, water, earth/fire, air

THE NUMEROLOGICAL INTERPRETATION
Tyler (NV = 8, CV = 5, VV = 3, FL = 2)

This is a person who will always be befriended. Tyler has a glowing smile and radiates joy and goodwill. It is no wonder that people like to be around Tyler, as he or she is usually so very optimistic. Money should flow easily to Tyler, who has a knack for realizing his or her creative visions and marketing and selling his or her products and services. An agreeable person, Tyler would rather keep quiet than waste energy on meaningless gossip. Tyler prefers to avoid social conflicts, and may have to learn to stand up for him- or herself in order to avoid more serious complications in the future.

DERIVATION: English, from the name of an Irish county. Gained prominence as a first name after the careers of two early twentieth-century film actors (who were father and son) named Tyrone Power.

PRINCIPAL COLORS: The entire range of yellow and green hues, also gold

GEMSTONES AND PRECIOUS METALS: Moonstones, pearls

BOTANICALS: Elder, hops, juniper

UNIQUE SPELLINGS: Tierone, Tiroan, Tiroane; Tirone, Tyerone, Tyroan, Tyroane

RELATED TO: Ty, Tylert, Tyson

A KABBALISTIC SYNOPSIS
טירען —TYRA'AN (Teth, Yod, Resh, Ayin, Nun)

Tyrone loves to surround himself with every possible trapping of consumerism, from the latest high-tech television to the fastest, most powerful car around. Tyrone's only problem is how on earth to get the money to provide the level of luxury he would love to have and feels, deep down, he deserves. However, the life of a successful city gent is not for Tyrone, as he is too unconventional by far to cope with a daily routine and the regulation suit and tie. Tyrone is a deeply creative guy, and he will try to make his mark using his talents. He is particularly suited to comedy, and given the appearance of the venomous letter Teth in both the spelling and the compression of his name, he may well be a genius at satire.

THE RUNIC INTERPRETATION
ᛖᚾᛟᚱᛃᛏ (Ehwaz, Nauthiz, Othila, Raido, Eihwaz, Teiwaz)

People think of Tyrone when they need to talk because he's been there and has a pretty good idea of what you are saying. Not that Tyrone has all the answers; he's the first to admit he likes to do things his own way, but the Teiwaz warrior energy and the powers of the four elements in his name make Tyrone brave enough to tell the truth. And that's precisely what makes people feel better. Tyrone also has the Raido rune, which gives him the gift of gab. He might be a radio announcer or class instructor. He's comfortable with himself, which comes across in his presentation. Yet Tyrone wasn't always like this. He does have the Nauthiz rune of constraint in his name, but he got over his insecurity. Now he inspires people with his confidence and good, old-fashioned common sense.

Elements: Air, fire, earth/fire, water, earth/fire, air

THE NUMEROLOGICAL INTERPRETATION
Tyrone (NV = 7, CV = 7, VV = 9, FL = 2)

Tyrone can be somewhat of a loner, a man who looks forward to long periods of solitude away from busy crowds of people. What does he do with himself? For one thing, Tyrone is a very dedicated researcher. He has a passion for science and technology and is very keen on perfecting his special interests. He does very well as an educator on the college level and is certainly at home in a research laboratory. It is difficult for him to be in intimate emotional contact with others, as he much prefers the life of the mind.

Uma

DERIVATION: Of Indic origin, meaning "bright."

PRINCIPAL COLORS: Black, dark blues and grays

GEMSTONES AND PRECIOUS METALS: Deep sapphires, dark stones

BOTANICALS: Angelica, shepherd's purse, marsh mallow

UNIQUE SPELLING: Umah

RELATED TO: Umalla, Umani

A KABBALISTIC SYNOPSIS
אמו —VMA (Vau, Mem, Aleph)

The number of all things magical is eleven, and as the total value of Uma's name can be reduced to this number, we should expect Uma to be quite an enigmatic individual. Uma may well find herself drawn to the fringes of occultism—and possibly even further! The initial letter Vau points to a strong intellect, and any investigations Uma makes into the unknown will be undertaken with a clear and objective mind. Uma is a fantastic mother if she chooses to have children, and if not, she will find other outlets for her nurturing and protective tendencies. The value of her name can be represented by the two letters Mem and Zayin. While Mem refers directly to the emotionally caring aspect of her personality, the letter Zayin means "sword" in Hebrew and tells us that while Uma may be warmhearted and affectionate, she will go to any lengths to protect those she loves. If you go out for an evening with Uma or, in fact, if you share an office with her, then you'd better be prepared for any eventuality. One of the correspondences with the value of her name is the Hebrew word for foolishness, and in Uma's case this should be interpreted as suggesting a love of practical jokes and other forms of amusement. Uma never plays nasty tricks on people, though, and invariably gets a laugh from her coworkers. In fact, whenever Uma moves on in her life to a new town or career, she leaves behind a group of people who are very sorry to see such a zany and warm person leave their lives.

THE RUNIC INTERPRETATION
ᚱᛗᚨ (Ansuz, Mannaz, Uruz)

Lovely Uma wants life to be heavenly, with people treating each other with delight and appreciation. Teaching and nurturing professions suit this idealistic woman well. She is tenderhearted and kind, and easily wounded. Rather than lose her sweet nature and toughen up in order to survive, perhaps Uma may find it best to be discriminating about where she works and who her friends are. The quality of life matters a great deal to Uma.

Elements: Air, air, earth

THE NUMEROLOGICAL INTERPRETATION
Uma (NV = 8, CV = 4, VV = 4, FL = 3)

The numbers in this name point to a very sensuous and earthy woman. Magnetic and sexually appealing, Uma is ambitious and full of physical vitality. She is very connected to her financial goals in life because personal economic security ranks very high on her list of priorities. Uma's life goals are very much connected to social status and material comforts. This is a woman who is very self-motivated. Her lessons come through the correct use of her extraordinary willpower to focus her many talents and abilities to achieve what she sets out to accomplish. The spiritual and religious facets of life will hold little interest or meaning for Uma unless she can apply the teachings in these doctrines to the practical world around her.

DERIVATION: English, German, and Scandinavian. Originally a Latin name meaning "little female bear." Saint Ursula, who lived in the fourth century, was a martyr. Most popular in the seventeenth century.

PRINCIPAL COLORS: Cream, white, green

GEMSTONES AND PRECIOUS METALS: Pearls, jade, moonstones

BOTANICALS: Plantain, chicory, lettuce, cabbage

UNIQUE SPELLINGS: Ursala, Ursella, Ursola

RELATED TO: Orsa, Orsala, Orsolla, Seula, Sula, Ulla, Ursa, Ursie, Ursule, Ursulina, Ursuline, Ursy, Urszuli

A KABBALISTIC SYNOPSIS

ורסולא —VRSVLA (Vau, Resh, Samech, Vau, Lamed, Aleph)

One thing is certain: Ursula will never be short of admirers. It is highly likely that Ursula will be absolutely stunning, and the total value of her name has associations with the tarot card the Lovers. Ursula is also a very intelligent woman. The letter Vau appears twice in her name, indicating a high concern with matters of the brain. The meaning of the letters Resh and Samech points to Ursula as being someone whose thoughts are often of others, since the letters relate to thought and supportiveness. However, they are followed in this name by the letter Lamed, meaning "ox goad." Lamed indicates a sense of duty and obligation, and Ursula needs to be careful not to ignore her own needs when considering those of everyone around her. Ursula will often wear her coworkers and friends out, as she seems to need only half the amount of sleep and rest time of anyone else. What's more, with all this activity, Ursula hardly ever seems to get irritable. This high energy is indicated by the presence of the letter Shin in the compression of her name, but once again Ursula needs to make sure that she isn't driving herself too hard due to the effect of the ox goad Lamed. Ursula's biggest problem in life is that despite being very intelligent, she is not at all practical and can often be utterly disorganized.

THE RUNIC INTERPRETATION

ᚨᛚᚢᛋᚱᚢ (Ansuz, Laguz, Uruz, Sowelu, Raido, Uruz)

The elements in Ursula's name give Ursula added balance and a zest for living. The double Uruz rune of the wild ox reminds us that once the ox was domesticated, it could pull enormous weight. Ursula needs to tame the illusions and urges that run her life out of control, and once she relinquishes the old life, the new one always has greater opportunities. So-called loss is truly a way to gain greater perspective and meaning in life. Fortunately, Ursula is flexible and has an excellent sense of humor, so that she can enjoy the comical aspects to any situation life presents her.

Elements: Air, water, earth, air, water, earth

THE NUMEROLOGICAL INTERPRETATION

Ursula (NV = 11, CV = 4, VV = 7, FL = 3)

Ursula is a name with an unusual combination of influences and energies. A gifted intuitive, Ursula often knows what is going to happen before it does. People will be prone to confide their secrets to her and get her advice. Ursula genuinely likes people and can communicate effectively with them in many ways. She is attracted to writing and is open to all the latest techniques that computer technology provides for people to be in touch with one another. But Ursula also has an introspective side to her nature, and will need a lot of time on her own to contemplate the many complexities of life. As a complement to her own nature, Ursula would most likely seek a partner who is a visionary, but who is also very much of a practical person with strong, earthly ambitions.

Valerie

DERIVATION: English and French, the Latin feminine form of the Roman name Valerius, from the root *valere*, meaning "to be strong." Especially popular in the middle of the twentieth century.

PRINCIPAL COLORS: Light pink to the deepest of reds

GEMSTONES AND PRECIOUS METALS: Bloodstones, rubies

BOTANICALS: Garlic, nettle, wormwood

UNIQUE SPELLINGS: Valaree, Valarey, Valari, Valarie, Valary, Valeree, Valerey, Valeri, Valery, Valorey, Valori, Valorie, Valory

RELATED TO: Val, Vale, Valeria, Vallie, Valry

A KABBALISTIC SYNOPSIS

ואלארי —VALARY (Vau, Aleph, Lamed, Aleph, Resh, Yod)

The value of this name reduces to fourteen, the number of the Temperance card in the tarot, and a sure sign of Valerie's inner sense of balance and harmony. If Valerie is a mom, which is highly likely, the energy of the Temperance card will be of great assistance to her when it comes to sorting out the usual disagreements between siblings. The R, or Resh, in her name shows Valerie to be a cheerful woman, and it is this sense of optimism that gives her immense energy and enables her to cope with the enormous number of jobs she takes on both in and outside the home. In this value of this name the number eight is featured as the final digit. This indicates that, despite her willingness to stay in the background, Valerie has a very strong character and forceful nature. Her strength of will comes into its own whenever anyone tries to take advantage of her.

THE RUNIC INTERPRETATION

MIRMLAF (Ehwaz, Isa, Raido, Ehwaz, Laguz, Ansuz, Fehu)

Valerie must choose a career wisely because her work is very important to her. She's unusually good with numbers, and a career in finance could be successful for her. Competitive and not especially patient, Valerie is also very intuitive. Eating carefully and keeping fit are important to her, and she almost feels ill when she neglects her exercise routine. Valerie enjoys dressing in expensive clothes and telling her friends about her latest adventures. The Ehwaz rune hints that Valerie could live and work abroad. Valerie is flexible, with the rune of flow in her name, and she has the power of the four elements.

Elements: Air, earth, water, air, water, air, fire

THE NUMEROLOGICAL INTERPRETATION

Valerie (NV = 9, CV = 7, VV = 2, FL = 4)

This is a woman with a brave heart and a noble spirit. Her name gives her these qualities plus a sincere interest in other people's welfare. It is common to find Valerie involved in charitable or humanitarian causes. Her pet projects may involve medical or sociological research, and she will be interested in finding cures for the ills that beset the world. Valerie's personal relationships have to be meaningful, as she is not given over to flings. Valerie prefers serious commitments and long-range projects.

Vanessa

DERIVATION: English, invented by the satirical writer Jonathan Swift (1667–1745) for his friend Esther Vanhomrigh. Mostly a literary name until the 1920s, when it became quite popular.

PRINCIPAL COLORS: The full range of red hues, particularly the richest shades

GEMSTONES AND PRECIOUS METALS: Rubies, garnets

BOTANICALS: Broom, onion, rape

UNIQUE SPELLINGS: Vanesa, Vannesa, Vannessa, Venesa, Venessa, Vennesa

RELATED TO: Nessa, Nessi, Nessie, Nessy, Van, Vana, Vanetta, Vania, Vannie, Vanya, Venetta

A KABBALISTIC SYNOPSIS

אססאנאו —VANASSA (Vau, Aleph, Nun, Aleph, Samech, Samech, Aleph)

Vanessa could brighten up the atmosphere in a morgue with her upbeat demeanor and ready wit! Her powerful voice plays an important part in all her dealings, good and bad. When she is not enjoying a bit of gossip, Vanessa prides herself on being efficient, and she is certainly capable of tackling a huge array of tasks with seeming ease and little supervision, thanks to her confidence in her own ability. In her relationships, Vanessa often looks for an older partner, as she has an essentially childlike view of the world and feels the need for a more mature and stabilizing influence in her life.

THE RUNIC INTERPRETATION

ᚨᛋᛋᛖᚾᚨᚠ (Ansuz, Sowelu, Sowelu, Ehwaz, Nauthiz, Ansuz, Fehu)

Vanessa is known as a perceptive woman. Double Sowelu is a most fortunate combination, signifying wholeness. No matter what comes her way, Vanessa has a sense of optimism and patience, and things do have a way of working out for her. She is good with finances but must be careful not to attract a partner who squanders money. Vanessa understands that how she packages herself makes an impression on others; therefore, marketing and promoting will be wonderful career options for her.

Elements: Air, air, air, air, fire, air, fire

THE NUMEROLOGICAL INTERPRETATION

Vanessa (NV = 9, CV = 11, VV = 7, FL = 4)

Vanessa is a woman with a definite sense of style. She is very much her own person when it comes to the way she dresses and to her political and social views about life. Vanessa tends to be very liberal and open-minded. She is a forgiving person and doesn't hold grudges; she is too busy investigating and experimenting with her own creative potential. People enjoy Vanessa's company. Vanessa is very innovative and not at all interested in taking the common, well-trodden path through life.

Velma

DERIVATION: English, of uncertain origin. Created in the twentieth century, possibly inspired by names such as Thelma and Selma. Commonly used since the 1920s.

PRINCIPAL COLORS: Black and dark gray, also deep shades of purple and blue

GEMSTONES AND PRECIOUS METALS: Black diamonds, sapphires, dull rubies

BOTANICALS: Marsh mallow, gravel root, shepherd's purse

UNIQUE SPELLINGS: Vellma, Vellmah, Velmah

RELATED TO: Delma, Selma, Thelma†

A KABBALISTIC SYNOPSIS
ואלמא —VALMA (Vau, Aleph, Lamed, Mem, Aleph)

The value of Velma's name is seventy-eight, and seventy-eight is a particularly important number, since it is the number of cards in a full tarot deck. In terms of personality, it suggests a well-rounded individual who likes to get out and experience as much of the world as possible rather than simply reading about it or seeing it on television. The initial Vau in this name marks Velma out as a thinker; she may not be a rational intellectual, but she has a genuine concern about a range of issues that face the population as a whole. Connected to her thoughtful nature is her preference for partners who like to sit and earnestly discuss the dynamics of their relationship. One equivalent of her name's value is the Hebrew phrase "to pity," which points to Velma's probable involvement with a number of charitable organizations.

THE RUNIC INTERPRETATION
ᚨᛗᛚᛖᚠ (Ansuz, Mannaz, Laguz, Ehwaz, Fehu)

Velma enjoys good food. She travels exhaustively and would enjoy gourmet tours in the south of France. Velma is confident and capable, with the Mannaz rune of self in her name. She has wealth in her future, and once she has financial security, Velma concentrates on developing her many talents. Her organizational ability and musical gifts serve her well in the performing arts. Velma can turn her talents in directions such as sculpting and cooking and enjoy the process immensely. Laguz, the rune of flow, indicates creativity and an open, original point of view. Even if fame eludes her, Velma knows what it is to feel creative and free, and to love life and enjoy the world around her.

Elements: Air, air, water, air, fire

THE NUMEROLOGICAL INTERPRETATION
Velma (NV = 8, CV = 11, VV = 6, FL = 4)

This is a name that gives a woman beauty and charisma. Velma is a very sensuous person with a need for intensely profound emotional experiences. This tendency can go to extremes with her lovers, and Velma has to take care that she doesn't compromise herself accordingly. If she is living up to the higher nature of the master number eleven in her name, she will use her feeling nature in a compassionate and impersonal manner. Velma can then become involved with social and community service work that serves to channel money and other resources to the people who most need them.

Vera

DERIVATION: Russian, from a word meaning "faith." Brought to the English-speaking world at the end of the nineteenth century. Also associated with the Latin *vera*, meaning "true." Especially popular in the 1920s.

PRINCIPAL COLORS: Brown, orange, the palest to the richest yellows, including gold

GEMSTONES AND PRECIOUS METALS: Citrine, topaz, amber

BOTANICALS: Chamomile, eyebright, borage

UNIQUE SPELLINGS: Veera, Veerah, Veira, Veirah

RELATED TO: Verena, Verene, Verina, Verla, Verochka, Veronica†, Veruschka, Verushka

A Kabbalistic Synopsis
וירא —VYRA (Vau, Yod, Resh, Aleph)

The main influence in Vera's name is the planet Jupiter. This Jovian influence, as it is known, has an extremely beneficial effect on nearly all aspects of her life. For starters, Jupiter is the planet of mirth and merriment, so we should all go round to Vera's whenever she has a party, as it is bound to be a memorable one! Vera loves all traditional holidays, and will pull together an extravagant gathering at the slightest provocation. Money is not often a concern; thanks again to the influence of Jupiter, Vera is likely to have a successful career. She is suited to jobs that are based on project work, as she is very good at ensuring tasks are completed. Vera has the rare fortune of being lucky both in money and in love. She is a hopeless romantic who could never marry for any reason other than true love, but she is more likely than most to marry her childhood sweetheart and be blissfully happy with him for a good many years.

The Runic Interpretation
ᚨᚱᛖᚠ (Ansuz, Raido, Ehwaz, Fehu)

Department store doors stay in motion when Vera is on the prowl. The Ehwaz rune for defense helps Vera spot a bargain and screen out poor-quality merchandise. Indeed, Vera may well pursue a career in fashion or merchandising. The Fehu rune of wealth hints that Vera could own her own mail-order catalog or work at designing clothes and/or putting on fashion shows. She has a great sense of humor, and the Ansuz rune of intuition helps her spot the people she can tease. Her keen eye makes her a bit sarcastic at times, but it's all in good fun. Vera must watch her figure because despite her interest in glamour, that sweet tooth of hers could create some difficulties. But sharp-eyed Vera will quickly detect any burgeoning curves in the dressing-room mirror.

Elements: Air, water, air, fire

The Numerological Interpretation
Vera (NV = 1, CV = 4, VV = 6, FL = 4)

Vera is a highly capable woman, one who can handle herself quite well in the world. She has a very direct nature and may not be the most diplomatic of people—but she does get the job done! Vera is able to take control and maintain her calm under a great deal of stress and chaos. She doesn't fall apart when challenged or threatened, but exudes a deep sense of inner poise and stands up to the test. Vera enjoys fine dining and good wines (and an attractive person to go with them). She makes a loyal friend and a fascinating lover.

Vernon

DERIVATION: English, originally a Norman baronial surname, from Gaulish roots meaning "alder tree." First used as a given name at the beginning of the nineteenth century, and most commonly used in the 1920s.

PRINCIPAL COLORS: Light to deep yellow and green

GEMSTONES AND PRECIOUS METALS: Pearls, cat's-eye, any white stones

BOTANICALS: Blackberry, juniper, hops

UNIQUE SPELLINGS: Vernen, Vernin, Vernyn

RELATED TO: Vern, Verne, Verney

A KABBALISTIC SYNOPSIS

ואַרנון —VARNVN (Vau, Aleph, Resh, Nun, Vau, Nun)

Immediately noticeable in this name is the fact that both the letters Vau and Nun appear twice. Consequently, the key features in Vernon's personality are bound up in emotions and the difficulties of decision making. As the emotional emphasis in this name is on the more negative aspects of our feelings, such as insecurity and self-doubt, it is likely that the problems Vernon experiences in making choices stem from this emotional conflict. However, all is not doom and gloom; the value of Vernon's name reduces to twenty, which is the number of the Judgment card in the tarot. The value of his name acts as a balance to the significance of the individual letters, and this gives Vernon a very discriminating nature. The net result is that while Vernon may be an emotionally sensitive man who likes to think very carefully before making a decision, he is not an emotional wreck rendered powerless by an inability to take positive action.

THE RUNIC INTERPRETATION

ᚺᛟᚺᚱᛖᚠ (Nauthiz, Othila, Nauthiz, Raido, Ehwaz, Fehu)

Nauthiz, the rune of constraint, strikes Vernon a mighty blow. Vernon is intelligent and capable, but he needs the help of the Ehwaz rune of defense to ward off the limitations and delays caused by the Nauthiz rune in his name. Vernon can separate himself from his cares, and as he breathes deeply, stress fades away. Vernon is very organized, and this, too, helps him stay in control. Money helps avert disaster, and as Vernon attracts money like a magnet, this is especially the case for Vernon. The Raido rune of good communication could incline Vernon toward writing a financial column; he'd also be a natural on the radio, offering tips on how to save. A likable fellow, Vernon tries harder than most to keep things running smoothly.

Elements: Fire, earth/fire, fire, water, air, fire

THE NUMEROLOGICAL INTERPRETATION

Vernon (NV = 7, CV = 5, VV = 11, FL = 4)

Personal freedom and the urge to explore life free from the restrictions of society are very significant elements in this name. Vernon can be a loner, and he certainly has a tendency to be a nonconformist. This is a man with a very distinct set of political and social opinions who can inspire others to come out of hiding and stand up for themselves. Vernon likes to share his beliefs, even broadcast them to others, but he is not receptive to being rebuked. He has to learn to consider views that contrast with his own and express more tolerance and compassion.

Veronica

DERIVATION: Latin form of Berenice, which is the Macedonian form of the Greek name Pherenike, meaning "victory bringer." Also from the Latin phrase *vera icon*, meaning "true image." Commonly used since the 1850s, and especially popular in the 1950s.

PRINCIPAL COLORS: Pale blue to rich shades of azure

GEMSTONES AND PRECIOUS METALS: Turquoise, emeralds

BOTANICALS: Dog rose, daffodils, walnuts

UNIQUE SPELLINGS: Verahnica, Veranica, Verohnica, Verohnicca, Verohnicka, Verohnika, Veronicka, Veronika

RELATED TO: Ronica, Ronna, Ronni, Ronnica, Ronnie, Ronny, Veera, Veira, Vera†, Vernice, Veronique

A KABBALISTIC SYNOPSIS

וארעניכא —VARA'ANYKA (Vau, Aleph, Resh, Ayin, Nun, Yod, Kaph, Aleph)

Veronica's name, when it is compressed, produces the letters Shin, Nun, and Cheth. The Shin tells us that Veronica is an active woman, as Shin is associated with the element of fire. We also can expect Veronica to have quite a stormy temperament and some pretty tempestuous relationships as well. The letter Nun may indicate the source of Veronica's stormy character; it relates to deep-seated emotional difficulties that Veronica prefers not to discuss or openly express. The final Cheth in the context of Veronica's name is important because of its value. It's number is eight, and as such, it is connected to the Strength card in the tarot, a definite indicator of impressive willpower. One Hebrew equivalent of Veronica's name is Nechesch. Nechesch is the name of the serpent who, according to the Bible, first tempted Eve. This is very positive news for any partner of Veronica's, since it gives a strong hint of a love of the forbidden—dangerous, sure, but fascinating.

THE RUNIC INTERPRETATION

ᛟᚲᛁᚺᛟᛇᛗᛖᚠ (Ansuz, Kano, Isa, Nauthiz, Othila, Raido, Ehwaz, Fehu)

The Raido rune of good communication makes Veronica so scrupulously honest that she sometimes steps on a few toes. Luckily, the Ehwaz rune of defense gives her a lot of ways of circumventing criticism. Money and opportunities come her way because Veronica is thorough in what she does and eager to go the extra mile. She is talented and intuitive, and could do well in sales or even become a successful astrologer. Veronica is also good at sports, and may prefer tennis and golf to water sports. When she's not on the court, she needs lots of solitude to stay in top form. As she is sensitive and finely balanced, news stories can quite upset Veronica, causing her to lose a good night's sleep. With Kano, the rune of openings, in her name, Veronica is sure to lead a rich and rewarding life. She is also blessed with the power of the four elements in her name.

Elements: Air, water, earth, fire, earth/fire, water, air, fire

THE NUMEROLOGICAL INTERPRETATION

Veronica (NV = 6, CV = 3, VV = 3, FL = 4)

The numbers in this name indicate a woman of strong intellectual gifts who has an easy way with words. Veronica is perfectly suited for a media career. She can handle herself well under all social circumstances, and puts people at their ease when communicating with them. Veronica knows how to embellish and decorate, but she does not do this to excess. Her name value of six gives Veronica an inner sense of balance and a definite orientation toward music and the arts. She sees value in everything and beauty in everyone, so although she is quite universal in her point of view, decision making can be quite problematic for her.

Vicky

A Kabbalistic Synopsis
ויכי —VYKY (Vau, Yod, Kaph, Yod)

Whenever the lottery jackpot is unusually high, you should get Vicky to buy a ticket for you. With all the good luck and generally benevolent influences crammed into her short name, Vicky stands a pretty good chance of hitting the jackpot. One Hebrew equivalent of her name is "tin," which may not sound that important until you realize that tin is the metal associated by tradition with the planet Jupiter, bringer of good fortune and happiness. In addition, her name's value reduces to ten and, as a result, brings the positive and lucky energies of the Wheel of Fortune tarot card into play. If Vicky ever does have a big win, it won't go to her head; the letter Kaph in her name tells us that she is a very practical person when she needs to be, and no doubt, any winnings would be very carefully invested.

The Runic Interpretation
ᛇᚲᛁᚠ (Eihwaz, Kano, Isa, Fehu)

When Vicky considers her life, there are a few things she might change, but basically she is satisfied. Kano, the rune of openings, sees to it that many opportunities cross her path. Early on, Vicky may make the common mistake of scattering her talents too thin, but once this becomes clear to her, she finds a few areas to concentrate on and then begins to bloom. The Isa rune of standstill helps Vicky get through this soul-searching time and emerge empowered. Vicky is willing to take risks because when she truly believes in a project, it can't help but succeed. Fehu, the rune of possessions, indicates that Vicky may be wealthy. This is fortunate because Vicky has a real appreciation of art and objects of quality. She'll live a prosperous and dynamic life surrounded by family and friends who admire her.

Elements: Earth/fire, water, earth, fire

The Numerological Interpretation
Vicky (NV = 7, CV = 9, VV = 7, FL = 4)

As Vicky is a contemplative and introspective woman, she may have a difficult time in social situations that demand a quick turn of phrase or a gregarious personality. She is much more the type of woman who considers her responses and actions seriously. When she does respond, you know that her answer comes from deep within her and is accompanied by a commitment to stand by her words and to fulfill her promises. Vicky can also be very religious, as she is aware that there is more to life than what is perceived through the senses.

DERIVATION: English, pet form of Victoria, which is from the Latin *victoria*, meaning "victory." Used independently, although more common as a nickname.

PRINCIPAL COLORS: The complete range of yellow and green hues

GEMSTONES AND PRECIOUS METALS: Pearls, moss agate

BOTANICALS: Elder, linseed, juniper

UNIQUE SPELLINGS: Vickee, Vickey, Vicki, Vickie, Vikie, Vikkey, Vikki, Vikkie, Vikky

RELATED TO: Vic, Victoriat, Victorie, Victorine, Viktoria, Viktorija, Viktorina, Vitoria, Vittoria

DERIVATION

DERIVATION: English, from the Latin *victor*, meaning "conqueror." Very popular among early Christians, and the name of several popes and saints. Especially popular in the United States in the 1950s.

PRINCIPAL COLORS: All but the brightest shades of blue

GEMSTONES AND PRECIOUS METALS: Blue and blue-green turquoise

BOTANICALS: Dog rose, vervain, violets

UNIQUE SPELLINGS: Vickter, Vicktor, Vicktyr, Vikter, Viktor, Viktyr

RELATED TO: Vic, Vick, Victorien, Vittorio, Vittorio

Victor

A KABBALISTIC SYNOPSIS

ויכטער —VYKTA'AR (Vau, Yod, Kaph, Teth, Ayin, Resh)

Victor likes to keep himself to himself, and when he is in the company of others, he doesn't really say very much at all. While he may give the impression of being incredibly lethargic, the letter Shin, which begins the compression of his name, is an indication of an energetic nature. In Victor's case, this energy is expressed through his mind rather than through any intensive physical activity. Victor never really stops thinking and may be a very light sleeper, a direct result of his ever active mind. The reduction of the value of Victor's name produces the number nine. This is the Hermit card in the tarot, and refers to an individual who has a considerable degree of wisdom and is seeking even more. However, the Hermit does not always indicate a truly solitary nature, and Victor is occasionally quite happy to go out and have a laugh—as long as he has time to complete all his work beforehand.

THE RUNIC INTERPRETATION

ᚱᛟᛏᚲᛁᚠ (Raido, Othila, Teiwaz, Kano, Isa, Fehu)

The presence of the four elements blesses Victor's name. This name is positive and suggests that Victor is a winner. With Teiwaz, the warrior rune, combining forces with Fehu, the rune of material possessions, Victor is sure to be financially comfortable and a good money manager. People feel secure around Victor because he has a built-in sense of abundance. The Raido rune of good communication gives Victor an eye for duplicity, and he can discard unreliable friends without looking back. Victor may marry late in life; he understands marriage is a big step, and won't take the plunge until he is sure he can provide his family with a comfortable foundation for years to come.

Elements: Water, earth/fire, air, water, earth, fire

THE NUMEROLOGICAL INTERPRETATION

Victor (NV = 6, CV = 9, VV = 6, FL = 4)

This is a man who cannot mask his feelings. He is very much in touch with the emotional context of every situation. Victor has to take care that all his actions and decisions are not made as a result of a mood or in response to a personal desire. He is a charitable and compassionate man, but he may have to work at including a fair amount of rational judgment in his way of dealing with others. This is not a man who enjoys being alone, and he sincerely appreciates the warmth of a loving friend.

Victoria

A KABBALISTIC SYNOPSIS
וויכטערייא —VYKTA'ARYA (Vau, Yod, Kaph, Teth, Ayin, Resh, Yod, Aleph)

Cheerful, energetic, intelligent, and business-minded, too—this woman has it all. Victoria is a deeply contented person with the confidence to take on any challenge that interests her. The central Ayin in her name is a key letter, as it indicates Veronica's business acumen will provide her with the money she needs to indulge the many and varied interests that make her such a contented individual. Victoria has very close ties to her parents and family, although they are not so close that they prevent her from forming commitments to more intimate relationships. Yet Victoria likes partners who can be genuinely honest and up-front about their feelings—but they must also know how to have fun! The value of her name reduces to eleven, the number most associated with magic and the unusual. It is not uncommon for Victoria to be interested in the mystical and supernatural once she has achieved her major goals in life and is looking for a new and stimulating interest.

THE RUNIC INTERPRETATION
ᚨᛁᚱᛟᛏᚲᛁᚠ (Ansuz, Isa, Raido, Othila, Teiwaz, Kano, Isa, Fehu)

Victoria is a powerful woman, as is indicated by the appearance of all four elements in her name. She has a sharp, analytical mind, and is ambitious because of the Teiwaz warrior energy that surges through her veins. Victoria reads the financial papers and knows how to position herself for success. The Kano energy brings her blessings, benefits, and opportunities. Victoria is one of those rare people who is both good at math and has considerable writing ability. Family and friends are important to her, and although Victoria leads a busy life, she always has time to listen to them.

Elements: Air, earth, water, earth/fire, air, water, earth, fire

THE NUMEROLOGICAL INTERPRETATION
Victoria (NV = 7, CV = 9, VV = 7, FL = 4)

Victoria is very attracted to nature and enjoys long walks alone among the trees or along the beach. She is not the easiest person to get to know. Some people think of her as being aloof and too detached, and this may be true to a point, as Victoria spends a lot of her time inside herself, contemplating the present and planning the future. She is a woman of considerable depth, and will seek a relationship that is very private. Although she is not the jealous type, Victoria is also not the most sociable of people, preferring to share herself with one person with whom she can build a stable and secure life.

DERIVATION: English and Spanish, from the Latin *victoria*, meaning "victory." Extremely popular among early Christians, and the name of a saint in the third century. Very popular in the 1950s and 1960s.

PRINCIPAL COLORS: Pale to deep green, light to rich yellow

GEMSTONES AND PRECIOUS METALS: Pearls, moss agate, cat's-eye

BOTANICALS: Linseed, juniper, grapes

UNIQUE SPELLINGS: Vicktoria, Vicktoriah, Vicktorya, Victoriah, Victorya, Victoryah, Viktoria, Viktoriah, Viktorya, Viktoryah

RELATED TO: Vic, Vickey, Vicki, Vickie, Vicky†, Victorie, Victorina, Viktorija, Viktorina, Vitoria, Vittoria

DERIVATION: Danish, Dutch, English, French, and Swedish, from the Latin *vincere*, meaning "to conquer." The name of several early saints associated with France. Popular from the 1840s on.

PRINCIPAL COLORS: Light to medium shades of blue

GEMSTONES AND PRECIOUS METALS: Emeralds, turquoise

BOTANICALS: Apricots, walnuts, almonds

UNIQUE SPELLINGS: Vincint, Vincynt, Vinczant

RELATED TO: Vicente, Vicenzio, Vin, Vince, Vincens, Vincents, Vincenz, Vincenzo, Vincien, Vinnie, Vinny

A KABBALISTIC SYNOPSIS

ויינסאנט —VYNSANT (Vau, Yod, Nun, Samech, Aleph, Nun, Teth)

More than anything, Vincent loves to indulge himself. His name's value reduces to fifteen, the number of the Devil card, and indicates Vincent's love of all forms of luxury. The double presence of the letter Nun in this name may suggest that his desire for an abundance of material goods originates from a desire to impress. If this is the case, Vincent need not concern himself; he is a popular guy. In the compression of his name we can see that he is both a witty individual and a good talker as well. While Vincent may worry about other people's opinions of him, the truth is that people love to chat with Vincent, and many would happily spend even more time with him. The only thing that will ever hold Vincent back from a fulfilling relationship is his own fear of rejection.

THE RUNIC INTERPRETATION

↑ᚾᛗᛋ↑ᛁᚠ (Teiwaz, Nauthiz, Ehwaz, Sowelu, Nauthiz, Isa, Fehu)

People appreciate Vincent's sunny disposition and quietly suffer through his insufferable antics, such as acting out his jokes with props and funny faces. Still, Vincent is a whiz at sales. With Sowelu, the rune of wholeness, combined with Teiwaz, the warrior, Vincent can close a deal faster than most. If he turns his persuasive personality to other areas, he could win elections or dream up advertising campaigns. Vincent is uninhibited and sincere. When people ask for his business card, he hands them two; he packages himself quite well. Vincent has the Fehu rune assuring him financial security and many friends throughout his life.

Elements: Air, fire, air, air, fire, earth, fire

THE NUMEROLOGICAL INTERPRETATION

Vincent (NV = 6, CV = 1, VV = 5, FL = 4)

Highly individualistic with a style all his own, Vincent is keen on asserting his personal identity in the world. He has his own way of dressing and is careful about his choice of friends. Vincent is warmhearted and quite generous with the people he loves. His abundant creativity comes from a source within himself that he is easily able to tap. Vincent is not so much a rebel or nonconformist as he is a unique individual with his own ways of dealing with life. He likes to travel, enjoys the challenge of one-on-one sports, and is eager to push ever beyond the limitations of his own boundaries.

Viola

DERIVATION: English, Italian, and Scandinavian, from the Latin *viola*, meaning "violet." Most notably the name of Sebastian's sister in Shakespeare's *Twelfth Night*. Commonly used since the 1860s.

PRINCIPAL COLORS: The full spectrum of lightly shaded hues

GEMSTONES AND PRECIOUS METALS: Diamonds, silver, platinum

BOTANICALS: Hazel, parsley, oats

UNIQUE SPELLINGS: Viohla, Viohlah, Violah, Vyohla, Vyohlah, Vyola, Vyolah

RELATED TO: Vi, Violaine, Viole, Violett, Violetta, Violette, Vyolet

A KABBALISTIC SYNOPSIS
וייעלא —VYA'ALA (Vau, Yod, Ayin, Lamed, Aleph)

Viola is a very refined woman who probably prefers to be referred to as a lady. She is both intelligent and intuitive. Success comes easily to her, which can be seen both in the Ayin of her name, which refers to corporate success, and in the value of her name, which ends in seventeen, the number of the Star card in the tarot, a symbol of protection by outside agencies. Traditionally the outside agency is seen as the divine spirit, but in Viola's case, it could well relate to the moral support and financial backing of her family. The reduction of Viola's name's value produces the number nine, which represents wisdom and experience.

THE RUNIC INTERPRETATION
ᚨᛚᛟᛁᚠ (Ansuz, Laguz, Othila, Isa, Fehu)

People who have the four elements represented in their name, as Viola does, seldom feel overwhelmed and are likely to lead balanced lives. Viola designs her life with plenty of rest and exercise, nutritious food, and free time in which to glean inspiration so that her life is both spontaneous and calm. Yet this takes planning and effort; Viola finds balance is a priority well worth striving for, not a given. Laguz, the rune of flexibility, gives Viola a sensitive and refined disposition. She'll enjoy the comforts of money, and she probably allocates a portion of her spending to support her fascination with culture and the humanities.

Elements: Air, water, earth/fire, earth, fire

THE NUMEROLOGICAL INTERPRETATION
Viola (NV = 5, CV = 7, VV = 7, FL = 4)

In order to live up to her creative best, Viola requires a frequent change of scenery and a lot of variety. She strongly believes in what she is doing and is an excellent salesperson and promoter. Viola will not get involved in anything unless she is convinced of its high quality. Her exacting attitude also extends into the realm of personal relationships. Although Viola will know a great many people and get along quite well with them on most superficial social levels, her personal life is another thing altogether. In truth, she has few close friends, but those who are dear to her are very treasured and highly respected.

Violet

DERIVATION: English, from the Latin *viola*, meaning "violet." One of the earliest popular flower names, Violet has been used since the 1830s.

PRINCIPAL COLORS: The full range of green and white hues

GEMSTONES AND PRECIOUS METALS: Moonstones, jade, cat's-eye

BOTANICALS: Colewort, plantain, cabbage

UNIQUE SPELLINGS: Violit, Violitt, Violyt, Violytt, Vyolet, Vyolit, Vyolitt, Vyolyt, Vyolytt

RELATED TO: Vi, Violat, Violaine, Violante, Viole, Violetta, Violette, Vyoletta, Vyolette

A KABBALISTIC SYNOPSIS

וייעהלאט —VYA'AHLAT (Vau, Yod, Ayin, Heh, Lamed, Aleph, Teth)

There is no doubt who is in charge when Violet is around; her name's value reduces to five, so we should not be surprised that Violet has a very definite air of authority about her. This matches the personality type indicated by the tarot card the Hierophant, whose value is also five. The letter Teth, meaning "serpent," concludes her name and gives a hint as to what can be expected by those who are foolish enough to challenge Violet's authority in the workplace or in the home. Whether she is in her office or her living room, Violet is confident enough in her position of authority not to need to wield a big stick, and she gets very good results. Part of her success is thanks to her very genuine interest in the people around her. This character trait is suggested by the letter Heh in her name, which means "window" and relates to a concern with the world outside one's self.

THE RUNIC INTERPRETATION

ᛏᛗᛚᛟᛁᚠ (Teiwaz, Ehwaz, Laguz, Othila, Isa, Fehu)

Shrinking Violet is a classic misnomer. With both the warrior rune and the rune of defense in her name, Violet is quite the opposite of fragile. She is passionate and has the courage required in a romantic liaison to know how to wait for her lover to come to her. Violet uses the rune of separation in her name to keep colleagues and lovers guessing. She is a wonderful ally in financial transactions because she can walk away from a deal and still get her price in the end. Kids enjoy Violet because she'll climb a tree or wade knee-deep in water to chase a toy sailboat. She has money and she has fun. While she tends to get carried away and live for the moment, no one could accuse Violet of lacking spontaneity—and she likes it that way. Violet enjoys the power of the four elements in her name.

Elements: Air, air, water, earth/fire, earth, fire

THE NUMEROLOGICAL INTERPRETATION

Violet (NV = 11, CV = 9, VV = 2, FL = 4)

Violet may be a social activist, as she is very much aware of political oppression and is a person who dislikes prejudice. Her name bestows an idealistic nature and the urge to see all people free to express their highest good. Violet is close to her religious faith and finds strength in her spiritual convictions. She is not a person who does well by herself, and she needs the loving companionship of a special partner and the support of a community who feel as she does about life. Violet is very group oriented and brings an element of harmony into all meetings and common endeavors.

748

Virgil

A Kabbalistic Synopsis
וירגיל —VYRGYL (Vau, Yod, Resh, Gimel, Yod, Lamed)

Virgil is a respected man, balanced and capable of holding high office and responsibility. He is definitely a man to be trusted. His career is likely to be influenced by his astrological chart in terms of the specific field he chooses, but he will always be found at the top of his profession. Politics would suit Virgil, as his name has strong connections to the seventeenth path, which is concerned with the breaking down of the established order and the creation of new systems and structures, on the Tree of Life. In his relationships, Virgil will be an understanding partner, without losing any sense of his own maleness in the process of being sensitive.

The Runic Interpretation
ᛚᛁᚷᚱᛁᚠ (Laguz, Isa, Gebo, Raido, Isa, Fehu)

Virgil can be independent, but if the truth be known, he much prefers company. The Gebo rune of partnership signifies that Virgil is flexible and eager to share his life with someone he admires. In business also Virgil is probably reluctant to strike out on his own. While it's true that the double Isa rune in his name suggests isolation, this refers to a spiritual need to meditate rather than a hermit's disposition. Virgil will travel and seek out the company of friends around the world. He'll E-mail them, remember their birthdays, and be a warm addition to their lives because he cares. He is a clear communicator and a success in his chosen career.

Elements: Water, earth, water, water, earth, fire

The Numerological Interpretation
Virgil (NV = 5, CV = 5, VV = 9, FL = 4)

Virgil is stimulated by change and has a hard time settling into any routine. His many friends all have one thing in common: the ability to accept each other regardless of race, religion, or lifestyle. Virgil is constantly educating himself and shares what he knows through the many fascinating discussions in which he loves to participate. He is a man who travels as much as possible and thrives in exotic and different surroundings. Virgil is more likely to have a number of intimate relationships during his life than one long-lasting and committed union.

DERIVATION: English, from the Roman clan name Vergilius. The name of the first-century B.C.E. Roman poet who wrote the *Aeneid*. Of unknown meaning, but perhaps related to the Latin meaning "stick." Often used to honor the poet.

PRINCIPAL COLORS: The palest shades of any color, especially light gray

GEMSTONES AND PRECIOUS METALS: Diamonds, silver

BOTANICALS: Hazel, oats, parsley, sea kale

UNIQUE SPELLINGS: Vergel, Verjel, Virgyl, Virjil, Vyrgel, Vyrgyl, Vyrjel, Vyrjil

RELATED TO: Verge, Vergilio

"Mind moves matter."
　　　　—VIRGIL (AUTHOR)

"Lucky is he who has been able to understand the causes of things."
　　　　—VIRGIL (AUTHOR)

DERIVATION: Danish, English, Italian, Spanish, and Swedish; the feminine form of the Roman name Verginius. Associated with the Latin *virgo*, meaning "maiden." Especially popular in the United States in the first half of the twentieth century.

PRINCIPAL COLORS: Dark shades of azure and purple, also gray and black

GEMSTONES AND PRECIOUS METALS: Carbuncles, black diamonds, amethyst

BOTANICALS: Shepherd's purse, ragwort, gravel root

UNIQUE SPELLINGS: Verginia, Verginnia, Verginnya, Verginya, Virgennya, Virgenya, Virginnia

RELATED TO: Geena, Geenia, Gina, Ginia, Ginni, Ginnie, Ginny, Vinny, Vinya, Virgie, Virgine, Virginie

Virginia

A KABBALISTIC SYNOPSIS

ווירגיניא—VYRGYNYA (Vau, Yod, Resh, Gimel, Yod, Nun, Yod, Aleph)

There are three Yods in Virginia's name, and this indicates huge amounts of fiery energy (although it is a more controlled form of fire energy than that represented by the letter Shin). All this energy means that Virginia will pursue any ambition no matter how unlikely, and there is a good chance that ultimately, through sheer persistence, she will succeed. In addition, the compression of her name produces the letters Resh and Tzaddi; Resh refers to a happy-go-lucky demeanor, and Tzaddi, meaning "fishhook," relates to a refusal to let go of any plan. One way Virginia will expend some of her lust for life is through travel, her favorite pastime, as indicated by the letter Gimel in her name.

THE RUNIC INTERPRETATION

ᚾᛁᚺᛁᚷᚱᛁᚠ (Ansuz, Isa, Nauthiz, Isa, Gebo, Raido, Isa, Fehu)

Virginia has the calm demeanor of a yoga teacher. Whether she gravitates toward meditation and spirituality or makes her living on the hectic floor of a stock exchange, Virginia is balanced and self-reliant. The triple Isa rune for isolation implies that no matter what Virginia does on the home and career fronts, she requires time to exercise and be alone with her own thoughts. Gebo, the rune of union, signifies that Virginia would work well in a romantic or business partnership. She is a team player, and with her love of travel, she undoubtedly has colleagues and friends in many parts of the country. Music is extremely important to Virginia. With Fehu, the rune of possessions, gracing her name, calm Virginia is sure to enjoy the benefits of wealth and success—although with Nauthiz and Isa, she could have problems managing her money and possessions. Virginia has the power of the four elements in her name.

Elements: Air, earth, fire, earth, water, water, earth, fire

THE NUMEROLOGICAL INTERPRETATION

Virginia (NV = 8, CV = 7, VV = 1, FL = 4)

"Believe in yourself!" is Virginia's motto. This is a woman who will tackle any challenge in order to prove her own self-worth, but there is a purpose behind her actions. Virginia just doesn't set off like Don Quixote, blindly fighting windmills. Her battles are well thought out, completely organized down to the smallest detail, and well executed. This is the name of a thinker and a planner, a woman who is careful about how she uses her energy and who intends to get positive results from her efforts. Virginia expects a great deal from herself, and has the stamina and drive to achieve her objectives.

Vivian

A Kabbalistic Synopsis
ויוין —VYVYVN (Vau, Yod, Vau, Yod, Vau, Nun)

Life with Vivian can be a bit confusing, to say the least. When her Yod personality dominates, she is energetic, enthusiastic, and at times, fairly rash when it comes to making a decision. However, when Vau takes over, her ability to make any decision at all is decidedly hampered by a wish to consider every possible angle. This process may be frustratingly slow at times, but it does have the advantage of ensuring that the right answer is produced. Vivian is aware that her behavior is less than consistent, and she can sometimes worry about her state of mind. This concern is mirrored in the fact that her name's value reduces to eighteen, the number of the Moon card in the tarot, and a symbol of anxiety and possible emotional loss.

The Runic Interpretation
ᚾᚨᛁᚠᛁᚠ (Nauthiz, Ansuz, Isa, Fehu, Isa, Fehu)

Vivian will have money tumble out of the sky into her upturned palms. She expects abundance, and it appears all around her. But her good fortune is not due to chance; Vivian understands that wise investment strategies are crucial, and she could well choose finance as a career. Isa makes her a cautious investor. She will certainly be successful at spotting trends in the market because she is highly intuitive and meticulous. Vivian's friends ask her for advice because she uses her calm, unassuming manner to help them see simple solutions and focus their thoughts. Vivian may wish she were more assertive and spontaneous, but once she finds the career direction that suits her, she will be less watchful and a bit looser. Vivian has high standards for herself, and is generous with her friends.

Elements: Fire, air, earth, fire, earth, fire

The Numerological Interpretation
Vivian (NV = 5, CV = 4, VV = 1, FL = 4)

"Foundation" is the key word in this name. Vivian requires a firm and solid base under her feet. She needs to know that her income is predictable and that her material needs are being met. "Foundation" is also very important to her emotionally. Vivian requires a partnership that is committed to a long-term future and whose objectives are clearly defined. Once these bedrocks are in place, the other part of Vivian's nature can emerge. This is a person who also has an adventurous soul, a perky disposition, and a need to enhance the scope of her knowledge and experience. Vivian loves to travel, but she needs to know that she has a return ticket in her pocket!

DERIVATION: English, from the Roman family name Vibianus. Related to the Latin *vivus*, meaning "alive." The name of a fifth-century French bishop who defended his people against the invading Visigoths. Both masculine and feminine.

PRINCIPAL COLORS: The full spectrum of very pale hues

GEMSTONES AND PRECIOUS METALS: Any pale stone, including silver and platinum

BOTANICALS: Oats, sweet marjoram

UNIQUE SPELLINGS: Viviane, Viviann, Vivianne, Vivien, Vivyan, Vyviane, Vyvianne, Vyvien, Vyvyan, Vyvyanne

RELATED TO: Bibi, Bibiana, Bibiane, Vi, Viv, Vivi, Vivia, Viviana, Vivianna, Vyvyana

Wade

DERIVATION: English, from the medieval English word meaning "ford." First used as a given name during the nineteenth century, and found most commonly in the southern United States.

PRINCIPAL COLORS: Pale to medium-rich shades of blue

GEMSTONES AND PRECIOUS METALS: Emeralds, turquoise

BOTANICALS: Violets, vervain, almonds

UNIQUE SPELLINGS: Waid, Waide, Wayde

RELATED TO: Wadleigh, Wadley, Wadly, Wadsworth, Walford

A KABBALISTIC SYNOPSIS

‏ואיד‎ —VAYD (Vau, Aleph, Yod, Daleth)

For Wade, getting a promotion is as easy as riding the escalator up to the next floor, since Wade's career progression is likely to be phenomenal. The value of Wade's name is twenty-one, which is the final card in the main tarot sequence and represents the completion of a plan or course of action. In other words, Wade is someone who can make things happen—usually by making sure that the job at hand is worked on until it is completely finished! If we reduce the total value of Wade's name further, we get three, the number of the Empress. This tarot card holds a promise of success—specifically, material comfort or even abundance.

THE RUNIC INTERPRETATION

ᛗᛞᚨᚾᚹ (Ehwaz, Dagaz, Ansuz, Wunjo)

The name Wade is a happy runic configuration. The Wunjo rune foretells the end of trials and tribulations and a time of verdant peacefulness. Wade has the sense to seize the moment and embrace his good fortune. But it's important for Wade to contribute frequently and generously to humanitarian causes, to bring balance to all his efforts. Art and imaginative and playful fields of endeavor suit Wade's joyful nature, and he offers a bit of sunshine that softens the harshness of day-to-day life.

Elements: Air, fire, air, earth

THE NUMEROLOGICAL INTERPRETATION

Wade (NV = 6, CV = 9, VV = 6, FL = 5)

Two of the most outstanding characteristics about Wade are his sensitivity and his ability to be intimate. Wade does not mind being vulnerable, and he walks through life with an open and caring heart. This is a man who puts other people ahead of himself; he cannot feel at ease unless he knows that his loved ones' emotional needs are being fulfilled. However, Wade has to be clear about his own emotional boundaries or else he will find himself codependent and compromised. It is important for him to balance his feeling nature with a clear sense of mental objectivity.

Wallace

A Kabbalistic Synopsis

וֹאלים —VALYS (Vau, Aleph, Lamed, Yod, Samech)

One Hebrew equivalent of the value of the name Wallace is the word "egg." This means that Wallace is skilled in the process of creating new ideas or products that are genuinely novel. It also suggests that he has a certain naïveté about him that, given the other factors in his name, is likely to prove an endearing quality when it comes to dating. The whole name is affected by the influence of the star sign Leo, and this gives Wallace a high degree of confidence and perceptible charisma.

The Runic Interpretation

ᛗᛋᚨᚾᚾᚨᛈ (Ehwaz, Sowelu, Ansuz, Laguz, Laguz, Ansuz, Wunjo)

Wallace is perfectly suited to a career in the fine arts. Music pulses through him, and as his feet move and his head bobs up and down, it's mesmerizing to watch. The Sowelu rune of wholeness lets him perform with remarkable grace and skill. Wallace is confident, talented, and imaginative. Ehwaz for defense lets him persevere, and criticism simply rolls off his back. Wallace exists to make people joyful; he has retained a childlike faith in the goodness of life, and he hopes to lift people up to share his inspiration. If Wallace doesn't pursue the arts as a career, he ought to use his leisure time to pursue his gifts. Wallace is also highly intuitive and could have premonitory dreams.

Elements: Air, air, air, water, water, air, earth

The Numerological Interpretation

Wallace (NV = 3, CV = 5, VV = 7, FL = 5)

A good sense of humor, a curious intellect, and an easy way with people are but three of the characteristics found in the numbers of this name. Wallace is very intellectual, and will find himself well suited for the media or any business where his communicative talents can be put to best use. Driven by an inner need for change and growth, Wallace definitely does not want to be tied down. He needs variety and opportunities to expand upon his storehouse of talents. He is not the most emotionally responsive person, and may find himself at a distinct disadvantage in relationships that require consistent emotional intimacy.

DERIVATION: Scottish and English, originally a surname referring to those of Celtic origin. First used in Scotland, and spread to other English-speaking countries during the late nineteenth and early twentieth centuries.

PRINCIPAL COLORS: Pale shades of purple to the richest violet hues

GEMSTONES AND PRECIOUS METALS: Amethyst, garnets

BOTANICALS: Dandelion, cherry, lungwort

UNIQUE SPELLINGS: Wallas, Wallice, Wallis, Wallys

RELATED TO: Wallach, Wallas, Wallie, Wally, Walwyn

Walter

DERIVATION: English and German, from the old Germanic roots *wald*, meaning "rule" and *heri*, meaning "army." Used from the eleventh century onward, and was especially popular during the early twentieth century.

PRINCIPAL COLORS: Gold, the full range of green and yellow hues

GEMSTONES AND PRECIOUS METALS: Moonstones, moss agate, pearls

BOTANICALS: Blackberry, hops, elder

UNIQUE SPELLINGS: Waltir, Waltirre, Waltyr

RELATED TO: Gaultier, Gautier, Gualterio, Valter, Valther, Wally, Walt, Walther, Walton, Watkins

❧

"I can't imagine a person becoming a success who doesn't give this game of life everything he's got."
—WALTER CRONKITE
(JOURNALIST)

A KABBALISTIC SYNOPSIS
ועלטא —VA'ALTA (Vau, Ayin, Lamed, Teth, Aleph)

Walter is his own biggest enemy, and he really needs a partner who is able to act as a monitoring force on the amount of time he spends pursuing his career goals. The combination of the letters Ayin and Lamed indicates that Walter is both committed and successful in his work, but there is a danger that he will work himself far too hard and end up having to take time off in order to overcome his sheer exhaustion. This potential problem is also suggested by the fact that the value of his name ends in a sixteen, the symbol of catastrophes from which one must learn for the future. While Walter is a great guy with a good sense of humor despite its sometimes cruel streak, partners of Walter's will have their work cut out for them. Trying to look after him will be difficult, since the value of his name reduces to eight, telling us that he has a very forceful character and a stubborn will.

THE RUNIC INTERPRETATION
ᚱᛖᛏᛚᚨᚹ (Raido, Ehwaz, Teiwaz, Laguz, Ansuz, Wunjo)

Walter is thoughtful and accommodating as well as brave and eager to forge new frontiers. He could be drawn to engineering, computers, or global technology. He may travel and work abroad, promoting his inventions or marketing concepts he is eager to share. The Wunjo rune of joy makes a jocular personality his trademark. Walter is a clear thinker. He is able to sense the preposterous aspects of events and step back and laugh in the face of catastrophe, which makes others relax and defuses the tension. People enjoy their jobs more when Walter is around.

Elements: Water, air, air, water, air, earth

THE NUMEROLOGICAL INTERPRETATION
Walter (NV = 7, CV = 1, VV = 6, FL = 5)

This is a name indicating a man of complex, and sometimes conflicting, personality characteristics. The strong bonds of family and sincere friendships are very important to Walter, yet he cannot be in a partnership in which there are constant demands upon his time and freedom. Walter needs to have space for himself. He is a strong-willed man with an urge to challenge his own creative boundaries. Walter's tests in life concern his ability to combine his need for closeness with others and his equally strong need to do his own thing in his own way.

❧

Wanda

A Kabbalistic Synopsis
ואנדא —VANDA (Vau, Aleph, Nun, Daleth, Aleph)

As friends go, you would have to go a very long way indeed to top Wanda. She is the most supportive individual you could meet, and is not the type to help you out and then remind you of it constantly for the next month. As far as she is concerned, there is no debt of gratitude owed Wanda, who is simply happy to be able to help. Her name's value is equivalent to the Hebrew for "healing," and this may suggest that medicine would be a perfect career for Wanda, especially as it is suited to her exceptionally caring nature. This equivalence could also refer directly to Wanda's emotionally supportive character rather than to any physical healing process. Wanda always makes sure that she saves some time for herself. She likes to spend it visiting her friends or possibly local areas of interest, particularly if they relate to the history of her community.

The Runic Interpretation
ᚹᛜᛏᛞᚨ (Ansuz, Dagaz, Nauthiz, Ansuz, Wunjo)

Wanda is prone to giggle in public and sob in private. The Nauthiz rune of constraint causes her some disappointments and delays. Yet as time goes by, Wanda develops an excellent spirit of resiliency. Wunjo, the rune of joy, means nothing can keep Wanda from being a happy camper. She loves sports and keeps her mood elevated with lots of exercise. Opportunities come her way, and the double Ansuz runes of intuition make Wanda a smart cookie. She anticipates trends and creates her own luck. Wanda's smart enough to recognize a good deal when she sees it, and is so charming in negotiations that even when people end up giving more than they receive at the bargaining table, they usually thank her for making the transaction pleasant for them!

Elements: Air, fire, fire, air, earth

The Numerological Interpretation
Wanda (NV = 7, CV = 5, VV = 2, FL = 5)

Wanda has a natural talent for diplomacy. She is a tactful and careful person who can be called upon to harmonize conflicting social circumstances. Wanda has a highly developed emotional nature, one that gives her a natural sense of connection to people. This special sensitivity permits her to develop cooperative conditions at home or in business so that people may work together and accomplish mutually beneficial projects. Wanda is careful about not hurting people's feelings, but in the process, she may compromise herself in her own personal relationships. It is important for Wanda to stand up for what and who she is and make her own needs clearly heard.

DERIVATION: English, of uncertain origin. Possibly from the medieval term *wend*, which was applied to the Slavonic people who lived in what is now northeast Germany. Other sources link Wanda to an Old German root meaning "wanderer." Especially common in the mid-twentieth century.

PRINCIPAL COLORS: Pale to bright and rich shades of yellow and green

GEMSTONES AND PRECIOUS METALS: Pearls, moss agate

BOTANICALS: Elder, hops, juniper

UNIQUE SPELLINGS: Wahnda, Wandah, Wannda, Wonda, Wonnda

RELATED TO: Vanda, Wandie, Wandy, Wenda, Wendaline, Wendeline, Wendy†

PRINCIPAL COLORS: The full gamut of green and yellow hues

GEMSTONES AND PRECIOUS METALS: Moss agate, white pearls, any other white stone

BOTANICALS: Blackberry, linseed

UNIQUE SPELLINGS: Warenn, Warinn, Warynn, Warrenn, Warrin, Warrinn, Warryn, Warrynn

RELATED TO: War, Ware, Warner, Warriner

Warren

A KABBALISTIC SYNOPSIS
ואָרון —VARVN (Vau, Aleph, Resh, Vau, Nun)

Change is most definitely the name of the game as far as Warren is concerned. Life is far too short to be restricted to some nine-to-five office job, or for that matter, to a long-term relationship with just one partner. Warren has a name whose value reduces to thirteen and whose total value also ends in thirteen. With such an emphasis on variety, as indicated by the double thirteen, Warren may manage to spend his whole life on the move. In the compression of his name we reveal the letter Tzaddi, which means "fishhook." Given the final Nun in his name, this lets us know that there are some emotional worries in Warren's personality. It may be that the Tzaddi is pointing to some emptiness that Warren is searching to fill, hence the constant moving. Warren is certainly set to have an interesting life, and thanks to the Resh in his name, he will also have a great time while he's at it!

THE RUNIC INTERPRETATION
ᛏᛖᚱᚱᚨᚹ (Nauthiz, Ehwaz, Raido, Raido, Ansuz, Wunjo)

Warren appreciates words. He's probably conscious of his own diction, and he notices the speech patterns of others. Warren's command of foreign languages is impressive. His humor is laced with the right nuance and sense of timing, and he's always ready with a joke. Warren loves to hear people snicker at his silliness. He knows that humor can chase away illness and make each day more satisfying. Warren could write or perform with his many gifts. His experiences with delays and disruptions seed his humor, which could have a sarcastic bite to it. His style is appropriate for stand-up comedy or greeting cards. Warren has the Wunjo rune of joy blessing his life.

Elements: Fire, air, water, water, air, earth

THE NUMEROLOGICAL INTERPRETATION
Warren (NV = 7, CV = 1, VV = 6, FL = 5)

Warren lives by certain codes and standards to which he is very closely attached. These beliefs may be quite correct for him, but they may not work as well for everybody else. Warren has a distinct sense of fair play, and he is a basically honest and just person. Deeply reflective, with a strong urge toward highly individualized interests, Warren enjoys spending time alone among his books, thoughts, and projects. He is also a family-oriented man, one who requires a loving partnership in order to make his life complete.

Wayne

A KABBALISTIC SYNOPSIS
ואין —VAYN (Vau, Aleph, Yod, Nun)

There are those of us who have to struggle hard for every break that we get, and then there are those who simply seem to land on their feet every time. Wayne certainly falls very firmly into the second category. When we look at the value of his name, we can see that it both begins and ends with a seven, so Wayne's life will begin and end in success. The evidence in his name of practical common sense and commitment suggest that he will have plenty of success in the middle of his life as well. Not everything in Wayne's life is a bed of roses, but because he seems to find life relatively easy, he has a difficult time understanding his partner's troubles and disappointments. He isn't heartless or unsympathetic; it's simply that he so rarely faces any setbacks in his own life that it is difficult for him to empathize.

THE RUNIC INTERPRETATION
ᛗᚾᛇᚨᚹ (Ehwaz, Nauthiz, Eihwaz, Ansuz, Wunjo)

Wayne views life as a giant chessboard, and he is careful and defensive. His name contains the Ansuz rune of intuition, which makes him vigilant and conscientious. Wunjo, the rune of joy, blesses his name with humor and optimism. Wayne is a man of few words and has a pleasant expression that masks his skepticism. He could work in surveillance or high-risk professions, careers which could suit his self-sufficient and practical approach to living. Wayne doesn't wear his heart on his sleeve, yet he is probably more sentimental than anyone in his family. He is the type who remembers the director and cast of old movies, has a collection of songs from twenty years ago, and keeps up with a few of his high school buddies over the years. Wayne is capable of deep devotion, and his friends and romantic partners will be well loved.

Elements: Air, fire, earth/fire, air, earth

THE NUMEROLOGICAL INTERPRETATION
Wayne (NV = 5, CV = 1, VV = 4, FL = 5)

This is a name indicating a progressive attitude and an eagerness to explore new possibilities. Wayne has an open mind and a desire to accept what life has to offer him. He is strong and stable, practical in his approach to life, and well organized. This inner stability allows him to adopt new concepts and expand his philosophy about life. Wayne his a pioneering spirit, one that brings him into contact with some very interesting entrepreneurial opportunities. He is an eagerly adventurous person who enjoys sports and outdoor activities.

DERIVATION: English, originally a surname referring to someone who made or drove wagons. Especially common in the United States during the mid-twentieth century, probably due to the popularity of film star John Wayne (1907–1979).

PRINCIPAL COLORS: Any very lightly shaded hue

GEMSTONES AND PRECIOUS METALS: Platinum, silver

BOTANICALS: Hazel, oats, parsley

UNIQUE SPELLINGS: Wain, Waine, Wane, Wayn

RELATED TO: Way, Waylan, Waylen, Waylin

❧

"One hundred percent of the shots you don't take don't go in."
—WAYNE GRETZKY (ATHLETE)

DERIVATION: English, originally a surname from an Old Germanic name meaning "one who wanders." Its usage as a first name has been enhanced by the fame of Supreme Court justice Oliver Wendell Holmes (1841–1935).

PRINCIPAL COLORS: Pale bluish purple to the richest shades of violet

GEMSTONES AND PRECIOUS METALS: Amethyst, garnets

BOTANICALS: Apple, mint, barberry

UNIQUE SPELLINGS: Wendel, Wendil, Wendill, Wendle, Wendyl, Wendyll, Wenndel, Wenndil, Wenndle, Wenndyl

RELATED TO: Wen, Wend

A KABBALISTIC SYNOPSIS

ואנדאל —VANDAL (Vau, Aleph, Nun, Daleth, Aleph, Lamed)

Wendell's name has a value that reduces to eleven. In addition, there is a strong lunar influence in his name. Combined, these two factors point to a very serious interest in the supernatural, particularly in established occult systems. The final half of Wendell's name suggests a possible motivation for this interest; it contains the letter Daleth, meaning "door," and the word AL, which is a Hebrew equivalent for God. In other words, Wendell's interest in the magical or supernatural is based on a desire to find a doorway to God. When he isn't poring over some mystical tome, Wendell enjoys surprisingly normal hobbies, and he may be particularly attracted to water sports such as sailing or windsurfing.

THE RUNIC INTERPRETATION

ᚾᚾᛗᛞᚾᛖᛗᛈ (Laguz, Laguz, Ehwaz, Dagaz, Nauthiz, Ehwaz, Wunjo)

Wendell has the ability to gaze into tomorrow, and he may even make a living off his rich imagination. Whether he chooses to aspire to the Supreme Court or turns to film to express his vision, he most definitely will leave his mark. Wendell is flexible, artistic, and always curious about the customs and politics of other cultures. He makes a wonderful dinner companion because he has good fashion sense and peppers his conversation with amusing trivia. He can speak intelligently on so many subjects that he develops an easy rapport with people. But it's not easy to be a visionary; Wendell isn't especially practical, and has been known to miss appointments or arrive in a country stylishly dressed—but all wrong for the climate. Wendell knows these are his weak points, and he encourages other people in his life to help him stay organized.

Elements: Water, water, air, fire, fire, air, earth

THE NUMEROLOGICAL INTERPRETATION

Wendell (NV = 3, CV = 2, VV = 1, FL = 5)

Wendell is an optimistic man, one who finds that life gives him a rich assortment of choices for his profit and enjoyment. It is Wendell's responsibility to develop the necessary discrimination to choose correctly. He has to take care that he does not spread himself too thinly, as there is also the tendency here to dissipate his vitality and not finish what he has begun. Wendell is a very socially oriented person, with a natural talent for putting people at their ease. He is welcomed and appreciated by his friends and associates, and will find that people naturally open doors for him and ask him inside.

Wendy

A Kabbalistic Synopsis
ואנדי —VANDY (Vau, Aleph, Nun, Daleth, Yod)

Nobody deliberately annoys Wendy. She is a lovely woman on the whole, but when she is angry, most people would rather be somewhere else! Apart from having a legendary short fuse, Wendy is a very affable person who is well liked and respected by all who know her. Her personality splits into two aspects on either side of the letter Nun, which reflects a certain amount of anxiety about which facet of her nature to follow. The first half of her name suggests a person with a strong imagination and the ability to creatively use that imagination to produce practical ideas. On the other hand, the second half of her name offers up a much more physically active side to her nature, one that is more at home in a business-type office environment than one conducive to creativity. Luckily for Wendy, at the end of the day she can follow either path with equal success.

The Runic Interpretation
ᛇᛞᚾᛖᚹ (Eihwaz, Dagaz, Nauthiz, Ehwaz, Wunjo)

Wendy's challenge is to find balance in her life. She longs to be free, but she is cautious. She faces delays and limitations, and yet wonderful and unusual opportunities are there for the asking. Wendy needs to learn to balance her impulses. Living in a foreign culture might help her to examine her personal values and discard worn-out belief systems. In the end, Wendy has the Wunjo rune of joy to fill her days with moments of great satisfaction.

Elements: Earth/fire, fire, fire, air, earth

The Numerological Interpretation
Wendy (NV = 8, CV = 5, VV = 3, FL = 5)

Wendy is a name indicating a highly productive person, a woman with long-range plans and goals and the stamina to achieve her envisioned ends. The people in her business circle find Wendy an asset to their ventures. She has practical insight plus an attractive personality that adds to her appeal. A highly organized person who manages to combine her many interests into a tightly woven package, Wendy can be overly materialistic and may find that she is too involved with the acquisition of money and status. Balance in this respect can come through some voluntary acts of service to the community.

DERIVATION: English, invented by author J. M. Barrie in 1904 for the name of the girl heroine in *Peter Pan*. The name then came into general use during the 1920s, and was especially popular in the 1960s and 1970s.

PRINCIPAL COLORS: Black, very dark hues, including blue, gray, and purple

GEMSTONES AND PRECIOUS METALS: Carbuncles, black diamonds, amethyst

BOTANICALS: Shepherd's purse, mandrake root, pilewort

UNIQUE SPELLINGS: Wendee, Wendey, Wendi, Wendie

RELATED TO: Gwen†, Gwendolyn, Wanda†, Wenda, Wendeline

DERIVATION: English, a place-name meaning "western meadow." The surname of the eighteenth-century founders of the Methodist Church, John and Charles Wesley. Initially, the first name was used only by members of the Methodist Church, but it is now found widely in all English-speaking countries.

PRINCIPAL COLORS: The deepest shades of azure and violet, also black, gray

GEMSTONES AND PRECIOUS METALS: Black pearls, sapphires, rubies

BOTANICALS: Angelica, marsh mallow, gravel root

UNIQUE SPELLINGS: Weslee, Wesleigh, Weslie, Wesly, Wessley, Wessly

RELATED TO: Wes, West, Westleigh, Westley

A KABBALISTIC SYNOPSIS
ואסלי —VASLY (Vau, Aleph, Samech, Lamed, Yod)

The key to Wesley's personality is in the central letters of his name, the Samech and the Lamed. These two letters indicate a great concern for his fellow man. Wesley wants to act as a support to society, and may well work in one of the caring professions such as nursing or social work. This desire is shown by the letter Samech, while the Lamed tells us that Wesley feels a sense of obligation to help others that is so strong that he has to act on it. It is possible, if Wesley is born under Pisces or Cancer, that this vocation will override all other concerns in his life. For a Wesley born under another sign, family and other close relationships will be deeply important, and Wesley will always make sure he has time to spend with his loved ones.

THE RUNIC INTERPRETATION
ᛇᛖᛚᛋᛖᛈ (Eihwaz, Ehwaz, Laguz, Sowelu, Ehwaz, Wunjo)

Welsey is a good companion because he makes his partner feel fascinating. Tender, charming, and accepting, Wesley has sophisticated taste that makes him attractive and unflappable. It's hard to win his heart, though, because he keeps it out of view. He's ambitious and studied, and could be accused of being opportunistic. Prosperous Wesley is in demand at business and social functions because he always knows the right thing to say to move the conversation along and he can easily laugh at himself. Someday Wesley will let his guard down enough to show people how vulnerable he really is. This is an especially powerful name, containing the strengths of all four elements.

Elements: Earth/fire, air, water, air, air, earth

THE NUMEROLOGICAL INTERPRETATION
Wesley (NV = 8, CV = 9, VV = 8, FL = 5)

This is a man who will establish himself in the world on a firm financial footing. Wesley wants to dress well, drive a fine automobile, and generally give the impression that he is successful. People respect him for his drive and perseverance. Even though Wesley is quite ambitious, there is a part of his nature that is distinctly humanitarian. Wesley has a strong ego, but he is not necessarily egotistical.

Whitney

A KABBALISTIC SYNOPSIS

ויטני —WYTNY (Vau, Yod, Teth, Nun, Yod)

Variety is very definitely the spice of life, as far as Whitney is concerned. Her name's value reduces to thirteen, which is the number of change. The double presence of the letter Yod in her name suggests that, as an energetic and dynamic woman, Whitney very much enjoys a bit of instability in her life. The value of her name is eighty-five, which can be represented as the two letters Peh and Heh. The Peh relates to her talking, or possibly singing, ability, and its union with Heh, which is concerned with the world outside the individual, suggests that Whitney may be drawn to speaking or performing in public. The central letter in her name is Teth, which means "serpent." While Teth can refer to a willingness to take revenge on or be spiteful toward those who cause offense, in Whitney's case, the implication is that at times, Whitney can be difficult to live or work with, as she insists that everything must be done her way.

THE RUNIC INTERPRETATION

ᛇᛖᚾᛏᛁᚺᚹ (Eihwaz, Ehwaz, Nauthiz, Teiwaz, Isa, Hagalaz, Wunjo)

The runes for chaos, defense, and limitation could create obstacles in Whitney's life, so she must be careful with choices in her life. She may find that her friends may not have her best interests at heart. On the bright side, the runes for warrior and joy also bless her name. Thus Whitney is multifaceted and creative. Given the proper guidance and opportunities, Whitney could rise to fame and fortune. She also has the courage to withstand the pressures of notoriety. The presence of the four elements in her name makes Whitney a powerful individual.

Elements: Earth/fire, air, fire, air, earth, water, earth

THE NUMEROLOGICAL INTERPRETATION

Whitney (NV = 5, CV = 2, VV = 3, FL = 5)

People with this name are prepared for all the surprises that life brings to them. They are resilient, versatile, and mutable. Whitney welcomes the opportunity to develop herself. She is not geared for a routine, humdrum life, but is excited by the possibilities that her creative talents attract. The numbers in this name suggest a socially adept individual, one who is at home with people from all different backgrounds and philosophical orientations. Success comes to Whitney due to a genuine openness and a freedom from preconceived attitudes about others.

DERIVATION: English, from the place-name meaning "white island." Originally used primarily for males, but has recently become almost exclusively a female name. In the United States, Whitney rose tremendously as a female name during the 1980s, in part due to the popularity of singer Whitney Houston.

PRINCIPAL COLORS: Light gray, any other very pale hue

GEMSTONES AND PRECIOUS METALS: Diamonds, platinum, silver

BOTANICALS: Hazel, parsley, sea kale

UNIQUE SPELLINGS: Whitnee, Whitni, Whitnie, Whitny

RELATED TO: Whit, Whitlee, Whitley, Whitly

DERIVATION: English, originally a surname, probably from the feminine German name Wilburg, which is from the Old English roots *wil*, meaning "desire," and *burh*, meaning "fortress." Commonly used in the United States since the middle of the nineteenth century.

PRINCIPAL COLORS: Electric colors, any hue of medium shade

GEMSTONES AND PRECIOUS METALS: Sapphires

BOTANICALS: Celandine, sage

UNIQUE SPELLINGS: Wilber, Wilburr, Willbur

RELATED TO: Wilbert, Wilford, Wilfred†, Wilfrid, Will, Willard, William†

A KABBALISTIC SYNOPSIS
וילבה —VYLBH (Vau, Yod, Lamed, Beth, Heh)

Wilbur is a forceful fellow, and this quality is very useful to him in his daily life. There are definite suggestions in his name of a connection to the construction industry, and the other elements of his name point to someone of a managerial level rather than a laborer. Wilbur's strong character and willpower will be very helpful to him in ensuring that work is done properly and on time. When he is away from the job, Wilbur is much more relaxed. He has quite traditional values, and enjoys spending the weekends with as many of his family as possible. He especially loves great big family reunions and holiday gatherings. Wilbur has a passionate side that his partner is very aware of and enjoys.

THE RUNIC INTERPRETATION
ᚱᚢᛒᛚᛁᚹ (Raido, Uruz, Berkana, Laguz, Isa, Wunjo)

Wilbur is sure to have a rich and productive life. He knows that the truest satisfaction in life comes from sharing love. Berkana, the rune of nurture and growth, combines with the runes for strength and good communication in this name. Wilbur is likely to gravitate toward a career or lifestyle that involves gardening or social services, including teaching, advocacy, or social work. Medicine and healing could be rewarding careers for Wilbur, too. Patience and compassion are unusual and valuable qualities, and Wilbur uses these strengths to bless the lives of those around him. Wilbur needs to toughen up a bit, though, because he is overly generous with his advice and time.

Elements: Water, earth, air/earth, water, earth, earth

THE NUMEROLOGICAL INTERPRETATION
Wilbur (NV = 4, CV = 1, VV = 3, FL = 5)

This is a man who takes care of his possessions, is responsible to his employer (or employees), and is faithful to his partner. Wilbur does not go off into a dreamland of possibilities and potential. He is a here-and-now type of person, one who fixes his attention on the value of the things and people in his immediate environment. For this reason, Wilbur has to take care not to wear blinders and restrict himself too much within his habits and routines. Friendship is a natural way for Wilbur to move outside of his own confines so that he may relax and enjoy the prosperity he is working so hard to achieve.

Wilfred

A KABBALISTIC SYNOPSIS
וילפריד —VYLPhRYD (Vau, Yod, Lamed, Peh, Resh, Yod, Daleth)

The most common phrase you will hear coming out of Wilfred's permanently smiling mouth is "Do you mind if I join you?" This man hates being on his own, even for just a short time. He craves company and has the self-confidence to start up a conversation with a complete stranger anywhere. Most people are happy to talk to Wilfred, as he is a friendly and interesting man. In addition, he is likely to have a fairly prosperous career, so he looks like the respectable sort of person you can trust. The only problem comes when Wilfred starts to talk about his career; he has a real desire to be seen as successful, and he can sometimes drone on about his latest business coup. Wilfred finds it easy to attract partners, and when he finally meets the right woman, he will be willing to go to extraordinary lengths to persuade her to stay with him long term.

THE RUNIC INTERPRETATION
ᛞᛖᚱᚠᛚᛁᚹ (Dagaz, Ehwaz, Raido, Fehu, Laguz, Isa, Wunjo)

Globe-trotting Wilfred has the resources to see the world, and he will collect memorabilia from all his trips. He is something of a conspicuous consumer. Luckily, he has the Dagaz rune signifying that opportunities come his way. Wilfred is generous with others and contributes time and money to philanthropy. He is well aware that he needs to lead a life of moderation in order to keep himself healthy and vigorous. Wilfred is confident and inspires others with his sweeping scope and global perspective on issues that affect our lives. He has the power of the four elements in his name.

Elements: Fire, air, water, fire, water, earth, earth

THE NUMEROLOGICAL INTERPRETATION
Wilfred (NV = 5, CV = 9, VV = 5, FL = 5)

One of the best qualities inherent in this name is the potential it gives to see the upside of things. Wilfred is a man who is basically free from personal repression. He greets life with exuberance and gratitude. This is a person who has always sought to have an adventurous attitude, and this gives him an outlook on life that is often broader than most other people's. Wilfred is a spiritual man, and his church and community life mean a great deal to him. However, he can be too idealistic and overly generous, and he may have to learn how to see others more realistically.

DERIVATION: English, from the Old Germanic roots *wil*, meaning "will," and *frid*, meaning "peace." The name was borne by two saints, but then hardly used in the Middle Ages. In the nineteenth century, it reappeared and became very popular.

PRINCIPAL COLORS: Any lightly shaded hue, particularly pale gray

GEMSTONES AND PRECIOUS METALS: Diamonds, silver

BOTANICALS: Oats, sweet marjoram

UNIQUE SPELLINGS: Wilfredd, Wilfrid, Wilfridd, Wilfryd, Wilfrydd, Willfred, Willfrid, Wylfred, Wylfrid

RELATED TO: Fred, Freddie, Wil, Wilford, Wilfredo, Wilfried, Will, Willfredo, Williet, Willy

In the absence of any direct equivalent to the letter *f* in the Hebrew alphabet, the letter Peh is used. Peh can function as either a hard or a soft letter, and as such, is one of the seven "doubles."

William

DERIVATION: English, from the Old German roots *wil*, meaning "desire," and *helm*, meaning "helmet." Entered Britain during the Norman Conquest, with the most common name bearer being William the Conqueror himself. From the Middle Ages to the twentieth century, William and John were the two most common names in English-speaking countries. William has also been used frequently as a royal name.

PRINCIPAL COLORS: The complete range of green and yellow hues

GEMSTONES AND PRECIOUS METALS: Moonstones, pearls, any other white stone

BOTANICALS: Blackberry, elder, juniper

UNIQUE SPELLINGS: Wiliam, Wiliamm, Willyam, Willyem, Willyum

RELATED TO: Bill†, Billiet, Billy, Guglielmo, Guillaume, Guillermo, Liam, Vilem, Vilhelm, Wilburt, Wilhelm, Wilkinson, Will, Willem, Williet, Willis, Willy, Wilmar, Wilmot, Wilson†

❧

"No bird soars too high, if he soars with his own wings."
—WILLIAM BLAKE (POET)

A KABBALISTIC SYNOPSIS
ויליאם —VYLYAM (Vau, Yod, Lamed, Yod, Aleph, Mem)

Success, success, and more success basically sums up William's life. The value of William's name adds up to ninety-seven, which can be represented by the letters Tzaddi and Zayin. The Tzaddi lets us know that William will doggedly pursue his goals until he is ultimately successful, while the letter Zayin indicates a willingness to drive a very hard bargain and force away any competition when it arises. William feels obligated to come out on top careerwise in order to provide the very best for his loved ones. He is a very affectionate man, and will make a great dad should he ever have children, what with his naturally supportive and understanding character. William's only irritating trait is due to the influence of Virgo in his name, which makes him somewhat preoccupied with hygiene.

THE RUNIC INTERPRETATION
ᛗᚨᛁᛚᛚᛁᚹ (Mannaz, Ansuz, Isa, Laguz, Laguz, Isa, Wunjo)

The runes in this name give William strength and balance. William is caring and sensitive. His flexibility inclines him toward a love of the arts. He could opt for this as a profession, or use his Isa rune of isolation to follow a precise and analytical profession such as law, engineering, or medicine. Still, creative impulses need an outlet, and playing music or being near water may relax William. As he matures, he gains confidence because the runes of intuition and the self are present in his name, and his somewhat introverted nature blossoms later in life. William enjoys prosperity, and his friends respect his calm and stable demeanor. The Wunjo rune of joy in his name emerges whenever he is around art.

Elements: Air, air, earth, water, water, earth, earth

THE NUMEROLOGICAL INTERPRETATION
William (NV = 7, CV = 6, VV = 1, FL = 5)

This name tends to indicate a sincere and genuine person. William takes his responsibilities to his home, business, and community seriously. He is an ethical man, one who seeks to separate truth from fiction and live by a code of right human relations. In this respect, William's philosophical side is very important to him. William is also sentimental and romantic. He tends to partner for the long term, for he is neither flirtatious nor fickle. It is important for him to find a hobby that is uplifting and exciting, as William does have the tendency at times to become a bit too somber.

❧

Willie

DERIVATION: A common nickname for William, which is also sometimes used as an independent name. Can also be a nickname for feminine forms of William, such as Willa, Williamina, and Wilhelmina.

PRINCIPAL COLORS: The palest to the richest shades of yellow and green

GEMSTONES AND PRECIOUS METALS: Pearls, moss agate

BOTANICALS: Juniper, linseed, hops

UNIQUE SPELLINGS: Wileigh, Willee, Willey, Willi, Willy

RELATED TO: Billt, Billiet, Billy, Guglielmo, Guillaume, Guillermo, Liam, Vilem, Vilhelm, Wilburt, Wilhelm, Wilkinson, Will, Willem, Williamt, Willis, Wilmar, Wilmot, Wilsont

A Kabbalistic Synopsis

ויללי —VYLLY (Vau, Yod, Lamed, Lamed, Yod)

Willie's name has a very significant numerical value, fifty-six, which points to the nature of Willie's character, in that we have the energy of success (seven) multiplied by the energy of willpower (eight). Willie's success is unlikely to be standard commercial success and may not even involve large amounts of money. He is a fairly unconventional man, and his talents lie very much in the avant-garde of the creative world. As such, his achievement may be in the recognition of his work by his peers rather than in financial reward. Willie would never contemplate a full-time job, as he is far too involved in his relationship with his partner for that. He is a real romantic, and what money he does earn is often blown in one go on some dramatic romantic gesture like filling the apartment with flowers.

The Runic Interpretation

MIⱤⱤIP (Ehwaz, Isa, Laguz, Laguz, Isa, Wunjo)

Willie has many of the same attributes as his namesake William. Willie is a good team player. He enjoys competitive sports and the performing arts rather than the fine arts. Willie is easygoing and loyal to his friends, whom he cares about like family. It's painful for him when his friends get caught up in the responsibilities of life and are no longer available to respond to his concerns. Willie is focused but not keenly ambitious; he holds the heartfelt and somewhat naive belief that his work will be discovered on its own merit. As time goes on, people help him promote his creations, and he spends as much time negotiating contracts as he does creating the product.

Elements: Air, earth, water, water, earth, earth

The Numerological Interpretation

Willie (NV = 7, CV = 11, VV = 5, FL = 5)

The strong combination of seven and eleven in this name indicates a person who can be quite psychic and intuitive. Willie is more concerned with the essential nature of a person than with what that person looks like or possesses. This is a man who is more at work developing his consciousness than his pocketbook, and in this respect, he should choose a partner who is more responsive to the pragmatic concerns of life.

Wilma

DERIVATION: English and German, a short form of Wilhelmina, which is from the Old German roots *wil*, meaning "desire," and *helm*, meaning "helmet." Also a feminine form of William. Common since the 1880s.

PRINCIPAL COLORS: Electric colors, the full spectrum of moderately toned hues

GEMSTONES AND PRECIOUS METALS: Sapphires

BOTANICALS: Sage, spinach, Solomon's seal

UNIQUE SPELLINGS: Willma, Willmah, Wilmah, Wilmma, Wilmmah, Wylma, Wylmah, Wylmma, Wylmmah

RELATED TO: Valma, Velmat, Vilma, Wilhelmina, Williamina, Wilmina

❧

"A lot of young girls have looked to their career paths and have said they'd like to be chief. There's been a change in the limits people see."
—WILMA PEARL MANKILLER (LEADER OF THE CHEROKEE NATION)

A KABBALISTIC SYNOPSIS
וילמא —VYLMA (Vau, Yod, Lamed, Mem, Aleph)

Wilma is a highly intelligent woman who is likely to settle down with her intellectual inferior, although this is in no way an obstacle to her or her partner's happiness. It's just as well Wilma has a good head on her shoulders, as she needs a very good job to provide the cash she needs for her various interests and acquisitions. Thankfully, Wilma will have no trouble in carving out a highly successful career for herself.

THE RUNIC INTERPRETATION
ᚨᛗᛚᛁᚹ (Ansuz, Mannaz, Laguz, Isa, Wunjo)

Wilma loves parties. With the Wunjo rune of joy in Wilma's name, she's a natural entertainer. Careers such as party planning and organizing fund-raisers are satisfying for Wilma. She's a born networker, and her client list is worth big money. Wilma has the rune of self in her name, and she can take on difficult clients and maintain her boundaries without being manipulated. The family enjoys coming to Wilma's house for the holidays because she genuinely wants people to relax and play, and her spirit infuses the group with love. Wilma has to curb her schedule and take time to rest and rejuvenate because she loves what she does so much, she can burn out if she's not careful. Wilma is a powerful woman.

Elements: Air, air, water, earth, earth

THE NUMEROLOGICAL INTERPRETATION
Wilma (NV = 4, CV = 3, VV = 1, FL = 5)

Wilma is a strong individual with an assertive and self-confident nature. She has no problem integrating herself with others. Wilma likes people, and she is appreciated by them in return. A bright light at any gathering, she is a good conversationalist and appreciates what other people have to say. Wilma has a very playful side to her personality, too, and requires a partner who is both intellectually gifted and knows how to enjoy life. A practical woman, Wilma will find her professional path is of great importance to her. She needs to know that her financial position is secure, and that her career offers her plenty of room to succeed.

Wilson

A KABBALISTIC SYNOPSIS
וליסון —VYLSVN (Vau, Yod, Lamed, Samech, Vau, Nun)

If you're ever next to a Wilson on a train, don't get into a serious discussion about anything! It's not so much that Wilson goes on, although he does, but more that what he has to say on a whole range of issues is so decidedly interesting that you could get so engrossed that you completely miss your stop. Most of all, Wilson loves a good debate about a thorny problem of the day, and he is ideally suited to a career in politics. Wilson is absolutely genuine in his beliefs, which is part of what makes him so interesting. His motivations are sincere, and he has a real desire to improve people's lives. He is even willing to sacrifice some of his own pleasures in order to try to work toward this goal.

THE RUNIC INTERPRETATION
ᛏᛟᛋᛚᛁᛈ (Nauthiz, Othila, Sowelu, Laguz, Isa, Wunjo)

Wilson is bound for success. True, he has the rune of delays in his name (Nauthiz and Isa), but Wilson will eventually rise to the top based on his own merit; he has the power of the four elements in his name to almost guarantee this! Once Wilson learns to bear the burdens of responsibility and develops tip-top organizational skills, he no longer feels weighed down by pressure. Othila, the rune of separation, teaches Wilson to be spontaneous, ignore the crowd, and follow his unique dream. He can do this by learning to follow his inner spirit through prayer and meditation. Yoga and the martial arts are good exercises for Wilson, who is a visionary, not a follower. He's flexible and creative, and his outstanding mental health helps him express the Wunjo rune of joy in his name.

Elements: Fire, earth/fire, air, water, earth, earth

THE NUMEROLOGICAL INTERPRETATION
Wilson (NV = 11, CV = 5, VV = 6, FL = 5)

Wilson has a special understanding of the more subtle facets of events that brings him close to the heart of every matter. He is much more concerned with unity and cooperation than with exclusivity and competition. Wilson is a caring man, and he enjoys the comforts and intimacy of family life. He is very good when it comes to working with groups, and is naturally inclined to be an active participant in community projects.

DERIVATION: English, transferred use of the surname. The surname probably developed in conjunction with the rise of the first name William.

PRINCIPAL COLORS: The full range of white and green hues

GEMSTONES AND PRECIOUS METALS: Moonstones, cat's-eye, pearls

BOTANICALS: Moonwort, lettuce, plantain, colewort

UNIQUE SPELLINGS: Willsen, Willson, Willsyn, Wilsen, Wilsenn, Wilsin, Wilsinn, Wilsyn

RELATED TO: Billt, Billiet, Wilhelm, Wilkinson, Will, Willem, Williamt, Williet, Wilmar, Wilos

Woodrow

DERIVATION: English, originally a place-name meaning "a row of houses by a wood." Most common in the United States due to the fame of President Woodrow Wilson (1856–1924).

PRINCIPAL COLORS: Any color that is very lightly shaded

GEMSTONES AND PRECIOUS METALS: Diamonds, silver

BOTANICALS: Hazel, sweet marjoram, parsley

UNIQUE SPELLINGS: Woodroe, Woodrowe

RELATED TO: Woodward, Woody†

A KABBALISTIC SYNOPSIS

ועדרעה —WA'ADRA'AH (Vau, Ayin, Daleth, Resh, Ayin, Heh)

Woodrow's name is quite unusual in that the letter Ayin appears twice in it. This is a clear indication of substantial material success, so perhaps it's not that surprising that a president of the United Sates was blessed with this name. In the compression of Woodrow we get the three letters Shin, Nun, and Heh. The Shin is a further indication of Woodrow's immense drive and energy, and also suggests that at times he may be quite a difficult person to work with. There is a danger that as Woodrow gains in stature, he will begin to suspect the motives of those around him. This possibility is shown by the Nun in his name's compression. When you have a schedule as busy as Woodrow's, you need to have some specific leisure activities to help you relax. In Woodrow's case, anything that involves observing others, such as photography or even bird-watching, will have a definite appeal, thanks to the presence of the letter Heh in his name.

THE RUNIC INTERPRETATION

ᛈᛟᚱᛞᛟᛟᛈ (Wunjo, Othila, Raido, Dagaz, Othila, Othila, Wunjo)

With three runes of separation in his name, Woodrow will not be bound by old belief systems. Woodrow is prone to peel away layers of worn-out habits and attitudes in order to find himself, and he is likely to own homes or land holdings in several locations. But he needs to be careful in dealing with people as he begins to sever old ties and redefine his relationships. He must be totally honest in his dealings, or he could damage himself and cause pain to others. After some struggles, he emerges triumphant, and the Wunjo rune of joy helps Woodrow find himself and enjoy a satisfying life. Dagaz, the rune of breakthrough, ensures that Woodrow will have many opportunities ahead, and helps him to break with old family traits or beliefs.

Elements: Earth, earth/fire, water, fire, earth/fire, earth/fire, earth

THE NUMEROLOGICAL INTERPRETATION

Woodrow (NV = 5, CV = 5, VV = 9, FL = 5)

Woodrow will reach certain turning points in life, times when he will ask himself if he is satisfied with the status quo. Invariably his answer will be "No, there has to be something more!" Woodrow seeks to break free from standard forms of behavior and move into those life experiences that are expanding, evolving, and growing. He is a curious person, and always ready to try something new. He wants to uncover those life situations that awaken new potentials within himself. Woodrow feels like a work of art that is always in the process of becoming. It is important for him to be open, but his constant restlessness can inhibit his appreciation of the present moment.

Woody

A Kabbalistic Synopsis
ועדי —VA'ADY (Vau, Ayin, Daleth, Yod)

The value of Woody's name is ninety, which means that when we compress his name we produce only one letter, Tzaddi, meaning "fishhook." This tells us that Woody is an extremely possessive man. The letter Tzaddi relates to the tendency to latch on to something and refuse to give it up, no matter the opposition. As this is the only letter in the compression of his name, it has a very major impact on Woody's personality. The presence of the letter Daleth indicates that Woody is always interested in trying out a new project or opportunity. It may also suggest that in relationships, he finds it hard to commit himself despite the fact that he is likely to be an extremely jealous lover. Woody really needs to feel secure, and if he has a lover who can supply this feeling, he will be able to let go a lot more and enjoy life considerably as a result.

The Runic Interpretation
ᛃᛞᛟᛟᛈ (Eihwaz, Dagaz, Othila, Othila, Wunjo)

Woody has many of the attributes of Woodrow. But the introduction of the Eihwaz rune to this name makes Woody defensive and well equipped to avert disaster. He could work in a high-stress field such as firefighting. But then again, Woody could go to the other extreme and be reclusive. He could live a neat and organized life and feel safe that way. If security is important to him, Woody will invest heavily in insurance and retreat into a safe and dependable job. Whichever scenario Woody chooses, he is fortunate that opportunities that enhance his vision come to him. Woody learns to empower himself by changing a tendency toward procrastination into focused goal-setting.

Elements: Earth/fire, fire, earth/fire, earth/fire, earth

The Numerological Interpretation
Woody (NV = 1, CV = 9, VV = 1, FL = 5)

Woody is definitely his own person, a man who has the need to express his talents and abilities in a very unique and singular fashion. His personal drive is very strong, and he has to take care that he doesn't become so involved with himself that he lives in a shell of total subjectivity. Woody can also be a pioneer, and if he develops his social consciousness more fully, he can open the doors to opportunity for many other people to enter. His original and innovative attitude to life can be the source of much admiration, but he does have to watch a certain tendency toward egocentricity.

DERIVATION: English, short form of Woodrow, which was originally a place-name meaning "a row of houses by a wood." Sometimes used to honor President Woodrow Wilson (1856–1924). Occasionally used as an independent name.

PRINCIPAL COLORS: Any yellow or russet shades, also orange

GEMSTONES AND PRECIOUS METALS: Citrine, amber, topaz

BOTANICALS: Lavender, eyebright, thyme

UNIQUE SPELLINGS: Woodey, Woodi, Woodie

RELATED TO: Woodrow†, Woodward

❧

"Some rob you with a six-gun and some with a fountain pen."
—WOODY GUTHRIE (MUSICIAN)

DERIVATION: English version of the French name Yolande, which derives from the Greek roots *ion*, meaning "violet" and *anthos*, meaning "flower." In the United States, Yolanda has been used primarily in the twentieth century, especially during the 1960s.

PRINCIPAL COLORS: The full range of red hues, from pink to rich crimson

GEMSTONES AND PRECIOUS METALS: Rubies, bloodstones, garnets

BOTANICALS: Garlic, nettle, broom

UNIQUE SPELLINGS: Yalonda, Yolandah, Yollanda, Yollandah, Yollonda, Yolonda, Yolondah

RELATED TO: Iola, Iolanda, Iolande, Iolanthe, Jola, Jolanda, Jolanne, Jolanta, Jolantha, Jolanthe, Yola, Yolande, Yolanthe

Yolanda

A KABBALISTIC SYNOPSIS
יעלאנדא —YA'ALANDA (Yod, Ayin, Lamed, Aleph, Nun, Daleth, Aleph)

This woman has a very impressive intellect indeed, so if you want to stand a chance of interesting Yolanda, you need to pack some pretty heavy academic credentials. Small talk with Yolanda can often include discussions about subjects such as the validity of Euclidean geometry in a three-dimensional world, so be prepared. Yolanda will almost definitely be employed as a top scientist, and despite her outstanding mind, she is happiest in a mainly supportive role, as indicated by the presence of the letter Samech in the compression of her name. This is largely so that she has plenty of mental space to think about her own interests and not just the company's. Yolanda has a strong social conscience and spends a lot of nights awake worrying about the potential impact of some technical innovations. However, she is also fascinated by new developments in technology.

THE RUNIC INTERPRETATION
ᚾᛞᚾᛏᚾᛚᛟᛇ (Ansuz, Dagaz, Nauthiz, Ansuz, Laguz, Othila, Eihwaz)

Yolanda likes to blend in with the crowd, but she knows that at her core she is really very different. The double Ansuz rune of intuition helps her sense the world around her surprisingly accurately. Things seem to run smoothly for Yolanda because she knows how to smell trouble coming and avert disaster. At some point in her life, she will have to overcome limitation either socially, financially, or in some other way, but Yolanda is flexible and can go with the flow. As long as Yolanda remains unprejudiced in her choice of friends and open to the many opportunities promised her by the Dagaz rune of breakthrough, she will have a rich and rewarding life. After all, Yolanda has the power of the four elements in her name to bless her.

Elements: Air, fire, fire, air, water, earth/fire, earth/fire

THE NUMEROLOGICAL INTERPRETATION
Yolanda (NV = 9, CV = 1, VV = 8, FL = 7)

The name Yolanda carries the qualities of compassion, understanding, and sincerity. She is a woman who is concerned with other people's welfare, and she often acts as a supportive friend to her loved ones. But Yolanda is also a very forthright woman, a person with her own agenda, goals, and visions. Financial and social success are very important to her, and she has the drive and determination to work through any challenges and adversities. A very emotional person, Yolanda has to take care that her better judgment is not swayed by the intensity of her passion.

Yvette

A Kabbalistic Synopsis
יואת —YVAT (Yod, Vau, Aleph, Teth)

Yvette's name has a value of twenty-six, which is a highly significant number in occult circles, and relates in a very broad way to the gaining of genuine enlightenment. Yvette is a real individual who will go her own way in everything she does. She tends to be very unconventional, but this is by nature rather than by a definite desire to shock; she simply wants to be her own person. The value of her name reduces to eight and in this case refers to the letter with a value of eight, Ch, or Cheth. Cheth means "fence" or "enclosure" and represents a person who feels a need to defend and maintain a very definite personal space. Yvette can be very forceful in a nonaggressive way, and would be ideal in a sales-related job, especially in dealing with corporate clients.

The Runic Interpretation
ᛖᛏᛏᛖᚠᛇ (Ehwaz, Teiwaz, Teiwaz, Ehwaz, Fehu, Eihwaz)

Yvette is on her way. The unusual double Ehwaz configuration for movement hints that Yvette could become a prizewinning dancer or athlete. She likes competitive sports because she has the double warrior rune (Teiwaz) in her name. She's brave, and she likes to win. It's certain from her name that Yvette will live and work in several locales during her exciting life. Fehu, the rune of money or property, ensures that Yvette will prosper no matter which career she chooses. She may even win trophies and prizes with her considerable talents. Yvette is a go-getter, and her self-assured personality and good physical health will win her the admiration of thousands of fans.

Elements: Air, air, air, air, fire, earth/fire

The Numerological Interpretation
Yvette (NV = 7, CV = 8, VV = 8, FL = 7)

A perfectionist in both mind and body, Yvette will not rest until she is certain that what she has created is the very best that it can be. She is quite concerned about her physical appearance, and can spend a lot of her resources on clothing, cosmetics, and personal possessions. Yvette wants the good life, and will invest the necessary time and effort to achieve it. When she focuses on developing the spiritual side of her nature, she will extend this need for perfection in the physical world to a more collective level. She will then be very ecologically oriented, and work to see that all people are well clothed and well fed.

DERIVATION: French feminine form of Yves or Ivo, which derives from an Old German root meaning "yew wood." In the twentieth century, it has been found in English-speaking countries as well.

PRINCIPAL COLORS: All yellow and green hues, including gold

GEMSTONES AND PRECIOUS METALS: Moonstones, moss agate, pearls

BOTANICALS: Elder, blackberry, juniper

UNIQUE SPELLINGS: Evett, Evette, Ivett, Ivette

RELATED TO: Evonne, Ivetta, Ivonna, Ivonne, Yevette, Yvetta, Yvonnet

DERIVATION: French feminine form of Ivon or Ivo, which derives from the Old German root meaning "yew wood." Has been used in English-speaking countries since the early twentieth century, and is extremely common in Britain.

PRINCIPAL COLORS: The full spectrum of very pale hues, particularly light gray

GEMSTONES AND PRECIOUS METALS: Diamonds, silver, platinum

BOTANICALS: Hazel, mushrooms, parsley

UNIQUE SPELLINGS: Evonn, Evonne, Ivonn, Ivonne

RELATED TO: Evana, Ivana, Ivanna, Ivonna, Yevette, Yvetta, Yvette†

A Kabbalistic Synopsis
יוען —YVA'AN (Yod, Vau, Ayin, Nun)

Yvonne seems to find something to worry about in everything she does, always convinced that the least little thing left unchecked could turn any project into a complete disaster. However, the value of her name reduces to twenty-one, and this should give her a good reason to relax, as the number twenty-one is deeply positive; it relates to the Universe card in the tarot. The Universe card is symbolic of the successful completion of all things, and as such, directly addresses Yvonne's key concerns. Yvonne is a very popular woman. The combination of the Nun and the Vau in her name means that despite her own worries, Yvonne always lends an understanding ear to anyone who needs a friend. Although Yvonne worries at work, she can be extremely reckless once outside the office and is attracted to all manner of adrenaline-inducing leisure activities.

The Runic Interpretation
ᛖᚾᚾᛟᚠᛇ (Ehwaz, Nauthiz, Nauthiz, Othila, Fehu, Eihwaz)

Yvonne is here to serve humanity. She is a healer, and if she follows her heart, she will board the next plane headed to a destination overcome by disaster and human suffering. The double Nauthiz rune hints that travel and accommodations on Yvonne's journeys could be inconvenient and test her patience, but she will overcome these obstacles with her calm and patient demeanor. Yvonne can weave in and out of difficult situations and avert disaster. Funding and contributions come her way because Yvonne works from her spirit and the work is for the highest good. The money rune, Fehu, assures Yvonne prosperity. She could establish a not-for-profit foundation in the future with her high vision and integrity. If Yvonne chooses another kind of career, she will still succeed, but charity work will still be a big part of her life.

Elements: Air, fire, fire, earth/fire, fire, earth/fire

The Numerological Interpretation
Yvonne (NV = 5, CV = 5, VV = 9, FL = 7)

Yvonne is curious, active, and ready to try anything that promises to enhance her life experience. She is a courageous person, a visionary who has a glimpse of what awaits her as soon as she puts her foot out the door. Yvonne avoids becoming entrapped by people and events, and is always in search of greater creative potentialities. She cannot let a day go by without trying to take advantage of what life has to offer. These characteristics make for a fascinating person, but Yvonne can also be an opportunist. It is important for her to assume a more profound sense of personal responsibility, so that her relationships deepen and her aspirations become realities.

Zachary

A Kabbalistic Synopsis

זאחארי —ZAChARY (Zayin, Aleph, Cheth, Aleph, Resh, Yod)

You never know what you'll be doing next with Zachary; he is full of surprises, and the Yod in his name means that he always has plenty of energy to get out there and do it. If he has a family, he will be in his element; taking the kids on surprise outings and arranging special birthday treats will be his forte. At work, though, he is a changed man, as he wants to get the promotions that will enable him to have the home life he desires. His name contains both the letters Zayin, meaning "sword," and Cheth, which refers to a concern for self-defense. In other words, work to Zachary is a battlefield, and he is just as efficient in attack as he is in defense; as he sees it, if he doesn't succeed, nobody will. Mind you, he is not disliked in the office. People realize that due to Zachary's enthusiasm and hard work, being on his team will give their own careers a boost.

The Runic Interpretation

ᛇᚱᚨᚺᚲᚨᛉ (Eihwaz, Raido, Ansuz, Hagalaz, Kano, Ansuz, Algiz)

Zachary is loaded with enthusiasm. He rushes around participating in numerous activities and working long hours. He is so involved with his business that he forgets that rest is also a valuable aspect of life. Zachary has such a hectic schedule, it's small wonder he incurs late fees on his bills; he's just not around to open mail! Confusion and overwork can lead Zachary to high stress levels. It's not that he is a melancholy type at all, but he experiences numerous highs and lows because he needs to reorganize his life. Zachary is surrounded by Algiz, the rune of protection. Before things get too out of line, Algiz teaches Zachary the important lesson that we can never lose as long as we try and we learn from our mistakes. This helps Zachary be more selective about where he spends his time and feel more relaxed and calm.

Elements: Earth/fire, water, air, water, water, air, air

The Numerological Interpretation

Zachary (NV = 1, CV = 1, VV = 9, FL = 8)

An outgoing individual, Zachary is very keen to develop his own mode of creative self-expression. He is an individualist who has to do things in life in his own way. No matter how many times he may fall down, Zachary will rise up and start all over again. He is a challenging person—quite confrontational, in fact—but he is also very open to helping others in distress, and he makes a very loyal friend. Even if he functions as a team leader, it is hard for Zachary to work in groups. He will contribute to the team effort but then has to continue creating his own path.

DERIVATION: English, from the biblical name Zacharias, which is a form of the Hebrew Zechariah, meaning "God has remembered." Zachariah is found in the Old and New Testaments, most notably as the father of John the Baptist in the New Testament. Zachary has become increasingly popular in the twentieth century, even as other "Zach" names have faded.

PRINCIPAL COLORS: All shades of yellow and brown, from the palest to the most brilliant

GEMSTONES AND PRECIOUS METALS: Citrine, amber, any other yellow stone

BOTANICALS: Eyebright, lavender, sorrel

UNIQUE SPELLINGS: Zacary, Zachery, Zackarie, Zackary, Zackery, Zakarie, Zakary, Zakery, Zekarie, Zekery

RELATED TO: Zacarias, Zaccheus, Zach, Zachariah, Zacharias, Zack, Zackariah, Zecheriah, Zeke

DERIVATION: English, from the Greek meaning "life." Especially popular among the early Christians, and the name of several martyrs of the second and third centuries. Commonly used in English-speaking countries since the middle of the nineteenth century.

PRINCIPAL COLORS: The palest yellow and brown to the richest golden and russet shades, also orange

GEMSTONES AND PRECIOUS METALS: Topaz, amber, yellow diamonds

BOTANICALS: Chamomile, borage, lavender

UNIQUE SPELLINGS: Zoee, Zoey, Zoi, Zoie, Zoiee, Zoiy, Zowee, Zowi, Zowie, Zowy

RELATED TO: Zoelee, Zoelie, Zoeline, Zoya

Zoe

A KABBALISTIC SYNOPSIS
זעי —ZA'AY (Zayin, Ayin, Yod)

They always say you should save the best for last, and the name Zoe is no exception! In the workplace, Zoe has been known to use her beguiling charm to advance her career, but as she will also use her wiles to get friends off the hook if necessary, she is a very popular woman around the office. Add her sense of humor, her willingness to help out her friends, and the additional bonus of being successful financially, and you can see why although Zoe may be last, she is very far from being least!

THE RUNIC INTERPRETATION
ᛗᛟᛉ (Ehwaz, Othila, Algiz)

Zoe has real acting ability. Whether she makes a career out of this or not, her acting ability still helps her to develop a good rapport with people. Zoe is capable and perceptive. The Algiz rune of protection makes her insightful, and she approaches challenges with a calm attitude and strives to simplify complex situations. People like Zoe, and by the end of her life, she's made friends internationally. She holds up well under stress and uses her humor to bring harmony and order to her dealings with family and friends. Zoe is a tad inclined to extremes, though, and she needs to curb those shopping sprees or late nights on the town when things threaten to get out of hand.

Elements: Air, earth/fire, air

THE NUMEROLOGICAL INTERPRETATION
Zoe (NV = 1, CV = 8, VV = 11, FL = 8)

This is a powerful name with tremendous potential. Zoe has the gift of the sixth sense: intuition. She can look at a fruit from the outside and see the level of its internal sweetness. Zoe can apply this gift to people as well. She is very aware of a person's inner resources, and can help them to focus on their strengths and transform their weaknesses. Zoe can do this because she has a firm grasp of her own reality. She is a person who, although very capable of intimate and passionate relationships, is not dependent upon intimacy nor overcome by her own passion. It is also easy for Zoe to achieve financial success. She has good organizational skills and knows how to make the most of her personal resources.

Alic. *See* Alexander
Alice, 76. *See also* Alicia; Allison; Alyssa
Alicia, 77. *See also* Alice; Allison; Alyssa
Alicin. *See* Allison
Alick. *See* Alex; Alexander
Alijandro. *See* Alejandro
Aliks. *See* Alex
Alin. *See* Alan; Allen
Aline. *See* Eleanor
Alisa. *See* Alice; Alicia; Allison; Alyssa
Alisabeth. *See* Elizabeth
Alise. *See* Alice; Alyssa
Alisha. *See* Alicia; Allison; Alyssa
Alison. *See* Alice; Alicia; Allison; Alyssa
Aliss. *See* Alice
Alissa. *See* Alice; Alicia; Alyssa
Alistair. *See* Alejandro; Alex; Alexander
Alix. *See* Alexandra; Alexis
Alixander. *See* Alexander
Alixandra. *See* Alexandra
Aliza. *See* Alyssa
Alizabeth. *See* Elizabeth
Allan. *See* Alan; Allen
Allayne. *See* Elaine
Allen, 78. *See also* Al; Alan
Allex. *See* Alex
Allexina. *See* Alexis
Allie. *See* Alexandra; Alice; Alicia; Allison;
   Alyssa
Allin/Allon. *See* Alan; Allen
Allison, 79. *See also* Alice; Alicia; Alyssa
Allonso/Allonsoe. *See* Alonzo
Allonzo. *See* Alonzo
Allun/Allyn. *See* Alan; Allen
Ally. *See* Alice
Allyson. *See* Alice; Alicia; Allison; Alyssa
Aloisa. *See* Louise
Alon. *See* Alan; Allen
Alonso. *See* Al; Alonzo; Lonnie
Alonzo, 80. *See also* Lonnie
Aloysia. *See* Louise
Alphie. *See* Alfonso
Alphonse. *See* Al; Alfonso; Alonzo
Alphonso/Alphonsus. *See* Alfonso; Alonzo
Alphonzo. *See* Alfonso
Alun/Alyn. *See* Alan; Allen
Alyce/Alyse. *See* Alice; Alicia; Allison; Alyssa
Alycia. *See* Alice; Alicia
Alycin/Alysin. *See* Allison
Alys/Alyss. *See* Alice
Alysa. *See* Alice; Alyssa
Alyson. *See* Alice; Alicia; Allison; Alyssa
Alyssa, 81. *See also* Alice; Alicia; Allison
Alyx. *See* Alex
Alyxandra. *See* Alexandra
Alyxice/Alyxis. *See* Alexis
Alyza. *See* Eliza
Ama. *See* Amy
Amala. *See* Amelia
Amalie. *See* Emily
Amalija. *See* Emily
Amanda, 82. *See also* Amy
Amandah. *See* Amanda
Amata. *See* Amanda; Amy
Amber, 83
Amberetta. *See* Amber
Ambir/Ambur. *See* Amber
Ambre. *See* Amber
Ambretta. *See* Amber

Ambrosina/Ambrosine. *See* Amber
Amela. *See* Amelia
Ameli. *See* Emily
Amelia, 84. *See also* Amy; Emily; Millie
Amelie. *See* Amelia; Emily
Amenda. *See* Amanda
Amey. *See* Amanda; Amy
Ami/Amia. *See* Amy
Amie. *See* Amelia; Amy
Amilia. *See* Amelia
Ammanda. *See* Amanda
Ammber/Ammbre. *See* Amber
Ammbur. *See* Amber
Ammela/Ammelia. *See* Amelia
Ammella. *See* Emily
Ammenda. *See* Amanda
Ammilia. *See* Amelia
Amy, 85. *See also* Amanda; Amelia
Amylia. *See* Amelia
Ana. *See* Anita; Ann; Anna; Anne; Roseanne
Anais. *See* Agnes
Anastasia. *See* Stacy
Andee/Andey. *See* Andy
Andera. *See* Andrea
Anders. *See* Andre; Andrew; Andy
Andi/Andie. *See* Andy
Andra. *See* Andrea
Andray. *See* Andre
Andre, 86. *See also* Andrew; Andy
Andrea, 87. *See also* Andy; Drew
Andreana. *See* Andrea
Andreas. *See* Andre; Andrew; Andy; Drew
Andree. *See* Andrea; Andy
Andreea/Andreia. *See* Andrea
Andrei/Andres. *See* Andy
Andrene. *See* Andrea
Andretta/Andrette. *See* Andrea
Andrew, 88. *See also* Andre; Andy; Drew
Andrewe. *See* Andrew
Andrewina. *See* Andrea; Ina
Andrey. *See* Andre
Andreya. *See* Andrea
Andria/Andrya. *See* Andrea
Andriana. *See* Andy
Andrianna. *See* Andrea
Andrina/Andrine. *See* Andy
Andris. *See* Andre
Andrue. *See* Andrew
Andy, 89. *See also* Andre; Andrew
Ane. *See* Ann; Anne
Aneeta. *See* Anita
Anet/Anete. *See* Annette
Aneta. *See* Anita
Anett/Anetta. *See* Annette
Anette. *See* Anita; Annette
Angel, 90. *See also* Angelica; Angelo
Angela, 91. *See also* Angel; Angelica
Angeleca. *See* Angelica
Angeles. *See* Angela; Angelica
Angelica, 92. *See also* Angel; Angela
Angelicka. *See* Angelica
Angelika/Angelike. *See* Angela; Angelica
Angeline. *See* Angelica
Angeliqua. *See* Angelica
Angelique. *See* Angel; Angela; Angelica
Angelita. *See* Angel; Angela; Angelica
Angella/Angello. *See* Angela
Angellica. *See* Angelica
Angelo, 93. *See also* Angel

Angie. *See* Angel; Angela; Angelica
Angil/Angyl. *See* Angel
Angila. *See* Angela
Angilica/Angilika. *See* Angelica
Angillica. *See* Angelica
Angillo/Angilo. *See* Angelo
Angus. *See* Gus
Angyla. *See* Angela
Anika. *See* Anita
Anita, 94. *See also* Ann; Anna
Anjel. *See* Angel
Anjil/Anjyl. *See* Angel
Ann, 95. *See also* Anita; Anna; Anne;
   Annette; Bethany; Hannah; Marianne;
   Mary Ann; Nancy; Nina; Roseanne
Anna, 96. *See also* Anita; Ann; Anne;
   Annette; Hannah; Marianne; Mary Ann;
   Nancy; Nina; Roseanne
Annabel/Annabella. *See* Anita; Ann; Anna;
   Anne; Roseanne
Annabelle. *See* Ann; Anna; Anne; Roseanne
Annah/Anneh. *See* Anna
Annalisa. *See* Anna
Anndrea/Anndria. *See* Andrea
Anndrue. *See* Andrew
Anne, 97. *See also* Anita; Ann; Anna;
   Annette; Bethany; Hannah; Marianne;
   Mary Ann; Nancy; Nina; Roseanne
Anneka. *See* Anita
Annelise. *See* Ann; Anna; Anne; Roseanne
Annemarie. *See* Marianne; Mary Ann
Anneta. *See* Anita
Annete. *See* Annette
Annetta. *See* Anita; Ann; Anne; Roseanne
Annette, 98. *See also* Anita; Ann; Anna;
   Anne; Hannah; Marianne; Mary Ann;
   Roseanne
Anngela. *See* Angela
Anngeleca/Anngelica. *See* Angelica
Anngeliqua. *See* Angelica
Anngello/Anngelo. *See* Angelo
Anngila/Anngyla. *See* Angela
Anni/Anny. *See* Bethany
Annice. *See* Anita; Annette
Annie. *See* Anita; Ann; Anna; Anne;
   Annette; Bethany; Nancy; Roseanne
Annika. *See* Ann; Anna; Anne; Roseanne
Annina/Anninka. *See* Nina
Annis. *See* Agnes
Annita. *See* Anita
Annthony. *See* Anthony
Anntoinette. *See* Antoinette
Anntoinnette. *See* Antoinette
Anntoney. *See* Anthony
Anntonia/Anntonya. *See* Antonia
Anntonio/Anntonyo. *See* Antonio
Antain. *See* Anthony
Anthonee/Anthoney. *See* Anthony
Anthony, 99. *See also* Antonio; Tony
Antionette. *See* Antoinette
Antoine. *See* Anthony; Antonio; Tony
Antoinete/Antoinett. *See* Antoinette
Antoinette, 100. *See also* Antonia; Toni;
   Tonya
Anton. *See* Anthony; Antonio; Tony
Antonea. *See* Antonia
Antonella/Antonello. *See* Toni
Antonette. *See* Antoinette; Antonia
Antoni/Antonin. *See* Anthony

Antonia, 101. *See also* Antoinette; Toni; Tonya
Antonie. *See* Antonia; Tonya
Antonina. *See* Antoinette; Antonia; Nina; Toni; Tonya
Antonino. *See* Tony
Antonio, 102. *See also* Anthony; Tony
Antony. *See* Anthony; Antonio; Tony
Antonya. *See* Antonia
Antonyo. *See* Antonio
Antwaine. *See* Antoinette
Anya. *See* Anita; Ann; Anna; Anne; Annette; Roseanne
Aprel. *See* April
April, 103
Aprill/Aprille. *See* April
Aprilla. *See* April
Apryl/Apryll. *See* April
Araldo. *See* Harold
Arch. *See* Archie
Archangela. *See* Angel
Archangelica. *See* Angela
Archee/Archey. *See* Archie
Archer. *See* Archie
Archi/Archy. *See* Archie
Archibald/Archibold. *See* Archie
Archie, 104
Archimbald. *See* Archie
Aren. *See* Aaron
Arina. *See* Irene
Arke. *See* Aaron
Arla. *See* Arlene
Arlean/Arleane. *See* Arlene
Arleen/Arleene. *See* Arlene
Arleine. *See* Arlene
Arlen/Arlena. *See* Arlene
Arlene, 105
Arletta/Arlette. *See* Arlene
Arline/Arlynn. *See* Arlene
Arlyn/Arlyne. *See* Arlene
Armand. *See* Armando; Herman
Armando, 106. *See also* Herman
Armandoe. *See* Armando
Armanndo. *See* Armando
Armendo. *See* Armando
Arn. *See* Aaron; Arnold
Arnald/Arnaldo. *See* Arnold
Arnaud/Arnauld. *See* Arnold
Arndt. *See* Arnold
Arne/Arno. *See* Arnold
Arnnold. *See* Arnold
Arnold, 107
Aroldo. *See* Harold
Aron. *See* Aaron
Arran/Arron. *See* Aaron
Arrnold. *See* Arnold
Art. *See* Arthur; Arturo
Artair. *See* Arthur; Artie; Arturo
Artero. *See* Arturo
Artey. *See* Artie
Arther. *See* Arthur; Artie
Arthur, 108. *See also* Artie; Arturo
Arthure. *See* Arthur
Artie, 109. *See also* Arthur; Arturo
Artor. *See* Artie
Artur. *See* Arthur; Arturo
Arturo, 110. *See also* Arthur; Artie
Arturoe. *See* Arturo
Arturro. *See* Arturo

Artus. *See* Artie
Arty. *See* Artie
Ash/Ashe. *See* Ashley
Ashlee/Ashlie. *See* Ashley
Ashleigh. *See* Ashley
Ashley, 111. *See also* Leigh
Aston. *See* Austin
Astra. *See* Estelle
Audie. *See* Audrey
Audra. *See* Audrey
Audree/Audreen. *See* Audrey
Audrey, 112
Audri/Audry. *See* Audrey
Audrie/Audria. *See* Audrey
Audrina. *See* Audrey
August. *See* Austin
Augustus. *See* Austin; Gus
Austen/Austyn. *See* Austin
Austin, 113
Avraham. *See* Abraham
Avril. *See* April
Awsten/Awstin. *See* Austin
Aybe. *See* Abe
Aylean/Ayleen. *See* Eileen
Ayn. *See* Ann; Anne; Bethany
Aypril. *See* April

Bab. *See* Barbara
Babette. *See* Barbara
Babs. *See* Barbara
Bahb/Bahbb. *See* Bob
Bahni/Bahnie. *See* Bonnie
Bahny. *See* Bonnie
Bahrbrah. *See* Barbara
Bairre. *See* Barry
Balinda/Balindah. *See* Belinda
Balynda. *See* Belinda
Bar/Bara. *See* Barbara
Barb. *See* Barbara
Barbara, 114
Barbarah. *See* Barbara
Barbra. *See* Barbara
Barbrah/Barbreh. *See* Barbara
Barby. *See* Barbara
Barbyra/Barbyrah. *See* Barbara
Bari/Barie. *See* Barry
Barnard/Barnardo. *See* Bernie
Barney/Barnie. *See* Bernie
Barnhard. *See* Bernie
Barra/Barrie. *See* Barry
Barry, 115
Bary. *See* Barry
Baubie. *See* Barbara
Bayrie/Bayry. *See* Barry
Baz/Bazza. *See* Barry
Bea. *See* Beatrice
Bear. *See* Bernie
Bearnard. *See* Bernard; Bernie
Bearnhard. *See* Bernard
Beatrice, 116
Beatriss. *See* Beatrice
Beatrix. *See* Beatrice
Beatryce. *See* Beatrice
Beatryse/Beatryss. *See* Beatrice
Beattie/Beattie. *See* Beatrice
Beca. *See* Becky
Becca/Becka. *See* Becky; Rebecca
Beckie. *See* Becky; Rebecca
Becky, 117. *See also* Rebecca

Beeatrice/Beetrice. *See* Beatrice
Beeatriss. *See* Beatrice
Beetryss. *See* Beatrice
Behn/Behnn. *See* Ben
Behnjamin/Behnjamyn. *See* Benjamin
Beht. *See* Betty
Behtey/Behtie. *See* Betty
Behtsey/Behtsy. *See* Betsy
Behttey. *See* Betty
Behtti/Behttie. *See* Betty
Behty. *See* Betty
Bekka. *See* Becky
Bel. *See* Isabelle
Belinda, 118
Belindah. *See* Belinda
Bell/Belle. *See* Isabelle
Bella. *See* Belinda; Isabelle
Belli. *See* Belinda
Bellita. *See* Isabelle
Belynda/Belyndah. *See* Belinda
Ben, 119. *See also* Benjamin
Benedict. *See* Ben
Bengemin. *See* Benjamin
Benjamen. *See* Benjamin
Benjamin, 120. *See also* Ben
Benjaminn. *See* Benjamin
Benjamon/Benjamyn. *See* Benjamin
Benjie. *See* Ben; Benjamin
Benjiman/Benjimon. *See* Benjamin
Benn. *See* Ben
Bennett. *See* Ben
Bennie/Benny. *See* Ben; Benjamin
Benson. *See* Ben
Bentley. *See* Ben
Benyamin. *See* Ben
Bern. *See* Bernie
Bernadetta. *See* Bernadette
Bernadette, 121
Bernadino. *See* Bernard
Bernard, 122. *See also* Bernie
Bernardetta/Bernardette. *See* Bernadette
Bernardo. *See* Bernard
Bernat. *See* Bernard
Bernette. *See* Bernadette
Berney/Berny. *See* Bernie
Bernhard/Bernhardt. *See* Bernard
Berni. *See* Bernadette; Bernie
Bernie, 123. *See also* Bernadette; Bernard
Bernt. *See* Bernard; Brett
Bert. *See* Albert; Robert; Roberto
Berta/Berti. *See* Roberta
Bertie. *See* Albert; Bob; Robert; Roberta; Roberto
Bess. *See* Betsy; Betty; Elizabeth
Bessie. *See* Beth; Betsy; Betty; Elizabeth
Bessy. *See* Beth; Betsy
Betey. *See* Betty
Beth, 124. *See also* Bethany; Betsy; Betty; Elizabeth
Bethan. *See* Bethany; Betsy
Bethani/Bethanie. *See* Bethany
Bethann/Bethanna. *See* Bethany
Bethanne. *See* Beth; Bethany
Bethanni/Bethannie. *See* Bethany
Bethanny. *See* Bethany
Bethany, 125. *See also* Ann; Anne; Beth; Betsy; Betty; Elizabeth
Bethe. *See* Beth
Bethi. *See* Betsy

Bethia. *See* Beth
Beti/Betie. *See* Betty
Betsey. *See* Beth; Betsy
Betsi/Betsie. *See* Betsy
Betsy, 126. *See also* Beth; Bethany; Betty;
  Elizabeth
Bette. *See* Betsy
Bettey/Bettie. *See* Betty
Betti. *See* Beth; Betsy; Betty
Bettina. *See* Betsy; Ina; Tina
Bettsi/Bettsy. *See* Betsy
Bettsie. *See* Betsy
Betty, 127. *See also* Beth; Bethany; Betsy;
  Elizabeth
Betty Ann. *See* Betty
Betty Jo. *See* Betty
Betty Lou. *See* Betty
Betty Mae. *See* Betty
Betty Sue. *See* Betty
Bety. *See* Betty
Bev/Bevah. *See* Beverly
Beverlea/Beverley. *See* Beverly
Beverleigh. *See* Beverly
Beverli/Beverlie. *See* Beverly
Beverly, 128
Bevi. *See* Beverly
Bhil/Bhill. *See* Bill
Bhilley. *See* Billie
Bhilli/Bhilly. *See* Billie
Bhyl/Bhyll. *See* Bill
Bhylley/Bhylly. *See* Billie
Bhylli/Bhyllie. *See* Billie
Bibi. *See* Vivian
Bibiana/Bibiane. *See* Vivian
Bil. *See* Bill
Bilinda. *See* Belinda
Bill, 129. *See also* Billie; William; Willie;
  Wilson
Billey/Billi. *See* Billie
Billie, 130. *See also* Bill; William; Willie;
  Wilson
Billy. *See* Bill; Billie; William; Willie
Bilynda. *See* Belinda
Bina. *See* Sabrina
Binyamin. *See* Benjamin
Biran/Biron. *See* Byron
Birnadet/Birnadett. *See* Bernadette
Blaike. *See* Blake
Blaine. *See* Blake
Blair. *See* Blake
Blaise. *See* Blake
Blake, 131
Blayke. *See* Blake
Bob, 132. *See also* Rob; Robert; Roberto
Bobb. *See* Bob
Bobbette. *See* Roberta
Bobbi. *See* Roberta
Bobbie. *See* Barbara; Bob; Rob; Roberta;
  Roberto
Bobby. *See* Bob; Rob; Robert; Roberto
Bonita. *See* Bonnie
Bonnee. *See* Bonnie
Bonni/Bonny. *See* Bonnie
Bonnie, 133
Bora. *See* Barbara
Brad. *See* Bradley
Braddick. *See* Bradley
Braddley. *See* Bradley
Braddock. *See* Bradley

Bradford. *See* Bradley
Bradlee/Bradlie. *See* Bradley
Bradley, 134
Bradli/Bradly. *See* Bradley
Bram. *See* Abraham
Branda. *See* Brenda
Brandan/Brandin. *See* Brandon
Brandee/Brandi. *See* Brandy; Brenda
Branden. *See* Brandon; Brian
Brandey/Brandie. *See* Brandy
Brando. *See* Brandon
Brandon, 135. *See also* Brian
Brandy, 136. *See also* Brenda
Brandyn. *See* Brandon
Brannden/Branndon. *See* Brandon
Branndin. *See* Brandon
Brant. *See* Brandon
Branton. *See* Brandon
Breand·n. *See* Brandon
Brehnda/Brehndah. *See* Brenda
Brehnnda. *See* Brenda
Brehnt/Brchntt. *See* Brent
Breht/Brehtt. *See* Brett
Brenda, 137. *See also* Brandy
Brendah. *See* Brenda
Brendan. *See* Brandon
Brendanna/Brendanne. *See* Brenda
Brenden. *See* Brandon; Brian
Brenna. *See* Brandy
Brennda. *See* Brenda
Brenne/Brenni. *See* Brandy
Brent, 138. *See also* Brandon; Brett; Bryant
Brentan. *See* Brent
Brenten/Brenton. *See* Brent
Brentt. *See* Brent
Bret/Brette. *See* Brett
Breton/Bretton. *See* Brett
Brett, 139. *See also* Brent; Brittany
Brian, 140. *See also* Brandon; Bryant; Byron;
  Ryan
Briant/Briantt. *See* Bryant
Brice. *See* Bruce
Brina. *See* Sabrina
Brion. *See* Brian
Brit. *See* Brittany
Britaney/Britani. *See* Brittany
Britany/Briteny. *See* Brittany
Britney. *See* Brittany
Britni/Britny. *See* Brittany
Britt. *See* Brittany
Britta. *See* Brittany
Brittan. *See* Brittany
Brittaney/Brittani. *See* Brittany
Brittany, 141
Britteny. *See* Brittany
Brittnee/Brittney. *See* Brittany
Brittni/Brittny. *See* Brittany
Brizio. *See* Bruce
Broderick. *See* Rod; Roderick
Brodrick. *See* Roderick
Brooce/Broose. *See* Bruce
Brook. *See* Brooke
Brooke, 142
Brookes/Brooks. *See* Brooke
Brookie. *See* Brooke
Broz. *See* Bruce
Bruce, 143
Brus. *See* Bruce
Bryan. *See* Brian; Bryant; Ryan

Bryant, 144. *See also* Brent; Brian; Byron
Bryce. *See* Bruce
Bryehnt. *See* Bryant
Bryen/Bryin. *See* Brian
Bryon. *See* Brian; Bryant; Byron
Bryont/Bryontt. *See* Bryant
Bullinda/Bullynda. *See* Belinda
Bunnie/Bunny. *See* Bonnie
Burt/Burtie. *See* Albert
Byford. *See* Byron
Byl. *See* Bill
Bylley/Bylly. *See* Billie
Bylli/Byllie. *See* Billie
Byram/Byrom. *See* Byron
Byran/Byren. *See* Byron
Byrin/Byryn. *See* Byron
Byrnadet. *See* Bernadette
Byrnadette. *See* Bernadette
Byrnard/Byrnhard. *See* Bernard
Byron, 145. *See also* Brian; Bryant

Caarle. *See* Carl; Karl
Caesar/Caezar. *See* Cesar
Cahleen/Cahlene. *See* Colleen
Cahlin/Cahlyn. *See* Colin
Cahnni/Cahnnie. *See* Connie
Cahnny. *See* Connie
Cahnstance. *See* Constance
Cairn. *See* Karen
Caitlin. *See* Catherine; Cathy; Kate;
  Katherine; Kathleen; Kathryn; Kathy;
  Katie; Katrina; Kay; Kitty
Caitriona. *See* Catherine; Cathy; Kate;
  Katherine; Kathleen; Kathryn; Kathy;
  Katie; Katrina; Kay; Kitty
Cal. *See* Calvin
Cale. *See* Caleb; Calvin
Caleb, 146
Caley. *See* Caleb; Calvin
Callib/Callyb. *See* Caleb
Callum. *See* Caleb
Cally. *See* Calvin
Calum. *See* Calvin; Colin
Calumba. *See* Caleb
Calven/Calvyn. *See* Calvin
Calvert. *See* Calvin
Calvin, 147
Calyb. *See* Caleb
Cam. *See* Cameron
Camerin/Cameryn. *See* Cameron
Cameron, 148
Camilla. *See* Millie
Camillus. *See* Cameron
Cammeron. *See* Cameron
Candace, 149
Candice. *See* Candace
Candis/Candiss. *See* Candace
Candy. *See* Candace
Candys/Candyss. *See* Candace
Cara. *See* Carol; Carolyn; Carrie; Charlotte;
  Kara
Caralin. *See* Carolyn
Caralyn. *See* Carolyn; Charlotte
Caralynne. *See* Carolyn
Careen. *See* Kara
Carel. *See* Carol; Charlie
Caren/Carin. *See* Karen
Carey. *See* Kara
Cari. *See* Carrie; Kerry

Curtiss. *See* Curtis
Curtt. *See* Kurt
Cyd. *See* Sidney; Sydney
Cydnee/Cydnie. *See* Sidney; Sydney
CydneyCydny. *See* Sidney; Sydney
Cyndi/Cyndy. *See* Cindy; Cynthia
Cyndie. *See* Cindy; Cynthia
Cynthea/Cynthya. *See* Cynthia
Cynthia, 200. *See also* Cindy; Cynthia

Daeman/Daemen. *See* Damon
Daemian/Daemien. *See* Damien
Daemin/Daemyn. *See* Damon
Daemon. *See* Damon
Daena. *See* Dana
Daevid. *See* David
Dahlia. *See* Daisy; Dale
Dahna. *See* Donna
Dai. *See* David
Daia. *See* Daisy
Dail/Daile. *See* Dale
Daina. *See* Dana
Daisey/Daisie. *See* Daisy
Daisy, 201
Daizy. *See* Daisy
Dale, 202
Daley/Daly. *See* Dale
Dalia. *See* Dale
Daman/Damen. *See* Damon
Damean/Dameon. *See* Damien
Damian/Damiano. *See* Damien; Damon
Damianos. *See* Damon
Damiao. *See* Damien
Damien, 203. *See also* Damon
Damin/Damyn. *See* Damon
Damio/Damion. *See* Damien
Damon, 204. *See also* Damien
Dan, 205. *See also* Daniel; Danny
Dana, 206. *See also* Danielle
Daneal. *See* Daniel
Danee. *See* Danny
Daneece/Daneese. *See* Denise
Daneen. *See* Dana
Danek. *See* Dan; Daniel; Danny
Danel. *See* Dan
Danella. *See* Dana
Danette. *See* Dana; Danielle
Dani/Dania. *See* Danielle
Danial. *See* Dan; Daniel; Danny
Daniale. *See* Danielle
Danica. *See* Danielle
Danice. *See* Denise
Daniel, 207. *See also* Dan; Danny
Daniela. *See* Danielle
Daniele. *See* Dan; Danielle
Danielita. *See* Danielle
Daniella. *See* Dana; Danielle
Danielle, 208. *See also* Dana
Danielo. *See* Danny
Danil. *See* Daniel; Danny
Danilo. *See* Dan; Daniel; Danny
Daniol. *See* Daniel
Danise. *See* Dana; Denise
Danita. *See* Dana
Dann. *See* Dan
Danna. *See* Dana; Danielle
Danne. *See* Dan; Diana
Dannee/Danney. *See* Danny
Danni/Dannie. *See* Danny

Danniel. *See* Daniel
Dannielle. *See* Danielle
Dannika. *See* Dana
Danny, 209. *See also* Dan; Daniel
Dannyelle. *See* Danielle
Danuta. *See* Dana
Danyel. *See* Daniel; Danielle
Danyele/Danyelle. *See* Danielle
Danyse. *See* Denise
Darell. *See* Darryl
Daren. *See* Darren; Darryl
Daril/Darill. *See* Darryl
Darin. *See* Darren
Darla. *See* Darlene
Darlean/Darleane. *See* Darlene
Darleen/Darleene. *See* Darlene
Darlein/Darleine. *See* Darlene
Darlena/Darlenna. *See* Darlene
Darlene, 210
Darlynn. *See* Darlene
Darol/Daroll. *See* Darryl
Darrel/Darrell. *See* Darren
Darren, 211. *See also* Darryl
Darril/Darrill. *See* Darryl
Darrin. *See* Darren
Darrol/Darroll. *See* Darryl
Darryl, 212. *See also* Darren
Darryll. *See* Darryl
Darryn/Daryn. *See* Darren
Daryl. *See* Darryl
Dasey/Dasie. *See* Daisy
Dasi/Dasy. *See* Daisy
Daun. *See* Dawn
Dauris. *See* Doris
Dave, 213. *See also* David
Daved. *See* David
Daven. *See* Dave
Davey. *See* Dave; David
David, 214. *See also* Dave; Devin
Davidd. *See* David
Davide. *See* Dave
Davidson. *See* Dave
Davie. *See* Dave
Davis. *See* Dave; David
Davon. *See* Dave
Davy. *See* Dave; David
Dawn, 215
Dawna. *See* Dawn
Dawne/Dawnn. *See* Dawn
Dawnetta. *See* Dawn
Dawnielle. *See* Dawn
Dawnysia. *See* Dawn
Dayanna. *See* Diana
Dayl/Dayle. *See* Dale
Dayman/Daymen. *See* Damon
Daymian/Daymien. *See* Damien
Daymin/Daymyn. *See* Damon
Daymon. *See* Damon
Dayn. *See* Dan
Dayna. *See* Dana
Daysie/Daysy. *See* Daisy
Dayv. *See* Dave
Dayved/Dayvid. *See* David
Dean, 216
Deana. *See* Diana
Deane. *See* Dean; Diana
Deanna, 217
Deanne. *See* Deanna
Debbi. *See* Debbie

Debbie, 218. *See also* Deborah
Debbora. *See* Deborah
Debbra. *See* Deborah
Debby. *See* Debbie; Deborah
Deberah. *See* Deborah
Debi/Deby. *See* Debbie
Debora. *See* Deborah
Deborah, 219. *See also* Debbie
Deborrah. *See* Deborah
Debra. *See* Debbie; Deborah
Debrah. *See* Deborah
Debs. *See* Debbie
Dede. *See* Diana
Dee. *See* Diana
Deeana/Deeanna. *See* Deanna
Deeloris. *See* Delores
Deen/Deene. *See* Dean
Deena. *See* Geraldine
Deenie. *See* Denise
Deiana. *See* Deanna
Deiniol. *See* Daniel
Dejuan. *See* Devin
Del. *See* Derek
Delina/Deline. *See* Adele
Delly. *See* Adele
Delma. *See* Velma
Delora/Deloria. *See* Lola
Delorcita. *See* Lola
Delores, 220. *See also* Doris; Lola; Lori
Deloris. *See* Delores
Delroy. *See* Leroy
Demion. *See* Damon
Demmoe. *See* Denise
Demyan. *See* Damien
Dena. *See* Deanna
Dene. *See* Dean
Deneice. *See* Denise
Denes/Denese. *See* Dennis
Deni. *See* Denise
Denice. *See* Denise
Denies. *See* Dennis
Denis. *See* Dennis
Denisa. *See* Denise
Denise, 221
Denize. *See* Denise
Dennes/Dennys. *See* Dennis
Dennis, 222
Dennise. *See* Denise
Dennison. *See* Dennis
Denny. *See* Dennis
Denton. *See* Dennis
Denys. *See* Dennis
Denyse. *See* Denise
Derec. *See* Derek
Derek, 223. *See also* Rick
Deric/Derick. *See* Derek
Derik. *See* Derek
Derreck/Derrek. *See* Derek
Derrick. *See* Derek; Rick
Deryck/Deryk. *See* Derek
Deseree. *See* Desiree
Desi. *See* Desiree
Desiderata. *See* Desiree
Desira/Desire. *See* Desiree
Desirae/Desiray. *See* Desiree
Desiree, 224
Desy. *See* Desiree
Desyree. *See* Desiree
Deven/Devon. *See* Devin

Devin, 225. *See also* David
Devinn. *See* Devin
Devonn/Devonne. *See* Devin
Devora/Devorah. *See* Debbie; Deborah
Dewain. *See* Dwayne
Dewayne. *See* Dwayne
Dhana. *See* Donna
Di. *See* Diana
Diahann. *See* Diana
Diana, 226. *See also* Deanna
Diane. *See* Deanna; Diana
Diann. *See* Diana
Dianna/Dianne. *See* Deanna; Diana
Dick. *See* Ricardo; Richard; Rick
Dickie/Dicky. *See* Ricardo; Richard; Rick
Diederick. *See* Derek
Diego. *See* Santiago
Dietrich. *See* Derek
Dill. *See* Dylan
Dillan. *See* Dylan
Dillen/Dillon. *See* Dylan
Dilys. *See* Dylan
Dina. *See* Geraldine
Dino. *See* Dean
Diogo. *See* Santiago
Dionysa. *See* Denise
Dirk. *See* Derek
Doireen/Doirene. *See* Doreen
Dolly. *See* Delores
Dolores/Deloris. *See* Delores
Dolorita. *See* Lola
Dolorris. *See* Delores
Dolph. *See* Rudolph; Rudy
Domenic/Domenik. *See* Dominic
Domenick. *See* Dominic
Domenico. *See* Dominic
Dominic, 227
Dominick/Dominik. *See* Dominic
Don. *See* Donald
Dona. *See* Donna
Donald, 228. *See also* Daniel
Donaleen. *See* Donna
Donall. *See* Donald
Donalld/Danauld. *See* Donald
Doneld. *See* Donald
Donelda/Donella. *See* Donna
Donita. *See* Donna
Donna, 229
Donnah. *See* Donna
Donnald/Donneld. *See* Donald
Donnauld. *See* Donald
Donnelle. *See* Donna
Donnie. *See* Donald
Donnita. *See* Donna
Donny. *See* Donald
Doogie. *See* Doug; Douglas
Dora. *See* Doreen; Doris; Dorothy
Dorathy/Dorethy. *See* Dorothy
Dorean/Doreane. *See* Doreen
Doreen, 230. *See also* Doris; Dorothy
Doreene/Dorene. *See* Doreen
Dorete. *See* Dorothy
Dorette. *See* Doreen
Dori. *See* Doris; Dorothy
Doria. *See* Doreen; Doris; Dorothy
Dorice. *See* Doris
Dorinda. *See* Doreen; Doris
Doris, 231. *See also* Delores; Doreen;
    Dorothy

Dorothea. *See* Doreen; Doris; Dorothy
Dorothee/Dorothey. *See* Dorothy
Dorothi/Dorothie. *See* Dorothy
Dorothy, 232. *See also* Doreen; Doris
Dorres. *See* Doris
Dorris/Dorrys. *See* Doris
Dory. *See* Doreen; Doris; Dorothy
Dorys. *See* Doris
Dosia. *See* Dorothy
Dot. *See* Dorothy
Dottie. *See* Dorothy
Doug, 233. *See also* Douglas
Dougal. *See* Doug; Douglas
Dougald. *See* Douglas
Dougie. *See* Doug; Douglas
Douglas, 234. *See also* Doug
Douglass. *See* Doug; Douglas
Dougles. *See* Douglas
Douglis/Douglys. *See* Douglas
Dougliss. *See* Douglas
Dousten. *See* Dustin
Doustin/Doustyn. *See* Dustin
Drena. *See* Andrea
Drew, 235. *See also* Andrew
Drewe. *See* Drew
Droo/Drue. *See* Drew
Duane. *See* Dwayne
Dubdara. *See* Dwayne
Dubhan. *See* Dwayne
Dug/Dugg. *See* Doug
Dugaid. *See* Doug
Dugal. *See* Doug; Douglas
Dugglas. *See* Douglas
Dugh. *See* Doug
Duncan, 236
Dunham. *See* Duncan
Dunkan/Dunkin. *See* Duncan
Dunky. *See* Duncan
Dunley. *See* Duncan
Dunlop. *See* Duncan
Dunmore. *See* Duncan
Dunn. *See* Duncan
Dunstan. *See* Duncan; Dustin
Dusten/Dustyn. *See* Dustin
Dustin, 237
Dustinn. *See* Dustin
Dusty. *See* Dustin
Duwain. *See* Dwayne
Dwain/Dwane. *See* Dwayne
Dwayne, 238
Dyan. *See* Diana
Dyana/Dyanna. *See* Diana
Dylan, 239
Dylann/Dyllen. *See* Dylan
Dylen/Dylin. *See* Dylan
Dylis. *See* Dylan

Eadwin/Eadwinn. *See* Edwin
Ean/Eann. *See* Ian
Earnest. *See* Ernest; Ernie
Earnist. *See* Ernest
Earrnest. *See* Ernest
Earv/Earve. *See* Irv
Earvin/Earving. *See* Irv; Irving
Earvyng. *See* Irving
Eave. *See* Eve
Ed, 240. *See also* Edgar; Edward; Edwin; Ted
Eda. *See* Edith
Edd. *See* Ed

Eddan. *See* Ed
Eddgar/Eddger. *See* Edgar
Eddie. *See* Ed; Edward; Edwin; Ted
Eddy. *See* Ed; Edward
Edelie. *See* Adele
Edgar, 241. *See also* Ed; Edward; Edwin
Edger. *See* Edgar
Edgir/Edgyr. *See* Edgar
Edie. *See* Edith
Edith, 242
Editha/Edithe. *See* Edith
Edlin. *See* Edward; Edwin
Edmund. *See* Ed; Edgar; Edward; Edwin
Edom. *See* Ed
Edouard. *See* Edward
Eduard. *See* Edward
Eduardo. *See* Ed
Edward, 243. *See also* Ed; Edgar; Ted
Edwerd. *See* Edward
Edwin, 244. *See also* Ed; Edgar; Edward
Edwinn. *See* Edwin
Edwyn. *See* Edward; Edwin
Edwyrd. *See* Edward
Edyth. *See* Edith
Edytha/Edythe. *See* Edith
Eeli/Eely. *See* Eli
Eena. *See* Ina
Eenes/Eenez. *See* Inez
Eeve. *See* Eve
Ehd. *See* Ed
Ehdwin/Ehdwyn. *See* Edwin
Ehdwinn/Ehdwynn. *See* Edwin
Eibe. *See* Abe
Eilean. *See* Eileen
Eileen, 245. *See also* Eleanor; Helene
Eilleen. *See* Eileen
Eily. *See* Eileen
Eireen/Eirene. *See* Irene
Eirik. *See* Eric
Eiris/Eirys. *See* Iris
Eister. *See* Esther
Eiv/Eive. *See* Eve
Ela/Elah. *See* Ella
Elaina. *See* Elaine; Elena; Ellen; Helene
Elaine, 246. *See also* Eleanor; Elena; Ellen;
    Helen; Helene
Elana. *See* Elaine; Elena; Helen
Elane/Elayne. *See* Elaine
Elayna. *See* Elena
Eleanor, 247. *See also* Eileen; Elaine; Elena;
    Ella; Ellen; Helen; Helene; Nell; Nellie;
    Nora
Eleanora. *See* Eleanor; Nora
Elen. *See* Eleanor; Ellen
Elena, 248. *See also* Elaine; Eleanor; Ellen;
    Helen; Nell; Nellie
Eleni. *See* Ellen
Elenna. *See* Elena
Elenora/Eleonora. *See* Eleanor
Elenore/Eleonore. *See* Eleanor
Eleshia. *See* Alicia
Elga. *See* Olga
Eli, 249. *See also* Elias
Elianora. *See* Eleanor
Elias, 250. *See also* Eli; Ellis
Elice. *See* Ellis
Elicia. *See* Alicia
Elie. *See* Elias; Ellis
Eliesa. *See* Eliza

Eliese. *See* Elyse
Elighza. *See* Eliza
Elihu. *See* Eli; Elias
Elijah. *See* Eli; Ellis
Elin. *See* Ellen
Elinor. *See* Eleanor; Helene
Elinore. *See* Eleanor
Eliot. *See* Elias
Elis. *See* Ellis
Elisa. *See* Alicia; Alyssa; Eliza; Elizabeth; Elyse
Elisabet/Elisabetta. *See* Betty; Eliza; Elizabeth
Elisabeth. *See* Beth; Betsy; Elizabeth; Elyse
Elise. *See* Alice; Alicia; Allison; Alyssa; Eliza; Elizabeth; Elyse
Elisha. *See* Alicia; Eli
Elissa. *See* Alicia; Alyssa; Elyse
Eliza, 251. *See also* Elizabeth; Elyse
Elizabeth, 252. *See also* Beth; Bethany; Betsy; Betty; Eliza; Elyse; Lisa
Elizabetta. *See* Betty; Eliza; Elizabeth
Elizahbeth. *See* Elizabeth
Elizer. *See* Eli
Ella, 253. *See also* Eleanor; Ellen; Helene; Nell; Nellie
Elladine. *See* Eleanor
Ellah. *See* Ella
Ellaine/Ellayne. *See* Elaine
Ellan. *See* Ellen
Elle. *See* Eleanor
Elleanor/Elleanora. *See* Eleanor
Ellen, 254. *See also* Eileen; Elaine; Eleanor; Elena; Ella; Helen; Helene; Marilyn; Nell; Nellie
Ellene. *See* Eleanor
Ellenor. *See* Ellen
Ellenore. *See* Eleanor
Elleonor. *See* Eleanor
Elletta/Ellette. *See* Ella
Elli. *See* Ella; Ellen
Ellias. *See* Elias
Ellice. *See* Ellis
Ellie. *See* Eleanor; Ella; Ellen; Helene; Nell; Nellie
Ellin/Ellon. *See* Ellen
Ellina. *See* Ella
Ellinor/Ellinore. *See* Eleanor
Elliot. *See* Elias
Ellis, 255. *See also* Elias
Elly. *See* Ella
Ellyas. *See* Elias
Ellyn. *See* Ellen; Helene
Ellys. *See* Ellis
Elna. *See* Eleanor
Elnora. *See* Eleanor
Eloi. *See* Ellis
Eloisa. *See* Lois; Louise
Eloise. *See* Louise
Elon. *See* Ellen
Eloy. *See* Ellis
Elroy. *See* Leroy; Roy
Elsbeth. *See* Betty; Eliza; Elizabeth
Else. *See* Eliza; Elizabeth
Elsie. *See* Chelsea; Eliza; Elizabeth
Elspeth. *See* Betsy; Betty; Eliza; Elizabeth
Ely. *See* Eli; Elias
Elyas. *See* Elias; Ellis
Elycia. *See* Alicia

Elyn. *See* Eleanor; Ellen
Elys. *See* Ellis
Elysa. *See* Alyssa
Elyse, 256. *See also* Alice; Allison; Alyssa
Elyssa. *See* Alicia; Allison; Elyse
Ema/Emah. *See* Emma
Emanuel. *See* Manuel
Emeli/Emilie. *See* Emily
Emelia. *See* Amelia
Emelina/Emeline. *See* Emily
Emely/Emelyn. *See* Emily
Emera. *See* Emily
Emila. *See* Emily
Emilee/Emiley. *See* Emily
Emileigh. *See* Emily
Emilia/Emilie. *See* Amelia; Emily
Emily, 257. *See also* Amelia; Emma; Millie
Emma, 258. *See also* Emily
Emmah. *See* Emma
Emmalina/Emmaline. *See* Emma
Emmanuel. *See* Manuel
Emme/Emmeh. *See* Emma
Emmelia. *See* Amelia
Emmeline. *See* Emma
Emmie. *See* Emma
Emmila. *See* Emma
Emmilia. *See* Amelia
Emylia. *See* Amelia
Ena. *See* Ina
Enora. *See* Eleanor
Enreke. *See* Enrique
Enreque/Enrike. *See* Enrique
Enric. *See* Enrique
Enrico. *See* Enrique; Henry
Enrikay. *See* Enrique
Enrique, 259. *See also* Hank; Henry; Rick
Era/Eri. *See* Erica
Ereca. *See* Erica
Erena/Erene. *See* Erin
Erenna. *See* Erin
Eric, 260. *See also* Rick
Erica, 261
Erich/Erick. *See* Eric
Ericka/Erika. *See* Erica
Erik. *See* Eric
Erin, 262
Erina/Erinn. *See* Erin
Erknee. *See* Ernie
Erma, 263. *See also* Irma
Ermah. *See* Erma; Irma
Ermando. *See* Armando
Ermanno/Ermano. *See* Herman
Ermma/Ermmah. *See* Irma
Ern. *See* Ernest
Erna. *See* Ernestine
Ernaline. *See* Ernestine
Ernastine/Ernastyne. *See* Ernestine
Ernee. *See* Ernie
Ernest, 264. *See also* Ernie
Ernestina/Ernestyna. *See* Ernestine
Ernestine, 265
Ernesto. *See* Ernest; Ernie
Ernestyne. *See* Ernestine
Ernie, 266. *See also* Ernest
Ernist. *See* Ernest
Erno. *See* Ernest
Ernst. *See* Ernest
Erny. *See* Ernie
Erric/Errick. *See* Eric

Errica/Erricka. *See* Erica
Errik. *See* Eric
Errika. *See* Erica
Errin/Errinn. *See* Erin
Errnest. *See* Ernest
Erryn/Errynn. *See* Erin
Erv. *See* Irv; Irving
Erving/Ervyng. *See* Irving
Eryn/Erynn. *See* Erin
Esperance. *See* Hope
Esperanza. *See* Hope
Essther. *See* Esther
Esta. *See* Esther
Esteban. *See* Stephen; Steve; Steven
Estel/Estele. *See* Estelle
Estell. *See* Estelle
Estella. *See* Estelle; Stella
Estelle, 267. *See also* Stella
Ester/Esterre. *See* Esther
Esteve. *See* Stephen; Steve; Steven
Esther, 268. *See also* Estelle
Estir. *See* Esther
Estrella. *See* Estelle; Stella
Estrellita. *See* Estelle
Eszter. *See* Esther
Etiénne. *See* Stephen; Steve; Steven
Eugene. *See* Gene
Eva, 269. *See also* Eve; Evelyn
Evah. *See* Eva
Evan, 270. *See also* Everett; Ian; Ivan; John; Scan; Shane; Shawn
Evana. *See* Yvonne
Evann. *See* Evan
Evans. *See* Evan
Eve, 271. *See also* Eva; Evelyn
Evelin. *See* Evelyn
Evelina. *See* Eva; Evelyn
Eveline. *See* Eve
Evelyn, 272. *See also* Eileen; Eva; Eve
Evelyna. *See* Evelyn
Evelyne/Evelynn. *See* Evelyn
Even/Evenn. *See* Evan
Everard. *See* Everett
Everet. *See* Everett
Everett, 273. *See also* Evan
Everit/Everitt. *See* Everett
Evett. *See* Yvette
Evette. *See* Eva; Eve; Evelyn; Yvette
Evie. *See* Eva; Eve; Evelyn
Evilina. *See* Eve
Evin/Evinn. *See* Evan
Eviret/Evirit. *See* Everett
Evita. *See* Eva; Eve; Evelyn
Evone. *See* Eve
Evonn. *See* Yvonne
Evonne. *See* Eva; Evelyn; Yvette; Yvonne
Evyn/Evynn. *See* Evan
Ewan. *See* Evan
Ewen. *See* Evan; Owen
Eyris. *See* Iris

Fae. *See* Faye
Faith. *See* Faye
Faleesha. *See* Felicia
Falesha/Falisha. *See* Felicia
Faleysha. *See* Felicia
Falicea/Falicia. *See* Felicia
Falycia. *See* Felicia
Fan. *See* Fannie

Gerardo. *See* Gerald
Gerda. *See* Gertrude
Gerhard. *See* Garrett; Gerald
Geri. *See* Geraldine; Gerry
Gerie. *See* Gerry
Gerilyn. *See* Gerry
Gerinimo. *See* Jerome
Gerlach. *See* Garrett; Gary
Germain/Germaine. *See* Jermaine
Germayne. *See* Jermaine
Geroam/Gerome. *See* Jerome
Gerold. *See* Gerald
Gerrald. *See* Gerald; Gerry
Gerrard. *See* Garrett; Gerry
Gerri. *See* Gerry; Jerome
Gerrie. *See* Gerry; Jerry
Gerrilyn. *See* Gerry
Gerrit. *See* Garrett; Gerald
Gerritt. *See* Garrett; Gary
Gerrold. *See* Gerald; Gerry; Jerry
Gerry, 302. *See also* Gerald; Geraldine;
   Jerome; Jerry
Gert/Gerta. *See* Gertrude
Gerti/Gertie. *See* Gertrude
Gertraud. *See* Gertrude
Gertrood. *See* Gertrude
Gertrud/Gertruda. *See* Gertrude
Gertrude, 303. *See also* Trudy
Gery. *See* Gerry; Jerry
Gi. *See* Guy
Giacobo. *See* Jacob
Giacomo/Giacopo. *See* Jacob
Gian. *See* John; Juan
Gillian. *See* Jill
Gina, 304. *See also* Jean; Regina; Virginia
Ginevra. *See* Genevieve
Ginia. *See* Virginia
Ginni/Ginny. *See* Virginia
Ginnie. *See* Virginia
Giordano. *See* Jordan
Giorgina. *See* Gina
Giorgio. *See* Jorge
Giovanni. *See* John; Juan; Sean; Shane;
   Shawn
Giraldo. *See* Gerald
Giulia. *See* Julia; Julie
Giulian/Giulius. *See* Julian
Giulio. *See* Julian; Julio; Julius
Giulya. *See* Julia
Giuseppe. *See* Joe; José; Joseph
Giusto. *See* Justin
Glen, 305. *See also* Glenn
Glendower. *See* Glen; Glenn
Glenn, 306. *See also* Glen
Glenton. *See* Glen; Glenn
Glentworth. *See* Glenn
Glenvil/Glenville. *See* Glen; Glenn
Glenworth. *See* Glen
Gloria, 307
Gloriah. *See* Gloria
Glorria/Glorriah. *See* Gloria
Glory/Glorya. *See* Gloria
Godfrey. *See* Geoffrey; Jeff; Jeffrey
Gordan/Gorden. *See* Gordon
Gordey/Gordie. *See* Gordon
Gordon, 308
Gordy/Gordyn. *See* Gordon
Grace, 309
Gracey/Gracie. *See* Grace

Graece/Graice. *See* Grace
Grant, 310
Grante/Grantt. *See* Grant
Grantley. *See* Grant
Granville. *See* Grant
Grayce. *See* Grace
Greeta. *See* Gretchen
Greg, 311. *See also* Craig; Gregory
Gregg. *See* Craig; Greg; Gregory
Greggory. *See* Gregory
Gregor. *See* Greg; Gregory
Gregory, 312. *See also* Greg
Grehg/Grehgg. *See* Greg
Greig. *See* Greg; Gregory
Gret. *See* Margaret; Margarita; Marguerite
Greta. *See* Gretchen; Margaret; Margarita;
   Marguerite
Gretchen, 313. *See also* Margaret; Margarita;
   Marguerite
Gretchin. *See* Gretchen
Gretel. *See* Gretchen; Margaret
Grethel. *See* Gretchen
Grettchen/Grettchin. *See* Gretchen
Grigor. *See* Gregory
Gualterio. *See* Walter
Guen/Guenne. *See* Gwen
Guglielmo. *See* William; Willie
Guhs/Guhss. *See* Gus
Guido. *See* Guy
Guillaume. *See* Bill; Billie; Guillermo;
   William; Willie
Guillermo, 314. *See also* Bill; Billie; William;
   Willie
Guinevere. *See* Jennifer
Guiyermo. *See* Guillermo
Gus, 315
Guss. *See* Gus
Gustaf/Gustaff. *See* Gus
Gustav/Gustave. *See* Gus
Gustavus. *See* Gus
Guy, 316
Gwen, 317. *See also* Gwendolyn; Wendy
Gwendolyn. *See* Gwen; Wendy
Gwenette. *See* Gwen
Gwenn. *See* Gwen
Gwenna/Gwenne. *See* Gwen
Gwenni. *See* Gwen
Gwyn. *See* Gwen
Gwyneth. *See* Gwen
Gwynna/Gwynne. *See* Gwen

Hadrian. *See* Adrian
Haervey. *See* Harvey
Hal. *See* Hank; Harold; Harry; Henry
Halina. *See* Helen
Hamish. *See* Jacob
Hana. *See* Annette; Hannah
Hanah. *See* Hannah
Hanck/Hankk. *See* Hank
Hank, 318. *See also* Enrique; Henry
Hanna. *See* Annette; Hannah; Marianne;
   Mary Ann
Hannah, 319. *See also* Bethany; Marianne;
   Mary Ann; Nancy
Hans. *See* Ian; John; Jonathan; Juan; Sean;
   Shane; Shawn
Harald/Haroldd. *See* Harold
Harbert. *See* Herb; Herbert
Hari/Harie. *See* Harry

Hariet/Hariett. *See* Harriet
Hariette. *See* Harriet
Hariot/Hariott. *See* Harriet
Harman. *See* Armando; Herman
Harmon. *See* Herman
Harold, 320. *See also* Harry
Haroldd. *See* Harold
Haroun. *See* Aaron
Harrald/Harraldd. *See* Harold
Harrey. *See* Harry
Harri/Harrie. *See* Harry
Harriet, 321. *See also* Hattie
Harriett/Harriette. *See* Harriet
Harrietta. *See* Harriet; Hattie
Harriot/Harriott. *See* Harriet
Harris. *See* Harry
Harrison. *See* Harry
Harrold/Harroldd. *See* Harold
Harry, 322. *See also* Enrique; Hank; Harold;
   Henry
Harv/Harve. *See* Harvey
Harvee/Harvie. *See* Harvey
Harvey, 323
Harvy. *See* Harvey
Hary. *See* Harry
Hatsie/Hatsy. *See* Harriet; Hattie
Hattey/Hatti. *See* Hattie
Hattie, 324. *See also* Harriet
Hatty. *See* Harriet; Hattie
Havier. *See* Javier
Heath. *See* Heather
Heathcliff. *See* Cliff
Heather, 325
Heatherre/Heathyrre. *See* Heather
Heathir/Heathyr. *See* Heather
Hecctor. *See* Hector
Heckie. *See* Hector
Hecktor/Hecktore. *See* Hector
Hecter. *See* Hector
Hector, 326
Hectore. *See* Hector
Hedda. *See* Heidi
Hedia. *See* Heidi
Hedy. *See* Heidi
Heida. *See* Heidi
Heidee. *See* Heidi
Heidelinde. *See* Heidi
Heidi, 327
Heidie/Heidy. *See* Heidi
Heindrick/Heindrik. *See* Hank
Heinrick. *See* Hank
Heinrik. *See* Henry
Heinz. *See* Henry
Heitor. *See* Hector
Helean/Heleane. *See* Helene
Heleanor. *See* Eleanor
Heleen. *See* Helene
Helen, 328. *See also* Eileen; Elaine; Eleanor;
   Elena; Ellen; Helene; Nell;
Nellie
Helena. *See* Helen; Helene; Nell; Nellie
Helene, 329. *See also* Eileen; Elaine; Ellen;
   Helen; Nell; Nellie
Helga. *See* Olga
Helin. *See* Helen
Helleen/Helleene. *See* Helene
Hellen. *See* Helen; Helene
Hellene. *See* Helene
Hellenor. *See* Helene

Hellin/Hellyn. *See* Helen
Heloisa/Heloise. *See* Louise
Helyn. *See* Helen
Hendrick. *See* Henry
Hendrik. *See* Enrique
Henning. *See* Henry
Hennrie/Hennry. *See* Henry
Henri. *See* Hank; Henry
Henrie. *See* Henry
Henrieta/Henrietta. *See* Harriet; Hattie
Henrik. *See* Enrique; Hank
Henrika. *See* Harriet; Hattie
Henry, 330. *See also* Enrique; Hank; Harry
Henryetta. *See* Harriet; Hattie
Herb, 331. *See also* Herbert
Herbb. *See* Herb
Herbbert/Herbertt. *See* Herbert
Herbert, 332. *See also* Herb
Herbie. *See* Herb; Herbert
Heriberto. *See* Herb; Herbert
Herman, 333. *See also* Armando
Hermann. *See* Herman
Hermie. *See* Herman
Hermin/Herminn. *See* Herman
Hermon. *See* Armando; Herman
Hermonn. *See* Herman
Hermyn/Hermynn. *See* Herman
Herold/Herrold. *See* Harold
Herrick. *See* Eric; Harold
Herve/Hervey. *See* Harvey
Hester. *See* Esther
Hesus. *See* Jesus
Hetha. *See* Heather
Hether/Hethir. *See* Heather
Hetta. *See* Heidi
Hetti/Hettie. *See* Harriet; Hattie
Hew/Hewe. *See* Hugh
Hewgo. *See* Hugo
Hewson. *See* Hugh; Hugo
Heydee. *See* Heidi
Heydi/Heydie. *See* Heidi
Hierome. *See* Jerome
Hilarey/Hilari. *See* Hillary
Hilaria/Hilarie. *See* Hillary
Hilario/Hilarion. *See* Hillary
Hilerey/Hilery. *See* Hillary
Hileri/Hilerie. *See* Hillary
Hilery *See* Hillary
Hillarey. *See* Hillary
Hillari/Hillarie. *See* Hillary
Hillary, 334
Hillerey/Hillerie. *See* Hillary
Hilleri/Hillery. *See* Hillary
Hilliary. *See* Hillary
Hoepe. *See* Hope
Hohmer. *See* Homer
Hohmir/Hohmyr. *See* Homer
Holla. *See* Holly
Hollee/Holley. *See* Holly
Hollena. *See* Holly
Holli/Hollie. *See* Holly
Holly, 335
Holmer. *See* Homer
Holmes. *See* Homer
Homer, 336
Homeros/Homerus. *See* Homer
Homir/Homyr. *See* Homer
Honora. *See* Nora
Hoolio. *See* Julio

Hope, 337
Hose. *See* José
Hosea. *See* Jesus; Joshua
How. *See* Howard
Howard, 338
Howell. *See* Howard
Howerd. *See* Howard
Howie. *See* Howard
Hudson. *See* Hugh; Hugo
Huegues. *See* Hugh; Hugo
Hugh, 339. *See also* Hugo
Hughes. *See* Hugh
Hughie. *See* Hugh; Hugo
Hugo, 340. *See also* Hugh
Huleo/Hulio. *See* Julio
Hulyo. *See* Julio
Huw. *See* Hugh
Hyacinth. *See* Cynthia
Hydee. *See* Heidi

Iacopo/Iacovo. *See* Jacob
Iago. *See* Jacob; Santiago
Iain/Iann. *See* Ian
Iakob/Iakov. *See* Jacob
Iakobos. *See* Jacob
Ian, 341. *See also* Ivan; Jack; Jan; John;
     Jonathan; Juan; Sean; Shane; Shawn
Ieronim. *See* Jerome
Igor. *See* Jorge
Ike/Ikey. *See* Isaac
Ilaine/Ilane. *See* Elaine
Ilana. *See* Helen
Ilean/Ileen. *See* Eileen
Ilecia. *See* Alicia
Ilene. *See* Eileen; Helen; Helene
Ilese. *See* Elyse
Ilicia. *See* Alicia
Ilise. *See* Alice; Alicia; Alyssa
Ilissa. *See* Alyssa
Illayne. *See* Elaine
Ilona. *See* Helen; Helene
Ilse. *See* Eliza; Elizabeth
Ilycia. *See* Alicia
Ilysa. *See* Elyse
Ilyse. *See* Alice; Alicia; Allison; Alyssa; Elyse
Ina, 342. *See also* Agnes
Ines. *See* Agnes; Inez
Inez, 343. *See also* Agnes
Inna. *See* Ina
Inrike. *See* Enrique
Inrique. *See* Enrique
Iola. *See* Yolanda
Iolanda/Iolande. *See* Yolanda
Iolanthe. *See* Yolanda
Ireen. *See* Irene
Irena *See* Irene
Irene, 344
Irenie. *See* Irene
Irina. *See* Erin; Irene
Irine. *See* Irene
Iris, 345
Irisa. *See* Iris
Irma, 346. *See also* Erma
Irmah. *See* Erma; Irma
Irmgard. *See* Erma; Irma
Irmigarde. *See* Erma; Irma
Irmina/Irmine. *See* Erma; Irma
Irmma/Irmmah. *See* Irma
Irmtraud. *See* Erma; Irma

Irv, 347. *See also* Irving
Irve. *See* Irv
Irvin/Irvine. *See* Irv; Irving
Irving, 348. *See also* Irv
Irvyng. *See* Irving
Iryne. *See* Irene
Irys. *See* Iris
Isa. *See* Isabelle
Isaac, 349
Isaak. *See* Isaac
Isabel. *See* Betsy; Eliza; Elizabeth; Isabelle
Isabela/Isabella. *See* Isabelle
Isabell. *See* Isabelle
Isabelle, 350. *See also* Eliza; Elizabeth
Isac/Isak. *See* Isaac
Isack. *See* Isaac
Iser. *See* Israel
Ishtar. *See* Esther
Isic. *See* Isaac
Isobel/Isobell. *See* Isabelle
Isobelle. *See* Isabelle
Israel, 351
Israell. *See* Israel
Issie. *See* Isabelle
Issur. *See* Israel
Issy. *See* Isabelle; Israel
Iva/Ivah. *See* Eva
Ivan, 352. *See also* Evan; Ian; Jack; Jan; John;
     Jonathan; Juan; Sean; Shane; Shawn
Ivana/Ivanna. *See* Yvonne
Ivann. *See* Ivan
Iven. *See* Ivan
Ivett. *See* Yvette
Ivetta/Ivette. *See* Yvette
Ivin/Ivinn. *See* Ivan
Ivonn. *See* Yvonne
Ivonna/Ivonne. *See* Yvette; Yvonne
Ivyn. *See* Ivan
Iwan. *See* Ian
Izabel/Izabela. *See* Isabelle
Izabell/Izabella. *See* Isabelle
Izabelle. *See* Isabelle
Izak/Izik. *See* Isaac
Izobel/Isobell. *See* Isabelle
Izobelle. *See* Isabelle
Izrael/Izraell. *See* Israel
Izzie/Izzy. *See* Isabelle

J. *See* Jay
Jac. *See* Jack
Jack, 353. *See also* Ian; Ivan; Jacob; Jake;
     John; Juan
Jackee/Jackey. *See* Jackie
Jacki. *See* Jackie; Jacqueline
Jackie, 354. *See also* Jack; Jacqueline
Jacklin. *See* Jacqueline
Jacklyn. *See* Jackie; Jacqueline
Jacko. *See* Jacob
Jackson. *See* Jack; Jake
Jacky. *See* Jackie; Jacob
Jaclyn. *See* Jackie; Jacqueline
Jaclynne. *See* Jacqueline
Jaco/Jacobo. *See* Jacob
Jacob, 355. *See also* Israel; Jake; James; Jay
Jacoline. *See* Jacqueline
Jacquee. *See* Jackie
Jacquelin. *See* Jacqueline
Jacquelina. *See* Jackie
Jacqueline, 356. *See also* Jackie

Jacquelyn. *See* Jackie; Jacqueline
Jacquelyne/Jacquelynne. *See* Jacqueline
Jacques. *See* Jack; Jacob; Jake; James
Jacquet. *See* Jacob
Jacquetta. *See* Jackie
Jacquey. *See* Jackie
Jacqui. *See* Jackie; Jacqueline
Jacquie. *See* Jackie
Jacquilen/Jacquilyn. *See* Jacqueline
Jacquiline. *See* Jacqueline
Jacub. *See* Jacob
Jae. *See* Jay
Jago. *See* Jacob; Santiago
Jaike. *See* Jake
Jaime, 357. *See also* Jacob; James; Jamie; Jim
Jaimee/Jaimi. *See* Jaime
Jaimes. *See* James
Jaimey. *See* Jaime; Jamie
Jaine. *See* Jane
Jaisen/Jaison. *See* Jason
Jak. *See* Jack
Jake, 358. *See also* Jacob
Jakie. *See* Jacob; Jake
Jakob. *See* Jacob; Jake
Jakov. *See* Jacob
Jakub. *See* Jacob
Jamaine. *See* Jermaine
Jamee. *See* Jaime; Jamie
Jamela. *See* Jamie
Jamell. *See* James
James, 359. *See also* Jacob; Jaime; Jamie; Jim; Santiago
Jamesie. *See* Jacob
Jamesina. *See* Jaime; Jamie
Jameson. *See* James; Jamie; Jim
Jamey/Jamez. *See* Jacob
Jami. *See* Benjamin; Jaime
Jamie, 360. *See also* Jacob; Jaime; James; Jim
Jamila. *See* Jaime
Jamille. *See* Jamie
Jamsey. *See* Jacob
Jan, 361. *See also* Ian; Jack; Janet; Janice; John; Juan; Sean; Shane; Shawn
Jana. *See* Jan; Jane; Janet; Janice
Jane, 362. *See also* Jan; Janet; Janice; Jean; Jeanette; Joan; Joanne
Janek. *See* Jack
Janelle. *See* Jan
Janet, 363. *See also* Jane; Janice; Jean; Jeanette
Janetta. *See* Janet
Janette. *See* Jan; Janet
Jani/Jania. *See* Janice
Janica. *See* Janice
Janice, 364. *See also* Jan; Jane; Janet
Janie. *See* Janice
Janina. *See* Nina
Janine. *See* Jan; Jane; Janet; Janice; Jean; Jeanette
Janis/Janiss. *See* Janice
Janit. *See* Janet
Jann/Janne. *See* Jan
Janna. *See* Janice
Jannel/Jannelle. *See* Janice
Jannet. *See* Janet
Janni. *See* Janice
Jannice. *See* Janice
Jannis/Janniss. *See* Janice
Jannit/Jannitt. *See* Janet
Janny/Jany. *See* Janice

Jannyce. *See* Janice
Janyce. *See* Janice
Jaquelin/Jaqueline. *See* Jacqueline
Jaquelyn. *See* Jacqueline
Jaquetta. *See* Jacqueline
Jarad/Jarid. *See* Jared
Jared, 365. *See also* Jordan
Jarman. *See* Jermaine
Jarod. *See* Jared
Jarrad. *See* Jared
Jarred/Jarrod. *See* Jared
Jase. *See* Jason
Jasen. *See* Jason
Jasin/Jasyn. *See* Jason
Jasmin. *See* Jasmine
Jasmine, 366
Jasmyn/Jasmyne. *See* Jasmine
Jason, 367. *See also* Jay
Javier, 368
Javierre. *See* Javier
Jay, 369. *See also* Jacob; Jake; Jason
Jaye. *See* Jay
Jayke. *See* Jake
Jayme. *See* Jacob; Jaime; Jamie
Jaymee. *See* Jaime; Jamie
Jaymes. *See* James
Jaymi/Jaymie. *See* Jaime
Jayne. *See* Jane; Janice
Jaysen. *See* Jason
Jaysin/Jayson. *See* Jason
Jazmine. *See* Jasmine
Jeafrey. *See* Jeffrey
Jean, 370. *See also* Genevieve; Jane; Janet; Jeanette; Joan; Joanne
Jeana. *See* Gina; Jean; Jeanette
Jeanc. *See* Genevieve; Jean
Jeanelle. *See* Jean
Jeanete. *See* Jeanette
Jeanette, 371. *See also* Genevieve; Janet; Jean
Jeanic. *See* Genevieve; Gina; Jean; Jeanette; Joanne
Jeanine. *See* Jean; Jeanette
Jeanne. *See* Genevieve; Jane; Jean
Jeannetta/Jeannette. *See* Jeanette
Jeannine. *See* Jeanette
Jeany. *See* Gina
Jed. *See* Gerald
Jeen/Jeene. *See* Gene; Jean
Jeena. *See* Gina; Regina
Jeesus. *See* Jesus
Jefery. *See* Geoffrey; Jeff
Jeff, 372. *See also* Geoffrey; Jeffrey
Jefferey/Jeffery. *See* Geoffrey; Jeffrey
Jefferies. *See* Geoffrey
Jefferson. *See* Geoffrey; Jeff; Jeffrey
Jeffree/Jeffrie. *See* Geoffrey; Jeffrey
Jeffrey, 373. *See also* Geoffrey; Jeff
Jeffry. *See* Geoffrey; Jeffrey
Jeffy. *See* Jeff
Jefree. *See* Jeffrey
Jefry. *See* Jeff
Jelena. *See* Helene
Jem. *See* Jeremiah; Jeremy; Jermaine
Jen. *See* Jennifer; Jenny
Jena. *See* Gina; Jenny; Regina
Jenaveave/Jenaveeve. *See* Genevieve
Jenavive. *See* Genevieve
Jenee. *See* Jenny
Jenefer. *See* Jennifer

Jenett/Jenette. *See* Jeanette
Jenetta. *See* Janet
Jeneveave/Jeneveeve. *See* Genevieve
Jenevive. *See* Genevieve
Jeney. *See* Jenny
Jeni/Jenie. *See* Jenny
Jenifer/Jeniffer. *See* Jennifer
Jeniveave/Jeniveeve. *See* Genevieve
Jenivive. *See* Genevieve
Jenn. *See* Jennifer; Jenny
Jenna. *See* Jennifer
Jennee/Jenney. *See* Jenny
Jennetta. *See* Janet; Jean
Jennette. *See* Jeanette
Jenni/Jennie. *See* Jennifer; Jenny
Jennica. *See* Jennifer; Jenny
Jennifer, 374. *See also* Jenny
Jenniffer. *See* Jennifer
Jenniver. *See* Jenny
Jenny, 375. *See also* Jennifer
Jennyfer. *See* Jennifer
Jenoveave/Jenoveeve. *See* Genevieve
Jenovive. *See* Genevieve
Jeny. *See* Jenny
Jenyfer. *See* Jennifer
Jenyveave/Jenyveeve. *See* Genevieve
Jenyvive. *See* Genevieve
Jeoffroi. *See* Jeff
Jeorge. *See* George
Jerad. *See* Jared
Jerald. *See* Gerald; Gerry
Jeraldean. *See* Geraldine
Jeraldeen/Jeraldene. *See* Geraldine
Jeramy. *See* Jeremy
Jeremaea. *See* Jeremiah
Jereme. *See* Jeremy
Jeremey/Jeremi. *See* Jeremy
Jeremia. *See* Jeremiah
Jeremiah, 376. *See also* Jeremy; Jerome; Jerry
Jeremie. *See* Jeremy
Jeremy, 377. *See also* Jeremiah; Jerome; Jerry
Jeremyah. *See* Jeremiah
Jeri. *See* Geraldine; Gerry
Jerie. *See* Gerry
Jerilene. *See* Gerry
Jerimy. *See* Jeremy
Jermain. *See* Jermaine
Jermaine, 378
Jermane/Jermayne. *See* Jermaine
Jeroam. *See* Jerome
Jerold. *See* Gerald; Gerry
Jerome, 379. *See also* Jeremiah; Jeremy
Jerrald. *See* Gerald
Jerrard. *See* Jeremy; Jerry
Jerremiah. *See* Jeremiah
Jerri. *See* Gerry; Jerome; Jerry
Jerrie. *See* Gerry; Jerry
Jerrold. *See* Gerald; Jared; Jerry
Jerry, 380. *See also* Gerald; Gerry; Jared; Jeremiah; Jeremy; Jermaine; Jerome
Jery. *See* Gerry; Jerry
Jes. *See* Jesse
Jesaca/Jesca. *See* Jessica
Jesica/Jesicah. *See* Jessica
Jess. *See* Jesse; Jessica; Jessie
Jessa. *See* Jessica; Jessie
Jessaca/Jesseca. *See* Jessica
Jessalin. *See* Jessica
Jessalyn. *See* Jessie

Jesse, 381. *See also* Jessie
JesSee. *See* Jesse
Jessey. *See* Jesse; Jessie
Jessi/Jessy. *See* Jessica; Jessie
Jessica, 382. *See also* Jessie
Jessicah. *See* Jessica
Jessie, 383. *See also* Jesse; Jessica
Jesus, 384
Jeulie. *See* Julie
Jeulius. *See* Julius
Jewelie. *See* Julie
Jey/Jeyes. *See* Jay
Jezus. *See* Jesus
Jil. *See* Jill
Jilian. *See* Jill
Jill, 385
Jille. *See* Jill
Jilleen. *See* Jill
Jillian/Jilliana. *See* Jill
Jillie/Jilly. *See* Jill
Jim, 386. *See also* Jacob; Jaime; James; Jamie
Jimi. *See* Jim
Jimm. *See* Jim
Jimmie. *See* Jacob
Jimmy. *See* Jaime; James; Jamie; Jim
Jina. *See* Gina
Jitta. *See* Judy
Jiulia. *See* Julia
Jiulian. *See* Julian
Jo. *See* Joanna; Joanne; Joe; Josephine; Joy
Jo Ann. *See* Joan; Joanna; Joanne
Jo Anne. *See* Joanna
Joady. *See* Jody
Joal. *See* Joel
Joan, 387. *See also* Jane; Janet; Joanne; Jodie; Jody; Juanita
Joana. *See* Joanna
Joane. *See* Joan
Joanie. *See* Joan; Joanne; Juanita
Joann. *See* Joanna; Joanne
Jo-Ann. *See* Joanne
Joanna, 388. *See also* Jane; Jean; Jeanette; Joan; Joanne; Juanita
Joanne, 389
Joanne. *See* Joan; Joanna
Jo-Anne. *See* Joanne
Joanne. *See also* Juanita
Jocelin/Joceline. *See* Jocelyn
Jocelyn, 390
Jock. *See* Jack; John
Jodee/Jodey. *See* Jodie; Jody
Jodi. *See* Jodie; Jody; Judith; Judy
Jodie, 391. *See also* Jody; Joe; Judith; Judy
Jody, 392. *See also* Jodie; Joe; Judith; Judy
Joe, 393. *See also* Joel; José; Joseph
Joeanne. *See* Joanne
Joel, 394
Joey. *See* Joe; Joel; José; Joseph
Johan. *See* Jack; Sean; Shane; Shawn
Johana. *See* Joan
Johann. *See* Ivan; Jan
Johanna. *See* Hannah; Jean; Joanna
Johannah. *See* Joanna
Johannes. *See* John; Juan; Sean; Shane; Shawn
John, 395. *See also* Evan; Ian; Ivan; Jack; Jan; Jonathan; Juan; Sean; Shane; Shawn
Johnathan. *See* John; Jonathan
Johnathon. *See* Jonathan

Johnn/Johnnie. *See* John
Johnny. *See* Jan; John; Jonathan; Juan
Johnson. *See* John
Joi/Joie. *See* Joy
Joice. *See* Joyce
Joise/Joisse. *See* Joyce
Joiye. *See* Joy
Jola. *See* Yolanda
Jolanda. *See* Yolanda
Jolanne. *See* Yolanda
Jolanta. *See* Yolanda
Jolantha/Jolanthe. *See* Yolanda
Jole. *See* Joel
Jolene. *See* Josephine
Jon. *See* Jan; John; Jonathan; Juan
Jona. *See* Joanne
Jonathan, 396. *See also* John
Jonathann. *See* Jonathan
Jonathen. *See* Jonathan
Jonathin/Jonathon. *See* Jonathan
Jone. *See* Joan
Joni. *See* Joan; Juanita
Jonn. *See* John
Jonna. *See* Jane
Jonny. *See* Jonathan
Jonothan. *See* Jonathan
Jonothen/Jonothon. *See* Jonathan
Joolia/Joolie. *See* Julia
Joon/Joone. *See* June
Joord. *See* Jordan
Jordaan. *See* Jordan
Jordan, 397
Jorden/Jordenn. *See* Jordan
Jordi. *See* Jordan
Jordin/Jordyn. *See* Jordan
Jordon. *See* Jordan
Jorg. *See* Jorge
Jorge, 398. *See also* George
Jorgen. *See* Jorge
Jorhe/Jorje. *See* Jorge
Jori. *See* Jorge
Jory. *See* Jordan
Josaline. *See* Jocelyn
Josay. *See* José
Joscelin/Joscelyn. *See* Jocelyn
Josceline. *See* Jocelyn
José, 399. *See also* Joe; Joseph
Josef. *See* Joe; José; Joseph
Josefa. *See* Josephine
Josefeen/Josefene. *See* Josephine
Joseff. *See* Joseph
Josefina. *See* Josephine
Josefine/Josefyne. *See* Josephine
Joseline/Joselyn. *See* Jocelyn
Joseph, 400. *See also* Jody; Joe; Joel; José
Josepheene/Josephene. *See* Josephine
Josephina. *See* Josephine
Josephine, 401
Josephyne. *See* Josephine
Josetta. *See* Josephine
Josey. *See* José
Josh. *See* Joshua
Joshooa. *See* Joshua
Joshua, 402. *See also* Jason; Jesus
Joshuah. *See* Joshua
Joshy. *See* Joshua
Josie. *See* Josephine
Josif/Josiff. *See* Joseph
Josiph. *See* Joseph

Josiphene. *See* Josephine
Josiphine/Josiphyne. *See* Josephine
Josline. *See* Jocelyn
Josselyn. *See* Jocelyn
Jossline/Josslyn. *See* Jocelyn
Josua. *See* Joshua
Josyf/Josyff. *See* Joseph
Josyph. *See* Joseph
Josyphene. *See* Josephine
Jourdain/Jourdan. *See* Jordan
Joy, 403. *See also* Joyce
Joya. *See* Joy; Joyce
Joyann/Joyanna. *See* Joy
Joyce, 404. *See also* Jocelyn; Joy
Joycela. *See* Joyce
Joycelyn. *See* Joyce
Joycie. *See* Joyce
Joye. *See* Joy
Joyse. *See* Joyce
Jozef. *See* Joe; José; Joseph
Jozua. *See* Jesus
Juan, 405. *See also* Ian; Ivan; Jack; John; Jonathan
Juana. *See* Jane; Juanita
Juaneeta. *See* Juanita
Juaneta. *See* Juanita
Juanita, 406. *See also* Joan; Joanna; Joanne
Juanito. *See* Juan
Juann. *See* Juan
Juanyta. *See* Juanita
Judd. *See* Jordan
Jude. *See* Jodie; Jody
Judee. *See* Judy
Judeth. *See* Judith
Judi. *See* Judith; Judy
Judie. *See* Jodie; Jody; Judith; Judy
Judita. *See* Judith; Judy
Judith, 407. *See also* Jodie; Jody; Judy
Juditha. *See* Judith; Judy
Judithe. *See* Judith
Judy, 408. *See also* Jodie; Jody; Judith
Judye. *See* Judy
Judyth/Judythe. *See* Judith
Juedith. *See* Judith
Juedy. *See* Judy
Juelia/Juelie. *See* Julia
Juelian. *See* Julian
Julea. *See* Julia
Julee. *See* Julia; Julie
Juleo. *See* Julio
Jules. *See* Julian; Julio; Julius
Juleus. *See* Julius
Juley/Juli. *See* Julie
Julia, 409. *See also* Julie
Julian, 410. *See also* Julio; Julius
Julianna/Julianne. *See* Julia; Julie
Julianus. *See* Julian
Julie, 411. *See also* Julia
Julie-Anne. *See* Julie
Julien. *See* Julian; Julio; Julius
Julienne. *See* Julia; Julie
Juliet/Juliette. *See* Julia; Julie
Julietta. *See* Julie
Julina. *See* Julia; Julie
Julio, 412. *See also* Julian; Julius
Julion. *See* Julian
Julita. *See* Julia; Julie
Julius, 413. *See also* Julian; Julio
July/Julya. *See* Julie

Julyan. *See* Julian
Julyanna. *See* Julia
Julyo. *See* Julio
Julyus. *See* Julius
Juna. *See* June
June, 414
Junella/Junelle. *See* June
Junette. *See* June
Junia. *See* June
Junina/Junine. *See* June
Jusstin. *See* Justin
Justen/Justenn. *See* Justin
Justin, 415
Justinius. *See* Justin
Justinn. *See* Justin
Justino. *See* Justin
Justo. *See* Justin
Justus. *See* Justin
Justyn. *See* Justin
Jutta. *See* Judith
Jyl. *See* Jill
Jyll/Jylle. *See* Jill
Jym. *See* Jim

K. *See* Kay
Ka. *See* Candace
Kaarle. *See* Carl; Carlos; Charles; Karl
Kacey. *See* Casey
Kacy. *See* Casey; Cassandra
Kahleen/Kahlene. *See* Colleen
Kahlin/Kahlinn. *See* Colin
Kahlyn/Kahlynn. *See* Colin
Kahnni/Kahnnie. *See* Connie
Kahnny. *See* Connie
Kahnrad. *See* Conrad
Kahnstance. *See* Constance
Kaleb/Kalebh. *See* Caleb
Kalleb/Kallib. *See* Caleb
Kalven. *See* Calvin
Kalvin/Kalvyn. *See* Calvin
Kamerin/Kameryn. *See* Cameron
Kameron/Kammeron. *See* Cameron
Kandace/Kandice. *See* Candace
Kara, 416
Karan. *See* Karen
Karel. *See* Carl; Carlos; Carol; Charles; Karl
Karen, 417. *See also* Catherine; Cathy; Kara;
   Kate; Katherine; Kathleen; Kathryn;
   Kathy; Katie; Katrina; Kay; Kitty
Karena. *See* Karen
Kari. *See* Carrie
Karin. *See* Catherine; Cathy; Karen; Kate;
   Katherine; Kathleen; Kathryn; Kathy;
   Katie; Katrina; Kay; Kitty
Karina. *See* Karen
Karl, 418. *See also* Carl; Carlos; Charles;
   Chuck
Karla/Karlah. *See* Carla
Karle. *See* Carl; Karl
Karleen/Karlene. *See* Carla
Karli/Karlie. *See* Carla
Karlos. *See* Carlos
Karmen. *See* Carmen
Karmin/Karmyn. *See* Carmen
Karol. *See* Carl; Carlos; Carol; Charles; Karl
Karolin/Karolyn. *See* Carolyn
Karoline/Karolyne. *See* Caroline
Karoly. *See* Carl; Carlos; Charles; Karl
Karon. *See* Karen

Karra/Karrah. *See* Kara
Karri/Karrie. *See* Carrie
Karrla. *See* Carla
Karrlos. *See* Carlos
Karry/Kary. *See* Carrie
Karyl. *See* Carol
Karyn. *See* Karen
Kasandra. *See* Cassandra
Kasey. *See* Casey
Kassandra/Kassandrah. *See* Cassandra
Katarina/Katerina. *See* Catherine; Cathy;
   Karen; Kate; Katherine; Kathleen;
   Kathryn; Kathy; Katie; Katrina; Kay; Kitty
Kate, 419. *See also* Catherine; Cathy; Karen;
   Katherine; Kathryn; Kathy; Katie;
   Katrina; Kay; Kitty
Katey. *See* Catherine; Cathy; Kate;
   Katherine; Kathleen; Kathryn; Kathy;
   Katie; Katrina; Kay; Kitty
Katharine. *See* Karen; Kate; Katherine;
   Kathleen; Kathryn; Kathy; Katie; Katrina;
   Kay; Kitty
Katheleen/Katheline. *See* Catherine; Cathy;
   Kate; Katherine; Kathleen; Kathryn;
   Kathy; Katie; Katrina; Kitty
Kathereen/Katherina. *See* Catherine; Cathy;
   Kate; Katherine; Kathleen; Kathryn;
   Kathy; Katie; Katrina; Kay; Kitty
Katherine, 420. *See also* Catherine; Cathy;
   Karen; Kate; Kathleen; Kathryn; Kathy;
   Katie; Katrina; Kay; Kitty
Katheryn/Katheryne. *See* Catherine; Cathy;
   Katherine; Kathryn; Kathy
Kathi. *See* Cathy; Kathy
Kathie. *See* Catherine; Cathy; Kate;
   Katherine; Kathleen; Kathryn; Kathy;
   Katie; Katrina; Kay; Kitty
Kathileen. *See* Catherine; Cathy; Kate;
   Katherine; Kathleen; Kathryn; Kathy;
   Katie; Katrina
Kathleen, 421. *See also* Catherine; Cathy;
   Karen; Kate; Katherine; Kathryn; Kathy;
   Katie; Katrina; Kay; Kitty
Kathleene/Kathlene. *See* Kathleen
Kathlyn/Kathlynn. *See* Catherine; Cathy;
   Kate; Katherine; Kathleen; Kathryn;
   Kathy; Katie; Katrina; Kay; Kitty
Kathrene. *See* Catherine; Cathy; Kate;
   Katherine; Kathleen; Kathryn; Kathy;
   Katie; Katrina; Kay; Kitty
Kathrine. *See* Catherine; Cathy; Katherine;
   Kathryn; Kathy
Kathryn, 422. *See also* Catherine; Cathy;
   Karen; Kate; Katherine; Kathleen; Kathy;
   Katie; Katrina; Kay; Kitty
Kathryne. *See* Catherine; Cathy; Katherine;
   Kathryn; Kathy
Kathy, 423. *See also* Catherine; Cathy; Karen;
   Kate; Katherine; Kathleen; Kathryn;
   Katie; Katrina; Kay; Kitty
Kathyrine. *See* Catherine; Cathy; Katherine;
   Kathryn; Kathy
Kati. *See* Katie
Katie, 424. *See also* Catherine; Cathy; Karen;
   Kate; Katherine; Kathleen; Kathryn;
   Kathy; Katrina; Kay; Kitty
Katina. *See* Catherine; Cathy; Kate;
   Katherine; Kathleen; Kathryn; Kathy;
   Katie; Katrina; Kay; Kitty

Katleen. *See* Catherine; Cathy; Kate;
   Katherine; Kathleen; Kathryn; Kathy;
   Katie; Katrina; Kay; Kitty
Katreena. *See* Katrina
Katrena. *See* Catherine; Cathy; Kate;
   Katherine; Kathleen; Kathryn; Kathy;
   Katie; Katrina; Kay; Kitty
Katrina, 425. *See also* Catherine; Cathy;
   Karen; Kate; Katherine; Kathleen;
   Kathryn; Kathy; Katie; Kay; Kitty
Katriona. *See* Catherine; Cathy; Kate;
   Katherine; Kathleen; Kathryn; Kathy;
   Katie; Katrina; Kay; Kitty
Katryna. *See* Catherine; Cathy; Kate;
   Katherine; Kathleen; Kathryn; Kathy;
   Katie; Katrina; Kay; Kitty
Kattrina. *See* Catherine; Cathy; Kate;
   Katherine; Kathleen; Kathryn; Kathy;
   Katie; Katrina; Kay; Kitty
Katy. *See* Catherine; Cathy; Kate; Katherine;
   Kathleen; Kathryn; Kathy; Katie; Katrina;
   Kay; Kitty
Kay, 426. *See also* Casey; Catherine; Cathy;
   Karen; Kate; Katherine; Kathleen;
   Kathryn; Kathy; Katie; Katrina; Kitty
Kaylee. *See* Kelly
Kayley. *See* Kay; Kelly
Kayte. *See* Kate
Kealey/Kealy. *See* Kelly
Keath. *See* Keith
Keelie. *See* Kelly
Keely. *See* Kelly; Kelsey
Keeth/Keethe. *See* Keith
Kehnt/Kehntt. *See* Kent
Kehnte. *See* Kent
Kehri/Kehrie. *See* Kerry
Kehrri/Kehrrie. *See* Kerry
Kehry. *See* Kerry
Kehvin/Kehvyn. *See* Kevin
Keighley. *See* Kelly
Keiley/Keily. *See* Kelly
Keilly. *See* Kelly
Keith, 427
Kelci/Kelcie. *See* Kelsey
Kelcy. *See* Kelsey
Kelda. *See* Kelly
Kelley/Kellie. *See* Kelly; Raquel
Kelli. *See* Kelly
Kelly, 428. *See also* Kelsey; Raquel
Kelsa. *See* Chelsea; Kelsey
Kelsey, 429
Kelsi/Kelsy. *See* Kelsey
Kelsie. *See* Chelsea; Kelsey
Ken, 430. *See also* Kenneth; Kent
Kendall. *See* Ken; Kenneth; Kent
Kendra, 431. *See also* Sandra
Kendrah. *See* Kendra
Kendrick. *See* Ken; Kenneth; Kent
Kenelm. *See* Ken; Kenneth; Kent
Keneth/Kenith. *See* Kenneth
Kenn. *See* Ken
Kennard. *See* Ken; Kenneth; Kent
Kennedy. *See* Ken; Kenneth; Kent
Kenneth, 432. *See also* Keith; Ken; Kent
Kennith. *See* Kenneth
Kenny. *See* Ken; Kenneth; Kent
Kent, 433. *See also* Ken; Kenneth
Kente/Kentt. *See* Kent
Kenton. *See* Ken; Kenneth; Kent

Kenward. *See* Ken; Kenneth; Kent
Kenway. *See* Ken; Kenneth; Kent
Kenyon. *See* Ken; Kenneth; Kent
Keri/Kerie. *See* Kerry
Kerk. *See* Kirk
Kerr/Kerrie. *See* Kerry
Kerri. *See* Carrie; Kerry
Kerry, 434
Kerstie. *See* Christine
Kerstin. *See* Christine; Kerry
Kert. *See* Kurt
Kertis/Kertiss. *See* Curtis
Kertt. *See* Kurt
Kery. *See* Kerry
Kevan. *See* Kevin
Keverne. *See* Kevin
Kevin, 435
Kevyn. *See* Kevin
Khanstance. *See* Constance
Khendra/Khendrah. *See* Kendra
Khim/Khimm. *See* Kim
Khiti/Khitie. *See* Kitty
Khitti/Khittie. *See* Kitty
Khitty. *See* Kitty
Khonstance. *See* Constance
Khora/Khorah. *See* Cora
Khrista. *See* Krista
Khristal. *See* Crystal
Khristeen/Khristene. *See* Christine
Khristian. *See* Christian
Khristina/Khristine. *See* Christina; Kristen; Kristina
Khristle. *See* Crystal
Khristofer/Khristopher. *See* Christopher
Khristyne. *See* Christine
Khrysta. *See* Krista
Khrystal. *See* Crystal
Khrystian. *See* Christian
Khrystina/Khrystyna. *See* Christina; Kristina
Khrystle. *See* Crystal
Khrystofer/Khrystopher. *See* Christopher
Khym/Khymm. *See* Kim
Kieley/Kieli. *See* Kelly
Kihm/Kihmm. *See* Kim
Kile. *See* Kyle
Kiley. *See* Kelly; Kyle
Kim, 436. *See also* Kimberly
Kimarie. *See* Kimberly
Kimba. *See* Kim; Kimberly
Kimba Lee. *See* Kim; Kimberly
Kimber. *See* Kim; Kimberly
Kimberlee/Kimberlei. *See* Kimberly
Kimberley. *See* Kim; Kimberly
Kimberli/Kimberlie. *See* Kimberly
Kimberly, 437. *See also* Kim
Kimberlyn. *See* Kim; Kimberly
Kimbley. *See* Kim; Kimberly
Kimette. *See* Kimberly
Kimiko. *See* Kimberly
Kimm. *See* Kim
Kimmie/Kimmy. *See* Kim; Kimberly
Kirby. *See* Kirk
Kirk, 438
Kirsten. *See* Christina; Krista; Kristen; Kristina
Kirsti. *See* Krista
Kirstie/Kirsty. *See* Christina; Kristen; Kristina

Kirstyn. *See* Christina; Krista; Kristen; Kristina
Kit. *See* Christopher
Kiti/Kitie. *See* Kitty
Kitti/Kittie. *See* Kitty
Kitty, 439. *See also* Catherine; Cathy; Karen; Kate; Katherine; Kathleen; Kathryn; Kathy; Katie; Katrina; Kay
Klaas/Klaes. *See* Nicholas
Klair/Klaire. *See* Claire
Klara. *See* Claire; Clara
Klarah. *See* Clara
Klare. *See* Claire
Klark/Klarke. *See* Clark
Klaudia/Klaudya. *See* Claudia
Klaus. *See* Nicholas
Klawdia. *See* Claudia
Kleday. *See* Kelly
Klif/Kliff. *See* Cliff
Klint/Klintt. *See* Clint
Kliph/Klyph. *See* Cliff
Klyf/Klyff. *See* Cliff
Klynt/Klyntt. *See* Clint
Kodee. *See* Cody
Kodey/Kody. *See* Cody
Kodi/Kodie. *See* Cody
Kolin/Kolinn. *See* Colin
Kolleen. *See* Colleen
Kollin/Kollinn. *See* Colin
Konni/Konnie. *See* Connie
Konny. *See* Connie
Konrad. *See* Conrad; Kurt
Konstance. *See* Constance
Kooper. *See* Cooper
Kora/Korah. *See* Cora
Korabell. *See* Cora
Korain. *See* Corey
Koreen. *See* Corey
Kori. *See* Corey; Courtney
Korin. *See* Corey
Korina/Korinne. *See* Cora
Korrey/Korrie. *See* Corey; Courtney
Korrina. *See* Corey
Korry. *See* Corey; Courtney
Korteni/Kortenie. *See* Courtney
Korteny. *See* Courtney
Kortnay/Kortney. *See* Courtney
Kory. *See* Corey; Courtney
Koryne. *See* Cora
Koryssa. *See* Cora
Kourtenay/Kourtenie. *See* Courtney
Kourteni/Kourteny. *See* Courtney
Kraig/Kraigg. *See* Craig
Kreg/Kregg. *See* Craig
Kris. *See* Chris; Christian; Christina; Christine; Christopher
Kriss. *See* Chris
Krista, 440. *See also* Christine; Kristen; Kristina
Kristal. *See* Crystal
Kristeen/Kristene. *See* Christine
Kristen, 441. *See also* Christine; Krista; Kristina
Kristian. *See* Christian
Kristie. *See* Christina; Crystal; Krista; Kristen; Kristina
Kristin. *See* Kristen
Kristina, 442. *See also* Christine; Krista; Kristen

Kristine. *See* Christina; Krista; Kristen; Kristina
Kristofer/Kristopher. *See* Christian; Christopher
Kristol. *See* Crystal
Kristy. *See* Christina; Crystal; Krista; Kristen; Kristina
Kristyan/Kristyne. *See* Christian
Kristyn. *See* Kristen
Kryss. *See* Chris
Krysta. *See* Krista
Krystal. *See* Crystal
Krystian. *See* Christian
Krystin. *See* Kristen
Krystina. *See* Christina; Kristina
Krystle. *See* Christine; Crystal
Krystofer/Krystopher. *See* Christopher
Krystyan. *See* Christian
Krystyn. *See* Kristen
Krystyna. *See* Christina; Christine; Kristina
Kuper. *See* Cooper
Kurk. *See* Kirk
Kurt, 443. *See also* Conrad; Curtis
Kurtis/Kurtiss. *See* Curtis
Kurtt. *See* Kurt
Kyhm/Kyhmm. *See* Kim
Kyle, 444
Kylee/Kylie. *See* Kelly
Kyly. *See* Kyle
Kym. *See* Kim
Kymberley/Kimberly. *See* Kimberly
Kyrsty. *See* Christina; Krista; Kristen; Kristina

Laetitia/Laetizia. *See* Leticia
Lahnie/Lahnnie. *See* Lonnie
Lahnny/Lahny. *See* Lonnie
Lance, 445
Lancelet. *See* Lance
Lancelot/Lancelott. *See* Lance
Lanny. *See* Alan; Allen
Lanz. *See* Lance
Laonsya. *See* Latoya
Lara/Larah. *See* Laura
Laraine. *See* Lorraine
Larehta. *See* Loretta
Larie. *See* Larry
Larrey/Larrie. *See* Larry
Larry, 446. *See also* Lawrence
Lars. *See* Larry; Lawrence
Lary. *See* Larry
Lasonia. *See* Latoya
Latanya. *See* Latoya
Latashia. *See* Leticia
Latia. *See* Leticia
Latisha. *See* Leticia
Latoia/Latoiah. *See* Latoya
Latonya. *See* Latoya
Latoya, 447
Latoyah. *See* Latoya
Latoyla. *See* Latoya
Launce. *See* Lance
Launcelet. *See* Lance
Laura, 448. *See also* Lauren; Laurie; Loretta; Lori; Lorraine
Laurah. *See* Laura
Lauree. *See* Laurie
Laureen. *See* Laura; Lauren; Loretta; Lori; Lorraine

Laurel. *See* Laura; Lauren; Loretta; Lori; Lorraine

Lauren, 449. *See also* Laura; Laurie; Loren; Loretta; Lori; Lorraine

Laurena. *See* Laura; Lauren; Laurie

Laurence. *See* Larry; Lawrence; Lorenzo

Laurene. *See* Laura; Lauren

Laurens. *See* Larry

Laurenso/Laurenzo. *See* Lorenzo

Laurent. *See* Lawrence

Lauretta. *See* Laura; Lauren; Loretta; Lori; Lorraine

Laurettah. *See* Loretta

Laurette. *See* Laura; Lauren; Laurie; Loretta

Lauri. *See* Laura; Lauren; Laurie; Lori

Lauriane. *See* Laura; Lauren; Loretta; Lori; Lorraine

Laurie, 450. *See also* Laura; Lauren; Lori

Laurin. *See* Lauren; Loren

Laurina. *See* Laura; Lauren; Laurie

Laurince. *See* Lawrence

Lauron. *See* Lauren

Laurraine. *See* Lorraine

Laury. *See* Laura; Lauren

Lauryn. *See* Lauren

Lawrence, 451. *See also* Larry; Loren; Lorenzo

Lawrie. *See* Larry

Lawrince. *See* Lawrence

Lawson/Lawton. *See* Lawrence

Laynce. *See* Lance

Laynz. *See* Lance

Layton. *See* Lee; Leland

Le roy. *See* Leroy

Lea. *See* Leah; Lee; Leigh

Leah, 452. *See also* Lee; Leigh

Leahn. *See* Leon

Leander. *See* Lee; Leland

Leandra. *See* Lee; Leigh

Leanne. *See* Leah

Leanor. *See* Nell; Nellie

Leanora. *See* Eleanor

Leda. *See* Leah; Leticia; Lydia

Lee, 453. *See also* Ashley; Bradley; Leah; Leigh; Leland; Leo; Leon; Leonard; Leroy; Leslie; Lionel

Leea/Leeah. *See* Leah

Leeahn. *See* Leon

Leeland. *See* Leland

Leena/Leenah. *See* Lena

Leeoh. *See* Leo

Leeohna. *See* Leona

Leeon. *See* Leon

Leeona/Leeonha. *See* Leona

Leeroi/Leeroy *See* Leroy

Leesa/Leeza. *See* Lisa

Lehs. *See* Les

Lehster. *See* Lester

Lehstir/Lehstyr. *See* Lester

Leicester. *See* Les; Leslie; Lester

Leigh, 454. *See also* Ashley; Leah; Lee; Leona; Leslie

Leighanne. *See* Leigh

Leighland. *See* Leland

Leigho/Leighoh. *See* Leo

Leighohna. *See* Leona

Leighon. *See* Leon

Leighona/Leighonha. *See* Leona

Leighton. *See* Lee; Leland

Leland, 455. *See also* Lee

Len. *See* Leon; Leonard

Lena, 456. *See also* Arlene; Eleanor; Helen

Lenard/Lenhard. *See* Leonard

Lenda. *See* Lena

Lene. *See* Arlene; Lena

Leni. *See* Lena

Lenna. *See* Lena

Lennard. *See* Leonard

Lennerd/Lennhard. *See* Leonard

Lennie/Lenny. *See* Leonard; Lonnie

Lenora. *See* Eleanor

Lenz. *See* Lawrence

Leo, 457. *See also* Lee; Leon; Leonard; Lionel

Leodegar. *See* Leo

Leoh. *See* Leo

Leoline. *See* Leona

Leon, 458. *See also* Lee; Leo; Leonard

Leona, 459. *See also* Leigh

Leonard, 460. *See also* Lee; Leo; Leon; Lonnie

Leonardo. *See* Leo; Leonard

Leone. *See* Leo; Leona

Leonhard. *See* Leonard

Leonia. *See* Leona

Leonicia. *See* Leona

Leonid. *See* Leonard

Leonidas/Leonides. *See* Leonard

Leonie. *See* Leona

Leonin. *See* Leona

Leonor/Leonora. *See* Nora

Leontine. *See* Leona

Leontios. *See* Leo; Leon

Leroi. *See* Leroy

Leroy, 461

Le'Roy. *See* Leroy

Leroy. *See also* Roy

Les, 462. *See also* Lee; Leslie; Lester

Leslea. *See* Leslie

Leslee. *See* Les; Leslie

Lesley. *See* Les; Leslie; Lester

Lesli. *See* Leslie

Leslie, 463. *See also* Les; Lester

Lesly. *See* Les; Leslie

Leslye. *See* Leslie

Less. *See* Les

Lesslie. *See* Leslie

Lester, 464. *See also* Les; Leslie

Lestir/Lestyr. *See* Lester

Leta/Letha. *See* Leticia

Letice. *See* Leticia

Leticia, 465

Letisha. *See* Leticia

Letitia. *See* Leticia

Letizia. *See* Leticia

Letta. *See* Leticia

Lettice. *See* Leticia

Lettie/Letty. *See* Leticia

Lew. *See* Lewis; Louis

Lewcile. *See* Lucille

Lewes. *See* Lewis; Louis

Lewie. *See* Lewis; Louis

Lewis, 466. *See also* Louis

Lewseal. *See* Lucille

Lexi/Lexy. *See* Alexandra; Alexis

Lexie. *See* Alexis

Leyland. *See* Leland

Lez. *See* Les

Lezly. *See* Les; Leslie

Lhea. *See* Leah; Lee; Leigh

Lhee. *See* Lee; Leigh

Lheea. *See* Leah

Lheena. *See* Lena

Lheesa/Lheesah. *See* Lisa

Lheigh. *See* Lee; Leigh

Lhiah. *See* Leah

Lhina. *See* Lena

Lhinda/Lhindah. *See* Linda

Lhynda/Lhyndah. *See* Linda

Lia. *See* Leah; Lee; Leigh

Liah. *See* Leah

Liam. *See* Guillermo; William; Willie

Liane/Lianne. *See* Leah; Lee; Leigh

Lianel/Lianyl. *See* Lionel

Lida. *See* Lydia

Lidia/Lidya. *See* Lydia

Lidija. *See* Lydia

Liesa. *See* Lisa

Liesebet. *See* Lisa

Lil. *See* Lily

Lila/Lile. *See* Lily

Lilac/Lilas. *See* Lily

Lili/Lilie. *See* Lily

Lilia. *See* Lillian; Lily

Lilian/Liliana. *See* Lillian

Lilias. *See* Lily

Lilibet. *See* Lily

Lilien. *See* Lillian

Lilith. *See* Lillian; Lily

Lility. *See* Lily

Lilla. *See* Lillian

Lilley. *See* Lily

Lilli/Lillia. *See* Lillian

Lillian, 467. *See also* Lily

Lillianna. *See* Lillian

Lillianne. *See* Lillian; Lily

Lillias. *See* Lillian

Lillie/Lilly. *See* Lillian; Lily

Lillyan. *See* Lillian

Lily, 468. *See also* Lillian

Lilyan. *See* Lillian

Lin. *See* Linda; Lindsey; Lynette; Lynn; Melinda

Lina. *See* Caroline; Lena

Linda, 469. *See also* Belinda; Lynn; Melinda

Lindah. *See* Linda

Lindee/Lindey. *See* Linda; Lindsey

Lindi. *See* Linda; Lindsey

Lindie. *See* Belinda; Linda; Lindsey

Lindsaye. *See* Lindsey

Lindsea. *See* Lindsey

Lindsey, 470

Lindsie/Lindsy. *See* Lindsey

Lindy. *See* Belinda; Linda; Lindsey; Melinda

Lindzi/Lindzy. *See* Lindsey

Linel. *See* Lionel

Linell. *See* Lynette; Lynn

Linette. *See* Lynette

Linn. *See* Linda; Lindsey; Lynette; Lynn

Linnell. *See* Lynette; Lynn

Linnett/Linnette. *See* Lynette

Linnie. *See* Melinda

Linsay/Linsey. *See* Lindsey

Linus. *See* Lionel

Linzey. *See* Lindsey

Linzi/Linzie. *See* Lindsey

Lion. *See* Leo; Leon

Lionel, 471. *See also* Lyle

Lionello. *See* Lionel
Lionyl. *See* Lionel
Lippo. *See* Felipe
Lis. *See* Eliza; Elizabeth; Lisa
Lisa, 472. *See also* Eliza; Elizabeth; Elyse
Lisabeth. *See* Beth; Lisa
Lisah. *See* Lisa
Lisbet. *See* Betty; Eliza; Elizabeth
Lisbeth. *See* Betsy; Lisa
Lise. *See* Alice; Eliza; Elizabeth; Elyse; Lisa
Liseta/Lisetta. *See* Lisa
Lisette. *See* Eliza; Elizabeth; Lisa
Lisle. *See* Lyle
Lissa. *See* Alice; Elyse; Lisa; Melissa
Lissah. *See* Lisa
Liszka. *See* Lisa
Littitia. *See* Leticia
Liv/Liva. *See* Olivia
Livia. *See* Olivia
Livvie/Livvy. *See* Olivia
Liz. *See* Eliza; Elizabeth; Lisa
Liza. *See* Eliza; Elizabeth; Elyse; Lisa
Lizabeth. *See* Lisa
Lize. *See* Elyse
Lizzi. *See* Lisa
Lizzie. *See* Eliza; Elizabeth; Lisa
Lleeah. *See* Leah
Llen. *See* Ellen
Llia. *See* Leah
Lloid. *See* Lloyd
Lloyd, 473. *See also* Floyd
Lloydd. *See* Lloyd
Loel/Loell. *See* Lowell
Lohis. *See* Lois
Lohla/Lohlah. *See* Lola
Lohlla. *See* Lola
Lohwel/Lohwell. *See* Lowell
Lohys. *See* Lois
Loid/Loidd. *See* Lloyd
Lois, 474. *See also* Louise
Loise. *See* Louise
Loiss. *See* Lois
Lola, 475. *See also* Delores
Lolita. *See* Delores; Lola
Loly. *See* Lola
Lon. *See* Larry; Lonnie
Loni. *See* Lonnie
Lonnard. *See* Leonard
Lonnie, 476
Lonny. *See* Larry; Leon; Leonard; Lonnie
Lonzo. *See* Lonnie
Loocas/Lookas. *See* Lucas
Looke. *See* Luke
Loother/Loothur. *See* Luther
Lora/Lorah. *See* Laura
Lorain. *See* Lorraine
Loraine. *See* Laura; Lauren; Lorraine
Lorane/Lorayne. *See* Lorraine
Loree. *See* Laura; Lauren; Laurie
Loreen. *See* Laura; Lauren; Loretta; Lori; Lorraine
Lorehta/Lorehtta. *See* Loretta
Loren, 477. *See also* Larry; Lauren; Lorenzo
Lorena. *See* Laurie; Loretta; Lori; Lorraine
Lorene. *See* Loretta; Lori; Lorraine
Lorenso. *See* Lorenzo
Lorenz. *See* Loren; Lorenzo
Lorenza. *See* Loretta; Lori; Lorraine
Lorenzo, 478. *See also* Lawrence; Loren

Loretta, 479. *See also* Laurie; Lori; Lorraine
Lorettah. *See* Loretta
Lorette. *See* Loretta; Lori; Lorraine
Lorey. *See* Laurie; Lori
Lori, 480. *See also* Delores; Laura; Lauren; Laurie; Lorraine
Lorie. *See* Gloria; Laurie; Lori
Lorin. *See* Lauren; Loren
Lorina. *See* Lorraine
Lorince. *See* Lawrence
Lorinda. *See* Loretta; Lori; Lorraine
Lorine. *See* Loretta; Lori; Lorraine
Lorita. *See* Loretta; Lori; Lorraine
Lorna. *See* Loretta; Lori; Lorraine
Loron. *See* Lauren
Lorraine, 481. *See also* Laura; Lauren; Loretta; Lori
Lorrane/Lorrayne. *See* Lorraine
Lorrehta. *See* Loretta
Lorren/Lorrin. *See* Loren
Lorri. *See* Laurie; Lori
Lorrie. *See* Laura; Lauren
Lorry. *See* Laura; Lauren; Laurie; Lori
Lory. *See* Gloria; Laura; Lauren; Laurie
Loryn. *See* Lauren
Lotario. *See* Luther
Lothair. *See* Luther
Lothar. *See* Luther
Lothario. *See* Luther
Lottie/Lotty. *See* Charlotte
Lou. *See* Lewis; Louis
Louie. *See* Lewis; Louis
Louis, 482. *See also* Lewis
Louisa. *See* Lois; Louise
Louise, 483. *See also* Lois
Louisetta/Louisette. *See* Louise
Louisiane. *See* Louise
Loukas. *See* Lucas
Lovel/Lovell. *See* Lowell
Lowel. *See* Lowell
Lowell, 484
Lowis/Lowiss. *See* Lois
Lowla/Lowlah. *See* Lola
Loyd/Loydd. *See* Lloyd
Loyise. *See* Louise
Loys. *See* Lois
Lu. *See* Louise
Luc. *See* Lucas; Luke
Lucas, 485. *See also* Luke
Luce. *See* Lucille; Lucy; Luz
Lucetta/Lucette. *See* Lucille; Lucy; Luz
Luci. *See* Lucille; Lucy
Lucia. *See* Lucille; Lucy; Luz
Lucian. *See* Lucas; Luke
Luciana. *See* Lucille; Lucy; Luz
Lucida. *See* Lucille; Lucy; Luz
Lucie. *See* Lucille; Lucy; Luz
Lucien. *See* Lucas; Luke
Lucienne. *See* Lucille
Lucila. *See* Lucille; Lucy; Luz
Lucile/Lucilia. *See* Lucille
Lucilla. *See* Lucille; Lucy; Luz
Lucille, 486. *See also* Lucy; Luz
Lucina/Lucine. *See* Lucille
Lucinda. *See* Cindy; Cynthia; Lucille; Lucy; Luz
Lucio. *See* Lucas; Luke
Lucita. *See* Lucille; Lucy; Luz
Lucius. *See* Lucas; Luke

Luck/Lucky. *See* Lucas; Luke
Lucy, 487. *See also* Lucille; Luz
Ludovica. *See* Louise
Luisa/Luise. *See* Louise
Lukas. *See* Lucas; Luke
Luke, 488. *See also* Lucas
Lula. *See* Louise
Lulita. *See* Louise
Luseal. *See* Lucille
Lutero. *See* Luther
Luther, 489
Luthur. *See* Luther
Luz, 490. *See also* Lucille; Lucy
Lyall. *See* Lyle
Lydia, 491
Lydiah. *See* Lydia
Lydie/Lydya. *See* Lydia
Lyell. *See* Lyle
Lyle, 492. *See also* Lionel
Lylian/Lylien. *See* Lillian
Lyllian/Lyllyan. *See* Lillian
Lylyan/Lylyen. *See* Lillian
Lyn. *See* Belinda; Linda; Lindsey; Lynette; Lynn
Lynda. *See* Belinda; Linda
Lyndah. *See* Linda
Lynde. *See* Linda; Lindsey
Lyndel/Lyndell. *See* Lynette; Lynn
Lyndie. *See* Belinda
Lyndsey/Lyndsy. *See* Lindsey
Lyndy. *See* Linda; Lindsey
Lynell/Lynelle. *See* Lynette; Lynn
Lynette, 493. *See also* Belinda; Lynn
Lynn, 494. *See also* Belinda; Linda; Lindsey; Lynette; Melinda
Lynna. *See* Lynette; Lynn
Lynndie. *See* Linda; Lindsey
Lynne. *See* Belinda; Linda; Lindsey; Lynette; Lynn; Melinda
Lynnelle. *See* Lynette; Lynn
Lynnett. *See* Lynette
Lynsay/Lynsday. *See* Lindsey
Lynsey/Lynsie. *See* Lindsey
Lyon. *See* Leo; Leon
Lysa/Lyssa. *See* Lisa
Lysbeth. *See* Lisa
Lysle. *See* Lyle

Maarten. *See* Martin; Marty
Maartin. *See* Martin
Mac. *See* Mack; Max
Macallister. *See* Mack
Macardle. *See* Mack
Macdonald. *See* Mack
Macdougal. *See* Mack
Mack, 495. *See also* Malcolm; Max
Mackenzie. *See* Mack
Mackey. *See* Mack
Macks. *See* Max
Macs. *See* Max
Madalaina. *See* Madeline
Madalena/Madalenne. *See* Madeline
Madalin/Madalyn. *See* Madeline
Madaline/Madalinne. *See* Madeline
Maddaline/Maddeline. *See* Madeline
Maddelyn/Maddelyne. *See* Madeline
Maddie/Maddy. *See* Madeline
Maddilin/Maddalyn. *See* Madeline
Maddiline/Maddilyne. *See* Madeline

Maddylen/Maddylin. *See* Madeline
Madelayne. *See* Madeline
Madeleine. *See* Madeline
Madelen. *See* Madeline
Madelin/Madelinne. *See* Madeline
Madeline, 496
Madella. *See* Madeline
Madelyn/Madelynne. *See* Madeline
Madge. *See* Madeline
Madilin/Madelyn. *See* Madeline
Madonna. *See* Donna
Madylen/Madylin. *See* Madeline
Mae, 497. *See also* May
Maergaret. *See* Margaret
Maervin. *See* Marvin
Mag. *See* Maggie; Megan
Magda. *See* Madeline; Maggie
Magdalena/Magdalene. *See* Madeline
Magdaline. *See* Marlene
Maggey/Maggi. *See* Maggie
Maggie, 498. *See also* Margaret; Megan;
   Peggy
Maggy. *See* Maggie
Magi/Magy. *See* Maggie
Magnilda. *See* Maggie
Magnolia. *See* Maggie
Maht. *See* Matt
Mai. *See* May
Maia. *See* Mae; May
Maiga. *See* Maggie
Mailie. *See* Melinda
Maire. *See* Maria; Marié; Marissa; Mary;
   Maureen; Rosemary
Mairee. *See* Mary
Mairey/Mairy. *See* Mary
Maisie. *See* Margaret
Maks. *See* Max
Malcolm, 499. *See also* Mack
Malcolum. *See* Malcolm
Malcom/Malcum. *See* Malcolm
Malia. *See* Molly
Malinda. *See* Melinda
Malisa/Malissa. *See* Melissa
Malkolm. *See* Malcolm
Malkom/Malkum. *See* Malcolm
Mallie. *See* Molly
Mallinda. *See* Melinda
Mallynda/Mallyndah. *See* Melinda
Malvin. *See* Melvin
Malynda. *See* Melinda
Malysa/Maylssa. *See* Melissa
Manda. *See* Amanda
Mandee/Mandie. *See* Amanda
Mandi. *See* Amanda
Mandy. *See* Amanda; Melinda
Manica/Manika. *See* Monica
Manka. *See* Monica
Mannica/Mannika. *See* Monica
Mannicka. *See* Monica
Manny. *See* Manuel
Manuel, 500
Manuele/Manuell. *See* Manuel
Manuwel. *See* Manuel
Manyuel. *See* Manuel
Mara. *See* Maria; Marianne; Marie; Marilyn;
   Marissa; Mary; Mary Ann; Rosemary
Marah. *See* Miriam
Maralen/Maralin. *See* Marilyn
Maralyn/Maralynne. *See* Marilyn

Marc. *See* Marco; Marcus; Mario; Marion;
   Mark; Martin; Marty
Marcea. *See* Marsha
Marcel. *See* Marco; Marshall; Martin;
   Marty
Marcelia. *See* Marsha
Marcella. *See* Marcia; Marsha
Marcelle. *See* Marcia
Marcellus. *See* Marshall; Martin; Marty
Marcene. *See* Marsha
Marci. *See* Marcia; Marsha
Marcia, 501. *See also* Marsha
Marciah. *See* Marcia; Marsha
Marcial. *See* Marshall
Marcie. *See* Marcia; Marsha
Marcille. *See* Marcia
Marcilynn. *See* Marsha
Marcita. *See* Marcia
Marck. *See* Mark
Marco, 502. *See also* Marcus; Mario; Marion;
   Mark
Marcoe/Marcos. *See* Marco
Marcus, 503. *See also* Marco; Mario; Marion;
   Mark; Marshall; Martin; Marty
Marcy. *See* Marsha
Mare. *See* Marianne; Marilyn; Mary Ann
Marea. *See* Maria
Maree/Mareea. *See* Marie
Marelin/Marelyn. *See* Marilyn
Marelynne. *See* Marilyn
Maren. *See* Maria; Marie; Marissa; Mary
Mareo. *See* Mario
Mareon/Mareonn. *See* Marion
Maret. *See* Martha
Marey. *See* Marie; Mary
Marga. *See* Margarita; Marguerite
Margaret, 504. *See also* Gretchen; Mae;
   Maggie; Margarita; Marguerite; Marjorie;
   May; Megan; Pearl; Peggy; Rita
Margareta. *See* Maggie; Margarita
Margarete. *See* Margaret; Marguerite
Margaretha. *See* Margarita
Margarett/Margarette. *See* Margaret
Margaretta. *See* Margaret; Margarita
Margarit. *See* Margaret
Margarita, 505. *See also* Maggie; Margaret;
   Marguerite; Marjorie; Megan; Rita
Margarite. *See* Margaret; Marguerite
Margaritte. *See* Marguerite
Margaryt. *See* Margaret
Margaryta. *See* Margarita
Margaryte. *See* Marguerite
Margaux. *See* Margaret; Margarita;
   Marguerite; Marjorie
Marge. *See* Margaret; Margarita; Marguerite;
   Marjorie
Margeree. *See* Marjorie
Margeret. *See* Margaret
Margerete. *See* Marguerite
Margeretha. *See* Margarita
Margerey. *See* Marjorie
Margeri/Margerie. *See* Marjorie
Margerita. *See* Margarita
Margery. *See* Maggie; Margaret; Margarita;
   Marguerite; Marjorie
Margeryta. *See* Margarita
Margeryte. *See* Marguerite
Margherita. *See* Margarita
Margherite. *See* Marguerite

Margie. *See* Maggie; Margaret; Margarita;
   Marguerite; Marjorie; Megan
Margireta. *See* Margarita
Margirite/Margiryte. *See* Marguerite
Margita. *See* Margarita; Marguerite
Margo. *See* Maggie; Margaret; Margarita;
   Marguerite; Marjorie; Megan
Margot. *See* Margaret; Margarita;
   Marguerite; Marjorie; Megan
Margret. *See* Margaret
Margrett/Margrette. *See* Margaret
Margrit/Margritte. *See* Margaret
Marguerita. *See* Margaret; Margarita
Marguerite, 506. *See also* Maggie; Margaret;
   Margarita; Marjorie; Megan; Rita
Marguerithe. *See* Marjorie
Margy. *See* Marjorie
Mari. *See* Maria; Marie; Marissa; Mary;
   May; Rosemary
Maria, 507. *See also* Marianne; Marie;
   Marilyn; Marissa; Mary; Mary Ann;
   Maureen; May; Miriam; Molly; Muriel;
   Myra; Rosemary
Mariah. *See* Maria; Marianne; Marie;
   Marilyn; Marissa; Mary; Mary Ann;
   Myra; Rosemary
Mariamm. *See* Miriam
Marian. *See* Marianne; Marilyn; Marion;
   Mary Ann
Mariana. *See* Marianne; Marilyn; Mary Ann
Mariane/Mariann. *See* Marianne; Mary Ann
Marianna. *See* Marianne; Marie; Marilyn;
   Marissa; Mary; Mary Ann
Marianne, 508. *See also* Maria; Marie;
   Marilyn; Marissa; Mary; Mary Ann; May;
   Rosemary
Mariano. *See* Marcus
Maribel. *See* Marianne; Marilyn; Mary Ann
Marie, 509. *See also* Maria; Marianne;
   Marilyn; Marissa; Mary; Mary Ann;
   Maureen; May; Miriam; Molly; Muriel;
   Myra; Rosemary
Mariea. *See* Maria
Mariel. *See* Maria; Marianne; Marie;
   Marilyn; Marissa; Mary; Mary Ann
Mariella. *See* Maria; Marianne; Marie;
   Marilyn; Marissa; Mary Ann
Marielle. *See* Maria; Marianne; Marie;
   Marilyn; Marissa; Mary; Mary Ann
Marien. *See* Marion
Marietta. *See* Maria; Marianne; Marie;
   Marilyn; Mary; Mary Ann
Marigold. *See* Marianne; Marilyn; Mary
   Ann
Marika. *See* Maria; Marianne; Marie;
   Marilyn; Marissa; Mary; Mary Ann
Marilee. *See* Maria; Marie; Marissa; Mary
Marilen/Marilenne. *See* Marilyn
Marilin. *See* Marilyn
Marilyn, 510. *See also* Maria; Marianne;
   Marie; Marissa; Mary; Mary Ann; May
Marilynne. *See* Marilyn
Mario, 511. *See also* Marco; Marcus; Marion;
   Mark
Marioe/Marioh. *See* Mario
Marion, 512. *See also* Marco; Marcus; Mario;
   Mark
Marionn. *See* Marion
Maris/Marise. *See* Marissa

Marisa. *See* Maria; Marie; Marissa; Mary
Marisah. *See* Marissa
Marisha. *See* Marissa
Marisol. *See* Marissa
Marissa, 513. *See also* Maria; Marianne; Marie; Marilyn; Mary; Mary Ann; May
Marissah. *See* Marissa
Marius. *See* Marco; Marcus; Mario; Marion; Mark; Marshall; Martin; Marty
Marjerey/Marjerie. *See* Marjorie
Marjeri/Margery. *See* Marjorie
Marjori/Marjory. *See* Marjorie
Marjorie, 514. *See also* Margaret; Margarita; Marguerite
Mark, 515. *See also* Marco; Marcus; Mario; Marion; Martin
Markis. *See* Marcus
Markita. *See* Margaret
Markk. *See* Mark
Marko. *See* Marco; Mark
Markoe. *See* Marco
Markus. *See* Marcus; Mark
Marla. *See* Marianne; Marilyn; Marlene; Mary Ann
Marlana/Marlane. *See* Marlene
Marlee. *See* Marlene
Marleen/Marleene. *See* Marlene
Marlena. *See* Madeline; Marlene
Marlene, 516. *See also* Madeline
Marline. *See* Marlene
Marlo. *See* Marlene
Marlynne. *See* Marlene
Marna. *See* Marlene
Marrcia. *See* Marsha
Marrelyn/Marrelynne. *See* Marilyn
Marreo/Marrio. *See* Mario
Marrilyn/Marrilynne. *See* Marilyn
Marrten/Marrtin. *See* Martin
Marrtha. *See* Martha
Marrvin. *See* Marvin
Marryoh. *See* Mario
Marschal/Marshall. *See* Marshall
Marsh. *See* Marshall
Marsha, 517. *See also* Marcia
Marshah. *See* Marcia; Marsha
Marshal. *See* Marshall
Marshall, 518. *See also* Marcus; Martin; Marty
Marshell. *See* Marshall
Marshella. *See* Marsha
Marshita. *See* Marsha
Mart/Marta. *See* Martha
Martee/Martey. *See* Marty
Martella/Martelle. *See* Martha
Marten. *See* Martin; Marty
Martha, 519
Marthah. *See* Martha
Marthe. *See* Martha
Marthena. *See* Martha
Marti/Martie. *See* Martha; Marty
Martia. *See* Marcia; Marsha
Martial/Martiall. *See* Marshall
Martin, 520. *See also* Marcus; Mark; Marshall; Marty
Martina. *See* Ina; Martha; Tina
Martinn. *See* Martin
Martino. *See* Martin; Marty
Martinus. *See* Marty
Marton. *See* Martin

Marty, 521. *See also* Marcus; Mark; Martha; Martin
Martyn. *See* Martin; Marty
Marv. *See* Marvin
Marven/Marvenn. *See* Marvin
Marvin, 522
Marvinn. *See* Marvin
Marvy. *See* Marvin
Marvyn/Marvynn. *See* Marvin
Marwin. *See* Marvin
Mary, 523. *See also* Mae; Maria; Marianne; Marie; Marilyn; Marissa; Marlene; Mary Ann; Maureen; May; Minnie; Miriam; Molly; Muriel; Myra; Rosemary
Mary Ann, 524. *See also* Marianne; May
Mary Anne. *See* Marianne; Mary Ann
Marya. *See* Maria
Maryan. *See* Marion
Mary-Ann/Maryann. *See* Marianne; Mary Ann
Mary-Anne/Maryanne. *See* Marianne; Mary Ann
Marye. *See* Marie
Maryen/Maryin. *See* Marion
Marylin/Marylinn. *See* Marilyn
Marylyn/Marylynne. *See* Marilyn
Maryo. *See* Mario
Maryon/Maryonn. *See* Marion
Marysa/Maryssa. *See* Marissa
Massima. *See* Maxine
Mat. *See* Matt
Mateo. *See* Matt; Matthew
Matheson. *See* Matt; Matthew
Matheu/Mathew. *See* Matt; Matthew
Mathewe. *See* Matthew
Mathias. *See* Matt; Matthew
Matias. *See* Matt; Matthew
Mats. *See* Matt; Matthew
Matt, 525. *See also* Matthew
Matteas. *See* Matt; Matthew
Matthew, 526. *See also* Matt
Matthewe. *See* Matthew
Matthias. *See* Matt; Matthew
Matti/Mattie. *See* Martha
Mattias. *See* Matt; Matthew
Mattieu. *See* Matt; Matthew
Matty. *See* Matt; Matthew
Matz. *See* Matt; Matthew
Maud. *See* Madeline
Maunike. *See* Monique
Maura. *See* Maria; Marianne; Marie; Marilyn; Marissa; Mary; Mary Ann; Maureen; Rosemary
Maurece. *See* Maurice
Maureen, 527. *See also* Maria; Marie; Mary; Molly
Maureene/Maureine. *See* Maureen
Maureese. *See* Maurice
Maurena/Maurene. *See* Maureen
Maurese. *See* Maurice
Maurice, 528. *See also* Moe; Morris
Mauricio. *See* Maurice
Maurine. *See* Maureen
Mauris/Mauriss. *See* Morris
Maurise. *See* Maureen; Maurice
Maurita. *See* Maureen
Maury. *See* Maurice; Morris
Mauryce. *See* Maurice
Mauryne. *See* Maureen

Maurys/Mauryss. *See* Morris
Max, 529
Maxeane. *See* Maxine
Maxeen/Maxeene. *See* Maxine
Maxena/Maxene. *See* Maxine
Maxi. *See* Maxine
Maxie. *See* Max; Maxine
Maxim/Maxime. *See* Max
Maximilian. *See* Max
Maximillian. *See* Max
Maximo. *See* Max
Maxina. *See* Maxine
Maxine, 530
Maxwell. *See* Max
Maxx. *See* Max
Maxy. *See* Max; Maxine
Maxyne. *See* Maxine
May, 531. *See also* Mae; Margarita; Maria; Marianne; Marie; Marilyn; Marissa; Mary; Mary Ann
Maya/Maye. *See* Mae; May
Maybelle. *See* May
Mayella. *See* May
Mayhew. *See* Matt; Matthew
Meagan/Meaghan. *See* Megan
Meariam. *See* Miriam
Mechele/Mechelle. *See* Michelle
Medgar. *See* Edgar
Meeriam. *See* Miriam
Meg. *See* Maggie; Margaret; Margarita; Marguerite; Marjorie; Megan; Peggy
Megan, 532. *See also* Maggie; Margaret; Margarita; Marguerite; Marjorie; Peggy
Megann. *See* Megan
Megen. *See* Megan
Meggi/Meggy. *See* Megan; Peggy
Meggie. *See* Maggie; Margaret; Margarita; Marguerite; Marjorie; Megan; Peggy
Meghan. *See* Megan; Peggy
Meghann/Meghanne. *See* Megan
Mehl/Mehll. *See* Mel
Mei. *See* May
Meichael/Maichal. *See* Michael
Meigh. *See* Mae
Meiriam. *See* Miriam
Mel, 533. *See also* Melanie; Melinda; Melissa; Melody; Melvin
Mela. *See* Melody
Melanee/Melaney. *See* Melanie
Melanie, 534. *See also* Mel
Melantha. *See* Mel; Melanie
Melany. *See* Melanie
Melbourne. *See* Mel
Melden. *See* Mel
Meldrick. *See* Mel
Melenie. *See* Melanie
Meli. *See* Melody
Melina. *See* Melinda
Melinda, 535. *See also* Linda; Lynn; Mel
Melindah. *See* Melinda
Melinde. *See* Melinda
Meline. *See* Melinda
Melinie/Meliny. *See* Melanie
Meliora. *See* Mel
Melisa/Melise. *See* Melissa
Melisande. *See* Mel
Melissa, 536. *See also* Mel; Misty
Melisse. *See* Melissa
Melita. *See* Melissa

Mell. *See* Mel
Mella. *See* Melinda; Melody
Mellaine. *See* Melanie
Mellane/Mellani. *See* Melanie
Mellanie/Mellannie. *See* Melanie
Mellany. *See* Melanie
Mellenie/Melleny. *See* Melanie
Melli. *See* Melody
Mellie. *See* Melanie; Melissa
Mellinda. *See* Melinda
Melliney/Melliny. *See* Melanie
Mellodey/Mellodie. *See* Melody
Mellodi/Mellody. *See* Melody
Melloney. *See* Melanie
Mellonie/Mellony. *See* Melanie
Mellven. *See* Melvin
Mellvin/Mellvyn. *See* Melvin
Melodee. *See* Melody
Melodey/Melodi. *See* Melody
Melodia/Melodie. *See* Melody
Melody, 537. *See also* Mel
Melony. *See* Melanie
Melosa. *See* Melissa
Melven/Melvenn. *See* Melvin
Melville. *See* Mel; Melvin
Melvin, 538. *See also* Mel
Melvina. *See* Mel
Melvinn. *See* Melvin
Melvy. *See* Melvin
Melvyn. *See* Mel; Melvin
Melvynn. *See* Melvin
Melwin. *See* Mel; Melvin
Melwyn. *See* Mel
Melynda/Melyndah. *See* Melinda
Melysa/Melyssa. *See* Melissa
Mer. *See* Meredith
Mera. *See* Meredith; Myra
Meradith. *See* Meredith
Merced. *See* Mercedes
Mercedes, 539. *See also* Sadie
Mercedies/Mercedys. *See* Mercedes
Merche. *See* Mercedes
Merci/Mercy. *See* Mercedes
Mercia. *See* Mercedes
Meredeth. *See* Meredith
Meredith, 540
Meredithe. *See* Meredith
Meredyth/Meredythe. *See* Meredith
Meri. *See* Meredith
Meria. *See* Myra
Merial. *See* Muriel
Merideth/Meridith. *See* Meredith
Meridyth/Meridythe. *See* Meredith
Meriel. *See* Muriel
Merisa/Merissa. *See* Marissa
Merradeth. *See* Meredith
Merradithe/Merredith. *See* Meredith
Merrelle. *See* Muriel
Merri. *See* Meredith
Merrideth. *See* Meredith
Merridie. *See* Meredith
Merridith/Merridythe. *See* Meredith
Merriol. *See* Muriel
Merry. *See* Meredith
Merrydith. *See* Meredith
Merryl. *See* Muriel
Mersaydes. *See* Mercedes
Mersedes. *See* Mercedes
Mersedies/Mersedys. *See* Mercedes

Merv. *See* Marvin
Mervin/Mervyn. *See* Marvin
Merwyn. *See* Marvin
Merydeth/Merydith. *See* Meredith
Meryl. *See* Muriel
Meta. *See* Margarita; Marguerite
Mey. *See* May
Mhel/Mhell. *See* Mel
Mia. *See* Marie; Mary; May
Mica. *See* Monica; Monique
Micaela. *See* Michelle
Micah. *See* Michael; Miguel
Michael, 541. *See also* Miguel; Mitchell
Michaela. *See* Michelle
Michal/Michel. *See* Michael; Michelle; Miguel
Micheal. *See* Michael
Michela/Michele. *See* Michelle
Michell/Michella. *See* Michelle
Michelle, 542. *See also* Shelly
Mick/Mickey. *See* Michael; Miguel; Mitchell
Micki. *See* Michelle
Micol. *See* Michael
Midge. *See* Michelle
Miera. *See* Myra
Migell. *See* Miguel
Miggel/Miggell. *See* Miguel
Miguel, 543. *See also* Michael; Mitchell
Mihail. *See* Mitchell
Mikael. *See* Michael
Mike. *See* Michael; Miguel; Mitchell
Mikel. *See* Michael
Mikey. *See* Michael; Miguel
Mikhail. *See* Michael; Miguel; Mitchell
Mikkel. *See* Michael; Miguel; Mitchell
Mikko. *See* Michael; Miguel
Mikol/Mikull. *See* Michael
Mikul/Milyl. *See* Michael
Mil. *See* Mildred
Milana. *See* Millie
Mildred, 544. *See also* Millie
Mildredd. *See* Mildred
Mildrid/Mildridd. *See* Mildred
Mildryd/Mildrydd. *See* Mildred
Milee. *See* Millie
Milena. *See* Millie
Mili. *See* Mildred; Millie
Milia. *See* Amelia
Milica. *See* Amelia; Emily
Milinda. *See* Melinda
Milissa. *See* Melissa
Milla. *See* Amelia; Mildred; Millie
Millee/Milli. *See* Mildred; Millie
Milley. *See* Mildred
Millicent. *See* Melissa; Millie
Millie, 545. *See also* Melissa; Mildred
Milly. *See* Mildred; Millie
Mily. *See* Millie
Mimi. *See* Maria; Marie; Mary; Miriam
Min. *See* Minnie
Minette. *See* Minnie
Minna/Minne. *See* Minnie
Minnee/Minney. *See* Minnie
Minni/Minny. *See* Minnie
Minnie, 546. *See also* Maria; Marie; Mary
Mique. *See* Monica; Monique
Miquela. *See* Michelle
Mira/Miri. *See* Miriam; Myra

Miram. *See* Miriam
Miranda. *See* Myra
Miream. *See* Miriam
Miriam, 547. *See also* Maria; Marianne; Marie; Marilyn; Marissa; Mary; Mary Ann; Myra; Rosemary
Mirian. *See* Miriam
Miriem. *See* Miriam
Miron. *See* Myron
Mirra. *See* Miriam
Mirream/Mirriam. *See* Miriam
Miryam/Miryem. *See* Miriam
Mischa. *See* Michael; Miguel
Misha. *See* Michelle; Mitchell
Mishel/Mishele. *See* Michelle
Mishelle. *See* Michelle
Missa. *See* Melissa
Missy. *See* Melissa; Misty
Mistey. *See* Misty
Misti/Mistie. *See* Misty
Misty, 548. *See also* Melissa
Mitch. *See* Michael; Miguel; Mitchell
Mitchel. *See* Mitchell
Mitchell, 549. *See also* Michael; Miguel
Mitchil/Mitchill. *See* Mitchell
Mitchyl/Mitchyll. *See* Mitchell
Mitzi. *See* Maria; Marie; Mary; Miriam; Misty
Mitzie. *See* Misty
M'lissa. *See* Melissa
Mo. *See* Maureen; Moe
Moana. *See* Mona
Moanike. *See* Monique
Moe, 550. *See also* Maurice
Moena. *See* Mona
Moh. *See* Moe
Moina. *See* Mona
Moira. *See* Maria; Marianne; Marie; Marilyn; Marissa; Mary; Mary Ann; Maureen; Rosemary
Moli. *See* Molly
Moll. *See* Molly
Mollee/Molley. *See* Molly
Molli/Mollie. *See* Molly
Molly, 551. *See also* Maria; Marianne; Marie; Marilyn; Mary; Mary Ann; Maureen
Mona, 552. *See also* Monica; Monique; Ramona
Monah. *See* Mona
Monca. *See* Monica
Moneca/Moneka. *See* Monica
Monica, 553. *See also* Mona; Monique
Monicah. *See* Monica
Monicka. *See* Monica
Monie. *See* Monica
Monika. *See* Monica; Monique
Monikah. *See* Monica
Monike. *See* Monique
Monique, 554. *See also* Mona; Monica
Monneca/Monnecka. *See* Monica
Monnica/Monnicka. *See* Monica
Mora. *See* Maureen
Morece. *See* Maurice
Moreen. *See* Maureen
Moreese. *See* Maurice
Morene. *See* Maureen
Morgan, 555
Morgana. *See* Morgan
Morgance. *See* Morgan

Morganica. *See* Morgan
Morgann/Morganne. *See* Morgan
Morgen. *See* Morgan
Morgin/Morginn. *See* Morgan
Morgyn/Morgynn. *See* Morgan
Moria. *See* Maureen
Morice. *See* Maurice; Morris
Moris/Moriss. *See* Morris
Morisa/Morissa. *See* Marissa
Moritz. *See* Maurice
Morrece/Morrice. *See* Maurice
Morreen. *See* Maureen
Morrell. *See* Maurice
Morris, 556. *See also* Maurice
Morrison. *See* Morris
Morriss. *See* Morris
Morrisson. *See* Morris
Morry. *See* Maurice; Morris
Morryce. *See* Maurice
Morse. *See* Morris
Morton. *See* Martin; Marty
Mory/Morys. *See* Morris
Moss. *See* Maurice
Mow. *See* Moe
Muiriel/Muiriele. *See* Muriel
Muirielle. *See* Muriel
Muri. *See* Muriel
Murial/Muriale. *See* Muriel
Muriall. *See* Muriel
Muriel, 557. *See also* Maria; Marianne;
    Marie; Marilyn; Mary; Mary Ann
Muriell. *See* Muriel
Muriella/Murielle. *See* Muriel
Murvynn. *See* Marvin
Muryal. *See* Muriel
Muryelle. *See* Muriel
Mya. *See* May
Mychael. *See* Michael
Mychal. *See* Michael
Myera. *See* Myra
Mykel/Mykol. *See* Michael
Mykul/Mykull. *See* Michael
Myldred/Myldrid. *See* Mildred
Myra, 558. *See also* Maria; Marie; Mary;
    Miriam
Myrah. *See* Myra
Myran/Myren. *See* Myron
Myria/Myriah. *See* Myra
Myriam. *See* Myra
Myrin/Myryn. *See* Myron
Myron, 559
Mystey/Mystie. *See* Misty
Mysti/Mysty. *See* Misty
Mytchell. *See* Mitchell

Nada. *See* Nadine
Nadeen. *See* Nadine
Nadege. *See* Nadine
Nadena/Nadene. *See* Nadine
Nadezhda. *See* Nadine
Nadia. *See* Nadine
Nadina. *See* Nadine
Nadine, 560
Nadiya. *See* Nadine
Nadja/Nadya. *See* Nadine
Nady. *See* Nadine
Nadyenka. *See* Nadine
Nadyna/Nadyne. *See* Nadine
Nadzia. *See* Nadine

Naida. *See* Nadine
Nainsi. *See* Nancy
Nan. *See* Ann; Anne; Annette; Nancy;
    Roseanne
Nana. *See* Ann; Anne; Annette; Roseanne
Nance. *See* Nancy
Nancee/Nancie. *See* Nancy
Nanci. *See* Nancy
Nancsi. *See* Nancy
Nancy, 561. *See also* Ann; Anne; Annette;
    Roseanne
Nanette. *See* Annette
Nani. *See* Ann; Anne; Roscanne
Nanice. *See* Nancy
Nanncey/Nanncy. *See* Nancy
Nannie/Nanny. *See* Nancy
NanSee/Nansey. *See* Nancy
Naoma. *See* Naomi
Naomi, 562
Naomia. *See* Naomi
Naomie/Naomy. *See* Naomi
Narumah. *See* Norma
Nastaliya/Nastalya. *See* Natasha
Nat. *See* Natalie; Natasha; Nate; Nathan;
    Nathaniel
Nata. *See* Nadine; Natalie; Natasha
Natacha/Natachah. *See* Natasha
Natala. *See* Natalie; Natasha
Natalee. *See* Natalie
Natalene/Nataline. *See* Natalie
Natalia. *See* Natalie; Natasha
Natalie, 563. *See also* Natasha
Natalja/Natalya. *See* Natalie; Natasha
Natanael. *See* Nathan; Nathaniel
Nataniel. *See* Nate; Nathaniel
Natascha/Nataschah. *See* Natasha
Natasha, 564. *See also* Natalie
Natashah. *See* Natasha
Natashenka. *See* Natasha
Nate, 563. *See also* Nathan; Nathaniel
Natelie. *See* Natalie
Nathalia/Nathalie. *See* Natalie; Natasha
Nathan, 566. *See also* Nate; Nathaniel
Nathaneal. *See* Nathan; Nathaniel
Nathanial. *See* Nate; Nathan; Nathaniel
Nathaniel, 567. *See also* Nate; Nathan
Nathanyal/Nathanyel. *See* Nathaniel
Nathen. *See* Nathan; Nathaniel
Nathin/Nathyn. *See* Nathan
Natilie. *See* Natalie
Natividad. *See* Natalie; Natasha
Natka. *See* Nadine
Nattailie. *See* Natalie
Nattalee/Nattalie. *See* Natalie
Nattelie. *See* Natalie
Nattie. *See* Natalie
Nattilie. *See* Natalie
Naurma. *See* Norma
Navit. *See* Naomi
Naydeen. *See* Nadine
Naydene/Naydyne. *See* Nadine
Nayomi/Nayomy. *See* Naomi
Nayomie. *See* Naomi
Nayt/Nayte. *See* Nate
Naythan. *See* Nathan
Naythen/Naythin. *See* Nathan
Neal/Neale. *See* Neil
Neall/Nealle. *See* Neil
Nealon. *See* Neil

Nealson. *See* Nelson
Ned/Neddy. *See* Edwin
Neel. *See* Neil
Neena/Neenah. *See* Nina
Neenna. *See* Nina
Nehl. *See* Nell
Nehllsohn/Nehllson. *See* Nelson
Nehlsohn/Nehlson. *See* Nelson
Nehlsson. *See* Nelson
Neight. *See* Nate
Neil, 568. *See also* Nelson
Neile. *See* Neil
Neill/Neille. *See* Neil
Neils. *See* Neil; Nelson
Nel. *See* Nell
Neli. *See* Nellie
Nelia. *See* Nell; Nellie
Nell, 569. *See also* Eleanor; Ellen; Helen;
    Nellie
Nella. *See* Nell; Nellie
Nelle. *See* Nell
Nelley. *See* Nell; Nellie
Nelli. *See* Nellie
Nellie, 570. *See also* Ellen; Nell
Nellsohn/Nellson. *See* Nelson
Nelly. *See* Eleanor; Helen; Nell; Nellie
Nels. *See* Neil; Nelson
Nelsohn. *See* Nelson
Nelson, 571. *See also* Neil
Nelsson. *See* Nelson
Nena/Nenah. *See* Nina
Nessa. *See* Agnes; Vanessa
Nessi/Nessy. *See* Vanessa
Nessie. *See* Vanessa
Nethaniel/Nethanyel. *See* Nathaniel
Nettie. *See* Natalie
Nial/Niall. *See* Neil
Nic. *See* Nicholas
Nicanor. *See* Nicholas
Niccolo. *See* Nicholas
Nichelle. *See* Nicole
Nichol. *See* Nicholas; Nicole
Nichola/Nichole. *See* Nicole
Nicholas, 572. *See also* Colin
Nicholette. *See* Nicole
Nicholl/Nichols. *See* Nicholas
Nicholle. *See* Nicole
Nicia. *See* Nicole
Nick. *See* Colin; Nicholas
Nicki. *See* Colin; Nicole
Nickie. *See* Nicholas
Nickol/Nickole. *See* Nicole
Nickolas/Nickolaus. *See* Nicholas
Nicky. *See* Colin; Nicholas
Nicol/Nicola. *See* Nicole
Nicolaas/Nicolas. *See* Nicholas
Nicolai/Nicolao. *See* Nicholas
Nicole, 573
Nicolea/Nicolie. *See* Nicole
Nicolene. *See* Nicole
Nicolette. *See* Nicole
Nicolina/Nicoline. *See* Nicole
Nicolis. *See* Nicholas
Nicoll/Nicolls. *See* Nicholas
Nicolla/Nicolle. *See* Nicole
Nicolo. *See* Nicholas
Niel. *See* Neil
Nik. *See* Nicholas
Nikki. *See* Nicole

Niklaas/Niklas. *See* Nicholas
Nikola. *See* Nicole
Nikolait/Nikolay. *See* Nicholas
Nikolas/Nikolaus. *See* Nicholas
Nikoleta. *See* Nicole
Nikolia. *See* Nicole
Nikolos. *See* Nicholas
Nikos. *See* Nicholas
Niles. *See* Neil; Nelson
Nilos. *See* Nicholas
Nils. *See* Nelson
Nilson/Nilsson. *See* Nelson
Nina, 574
Ninacska. *See* Nina
Ninah. *See* Nina
Nineta/Ninete. *See* Nina
Ninetta. *See* Nina
Ninette. *See* Annette; Nina
Ninian. *See* Nina
Ninnette. *See* Nina
Ninochka/Ninotchka. *See* Nina
Ninon. *See* Nina
Nita. *See* Juanita
Noa. *See* Noah
Noach. *See* Noah
Noah, 575
Noak. *See* Noah
Noami. *See* Naomi
Noé. *See* Noah
Noel, 576
Noela. *See* Noel
Noeleen. *See* Noel
Noelene/Noeline. *See* Noel
Noella/Noelle. *See* Noel
Noelleen. *See* Noel
Noelynn. *See* Noel
Noemi/Noemie. *See* Naomi
Noha. *See* Noah
Nohra/Nohrah. *See* Nora
Nole. *See* Noel
Noll. *See* Noel; Oliver
Nora, 577. *See also* Eleanor
Norah. *See* Nora
Noreen. *See* Nora
Norina/Norine. *See* Nora
Norm. *See* Norman
Norma, 578
Normah. *See* Norma
Norman, 579
Normand. *See* Norman
Normen. *See* Norman
Normi/Normie. *See* Norma
Normin/Normyn. *See* Norman
Norra/Norrah. *See* Nora
Norris. *See* Norman
Nowel/Nowell. *See* Noel
Noweleen. *See* Noel

Ohlga/Ohlgah. *See* Olga
Ohwin/Ohwyn. *See* Owen
Ohwinne. *See* Owen
Ola. *See* Olga
Olenka. *See* Olga
Olga, 580
Olgah. *See* Olga
Olia. *See* Olga; Olivia
Oliva/Olive. *See* Olivia
Oliver, 581
Oliverio/Olivero. *See* Oliver

Olivet/Olivette. *See* Olivia
Olivia, 582
Oliviah. *See* Olivia
Olivier/Oliviero. *See* Oliver
Olivine. *See* Olivia
Olivor. *See* Oliver
Olivya. *See* Olivia
Olley/Ollie. *See* Oliver
Olliver/Ollivor. *See* Oliver
Olva. *See* Olivia
Olyvia. *See* Olivia
Olyvyva. *See* Olivia
Omero. *See* Homer
Orsa. *See* Ursula
Orsala. *See* Ursula
Orsolla. *See* Ursula
Oscar, 583
Oshea. *See* Joshua
Oskar/Osker. *See* Oscar
Ossie. *See* Oscar
Owain. *See* Owen
Owen, 584
Owin/Owyn. *See* Owen
Owinne. *See* Owen
Ozzy. *See* Oscar

Paavo. *See* Pablo; Paul
Pablo, 585. *See also* Paul
Pabloh/Pablow. *See* Pablo
Paddie. *See* Pat
Paddy. *See* Pat; Patrick
Padraig. *See* Patrick
Padriac. *See* Patrick
Pahblo. *See* Pablo
Pahbloh/Pahblow. *See* Pablo
Palie. *See* Paul
Pall. *See* Paul
Palla. *See* Paula
Pam. *See* Pamela
Pamala/Pamalla. *See* Pamela
Pamela, 586
Pamelia. *See* Pamela
Pamella/Pamilla. *See* Pamela
Pammela. *See* Pamela
Pammie/Pammy. *See* Pamela
Paola. *See* Paula; Pauline
Paolo. *See* Pablo; Paul
Parry. *See* Perry
Pat, 587. *See also* Patricia; Patrick; Patty
Patreece. *See* Patricia; Patty
Patric. *See* Pat; Patrick
Patrice. *See* Pat
Patricia, 588. *See also* Pat; Patty
Patricio. *See* Pat
Patrick, 589. *See also* Pat
Patrik. *See* Pat; Patrick
Patrisha. *See* Patricia
Patrizia/Patrizio. *See* Patricia
Patrizius. *See* Patrick
Patryck/Patryk. *See* Patrick
Pats. *See* Pat
Patsy. *See* Patricia
Patt. *See* Pat
Patti. *See* Pat; Patty
Pattie. *See* Pat; Patricia; Patty
Patton. *See* Pat; Patrick
Patty, 590. *See also* Pat; Patricia
Paul, 591. *See also* Pablo
Paula, 592. *See also* Pauline

Paulah. *See* Paula
Paule. *See* Pauline
Pauleen/Paulene. *See* Pauline
Pauletta/Paulette. *See* Paula; Pauline
Paulie. *See* Pablo; Pauline
Paulina. *See* Paula; Pauline
Pauline, 593. *See also* Paula
Paulus. *See* Pablo; Paul
Pauly. *See* Pablo; Paul
Paulyne. *See* Pauline
Pavel. *See* Pablo; Paul
Pawel/Pawl. *See* Paul
Pawela/Pawelah. *See* Paula
Pawla/Pawlah. *See* Paula
Pawleen/Pawlene. *See* Pauline
Pawline/Pawlyne. *See* Pauline
Paydro/Paydroh. *See* Pedro
Peadar. *See* Pete; Peter
Pearce. *See* Pedro; Pete; Peter
Pearie. *See* Pearl
Pearl, 594
Pearla/Pearle. *See* Pearl
Pearleen/Pearlena. *See* Pearl
Pearlette. *See* Pearl
Pearley/Pearlie. *See* Pearl
Pearline. *See* Pearl
Pearly. *See* Pearl
Peder. *See* Pedro
Pedro, 595. *See also* Pete; Peter
Pedroh. *See* Pedro
Peet. *See* Pete
Peeter. *See* Peter
Peetir/Peetyr. *See* Peter
Peg. *See* Margaret; Margarita; Marguerite;
    Megan; Peggy
Pegeen. *See* Peggy
Peggey/Peggi. *See* Peggy
Peggie. *See* Peggy
Peggy, 596. *See also* Margaret; Margarita;
    Marguerite; Megan
Pehggey/Pehggy. *See* Peggy
Pehggie. *See* Peggy
Pehnee/Pehnnee. *See* Penny
Pehnney/Pehnny. *See* Penny
Pehnnie/Pehnni. *See* Penny
Pen. *See* Penny
Penee. *See* Penny
Penelopa. *See* Penelope; Penny
Penelope, 597. *See also* Penny
Penelopea. *See* Penelope
Penelopee. *See* Penelope
Penelopi. *See* Penelope
Penelopie. *See* Penelope
Penelopy. *See* Penelope
Penelopye. *See* Penelope
Penilope. *See* Penelope
Penina. *See* Penelope; Penny
Penna. *See* Penelope; Penny
Pennee. *See* Penny
Pennelope. *See* Penelope
Pennelopie/Pennelopi. *See* Penelope
Penney. *See* Penny
Penni/Pennie. *See* Penelope; Penny
Penny, 598. *See also* Penelope
Pepe. *See* Joe; José; Joseph
Peppi. *See* Joe
Peregrin/Peregryn. *See* Perry
Peregrine. *See* Perry
Perl. *See* Pearl

Perla/Perle. *See* Pearl
Perline. *See* Pearl
Perlita. *See* Pearl
Perly. *See* Pearl
Perree/Perrey. *See* Perry
Perri/Perrie. *See* Perry
Perry, 599. *See also* Pete; Peter
Pete, 600. *See also* Peter
Peter, 601. *See also* Pedro; Pete
Petey. *See* Pete; Peter
Petir/Petyr. *See* Peter
Petricia. *See* Patricia
Petrisha. *See* Patricia
Phalicia/Phalycia. *See* Felicia
Phelecia/Phelycia. *See* Felicia
Phelps. *See* Phil; Phillip
Phernando/Phernendo. *See* Fernando
Phil, 602. *See also* Phillip
Philip. *See* Felipe; Phil; Phillip
Philipp/Philippe. *See* Phil; Phillip
Philis. *See* Phyllis
Phill. *See* Phil
Phillie. *See* Phyllis
Phillip, 603. *See also* Phil
Phillipa. *See* Phyllis
Phillipina. *See* Phyllis
Phillips. *See* Phil; Phillip
Phillyda. *See* Phyllis
Phillyp/Philyp. *See* Phillip
Phillys/Philys. *See* Phyllis
Phlora/Phlorah. *See* Flora
Phlorance/Phlorence. *See* Florence
Phlorince/Phlorynce. *See* Florence
Phlorrance. *See* Florence
Phlycia. *See* Felicia
Phrances/Phrancis. *See* Frances; Francis
Phrancisco. *See* Francisco
Phrancys. *See* Frances
Phrank. *See* Frank
Phransis/Phransys. *See* Frances
Phred. *See* Fred
Phrederick. *See* Frederick
Phyl. *See* Phil
Phylecia/Phylesha. *See* Felicia
Phylip. *See* Phillip
Phylis. *See* Phyllis
Phylisha. *See* Felicia
Phyll. *See* Phil
Phyllida. *See* Phyllis
Phyllip. *See* Phillip
Phyllis, 604
Phylliss. *See* Phyllis
Phyllyp/Phylyp. *See* Phillip
Phyllys/Phylys. *See* Phyllis
Pierce. *See* Pete; Peter
Piero. *See* Pedro; Pete; Peter
Pierre. *See* Pedro; Pete; Peter
Pierro. *See* Pete; Peter
Piet. *See* Pete; Peter
Pieter. *See* Pedro; Peter
Pietro. *See* Pedro; Pete; Peter
Pietyr. *See* Peter
Pino. *See* Joe
Piotr. *See* Pedro
Pip. *See* Felipe
Pippa/Pippy. *See* Phyllis
Pippo. *See* Felipe; Phil; Phillip
Pitricia. *See* Patricia
Pitrisha. *See* Patricia

Poll. *See* Molly
Pollie. *See* Paula
Polly. *See* Mary; Molly; Paula; Pauline
Presleigh. *See* Preston
Presley. *See* Preston
Prestan/Presten. *See* Preston
Prestin/Prestyn. *See* Preston
Preston, 605
Priestley/Priestly. *See* Preston
Pris. *See* Priscilla
Prisca. *See* Priscilla
Priscella. *See* Priscilla
Priscila. *See* Priscilla
Priscilla, 606
Prisilla. *See* Priscilla
Prissie/Prissy. *See* Priscilla
Pryscila. *See* Priscilla
Prysila/Prysilla. *See* Priscilla
Purl/Purle. *See* Pearl
Purly. *See* Pearl
Pyotr. *See* Pete; Peter

Raalf/Raalff. *See* Ralph
Raalph. *See* Ralph
Rabertah. *See* Roberta
Rach/Rache. *See* Rachel
Rachael/Racheal. *See* Rachel; Raquel
Rachel, 607. *See also* Raquel; Shelly
Rachele. *See* Rachel
Rachelle. *See* Rachel; Raquel
Rachil. *See* Rachel
Rae. *See* Rachel; Ray; Raymond
Raemond. *See* Ramón; Raymond
Raemund. *See* Raymond
Rafael, 608
Rafayal/Rafayel. *See* Rafael
Rafe. *See* Rafael; Ralph; Raul
Rafel. *See* Rafael
Rafello. *See* Rafael
Raff. *See* Ralph; Raul
Raffaelo. *See* Rafael
Ragena/Ragina. *See* Regina
Rahb/Rahbb. *See* Rob
Rahbbert/Rahbberto. *See* Robert
Rahbert/Rahberto. *See* Robert
Rahberta/Rahbertah. *See* Roberta
Rahd/Rahdd. *See* Rod
Rahel. *See* Rachel; Raquel
Rahger/Rahjer. *See* Roger
Rahil. *See* Rachel; Raquel
Rahmiro. *See* Ramiro
Rahmon. *See* Ramón
Rahmona. *See* Ramona
Rahn. *See* Ron
Rahnald. *See* Ronald
Rahool/Rahul. *See* Raul
Rahwul. *See* Raul
Rai. *See* Ray; Raymond
Raigh. *See* Ray; Raymond
Raimond/Raimondo. *See* Raymond
Raimund. *See* Ray; Raymond
Raimundo. *See* Ramón; Ray; Raymond
Raina. *See* Regina
Rajeena/Rajena. *See* Regina
Rajer. *See* Roger
Rakel. *See* Rachel; Raquel
Rakelle. *See* Raquel
Ralf. *See* Ralph; Raul
Ralff. *See* Ralph

Ralph, 609. *See also* Raul
Rameero/Rameeroh. *See* Ramiro
Ramirez. *See* Ramiro
Ramiro, 610
Ramiroh. *See* Ramiro
Ramoan. *See* Ramón
Ramón, 611. *See also* Ramiro; Ray; Raymond
Ramona, 612
Ramond. *See* Ramón; Ray; Raymond
Ramonda/Ramonde. *See* Ramona
Ramone. *See* Ramón; Raymond
Ramonna. *See* Ramona
Ranald. *See* Ron; Ronald
Randal. *See* Randall; Randolph; Randy
Randalf. *See* Randolph
Randall, 613. *See also* Randolph; Randy
Randalph. *See* Randolph
Randel/Randell. *See* Randall; Randolph; Randy
Randey. *See* Randy
Randi/Randie. *See* Randy
Randle. *See* Randall; Randolph; Randy
Randolf. *See* Randall; Randolph; Randy
Randolph, 614. *See also* Randall; Randy
Randy, 615. *See also* Randall; Randolph
Raool/Raoul. *See* Raul
Raphael/Raphaell. *See* Rafael
Raphayal/Raphayel. *See* Rafael
Raquel, 616. *See also* Rachel
Raquela. *See* Rachel
Raquele. *See* Raquel
Raquelinda. *See* Rachel
Raquelita. *See* Rachel
Raquelle. *See* Rachel; Raquel
Rashell. *See* Rachel; Raquel
Rashelle. *See* Raquel
Rasia. *See* Rosa; Rosalie; Rose; Roseanne; Rosemary
Raul, 617. *See also* Ralph
Rauquella. *See* Rachel
Ray, 618. *See also* Rachel; Ramón; Raymond
Raychael/Raycheal. *See* Rachel
Raychel/Raychil. *See* Rachel
Raychelle. *See* Rachel; Raquel
Raye. *See* Ray
Raymond, 619. *See also* Ramón; Ray
Raymondo. *See* Ray; Raymond
Raymund/Raymunde. *See* Raymond
Raymundo. *See* Ramón; Raymond
Reba. *See* Becky; Rebecca
Rebbecca. *See* Rebecca
Rebbie. *See* Rebecca
Rebeca/Rebecah. *See* Rebecca
Rebecca, 620. *See also* Becky
Rebecka. *See* Becky; Rebecca
Rebeckah. *See* Rebecca
Rebeka. *See* Becky; Rebecca
Rebekah. *See* Rebecca
Rebekka/Rebekkah. *See* Rebecca
Recks. *See* Rex
Ree. *See* Rebecca
Reeba. *See* Rebecca
Reena. *See* Andrea
Reeta/Reetah. *See* Rita
Reg. *See* Reginald
Regan. *See* Regina
Reggie. *See* Reginald

Regina, 621. *See also* Gina; Ina
Reginal. *See* Rex
Reginald, 622. *See also* Rex; Ronald
Reginauld. *See* Reginald
Regine. *See* Regina
Reginold. *See* Reginald
Reina/Reine. *See* Regina
Reinaldo. *See* Reginald
Reinhold. *See* Reginald
Reinwald. *See* Reginald
Reita/Reitah. *See* Rita
Rejeena. *See* Regina
Reks. *See* Rex
Rena. *See* Andrea; Irene
Renae/Renay. *See* Rene; Renee
Renata. *See* Renee
Renault. *See* Reginald
René. *See* Rene; Renée
Rene, 623
Renee, 624
Renell/Renelle. *See* Rene; Renee
Renie. *See* Irene; Rene; Renee
Rennie/Renny. *See* Rene; Renee
Renzo. *See* Lorenzo
Reuban. *See* Ruben
Reuben/Reubin. *See* Ruben
Revah. *See* Rebecca
Reven. *See* Ruben
Rex, 625. *See also* Reginald
Reynaldo. *See* Reginald
Reynold/Reynolds. *See* Reginald
Rheeta/Rheetah. *See* Rita
Rhoda. *See* Rhonda
Rhona. *See* Rhonda
Rhonda, 626
Rhondah. *See* Rhonda
Rhonnda/Rhonndah. *See* Rhonda
Rian. *See* Ryan
Rica. *See* Erica
Ricardo, 627. *See also* Richard; Rick
Riccardo. *See* Ricardo
Rich. *See* Ricardo; Richard; Rick
Richard, 628. *See also* Ricardo; Rick
Richardo. *See* Ricardo; Richard
Richart. *See* Ricardo; Richard
Richerd. *See* Richard
Richie. *See* Ricardo; Richard
Rick, 629. *See also* Enrique; Eric; Ricardo; Richard
Rickard. *See* Ricardo; Richard
Rickardo. *See* Ricardo
Rickey. *See* Ricardo; Richard; Rick
Ricki. *See* Erica
Rickie. *See* Ricardo; Richard
Ricky. *See* Enrique; Eric; Ricardo; Richard; Rick
Rihck/Rihk. *See* Rick
Rik. *See* Rick
Rika. *See* Erica
Rikardo/Rikkardo. *See* Ricardo
Rina. *See* Regina
Rine. *See* Ryan
Riobard. *See* Bob; Robert; Roberto
Riocard. *See* Ricardo; Richard
Risa. *See* Iris
Rita, 630. *See also* Margaret; Margarita; Marguerite; Marjorie
Ritchard. *See* Richard
Ritcherd/Ritchyrd. *See* Richard

Ritshard/Ritsherd. *See* Richard
Riva/Rivah. *See* Rebecca
Rivi/Rivy. *See* Rebecca
Rivkah. *See* Rebecca
Roana. *See* Rhonda
Rob, 631. *See also* Bob; Robert; Roberto; Robin
Robb. *See* Rob
Robben. *See* Robin
Robbert/Robbertt. *See* Robert
Robberta. *See* Roberta
Robberto/Robbertto. *See* Roberto
Robbi. *See* Roberta; Robin
Robbie. *See* Bob; Rob; Robert; Roberta; Roberto
Robbin. *See* Rob; Robin
Robbins. *See* Rob
Robby. *See* Bob; Robert; Roberto; Robin
Robbyn. *See* Robin
Roben. *See* Robin
Robena/Robenia. *See* Roberta; Robin
Robert, 632. *See also* Bob; Rob; Roberto; Robin
Roberta, 633. *See also* Robin
Robertah. *See* Roberta
Robertain. *See* Roberta
Robertena. *See* Roberta
Roberto, 634. *See also* Bob; Rob; Robert; Robin
Robertson. *See* Rob
Robertt. *See* Robert
Robertta/Robertto. *See* Roberta
Robin, 635. *See also* Bob; Rob; Robert; Roberta; Roberto
Robina. *See* Roberta; Robin
Robinette. *See* Robin
Robinia. *See* Robin
Robinson. *See* Bob; Rob; Robert; Roberto
Roby. *See* Rob
Robyn. *See* Roberta; Robin
Rochelle. *See* Shelly
Rod, 636. *See also* Roderick; Rodney
Rodd. *See* Rod; Roderick; Rodney
Rodderick. *See* Roderick
Roddie. *See* Rod; Roderick; Rodney
Roddnee. *See* Rodney
Roddney/Roddnie. *See* Rodney
Roddrick. *See* Roderick
Roddy. *See* Rod; Roderick
Roderic. *See* Roderick
Roderich. *See* Rod
Roderick, 637. *See also* Rod; Rodney
Roderigo. *See* Roderick
Roderyck/Roderyk. *See* Roderick
Rodge/Rodger. *See* Roger
Rodman. *See* Rodney
Rodnee/Rodnie. *See* Rodney
Rodney, 638. *See also* Rod; Roderick
Rodolfo. *See* Rudolph; Rudy
Rodolphe. *See* Rudolph; Rudy
Rodrick. *See* Roderick
Rodrigo. *See* Rod; Roderick
Rodrik. *See* Rod; Roderick
Rodrique. *See* Rod
Rodryck/Rodryk. *See* Roderick
Rog. *See* Roger
Roger, 639
Rogerio. *See* Roger

Rogers. *See* Roger
Rogiero. *See* Roger
Rohz/Rohza. *See* Rose
Roi. *See* Roy
Rojer. *See* Roger
Roksane. *See* Roxanne
Roksann/Roksanne. *See* Roxanne
Rolf. *See* Ralph; Raul; Rudolph; Rudy
Rolfe. *See* Rudolph; Rudy
Rolph. *See* Ralph; Raul
Romona. *See* Ramona
Romonda/Romonde. *See* Ramona
Romy. *See* Rosemary
Ron, 640. *See also* Aaron; Myron; Ronald
Rona. *See* Rhonda
Ronald, 641. *See also* Reginald; Ron
Ronan. *See* Ron
Ronda/Rondah. *See* Rhonda
Roni. *See* Rhonda
Ronica. *See* Veronica
Ronit. *See* Ron
Ronn. *See* Ron
Ronna. *See* Veronica
Ronnda. *See* Rhonda
Ronney. *See* Ronald
Ronni. *See* Rhonda; Veronica
Ronnica. *See* Veronica
Ronnie. *See* Aaron; Rhonda; Ron; Ronald; Veronica
Ronny. *See* Aaron; Ron; Ronald; Veronica
Ronson. *See* Ronald
Roobey/Roobie. *See* Ruby
Roobi/Rooby. *See* Ruby
Roodey/Roodie. *See* Rudy
Roodi/Roody. *See* Rudy
Rooth/Roothe. *See* Ruth
Rosa, 642. *See also* Rosalie; Rose; Roseanne; Rosemary
Rosalba. *See* Rosa; Rosalie; Rose; Roseanne; Rosemary
Rosalee/Rosaley. *See* Rosalie
Rosaleen. *See* Rosa; Rosalie; Rose
Rosalia. *See* Rosa; Rosalie; Rose; Roseanne; Rosemary
Rosalie, 643. *See also* Rosa; Rosalie; Rose; Roseanne; Rosemary
Rosalin/Rosaline. *See* Rosa; Rosalie; Rose; Roseanne; Rosemary
Rosalind. *See* Rosa; Rosalie; Rose; Roseanne; Rosemary
Rosalyne. *See* Rosa; Rosalie; Rose
Rosanna/Rosannah. *See* Rosa; Rosalie; Rose; Roseanne; Rosemary
Rosanne. *See* Roseanne
Roscoe. *See* Ross
Rose, 644. *See also* Rosa; Rosalie; Roseanne; Rosemary
Roseane. *See* Roseanne
Roseann/Roseanna. *See* Roseanne
Roseanne, 645. *See also* Rosa; Rosalie; Rose; Roseanne; Rosemary
Roseayn. *See* Roseanne
Rosehannah. *See* Roseanne
Roselina. *See* Rosa; Rosalie; Rose; Roseanne; Rosemary
Rosella. *See* Rosa; Rosalie; Rose
Rosemaree/Rosemarey. *See* Rosemary
Rosemari. *See* Rosemary
Rosemaria/Rosemarie. *See* Rosemary

Thurstan. *See* Dustin
Tieler. *See* Tyler
Tierone. *See* Tyrone
Tifaney. *See* Tiffany
Tifani/Tifany. *See* Tiffany
Tiff. *See* Tiffany
Tiffaney. *See* Tiffany
Tiffani/Tiffanie. *See* Tiffany
Tiffany, 719
Tiffeney/Tiffenie. *See* Tiffany
Tiffeni/Tiffeny. *See* Tiffany
Tiffie. *See* Tiffany
Tilar. *See* Tyler
Tiler/Tilerr. *See* Tyler
Tilyr. *See* Tyler
Tim, 720. *See also* Timothy
Timm. *See* Tim
Timmi/Timmie. *See* Tim; Timothy
Timmothey/Timmothy. *See* Timothy
Timmy. *See* Tim; Timothy
Timo. *See* Tim; Timothy
Timofei/Timofey. *See* Tim; Timothy
Timofeo. *See* Tim; Timothy
Timon. *See* Tim; Timothy
Timoteo/Timotheo. *See* Tim; Timothy
Timotheus. *See* Tim; Timothy
Timothey/Timothie. *See* Timothy
Timothy, 721. *See also* Tim
Tina, 722
Tinah. *See* Tina
Tine. *See* Tina
Tiphaney/Tiphanie. *See* Tiffany
Tiphani/Tiphany. *See* Tiffany
Tiroan/Tiroane. *See* Tyrone
Tirone. *See* Tyrone
Tish/Tisha. *See* Leticia
Tod/Todde. *See* Todd
Todd, 723
Todor. *See* Todd
Tohnya. *See* Tanya
Tom, 724. *See also* Thomas
Tomas. *See* Thomas; Tom
Tomaso/Tomasso. *See* Thomas; Tom
Tomie. *See* Thomas; Tom
Tomis. *See* Thomas
Tomkin. *See* Thomas; Tom
Tomlin. *See* Thomas; Tom
Tomm. *See* Tom
Tommey/Tommie. *See* Thomas; Tom
Tommis. *See* Thomas
Tommy. *See* Thomas; Tom
Tomson. *See* Thomas; Tom
Tomys/Tomyss. *See* Thomas
Tonea. *See* Tonya
Tonee/Tonie. *See* Toni; Tonya
Toney. *See* Toni; Tony
Toni, 725. *See also* Antoinette; Antonia; Tonya
Tonia. *See* Antoinette; Antonia; Toni; Tonya
Toniah. *See* Tonya
Tonio. *See* Anthony; Antonio
Tonja. *See* Toni; Tonya
Tony, 726. *See also* Anthony; Antonio; Toni; Tonya
Tonya, 727. *See also* Antoinette; Antonia; Tanya; Toni; Tonya
Tonyah. *See* Tanya; Tonya
Torr. *See* Troy
Torrence. *See* Troy

Torrey. *See* Troy
Torrin. *See* Troy
Totty. *See* Charlotte
Tracee/Tracey. *See* Tracy
Traci. *See* Tracy
Tracie. *See* Terri; Terry; Theresa; Tracy
Tracy, 728. *See also* Terri; Terry; Theresa
Trav. *See* Travis; Trevor
Traver. *See* Travis; Trevor
Travers. *See* Trevor
Travess/Traviss. *See* Travis
Travis, 729. *See also* Trevor
Travys/Travyss. *See* Travis
Treena. *See* Catherine; Kate; Katherine; Kathleen; Kathryn; Katie; Katrina; Kitty
Trefor. *See* Trevor
Tresa. *See* Terri; Terry; Theresa; Tracy
Tressa. *See* Theresa; Tracy
Trev. *See* Trevor
Trevar/Trevir. *See* Travis
Trever. *See* Travis; Trevor
Trevor, 730. *See also* Travis
Trevver/Trevvor. *See* Trevor
Trevvyr/Trevvir. *See* Trevor
Trevyr. *See* Trevor
Trey. *See* Troy
Tricia. *See* Pat; Patricia
Trina. *See* Catherine; Kate; Katherine; Kathleen; Kathryn; Katie; Katrina; Kitty
Trish. *See* Pat; Patricia
Trisha. *See* Patricia
Trissie. *See* Beatrice
Trixie. *See* Beatrice
Troi. *See* Troy
Troodi/Troodie. *See* Trudy
Troy, 731
Troye. *See* Troy
Truda. *See* Trudy
Trude. *See* Gertrude
Trudee/Trudey. *See* Trudy
Trudi/Trudie. *See* Gertrude; Trudy
Trudina. *See* Trudy
Trudy, 732. *See also* Gertrude
Ty. *See* Tyler; Tyrone
Tyeler. *See* Tyler
Tyerone. *See* Tyrone
Tyfaney. *See* Tiffany
Tyffani/Tyffany. *See* Tiffany
Tyffanie. *See* Tiffany
Tylar. *See* Tyler
Tyler, 733. *See also* Tyrone
Tylerr. *See* Tyler
Tylir/Tylyr. *See* Tyler
Tym/Tymm. *See* Tim
Tymmothy/Tymothy. *See* Timothy
Tynan. *See* Tyler
Tyroan/Tyroane. *See* Tyrone
Tyrone, 734
Tyson. *See* Tyler; Tyrone

Ugo. *See* Hugh; Hugo
Ulla. *See* Ursula
Uma, 735
Umah. *See* Uma
Umalla. *See* Uma
Umani. *See* Uma
Una. *See* Agnes
Ursa/Ursie. *See* Ursula

Ursala/Ursola. *See* Ursula
Ursella. *See* Ursula
Ursula, 736
Ursule. *See* Ursula
Ursulina/Ursuline. *See* Ursula
Ursy. *See* Ursula
Urszuli. *See* Ursula

Val. *See* Valerie
Valaree/Valarey. *See* Valerie
Valari/Valarie. *See* Valerie
Valary. *See* Valerie
Vale. *See* Valerie
Valeree/Valerey. *See* Valerie
Valeri/Valeria. *See* Valerie
Valerie, 737
Valery. *See* Valerie
Vallie. *See* Valerie
Valma. *See* Wilma
Valorey/Valorie. *See* Valerie
Valori/Valory. *See* Valerie
Valry. *See* Valerie
Valter/Valther. *See* Walter
Van/Vana. *See* Vanessa
Vanda. *See* Wanda
Vanek. *See* Ivan
Vanesa. *See* Vanessa
Vanessa, 738
Vanetta. *See* Vanessa
Vania/Vanya. *See* Vanessa
Vannesa/Vannessa. *See* Vanessa
Vannie. *See* Vanessa
Veera/Veira. *See* Vera; Veronica
Veerah/Veirah. *See* Vera
Vellma/Vellmah. *See* Velma
Velma, 739. *See also* Thelma; Wilma
Velmah. *See* Velma
Venesa/Venessa. *See* Vanessa
Venetta. *See* Vanessa
Vennesa. *See* Vanessa
Venyamin. *See* Benjamin
Vera, 740. *See also* Veronica
Verahnica. *See* Veronica
Veranica. *See* Veronica
Verene. *See* Vera
Verge/Vergel. *See* Virgil
Vergennya/Vergenya. *See* Virginia
Vergilio. *See* Virgil
Verginia/Verginya. *See* Virginia
Verginnia/Verginnya. *See* Virginia
Verina. *See* Vera
Verjel. *See* Virgil
Verla. *See* Vera
Vern/Verne. *See* Vernon
Vernen/Verney. *See* Vernon
Vernice. *See* Veronica
Vernin/Vernyn. *See* Vernon
Vernon, 741
Verochka. *See* Vera
Verohnica/Verohnica. *See* Veronica
Verohnicka/Verohnika. *See* Veronica
Veronica, 742. *See also* Vera
Veronicka/Veronika. *See* Veronica
Veronique. *See* Veronica
Veruschka/Verushka. *See* Vera
Vi. *See* Viola; Violet; Vivian
Vic. *See* Vicky; Victor; Victoria
Vicente. *See* Vincent
Vicenzio. *See* Vincent

Vick. *See* Victor
Vickee. *See* Vicky
Vickey. *See* Vicky; Victoria
Vicki/Vickie. *See* Vicky; Victoria
Vickter/Vicktor. *See* Victor
Vicktoria/Vicktorya. *See* Victoria
Vicktoriah. *See* Victoria
Vicktyr. *See* Victor
Vicky, 743. *See also* Victoria
Victor, 744
Victoria, 745. *See also* Vicky
Victoriah. *See* Victoria
Victorie. *See* Vicky; Victoria
Victorien. *See* Victor
Victorina. *See* Victoria
Victorine. *See* Vicky
Victorya/Victoryah. *See* Victoria
Vikie. *See* Vicky
Vikkey/Vikkie. *See* Vicky
Vikki/Vikky. *See* Vicky
Vikter/Viktor. *See* Victor
Viktoria. *See* Vicky; Victoria
Viktoriah. *See* Victoria
Viktorija. *See* Vicky; Victoria
Viktorina. *See* Vicky; Victoria
Viktorya/Viktoryah. *See* Victoria
Viktyr. *See* Victor
Vilem. *See* William; Willie
Vilhelm. *See* William; Willie
Vilma. *See* Wilma
Vin. *See* Calvin; Vincent
Vince. *See* Vincent
Vincens. *See* Vincent
Vincent, 746
Vincents. *See* Vincent
Vincenz/Vincenzo. *See* Vincent
Vincien. *See* Vincent
Vincint/Vincynt. *See* Vincent
Vinczant. *See* Vincent
Vinnie. *See* Calvin; Melvin; Vincent
Vinny. *See* Vincent; Virginia
Vinya. *See* Virginia
Viohla/Viohlah. *See* Viola
Viola, 747. *See also* Violet
Violah. *See* Viola
Violaine. *See* Viola; Violet
Violante. *See* Violet
Viole. *See* Viola; Violet
Violet, 748. *See also* Viola
Violetta/Violette. *See* Viola; Violet
Violit/Violitt. *See* Violet
Violyt/Violytt. *See* Violet
Virgie. *See* Virginia
Virgil, 749
Virgine/Virginie. *See* Virginia
Virginia, 750
Virginnia. *See* Virginia
Virgyl. *See* Virgil
Virjil. *See* Virgil
Vitoria/Vittoria. *See* Vicky; Victoria
Vitorio/Vittorio. *See* Victor
Viv. *See* Vivian
Vivi/Vivia. *See* Vivian
Vivian, 751
Viviana/Viviane. *See* Vivian
Viviann. *See* Vivian
Vivianna/Vivianne. *See* Vivian
Vivien. *See* Vivian
Vivyan. *See* Vivian

Vyohla/Vyohlah. *See* Viola
Vyola/Vyolah. *See* Viola
Vyolet. *See* Viola; Violet
Vyoletta/Vyolette. *See* Violet
Vyolit/Vyolitt. *See* Violet
Vyolyt/Vyolytt. *See* Violet
Vyrgel/Vyrgyl. *See* Virgil
Vyrjel/Vyrjil. *See* Virgil
Vyviane/Vyvienne. *See* Vivian
Vyvien/Vyvyan. *See* Vivian
Vyvyana/Vyvyanne. *See* Vivian

Wade, 752
Wadleigh. *See* Wade
Wadley/Wadly. *See* Wade
Wadsworth. *See* Wade
Wahnda. *See* Wanda
Waid/Waide. *See* Wade
Wain/Waine. *See* Wayne
Walford. *See* Wade
Wallace, 753
Wallach. *See* Wallace
Wallas. *See* Wallace
Wallice. *See* Wallace
Wallie. *See* Wallace
Wallis/Wallys. *See* Wallace
Wally. *See* Wallace; Walter
Walt. *See* Walter
Walter, 754
Walther. *See* Walter
Waltir/Waltyr. *See* Walter
Waltirre. *See* Walter
Walton. *See* Walter
Walwyn. *See* Wallace
Wan. *See* Juan
Wanda, 755. *See also* Wendy
Wandah. *See* Wanda
Wandie/Wandy. *See* Wanda
Wane. *See* Wayne
Waneeta. *See* Juanita
Waneta/Wanita. *See* Juanita
Wann. *See* Juan
Wannda. *See* Wanda
Wanyta. *See* Juanita
War/Ware. *See* Warren
Ward. *See* Howard
Warenn/Warinn. *See* Warren
Warner. *See* Warren
Warren, 756
Warrenn/Warrinn. *See* Warren
Warrin/Warryn. *See* Warren
Warriner. *See* Warren
Warrynn/Warynn. *See* Warren
Watkins. *See* Walter
Way. *See* Wayne
Wayde. *See* Wade
Waylan. *See* Wayne
Waylen/Waylin. *See* Wayne
Wayn. *See* Wayne
Wayne, 757. *See also* Dwayne
Wen/Wend. *See* Wendell
Wenda. *See* Wanda; Wendy
Wendaline. *See* Wanda
Wendee/Wendey. *See* Wendy
Wendel. *See* Wendell
Wendeline. *See* Wanda; Wendy
Wendell, 758
Wendi/Wendie. *See* Gwen; Wendy
Wendil/Wendill. *See* Wendell

Wendle. *See* Wendell
Wendy, 759. *See also* Gwen; Wanda
Wendyl/Wendyll. *See* Wendell
Wennodel/Wenndle. *See* Wendell
Wenndil/Wenndyl. *See* Wendell
Wes. *See* Wesley
Weslee. *See* Wesley
Wesleigh. *See* Wesley
Wesley, 760
Weslie/Wesly. *See* Wesley
Wessley/Wessly. *See* Wesley
West. *See* Wesley
Westleigh. *See* Wesley
Westley. *See* Wesley
Whit. *See* Whitney
Whitlee. *See* Whitney
Whitley/Whitly. *See* Whitney
Whitnee/Whitnie. *See* Whitney
Whitney, 761
Whitni/Whitny. *See* Whitney
Wido. *See* Guy
Wil. *See* Wilfred
Wilber. *See* Wilbur
Wilbert. *See* Wilbur
Wilbur, 762. *See also* William; Willie
Wilburr. *See* Wilbur
Wileigh. *See* Willie
Wilford. *See* Wilbur; Wilfred
Wilfred, 763. *See also* Wilbur
Wilfredd. *See* Wilfred
Wilfredo. *See* Wilfred
Wilfrid. *See* Wilbur; Wilfred
Wilfridd/Wilfried. *See* Wilfred
Wilfryd/Wilfrydd. *See* Wilfred
Wilhelm. *See* Bill; Billie; William; Willie;
    Wilson
Wilhelmina. *See* Minnie; Wilma
Wiliam/Wiliamm. *See* William
Wilkinson. *See* Bill; Billie; William; Willie;
    Wilson
Will. *See* Bill; Billie; Wilbur; Wilfred;
    William; Willie; Wilson
Willard. *See* Wilbur
Willbur. *See* Wilbur
Willee/Willey. *See* Willie
Willem. *See* William; Willie; Wilson
Willfred/Willfrid. *See* Wilfred
Willfredo. *See* Wilfred
Willi. *See* Willie
William, 764. *See also* Bill; Billie; Guillermo;
    Wilbur; Willie; Wilson
Williamina. *See* Wilma
Willie, 765. *See also* Bill; Billie; Wilfred;
    William; Wilson
Willis. *See* Bill; Billie; William; Willie
Willma/Willmah. *See* Wilma
Willsen/Willson. *See* Wilson
Willsyn. *See* Wilson
Willy. *See* Bill; Billie; Wilfred; William;
    Willie
Willyam/Willyem. *See* William
Willyum. *See* William
Wilma, 766
Wilmah. *See* Wilma
Wilmar. *See* William; Willie; Wilson
Wilmina. *See* Wilma
Wilmma/Wilmmah. *See* Wilma
Wilmot. *See* William; Willie
Wilmott. *See* Bill; Billie

Wilos. *See* Wilson
Wilsen/Wilsenn. *See* Wilson
Wilsin/Wilsinn. *See* Wilson
Wilson, 767. *See also* Bill; Billie; William;
    Willie
Wilsyn. *See* Wilson
Win. *See* Gwen
Winnie. *See* Gwen
Wonda/Wonnda. *See* Wanda
Woodey. *See* Woody
Woodi/Woodie. *See* Woody
Woodroe. *See* Woodrow
Woodrow, 768. *See also* Woody
Woodrowe. *See* Woodrow
Woodward. *See* Woodrow; Woody
Woody, 769. *See also* Woodrow
Wylfred/Wylfrid. *See* Wilfred
Wylma/Wylmah. *See* Wilma
Wylnma/Wylmmah. *See* Wilma
Wynne. *See* Gwen

Xavier. *See* Javier; Salvatore
Xever. *See* Javier

Yakov. *See* Jacob
Yalonda. *See* Yolanda
Yan. *See* Jan; John; Juan
Yaron. *See* Aaron

Yasmin. *See* Jasmine
Yasmina/Yasmine. *See* Jasmine
Yehoshua. *See* Jesus; Joshua
Yevette. *See* Yvette; Yvonne
Yisrael. *See* Israel
Yitzhak. *See* Isaac
Yola. *See* Yolanda
Yolanda, 770
Yolandah. *See* Yolanda
Yolande. *See* Yolanda
Yolanthe. *See* Yolanda
Yollanda/Yollonda. *See* Yolanda
Yollandah. *See* Yolanda
Yolonda/Yolondah. *See* Yolanda
Yosef. *See* José; Joseph
Yousef. *See* Joe
Yusuf. *See* Joseph
Yvetta. *See* Yvette; Yvonne
Yvette, 771. *See also* Yvonne
Yvonne, 772. *See also* Yvette

Zacarias. *See* Zachary
Zacary. *See* Zachary
Zaccheus. *See* Zachary
Zach. *See* Isaac; Zachary
Zachariah. *See* Zachary
Zacharias. *See* Zachary
Zachary, 773

Zachery. *See* Zachary
Zack. *See* Isaac; Zachary
Zackariah. *See* Zachary
Zackarie. *See* Zachary
Zackary/Zackery. *See* Zachary
Zakarie. *See* Zachary
Zakary/Zakery. *See* Zachary
Zandra. *See* Sandra
Zane. *See* Ivan; John; Juan
Zara. *See* Sarah
Zavier. *See* Javier; Salvatore
Zecheriah. *See* Zachary
Zekarie. *See* Zachary
Zeke. *See* Zachary
Zekery. *See* Zachary
Zilvia. *See* Sylvia
Zoe, 774
Zoee. *See* Zoe
Zoelee/Zoelie. *See* Zoe
Zoeline. *See* Zoe
Zoey. *See* Zoe
Zofi/Zofia. *See* Sophia
Zoi/Zoiy. *See* Zoe
Zoie/Zoiee. *See* Zoe
Zowee/Zowie. *See* Zoe
Zowi/Zowy. *See* Zoe
Zoya. *See* Zoe
Zylvia. *See* Sylvia

About the Nomenology Project

The Nomenology Project is a team of writers and editors led by internationally renowned practitioners Alan Oken, Kathleen Deyo, Jonathan Sharp, and Edward Aviza.